CCH BUSINESS OWNER'S TOOLKIT™

BUSINESS PLANS THAT WORK

FOR YOUR SMALL BUSINESS

Second Edition

A *CCH Business Owner's Toolkit*™ Publication

Alice H. Magos

Steve Crow

CCH INCORPORATED
Chicago
A WoltersKluwer Company

Cover designed by Tim Kaage, Laurel Graphx, Inc.

Books may be purchased at quantity discounts for educational, business or sales promotion use. For more information please contact:

Consumer Media Group
CCH INCORPORATED
2700 Lake Cook Road
Riverwoods, Illinois 60015

ISBN 0-8080-0858-7

Printed in the United States of America

THE CCH BUSINESS OWNER'S TOOLKIT TEAM

Drew Snider, Publisher, Consumer Media Group (*dsnider@cch.com*) has over 25 years experience with business-information services (SRDS), consumer magazines (*Golfweek*), and home-based software applications (Parsons Technology).

Alice H. Magos (*amagos@cch.com*) has over 35 years of experience running the operations of numerous small businesses. She is the author of the *CCH Business Owner's Toolkit*™ online advice column "Ask Alice." Alice is a popular instructor at small business seminars on accounting, financial planning, and using the Internet; is an accountant and a Certified Financial Planner; and holds degrees from Washington University in St. Louis and Northwestern University.

Joel Handelsman (*jhandels@cch.com*) has almost 25 years of experience writing about business, tax, and financial topics. He has been involved in multiple new product and business ventures in the publishing industry, and has held a variety of management positions. Joel holds degrees from Northwestern University's Medill School of Journalism and DePaul University College of Law.

John L. Duoba (*jduoba@cch.com*) has more than 15 years of small business experience in book and magazine publishing, fulfilling various roles in editorial and production management. He has been involved in the publication of scores of titles, with multiple editions and issues raising the total well into the hundreds. John is a professional journalist and holds a degree from Northwestern University's Medill School of Journalism.

Paul N. Gada (*pgada@cch.com*) has over eight years of legal publishing experience, primarily in dealing with federal and state tax issues. He has helped create numerous editorial products, including newsletters, journals, books and electronic information systems. Paul is an attorney and holds degrees from the John Marshall Law School (LLM. - Tax and Employee Benefits), Southern Illinois University (JD), Northern Illinois University (MBA) and Loyola University of Chicago (BA).

Catherine Gordon (*cgordon@cch.com*) has over 15 years of experience in the tax, business, and financial publishing field and has worked as a tax consultant providing services to individuals as well as large and small companies. Catherine holds a juris doctorate degree from the State University of New York at Buffalo School of Law and a BA in sociology from the State University of New York at Stony Brook.

Steve Crow is a business plan writer, consultant and teacher in Colorado Springs, Colorado. He has 20 years of experience in business planning, management, marketing, sales, and training, and has provided advice, support and direction to a broad range of businesses, from small startups to multi-million dollar expansions. Not only an author of business plans, related documents, and articles on business planning, Steve also regularly presents seminars on the importance and the process of business planning.

We would also like to acknowledge the significant efforts of Susan M. Jacksack, J.D., for her contributions to this book.

FOREWORD

There are dozens of articles and books being written about business plans today. Many provide very good, thorough advice about the process of writing a planning document and, incidentally, how to run your business effectively.

But very few of them are willing to show you what an actual business plan, for a real business, looks like. Most of the business plans that have been published are works of fiction, created as an illustration of an "average" small business, rather than real, working plans created by the business people who will actually have to live with those plans.

Yet knowing what a real business plan looks like is *exactly* the information that you need most, in order to write your first plan. In fact, what you really need to see are plans that have performed successfully for their business owners – plans that have helped the owner obtain needed financing, get a new business started, or embark on an expansion or change in direction.

Why are real business plans so difficult to find? One reason is that it takes a substantial amount of time and effort to create a high-quality plan. Much research and thinking goes into the process. Once the work is done, the creators are often unwilling to share the fruit of their efforts.

In view of these facts, we are grateful for the assistance of Steve Crow, a professional business consultant and planner in Colorado Springs, Colorado. Steve was willing to share his expertise with us in the form of five plans developed for real, live businesses that are starting up or already operating. By reading through these plans, you can get a clear sense of the type of information and the level of detail that you'll need to include in your own plans.

Business Plans that Work for Small Business, second edition, will also help you understand the elements that must be included in a planning document, and the information you need to gather to create your own plan. You'll see that creating a business plan need not be difficult, and the time you spend planning will save you many, many hours of time you'd otherwise spend dealing with major problems in the future.

Why should you turn to us? CCH INCORPORATED is a leading provider of information and software to the business and professional community. More than four generations of business advisors have trusted our products, and now you can too.

A caution and an invitation—the discussions and plans contained in this book are current as of the date of publication. But remember, things change. To keep abreast of the latest news affecting your business, visit *CCH Business Owner's Toolkit* on the Internet (www.toolkit.cch.com).

While you're there, take a look at the other interactive information and tools we offer to assist you in running your business. You can also ask follow-up questions of our team of small business experts. We welcome and look forward to your questions and comments.

Drew Snider

Publisher, Consumer Media Group

Table of Contents

Table of Contents

Part I

Creating A Business Plan That Works

Coming up with a great idea for a new business, or for a way to turn around or expand an existing business, can be a tremendous challenge in itself. While there's never a shortage of raw ideas, finding one that's solid enough to support a successful company for an extended period of time takes a great deal of investigation and research, good judgment, timing, and even luck.

But coming up with a great idea, difficult as it may be, is not enough. Countless businesses have started out well, sailed through the first few months or even years, and then foundered as soon as the first real problems cropped up.

How can you make sure this won't happen to you? You can't, of course. But you can greatly improve your chances by taking the time to thoroughly research your business idea before plunging into it. Then you can take the most important step: using what you've learned to create a detailed plan that plots out your objectives, your marketing strategy, operations procedures, and the right combination of expertise, equipment, location, and sheer capital that will be required to convert your ideas into reality.

Creating a business plan need not be difficult. However, it does require a step-by-step approach, and a willingness to persist in digging for information and thinking through all the essential factors that will contribute to your operation. You'll find that the time you spend creating your plan will be some of the most valuable hours in your entrepreneurial career. By creating a business plan, you'll know exactly what pieces must come together at the right time, place, and amount to make your project a success. What's more, you'll be able to explain your idea to others whom you must convince to write a loan, invest in your business, or join you as a partner or co-owner.

While the planning document itself can be important, particularly if you're going to use it to obtain necessary capital, the planning process is even more important. It's during the process of creating the plan that you round out your knowledge base by gathering information, consider numerous alternatives, and make dozens, if not hundreds, of decisions about how to proceed.

Where available, you can and should enlist the help of others (e.g., your accountant, lawyer, consultant, or even a professional business plan developer) to help you pull together the physical document. A review of the financial section by an accountant can be particularly helpful. But *you* must ultimately do the essential thinking and decisionmaking yourself. Your plan must reflect your own individual strengths, personality, and intentions for your business, and no one knows them as well as you.

In Part I, we'll describe the process of creating a plan, and the important elements you need to include in the formal document. We'll also describe some ways that you can use your plan in the future to manage your business more effectively.

Chapter 1: Preparing to Put Your Plan Together shows how to shape your plan to match your reason for creating it, and the audience to whom your plan is directed.

Chapter 2: Format and Introductory Elements presents an overview of your written plan, discusses format and presentation issues, and describes the executive summary, table of contents, and appendix portions of the plan.

Chapter 3: The Company Summary discusses the parts of your plan that will describe the ownership, mission, objectives, and keys to success of your company. Where appropriate, it may include descriptions of your facilities and your company history.

Chapter 4: Market Analysis explains the portions of your plan that describe your industry, your target market, and your competition. We suggest you include a Strengths, Weaknesses, Opportunities, and Threats (SWOT) Analysis and a Needs Analysis.

Chapter 5: Product or Service Description discusses the part of your plan that provides a detailed description of what your company's offerings are or will be.

Chapter 6: Marketing and Sales Plans explains how to present your marketing strategy and plans for implementing that strategy.

Chapter 7: Operations and Management Plans discusses the portions of the plan that address your management team and employees, important processes, and other operations issues that are important to your business.

Chapter 8: Financial Plans, discusses the financial statements that must be included, as well as the assumptions and projections you must make in order to complete them.

Chapter 9: Using the Completed Plan explains how a business plan can become an important tool for keeping your business on track, long after the plan is completed.

Chapter 1

Preparing To Put Your Plan Together

Before you sit down to write your business plan, it's important to think about your reasons for doing it, and what you hope to get out of the process and the plan itself.

Remember that no two business plans will look alike. There are a number of key considerations that will play an important role in shaping the scope and contents of your particular plan. What's more, your plan should reflect your personality and your management style. You'll want the readers to feel as if they know you, and have a good handle on what your business is all about.

Work Smart

Try to avoid the cookie-cutter template effect that you can get by using some business planning software. Software can be a tremendous time-saver, certainly, but some business owners are tempted to just "fill in the blanks" without attempting to consider whether another organization or style might be more appropriate for their business.

This can be a serious error if you're applying for a loan, and your banker has read dozens of plans using the same software (and boilerplate language) already. Resist the temptation — make sure that your plan expresses your creativity and individuality.

Obviously, your business's position in its life cycle will have a significant impact on the type of planning that's needed. A startup may need extensive planning of all its aspects, while an ongoing business might require a plan that relates primarily to a new market that it wants to enter, or a new product that it wants to introduce.

The most important consideration will be the uses to which you expect to put your plan, and the audience who will read it. Will people outside the business see your plan? Will you be seeking outside financing, and if so, from whom? The type of lender or investor you're pursuing will dictate the type of information and details you need to include. On the other hand, if the plan is to be used primarily as a management tool for yourself and/or other owners or key employees, you can be more flexible about the length and contents of the plan.

A PLAN FOR AN OUTSIDE AUDIENCE

Just as a person seeking a job prepares a resume that outlines qualifications, experience, and other relevant information, a business that is seeking debt financing or an infusion of capital from an outside investor will benefit from having a "resume" of its own.

You can think of your business plan as a rather lengthy resume. To the extent that it reflects the reasonable plans of a good manager, it gives your audience a positive image of what your business is and what it can be expected to do.

For Lenders and Investors

Starting a new business, or expanding an existing one, may require more money than you can get together on your own. This means turning to an outside source for financing. While you might consider taking on a partner or finding an investor, you also might go to a bank to apply for a loan.

If you're just starting out, you obviously won't have a history of profitable operations to indicate that you can function successfully enough to make all your loan payments. In the past, this lack of a history made most banks extremely hesitant to lend money to new, unproven businesses. However, there are indications that bankers are becoming somewhat more open to financing startup operations.

Nevertheless, with the majority of conventional lenders, a workable business plan is essential to getting startup financing. It is one of the first things that a potential lender will want to examine (along with a list of your *personal* assets).

If you've been in business for a while and you need financing to expand or introduce a new product or service, your lender might not require you to submit a full-fledged business plan. However, a solid plan that illustrates a successful track record can provide strong support for your loan request, and should increase your chances of getting the amount and type of loan you want.

Venture capitalists, prospective partners or shareholders, and even relatives who might loan money or invest in your business will want some assurances that they have used their money wisely. A business plan demonstrates how their money will be used and what they, and the business, can expect in return.

Finally, if you expect an ongoing need for funding, showing that the business is meeting or exceeding planned goals can help you build a history that might let you borrow under more desirable rates and conditions in the future.

For Prospective Employees

In some cases, portions of a business plan can serve to introduce prospective employees to your business. Particularly if you intend to hire long-term or high-level employees, you'll want to present a fair picture of what your business is and what types of work need to be performed. You can also establish expectations regarding income and growth opportunities based on the plan's projections.

Shaping the Plan for an External Audience

If you are writing a plan primarily to be shown to an external audience, you'll want to pay close attention to the established conventions of business plan documents. There are certain elements and types of information that your lender or potential investors will expect to see, and it doesn't pay to disappoint them. Similarly, a business plan is expected to have a "professional" appearance, which means that it must look somewhat like every other business plan.

For any outside lender or investor, the executive summary is the most important part of your plan. Venture capitalists, in particular, typically receive hundreds of plans and don't have time to read them all cover to cover. If your summary doesn't capture their attention, they won't go any farther.

A plan destined to be shown to a banker must include a financing proposal or statement that succinctly describes the type of loan(s) you are seeking, the purposes to which the funds will be put, and how you will pay the money back. In the lender's view, this is the most important part of the plan, so place it up front, in the executive summary or immediately afterward.

Any plan for an outside investor will have to emphasize the financial side of your business. The section that includes your financial statements is often the second section a banker will turn to, so make sure that it is complete, accurate, and reasonable in its assumptions.

Venture capitalists and outside investors will want all the financial information that a banker would need, plus a good deal of marketing, operational, and personnel information. These types of investors view themselves as owners, so they tend to want a lot of detail. They also need to get a strong sense of your vision, experience, and commitment to the company.

Venture capitalists tend to be short-term investors, and it's important that you include an exit plan if you are seeking VC backing. You'll need to show that you have a workable plan for cashing out the investor, generally by selling stock to the public or by selling the business to a larger company. There may be some other options, depending on the particular investor, but you should at least consider the possibility that your own involvement in the company's management will be greatly reduced within the foreseeable future.

However, with any plan for an outside audience, keep the reader's attention span in mind. If the plan is too short, it won't provide all the answers that the reader is looking for; if it is too long, the reader may give up before coming to the conclusion. Somewhere around 20 to 30 pages should be the right length for most small businesses.

For an example of a plan that was created for the purpose of getting financing, see the Plan for Commercial Fitness Equipment on page 233.

THE BUSINESS PLAN AS A MANAGEMENT TOOL

An extremely important, but too-often overlooked, reason for creating a business plan is to help you manage vital business activities better.

If you're just starting out in business, the time it takes to create your first plan will be more than repaid by the insight you gain. If you're in business already but have never created a business plan, you'll be in a much better position to assess opportunities and risks that accompany the various changes you may be considering.

You should consider creating a business plan if:

- You want to open a new business.

- Your business has grown significantly since you last did any significant planning.

- You want to introduce a new product.

- You want to enter a new market.

- You want to acquire a new business or a franchise.

A Business Plan for a New Business

For most entrepreneurs, it's only when you take the time to create a written document that embodies your thoughts that you realize the scope and magnitude of what's involved in running a business. In your head, you've concentrated on the idea. In your plan, you can examine the nuts and bolts of running a business to exploit your idea.

Since you're considering a wholly new business, a big part of the planning process is going to involve developing an initial set of assumptions. You'll have to make assumptions regarding costs, labor, the number of potential customers, pricing, and many other factors.

Your business plan will also identify the essential events that must occur and actions that must be taken, and set forth a clear timetable for accomplishing them. You may want to show these important activities in a chart.

Perhaps the most important component of the business plan is your marketing plan, which identifies your target audience and explains how you will position your product or service to reach that audience. Your specific advertising and promotional activities will be linked to sales targets. Your operational plans will explain how your business will conduct its day-to-day activities. The timing of these activities in relation to marketing plans is crucial; for example, there is little point in running ads for a product that isn't available for sale.

A good business plan also includes a substantial amount of detail regarding cash flow projections that set forth the projected timing of revenues and expenses. These projections help establish whether and how the business will meet its obligations to vendors and others who provide the business with goods or services. Most of these projections are tied directly to planned operational results. For example, the sales projected to occur in one month are supposed to generate the income necessary to pay expenses that are due the following month.

Work Smart

If you work hard to create a business plan and your plan demonstrates that you can't profitably exploit your idea without making some pretty wild assumptions, you haven't lost anything. To the contrary, you've saved yourself the time, money, and heartache you would have expended on a hopeless cause. It is far better to realistically appraise your chance for success before you commit your time and money to a new enterprise.

In a well-crafted plan, the overall rhythm of the business will be realistically reflected. If some portion of the business is cyclical, as is often the case, the cycle will be identified and accounted for. For example, many retail outlets rely on the Thanksgiving-to-Christmas period for a substantial part of their annual sales volume. This cycle is reflected in the plan by, for example, increasing inventory as November approaches, planning for the addition of temporary workers to handle the expanded sales volume, and clumping expense payments directly following the busy season when cash is most available.

For examples of business plans that were created to get a new business off the ground, see the plans for Latina Media on page 139, All About the Home on page 189, Commercial Fitness Equipment on page 233, and Emma's Espresso on page 279.

Business Expansion

If your business experiences gradual growth, at some point that expansion alone will make it worth your while to create a plan to explore the opportunities that growth might provide. For example, a production-based business might be able to acquire additional or better production equipment because the volume of business has reached a level that justifies the expense. Or, it might be time for a retail establishment to consider the costs, benefits, and risks of opening a second business location.

Planning for growth also can reveal some of the disadvantages of getting bigger. For example, as your sales volume increases, your need for working capital may increase correspondingly. Careful planning can help you to become aware of the magnitude of your future cash needs, and make arrangements to meet them. As another example, as your business expands you may need to hire more employees, or train your existing employees for expanded duties. By thinking through your needs ahead of time, you'll be able to make better hiring decisions.

Ideally, before launching a new product, moving into a new market, or developing a new distribution channel, you would revisit your existing business plan and integrate the new product or project into the overall plan. As an alternative, you might create a plan that is limited in scope to the impact that the change will have on your existing operations.

For an example of a business plan that was created to help an existing business expand, see the plan for Elevator DataCommand on page 91.

Acquisitions and Franchise Opportunities

If you're considering the purchase of an existing business, how do you know how much to pay? Will the business provide you with the income you need three years down the road? While there's no substitute for a thorough investigation, a business plan can be a useful tool to help you assess whether you should buy a business or let the opportunity go by. In fact, many sellers will create a selling memorandum, which is really a business plan in reverse, to fully acquaint prospective buyers with their business and convince them that the opportunity is a good one. You can use this as a starting point for creating your own plan for the future.

Similarly, deciding whether to purchase a franchise is a serious issue. By becoming a franchisee, you agree to conform to a wide variety of very specific requirements. A business plan provides the framework for considering whether the benefits of holding a franchise outweigh the associated costs and restrictions. The plan is the perfect tool for modeling how your business will perform as a member of the franchise. If you're already operating as an unaffiliated business, you can compare your current operations to the costs and opportunities presented by joining the franchisor.

Managing an Existing Business

Obviously, no one likes to take big risks to obtain a small return. A business plan can be used as a modeling tool to look at a variety of scenarios.

Suppose you decide to drop your prices, which generally means that you'll accept a somewhat lower gross margin in exchange for greater sales volume. How much will sales increase? Will you have enough production capacity? Will you need additional help, or storage space? Can your suppliers provide the raw materials you need? Will lower prices fit your mission and image? Answers to these questions are more readily available if your business plan is used as a baseline, so you can see what happens as you change some of the variables.

For a plan that was created to help an existing business take stock of its current situation and make some changes in direction, see the plan for Elevator DataCommand on page 91.

Tracking Your Progress

It probably comes as no surprise to you that, until recently, even some very large companies used a "cigar box" approach to tracking business results. That is, every dollar that comes in to the business goes *into* the cigar box. All the expenses are paid *from* the cigar box. As long as the box isn't empty and there's adequate money left over for the business owner, everything is just fine.

But there are better ways to stay on top of how your business is doing.

A business plan can provide the foundation for a tracking system that lets you evaluate your business's progress. This tracking function gives you, as the business owner, real-time feedback regarding operations. Deviations between actual and planned results provide clues that you can use to tweak or fine-tune certain elements of the plan.

Shaping the Plan for an Internal Audience

If your primary reason for business planning is to use the planning process and the document itself as management tools, you can be quite flexible about the length, scope, and style of your plan.

While you'll want to include all the elements that are customarily found in a plan for an outside audience, you may choose to emphasize certain areas where you feel your business is weak. You may also decide to create a longer plan that provides more detail in terms of the specific tasks you want to undertake during the year. For example, you may want to use your cash-flow statement as the basis for a more detailed budget that you'll attempt to adhere to during the year.

You may also want to do more thinking about various contingencies that may occur during the year, and create a plan to deal with the most likely scenarios. For example, you may want to consider what you'll do if a major new competitor enters your market, if a key supplier goes out of business, or if a natural disaster forces you to close down for a while. The time to unearth all the potential pitfalls is in the planning stage, not later on when unexpected events tend to be unfavorable and costly.

There may be others within the business with whom you will share the business plan, or substantial pieces of it. Clearly, if you have partners, co-owners, or a Board of Directors, those individuals should see the plan after its completion. They may also be able to provide you with significant input into the plan as it's being developed.

If you have employees, many of the goals that you set for them will be derived from the plan. For example, your sales projections might translate directly into the level of sales your representatives must achieve. In general, your people will be able to do a better job if they see exactly where they fit in with your business objectives.

Example

Let's say that your business plan provides a detailed strategy for achieving a 50 percent increase in sales over the next 12 months. It would be a good idea to share the strategic analysis and your mission statement with your sales people. Your sales force will have a much better idea of what is expected of them, and they'll have a solid understanding of where they fit within your organization.

Obviously, there may be parts of the plan that you won't want to share with your employees. This is particularly true of portions that might reveal more than you want them to know about your personal finances. Similarly, you may not choose to share information regarding how the business finances its operations.

You'll have to use your judgment regarding the type and amount of detail that will be relevant to each of your employees. In many cases, you may want to share with them only your executive summary and the top-line goals for the year. In other cases, greater detail will be necessary and helpful in motivating key employees to "get with the plan."

How Far Out Can You Plan?

When you hear an extended weather report, you know that the predictions for today and tonight are more likely to be accurate than the five-day forecast. Similarly, many of the variables that can affect businesses in general or your business in particular aren't easily predicted. The value of the dollar compared to foreign currencies, interest rates, and many other factors that can affect a business's profitability change constantly. There are no guarantees. So how far out do you plan?

The answer is: *it depends.* For example, there were no doubt dozens of aspiring entrepreneurs in Atlanta who figured out a way to profit from the Olympic Games held there in 1996. Some of these businesses came into being and shut down in less than a year, as one-time opportunities.

On the other hand, some businesses may spend months or years in a product development stage before any sales activities begin. A software business may expend tremendous amounts of money and time developing a product, with the expectation that the product will be sold, and upgraded, for a number of years to come. Obviously, the planning horizon for the software business would be far longer than a business designed around the Olympics.

As a general rule, for an "average" business, a three-year plan is a reasonable starting point. But that doesn't mean that you need to map out, month-by-month, or week-by-week, what is going to happen over the next 36 months. The level of detail will drop as your plan covers periods further into the future. The cash flows that are tracked monthly during the first year of operation may be projected by quarter or by year for the second and third years. Just how this transition from detail to the big picture is managed will depend on your specific situation.

Example

If your goal is to obtain a five-year term loan, you may want to project your plan out for five years to better convince your banker that the loan will be paid off on time.

Predicting your sales, costs of goods, or what the prevailing wage rates will be one, two or five years down the road is no easy matter. Obviously, the assumptions relating to the very near future are more likely to be accurate than those relating to periods further out. For example, if interest rates have held reasonably steady for the past year or so, assuming that the interest rate on a variable-rate loan won't increase by more than a point in the next six months is a fairly safe bet. But you would be much less certain where the rates might be in 12 or 24 months.

PLANNING FOR YOUR TYPE OF BUSINESS

Very few businesses deal exclusively in the provision of goods *or* in the performance of services. For planning purposes, however, it is useful to consider whether your business is primarily a service provider, a seller of goods, or both. Issues that might be extremely important to a product-based business, such as inventory, can have vastly less significance for a service provider.

Service Businesses

One of the first things the owner of a service business must consider will be the question of who, exactly, who will be providing the services that your business sells? Will you be the sole provider, or will you need to recruit other employees or independent contractors to serve your customers?

If someone other than yourself will be providing the services, you'll need to build in some procedures to ensure that the quality is up to your standards. This may involve screening prospective employees very carefully, providing special training to workers, and following up to check on their work.

Many personal service businesses require the owner to spend substantial time doing presentations, preparing bids or estimates, or doing other sales-related activities to acquire future business. To the extent that your time must be spent on sales activities, you can't devote time to actually providing the services. If performing services is what you do best (or even, what you *like* to do best), you may need to plan to hire a manager, or at least an administrative assistant, at some point down the road.

Another issue service providers face relates to billing and collections policies. When goods are sold, there is a clear event that triggers the need for payment. For some service providers, the event that should trigger payment might not be so clear. For example, a contractor may feel that payment should be made when he or she informs the homeowner that the job is complete. The homeowner, however, may feel that he or she has a right to have the work inspected before tendering payment.

One way to reduce the possibility of this type of problem is to include clauses in all your contracts for larger jobs stating that customers must make progress payments of a specific percentage of the total price as a job proceeds. Another is to establish credit terms and consider offering a discount to customers who pay earlier than required. Ultimately, you must plan your cash flow requirements realistically, allowing for the possibility that a certain portion of what you are owed might not be immediately forthcoming. For examples of business plans for service businesses see the plans for Latina Media on page 139 and All About the Home on page 189.

Product-Based Businesses

Retailers, wholesalers, and manufacturers can all be considered product-based businesses. In each case, the business plan will have to include some type of inventory planning. Even if you intend to carry little inventory but order it from suppliers as you make a sale, you'll need to state that fact in your business plan. In some cases, you'll have a lot of money tied up in inventory, and your financing needs may be more extensive.

Your needs for employees may also be an important issue that needs to be addressed in your business plan. Will you use part-timers or full-timers? How will you recruit and retain these workers? What pay and benefits will you need to offer, and what raises should you budget within the time frame that your plan will cover?

Businesses engaged in manufacturing typically need a good deal of equipment in order to operate. Leasing or buying, maintaining, repairing, and insuring your equipment must all be part of your plan. You'll also need to plan for the eventual replacement of obsolete equipment. Similarly, retailers and, to a lesser extent wholesalers, must plan for the shelving, counters, lighting, and other fixtures and decorating their particular business will need.

Since a retailer's business can sink or swim based on its location, a business plan for a retailer must place some importance on this issue. Your plan should explain what a "good" location means in your industry, and how the location you've chosen fits the bill.

For an example of a business plan for a small manufacturer, see the plan for Elevator DataCommand on page 91.

Mixed Goods and Services

A business that provides its customers with both goods and services will probably have a somewhat more complicated business plan than a business that primarily provides either goods or services. There are many logistical considerations relating to managing the interaction between the delivery of goods and the performance of services.

Example

Take the case of a restaurant, where customers expect to receive good food and to be served by an attentive wait staff. Everything has to come together for each customer in order to meet his or her expectations. This is no mean feat for the business owner.

Probably everyone has experienced an "almost good" meal, where one small aspect of the meal didn't go quite right. Perhaps the food was excellent but too long in coming, or maybe you had to ask for the check three times before you finally got it. Whatever the reason, it is clear that people expect both the product and the service to meet their standards. If either fails, customer satisfaction will suffer.

The financial aspects of a mixed goods and services business require careful scrutiny. The relative mix between goods and services must be managed to maintain a reasonable return on the entire enterprise. Pricing is more of an issue because you are trying to cover the wide variety of components that make up the entire package. The business planning process affords you with an opportunity to examine this and other relationships that can impact on the profitability of your business. For an example of a plan for a mixed goods-and-services business, see the plan for Commercial Fitness Equipment on page 233.

Chapter 2

Format and Introductory Elements

After you've considered the purpose of your plan and done some background preparation, it's time to consider the actual elements that you'll include in the written document, and the format your plan will take.

A business plan customarily has a number of major elements or sections. Each of these elements serves a particular purpose in the overall presentation of your plan. The following list identifies and briefly describes each of the documents or document categories that will make up your plan.

Components of a Written Business Plan

Cover page: *This page identifies you and your business, and dates the plan.*

Table of contents: *This element makes it easy for readers to find and examine particular documents.*

Executive summary: *This is arguably the most important single part of your document. It provides a high-level overview of the entire plan that emphasizes the factors that you believe will lead to success.*

Company summary: *This section provides company-specific information, describing the business organization, ownership, mission, objectives, and history. If location is important in your business, you can include a description of your business facilities here.*

Market analysis: *This section or sections presents an analysis of the industry, target market, and competition that the business faces.*

Product or service description: *This section describes exactly what your company will offer its customers.*

Marketing and sales plans: *These sections set forth the marketing strategy that the business will follow, and provide details of your marketing activities to support sales.*

Operations and management plans: *Depending on your type of business, your operations and management plans may include production and inventory plans, customer service and order fulfillment plans, facilities and equipment plans, management and personnel plans, expansion plans, and any other pertinent issues.*

Financial plans: *This section includes your projections (and historical financial information, if you have it) that demonstrate how the business can be expected to do financially if the business plan's assumptions are sound.*

Appendix: *This is the place to present supporting documents, statistical analysis, product marketing materials, resumes of key employees, etc.*

These items are presented in the order in which they *usually* appear in the plan. But don't feel constrained to follow this exact format if another way makes more sense because of the nature of your business.

Work Smart

Remember that there is no requirement that these items be created in the order shown. In fact, conventional wisdom has it that the executive summary, which is preceded only by the cover sheet and table of contents, should be prepared after the rest of the plan is complete.

The relative mix of product and services to be offered will affect the content of a plan. For example, a business that relies on the services of many professional employees would provide substantial details about acquiring and retaining these vital workers. Issues relating to suppliers, production, inventory, etc., become more significant as the product/service mix moves toward a purely product-based business.

In any event, it pays to at least mention all the major issues discussed here, even the ones that are relatively less significant to your particular business. This is particularly true if you're developing a plan with the object of obtaining financing. Someone who's reading your plan will be more confident about your assessment of the situation if you identify such issues and resolve them, however quickly.

If you plan to work alone and perform all services personally, you might note that you don't anticipate a need to hire employees or engage independent contractors if the business succeeds at the levels projected in the plan. You don't want to raise any questions in the mind of your audience that aren't resolved somewhere within the plan document.

FORMAT AND PRESENTATION ISSUES

First of all, remember that the business plan is a clearly recognizable type of document, and your audience will have some expectations with respect to style and contents. Just as your teachers in school expected you to conform to certain standards, the people who will look at your business plan will have certain expectations.

You want your plan to look professional and be a useful tool. There are a number of things you can do to ensure that is the case:

- Print the plan on a high-quality white or cream colored paper. Print on one side of the paper only.

- Incorporate a cover page that includes your logo, company motto, or other identifying information or graphic. Be sure to include an address and phone number for the business and to name the person who should be contacted about the plan.

- Use a typeface that is easy to read, and a font size that is large enough to prevent eyestrain. This may require financial projections to be spread over several pages in order to maintain readability.

- Maintain reasonable borders for your pages. Allowing one inch of white space all around is a good rule of thumb.

- If those in your business use specialized language or acronyms, use them sparingly and be sure to define any terms that someone outside your area of expertise wouldn't readily know.

- Number the pages, and be sure that the page numbers are accurately reflected in the table of contents.

- Keep the plan short and concise: 20 to 30 pages should be sufficient for most small businesses. You can always provide additional details in an appendix, if required.

- Be certain to carefully edit the document. Spelling and grammatical errors do not make a good impression.

- Don't go overboard on expensive binders, paper, printing, etc. Elevating the form of the plan over its substance can raise doubts among those reading the plan. If the plan is for an outside audience, a simple plastic spiral binding will allow your plan to lie flat while opened, without adding too much to the weight and bulk of the plan. If the plan is for internal use, you may want to use a three-ring binder so that you can insert additional materials as needed.

THE COVER PAGE

If you have spent any time and effort at all on a company logo, slogan, or other identifying graphic or text, the cover page is the place to highlight it.

If you haven't considered these basic marketing tools, we strongly suggest that you do so. Building an identity is vital if you want people to recognize and remember your business.

In addition, the cover sheet contains all the usual and appropriate identification information about the business. This includes business address, telephone numbers, facsimile numbers, etc.

The cover sheet should state the date that the plan was prepared. It should identify the person to contact regarding any questions about the plan (generally, you). If you have prepared multiple copies of your business plan, you might also put a copy number on the cover page to help you ensure that none go astray.

THE TABLE OF CONTENTS

The table of contents should clearly and simply lead a reader to each of the documents in the plan. Be sure that page numbers are accurately reflected. If the plan is long, consider dividing it up into subsections, if that will make it easier for readers to find specific documents. For shorter plans, just numbering the pages in sequence is fine.

If your table of contents is more than two pages long, reconsider the length of the section headings, the length of your plan, and the number of documents you've included.

THE EXECUTIVE SUMMARY

The executive summary is one of the most important sections of the business plan. Its purpose is to summarize the highlights of the plan and to provide a brief snapshot of the business. It must be concise, specific, and well-written.

The summary emphasizes those factors that will make the business a success. It must give the reader a fix on the size and type of company for which the plan is written, its management, and the types of products or services it offers. It should briefly present some basic information about the industry, the size of the target market, and company financial goals in terms of revenue and profits, and indicate any funding required.

For new businesses or businesses seeking funding, credibility and excitement are key elements of the executive summary. Venture capitalists receive hundreds of plans each month, and just a few are actually read from cover to cover. A quick 20-second scan of the executive summary is often the basis for determining whether the plan will be read and whether your company may be considered for investment. When the plan is the vehicle used to attract financing or investment, the executive summary should make it clear to the reader who is a potential source of funds why the company is a sound investment.

If your business plan is designed to help you get a loan, the executive summary should include some information on the amount and purpose of the funds you are seeking, and indicate how you intend to pay the money back. The more specific you can be about the type(s) of loan you are seeking (e.g., a term loan, a working capital line of credit, a mortgage on real estate), the more you will favorably impress the lender. Some business owners choose to highlight this information by placing it in a separate subsection, entitled "Financing Proposal" or something similar.

THE APPENDIX

The appendix is the repository for those items that aren't part of the plan itself but that are helpful or persuasive to someone reading the plan. While it will appear at the very end of your plan, we mention it here to remind you that you can add to it as you develop each section of your plan.

Your plan document is intended to present a concise summary of your business; in the process of creating it, you'll uncover a lot of interesting information that won't actually be included in the plan itself. If you think it is likely that a reader will seek further information regarding some portion of your plan, you can include the appropriate supporting material in the appendix.

The appendix may also house sample marketing materials such as brochures, ads, sales scripts, letters of reference from customers, and good product reviews. If you are just starting out, consider including resumes of key employees if you are relying on their skill and experience. Consider material for inclusion only if you believe that it adds to or clarifies the rest of the plan.

Chapter 3

The Company Summary

The company summary section of your business plan generally consists of four to six subsections that, when considered together, present information that gives a general overview of the nature, structure, and goals of your business.

For many businesses, the information that needs to be presented is your company's ownership and organization structure, a mission statement, and a list of your business objectives. Depending on your business, you may need to include a description of your location and facilities, your company's history, and/or startup information. For all businesses, we recommend that you include a listing of what you perceive to be the keys to your business's success. This will help you to prioritize your goals and your activities throughout the year.

Note that startup businesses face a special challenge when drafting the company summary. In the absence of an existing operation, the background will be couched in terms of what the business *will do*, not what it has done. This makes it even more important to have a clear picture in mind as to how your business will look and operate once it's up and running. When you have a track record, it's easy to point at the results you've achieved as an indication of your potential for success. Without any history, you'll have to work a little harder to make sure that you've developed, and presented, a realistic idea of what it will take to make your business work.

COMPANY OWNERSHIP

The company ownership portion of the plan provides information that describes the form of organization of your business — that is, whether it is a sole proprietorship, partnership, corporation, or limited liability company.

For a sole proprietorship, a simple one-line statement to that effect may be all you need. If the business has more than one owner, this subsection should list the owners and the percentage or number of shares that they own. If the owners are active in the business, you may want to briefly describe their role, although you should also include a lengthier description of each principal's responsibilities in the "management and employees" section of the plan (see page 59).

If the structure of your business has changed over the years, you may want to include that information and a brief statement as to why you decided to make the change. For example, you might say that "in 1997 the business was incorporated to facilitate succession planning for the owner."

THE MISSION STATEMENT

A company mission statement can be a powerful force to clearly define your company's purpose for existence, and to determine the direction that all future activity should take.

Your mission statement will not necessarily describe what your business provides to customers, right now, but rather expresses your vision for the company. It should focus on the future and present an expansive view of what your company is all about.

The most successful company missions are measurable, definable, and actionable project statements, with emotional appeal, that everyone involved with the company knows and can act upon. For an example from corporate America, a mission to "be the best health-care provider in the world" for a multi-national HMO organization sounds good. But a simple mission statement from Honda — "beat GM!" — is better because it's a project statement that can be measured every day by every employee.

Case Study — Creating a Company Mission Statement

As an example of how a company mission statement can serve as a focus for improvement in your business's performance, consider the case of Fred's Grocery, a small one-store business, which suffered sales declines when a large chain supermarket opened in the neighborhood.

Fred initially considered lowering prices and adding many new items to compete, at great expense and lower margins. However, a family discussion about the "mission" of Fred's Grocery caused Fred to respond in a less direct, less costly, and less risky manner.

Fred and his family realized that their mission was to serve the convenience needs of local, upscale neighborhood shoppers for specialty items and "fill-in" grocery items that they needed.

The majority of Fred's shoppers spent an average of only $12 ($5-$25 per visit), considerably less than at the larger chain store. Fred and his family decided they would offer more services and specialty items than the larger chain store. Their array of specialty goods, prices, and services also separated them from convenience store chains like Seven-Eleven.

Fred's carried all groceries to the shoppers' cars and apartments and delivered gift baskets/flowers, at no extra charge within a five-block radius of the store. They also added specialty items to their store, putting in an espresso coffee bar, wine kiosk, and food/flower gift assortments. They upgraded and limited the amount of fruits and fresh vegetable selections and added fresh, warm breads and cookies.

After one year, Fred's Grocery realized its best year ever and increased both shopper traffic and average sale by 100 percent to an average of over $25 per shopper. Fred felt the new chain store was the best thing that ever happened to his business, thanks to the time he took to discuss and refine his mission statement!

YOUR COMPANY OBJECTIVES

The statement of objectives in your business plan is basically your short list of goals for the year, or for the time period covered by the plan. In order to be meaningful, an objective should meet three standards.

First, it must be *specific*, not vague or general. For instance, "grow the business" is vague, while "increase sales" is specific. Second, the objective must be *quantified*. As an example, "increase sales significantly" is not quantified, while "increase sales by 10 percent" is quantified. Finally, an objective must be *time-limited*. "Increase sales by 10 percent in record time" is not time-limited, but "increase sales by 10 percent in 2004 over 2003" is time-limited, and meets all three of the standards.

Most business owners find it helpful to set a number of annual financial goals. For example, you may set goals of hitting a certain volume of sales in dollars or units, maintaining a certain percentage of gross margin, achieving a certain inventory turnover rate, or increasing your market share to a certain percentage. For a startup business, one of your goals may simply be to become profitable within a certain number of months (or years) after you open for business.

You may also have some non-financial goals, such as opening a new location, establishing a training program for employees, reducing customer complaints to a certain number per month, introducing a certain number of new products, or modifying your customer base (for example, transforming a 50/50 split between retail and wholesale, to a 35/65 split in favor of wholesale).

It's important to keep your goals realistic and limited in number. If outsiders are reading your plan, they will generally expect to see at least three financial goals, and they will expect you to set goals that are reasonably achievable.

But even if you are writing a plan that no one but yourself will see, your goals should be set high enough to motivate you into action, but not so high that you'll give up in disgust after three or four months.

Work Smart

One of the most difficult parts of running a small business can be prioritizing your time. Particularly if you're just starting out, it can be tempting to get caught up in the thousands of details that go into the business's operation, and to feel overwhelmed by all the decisions you need to make. It can be extremely helpful to keep your goals in sight at all time, to remind yourself of what's really important, and to stay focused on relentlessly pursuing those tasks that will help you reach your goals.

KEYS TO SUCCESS

While not absolutely essential to every plan, we believe that an effective business plan should list, early on, the most important of the actions that you must take to reach your goals.

Identifying these key activities can itself be an art, not a science, and the keys to success portion of your plan will illustrate your style as a manager as much as it will tell the reader about your business. You may find it useful to hold off on writing the keys to success until you have completed the rest of your plan. When you know how all the pieces of the plan fit together, you can identify those tasks that are most crucial.

One important point: your keys to success should be things that you can control.

Example

As a very simple example, a snow removal company may know that it will have more work if there is a heavier than normal amount of snowfall this year, but there's obviously nothing the business owner can do to control the weather! There's little point in listing, as a key to success, "snow on at least 40 days this winter."

In this instance, the key to success might be to increase the percentage of sales made to customers who are willing to pay a monthly charge for snow removal, regardless of the number of times that the plowing must actually be done. That way, the uncontrollable but important factor can be effectively neutralized.

COMPANY LOCATION AND FACILITIES

The company summary section of your business plan may include information about your business's location and facilities (e.g., your retail store, manufacturing plant, etc.), although you may need to devote a separate section to this subject if your facilities are very important to your business (see page 57).

At a minimum, the facilities description should list the type, address, and size of each business location you own or rent. It should also briefly describe the surrounding area (i.e., is your store located in a commercial strip mall with off-street parking, or are you located on the second floor of an indoor shopping galleria). Is the area zoned residential, commercial, or light industrial? Is it convenient to major transportation routes? Is there adequate parking? What are your hours of operation?

You may want to describe your most immediate neighbors, if relevant. For example, if you have a small retail store, the presence of a major department or food store in the vicinity may be an important source of walk-in business, and a major advantage to your company.

COMPANY BACKGROUND AND CURRENT STATUS

For a business that has been in operation for a while, you need to set the stage for the business plan with a narrative that explains how your company came into being and what were the major milestones you've passed along the way.

This will give the reader a sense of why you chose the business you're in, where you currently stand in the business lifecycle, and a general overview of your major strengths and weaknesses.

This section of the business plan need not be lengthy and filled with facts and figures — those will have their place later on, in the marketing, operations, and financial sections. The emphasis here should be on conveying the broad outlines, in a way that presents a very positive image of your company. It's a good opportunity for you to express your personal style.

STARTUP SUMMARY

If your business is in the startup phase, you should include a section that provides detailed information about the costs you expect to incur in starting your business. The chart that follows can be used as a starting point to determine your business startup costs.

Initial Cash Requirements for the New Business
One-Time Startup Expenses

Startup Expenses	Amount	Description
Advertising		Promotion for opening the business.
Building/Remodeling		The amount per contractor bid, materials, etc.
Decorating		Estimate based on bid if appropriate.
Deposits		Check with the utility companies.
Equipment Lease Payments		The amount to be paid before opening.
Insurance		Bid from insurance agent.
Licenses and Permits		Check with city or state offices.
Miscellaneous		All other.
Professional Fees		Include CPA, attorney, engineer, etc.
Rent		The amount to be paid before opening.
Services		Cleaning, accounting, etc.
Signs		Use contractor bids.
Supplies		Office, cleaning, etc. supplies.
Unanticipated Expenses		Include an amount for the unexpected.
Total Startup Expenses		Total amount of expenses before opening.
Cash		Requirements for the first 90 days.
Beginning Inventory		The amount of inventory needed to open.
Other Short-Term Assets		
Total Short-Term Assets		
Building		Use the actual price of the property you want.
Fixtures and Equipment		Use actual bids.
Installation of Fixtures and Equipment		Use actual bids.
Other Long-Term Assets		
Total Long-Term Assets		
Total Startup Expenses		Total expenses and assets before opening.
Left to Finance		Amount of financing still needed.

You'll also need to explain how you expect to finance these costs. If you are seeking a short-term line of credit, equipment financing, a mortgage, or other type of loan, this should be explained in your startup summary. If the initial costs will be borne by yourself and any other owners, be sure to state that fact.

The amount that you've invested in the business will be a point of interest to any prospective lenders, since owners with significant personal investment are considered to be much stronger credit risks. This information may also be presented in the form of a "sources and uses of funds" statement that you include in the financial statement section of the plan.

Funding Plan for the New Business
One-Time Startup Expenses

Funding Source	Amount	Description
Investment		
Investment from Owner A	_____	Investment by individual owner, if appropriate.
Investment from Owner B	_____	Use if necessary.
Investment from Owner C	_____	Use if necessary.
Total Investment	_____	Total investment by business owners.
Short-Term Borrowing		
Unsecured Short-Term Loans	_____	Often, credit cards are used for fill-in cash.
Line of credit	_____	
Other Short-Term Loans	_____	
Total Short-Term Borrowing	_____	
Long-Term Borrowing		
Mortgage	_____	On business property or on your home.
Equipment Loans	_____	
Other Long-Term Loans	_____	
Total Long-Term Loans	_____	
Total Borrowing		Total amount of short and long-term loans.
Loss at Startup	( )	Total amount of startup expenses (not assets)
Total Equity		Total investment
Total Debt and Equity		Add your total investment to total borrowing.

Chapter 4

Market Analysis

A business plan is the blueprint for taking an idea for a product or service and turning it into a commercially viable reality. The Market Analysis section provides the evidence that there is a niche in the market that your company can exploit. It consists of:

- an industry analysis, which assesses the general industry environment in which you compete

- a target market analysis, which identifies and quantifies the customers that you will be targeting for sales

- a competitive analysis, which identifies your competitors and analyzes their strengths and weaknesses

- a SWOT and/or needs analysis may be included to further describe the Strengths and Weaknesses of your business and the market Opportunities and Threats you face (SWOT), or the met and unmet needs that you perceive in the marketplace

The precise way in which you choose to organize this information is up to you. As long as you include all the basic facts, there are a number of outline forms that can work well. Just keep the purpose of your plan in mind, and highlight or expand the sections that have the greatest application to what you're trying to accomplish.

It's also important to realize that as you go about planning a business startup or expansion, you should be doing a lot of research and learning an enormous amount about its marketing environment. Your business plan is not intended to include everything you've learned. It will just summarize the highlights, in a way that shows the reader that you understand your industry, market, and individual business.

THE INDUSTRY

The industry analysis is the section of your business plan in which you demonstrate your knowledge about the general characteristics of the type of business you're in. You should be able to present some statistics about the size of the industry (e.g., total U.S. sales in the last year) and its growth rate over the last few years. Is the industry expanding, contracting, or holding steady? Why?

Who are the major industry participants? While you might not compete directly against these companies (they are likely to be large national or international corporations), it's important that you can identify them, and have a good understanding of their market share and why they are or aren't successful.

You should also be able to discuss the important trends that may affect your industry. For example, significant changes in the target market, in technology, or in other related industries may affect the market's perception of your product or your profitability.

This kind of information is often available for free from the following sources:

- trade association data

- industry publications and databases

- government databases (e.g., Census Bureau, state trade measurements)

- data and analysts' opinions about the largest players in the industry (e.g., Standard & Poor's reports, quotes from reputable news sources)

The *Directory of On-Line Resources* and the *Data Base Catalog* are popular services listing many resources available over your computer modem. Or, if your prefer to do research the old-fashioned (print-based) way, consult a book called *Knowing Where to Look: The Ultimate Guide to Research* by Louis Horowitz, published by the Writer's Digest. The American Marketing Association (the "other" AMA) may be able to help you as well. You can reach it by phone at 1-800-AMA-1150, or on the Internet at http://www.ama.org.

THE TARGET MARKET

How do you determine if there are enough people in your market who are willing to purchase what you have to offer, at the price you need to charge to make a profit? The best way is to conduct a methodical analysis of the market you plan to reach.

You need to know precisely who your customers are, or will be. If you've been in business for a while, you may know many of them by name, but do you really know what type of people or businesses they are?

For example, if you sell to consumers, do you have demographic information (e.g., what are their average income ranges, education, typical occupations, geographic location, family makeup, etc.) that identifies your target buyers? What about lifestyle information (e.g., hobbies, interests, recreational/entertainment activities, political beliefs, cultural practices, etc.) on your target buyers?

You may very well sell to several types of customers — for example, you may sell at both retail and wholesale, and you may have some government or nonprofit customers as well. If so, you'll want to describe the most important characteristics of each group separately.

Directly surveying your current customers can be expensive. For planning purposes, it's acceptable to substitute published industry-wide information; for example, "the average U.S. household computer owner is between the ages of 31 and 42, has graduated from college, and earns $40,000 to $60,000 per year."

Once obtained, this type of information can help you in two very important ways. It can help you develop or make changes to your product or service itself, to better match what your customers are likely to want. It can also tell you how to reach your customers through advertising, promotions, etc.

Example

A company that sells athletic shoes may know that its typical customer is also a sports fan. Thus, if it can build shoes good enough to be worn by professional athletes, it will have a convincing story about quality to tell. It can also benefit by using well-known athletes as spokespersons in its advertising, and by placing advertisements in sports magazines where its customers are likely to see them.

It is also important to be able to estimate the size of your target market, particularly if you're thinking about a new venture, so that you can tell if the customer base is large enough to support your business or new product idea. Remember that it's not enough that people like your business concept. There must be enough target buyers on a frequent enough basis to sustain your company revenues and profits from year to year. Small businesses have a strong advantage here, in that they can often be profitable while serving a relatively small niche

— one that a Fortune 500 company would consider too small to pursue.

Niche Marketing

Most marketers know that "20 percent of buyers consume 80 percent of product volume." If you could identify that key 20 percent and find others like them, you could sell much more product with much less effort.

The heaviest users of your product or service can be thought of as a market "niche" that you should attempt to dominate. The driving force behind niche marketing is the need to satisfy and retain those consumers who really love your products or services. It is much more efficient to continue selling to the same customers, than it is to continually go out and find new ones.

Therefore, in your target market analysis, you'll want to identify your ideal customer niche as narrowly as possible, keeping in mind that your niche must be large enough to profitably support your company.

Influences on Consumer Behavior

If your customers are primarily the ultimate consumers or end users of your product or service, identification of your target market is generally done in terms of demographic and lifestyle factors.

Demographics are tangible, measurable facts that distinguish one group of people from another, whereas lifestyle analysis is more concerned with the intangibles.

Demographic Factors

- ethnic background
- age
- income
- education
- sex

- location
- occupation
- number of people in family
- children's ages

Lifestyle Factors

- cultural background
- religious beliefs
- political beliefs

- music preferences
- literature preferences
- food or menu preferences

- *value systems*
- *recreation and hobbies*
- *social interaction patterns*

- *entertainment preferences*
- *travel preferences*
- *media habits*

For example, heavy coffee, liquor, and tobacco users are not easily identified with demographic information. They may be found in any age group or socio-economic category. However, lifestyle analysis shows high correlation with certain characteristics, including media habits, recreational pursuits, social interaction patterns, music, and other attributes.

Influences on Channel Buyers

If you sell to other businesses that turn around and resell your products and services, your buyers are predominantly channel buyers. Examples of channel buyers from the grocery and drug industry are:

- national master distributors

- local/regional distributors

- chain store wholesaler buyers

- individual retail store buyers

Influences on channel buyers may include things that have little to do with what you consider the key benefits of your products.

Influences on Channel Buyer Decisions

- ***Profitability of the item*** — *the higher the margin and dollar profit per item as compared to competitive category products, the more likely the trade will accept it, regardless of product quality.*

- ***Availability of discount deals*** — *they can increase margin, volume, and velocity of the item. For example, 10 percent to 25 percent off invoice for all purchases during a quarter is a typical discount range for grocery and drug retailers.*

- ***Advertising and promotion support programs*** — *multi-media TV, radio, print, and PR support, plus heavy consumer couponing, sweepstakes, or contests are typical consumer packaged goods programs that may be run one to four times per year.*

- **Other cash deals** — for example, new item "slotting fees" are the subject of controversy and frustration for many manufacturers supplying grocery, drug, and mass merchandiser retailers. Slotting fees are cash payments and/or free goods that are not refundable, even if the products are dropped after six months by the retailer. Slotting fees range from a few hundred dollars to over $25,000 per item in some chains.

- **Availability of free goods** — for example, one free case per store is common for new grocery item distribution.

- **Personal buyer/seller relationships** — there will always be personal relationships influencing buying decisions as long as there are people selling to people. That's why you hire good salespeople!

- **Sales incentive programs** — these programs may spur salespeople on to greater productivity and sales of a particular item or offering.

THE COMPETITION

Once you've identified what's unique about your business and who your target buyers are, you need to take a good, long look at your competition.

In the industry overview section of your business plan, you may have identified the largest players in your industry. Not all of these businesses will be directly competing with you, however. Some may be located in geographically distant locations, and others may have pricing or distribution systems that are very different from those of a small business.

Therefore, in your competition analysis, you'll focus on those businesses that directly compete with you for sales.

Levels of Competition

It may help to think of your competitors as a series of levels, ranging from your most direct competitors to those who are more remote.

- **First level** — the specific companies or brands that are direct competitors to your product or service, in your geographic locality. In many cases, these competitors offer a product or service that is interchangeable with yours in the eyes of the consumer (although, of course, you hope you hold the advantage with better quality, more convenient distribution, and other special features). For example, if you operate a local garden center, you may compete against the other garden centers within a 10-mile radius.

- **Second level** — competitors who offer similar products in a different business category or who are more geographically remote. Using the example of the garden center, a discount chain that sells garden supplies and plants in season is also your competitor, as is a landscaping contractor who will provide and install the plants, and a mail-order house who sells garden tools and plants in seed or bulb form. None of these competitors provides exactly the same mix of products and services as you, but they may be picking off the most lucrative parts of your business.

- **Third level** — competitors who compete for the "same-occasion" dollars. Inasmuch as gardening is a hobby, third-level competitors might be companies that provide other types of entertainment or hobby equipment; inasmuch as gardening is a type of home-improvement, competitors might be providers of other home-improvement supplies and services.

The point of this analysis is to consider carefully, from the buyer's point of view, all the alternatives that there are to purchasing from you. Knowing that, you can attempt to make sure that your business provides advantages over your competitors, beginning with those who are the most directly similar to you. In fact, you can even borrow ideas from second- or third-level competitors in order to compete more effectively against your first-tier competitors.

Competitors' Strengths and Weaknesses

It's to your advantage to know as much as you reasonably can about the identity of your competitors, and the details of your competitors' businesses. Study their ads, brochures, and promotional materials. Drive past their location (and if it's a retail business, make some purchases there, incognito if necessary). Talk to their customers and examine their pricing. What are they doing well that you can copy, and what are they doing poorly that you can capitalize on?

Secondary data, as well as information from your sales force or other contacts among your suppliers and customers, can provide rich information about competitors' strengths and weaknesses. Basic information every company should know about their competitors includes:

- each competitor's size and market share, as compared to your own

- how target buyers perceive or judge your competitors' products and services

- your competitors' financial strength, which affects their ability to spend money on advertising and promotions, among other things

- each competitor's ability and speed of innovation for new products and services

There may be a wealth of other facts that you need to know, depending on the type of business you have. For example, if you're in catalog sales, you'll want to know how fast your competitors can fulfill a typical customer's order, what they charge for shipping and handling, etc.

Even for new businesses, company data from competitors may be available by interviewing competitor company executives, attending industry trade shows, and asking the right questions from industry "experts." They may be unaffordable as consultants but willing to direct you to free databases that you would not ordinarily know of or have access to. And don't overlook your competitor's suppliers. They can be excellent sources of information to aid your research.

Future Competition

Along with your current competitors, your business plan should give some consideration to the possibility that other competition will arise in the near future.

So, you should discuss the barriers to entry for a new business in your industry and market. Is it relatively easy, or relatively difficult, to join the fray in terms of capital, staffing, inventory, distribution control, workforce, relationships with suppliers, etc.?

If your business is new, you'll have to show how you can overcome these hurdles yourself.

What other types of businesses (or other entities) are most likely to be able to overcome these hurdles? What is the likelihood of new entrants to the market in the next few years? Remember that, with the increasing influence of the Internet and catalog merchants, companies that are geographically remote from you may already be selling directly to your customers.

(SWOT) ANALYSIS

One useful way to organize information about your company and its marketing environment is to do a Strengths, Weaknesses, Opportunities, and Threats (SWOT) analysis. While this section is not mandatory for all business plans, it can help you to think more creatively about the factors that will affect your business.

Strength and weakness analysis is an internal company exercise to gauge your ability to compete effectively. Opportunity and threat analysis is an external exercise centered on competitors and the external environment that affect your company's ability to compete. Almost every business can come up with a list of at least five or six items, for each of these four categories. Some key questions are:

Strengths and weaknesses:

- What are your company's greatest strengths in terms of product or service, name recognition and reputation, production processes, workforce, location, distribution channels, favorable supplier relationships, management knowledge and experience, and creativity?

- What are your greatest weaknesses in these areas?

- Are some or all of the items you sell subject to varying product life cycles? How do your products compare to competitors' product life cycles?

Opportunities and threats:

- How does the overall economic outlook, and the economic outlook in your geographical area, affect you? Is the local population growing? Is the job market growing? Are income levels increasing?

- How big are your competitors, and what are their financial resources? Is your competition actively seeking to grow through new product or service introductions, new outlets, new distribution channels, or acquisitions?

- Are competitors' market shares growing, or are they loosing their grip on your target buyers? What types of competitive spending, promotions, advertising, and field sales response will your business encounter?

You may need to network with potential customers, industry associations, suppliers, and competitors to answer these questions.

In the case of weaknesses and threats, you should give a considerable amount of thought to how you'll go about compensating for (or better yet, eliminating) the problem, and discuss that in your plan. In the case of positive factors, you may want to give some thought to how you'll preserve your edge.

For an example of how SWOT analysis might be conducted for a small service company, consider the following case study.

Case Study — Life Designs Architecture

An independent architect who specializes in designing residential homes, Life Designs, has a strengths, weaknesses, opportunities, and threats (SWOT) list that includes:

Strengths:

- *ability to respond quickly to customer demands and changes*
- *ability to make acceptable margins on small jobs, with low overhead*
- *high quality of work and experience*
- *reputation for being affable, honest, and easy to work with*
- *reputation for good value of services and prices*
- *appeal to customers of working directly with the architect/principal*

Weaknesses

- *very limited financial, personnel, and time resources*
- *a limit of three to four projects at any given time*
- *inability to sell and work on a project at the same time*
- *not having a personal relationship with influential local business leaders*
- *being known for a limited number of architectural design "styles"*

Opportunities

- *a growing market for new homes and more upscale homeowners moving to the area, fostered by a growing local economy*
- *a chance to contract with a local developer for an exclusive agreement*
- *a chance to work with the university architectural design department as a visiting lecturer*
- *a chance to relocate his office from his home to a co-op business office center, with shared secretaries, receptionist, conference rooms, and computers*
- *the availability of hiring independent sales reps to work with residential owners, real estate firms, and contractors*

Threats

- *a growing amount of advertising and business inroads by outside regional and national firms in the local area*

- *new local zoning codes and state/federal legislation increasing the cost of new home and remodeling/addition work*

- *increasing costs of building materials*

- *a possible shortage of skilled building trade people in the area*

- *a new competitor in the area specializing in residential home design, especially in his known "style" of design*

NEEDS ANALYSIS

While not absolutely essential for all business plans, a needs analysis can help you to further refine your expectations for the success of your business.

Particularly for new business owners, it's important to remember that, while you may be drawn to a particular type of business because of your knowledge of its operations or your affinity with the type of product or service you're planning to offer, ultimately your success will depend on how well you satisfy your customers' needs.

Example

A small business that operates an auto repair shop must remember that customers patronize the shop because they need reliable transportation. Everything that the shop does must come together to serve that need.

By focusing on the customer's need, the shop owner can devise ways to improve service in the eyes of the customer, such as by offering loaner cars, providing free rides to the customer's workplace, or guaranteeing the service performed for a specified period. The typical auto shop customer is less likely to be concerned about the decor of the shop or about bargain-basement prices, since those don't immediately impact on the need for transportation.

Once you've come up with what you believe to be the customer's most important needs in relation to your products or service, and to your category of business in general, you can divide your list into two parts: needs that are already being successfully met in the marketplace, and needs that remain unfilled. You can then describe how your business will fill these gaps in the marketplace.

You need to be aware of the needs that are already being filled, so that you can avoid being simply a "me-too" business with little chance of breaking down your customers' already established loyalty to another provider. Particularly if the competition is well-established with a substantial market share, it will be difficult to break in unless you do a noticeably better job of meeting more of your customers' needs.

On the other hand, there are few customer needs that go unnoticed and unserved for long. If you believe that you've discovered a huge, gaping hole in the marketplace, chances are that either (a) the need isn't as large as it appears, (b) the need can't be profitably satisfied, or (c) your competitors are already making plans to move into the market.

Although there are a few exceptions, particularly where new technology is being employed, most small businesses can thrive by becoming more closely attuned to their customers' needs, and offering a product or service combination that meets those needs in a significantly superior way.

Warning

You may discover that virtually all of the customer's needs are already being filled. If so, you'll have to reexamine the situation a bit. Either you must dig deeper to uncover more unmet needs, or rethink your business plan more dramatically. Perhaps going into a slightly different type of business would allow you to function in a marketplace that's not quite as saturated.

Chapter 5

Product or
Service Description

If you've reached the point where you are trying to write a description of what it is that your business actually does or sells, you've probably been thinking about your product or service for quite some time. Now is the time to take a step back and reflect.

What's the view from 40,000 feet? What's the big picture overview of your product lines or the services you offer? How would you categorize them and describe them for a reader who's unfamiliar with the terrain?

Remember that the product or service idea you have hasn't been kicking around for months in the heads of the people who might read your plan. You may have to set the stage a little bit to make sure that a reader understands exactly what your product or service is. On the other hand, don't go overboard with detail. For example, you won't need to list every single product that will be carried in a retail store, or every item that will be on the menu for a restaurant.

The starting point is a clear statement of what the product is or what service your business will provide. Focus on those factors that make your offering unique and desirable to customers. Explain what it does, how it works, how long it lasts, what options are available, etc. Especially if your plan is being written for an external audience, be sure that you explain any special terms with which people outside your industry might be unfamiliar.

If you're a service provider, what categories of services do you offer, and approximately how long does it take to provide each unit of service? Are packages available?

Explain whether you are selling a standalone product (e.g., lunch) or a product that must be used with other products (e.g., computer software or peripheral devices). Be sure to describe the requirements for any associated products (especially vital for software). And, if there are special requirements for successful sales, say so.

Another issue to consider is whether you hope to sell items on a one-time or infrequent basis, or whether repeat sales are the goal. If you're opening a bakery or restaurant, you're going to count on the same customers returning on a regular basis. But a heating contractor installing a new furnace or a consultant helping to implement a new order processing system probably isn't going to do that again for the same client any time soon (we hope!). ·

If there are certain products or services that your competitors carry but you don't, take some time to explain why so that the reader isn't left to question your judgment.

If you will be operating a retail environment, you'll want to describe the store or restaurant, as well as the items you'll offer there. You might consider adding a picture or a diagram of the layout in your appendix, as well, unless you'll be discussing these things in detail in a separate "Business Facilities" section of your plan (see page 57).

COMPETITIVE COMPARISONS

Your product or service description should give the reader a complete picture by comparing your offering to similar services or products offered by others. This is especially important for a new business seeking financing. The potential lender or investor will want to mentally position you among the other companies in your category, with which he or she is more familiar.

In the competitive comparison section, it's natural to focus on how your products are bigger, better, longer lasting, better tasting, or generally more exciting that those of your competitors. There's nothing wrong with being very positive about your business's offerings. However, if your competitor's products are clearly superior in some respects, you should mention that as well. Your business plan is a planning document, not a sales brochure, and readers will not be favorably impressed by unrealistic hyperbole.

As a general rule, your plan should always address potential problems, including the strengths of your competition, rather than avoiding all mention of them. The fact that you can recognize where legitimate problems might exist reflects well on your management abilities. Most lenders and outside investors will be more impressed by the fact that you can identify problems and deal with them, than they would be if no problems existed in the planning document.

SOURCING

To some extent, all businesses are dependent on their relationships with suppliers. Even if you make nearly all the products you sell, you'll need to get your raw materials from somewhere. Service providers must locate sources of supplies used in rendering those services. And if you resell products, the source of those products can be extremely important.

Your business plan should address the type of vendors you will use, and if possible, identify them by name. You'll want to show that the issues of price, quality, and availability have been covered. Knowing which vendors you want to use, what products or services they can provide, and what business terms they require is an important part of getting your business on its feet.

In some cases, the readers of your plan will be more familiar with the vendors you use than they are with you, and you have the opportunity to gain favorably by association. You might include copies of important contracts in the appendix of your business plan, to reinforce this favorable impression.

FUTURE PRODUCTS AND SERVICES

Successful small businesses generally find that other businesses will eventually discover their formula and attempt to imitate them. Particularly if you've done a good job of identifying an important unmet need of your target market, you'll find that copycats seem to spring out of the woodwork all too quickly, and some of them may even threaten your hard-won market share.

So, small business owners need to embrace and seek out change, rather than avoid it or wait until change is forced upon them by competitors. One way to do this is to constantly be on the lookout for ways to expand your business by offering new products or services to your customers, or by combining products or services in new ways.

Your business plan should address the future in some fashion, by outlining the opportunities you see for growth beyond your current capabilities. To some extent, you've done that by creating an expansive mission statement (see page 24). But you should also include at least a few paragraphs, in the product or service section of the plan, that describe your expectations for the next round of new products or services, or an update/upgrade of your current ones.

Work Smart

Timing is also an issue to address. Be realistic about the time it will take to develop the new product or service.

It's generally better to set a far-off deadline and come in early, than to continually have to revise and extend your introduction date (witness the credibility gap that some giant software companies have experienced when promised software takes months or years longer than expected to materialize).

Chapter 6

Marketing and Sales Plans

Your marketing and sales plans explain how you plan to reach your targeted customers and how you will effectively market your product or service to those customers. In essence, the marketing plan provides an answer to the market analysis that you've done. It sets forth the specific steps you will take to promote and sell your product or service and provides a timetable for those actions to occur.

Traditionally, the marketing plan portion of the business plan addresses four main topics: product, price, place, and promotion.

PRODUCT

What are the goods or services that your business will offer? How are your offerings better than those against which they will compete? Why will people buy from you? These questions will be answered in the "product" section of your marketing and sales plan.

First, you'll want to provide a very brief overview of your products or services, primarily to set the stage for readers who may not yet have read the detailed product or service description that you've provided in a separate section of the business plan (see Chapter 5).

Then, highlight the aspects of your offerings that will surpass those of your competitors. For example, if you offer a superior warranty or a broader range of services, this is the place to say that.

PRICE

How much will you charge? How will you strike a balance between sales volume and price to maximize net income? Will you be testing a variety of price points? Will you offer discounts and, if so, under what circumstances? This section of your business plan will discuss your pricing policy in some detail.

All pricing strategies depend on balancing three influences:

- Cost — to produce the item and to cover your overhead

- Competition — what other businesses are charging for comparable offerings

- Demand — what customers are willing to pay, and how many of them are willing to pay it

The basic concern for almost all small businesses is to price products at a level that will cover all expenses and that customers will accept, which generally means pricing that's fairly close to that of your competitors.

Analyzing Market Size and Composition

In setting prices for your product or service, one of the first calculations you must do is to estimate approximately how large your potential sales volume could be, based on a reasonable assessment of your potential market share in the product category, at different price levels. Knowing the size of the existing market is critical to determining if there are enough customers to establish and grow a business.

In an established market, in order to sell your product you must cut into your competitors' market shares. Who will you compete against? What are their strengths and weaknesses? Are any direct competitors vulnerable to your products? Are any competitive products priced too high or not providing product "value" for the price? The competitive analysis, described on page 36, should help you to answer these questions.

Researching Product Price Elasticity

If demand for your product or service changes significantly with slight changes in price, the product category is considered to be *elastic* with respect to price.

If no significant volume changes occur, even with significant price changes, the category is *inelastic*.

Example

Grocery store items are often very price sensitive, with a 10 percent price increase or decrease resulting in significant share and volume changes per brand. Consumers are less price-conscious when shopping for gourmet foods, and a price increase or decrease of 50 percent may be required to create any perceptible changes in consumers' behavior.

The greater the price elasticity for a product you offer, the closer you should price your products to similar competitive products and vice versa. While your product may be unique, consumers will not pay much of a premium for it if there are similar competitive choices at lower prices.

To find out more about price elasticity, you might study secondary data sources for your industry or talk to trade association experts.

Evaluating Your Product's Uniqueness

The closer your product resembles competitive products, the smaller the price differences that buyers will tolerate. And the closer the product differences between brands, the greater the likelihood that brand-switching will occur when products go on sale.

Product uniqueness does not guarantee a significant price premium over a competitive product, if the product differences aren't recognizable and meaningful to consumers. And depending on the category of product or service, even recognizable and meaningful product differences may not be enough to get buyers to switch to the new product at equivalent pricing, let alone at a premium price over the competition.

Field testing on a small market basis is highly recommended for testing new product differences or unique new products.

Analyzing Your Costs and Overhead

The most common errors in pricing are:

- pricing products or services based only on the cost to produce them

- pricing products based only on competitors' prices

Instead, you need to take both of these strategies into account and find the proper balance between them. At the very least, your pricing policy must allow you to meet your breakeven point. For more on how to calculate breakeven, see page 66.

Wholesaling and Retailing Markups

Retailers and wholesalers need to consider the issue of markups in their pricing structure, and manufacturers or other product producers need to be aware of the average markup in their industry.

A Few Definitions

- *"Markup" is the percentage of the selling price (or sometimes the cost) of a product which is added to the cost in order to arrive at a selling price.*

- *"Markdown" is a percentage reduction from the selling price.*

Be aware that there are two different ways to calculate markup — on cost or on selling price. So when someone asks you about your markup on an item, you must specify whether it is "20 percent of *cost*" or "20 percent of *selling price*." In retailing, the industry standard is to compute markup as a percentage of selling price.

Example

Joel received a shipment of clocks that he will sell in his gift store. He paid $12.00 for each clock and plans to make $4.00 on each one. The selling price is then $16.00.

The markup percentage on cost is the dollar markup (4.00) divided by cost (12.00) = **33%.**

However, the markup percentage on selling price is the dollar markup (4.00) divided by selling price (16.00) = **25%.**

As a product wends its way through a distribution channel, each step along the journey adds a "markup" before selling the product to the next step. Here's an example of how markups work based on selling price:

Level	Category	$	%
Producer	Cost	20.00	80.0
	Markup	5.00	20.0
	Selling Price	25.00	100.0

Level	Category	$	%
Wholesale Outlet	Cost	25.00	71.5
	Markup	10.00	28.5
	Selling Price	35.00	100.0
Retailer	Cost	35.00	70.0
	Markup	15.00	30.0
	Selling Price	50.00	100.0

Markups vary widely among industries. For example, average retail markups (on selling price) are 14 percent on tobacco products, 50 percent on greeting cards, 8 percent on baby food, and often more than 50 percent on high-end meats.

Considering Other Pricing Strategies

In addition to the primary goal of making money, a company can have many different pricing objectives and strategies. Larger companies may utilize product pricing in a predatory or defensive fashion, to attack or defend against a competitor.

Example

Maxwell House Coffee introduced a second, low-priced brand into their own dominant eastern United States markets during the 1970s to slow and confuse the introduction of Folger's Coffee into their markets. This new product was packaged and designed to resemble Folger's familiar red can, with pricing set below Folger's Coffee. The new temporary product clogged grocer shelves and made it more difficult and expensive for Folger's to introduce their coffee into new eastern markets.

If you have a premium quality product, with premium packaging, graphics, and unique features and benefits, perhaps a premium price is necessary to reinforce the premium brand image. Higher margins than normal may be one benefit. High prices confirm perceptions of high value in consumer minds.

A good pricing strategy will also indicate guidelines for action in the case of price increases or decreases. For example, "We will price at or near the share leader's pricing on a per unit basis. We will increase prices to follow a share leader price increase, but only if we can preserve margin objectives."

Work Smart

Be sure to consider variations that may come up to affect your pricing. You may wish to use discounting for prompt cash payment or for quantity purchases. Seasonal items may warrant special pricing from time to time. How about senior citizen and student discounts? And promotional incentives may motivate your dealers. These are but a few of many variables you'll want to consider when you formulate your pricing strategy.

The pricing levels you finally select for your products should have flexibility for both increases and discounts to customers. Price increases may be inevitable because of component, ingredient, and processing cost increases. The market may or may not absorb price increases without decreasing volume effects.

Work Smart

If in doubt, price on the high side, where possible. It is always easier to discount prices than to raise them.

PLACE

Which sales channels will you use? Will you sell by telephone or will your product be carried in retail outlets? Which channel will let you economically reach your target audience? The "place" discussion in your marketing plan should explain the distribution choices you've made, and how you will go about implementing those choices.

Small businesses may have products that would appeal to many different markets, or channels of distribution in a single market. However, when you have limited resources, it's often best to select a single distribution channel or a limited number of distribution channels that offer:

- greatest ease of entry against the competition

- least financial risk and long-term commitment

- sufficient volume potential to reach short-term company goals

- pricing levels to provide acceptable profit margins

PROMOTION

Whatever you're selling, you'll need to communicate about it with your target buyers. Most businesses find that they need all three components of marketing communications (promotion, advertising, public relations), in some combination. But how do you narrow down the available choices and build a communications program that makes sense? Here's how:

1. **Know who the target buyer is.** Identify the target buyer in demographic, lifestyle, and other descriptive terms.

2. **Determine what is meaningfully unique about your product.** "Meaningful" differences are those business or brand attributes *that buyers or end users consider in making purchase decisions* among different available choices.

3. **Construct a business positioning strategy statement.** It is important to be consistent in all promotion, advertising, and PR programs, particularly with the scarce resources of most small businesses. A good business positioning strategy statement will address who the target buyer or end user is, what the competitive environment is, and what the meaningful differences in the products or services are when compared to the competition. The statement might also communicate some idea of a business "personality" that will be created and fostered in all marketing programs.

4. **Determine the best message to communicate your product positioning to target buyers.** Use your positioning statement to construct a memorable "slogan" or ad message that correlates with the needs and wants of your target buyer.

5. **Determine promotion options and costs in terms of available budget.** There is never enough money to do everything desirable to build the business. Often a promotional budget reality check means a choice between a little promotion, advertising, or PR, but not all three at the same time. Here are some options to consider.

   — Advertising — consider print, radio, cable television, billboard, and Internet ads; packaging; display and point-of-purchase signs; direct mail; catalogs; brochures and flyers; doorhangers; posters; and the yellow pages and other directories.

— Sales promotions — consider grand openings, games and contests, premiums and gifts, coupons, rebates or "frequent buyer" programs, product demonstrations, low-interest financing, and trade shows.

— Publicity and public relations — consider press releases and press kits; public service activities; and speeches or seminars. These types of activities are often "free" except for the time you'll spend on them.

The marketing and sales plan usually includes a calendar that ties marketing and sales activities to specific operational events. For example, an advertising campaign may begin some months before a new product is ready to be sold. As the date of the new product introduction approaches, the ad campaign would be stepped up. Once the new product hits the market, additional advertising is used to support specific sales objectives.

If your target market is divided among several different types of customers (for instance, you sell both wholesale and retail), you may find it necessary to address promotions for each group separately.

YOUR SALES PLANS

Your sales plans may be included in the "promotions" part of your marketing plans; however, if personal selling is a large part of your strategy and especially if your business will have a sales force, you may wish to devote a separate section to your sales plans.

One challenge that you face in developing your business plan is selecting the sales channel that is most effective. For instance, if you're in a business where you provide services personally, your participation in the sales process can be extensive. In contrast, if your business deals in the sale and production of large quantities of product with little associated service, then you face a different challenge. Customers may not know or care who you are.

Planning for selling is, therefore, based on the particular mix of goods and services that you plan to offer and on the way you intend to reach potential customers. Some tools to consider are sales presentations, product samples and giveaways, and incentive programs for sales reps.

If you are going to have a sales force of some kind, be sure you know what you will expect them to do. When making hiring decisions, do your best to find people who can do what you want. If *you* will be the entire sales force, at least initially, try to quantify the activities and time involved.

Chapter 7

Operations and Management Plans

The operations and management portions of your business plan will explain how you will actually produce the goods and services your business will deliver to its customers. These sections also address the back office or "overhead" activities that all businesses must undertake.

Operations and management include activities such as:

- hiring and managing employees or contract workers

- choosing and maintaining your business facility

- supervising and improving your production processes

- filling orders

- collecting money from customers

- providing customer service and support after the sale

- dealing with unexpected occurrences or changing conditions

These types of issues can be grouped into two major categories for purposes of dealing with them in your plan. The categories are: the operations plan, and the management and human resources plan.

PLANNING YOUR OPERATIONS

Creating the operations plan forces you to think through each step that must be completed before your customers receive whatever it is that they purchase from you, and also how you will interface with customers after the sale. For the reader of your business plan, the operations planning section should provide a good overview of the types of activities your business must routinely perform in its core business activities.

The types of operational issues that you'll face will vary tremendously based on the type of business you own. For example, a consultant who deals primarily in assisting customers with network communications isn't going to have an extensive manufacturing or inventory control plan.

For some service businesses, the operations issues may be adequately addressed in the section of your business plan in which you describe your services. It may be most efficient to describe how you're planning to provide services in the same place where you describe exactly what they are. In that case, the services description section (see page 43), in combination with the human resources section (see page 59), may avert the need for a separate operations section.

Production Plans

A fast food vendor, in contrast, will have to carefully plan for purchasing the food and related supplies, inventory storage and turnover, the cooking process, employee sanitation, disposal, etc. Similarly, a manufacturer will generally have to plan for facilities, equipment, and inventories of raw materials and finished goods, not to mention the production processes themselves. Owners of these types of businesses should include a fairly detailed operations section in their business plan. They may even want to divide the operations section into several subsections, such as production, facilities, inventory control, and customer service/order fulfillment.

In writing the production section of the business plan, you may find it useful to look at your business as if it were a linear process that starts with raw materials and ends with a delivery to a satisfied customer. You'll probably be surprised at how many steps there are and how critical the timing and duration of each step is.

While it is easy to relate to production issues in a manufacturing process where goods are fabricated, the concept may also be applicable to other types of businesses.

Example

As a consultant you are engaged to help a company convert from a paper-based billing system to a computer-based system. The end "product" that you will deliver is assistance in selecting the appropriate software and hardware, training on that new equipment, and supervision of the process by which the data is converted to electronic format.

You can do a great job without "producing" anything tangible beyond, perhaps, documentation of the process. This doesn't mean that you can ignore "production." Consider all the work that you would have to do. First, a working knowledge of the client's existing system has to be acquired. Then, software and hardware combinations are evaluated in light of the client's needs and budget. A conversion process has to be developed so that those portions of the existing data that carry over to the new system are available in the new format. Documentation must be prepared to train the client's employees in using the new system. Whether you thought of them that way or not, each of these activities would be part of your production process.

Business Facility Assessment

There are a number of issues you should address in your business plan regarding the choice of a facility.

The first question to address is why you need a business facility, and what kind. At one extreme, a consultant may perform most services in space provided by clients. That consultant may not need a facility at all and may maintain a small home office to store reference materials and business records. At the other extreme, a manufacturing business may require access to rail transport, room for manufacturing operations and storage, parking facilities for a lot of employees, etc.

The success of a retail outlet or a restaurant may depend to a large extent on its location. Is it situated in the right part of town, on a street with sufficient foot traffic, parking, or public transportation? Are the neighbors conducive to drawing customers who might also patronize your business? Don't give these issues short shrift, either in actually choosing your location, or in explaining your choice in your business plan.

Your business plan should also describe the basic aspects of your facility (age, square footage, location on first or second floor, etc.), as well as the important aspects of any equipment, furniture, or fixtures that you may need for operation. You may want to augment your explanations with maps, site plans, floor plans, or even architectural drawings.

If you've already obtained a lease, you may want to attach a copy to the plan in an appendix. If you're seeking financing in order to purchase a facility, you'll want to include a lot of detail about the property you're considering and how it suits your needs.

Inventory Control

Businesses that are required to carry an inventory often find that a significant amount of their working capital is tied up in inventory. This applies to those engaged in retailing, wholesaling, and manufacturing, but may also apply to some service businesses. For example, restaurants must maintain inventory of the food they will be serving and perhaps also supplies such as napkins, straws, sugar packets, etc.

If your business maintains an inventory, we suggest that your business plan should discuss how you plan to manage it. For example, how many weeks' or months' worth of raw materials will you attempt to keep on hand? How many months' supply of finished or retail products? Who will be in charge of keeping track? Will you have a computerized system? Will your suppliers help you to stay on top of your inventory?

Being able to answer these questions in your plan will show that you've considered the implications of maintaining adequate stock, without tying up too much money in inventory that may become obsolete or unsalable. If you're just starting out, your suppliers should be able to give you ballpark estimates of what you'll need; trade associations may also provide some helpful information.

Order Fulfillment and Customer Service

Providing superlative customer service is often the most important way in which small businesses can distinguish themselves from the competition. If you've established a customer service policy, be sure to include it in your plan. Your policy may be as simple as saying that "all customers will be treated in a friendly, professional manner" — and if you have employees, you may need to reinforce it often.

If your business is one in which customers place advance orders and then receive their products later, consider including a section in your business plan that discusses your procedures for taking and fulfilling orders. What shipping methods will you use? Will you charge a flat rate for shipping, or will you base your shipping charges on what the carrier charges, plus (or minus) a fixed percentage?

Will you set a target fulfillment period within which the customer should receive the order? Will you set a time limit on returns, or will you state that only exchanges are available (i.e., no cash returns)?

MANAGEMENT AND HUMAN RESOURCE PLANS

A business plan should help you to organize the roles and responsibilities of all the people involved in your business. Therefore, virtually every plan will have a section describing its management. Some businesses will also need a description of their other staffing or the independent contractors they plan to use.

Management Plans

Whether your business has one owner/employee — you — or dozens, you'll need to describe the management strengths and expertise of your business in your business plan.

If your plan is designed to be shown to an outside investor or lender, the quality of management can be a deciding factor in whether you get the desired capital or not. Generally "quality" is interpreted as meaning "experience," so be sure to explain any previous related job experience, any pertinent experience working for community or other voluntary organizations, and even your family background if that will indicate that you know what you are doing in running the business. Also highlight any special skills or education you have. You may wish to include a formal resume in your appendix.

If your business has more than one owner or manager, you should explain how the important roles and duties will be divided between you. For example, will one of you focus on sales, while the other takes care of the production plant? Or will each of you be in charge of a separate business facility, such as a store or restaurant?

It's generally better to establish business roles with some definition, rather than just assuming that "everyone will pitch in with whatever needs doing." Although in fact you may all need to cover each other's roles from time to time, most owners find that the business runs more smoothly if everyone knows what their primary responsibilities are.

Also consider the "key person" concept. Is there anyone whose presence in the business is vital? For instance, yourself? If so, it makes sense to consider what your business would do in the event that a key player is lost. This may be especially important to lenders who would be concerned if the business's revenue stream were interrupted.

Management Gaps

For some businesses, particularly those just starting out, there may be important positions in the business that remain to be filled, or there may be some gaps in the owner's experience or skills that need to be addressed.

If that's true in your case, your plan should explain the situation. If, for example, you're launching a new magazine but are still searching for the right managing editor, you should explain the importance of the position and the fact that finding the right person is crucial to your success. You may want to outline the qualities and experience you're looking for. Be sure to list a ballpark salary that you expect to pay — you'll need it to complete your financial projections.

If you recognize gaps in your own experience, you should explain what they are and how you expect to compensate. In many cases, you can hire a business or an individual to take care of the tasks that are not your strengths. For instance, you can hire an accountant if you don't know much about recordkeeping, and you can hire a salesperson if personal selling is not your strong suit. The fact that you admit your potential weaknesses will generally not diminish your business's potential in the eyes of an outside reader, as long as you have a realistic plan to fill the gaps.

Staffing Plans

It can be difficult to predict how many people your business is going to need, particularly if you're in a new business. You should find that the process of creating a business plan will be very helpful in this respect. As you consider each of the key areas, you'll develop a picture of all the activities that go into running your business. Then you can estimate how many and what kind of employees you'll need, how much you'll need to pay them, and what your total payroll and contractor costs will be.

At one extreme, your business plan can make it clear that you won't ever have any employees. What little you can't do, you'll contract out. Many businesses built around performing services tend to be near this end of the spectrum. At the other extreme, your plan may reveal a need for an exponentially expanding sales force until you have reps in every major city in the United States.

Even if it's just for your own benefit, a description or even a checklist of all the different tasks performed by individuals (or classes of individuals, if you have many employees) may be useful. You may want to include an organization chart to show who reports to whom, if that is a part of your business's structure.

Chapter 8

Financial Plans

Unless you are thinking of starting a religious or charitable organization, the main reason you're starting a business is because you think you can make money at it. The drive to be your own boss might have caused you to quit being an employee and *start* your business, but the quest for income is what keeps it going. When you develop a business plan, financial projections and cash flow analysis are among the most critical elements.

You have a close personal interest in the financial performance of your business. So does everyone else who might be looking at your business plan. Not surprisingly, the portions of your plan dealing with expected financial performance will usually come under the closest scrutiny. A potential lender will want to know what you'll be doing with the money it lends you and how you plan to generate the necessary income to pay the money back.

Fortunately, or perhaps unfortunately, the financial projections are the most formalistic and stylized documents that you will have to prepare. There are certain accounting conventions that you are expected to follow. Simple accounting or business planning software can be extremely helpful in formatting the statements and doing the math. For example, four of the plans in this book were originally formatted using Business Plan Pro™ from Palo Alto Software. You can generally purchase such software for under $100, and it's well worth the price.

In some cases, you may need to prepare the financial portions of your plan in conformance with "generally accepted accounting principles" (GAAP). This usually occurs when the business owner is creating a plan in an effort to obtain a loan or line of credit, and the bank or potential investor requests that you follow these formally established accounting rules. It also means that you'll need to get an accountant involved in preparing that portion of the plan. If the financial material was created in conformance with GAAP, that should be noted within the plan. The same is true if the financial statements have been audited.

Important Financial Information to Include

- ***Important assumptions*** — *statements that must be assumed to be true as the premise for all your projections*

- ***Breakeven analysis*** – *a description of the sales volume needed to cover all your costs (may be omitted for businesses that have been operating for some time)*

- ***Projected sales volume*** – *your assessment of how much you can realistically sell at your chosen price points, in a given period of time*

- ***Projected profit and loss*** – *the statement that details your income, your expenses, and the difference between the two which equals your profit or loss*

- ***Projected cash flow budget*** – *the statement that shows the timing of cash inflows and outflows for your business*

- ***Projected balance sheet*** – *the statement that shows your business's projected net worth after operating for a specified period of time*

The type of financial information that you're going to need to prepare your analysis will depend on whether your business is an established enterprise or is just starting out.

As a general rule, however, you should plan to include three years of projected financial statements, unless your lender requests five years. The first year's statements should be broken down by month; later years' information can be presented on a quarterly or annual basis.

Startup Business Financial Information

If you're just starting out, you face a special challenge because there is no history of operations, profitable or otherwise. You're going to have to rely almost entirely on financial projections; that is, *prospective* ("pro-forma") statements based on assumptions that you've made as to how your business will perform in the future.

You'll also have to rely heavily on your ability to sell yourself as a potentially successful business owner. In large part, your ability to capture the readers' imagination and get them excited about the possibilities is a substitute for the historical information that doesn't exist.

Startup businesses, or business expansions, frequently involve a startup budget that is different in character from the operating budget of an ongoing business. These startup costs will be detailed separately, in the startup summary of the company summary section of your plan (see page 23).

The startup funding plan will show how your personal investment will be used to fund the business (see page 27). If you plan to contribute any personal assets to the business, such as a car, truck, office machines or computers, etc., you should provide specific details on that as well. Other documents that may be required, particularly if you're trying to obtain outside financing, are a personal financial statement and your income tax returns for the last few years.

As with an established business, you're also going to need to provide a statement of important assumptions, a breakeven analysis, and projected sales forecasts, profit and loss statements, cash flow budget worksheets, and balance sheets. These documents quantify the results you expect to achieve through your operations.

Historical Financial Information

An existing business can bolster the credibility of its business plan by documenting the results of its ongoing operations. A proven track record is very persuasive evidence of your chances for continued success.

Hopefully, you've been creating and maintaining financial records since the inception of your business. If so, most of your work is done. You'll already have balance sheets, income statements, and cash flow budgets for the last three to five years (or since inception if your business is less than three years old). As always, the relative importance of each type of document will vary with the characteristics of your particular business.

These financial statements are the most objective pieces of evidence that lenders will look at to either support or contradict your forecasts for future performance. Generally speaking, the reader of your plan will expect that "history will repeat itself" and that your business's future will be an extension of the trends that are shown in your historical statements. Therefore, if you expect that the picture will improve dramatically, be sure your plan provides solid evidence as to why that will happen.

Our sample business plans (beginning on page 87) have left out the historical financial statements, in the interest of saving space. But be sure to include them in your own finished plan.

ESTABLISHING REASONABLE ASSUMPTIONS

When you draft a business plan, you need to make many different types of assumptions. Some of these are so basic that they remain, appropriately, unstated. For example, although the U.S. economy might cease to function predictably if the country were invaded by Canadian armed forces, it's safe to assume that no such invasion will occur.

Beyond that, there are several broad types of assumptions that you're going to have to make. These assumptions are what support and quantify the financial projections that you'll make in the plan.

Assumptions About the Business Environment

As you draft your business plan, you may feel somewhat overwhelmed by the sheer number of external factors that can dramatically impact your business. Most of these factors are simply beyond your control. For example, if you're planning to take out a variable-rate loan, you'll have to make an assumption about the interest rate during the planning period, which may be dependent upon the general state of the economy.

Work Smart

If you feel very uncomfortable predicting an average interest rate, you may want to draw up several sets of financial projections using best-case, worst-case, and most-likely-case interest rate assumptions. However, this is rather time-consuming and most business owners will simply choose the most-likely-case scenario, for initial planning purposes.

As another example, while Census data may tell you how many people are physically located in your geographic market, the percentage of people who will actually buy your product or service isn't so easy to nail down. But such assumptions are an absolute requirement when it comes time to project sales.

Besides the assumptions about interest rates and about market demand for your product, your business plan should list any other assumptions on which the financial statements depend. For the reader, and for yourself as well, the list serves as a warning that if an assumption later turns out to be false, your business may not perform as expected.

Examples

Here are some examples of the wide variety of types of statements you may want to include in your assumptions:

- *We assume continued stable government and political structure in the African countries we will tour.*

- *There will be no major competitive threat from a currently unknown source.*

- *No sales will be made on credit.*

- *Fifty percent of sales in our retail gift shop will occur during the last three months of the year.*

- *Personnel burden (the extra costs of payroll taxes and benefits for employees) will be 15% of total payroll.*

Despite the difficulty in ensuring that your assumptions are reasonable, there is a lot of help available. For example, a bank can provide you with historical information regarding rate changes, and possibly even a prediction about future rates. Vendors can tell you about product availability issues. Get as much information as you need to feel comfortable with your ability to make reasonable assumptions. Remember, however, that no one is likely to be right all the time. If the assumptions on which you base your planning are generally "in the ballpark," you have done a good job.

Assumptions About Your Business

As you work your way through the planning process, you will be called on to take your best guess regarding the key operational issues facing any business. You'll have to make estimates regarding productivity, capacity, cash flow, costs, and a hundred other interrelated factors. For example, if you are considering a manufacturing business, how many units of product can you expect a particular piece of equipment to produce? What assumptions can you make about the equipment's reliability and potential down-time?

From a practical standpoint, there are two potential sources for the information you need to make reasonable assumptions. If you have an existing business, you have your personal experience on which to rely. You know how much to expect from an employee or how reliable your production equipment is. Even if you're taking on a new product or trying to enter a new market, your experience in the industry in general will serve you well.

But what about the business owner who has relatively little experience in a particular field? The best bet is to tap into existing sources of information. One excellent source is industry groups or associations. These organizations exist to further the aims of business owners within a specific industry or field of endeavor. They can provide information regarding a wide variety of topics. Local chambers of commerce and other civic organizations can often provide valuable demographic information regarding the specific geographic market in which you will compete.

Potential vendors and suppliers can also be consulted to get information regarding costs, product availability, timing requirements, etc.

While there is no substitute for personal experience, you can learn a lot by drawing on the experience of those around you. Unless you're starting a wholly new type of business, there will be someone around with experience at what you're planning to do. You'd be surprised how willing even potential competitors are to share information, if asked in the right way. This is particularly true if your business will serve a limited geographic market and won't directly compete with a similar business located some distance away.

BREAKEVEN ANALYSIS

The "breakeven point" for your business is the sales volume you need to achieve in order to cover all the costs of your business. It's extremely important for you to know what your breakeven point is, and to have confidence that you can achieve that volume of sales within a reasonable period of time — otherwise, you need to do more work on the marketing portion of the plan, or to rethink your business idea altogether!

Also, it's a good idea to recalculate your breakeven point periodically, because it will change whenever your costs or your pricing structure changes. Knowing your breakeven point is a good way to keep a handle on all your costs over time.

Fixed and Variable Costs

So, how do you calculate breakeven? Start by determining all the costs of doing business. You may want to use your income statement form as an aid (see page 72).

Virtually all of your business's costs will fall, more or less neatly, into one of two categories:

- "Variable costs" increase directly in proportion to the level of sales in dollars or units sold. Depending on your type of business, some examples of variable costs would be the price you paid for the items you sold (cost of goods sold), sales commissions, shipping charges, delivery charges, costs of direct materials or supplies, wages of part-time or temporary employees, and sales or production bonuses.

- "Fixed costs" remain the same, at least in the short term, regardless of your level of sales. Depending on your type of business, some typical examples would be rent, interest on debt, insurance, plant and equipment expenses, business licenses, and salary of permanent full-time workers.

Your accountant can help you determine which of your costs are fixed and which are variable, but here the key word is "help." In order to be accurate, the ultimate classification has to be done by someone who's intimately familiar with your business operations—which probably means you.

Combination Costs

Some costs are a combination of fixed and variable: a certain minimum level will be incurred regardless of your sales levels, but the costs rise as your volume increases. As an analogy, think about your phone bill: you probably pay an access or line charge that is the same each month, and you probably also pay a charge based on the volume of calls you make. Strictly speaking, these costs should be separated into their fixed and variable components, but that may be more trouble than it's worth for a small business.

Save Time

To simplify things, just decide which type of cost (fixed or variable) is the most important for the particular item, and then classify the whole item according to the more important characteristic. For example, in a telemarketing business, if your phone call volume charges are normally greater than your line access charges, you'd classify the entire bill as variable.

Variable Costs Per Unit

If you add up all your variable costs for the accounting period, and divide by the number of units sold, you will arrive at the cost per unit. This cost should remain constant, regardless of how few or how many units you sell. If yours is a service business, you may be able to divide your variable costs by the number of jobs performed (if the jobs are essentially similar) or by the hours spent on all jobs (if the jobs vary greatly in size).

Calculating the Breakeven Point

Once you know what your variable costs are, as well as your overall fixed costs for the business, you can determine your breakeven point: the volume of sales needed to at least cover all your costs. You can also compute the new breakeven point that you'd need to meet if your cost structure changed (for example, if you undertook a major expansion project or bought some new office equipment, thus increasing your fixed costs). The computation is best explained through an example.

Example

 Assume that the financial statements for Lillian's Bakery reveal that the bakery's total fixed monthly costs are $4,900, and its variable costs per unit of production (loaf of raisin coffee cake) are $.30.

Further assume that each loaf sells for $1.00. Therefore, after the $.30 per loaf variable costs are covered, each loaf sold can contribute $.70 toward covering fixed costs.

Dividing fixed costs by the contribution to those costs per unit of sales tells Lillian's Bakery at what level of sales it will break even. In this case: $4,900/$.70 = 7,000 loaves.

As sales exceed 7,000 loaves per month, Lillian's Bakery earns a profit. Sales of less than 7,000 loaves produce a loss.

Lillian's Bakery can see that a 1,000-loaf increase in sales over the break-even point to 8,000 loaves will produce a $700 profit, and a 3,000-loaf increase to 10,000 will produce a $2,100 profit. On the other hand, a decline in sales of 1,000 loaves from break-even to 6,000 loaves will produce a loss of $700, and a 3,000 decrease from the 7,000 break-even point produces a $2,100 loss.

Presenting this information in your business plan is generally done in the form of a graph, with sales units (or dollars) forming one axis of the graph and profits (and losses) forming the other axis. (For an example, see Emma's Espresso on page 279). The reader can immediately see the effect that various sales levels will have on your bottom line.

PROJECTED SALES FORECAST

Every financial plan must include a forecast of sales for the business. Any forecast will include some uncertainty. Your sales forecast probably won't match your actual sales because of the many variables that ultimately affect the final amount. The economy, inflation, competitive influences, and a whole range of other variables will affect your actual sales. No matter how much uncertainty you associate with these variables, you must come up with an estimate of future sales.

Projecting Sales for an Existing Business

If your business has been operating for a number of years, your sales reports for the last few years are the best starting point for estimating sales for the coming year. Simply adjust last year's sales figures as necessary to reflect the conditions you expect next year.

If you anticipate making changes that will affect your sales volume in the future, the sales forecast section of the plan should explain those changes, and why they will have the effect you state. Similarly, if you expect that external changes will have an effect on your sales volume, such as a new highway, a plant closing, changing demographics in your area, or new competition entering the market, this is the place to say so.

You might also want to explain your strategy for meeting the challenges you foresee — for instance, will you hire an additional salesperson if you expect sales would otherwise drop, or will you need more production capacity if you expect sales revenue to increase dramatically?

Case Study — Sales Forecasting

John Divot owns a golf supply retail store. John will use last year's sales figures to prepare his sales forecast for the next six months. Here is the sales information from the first six months of last year:

January	$18,000
February	$18,500
March	$20,500
April	$28,900
May	$32,300
June	$36,600

John expects sales for this year to be 1 percent higher in the off season and 1.5 percent higher during the golf season, which begins in April. John forecasts his sales for the first six months of this year to be as follows:

January	$18,180
February	$18,685
March	$20,705
April	$29,333
May	$32,785
June	$37,150

Projecting Sales for a New Business

Before we take a look at some ways to estimate revenues for a startup business, a word of caution. Estimating your sales will be an inexact science. Don't count too heavily on your projections and, if you're going to err, err on the conservative side in predicting how much business you'll do in your first year.

Product vendors may be an excellent source of sales data. If your new business is one that will have high inventory levels, suppliers or warehouse facilities may be a potential source of sales data.

For example, assume you plan to open a grocery store. You would purchase the majority of your product from a primary grocery distributor. Usually a distributor of any significant size will have access to other grocery stores' sales in your trade area. This could be your starting point for your sales potential. You will have to make adjustments to the sales figure based, for example, on site selection, competition, and marketing.

Warning

Be careful when dealing with product vendors to determine sales potential. Some may just tell you what you want to hear in order to get your business. Back up their forecasts with other sources.

Most libraries have a wide range of information available for specific types of enterprises. The trade publications and trade associations are good sources of overall sales information for your specific industry. These publications will generally break out sales by geographic region and by business type.

The Bureau of the Census publications, available in larger libraries, can provide you with a lot of information on sales volume for various business types by geographic location. This information is usually a few years out of date, so if your new business is one that will be greatly affected by the time lag, you'll want to make adjustments for it. Remember that your sales figure will still be just an educated guess. Along with the sales figure, Census publications will provide other financial details, such as average cost of goods sold and payroll.

Example

Let's say you want to estimate sales for a fictitious submarine sandwich shop in Cedar Rapids, Iowa.

The Census of Retail Trade, a Census Bureau publication, showed that there were 284 eating and drinking establishments in Cedar Rapids. The average sales volume per eating establishment was $548,866. Based on other research, it was determined that this in itself was not a realistic number for the planned sub shop, and adjustments need to be made for other known facts.

Assume that the average customer will spend $4.50 per meal. Also assume that the restaurant will have between 150 to 200 customers on an average day. Multiplying the $4.50 times 175 customers (average of 150 and 200) times 365 days, the sales will compute to $287,438 per year.

PROJECTED PROFIT AND LOSS STATEMENT

Also called an income statement, a profit and loss statement lists your income, expenses, and the difference between the two, which is your net income (or loss). Your business's tax return will use a variation of the profit and loss statement to determine your potentially taxable income.

The profit and loss statement shows you a summary of the flow of transactions your business has over the entire accounting period. In other words, the statement shows you what happens during the period between balance sheets.

Three years' worth of projected income-statement data is normally presented, so that you can make comparisons and identify trends.

For a sample form that you can use to construct your own statement, see the next page. The categories provided are the ones that are most common for the average small business — be sure to add or subtract categories as appropriate to your particular company.

	JAN	FEB	MAR	APR	MAY	JUN
Your Company						
Projected Profit and Loss Statement - Annual by Month						
Revenue:						
Gross Sales						
Less: Sales Returns						
Net Sales						
Cost of Goods Sold:						
Materials						
Labor						
Other Direct Expenses						
Indirect Expenses						
Total Cost of Goods Sold						
Gross Profit (Loss)						
Expenses:						
Advertising						
Bad Debts						
Bank Charges						
Credit Card Fees						
Delivery Expenses						
Depreciation						
Dues and Subscriptions						
Equipment Rental						
Insurance						
Interest						
Maintenance						
Miscellaneous						
Office Expenses						
Operating Supplies						
Payroll Taxes						
Permits and Licenses						
Postage						
Rent						
Telephone						
Travel						
Utilities						
Wages and Benefits						
Total Expenses						
Net Operating Income						
Other Income:						
Gain (Loss) on Asset Sales						
Interest Income						
Total Other Income						
Net Income Before Tax						
Net Income After Tax						

Your Company						
Projected Profit and Loss Statement - Annual by Month						
JUL	**AUG**	**SEP**	**OCT**	**NOV**	**DEC**	**TOTAL**

The data on your projected profit and loss consist of the following:

- sales revenue

- sales returns and allowances

- cost of goods sold

- selling, general, and administrative expenses

- depreciation and amortization expenses

- interest expense

A detailed, month-by-month P & L should be provided for the first year. For later years, you may want to break down the information by quarter, or you may decide to provide an annual summary.

Depending on whether you are preparing a projected profit and loss statement for an existing business or a startup enterprise, you may have some difficulty coming up with reliable estimates for some of these figures. Dun & Bradstreet and other financial information purveyors may be able to provide information regarding industry average expenditures for cost of goods sold, general and administrative expenses, and other major categories as a percentage of sales. As you talk to suppliers and receive bids from them, sign leases for equipment or facilities, find out the going rate for employees in the jobs you'll be hiring for, etc., you should be able to fill in the blanks.

PROJECTED CASH FLOW BUDGETS

In its simplest form, cash flow is the movement of money in and out of your business. It could be described as the process in which your business uses cash to generate goods or services for the sale to your customers, collects the cash from the sales, and then completes this cycle all over again.

"Inflows" are the movement of money into your business, and are most likely from the sale of your goods or services to your customers. If you extend credit to your customers and allow them to charge the sale of the goods or services to their account, then an inflow occurs as you collect on the customers' accounts. The proceeds from a bank loan are also a cash inflow.

"Outflows" are the movement of money out of your business, and are generally the result of paying expenses. If your business involves reselling goods, your largest outflow is most likely to be for the purchase of retail inventory.

A manufacturing business's largest outflows will most likely be for payroll and for the purchases of raw materials and other components needed for the manufacturing of the final product. Purchasing fixed assets, paying back loans, and paying accounts payable are also cash outflows.

A good way to learn respect for the concept of cash flow is to compare it to the idea of profit. If a retail business is able to buy a retail item for $1,000 and sell it for $2,000, then it has made a $1,000 gross profit. But what if the buyer of the retail item is slow to pay his or her bill, and six months pass before the bill is paid? Using accrual accounting, the retail business still shows a profit, but what about the bills it has to pay during the six months that pass? It will not have the cash to pay them, despite the profit earned on the sale.

As you can see, profit and cash flow are two entirely different concepts, each with entirely different results. The concept of profit is somewhat narrow, and only looks at income and expenses over an entire accounting period. Cash flow, on the other hand, is more dynamic. It is concerned with the movement of money in and out of a business. More importantly, it is concerned with the time at which the movement of the money takes place. You might even say the concept of cash flow is more in line with reality!

Therefore, your cash flow projections will be the most important financial statements in your business plan. You need to include a month-by-month cash flow projection for at least the first year. For a sample form on which you can compute your own cash flow, see page 76. In using the form, note that the cash that remains at the end of the first month will become the beginning cash balance for the second month, and so on through all the months of the year.

For later years, you can project annually by quarter, or even annually by year, as you'll see in our sample business plans.

If you are preparing a cash flow budget worksheet for an existing business, you can base your estimates of cash inflows and outflows on historical information. On the other hand, if you're a startup business, you should base your estimates of cash sources and uses on the revenues and expenses listed in the projected profit and loss statements. Accordingly, we recommend that you complete a projected profit and loss statement before completing the cash flow budget worksheet.

If you are seeking a loan, an important feature of your cash flow statement is that it will show the lender exactly how you're going to afford the loan payments.

Your Company Cash Flow Budget Worksheet - Annual by Month						
	JAN	**FEB**	**MAR**	**APR**	**MAY**	**JUN**
Beginning Cash Balance						
Cash Inflows (Income):						
Accounts Receivable Collections						
Loan Proceeds						
Sales & Receipts						
Other						
Total Cash Inflows						
Available Cash Balance						
Cash Outflows (Expenses):						
Advertising						
Bank Service Charges						
Credit Card Fees						
Delivery						
Health Insurance						
Insurance						
Interest						
Inventory Purchases						
Miscellaneous						
Office						
Payroll						
Payroll Taxes						
Professional Fees						
Rent or Lease						
Subscriptions & Dues						
Supplies						
Taxes & Licenses						
Utilities & Telephone						
Other						
Travel						
Maintenance						
Subtotal						
Other Cash Outflows:						
Capital Purchases						
Loan Principal						
Owner's Draw						
Other:						
Subtotal						
Total Cash Outflows						
Ending Cash Balance						

Your Company						
Cash Flow Budget Worksheet - Annual by Month						
JUL	AUG	SEP	OCT	NOV	DEC	TOTAL

Planning Your Cash Flow

If you were able to do business in a perfect world, you'd probably like to have a cash inflow (a cash sale) occur every time you experience a cash outflow (pay an expense). But you know all too well that business takes place in the real world, and things just don't happen like that.

Instead, cash outflows and inflows rarely occur together. More often than not, it seems, cash inflows lag behind your cash outflows, leaving your business short of money. Think of this money shortage as your cash flow gap.

When creating your business plan, you have the time and opportunity to adjust your projected cash flow statements. If you notice a gap, and especially if the gap is large, try to change your operating plans until the gap disappears. For instance, if you expect a gap in October as you load up on inventory for the December selling season, consider reducing or postponing some of the expenses you'd normally pay that month. You might be able to reduce your travel expenses that month, or avoid purchasing office supplies, or change your insurance payment due dates so that none fall in October.

The point is not only to make your business plan look good (although that's important, obviously) but also to do as much as you can ahead of time to avoid any cash flow gaps and the havoc they can wreak upon your business.

PROJECTED BALANCE SHEETS

The balance sheet is a statement of your company's relative wealth or financial position *at a given point in time*. It's often referred to as a "snapshot," because it gives you a fairly clear picture of the business at that moment, but does not in itself reveal how the business arrived there or where it's going next. That's one reason why the balance sheet is not the whole story — you must also look at the information from each of the other financial statements (and at historical information as well) to get the most benefit from the data.

In your business plan, you'll want to provide at least three years of projected balance sheet information. You may want to provide detailed, month-by-month information for the first year, as our sample business plans have done.

The balance sheet consists of three categories of items: assets, liabilities, and stockholders' or owners' equity.

Assets. Assets are generally divided into two groups: current assets and noncurrent (long-term) assets. They are usually presented in order of liquidity, with current assets (cash and those that will be converted to cash within one year) appearing first. Current assets include cash, accounts and notes receivable, inventories, prepaid expenses, and any other short-term investments. Long-term assets include land, buildings, machinery and equipment, and capitalized leases, less any accumulated depreciation and amortization.

Liabilities. Liabilities are normally presented in order of their claim on the company's assets (i.e., liabilities due within one year are presented before liabilities due several years from now). Liabilities include accounts payable, notes payable, income taxes payable, the current portion of any long-term debt, and any other liabilities due within the accounting period. Long-term liabilities include a mortgage or any other debt that will become due after the relevant accounting period, deferred income taxes, or other deferred debts.

Equity. For sole proprietorships, equity is usually a one-line entry that represents the difference between the business's assets and its liabilities.

For co-owned businesses such as partnerships or limited liability companies, the statement should show the division of equity between or among the co-owners.

For corporations, stockholders' equity is presented properly when each class of stock is presented with all its relevant information (for example, number of shares authorized, shares issued, shares outstanding, and par value). If retained earnings are restricted or appropriated, this also should be shown.

See page 80 for a sample balance sheet form that you can adapt for your company. We've filled in the blanks for a fictitious company, to show you how the numbers should add up. You can also use other formats, as illustrated in the sample business plans.

SOURCES AND USES OF FUNDS STATEMENT

If your business is seeking a loan or investment by an outsider, it's important to show prospective financiers exactly how much money you need and how you expect to spend it. The sources and uses of funds statement is the best way to highlight this information. It will also indicate the extent to which you're investing your own funds in the business – something that is highly important to an investor. With your own assets on the line, you'll certainly be more motivated to make sure the business succeeds.

Joel's Chocolate Company, Inc.
Projected Balance Sheet - December 31, ____

Assets			Liabilities and Capital		
Current Assets:			**Current Liabilities:**		
Cash		$815,840	Accounts Payable	$7,500	
Accounts Receivable	$22,000		Sales Taxes Payable	800	
Less: Reserve for Bad Debts 1,980		20,020	Payroll Taxes Payable	17,500	
Merchandise Inventory		15,000	Accrued Wages Payable	60,000	
Prepaid Expenses		5,200	Unearned Revenues	78,000	
Notes Receivable		0	Short-Term Notes Payable	0	
Total Current Assets		$856,060	Short-Term Bank Loans Payable	0	
			Total Current Liabilities		$163,800
Fixed Assets:					
Vehicles	0		**Long-Term Liabilities:**		
Less: Accumulated Dep.	0	0	Long-Term Notes Payable	50,000	
Furniture and Fixtures	25,000		Mortgages Payable	0	
Less: Accumulated Dep.	9,000	16,000	**Total Long-Term Liabilities**		50,000
Equipment	160,000				
Less: Accumulated Dep.	60,000	100,000	**Total Liabilities**		213,800
Buildings	0				
Less: Accumulated Dep.	0	0	**Capital:**		
Land	0		Paid-in Capital	758,260	
Total Fixed Assets		116,000	Additional Capital	0	
Other Assets:			**Total Capital**		758,260
Goodwill		0			
Total Other Assets		0			
Total Assets		$972,060	**Total Liabilities and Capital**		$972,060

The sources and uses of funds document should start by stating the total amount of capital you need to start operations, to finance your expansion project, or to do whatever else it is that you want to accomplish with your plan.

It should detail how you expect to spend the money, in categories such as: working capital, facilities, equipment, marketing expenses, staff hiring, initial inventory, etc.

Then, it should detail how you expect to obtain the money: investment by you, sale of stock in the company, a short-term line of credit, long-term debt, a mortgage, etc. The total funds needed should equal the total funds to be sourced, of course!

Chapter 9

Using The Completed Plan

Your completed business plan is a document that you can use as a blueprint as you begin or continue to operate the company. It's also a document that you can use to communicate with both internal and external audiences.

But creating a business plan should yield many benefits over and above the actual document. Most importantly, you will have established a planning process that you can use over and over again, improving it each time by incorporating the experience you have gained. The existence of both the *document* and the *process* enable you to derive the maximum benefit from the work you put into creating the plan.

The plan can also become a tracking and evaluation tool. Because your plan will set forth a number of marketing, operational, and financial milestones, you can meaningfully interpret your actual operating results against the baseline established by the plan.

Let's take a look at how you can effectively use your business plan to run your company.

MONITORING YOUR PROGRESS

A well-written business plan defines the goals and objectives that you wish to achieve over the next few years in specific, quantifiable terms. It may project a certain level of sales by a given date, the acquisition of a certain number of clients, or any of a number of other objective measures of success. Whatever the conditions that spell success, you'll want to watch your progress toward those goals over time. If you're on track, great!

If not, you're in a position to take steps to get back on track before it's too late.

The process of monitoring your business's performance can be relatively painless. The following pages discuss the issues to consider.

How Frequently Should You Look?

As a practical matter, you'll probably have a feel for how you're doing because of your involvement with the day-to-day activities of your business. If you make the bank deposits each night, if you pay the bills each month, if you balance the books at the end of the month, then you already know a lot about how your business is doing. But it's worthwhile to supplement this familiarity with some hard and fast milestones.

Using milestones is simply a decision to take a look at a specific performance measure at a particular point in time. You should select your milestones to accommodate two competing considerations. On the one hand, milestones should be infrequent enough so that there is a meaningful amount of information available to analyze. On the other hand, milestones must occur frequently enough so that you can take appropriate action if you see that interim goals aren't being reached. With luck, you'll be able to schedule these periodic business check-ups to coincide with activities you would do anyway, such as balancing your checking account.

Many larger businesses take a look, each month, at certain performance measures that they deem especially important. We suggest that your business do the same, so that you can make any necessary corrections quickly and avoid major problems. Waiting until the end of the year, or even the calendar quarter, to check your progress may be too late.

Selecting Performance Measures

Almost every aspect of your business can probably be measured against some objective yardstick of success. The ability of a salesperson can be measured by the number of sales per month or by the cumulative amount of sales, year-to-date. If your business gets most of its profit from the more expensive products or services you provide, sales revenue (or dollar amount per sale) will be of far more interest than the raw number of sales.

If possible, try to integrate all of your performance measures into the routine of your operations. For example, if a lender requires monthly statements of income and expense, use them to monitor performance. You may want to track information the lender doesn't want, but you can piggyback that data-gathering onto your required reports.

Assessing Your Performance

Once you begin operations according to your business plan, there are two possible outcomes. One is that your projections and assumptions prove to be relatively accurate. In that case, it's likely that your business will be performing as you had hoped. More likely, however, things aren't going exactly as projected. These departures from your plan may be small and not a source of concern, or they may be substantial and require immediate action on your part.

When Things Go According to the Plan

Let's consider the first outcome: you did a good job of planning and, basically, your business is operating the way you'd like to see it. Your performance measurement system is generating data showing that the goals and objectives set forth in your business plan are being met. Congratulations! As many race car drivers say, "I'd rather be lucky than good any day." If you've written a plan and your business developed just as you projected, you're definitely one or the other. So, what do you do about it?

First, make an effort to extend your planning horizon further out in time. Begin to "firm up" the numbers for periods beyond the initial planning window. Fine-tune the plan to get an even better picture of where you're heading. For you, keeping the plan current is easy.

Second, and more importantly, begin looking for ways to improve on what you've done so far. You've begun to build a track record of success and you want to keep on building. Your basic business idea was, most likely, sound (never completely discount the luck factor), and you now have an opportunity to expand, refine, and innovate. If you haven't considered the long-term future of your business, start thinking. If you've set aggressive goals (and most business owners do), consider what you'll have if your business stays on track for three years, or five.

When Things Go Wrong

Despite your best efforts, sometimes a business just doesn't take off the way you expected. The unfortunate fact is that a large percentage of new small businesses fail. But then, most small business owners don't bother to create a written business plan unless they are absolutely required to (as is usually the case if you need outside investors or bank financing). Without a written plan, it's just that much harder to cope when your business isn't meeting your goals.

You, however, will have a written plan, so let's see how it can help you out when things go wrong.

Deviation Analysis

We've included a chart, below, that you can use to compare your expected results against your actual results for any given month, and for the year to date. The difference between the actual and expected results is the deviation — and it can be positive (in your favor) or negative. In the columns labeled "Budget," you can insert the data from the pro-forma income statements in your business plan. Comparing the "actual" data with the "budget" will tell you the deviation, either positive or negative. Once you know the extent of your deviation from what you had hoped to achieve, you can decide what to do about it.

Financial Results	This Month	This Month	This Month	Year to Date	Year to Date	Year to Date	Prior Year to Date
(In 1000's)	Actual	Budget	Deviation	Actual	Budget	Deviation	Actual
Sales Revenue							
Direct Costs							
Marketing Costs							
Marketing Contribution							
New Units Sold: Line A							
New Units Sold: Line B							

When things don't go well for a business, it isn't always easy to figure out why. It could be that your business plan contains some faulty assumptions or conclusions. Or it could be that your business is having operational difficulties of some sort. In either event, you have to isolate the cause of the problem before you can correct it.

Some problems will be internal to your business, while others will result from external factors beyond your direct control.

External factors can be very widespread, such as a downturn in the entire local economy, or they can be specific to your business, such as a vendor's failure to deliver on time. Internal factors relate to the specific processes and activities that you use in running your business. An employee may not be performing as you'd like, or operating cost estimates contained in the business plan might have been too low.

In all probability, there won't be just a single root cause for your business's problems. As you look for the source of your problems, don't be surprised if you have to address several issues. The key concern is to identify all of the reasons why your business isn't going the way you'd like. Then you can consider what to do about them.

KEEPING YOUR PLAN CURRENT

You should treat your business plan as a dynamic document that should be kept current as your business evolves. You've invested a good deal of your time and effort to create the plan in the first place. If you don't keep the plan current, you can look forward to a similar effort the next time you need a written plan. Remember, it's almost always easier to edit an existing document than to create a new one from scratch.

Planning Interval

Many people think of "planning" as an annual process. Thousands of companies publish an annual plan each year, outlining their expectations about operating results for the coming 12 months.

Realistically, though, you're probably planning all the time. Most business owners are always thinking about ways to make their business better. In discussing a "planning interval," what we're really suggesting is periodically setting aside a certain amount of time to create or update your written business plan.

So how do you select a reasonable planning interval? Start with the assumption that you'd like to have at least one planning period each year. Many factors that affect your business will be tied to some annual cycle. For example, income taxes are due yearly, and federal safety rules require posting annual summaries of information. Also, many employees will expect annual raises or bonuses. This and other factors make annual planning after tax time a reasonable starting point, though your circumstances may require a different planning interval.

Example

 Consider a business located on a small chain of lakes. It operates a marina and boat repair facility from spring to fall. As the boating season ends, the business switches to servicing snowmobiles and supporting ice fishers. Even though the results of marina operations are available as of the end of the season, that information is of limited value in planning for the coming winter.

The information that is meaningful to the business owner trying to plan for winter relates to the prior winter's operations. Planning for summer operations and for winter operations wouldn't have to occur at the same time, and there would likely be benefits from scheduling two planning sessions.

Part II

Five Sample Business Plans

Now that you have a good understanding of the elements that a good business plan should include and the purposes that each section serves, it's time to take a look at some real, live business plans that have been created by and for entrepreneurs like yourself.

In Part II, we provide you with five sample business plans written for different types of businesses, in various stages of the business lifecycle. We include a plan for a small service business, a growing manufacturer, a three-person retail operation, a specialty coffee retailer, and a new media company. Four of the plans are for startups, and one is for a business that is already operating but wants to expand its scope (and profitability).

Elevator DataCommand. The plan for Elevator DataComand is designed to gain $200,000 in funding for a significant expansion of this young business. The principals of the company have many years of experience designing industrial controls providing vertical and horizontal automated positioning systems. Elevator DataCommand owns and controls unique technology that is employed in its state-of-the-art product.

The Elevator DataComand plan is instructional in several areas:

- This is a good example of a plan for a manufacturing business.

- This is a young business with break-through technology entering an old industry.

- The business is national in geographic scope, and is strategic in its roll-out.

- This is a business attempting a significant expansion.

- This plan is designed to gain new funding.

Latina Media. This is an exciting company built on the skill, experience and creative mind of its owner, Elena Trujillo. Elena is a recent immigrant to the United States from Mexico, and is quickly exhibiting her entrepreneurial spirit on this side of the border. Elena is really launching two businesses under one name, although the two businesses use the same equipment and are marketed to the same target.

The plan for Latina Media provides several important insights:

- This business targets the fastest growing (and now largest) minority market in the U.S.—the Hispanic population.

- The plan demonstrates a logical approach to presenting two business ideas in one plan.

- This plan offers a strategy for presenting a business built primarily on the creative skill of its owner—Elena's education, experience and contacts are prominently featured early in the plan.

- This business sells creative art products, a unique challenge.

All About the Home. This plan is a wonderful example of what can be accomplished by two determined young business owners. Aaron Horner and Ed Edmonson live in suburban Colorado Springs, and were students in an intensive business plan writing course presented by the local Small Business Development Center. Using material from *NxLevel*™, and meeting one evening per week for 12 weeks, the class participants write their complete business plan.

Neither Aaron nor Ed had any previous experience in writing a business plan. Nevertheless, they completed their thorough and well-written plan—a runner-up award winner at the Colorado state competition—during the 12-week class.

Like the other plans presented here, the plan for All About the Home has much to offer:

- An inexperienced plan writer really CAN create a great plan!

- This plan uses the *NxLevel*™ format—a format that's different from that used in the other four plans included here. It's not the format that's important; it's the information!

- This business is oriented to provide a service, and the plan is a good example of one designed for service businesses.

- This plan, like the plan for Emma's Espresso, uses a novel approach to sales forecasting. If you're struggling to forecast sales for your new business, be sure to check these plans.

Commercial Fitness Equipment. This is a great example of success in business planning. Three young entrepreneurs joined forces to create this interesting retail concept—a commercial fitness equipment vendor with aggressive outside sales activity *plus* a brick-and-mortar storefront.

It's a well-structured plan with some important lessons:

- The owners all left a single employer to launch their new business. If this is your situation, take a few minutes to see how these owners approach the challenge.

- This plan was completed in 30 days. Plans often take 60-90 days to finish.

- This plan has a strong, aggressive style, just like the three owners.

- This business needed $150,000 in startup capital from an outside source. The plan was finished on a Friday afternoon, presented to the angel investor that evening, and the full $150,000 was approved and available the next day!

Emma's Espresso. This is a plan that should appeal to you if you're entertaining an idea for a "microbusiness." Emma's Espresso is a one-person coffee cart planning to set up shop in a permanent indoor location. This is a simple, basic business, but it still requires careful thinking and planning. Emma has done that planning, and created a thorough and workable plan. If you're looking for a straightforward, easily understood plan with all the right parts, this may be the place to start.

Emma's plan offers several important elements:

- The business is dependent on a host location.

- The plan does a good job of addressing "the Four P's of Marketing:" Product, Price, Place and Promotion.

- The plan includes a well-organized SWOT analysis.

- Like the plan for All About the Home, Emma has generated a logical sales forecast based on a top-down (market-based) analysis *and* a bottom-up (breakeven) analysis.

Clearly, all of these companies have benefited greatly from the business planning process. We'd like to note that the names and addresses of Elevator DataComand, Latina Media, Commercial Fitness Equipment and Emma's Espresso, and their owners, have been changed, to protect their privacy.

The Plan For
Elevator DataCommand

NICK EIDEN, Director of Marketing

MATT WOLF, Director of Engineering

DALE CROCKETT, Director of Finance

New York, NY

(212) 956-4812

Copy Number __ of Five.

THE PLAN FOR ELEVATOR DATACOMMAND

1.0 EXECUTIVE SUMMARY

MISSION

The Mission of Elevator DataCommand is to provide the owners of commercial buildings precise, efficient and virtually maintenance-free elevator performance. Elevator DataCommand will become America's premier provider of precise, efficient, and minimal-maintenance elevator control systems.

THE ED20-20

The unique technology owned and controlled by Elevator DataCommand is contained in the ED20-20, the state-of-the-art elevator control system. The ED20-20 is *precise, efficient, and virtually maintenance-free*. Unlike traditional elevator control systems, the ED20-20 doesn't use any mechanical parts for positioning the car. Instead, the ED20-20 uses a state-of-the-art, computerized Electronic Distance Meter (EDM). Very simply, the EDM is able to determine the exact location of the car at all times, and can position the car to predetermined floor locations with extreme accuracy and unfailing consistency. This precise, computerized system allows faster and more efficient use of the elevator. No other elevator service company offers a control system that can approach the ED20-20 in key benefit areas.

OWNERSHIP AND BACKGROUND

Elevator DataCommand (ED) was formed in July of 2001 as a Limited Liability Company in New York, New York. The members of the Company, with equal ownership shares, are Nick Eiden, Director of Marketing; Dale Crockett, Director of Finance; and Matt Wolf, Director of Engineering. Each of the three members is active in the day-to-day operation of the Company and makes a significant contribution to the success of the operation.

Although Elevator DataCommand is a young company, it is grounded on a firm foundation of experience and accomplishment. The engineering, sales and support departments have over 35 years of experience designing industrial controls, providing vertical and horizontal automated positioning systems for companies around the globe. United Airlines, American Airlines, General Motors, Ford, IBM, NASA, the U.S. Navy and U.S. Steel are just a few of the hundreds of companies that have, through the expert assistance of current ED staff, implemented the superior technology incorporated into the ED20-20.

Elevator DataCommand currently conducts all operations at its headquarters in New York, New York. This facility consists of a modern 2,000 sq.ft. building in a professional/industrial business park.

2002 EXPANSION PLAN

Elevator DataCommand will build its sales and profit via a disciplined expansion throughout 2002 and 2003, and will enter the year 2004 with its initial beachhead firmly established. The 2002 Expansion is built upon five key components:

-4-

1. The identification of limited and specific geographic target market penetration points. These areas have been identified as the Mid-Atlantic Region, focused on New York; the South Atlantic Region, focused on Miami; and the Midwest Region, focused on Chicago/Milwaukee.

2. The installation of real-life, commercially active demonstration systems in each of the target areas.

3. The development and successful execution of an effective and efficient marketing strategy to generate sales in each target area.

4. The deployment of an adequate installation and technical support base in each geographic target area.

5. The assurance of sufficient engineering and production capacity to accommodate increased demand.

OBJECTIVES 2002-2003

The primary objectives for 2002 are:

1. Complete an appropriate and actionable business plan by September 30.

2. Secure funding for the 2002 Expansion by November 30.

3. Complete demonstration site installations by October 31.

4. Achieve patent approval on the ED20-20 technology by October 31.

5. Achieve $2,000,000 in sales, with $200,000 net profit before taxes.

Primary objectives for 2003 are:

1. Open a full-service office in Miami, and expand offices in New York and Chicago/Milwaukee. Each office will be staffed with sales and engineering personnel sufficient to sell and service customers in the area.

2. Generate $8,000,000 in sales, with $850,000 net profit before taxes.

Business Plan Highlights

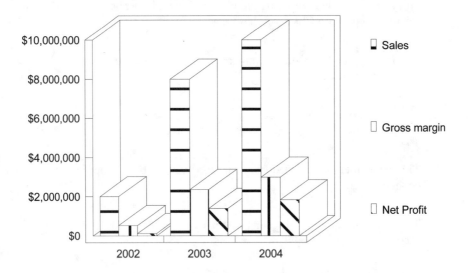

2.0 COMPANY SUMMARY

2.1 Company Mission & Philosophy

The Mission of Elevator DataCommand is to provide the owners of commercial buildings precise, efficient and virtually maintenance-free elevator performance. ED uses its unique <u>technology</u> and its extraordinary <u>service philosophy</u> to provide these elevator control systems to building owners throughout the world.

The <u>unique technology</u> owned and controlled by Elevator DataCommand is contained in the ED20-20, the state-of-the-art elevator control system—The ED 20-20 is *precise, efficient, and virtually maintenance-free.* No other elevator service company offers a control system that can approach the ED20-20 in these three key benefit areas.

The <u>service philosophy</u> of Elevator DataCommand is straightforward: Elevators should not be built with the assumption of the need for constant maintenance and adjustment, they should be built to operate precisely and efficiently for years, with only minimal care. The elevators of the year 2000 and beyond should be so technologically advanced, so standardized in their individual components, and so easily monitored and maintained, that a competent building maintenance team can perform 95% of the work required to service a building's elevators. In addition to creating and installing such control systems, Elevator DataCommand can also provide complete elevator maintenance service to those building owners who wish to use an outside provider. In fact, ED is developing a new and totally unique system of elevator maintenance contracting that may revolutionize the entire elevator service sector.

This philosophy is diametrically opposed to the operating plans of other elevator companies, which seek to build their business on the opposite premise: By selling and installing proprietary components (those that can realistically only be serviced by the original manufacturer) that operate on a failure-prone primitive mechanical basis, building owners can be convinced to buy expensive, never-ending service contracts which form the long-term profit basis for the elevator company. In other words, ED's competition sells the original elevator (at a loss if necessary) in order to get the owner/manager locked into a highly profitable service/maintenance contract.

2.2 Company Ownership

Elevator DataCommand (ED) was formed in July of 2001 as a Limited Liability Company in New York, New York. The members of the Company, with equal ownership shares, are Nick Eiden, Director of Marketing; Dale Crockett, Director of Finance; and Matt Wolf, Director of Engineering. Each of the three members is active in the day-to-day operation of the Company and makes a significant contribution to the success of the operation.

2.3 Company History

Although Elevator DataCommand is a young company, it is grounded on a firm foundation of experience and accomplishment. The engineering, sales and support departments have over 35 years of experience designing industrial controls, providing vertical and horizontal automated positioning systems for companies around the globe. United Airlines, American Airlines, General Motors, Ford, IBM, NASA, the U.S. Navy and U.S. Steel are just a few of the hundreds of companies that have, through the expert assistance of current ED staff, implemented the superior technology incorporated into the ED20-20.

In addition to elevators used in industry, projects have included the design, assembly and installation of technologically advanced positioning systems for tunneling, coal mining, steel production, nuclear refueling, nuclear waste handling, and material and cargo handling. The unique technology designed to accomplish precise, efficient and maintenance-free positioning has been proven in the most vital and difficult industrial applications imaginable. As owner Matt Wolf puts it, "If we can design, manufacture and install a personnel/material transportation and positioning system that is precise, efficient and low-maintenance, a mile and a half deep inside a dusty Australian coal mine, we can do it anywhere!"

In 1999, the Federal Government requested that this advanced positioning technology be applied to the 30-year old personnel elevator in a key building. The installation was accomplished, and the elevator now operates faster, smoother and more accurately than ever before. Additionally, it has not had a single failure since its state-of-the-art update.

The success of this installation, and the overwhelming response of the onsite staff, prompted the founders of Elevator DataCommand to design a control system for direct commercial application. This initial product design has been installed in the elevators in the OfficeSuites in New York. Furthermore, ED is currently installing a refined version of the ED20-20 in a parking facility in Atlanta, the Charles Sprague Building in Chicago, and the Department of Defense in Washington, D.C. Signed contracts for each of these assignments are included in the Supporting Documents.

2.4 The ED20-20 Control System

In order to clearly define the role of the ED20-20, a brief review is appropriate.

All elevators operate with four basic components. First, the Elevator Car, with its doors, is the enclosure which holds the people or freight which is moved from one building level to another. Second, the elevator shaft, or Hoistway, with its doors, provides a vertical path through which the car moves. Third, a Power Source (with its ropes, pulleys or hydraulic pistons) is required that is sufficient to move a fully loaded car through the complete range of floors. Fourth, an electronic system called the Control System is necessary to govern the operation of the elevator, e.g. where is the car now?, what floor is calling?, how many stops will the car make along the way?, how fast will the car travel?, how smoothly will it stop?, how accurately will it stop?, etc.

This fourth component, the Control System, is where the ED20-20 makes its impact. The ED20-20 is a new and unique elevator control system which has the potential to revolutionize the way elevators are controlled worldwide. Traditional primitive control systems all use some form of external measurement. They use a mechanical device to count pulses or rotations. This data is then used to position the elevator. In other words, the control system is never in direct communication with the car; it depends on rotary encoders, cams, switches and/or steel tape that count incrementally. This gap in data transfer, these indirect control mechanisms, all leave too much room for error and failure. For example, if the control system knows that it needs to count 729 revolutions to move from the first floor to the second, what happens if the cable has stretched and the revolutions needed to make a one-floor move have increased? The elevator will be mispositioned at each stop until an elevator service technician corrects the problem. Even then, the problem is ongoing, and maintenance is a constant necessity.

Unlike traditional elevator control systems, the ED20-20 doesn't use any mechanical parts for positioning the car. Instead, the ED20-20 uses a state-of-the-art, computerized Electronic Distance Meter (EDM). Very simply, the EDM uses optic technology to determine the exact location of the car at all times, and can position the car to predetermined floor locations with extreme accuracy and unfailing consistency. This precise, computerized system allows faster and more efficient use of the elevator.

The ED20-20 Control System offers exceptional operational and economic advantages over competitive control systems. These advantages cluster around the three core areas:

PRECISION

- True closed loop positioning system—the only one in the industry.

- No mechanical positioning parts.

- Positioning with accuracy of +/- 1 millimeter.

-8-

EFFICIENCY

- Car down time during installation is only 5-7 days vs. 14-21 days for primitive systems.

- "Creep zone" is eliminated, making floor-to-floor moves faster and smoother.

- Up to 33% increase in the number of passengers handled per hour vs. primitive systems.

- Energy savings of $3,000 to $5,000 per year per elevator vs. primitive systems.

MINIMAL MAINTENANCE

- Uses all industrial grade vs. commercial grade components—longer service life.

- Simple setup and adjustment of floor positions.

- All maintenance diagnostics are done on a simple-to-use computer screen.

- System will self-diagnose any malfunction and call for service.

- Significantly reduced maintenance costs compared to primitive systems.

ED has exclusive license to sell and install this technology in the United States, and is currently in the patenting process. Although the ED20-20 is currently on the leading edge of technology, management will not be satisfied with ED as a simple, product-focused company. Therefore, they are strategically positioning the Company to maintain its technological edge in elevator positioning systems into the future. The details of these intellectual and technological strategic plans are detailed in later chapters.

2.5 Company Locations and Facilities

Elevator DataCommand currently conducts all operations at its headquarters in New York, New York. This facility consists of a modern 2,000 sq.ft. building in a professional/industrial business park; further detail on the engineering and manufacturing facility is included in Chapter 8, Manufacturing.

2.6 Current Situation

Elevator DataCommand has developed a product and a philosophy that fills a distinct need of building owners—the need for precise, energy-efficient and maintenance-free elevators. Because ED is able to fill this need, building owners have been eager to learn about the company and technology, and to invest their elevator dollars in the ED20-20. The following projects are currently underway:

- **The Charles Sprague Building in Chicago** — This is a standard installation of the ED20-20 in one elevator in a 10-story commercial building. Completion is expected by August 31.

- **The Department of Defense Kirtzner Building in Washington, D.C.** — This is also a standard installation of 12 elevators in a 10-story office building. The project should be complete by September 30.

- **The New Concept Parking in Atlanta, Georgia** — This is a complicated installation in a 12-story vertically-oriented parking facility. The ED20-20 is being used to control and position vehicle-sized elevators that move both vertically and horizontally in order to place and retrieve vehicles in this vertical "honey-combed" parking garage. The installation is proceeding as planned, and should be complete by July 31.

- **Showcase Casino, Las Vegas, Nevada.** — This business has contacted ED to install an ED20-20 system in one of its two side-by-side showcase elevators at the main entrance. Once they have observed the superior performance of the ED20-20, they will immediately have the other of the pair updated. Additional units will follow.

It is important to note that these jobs were obtained by a fledgling company, without "corporate offices" or high-priced marketing and sales campaigns, in an industry that is dominated by big-name corporate giants such as Otis and Montgomery KONE. The capture of this business addresses and answers one of the most fundamental questions facing a new business: "Does the target market have a need for the product being offered; and are they ready, willing and able to buy it?" In the case of Elevator DataCommand and the ED20-20, the answer is a resounding "YES!"

Based on the positive market response to the unique technology of the ED20-20 and to the extraordinary service philosophy of Elevator DataCommand, the owners of the Company have created a plan for the prompt and significant expansion of Elevator DataCommand.

2.7 Long-Term and Medium-Term Vision

Elevator DataCommand has begun to establish a niche in the elevator market. Because of its unique technology and extraordinary service philosophy, ED has the long-term potential to become a worldwide provider of precise, efficient and virtually maintenance-free elevator performance. The long-term Company Vision is:

Elevator DataCommand will become the <u>world's</u> premier provider of the most precise, efficient, and minimal-maintenance elevator control systems.

The accomplishment of this vision will take years, if not decades, and is absolutely dependent on the Company's ability to maintain its technological and philosophical advantages over the competition. It also will come only after the realization of the Company's medium-term vision:

-10-

Elevator DataCommand will become the <u>USA's</u> premier provider of the most precise, efficient, and minimal-maintenance elevator control systems.

This is a vision that will take shape over the next five to ten years, and will be the result of the successful execution of a well-conceived plan that moves the Company forward in a logical and sustainable manner. In essence, Elevator DataCommand must 1) establish a beachhead from which it can build credibility, sales and profit, 2) expand from the beachhead to a nationwide market presence, 3) develop its U.S. position as the premier provider of state-of-the-art systems, and 4) move into international markets.

The establishment of an initial beachhead involves a targeted and well-executed thrust into a limited geographical market, the "Elevator DataCommand 2002 Expansion Plan".

2.8 2002 Expansion Plan

Elevator DataCommand will build its sales and profit via a disciplined expansion throughout 2002 and 2003, and will enter the year 2004 with its initial beachhead firmly established. The 2002 Expansion includes new long-term debt of $200,000, and is built upon five key components:

1. The identification of limited and specific geographic target market penetration points. These areas have been identified as the Mid-Atlantic Region, focused on New York; the South Atlantic Region, focused on Miami; and the Midwest Region, focused on Chicago/Milwaukee.

2. The installation of real-life, commercially active demonstration systems in each of the target areas.

3. The development and successful execution of an effective and efficient marketing strategy to generate sales in each target area.

4. The deployment of an adequate installation and technical support base in each geographic target area.

5. The assurance of sufficient engineering and production capacity to accommodate increased demand.

Each of these components will be examined in detail throughout this plan.

2.9 Company Objectives

The primary objectives for 2002 are:

1. Complete an appropriate and actionable business plan by September 30.

2. Secure funding for the 2002 Expansion by November 30.

3. Complete demonstration site installations by October 31.

4.   Achieve patent approval on the ED20-20 technology by October 31.

5.   Achieve $2,000,000 in sales, with $200,000 net profit before taxes.

Primary objectives for 2003 are:

1.   Open a full-service office in Miami, and expand offices in New York and Chicago/Milwaukee. Each office will be staffed with sales and engineering personnel sufficient to sell and service customers in the area.

2.   Generate $8,000,000 in sales, with $850,000 net profit before taxes.

3.0 INDUSTRY ANALYSIS

3.1 Industry Overview

Elevators are the dominant mode of transportation in buildings worldwide, and the development of safe and efficient elevators has made tall buildings feasible. Since its beginning in the 1800s, the U.S. "Elevator Industry" has grown to its current sales of more than $5 billion per year. The industry is divided into four distinct activities:

1. New Installations — As new buildings are erected, new elevators are included. New elevator installations currently number approximately 14,000 to 16,000 units per year nationwide, generating $1 billion, or about 20% of total elevator industry market sales. This field is dominated by major producers that manufacture proprietary equipment and install it using their own staff. The five major U.S. elevator companies are Otis, Dover, Schindler, Montgomery KONE and Thyssen. In addition to the major players, roughly 300 smaller independent contractors install new equipment. These contractors may manufacture some parts, but the majority of the equipment they install is supplied by component manufacturers. Elevator contractors use their own labor or hire workers on a per job basis. Elevator DataCommand participates in the new installations market.

2. Modernization — Elevators have been used in the U.S. for over 150 years. Throughout that time, there has been continuous growth in technology, creating a vast opportunity to upgrade existing installations. In fact, building owners who choose not to modernize their elevators are often taking serious safety and business risks. The safety risk of continuing to use old, outdated equipment is obvious, and the risk of losing residential and commercial tenants due to slow or out-of-service elevators is a major stimulant to modernization. Modernization can be carried out in degrees ranging from simple cosmetics such as a new or upgraded car enclosure, to full replacement of all operating systems. As building owners/managers develop their modernization plans, computerization and energy utilization are prominent concerns.

Again, the major companies such as Otis, etc., dominate the modernization market. These majors have several advantages over the independents. They bid in-house material and labor on the entire job, they have numerous advantages of scale, and they are well-known nationwide. In the modernization market, it seems logical to many building managers to call the original manufacturer to conduct a modernization campaign. A pleasant distinction of the modernization market is that it may be directly impacted by the efforts of the participating companies—good selling can, and does, generate new business.

There are over 600,000 elevators in use in the U.S. today, and all except those built in the last five to ten years are potential candidates for some type of modernization. It is estimated that modernization occurs annually on roughly 10% of the existing installations over 20 years of age (370,000 total estimated count), with additional modernization occurring on many units in the 10-20 year old range. According to the 2001 Experience Exchange Report published by the Building Owners and Managers Association (BOMA), the average age of a U.S. private-sector building is 28 years in downtown locations, and 14 years in suburban locations. At an average cost of $40,000 to $50,000 per unit, this market equals about $2 billion annually, or twice the potential of the new installation market. The modernization market is a key area for Elevator DataCommand.

3. Maintenance — The third primary revenue generator in the elevator industry is maintenance of existing units. For many companies, the maintenance market represents the best opportunity for revenue and profit growth. The world's largest elevator manufacturer, Otis, has learned how to skew its business toward maintenance, as noted in an article entitled, "Otis: The Ups and Downs of Business," in the November 1999 issue of *Management Review.*

> Long ago, Otis found that its real, long-term profits come not from selling new elevators, but from servicing older ones. "Just like appliances," says William Sheeran, senior V.P. for worldwide engineering, who learned this lesson at his last employer, General Electric, "you sell new equipment to build up your base of service. Most appliance manufacturers don't make money off selling you a refrigerator; they make it off service."

Perhaps more than any other industry activity, maintenance offers the opportunity for the financial abuse of building owners, who know very little about how elevators are built or how they work. They depend on elevator companies, elevator technicians and elevator consultants to keep their elevators running properly, and the service providers depend on the building owners for revenue. The less building owners know about their elevators, the more dependent they are on the elevator service companies. Therefore, the strategy that the elevator industry has adopted is 1) Install proprietary equipment using specially-built components that is difficult to maintain and/or repair, 2) Use primitive technology with mechanical parts that have high maintenance needs and short useful lives, and 3) Avoid at all costs the adoption of advanced technology that would provide standardized, industrial-grade components that offer long life, low maintenance requirements and easy service. For now, there is a lot of money to be made in the elevator maintenance business.

Maintenance service has a highly diffused group of providers. On one end of the spectrum, Otis and other industry leaders have offices in practically every major city, and maintain thousands of elevators with hordes of mechanics, each responsible for up to a hundred units. At the other end, there are more than 300 companies in the U.S. whose primary business is elevator maintenance. These may be one- or two-person firms maintaining a total of only 50-100 units. Generally, each elevator maintenance technician needs to generate approximately $18,000 in monthly gross revenue in order to be "profitable". Much of the revenue generated in the maintenance arena is billed in the form of ongoing maintenance contracts, which allows controlled costs for the building owner and dependable income for the service provider.

The total revenue generated by the maintenance segment is hard to establish, since there is no clearinghouse for companies' sales figures. Nevertheless, the latest edition of the Vertical Transportation Industry Profile estimates the maintenance market at roughly equal to the modernization market, $2 billion annually, or 40% of the total market.

Elevator DataCommand plans to pursue maintenance contracts for ED-installed or modernized units. An important part of the Company's maintenance strategy is to buy existing elevators from building owners; modernize them, monitor them, maintain them, and rent them back to the building owner at a profitable monthly payment. This concept is not uncommon in other industries, but it is ground-breaking in the elevator industry. Details are included in a later chapter of this plan.

4. Supply of Components — Many elevator components are commonplace items such as ventilation fans, lighting systems, electric motors, etc. These are made by a worldwide network of manufacturers. Other components are highly specific to the elevator industry, such as cars, door systems, hydraulics, gear and pulley systems, and the electronic control systems. Manufacturers may be broadly divided into two groups: the Major Elevator Companies and the Component Manufacturers.

The Major Elevator Companies have already been identified as Otis, Dover, Schindler, Montgomery KONE and Thyssen. The "Big Five" account for about half of the manufacturing and new installations done in the U.S. each year. These have the design and manufacturing capacity; the marketing skill and power; and the installation and service network necessary to dominate the manufacturing portion of this industry. They also install their own proprietary equipment, and rarely sell to other service companies.

Almost 1,000 smaller companies compete as Component Manufacturers, building one or more of the key components needed in the installation of a new elevator or the modernization of an existing unit. Most of these businesses sell their components to the on-site installers and modernizers.

Since the cost of components is included in the totals for New Installations, Modernization and Maintenance, there is no separate estimate of market share for this segment of the market. Elevator DataCommand will participate in the component supply market by selling the ED20-20 to elevator manufacturers and to other full-service elevator contractors.

-14-

Building Owners/Managers, Regulators and "The Public" — An overview of the elevator industry would not be complete without mentioning the three groups of people which create the demand for all of the previously mentioned activities.

Building owners and managers are the individuals responsible for the elevators in use in buildings throughout the country. They make the decisions regarding which company will perform the initial elevator installations, modernizations, repairs and maintenance.

Regulators include federal, state and local governmental agencies and elevator industry agencies which work together to provide standards for the industry. The primary document used to regulate elevator safety is the A17.1 Safety Code for Elevators and Escalators, instituted in 1992. In addition to the A17.1, the A17.2 and A17.3 relate to enforcement guidelines and regulations for existing elevators. The Americans With Disabilities Act (ADA) has also had an impact on the elevator industry.

Finally, it is the citizens working and living in commercial and residential buildings nationwide, who use elevators every day, who are the final judge of the service provided by these elevators. Every building owner and/or manager knows how important elevator service is. There are few building malfunctions that will cause a building manager's phone to ring more quickly than an out-of-service or malfunctioning elevator. Attractive, fast, and dependable elevators are vital to the process of generating new tenants and holding established tenants.

3.2 Elevator Equipment Types

There are three dominant mechanical formats for elevators: Hydraulic, Geared, and Gearless.

Hydraulic — This is the simplest and least expensive type of elevator, and is common in low-rise buildings from two floors up to a maximum of five or six. The basic mechanism is a large hydraulic cylinder that raises and lowers the car from below. The average speed of hydraulic elevators is a relatively slow 150 feet per minute (fpm). Since most buildings have fewer than six floors, the hydraulic elevator has become the dominant type, accounting for about 75% of current new installations. However, since the hydraulic systems did not become dominant until the 1950s, the bulk of elevators in the "modernization pool" are geared and gearless. The dominant major company installing hydraulic elevators is Dover. Complete installations can be supplied by any elevator contractor such as CEMCO, ESCO, Canton and Schumacher, as well as others. An "average" newly installed hydraulic elevator costs $65,000. The installation cycle (time from contract signature to completed installation) is short; one year is average. Although it is traditional to get partial payments during an installation, the profit usually isn't gained until the final settlement.

Geared — This elevator mechanism uses cables and pulleys, and offers speeds up to 450 fpm. Geared elevators are more common in suburban-type office buildings up to ten or twelve floors, apartments up to about 25 floors, and various low-rise buildings where a high quality of service is needed, such as hospitals and high-end buildings.

These are the second most common new installations, and cost an average of $200,000. The average installation cycle can be as long as two years. Geared units are sold and installed by the major companies like Otis and Schindler, and by independent elevator contractors as well. Components are supplied to the contractors by a number of manufacturers such as Hollister-Whitney and Titan Machine.

Gearless — These are the true high-performance machines, reaching speeds from 500 fpm to a blistering 2,000 fpm. The higher the speed, the more travel distance is needed to attain maximum speed and perform a comfortable slowdown to a stop. This implies an express run of a number of floors before the higher maximum speed becomes practical. Most elevators in major buildings serve a maximum of 15 floors, so the high-speed gearless unit will have an express run up to its "cluster" of 15 stops. A high-rise residential building may use elevators with as many as 30 stops. These high-speed gearless elevators account for about 5% of new installations, and can cost upward of $300,000 to install. The installation cycle for these machines is the longest in the industry, up to three years (although Elevator DataCommand can shorten the timeline substantially). They are usually installed by the major manufacturers, although gearless machines can be supplied to independent elevator contractors by General Electric, Imperial Electric and Leroy Sommers.

4.0 TARGET MARKET

4.1 The Selected Market

The management team at Elevator DataCommand is aware of the high level of competition within the four key activities that comprise the elevator industry: New Installations, Modernization, Maintenance, and Supply of Components. Therefore, the Company must be strategic in its approach to targeting markets. Before discussing the specifics of the markets that Elevator DataCommand targets, two definitions may be useful. A *market* is defined here as the set of all actual and potential buyers of a product. A *target market* is that market subset which the company decides to pursue. The members of the target market must have interest, income, access and qualifications for the particular market offer.

The ED management team believes that the markets targeted must be selected based on six key elements. The first is *history*. Every company has a history of goals, policies, achievements and failures. That history becomes a platform upon which the future is to be built, and will certainly impact on the selection of the markets to be targeted. The second consideration is the *current preferences* of the owners and management team. The individuals guiding the enterprise into uncharted territory have a clear vision of what they want the company to be, and who its customers will be. The third element that impacts on a company's selection of its target markets is an evaluation of each *potential market segment's size, growth and attractiveness*. Clearly, the company must select market segments that can provide sufficient sales opportunity. Fourth, a company must consider *environmental factors*. These are the opportunities and threats that exist in the marketplace, including the competition, which must be carefully assessed during the selection of a business's target market. Fifth, the organization must take a realistic inventory of its *resources* before it solidifies the list of potential customers it wishes to target. Finally, a company should base its target market selection based on its own *distinctive competencies*.

After extensive evaluation of the history; current preferences; potential market segment size, growth and attractiveness; environmental factors; resources; and distinctive competencies of Elevator DataCommand, the management team has determined that the Company will participate to some degree in three of the four key industry activities. This is a strategic decision based upon a logical understanding of what will be required of Elevator DataCommand for it to achieve its objectives and vision. In order for building managers to recognize Elevator DataCommand as a full-fledged member of the elevator industry, ED must be prepared to fulfill a wide range of elevator service needs. It is not enough to be able to assemble and install a new unit in a new building. It is not enough to be able to modernize an old unit. It is not enough to offer a standard maintenance agreement. Building managers want, and often <u>demand</u>, one-stop shopping from their elevator service company. Elevator DataCommand will serve the needs of its customers.

At the broadest level, Elevator DataCommand targets one industrial target market group: Building Owners/Managers. Specifically, Elevator DataCommand has further segmented the market into the following three target market groups:

1. **New Installation** — The Company targets the Owners/Architects/Engineers involved in the planning and construction of new buildings with elevators with more than eight stops, within the geographic target area.

2. **Modernization** — The Company targets the Owners/Managers of buildings with elevators with more than eight stops and with control systems more than 20 years old, within the geographic target area.

3. **Maintenance** — The Company targets the Owners/Managers of buildings with elevators installed or modernized by Elevator DataCommand.

In order to compete effectively in the New Installation market, the Modernization market and the Maintenance market in any given geographic area, Elevator DataCommand must be able to generate "critical mass" in that location. Critical mass, in this case, consists of a regional sales office; permanent management personnel; a "market presence" e.g. contacts, installed systems and a satisfied customer base; and a pool of qualified installation and maintenance technicians. Management has divided the nation into six geographic regions: North Atlantic, Mid-Atlantic, South Atlantic, Midwest, Rocky Mountain and West Coast. These six regions are roughly equal in sales potential, with each one representing between 13% and 21% of the nation's urban and suburban population, as represented in the Top 100 Metropolitan Statistical Areas (MSA). A table listing each of the regions and their MSAs, and a map depicting the regional structure, are located in the Appendix (but not included in this sample plan).

-17-

Initially, Elevator DataCommand will limit its marketing focus to three regions; the Mid-Atlantic, the South Atlantic, and the Midwest. These three combined include 53 of the top 100 MSAs, with a total population of 83,211,000. This is roughly 50% of the 164,904,000 people living in the top 100 MSAs nationwide.

As sales, profit and cash flow permit, the Company will expand its target market first to include the North Atlantic Region, then the West Coast Region, and finally, the Rocky Mountain Region.

The decision to focus the 2002 expansion on only three of the six sales regions, and on the Mid-Atlantic, South Atlantic and Midwest Regions specifically, is based on sound strategic and logistical reasoning:

- Attempting to attack the entire nation at once is simply not reasonable based on the Company's current market position and resources. Therefore, management must select appropriate geographic market segments for the initial thrust.

- The nation has been divided into geographic regions, approximately equal in sales potential, and each being of a size that can be initially managed by one salesperson. The result of this process are the six sales regions identified above. The question then becomes, how many regions may be successfully targeted initially?

- Management believes that Elevator DataCommand can successfully establish a market presence in the Mid-Atlantic, Midwest and South Atlantic Regions simultaneously.

  — The Mid-Atlantic Region is an obvious choice because, 1) the Company is located in New York. The Company headquarters building is a strong marketing tool. 2) Company management and engineering personnel are based in this region, allowing efficient operation. 3) Functional, commercially active ED20-20 systems are already installed. This is a vital marketing factor.

  — The Midwest Region is also an obvious choice because a commercially active demonstration system is being installed in Chicago.

  — The South Atlantic Region is a logical choice because, 1) Several commercially active demonstration sites are already installed. 2) This "non-management" location gives ED the opportunity to develop a prototype of a joint-venture approach to local sales, installation and service. The joint-venture program is detailed later in the plan. Once the joint-venture program has been established and debugged, it will serve as the model for expansion to the remaining three regions, then to further geographic subdivisions.

-18-

4.2 Market Size and Trends

The following statistics help to establish the size and scope of the Elevator DataCommand target market.

NEW INSTALLATIONS

- Roughly 15,000 new elevators are installed in the U.S. each year. 3,750 (25%) of new installations are geared or gearless, appropriate for the ED20-20.

- ED estimates that new installations will continue to number roughly 15,000 per year, although economic events may impact on that rate.

- At $200,000 per unit, these 3,750 new installations represent $750 million in sales potential.

- The Mid-Atlantic, South Atlantic and Midwest Regions represent 50% of this potential, or $375 million annually.

MODERNIZATION

- There are currently 600,000 operating elevators in the country.

- 370,000 of these are 20 years old or older.

- Approximately 10% of these 370,000 are modernized each year.

- Additional modernizations occur on units 10-20 years old.

- At a cost ranging from $40,000 to $200,000 per unit, modernizations represent a total market of almost $2 billion annually.

- ED estimates that half of this total, or $1 billion annually, is spent to modernize geared and gearless units appropriate for the ED20-20.

- ED estimates that the Mid-Atlantic, South Atlantic and Midwest Regions, with their older buildings, account for 60% of the modernization market potential, or a total of $600 million annually.

- Industry forecasts call for continuing growth in the modernization backlog "pool." As units age, they must be modernized repeatedly (at least every 10-20 years) in order to meet safety standards and tenant demands. Therefore, the modernization pool will continue to grow roughly 10% per year. Note: This 10% growth forecast is based on the use of primitive control systems. The superior technology of the ED20-20 will make modernization even more beneficial to building owners.

-19-

MAINTENANCE

- Since the maintenance target market for Elevator DataCommand includes only the owners and managers of buildings with elevators installed or modernized by Elevator DataCommand, this is a market that is small and very specific, currently consisting of the building installations described earlier.

- As new installations and modernizations grow, the sales potential for maintenance revenue will increase dramatically.

4.3 Unmet Market Needs

Building owners and managers generally know little or nothing about elevators—elevators either work or they don't work. Owners depend, almost blindly, on elevator consultants, companies and technicians to recommend and install the right equipment for new or modernized units, and to keep their elevators running smoothly. Conversely, the elevator industry depends on building owners for 100% of their revenue. The conflict here is obvious—it is in the "best interest" of everyone in the elevator manufacturing, installation and maintenance business to keep their customers dependent upon the "elevator experts" for every aspect of elevator service. The more specialized and utterly incomprehensible the elevator suppliers can make elevators, the more dependent on them the building owners become. This is very expensive for the building owners, and it never ends. The situation is somewhat analogous to today's new car owner, who hasn't the knowledge or equipment to maintain or repair (or even adjust) his car's fuel-injection system—he is totally dependent on an "expert" to provide the service. Perry Burch, president of the National Association of Elevator Contractors (NAEC) puts it, "There's been a trend going on in our industry over the last several years where the majors proprietarize the equipment they're installing so they can be guaranteed the maintenance on it." They then try to guard the technical data with which they program the unit, so that the building owner, or any other elevator company, cannot properly service it.

The end result of such a supplier-dominated industry is the tendency of the elevator companies to actively avoid any technological advancements that would make life easier, simpler and less expensive for the building owners. After all, if an elevator could be built that was precise, efficient and virtually maintenance-free, what would happen to the elevator replacements, the repairs, and the service contracts?!

A rapidly emerging need in building ownership is the need for energy savings. The financial and public relations benefit of reducing energy consumption is becoming more and more important to building owners and managers. Landis & Staefa, a prominent provider of building management systems, states that the push for energy conservation has recently and quickly begun to move beyond the basics such as lighting, heating and cooling, and now includes a building's elevator system as well. In fact, a Landis & Staefa representative recently noted that 30-40% of their energy conservation customers now specifically request information on how they can reduce their elevator energy use. And PEPCO, the Washington, D.C.-based electric utility, has begun to work toward energy reduction in elevator usage. Although this is a relatively new phenomenon, the push for elevator energy savings may eventually become the driving impetus for growing sales of the ED20-20 and its progeny.

4.4 Purchase Patterns/Process

Elevator DataCommand has identified three distinct target groups, and it is reasonable to examine the purchase patterns and processes for each of these groups separately.

1. **New Installation** — Decisions regarding elevator components and performance expectations are determined throughout the process of designing a new building. The owner, architect and engineers work together to ensure adequacy of service and code compliance for all of the building's elevators. Building owners place great faith in their architects and engineers, and usually accept their expert recommendations.

2. **Modernization** — This situation is not as straightforward as the New Installation scenario. These target customers are in a pitched battle between two opposite driving forces. On one hand, they must keep building operational costs to an absolute minimum. On the other hand, they must create a building and workspace so modern and attractive that they can hold current tenants and attract new tenants. With regard to elevator service, cost control generally wins the battle. A building owner will do his or her best to limp along for as long as possible, delaying any significant modernization program until it is <u>absolutely</u> necessary. When tenants threaten to leave because of poor elevator service—or worse, when they actually <u>do</u> leave—the owner knows that it's time to bite the bullet and spend the money. Interestingly, elevator service is one of the most important building features to commercial tenants.

   Once an owner is convinced that delay is no longer an option, he will generally take one of two courses of action. Some will contact an elevator consultant; an expert who, for a fee, will examine the building and make specific recommendations regarding how to modernize. Others will turn to an elevator company—perhaps the company who installed the units originally; perhaps the company which did the modernization 15 years ago; perhaps the company which holds the current maintenance contract; or perhaps a young company that offers a better alternative to the traditional, primitive control system that has caused the problem in the first place.

   Alternatively, if a building owner/manager is working with an electric utility or an energy conservation consultant to reduce energy use and cost, they may approach the issue of elevator modernization from a strict energy use perspective. In this case, the knowledge and expertise of the consultant will determine the direction the modernization may take.

3. **Maintenance** — The ED20-20 provides precise, efficient and virtually maintenance-free service, and can be maintained by a trained building maintenance team. However, some building owners want the security of using outside elevator professionals to perform their routine maintenance. Maintenance contracts may be arranged during the initial negotiations for the new installation/modernization, or they may be added at the completion of the

installation/modernization. In either case, the maintenance agreement is almost always awarded to the company that has done the primary work. With regard to the ED20-20, it is likely that an owner who wants a maintenance contract on an ED-installed unit will view Elevator DataCommand as the safest and most logical choice.

5.0 COMPETITION

5.1 Competitive Situation

There is no question that competition between companies in the elevator industry is aggressive and ongoing. With five major suppliers, plus hundreds of smaller players, competition is a certainty. However, most of the competition—especially in the modernization and maintenance markets—is focused on price. The reason for building managers' inordinate preoccupation with the price of elevator components and maintenance reflects on the role that the building manager plays in the business of building ownership. The manager's job is to keep the building operating at a functional level, at an absolute minimum cost, with a limited number of tenant complaints. Nowhere in this job description does it direct the building manager to make the elevators <u>100%</u> efficient, or to have <u>no</u> breakdowns, or even to get <u>no</u> elevator complaints. The job is to keep things running at the lowest cost possible. This fact means that suppliers of elevator services are always pressed to offer the lowest price—to respond correctly to the "What's the least I can do to get by?" mentality.

It is precisely this mindset, combined with the obvious supplier benefits of planned obsolescence, that has brought us to the competitive situation in which we find ourselves today: hundreds of companies—especially the small modernization, repair and maintenance companies—fighting to win contracts by cutting every possible corner, and using the least expensive, lowest quality components available.

Elevator DataCommand provides an elevator control system that offers the most precise positioning on earth. In addition, for all elevators of 10-12 stops or more, the ED20-20 is less expensive to buy, is easier and less expensive to install, and substantially less expensive to operate and maintain than any other control system on the market.

5.2 Primary Competitors

The five prominent elevator manufacturers in the U.S. market are Otis, Dover, Schindler, Montgomery KONE and Thyssen. These five companies combine to generate 80% of the industry's sales each year. They all sell, install and perform maintenance nationwide. These five clearly represent the most direct and formidable competition faced by Elevator DataCommand. Although each major metropolitan area brings its own local niche players, the management team at Elevator DataCommand has chosen to build its competitive strategy around these five key companies. The Company will focus its competitive strategy on the "big five" for four specific reasons. First, they are clearly the dominant players, with a combined 80% market share. Second, they are not only dominant on a <u>national</u> scale, they are also dominant in the three <u>regional</u> markets that ED has chosen to target first: the Mid-Atlantic, the South Atlantic, and the Midwest Regions. Third, they are the companies that are most able to mount a competitive response to ED's 2002 Expansion Plan. These five companies have the financial and marketing strength to defend their positions. Finally, these five companies represent the best exit strategy for the Elevator DataCommand management team and for the Company's investors. The elevator industry is filled with examples of a smaller company with valuable assets, customers and ideas being purchased by one of the larger elevator companies. The intent with Elevator DataCommand is to create such value—technological value, patent value, human resource value, and installed-base value—that the Company will be an irresistible takeover target within five to seven years. The following reviews of the "big five" detail some of the takeovers that have been a part of their growth.

Otis Elevator Company is the world's largest elevator company, a wholly owned subsidiary of United Technologies Corporation. Although Otis is a U.S. corporation, most of its revenue is generated outside the country. Worldwide sales are $4.6 billion, with 50,000 employees. In the U.S., Otis generates roughly $1.1 billion annual sales with about 8,000 employees. Otis participates in virtually every phase of the vertical transportation industry and is the undisputed industry leader. As the market leader, Otis has an especially difficult challenge. Unlike market leaders such as Kodak or Coke, which can grow sales by creating new demand, it is difficult for Otis to create demand for new elevators, or even modernizations. Moreover, virtually all installed elevators are already contracted for ongoing maintenance, leaving little potential to create new business. Therefore, Otis is left with two realistic options to maintain and grow its business. First, they must ferociously defend their current maintenance contract business, the life blood of their revenue stream. Second, they must aggressively pursue new installations and modernizations, not only for their direct revenue, but to establish new opportunities for maintenance contracts. Remember the quote from earlier in this plan regarding how Otis has learned to skew its business toward maintenance, as noted in an article entitled, "Otis: The Ups and Downs of Business," in the November 1995 issue of *Management Review*:

> *Long ago, Otis found that its real, long-term profits come not from selling new elevators, but from servicing older ones. "Just like appliances," says William Sheeran, senior V.P. for worldwide engineering, who learned this lesson at his last employer, General Electric, "you sell new equipment to build up your base of service. Most appliance manufacturers don't make money off selling you a refrigerator; they make it off service."*

Otis is not shy about using aggressive tactics to defend its territory. Earlier this year, Otis used its muscle to virtually steal a modernization contract from ED at Northern Indiana University. In spite of a bad reputation at NIU, Otis managed to force its way into the "accepted vendor" group, and then presented a below-cost bid to win business that would have gone to ED. Otis is an aggressive defender. However, because of its absolute dependence on long-term maintenance contracts, it cannot be aggressive in technological advancements that would reduce building costs and reduce or eliminate expensive maintenance agreements. This is its weakness.

Dover Elevator is a U.S. corporation that is currently being spun off from its parent, Dover Corporation. Dover Elevator generates U.S. revenue of $880 million annually with its roughly 10,000 employees. Dover is substantially different from Otis and the other major companies in two specific ways. First, Dover focuses its operations in North America, having sold its European operations in 1997. Second, Dover's product strength lies in its dominance of the hydraulic elevator market.

Schindler is a Swiss company that claims to be the world's second largest elevator manufacturer, with 35,000 employees worldwide. Schindler boasts U.S. sales of $650 million with 5,700 employees. The company is involved in all types of vertical transportation.

Montgomery KONE is the U.S. subsidiary of Finnish KONE. With worldwide sales of $2.25 billion and 22,500 employees, KONE stands with Schindler and Thyssen as the European triad of elevator manufacturers. KONE's purchase of Moline, IL-based Montgomery Elevator Company gave the company the U.S. presence it sought. Current U.S. sales are $667 million with 5,100 employees.

Thyssen Industrie A.G. is a German company with U.S. operations consisting of Payne Elevator in New England and U.S. Elevator covering the rest of the country. Although they are a very large international player, with worldwide sales of $2 billion annually, U.S. sales are less than 10% of the total; about $150 million annually with roughly 1,300 employees. Thyssen manufactures and installs all types of vertical transportation products.

Elevator DataCommand also competes with other companies that are focused on manufacturing and selling elevator Control Systems. The three companies specializing in control systems are Motion Control, with an estimated 35% market share; Swift, 20%; and Thompson, 15%.

None of these—none of the "big five," nor any of these final three—have a control system that matches the features and benefits of the ED20-20.

5.3 Barriers to Competition

The ED20-20 relies on a state-of-the-art interface between a computer-driven elevator controller and an industrial optical positioning system. This state-of-the-art interface is the key to the uniqueness of the ED20-20. There are four specific and formidable barriers to any technology-based competitive response.

1. No other company—not even Otis—can match the experience of the Elevator DataCommand team with regard to the industrial application of optical positioning systems. The ED engineering, sales and support departments have over 35 years of experience designing industrial controls, providing vertical and horizontal automated positioning systems for companies around the globe. This unmatched experience gives ED a substantive competitive advantage.

-24-

2. The software code and algorithms required to accomplish what the ED20-20 does are currently being patented. With patent approval expected by Fall, 2002, Elevator DataCommand will effectively control the only known and tested optical interface on earth. ED engineers estimate that even a major company, if it decided to develop a competitive system, would need a minimum of two years to develop and test a comparable system that would not infringe on ED's patent.

3. Much of the programming for the optical positioning system used in the ED20-20 was developed, tested and perfected by Tom Baconrind, currently the Chief of R&D for Spectrum Technology, Miltown, NY. Tom is available to Elevator DataCommand as a consultant for ongoing projects in which his special expertise is needed.

4. The entire premise of optically controlled, highly precise, extremely efficient and virtually maintenance-free elevator control systems is antithetical to the current primitive systems sold and maintained by the major elevator companies. It is important to remember that expensive ongoing maintenance contracts are a primary profit center for all of ED's major competitors, including all of the "big five." Therefore, unless and until Elevator DataCommand begins to make major inroads into their business, the most logical response of the majors is to ignore ED and its technological superiority.

6.0 SWOT ANALYSIS

6.1 Company Strengths

Elevator DataCommand enjoys a number of market strengths.

1. **Unmatched experience in optical positioning systems** — With their 35 years of combined experience in industrial optical positioning, Nick and Matt possess industry-leading knowledge of the application of this technology to the commercial elevator industry. No other company has the knowledge and experience of Elevator DataCommand.

2. **Ownership of a functional and debugged product and system** — Elevator DataCommand enjoys a clear market advantage because it owns a product and system that has been proven in the marketplace. All other elevator companies are at a competitive disadvantage since they have only mechanical positioning systems developed and in place.

3. **Elevator DataCommand is not reliant on maintenance sales for sustainable revenue and profit** — Because the Company can produce adequate gross profit on new installations and on modernizations with the ED20-20, ED is not forced to continuously sell maintenance contracts. This allows ED to focus on its real strength, the technological advantages of true optical positioning.

4. **Small size** — Because Elevator DataCommand is a small company, especially compared to industry giants like Otis, ED is able to focus more directly and quickly to customer needs. There are no executive committees, no approval teams, and no corporate red tape.

6.2 Company Weaknesses

1. **Small size** — Because Elevator DataCommand is a new and small company, there is a natural lack of recognition and respect in the marketplace. This weakness is being overcome through continued marketing and marketplace success.

2. **Lack of installed demo sites** — In each targeted market area, ED must develop successful demonstration installations. The Mid-Atlantic and South Atlantic Regions have the use demonstration sites up and operational, but the Midwest Region has yet to see its demonstration sites established.

3. **Minimal competitive financial strength** — The marketplace reality is that Elevator DataCommand is competing in an industry dominated by corporate giants. If Otis or Montgomery/KONE decided that it was in their best interest to compete in the optical positioning segment of the market, they certainly have the financial capacity to do so. However, this is a threat that does not appear to be in any way imminent. In fact, the Company views competitive inaction as an opportunity, as detailed in the following chapter.

6.3 Market Opportunities

1. **Lack of competitive response** — Elevator DataCommand has evaluated the potential for an aggressive competitive response to state-of-the-art optical positioning, and believes the following: 1) no competitor has thus far attempted to duplicate or imitate Elevator DataCommand technology; 2) none of the major companies have indicated any intention of developing optical positioning technology; 3) if a major company does initiate an optical positioning development program, it would be at least two years before they could have a functional system ready for the marketplace; 4) this lack of competitive response indicates the desire and intention of these market leaders to continue to support, sell, and maintain current primitive positioning technology; 5) the need for continuing support of primitive technology is based upon the need to continue selling highly labor-intensive maintenance contracts; 6) unless and until Elevator DataCommand begins to capture substantial market share, the major elevator companies simply see no need for a direct competitive response. These companies do not currently view Elevator DataCommand as a threat of any significance. Their lack of concern will give ED adequate competitive space to grow its business in the near- and medium-term. Long-term prospects for the acquisition of Elevator DataCommand by one of the majors is reasonable to anticipate.

2. **Energy initiatives** — The drive to conserve energy in the American industrial and commercial environment is gaining momentum. Numerous companies, such as Landis-Steafa and Johnson Controls, are dedicated to creating efficient energy use and substantial energy savings in commercial buildings. Certain governmental agencies across the country are mandating strict energy management codes. At several levels, optical elevator positioning systems in general, and the ED20-20 specifically, represent the potential for substantial energy savings. This is an arena which presents great opportunity for Elevator DataCommand.

6.4 Market Threats

1. **Patent difficulties** — At this time, the use patent affiliated with the ED20-20 is in process. No difficulties are anticipated, and the Company anticipates patent approval before year-end 2002. However, if difficulties and delays arise during the patent process, there could be opportunity for competitive encroachment. In that event, Elevator DataCommand would need to rely on the intellectual property that it already owns, namely, the knowledge and experience of Nick Eiden and Matt Wolf. In addition, the Company has established a close and strong relationship with the individual who designed the original and still-used algorithm which enables the successful operation of the ED20-20. Technologically, the Company is well prepared to maintain its marketplace advantage.

2. **Direct competitive response from a major competitor** — In spite of the Company's firm belief that none of the major elevator companies will mount a direct competitive response to Elevator DataCommand, the potential still remains for that to happen. This is a threat that cannot be ignored, nor can be a threat that causes the Company to freeze, motionless, in fear. The founders and owners of Elevator DataCommand firmly believe that the Company will be launched successfully and will eventually represent a viable buyout opportunity for one of the majors.

7.0 PRODUCTS

7.1 Product Description

Unlike traditional elevator control systems, the ED20-20 doesn't use any mechanical parts for positioning the car. Instead, the ED20-20 uses a state-of-the-art, computerized Electronic Distance Meter (EDM). Very simply, the EDM is able to determine the exact location of the car at all times, and can position the car to predetermined floor locations with extreme accuracy and unfailing consistency. This precise, computerized system allows faster and more efficient use of the elevator.

The ED20-20 Control System offers exceptional operational and economic advantages over competitive control systems. These advantages cluster around the three core areas:

PRECISION

- True closed loop positioning system—the only one in the industry.

- No mechanical positioning parts.

- Positioning with accuracy of +/- 1 millimeter.

EFFICIENCY

- Car downtime during installation is only 5-7 days vs. 14-21 days for primitive systems.

- "Creep zone" is eliminated, making floor-to-floor moves faster and smoother.

- Up to 33% increase in the number of passengers handled per hour vs. primitive systems.

- Energy savings of $3,000 to $5,000 per year per elevator vs. primitive systems.

MINIMAL MAINTENANCE

- Uses all industrial grade vs. commercial grade components—longer service life.

- Simple setup and adjustment of floor positions.

- All maintenance diagnostics are done on a simple-to-use computer screen.

- System will self-diagnose any malfunction and call for service.

- Significantly reduced maintenance costs compared to primitive systems.

ED has exclusive license to sell and install this technology in the United States, and is currently in the patenting process. Although the ED20-20 is currently on the leading edge of technology, management will not be satisfied with ED as a simple, product-focused company. Therefore, they are strategically positioning the Company to maintain its technological edge in elevator positioning systems into the future. The details of these intellectual and technological strategic plans are detailed in later chapters.

The ED20-20 uses a state-of-the-art computerized PLC with a touch screen for three key functions: setup, diagnostics and modification of elevator operation. With a built-in modem and diagnostics software, the ED20-20 can notify building management of a developing problem before the unit fails. The ED20-20 can be accessed any time via modem for software updates, diagnostics or status reports. Every ED20-20 comes with a digital, self-tuning, energy efficient motor drive installed in a U.L.-approved panel.

Specifically, Elevator DataCommand divides its market offerings into four categories:

- **Design/Engineering** — Each project requires a design and engineering phase to create a project plan that will create a system to meet the customer's needs. Although there is some customization necessary to accommodate each situation, the interface between the distance meter, the motor drive and the PLC is standardized and duplicatable. This interchangeability will greatly reduce costs over time.

- **Assembly** — Elevator DataCommand assembles the sub-panels and enclosures, including all of the software and programming necessary to ensure flawless integration with the distance meter.

- **Installation** — Using either an in-house installation team or a subcontracted installer, Elevator DataCommand completes the system installation.

- **Maintenance** — Elevator DataCommand will contract to perform ongoing maintenance on ED systems.

7.2 Competitive Comparison

The ED20-20 Control System offers exceptional operational and economic advantages over competitive control systems. These advantages cluster around the three core areas:

PRECISION

- True closed loop positioning system—the only one in the industry.

- No mechanical positioning parts.

- Positioning with accuracy of +/- 1 millimeter.

EFFICIENCY

- Car downtime during installation is only 5-7 days vs. 14-21 days for primitive systems.

- "Creep zone" is eliminated, making floor-to-floor moves faster and smoother.

- Up to 33% increase in the number of passengers handled per hour vs. primitive systems.

- Energy savings of $3,000 to $5,000 per year per elevator vs. primitive systems.

MINIMAL MAINTENANCE

- Uses all industrial grade vs. commercial grade components—longer service life.

- Simple setup and adjustment of floor positions.

- All maintenance diagnostics are done on a simple-to-use computer screen.

- System will self-diagnose any malfunction and call for service.

- Significantly reduced maintenance costs compared to primitive systems.

-29-

8.0 Manufacturing

8.1 Facilities & Equipment

As noted earlier in the plan, all engineering and assembly operations occur at the headquarters building in New York. This industrial facility has the capacity to house the equipment and personnel necessary to accomplish the 2002-2003 sales objectives.

8.2 Component Sourcing

There are four key components involved in the assembly of the ED20-20 system.

1. **The Distance Meter** — This is currently sourced from Spectrum Technology.

2. **The PLC (Programmable Logic Controller)** — These are currently sourced from Northrup, the leading producer of this technology. ED engineers believe that Northrup is the state-of-the-art; numerous other companies also make high quality PLCs.

3. **Motor Drives** — ED sources motor drives from GE and Rockwell.

4. **Other miscellaneous components** — Available from numerous suppliers.

In the scope of generating sales, Elevator DataCommand will find it necessary to sell and install complete elevator systems. This may include cars, interiors, door systems, and complete lifting systems including motors, pulleys, and cables. All of these components are widely available from a great number of suppliers.

It should be understood that Elevator DataCommand is not dependent on any individual supplier for the ability to continue and expand operations.

8.3 Operations

The production of each ED20-20 system follows a straightforward pattern from sales to engineering to production. The primary components of each system are standardized and non-customized. There is some slight customization required based on the individual installation needs. The basic process is as follows:

1. The design is developed by the engineering personnel in conjunction with field sales and delivered to the purchasing supervisor so he can order the necessary components required to build the specified unit.

2. Components are received over a period of time until enough material is available to begin work on the job. Because the Company can handle several jobs at once, the production workload is carefully balanced to maximize efficiency.

-30-

3. Assembly of the unit progresses in three steps: a) computer sub-panels are laid out and the components mounted and wired before the sub-panel is mounted in the unit enclosure; b) each unit enclosure is prepared for the sub-panel and any painting or external components (transformers, friends, warning lights, user interfaces, etc.) are mounted; c) the sub-panel is mounted in the unit enclosure and wired to any external devices. Terminals are provided for field connections such as limit switches and primary power.

4. Once the unit enclosure is assembled, it can be tested. Because a majority of the Company's sales are a replacement of old control systems, the controls must interface with existing motors and feed devices. Therefore, it is not possible to fully test every component in the factory. All designs are developed around proven components. All enclosure wiring is checked to ensure accuracy before the unit is powered up using the design supply voltage.

5. The unit enclosure is then prepared for shipping. Any loose devices are secured in the enclosure or packaged in another carton. The unit enclosure is then crated and shipped to the site for installation.

When the Company acquires a contract which includes installation of components beyond the normal optical positioning system previously described, the process for all non-positioning components is as follows:

1. The design is developed by the engineering team in conjunction with sales staff and delivered to our purchasing supervisor so he can order the necessary components required for the job.

2. Components are delivered to the appropriate regional installation arm of the Company for partial assembly and installation preparation.

3. The installation is completed at the job site.

9.0 MARKETING PLAN

9.1 Positioning Statement

Positioning is the act of designing the company's image and offer so that the target customers understand and appreciate what the company stands for in relation to its competitors. In the case of Elevator DataCommand, this relates directly to the Company's expertise in the development and production of the most technologically advanced elevator positioning systems. With that focus in mind, ED has established the following positioning statement:

Elevator DataCommand is the USA's premier provider of the most precise, efficient, and minimal-maintenance elevator control systems.

9.2 Product

The concept of actually designing a product to fit the needs of customers is an oft-repeated mantra, but it is too seldom really implemented. In the case of the ED20-20, the "find a need and fill it" marketing philosophy has been at work from the very beginning. In fact, it was a specific request that first led the Elevator DataCommand team toward the commercial elevator market. Since then, every product development decision has been made with the sole purpose of fulfilling customer needs—for smooth and precise elevator positioning; for quick and efficient installation; for energy savings; for low initial cost; and for long-term service with minimal maintenance.

This initial and continuing focus on real customer needs (in contrast to the "service contract" mentality of the primitive companies) has been the foundation of the Elevator DataCommand marketing plan.

9.3 Price

There are three primary approaches to pricing policy, and ED has used a combination of the three to arrive at its pricing. First, price may be based on cost of components, with additions for overhead and profit. Obviously, the selling price must be higher, in the long run, than fully loaded cost. Second, price may be based on what the competition is charging. Third, price may be based—in fact will be based—on what the customer is willing and able to pay.

Elevator DataCommand has included each of these three in developed its pricing. Costs are well-covered, with gross margins on individual projects ranging from 25-30%, and net margins before tax of 5-10%.

Regarding competition, ED prices are more than competitive with the primitive companies. Remember, because it is an optical positioning system, the ED20-20 costs basically the same to install in a 50-story building as it does in a 5-story building. With primitive mechanical positioning systems using steel tape and multiple location sensors for each stop, costs escalate with each additional floor. It should be noted that the installed cost of an ED20-20 system in a 2-story building would be slightly higher than a primitive system, since the basic components of the ED20-20 are more expensive industrial-grade components. However, the cost advantage of the traditional systems disappears quickly as the number of floors increases. At a level of 10-12 stories, the cost advantages of optical positioning begin to dominate, and from that point upward, the ED20-20 is increasingly less expensive than primitive systems. And these cost savings don't even include the savings of time and aggravation associated with the faster installation times possible with the ED20-20. As noted earlier, Elevator DataCommand specifically targets owners of buildings with more than eight stops.

Are customers willing to pay? Experience is demonstrating that customers are very willing to pay the price for the ED20-20. Price is generally not one of the major objections. Rather, potential customers are more concerned about the functionality and durability of the technology, the longevity of Elevator DataCommand, and future maintenance service.

All equipment is shipped F.O.B. New York, NY.

Currently, Elevator DataCommand offers two types of payment terms:

1. **Standard** — 30% of contract estimate is paid at order placement; 50% at shipping; and the balance at project completion. Delivery is promised within eight weeks of the signed order and 30% deposit.

2. **Financed** — For qualifying companies, ED offers 100% financing through Spectrum Credit Corporation. Payments can be delayed or adjusted to meet the customer's requirements. This option is a direct agreement between the customer and Spectrum, and does not impact the pricing or profit on the project. Under this program, ED is paid in full at project completion by Spectrum.

9.4 Place (Distribution)

Company management is well aware of the importance of achieving "critical mass" in the three geographic regions it has chosen to penetrate. In order to accomplish the sales and profit goals, the Company must create a substantial presence in each of the three regions. This presence will consist of 1) commercially active demonstration systems; 2) an effective and efficient promotional campaign; and 3) an adequate installation and technical support base—either in-house or sub-contracted.

While the Company will not directly solicit business outside its targeted marketing areas prior to the nationwide marketing roll-out, it is inevitable that ED will generate sales geographically outside of the Mid-Atlantic, South Atlantic and Midwest Regions. When this occurs, ED will make project-specific decisions regarding the most effective and cost-effective ways to accomplish installation and maintenance requirements.

9.5 Promotion

This last of the four key components of the marketing plan, Promotion, should be viewed as a constellation of four sub-topics. Each of these is unique and important to the overall promotional plan and to the entire marketing plan.

9.5.1 Public Relations

ED has learned to use the media to announce important events.

- Frequent press releases detailing contracts and/or completions.

- A major article regarding the ED20-20 will appear in the Fall '02 issue of *Elevator World*.

- A secondary article will appear in *Parking Today*.

9.5.2 Sales Promotion

The Company uses a variety of sales promotion tools to reinforce its message in the marketplace.

- Building management tradeshows in New York and other markets

- Live, commercially active demonstration sites in each targeted region

- Scratch pads with ED logo and message

- Pens with ED logo

9.5.3 Advertising

Elevator DataCommand uses print advertising to create awareness and generate leads.

- Yellow Pages online ads in New York, Washington and Miami

- *Elevator World*'s "World Source," an annual industry source book

- *Skylines Magazine*, the official journal of BOMA, Building Owners and Managers Association

- Various architectural journals are under investigation

- High-quality, professionally designed and executed 4-color brochure

- Six professionally designed technical brochures

- Limited direct mail to building owners

- Demonstration video is in process

9.5.4 Personal Selling

Personal selling is the arena in which all of the other marketing activities pays off. All of the Company's sales are ultimately the result of effective application of professional selling skills. The sales team currently consists of four people, each fully trained and impacting his market.

- Nick Eiden, Director of Sales.

- Dave Conway, Midwest Regional Sales Manager.

- Freddie Hart, Mid-Atlantic and South Atlantic Regional Sales Manager.

- Kevin McConnell, South Atlantic Independent Sales Rep.

10.0 MANAGEMENT SUMMARY

10.1 Management Team

Elevator DataCommand is a company that grew out of what was originally simply a strong working relationship between Nick Eiden and Matt Wolf. In 2001, Elevator DataCommand, a limited liability company, was formed with Nick and Matt along with CPA Dale Crockett. Each of these three owners brings a unique set of talents and experiences to the Company.

- **Nick Eiden** — Nick has over 20 years experience in the industrial automation field. In 1976, he worked as an application engineer and programmer for flexible manufacturing systems. These systems produced precision machine parts for the aerospace industry. From engineering, Nick went into the sales side of the industry in 1982, selling sophisticated computer systems for programming and communications. In 1986, he began working for Worldtronics (the company that originally manufactured and sold the optical positioning system used in the ED20-20) selling control systems for the plating industry and positioning systems for material handling and steel production. In 1995 Nick founded The Eiden Company, which engineers solutions for major companies needing to automate production and/or accurately place product in specific locations, e.g. nuclear reactors, air cargo facilities, steel mills, storage and retrieval systems. This business depends almost entirely on repeat and referral business, and Nick has built a solid reputation in the industry.

- **Matt Wolf** — Matt brings his 27-year career to lead the Elevator DataCommand technical team. After receiving his Bachelor's in Electrical Engineering from Triton University, he worked as a maintenance engineer in a highly automated production facility owned by Honeywell. In 1972, Matt joined a division of Rockwell Automation, as a product manager for variable speed, solid state motor/drive products. As a manager in an electrical systems integration company, he was responsible for overseeing the design and manufacture of a line of solid state motor/drive equipment for use in the bulk conveyor handling industry. In 1983, Matt formed his own electrical systems integration company, Mid-Atlantic Controls, Inc., in New York. This company focused on designing and manufacturing custom electrical control systems for the automated material handling industry. As Director of Engineering for Elevator DataCommand, Matt is responsible for new product development, application engineering, and manufacturing.

- **Dale Crockett** — Dale earned his Bachelor of Science in Accounting and Finance from Missouri State University, and has been a private-practicing CPA for more than 20 years. Dale is currently the Director of Finance for Elevator DataCommand.

10.2 Personnel Plan

The company currently has six employees: the three principals; sales professionals Dave Conway and Freddie Hart; and engineer Paul Langford.

The 2002 Expansion Plan calls for substantial increases in personnel across several functional lines. Each of these will be phased in as sales grow.

- Sales

  — Full-time sales manager for the South Atlantic Region. Telecommuting position.

- Engineering

  — Engineer for in-house engineering, CAD drawings, and site engineering. Headquarters position.

  — Software engineer to manage the development of ED20-20 Plus. Headquarters position.

- Installation

  — Manager of Installation Operations to oversee installations nationwide. Telecommuting position.

Personnel Plan

Production	2002	2003	2004
Paul Langford	$48,000	$50,400	$52,920
Engineer	$32,000	$50,400	$52,920
Software Engineer	$16,000	$50,400	$52,920
Installation Manager	$16,000	$50,400	$52,920
Other	$0		
Subtotal	$112,000	$201,600	$211,680

Sales and Marketing Salaries	2002	2003	2004
Dave Conway	$12,000	$12,600	$13,230
Freddie Hart	$12,000	$12,600	$13,230
South Atlantic Sales Manager	$6,000	$12,600	$13,230
Other	$0		
Subtotal	$30,000	$37,800	$39,690

-36-

General and Administrative Salaries	2002	2003	2004
Nick Eiden	$60,000	$63,000	$66,150
Matt Wolf	$60,000	$63,000	$66,150
Dale Crockett	$60,000	$63,000	$66,150
Other	$0		
Subtotal	$180,000	$189,000	$198,450

Other Salaries	2002	2003	2004
Name or title	$0		
Other	$0		
Subtotal	$0	$0	$0

Total Headcount	2002	2003	2004
Total Payroll	$322,000	$428,400	$449,820
Payroll Burden	$64,400	$85,680	$89,964
Total Payroll Expenditures	$386,400	$514,080	$539,784

11.0 FINANCIAL PLAN

11.1 Important Assumptions

The vital competitive assumptions are detailed elsewhere in this plan. The remaining key assumptions are straightforward: 1) that the U.S. economy continues steady long-term growth, and 2) that tall buildings continue to be an important part of the American landscape.

11.2 Sales Forecast

The forecast for sales growth in 2002 is for steady growth. With the influx of cash at the end of 2002 as part of the 2002 Expansion Plan, significant sales growth will occur in 2003. The chart below details 2002 sales. The table below includes sales in out-years.

Sales Forecast

Sales	2002	2003	2004
New Installations	$1,000,230	$4,000,000	$5,000,000
Modernizations	$800,545	$3,200,000	$4,000,000
Maintenance	$200,045	$800,000	$1,000,000
Supply of Components	$0		
Other	$0		
Total Sales	$2,000,820	$8,000,000	$10,000,000

Cost of sales	2002	2003	2004
New Installations	$700,163	$2,800,000	$3,500,000
Modernizations	$560,382	$2,240,000	$2,800,000
Maintenance	$100,021	$400,000	$500,000
Supply of Components	$0		
Other	$0		
Subtotal Cost of Sales	$1,360,566	$5,440,000	$6,800,000

Total Sales by Month in Year 1

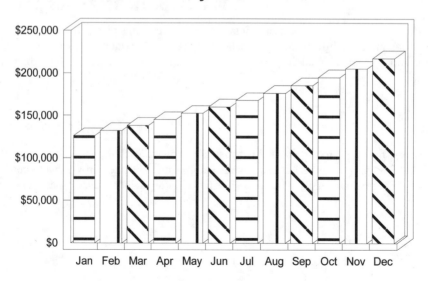

11.3 Projected Profit and Loss

The table below includes highlights of the Projected Income Statement. Full details are included in the Appendix.

Pro-Forma Income Statement

Category	2002	2003	2004
Sales	$2,000,820	$8,000,000	$10,000,000
Direct Cost of Sales	$1,360,566	$5,440,000	$6,800,000
Production	$112,000	$201,600	$211,680
Other	$0	$0	$0
Total Cost of Sales	$1,472,566	$5,641,600	$7,011,680
Gross Margin	$528,254	$2,358,400	$2,988,320
Gross Margin Percent	26.40%	29.48%	29.88%
Operating Expenses			
Sales and Marketing Salaries Expenses			
Sales and Marketing Salaries	$30,000	$37,800	$39,690
Advertising/Promotion	$21,000	$60,000	$75,000
Travel	$16,000	$48,000	$60,000
Miscellaneous	$6,000	$10,000	$12,500
Other	$0	$0	$0
Total Sales and Marketing Salaries Expenses	$73,000	$155,800	$187,190
Sales and Marketing Salaries Percent	3.65%	1.95%	1.87%
General and Administrative Salaries Expenses			
General and Administrative Salaries	$180,000	$189,000	$198,450
Leased Equipment	$9,000	$12,000	$12,600
Utilities	$6,000	$6,000	$6,000
Insurance	$3,000	$3,000	$3,000
Rent	$30,000	$30,000	$30,000
Depreciation	$0	$0	$0
Payroll Burden	$64,400	$85,680	$89,964
Other	$0	$0	$0

Total General and Administrative Salaries Expenses	$292,400	$325,680	$340,014
General and Administrative Salaries Percent	14.61%	4.07%	3.40%
Other Salaries Expenses			
Other Salaries	$0	$0	$0
Contract/Consultants	$0		
Other	$0		
Total Other Salaries Expenses	$0	$0	$0
Other Salaries Percent	0.00%	0.00%	0.00%
Total Operating Expenses	$365,400	$481,480	$527,204
Profit Before Interest and Taxes	$162,854	$1,876,920	$2,461,116
Interest Expense ST	$0	$0	$0
Interest Expense LT	$1,500	$18,000	$18,000
Taxes Incurred	$40,339	$464,730	$610,779
Net Profit	$121,016	$1,394,190	$1,832,337
Net Profit/Sales	6.05%	17.43%	18.32%

11.4 Projected Cash Flow

The table and chart below include highlights of the Cash Flow Forecast. Full details are included in the Appendix.

Pro-Forma Cash Flow

Category	2002	2003	2004
Net Profit	$121,016	$1,394,190	$1,832,337
Plus:			
Depreciation	$0	$0	$0
Change in Accounts Payable	($51,200)	$0	$0
Current Borrowing (repayment)	$0	$0	$0
Increase (decrease) Other Liabilities	$0	$0	$0
Long-term Borrowing (repayment)	$200,000	$0	$0
Capital Input	$0	$0	$0
Subtotal	$269,816	$1,394,190	$1,832,337

Less:			
Change in Accounts Receivable	($167,125)	$0	$0
Change in Inventory	$0	$0	$0
Change in Other ST Assets	$0	$0	$0
Capital Expenditure	$0	$0	$0
Dividends	$0	$0	$0
Subtotal	($167,125)	$0	$0
Net Cash Flow	$436,941	$1,394,190	$1,832,337
Cash Balance	$445,358	$1,839,548	$3,671,885

Cash Analysis

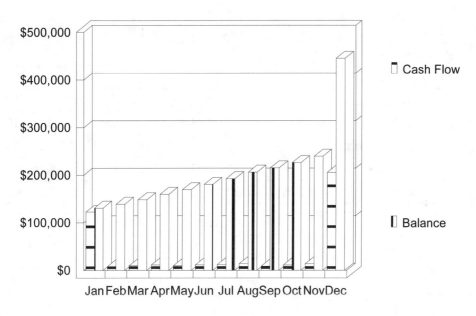

11.5 Projected Balance Sheet

The table and chart below include highlights of the Company's financial history and the Balance Sheet Forecast. Full details are included in the Appendix.

Pro-Forma Balance Sheet

Category	2002	2003	2004
Short-Term Assets			
Cash	$445,358	$1,839,548	$3,671,885
Accounts receivable	$0		
Inventory	$0		
Other Short-Term Assets	$0	$0	$0
Total Short-Term Assets	$445,358	$1,839,548	$3,671,885
Long-term Assets			
Capital Assets	$12,489	$12,489	$12,489
Accumulated Depreciation	$5,000	$5,000	$5,000
Total Long-term Assets	$7,489	$7,489	$7,489
Total Assets	$452,847	$1,847,037	$3,679,374
Debt and Equity			
Accounts Payable	$0		
Short-term Notes	$0	$0	$0
Other ST Liabilities	$0	$0	$0
Subtotal Short-term Liabilities	$0	$0	$0
Long-term Liabilities	$200,000	$200,000	$200,000
Total Liabilities	$200,000	$200,000	$200,000
Paid in Capital	$45,000	$45,000	$45,000
Retained Earnings	$86,831	$207,847	$1,602,037
Earnings	$121,016	$1,394,190	$1,832,337
Total Equity	$252,847	$1,647,037	$3,479,374
Total Debt and Equity	$452,847	$1,847,037	$3,679,374
Net Worth	$252,847	$1,647,037	$3,479,374

Past Financial Performance

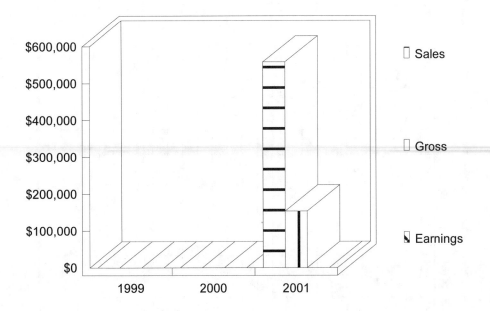

Pro-Forma Balance Sheet

Category	Jan-02	Feb-02	Mar-02	Apr-02	May-02	Jun-02	Jul-02	Aug-02	Sep-02	Oct-02	Nov-02	Dec-02	2002	2003	2004
Short-term Assets															
Cash	$130,995	$139,087	$148,674	$159,909	$169,309	$180,544	$192,366	$206,232	$215,061	$226,187	$239,745	$445,358	$445,358	$1,839,548	$3,671,885
Accounts Receivable													$0		
Inventory													$0		
Other Short-term Assets	$0	$0	$0	$0	$0	$0	$0	$0	$0	$0	$0	$0	$0	$0	$0
Total Short-term Assets	$130,995	$139,087	$148,674	$159,909	$169,309	$180,544	$192,366	$206,232	$215,061	$226,187	$239,745	$445,358	$445,358	$1,839,548	$3,671,885
Long-term Assets															
Capital Assets	$12,489	$12,489	$12,489	$12,489	$12,489	$12,489	$12,489	$12,489	$12,489	$12,489	$12,489	$12,489	$12,489	$12,489	$12,489
Accumulated Depreciation	$5,000	$5,000	$5,000	$5,000	$5,000	$5,000	$5,000	$5,000	$5,000	$5,000	$5,000	$5,000	$5,000	$5,000	$5,000
Total Long-term Assets	$7,489	$7,489	$7,489	$7,489	$7,489	$7,489	$7,489	$7,489	$7,489	$7,489	$7,489	$7,489	$7,489	$7,489	$7,489
Total Assets	$138,484	$146,576	$156,163	$167,398	$176,798	$188,033	$199,855	$213,721	$222,550	$233,676	$247,234	$452,847	$452,847	$1,847,037	$3,679,374
Debt and Equity															
Accounts Payable													$0		
Short-Term Notes	$0	$0	$0	$0	$0	$0	$0	$0	$0	$0	$0	$0	$0	$0	$0
Other ST Liabilities	$0	$0	$0	$0	$0	$0	$0	$0	$0	$0	$0	$0	$0	$0	$0
Subtotal Short-term Liabilities	$0	$0	$0	$0	$0	$0	$0	$0	$0	$0	$0	$0	$0	$0	$0
Long-term Liabilities	$0	$0	$0	$0	$0	$0	$0	$0	$0	$0	$0	$200,000	$200,000	$200,000	$200,000
Total Liabilities	$0	$0	$0	$0	$0	$0	$0	$0	$0	$0	$0	$200,000	$200,000	$200,000	$200,000
Paid in Capital	$45,000	$45,000	$45,000	$45,000	$45,000	$45,000	$45,000	$45,000	$45,000	$45,000	$45,000	$45,000	$45,000	$45,000	$45,000
Retained Earnings	$86,831	$86,831	$86,831	$86,831	$86,831	$86,831	$86,831	$86,831	$86,831	$86,831	$86,831	$86,831	$86,831	$207,847	$1,602,037
Earnings	$6,653	$14,745	$24,332	$35,567	$44,967	$56,202	$68,024	$81,890	$90,719	$101,845	$115,403	$121,016	$121,016	$1,394,190	$1,832,337
Total Equity	$138,484	$146,576	$156,163	$167,398	$176,798	$188,033	$199,855	$213,721	$222,550	$233,676	$247,234	$252,847	$252,847	$1,647,037	$3,479,374
Total Debt and Equity	$138,484	$146,576	$156,163	$167,398	$176,798	$188,033	$199,855	$213,721	$222,550	$233,676	$247,234	$452,847	$452,847	$1,847,037	$3,679,374
Net Worth	$138,484	$146,576	$156,163	$167,398	$176,798	$188,033	$199,855	$213,721	$222,550	$233,676	$247,234	$252,847	$252,847	$1,647,037	$3,479,374

Pro-Forma Cash Flow

Category	Jan-02	Feb-02	Mar-02	Apr-02	May-02	Jun-02	Jul-02	Aug-02	Sep-02	Oct-02	Nov-02	Dec-02	2002	2003	2004
Net Profit	$6,653	$8,093	$9,587	$11,235	$9,401	$11,235	$11,822	$13,865	$8,830	$11,126	$13,558	$5,613	$121,016	$1,394,190	$1,832,337
Plus:															
Depreciation	$0	$0	$0	$0	$0	$0	$0	$0	$0	$0	$0	$0	$0	$0	$0
Change in Accounts Payable	($51,200)	$0	$0	$0	$0	$0	$0	$0	$0	$0	$0	$0	($51,200)	$0	$0
Current Borrowing (repayment)	$0	$0	$0	$0	$0	$0	$0	$0	$0	$0	$0	$0	$0	$0	$0
Increase (decrease) Other Liabilities	$0	$0	$0	$0	$0	$0	$0	$0	$0	$0	$0	$0	$0	$0	$0
Long-term Borrowing (repayment)	$0	$0	$0	$0	$0	$0	$0	$0	$0	$0	$0	$200,000	$200,000	$0	$0
Capital Input	$0	$0	$0	$0	$0	$0	$0	$0	$0	$0	$0	$0	$0	$0	$0
Subtotal	($44,548)	$8,093	$9,587	$11,235	$9,401	$11,235	$11,822	$13,865	$8,830	$11,126	$13,558	$205,613	$269,816	$1,394,190	$1,832,337
Less:															
Change in Accounts Receivable	($167,125)	$0	$0	$0	$0	$0	$0	$0	$0	$0	$0	$0	($167,125)	$0	$0
Change in Inventory	$0	$0	$0	$0	$0	$0	$0	$0	$0	$0	$0	$0	$0	$0	$0
Change in Other ST Assets	$0	$0	$0	$0	$0	$0	$0	$0	$0	$0	$0	$0	$0	$0	$0
Capital Expenditure	$0	$0	$0	$0	$0	$0	$0	$0	$0	$0	$0	$0	$0	$0	$0
Dividends	$0	$0	$0	$0	$0	$0	$0	$0	$0	$0	$0	$0	$0	$0	$0
Subtotal	($167,125)	$0	$0	$0	$0	$0	$0	$0	$0	$0	$0	$0	($167,125)	$0	$0
Net Cash Flow	$122,578	$8,093	$9,587	$11,235	$9,401	$11,235	$11,822	$13,865	$8,830	$11,126	$13,558	$205,613	$436,941	$1,394,190	$1,832,337
Cash Balance	$130,995	$139,087	$148,674	$159,909	$169,309	$180,544	$192,366	$206,232	$215,061	$226,187	$239,745	$445,358	$445,358	$1,839,548	$3,671,885

Personnel Plan

Category	Jan-02	Feb-02	Mar-02	Apr-02	May-02	Jun-02	Jul-02	Aug-02	Sep-02	Oct-02	Nov-02	Dec-02	2002	2003	2004
Production															
Paul Langford	$4,000	$4,000	$4,000	$4,000	$4,000	$4,000	$4,000	$4,000	$4,000	$4,000	$4,000	$4,000	$48,000	$50,400	$52,920
Engineer					$4,000	$4,000	$4,000	$4,000	$4,000	$4,000	$4,000	$4,000	$32,000	$50,400	$52,920
Software Engineer									$4,000	$4,000	$4,000	$4,000	$16,000	$50,400	$52,920
Installation Manager									$4,000	$4,000	$4,000	$4,000	$16,000	$50,400	$52,920
Other													$0		
Subtotal	$4,000	$4,000	$4,000	$4,000	$8,000	$8,000	$8,000	$8,000	$16,000	$16,000	$16,000	$16,000	$112,000	$201,600	$211,680
Sales and Marketing Salaries															
Dave Conway	$1,000	$1,000	$1,000	$1,000	$1,000	$1,000	$1,000	$1,000	$1,000	$1,000	$1,000	$1,000	$12,000	$12,600	$13,230
Freddie Hart	$1,000	$1,000	$1,000	$1,000	$1,000	$1,000	$1,000	$1,000	$1,000	$1,000	$1,000	$1,000	$12,000	$12,600	$13,230
South Atlantic Sales Manager							$1,000	$1,000	$1,000	$1,000	$1,000	$1,000	$6,000	$12,600	$13,230
Other													$0		
Subtotal	$2,000	$2,000	$2,000	$2,000	$2,000	$2,000	$3,000	$3,000	$3,000	$3,000	$3,000	$3,000	$30,000	$37,800	$39,690
General and Administrative Salaries															
Nick Elden	$5,000	$5,000	$5,000	$5,000	$5,000	$5,000	$5,000	$5,000	$5,000	$5,000	$5,000	$5,000	$60,000	$63,000	$66,150
Matt Wolf	$5,000	$5,000	$5,000	$5,000	$5,000	$5,000	$5,000	$5,000	$5,000	$5,000	$5,000	$5,000	$60,000	$63,000	$66,150
Dale Crockett	$5,000	$5,000	$5,000	$5,000	$5,000	$5,000	$5,000	$5,000	$5,000	$5,000	$5,000	$5,000	$60,000	$63,000	$66,150
Other													$0		
Subtotal	$15,000	$15,000	$15,000	$15,000	$15,000	$15,000	$15,000	$15,000	$15,000	$15,000	$15,000	$15,000	$180,000	$189,000	$198,450
Total Payroll	$21,000	$21,000	$21,000	$21,000	$25,000	$25,000	$26,000	$26,000	$34,000	$34,000	$34,000	$34,000	$322,000	$428,400	$449,820
Payroll Burden	$4,200	$4,200	$4,200	$4,200	$5,000	$5,000	$5,200	$5,200	$6,800	$6,800	$6,800	$6,800	$64,400	$85,680	$89,964
Total Payroll Expenditures	$25,200	$25,200	$25,200	$25,200	$30,000	$30,000	$31,200	$31,200	$40,800	$40,800	$40,800	$40,800	$386,400	$514,080	$539,784

Pro-Forma Income Statement

Category	Jan-02	Feb-02	Mar-02	Apr-02	May-02	Jun-02	Jul-02	Aug-02	Sep-02	Oct-02	Nov-02	Dec-02	2002	2003	2004
Sales	$126,000	$132,000	$138,216	$145,101	$152,462	$160,113	$167,851	$176,365	$185,384	$194,948	$205,084	$217,296	$2,000,820	$8,000,000	$10,000,000
Direct Cost of Sales	$85,680	$89,760	$93,984	$98,671	$103,678	$108,883	$114,138	$119,928	$126,061	$132,564	$139,457	$147,762	$1,360,566	$5,440,000	$6,800,000
Production	$4,000	$4,000	$4,000	$4,000	$8,000	$8,000	$8,000	$8,000	$16,000	$16,000	$16,000	$16,000	$112,000	$201,600	$211,680
Other												$0	$0		
Total Cost of Sales	$89,680	$93,760	$97,984	$102,671	$111,678	$116,883	$122,138	$127,928	$142,061	$148,564	$155,457	$163,762	$1,472,566	$5,641,600	$7,011,680
Gross Margin	$36,320	$38,240	$40,232	$42,430	$40,784	$43,230	$45,713	$48,437	$43,323	$46,384	$49,627	$53,534	$528,254	$2,358,400	$2,988,320
Gross Margin Percent	28.83%	28.97%	29.11%	29.24%	26.75%	27.00%	27.23%	27.46%	23.37%	23.79%	24.20%	24.64%	26.40%	29.48%	29.88%
Operating expenses:															
Sales and Marketing Salaries Expenses															
Sales and Marketing Salaries	$2,000	$2,000	$2,000	$2,000	$2,000	$2,000	$3,000	$3,000	$3,000	$3,000	$3,000	$3,000	$30,000	$37,800	$39,690
Advertising/Promotion	$1,000	$1,000	$1,000	$1,000	$1,000	$1,000	$1,000	$1,000	$1,000	$1,000	$1,000	$10,000	$21,000	$60,000	$75,000
Travel	$1,000	$1,000	$1,000	$1,000	$1,000	$1,000	$1,000	$1,000	$1,000	$1,000	$1,000	$5,000	$16,000	$48,000	$60,000
Miscellaneous	$500	$500	$500	$500	$500	$500	$500	$500	$500	$500	$500	$500	$6,000	$10,000	$12,500
Other												$0	$0		
Total Sales and Marketing Salaries Expenses	$4,500	$4,500	$4,500	$4,500	$4,500	$4,500	$5,500	$5,500	$5,500	$5,500	$5,500	$18,500	$73,000	$155,800	$187,190
Sales and Marketing Salaries Percent	3.57%	3.41%	3.26%	3.10%	2.95%	2.81%	3.28%	3.12%	2.97%	2.82%	2.68%	8.51%	3.65%	1.95%	1.87%
General and Administrative Salaries Expenses															
General and Administrative Salaries	$15,000	$15,000	$15,000	$15,000	$15,000	$15,000	$15,000	$15,000	$15,000	$15,000	$15,000	$15,000	$180,000	$189,000	$198,450
Leased Equipment	$500	$500	$500	$500	$500	$500	$1,000	$1,000	$1,000	$1,000	$1,000	$1,000	$9,000	$12,000	$12,600
Utilities	$500	$500	$500	$500	$500	$500	$500	$500	$500	$500	$500	$1,000	$6,000	$6,000	$6,000
Insurance	$250	$250	$250	$250	$250	$250	$250	$250	$250	$250	$250	$250	$3,000	$3,000	$3,000
Rent	$2,500	$2,500	$2,500	$2,500	$2,500	$2,500	$2,500	$2,500	$2,500	$2,500	$2,500	$2,500	$30,000	$30,000	$30,000
Depreciation													$0		
Payroll Burden	$4,200	$4,200	$4,200	$4,200	$5,000	$5,000	$5,200	$5,200	$6,800	$6,800	$6,800	$6,800	$64,400	$85,680	$89,964
Other													$0		
Total General and Administrative Salaries Expenses	$22,950	$22,950	$22,950	$22,950	$23,750	$23,750	$24,450	$24,450	$26,050	$26,050	$26,050	$26,050	$292,400	$325,680	$340,014
General and Administrative Salaries Percent	18.21%	17.39%	16.60%	15.82%	15.58%	14.83%	14.57%	13.86%	14.05%	13.36%	12.70%	11.99%	14.61%	4.07%	3.40%
Other Salaries Expenses															
Other Salaries	$0	$0	$0	$0	$0	$0	$0	$0	$0	$0	$0	$0	$0	$0	$0
Contract/Consultants													$0		
Other													$0		
Total Other Salaries Expenses	$0	$0	$0	$0	$0	$0	$0	$0	$0	$0	$0	$0	$0	$0	$0
Other Salaries Percent	0.00%	0.00%	0.00%	0.00%	0.00%	0.00%	0.00%	0.00%	0.00%	0.00%	0.00%	0.00%	0.00%	0.00%	0.00%

	Jan-02	Feb-02	Mar-02	Apr-02	May-02	Jun-02	Jul-02	Aug-02	Sep-02	Oct-02	Nov-02	Dec-02	2002	2003	2004
Total Operating Expenses	$27,450	$27,450	$27,450	$27,450	$28,250	$28,250	$29,950	$29,950	$31,550	$31,550	$31,550	$44,550	$365,400	$481,480	$527,204
Profit Before Interest and Taxes	$8,870	$10,790	$12,782	$14,980	$12,534	$14,980	$15,763	$18,487	$11,773	$14,834	$18,077	$8,984	$162,854	$1,876,920	$2,461,116
Interest Expense ST	$0	$0	$0	$0	$0	$0	$0	$0	$0	$0	$0	$1,500	$1,500	$0	$0
Interest Expense LT	$0	$0	$0	$0	$0	$0	$0	$0	$0	$0	$0	$0	$0	$18,000	$18,000
Taxes Incurred	$2,218	$2,698	$3,196	$3,745	$3,134	$3,745	$3,941	$4,622	$2,943	$3,709	$4,519	$1,871	$40,339	$464,730	$610,779
Net Profit	$6,653	$8,093	$9,587	$11,235	$9,401	$11,235	$11,822	$13,865	$8,830	$11,126	$13,558	$5,613	$121,016	$1,394,190	$1,832,337
Net Profit/Sales	5.28%	6.13%	6.94%	7.74%	6.17%	7.02%	7.04%	7.86%	4.76%	5.71%	6.61%	2.58%	6.05%	17.43%	18.32%

Sales Forecast

Sales	Jan-02	Feb-02	Mar-02	Apr-02	May-02	Jun-02	Jul-02	Aug-02	Sep-02	Oct-02	Nov-02	Dec-02	2002	2003	2004
New Installations	$63,000	$66,000	$69,180	$72,551	$76,124	$79,911	$83,926	$88,182	$92,692	$97,474	$102,542	$108,648	$1,000,230	$4,000,000	$5,000,000
Modernizations	$50,400	$52,800	$55,200	$58,040	$61,113	$64,220	$67,140	$70,547	$74,154	$77,979	$82,034	$86,918	$800,545	$3,200,000	$4,000,000
Maintenance	$12,600	$13,200	$13,836	$14,510	$15,225	$15,982	$16,785	$17,636	$18,538	$19,495	$20,508	$21,730	$200,045	$800,000	$1,000,000
Supply of Components															
Other													$0	$0	
Total Sales	$126,000	$132,000	$138,216	$145,101	$152,462	$160,113	$167,851	$176,365	$185,384	$194,948	$205,084	$217,296	$2,000,820	$8,000,000	$10,000,000

Cost of sales	Jan-02	Feb-02	Mar-02	Apr-02	May-02	Jun-02	Jul-02	Aug-02	Sep-02	Oct-02	Nov-02	Dec-02	2002	2003	2004
New Installations	$44,100	$46,200	$48,426	$50,788	$53,287	$55,938	$58,748	$61,727	$64,884	$68,232	$71,779	$76,054	$700,163	$2,800,000	$3,500,000
Modernizations	$35,280	$36,960	$38,640	$40,628	$42,779	$44,954	$46,998	$49,383	$51,908	$54,585	$57,424	$60,843	$560,382	$2,240,000	$2,800,000
Maintenance	$6,300	$6,600	$6,918	$7,255	$7,612	$7,991	$8,392	$8,818	$9,269	$9,747	$10,254	$10,865	$100,021	$400,000	$500,000
Supply of Components															
Other													$0	$0	
Subtotal Cost of Sales	$85,680	$89,760	$93,984	$98,671	$103,678	$108,883	$114,138	$119,928	$126,061	$132,564	$139,457	$147,762	$1,360,566	$5,440,000	$6,800,000

The Plan For
Latina Media, LLC

ELENA TRUJILLO

5927 Michigan Avenue

Chicago, IL

(312) 841-5894

Copy Number __ of Five.

THE PLAN FOR LATINA MEDIA, LLC

1.0 Executive Summary

Latina Media, LLC, is a new company dedicated to the production and distribution of substantive, superior-quality, socially uplifting, and sellable television and video productions for the Chicagoland Hispanic market. The establishment of the Company marks the culmination of a lifelong journey for the company's founder, Elena Trujillo.

Latina Media will be successful because it is being built on three solid foundational strengths: Elena Trujillo; technological excellence; and properly targeted market offerings.

ELENA TRUJILLO

The heart and soul of Latina Media is its owner and founder, Elena Trujillo. Bright and energetic, Elena was raised in Monterey, Mexico. She conducted her post-secondary education in Advertising, Journalism, and Arts and Theater. Elena wrote, directed and acted in numerous theatrical productions throughout her college years. 1992-1995 saw Elena develop video training programs for a number of corporate clients, including Redken and Mary Kay. During this time she also produced dozens of high-quality videos, feature programs, and commercials for institutional and corporate customers including Coca-Cola, Mexicana Airlines, and the University of Monterey.

In 1995 Elena and her family made the bold move from Monterey to Chicago to begin their new life in America. 1997 saw the debut of Elena's new Spanish-language television program, *Estilo Latino*, or *Latin Style*. *Estilo Latino* is currently carried on Cook County TCI's public-access commercial-free Channel 17.

TECHNOLOGICAL EXCELLENCE

In order for Latina Media to be competitive in its chosen markets, technological excellence is of paramount importance. The quality of any video product is determined technologically by the camera and editing equipment.

Recent advances in digital video technology have made it possible for Latina Media to acquire an outstanding digital video camera and editing package at a very reasonable cost. This professional-level equipment, at this low price, has not been available previously. In the hands of a professional, this equipment moves Latina Media to the head of the class.

MARKET OFFERINGS

Elena has identified two specific unfilled needs in the Chicagoland Hispanic marketplace. First, Elena realizes that many Cook County Hispanic families are interested in purchasing professional-quality videotaping of important social events—specifically, Sweet 15 Parties and Weddings. Second, Elena's experience with *Estilo Latino* suggests that there are many opportunities for Spanish-language television programs in the Chicago marketplace.

-4-

<u>Social Event Videos</u>: Hispanic families want to capture important social events in a professionally produced video. Latina Media has already begun to sell this service to the Cook County Hispanic community, and there is great potential left to be developed.

<u>Spanish-language Television</u>: The six-county Chicago metro area is home to almost 200,000 Hispanic youth in the 10-19 age range. Yet throughout all of Chicagoland, there are <u>no</u> local television programs designed to reach this target group. To fill this need, Latina Media will introduce <u>*Juventud Hispana,* a weekly situation-based television program centered on the lifestyle and events of Chicagoland Hispanic youth.</u>

The setting for the program is the fictional Arts and Literature class of Teacher Perez at a Chicago-area high school. He is surrounded by 6 student lead characters. With each new school year, Teacher Perez will "select" from his Arts and Literature class six students to operate the school's "television production team." Through the school year, this team of 6, along with Teacher Perez, "produce" a weekly television program featuring issues of importance to Chicagoland Hispanic youth. Topics may include music, dancing, cars and driving, education, sex, pregnancy, drug and alcohol awareness, sexually transmitted diseases awareness, college, general health, finances, Chicagoland cultural attractions, etc.

Juan Gonzalez, Vice President and General Sales Manager of Chicago's Channel 46, responded very positively to Elena's experience and background, and to the *Juventud Hispana* programming concept. According to Gonzalez, "Elena has much more industry experience than many of the producers I deal with now." Regarding the show itself, he noted, "This program fits very well into our goals for Channel 46."

ROLLOUT STRATEGY

Immediately upon acquisition of the selected digital camera and editing package, Latina Media will begin aggressive marketing of the Social Event Video product. This business will grow quickly, achieving breakeven within the first quarter. These video events will provide not only revenue (and profit), they will also provide the opportunity for Elena to develop her skill in using the new digital camera and editing equipment.

In the second half of 2002, the Company will be prepared financially and technologically to begin producing and selling *Juventud Hispana*, and intends to begin airing in September, 2002.

The graph below depicts the 3-year forecast for sales and profits of Latina Media.

Business Plan Highlights

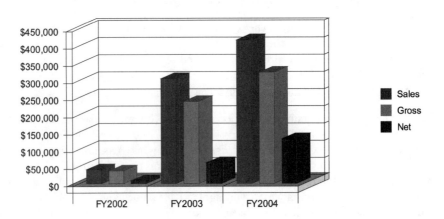

2.0 COMPANY SUMMARY

2.1 Ownership

Latina Media is registered as an Illinois Limited Liability Company, owned by its founder, Elena Trujillo.

2.2 Mission

Latina Media is dedicated to the production and distribution of substantive, superior-quality, socially uplifting, sellable television and video productions for the Chicagoland Hispanic market.

There are three primary keys to the accomplishment of the Company's Mission. First, Elena Trujillo. Her skills and community position are vital components of future success. Second, Technological Excellence. In order to create the video and television products that will capture market share, Latina Media must initiate operations with the right advanced equipment. Finally, the Company must create the correct Market Offerings. These keys to success are detailed in the next chapter.

-6-

2.3 Keys to Success

2.3.1 Elena Trujillo

The heart and soul of Latina Media is its owner and founder, Elena Trujillo. Bright and energetic, Elena completed her elementary and secondary education in her hometown of Monterey, Mexico. She then went on to continue her post-secondary education, majoring in Advertising at the prestigious Center for Studies in Communications Science. In addition, she studied Journalism and Arts and Theater. These years of training in the communication arts and sciences developed in Elena a love for television and video production that would stay with for throughout her career. Elena wrote, directed and acted in numerous theatrical productions throughout her college years.

1991 saw the beginning of Elena's professional career, producing advertising campaigns for a number of corporate sponsors. In 1992, she broke into the video world developing video training programs for a number of corporate clients, including Redken and Mary Kay.

1993 through 1995 was a period of dramatic expansion of Elena's television production career. During this time she produced dozens of high-quality videos, feature programs, and commercials for a variety of institutional and corporate customers, including Coca-Cola, Mexicana Airlines, Mary Kay, Redken and the University of Monterey.

In 1995 Elena and her family made the bold move from Monterey to Chicago to begin their new life in America. She immediately went to work in the communication industry by cofounding and co-editing the first Hispanic weekly newspaper in Cook County, *Periodico*. Elena was responsible not only for editorial content, but also for advertising revenue. In this capacity she quickly learned which businesses and institutions in Cook County were interested in supporting the Hispanic community and advertising in Hispanic and Spanish-language communication vehicles. *Periodico* has since been purchased by a separate group of investors, allowing Elena to apply her talent and energy to her first love, television production.

1997 saw the debut of Elena's new Spanish-language television program, *Estilo Latino,* or *Latin Style.* This program is a lively mix of interviews, public issues, and personal interest stories about and for Cook County Hispanics. *Estilo Latino* is currently carried on Cook County TCI's public-access commercial-free Channel 17.

As evidenced by her career to date, Elena Trujillo is an individual of unusual talent, experience, determination, and spirit. She is, without question, the singular driving force that will propel Latina Media into the future. She has already established herself as a member of the **Coalicion Latinas Unidos of Cook County**, a coalition of Hispanic leaders in Cook County. In addition, she is one of the founding members of a currently forming **Chicago Hispanic Film, Television and Fine Arts Coalition.** Both of these represent outstanding opportunities for Elena and Latina Media.

-7-

Three specific attributes provide Elena with the unique qualifications to move Latina Media to successful operation: 1) Her video production skill, 2) Her determination, and 3) Her position within the Chicagoland Hispanic community.

Elena has committed herself to the establishment and profitable operation of a Cook County-based television and video production business. She is absolutely dedicated to the long-term success of this operation.

2.3.2 Technological Excellence

In order for Latina Media to be competitive in its chosen markets, technological excellence is of paramount importance. The quality of any video product is determined technologically by the camera and editing equipment.

To achieve its mission, the Company must initiate operations with camera and editing equipment sufficient to accomplish its immediate goals. Specifically, the equipment must be adequate to meet the highest technological demands that will be placed upon it—in this case, a demand for broadcast television quality. Elena has selected a package of excellent <u>digital</u> equipment that provides Latina Media with the technological capacity to serve its customers now and into the foreseeable future. Anything less is unacceptable, and anything more is unnecessary. The cost of this equipment is included in the Startup Summary in Chapter 2.5, and a detailed review of the equipment is included in a Chapter 6, Operations.

2.3.3 Market Offerings

The final key to success is the development of the right product offerings. Elena is confident that she has correctly developed two prime products for the Chicagoland Hispanic market: a broadcast television program called *Juventud Hispana*, and professional video production of important social events. Each of these is fully addressed in this plan.

The merging of the right person (Elena Trujillo), the right technology (digital video), and the right products (*Juventud Hispana* and Social Event Videos) create a winning formula for Latina Media.

2.4 Concept Testing

With the successful introduction of her first American television/video venture, *Estilo Latino*, Elena began a diligent search for programming opportunities that would allow her to move from the realm of public-access, commercial-free television into the world of commercially viable video and television production.

Two specific opportunities were quickly identified. First, Elena's experience with *Estilo Latino* suggested that there were many opportunities for <u>Spanish-language television programs</u> in the Chicago marketplace. Second, Elena was aware that many Cook County Hispanic families are interested in purchasing <u>professional-quality videotaping of important social events—specifically, Sweet 15 Parties and Weddings</u>.

-8-

2.4.1 Commercial Television Programming

Elena tested three substantially different program ideas in Cook County in order to determine which was the most commercially viable. The first was the original program, *Estilo Latino*. The second was a program aimed at children, entitled *La Pequenita de Estilo Latino*, or *Little Miss Hispanic Style*. The third was a program targeted at Hispanic youth aged 10-19 years, *Juventud Hispana*, or *Hispanic Youth*.

While all three program concepts were well received by Hispanic viewers and potential sponsors, *Juventud Hispana* was universally viewed as the program of greatest interest to the viewing audience, and was the strongest commercially. A pilot of *Juventud Hispana* was produced and used throughout the testing of consumer acceptance, sponsor/advertiser acceptance, and network-acceptance.

Preliminary selling to potential sponsors was conducted using the pilot program and Elena's energy and presentation ability. With Elena's diligent effort, the pilot episode ran on TCI Channel 17 under corporate sponsorship. Each of the sponsors was more than satisfied with the investment they made. These will be the first targeted sponsors for the beginning of the series.

Viewer testing with demographically appropriate subjects was also strongly positive. The Hispanic teenagers that were involved with the program are eagerly awaiting the continuation of the series, and teens from throughout Cook County continue to ask (in person and via phone calls) when the next episodes will be on T.V.

Finally, the pilot program was presented to Juan Gonzalez, Vice President and General Sales Manager of Chicago's Channel 46, one of the city's primary foreign-language television stations. He responded very positively to Elena's experience and background, and to the *Juventud Hispana* programming concept. According to Gonzalez, "Elena has much more industry experience than many of the producers I deal with now." Regarding the show itself, he noted, "This program fits very well into our goals for Channel 46." He stated that he would like to position *Juventud Hispana* in the time slot just after the station's number one spanish-language program, *El Show de Angelo Lopez*. Mr. Gonzalez' letter of support is included in the Appendix (not included in this sample plan). Further negotiations will finalize an agreement for weekly airing.

2.4.2 Social Event Video

Increasingly, Hispanic families want to capture important social events in a professionally produced video. The reasons are many and varied, but generally there are two primary reasons why these videotapes are so important to the family. First, they want to have and keep the video as a private memory of this important event. Second, they want to have a video record to send to family and friends in their country of origin and who could not attend the event. Both of these are very powerful motivators to the purchase of professional-quality video production.

The demand for professional quality videos of these social events has become very evident to Elena very quickly. In spite of the fact that she has previously used inferior home-video technology, Elena's proven skill and community position has already allowed her to schedule numerous social event projects at an average price of almost $500 per event. It should be noted that these contracts have been booked with **no marketing**—these customers found Elena because of her television work and community contacts. In the Social Video category, demand is real, it is growing, and it is ready for Latina Media.

Currently, Elena is turning down work, since she wants to establish her business as a top-quality producer using top-quality equipment. She believes it is better to turn down work now, and develop her business after she acquires the digital equipment detailed in this plan.

In addition to building her own social event videography business, Elena has a standing opportunity to do freelance videography and editing work on an ongoing basis (once she has acquired digital equipment) for two large Hispanic-owned video companies in Chicago. This represents an excellent support base for Latina Media during the startup phase, and is detailed later in the plan.

2.5 Startup Summary

With strong confirmation of the market's acceptance of both of its concepts—Social Video and *Juventud Hispana*—Latina Media stands ready to move to the next phases of implementation; funding and production.

Startup expenses are detailed in the table below, and represent a realistic expectation of the costs of establishing the Company on firm financial footing.

Startup Requirements Plan

Startup Expenses		Startup Assets Needed	
Legal	$ 0	Cash Requirements	$7,500
Stationery etc.	100	Other Short-Term Assets	0
Menus	100	Total Short-Term Assets	7,500
Consultants	0	Long-Term Assets	17,000
Insurance	100		
Rent	0		
Research and Development	0		
Expenses Equipment	200		
Other	0		
Total Startup Expense	**$500**	**Total Assets**	**$24,500**
	Total Startup Requirements	**$25,000**	

-10-

Startup Funding Plan

Investments		Short-Term Liabilities	
Investor 1	$ 0	Unpaid Expenses	$ 0
Investor 2	0	Short-Term Loans	0
Other	0	Interest-Free Short-Term Loans	0
		Subtotal Short-Term Liabilities	0
		Long-term Liabilities	25,000
Total Investment	**$ 0**	**Total Liabilities**	**$25,000**

Loss at Startup	**($500)**
Total Capital	**($500)**
Total Capital and Liabilities	**$24,500**

2.6 Near-Term Objectives

Elena has established the following objectives for Latina Media for its first fiscal year, July '01 - June '02:

- Achieve full funding by May 31, 2001.

- Purchase camera and editing package by June 15, 2001.

- Contract 2 social videos and 3 freelance jobs per month during the three months Jul-Sep, 2001.

- Contract 4 social videos and 2 freelance jobs per month during the four months Oct 99-Jan 2002.

- Purchase a second digital camera ($5,000) in Feb, 2002, from cash flow.

- Contract 6 social videos and 2 freelance jobs per month during the five months Feb-Jun 2002.

- Sign contract with Channel 46 by Dec 31, 2001 to broadcast an initial four months of *Juventud Hispana*, first airing on September 9, 2002.

- Achieve four-month (Sep-Dec, 01) funding commitment from inaugural advertisers and sponsors by June 30, 2002.

- Achieve 2001 sales of $40,000.

- Achieve a net profit on operations in FY 2002.

- Retire all debt within 3 years.

With these objectives in place, the plan now moves to a detailed review of each business segment. Chapter 3 discusses the rationale and plan for *Juventud Hispana*, while Chapter 4 includes the specifics for the Social Video products.

3.0 "JUVENTUD HISPANA" (JH)

3.1 JH Industry Analysis

3.1.1 U.S. Television & Hispanic Demographics

Juventud Hispana participates in a marketplace with enormous growth potential for the next 30-50 years—the Hispanic television industry. This industry represents the intersection of two rapidly expanding opportunities—the overall U.S. television industry and the exploding U.S. Hispanic demographic.

To characterize the United States television industry as a runaway success would not be an overstatement. Standard & Poor's forecasts a strong 8% annual growth rate for broadcast television ad revenues through the 1995-2000 time period. For cable television, the 1995-2000 annual growth rate is forecast to be an incredible 21.4%. The basic facts are quite simple: Americans love to watch TV, and because they watch so much TV, television advertising has become the dominant advertising medium used by corporate America to promote its products. Witness the continually escalating prices of premier-event advertising slots—$1 million for 30 seconds! Observe the continual proliferation of new channels, cable systems, and satellite viewing options. There can be no doubt that television, love it or loathe it, will be with us for the foreseeable future.

What may not be quite so obvious is that the United States Hispanic population is also poised for rapid growth over the next several decades. Today, at over 30 million individuals, Hispanics make up more than 13 percent of the total U.S. population. In 50 years though, by some estimates, one out of every four Americans—that's an incredible 25%—will be of Hispanic origin. The Hispanic market is the fastest growing market in the country. In fact, by 2025, the United States will be second in Hispanic population only to Mexico. This single demographic statistic—the rapid increase in Spanish-speaking Americans—is enough to make any marketer's heart beat faster.

But overall growth is not the only impressive Hispanic market factor. Consider these additional demographic and psychographic statistics:

-12-

- The average family income of Hispanic families in the U.S. is $37,500, compared to the U.S. median household income of $38,135.

- The buying power of Hispanic households in 1996 was $228 billion.

- Hispanic households are significantly larger than the non-Hispanic U.S. average; 3.41 persons vs. 2.63.

- Hispanics prefer brand-name products.

- Hispanic consumers are more brand-loyal than the average consumer.

- Hispanic watch more television: an average of 3.6 hours on weekdays vs. 3.2 hours for non-Hispanics.

The convergence of the rapidly expanding television and video industry with these overwhelming Hispanic demographic and psychographic statistics leads to an almost inevitable conclusion—Hispanic television and video will experience rapid growth in the United States. The prudent business course is to attempt to capitalize on this opportunity.

3.1.2 U.S. Hispanic Television

U.S. Spanish-language television is led by two industry behemoths, Univision and Telemundo.

Univision is the undisputed national market leader with an incredible 88% prime-time market share. Founded in 1962, Univision has recently enjoyed, 1) rapidly expanding ad dollars, 2) its first successful "up-front" sell-in of advertising space, 3) a greater audience share, and 4) rave reviews from Wall Street. "We anticipate that this (Univision) will be one of the best performing stocks in the broadcast industry," says Merrill Lynch Global Securities stock analyst Jessica Reif in a report to shareholders. "I think they are tapping into the fastest growing segment of the population that is incredibly attractive to advertisers and who are becoming bigger and better consumers. They have hired very good people from the Anglo marketplace to help run the company."

Univision reaches 93% of U.S. Hispanic households via 12 full power stations covering nine of the top 10 Hispanic viewer-designated market areas, as well as an additional seven low-power stations, 29 affiliated television stations and 826 cable systems. Univision has become so powerful, in fact, that it now touts itself as the "fifth full-time network," delivering close to two million viewers every hour of prime time.

Univision's success began in 1992 when two Latin America-based programmers, Televisa and Venevision, joined media mogul Jerrold Perenchio to buy Univision from Hallmark, the greeting card company. These two Latin American networks provide Univision with two-thirds of its programming, including the popular "novelas," nightly soap operas.

-13-

At least part of the credit for Univision's recent rapid rise goes to Henry Cisneros, former U.S. Secretary of Housing and Urban Development, who became president and chief operating officer of Univision in early 1997. Cisneros' position as a powerful and leading Hispanic figure has created for the network a higher level profile than previously possible. To further heighten its visibility, the network recently signed WBC welterweight champion Oscar De La Hoya as its spokesman.

Telemundo, a distant second place with roughly 13 percent of the prime-time Hispanic audience, is not about to give up without a fight. The owners of Telemundo sought and found a deep-pocketed buyer for the network. In November, 1997 Sony Corp. led a $440 million buyout of the network, believing that it has the cash, expertise and vision to make Telemundo work.

Since it does not have access to low-priced Latin America-produced programming as does Univision, Telemundo has been forced to generate its own programming, featuring talk shows, news magazines, and a broad variety of sports, comedy and drama programming. Telemundo management is seeking a partnership with one of the big U.S. television programmers that will give the network access to the entertainment formats of hit English-language shows. Telemundo would then create Spanish-language versions of those shows. "We want to break the historic programming models that have been used in the U.S. (Spanish-language market) and take a new direction that addresses the lifestyles of the U.S. audience. There is a huge opportunity here because the U.S. Hispanic audience, particularly in prime time, hasn't had the benefit of large quantities of non-telenovela product."

Telemundo reaches 85% of U.S. Hispanic households via its 7 full-power owned and operated stations in the top seven markets, 43 affiliated broadcast stations, 91 satellite-direct cable systems and more than 513 cable systems.

Beyond these two primary players, there are dozens of local Spanish-language stations located geographically in areas of Hispanic concentration.

3.1.3 Chicago Hispanic Television

The Chicago metropolitan area is home to 1.2 million Hispanic residents, fifth in the nation after Los Angeles, Miami/Fort Lauderdale, New York and San Francisco/Oakland/San Jose. These residents constitute a ready market for Hispanic television programming, and the industry has not disappointed them.

Chicago is home to five significant Spanish-language stations:

- **Univision, Channel 66** — This network has already been described in detail. All programming, except for some news, is national.

- **Telemundo, Channel 44** — This network has already been described in detail. All programming, except for some news, is national.

- **Galavision** — Galavision is a secondary national cable Spanish-language network owned by Univision. All programming, except for some news, is national.

- **Channel 25/Showcase Chicago** — Channel 25 is a local cable station (carried in Chicago only) providing a variety of locally produced programs, some of which are Spanish-language.

- **Channel 46** — Channel 46 is a local broadcast station that "serves the unique and diverse multi-cultural community in Chicago." The station broadcasts from an antenna atop the Sears Tower, and reaches the overwhelming majority of Chicagoland Hispanic residents. It carries a great variety of programs in more than 15 languages throughout the day. There is one Spanish-language program aired on Saturday afternoon. This is the station with which Latina Media is negotiating for the broadcasting of *Juventud Hispana*.

3.2 JH Target Market

3.2.1 JH Target Customer

In the reality of the Chicago Hispanic Television Industry, as is the case in most of the television industry and much of the publishing industry, Latina Media finds itself with an odd juxtaposition between its target customer group and its "product."

In order to accurately develop the growth plan for the Company, it is vitally important to understand the true relationship between Latina Media, the viewing audience, and the advertisers/sponsors. The "product" that Latina Media sells is <u>not</u> the program that is viewed by the audience. The programming simply provides a mechanism through which Latina Media is able to develop a television audience that can then be sold for its value to advertisers and sponsors. The reality, then, is that:

- The Company's target customers are *advertisers and sponsors* that want to reach Chicagoland Hispanics aged 10-19 years of age.

- The "product" the Company sells is access to the *viewing audience*—the opportunity for advertisers and sponsors to reach a specific target audience (Chicagoland Hispanics 10-19 years) with an appropriate message. The overall advertising market potential may be measured as total annual spending on Chicagoland Spanish-language advertising. What is the total annual Chicagoland Hispanic ad spend? <u>The *1997 Hispanic Business* reports 1997 advertising expenditures in the Chicago Hispanic market totaled over $62 million, led by television at $27.3 million,</u> then radio with $22.5 million, and print at $12.5 million.

- The programming represents the vehicle through which Latina Media generates the audience, which it then sells to the advertisers and sponsors.

Defining the customer as the advertiser/sponsor does not in any way diminish the vital importance of creating television programming that is appropriate for, and appealing to, the intended viewing audience. On the contrary, the fact that the Company's programs are the <u>sole</u> vehicle through which Latina Media generates its audience serves to underscore the fact that the presentation of appealing and effective programming is the most important element in developing our "product," the viewing audience. In other words, the Company must develop programs that appeal to the viewing audience in order to create an audience large enough to appeal to its sponsors and advertisers. A detailed review of the targeted viewing audience appears in Chapter 5. The remainder of <u>this</u> chapter details the advertisers and sponsors that Latina Media will pursue.

To this point, the term "sponsors/advertisers" has been used as if these target customers are a monolithic group. The fact is, of course, that advertisers and sponsors share commonalities but have substantial differences as well.

TARGETED ADVERTISERS

Latina Media targets businesses that have demonstrated interest in reaching Chicagoland Hispanics. These businesses have been identified by logging the names of current advertisers on Chicago's Hispanic stations. The initial list includes:

- McDonald's

- Burger King

- Revlon

- Toys 'R Us

- L'Oreal

- Coca Cola

- Domino's Pizza

Each of these businesses, as well as many others, will be directly targeted by Latina Media to buy advertising time on *Juventud Hispana*.

TARGETED SPONSORS

The concept of program sponsorship introduces a different group of institutions than those targeted for advertising. Sponsorship of *Juventud Hispana* is viewed as the role of major corporations, foundations, and public or non-profit institutions. Sponsorship involves a higher level of financial commitment; a more "noble" intent; an interest in deploying the institution's resources to support a cause in which the institution has a constituency or special interest. Several institutions already currently sponsor other similar Hispanic-oriented programs, and are primary targets for Latina Media. However, there are dozens, if not hundreds, of additional corporations, foundations, and institutions in Chicagoland that would, by their nature and interest, be appropriate targets for Latina Media and *Juventud Hispana*. The following potential sponsors represent the initial target list:

-16-

- Chicago Park District

- Chicago Public Schools

- Sears

- Abbott Laboratories

- Chicago Catholic Archdiocese

3.2.2 JH Purchase Patterns & Process

Because of their differing functions and objectives, it is appropriate to examine the purchase patterns of advertisers and sponsors separately.

ADVERTISERS

Commercial advertisers select their advertising venues based on a simple concept. They try to maximize the number of target customers "hit," and maximize the frequency of hits on each target customer. Advertisers are always seeking new and better ways to accomplish this goal. Large, mainstream businesses often use the services of an advertising agency. These agencies provide support to the advertiser in the conceptual and design phases of their advertising campaign, as well as the specific placement of advertising into various media.

Smaller businesses, however, must rely on their own creativity and judgment. They often rely on the representatives of the various media for advice and support with regard to their advertising campaigns. For instance, newspapers will often help small-business owners design the advertisement placed in their paper. Likewise, television and radio stations often assist small customers in the design and production of their advertising spots.

SPONSORS

Sponsors, like advertisers, seek to optimize their influence with the target audience. However, sponsors often take a more direct interest in assuring that the vehicle selected "fits" the mission of the sponsoring organization. Decisions regarding sponsorship of broadcast television programming is usually made on a case-by-case basis.

3.3 JH Targeted Television Audience

3.3.1 The Chicagoland Hispanic Community

The Chicagoland Hispanic community is large, financially strong, and growing. Consider:

-17-

- Chicago is home to 1.2 million Hispanics; fifth in the nation after Los Angeles, Miami/Fort Lauderdale, New York and San Francisco/Oakland/San Jose.

- Chicago Hispanics comprise 288,300 households.

- The average Chicago Hispanic household is composed of 3.84 individuals, compared to 2.71 persons in Chicago non-Hispanic households.

- The mean household income for Chicago area Hispanics is $39,332.

- The total buying power for Chicagoland Hispanics is $9,071,456,000.

While the statistics clearly support the current importance of the Hispanic community to the Chicagoland area, they do not adequately represent the <u>future</u> impact that the Hispanic community will have in Chicagoland. Consider the following excerpt from *American Demographics*, January 1998:

> It's <u>where</u> Illinois is growing that makes it worth watching. The state's future is suburban, and to a lesser extent, Hispanic, according to 1997 County population projections prepared for the Illinois bureau of the budget... Much of the urban and suburban growth in Illinois will probably belong to the state's burgeoning Hispanic population. Hispanics are expected to increase their numbers much faster than non-Hispanics. Hispanics may account for 52% of newcomers to Illinois to 2020...Cook County would probably decline in population if it weren't a magnet for Hispanic immigrants. Three-fourths of the state's Hispanics lived in Cook County in 1995, and 92% lived in Cook and five other Chicago-area counties. In Cook County, newly arriving Hispanics should offset projected declines in the non-Hispanic population between 1995 and 2020. The number of non-Hispanics in the County is projected to decline 6% during the period. But **<u>a 65% increase in the Hispanic population will add 530,000 newcomers to the County between 1995 and 2020</u>**."

It seems clear that the Hispanic influence in Chicago will continue to gain strength for at least the next several decades. The timing of the establishment of Latina Media could hardly be better.

3.3.2 The Selected JH Audience

Juventud Hispana **is television programming specifically designed to reach Chicagoland Hispanic youth aged 10 to 19 years.** In 1996, the six County area was home to almost 200,000 Hispanic youth in the target age range. The county-specific breakdown is as follows:

-18-

Hispanic Youth Demographics

County	Population	% of Target Market
Cook	159,525	81
DuPage	8,340	4
Kane	12,100	6
Lake	10,088	5
McHenry	1,599	1
Will	5,863	3
Total	197,515	100

As noted earlier, *Juventud Hispana* was universally viewed as the program of greatest interest to the viewing audience and the most supportable commercially. Research has demonstrated a strong interest in *Juventud Hispana* on the part of advertisers, sponsors, and Hispanic viewing youth.

3.3.3 JH Demographics & Psychographics

The Hispanic youth market (under age 20) is the fastest-growing segment in the nation, and it is expected to grow to 12.7 million by 2005 (from 8.4 million in 1990, a 52% increase in 15 years), while the non-Hispanic youth market is expected to decrease during the same period. Demographic trends in the Chicagoland Hispanic market should parallel the national direction.

As the Hispanic youth market grows it will become increasingly important. Major market players in the toy, apparel, soft drink, food, and media industries have noticed this trend and are targeting Hispanic youth and their parents.

What do we know about this rapidly expanding group called Hispanic youth? First, they follow the strong tendency of their parents and grandparents to be closely associated with family and involved in family activities. Hispanic culture stresses child dependency on parents, whereas traditional American culture stresses independence. Hispanic children and teens follow developmental stages like any other child or teen in the world. However, their unique familial context and ways of social interaction require marketers to recognize the differences between Hispanic culture and middle-class Anglo culture.

Generally, Hispanic children and teens:

- Speak Spanish at home

- Are mostly Catholic, but Protestants are increasing

- Are family-oriented

- Are group-oriented

Loretta Adams, president of Marketing Development Inc., says her research company conducted a survey among 500 Hispanic teenagers ages 12-17 last October. Results showed 88% of the teens surveyed were born in the United States. Half of those had at least one parent who was born outside the U.S.. About 34% speak Spanish at home while 4% speak Spanish with friends. About 14% speak English at home and 37% speak English with their friends. The data also indicate Hispanic teens are closely identified with their family, heritage and culture.

"Culture defines attitudes," says Ms. Adams. Hispanic teens are not rebels. In general, their attitudes tend to reflect the morals and values of their parents. Family relationships are valued and, according to the MDI survey, more than 75% of those surveyed perceive their parents or family members as heroes.

Tony Dieste, president of Dieste & Partners, Dallas, says the Hispanic teens are "on top of trends and constantly changing their opinions." Hispanic teens tend to navigate between two languages and two cultures. It is a marketing challenge to develop a creative strategy to reach this group because they are both a bicultural and bilingual group. "Music is one of the major in-culture attributes of Hispanic teens that binds them together," says Mr. Dieste, who adds that Hispanic teens share a passion for Latin music. The styles of music differ from salsa to Latin pop, but are all based on Latin roots, he adds.

The tendency of Hispanic youths to feel as if they are being pulled between two cultures and two languages may be the impetus for a new hybrid style of speech and language called "Spanglish," an aptly named mixture of English and Spanish. An increasing number of Hispanic youths recognize Spanglish as a language option.

3.4 The Program, "Juventud Hispana"

3.4.1 JH Program Description

Juventud Hispana **is a weekly situation-based television program centered on the lifestyle and events of Chicagoland Hispanic youth.**

The setting for the program is the fictional Arts and Literature class of Teacher Perez at a Chicago-area high school. Teacher Perez is the show's sole adult lead character. He is surrounded by 6 student lead characters; a mix of gender and ethnicity. These seven characters are the permanent cast members of the show (although the six students will be recast each academic year), and offer week-to-week cast continuity. All other cast members are interchangeable students representing the high school student body. (Note: this theme and setting represents slight changes introduced since the pilot was produced.)

-20-

The program will be taped at an actual Chicago-area high school, with the ability to use exterior and interior real-life crowd shots; and the use of one classroom, the cafeteria, and the auditorium for cast-only shots.

With each new school year, Teacher Perez will "select" from his Arts and Literature class six students to operate the school's "television production team." Through the school year, this team of 6, along with Teacher Perez, "produce" a weekly television program featuring issues of importance to Chicagoland Hispanic youth. This program, "La Juventud de la Chicago," "The Youth of Chicago," is supposedly "broadcast" to all of Chicagoland via a local access channel. Therefore, the "programming" is targeted toward all Chicagoland youth, not just students of this local high school. Topics may include music, dancing, cars and driving, education, sex, pregnancy, drug and alcohol awareness, sexually transmitted diseases awareness, college, general health, finances, Chicagoland cultural attractions, etc.

Each weekly episode will include real, local musical talent. Chicagoland high school performers, including soloists, groups, private bands, etc., will be able to submit audition tapes to Latina Media. Selected artists will be invited to the program set for video taping.

This "situation setting" offers Latina Media the opportunity to create a fast-moving, entertaining, issues-oriented program with tremendous appeal to advertisers and sponsors.

3.4.2. JH Production Plan

It is generally accepted that television programs are produced in two separate 13-episode groups each year—13 fall-season episodes plus 13 spring-season episodes. In order to enter the market strongly, *Juventud Hispana* will produce 15 episodes in the Fall '00 season and 17 episodes in the Spring '01 season. Following this inaugural year, Juventud Hispana will produce 26 total episodes each year, 13 in each season. The show will, of course, be broadcast each week, using reruns to fill the remaining 26 weeks per year.

The writing/shooting schedule for each seasonal group will be broken into respective blocks of 3-5 episodes each. A brief description of the production plan is as follows:

- Scripts will be developed in blocks of three to five programs, yielding continuity and connectedness from show to show. The primary writer will be Elena herself. Elena has written dozens of programs, and will write at least the first and second episodes herself. If time constraints require it (due to stronger than expected bookings for social event videos), Elena has made arrangements to subcontract writing services from three experienced Hispanic writers in Chicagoland. Ricardo Isles is a writer and director who is a primary figure in the Chicagoland Hispanic television/video marketplace. In addition, Elena has a writing commitment from two writers who previously wrote for "Television Azteca," one of the primary Mexican television production companies. When outside writers are required, Latina Media will pay a flat $500 per one-hour episode, including all necessary revisions.

-21-

- Elena will break each script into a shooting schedule, then combine the shooting schedules of the entire multiple-episode block in order to produce an optimized master shooting schedule for that block of programs.

- Shooting will be done on each block of programs in a four- to six-day shoot. All of the episodes will be completely shot during this single multi-day shoot.

- Elena will edit all programs, estimating one editing day per episode.

- Final programs will be delivered to Channel 46 according to the final agreement.

- Production costs for each episode will consist of:

Writers	$ 500
Editors	300
Production Crew	1,700
Cast	350
Misc. expense	100

The writing, editing, production and cast expenses will not be paid at the time of shooting. Instead, they will be paid to coincide with receipt of revenue from the advertisers/sponsors for each specific episode. All revenue from each episode will be received from advertisers/sponsors prior to the airing of that episode.

3.5 JH Competition

3.5.1 JH Competitive Situation

As noted earlier, the Company's customers are advertisers and sponsors trying to reach Hispanic youth. They have a multitude of options available, all of which represent some level of competition for Latina Media. These include television, radio, newspapers, billboards, posters and leaflets, direct mail, etc.

Each of the potential media listed above has its own advantages. However, television is a unique medium, offering advertisers and sponsors the ability to impact their target audience with more power and more senses (sight _and_ sound) than any other medium. Therefore, Elena is convinced that the proper competitive comparisons must be made between _Juventud Hispana_ and other Spanish-language, youth-oriented television programming available in Chicagoland Hispanic homes.

Juventud Hispana **will be groundbreaking programming for Spanish-speaking young people in the Chicago marketplace. Why? Because throughout all of Chicagoland, there are <u>no</u> other local television programs designed to reach this target group.** As described previously, the vast majority of Hispanic programming is national or international in scope.

_-22-_

Univision, Telemundo and Galavision all include certain program elements targeted to Hispanic youth. These are high-quality programs modeled after similar English-language programs. But they are all national or even international in scope and content.

Why will *Juventud Hispana* be able to compete successfully with these industry titans? The answer relates back to the unique distinctions that mark Hispanic culture—family-orientation and group-orientation. Hispanics affiliate with their local cultural group to a significantly greater extent than do their Anglo counterparts. They are deeply involved in their community and in each other's lives. The nature of *Juventud Hispana* directly and intentionally appeals to this desire for community and togetherness that permeates Hispanic culture. It is this local affiliation—this real-life connection to the Chicagoland community—that will continue to allow *Juventud Hispana* to occupy a distinct niche in Chicagoland Hispanic television programming.

Channel 46 carries one Saturday afternoon program that offers both competition and potential synergy. *El Show de Angelo Lopez* presents a weekly review of live Hispanic music events in the Chicagoland area. The producer, Angelo Lopez, has enjoyed great success in attracting advertisers for his program. Since *Juventud Hispana* will be slotted immediately following Angelo's show, the synergy opportunities are obvious.

3.5.2 JH Potential Competitors

Will television competitors create local programs to compete with *Juventud Hispana*? New direct competition would almost certainly come from one of two venues. First, new television competition could come from the established national networks, Univision, Telemundo or Galavision. While this is theoretically possible, there is no anticipation of any change in programming philosophy forthcoming from the major national Hispanic networks. Their strength is in "macro-programming"—national or international programming distributed via local affiliates. Local programming is neither their forte nor their future.

Second, direct television competition could come from local Hispanic independent television producers with skills similar to Elena's. There is no current indication of, nor any anticipation of, any competitive Hispanic independent producer capable of and interested in producing any program that would compete with *Juventud Hispana*. It is Elena's intent to establish *Juventud Hispana* so firmly in the mind and viewing habits of Chicagoland Hispanic youth that the program becomes the medium of choice for top-level advertisers and sponsors. Producers of new competitive programs would be forced to develop other, second-tier advertisers and sponsors.

3.6 JH Marketing Plan

3.6.1 JH Positioning Statement

Juventud Hispana is the first and best locally produced and locally oriented television program targeting Chicagoland Hispanic youth aged 10-19 years. It is the most effective and efficient television vehicle available to reach this important and growing audience.

3.6.2 Four P's—Product

Every aspect of *Juventud Hispana* has been designed to appeal to the target customer (the advertisers and sponsors) and the target viewing audience (Hispanic youth). The program name, setting, content, music, issues and format have all been created to maximize the impact on the audience and the appropriateness for advertisers and sponsors. Careful and continuous attention to customer and viewer needs and wants will ensure that *Juventud Hispana* remains a viable program for years to come.

3.6.3 Four P's—Price

Pricing for advertising space on *Juventud Hispana* will initially be established in a range comparable to that for other similar programming on Channel 46. For instance, the program *El Show de Angelo Lopez* is carried each Saturday afternoon, with a 30-second spot selling for $150. Although initial pricing on *Juventud Hispana* will be $150 per 30-second spot, Elena believes that the program will eventually be able to command a higher rate.

In addition to standard advertising, *Juventud Hispana* will secure institutional sponsors for each episode. As described earlier, these sponsors may be large corporations, foundations, public institutions or governmental bodies. The sponsors will be recognized during the program, and may sponsor specific episodes in which the programming issues have particular interest to the sponsoring institution. Sponsorship rates will begin at $500 per episode, and may range up to $1,000 or more per episode. It is possible that one sponsor, or a small group of sponsors, may wish to underwrite the entire program.

3.6.4 Four P's—Place (Distribution)

Latina Media will sell directly to its institutional sponsors and advertisers through a professional sales staff. The program will not be "bundled," distributed or sold through a secondary network affiliation.

3.6.5 Four P's—Promotion

Promotion will be comprised of an assertive combination of three primary components:

1. **Personal selling** — Properly targeted potential sponsors and advertisers will be contacted by a professional sales team. At launch, the sales team will consist of two strongly bilingual experienced salespeople:

   - **Martinez Delatorre** — Martinez has been a part of the Chicagoland Hispanic media for years. He currently sells advertising for the largest Hispanic newspaper in Chicagoland, *La Raza*. In addition, he has experience in selling radio and television to local advertisers. Martinez will be responsible for generating sales in the city of Chicago (representing roughly 65% of the Chicagoland Hispanic population.)

-24-

- **Pat Guzman** — Pat is an experienced sales professional who has a strong desire to become a part of the Hispanic media business. Pat will take responsibility for the non-Chicago area, representing about 35% of the Hispanic community.

A media kit is in development which will include high-quality selling materials along with a demo tape of the program.

2. **Aggressive networking** — As noted earlier in this plan, Hispanics tend to be group-oriented and family-oriented. Elena will expand her already substantial network within the Chicagoland Hispanic community in order to contact and convince key sponsor and advertiser targets that Juventud Hispana is the best way to reach the 10-19 year old Chicagoland Hispanic youth.

3. **On-air advertising** — Initially, spots will be produced to sell advertisers on the benefits of advertising on *Juventud Hispana*.

Of course, there will be additional elements within the marketing plan, but these three form the foundation.

3.6.6 JH Sales Plan

Each 60-minute program includes 14 minutes of advertising time slots (28 x 30-second slots) including two minutes of sponsorship recognition. **The initial sales plan calls for the first four programs to air with 14 x 30-second advertising time slots filled, the next four episodes to run with 21 x 30-second slots sold, and all future episodes to run with all 28 slots sold.** At the initial rate of $150 per 30-second spot, this represents a final potential of $4,200 of advertising revenue per episode (28 spots @ $150).

The initial pool of targeted advertisers will consist of local businesses currently running spot television advertisements targeted to the Hispanic market. These have been collected by direct observation.

In addition to standard advertising, *Juventud Hispana* will begin airing with a minimum of two institutional sponsors for each of the first four episodes, three sponsors for each of the next four episodes, and four sponsors each for all future episodes. With first-year sponsorship rates of $500 per episode, these sponsorships have the potential to contribute an additional $1,000 to $2,000 per episode, or more.

The initial pool of targeted sponsors will be selected from two sources. First, local Hispanic television is being monitored to identify those institutions and organizations currently using television to reach their target audience. This will constitute the A-list. Second, a data search is underway to identify additional potential sponsors that are not currently using television to reach their target audience. This group will form the B-list.

As delineated in chapter 2.6, Near-Term Objectives, Elena has established the following first year objectives for *Juventud Hispana*:

- Sign contract with Channel 46 by Dec 31, 2001 to broadcast an initial four months of *Juventud Hispana*, first airing on September 9, 2002.

- Achieve four-month (Sep-Dec, 01) funding commitment from inaugural advertisers and sponsors by June 30, 2002.

In order to accomplish these goals, Elena will take the following action steps:

1. Complete initial lists of potential advertisers and sponsors by December 31, 2001.

2. Complete all permanent promotional items (media kit, business cards, brochures, demo tape) by December 31, 2001.

3. Contract and train Martinez Delatorre and Pat Guzman by December 31, 2001.

4. Initiate customer calls by January 1, 2002.

Latina Media will buy its time slot on Channel 46 for $650 per week. Latina Media will deliver to Channel 46 a one-hour tape for each week's programming slot. This tape will include the program, with its advertisers' and sponsors' messages incorporated into the program. In other words, Channel 46 will have no responsibility for, nor control of, the advertising and sponsorship messages included in each week's program. Channel 46 derives its revenue solely from the $650 payment made by Latina Media.

4.0 SOCIAL EVENT VIDEO (SV)

4.1 SV Target Market

4.1.1 SV Target Customer

Hispanics are traditionally highly family-oriented. This tendency has continued unabated in Hispanic families that are located in Chicagoland. There are four primary social events in the life of Hispanic females. Each of the four spans issues of family, culture and religion. In chronological order, they are 1) Christian Baptism, 2) First Communion, 3) Sweet 15 Party, and 4) Wedding. Although each of these is important, the last two in particular are planned for, dreamed of, and treated with utmost respect. The first of these two is the Sweet 15 Party. This is the Hispanic version of the "coming out" party—the passage to adulthood for Hispanic girls. There should be no mistake, this is a major event in the life of these young ladies. No cost is spared in making this the party of a lifetime. Families sometimes save for years in order to produce the type of Sweet 15 Party their daughter wants and deserves. The second major event in the Hispanic girl's life is her wedding. Again, no expense is spared in providing the wedding of her dreams.

Based on the pre-existing need and desire for professional quality video taping of Sweet 15 Parties and weddings, Latina Media **targets Cook County Hispanic girls aged 13-24, and their families**. This demographic group targets girls as they begin to dream and prepare for their Sweet 15 Party, and follows them through the typical marriage years.

-26-

The decision to restrict the geographic target area, rather than purse to the entire Chicagoland area is based on the following rationale:

1. Restricting the target market to Cook County minimizes travel costs to meet customers and to tape events. Since these are one-time events, it makes logistical sense to restrict the travel area.

2. The entire Chicagoland market is too large and diverse to be effectively or efficiently reached. Elena is aware that the television program *Juventud Hispana* will provide a valuable marketing vehicle to promote Social Video throughout the entire Chicago area. This opportunity may be captured in the future.

3. Evidence suggests that Cook County alone will provide the base of business desired.

Quantifying the number of Sweet 15 Parties and weddings each year in the target area is difficult, since there is no organized collection of the data. In order to create a reasonable estimate of the potential number, Latina Media was able to obtain a report of the number of events held at one church, Sagrada Familia (Sacred Family) Catholic Church, a large, predominantly Hispanic church in Chicago. **In 1999 alone, this <u>one church</u> conducted 546 baptisms, 148 First Communions, 70 weddings and 45 Sweet 15 Parties.** The church secretary noted that the number of Sweet 15s was low, and the 2002 number should be at or above the number of weddings.

Latina Media estimates the number of target area Hispanic females aged 13-24 at between 7,500 and 8,000. Based on an estimate of 750-800 target area Hispanic girls in each yearly cluster, the Company further estimates that each year the area is host to approximately 600 Sweet 15 Parties and 500 Hispanic weddings. These 1,100 events provide an opportunity to videotape roughly <u>90 events per month</u>, or almost <u>23 events per weekend</u>. Because of the increasing number of these events, they are being held on Fridays, Saturdays and Sundays, virtually every week of the year.

4.1.2 SV Purchase Patterns & Process

There is a strong word-of-mouth network that permeates these neighborhoods, and buying decisions are often made based on recommendations from friends and family. With specific regard to Sweet 15 Parties and weddings, there is a significant amount of peer pressure brought to bear on parents to provide a certain "level" of event.

4.2 SV Products

4.2.1 SV Product Description

Latina Media applies its professional talents and technologically superior equipment to create social event videos so exceptional that they rival some television programming. The event is captured on video from start to finish, then masterfully edited and dubbed to create a lifetime memory.

Elena has created five separate products representing five different levels of cost and value. Each successive level includes all features of the previous level, plus the noted additions, as follows:

- **Economy** — This basic level includes live taping at the church and the reception; professional editing; music over-dubbing; and special effects. The final product is one complete professional two-hour videotape, labeled and boxed. The delivered price is $400. Additional copies of the tape are available for $25 each.

- **Basic** — Add: special videotaping of key participants at a park or other site between the ceremony and the reception (this additional photo opportunity is often staged for the still photographer, but yields excellent video footage as well). The final tape is 2 1/2 hours long, priced at $500.

- **First Class** — Add: special videotaping at the honoree's home on the morning of the event. This captures the excited preparation for this important day in the girl's life. The final edited tape is 2 3/4 hours long. Also add: a special 25-minute condensed highlight film of the entire day's activities, for the client to show to family and friends. This package sells for $650.

- **Deluxe** — Add: a unique 20-minute video montage, with sound over-dubbing, created from childhood and family photographs of the honoree. This video is produced before the event, and shown during the event reception. Add: additional candid taping of the honoree in a setting of her choice on a day prior to the event. This package sells for $750.

- **Super Deluxe** — Add: complete two-camera shooting at all venues (special candid shoot of honoree, shooting at honoree's home, shooting the event at the church, shooting at the park, and shooting at the reception). This package sells for $950.

4.2.2 SV Production Plan

The specific production plan for each event depends on the product package purchased. The following is a review of the production of a First Class package.

Elena arrives early on the morning of the event at the client's home and captures on tape the family's preparation for the day. She then moves to the church and performs a "walk through" with the client prior to the event. With that information in hand, Elena establishes light and camera positions to properly capture each important phase of the event. Since the production is a one-camera shoot, Elena must constantly anticipate the action and its flow. The taping then moves on to the post-ceremony park shoot, party and dance. Unlike some competitors, Elena always stays through the entire event, so that she can capture all of the planned and unplanned important moments. All of the major elements of the event are captured on tape.

-28-

With the raw tape completed, Elena spends the next several hours in the editing booth. Editing work is broken into three primary segments. First, the video images are cut and spliced for the full video and the 25-minute highlight tape, with the appropriate fades and effects, to produce the finished video presentation. Second, the sound tracks are produced to match the video tracks. This not only involves the sound taken at the live event, but often includes additional music or voice dubbed onto the finished videos. Finally, video script (titles, dates, intro, credits, etc.) is superimposed onto the final master videos. The final masters are then copied onto VHS tapes for presentation to the client.

4.3 SV Competition

4.3.1 SV Competitive Situation

There are numerous Anglo companies selling video services in Cook County. These provide service to both personal and business customers. However, Hispanic families almost unanimously choose to do business with Hispanic providers of video services. This may be due to simple language barriers, a desire to support the Hispanic community, or other reasons. Nevertheless, the Anglo video companies do not impact in the Hispanic community.

The Cook County Hispanic community is served by just three Hispanic companies that provide social videotape services; Latina Media and two others, Mark Productions and Latino Video.

4.3.2 SV Primary Competitors

Mark Productions is a one-man operation run by a 30-year-old Waukegan man whom Elena personally trained to produce social event video. Elena's initial intent was to employ Mark as a secondary cameraman for her own social video business. After being trained by Elena, Mark began his own company in 1996.

Mark uses a home-model VHS camera, and has no editing equipment. Therefore, he provides his clients with a simple, home-quality, non-edited tape of their event. He charges his customers $380 for a completed 2-hour tape. Mark has a cousin who is affiliated with one of the large Catholic churches in Waukegan, and this relationship generates much of his business. In addition, he pays $40 to a local still photographer for each referral event captured. Mark recently purchased an additional camera, and is training his cousin in videotaping skills. It is estimated that Mark Productions is currently capturing an astounding 1-3 events per week.

Recently, Elena has become aware that Mark has attempted to break into the still photography market for social events, in spite of the fact that he has no training or proper equipment. The "word on the street" is that Mark is beginning to suffer from a bad reputation for his still photography work and for his video productions. It seems that his inattention to professional equipment and high production quality may be starting to take its toll.

-29-

Latino Video is a Waukegan-based business run from a storefront clothing boutique. Latino Video uses a VHS camera better than Mark's, but well below the quality of Latina Media. Latino Video does have an expensive effects generator (editing computer) that allows him to do some nice post-production work. In spite of possessing decent equipment, this company produces an inferior product—using their current equipment, Latino Video produced a television program pilot that was turned down by local TCI channel 17 (the "take all" public access channel).

Latino Video produces a 2-hour final video, and charges its clients from $300-$1,000, depending on the client's ability to pay. It has been difficult to determine how many events Latino Video produces, but an educated guess is 2-4 events per month.

4.4 SV Marketing Plan

4.4.1 SV Positioning Statement

Latina Media is the leading provider of special event videotaping services to Cook County Hispanics.

4.4.2 Four P's—Product

Latina Media believes that the most effective marketing device is to provide a superior product. Therefore, the Company pledges to deliver to its customers a finished video product that is beyond their expectations, and significantly superior to the product offered by the competition. To the trained eye, and the untrained as well, video projects generated by Latina Media are the leaders in the marketplace. Quality is the Company's first and foremost marketing tool.

First, Latina Media video products are created using superior-quality camera and editing equipment. Second, the camera and editing work is completed by an established professional, Elena Trujillo. Her skill, combined with professional equipment and exceptional attention to detail, results in a final video product that stands head and shoulders above the local competition.

As described in detail in Chapter 4.2.1, Latina Media has developed multiple packages that appeal to the variety of needs and budgets of clients. The development of specific products to meet specific needs demonstrates Elena's commitment to the customer.

4.4.3 Four P's—Price

The pricing of the video packages has been developed based on three primary determinants. First, the price for each package must cover the direct cost of the product and produce gross profit to cover fixed costs. Second, the pricing considers the prices being charged by the competition. Third, the prices must be within a range that customers are willing to pay.

-30-

In every case, for all five product levels, Elena is convinced that the prices selected are appropriate and sustainable in the marketplace.

4.4.4 Four P's—Place (Distribution)

Latina Media sells its social event video taping service directly to its customers. The Company does not use agents, retail location distribution, or independent sales representatives to promote its services.

4.4.5 Four P's—Promotion

Latina Media will use a cluster of promotional tools to reach its market. These may be grouped as follows:

ADVERTISING

The Company will advertise in those vehicles that provide direct and specific access to the target audience. These include primarily Yellow Pages; radio; and posters and leaflets displayed at appropriate retailers.

SALES PROMOTION

The Company will use appropriate exhibits and demonstrations at fairs and trade shows; discount coupons; and tie-ins with affiliated businesses such as churches, still photographers, florists, caterers, retail bridal stores, and wedding and party consultants.

PUBLICITY

The Company will seek publicity through press releases and the targeted provision of free services. Specifically, Elena will offer free taping and editing of certain high-profile public events of importance to the Hispanic community. Through this process, the Company will be able to demonstrate its skill to the target audience, and distribute promotional material on-site. Finally, Elena will use her position within the *Coalicion Latinas Unidos of Cook County* to promote the Company.

PERSONAL SELLING

All of the previously discussed promotional efforts will generate interest in, and calls to, Latina Media. Elena will personally follow-up on each call to complete the sale. Sales tools will include demonstration tapes, professional brochures and price lists, and professional business cards.

4.4.6 SV Sales Plan

Elena has established the FY 2002 goal of producing two social event videos per month in July, August and September, 2001; four per month from October '01 through January '02; and six per month thereafter. This yields a total of 52 social events in FY 2002, at an average of $600 per event.

In addition, she has been recruited (subject to obtaining the new video equipment) to work as a freelance videographer for two large Hispanic-owned video production companies in Chicago. In each case, Elena will be responsible to attend and tape a specific event (social events such as weddings and Sweet 15 Parties) using her own equipment, and deliver an edited tape. She has set a target of three freelance events in July through September '01; and two per month thereafter, for a total of 27 freelance events for the year. These pay a flat $350 per event.

In order to accomplish this goal, Elena will take the following action steps:

1. Finalize the agreements with both freelancing studios by June 15, 2001.

2. Complete all permanent promotional items (business cards, brochures, demo tape, posters and flyers) by June 15, 2001.

3. Arrange a reciprocal referral agreement with key affiliated businesses by June 15, 2001.

4. Complete distribution and posting of flyers and posters in appropriate retail locations by June 15, 2001.

5.0 SWOT ANALYSIS

5.1 Company Strengths

Latina Media will initiate operations with several important strengths:

- **Elena Trujillo** — Elena offers Latina Media knowledge and experience that clearly set it apart from similar Chicagoland Hispanic television and video production companies. This is an irreplaceable strength.

- **Network with Chicagoland Hispanics** — This is a strength related to Elena personally, but one that reaches beyond the the personal contribution. As the Company strengthens its credibility in the marketplace, the network strength that began with Elena will deepen and solidify.

- **Strong staff of sales, production, and writing professionals** — Beyond Elena herself, Latina Media will start up with solid professionals in these key positions.

5.2 Company Weaknesses

- **Shortage of capital** — Having just recently moved to the United States, Elena has little cash to invest in the business. Therefore, Latina Media must secure outside funding for initial equipment and working capital.

-32-

- **Inexperience selling advertising and sponsorships for *Juventud Hispana*** — Although all indicators suggest that *Juventud Hispana* will be openly received by targeted customers, the final test will come only when the program is rolled out in actual production.

- **Latina Media is a new company in the Chicago market** — As a new company competing against established companies in the social video market and the television market, Latina Media will face resistance. The Company's resilience and determination will be tested early and often.

5.3 Market Opportunities

- **Rapidly growing customer base** — The growth of the Chicagoland Hispanic community is unmistakable, and will continue for decades to come. This singular opportunity will provide a growing source of revenue for Latina Media for the foreseeable future.

- **No substantive local television competition** — This gap in television programming represents an opportunity waiting to be seized. Latina Media will be the best at capitalizing on it.

- **Weak competition for Social Video** — The apparent weakening of Mark Productions offers an immediate opportunity for Latina Media to capture a major share of the social video market.

5.4 Market Threats

- **New television competition from major players** — Although there is no sign of it currently, any decision by one of the major Hispanic networks (Univision or Telemundo) to seriously develop local programming would represent a serious challenge to *Juventud Hispana*. It is clear that local programming is not the strength of these networks, and there is no reason to believe that local programming will become a strength in the future. In the extremely unlikely event of this national competition occurring, Latina Media could and would remain the low-cost provider.

- **Failure of ability to broadcast on Channel 46** — Channel 46 currently represents the clearly best broadcast medium for *Juventud Hispana*. If Channel 46 failed, or if the relationship between Channel 46 and Latina Media failed, continuing airing of *Juventud Hispana* would be in jeopardy. In that event, options would include 1) contracting with Channel 25, 2) contracting with local cable companies, 3) contracting with Univision or Telemundo for local broadcasting.

- **General economic downturn** — A broad recession that would seriously damage the spending capacity of Chicagoland Hispanic families would represent a threat to Social Video and potential sales of advertising and sponsorships for *Juventud Hispana*. To defend against this possibility, the Company intends to 1) quickly retire all debt, 2) continuously build a low-cost operation, and 3) develop a core group of substantial advertisers and sponsors that will enable continued operation.

6.0 OPERATIONS

6.1 Equipment and Facilities

Latina Media will initiate operations with adequate camera and editing equipment. Elena's professional expertise, combined with high-quality equipment, will establish the Company as one of the leading players in the Chicagoland Hispanic television and video marketplace.

Specifically, the equipment must be of a quality that 1) meets Elena's personal standards, 2) generates a product that is appealing to the viewing audience, and 3) is acceptable to Channel 46.

Elena has selected a digital camera and editing package in which all components are perfectly integrated. The list of initial equipment, with prices, appears in the Appendix (not included in this sample plan). The three key components of the package are the camera, the video editing suite, and a custom-designed IBM-compatible desktop computer. Full documentation of the selected equipment is available, and cost quotes for each element is included in the appendix. This package, although quite reasonably priced, affords Latina Media the ability to produce programs of a quality that exceeds both current standards <u>and</u> standards anticipated within the next five years.

Latina Media is a home-based business, and all business activities, with the exception of location shoots, will be conducted from the Company office in Elena's residence.

6.2 Operational Plan

Operationally, Latina Media will focus its energies on two fronts simultaneously.

- **Program Quality** — In order to grow a successful business, Latina Media must produce high-quality video programming. Whether in the broadcast television program *Juventud Hispana*, or in the social event videos produced for individual clients, the Company realizes that its short-term and long-term success depends, to a great extent, on creating superior-quality programs. In order to accomplish this, Elena will take personal responsibility for program quality. Programming is Elena's strength, and it is in this area where her ability and experience will have the greatest impact. Quantifying "quality" is difficult, and Latina Media believes that the best evidence of quality is the acceptance of the Company's products by its target customers.

- **Selling** — The production of a quality program does not guarantee a successful business enterprise. The second, and equally important, operational requirement is to successfully sell *Juventud Hispana* and social event videos to their respective audiences. In order to maximize sales of advertising and sponsorship of *Juventud Hispana*, Elena has already established contract selling agreements with Pat Guzman and Martinez Delatorre. These are selling professionals that are ready to bring their expertise to Latina Media.

The selling of Social Video is somewhat different, for two primary reasons: 1) the target customers are geographically concentrated in Cook County, and 2) the marketing strategy uses non-personal marketing tools to generate calls to Latina Media, then finalize the sale through personal sales efforts. These two facts create a selling situation in which there is little or no prospecting, and the closing rate can be very high (50-70%). In this case, Elena herself will manage the sales effort. Why should Elena use her time to generate Social Video sales? For several reasons:

1. The Social Video segment of the business represents the foundational cash flow generator of the Company. This is vital business, and Elena is the best person to fulfill the role.

2. By their nature, these target customers are not sophisticated buyers, and do not need or want to be sold by "professional" sales people.

3. Because of the high closing rate with no prospecting, paying outside sales people would be unnecessary and too costly.

4. "Elena Trujillo" is becoming a very well-known and respected name in and around the Cook County Hispanic community. Since Social Video events are very public, they represent a great opportunity for Elena to heighten her personal and business reputation. When Elena personally visits with these families to finalize their video programming needs, the closing rate could go as high as 90%.

5. The revenue per call and per hour will be very high. This is good use of Elena's time and effort.

7.0 MANAGEMENT SUMMARY

7.1 Personnel Plan

It should be noted that the video production industry is somewhat different than most other businesses, in that many, if not most, of the staff work as freelancers. This will be true in the case of Latina Media—each of the following people/positions will be on a freelance basis (independent contractor status).

1. **Writers/Editors** — As time constraints require it, Elena will subcontract writing and editing services from three experienced Hispanic professionals in Chicagoland. Ricardo Isles is a writer and director who is a primary figure in the Chicagoland Hispanic television/video marketplace. In addition, Elena has a writing commitment from two writers who previously wrote for "Television Azteca" one of the primary Mexican television production companies.

2. **Sales Staff** — As noted previously, selling advertising for *Juventud Hispana* will be the primary role of two sales professionals. Martinez Delatorre has been a part of the Chicagoland Hispanic media market for years. He currently sells advertising for the largest Hispanic newspaper in Chicagoland, *La Raza*. In addition, he has experience in selling radio and television to local advertisers. Martinez will be responsible for generating sales in the city of Chicago (representing roughly 65% of the Chicagoland Hispanic population.) Pat Guzman is an experienced real estate sales professional who has a strong desire to become a part of the Hispanic media business. Pat will take responsibility for the non-Chicago area, representing about 35% of the Hispanic community.

3. **Camera Operators** — Elena will initially do all of the camera work for Social Videos. However, for taping of *Juventud Hispana*, she will be directing, not shooting. Therefore, she must have excellent camera operators during taping of the television program. Roberto Isles is an outstanding videographer, and has agreed to work on the production of *Juventud Hispana*.

Note that each of these will affiliate with Latina Media as independent contractors. This is standard operating procedure in the television and video industry. Only Elena herself is carried as a salaried employee of the Company.

Personnel Plan

Personnel	FY2002	FY2003	FY2004
Elena Trujillo	$13,000	$19,800	$21,780
Other	$0	$0	$0
Total Payroll	$13,000	$19,800	$21,780
Total Headcount	1	1	1
Payroll Burden	$1,950	$2,970	$3,267
Total Payroll Expenditures	$14,950	$22,770	$25,047

8.0 FINANCIAL PLAN

8.1 Juventud Hispana Sales Forecast

8.1.1 Market Opportunity Analysis

1997 Hispanic Business reports Chicagoland advertising targeted at Hispanics totaled $62 million, $1.2 million per week. This is a total of television, radio and print spending, and is a reasonable total for this analysis, since *Juventud Hispana* will be one of the very few television advertising opportunities that will offer local advertisers a reasonable alternative to radio or print advertising. Based on this total, three different approaches are used to confirm a reasonable market potential for *Juventud Hispana*.

1. **Simple market penetration rate** — If *Juventud Hispana* captured just 1/2 of 1% (.005) of this $62 million annual expenditure, the weekly revenue for Latina Media would be $6,000. Is $6,000 a reasonable possibility, based on other experiences? Fortunately, two test cases (below) demonstrate that this level of penetration is a reasonable expectation.

2. **Advertising on a comparable program** — The 1 1/2 hour program *El Show de Angelo Lopez* is carried on Channel 46 each Saturday afternoon, with a 30-second spot selling for $150, and all spots are sold each week (in fact, Angelo reports that he is hoping to double his show in 2001 to a full <u>three hours</u> each week, based on advertising demand). Since *Juventud Hispana* is a higher quality show, carried on the same channel in a similar time slot, it is reasonable to expect that JH will be able to command at least $150 per 30-second spot. With 28 x 30-second spots available on each one-hour program, this totals $4,200 per one-hour episode. Additional revenue will come from sponsors. The experience of Angelo Lopez confirms the market potential of $5,000-6,000+ in weekly revenue.

3. ***Juventud Hispana* pilot sell-in** — As noted previously, the pilot of JH received corporate sponsorship totaling $5,850. It must be noted that two-thirds of the total was in trade value. However, $1,850 was <u>cash</u>, including $200 for a 30-second spot. It should also be noted that these sponsors were relatively small, local sponsors. Each of these sponsors was more than satisfied with the investment they made. One can only imagine the sponsorship potential of large Chicago-based sponsors such as Chicago Public Schools, the Chicago Park District, McDonald's Corp., the Abbott Foundation, or The Art Institute of Chicago. The experience of the pilot program confirms the market potential of $5,000-6,000 in weekly revenue.

8.1.2 Breakeven Analysis

The breakeven point for *Juventud Hispana* is defined as the amount of advertising/sponsorship revenue required <u>per episode</u> to cover all of the Company's production costs plus fixed costs. In order to calculate the breakeven, we must assign a direct cost of producing each dollar of revenue, as well as establishing the production cost per episode and the fixed costs of running the business:

1. **Direct cost of generating each dollar of advertising/sponsorship revenue** — For purposes of the analysis, the direct cost of generating each dollar of revenue is limited to the sales commission paid to the salesperson who sells the advertising. The analysis assumes that <u>all</u> advertising and sponsorships will be sold by outside sales agents Martinez Delatorre and Pat Guzman at a full commission of 25% of gross sales generated. **Therefore, each $1.00 of revenue has a direct cost of $0.25**.

2. **Production Costs per Episode** — *JH* production expenses include writing, editing, production crew, and cast: a total of **$2,950 per episode**. This total represents fully loaded costs, and three important points must be noted: 1) $500 of writing expense per episode has been included in the estimate, even though Elena intends to do most of the writing herself. 2) The total includes $300 per episode for outside editing expense, enough to fully compensate an outside editor. However, as in the case of writing, Elena intends to do all or most of the editing herself. 3) <u>Most importantly, it is vital to remember that this analysis assumes that each episode is newly produced each week. In reality, once the program is established, fully one-half of each year's episodes will be reruns, with no production costs</u>.

3. **Assigned Fixed Expenses per Episode** — Fixed monthly <u>administrative</u> expenses are taken from the Income Statement, and include advertising/promotion, travel, office expense, telephone, insurance, Elena's salary and tax burden, and depreciation, totalling $2,300 per month, or **$575 per episode** in a four-episode month. This analysis assumes that *JH* will be responsible for 100% of this monthly expense, when, in reality, this cost will be shared with Social Video.

As depicted in the following table and graph, the breakeven point for *Juventud Hispana* is $4,406 of advertising/sponsorship revenue per episode. Accepting the stringent assumptions used in this analysis, and assuming that revenue is generated according to the *Juventud Hispana* Sales Plan presented in Chapter 3.6.6, the program should approach breakeven status by the fifth episode (21 x 30-second advertising spots @ $150; plus 2 sponsors @ $500). In reality, breakeven should occur quickly, since:

- Elena will do all or most of the writing.

- Elena will do all or most of the editing.

- *Juventud Hispana* will only <u>share</u> in the coverage of fixed monthly administrative expenses of $2,300.

Breakeven Analysis

Assumptions	
Production Costs per Episode	$2,950
Fixed Costs per Episode	$575
Total Average Cost per Episode	$3,525
Sales Commissions	25% of ad revenues (approx. $881 for $3,525 of ad sales)
Breakeven Ad Revenue per Episode	$4,406

8.2 Social Video Sales Forecast

8.2.1 Market Opportunity Analysis

Latina Media estimates the number of target area Hispanic females aged 13-24 at between 7,500 and 8,000. Based on an estimate of 750-800 target area Hispanic girls in each yearly cluster, the Company further estimates that each year the area is host to approximately 600 Sweet 15 Parties and 500 Hispanic weddings. These 1,100 events provide an opportunity to videotape roughly <u>90 events per month</u>, or almost <u>23 events per weekend</u>. Because of the increasing number of these events, they are being held on Fridays, Saturdays and Sundays, virtually every week of the year.

With only weak competition from Mark Productions and Latino Video, it should be possible for Latina Media to capture up to 50% of this market, or 12 events per weekend. The current plan for the Company does not provide the capacity to capture 12 events per weekend, but long-term growth potential certainly exists.

8.2.2 Breakeven Analysis

In order to calculate a breakeven point for each Social Event, three key values are required—average revenue generated per event, direct cost of producing that revenue, and monthly fixed costs of running the business:

1. **Revenue per event —** This analysis assumes a modest revenue of **$600 per event**. The Company expects actual revenue to be closer to $700.

2. **Direct cost of producing the event —** The direct production cost for each event consists of videotape and travel expense—**a maximum total of $50 per event.**

3. **Monthly fixed expense —** Fixed monthly expenses are taken from the Income Statement, and include advertising/promotion, travel, office expense, telephone, insurance, Elena's full salary and tax burden, and depreciation, totaling **$2,300 per month.**

As depicted in the following table and graph, the breakeven point for Social Video is 4 events per month. In spite of the stringent assumptions used in this analysis, Social Video should achieve breakeven status in October, 2001. It is also necessary to bear in mind that breakeven should actually occur much sooner, since this analysis completely disregards the freelancing video work that Elena will be conducting. Each freelance event generates $350 revenue and $300 of gross profit. Adjusting the calculation by 1) including the stair-stepping of Elena's salary over the first seven months, and 2) including the expected freelancing revenue, breakeven occurs in month one.

Breakeven Analysis

Monthly Units Breakeven	4
Monthly Sales Breakeven	$2,509
Assumptions	
Average Per-Unit Revenue	$600.00
Average Per-Unit Variable Cost	$50.00
Estimated Monthly Fixed Cost	$2,300

Breakeven Analysis

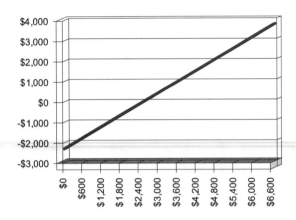

8.3 Resultant Sales Forecast

The following table and chart depict the resultant sales forecast for all four segments of revenue. The complete monthly schedule may be found in the Appendix.

FY 2002 Social Event revenue and Freelancing revenue are presented as detailed in the Sales Plan, Chapter 4.4.6. Social Video is calculated at $600 per event, with a Cost of Sales of $50 per event. Freelancing events are calculated at $350 per event, with a Cost of Sales of $50 per event. Outyears are forecast for steady volume (six social events and two freelance events per month) plus 10% annual price increases.

FY 2002 includes no revenue from *Juventud Hispana*, as detailed previously. Revenue in FY 2003 is presented as detailed in Chapter 3.6.6. Cost of Sales is calculated as 25% of revenue, paid as direct commission to sales staff. FY 2003 assumes a 10% price increase for advertising and sponsorships.

Sales Forecast

Sales	FY2002	FY2003	FY2004
Juventud Hispana Advertising	$0	$168,000	$240,240
Juventud Hispana Sponsorships	$0	$80,000	$114,400
Social Video	$31,200	$47,520	$52,272
Social Video Freelancing	$9,450	$9,240	$10,164
Other	$0	$0	$0
Total Sales	$40,650	$304,760	$417,076

Direct Cost of Sales	FY2002	FY2003	FY2004
Juventud Hispana Advertising	$0	$42,000	$60,600
Juventud Hispana Sponsorships	$0	$20,000	$28,600
Social Video	$2,600	$3,600	$3,600
Social Video Freelancing	$1,350	$1,200	$1,200
Other	$0	$0	$0
Subtotal Cost of Sales	$3,950	$66,800	$94,000

Total Sales by Month in Year 1

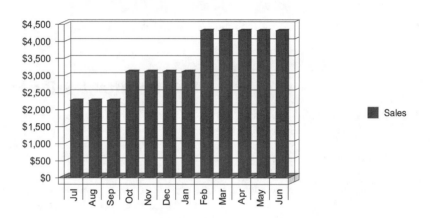

8.4 Projected Profit and Loss

The following table and chart depict the profit forecast for 2002, 2003 and 2004. The complete monthly schedule may be found in the Appendix. Depreciation on camera and editing equipment is taken on a straight 5-year schedule, with depreciation on the second camera commencing in March, 2002. Interest on the original $25,000 loan is calculated at 10.5% for 36 months.

FY 2003 costs for *Juventud Hispana* include the production of 32 new episodes and the airing of 43 episodes (one episode per week beginning September 9, 2002). FY 2004 *JH* costs include production of 26 episodes and airing of 52 episodes. Fees to Channel 46 assume a 10% increase per episode in 2004.

Profit and Loss (Income Statement)

Category	FY2002	FY2003	FY2004
Sales	$40,650	$304,760	$417,076
Direct Cost of Sales	$3,950	$66,800	$94,000
Other	$0	$0	$0
Total Cost of Sales	$3,950	$66,800	$94,000
Gross Margin	$36,700	$237,960	$323,076
Gross Margin %	90.28%	78.08%	77.46%
Operating expenses:			
Advertising/Promotion	$2,500	$2,640	$2,904
Travel and Entertainment	$600	$660	$726
Office Expense	$600	$660	$726
Payroll Expense	$13,000	$19,800	$21,780
Payroll Burden	$1,950	$2,970	$3,267
Depreciation	$4,520	$5,160	$5,160
Telephone	$600	$1,200	$1,320
Insurance	$300	$300	$300
JH Production Costs	$0	$0	$0
JH Writers	$0	$16,000	$13,000
JH Editing	$0	$9,600	$7,800
JH Production Staff	$0	$54,400	$44,200
JH Cast	$0	$11,200	$9,100
Misc. Production Expenses	$0	$3,200	$2,600
Channel 23 air fee	$0	$27,950	$37,180
Total Operating Expenses	$24,070	$155,740	$150,063
Profit Before Interest and Taxes	$12,630	$82,220	$173,013
Interest Expense Short-Term	$0	$0	$0
Interest Expense Long-Term	$2,206	$1,404	$484
Taxes Incurred	$2,606	$20,204	$43,132
Net Profit	$7,818	$60,612	$129,397
Net Profit/Sales	19.23%	19.89%	31.02%

Net Profit Monthly

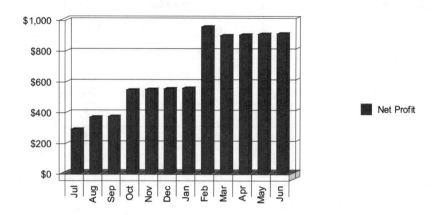

8.5 Projected Cash Flow

The following table and chart depict the cash flow forecast for 2002, 2003 and 2004. The complete monthly schedule may be found in the Appendix. The repayment of principal on the original long-term $25,000 loan is fully accomplished by the end of FY 2004. The unusual negative cash flow in February 2002 is a result of a capital expenditure of $5,000 for the purchase from cash flow of a second digital camera.

Pro-Forma Cash Flow

Category	FY2002	FY2003	FY2004
Net Profit	$7,818	$60,612	$129,397
Plus:			
Depreciation	$4,520	$5,160	$5,160
Change in Accounts Payable	$0	$0	$0
Current Borrowing (repayment)	$0	$0	$0
Increase (decrease) Other Liabilities	$0	$0	$0
Long-Term Borrowing (repayment)	($7,480)	($8,305)	($9,215)
Capital Input	$0	$0	$0
Subtotal	$4,858	$57,467	$125,342

Less:			
Change in Other Short-term Assets	$0	$0	$0
Capital Expenditure	$5,000	$0	$0
Dividends	$0	$0	$0
Subtotal	$5,000	$0	$0
Net Cash Flow	($142)	$57,467	$125,342
Cash Balance	$7,358	$64,825	$190,167

Cash Analysis

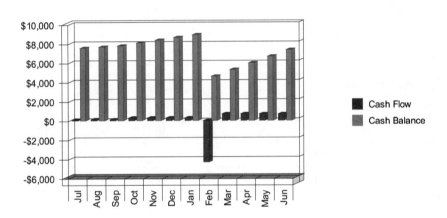

8.6 Projected Balance Sheet

The following table depicts the balance sheet forecast for 2002, 2003 and 2004. The complete monthly schedule may be found in the Appendix.

Pro-Forma Balance Sheet

Category	Starting Balances	FY2002	FY2003	FY2004
Short-term Assets				
Cash	$7,500	$7,358	$64,825	$190,167
Other Short-term Assets	$0	$0	$0	$0
Total Short-term Assets	$7,500	$7,358	$64,825	$190,167
Long-term Assets				
Capital Assets	$17,000	$22,000	$22,000	$22,000
Accumulated Depreciation	$0	$4,520	$9,680	$14,840
Total Long-term Assets	$17,000	$17,480	$12,320	$7,160
Total Assets	$24,500	$24,838	$77,145	$197,327
Liabilities and Capital				
Accounts Payable	$0	$0	$0	$0
Short-term Notes	$0	$0	$0	$0
Other Short-term Liabilities	$0	$0	$0	$0
Subtotal Short-term Liabilities	$0	$0	$0	$0
Long-term Liabilities	$25,000	$17,520	$9,215	$0
Total Liabilities	$25,000	$17,520	$9,215	$0
Paid in Capital	$0	$0	$0	$0
Retained Earnings	($500)	($500)	$7,318	$67,930
Earnings	$0	$7,818	$60,612	$129,397
Total Capital	($500)	$7,318	$67,930	$197,327
Total Liabilities and Capital	$24,500	$24,838	$77,145	$197,327
Net Worth	($500)	$7,318	$67,930	$197,327

APPENDIX

Pro-Forma Balance Sheet

Category	Starting Balances	Jul	Aug	Sep	Oct	Nov	Dec	Jan	Feb	Mar	Apr	May	Jun	FY2000	FY2001	FY2002
Short-Term Assets																
Cash	$7,500	$7,546	$7,666	$7,784	$8,070	$8,354	$8,638	$8,920	$4,594	$5,287	$5,979	$6,669	$7,358	$7,358	$64,825	$190,167
Other Short-Term Assets	$0	$0	$0	$0	$0	$0	$0	$0	$0	$0	$0	$0	$0	$0	$0	$0
Total Short-Term Assets	$7,500	$7,546	$7,666	$7,784	$8,070	$8,354	$8,638	$8,920	$4,594	$5,287	$5,979	$6,669	$7,358	$7,358	$64,825	$190,167
Long-Term Assets																
Capital Assets	$17,000	$17,000	$17,000	$17,000	$17,000	$17,000	$17,000	$17,000	$22,000	$22,000	$22,000	$22,000	$22,000	$22,000	$22,000	$22,000
Accumulated Depreciation	$0	$350	$700	$1,050	$1,400	$1,750	$2,100	$2,450	$2,800	$3,230	$3,660	$4,090	$4,520	$4,520	$9,680	$14,840
Total Long-term Assets	$17,000	$16,650	$16,300	$15,950	$15,600	$15,250	$14,900	$14,550	$19,200	$18,770	$18,340	$17,910	$17,480	$17,480	$12,320	$7,160
Total Assets	$24,500	$24,196	$23,966	$23,734	$23,670	$23,604	$23,538	$23,470	$23,794	$24,057	$24,319	$24,579	$24,838	$24,838	$77,145	$197,327
Liabilities and Capital																
Accounts Payable	$0	$0	$0	$0	$0	$0	$0	$0	$0	$0	$0	$0	$0	$0	$0	$0
Short-Term Notes	$0	$0	$0	$0	$0	$0	$0	$0	$0	$0	$0	$0	$0	$0	$0	$0
Other Short-Term Liabilities	$0	$0	$0	$0	$0	$0	$0	$0	$0	$0	$0	$0	$0	$0	$0	$0
Subtotal Short-Term Liabilities	$0	$0	$0	$0	$0	$0	$0	$0	$0	$0	$0	$0	$0	$0	$0	$0
Long-term Liabilities	$25,000	$24,406	$23,807	$23,203	$22,593	$21,978	$21,358	$20,732	$20,101	$19,464	$18,822	$18,174	$17,520	$17,520	$9,215	$0
Total Liabilities	$25,000	$24,406	$23,807	$23,203	$22,593	$21,978	$21,358	$20,732	$20,101	$19,464	$18,822	$18,174	$17,520	$17,520	$9,215	$0
Paid in Capital	$0	$0	$0	$0	$0	$0	$0	$0	$0	$0	$0	$0	$0	$0	$0	$0
Retained Earnings	($500)	($500)	($500)	($500)	($500)	($500)	($500)	($500)	($500)	($500)	($500)	($500)	($500)	($500)	$7,318	$67,930
Earnings	$0	$290	$659	$1,031	$1,577	$2,126	$2,680	$3,238	$4,193	$5,093	$5,997	$6,905	$7,818	$7,818	$60,612	$129,397
Total Capital	($500)	($210)	$159	$531	$1,077	$1,626	$2,180	$2,738	$3,693	$4,593	$5,497	$6,405	$7,318	$7,318	$67,930	$197,327
Total Liabilities and Capital	$24,500	$24,196	$23,966	$23,734	$23,670	$23,604	$23,538	$23,470	$23,794	$24,057	$24,319	$24,579	$24,838	$24,838	$77,145	$197,327
Net Worth	($500)	($210)	$159	$531	$1,077	$1,626	$2,180	$2,738	$3,693	$4,593	$5,497	$6,405	$7,318	$7,318	$67,930	$197,327

Pro-Forma Cash Flow

Category	Jul	Aug	Sep	Oct	Nov	Dec	Jan	Feb	Mar	Apr	May	Jun	FY2000	FY2001	FY2002
Net Profit	$290	$369	$373	$545	$550	$554	$558	$956	$900	$904	$908	$913	$7,818	$60,612	$129,397
Plus:															
Depreciation	$350	$350	$350	$350	$350	$350	$350	$350	$430	$430	$430	$430	$4,520	$5,160	$5,160
Change in Accounts Payable	$0	$0	$0	$0	$0	$0	$0	$0	$0	$0	$0	$0	$0	$0	$0
Current Borrowing (repayment)	$0	$0	$0	$0	$0	$0	$0	$0	$0	$0	$0	$0	$0	$0	$0
Increase (decrease) Other Liabilities	$0	$0	$0	$0	$0	$0	$0	$0	$0	$0	$0	$0	$0	$0	$0
Long-term Borrowing (repayment)	($594)	($599)	($604)	($610)	($615)	($620)	($626)	($631)	($637)	($642)	($648)	($654)	($7,480)	($8,305)	($9,215)
Capital Input	$0	$0	$0	$0	$0	$0	$0	$0	$0	$0	$0	$0	$0	$0	$0
Subtotal	$46	$120	$119	$285	$285	$284	$282	$675	$693	$692	$690	$689	$4,858	$57,467	$125,342
Less:															
Change in Other Short-term Assets	$0	$0	$0	$0	$0	$0	$0	$0	$0	$0	$0	$0	$0	$0	$0
Capital Expenditure	$0	$0	$0	$0	$0	$0	$0	$5,000	$0	$0	$0	$0	$0	$0	$0
Dividends	$0	$0	$0	$0	$0	$0	$0	$0	$0	$0	$0	$0	$5,000	$0	$0
Subtotal	$0	$0	$0	$0	$0	$0	$0	$5,000	$0	$0	$0	$0	$5,000	$0	$0
Net Cash Flow	$46	$120	$119	$285	$285	$284	$282	($4,325)	$693	$692	$690	$689	($142)	$57,467	$125,342
Cash Balance	$7,546	$7,666	$7,784	$8,070	$8,354	$8,638	$8,920	$4,594	$5,287	$5,979	$6,669	$7,358	$7,358	$64,825	$190,167

Personnel Plan

Personnel	Jul	Aug	Sep	Oct	Nov	Dec	Jan	Feb	Mar	Apr	May	Jun	FY2000	FY2001	FY2002
Elena Trujillo	$500	$500	$500	$1,000	$1,000	$1,000	$1,000	$1,500	$1,500	$1,500	$1,500	$1,500	$13,000	$19,800	$21,780
Other	$0	$0	$0	$0	$0	$0	$0	$0	$0	$0	$0	$0	$0	$0	$0
Total Payroll	$500	$500	$500	$1,000	$1,000	$1,000	$1,000	$1,500	$1,500	$1,500	$1,500	$1,500	$13,000	$19,800	$21,780
Total Headcount	1	1	1	1	1	1	1	1	1	1	1	1	1	1	
Payroll Burden	$75	$75	$75	$150	$150	$150	$150	$225	$225	$225	$225	$225	$1,950	$2,970	$3,267
Total Payroll Expenditures	$575	$575	$575	$1,150	$1,150	$1,150	$1,150	$1,725	$1,725	$1,725	$1,725	$1,725	$14,950	$22,770	$25,047

Profit and Loss (Income Statement)

Category	Jul	Aug	Sep	Oct	Nov	Dec	Jan	Feb	Mar	Apr	May	Jun	FY2000	FY2001	FY2002
Sales	$2,250	$2,250	$2,250	$3,100	$3,100	$3,100	$3,100	$4,300	$4,300	$4,300	$4,300	$4,300	$40,650	$304,760	$417,076
Direct Cost of Sales	$250	$250	$250	$300	$300	$300	$300	$400	$400	$400	$400	$400	$3,950	$66,800	$94,000
Other	$0	$0	$0	$0	$0	$0	$0	$0	$0	$0	$0	$0	$0	$0	$0
Total Cost of Sales	$250	$250	$250	$300	$300	$300	$300	$400	$400	$400	$400	$400	$3,950	$66,800	$94,000
Gross Margin	$2,000	$2,000	$2,000	$2,800	$2,800	$2,800	$2,800	$3,900	$3,900	$3,900	$3,900	$3,900	$36,700	$237,960	$323,076
Gross Margin %	88.89%	88.89%	88.89%	90.32%	90.32%	90.32%	90.32%	90.70%	90.70%	90.70%	90.70%	90.70%	90.28%	78.08%	77.46%
Operating expenses:															
Advertising/Promotion	$300	$200	$200	$200	$200	$200	$200	$200	$200	$200	$200	$200	$2,500	$2,640	$2,904
Travel and Entertainment	$50	$50	$50	$50	$50	$50	$50	$50	$50	$50	$50	$50	$600	$660	$726
Office Expense	$50	$50	$50	$50	$50	$50	$50	$50	$50	$50	$50	$50	$600	$660	$726
Payroll Expense	$500	$500	$500	$1,000	$1,000	$1,000	$1,000	$1,500	$1,500	$1,500	$1,500	$1,500	$13,000	$19,800	$21,780
Payroll Burden	$75	$75	$75	$150	$150	$150	$150	$225	$225	$225	$225	$225	$1,950	$2,970	$3,267
Depreciation	$350	$350	$350	$350	$350	$350	$350	$350	$430	$430	$430	$430	$4,520	$5,160	$5,160
Telephone	$50	$50	$50	$50	$50	$50	$50	$50	$50	$50	$50	$50	$600	$1,200	$1,320
Insurance	$25	$25	$25	$25	$25	$25	$25	$25	$25	$25	$25	$25	$300	$300	$300
JH Production Costs:	$0	$0	$0	$0	$0	$0	$0	$0	$0	$0	$0	$0	$0	$0	$0
JH Writers	$0	$0	$0	$0	$0	$0	$0	$0	$0	$0	$0	$0	$0	$16,000	$13,000
JH Editing	$0	$0	$0	$0	$0	$0	$0	$0	$0	$0	$0	$0	$0	$9,600	$7,800
JH Production Staff	$0	$0	$0	$0	$0	$0	$0	$0	$0	$0	$0	$0	$0	$54,400	$44,200
JH Cast	$0	$0	$0	$0	$0	$0	$0	$0	$0	$0	$0	$0	$0	$11,200	$9,100
Misc. Production Expenses	$0	$0	$0	$0	$0	$0	$0	$0	$0	$0	$0	$0	$0	$3,200	$2,600
Channel 46 air fee	$0	$0	$0	$0	$0	$0	$0	$0	$0	$0	$0	$0	$0	$27,950	$37,180
Total Operating Expenses	$1,400	$1,300	$1,300	$1,875	$1,875	$1,875	$1,875	$2,450	$2,530	$2,530	$2,530	$2,530	$24,070	$155,740	$150,063
Profit Before Interest and Taxes	$600	$700	$700	$925	$925	$925	$925	$1,450	$1,370	$1,370	$1,370	$1,370	$12,630	$82,220	$173,013
Interest Expense Short-term	$0	$0	$0	$0	$0	$0	$0	$0	$0	$0	$0	$0	$0	$0	$0
Interest Expense Long-term	$214	$208	$203	$198	$192	$187	$181	$176	$170	$165	$159	$153	$2,206	$1,404	$484
Taxes Incurred	$97	$123	$124	$182	$183	$185	$186	$319	$300	$301	$303	$304	$2,606	$20,204	$43,132
Net Profit	$290	$369	$373	$545	$550	$554	$558	$956	$900	$904	$908	$913	$7,818	$60,612	$129,397
Net Profit/Sales	12.88%	16.39%	16.57%	17.60%	17.73%	17.86%	17.99%	22.22%	20.92%	21.02%	21.12%	21.22%	19.23%	19.89%	31.02%

Sales Forecast

Sales	Jul	Aug	Sep	Oct	Nov	Dec	Jan	Feb	Mar	Apr	May	Jun	FY2000	FY2001	FY2002
Juventud Hispana Advertising	$0	$0	$0	$0	$0	$0	$0	$0	$0	$0	$0	$0	$0	$168,000	$240,240
Juventud Hispana Sponsorships	$0	$0	$0	$0	$0	$0	$0	$0	$0	$0	$0	$0	$0	$80,000	$114,400
Social Video	$1,200	$1,200	$1,200	$2,400	$2,400	$2,400	$2,400	$3,600	$3,600	$3,600	$3,600	$3,600	$31,200	$47,520	$52,272
Social Video Freelancing	$1,050	$1,050	$1,050	$700	$700	$700	$700	$700	$700	$700	$700	$700	$9,450	$9,240	$10,164
Other	$0	$0	$0	$0	$0	$0	$0	$0	$0	$0	$0	$0	$0	$0	$0
Total Sales	$2,250	$2,250	$2,250	$3,100	$3,100	$3,100	$3,100	$4,300	$4,300	$4,300	$4,300	$4,300	$40,650	$304,760	$417,076

Direct Cost of sales	Jul	Aug	Sep	Oct	Nov	Dec	Jan	Feb	Mar	Apr	May	Jun	FY2000	FY2001	FY2002
Juventud Hispana Advertising	$0	$0	$0	$0	$0	$0	$0	$0	$0	$0	$0	$0	$0	$42,000	$60,600
Juventud Hispana Sponsorships	$0	$0	$0	$0	$0	$0	$0	$0	$0	$0	$0	$0	$0	$20,000	$28,600
Social Video	$100	$100	$100	$200	$200	$200	$200	$300	$300	$300	$300	$300	$2,600	$3,600	$3,600
Social Video Freelancing	$150	$150	$150	$100	$100	$100	$100	$100	$100	$100	$100	$100	$1,350	$1,200	$1,200
Other	$0	$0	$0	$0	$0	$0	$0	$0	$0	$0	$0	$0	$0	$0	$0
Subtotal Cost of Sales	$250	$250	$250	$300	$300	$300	$300	$400	$400	$400	$400	$400	$3,950	$66,800	$94,000

The Plan For
All About the Home

AARON HORNER & ED EDMONSON

2054 Rampart Range Road

Woodland Park, CO

(719) 686-8974

Copy Number __ of Five.

THE PLAN FOR ALL ABOUT THE HOME

1.0 EXECUTIVE SUMMARY

1.1 Executive Summary

All About The Home, LLC (AAH) intends to assist customers with interior and exterior home improvement projects. What makes this company unique is the method of customer service. Our vision is to construct the framework for customer loyalty by providing quality service, as well as build customer confidence in the finished product. Loyalty is attained when the customer sees that licensed AAH owners are performing the work, unlike other landscape and remodeling companies. Thus, the customer is ensured of an owner/operator on site working on the project, giving him/her the opportunity to address any issues directly. The latter is furnished by educating the customer on exactly what is being done and why, in addition to proper maintenance procedures.

AAH believes the home consists of the 'Total Package,' which is inherent in our landscape and remodeling designs. This means that the interior, exterior, and surrounding landscape all contribute to beauty and function.

All About The Home is Aaron and Julie Horner, Jamie and Bridget Bridge, and Ed and Sunshine Edmonson. This 'family business' affords the luxury of close friends with similar ideas and principles to operate in an atmosphere that will ensure pride and integrity in all our work.

AAH will operate under the legal structure of a Limited Liability Company, under the laws and guidance of the State of Colorado. It is this business unit that enables the company to acquire legal protection of personal assets. Furthermore, AAH will perform work with general liability insurance, which will enhance customer confidence and enable AAH the opportunity to work with many of Colorado Springs' homebuilders.

Initial startup consists of initial equitable financial contributions by each member family. As well, each owns the tools and skill sets to perform all aspects of the business. This includes the administrative and technical functions of the organization. Our estimated monthly and yearly revenue are based on sound logical principles, and backed by documented statistics provided by current economic and historical conditions. These numerous factors will show that All About The Home is a viable organization that will instantly compete, and succeed, in the Pikes Peak region.

2.0 MISSION, GOALS & OBJECTIVES

2.1 Business Description

The home is central to life. It provides a sanctuary for all members of the family. The home is where the majority of homeowners express who they are. It is used by some to

-4-

show off individual wealth. To others, it is a safe place to raise children. In all cases, the home is more than what is inside it. The home is comprised of the interior, the exterior, and the yard surrounding it. No single aspect makes a house a good home. It is this total package which brings out the true value of the home.

In many cases, a house will have one, or even two, parts of the total package. In these cases, homeowners will look to improve on the rest of the total package, increasing its value. Each part of the total package can be further dissected. It is very rare for a single company to provide services for all aspects of even a single piece of the total package, let alone all the pieces.

Homeowners can experience difficulties when trying to complete home improvement projects. Examples include installing a sprinkler system and installing sod and rock landscaping. If the sprinklers are installed first, the process of installing the sod and rock has a reasonably good chance of damaging the sprinklers. Likewise, if the sod and rock is installed first, then the sprinkler installation will tear up some of the yard. Homeowners can save time, money and headaches by contacting a single company that can complete all tasks while coordinating its actions to ensure minimum cost and impact.

The driving idea behind All About the Home (AAH) is to provide homeowners with a single source of contact for all improvements to the total package. AAH plans to fill the need in Colorado Springs for an affordable general contractor who is willing and able to do repair, remodeling, and landscaping jobs regardless of size or diversity of tasks. AAH will also pursue the purchase, repair, and resale of existing homes in the area. This will allow AAH to improve all aspects of the total package for these houses before returning them to the market. This will not only improve the value of the home for the consumer, but it will improve the aesthetic value to the community. AAH intends to make a profit on these types of opportunities. There are many properties, such as bank foreclosures, that can benefit from this operation.

AAH will offer convenient and direct contact for homeowners that need both indoor and outdoor projects completed. The versatility of AAH in this endeavor will provide work year-round, which will not limit the company to the traditional summer construction-working season. AAH is not limited to specific tasks, such as drywall or irrigation. Therefore, AAH will enjoy opportunities not afforded to specialized contractors.

Initially, AAH will focus its efforts in the Colorado Springs and Woodland Park area. Both of these cities have many competitors. However, most are contractors that specialize in one field or another, such as a concrete specialist. The AAH team offers a 'jack-of-all-trades' approach, where direct contact is a trademark. Both will distinguish AAH from other 'referral' service and 'general contracting' companies.

The premise will be to help new and experienced homeowners, either by remodeling and enhancing occupied homes, or buying, refurbishing, and selling used homes.

AAH will be set up as a Limited Liability Company (LLC), which will work on typical, and not so typical home issues. In today's society, particularly in Colorado Springs, many individuals spend much of their time at desk jobs for large corporations or performing work for the military. The Colorado Springs area enjoys the benefits of a diversified work force, including a high degree of technology and military economic presence. These professionals do not have the time nor, in many cases, the knowledge to perform home maintenance and upgrades yet still want to have the most attractive house in the neighborhood. AAH will address this market segment.

The presence of large corporations notwithstanding, the Front Range is conducive to small business ventures such as AAH. The state of Colorado is dominated by small business. Over 87% of all business establishments have fewer than 20 employees, and they employ about 28% of the state's workforce.[1] Construction and the Services sector, together, combined for 29% of Colorado's Gross Domestic State Product (GSP) in 1999, with forecasted growth that will place Colorado in the top ten states for GSP growth through the first decade of the 21st century.

AAH will be a single direct contact for both indoor and outdoor home maintenance and remodeling. Projects include custom remodeling, interior and exterior repairs, decorative landscaping, sprinkler systems, and custom outdoor play sets. These are items deemed by homeowners to be 'upgrades'.

AAH will also pursue the purchasing, repairing, and selling of existing homes. Through this avenue AAH will look at "fixer-uppers" and foreclosures. These homes present an opportunity to acquire them at or below cost to be resold at a profit, provided that repairs are completed. Property management could be a future result of this endeavor.

All of the partners in AAH have had extensive exposure to the aspects of home improvement. All have completed remodeling projects in several homes, including those in which they currently reside. This knowledge and experience will be used as a starting point to acquire jobs and to build a portfolio of completed projects. As the company gets underway and time allows, the owners will continue their education through classes and other training opportunities.

AAH plans to keep operations small at the beginning in order to provide the best quality service possible. As the business develops, AAH will grow by acquiring a greater market share through expanded services and through an expanded demographic market area. All growth opportunities will be assessed as they are presented to ensure AAH can incorporate the new growth into the business without losing focus on quality and customer satisfaction. All owners of AAH are dedicated to their work and are willing to stand behind every job. Timeliness, good communication, and dedication to quality will be leveraged to gain jobs where AAH may not have the lowest price.

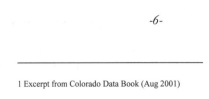

-6-

1 Excerpt from Colorado Data Book (Aug 2001)

2.2 Mission

All members of AAH believe in the same basic set of values. These values not only govern how business is done, but are also used to govern the lives of company members. The belief that every job worth doing is worth the effort required to do it right is fundamental. Quality work speaks for itself in how long it lasts under all conditions. The belief in providing honest estimates and honest work for fair prices is also central. AAH does not employ the practices of cutting corners on materials to save cost or under-estimating a bid to get a contract and then raising the cost part way through the project.

The vision driving AAH is to build a company willing and able to perform all manner of landscaping and remodeling jobs for homeowners while maintaining a strong dedication to quality work and customer satisfaction. Through this AAH will achieve a quality of life for its members, derived from pride in quality craftsmanship and satisfied customers, and through providing an income to support all members and their families and the time for all members to pursue fulfilling family lives.

The mission of AAH is to provide quality work for honest prices backed with the support necessary to ensure absolute customer satisfaction.

2.3 Goals & Objectives

AAH has set up a series of goals and objectives designed to guide the business to success. These goals will continue to be readdressed as the company grows to ensure there is always a plan giving AAH direction for the future.

For the immediate future AAH has set up some short-term goals designed to establish a firm foundation to build the company on.

- Form an LLC and draft an operating agreement to be signed by all members. This agreement will establish the policies by which the company will be run. It is intended to provide a set of rules, written prior to any disagreements or emotional involvement, which can be referred to when issues arise. The agreement will address issues of membership, salaries, accounting, selling, votes, dividends, task assignments, training, employees, and amendment procedures. This agreement will be written and signed by all members by October 2002.

- Establish business foundation on which AAH can build. This includes registering the business name, writing a complete business plan, obtaining all licensing, procuring insurance, and setting up a business phone line with either voice mail or an answering machine. This foundation will be established by December 2002.

- Establish an array of contacts and professional advisors who can assist in making the business successful. These include suppliers, inspectors, accountants, tax specialists, and lawyers. Additional contacts that can help promote the business will also be established. These contacts include several different realtors. These contacts will be established by February 2003.

- Gain business. By July 2003 AAH will be successfully bidding and acquiring the contracts for two jobs every month. AAH will also be submitting bids on at least four contracts every month.

To establish a direction for growth, AAH has also set up several long-term goals.

- Establish consistent revenue that will allow for company growth. Within two years from the launch date, AAH will have become recognized as a reliable company with enough work to support each of its members financially. The company will also be making enough surplus income to invest in expansion.

- Expand business into buying, fixing and reselling houses. Within three years of establishment, AAH will financially be in a position to acquire houses in need of repairs, perform the repairs, and sell the house for a profit. By the end of four years, the business will be turning a house around every two to three months.

- Expand business into property management. Within five years after establishment AAH will be in a position to expand operations into rental properties. Properties that will be considered for rental purposes will be single-family residences, duplexes, town homes, and condominiums. Rentals will be on a long-term basis only. Two years after entering the rental business, AAH will be managing six to ten properties.

3.0 MARKETPLACE ANALYSIS

3.1 Historical Background

Colorado's population has grown faster than the national average since the 1940s. Its population of 4.3 million makes Colorado the 24th largest state in the country.[2] 2010 projections place the Front Range with the largest percentage increase in the state.[3] Despite the population rankings, Colorado ranks first in the nation in the percentage of residents who have college and graduate school degrees. An astounding 34.6% of Colorado residents have a bachelor's degree or higher[4]. This supports the American Electronics Association 2001 report that maintains Colorado as first in the nation in the number of skilled high-tech professionals, 97 per 1,000 workers, and fourth in the nation for high-tech job growth.

-8-

---

2 From Colorado Data Book (Aug 2001)

3 From Colorado Data Book (Aug 2001)

4 From US Census Bureau (Mar 2000)

The Front Range of Colorado, in particular Colorado Springs, has seen tremendous growth. The Springs' eastward expansion continues today and can be attributed to the growing military presence. Schriever Air Force Base now houses the hub of the Space Command Satellite Control Network, working in conjunction with the Cheyenne Mountain Complex and Peterson Air Force Base to secure our nation's global threats.

Construction had to keep pace with the rapidly growing technically oriented population, with expansion into eastern El Paso County. The construction industry, by far, was the leading sector in Colorado's Gross State Product (GSP) with over 200% growth during the 1990's. [5]Wages for this industry type reflect that. In El Paso County alone, the average wage for almost 1700 specialty construction employees was over $33,000 a year in 2000. Total expenditures for Owner-Occupied One-Unit properties for contractors or hired labor grew by 21 million dollars since 1995[6]. In 1999, net-housing permits reached the 5500 level, as evidenced by the expansion of Powers Blvd. It now reaches Research Pkwy and onward to I-25 north, and is now home to Lowe's Home Improvement, IMAX movie theatres, and countless restaurants and shops. With more houses being built, more homeowners are looking to remodel to suit their individual preferences.

Traditionally, almost half of the grounds maintenance work force is employed in companies providing landscape and horticultural services. Others work for larger firms that build real estate, amusement and recreational facilities, as well as parks, schools, and hospitals. More than 1 in 6 are self-employed, providing landscape services directly to customers on a contract basis.[7]

With society slumping and constant news of layoffs in technical industries, more than 5,000 in the Colorado Springs' IT industry alone, homeowners are no longer considering a move to the perfect home. This, in turn, results in more homeowners looking at ways to make their existing home better. As more people decide upon improvements, more demand is placed upon general contractors, such as AAH, to complete these upgrades and repairs in a timely manner.

When the economy rebounds, many homeowners will change from looking at ways to improve their older home and will again start looking to buy the perfect home. In this ever-changing environment, AAH will provide the landscaping and finishing work required by covenants in new housing developments. Still, for those homeowners who do not desire the hassles of a new house, there will still be expansions and projects on older existing houses. AAH will buy, repair, and resell the older houses left unoccupied by the homeowners, due to changes in the economy.

-9-

---

5 From Colorado Data Book (Aug 2001)

6 US Census (2000)

7 2002-2003 edition of Occupational Outlook Handbook

Loan defaults are another trend that results from the economic downturn. This, inevitably, results in more foreclosures. According to one *Gazette* article, there were more foreclosures as a result of the March 2001 recession than the one occurring more than a decade before, in the late 1980s that preceded Desert Storm. As more foreclosed homes enter the market, and interest reductions are enacted by the Department of Treasury, prices will be kept low. AAH will also take advantage of this new economic opportunity.

As the economy turns around, general contractors who are established and diversified will be able to ride the new wave of prosperity as people look at building and finishing new homes.

3.2 Emerging Trends

Coloradoans are spending more of their income than ever before to pay for their homes, according to data from the U.S. Census Bureau. In fact, less than one of every four owner-occupied Colorado homes is debt-free, according to the figures, which are based on 2000 census data released today. That ranks Colorado second only to Nevada—home to Las Vegas, the fastest-growing U.S. city—in the percentage of homes with mortgages. [8]The hi-tech and military segments usually employ young college graduates, and Colorado Springs continues to be among the leading cities in this area. The July 3rd 2001 issue of the *Gazette Telegraph* reported the trend of homeownership among the younger generation, reiterating the Census forecasts. In addition, the *Occupational Outlook Handbook* reports that job opportunities are expected to be excellent, as increased demand for these skills is expected to outpace the supply of workers.[9] Employment is expected to grow about as fast as the average for all occupations through the year 2010.

The rapidly growing hi-tech industry has had to face the recent economic difficulties. With over 5,000 people losing jobs in the Pikes Peak region this past year, and home foreclosures on the rise, many families are choosing to stay and remodel their current home. The economic forecasts for Lowe's and other home improvement shops attest to this recent trend. Despite the layoffs, retail home improvement stock continues to rise. Landscaping companies abound, with over 50 sprinkler technicians listed in the El Paso County Yellow Pages alone.

3.3 Business Fit Considerations

Continuing economic dependency and a willingness to offer an 'honest days work for an honest days pay' has become the foundation upon which All About the Home, LLC is

-10-

---

8 Aug 6, 2001 edition of Gazette/Telegraph

9 Occupational Outlook Handbook

built. The company will grow from mere ideas between 3 couples to an organization that has established relationships with various suppliers to conduct business on a part-time basis. The customer satisfaction provided by AAH has resulted in several letters of reference as well as 'word of mouth' advertising. AAH plans to build upon these relationships to secure loyal customers.

The services provided by AAH are a good fit for the construction industry. Market analysis shows that most residential work is performed by small, individually owned contracting companies. AAH will perform the same, albeit with more customer interaction. AAH proposes to educate the homeowner in the design and maintenance of their landscape and remodeling projects. AAH will use this customer relationship to compete against larger companies. This same loyalty will enable AAH to compete against the smaller organizations as well. AAH will work to anticipate future demographic and economic trends to continually seek new customers.

3.4 Customer Considerations

Customers today are picky. They know exactly what they want, but in many cases are unable to express that desire. AAH will talk with customers several times prior to performing any service to ensure what is offered is exactly what is desired. Once we have a complete understanding of customer requirements, we will start work on the project. This customer support, both before and during a project, will ensure a satisfied customer at project completion.

Customer support does not end with the project though. Once a project has been completed, the customer will need to be educated in its maintenance. This is especially important with landscaping and sprinkler system projects.

3.5 Supplier Considerations

Initially, tools and supplies from Home Depot and Lowes will be comparison-shopped for the lowest prices. Specific plumbing, sprinkler, and heating parts will be purchased from ABC Plumbing and Heating. As business increases, company deals and other incentive options will be pursued with all companies.

3.6 Competition

Competition in this market is fierce. Many customers look at price as the deciding factor in choosing which company to sign with. They do not always consider the benefits derived from quality. Also, in the construction business, there are many areas where a company can cut corners to save money. An unknowledgeable customer will not realize what has been done until it's too late. With these companies, AAH will only be able to compete by educating customers as to what they are purchasing and describing the benefits of quality.

-11-

There are also many other companies and individuals who provide quality work. With these companies, AAH will have to win bids based on personality and willingness to work with the customer to ensure he or she gets exactly what is desired.

4.0 LEGAL STRUCTURE & ORGANIZATIONAL MATTERS

4.1 Legal Entity

All About the Home will take on the legal structure of a Limited Liability Company (LLC), under the laws and auspices of the State of Colorado. The primary, and perhaps the most appealing, advantage of operating under this legal entity is to separate personal and business assets. Liability protection is the single most important criteria for small business peace of mind. The construction/grounds maintenance industry, more so than most, is susceptible to legal claims. A second advantage is the formal technicalities of this legal operation are somewhat lenient. This allows small business to focus on providing quality services and support to customers instead of on bureaucratic procedures.

AAH, LLC consists of three members (with an additional three spouses that will, ultimately, have a vote). All three families will have an equitable financial share in the company. Further discussion will follow in terms outlined in a future Operating Agreement.

4.2 The AAH Team

The management team consists of Aaron and Julie Horner, Jamie and Bridget Bridge, and Ed and Sunshine Edmonson. Aaron, Jamie, and Ed will be the primary managers and perform the majority of the contract operations. Julie, Bridget, and Sunshine will start out performing more of the administrative roles, including budgeting and advertising. Everyone, while not necessarily performing all tasks, will have the knowledge of the individual and varied operating functions. The primary roles, however, will be to maintain customer, vendor/supplier, and regulatory relationships. In addition, each member brings extensive technical and administrative experience to benefit the company. AAH does recognize, nonetheless, that individuals not part of the company will have to perform some tasks that are beyond AAH's experience level. Those tasks may include accounting and legal counsel, not to mention local SBA assistance.

4.3 Personnel

At the time of startup AAH members will be the only employees. The owners will be performing the entire range of tasks, from contract bids to maintaining external relationships, as well as the actual contractual labor. The company will address additional employees as growth allows.

-12-

4.4 Risk Management

AAH will be protected by general liability insurance. This coverage will be initially set at $300,000, as that is the estimated value of the higher end houses AAH will be working on. Within two years, as the business becomes firmly established, this coverage will be raised to $500,000. Within three years insurance will be raised again to $1,000,000. This additional coverage will protect AAH against the costs of any unintentional damage to customer property as the business grows and prospers.

As AAH starts out, vehicles and tools will be rented from the owners for reasonable compensation. As business grows, AAH will purchase its own vehicles and tools. AAH will then acquire insurance to protect the vehicles, drivers, and tools.

Each owner, for the first year, will be employed at his current job as well. We will maintain personal insurance through this avenue, or through coverage provided by the respective spouses. AAH will obtain medical, dental, vision, and disability insurance for each of the owners after the initial year of operation. Whether or not this is done through a group health plan or through individual coverage will be based on overall cost. Initial investigation indicates that a group plan usually costs more but has less stringent criteria on who can be covered based on health and occupational risks.

AAH has taken steps to minimize as many of the internal and external risks as possible. As the business is getting started, it is borrowing the tools required, through a loan agreement, from the owners personal collections. In many cases, AAH is able to borrow duplicates of the most business critical tools in case one is broken or lost. Tools will be documented and accounted for, thus preventing theft. Risks that cannot directly be controlled, such as competition for the same customer base, will be addressed through marketing strategies and dedication to quality work and the customer.

4.5 Recordkeeping Functions

Keeping records is a necessary business function. Tracking accounts receivable and accounts payable will allow AAH to ensure a positive cash flow and identify unnecessary cash drains. The accurate bookkeeping activities are a way of assessing the current business climate, as well as forecasting future sales. Initially, AAH will strive to keep its accounts receivable simple and its accounts payable to a minimum. Most projects would be cash-only at time of completion.

4.5.1 Accounts Receivable

AAH will operate on a simple payment schedule, similar to those used by many other construction companies. Homeowners who sign a contract with AAH will be required to pay half of their bill upfront and the second half upon completion of the job. The upfront half of the money will be used to purchase required material,s and the second half will be used to cover the rest of the materials and labor costs. AAH will operate on a cash or check basis. All contracts will be tracked along with payments by Julie Horner.

-13-

By accepting personal checks, AAH must consider the possibility of bounced checks. To make it easier to collect on these, drivers' license numbers will be required. Customers will also be held responsible for any penalties and fees associated to their bounced check. AAH will also pursue liens on property as a means to ensure monies owed are collected.

After AAH has built up a cash reserve, the possibility of accepting credit cards and payment invoices will be reconsidered. Both of these methods incur additional costs, delaying when AAH actually receives money, and it is necessary for the business to have cash on hand to cover its expenses.

4.5.2 Account Reconciliation & Cash

Maintaining accurate cash flow records will allow AAH to operate in the black. Julie Horner will reconcile bank accounts and manage petty cash expenses for the business. By analyzing these records on a daily basis she will be able to identify discrepancies and other issues in such a manner that they can be addressed immediately.

4.5.3 Accounts Payable

As with any business, AAH will have expenses in order to operate effectively. In the landscape and remodeling business, it is necessary to be licensed and insured. Licenses must be purchased for every member who will be performing the work and must be renewed every one to three years depending on the license. General liability insurance is also required to operate and will require monthly payments. AAH will also incur monthly expenses in phone bills, cell phone bills, and Internet connectivity. All of these expenses will be tracked and handled by Julie Horner.

4.5.4 Payroll

AAH will not have employees for at least the first year of operation. All aspects of the business will be handled by the three member families. The members of AAH will consider collecting salary from the company only after the business is established. Until AAH is secure, its members will not burden the company with the expense of regular paychecks independent of jobs performed. Instead they will collect wages based upon the hours spent working on each job.

4.6 Operational Controls

Operational controls include environmental controls, authorization, physical and processing controls, and monitoring and training. These controls are to ensure that employees of the company perform all tasks up to the standards set by the members. AAH will evaluate each of these controls at the time when it evaluates the need for employees.

-14-

At a high level operation, controls are necessary even for the members of AAH. Such controls will ensure that all members are commited to the same standards of quality. These controls will be addressed in the operating agreement, approved by signatures of all members of AAH.

5.0 MARKETING PLAN

5.1 Market Analysis

The market consists of the customer, the competition, and the market potential. Establishing a profile of the customer allows AAH to specifically focus limited resources to have the greatest effect. Analyzing the competition ensures AAH is providing comparable and competitive services in cases where services overlap. This also provides knowledge to allow AAH to focus resources on services it uniquely provides. Researching and understanding the market potential gives AAH the ability to set realistic goals for the business. It also allows AAH to act on up-and-coming changes in the market before they occur instead of having to react after the change happens.

5.1.1 Customer Profile

A customer profile consists of both demographic and psychographic considerations. Demographics for AAH are limited to the area surrounding the business. With the limited number of partners in AAH, it becomes ineffective to attempt to provide services far from the center of business. Psychographics are important at the outset of AAH since these lead to an understanding of the customer mentality. Using this analysis to understand the desires of the customer market will allow AAH to cater specifically to each customer.

DEMOGRAPHIC CHARACTERISTICS

Creating a customer profile is an important step to business success. Members of society who own one or more homes could potentially benefit from the services offered by AAH. Since renters are not usually responsible for property maintenance, AAH will not focus landscape and remodeling advertising toward them. As AAH expands into the property resale and rental business, advertising to this group will be reevaluated.

In 2000, there was almost $85 million spent on payments to contractors or hired labor, with maintenance and repairs contributing over $22 million of the total. [10] The specific target customer, then, is one who is conscientious about the upkeep of his dwelling and can afford to achieve it.

-15-

---

10 Taken from 2000 edition of the Colorado Data Book

Gender has not been considered due to changes in the demographics of society. There are more single females purchasing homes on their own either due to a desire to be independent or because of divorce.

The age of the home owner is considered a secondary criterion. It will be used to determine the type of advertising approach used more than the demographics. Younger homeowners are busy working and in their spare time enjoying their lives. These individuals do not want to spend the time landscaping or repairing their home. To them their time is more important, and they would rather pay others to do such work than spend their time on it. Older middle-aged people are caught up in work and families. They don't have enough spare time to devote to landscaping and remodeling projects. In many cases age is also starting to catch up to them in the manner of back pains, carpal tunnel syndrome, arthritis, and other ailments that make manual labor difficult. Elderly individuals do not have the endurance or the strength required for many such projects. Overall, age does not impact the need for the services offered by AAH. It will impact the strategy that needs to be used to target the consumer groups.

In general all houses can benefit from the services offered by AAH. New houses, while in need of very little in the way of remodeling and repairs, need much work in the way of landscaping. Older houses, for the most part, have established yards but are in greater need of remodeling and repairs. For these reasons AAH will focus efforts primarily on new housing developments and houses that are ten to twenty years old. Houses less than ten years old, for the most part, need little in the way of work, and houses greater than twenty years old have a much greater potential of needing major and costly repairs. There are exceptions to both of these cases that AAH will watch for, but they will not be a focus of the business.

PSYCHOGRAPHIC CHARACTERISTICS

Psychographic information demonstrates the lifestyle, really the habits, of potential customers. AAH has decided to target the working professional.

Professionals, such as those employed in the IT industry, generally spend much time working, either at home or at the office. This does not afford time for upkeep of the house. Based on demographic data, they tend to earn more than the average worker, thus can afford to have landscape services performed. Based on experience, this particular group does not have the skill or expertise to perform the necessary repairs and enhancements, despite their educational background.

5.1.2 Competitive Analysis

The construction industry has many competitors. In El Paso County alone, based on just Yellow Page entries, there are more than 50 competitors for sprinkler systems.

Randy's Landscaping, Inc. is the competitor most like AAH, in that they offer sprinkler repair, design, and installation as well as other landscaping services. They are located on Valley St., which puts them in a central location for easy access to the eastern and western parts of Colorado Springs. They perform both commercial and residential work, but maintain that most of their sales volume comes from residential customers. Randy's, however, does not target a particular customer, so it is assumed that they have the same customer profile as AAH.

Randy's key features for sprinkler services are a 3-year winterization routine whereby a crew will come and properly drain the system. A 3-year warranty on parts, primarily through the Toro manufacturer's guarantee, is also offered. They believe the warranties, in addition to their customer attention, is the competitive advantage they seek.

Randy's Landscaping, Inc. has a total gross sales volume of $300,000 to $350,000 per year. However, Randy's can charge $3,000 to $5,000 for design and installation of an average yard using Toro sprinkler parts. AAH, in comparison, would beat the price while using Irritrol parts, which has been rated higher in customer satisfaction. Randy's admits that Toro products have been disappointing during the current season, to the benefit of AAH.

5.1.3 Market Potential

Market analysis allows AAH to plan for future considerations. This encompasses areas such as product, place, price, and promotion. In addition, there are numerous subsets that make up the marketing strategy. Describing market potential is an important aspect that will be addressed here.

Geographic boundaries limit AAH to Colorado Springs and the surrounding areas. This would include Woodland Park to the west, Black Forest to the north, Calhan to the east, and Fountain/Security to the south. As anticipated growth progresses, AAH plans to service all of Southern Colorado.

Market size, based on population and demographic information, can currently comprise almost 100,000 people. The Front Range has experienced a growth rate of 25% during the decade of the 1990s. Census information has recorded over 525,000 residents living in El Paso County. The Pikes Peak region has forecasted a projected population of 625,000 residents by 2010.[11] The military presence continues to grow, too. Space Command, which comprise Cheyenne Mt., Peterson, and Schriever Air Force Bases is now preparing for a larger role in homeland protection.

The number of potential customers, as derived from our target customer profile, can be estimated at 30,000 people. AAH's first sales volume projection was roughly calculated by multiplying the predicted number of 'actual buy' customers with expected price per project. AAH expects that 5,000 people (out of the 30,000 potential customers) actually fit the customer profile to some degree. Then, out of the remaining 5,000, AAH calculates that 4% (roughly 200 people) would hire our services. The average expected

-17-

---

11 2002 edition of Colorado Edge

price for our landscape, primarily sprinklers, is $2,500. The resulting product equates to an expected sales volume of approximately $500,000 per year.[12] Forecasts based on population and demographics indicate that the customer base will increase by almost 20% in the next decade. A semi-annual routine maintenance service provided to customers has the potential of keeping 20 customers per year [13] loyal to AAH, sustaining the customer base.

5.2 Products & Services

AAH plans to provide a single source for customers and their total package needs. Unlike services such as The Handyman Connection, AAH will be the ones performing the work instead of being a middleman between the customer and the contractor. In order to establish the business as a single source for homeowners, AAH will start by providing a wide range of services. This will not only create the first impresion that AAH can handle all types of requests, but will create fewer questions when additional services are added as the business grows.

As AAH grows it will start looking for houses to purchase and repair. Initial house hunting will involve HUD homes and other foreclosures. AAH will also investigate working with a realty company to find houses listed within our capital budget.

To enforce the commitment to quality upheld by every member of AAH, there are many features and benefits that are included with all of the services provided. Many of these features and benefits that AAH believes to be a right of the customer are lacking in many businesses providing similar services.

Due to the nature of the services offered by AAH, there are lifecycle and seasonality issues that must be analyzed and understood. Addressing these issues will allow AAH to see how demand for each service will wax and wane over time and compensate for the fluctuations with other aspects of the business.

5.2.1 Services

The majority of homeowners want to make improvements and or modifications to their homes, but are incapable of doing so on their own. This is a result of not having the knowledge or not having the time. Either way, AAH will be able to make the improvements for the homeowner, beautifying the Front Range in the process.

AAH will offer a variety of landscape and home remodeling services. First, the core business, at this point, is sprinklers. AAH offers installation of well-designed residential sprinkler systems using contractor-grade Irritrol sprinkler parts. Sprinkler systems are designed for maximum efficiency that considers climate, terrain, and coverage.

-18-

---

12 Statistics based on residential customers only

13 Statistics based on AAH analysis

AAH also offers an extensive array of landscape and home remodeling upgrades. AAH will design and create residential landscapes, using a 'common sense' approach that will consider drainage, structural integrity, and physical attractiveness issues. Landscape designs can include projects such as wood decks, stone pathways, and fences/gates. This can also include yard maintenance like aeration, sod installation, and trimming/pruning.

AAH, unlike other competitors, also offer design and expertise of home remodeling projects. Drywall repair and texture, interior painting, flooring, and basement remodeling are just some of the services that AAH provides.

Services Provided by AAH

Service	Description
Custom Deck Design & Installation	Designing and building decks to fit customer desires.
Custom Swing Set & Jungle Gym Design & Installation	Designing and building play sets to fulfill customer desires to give their children something unique and special.
Decorative Landscaping	Designing and constructing decorative flower gardens and planters. Installing grass and rock.
Decorative/Functional Retaining Wall Construction	Building retaining walls for terracing, erosion control, and decoration.
Fence Installation & Repair	Installation of picket, split rail, and privacy fences including gates.
Finishing Basements	Designing and finishing basements to fit customer desires.
Interior Remodeling	Performing alterations to the inside of a house based on customer requests.
Painting – Custom Interior	Custom painting such as sponge painting, faux painting, stenciling and other stylized decorating.
Painting – Exterior	Includes primer coats, spray and brush painting both the exterior and the trim.
Painting – Standard Interior	Painting interior rooms and ceilings with either a roller or large brush in single colors.
Project Consulting	Individual advise for do-it-yourselfers on how to complete their projects.
Repair – Electrical	Repairing faulty outlets, switches, and fixtures.

-19-

Repair — Exterior	Repairing siding and trim.
Repair — Interior	Repairing damaged molding, sheetrock, railing, etc.
Repair — Plumbing	Repairing leaks in water lines and fixtures.
Roof Installation & Repair	Repairing and installing cedar shake and asphalt shingle roofs.
Sprinkler System Design & Installation	Designing and installing sprinkler systems to maximize watering efficiency.
Sprinkler System Repair	Repairing existing sprinkler systems.
Xeriscape Design and Installation	Designing and installing Xeriscape yards to help customers conserve water.

In addition to the services initially offered by AAH, there are plans to expand the services provided. These services initially will not be offered due to licensing and training which will be required for the members of the business.

Future Services Provided by AAH

Service	Description	Notes
Custom Addition Construction	AAH will work with each customer to design and build additions to existing houses based on customer desires.	As AAH expands into working on large-scale house projects for itself, it is only logical to make such a service available to consumers.
Custom Home Construction	AAH will work with each customer to design and build a house based on customer desires.	As AAH expands into working on large-scale house projects for itself, it is only logical to make such a service available to consumers.

As AAH grows there are plans to acquire properties which are in need of repairs. These properties will be fixed and either resold or rented. Resale of homes will allow AAH to make larger returns on capital investments which will provide greater profits and more opportunities for growth. Property management of rental properties will provide a constant income throughout the year.

-20-

Products Provided by AAH

Product	Description	Notes
Home Repair & Resale	AAH purchase homes from the real estate market, specifically looking at foreclosures and other under valued residences, that are in need of repairs. AAH will make the necessary repairs on these homes and make other improvements to make the house have a better first impression. These houses will then be returned to the housing market through a realtor who works with AAH.	Many properties on the market today sell for less than they could and/or stay on the market longer than necessary for want of a few repairs. AAH will specifically look for these homes in order to repair and provide more curb appeal, thus returning them to the market in a better condition. By purchasing these homes, AAH will be able to make the improvements under its own supervision and its own timeline.
Property Management	AAH purchase homes from the real estate market, specifically looking at foreclosures and other under valued residences, that are in need of repairs. AAH will make the necessary repairs on these homes and make other improvements to make the house have a better first impression. These houses will then be rented.	Due to the semi-transient nature of today's society, many people choose to rent their homes instead of buying them. This is especially the case with military personnel and students in colleges and universities. Colorado Springs has a large population of both military and students making rental property a favorable market.

5.2.2 Features & Benefits

Services rendered by AAH include many features and benefits. These features and benefits are a standard part of project completed by AAH. All members of the business believe any job worth doing is worth doing right, and that any job done right is easy to support with guarantees.

Features & Benefits Provided on Services by AAH

Feature	Description	Benefit
Fully Licensed	Every member of AAH will be fully licensed to perform all of the services offered.	Full licensing ensures every member can perform every service and that a customer will always be dealing with a licensed individual.
Labor Guarantee	AAH guarantees all of its labor for one year after a service is rendered.	AAH stands behind all of its work demonstrating a belief in the quality of the job it does.
Optional Extended Maintenance Plan	AAH will offer extended maintenance plans for only a small additional cost in varying time increments	Customers are willing to pay extra for the peace of mind offered by extended warranties and maintenance plans. Quality work makes extended coverage plans easy to offer.
Quality Designs & Construction	High quality designs supported by quality construction using quality materials ensures structural integrity efficiency and lasting beauty.	Quality from beginning to end on a project will speak for itself for years to come.
Sprinkler Manufacturer's Guarantee	AAH uses Irritrol sprinkler products which include a standard one year manufacturer's guarantee.	AAH only uses quality materials to ensure a quality job.
Timeliness	AAH will give a window that is between 30 minutes and 1 hour in which a member will be at a customer location and will strive to always have the member arrive at the beginning of the window.	Time is as important to a customer as it is to AAH. Giving large windows in which AAH will arrive not only wastes valuable customer time it creates an impression of an uncaring company.

AAH is built on two fundamental philosophies: Any job should be done right the first time, and an honest day's work for an honest day's pay. These philosophies are reflected in the way AAH does business and stands behind its work.

5.2.3 Lifecycle and Seasonality

The lifecycle of landscape and home remodeling services are difficult to gauge. According to the latest Census figures, new home construction has been rising steadily for the past few years, despite the recent economic downturn. The state's construction industry, in particular the grounds' maintenance and home remodeling fields, has prospered. Even in the mature stages of the technology, landscape and remodeling remains more labor-intensive. Nonetheless, as home construction continues to grow, new homeowners will desire green lawns and beautiful landscape. That is the epitome of the American Dream.

Well-designed sprinkler systems, with the proper maintenance and care, should last 8 to 10 years. The drawback, however, is that sprinkler installation and maintenance can only occur in the warmer months. In Colorado, that could be from March to October. Peak sales, undoubtedly, will occur during mid-April to mid-July. The subsequent months will show that business will wane somewhat.

AAH plans to compensate for the seasonality of the landscaping industry by supplementing the business with home remodeling. Home remodeling can be performed in the winter season, when the sprinkler business lies dormant. AAH will expect peak sales from October to November, then sales should drop during the Christmas season. The beginning of the year, according to human nature, will again show a rebound in home remodeling sales.

5.3 Marketing Strategies

Marketing strategies are a combination of the location of the business, the price and quality of the product or service, and the methods used to notify the public of the business. By analyzing each of these areas, AAH has determined its needs and is able to focus its strategy for maximum effect at a minimum cost.

5.3.1 Location & Distribution

As AAH starts out, the business will be based out of the homes of its members. This will reduce the rental and storage costs associated with maintaining a separate facility to a nominal amount. AAH can make this work since the facility is not one that customers will see. The majority of business will be conducted at the customers' home. Working out of the homes of it members allows AAH to maintain its operations in multiple locations. Customer calls will be handled in one place while tools and equipment will be stored in another.

As the business grows and requires additional staff to handle customer calls and additional storage for necessary equipment, it will become necessary to acquire a facility to work out of. Since this need is at least five years out, AAH is not going to base itself at a fixed location in order to minimize overhead costs.

5.3.2 Price-Quality Relations

AAH is founded on high quality. In order to do a job right, quality materials and quality craftsmanship must be used. Due to the fact that many of the services AAH offers will not be directly visible to the homeowner, AAH will generate a perception of quality through price. Examples of our services that customers will not see everyday include underground sprinkler systems and wall framing hidden behind sheet rock. In the landscaping and remodeling business, the only work that homeowners talk about is work that is poor quality and causes problems. The goal of AAH is to produce quality work that a homeowner never needs to worry about.

By not charging the lowest price, advertising quality work done right the first time, and backing all work with a guarantee, AAH will support the true quality of its work with a perceived quality. Also when price is brought into question, AAH is willing to show consumers what their money is buying. Each bid and contract will contain a breakdown of all materials and their costs, and AAH will discuss with each potential customer why higher quality components are being used.

5.3.3 Promotional Strategies

Promoting the business involves more than just advertising. Presentation, public relations, and customer service are all equally important to AAH. Every member of AAH believes in presenting the company to every consumer in such a way as to leave them with a lasting positive impression.

PACKAGING & PRESENTATION

Presenting a clean positive image to all potential customers is important to AAH. First impressions of individuals are hard to change. It is no different for small businesses. By showing up to provide an estimate in professional attire, AAH will present itself as a business that is concerned with details, quality, and appearances. Attentively addressing every question in an honest manner and at a level the customer can understand will further support the image.

Discussing design plans and possible differing style issues with each customer will create an image of a caring company. Giving each potential customer a neat and easy-to-read estimate that outlines all of the expenses and walks the individual through it will assist in furthering the lasting image.

PUBLIC RELATIONS

AAH is actively considering several activities to aid public relations. Assisting with or even solely contributing to new school playgrounds and community parks are a strong motivation to the members of AAH. By unselfishly donating time, expertise, and materials to projects to better the community, an image of caring will be built.

Members of AAH will also look for opportunities to share their knowledge with the public for the benefit of everyone. This will include writing articles for the local newspaper discussing benefits of Xeriscaping in the desert climate. Other topics will include water saving measures for both inside and outside the house, and how to identify minor problems before they become major.

ADVERTISING

Mass advertising is necessary to promote a business to the public. Unfortunately such advertising cannot be directed solely at the intended audience. For this reason AAH will start with only limited mass advertising. In many cases, people looking for services, such as those offered by AAH, are in need of a company who can help them immediately. For these individuals, the phone book or Yellow Pages are the most frequently used resource. AAH will be listed in both the published Yellow Pages and in the online Yellow Pages.

Another source that people turn to in today's technologically driven world is the Internet. This resource is used to research the services provided by companies and compare the quality of the services offered. AAH will maintain a web site which will promote the company and display a portfolio of jobs that have been completed. This web site will be listed on business cards and other forms of advertising.

As business grows, AAH will investigate advertising on company vehicles and the possibility of using television and the Internet to get the company name into the minds of the public.

AAH will maintain a record of each customer who purchases services. Such a database will allow reminders for maintenance to be sent out. For sprinkler system customers, AAH will send out notes telling customers when it is time to turn sprinkler systems on and off. Combining this kind of advertising with customer service will help create the customer referrals that no company can survive without.

Once AAH is established, additional avenues for advertising will be investigated. AAH will look into partnering with construction companies such as Keller Homes and Classic Homes to become a recommended landscaping company to individuals who purchase new homes. AAH will also investigate partnering with some realty companies to provide remodeling and repair services to people who are buying and selling homes. A third partnership opportunity that AAH will research is with existing property management companies. Through this arrangement AAH would repair rental properties and handle service calls for the property manager.

CUSTOMER SERVICE

Customers are what keep AAH in business. They expect quality customer service and in many cases are willing to pay for it. They deserve to be treated with respect and honesty. To show this, AAH strives always to be on time to every appointment and will not give a customer a time window greater than one hour for arrival. AAH will also offer discounts on services if a member of the business does not arrive within the given window for an estimate.

-25-

It is also important that both customers and consumers be able to contact AAH. The business will strive to have a knowledgeable person who can answer the phone during standard business hours. If a customer or consumer must leave a message, AAH will promptly return the call.

Providing consumers with quality customer service will promote positive relations. When combined with honest quality work and continuing support afterwards AAH strives for complete customer satisfaction.

6.0 FINANCIAL PLANS

6.1 Sales Forecast

The sales forecast is built on two principles. Using a "top-down" approach, the total market share is determined. Then it is narrowed down through facts and logical assumptions to determine the amount of the market available to AAH. This approach will determine the number of jobs available for AAH and the money AAH can expect to generate.

The second principle uses a "bottom-up" approach to determine the cost for AAH to do business. This approach takes into consideration the fixed recurring costs of operation and the variable costs which change with job volume. The sunk costs involved in startup are also included to assist in determining the point at which AAH has paid for itself.

6.1.1 Initial Assumptions

Every forecast must be built on some initial assumptions. From these assumptions, a logical progression will be made to either support or refute the assumption that there is a place in the market for AAH. The following list contains AAH's initial assumptions.

- Every house will, at several points in its life, need work. This work ranges from landscaping at new homes, to repairs due to weather and other damage at middle-aged homes, to repairs due to old age at older homes.

- The total population of home owners in Colorado Springs are potential customers. If every home will eventually need work, it is logical to assume that every homeowner will at some point need work done on his home.

- Homeowners living in mobile homes will be factored out of the potential clientele. Three percent of homeowners in Colorado Springs live in mobile homes. AAH is not qualified to work on these types of homes.

- A percentage of homeowners are dedicated do-it-yourselfers. These individuals will not pay someone else to do the work they can do. They will have to be factored out of the potential clientele. This percentage varies depending on the type of job. For the jobs perceived as easier, such as decorative landscaping, the percentage will be higher. For the jobs perceived as much more difficult or dangerous, such as sprinkler system installation and framing, the percentage will be lower. For our services, it is assumed that no more than 10 percent of the population are do-it-yourselfers. This value takes into consideration the homeowners with access to the knowledge, the tools, the time, and the physical abilities to perform the job.

- A percentage of homeowners just don't care about the conditions they live in. These individuals cannot be convinced to better their living arrangements under any circumstance. AAH assumes that 1 percent of homeowners will fall into this category. These will also need to be factored out of the potential clientele.

- AAH is not performing the type of work at a price that would interest individuals of lower incomes. Households with an income less than $15,000 will be removed from the potential clientele.

By starting with these basic assumptions AAH has narrowed the scope of potential customers down to a reasonable base.

6.1.2 Market Potential

A total of 202,428 housing units are in Colorado Springs per the 2000 census data on housing characteristics. 6,807 of these units are mobile homes and 200 others are recreational vehicles, boats, and other non-house type homes. This leaves 195,421 homes as the available market.

Per the Colorado Springs 2000 census on economic characteristics, there are 201,265 total households. Of these households 24,753 have an income less than $15,000 annually. This calculates out to 12.30% of households earn less than $15,000 per year.

From the initial assumptions, households with incomes below $15,000 are not interested in the services offered by AAH. This means 24,037 of houses in the available market make below $15,000, leaving 171,384 households to make up the available market.

From the available market, the do-it-yourselfers and the homeowners who do not care about their houses have to be removed. These two categories together are assumed to make up 11% of the market or 18,852 households in Colorado Springs. This reduces the available market to 152,532 households.

According to the 2000 Colorado Springs census data approximately 20% of houses were built prior to 1960. Since the building standards are much different on older houses, AAH is not, at this time, prepared to assume the risks of working on these houses. This further reduces the available market to 122,026 households.

Assuming that all 122,026 households are in the process of researching improvements but only 25% of these individuals will have the money and the time to pursue their desired improvements in any one given year. This further reduces the prospective market to 30,507 households.

It is assumed that the available market will divide itself fairly evenly among the available businesses offering landscape and remodeling services. This assumption is based on the natural human desire to want things done quickly. Statistically very few individuals are willing to wait for a service when they can get the service sooner if they go elsewhere. Since AAH is one of very few businesses offering the total package of interior and exterior repair and remodeling and landscape design and installation, the market needs to be analyzed in separate pieces. There are 590 entries in the Colorado Springs phone book for businesses offering some form of interior and exterior remodeling and repair. Assuming that about 10% of businesses are not listed in the phone book, this means there are 650 businesses offering competition to AAH on remodeling and repair services. Similarly there are 10 businesses listed under sprinkler systems and 127 listed under landscape design and contractors. Assuming about 10% of these businesses are also not listed, that brings the total competition to 11 sprinkler system businesses and 140 landscaping businesses.

It is not logical to assume that every business listed is offering similar services to a similar market. This is especially true for the repair and remodeling services. Assuming that 25% of the repair and remodeling competition deals only in large commercial projects for businesses, and that once a business starts to deal with commercial businesses it will not want to take a step back to deal with the smaller contracts offered by residential homeowners, these can be factored out. This leaves 488 businesses as competition. Similarly for sprinkler systems and landscape design and installation, the percentage is also assumed to be 25%. This leaves 8 competitors for sprinkler systems and 105 competitors for landscaping.

Of all the competition in the market it assumed that approximately 5% of the listed businesses are support for the business and not actually into performing the work. Factoring these businesses out leaves 464 repair and remodeling competitors, approximately 8 sprinkler system competitors, and 100 landscaping competitors.

From the 2000 Colorado Springs housing characteristic census data, there are 4,007 houses built between 1999 and 2000. Of the 202,428 total housing units this equates to approximately 2%. Assuming that growth remained constant, it can be assumed that about 2% of the market is interested in sprinkler system installations. It is also assumed that about 20% of the available market is interested in landscaping services. Approximately 80% of the market is interested in repair and remodeling services.

Applying these percentages to the available market determined above evaluates to 24,406 households interested in repair and remodeling services. 610 households interested in sprinkler systems, and 6,101 households interested in landscaping services. Evenly dividing these jobs among the market competitors results in 53 repair and remodeling jobs per business, 76 sprinkler system jobs per business, and 61 landscaping jobs per business per season. Assuming that, on average, these jobs are spread evenly throughout the working season and that a season is 12 months for repair and remodeling, 3 months for sprinkler systems, and 6 months for landscaping, this equates to about 4 repair and remodeling jobs per month, 25 sprinkler system jobs per month, and 10 landscaping jobs per month.

-28-

These numbers are based on the assumption that AAH can gain an equal share of the market with the rest of the competition. This in itself is not a logical assumption for a business starting out, but AAH plans to work on marketing its willingness to accept the smaller jobs which the majority of other businesses will not accept and offering non-typical services such as drip sprinkler systems and Xeriscaping. It is assumed that these niche services can account for the difference in market share. This assumption is based on the difficulty consumers have in finding a company willing to do smaller jobs and the persistent drought conditions combined with the restrictions the city of Colorado Springs is placing on homeowners.

As business grows AAH will also selectively target it services to commercial and government businesses to enlarge its market share. These engagements will only be made after much research and will specifically target the needs of the particular business. This will allow AAH to enlarge its market without the costs associated to mass marketing.

6.1.3 Breakeven Analysis

At the breakeven point, the costs of doing business are equal to the revenue from doing business. Determining this point requires an analysis of fixed business costs that reoccur every month or every year, and of the variable costs that change with each job. Together these determine the cost of doing business. Sunk costs, money that has already been invested in the business, is not included in determining the breakeven point because it is invested whether or not AAH reaches the breakeven point. It is included here only to help determine at what point after the breakeven point AAH has truly made money.

Initial fixed costs for AAH include insurance, phone service, licenses, CPA services, and advertising. Research indicates insurance will cost between $1,000 and $2,000 annually. The current quote AAH has from State Farm is for $1,168 per year for liability. This is based on a $1,000,000 coverage policy, which is the standard offered by many agencies. The minimum coverage required by the state of Colorado is $300,000 but many housing companies such as Classic Homes and Vantage require between $500,000 and $1,000,000 coverage. Health insurance will be added once AAH has been in business for a year. Initial investigation has found rates of $311 per family per month for individual policies and $2,442 per month for a group policy. For the first two years AAH will not offer health insurance as a benefit. During this time members will find their own health coverage through other means.

Phone service initially will be through Qwest. It will cost between $40 and $80 per month for a single line with voice mail that will answer when the line is busy. The difference in cost depends on whether or not the line is ordered as residential or business. The business line rate includes a free listing in both the yellow and the white pages of the Qwest phone book. AAH is starting with the business line for $80. After six to twelve months of operation, AAH will investigate a cell phone policy for its owners. At this time cell phones are not included.

The state of Colorado requires all people performing contract labor on new or existing structures greater than 120 square feet to be licensed. They also require individuals to be licensed in order to connect to the main water supply inside a house. The type E Repair/Maintenance license offered by the state covers all of the remodeling and repair work that AAH offers at this time. This license costs $75 per person per year. AAH will eventually grow into the type C Homebuilder license which costs $150 per person per year. At this time the state of Colorado does not require licenses to perform landscaping nor to install sprinkler systems assuming the stub out from the main water supply is already installed. In order to install the stub out for sprinkler systems, the Water Connected Appliance license is required. This license costs $100 per person per year. AAH will license its members with both the type E and Water Connected Appliance licenses for a cost of $175 per person per year. Since AAH emphasizes that its members performing contract work are licensed, three sets will be required for a total of $525 per year.

AAH will require CPA services to ensure taxes are filed correctly each year. These services will cost between $70 and $100 per year.

The final fixed cost for AAH is advertising. AAH has worked at building a network of contacts, including realtors and other general contractors, that have offered resources to help minimize advertising costs. Also by purchasing a business phone line, a listing in the phone book is included. On top of all this AAH plans to spend $1,200 per year on additional advertising.

Salaries are not included as a fixed cost since, for the first two years of operation the members of AAH will be paid on a per-hour-on-the-job basis. This will encourage members to work harder during the first years and will save overhead costs during lean months when there are not as many jobs. Each member will be paid $18 per hour on each job site. After two years members will be switched to salaries, allowing for more money to be invested back into the business.

Calculating these fixed expenses, AAH expects $3,953 per year in fixed expenses or approximately $329.42 in fixed expenses each month.

Variable costs are another part of business. These costs change for each job and with the number of jobs. These costs include the cost of materials, fuel, and office supplies. For the first two years, compensation will also be a variable cost since members of AAH will collect hourly wages.

Materials are part of every job. AAH offers four basic types of services, each with a different average cost for materials. Home repair jobs average approximately $500 in materials. Home remodeling jobs average about $3,000 in materials. Sprinkler systems average $1,100 in materials, and landscaping jobs average $2,000 in materials. These costs are passed on to the customer who only incurs them when the bid is accepted. AAH will only assume the costs of materials that exceed the amount included in the estimate. AAH estimates high on quantities for materials preferring to refund customers the costs of unused materials than to either have to ask for more money or cover material overruns.

-30-

Standard fuel reimbursement rates for business travel are currently $0.32 per mile. Since AAH relies on being able to reach a customer at their home, it will pay members fuel costs for travel. The majority of AAH's jobs will come from homeowners in Colorado Springs and the area immediately surrounding it. On average each job will require one trip to the residence for an estimate, one supply run, and trips to the residence over two and a half days to complete the job. Assuming that 25% of bids result in jobs, then each job must cover the costs of three additional estimate trips. On average each residence will be 15 miles away. The stores for supplies are within 15 miles of AAH's center of operations. This figures out to each job will require approximately 135 miles of driving. The additional estimate trips will require another 45 miles of driving. Using these calculations each job will need to support 180 miles of driving for a cost of $58 per job.

Office supplies include paper and printer cartridges for printing contracts and other business analysis documents. It also includes pencils and paper for estimates and business cards. Every contract is two pages, and for every job a two-page analysis document is produced. Each estimate form is one page. Assuming 25% of bids submitted are accepted this means each job must cover thirteen pieces of printer paper. Therefore a ream of paper will cover 38 jobs. At Office Depot a ream of paper cost $6. Printer cartridges at Office Depot cost $35. Each cartridge should last through two and a half reams of paper or about 95 jobs. Other miscellaneous office supplies such as pencils and stables will cost about $10 for every 200 jobs. Business cards cost $13 for 250 cards which will cover 60 jobs. This equates to a cost of $0.80 per job to cover office supplies.

For the first two years, members of AAH will work for an hourly wage instead of burdening the business with salaries to support. After two years of operation, hourly wages will be reevaluated to determine if salaries are a viable and better option. The industry average for general contract type labor is $18.75 per hour. The AAH partnership agreement dictates that 20% of labor costs must be returned to the business for growth and expenses. To cover wages and growth/expense money, AAH will need to charge $24 per person per hour.

From previous assumptions each job will average two and a half days for two people both working ten-hour days. This calculates out to 25 hours per person per job or 50 man-hours per job. At $24 per person per job, AAH will charge an average of $1,200 in labor per job. Twenty percent, or $240, of this will be invested in the business to cover growth and expenses.

6.1.4 Forecast Analysis

Analysis of the Colorado Springs market potential revealed 4 repair and remodeling jobs per month over a 12-month year. Of these jobs, three are assumed to be the less expensive repair jobs and one will be the more expensive remodeling job. Market potential also revealed 25 sprinkler system jobs per month over a 3-month season, and 10 landscaping jobs per month over a 6-month season. This figures out to 4 jobs per month for six months of the year, 14 jobs per month for 3 months of the year and 39 jobs per month for three months of the year, or 183 jobs per year. AAH estimates an average repair job, including materials, costs $1,700, remodel job costs $4,200, landscaping job costs $3,200, and sprinkler system costs $2,300. This calculates to a gross income of $399,300 annually including materials or $219,600 without materials.

From the breakeven analysis, the monthly expenses for AAH are $329.42 for fixed costs and $959 per job variable expenses, excluding materials. Comparing this to the $1,200 in labor charges per job, if AAH completes two jobs per month a net revenue of $2,400 will be realized which will more than cover expenses.

In three years when the member families convert to salaries, of $3,600 each, instead of hourly wages, the fixed costs of AAH will become $11,129.42 and the variable costs will become $59 per job plus materials. On a per month basis there will be some months of the year where expenses exceed revenue. Annually the fixed costs are $133,553.04. At $59 in variable costs per job and $1,200 in labor charges per job there is $1,141 per job put toward covering fixed costs. Dividing $1,141 into the annual fixed costs of $133,553.04 it figures out to 117 per year.

Based on the analysis of the market potential AAH expects to have 183 jobs per year. During the first two years of operation AAH only requires 24 jobs per year to cover expenses leaving 159 jobs to figure towards profit. This figure also allows for some leeway in the very real case that AAH cannot acquire its share of the market immediately. After two years when AAH converts its members to salaries, 117 jobs will be required to cover annual expenses. This will leave 66 jobs to go towards business improvements, growth, and profit.

6.2 Cash Flow Projections

Cash flow worksheets for the years 2002, 2003, and 2004 are included in here.

Monthly Cash Flow Projections for the Year 2002   All About the Home

Months	1 Jan	2 Feb	3 March	4 April	5 May	6 June	7 July	8 Aug	9 Sept	10 Oct	11 Nov	12 Dec	Yearly Total
1. (A) Beginning Cash Balance	$0.00	$0.00	$0.00	$0.00	$0.00	$0.00	$0.00	$145.00	$346.20	$281.60	$751.40	$881.20	$0.00
Cash Receipts													
2. Cash Sales							$316.00	$3,200.00	$3,400.00	$9,300.00	$9,300.00	$9,300.00	$34,816.00
3. Collect Accounts Receivable							$0.00	$0.00	$0.00	$0.00	$0.00	$0.00	$0.00
4. Sale of Fixed Assets							$0.00	$0.00	$0.00	$0.00	$0.00	$0.00	$0.00
5. Miscellaneous Income							$0.00	$0.00	$0.00	$0.00	$0.00	$0.00	$0.00
(B) Total Cash Receipts	$0.00	$0.00	$0.00	$0.00	$0.00	$0.00	$316.00	$3,200.00	$3,400.00	$9,300.00	$9,300.00	$9,300.00	$34,816.00
Cash Disbursements													
6. Cash Purchases (Merchandise)							$0.00	$0.00	$0.00	$0.00	$0.00	$0.00	$0.00
7. Pay Accounts Payable													
7 a. Phone							$0.00	$0.00	$80.00	$80.00	$80.00	$80.00	$320.00
8. Salaries/Wages & Benefits							$100.00	$900.00	$1,800.00	$3,600.00	$3,600.00	$3,600.00	$13,600.00
9. Owner Withdrawal							$0.00	$0.00	$0.00	$0.00	$0.00	$0.00	$0.00
10. Outside Services - Prof. Services													
10 a. CPA							$0.00	$0.00	$0.00	$0.00	$0.00	$100.00	$100.00
11. Insurance													
11 a. Liability							$0.00	$0.00	$292.00	$115.00	$115.00	$115.00	$637.00
11 b. Health							$0.00	$0.00	$0.00	$300.00	$600.00	$600.00	$1,500.00
12. Advertising							$0.00	$0.00	$0.00	$0.00	$0.00	$0.00	$0.00
13. Occupancy Expenses							$0.00	$0.00	$0.00	$0.00	$0.00	$0.00	$0.00
14. Miscellaneous Expenses													
14 a. Business Name Registration							$8.00	$0.00	$0.00	$0.00	$0.00	$0.00	$8.00
14 b. License Application Fee							$0.00	$40.00	$0.00	$0.00	$40.00	$0.00	$80.00
14 c. License Fee (Aaron in Sept., Ed in Dec.)							$0.00	$0.00	$175.00	$0.00	$0.00	$175.00	$350.00
14 d. Office Supplies							$0.00	$0.80	$1.60	$3.20	$3.20	$3.20	$12.00
14 e. Fuel Reimbursement							$0.00	$58.00	$116.00	$232.00	$232.00	$232.00	$870.00
14 f. Materials							$63.00	$2,000.00	$1,000.00	$4,500.00	$4,500.00	$4,500.00	$16,563.00
15. Purchase of Fixed Assets							$0.00	$0.00	$0.00	$0.00	$0.00	$0.00	$0.00
15. Debt Payment - Old							$0.00	$0.00	$0.00	$0.00	$0.00	$0.00	$0.00
(C) Total Cash Disbursements	$0.00	$0.00	$0.00	$0.00	$0.00	$0.00	$171.00	$2,998.80	$3,464.60	$8,830.20	$9,170.20	$9,405.20	$34,040.00

Net Cash Flow (B - C)	$0.00	$0.00	$0.00	$0.00	$0.00	$0.00	$145.00	$201.20	($64.60)	$469.80	$129.80	($105.20)	**$776.00**
Adjustments to Net Cash Flow													
17. (+) New Debt						$0.00	$0.00	$0.00	$0.00	$0.00	$0.00	$0.00	$0.00
18. (+) New Owner Investment						$0.00	$0.00	$0.00	$0.00	$0.00	$0.00	$0.00	$0.00
19. (-) New Debt - Interest payments						$0.00	$0.00	$0.00	$0.00	$0.00	$0.00	$0.00	$0.00
20. (-) New Debt- Principal payments						$0.00	$0.00	$0.00	$0.00	$0.00	$0.00	$0.00	$0.00
21. (-) New Owner Withdrawals						$0.00	$0.00	$0.00	$0.00	$0.00	$0.00	$0.00	$0.00
(D) Adjusted Net Cash Flow	$0.00	$0.00	$0.00	$0.00	$0.00	$0.00	$145.00	$201.20	($64.60)	$469.80	$129.80	($105.20)	$776.00
Ending Cash Balance (A + D)	$0.00	$0.00	$0.00	$0.00	$0.00	$0.00	$145.00	$346.20	$281.60	$751.40	$881.20	$776.00	**$776.00**

Monthly Cash Flow Projections for the Year 2003   All About the Home

Months	1 Jan	2 Feb	3 March	4 April	5 May	6 June	7 July	8 Aug	9 Sept	10 Oct	11 Nov	12 Dec	Yearly Total
1. (A) Beginning Cash Balance	$839.00	$808.80	$778.60	$823.40	$2,099.20	$10,611.00	$19,097.80	$27,609.60	$30,131.40	$32,103.20	$33,419.00	$33,528.80	$839.00
Cash Receipts													
2. Cash Sales	$9,300.00	$9,300.00	$9,300.00	$25,300.00	$98,800.00	$98,800.00	$98,800.00	$41,300.00	$41,300.00	$25,300.00	$9,300.00	$9,300.00	$476,100.00
3. Collect Accounts Receivable	$0.00	$0.0C	$0.00	$0.00	$0.00	$0.00	$0.00	$0.00	$0.00	$0.00	$0.00	$0.00	$0.00
4. Sale of Fixed Assets	$0.00	$0.0C	$0.00	$0.00	$0.00	$0.00	$0.00	$0.00	$0.00	$0.00	$0.00	$0.00	$0.00
5. Miscellaneous Income	$0.00	$0.0C	$0.00	$0.00	$0.00	$0.00	$0.00	$0.00	$0.00	$0.00	$0.00	$0.00	$0.00
(B) Total Cash Receipts	$9,300.00	$9,300.00	$9,300.00	$25,300.00	$98,800.00	$98,800.00	$98,800.00	$41,300.00	$41,300.00	$25,300.00	$9,300.00	$9,300.00	$476,100.00
Cash Disbursements													
6. Cash Purchases (Merchandise)	$0.00	$0.00	$0.00	$0.00	$0.00	$0.00	$0.00	$0.00	$0.00	$0.00	$0.00	$0.00	$0.00
7. Pay Accounts Payable													
7 a. Phone	$80.00	$80.00	$80.00	$80.00	$80.00	$80.00	$80.00	$80.00	$80.00	$80.00	$80.00	$80.00	$960.00
8. Salaries/Wages & Benefits	$3,600.00	$3,600.00	$3,600.00	$8,100.00	$35,100.00	$35,100.00	$35,100.00	$12,600.00	$12,600.00	$8,100.00	$3,600.00	$3,600.00	$164,700.00
9. Owner Withdrawal	$0.00	$0.00	$0.00	$0.00	$0.00	$0.00	$0.00	$0.00	$0.00	$0.00	$0.00	$0.00	$0.00
10. Outside Services - Prof. Services													
10 a. CPA	$0.00	$0.00	$25.00	$0.00	$0.00	$25.00	$0.00	$0.00	$25.00	$0.00	$0.00	$25.00	$100.00
11. Insurance													
11 a. Liability	$115.00	$115.00	$115.00	$115.00	$115.00	$115.00	$115.00	$115.00	$115.00	$115.00	$115.00	$115.00	$1,380.00
11 b. Health	$600.00	$600.00	$600.00	$600.00	$600.00	$600.00	$600.00	$600.00	$600.00	$600.00	$600.00	$600.00	$7,200.00
12. Advertising	$200.00	$200.00	$100.00	$100.00	$100.00	$100.00	$100.00	$60.00	$60.00	$60.00	$60.00	$60.00	$1,200.00
13. Occupancy Expenses	$0.00	$0.00	$0.00	$0.00	$0.00	$0.00	$0.00	$0.00	$0.00	$0.00	$0.00	$0.00	$0.00
14. Miscellaneous Expenses													
14 a. Business Name Registration	$0.00	$0.00	$0.00	$0.00	$0.00	$0.00	$0.00	$0.00	$0.00	$0.00	$0.00	$0.00	$0.00
14 b. License Application Fee	$0.00	$0.00	$0.00	$0.00	$0.00	$0.00	$0.00	$0.00	$0.00	$0.00	$0.00	$0.00	$0.00
14 c. License Fee (Aaron renewal in Sept. 3yr & Ed renewal in Dec. 3yr)	$0.00	$0.00	$0.00	$0.00	$0.00	$0.00	$0.00	$0.00	$525.00	$0.00	$0.00	$525.00	$1,050.00
14 d. Office Supplies	$3.20	$3.20	$3.20	$7.20	$31.20	$31.20	$31.20	$11.20	$11.20	$7.20	$3.20	$3.20	$146.40
14 e. Fuel Reimbursement	$232.00	$232.00	$232.00	$522.00	$2,262.00	$2,262.00	$2,262.00	$812.00	$812.00	$522.00	$232.00	$232.00	$10,614.00
14 f. Materials	$4,500.00	$4,500.00	$4,500.00	$14,500.00	$52,000.00	$52,000.00	$52,000.00	$24,500.00	$24,500.00	$14,500.00	$4,500.00	$4,500.00	$256,500.00
15. Purchase of Fixed Assets	$0.00	$0.00	$0.00	$0.00	$0.00	$0.00	$0.00	$0.00	$0.00	$0.00	$0.00	$0.00	$0.00
15. Debt Payment - Old	$0.00	$0.00	$0.00	$0.00	$0.00	$0.00	$0.00	$0.00	$0.00	$0.00	$0.00	$0.00	$0.00
(C) Total Cash Disbursements	$9,330.20	$9,330.20	$9,255.20	$24,024.20	$90,288.20	$90,313.20	$90,288.20	$38,778.20	$39,328.20	$23,984.20	$9,190.20	$9,740.20	$443,850.40

Net Cash Flow (B - C)	($30.20)	($30.20)	$44.80	$1,275.80	$8,511.80	$8,486.80	$8,511.80	$2,521.80	$1,971.80	$1,315.80	$109.80	($440.20)	**$32,249.60**
Adjustments to Net Cash Flow													
17. (+) New Debt	$0.00	$0.00	$0.00	$0.00	$0.00	$0.00	$0.00	$0.00	$0.00	$0.00	$0.00	$0.00	$0.00
18. (+) New Owner Investment	$0.00	$0.00	$0.00	$0.00	$0.00	$0.00	$0.00	$0.00	$0.00	$0.00	$0.00	$0.00	$0.00
19. (-) New Debt - Interest payments	$0.00	$0.00	$0.00	$0.00	$0.00	$0.00	$0.00	$0.00	$0.00	$0.00	$0.00	$0.00	$0.00
20. (-) New Debt- Principal payments	$0.00	$0.00	$0.00	$0.00	$0.00	$0.00	$0.00	$0.00	$0.00	$0.00	$0.00	$0.00	$0.00
21. (-) New Owner Withdrawals	$0.00	$0.00	$0.00	$0.00	$0.00	$0.00	$0.00	$0.00	$0.00	$0.00	$0.00	$0.00	$0.00
(D) Adjusted Net Cash Flow	($30.20)	($30.20)	$44.80	$1,275.80	$8,511.80	$8,486.80	$8,511.80	$2,521.80	$1,971.80	$1,315.80	$109.80	($440.20)	$32,249.60
Ending Cash Balance (A + D)	$808.80	$778.60	$823.40	$2,099.20	$10,611.00	$19,097.80	$27,609.60	$30,131.40	$32,103.20	$33,419.00	$33,528.80	$33,088.60	**$33,088.60**

Monthly Cash Flow Projections for the Year 2004   All About the Home

Months	1 Jan	2 Feb	3 March	4 April	5 May	6 June	7 July	8 Aug	9 Sept	10 Oct	11 Nov	12 Dec	Yearly Total
1. (A) Beginning Cash Balance	$33,088.60	$32,718.40	$31,863.20	$31,608.00	$32,583.80	$40,795.60	$48,982.40	$57,194.20	$59,416.00	$61,612.80	$62,628.60	$62,438.40	$33,088.60
Cash Receipts													
2. Cash Sales	$9,300.00	$9,300.00	$9,300.00	$25,300.00	$98,800.00	$98,800.00	$98,800.00	$41,300.00	$41,300.00	$25,300.00	$9,300.00	$9,300.00	$476,100.00
3. Collect Accounts Receivable	$0.00	$0.00	$0.00	$0.00	$0.00	$0.00	$0.00	$0.00	$0.00	$0.00	$0.00	$0.00	$0.00
4. Sale of Fixed Assets	$0.00	$0.00	$0.00	$0.00	$0.00	$0.00	$0.00	$0.00	$0.00	$0.00	$0.00	$0.00	$0.00
5. Miscellaneous Income	$0.00	$0.00	$0.00	$0.00	$0.00	$0.00	$0.00	$0.00	$0.00	$0.00	$0.00	$0.00	$0.00
(B) Total Cash Receipts	$9,300.00	$9,300.00	$9,300.00	$25,300.00	$98,800.00	$98,800.00	$98,800.00	$41,300.00	$41,300.00	$25,300.00	$9,300.00	$9,300.00	$476,100.00
Cash Disbursements													
6. Cash Purchases (Merchandise)	$0.00	$0.00	$0.00	$0.00	$0.00	$0.00	$0.00	$0.00	$0.00	$0.00	$0.00	$0.00	$0.00
7. Pay Accounts Payable													
7 a. Phone	$80.00	$80.00	$80.00	$80.00	$80.00	$80.00	$80.00	$80.00	$80.00	$80.00	$80.00	$80.00	$960.00
8. Salaries/Wages & Benefits	$3,600.00	$3,600.00	$3,600.00	$8,100.00	$35,100.00	$35,100.00	$35,100.00	$12,600.00	$12,600.00	$8,100.00	$3,600.00	$3,600.00	$164,700.00
9. Owner Withdrawal	$0.00	$0.00	$0.00	$0.00	$0.00	$0.00	$0.00	$0.00	$0.00	$0.00	$0.00	$0.00	$0.00
10. Outside Services - Prof. Services													
10 a. CPA	$0.00	$0.00	$25.00	$0.00	$0.00	$25.00	$0.00	$0.00	$25.00	$0.00	$0.00	$25.00	$100.00
11. Insurance													
11 a. Liability	$115.00	$115.00	$115.00	$115.00	$115.00	$115.00	$115.00	$115.00	$115.00	$115.00	$115.00	$115.00	$1,380.00
11 b. Health	$900.00	$900.00	$900.00	$900.00	$900.00	$900.00	$900.00	$900.00	$900.00	$900.00	$900.00	$900.00	$10,800.00
12. Advertising	$200.00	$200.00	$100.00	$100.00	$100.00	$100.00	$100.00	$60.00	$60.00	$60.00	$60.00	$60.00	$1,200.00
13. Occupancy Expenses													
14. Miscellaneous Expenses													
14 a. Business Name Registration	$0.00	$0.00	$0.00	$0.00	$0.00	$0.00	$0.00	$0.00	$0.00	$0.00	$0.00	$0.00	$0.00
14 b. License Application Fee	$40.00	$0.00	$0.00	$0.00	$0.00	$0.00	$0.00	$0.00	$0.00	$0.00	$0.00	$0.00	$40.00
14 c. License Fee (3yr license for Jamie)	$0.00	$525.00	$0.00	$0.00	$0.00	$0.00	$0.00	$0.00	$0.00	$0.00	$0.00	$0.00	$525.00
14 d. Office Supplies	$3.20	$3.20	$3.20	$7.20	$31.20	$31.20	$31.20	$11.20	$11.20	$7.20	$3.20	$3.20	$146.40
14 e. Fuel Reimbursement	$232.00	$232.00	$232.00	$522.00	$2,262.00	$2,262.00	$2,262.00	$812.00	$812.00	$522.00	$232.00	$232.00	$10,614.00
14 f. Materials	$4,500.00	$4,500.00	$4,500.00	$14,500.00	$52,000.00	$52,000.00	$52,000.00	$24,500.00	$24,500.00	$14,500.00	$4,500.00	$4,500.00	$256,500.00
15. Purchase of Fixed Assets	$0.00	$0.00	$0.00	$0.00	$0.00	$0.00	$0.00	$0.00	$0.00	$0.00	$0.00	$0.00	$0.00
15. Debt Payment - Old	$0.00	$0.00	$0.00	$0.00	$0.00	$0.00	$0.00	$0.00	$0.00	$0.00	$0.00	$0.00	$0.00
(C) Total Cash Disbursements	$9,670.20	$10,155.20	$9,555.20	$24,324.20	$90,588.20	$90,613.20	$90,588.20	$39,078.20	$39,103.20	$24,284.20	$9,490.20	$9,515.20	$446,965.40

Net Cash Flow (B - C)	($370.20)	($855.20)	($255.20)	$975.80	$8,211.80	$8,186.80	$8,211.80	$2,221.80	$2,196.80	$1,015.80	($190.20)	($215.20)	**$29,134.60**
Adjustments to Net Cash Flow												
17. (+) New Debt	$0.00	$0.00	$0.00	$0.00	$0.00	$0.00	$0.00	$0.00	$0.00	$0.00	$0.00	$0.00
18. (+) New Owner Investment	$0.00	$0.00	$0.00	$0.00	$0.00	$0.00	$0.00	$0.00	$0.00	$0.00	$0.00	$0.00
19. (-) New Debt - Interest payments	$0.00	$0.00	$0.00	$0.00	$0.00	$0.00	$0.00	$0.00	$0.00	$0.00	$0.00	$0.00
20. (-) New Debt- Principal payments	$0.00	$0.00	$0.00	$0.00	$0.00	$0.00	$0.00	$0.00	$0.00	$0.00	$0.00	$0.00
21. (-) New Owner Withdrawals	$0.00	$0.00	$0.00	$0.00	$0.00	$0.00	$0.00	$0.00	$0.00	$0.00	$0.00	$0.00
(D) Adjusted Net Cash Flow	($370.20)	($855.20)	($255.20)	$975.80	$8,211.80	$8,186.80	$8,211.80	$2,221.80	$2,196.80	$1,015.80	($190.20)	($215.20)	$29,134.60
Ending Cash Balance (A + D)	$32,718.40	$31,863.20	$31,608.00	$32,583.80	$40,795.60	$48,982.40	$57,194.20	$59,416.00	$61,612.80	$62,628.60	$62,438.40	$62,223.20	**$62,223.20**

6.3 Projected Income Statements

The income statement is a basic record for reporting a company's earnings. Total sales of AAH services for the partial year ending December 31, 2002 are forecasted to be over $18,000. Total cost of services provided is $0. AAH provides landscape and remodeling services, therefore, the cost of materials is passed to the customer without incurring mark up. Transportation costs are based on the standard 32 cents per mile. As well, taxes were assumed to be 20% of net operating profit. The income statement worksheet is included here.

Initial Income Statement

Category	Deductions	Balance
Sales		$18,316.00
Less: Cost of Services Sold	$0.00	
Gross Margin		**$18,316.00**
Less: Operating Expenses		
Member Wages	$13,600.00	
Insurance	$637.00	
Licenses	$430.00	
Advertising	$940.40	
Phone	$320.00	
Office Supplies	$12.00	
Transportation	$870.00	
Total Operating Expenses	$16,809.40	
Net Operating Profit		**$1,506.60**
Net Income Before Taxes		$1,506.60
Less: Income Taxes	$301.32	
Net Income		**$1,205.28**

6.4 Initial Balance Sheet

A balance sheet is a snapshot of a business' financial condition at a specific moment in time. For the year ending December 31, 2002, total assets of AAH are cash only. AAH is a mobile and phone contact-only business, with members responsible for their own tools. Therefore, PP&E has a value of $0. At this time, AAH incurs no liabilities, so total liabilities and equity equal total net income. The initial balance sheet worksheet is included here.

Initial Balance Sheet

Current Assets	Balance
Cash	$1,205.28
Property, Plant, and Equipment	
Land	$0.00
Buildings	$0.00
Equipment	$0.00
Less: Accumulated Depreciation	$0.00
Intangible Assets	$0.00
Total Assets	$1,205.28

Liabilities	
Current Liabilities	$0.00
Long-Term Liabilities	$0.00
Notes Payable	$0.00
Licenses Payable	$0.00
Total Liabilities	$0.00
Owner's Equity	$1,205.28
Total Liabilities and Equity	$1,205.28

6.5 Owner Equity Statement

Total retained earnings for the year ending December 31, 2002, is equal to the total net income of $1,205.28. At this time, AAH issues no stocks and pays no dividends to members. The owner equity worksheet is included here.

-40-

Owner Equity Statement

Beginning Equity	$1,205.28
New Income	$0.00
Less: Dividends	$0.00
Ending Equity	**$1,205.28**

6.6 Additional Financial Information

At this time personal financial statements for each member of AAH are not included since AAH does not plan to seek financing from outside institutions. At such time when outside financing is required, AAH will include financial statements for each of its members as required.

7.0 BUSINESS LOCATION & EQUIPMENT

7.1 Site & Facility Location

AAH is a mobile business. It is intended to go to a home and work from there. With this in mind, the business will be based out of the company truck and trailer. When not on a project site, the truck and tools will need to be stored. It will be stored at one of the members' homes to begin with. Once the business is profitable enough, other facilities will be investigated.

One option for storage is in Colorado Springs, which is closer to the majority of expected business but space is at a premium and may have covenant issues. A second option is in Woodland Park, which is further from the majority of business but a storage barn can be built to store the equipment.

7.2 Equipment Description

In order to perform the services AAH offers, the tools in the following table are required. As AAH initially starts up, these tools will either be purchased or borrowed from the owners. As profits allow, all of the tools on the list will be purchased. Rental companies will be utilized to rent equipment deemed necessary to complete projects.

Necessary Tools and Equipment

Equipment/Tool	Price	Description
Air Compressor		
Bar		
Caulking Gun		
Channel Locks		
Circular Saw		
Drill – cordless		
Drill Bits		
Drill w/ cord		
Extension cords		25 foot, 50 foot, 100 foot
Hammers		
Jig Saw		
Ladder – 12 foot		
Ladder – 16 foot		
Ladder – 25 foot extension		
Ladder – 6 foot		
Levels		
Linemen's Pliers		
Nail Gun		
Needle Nose Pliers		
Paint Scrappers		
Paint Sprayer		
Pipe Cutter		
Power Miter Box		
Power Washer		
Putty Knives		Wide, Small, Corner,
Radial Arm Saw		
Sander – belt		
Sander – disc		
Sander – Finishing		

-42-

Sander — vibrating		
Screwdrivers — Flat		
Screwdrivers — Hex		
Screwdrivers — Philips		
Screwdrivers — Star		
Sheet Rock Knife		
Sheet Rock Square		
Shovels		
Side cutters		
Socket Set		
Soldering Torch		
Speed Bits		
Squares		
Tape Measures		
Texture Gun		
Tin Snips		
Trailer		
Trouble Light		
Trowel		Grout
Truck		¾ ton or 1 ton
Utility Knives		
Wire Strippers		
Wrench Set — American		
Wrench Set — metric		

The following table contains the tools which are not mandatory to perform the offered services, but ones which it would be useful to have. These tools will not be acquired initially but over time as profits allow.

Optional Tools and Equipment

Equipment/Tool	Price	Description
Cell Phones		
Cooler		
Generator		
Gloves		
Laptop		For estimates and bids w/ printer
Pencils		#2 & Chalk
Post Hole Digger		
Radio		
Saw Horses		
Skid Loader		
Tool Belts		
Water Barrel		
Weight Belts		

-44-

The Plan For
Commercial Fitness Equipment, Inc.

KEN ACKERMEN, TED WHITE and MIKE BRENNAN

Dallas, TX

(219) 228-0729

Copy Number __ of Five.

THE PLAN FOR COMMERCIAL FITNESS EQUIPMENT, INC.

1.0 EXECUTIVE SUMMARY

THE BACKGROUND

Picture three men, each of them a top performer in their shared field of expertise, working together in a young company. Sales are strong, and profits grow every year. Life is good. Yet these three young men aren't satisfied. They see how sales could be still stronger, how profits could grow even more each year, how customer needs could be truly paramount. So they form a company and strike out on their own, eventually overtaking their previous employer as the dominant player in the market. Is it Apple Computer? Or Southwest Airlines? Or Pizza Hut? It could be any of these, but, in this case, it's the newest, and soon-to-be leading, seller of commercial fitness equipment in the Dallas metroplex—Commercial Fitness Equipment. Three distinct characteristics will combine to propel this new company to market leadership: Outstanding People, Outstanding Products, and Outstanding Customer Service.

OUTSTANDING PEOPLE

The founders and principals of Commercial Fitness Equipment (CFE) are three men who share a combined 30 years of experience in the fitness industry. In just three short years, Ken Ackerman, Ted White and Mike Brennan created a Dallas-area commercial sales team at Workouts Work that consistently blew away the old sales records! In fact, this trio of overperformers singlehandedly generated 25% of the sales of the entire nationwide Workouts Work Commercial Division! As they built their business together at Workouts Work, Ken, Ted and Mike developed a confidence in each other—a shared belief that each of the three were outstanding individuals, and that the three combined into a team were virtually unstoppable.

OUTSTANDING PRODUCTS

Over the past years, Ken, Ted and Mike have worked to develop strong relationships with key individuals at all of the leading manufacturers. Now, with the launch of Commercial Fitness Equipment, those relationships have become very important indeed. CFE intends to begin operations with the following four primary lines:

1. **Life Fitness** — This will be the Company's flagship cardiovascular line. Life Fitness is a clear industry leader, and one that should continue to grow in the future under the Brunswick banner.

2. **Paramount Fitness** — Paramount will be the premier strength-conditioning line. A major player in the strength area, Paramount makes a great pairing with Life Fitness on the cardiovascular side.

3. **Schwinn Fitness** — Schwinn will be the company's cardiovascular step-down line, with a slightly lower price point than Life Fitness.

4. **Muscle Dynamics** — MD will be the step-down line in the strength area.

-4-

The company will also carry several complementary lines that have already made commitments to do business with CFE, including Parabody, Troy and Polar. This combination of primary and secondary manufacturer relationships gives CFE complete coverage of the different equipment types, and enables the company to fill virtually any equipment need a facility may have.

OUTSTANDING CUSTOMER SERVICE

Outstanding service is the bedrock foundation of Commercial Fitness Solutions. Service is more important than product line. Service is more important than product knowledge. Service is more important than good selling skills. Service is even more important than price. Everyone at CFE believes that providing absolutely outstanding customer service will make the company successful and keep the company successful. CFE will meet the four specific outstanding needs of its customers:

1. Customers need a supplier who really cares.

2. Customers need a one-stop shop.

3. Customers need a fast and effective way to learn about the equipment, order it, receive it and set it up.

4. Customers want all of their machines working perfectly all the time.

THE MARKET

CFE targets Dallas-area commercial businesses and institutions that purchase commercial-quality exercise and fitness equipment for use by their members, patients, employees, students and associates. Sales efforts will be focused on health/fitness clubs, corporate fitness facilities, park districts, condominium associations, schools, YMCA/JCCs, hospitals, and hotels. CFE management estimates annual market sales of $14 million, of which CFE will capture approximately 14% in the first year.

THE FINANCIAL PLAN

The financial health of CFE will be reflected in four measurable areas: 1) Sales, 2) Gross Margin, 3) Accounts Receivable Management, and 4) Cost Control. First-year financial objectives are:

1. Achieve sales of $1,991,000. This is roughly one-half of the team's 2001 WW sales.

2. Maintain a 25% gross margin on equipment sales.

3. Collect 90% of accounts within 30 days of delivery; 100% within 60 days.

4. Maintain operating expenses at or below 15% of sales.

5. End the year with a profit.

Business Plan Highlights

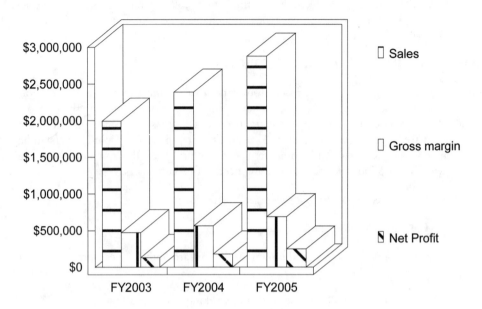

2.0 COMPANY SUMMARY

2.1 Mission

The company's mission:

Commercial Fitness Equipment is a company dedicated to providing solutions for the fitness equipment needs of our clients. We are committed to selling service first, and products second. We plan to serve the commercial fitness industry with integrity and honesty. To accomplish this, we must not over-promise, but instead over-deliver.

Commercial Fitness Equipment is built upon three essential cornerstones: Outstanding People, Outstanding Products, and Outstanding Customer Service. Like the three legs of a stool, each of these three is absolutely necessary for the company to succeed. When all are strongly in place, the whole is strong as well.

2.2 Outstanding People

The founders and principals of Commercial Fitness Equipment are three young men who share a combined 30 years of experience in the fitness equipment industry. Using their combined experience, knowledge and ability, in just three short years, Ken

-6-

Ackerman, Ted White, and Mike Brennan created a Dallas-area commercial sales team at Workouts Work that consistently blew away the old sales records! In fact, this trio of overperformers singlehandedly generated 25% of the sales of the entire nationwide Workouts Work Commercial Division! As they built their business together at Workouts Work, Ken, Ted and Mike developed a confidence in each other—a shared belief that each of the three were outstanding individuals, and that the three combined into a team were virtually unstoppable. Chapter 11 details the tremendous sales, management, and life achievements of these three men.

As their sales grew, the team grew stronger, and they began to see opportunities that Workouts Work was missing; customer needs that WW didn't recognize. Gradually, they began to dream together about the possibility of striking out on their own. What did customers really want from a fitness equipment supplier? Could three guys in a startup operation make it against the big boys? What were the foundational issues that must be in place in order to be successful? The answers to these questions, and many more, are detailed in this plan.

2.3 Outstanding Products

The second of the three "stool legs" is outstanding products. In order to be ultimately successful, Commercial Fitness Equipment must acquire and maintain access to sell a complete line of commercial fitness equipment. There must be a high-end line of both cardiovascular and strength equipment, and a secondary line of each for those customers who want it. Additional accessory lines are needed as well, such as barbells, mats, etc.

CFE management has successfully cultivated the relationships necessary to complete those supplier agreements. The four primary product lines at launch will be Life Fitness, Schwinn Fitness, Paramount Fitness and Muscle Dynamics. Complete details are located in Chapter 7.1.

2.4 Outstanding Customer Service

The third foundation of success is outstanding customer service. In order to be truly successful, Commercial Fitness Equipment must create a level of service that is unmatched in the industry. As veterans of this business and this market, the management of CFE is keenly aware of the expectations of its customers. In response to those needs, detailed in Chapter 6, CFE has built its operation around the concept of unsurpassed customer service. These service plans and standards are outlined in Chapter 7.2.

2.5 Company Ownership

Commercial Fitness Equipment, Inc., is a Texas subchapter S corporation. All stock is owned, in equal shares, by the founders; Ken Ackerman, Ted White and Mike Brennan.

-7-

2.6 Company Location and Facilities

The company will initially be based in a small facility. This facility will consist of 300-600 sq. ft., and should rent for approximately $600 per month. CFE does not require grand work space, nor a public showroom. From time to time, customers wish to see equipment in operation. In those instances, they want to see the equipment in a real-use setting, so CFE will simply arrange a visit for the prospective buyer at a nearby club that already owns that piece. At Workouts Work, onsite visits were an effective selling tool—happy customer, happy patrons, a lot of smiling, etc. The same system will work for CFE.

2.7 Objectives

Objectives for 2002 are:

1. Initiate operations February 1.

2. Achieve 2002 sales of $1,991,000 (50% of the team's 2001 sales).

3. Maintain a 25% gross margin on equipment sales.

4. Collect 90% of accounts within 30 days of delivery; 100% within 60 days.

5. Maintain operating expenses at or below 15% of sales.

6. End the year with a net profit.

2.8 Startup Summary

The startup events are relatively simple and straightforward, and the costs relatively minor. The table below specifies the costs involved.

Startup Costs

Working Capital	$119,500
Service Van; painting/lettering	12,000
Computer Hardware and Software	10,000
Legal, Accounting, Business Plan	6,000
Expensed Equipment; furniture, etc.	1,000
Rent	600
Stationery	500
Utilities Deposits	400
Total Startup Capital Required	$150,000

3.0 INDUSTRY ANALYSIS

3.1 Industry Overview

Commercial Fitness Equipment is part of the multi-billion dollar "commercial fitness equipment" industry. To gain a clear perspective on this industry, it is necessary to take a step back and examine the entire U.S. sports/fitness/exercise business picture.

According to a 2000 National Sporting Goods Association (NSGA) survey, more than 70 million Americans over the age of seven now participate in some form of deliberate sporting activity each year. These range from exercise walking (73 million) to swimming (60 million) to wind surfing (0.7 million). The participation rate is growing—of the NSGA's 52 established sports categories, 42 saw increased participation over 1999 levels. One of the primary reasons for the continued growth in the U.S. fitness industry, now and into the future, is that great demographic bulge of humanity—Baby Boomers. These middle-agers, born from 1946 to 1964, are beginning to have a significant positive impact on the fitness industry. In fact, Tom Doyle, the NSGA's vice president of information and research, authored a July 21, 2001 article in *Sporting Goods Business* entitled, "Why the Fitness Boom Won't Disappear." He goes to great lengths to document the impact that Baby Boomers have already had on the fitness business, and how their impact will continue to grow into the future. Author and futurist Gerald Celente agrees. In his 1997 book *Trends 2000*, Celente predicts that, driven by aging Baby Boomers, health will become a higher priority in the years beyond 2000.

The continuing growth in sports participation translates into big business. The Sporting Goods Manufacturers Association (SGMA) reports that in 2000 total sports and recreation spending surpassed $60 BILLION for the first time ever; a 31% increase over 1996, and 6% higher than 1999. It should be noted that the SGMA estimate of spending is very conservative; it includes only the wholesale cost of tangible merchandise, and excludes any spending on services such as consulting, training, health club membership costs, etc.

As noted at the beginning of this chapter, Commercial Fitness Equipment is part of the commercial fitness equipment industry, a subset of the overall sports and fitness industry. The SGMA has identified a subset of the total sports merchandise industry called "Total Exercise," and it is in this equipment arena that DFS operates. Sales in this group have grown each year since 1992. SGMA reports the following sales statistics for its Total Exercise group in 2000:

-9-

2000 Sales of Exercise Equipment

(U.S., millions of $$)

Exercise Cycles	$ 170
Free Weights	125
Home Gyms	205
Treadmills	725
Exercise Benches	107
Step Climbers	130
Ab Machines	225
Aero Gliders	480
Other Retail	100
Exercise Institutional	170
TOTAL	$2,437

This total sales volume, $2.4 billion, is more than the amount spent on Camping ($1.5B), Firearms/Hunting ($1.7B), and even Golf ($2.2B). Without question, exercise machines are Big Business, and getting bigger. NSGA surveys show that in 2000, 47.8 MILLION Americans participated in "Exercising with Equipment," up a full 8% over 1999. This category now ranks FOURTH in total number of participants (behind exercise walking, swimming, and bicycle riding).

Sales of exercise equipment are split almost evenly between two fairly well-defined subsets: the home market and the commercial market. While there is some crossover, the home market generally consists of individuals buying low-priced and relatively low-quality machines for home use; while the commercial market is made up of health clubs, corporate health facilities, and other institutional users purchasing high-priced and high-quality machines for heavy commercial use. CFE sells to the commercial market, which will be examined in detail in later chapters. The next chapter identifies the primary participants in the exercise equipment industry.

3.2 Industry Participants

The most appropriate way to examine the industry participants is to divide them into the three natural subgroups: 1) Manufacturers; 2) Distributors, and 3) End Users.

-10-

MANUFACTURERS

The *2001 Sports Marketplace Directory*, the most complete reference source for sporting equipment suppliers, lists more than 60 different manufacturers of exercisers and exercise machines. These range in size from industry giant ICON, with sales approaching $750 million annually, to small players generating only marginal sales. The complete list from *Sports Marketplace Directory* is included in the Appendix (not included in this sample plan). While many of the manufacturers (including the three top makers, ICON, Nordick Track, and DP) focus on low-end products for the home market, CFE is building its reputation and relationships with those producers that create the high-quality, durable machines used in clubs and other commercial facilities. High-end manufacturers include:

1. **Life Fitness** — Life Fitness is a Franklin Park, Illinois-based subsidiary of Brunswick Corporation, an emerging deep-pocketed giant in the leisure/sports/fitness arena. With sales of $180 million, Life Fitness ranks fourth in overall U.S. annual fitness sales, and is a true market leader in the professional/commercial cardiovascular market. As stated in a June 23, 1997 article in *Sporting Goods Business*, "...of the high-end branded players in the exercise equipment arena, Life Fitness is the hands-down sales leader, and should see significant sales growth..."

2. **Paramount** — Based in Los Angeles, Paramount Fitness Corp. specializes in strength conditioning, and now offers more than 90 commercial-grade strength-training products.

3. **Precor** — Enjoying sales of over $70 million, Precor has established itself as another of the big players in the cardiovascular segment of the commercial market. In fact, Precor makes the most-in-demand elliptical trainer currently on the market.

4. **Cybex/Trotter** — Cybex is a leader in both the strength and cardiovascular equipment field, with a focus in the rehabilitation segment. Annual sales are $81 million.

5. **Schwinn Fitness** — Schwinn Fitness is a special division of the giant bicycle maker focusing on commercial and home-use stationary bikes. Their commercial products fill a slightly lower-priced niche than Life Fitness and Precor.

6. **Muscle Dynamics** — Another builder of strength-training equipment, Muscle Dynamics is slightly lower in price than Paramount.

7. **TechnoGym** — Strength and cardiovascular equipment.

8. **Keiser** — Air-resistance bikes and strength equipment.

9. **Stairmaster** — Strength and cardiovascular equipment.

10. **Pacific Fitness** — Strength equipment.

11. **Star Trac** — Cardiovascular equipment—treadmills, bikes, and stairclimbers.

DISTRIBUTORS

Exercise equipment is sold primarily through three channels: Large Sporting Goods Retailers, Specialty Fitness Chains, and Independent Sales Teams.

1. **Large Sporting Goods Retailers** — These are general sporting goods retailers such as Sportmart and Sports Authority, selling sports equipment, clothing and accessories primarily to the public.

2. **Specialty Fitness Chains** — These are retailers that focus specifically on the fitness and exercise market. These often have both "brick and mortar" retail stores AND an outside commercial sales team. Examples of this group include Busy Body, Fitness Experience, Push Pedal Pull, Workouts Work, and Fitness Works.

3. **Independent Sales Teams** — These are retailers that sell to the commercial market only, via an outside sales team, and generally do not have a public showroom. Examples include Commercial Fitness Equipment, Ortho Tech in the St. Louis area, and Midwest Fitness Equipment in suburban Dallas. These will be examined in more detail in the chapter on Competition.

END USERS

Home-use purchasers account for about half of all exercise equipment sales. The other half of purchases are for use in commercial settings. The number of commercial users is large and growing, and includes:

1. Health and Fitness Clubs

2. Hospitals

3. Physical Therapy Centers

4. Corporate Fitness Facilities

5. Hotels

6. Colleges and Universities

7. High Schools

8. Municipalities/Park Districts

9. Martial Arts Studios

10. Property Management Groups

11. Golf Course Clubs

12. Retirement Centers

13. Athletic Teams

14. Condominium Associations

15. Commercial Development Companies

-12-

4.0 TARGET MARKET

4.1 The Selected Market

Commercial Fitness Equipment has identified a large, well-defined and reachable group of target customers. The CFE target customer is defined as follows:

CFE targets Dallas-area commercial businesses and institutions that purchase commercial-quality exercise and fitness equipment for use by their members, patients, employees, students and associates.

The Company has selected this specific target group for several reasons. First, and most importantly, the three principals of the company have extensive first-hand knowledge of this market, and have demonstrated outstanding success in generating sales of these products to this target group. Second, this market is expected to experience substantial growth through the foreseeable future. Third, CFE knows the competition in this market—its strengths and weaknesses—and has developed strategies to overtake these competitors. Fourth, CFE management has developed excellent relationships with the manufacturers of the commercial-quality equipment sought by these target customers.

Specifically, the targeted customer base is defined below by type of business/institution. The reader will note that for each sub-segment, a percentage of sales is reported. These sales share statistics reflect the 2001 sales results of the Dallas-area commercial division of Workouts Work. These real, historic sales results have been used throughout this plan as the basis for market potential and anticipated CFE revenue. In choosing to use real historic statistics rather than hypothetical and unsupportable hopes, the principals of CFE wish to demonstrate that this is a business with responsible expectations based on real data.

1. **Health and Fitness Clubs** — As one would expect, this group of target customers represents the largest concentration of business, currently accounting for 30% of sales. There are currently about 200 fitness clubs in the target group, including both strictly commercial clubs and hospital-owned or hospital-affiliated clubs. This group represents not only the largest overall volume share, but also the largest average sale per transaction, $11,600. CFE already knows these clubs and has excellent rapport with the owner/manager of many of them.

2. **Corporate Facilities** — An increasing number of employers now make exercise equipment available to their employees. Some are giant companies that provide complete workout facilities, but most are smaller firms that set aside a room equipped with a small number of machines. Unlike most of the other CFE target groups, this customer group consists of an extremely large group of business targets—tens of thousands throughout the target area—and therefore requires a different marketing approach. Corporate facilities currently generate 19% of sales.

-13-

3. **Park Districts and Other Government** — Park Districts throughout the state own and operate almost 200 Recreation Centers, many of which are in the target area. These look and feel like commercial clubs, but are operated by public employees. They generated 26% of 1997 sales. Park Districts are easily identified and well-known to CFE.

4. **Condominium Associations** — Currently accounting for 10% of sales, these residential associations often provide an on-site workout facility as one of the amenities of high-density urban living. There are hundreds of these associations throughout the target area.

Together, these four subsets of the target market account for 85% of current sales and will be the primary CFE focus at the outset of operations. The remaining groups, representing 15% of sales, will be secondary targets.

5. **Education** — There is opportunity in this arena as well, since every high school, college and university maintains one or more exercise facilities for its staff, students and athletic teams. Currently 6% of sales, this is expected to be an area of strong growth.

6. **YMCA/JCC** — The YMCAs and Jewish Community Centers throughout the target market are also buyers of commercial-grade exercise equipment, and provided 5% of sales in 2001.

7. **Medical** — Separate from their fitness clubs, most hospitals now maintain fairly sophisticated exercise facilities for use in physical and cardiovascular evaluation and rehabilitation. 2% of 2001 sales.

8. **Hotel** — Virtually all full-service hotels now offer well-equipped workout facilities, and some are even making some machinery available for in-room exercising. 2% of 2001 sales.

Commercial Fitness Equipment estimates the total sales within the target market at $14 million annually. The graph below depicts the target market segments and their relative potential.

Potential Market

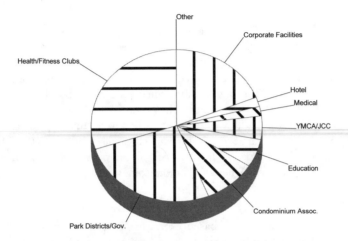

4.2 Market Trends

CFE believes that the trend for future sales of commercial exercise equipment within the target market is a function of two specific trends, as follows:

1.   Trends in target market population and income level.

It seems obvious that a growing target market population will have a positive impact on sales opportunities, and the CFE target market should provide that positive impact.   The Dallas metropolitan area is experiencing substantial growth, and many suburban cities are seeing almost explosive growth.   The North Texas Planning Commission (NTPC) reports the 1994 six-county metro population at 7,261,074.   NTPC estimates that the 2020 census will show 9,044,913 residents, an increase of almost 1.8 million people, or 25% over the period (1.8 million is about the size of the entire Denver metro area).   Growth will be spread over the entire region, including Dallas but will be fastest in outlying counties.   And the expected growth is not some hoped-for phenomenon that should arrive between 2010 and 2020; the growth rate is already accelerating.   NTPC reports that the area population grew by less than 300,000 between 1970 and 1990, but added more than 300,000 residents in just the next five years.   It is reasonable to expect that target market population growth will provide a growing customer base.

With regard to target market household income level, CFE understands that the ongoing success of many of its target subgroups depends, at least in part, on the income of their members/customers. In fact, the International Health, Recreation and Sports Association (IHRSA) reports that fully half the members of commercial health clubs have household incomes above $50,000, well above the national average of $33,472 (TRAC, Transactional Records Access Clearinghouse). In contrast, TRAC reports that the CFE target market had median incomes ranging from $39,060 to $62,740. Clearly, the Dallas metropolitan area enjoys income levels substantially above the national average. How will incomes fair in the future? The best gauge would seem to be anticipated job growth, and the area looks strong in this area as well. NTPC projects that between 1990 and 2020, the number of jobs in the Dallas area will swell from 3.8 million to 5.3 million, 37% overall growth for the period, compared to a comparatively smaller 25% growth in population. With more jobs competing for relatively fewer people, the law of supply and demand should dictate higher wages and incomes over time.

2. Trends in club-based machine exercising.

The national trend in club-based exercising is quite promising. The Fitness Products Council reports that in 2000 the number of health club members climbed to an all-time high of 20.8 million, 9% higher than in 1999 (includes commercial clubs, park district recreation centers, hospital fitness centers, college centers and YMCAs).

Part of this growth may reflect the trend toward more people exercising with equipment rather than participating in walking, swimming, bicycling, aerobic/dance, etc. The 2000 NSGA statistics reveal that of the top 5 sports participation activities, "exercising with equipment" was the fastest growing, increasing 8% from 1999 to now include 47.8 million people per year. That growth may be seen in the expansion plans of clubs nationwide. In 2000 (the most recent data), machine-related expansion was the highest priority:

Planned 2000 Expansion
(Percent of clubs planning expansion)

Cardiovascular Equipment Area	29.6%
Resistance Equipment Area	27.8
Free-Weight Area	25.0
Office Space	20.4
Childcare Area	28.7
Aerobics/Dance Area	20.4
Locker Rooms	20.4
Children's Recreation Area	25.9

-16-

What's the bottom line? CFE believes that the trends within the target market are clear: Growing population + high and growing target market income + record-high club membership + high and growing rates of exercising with equipment + high rate of club expansion of cardiovascular and resistance equipment areas = a strong and growing market that is ready to spend money with top-level suppliers.

4.3 Purchase Patterns/Process

The patterns by which contacts are made in this market are generally simple and direct.

1. **Customer calls a manufacturer** — If a customer wants or knows of a specific brand, they may call directly to that manufacturer to gain information. Since most of the major manufacturers sell through retailers, the manufacturer will forward that lead to its retail distributor in that geographic area.

2. **Customer calls a local retail distributor** — In this case, a customer that needs equipment and/or service locates and contacts a local distributor directly.

3. **Cold calling by distributor** — Here, a sales representative or a telephone salesperson makes a cold call on a business or institution within the target group.

4. **Referrals from satisfied customers** — This is the most desired situation, in which a satisfied customer refers another potential customer to a high-quality retail distributor. CFE has designed a marketing strategy to maximize these referrals.

Although the contacts are relatively straightforward, the actual selling process is often a lengthy and difficult process. Some small sales are culminated in the first or second visit, although this is not the norm. Usually, there is a formal progression of meetings to establish needs; draw up a list of equipment options; and generate price quotes for machines, delivery, setup and preventative maintenance. After that, like in any other large-ticket sale, it's follow-up, follow-up, and more follow-up.

5.0 COMPETITION

5.1 Primary Competitors

The competition within the Dallas-area commercial exercise machine market is substantial, but limited to a few specific players that are clearly identified and well known to the management team of CFE.

1. **Southwest Fitness Equipment** — This is a one-man operation run from a small commercial office, and is owned by Rod Sparks. Rod carries equipment from Precor, Body Master, Tetrix and Quinton. Rod has generally good

relationships with these manufacturers, although CFE management believes that he will lose the Precor line in Jan. 2002. He has been successful in selling to large clubs, and has a strong foothold in a number of the clubs he services. The strength of Southwest Fitness in the market is that it is home-based, with very low overhead and no employees. However, Rod's strength is also his weakness, since his small size prevents him from growing to serve more of the market more successfully. Nevertheless, Southwest Fitness accounts for roughly 20% of market sales.

2. **Fitness Expertise** — Another local dealer that also operates a retail presence, Fitness Expertise generates most of its commercial business from condominium/apartment buildings and park district recreation centers. They currently account for 20-25% of market sales.

3. **Wachman Industries** — This local retail business is a minor player, capturing perhaps 5% of sales. Wachman focuses primarily on apartments and small corporate sales.

4. **Workouts Work** — This is an unusual situation, since the formation of Commercial Fitness Equipment has cost Workouts Work its award-winning triple-team local sales staff of Ken Ackerman, Ted White and Mike Brennan. Workout Works is a Dallas-based retail chain with 50 stores in nine metropolitan areas. Their primary market is home-use equipment, although they have established outside commercial sales teams in several of its market cities. By far the most successful of the commercial sales teams has been the three-man team of Ackerman, White and Brennan, which alone generated 25% of Workouts Works' national commercial sales. As detailed in the Target Market section, WW's sales strength has been in the fitness clubs, corporate facilities, park district recreation centers and condominium/apartment buildings. Historically, Workouts Work has controlled 25-30% of the local market. However, with the simultaneous departure of all three members of the sales team, WW is seriously wounded, and will be hard-pressed to maintain a substantial share of the business in the immediate future. It will have little chance to grow its Dallas-area commercial sales over the next year or more.

5. **Manufacturers' Representatives** — Many of the manufacturers sell through in-house reps as well as dealers. These reps have very large territories, sometimes several states (one recently reported an 11-state territory). They usually get all leads that come to the manufacturer, handle some, and pass others on to their dealers. Generally, the relationship between manufacturer's rep and the dealers is positive and helpful. Often, leads are split between them based on customer type, with manufacturer's reps usually holding onto the large club business. The manufacturer's reps are usually paid a discounted commission on product sold by dealers.

5.2 Barriers to Entry

Commercial Fitness Equipment believes that any newcomer to the Dallas-area commercial fitness equipment market will be forced to overcome a number of significant barriers, as noted below. Although the barriers are not necessarily costly in dollar terms, they are significant in that they include skills, knowledge and relationships that take years to develop.

- **Customer Knowledge** — The current suppliers in the market have a detailed knowledge of the customers and their needs. Any newcomer must build that knowledge base and come from behind to develop the rapport that is essential in this type of selling.

- **Sales Ability** — This is a business in which exceptional sales ability is vital to long-term success. Any newcomer that intends to capture substantial market share must have outstanding motivation, success orientation, communication skills and follow-up ability.

- **Industry and Market Experience** — A new company entering this market must demonstrate exceptional experience within this industry and market. With respect to clubs and park district centers in particular, these are specific markets in which the owners/managers know each other and talk with each other on a regular basis. Therefore, inexperienced or inadequate suppliers quickly gain a negative reputation. There are few individuals, let alone teams of professionals like CFE, which have the needed level of experience to penetrate this market.

- **Relationship to Manufacturers** — A fitness equipment retailer is only as good as the products it represents. Any new entrant into this market will be required to establish a dealer relationship with the premier suppliers, and CFE does not intend to let that happen. The three principals of CFE intend to provide such outstanding representation to the top-level manufacturers, e.g. Life Fitness, Precor, Cybex, that no other dealers will be approved in the CFE market area.

5.3 Future Competition

CFE anticipates possible future competition from three specific areas:

1. It is possible that established independent sales teams from other geographic areas may try to encroach on the Dallas market. Specifically, Ortho Tech from St. Louis may try to come in. There is no indication of that at this time. If it should happen, CFE would have clear the advantages of home field, established relationships and low fixed costs.

2. Manufacturers could decide to sell only through in-house sales personnel. This would obviously be devastating to all dealers, including CFE. However, manufacturers have found it to be more efficient and effective to sell through a dealer network, since independent dealers are able to represent a broad line of complimentary products that answer the many needs of facility managers. An in-house representative has only one line to sell, and can't really meet the needs of the customer. The likelihood of manufacturers dropping the dealer distribution channel are slim to none.

3. Workouts Work retribution. It is possible that Stan Eikner, the founder of Workouts Work, will be so angry with the departure of Ken, Ted and Mike that he will go out of his way to try to stop CFE from being successful. Two ideas suggest that that will not happen. First, Stan has not exhibited vindictive behavior in the past. He is competitive and will try to defend his business, but it is very unlikely that he will risk serious damage to his own company and margins just to drive CFE out of the market. Second, in the six to twelve months following the departure of "the team," Workouts Work will be scrambling just to hold and service its old customers—they will have little time or means of stopping the massive selling effort that CFE will put forth.

6.0 NEEDS ANALYSIS

The principals of CFE have a combined 30 years of experience in the exercise equipment business. They spend all day, every day, with the customers who buy commercial equipment. They constantly ask their customers what the customer's needs are. They have become top producers in this field because they know how these customers think and what they need from equipment suppliers. CFE has identified the following four needs as the primary needs that, when met, create satisfied repeat customers.

1. Customers want a one-on-one relationship. These customers want to know the face and the name of their equipment supplier. A facility's life depends on top-level equipment operating at top-level effectiveness. And the facility owner/manager needs to know that their supplier cares about them and their facility enough to maintain an ongoing relationship. They want "face time." They want a supplier that doesn't show up only when there's a sale to be made, but one who shows a real interest in that customer's operation. THEY WANT A SUPPLIER WHO REALLY CARES.

2. Customers want their supplier to have a broad line of top-level products. It should be obvious that once an owner/manager has found a supplier who cares, they will want to concentrate their buying on that one supplier. These customers ideally would like to be able to buy all of their equipment from one supplier that they can count on. THEY WANT A ONE-STOP SHOP.

-20-

3. Customers want a fast and effective way to learn about the equipment, order it, receive it and set it up. No one likes a lot of hassles when they're trying to buy something from a supplier. They want the information and ordering process to be simple and efficient. They want to get their machine ASAP, and they want it set up right and right away. THEY WANT GOOD INFORMATION, EASY ORDERING, FAST DELIVERY, AND COMPETENT SETUP.

4. Customers want all their machines to be working perfectly all the time. There are two steps to get close to this ideal: 1) perform excellent ongoing maintenance, and 2) when a machine breaks down, get it repaired instantly. Facility owner/managers are not engineers, technicians, or computer experts. They depend on their supplier to keep their machines in working order. What these customers want is instant response and repair, so that the down time is so short that nobody even knows the machine was down. THEY WANT EXPERT MAINTENANCE AND INSTANT SERVICE RESPONSE.

7.0 SERVICES AND PRODUCTS

In its simplest essence, Commercial Fitness Equipment is a retail dealer of commercial-grade exercise equipment, selling through personal sales calls. However, what CFE really offers its customers are answers to their four most critical needs, as detailed in the previous chapter. In fact, every service CFE offers has been developed in DIRECT response to these four key customer needs:

- They want a supplier who really cares.

- They want a one-stop shop.

- They want good information, easy ordering, fast delivery, and competent setup.

- They want expert maintenance and instant service response.

If these four needs are examined closely, it becomes clear that each of them relates directly to the desire for OUTSTANDING SERVICE. Outstanding service is the bedrock foundation of Commercial Fitness Equipment. Every decision made is made with outstanding customer service in mind. A secondary need expressed in the "top four" is the need for a broad selection of top-quality products, and CFE will fill that need as well. The next two chapters deal specifically with service and product line.

7.1 The CFE Products

Commercial Fitness Equipment intends to be the one-stop shop that customers want. In order to accomplish that goal, CFE needs to be able to offer machines in several different categories, some of which require two different price levels. Categories include:

- Treadmills

- Gyms (weight training machines)

- Elliptical Trainers

- Free Weights

- Upright Bikes

- Recumbent Bikes

- Steppers

- Flooring

- TV/Monitoring Systems

Over the past several years, Ken, Ted and Mike have worked to develop strong relationships with key individuals at all of the leading manufacturers. Each of them is always in search of high-quality dealers. Now, with the imminent launch of Commercial Fitness Equipment, those relationships have become very important indeed. As detailed in the Chapter 3.2, Industry Participants, there are a number of leading manufacturers in this industry, along with several secondary providers. CFE intends to begin operations with the following four primary lines:

1. **Life Fitness** — This will be the Company's flagship cardiovascular line. Life Fitness is a clear industry leader, and one that should continue to grow in the future under the Brunswick banner. Negotiations with Life Fitness have been very successful and should be finalized in early 2002. Based on expectations of high CFE sales productivity, Life Fitness intends to initiate CFE dealer status at the Platinum level, the highest level possible. Only 15 dealers nationwide are expected to be awarded the Platinum Level, which guarantees an exclusive selling area. In the case of CFE, the exclusive area includes all of Texas. Life Fitness now also includes the Hammer Strength line.

2. **Paramount Fitness** — Paramount will be the premier strength-conditioning line. A major player in the strength area, Paramount makes a great pairing with Life Fitness on the cardiovascular side. Paramount has agreed to a dealership arrangement with CFE.

3. **Schwinn Fitness** — Schwinn will be the company's cardiovascular step-down line, with a slightly lower price point than Life Fitness. Schwinn has agreed to CFE dealer status. Includes Airdyne, Spinning.

4. **Muscle Dynamics** — MD will be the step-down line in the strength area. MD has agreed to CFE dealer status.

The Company will also carry several complementary lines which have already made commitments to do business with CFE, including Parabody, Troy and Polar. This combination of primary and secondary manufacturer relationships gives CFE complete coverage of the different equipment types, and enables the company to fill virtually any equipment need a facility may have.

All products come with a manufacturer's warranty, and CFE will manage any in-warranty repairs that are necessary.

7.2 The CFE Services

Outstanding service is the bedrock foundation of Commercial Fitness Equipment. Service is more important than product line. Service is more important than product knowledge. Service is more important than good selling skills. Service is even more important than price. Everyone at CFE believes that providing absolutely outstanding customer service will make the company successful and keep the company successful.

This is how CFE will meet the four specific outstanding needs of its customers:

1. Customers need a supplier who really cares. It's easy for every dealer and manufacturer's rep to SAY that he or she cares about a customer. But how does Commercial Fitness Equipment PROVE that it cares? First, by assigning one key CFE contact person that has responsibility for knowing everything about that customer. This step gives each of these customers that one-on-one relationship they're looking for. Once that relationship is established, CFE will prove it cares by being there! Ken, Ted or Mike plan to personally call on every commercial club, every hospital-affiliated club, every park district club every YMCA/JCC club, and ALL previous customers from all target groups (these are all "Class A Targets," roughly 300 at the outset) in the target area at least six times per year. For these key targets, whether they are current customers or not, CFE will be there to prove that we care! For Class B targets (non-customer corporations, condominium associations, schools and medical facilities), visits will be made based on leads, referrals, or on a time-available basis. A customer's CFE Key Account Manager will be present at any special events, such as Grand Openings, Customer Appreciation Days, etc. CFE customers will know that their supplier cares about them because they will get face time.

    In addition, Class A customers will receive periodic mailings from CFE in the form of a high-quality, informative, equipment-oriented newsletter. Not face time, but it shows that CFE cares.

    Finally, customers will also know that CFE cares because they'll have easy access to the company. All Class A customers will be given not only the CFE office phone number, but their Key Account Rep's cellular phone number and their pager number. Now that's access!

-23-

2. Customers need a one-stop shop. CFE knows the importance of simplicity to a facility owner/manager. As detailed in the previous chapter, the company has already gained commitments from key manufacturers in the industry, and will be able to provide virtually any type and price level of equipment a customer would need. When customers choose CFE, they won't need to look elsewhere to fill their equipment needs. One sales rep relationship, one credit relationship, one invoice, one check, one company to deal with.

3. Customers need a fast and effective way to learn about the equipment, order it, receive it and set it up. With 30 years in the business, CFE understands this need very well, and the management team has devised the most advanced ways to fill these customer needs, as follows:

   — Learning about the equipment. Depending on the customer's level of technological expertise and their time constraints, CFE will use one or more of the following methods of information exchange. Personal presentation, phone conversation, mail, overnight delivery, fax, e-mail, CFE website. Obviously, personal presentation is optimal, but not always possible. Part of this information phase includes not only free price quotes, but also free floor design and space planning, and free C.A.D. drawings.

   — Ordering product. Each of the options above is available. Every situation is unique, and the Key Account Rep involved will find the best way to get the order.

   — Receiving product and setting it up. All equipment will be drop-shipped from the manufacturer's warehouse directly to the customer. This cuts delays and reduces shipping damage. A member of the CFE Delivery Team, consisting of a full-time and a part-time Service Technician, will meet the manufacturer's delivery at the customer's location and complete the installation (Each of the three principals will also be certified technicians as well, and may be used in times of peak demand).

4. Customers want all of their machines working perfectly all the time. This is the ideal that customers want to achieve, and CFE is determined to get as close to this ideal as possible. CFE believes that the best repairs are repairs that never have to happen. The first CFE service goal is to prevent breakdowns, and the first two items in this area are strictly preventive.

   – At the time of delivery (or at the customer's convenience), CFE will conduct a free in-service to teach facility personnel how to use the equipment correctly and how to conduct simple routine maintenance. The in-service package includes a maintenance kit containing the correct supplies for cleaning and lubricating the item. Proper simple maintenance prevents many breakdowns.

-24-

— CFE will also sell and perform routine preventive maintenance. This is not a repair service; this is ongoing routine maintenance on a scheduled basis that is intended to eliminate breakdowns. Does it cost the customer to have this service? You bet it does. Is it worth it? Anyone who has ever seen the reaction of a daily patron whose favorite machine is on the blink knows the value of keeping those machines operating 100% of the time.

— Regardless of the best preventive maintenance, equipment does break down occasionally. Repair calls will be taken at CFE headquarters (or customers may call their Key Account Rep), and the Service Technician will be dispatched via cellular phone and/or pager. CFE guarantees a service call within 24 hours of notification of a problem. CFE will have a full-time Service Technician who is fully trained and capable of repairing every piece of equipment sold, plus a part-time helper. This Service Technician will conduct business from a CFE service van fully stocked with vital equipment and parts adequate to conduct virtually any repair immediately. On any repair job requiring parts not stocked, CFE will have the part sent from the manufacturer overnight, and meet the part at the customer the next day to complete the repair.

— CFE will also develop and sell an extended warranty program to take over when the original manufacturer's warranty ends. This should eventually be its own profit center.

To solidify the company's commitment to absolutely outstanding customer service, Commercial Fitness Equipment will go even one step further—CFE will establish a 24-hour Service Hotline phone number. Any call to that number will get either service response on the spot or a GUARANTEED return phone call from one of the three principals of the company within ONE HOUR, plus an in-person service call within 24 hours, 24 hours-a-day, seven days-a-week, 365 days-a-year. If CFE misses either the one-hour return call deadline or the 24-hour service call deadline, the service call is FREE.

7.3 Competitive Comparison

None of the market competitors has taken the same care as CFE to meet the most important needs of the customers. They try to offer a broad line and outstanding customer service, but they just aren't as committed to it as the owners of CFE. For example:

- No manufacturer can provide the one-stop shopping that customers want and need.

- No competitor has a web site detailing a broad product line and services to meet customers' needs.

-25-

- No competitor can provide the same face time as CFE. They simply don't have the personnel to do it.

- No competitor provides a newsletter to keep its customers informed and entertained.

- No competitor can match the skill of CFE technicians—most hire outside companies to do their work.

- No competitor guarantees 24-hour response on service calls. They need 48 hours or longer.

7.4 Future Services

Commercial Fitness Equipment currently anticipates offering two additional services within two years:

1. **Full Facility Consulting** — Many individuals planning to open a club, corporate facility, or some other venue need a great deal of direction in order to build their business plan and facility plan. CFE intends to develop a reputation so strong that companies will come to us for help in the planning process. In fact, as part of Workouts Work, the CFE team has already been asked to provide professional assistance in organizing a new club. This can be very profitable business.

2. **Personal Training Seminars in Unstaffed Facilities** — Many corporate and condominium/apartment facilities are unstaffed. There may be a need for occasional training seminars in these facilities to teach users how to get the most out of their equipment use. This will be a secondary priority to consulting.

8.0 SWOT ANALYSIS

As Commercial Fitness Equipment takes its first steps toward success, it is prudent to analyze the internal strengths and weaknesses of the Company, as well as the external opportunities and threats facing the Company.

8.1 Company Strengths

1. **Management Team** — Without question, the most apparent and important strength of CFE is its team of founders and principals, Ken Ackerman, Ted White, and Mike Brennan. These men have more than just 30 years of combined experience in this field; they have demonstrated individually and collectively an incredible ability to get the job done—to create rapport with customers, to determine their needs, to find products to fill those needs, to close the sale, and to provide the outstanding customer service to create and keep satisfied customers. These men—their knowledge, attitude, skills and effort—are the critical mass that will drive Commercial Fitness Equipment forward to success.

-26-

2. **Supplier Relationships** — The CFE management team has carefully nurtured its relationships with key manufacturers throughout several years. These relationships now become a real and demonstrable strength at launch.

3. **Low Fixed Costs** — Because CFE is a dealer selling through an outside sales team, with no public showroom, the company will enjoy a lower overhead than the competition. Lower fixed costs allows for lower gross margins if price competition becomes an issue.

8.2 Company Weaknesses

1. **New Company** — As a new company, CFE is obviously weak in its development of systems to accomplish its goals. Although management has diligently planned each phase of the business, nothing is proven until the company initiates operations and tests each system in the real world of day-to-day competition. This weakness will be gradually eliminated as the company grows.

2. **Management Team Lacks Financial Expertise** — The three principals of the company have outstanding expertise in two of the three vital areas, Sales and Service. However, none of them has a strong background in the third area, Finance. Recognizing this initial weakness, management has considered the most effective and cost-efficient way to gain this expertise at launch. They have decided that Ken will take responsibility for the day-to-day bookkeeping, thereby keeping one of the principals intimately involved with the financial management of the company. In addition, CFE has selected a C.P.A., David Price, who specializes in small business accounting. David has the ability to monitor the financial condition of CFE each month and suggest corrective measures when necessary.

8.3 Market Opportunities

1. **Lackluster Customer Service** — As insiders, the management team is quite aware of the lack of truly outstanding customer service in this business, and how badly customers want outstanding service. This represents a clear opportunity—one that CFE will exploit fully.

2. **Workouts Work Downtime** — CFE management knows that the departure of Ken, Ted and Mike will leave a gaping hole in the ability of WW to maintain its commercial business. This is another opportunity that CFE will maximize.

3. **Market Expansion** — Quite simply, commercial fitness equipment is a growing industry that should see growing sales for the foreseeable future. CFE will be perfectly positioned to capitalize on that growth.

8.4 Market Threats

1. The largest and most problematic threat is the threat of losing dealer status with key manufacturers. There are only two realistic ways that would happen: 1) If CFE fails profoundly in its sales efforts, manufacturers would be justified in pulling their line, and 2) If an individual company changes policies because of internal politics or changes its distribution strategies, they may decide to withdraw dealer status. Regarding option #1, CFE is responsible to make its sales goals, and has every intention of exceeding them. Regarding #2, if a manufacturer withdraws dealer status from CFE because of a change in its distribution strategy, the company will immediately replace that line with another similar line. CFE will always maintain good relationships with all manufacturers so that a shift may be made quickly if necessary.

2. Competition is always a threat, and an unforeseen competitive entry is theoretically possible. However, CFE management currently assesses the competitive situation as detailed in Chapter 5, and is prepared to deal with any competitive threats as they arise.

9.0 MARKETING PLAN

CFE has developed its marketing plan using the "Four P's" approach popularized by the world-renowned professor of marketing at Northwestern University, Philip Kotler.

9.1 Product

According to Kotler, "The marketing concept holds that the key to achieving organizational goals consists in determining the needs and wants of target markets and delivering the desired satisfactions more effectively and efficiently than competitors." The CFE shortened version is "Find a need and fill it." And that's just what the company has done—found a need for a broad product line and outstanding service, then built a company to fill that need. Mr. Kotler would be proud.

Every part of the product and service mix offered by CFE is designed to fill specific customer needs. Since these have been detailed at length in Chapter 7, it is not necessary to state them again here. Suffice it to say that CFE management believes that the first part of successful marketing is the creation of products and services that meet the needs of customers, and that has been accomplished in the launch of CFE.

9.2 Price

Commercial Fitness Equipment believes that price is secondary in customer priority to product quality and customer service. The company will always sell quality and service first, and will not be the low price leader in the market. CFE will establish its prices based on a constant balance between three factors: adequate gross margin to cover fixed costs; competitive prices; and customer willingness to pay. Years of experience in this industry and market have established the real pricing parameters possible.

Generally, CFE will quote major clubs and other high-potential sales at a calculated gross margin of 10-25%. This may seem to be a broad range, but it is reasonable considering the variations in brands, quality, value of the total sale, customer pressure, and competitive pressure. Bids to other, lower volume customers with less competitive pressure will generally allow higher margins; 30-40% is probable. Overall gross margin will be 23-25% of the selling price, not including freight and installation.

Freight and installation will be added to the final price, and will range from 3-7% of the selling price. Again, experience shows that this variation is appropriate, depending on the items, their price, weight, and distance to be shipped. Overall, freight and installation will average 6%, and will cover the outside billed freight charges that CFE must pay, plus the cost of the Service Technician time for setup.

9.3 Place

The distribution design for Commercial Fitness Equipment is quite simple and straightforward. CFE will sell its products through its three-man management team, primarily via direct calls on customers. No showroom is required; no posh office is necessary to impress customers or suppliers. When customers wish to see equipment in action, they much prefer to see it in the real-life setting of club use, not a sterile showroom. It is simple and effective to arrange a site visit to observe a machine in use. Of course, our sales team will always set up the site visit with a well-satisfied and vocal CFE customer. The delivery of products will be by direct shipment from manufacturers.

9.4 Promotion

Following Kotler's model, the fourth "P" of marketing, Promotion, is further divided into its core components, Personal Selling, Advertising, Sales Promotion, and Publicity.

9.4.1 Personal Selling

Commercial Fitness Equipment will build its promotion around personal selling. This is the oldest and most effective form of promotion, and it still works the best in this industry and market. To avoid confusion, it is wise to describe what selling is and what it is not. First, selling is not fast-talking people into doing something they really don't want to do. Selling is not price-gouging or taking advantage of people against their will or knowledge. Selling is not telling lies to customers or promising things that can't be delivered in order to get the order. Selling is a careful and thoughtful method of determining a customer's needs, developing a solution to those needs at a reasonable and profitable price, convincing the customer your solution is correct and sensible, and helping the customer take the action needed to actually buy the product.

-29-

Given the establishment of the right product line and outstanding customer service; if there is a single skill that must be abundant within CFE in order to make the company successful, it is the skill of personal selling. Fortunately, the skill of personal selling IS in great abundance at CFE. Each of the three principals of CFE is a true and proven sales professional. Their resumes are included in the Appendix to this plan (not included in this sample plan).

These three sales professionals have divided the target area geographically into areas of responsibility similar to those they had at Workouts Work. In addition to one-on-one sales calls, the team will also attend all available and appropriate area conventions and trade shows.

9.4.2 Advertising

Advertising will be the second key component to the CFE promotional mix. Management currently forecasts the following primary advertising venues:

- **Yellow Pages** — The current Dallas Business-to-Business Directory (circulation approximately 600,000) carries 15 different companies under the most appropriate heading, "Exercise Equipment—Sales and Service." Several competitors are listed, but no manufacturers. Only two of the listed companies have anything more than a single line with their name, address and phone number. CFE will use this vehicle to make itself known to buyers actively seeking new equipment.

- **Newsletter** — A high-quality and entertaining newsletter is a perfect vehicle for CFE for two important reasons. First, CFE is able to identify entire groups of key target customers, by name and address, that have significant continuous business potential—specifically fitness clubs, park district recreation centers, YMCAs and JCCs. This is the perfect setting for a successful newsletter. Second, none of the other competitors in the market currently produce such a newsletter. Cooperative advertising dollars may be available from manufacturers.

- **Service Van** — In addition to providing transportation for the CFE service team, the service van will be a travelling billboard.

- **Trade Journal Ads** — These will be considered based on cost and potential response.

9.4.3 Sales Promotion

Sales promotion includes a diverse mix of short-term incentive tools designed to stimulate quicker and/or greater purchase of product. Sales promotions offer an incentive to buy now! CFE will use a number of sales promotion ideas, including premiums and gifts such as squeeze balls, T-shirts, water bottles and pens; as well as special finance promotions, rebates, discount coupons, contests, etc. The CFE newsletter will be an excellent vehicle in which to promote the sales promotions.

-30-

9.4.4 Publicity

Publicity generally includes press releases, speeches, seminar presentations, publicity-oriented charitable donations. Realizing the power that good publicity can have for a company, and the impact it can have on sales, CFE will begin to develop opportunities for these avenues at launch. CFE plans to donate 2% of net profit to a variety of charities, and may derive some public relations benefit from this philanthropy.

10.0 OPERATIONS

10.1 Generating Sales

Each of the principals of CFE is a key account manager and has the responsibility to generate sales. Each has proven himself with regard to Knowledge, Attitude, Skill and Effort (KASE) as a top-performing sales professional. The sales plan for CFE is designed as follows:

1. Manufacturers provide leads to their dealers based on phone inquiries they receive at their headquarters. All leads will be followed-up within 24 hours of receipt.

2. Roughly 300 "Class-A Targets" have been identified. These are the commercial fitness clubs, the hospital-affiliated fitness clubs, YMCAs and JCCs, and all previous CFE customers; the busiest and highest-potential accounts in the market. Each of the three Key Account Managers (KAM) will be responsible to personally visit one-third of the Class-A Targets every 60 days. This means that all of these target accounts will receive a personal call from CFE at least 6 times per year. At 20 work days per month, this call rate equates to 2.5 Class-A Target calls per day per man, a doable job.

3. All remaining target customers; condo/apartment complexes, schools, hospitals, corporations, etc. will be contacted initially via networking and/or cold phone contact. There are thousands of these potential customers in the market area. Again, it should be noted that the three CFE principals have built their reputation by selling. They know how to initiate contact, determine customer needs, and finalize the sale. Current estimates are for 15 phone calls per day per man.

4. Non-personal marketing activities such as advertising, newsletter and web site will generate contacts from customers. These will all receive immediate response.

5. Repeat calls from previous clients (Workouts Work and CFE) will receive immediate response as well.

6. Finally, CFE will immediately take steps to be included on all county bid lists. This will ensure that the company is included in any county government purchasing opportunities.

This sales plan is similar to the plan pursued at WW, but it is more structured with regard to the focus on high-frequency calls with high-potential target customers. It is an achievable plan and will generate the projected sales.

Customers who need planning assistance are able to use CFE consulting experience and CFE expertise in facility layout design. All quotes and correspondence will be on company letterhead and forms. Most sales will be made with 50% down at the time of order placement, 50% due on delivery.

10.2 Processing Orders

All orders will be processed and tracked through headquarters. The Office Manager has responsibility to follow each order to ensure that the product is in stock at the manufacturer and that delivery is on time. In case of delivery delay, the Office Manager will alert the KAM responsible, who will notify the customer. All customer contact will be made by the KAM, thus maintaining the one-on-one communication that customers want so badly.

10.3 Delivery and Installation

Product will be delivered to the customer in one of three primary ways:

1. **Direct Manufacturer Delivery**

2. **North American Van Lines** (or equivalent service) — There are several professional delivery and setup firms in the market, qualified to deliver AND set up equipment, if necessary.

3. **CFE Service Van** — For orders of one treadmill or one bike, management may decide to use the CFE Van to deliver the item.

In any of the three scenarios, the CFE Service Technician will be at the facility at or near the time of delivery to professionally install and set up the equipment.

10.4 Ongoing Service

As noted in an earlier chapter, the management team of CFE believes that outstanding customer service is absolutely vital to the company's long-term success. With that goal in mind, CFE has designed three specific programs to provide outstanding customer service.

1. CFE will sell and perform routine preventive maintenance. This is not a repair service, this is ongoing routine maintenance on a scheduled basis that is intended to eliminate breakdowns. This is the first layer of protection for the customer.

2. CFE will also develop and sell an extended warranty program to take over when the original manufacturer's warranty ends. 24-hour response time guaranteed.

-32-

3. Regardless of the best preventive maintenance, equipment does break down occasionally. Repair calls will be taken at CFE headquarters (or customers may call or page their Key Account Manager), and the Service Technician will be dispatched via cellular phone and/or pager. CFE guarantees a service call within 24 hours of notification of a problem. CFE will have a full-time Service Technician who is fully trained and capable of repairing every piece of equipment sold, plus a part-time helper. This Service Technician will conduct business from a CFE service van fully stocked with vital equipment and parts adequate to conduct virtually any repair immediately. On any repair job requiring parts not stocked, CFE will have the part sent from the manufacturer overnight, and meet the part at the customer the next day to complete the repair.

To solidify the Company's commitment to absolutely outstanding customer service, Commercial Fitness Equipment will go even one step further—CFE will establish a 24-hour Service Hotline phone number. Any call to that number will get either service response on the spot or a GUARANTEED return phone call from one of the three principals of the company within ONE HOUR, plus an in-person service call within 24 hours, 24 hours-a-day, seven days-a-week, 365 days-a-year. If CFE misses either the one-hour return call deadline or the 24-hour service call deadline, the service call is FREE.

10.5 Risk Management

The management team of Commercial Fitness Equipment recognizes that there are risks involved in operating this business. In order to limit the liability of the owners of the company, CFE has been formed legally and appropriately as a corporation. Great care will be taken to ensure that all corporation-associated requirements are met. Listed below are several of the risks involved in this business, and a brief statement of how they will be managed.

- **Damage to CFE property** — Covered by business owners' policy.

- **Bodily injury and property damage liability** — Business owners' policy.

- **Product liability** — All manufacturers carry coverage for their equipment. Nevertheless, CFE management is consulting legal and insurance experts for counsel with regard to the need for separate CFE product liability insurance.

- **Death or disability of one of the principals** — Key employee life insurance and disability insurance is being investigated.

- **Workouts Work breach-of-contract claim** — None of the principals had an employment contract with Workouts Work. CFE legal counsel states that this risk is low.

-33-

11.0 THE CFE MANAGEMENT TEAM

As noted throughout the plan, the three men who own and manage Commercial Fitness Equipment are successful sales and management professionals. Each of these men has built exciting careers filled with achievements and awards that would take most salespeople a lifetime to accumulate. A brief review of their career accomplishments is included here. Their complete resumes are included in the Appendix (not included in this sample plan).

11.1 Ken Ackerman

Ken received his B.A. in Exercise Science/Physiology from the University of Kansas, and will receive his Master's in Exercise Science/Physiology from University of Texas Medical School in 2002. He joined Workouts Work in 1995 in a retail sales role, and in 1996 achieved $1.5 million in retail sales. In 1997, Ken was asked to open and manage a new store in Dallas, which became the most profitable store in the Dallas Region that very same year. In 1998, he earned the Workouts Work Inspiration Award, given to the employee who best models what the ideal WW employee should be. In 1999 Kevin was promoted to National Sales Trainer, where he wrote the training text for all new employees and was part of a select task force charged with implementing positive changes in the company. In 2000 and 2001, as a commercial sales manager in Dallas, Ken joined five others nationwide as a member of the Million Dollar Club.

11.2 Ted White

Ted received his B.S. in Exercise Science from Texas Christian University. Since graduation, Ted has been involved in virtually every aspect of the fitness industry: as a university-level strength coach; as a commercial fitness center membership coordinator and personal trainer; as a manufacturer's sales rep for Nordick Track; as a manager of a Workouts Work retail store; and as a top-performing WW commercial salesperson. Exceptional WW accomplishments include: 1999 AND 2000, ranked #1 nationwide in sales; 1998, Manager of the Year; 1997, Motivator of the Year; and 2001, ranked #3 nationwide in sales.

11.3 Mike Brennan

With a B.S. in History from Texas A&M, Mike is the consummate sales professional. Mike began his career with WW in 1995, responsible to hire, train, schedule and support store sales staff, resulting in the Denton store finishing #1 in sales every month from October 1995 through October 1997. From October 1997 until 1999, Mike served as General Manager of the Eastern Region for Workouts Work (Maryland/Virginia), establishing three new stores in this new area. Two of the stores were #1 and #2 in the nation in 12/97-1/98. As a commercial sales rep starting in 1999 (year ending in 2000), Mike broke the commercial Million Dollar mark for the first time in the company's history. In the year ending June 2001, Mike ranked #1 of 20 commercial sales reps nationwide with $1.4 million in sales; and is on track to hit $1.6 million in fiscal 2002.

12.0 FINANCIAL PLAN

12.1 Important Assumptions

The following assumptions have been made in the preparation of the pro forma financial statements:

1. The U.S. economy will continue to grow within a normal range.

2. The Dallas area economy will continue to grow at or near forecast.

3. Fitness spending growth will continue as forecast.

4. CFE expectations of competition are reasonably accurate.

12.2 Key Financial Indicators

CFE management firmly believes that because of the retail nature of this business, the financial indicators are few and specific, and must be examined continuously in order for the company to remain on course. Each of these indicators is reflected directly in the company's stated objectives.

1. **Sales** — Everything begins with the generation of sales.

2. **Gross margin** — Pricing must be held high enough to make the gross margin target.

3. **Collections** — Cash is king. Collections cannot fall behind.

4. **Costs** — Constant control of costs is required in order to generate profit.

12.3 Breakeven Analysis

The breakeven analysis uses three key numbers to calculate the number of individual sales required to achieve the breakeven point. The average sale is expected to be $8,028. With the anticipated cost-of-goods percentage of 75%, the cost of creating that average sale will be $6,021. Fixed costs from the P&L table are $25,700 per month. The resulting breakeven analysis demonstrates the need to generate 13 sales per month, totaling $102,800 per month, in order to reach breakeven. Sales are projected to surpass that level in month 2. The graph on the next page depicts the breakeven point.

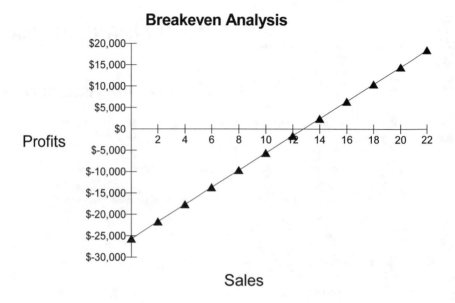

Breakeven Analysis

Profits

Sales

12.4 Projected Sales

The sales forecast shown on the following page is based on the following:

1. In order to build reasonable and justifiable financial expectations, the CFE management team has forecast 2002 sales of only one-half of their own 2001 Workouts Work sales volume. Although each of the three principals is fully convinced that actual sales will be significantly higher than this forecast, they feel that it is prudent to use a lower expectation, and design a profitable operation based on lower expectations. Therefore, first year sales are pegged at $1,991,000.

2. Sales will begin in the first month. Most customers buy from the sales person, not the company he represents. This means that once CFE is established, customers will immediately want to process sales in progress through CFE rather than WW. CFE WILL NOT attempt to shift sales away from WW, nor will we encourage customers to "wait another month or so" in order to steal business from WW. However, as detailed throughout this plan, customers want outstanding service, and as soon as they are aware that Ken, Ted and Mike have formed their own company, many will want to shift their purchases to CFE immediately. Within 30 days, sales will be on a steady growth pattern.

3. There is no seasonality in sales patterns.

4. Year 2 and 3 sales forecasts are also quite modest; just 20% growth year over year. Actual performance should be much higher.

5. Year three includes minor consulting revenue.

Sales Forecast

Sales	FY2003	FY2004	FY2005
Equipment	$1,810,000	$2,172,000	$2,606,400
Freight/Install/Setup (6% of equip)	$108,600	$130,320	$156,384
Maintenance Contracts (2% of equip)	$36,200	$43,440	$52,128
Service (2% of equip)	$36,200	$43,440	$52,128
Other	$0	$0	$10,000
Total Sales	$1,991,000	$2,389,200	$2,877,040

Cost of sales	FY2003	FY2004	FY2005
Equipment (75.00%)	$1,357,500	$1,629,000	$1,954,800
Freight/Install/Setup (100.00%)	$108,600	$130,320	$156,384
Maintenance Contracts (75.00%)	$27,150	$32,580	$39,096
Service (75.00%)	$27,150	$32,580	$39,096
Other (10.00%)	$0	$0	$1,000
Subtotal Cost of Sales	$1,520,400	$1,824,480	$2,190,376

Total Sales by Month in Year 1

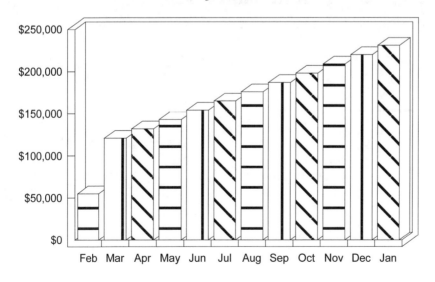

-37-

12.5 Personnel Plan

The personnel and salary plan is shown below and in the Appendix.

- Personnel burden is calculated at 15% of salaries.

- Employees will share in a year-end bonus payment equal to 2% of all revenue over the objective of $1,991,000.

Personnel Plan

Job Title	FY2003	FY2004	FY2005
Ken Ackerman	$48,000	$52,800	$58,080
Mike Brennan	$48,000	$52,800	$58,080
Ted White	$48,000	$52,800	$58,080
Office Manager	$30,000	$33,000	$36,300
Service Tech	$30,000	$33,000	$36,300
Other	$0	$0	$0
Subtotal	$204,000	$224,400	$246,840

12.6 Projected Profit and Loss

The projections of profit are depicted in the graph nearby, the table on the next page, and in the Appendix. The management team has called for an average of 30 days collection time on accounts receivable.

-38-

Pro-Forma Income Statement

Category	FY2003	FY2004	FY2005
Sales	$1,991,000	$2,389,200	$2,877,040
Direct Cost of Sales	$1,520,400	$1,824,480	$2,190,376
Other	$0	$0	$0
Total Cost of Sales	$1,520,400	$1,824,480	$2,190,376
Gross Margin	$470,600	$564,720	$686,664
Gross Margin Percent	23.64%	23.64%	23.87%
Operating Expenses:			
Advertising/Promotion	$3,600	$4,320	$5,184
Travel	$14,400	$17,280	$20,736
Entertainment	$14,400	$17,280	$20,736
Service Van	$4,800	$5,760	$6,912
Payroll Expense	$204,000	$224,400	$246,840
Cellular Phones	$2,400	$2,400	$2,400
Utilities	$2,400	$2,880	$3,456
Insurance	$15,000	$15,000	$15,000
Rent	$7,200	$7,920	$8,712
Depreciation	$3,600	$3,600	$3,600
Payroll Burden	$30,600	$33,660	$37,026
Accounting/Consultant	$4,200	$4,620	$5,082
Telephone Service	$1,800	$1,980	$2,178
Other	$0	$0	$0
Total Operating Expenses	$308,400	$341,100	$377,862
Profit Before Interest and Taxes	$162,200	$223,620	$308,802
Interest Expense ST	$0	$0	$0
Interest Expense LT	$0	$0	$0
Taxes Incurred	$32,440	$44,724	$61,760
Net Profit	$129,760	$178,896	$247,042
Net Profit/Sales	6.52%	7.49%	8.59%

Business Plan Highlights

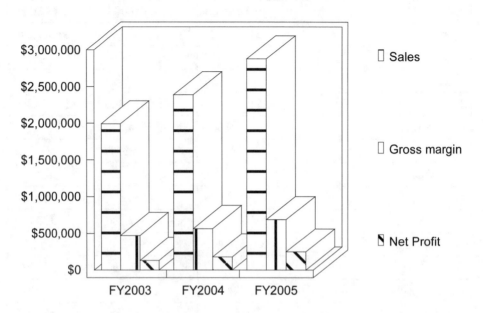

12.7 Projected Cash Flow

Cash flow is depicted in the graph nearby, the table below, and in the Appendix.

Pro-Forma Cash Flow

Category	FY2003	FY2004	FY2005
Net Profit	$129,760	$178,896	$247,042
Plus:			
Depreciation	$3,600	$3,600	$3,600
Change in Accounts Payable	$177,680	$34,921	$42,002
Current Borrowing (repayment)	$0	$0	$0
Increase (decrease) Other Liabilities	$0	$0	$0
Long-term Borrowing (repayment)	$0	$0	$0
Capital Input	$0	$0	$0
Subtotal	$311,040	$217,417	$292,643

-40-

Less:	FY2003	FY2004	FY2005
Change in Accounts Receivable	$231,000	$46,200	$56,600
Change in Inventory	$0	$0	$0
Change in Other ST Assets	$0	$0	$0
Capital Expenditure	$0	$0	$0
Dividends	$0	$0	$0
Subtotal	$231,000	$46,200	$56,600
Net Cash Flow	$80,040	$171,217	$236,043
Cash Balance	$199,540	$370,757	$606,800

Cash Analysis

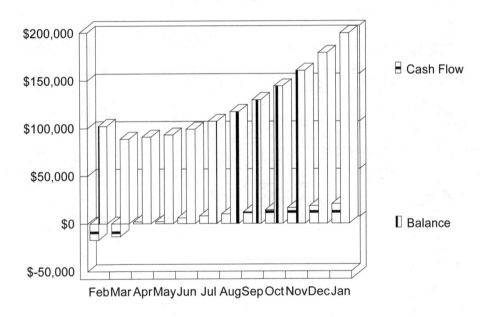

12.8 Projected Balance Sheet

The projected balance sheet is presented in the table below and in the Appendix.

Pro-Forma Balance Sheet

Category	FY2003	FY2004	FY2005
Short-term Assets			
Cash	$199,540	$370,757	$606,800
Accounts Receivable	$231,000	$277,200	$333,800
Inventory	$0	$0	$0
Other Short-term Assets	$0	$0	$0
Total Short-term Assets	$430,540	$647,957	$940,600
Long-term Assets			
Capital Assets	$12,000	$12,000	$12,000
Accumulated Depreciation	$3,600	$7,200	$10,800
Total Long-term Assets	$8,400	$4,800	$1,200
Total Assets	$438,940	$652,757	$941,800
Debt and Equity			
Accounts Payable	$177,680	$212,601	$254,603
Short-Term Notes	$0	$0	$0
Other ST Liabilities	$0	$0	$0
Subtotal Short-Term Liabilities	$177,680	$212,601	$254,603
Long-Term Liabilities	$0	$0	$0
Total Liabilities	$177,680	$212,601	$254,603

Paid in Capital	$150,000	$150,000	$150,000
Retained Earnings	($18,500)	$111,260	$290,156
Earnings	$129,760	$178,896	$247,042
Total Equity	$261,260	$440,156	$687,198
Total Debt and Equity	$438,940	$652,757	$941,800
Net Worth	$261,260	$440,156	$687,198

APPENDIX

Pro-Forma Balance Sheet

Category	Feb-02	Mar-02	Apr-02	May-02	Jun-02	Jul-02	Aug-02	Sep-02	Oct-02	Nov-02	Dec-02	Jan-03	FY2003	FY2004	FY2005
Short-term Assets															
Cash	$102,259	$88,839	$90,865	$93,013	$99,049	$107,165	$117,361	$129,637	$143,992	$160,428	$178,944	$199,540	$199,540	$370,757	$606,800
Accounts receivable	$54,247	$119,342	$130,192	$143,000	$154,000	$165,000	$176,000	$187,000	$198,000	$209,000	$220,000	$231,000	$231,000	$277,200	$333,800
Inventory	$0	$0	$0	$0	$0	$0	$0	$0	$0	$0	$0	$0	$0	$0	$0
Other Short-term Assets	$0	$0	$0	$0	$0	$0	$0	$0	$0	$0	$0	$0	$0	$0	$0
Total Short-term Assets	$156,506	$208,181	$221,057	$236,013	$253,049	$272,165	$293,361	$316,637	$341,992	$369,428	$398,944	$430,540	$430,540	$647,957	$940,600
Long-term Assets															
Capital Assets	$12,000	$12,000	$12,000	$12,000	$12,000	$12,000	$12,000	$12,000	$12,000	$12,000	$12,000	$12,000	$12,000	$12,000	$12,000
Accumulated Depreciation	$300	$600	$900	$1,200	$1,500	$1,800	$2,100	$2,400	$2,700	$3,000	$3,300	$3,600	$3,600	$7,200	$10,800
Total Long-term Assets	$11,700	$11,400	$11,100	$10,800	$10,500	$10,200	$9,900	$9,600	$9,300	$9,000	$8,700	$8,400	$8,400	$4,800	$1,200
Total Assets	$168,206	$219,581	$232,157	$246,813	$263,549	$282,365	$303,261	$326,237	$351,292	$378,428	$407,644	$438,940	$438,940	$652,757	$941,800
Debt and Equity															
Accounts Payable	$46,866	$95,921	$104,097	$112,273	$120,449	$128,625	$136,801	$144,977	$153,152	$161,328	$169,504	$177,680	$177,680	$212,601	$254,603
Short-term Notes	$0	$0	$0	$0	$0	$0	$0	$0	$0	$0	$0	$0	$0	$0	$0
Other ST Liabilities	$0	$0	$0	$0	$0	$0	$0	$0	$0	$0	$0	$0	$0	$0	$0
Subtotal Short-term Liabilities	$46,866	$95,921	$104,097	$112,273	$120,449	$128,625	$136,801	$144,977	$153,152	$161,328	$169,504	$177,680	$177,680	$212,601	$254,603
Long-term Liabilities	$0	$0	$0	$0	$0	$0	$0	$0	$0	$0	$0	$0	$0	$0	$0
Total Liabilities	$46,866	$95,921	$104,097	$112,273	$120,449	$128,625	$136,801	$144,977	$153,152	$161,328	$169,504	$177,680	$177,680	$212,601	$254,603
Paid in Capital	$150,000	$150,000	$150,000	$150,000	$150,000	$150,000	$150,000	$150,000	$150,000	$150,000	$150,000	$150,000	$150,000	$150,000	$150,000
Retained Earnings	($18,500)	($18,500)	($18,500)	($18,500)	($18,500)	($18,500)	($18,500)	($18,500)	($18,500)	($18,500)	($18,500)	($18,500)	($18,500)	$111,260	$290,156
Earnings	($10,160)	($7,840)	($3,440)	$3,040	$11,600	$22,240	$34,960	$49,760	$66,640	$85,600	$106,640	$129,760	$129,760	$178,896	$247,042
Total Equity	$121,340	$123,660	$128,060	$134,540	$143,100	$153,740	$166,460	$181,260	$198,140	$217,100	$238,140	$261,260	$261,260	$440,156	$687,198
Total Debt and Equity	$168,206	$219,581	$232,157	$246,813	$263,549	$282,365	$303,261	$326,237	$351,292	$378,428	$407,644	$438,940	$438,940	$652,757	$941,800
Net Worth	$121,340	$123,660	$128,060	$134,540	$143,100	$153,740	$166,460	$181,260	$198,140	$217,100	$238,140	$261,260	$261,260	$440,156	$687,198

Pro-Forma Cash Flow

Category	Feb-02	Mar-02	Apr-02	May-02	Jun-02	Jul-02	Aug-02	Sep-02	Oct-02	Nov-02	Dec-02	Jan-03	FY2003	FY2004	FY2005
Net Profit	($10,160)	$2,320	$4,400	$6,480	$8,560	$10,640	$12,720	$14,800	$16,880	$18,960	$21,040	$23,120	$129,760	$178,896	$247,042
Plus:															
Depreciation	$300	$300	$300	$300	$300	$300	$300	$300	$300	$300	$300	$300	$3,600	$3,600	$3,600
Change in Accounts Payable	$46,866	$49,056	$8,176	$8,176	$8,176	$8,176	$8,176	$8,176	$8,176	$8,176	$8,176	$8,176	$177,680	$34,921	$42,002
Current Borrowing (repayment)	$0	$0	$0	$0	$0	$0	$0	$0	$0	$0	$0	$0	$0	$0	$0
Increase (decrease) Other Liabilities	$0	$0	$0	$0	$0	$0	$0	$0	$0	$0	$0	$0	$0	$0	$0
Long-term Borrowing (repayment)	$0	$0	$0	$0	$0	$0	$0	$0	$0	$0	$0	$0	$0	$0	$0
Capital Input	$0	$0	$0	$0	$0	$0	$0	$0	$0	$0	$0	$0	$0	$0	$0
Subtotal	$37,006	$51,676	$12,876	$14,956	$17,036	$19,116	$21,196	$23,276	$25,356	$27,436	$29,516	$31,596	$311,040	$217,417	$292,643
Less:															
Change in Accounts Receivable	$54,247	$65,096	$10,849	$12,808	$11,000	$11,000	$11,000	$11,000	$11,000	$11,000	$11,000	$11,000	$231,000	$46,200	$56,600
Change in Inventory	$0	$0	$0	$0	$0	$0	$0	$0	$0	$0	$0	$0	$0	$0	$0
Change in Other ST Assets	$0	$0	$0	$0	$0	$0	$0	$0	$0	$0	$0	$0	$0	$0	$0
Capital Expenditure	$0	$0	$0	$0	$0	$0	$0	$0	$0	$0	$0	$0	$0	$0	$0
Dividends	$0	$0	$0	$0	$0	$0	$0	$0	$0	$0	$0	$0	$0	$0	$0
Subtotal	$54,247	$65,096	$10,849	$12,808	$11,000	$11,000	$11,000	$11,000	$11,000	$11,000	$11,000	$11,000	$231,000	$46,200	$56,600
Net Cash Flow	($17,241)	($13,420)	$2,027	$2,148	$6,036	$8,116	$10,196	$12,276	$14,356	$16,436	$18,516	$20,596	$80,040	$171,217	$236,043
Cash Balance	$102,259	$88,839	$90,865	$93,013	$99,049	$107,165	$117,361	$129,637	$143,992	$160,428	$178,944	$199,540	$199,540	$370,757	$606,800

Personnel Plan

Job Title	Feb-02	Mar-02	Apr-02	May-02	Jun-02	Jul-02	Aug-02	Sep-02	Oct-02	Nov-02	Dec-02	Jan-03	FY2003	FY2004	FY2005
Ken Ackerman	$4,000	$4,000	$4,000	$4,000	$4,000	$4,000	$4,000	$4,000	$4,000	$4,000	$4,000	$4,000	$48,000	$52,800	$58,080
Mike Brennan	$4,000	$4,000	$4,000	$4,000	$4,000	$4,000	$4,000	$4,000	$4,000	$4,000	$4,000	$4,000	$48,000	$52,800	$58,080
Ted White	$4,000	$4,000	$4,000	$4,000	$4,000	$4,000	$4,000	$4,000	$4,000	$4,000	$4,000	$4,000	$48,000	$52,800	$58,080
Office Manager	$2,500	$2,500	$2,500	$2,500	$2,500	$2,500	$2,500	$2,500	$2,500	$2,500	$2,500	$2,500	$30,000	$33,000	$36,300
Service Tech	$2,500	$2,500	$2,500	$2,500	$2,500	$2,500	$2,500	$2,500	$2,500	$2,500	$2,500	$2,500	$30,000	$33,000	$36,300
Other	$0	$0	$0	$0	$0	$0	$0	$0	$0	$0	$0	$0	$0	$0	$0
Subtotal	$17,000	$17,000	$17,000	$17,000	$17,000	$17,000	$17,000	$17,000	$17,000	$17,000	$17,000	$17,000	$204,000	$224,400	$246,840

Sales Forecast

Sales	Feb-02	Mar-02	Apr-02	May-02	Jun-02	Jul-02	Aug-02	Sep-02	Oct-02	Nov-02	Dec-02	Jan-03	FY2003	FY2004	FY2005
Equipment	$50,000	$110,000	$120,000	$130,000	$140,000	$150,000	$160,000	$170,000	$180,000	$190,000	$200,000	$210,000	$1,810,000	$2,172,000	$2,606,400
Freight/Install/Setup 6% of equip	$3,000	$6,600	$7,200	$7,800	$8,400	$9,000	$9,600	$10,200	$10,800	$11,400	$12,000	$12,600	$108,600	$130,320	$156,384
Maintenance Contracts 2% of equip	$1,000	$2,200	$2,400	$2,600	$2,800	$3,000	$3,200	$3,400	$3,600	$3,800	$4,000	$4,200	$36,200	$43,440	$52,128
Service 2% of equip	$1,000	$2,200	$2,400	$2,600	$2,800	$3,000	$3,200	$3,400	$3,600	$3,800	$4,000	$4,200	$36,200	$43,440	$52,128
Other	$0	$0	$0	$0	$0	$0	$0	$0	$0	$0	$0	$0	$0	$0	$10,000
Total Sales	$55,000	$121,000	$132,000	$143,000	$154,000	$165,000	$176,000	$187,000	$198,000	$209,000	$220,000	$231,000	$1,991,000	$2,389,200	$2,877,040

Cost of sales	Feb-02	Mar-02	Apr-02	May-02	Jun-02	Jul-02	Aug-02	Sep-02	Oct-02	Nov-02	Dec-02	Jan-03	FY2003	FY2004	FY2005
Equipment 75.00%	$37,500	$82,500	$90,000	$97,500	$105,000	$112,500	$120,000	$127,500	$135,000	$142,500	$150,000	$157,500	$1,357,500	$1,629,000	$1,954,800
Freight/Install/Setup 100.00%	$3,000	$6,600	$7,200	$7,800	$8,400	$9,000	$9,600	$10,200	$10,800	$11,400	$12,000	$12,600	$108,600	$130,320	$156,384
Maintenance Contracts 75.00%	$750	$1,650	$1,800	$1,950	$2,100	$2,250	$2,400	$2,550	$2,700	$2,850	$3,000	$3,150	$27,150	$32,580	$39,096
Service 75.00%	$750	$1,650	$1,800	$1,950	$2,100	$2,250	$2,400	$2,550	$2,700	$2,850	$3,000	$3,150	$27,150	$32,580	$39,096
Other 10.00%	$0	$0	$0	$0	$0	$0	$0	$0	$0	$0	$0	$0	$0	$0	$1,000
Subtotal Cost of Sales	$42,000	$92,400	$100,800	$109,200	$117,600	$126,000	$134,400	$142,800	$151,200	$159,600	$168,000	$176,400	$1,520,400	$1,824,480	$2,190,376

Pro-Forma Income Statement

Category	Feb-02	Mar-02	Apr-02	May-02	Jun-02	Jul-02	Aug-02	Sep-02	Oct-02	Nov-02	Dec-02	Jan-03	FY2003	FY2004	FY2005
Sales	$55,000	$121,000	$132,000	$143,000	$154,000	$165,000	$176,000	$187,000	$198,000	$209,000	$220,000	$231,000	$1,991,000	$2,389,200	$2,877,040
Direct Cost of Sales	$42,000	$92,400	$100,800	$109,200	$117,600	$126,000	$134,400	$142,800	$151,200	$159,600	$168,000	$176,400	$1,520,400	$1,824,480	$2,190,376
Other	$0	$0	$0	$0	$0	$0	$0	$0	$0	$0	$0	$0	$0	$0	$0
Total Cost of Sales	$42,000	$92,400	$100,800	$109,200	$117,600	$126,000	$134,400	$142,800	$151,200	$159,600	$168,000	$176,400	$1,520,400	$1,824,480	$2,190,376
Gross Margin	$13,000	$28,600	$31,200	$33,800	$36,400	$39,000	$41,600	$44,200	$46,800	$49,400	$52,000	$54,600	$470,600	$564,720	$686,664
Gross Margin Percent	23.64%	23.64%	23.64%	23.64%	23.64%	23.64%	23.64%	23.64%	23.64%	23.64%	23.64%	23.64%	23.64%	23.64%	23.87%
Operating expenses:															
Advertising/Promotion	$300	$300	$300	$300	$300	$300	$300	$300	$300	$300	$300	$300	$3,600	$4,320	$5,184
Travel	$1,200	$1,200	$1,200	$1,200	$1,200	$1,200	$1,200	$1,200	$1,200	$1,200	$1,200	$1,200	$14,400	$17,280	$20,736
Entertainment	$1,200	$1,200	$1,200	$1,200	$1,200	$1,200	$1,200	$1,200	$1,200	$1,200	$1,200	$1,200	$14,400	$17,280	$20,736
Service Van	$400	$400	$400	$400	$400	$400	$400	$400	$400	$400	$400	$400	$4,800	$5,760	$6,912
Payroll expense	$17,000	$17,000	$17,000	$17,000	$17,000	$17,000	$17,000	$17,000	$17,000	$17,000	$17,000	$17,000	$204,000	$224,400	$246,840
Cellular Phones	$200	$200	$200	$200	$200	$200	$200	$200	$200	$200	$200	$200	$2,400	$2,400	$2,400
Utilities	$200	$200	$200	$200	$200	$200	$200	$200	$200	$200	$200	$200	$2,400	$2,880	$3,456
Insurance	$1,250	$1,250	$1,250	$1,250	$1,250	$1,250	$1,250	$1,250	$1,250	$1,250	$1,250	$1,250	$15,000	$15,000	$15,000
Rent	$600	$600	$600	$600	$600	$600	$600	$600	$600	$600	$600	$600	$7,200	$7,920	$8,712
Depreciation	$300	$300	$300	$300	$300	$300	$300	$300	$300	$300	$300	$300	$3,600	$3,600	$3,600
Payroll Burden	$2,550	$2,550	$2,550	$2,550	$2,550	$2,550	$2,550	$2,550	$2,550	$2,550	$2,550	$2,550	$30,600	$33,660	$37,026
Accounting/Consultant	$350	$350	$350	$350	$350	$350	$350	$350	$350	$350	$350	$350	$4,200	$4,620	$5,082
Telephone Service	$150	$150	$150	$150	$150	$150	$150	$150	$150	$150	$150	$150	$1,800	$1,980	$2,178
Other	$0	$0	$0	$0	$0	$0	$0	$0	$0	$0	$0	$0	$0	$0	$0
Total Operating Expenses	$25,700	$25,700	$25,700	$25,700	$25,700	$25,700	$25,700	$25,700	$25,700	$25,700	$25,700	$25,700	$308,400	$341,100	$377,862
Profit Before Interest and Taxes	($12,700)	$2,900	$5,500	$8,100	$10,700	$13,300	$15,900	$18,500	$21,100	$23,700	$26,300	$28,900	$162,200	$223,620	$308,802
Interest Expense ST	$0	$0	$0	$0	$0	$0	$0	$0	$0	$0	$0	$0	$0	$0	$0
Interest Expense LT	$0	$0	$0	$0	$0	$0	$0	$0	$0	$0	$0	$0	$0	$0	$0
Taxes Incurred	($2,540)	$580	$1,100	$1,620	$2,140	$2,660	$3,180	$3,700	$4,220	$4,740	$5,260	$5,780	$32,440	$44,724	$61,760
Net Profit	($10,160)	$2,320	$4,400	$6,480	$8,560	$10,640	$12,720	$14,800	$16,880	$18,960	$21,040	$23,120	$129,760	$178,896	$247,042
Net Profit/Sales	-18.47%	1.92%	3.33%	4.53%	5.56%	6.45%	7.23%	7.91%	8.53%	9.07%	9.56%	10.01%	6.52%	7.49%	8.59%

The Plan For
Emma's Espresso

EMMA HART

546 College Lane

Racine, WI

(414) 520-0006

Copy Number __ of Five.

THE PLAN FOR EMMA'S ESPRESSO

1.0 EXECUTIVE SUMMARY

Emma's Espresso is a sole proprietorship owned by its founder, Emma Hart. The Company will own and operate a free-standing espresso cart placed in a permanent host location with a minimum of 2,000 demographically correct daily potential customers and additional walk-by potential customers. The Company is focusing its search for potential locations in a five-county area including Lake and McHenry Counties in Illinois, and Kenosha, Racine and Walworth Counties in Wisconsin.

Emma's Espresso provides real value to its customers far beyond simply providing a good cup of coffee. Customers will find that Emma's offers:

1. **Convenience** — Emma's will be located right in their building. How much simpler will it be to walk down the hall, versus driving to a distant outside retailer? This clearly will be the primary value to most customers.

2. **Quality** — Emma's will offer the highest quality food and beverages available, all freshly prepared.

3. **Attentive, Caring Service** — This is an intangible value, yet it is very real. Buying coffee each day from someone who knows you—who knows what you drink, who knows you were on vacation last week, who knows whether you like to chat or just buy 'n run—these are things that make a difference to people. A difference that they are willing to pay for. In fact, for some customers, a conversation with the barrista at Emma's Espresso may be the friendliest encounter of the day.

4. **Emotional Uplift** — Emma's Espresso will offer customers a small indulgence, a little "life-enhancer," a simple pleasure.

Sales forecast: July sales of 100 cups per day; August sales of 150 cups; September-December sales of 200 cups per day; and sales for January-June 1999 sales of 220 cups per day. Fiscal years 2004 and 2005 are forecast for additional 10% growth per year, all calculated on a monthly basis. Food sales remain a steady 15% of beverage sales. The nearby tables and charts depict the actual sales forecast.

The Income Statement assumes a 20% cost-of-goods-sold on drinks (12% for actual cost-of-goods-sold plus 8% rent), and 50% cost-of-goods-sold on food (42% actual product cost plus 8% rent). The 12% cost-of-goods-sold estimate results in average cost per cup of $.25 ($2.10 x 12%); with $.16 for cost of coffee, $.08 for the cup, and $.01 for the lid. Long-term interest expense represents interest paid on the $14,050 loan at startup, paid off over 36 months. Salaries include a $1,700 per month first-year salary for Emma Hart, plus two additional staff each earning $6 per hour for a combined total of 45 hours per week, or $1,080 per month. Personnel burden is carried at 10% of salaries to cover employment taxes.

This plan includes lease payments of $645 per month on a lease of $20,000 for fixtures and equipment at 10% interest. Alternatively, if adequate initial financing was available, the capital needed to purchase these assets could be taken on as additional long-term debt and paid out as interest expense and return of principle. Purchase negotiations will determine which strategy will be most cost-effective.

The following chart provides highlights of the three-year plan.

Business Plan Highlights

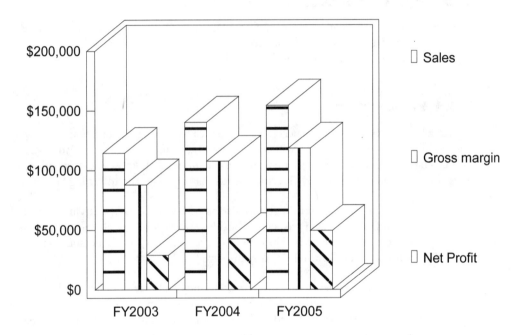

2.0 COMPANY SUMMARY

2.1 Ownership

Emma's Espresso is a sole proprietorship owned by its founder, Emma Hart. The company was established in 2002, and is based in Emma's home at 546 College Lane, Racine, Wisconsin.

-5-

2.2 Mission

The mission of the company is straightforward:

Emma's Espresso is dedicated to providing its customers a source for consistently high-quality specialty drinks (focused on espresso-based coffee) and snacks. Our business will be known for its knowledgeable, friendly staff and convenient, clean environment. The host, customers, employees and owner of Emma's Espresso will be rewarded both emotionally and financially.

2.3 Keys to Success

In every business endeavor, there are a few vital issues that are paramount to success. The ultimate success of Emma's Espresso will be determined in large part by just three key issues: Management, Product Quality, and Location.

2.3.1 Management

In virtually every business, the success of the endeavor is dependent upon its people. The success of Emma's Espresso will be primarily the result of the energy and effort of Emma Hart. Emma brings into this business a lifetime of knowledge, experiences, skills, attitudes and observations. Specifically, Emma possesses the following key traits:

- An absolute dedication to high morals and integrity. This is a driving force and will be reflected in every aspect of business operation. In all dealings with the host location, employees, suppliers and customers, Emma's personal integrity and moral standards will be clearly displayed.

- A lifetime of experience of hard work. Nothing has ever been handed to Emma. No silver spoon, no trust fund, no Ivy League education. She's had to work for everything she's ever had, and she's prepared to work to make Emma's Espresso a success. "Success is 10% inspiration and 90% perspiration."

- A deep knowledge of the specialty coffee business. Throughout two years of employment in the specialty coffee industry, Emma has learned first-hand the dos and don'ts of the business. This is an education that can't be gained in schools and can't be learned from books.

- A thorough understanding of successful coffee cart operation. The successful operation of a coffee cart has its own specific nuances. It is a different business, and it is one that Emma knows well. There is no need to hope that Emma will enjoy the day-to-day operation of a coffee cart, or to hope that she can run one successfully. She has been the full-time manager of a cart operation, she's good at it, and she enjoys it.

- A natural desire to "delight the customer." Emma has an inherent desire to provide outstanding customer service—to go beyond simply offering a high-quality product. She wants each customer to be truly pleased and delighted with every aspect of their interaction with Emma's Espresso.

- An innate focus on structure, work flow and processes. Emma is an organizer and planner. She finds it normal and easy to manage the daily affairs of a retail business—staffing, inventory, cash management, quality assurance, maintenance, etc.

- An unstoppable drive to succeed. Above all else, Emma has the will to make this business a success. She will pour her heart and mind and soul into it. This dogged determination to succeed is a vital part of any new business, and it will be in this one as well.

2.3.2 Product Quality

The second key to success is the presentation of quality products. Emma's Espresso will serve espresso drinks (hot and cold), drip-brewed coffee, hot chocolate, various teas (hot and cold), blender drinks, granita drinks, bagels and muffins. All products will be fresh. All staff will be fully trained and fully competent. Baked goods will be fresh each morning from top-of-the-line local bakeries, and never held over to the next day. Drip-brewed coffees will be freshly brewed every one to one-and-a-half hours throughout the day. Espresso beans will be delivered fresh from the roaster each week, and ground fresh for each cup. Specialty coffee customers appreciate the value of good products, well-made and well-served. Emma's Espresso will satisfy the need for quality products.

2.3.3 Location

As with most retail businesses, location of the cart in an appropriate host is absolutely essential to success. Generally, there are two approaches to the strategy of cart location selection: permanent and temporary.

Permanent location strategy calls for locating the cart in a single, specific position, on a contract basis, for a year or longer. The advantages are many:

1. A single long-term agreement. No continuous contacting and contracting for space.

2. No need to constantly transport the cart to a new venue.

3. Loyal customer relationships may be built, solidifying profit.

4. Revenue may be more accurately predicted.

5. Staffing needs are straightforward.

6. Potential insulation from direct competition.

-7-

There are also disadvantages to a permanent location:

1. Long-term contracts limit ability to leave an unprofitable venue.

2. The host may dictate or change conditions.

3. There may be limited ability to respond to new competition.

Within the permanent location group, there are two somewhat defined subsets. Some permanent locations offer predominantly a single group of potential customers; the same people every day, with many daily (or even multiple times per day) customers. Examples would include office buildings and colleges. Other permanent locations see a constantly changing flow of customers, with only a relative few "daily regulars." These would include airports, bookstores, malls, shopping centers, supermarkets, court houses and car dealers.

Using a temporary location strategy requires a very different mindset. This is a fast-moving, on-the-go style of doing business where the owner/manager is always looking forward to the next event. Each event is a new risk, with the chance for utter failure, or for tremendous success! Coffee carts located at busy outdoor festivals have been known to operate at maximum capacity for hours on end. Carts have been used very successfully in temporary settings such as conventions, art/craft shows, sporting events, festivals, etc.

In essence, a cart can be profitably placed wherever there will be an adequate number of target customers. What is an adequate number of target customers? The answer to that question is, "It varies." Some carts operate well in a closed office building with only 2,000 workers. Colleges with 15,000 college students passing by each day can generate excellent sales, but a poor location within the campus can reduce sales to only marginal levels. It is clear that a cart owner would want to maximize the cart's exposure to potential customers.

Industry experts seem to agree that a minimum pool of 2,000 daily potential demographically correct customers is required to achieve a reasonable opportunity for success. Other location-specific factors for site success include specific cart location within the host, traffic flow near the cart, time constraints on potential customers, and the general ambiance (seating, etc.) around the cart location.

Emma's Espresso will locate in a permanent location with a minimum of 2,000 regular, daily potential customers and additional walk-by potential customers. The company is focusing its search for potential locations in a five-county area including Lake and McHenry Counties in Illinois, and Kenosha, Racine and Walworth Counties in Wisconsin. These five counties contain dozens of potential sites. Each potential site will be examined for suitability and availability, yielding a pool of final candidates. Negotiations with the owner/manager of each of the finalists will determine the location selected.

As is the case with almost every retail business, selecting the proper location will be critical to the success of Emma's Espresso. Great care is being taken to create a set of criteria that any potential location must meet. The ideal location would include the following:

-8-

1. Be currently established within the five-county area.

2. Provides adequate "gross traffic" on site.

3. Provides the correct demographic customers.

4. Provides proper traffic flow to cart site.

5. Offer a multi-year exclusive contract.

6. A rent royalty that allows profitable operation.

The search for this ideal location is underway. A number of potential locations have been identified, and contacts are being made. Current sites under consideration include:

- Kemper; Long Grove, IL

- VA Medical Center; Milwaukee, WI

- Chicago Medical School; North Chicago, IL

- Columbia College; IL

- Gateway Technical College; WI

- Various Car Dealers

- Various Hospitals

Once a contingent commitment for startup funding has been arranged, negotiations with potential hosts will begin in earnest.

2.4 Objectives

Objectives are:

1. Open for business by July 1, 2002.

2. Achieve sales of $115,000 in the first 12 months of operation.

3. Achieve net profit before taxes of $20,000 in the first 12 months of operation.

4. Be debt-free after 24 months of operation.

2.5 Startup Summary

Estimated startup costs are detailed in the following table. True startup costs are primarily limited to one-time startup expenses, working capital, and miscellaneous assets. The category "Other Short-Term Assets" includes $1,000 for small wares. The cart itself, usually a fully complete and self-contained unit, may be obtained through a lease arrangement with the manufacturer. Likewise, the major equipment items such as the espresso machine, drip brewer, grinders, blenders, granita machine and air pots may be attainable through a lease agreement. The cart and brewing equipment are detailed later in the plan.

Startup Requirements Plan

Startup Expenses		Startup Assets Needed	
Legal	$ 500	Cash Requirements	$5,000
Stationery etc.	100	Startup Inventory	$1,000
Menus	200	Other Short-Term Assets	$1,000
Business Plan Consultant	1,200	Total Short-Term Assets	$7,000
Computer, Fax, Phone, Copier	3,000	Long-Term Assets	$0
Consultants, Accounting/Bookkeeping	500		
Insurance	500		
Licensing, Memberships	1,050		
Other	0		
Total Startup Expense	**$7,050**	**Total Startup Assets**	**$7,000**

Total Startup Requirements	**$14,050**

Startup Funding Plan

Investments		Short-Term Borrowing	
Investor 1	$ 0	Unpaid Expenses	$ 0
Investor 2	0	Short-Term Loans	0
Other	0	Interest-Free Short-Term Loans	0
		Subtotal Short-Term Borrowing	0
		Long-Term Borrowing	14,050
Total Investment	**$ 0**	**Total Borrowing**	**$14,050**

Startup Loss	**($7,050)**
Startup Debt	**($7,000)**
Total Debt and Net Loss	**($14,050)**

-10-

3.0 INDUSTRY ANALYSIS

3.1 Industry Overview

The business of growing, roasting, brewing, and selling coffee is one of the oldest and largest industries in the world. In fact, the statistics regarding the coffee business are astounding. The Specialty Coffee Association of America (SCAA) reports that:

- Coffee is the world's most popular drink.

- The coffee industry is second in total dollars in worldwide trade only to the petroleum industry.

- More than 20 million people are employed in the global coffee industry.

- 400 billion cups per year are sold worldwide.

The National Coffee Association's statistics show that Americans drink 400 million cups of coffee PER DAY, one third of all the coffee grown in the world. This equals 1.87 cups per person over the age of 10. While total U.S. coffee sales remain at close to $5 billion annually, growth has come in a unique subset of the coffee trade, specialty coffee. Specialty coffee is differentiated from supermarket brand "commercial" coffee and has grown in its share of the total coffee market from less than 5% in 1983 to an expected 28.9% in 1997. The SCAA projects that specialty coffee controlled $3 billion of the entire $8 billion U.S. coffee trade as we began the new century, a 37.5% market share.

Specialty coffee is available through a variety of retail channels, but the fastest growing channel is the coffee cart. A coffee cart is a self-contained retail store focused on the brewing and selling of ready-to-drink specialty coffee from a cart that usually measures roughly 4 feet wide by 6 feet long. The offerings include drip-brewed coffee and tea; espresso-based drinks such as cafe latte, cafe mocha, etc. (espresso is coffee brewed one cup at a time through a high-pressure espresso machine); other miscellaneous drinks; and a limited selection of food items to accompany the drinks. The best-known of the coffee cafes is Starbucks, with stores across the U.S. SCAA estimates that there were about 200 specialty coffee outlets nationwide in 1989, but that by 2000, there were over 10,000! This is phenomenal growth, which began on the East and West Coasts and is now moving to fill in the center of the country.

Reasons for the rapid growth of the specialty coffee retail trade include:

-11-

- Specialty coffee is SUPERIOR COFFEE!

- Selling coffee by the cup offers a high-gross margin.

- Espresso-based coffees are difficult for consumers to prepare correctly at home.

- Existing food-service locations will be slow to upgrade their product quality to the level of specialty coffees.

- Customers truly appreciate friendly, personal service from a familiar face—an experience that is less and less common in today's computerized world.

It is apparent that this change toward gourmet coffee is a permanent one. Just as the technologically superior compact disc changed the music industry forever, the availability of technologically superior coffee—espresso-based, fresh-ground and pressure-brewed—has changed the coffee industry forever. The message is clear—the specialty coffee industry and coffee carts are here for the foreseeable future.

3.2 Industry Participants

There are a number of important players in the specialty coffee cart industry.

- **The Coffee Suppliers** — For a coffee cart to succeed, it must serve outstanding coffee products, and that necessitates the procurement of outstanding roasted coffee. There are now hundreds of specialty coffee roasters in the U.S. In fact, the number of "microroasteries" has grown from 40 in 1979, to 385 by 1989, and expanded to roughly 1400 by 1999. Suppliers are not in short supply. Suppliers of other inventory products are also abundant.

- **The Cart Manufacturers** — As this industry has developed over the last decade, a number of high-quality cart manufacturers have emerged to accommodate the demand. Today, there are numerous providers, including Burgess Enterprises, Bridge Industries, Elliott Bay Espresso and others.

- **The Equipment Suppliers** — These companies manufacture and service the specialized grinders, brewers and mixers that are a key part of every specialty coffee server. The most important piece of equipment is, of course, the espresso machine itself. There are many high-quality espresso machine manufacturers, including Saporitalia, Espresso Specialist, LaMarzocco, Fetco, Sorrento and Nuova Simonelli.

- **The Cart Operators** — These are the entrepreneurs who buy, equip, place and staff the retail carts. Obviously, they are important to the industry.

- **The Host Locations** — These are the public and private venues which lease or lend space to cart operators in an effort to provide a valuable product to their employees, patrons, customers, students, visitors, etc. These are vitally important participants in the industry, since without a host location, there is no access to customers. Host locations will be discussed in detail in a later chapter.

- **The Customers** — These are the individuals who buy the product at the cart. Clearly, the success of the cart is determined to a large degree by its placement in a host location that collects a sufficient number of target customers. Again, the targeted customer group will be discussed in detail in a later chapter.

4.0 TARGET MARKET

4.1 The Selected Market

The most common specialty coffee patrons are demographically definable and reachable: Baby Boomers, young adults, teens, metropolitan/suburban, upscale, well-educated, light drinkers or nondrinkers, medium-to-high household income level (over $35,000 per year).

Beyond the simple demographic target identification, the nature of the specialty coffee cart business demands a secondary level of consideration. The cart must be placed in a location that puts it in front of a sufficient number of target customers. As in most retailing, it can be said of the specialty coffee cart business (only partially tongue-in-cheek) that the three most important factors for success are Location, Location, and Location.

Emma's Espresso will locate in a permanent location with a minimum of 2,000 demographically correct daily potential customers and additional walk-by potential customers. As noted previously, the company is focusing its search for potential locations in a five-county area including Lake and McHenry Counties in Illinois, and Kenosha, Racine and Walworth Counties in Wisconsin. These five counties contain dozens of potential sites. Each potential site will be examined for suitability and availability, yielding a pool of final candidates. Negotiations with the owner/manager of each of the finalists will determine the location selected.

4.2 Market Trends

Because Emma's Espresso will be located in a permanent host location, the "market trends" will depend primarily on the specific host in which the cart is finally located. A well-chosen host location may be able to create its own "trends," regardless of the economic trends in the surrounding area.

-13-

Nevertheless, it is prudent to examine the five-county area in which the cart will ultimately locate in order to be assured that it is an area with adequate population, appropriate income level, and prospects for future vitality and growth.

Each year, the journal *Sales and Marketing Management* publishes a national survey of economic trends and buying power. The 2001 edition of this survey is the source for the following market statistics.

The five-county area (Lake and McHenry in Illinois, and Racine, Kenosha and Walworth in Wisconsin) boasts a total 2001 population of 1.235 million (824,000 in Illinois), and is expected to grow to 1.341 million by the year 2006, an exceptional growth of 8.5% over the five-year period. This growth is more than *triple* the rate of growth for Illinois and Wisconsin overall, just 2.4% for the same period. Most of this growth will occur in Lake and McHenry counties. Clearly, the target area will continue to be an area of strong population growth well into the future.

Generally, specialty coffee drinkers are young. Therefore, a young population would be generally more receptive to a specialty coffee cart. The data show that the target area is an area of relative youth. Lake and McHenry counties report that roughly 79% of their residents are under the age of 50, compared to a state average of just 74%. This 5% gap is substantial, and demonstrates a significantly youthful slant to the local population. The Wisconsin target counties also show a younger population than the state as a whole; the target counties have 74% under 50, while the state average is 73%.

Another characteristic that supports the purchase of specialty coffee is a medium-to-high household income. Here again, the target area shows strong potential. Nationally, the median household Effective Buying Income (EBI), essentially after-tax income, in 2001 was $33,482. All five of the target counties exceed the national average. In fact, Lake County reports an astounding household EBI of $53,805, 61% above the national average. McHenry County isn't far behind, with an average of $47,323. The Wisconsin counties follow, with Racine at $37,379; Kenosha at $34,571; and Walworth at $34,391. It is clear that the entire target area enjoys a relatively high income level. These data also demonstrate that the two Illinois counties have extremely high income levels, offering the best potential for specialty coffee drinkers.

These statistics substantiate Emma's initial sense that these five counties represent a solid target for placement of her coffee cart. They also point out that Lake and McHenry Counties in Illinois are clearly the leaders with regard to population, growth, youth, and income. The combination of these factors lead to the conclusion that Lake and McHenry counties offer the strongest potential for cart success. The search for the final cart host location will focus more intently on these two counties, but not to the exclusion of the three Wisconsin counties.

-14-

4.3 Purchase Patterns/Process

Individuals who have developed an appreciation for high-quality specialty coffee are often not only buying a hot drink with caffeine, they are also buying a feeling, an ambience, a connection to a time when life was simpler and more personal. There is something special about having your drink made personally, just for you, by a friendly and attentive barrista (a person trained to brew espresso).

Purchase patterns vary, but there is clear evidence to suggest that customers buy specialty coffee drinks from people they like and with whom they feel comfortable. They provide repeat business (even multiple times within the same day) to coffee sellers that provide a high-quality product *and* true personal attention.

5.0 COMPETITION

5.1 Primary Competitors

For Emma's Espresso, competition currently exists in two different forms.

First, there is competition to identify and occupy the best locations. It is clear that there are other companies in the coffee cart business, and they are also trying to find the best locations. However, during extensive research and reviews of potential hosts, no competitors have been observed attempting to negotiate with target sites. Emma's Espresso will continue to move forward to locate and contract with a high-potential location. If competing companies begin to become an issue, Emma will market aggressively to win a prime location.

Second, there will be competition for sales once the cart has been established. An examination of the competition for a host-based location is fairly straightforward. In its broadest sense, competition would be any other provider of hot or cold drinks, especially caffeinated drinks, at or near the host site. That could include the office water fountain, vending machines, company coffee shop or cafeteria, etc. We have identified potential primary competitors (depending on the host site) as:

1. Company coffee shop/cafeteria.

2. Vending machines.

3. Coffeehouse within 5 minutes.

4. Local fast food.

5. Local gas/convenience station.

-15-

5.2 Barriers to Entry

Once Emma's Espresso has established itself in a host location, there are several barriers that create problems for new competitors:

1. **Exclusive Contract** — First, and most importantly, Emma's Espresso plans to sign a long-term contract for exclusive rights to sell specialty drinks within the host location. This is paramount, as it will insulate Emma's from direct competition on-site. Any competitor must then compete from a distance.

2. **Knowledge** — Any potential competitor off-site must have adequate knowledge of the specialty coffee industry in order to be viable competition.

3. **Capital Financing** — Any competitor that would represent a serious challenge for the bulk of customers on a day-to-day basis would need to be located within close proximity to the host location—probably no more than a 5-minute drive. It takes real money to open and operate a full-scale brick-and-mortar specialty coffee house—money most startups don't have.

5.3 Future Competition

Possible future competition would come from coffeehouses not yet established near the host location. These may include, but would not be limited to, Starbucks, Brewster's, Caribou Coffee.

6.0 THE OFFERINGS

6.1 Description of Offerings

In this section, we will detail the specific products that will be sold at Emma's Espresso. In the following sub-chapter, "Value to the Customer," we will address the emotional issues that relate to what Emma's Espresso has to offer.

The menu at Emma's Espresso will be limited and simple. It will also be modified to match the desires of the host clientele. Initially, the following food and drink items will be available:

1. **Freshly brewed high-quality coffee** — Four different coffees will be offered each day: the house blend; a lighter blend; a decaffeinated blend; and a single-origin coffee.

2. **Espresso-based coffee drinks** — These include:

-16-

- — Espresso

- — Americano

- — Cappuccino

- — Latte

- — Mocha

- — Beve

- — Cafe Au Lait

- — Signature Drink.

- — Specialty Drink of the Month.

3. **Blender drinks** — These are primarily cold drinks using ground ice plus coffee, milk, chocolate, etc.

4. **Teas, hot and cold** — Teas generally fall into three categories: Black, Oolong, and Green. Emma's will carry at least one of each, plus a decaffeinated herbal tea (really a blend of fruits, spices and aromatic roots).

5. **Chai** — This is a blend of rich black teas combined with spices and sugar crystals.

6. **Bagels/Muffins/Biscotti/Scones** — Fresh daily, these will be selected to match the desires of customers.

7. **Mineral Water, Water Joe, Juices**

6.2 Value to the Customer

Emma's Espresso provides real value to its customers far beyond simply providing a good cup of coffee. Customers will find that Emma's offers:

1. **Convenience** — Emma's will be located right in their building. How much simpler to walk down the hall, versus driving to a distant outside retailer. This clearly will be the primary value to most customers.

2. **Quality** — Emma's will offer the highest quality food and beverages available, all freshly prepared.

3. **Attentive, Caring Service** — This is an intangible value, yet it is very real. Buying coffee each day from someone who knows you—who knows what you drink, who knows you were on vacation last week, who knows whether you like to chat or just buy 'n run—these are things that make a difference to people. A difference that they are willing to pay for. In fact, for some customers, a conversation with the barista at Emma's Espresso may be the friendliest encounter of the day.

-17-

4. **Emotional Uplift** — Emma's Espresso will offer customers a small indulgence, a little "life-enhancer," a simple pleasure.

7.0 SWOT ANALYSIS

7.1 Company Strengths

The company has a number of strengths at launch.

1. Emma Hart — This is the first and foremost strength of the company. Emma brings:

   — absolute dedication to high morals and integrity

   — lifetime of experience of hard work

   — deep knowledge of the specialty coffee business

   — thorough understanding of successful coffee cart operation

   — natural desire to "delight the customer"

   — innate focus on structure, work flow and processes

   — unstoppable drive to succeed

2. Excellent planning and professional advice — This business has been built on a thorough plan, strong research and thought, and a great deal of input from outside experts. As demonstrated by history and scientific research, businesses that begin with a *specific written plan*, along with the support and *counsel of professional advisor*s, are statistically more likely to succeed than those who do not have specific plans and outside counsel. In fact, as demonstrated by Robert Lussier in his research presented in the *Journal of Small Business Management*, these two variables are the *primary controllable variables which have a direct and positive impact on success in young businesses*. Emma has taken great care to involve a group of advisors from whom she seeks counsel before making key decisions, and she has dedicated hundreds of hours of time and effort to the preparation on this business plan. However, it is important to point out that Emma does not seek counsel because she is indecisive or unsure of where it is she wants to go. On the contrary, she uses advisors to confirm her own ideas, and uses the advice she solicits to make more informed decisions. Likewise, she doesn't plan and replan in order to avoid *doing*. Emma is a doer, and the planning process is a disciplined effort on her part to "do" smartly, rather than to "do" sloppily.

3. The company will have adequate capitalization to build a successful operation.

4. The cart will be placed in a prime host location.

5. Emma's Espresso will own top-quality equipment, designed and built to allow the company to provide its customers with outstanding products and services.

6. The company will have outstanding employees, expertly trained.

7.2 Company Weaknesses

The company will initiate operations with several recognized weaknesses.

1. Emma has not yet run her own business. This perceived weakness will be quickly converted into a strength.

2. Emma has little experience with financial operations, bookkeeping, etc. To remedy this weakness, she has already taken an SBA course that includes a section on business accounting. In addition, she plans to take a course in using Quicken software. She also has contacted a recommended business accountant, and will use an accounting service for needed assistance.

3. Emma has little legal experience. To correct this deficiency, she has contacted a business attorney, and will use legal advice to establish and run her business.

4. Emma has no experience with business bankers. In order to build a solid banking relationship, she has begun investigating local banks.

7.3 Market Opportunities

Opportunities include:

1. As detailed earlier, the specialty coffee industry continues to exhibit strong growth. This growth offers Emma's Espresso an opportunity to fill a specific need in a specific location.

2. Businesses and government agencies are always looking for ways to offer their employees/customers/students added value. A high-quality coffee cart in a busy lobby location is certainly "added value." This desire represents an opportunity for Emma's Espresso to fill a need within the host location.

3. The local economy continues to grow, giving individuals throughout the five-county area the discretionary income that allows free spending on specialty coffee. This is an opportunity that the Company can take advantage of.

4. Businesses and government agencies are always looking for ways to create additional profit centers within their operations. This desire creates an opportunity for Emma's Espresso, since the cart pays a high rental rate per square foot.

7.4 Market Threats

In several cases, threats are a reflection of an opportunity gone awry:

1. A sudden and severe downturn in the public's demand for specialty coffee would be a threat to success. There is no indication of this happening.

2. If the local economy took a sudden and substantial downward turn, leaving customers unable to freely devote dollars to specialty coffee, the business would perhaps be threatened. First, there is no indication of such a downward turn coming any time soon. Second, it is reasonable to expect that an "indulgence" in something as innocent and inexpensive as a cup of high-quality coffee would not be high on a customer's "hit list" of expenses that must be cut out immediately. Other, larger expense items would likely be the first to be cut.

3. There are other companies interested in placing coffee carts in host locations. These companies are threats to the current location search, and are potential threats to renegotiating the contract with Emma's ultimate initial location.

4. Once a host location is contracted, and operations begin, any disruption to an ongoing positive relationship with the host location would certainly be a threat to success.

5. Any unrealized or unsustained host location traffic flow would be a threat.

6. Any substantial increase in labor or inventory cost could threaten success.

7. A potential threat exists in that the company will be serving hot drinks. There may be a liability threat implicit in this business.

OPERATIONS

8.1 The Cart

There are many cart manufacturers in this growing industry. Free-standing coffee carts are truly technological wonders—they contain, in a very small space, all of the equipment, supplies and inventory necessary to operate a fully functional coffee business for an entire day. This may sound simple to the untrained, but it is a major challenge. These manufacturers stay current with trends in durability, style, color, options and health department regulations.

-20-

Cart manufacturers offer options that allow the cart owner to match the needs of the host location. Some options include: Cart size (4 ft., 5 ft. or 6 ft.), side carts, display cases, awnings/canopies, track lights and power supply requirements. Power supply is an important consideration for future product offerings. It is important that the cart has the ability to handle enough current for additional equipment. Carts are usually constructed of plywood attached to a steel or aluminum frame. Clearly, a heavier frame will sustain longer and more frequent moving within the host site or from site to site. Standard features on most carts include:

- 50-amp electrical panel
- 6.2-cubic-foot refrigerator
- Two five-gallon stainless steel water tanks
- One twelve-gallon waste tank
- Water pump
- 1300-watt water heater
- Pull-out hand sink

Options available on many carts include:

- Extra-long power cable
- Custom canopy
- Sneeze guard
- Sneeze guard lettering
- Cup storage
- Balloon tires
- Ice bin
- Water filtration system
- Water softener system

Cart dimensions are usually:

- Height — 42 inches
- Width — 36 inches
- Length — 4 feet, 5 feet or 6 feet
- Wings — 18 inches each (collapsible)
- Total maximum length with wings extended — 9 feet

Side carts can be added for additional storage and merchandising space. Some include lockable storage areas. Side carts are usually 2 feet wide and up to 6 feet long. They extend at a 90-degree angle to the cart itself, and add substantial "presence" to the cart appearance. In fact, a cart with two 6-foot side carts almost takes on the appearance of a mini-store.

Most cart manufacturers can assemble and ship a standard cart within 5 days, with an additional week of shipping time (two weeks total delivery time). Costs for crating and shipping from the West Coast (where most come from) is approximately $320.

Emma's Espresso will select its cart from one of several vendors, depending on the needs and space available at the host location. We will intentionally invest in a cart with adequate capabilities for current sales expectations, plus the capacity for expansion with side carts, etc. if necessary.

8.2 The Coffee

Commercially speaking, there are two main species of coffee: coffea arabica and coffea robusta. These trees and beans are referred to as arabica and robusta. Arabica beans are grown at higher altitudes, have a slower growing cycle, and are much more flavorful. Robusta beans are lower quality beans often used in commercial-grade coffee. Emma's Espresso uses only arabica beans in all its coffees.

Arabica beans come from three primary world areas: Central/South America, Africa, and Indonesia. The unique qualities of a coffee are determined by the geographic region where it is grown. Each region has its own growing conditions and harvesting methods that affect the taste of the bean. In order to create coffees that appeal to the largest audience possible, coffee roasters develop mixtures, or blends, of different coffees. Most coffee served in the U.S. uses Central and South American coffees as its base, since these coffees generally have a smooth texture and clean flavor. Other coffees are then added to the base to add variety and body.

Fine-quality green coffee beans must be roasted properly in order to create fine-quality coffee. The length of time a bean is roasted will determine its appearance and flavor. Cinnamon, City, Full City, Italian and French are all terms used to describe the degree to which a bean has been roasted. A cinnamon roast, yielding a light brown color, would resemble a light commercial coffee roast, while a french roast yields the darkest of coffees, one that appears and tastes almost burnt.

Emma's Espresso will use fine arabica beans from around the world, roasted by expert roasters, to produce outstanding coffees designed to match the tastes and needs of the customer group at the host location.

-22-

8.3 The Water

Since coffee is 99% water, good quality water is a key component in the flavor of coffee. Therefore, Emma's Espresso will use whatever reasonable accommodation is needed to ensure clean, high-quality water is used in its drinks. The measures taken will be determined by the final host location and its water supply. Actions required will probably be limited to a simple filtration system using activated charcoal. This type of filtration is simple, effective and inexpensive. A positive by-product of using filtered water is that it causes much less calcium scale buildup in and on the brewing equipment. This saves cleaning and maintenance time, and repair dollars.

8.4 Brewing Equipment

Emma's will use two primary types of brewing equipment—the espresso machine and a drip-brewing system.

The espresso machine is the heart of all specialty coffee operations, and it is the most important piece of equipment to be selected. It is used to create all of the espresso-based drinks, and its performance must be consistently superb. The primary points to consider when selecting an espresso machine are the boiler capacity and the ability to maintain consistent water temperature.

After thoroughly researching the options available, Emma has chosen to use the "La Marzocco" by Espresso Specialists, Inc. of Seattle. This is a premium machine that features double stainless steel boilers for high volume output and brewing temperature stability. It comes highly recommended by multiple industry experts.

The drip-brewing system is used to brew large quantities of coffee at one time which is stored and sold from airpots. Emma's will use the Fetco CBS-52HAP, a two-pot multi-volume brewing system that allows half-batch options and brews directly into the airpots. Like the La Marzocco espresso machine, this drip-brew system offers Emma's Espresso the quality equipment that is required to produce consistently excellent coffee.

In addition to the espresso machine and the high-volume drip-brewing system, the coffee grinders used must be of the highest quality. The grind needed to create excellent-quality coffee will vary with temperature and humidity, often several times within one day. Grinders must be efficient, easily adjustable, and durable. Emma's will use Rio Grinders from Espresso Specialists. These are industrial quality "burr" grinders that have the capacity to grind a high volume of coffee with precision and ease.

8.5 Product Sourcing

Emma's Espresso will source its whole-bean coffee from Ancora Coffee Roasters of Madison, Wisconsin. Ancora is owned and operated by Jim and Sue Krug, people who are fanatical about the quality and freshness of their coffees. Less than 8% of the world's arabica coffee qualifies as specialty-grade coffee. Only the finest tasting coffees from that 8% are chosen to become Ancora coffee. Ancora not only offers great coffee, they also offer comprehensive training and support in the specialty coffee business. Jim and Sue have been eager to answer questions, ready to provide information, and willing to allow Emma to visit their roasteria for roasting training. Their coffee prices are comparable to the industry, and their proximity to Emma's target area make Ancora Coffee Roasters an excellent choice for a coffee source. Ancora could also be a source for teas.

Other inventory and supply items will be sourced as follows:

- **Small Wares** — Service Ideas; Visions.

- **Paper Products** — Sun Source Paper; Dixie; Solo.

- **Dairy** — Dean's; Becker's.

- **Cocoa Products** — Mont Blanc; Ghirardelli Chocolate.

- **Syrups** — Torani; Folklore; Sterling.

- **Pastries** — Local bakeries, to be determined once host site has been established.

8.6 Staffing

All employees working the cart will have an open and engaging personality. They will know and agree with the philosophy of the business, understand specialty coffee, be trained to make excellent drinks, and exude the true meaning of customer service. The personal appearance of all staff will be in accordance with the accepted social and business standards of the host location, and will also be compliant with health department regulations.

The staffing objective is to provide enough staff to give customers professional service with an efficient flow of product, but without overstaffing. Generally speaking, one barrista can handle up to 25 customers per hour, not including breaks, restocking, problems, cleaning, etc. The current plan calls for average sales throughout the day of 200 cups in 8 hours, or 25 cups per hour. Therefore, in order to provide top-level service for all customers, the initial plan includes 2 people on duty during all service hours.

The table below details the current plan for three total workers (Emma plus two others) and the anticipated salary expense per person. This salary schedule assumes that the cart will be open from 7:00 - 3:00 Monday through Friday (staff in place from 6:30 - 3:30), and that the volume of sales meets the anticipated 200 cups per day. Shifts will be designed as follows:

-24-

Emma — 6:30 - 3:30 daily = 9 hours per day x 5 days = 45 hours per week

Person 2 — 7:00 - 12:00 daily = 5 hours per day x 5 days = 25 hours/week x $6 = $150 per week

Person 3 —   11:30 - 3:30 daily = 4 hours per day x 5 days = 20 hours/week x $6 = $120 per week

Years 2 and 3 include 5% salary increases.

Personnel Plan

Job Title	FY2003	FY2004	FY2005
Emma Hart	$20,400	$21,420	$22,491
Person 2	$7,200	$7,560	$7,938
Person 3	$5,760	$6,048	$6,350
Other	$0	$0	$0
Total	$33,360	$35,028	$36,779

8.7 Training

Training will be divided into two vital areas—technical training and customer service training.

Customer service is the hallmark of Emma's Espresso, and training in this area will be prominent. If a staff member makes outstanding drinks, but doesn't care for the customers, all is in vain. Emma's personal attitude toward customer service will be instilled in each employee. From the initial greeting, through the opportunity to help a customer understand specialty coffee terms, to the final "see you tomorrow!", customer service will be impeccable.

Technical training is much more objective, and just as important. All staff will be trained in the following areas:

1. Familiarity with the host location, its business, and the type of people it serves

2. Familiarity with the immediate cart surroundings, the cart, supply room and kitchen

3. Daily task list and reports

4. Cash register and cash systems

5. Menu memorization and drink-making proficiency

6. Coffee basic training

7. The espresso machine

8. Handling peak demand

9. Opening procedures

10. Closing procedures

11. Training other employees

8.8 Quality Control

Quality control ultimately comes down to two basic elements: quality materials and quality workmanship. Chapters 8.1 through 8.7 have detailed the careful attention Emma has paid to the issue of quality materials—staffing, training, equipment, water and inventory will all be top-of-the-line. That leaves workmanship. In addition to these, Emma has established systems and procedures that will ensure a high-quality product for every customer. Some of these systems and procedures include:

- Training, training, training.

- The espresso machine will be cleaned every week. This guarantees clean tasting coffee.

- Ancora packages all their coffee in specially made bags that feature a one-way valve that allows gasses to escape, but no air or moisture to enter. This system effectively controls the worst enemies of coffee—air and moisture—until the bag is opened. Coffee will be ordered each week, and all coffee should be used within one week of its arrival. Once a new bag of coffee is opened, it will be stored in airtight containers, and will be used within one week.

- Brewed coffee will be kept for only 1 to 1.5 hours, then any left is thrown out.

- No bakery goods will be carried over to the second day.

- Dairy products will be delivered twice a week, and will be kept out of the temperature danger zone of 40 degrees F. to 140 degrees F. This means that all dairy will be kept at less than 40 degrees, in the refrigerator; or higher than 140 degrees, ready to serve. Every 2-3 hours, all pitchers will emptied and washed. Milk is never frothed more than once nor steamed more than twice.

- The barrista should always remember the four principle goals of good coffee preparation:

-26-

— The coffee should *smell* good.

— The coffee should *look* good.

— The coffee should *feel* good.

— The coffee should *taste* good.

8.9 Inventory Control

The proper monitoring and control of inventory is essential to profitable operation. Emma's Espresso has developed a logical and manageable method to accomplish this goal.

First, the cash register used will be one that allows automatic and tamper-proof capture of all pertinent information such as product category sales, sales tax, time of sale, employee ringing the sale, etc.

Second, a Daily Information Sheet will be completed at the close of business each day. The sheet will record key information including:

1. Cash report, with explanations of any deviations

2. Number of transactions

3. Number of drink transactions and dollar amount

4. Number of food transactions and dollar amount

5. Grinder count   (t6he coffee grinder/dispenser maintains a count of espresso shots ground)

6. Milk usage count

7. Cup inventory reconciliation

8. Pastries count

9. List of any items purchased from cash

10. Number of hours worked, by employee

Third, a Weekly Inventory Sheet will be produced to track the inflow and outflow of each inventory item. For each inventory item, the following process will be used:

Starting Inventory + New Product = Total Available - Ending Inventory
= Inventory Used.

The register tape and these two forms provide the foundation of the inventory control system. Other provisions include:

-27-

1. Employees will pay for products used personally, and will place the receipt in the drawer with their name on it.

2. Random drawer checks will be conducted to confirm the accuracy of the drawer at all times during the day.

3. Any wasted food or cups will be collected in a Waste Bin, and logged on a Waste Record.

4. Each shift will start with a new cash drawer.

Through diligent effort and frequent inspection, Emma's Espresso will maintain control of the inventory and supplies necessary to conduct business profitably.

9.0 MARKETING PLAN

9.1 Company Image

Specialty coffee retailers are able to choose the image that they wish to portray to their customers. Some strive for a very strong upscale feeling—approaching the "coffee snob" experience. Others want a high-tech, educated sort of ambience. In the case of a coffee *cart*, there is very little space in which to create the desired image. Since the entire operation occupies less than 100 sq. ft., the cart and the staff must speak clearly and strongly.

Emma's Espresso will have an image that reflects the personality of its owner, Emma Hart. A group of adjectives may be the best way to describe the image: friendly, kind, non-threatening, fun, comforting, clean, organized, unpretentious, personal. Even the name fits the image—Emma's Espresso—simple, straightforward, understandable.

9.2 The "Four P's"

The marketing function may be segmented into four basic components: Product, Price, Place and Promotion—the "Four P's" of marketing.

9.2.1 Product

The products offered by a company are a vital part of the marketing strategy. There are a number of product-oriented steps that can be taken to effectively present a company's offerings to the target market.

At Emma's Espresso, the specific drinks and pastries offered will be selected and adjusted based on customer needs, and they will always be *clearly superior in quality*. A wide variety of options will be available to customize each drink: flavors, cream, skim/whole milk, whipped cream, foam, etc.

-28-

The Company is investigating a variety of packaging options, including paper or "rubber-coated" cups for hot drinks with or without the Company logo, java jackets with or without the logo. This decision will also possibly depend on the final location and their recycling needs/policy. Cold drink cups will be clear plastic with logo.

All hot and cold drinks will be sold in 16 oz. and 20 oz. sizes. These are the most popular and most profitable sizes available, and limiting the selection to just two sizes will simplify the menu, storage, etc.

Emma's Espresso will make the "2-Minute Pledge." A customer's order will be processed, prepared and delivered within 2 minutes of order placement. Since every drink is made-to-order, this is an exceptional pledge. If the order takes longer than two minutes, it's free.

Emma's will feature a liberal and customer-oriented return policy. If a customer is unhappy with their drink, they can simply return it for a remake. If the drink is a specialty drink, and the customer tries it but doesn't like it, they can switch to another drink they know and like.

9.2.2 Price

The establishment of product prices is generally a process dominated by three different approaches. First, prices can be based on the cost of the components. In fact, if the selling price doesn't cover the cost of producing the product, the business will fail quickly. Second, prices can be based upon the prices charged by market competition. Third, prices can be based on what customers are willing to pay.

Emma's Espresso has used each of the three bases to establish its prices. Clearly, the retail prices are sufficient to cover the cost of goods sold, and provide a substantial gross margin to cover fixed costs. The prices of Emma's products are similar to those charged by other specialty coffee retailers in the market area. Finally, the prices are established at a level that customers are willing to pay. This final basis, customers' willingness to pay, is the dominant basis used. Pricing will be adjusted, if necessary, to accurately match the customers' willingness to pay. Emma's will not attempt to be the price leader on the high end or on the low end, but will follow the leadership of dominant coffee sellers such as Starbucks, Brewsters, etc.

Emma's will open for business with the following menu and prices:

Emma's Menu

Item	16 oz.	20 oz.	Item	Price
Espresso	$1.25	$1.52	Mineral Water	1.40
Americano	1.40	1.60	Water Joe	1.40
Cappuccino	2.20	2.90	Juice	1.59
Latte	2.20	2.90	Biscotti	1.25
Mocha	2.48	3.23	Bagel	.65
Beve	2.48	3.18	Bagel/cr chs	1.26
Cafe Au Lait	1.52	1.78	Muffin	1.54
Special	2.88	3.62	Scone	1.54
Hot Tea	1.25	1.52	Wh. Crm	.35
Hot Chai	2.20	2.90	Flavor	.35
Steamers	1.65	1.90	Xtra shot	.35
Hot Choc.	2.06	2.43		
Iced Coffee	1.45	1.69		
Iced Latte	2.90	3.09		
Iced Mocha	3.05	3.41		
Iced A'cano	1.52	1.78		
Iced Chai	2.90	3.09		
Iced Tea	1.26	1.45		
Italian Soda	1.75	2.05		
Ital Soda	1.95	2.25		
Granita	3.08	3.31		
Esprso Granita	3.41	3.88		
Mocha Granita	3.41	3.88		
Coffee/Muffin	2.48	2.71		
Latte/Muffin	3.46	4.16		
Cappuc/Muffin	3.46	4.16		
Mocha/Muffin	3.64	4.36		

-30-

9.2.3 Place

In examining the marketing strategy for Emma's Espresso, it is clear that location is an important part. In fact, location may be *the most important* part of marketing. If one looks at marketing through the eyes of the typical employee or student at the host location, the value of location is obvious. The convenience, lack of travel required, and simplicity of the "Emma's Experience" all combine to make buying from Emma's an easy choice. Most importantly, these "convenience factors" are all related directly and specifically to the issue of location. Just by *being there*, Emma's has a great advantage over all other caffeine vendors.

The old adage in the retail world has never been more appropriate than it is for a specialty coffee cart: The three most important components for success are location, location and location. Being there is 80% of the battle. Product quality, pricing and promotion make up the remaining 20%.

9.2.4 Promotion

Although the marketing plan for Emmas Espresso is driven by the Place, the Product and the Pricing, there is still a place for Promotion as well. Promotion is a broad term that really includes four specific activities: advertising, sales promotion, publicity and personal selling. The following is a brief description of how Emma's will address the four aspects of Promotion.

- **Advertising** — Since Emma's is a host location-based business, the advertising will be focused entirely on "in-house" vehicles such as cart, cup and apron signage; attractively printed menus and business cards; and posters and leaflet distribution (as allowed by the host).

- **Sales promotion** — This is an area where Emma's will really have some fun! Frequent games and contests will stimulate awareness and add to the image Emma wants to develop; sampling of new products and/or flavors will draw a positive response; "Coffee 101" is a class that may be offered to host employees to teach them the basics of specialty coffee; "frequent buyer cards" will stimulate repeat sales; and tie-ins with the host cafeteria will expand sales opportunities.

- **Publicity** — Emma's Espresso will work to build publicity within the host location. This could take the form of a write-up in the host company's newsletter or company e-mail system. Other opportunities for publicity may occur, depending on the host.

- **Personal selling** — Personal selling may be possible and profitable at the beginning of the relationship with the host location. Emma will attempt to meet and befriend as many potential customers as possible. She will present herself and her business as a great place for great coffee and great service. Once the business is established, personal selling will primarily consist of "across the bar" conversations.

-31-

10.0 FINANCIAL PLAN

10.1 Important Assumptions

The following forecasts of sales, profit, cash flow and balance sheet have been developed based on several fundamental assumptions, all of which are logical and valid.

1. The economy of the target market area remains strong and stable.

2. The consumer interest in and demand for gourmet ready-to-drink coffee remains strong.

3. The host location will continue to provide the necessary pedestrian traffic at the cart site.

4. An agreement can be reached with a host location that will limit "rent royalties" to no more than 8% of gross sales.

10.2 Sales Forecast

The development of the sales forecast includes a "top-down view" and a "bottom-up view." Chapter 4.2.1, "Analysis of Market Potential," evaluates sales potential using appropriate market penetration assumptions. Chapter 4.2.2, "Analysis of Breakeven Requirements," uses reasonable cost-of-doing-business estimates to arrive at a minimum level of sales that will support the ongoing operation. Finally, Chapter 4.2.3, "Actual Sales Forecast," provides a solid, achievable, realistic expectation of sales based on market potential, breakeven analysis and documented past experience.

10.2.1 Analysis of Market Potential

As noted in the opening chapter, the average American over the age of 10 drinks 1.87 cups of coffee per day. This statistic is solid, well-documented, and trustworthy. Using this number, it is simple to calculate sales potential for a coffee cart in a business or school setting with 2,000 daily captive customers (2,000 is the current target location customer threshold).

*   If the average is 1.87 cups per day per person, then 2,000 people will drink 3,740 cups per day.

*   Assume that two-thirds of the coffee is purchased off-site (home-brewed, restaurants, drive-throughs, etc.), and that the remaining one-third is purchased from 7:00 a.m. to 8:00 p.m. at the host location (These thirteen hours represent the bulk of the waking, working, studying hours each day). This results in 1,247 cups per day purchased on-site.

-32-

- Assume that one-third of the coffee consumed is specialty coffee. This is roughly the national average market share for specialty coffee, and results in 416 cups of specialty coffee being purchased on-site. Since Emma's Espresso has exclusive rights to sell specialty coffee on-site, we capture 100% of these 416 cups. At an average of $2.10 per cup, the market potential is $874 per day, plus food sales.

10.2.2 Analysis of Breakeven Requirements

The breakeven analysis displayed in the table and chart below are based on a three key numbers.

First, we have calculated the average price per sale as one cup of coffee at $2.10. This is a conservative assumption based on historical sales data. There are three factors that make this estimate very conservative. First, the historical data (from which this $2.10 average was generated) was gathered in a cold weather period, and therefore does not accurately reflect the full impact of sales of high-priced iced drinks. Second, Emma will be working diligently to shift customer demand to the more expensive espresso-based drinks. Third, this estimate does not include any food sales. Emma estimates that food sales will add 15% to the average sale (historical average). Nevertheless, we have used $2.10 as the average sale.

Second, we have established the average cost of this average sale to be 20% of the sale price, or $.42. This includes 12% for the true cost of the coffee, cup, lid, etc., plus 8% of gross sales to be paid as rent to the host location.

Finally, the monthly fixed costs of operation are $3,933 (taken from the Income Statement Forecast) plus $453 per month in principal and interest to repay the startup loan of $14,050.

The calculation yields a breakeven point of 2,341 sales (cups) per 20-day month, or 117 cups per day. This is less than one-third of the market potential of 416 cups per day, and should be readily attainable.

Breakeven Analysis

Monthly Units Breakeven	2,341
Monthly Sales Breakeven	$4,916
Assumptions:	
Average Unit Sale	$2.10
Average Per-Unit Cost	$0.42
Fixed Cost	$3,933

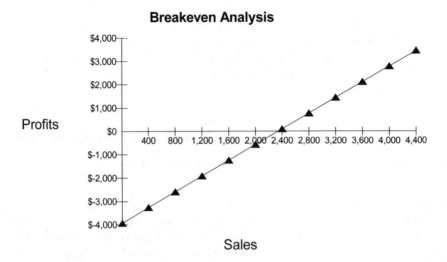

Breakeven Analysis

10.2.3 Resultant Sales Forecast

Based on a careful evaluation of the market potential, breakeven analysis, and documented personal observations from three different specialty coffee locations, the actual sales forecast is for July sales of 100 cups per day; August sales of 150 cups; September-December sales of 200 cups per day; and sales for January-June 1999 sales of 220 cups per day. Fiscal years 2004 and 2005 are forecast for additional 10% growth per year, all calculated on a monthly basis. Food sales remain a steady 15% of beverage sales. The following table and chart depict the actual sales forecast.

Sales Forecast

Sales	FY2003	FY2004	FY2005
Beverages	$99,540	$121,968	$134,165
Food	$14,931	$18,295	$20,124
Other	$0	$0	$0
Total Sales	$114,471	$140,263	$154,289
Cost of sales	**FY2003**	**FY2004**	**FY2005**
Beverages	$21,330	$26,136	$28,750
Food	$5,333	$6,534	$7,188
Other	$0	$0	$0
Total Cost of Sales	$26,663	$32,670	$35,938

Total Sales by Month in Year 1

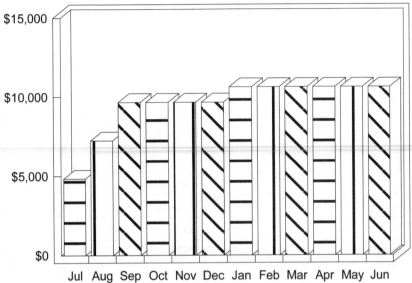

10.3 Projected Profit and Loss

The Income Statement assumes a 20% cost-of-goods-sold on drinks (12% for actual cost-of-goods-sold plus 8% rent), and 50% cost-of-goods-sold on food (42% actual product cost plus 8% rent). The 12% cost-of-goods-sold estimate results in average cost per cup of $.25 ($2.10 x 12%); with $.16 for cost of coffee, $.08 for the cup, and $.01 for the lid.

This plan includes lease payments of $645 per month on a lease of $20,000 for fixtures and equipment at 10% interest. **Alternatively, if adequate initial financing was available, the capital needed to purchase these assets could be taken on as additional long-term debt and paid out as interest expense and return of principle.** Purchase negotiations will determine which strategy will be most cost-effective.

Long-term interest expense represents interest paid on the $14,050 loan at startup, paid off over 36 months.

Salaries include a $1,700 per month first-year salary for Emma Hart, plus two additional staff each earning $6 per hour for a combined total of 45 hours per week, or $1,080 per month.

Personnel burden is carried at 10% of salaries to cover employment taxes.

The following table and chart demonstrate the projected profit.

-35-

Pro-Forma Income Statement

Category	FY2003	FY2004	FY2005
Sales	$114,471	$140,263	$154,289
Direct Cost of Sales	$26,663	$32,670	$35,938
Other	$0	$0	$0
Total Cost of Sales	$26,663	$32,670	$35,938
Gross Margin	$87,808	$107,593	$118,351
Gross Margin Percent	76.71%	76.71%	76.71%
Operating expenses:			
Advertising/Promotion	$1,200	$1,100	$1,210
Accounting/Legal	$480	$480	$480
Payroll Expense	$33,360	$35,028	$36,779
Leased Equipment	$7,740	$7,744	$7,744
Utilities	$0	$0	$0
Insurance	$600	$600	$600
Rent	$0	$0	$0
Depreciation	$0	$0	$0
Payroll Burden	$3,336	$3,503	$3,678
Licenses, etc. (SCAA, Health Bd.)	$480	$480	$480
Contract/Consultants	$0	$0	$0
SCAA Convention	$1,000	$1,000	$1,000
Total Operating Expenses	$48,196	$49,935	$51,971
Profit Before Interest and Taxes	$39,612	$57,658	$66,380
Interest Expense ST	$0	$0	$0
Interest Expense LT	$1,210	$865	$505
Taxes Incurred	$9,601	$14,198	$16,469
Net Profit	$28,802	$42,595	$49,406
Net Profit/Sales	25.16%	30.37%	32.02%

-36-

Business Plan Highlights

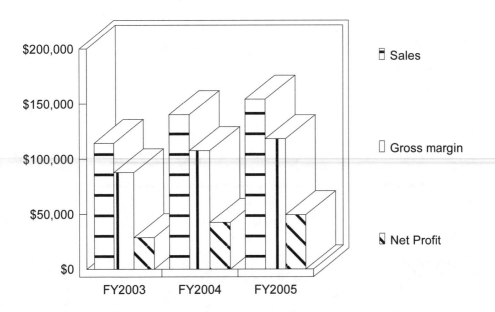

10.4 Projected Cash Flow

The table and chart below demonstrates the elimination of long-term debt and accumulation of cash in the business.

Pro-Forma Cash Flow

Category	FY2003	FY2004	FY2005
Net Profit	$28,802	$42,595	$49,406
Plus:			
Depreciation	$0	$0	$0
Change in Accounts Payable	$3,261	$505	$289
Current Borrowing (repayment)	$0	$0	$0
Increase (decrease) Other Liabilities	$0	$0	$0
Long-term Borrowing (repayment)	($3,600)	($3,600)	($3,600)
Capital Input	$0	$0	$0
Subtotal	$28,462	$39,500	$46,095

-37-

Less:			
Change in Accounts Receivable	$0	$0	$0
Change in Inventory	$238	$279	$152
Change in Other ST Assets	$0	$0	$0
Capital Expenditure	$0	$0	$0
Dividends	$0	$0	$0
Subtotal	$238	$279	$152
Net Cash Flow	$28,225	$39,221	$45,943
Cash Balance	$33,225	$72,446	$118,389

Cash Analysis

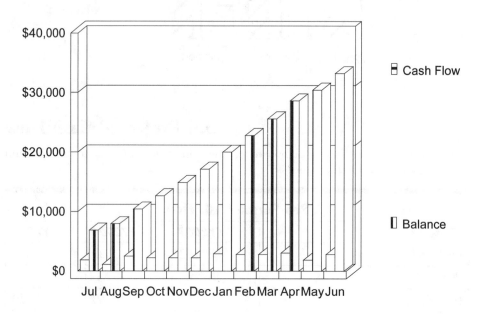

10.5 Projected Balance Sheet

The table below demonstrates the accumulation of cash on the balance sheet.

Pro-Forma Balance Sheet

Category	FY2003	FY2004	FY2005
Short-term Assets			
Cash	$33,225	$72,446	$118,389
Accounts receivable	$0	$0	$0
Inventory	$1,238	$1,516	$1,668
Other Short-term Assets	$1,000	$1,000	$1,000
Total Short-term Assets	$35,462	$74,962	$121,057
Long-term Assets			
Capital Assets	$0	$0	$0
Accumulated Depreciation	$0	$0	$0
Total Long-term Assets	$0	$0	$0
Total Assets	$35,462	$74,962	$121,057
Debt and Equity			
Accounts Payable	$3,261	$3,766	$4,054
Short-term Notes	$0	$0	$0
Other ST Liabilities	$0	$0	$0
Subtotal Short-term Liabilities	$3,261	$3,766	$4,054
Long-term Liabilities	$10,450	$6,850	$3,250
Total Liabilities	$13,711	$10,616	$7,304
Paid in Capital	$0	$0	$0
Retained Earnings	($7,050)	$21,752	$64,346
Earnings	$28,802	$42,595	$49,406
Total Equity	$21,752	$64,346	$113,753
Total Debt and Equity	$35,462	$74,962	$121,057
Net Worth	$21,752	$64,346	$113,753

APPENDIX

Pro-Forma Balance Sheet

Category	Jul-02	Aug-02	Sep-02	Oct-02	Nov-02	Dec-02	Jan-03	Feb-03	Mar-03	Apr-03	May-03	Jun-03	FY2003	FY2004	FY2005
Short-Term Assets															
Cash	$6,827	$7,928	$10,419	$12,647	$14,876	$17,107	$20,002	$22,793	$25,586	$28,603	$30,426	$33,225	$33,225	$72,446	$118,389
Accounts receivable	$0	$0	$0	$0	$0	$0	$0	$0	$0	$0	$0	$0	$0	$0	$0
Inventory	$563	$844	$1,125	$1,125	$1,125	$1,125	$1,238	$1,238	$1,238	$1,238	$1,238	$1,238	$1,238	$1,516	$1,668
Other Short-Term Assets	$1,000	$1,000	$1,000	$1,000	$1,000	$1,000	$1,000	$1,000	$1,000	$1,000	$1,000	$1,000	$1,000	$1,000	$1,000
Total Short-Term Assets	$8,390	$9,772	$12,544	$14,772	$17,001	$19,232	$22,240	$25,031	$27,823	$30,841	$32,664	$35,462	$35,462	$74,962	$121,057
Long-term Assets															
Capital Assets	$0	$0	$0	$0	$0	$0	$0	$0	$0	$0	$0	$0	$0	$0	$0
Accumulated Depreciation	$0	$0	$0	$0	$0	$0	$0	$0	$0	$0	$0	$0	$0	$0	$0
Total Long-term Assets	$0	$0	$0	$0	$0	$0	$0	$0	$0	$0	$0	$0	$0	$0	$0
Total Assets	$8,390	$9,772	$12,544	$14,772	$17,001	$19,232	$22,240	$25,031	$27,823	$30,841	$32,664	$35,462	$35,462	$74,962	$121,057
Debt and Equity															
Accounts Payable	$1,947	$2,495	$3,042	$3,042	$3,042	$3,042	$3,261	$3,261	$3,261	$4,234	$3,261	$3,261	$3,261	$3,766	$4,054
Short-Term Notes	$0	$0	$0	$0	$0	$0	$0	$0	$0	$0	$0	$0	$0	$0	$0
Other ST Liabilities	$0	$0	$0	$0	$0	$0	$0	$0	$0	$0	$0	$0	$0	$0	$0
Subtotal Short-term Liabilities	$1,947	$2,495	$3,042	$3,042	$3,042	$3,042	$3,261	$3,261	$3,261	$4,234	$3,261	$3,261	$3,261	$3,766	$4,054
Long-term Liabilities	$13,750	$13,450	$13,150	$12,850	$12,550	$12,250	$11,950	$11,650	$11,350	$11,050	$10,750	$10,450	$10,450	$6,850	$3,250
Total Liabilities	$15,697	$15,945	$16,192	$15,892	$15,592	$15,292	$15,211	$14,911	$14,611	$15,284	$14,011	$13,711	$13,711	$10,616	$7,304
Paid in Capital	$0	$0	$0	$0	$0	$0	$0	$0	$0	$0	$0	$0	$0	$0	$0
Retained Earnings	($7,050)	($7,050)	($7,050)	($7,050)	($7,050)	($7,050)	($7,050)	($7,050)	($7,050)	($7,050)	($7,050)	($7,050)	($7,050)	$21,752	$64,346
Earnings	($257)	$877	$3,403	$5,930	$8,459	$10,991	$14,079	$17,170	$20,263	$22,607	$25,703	$28,802	$28,802	$42,595	$49,406
Total Equity	($7,307)	($6,173)	($3,647)	($1,120)	$1,409	$3,941	$7,029	$10,120	$13,213	$15,557	$18,653	$21,752	$21,752	$64,346	$113,753
Total Debt and Equity	$8,390	$9,772	$12,544	$14,772	$17,001	$19,232	$22,240	$25,031	$27,823	$30,841	$32,664	$35,462	$35,462	$74,962	$121,057
Net Worth	($7,307)	($6,173)	($3,647)	($1,120)	$1,409	$3,940	$7,029	$10,120	$13,213	$15,557	$18,653	$21,752	$21,752	$64,346	$113,753

Pro-Forma Cash Flow

Category	Jul-02	Aug-02	Sep-02	Oct-02	Nov-02	Dec-02	Jan-03	Feb-03	Mar-03	Apr-03	May-03	Jun-03	FY2003	FY2004	FY2005
Net Profit	($257)	$1,134	$2,526	$2,527	$2,529	$2,531	$3,089	$3,091	$3,093	$2,344	$3,096	$3,098	$28,802	$42,595	$49,406
Plus:															
Depreciation	$0	$0	$0	$0	$0	$0	$0	$0	$0	$0	$0	$0	$0	$0	$0
Change in Accounts Payable	$1,947	$548	$547	$0	$0	$0	$219	$0	$0	$973	($973)	$0	$3,261	$505	$289
Current Borrowing (repayment)	$0	$0	$0	$0	$0	$0	$0	$0	$0	$0	$0	$0	$0	$0	$0
Increase (decrease) Other Liabilities	$0	$0	$0	$0	$0	$0	$0	$0	$0	$0	$0	$0	$0	$0	$0
Long-Term Borrowing (repayment)	($300)	($300)	($300)	($300)	($300)	($300)	($300)	($300)	($300)	($300)	($300)	($300)	($3,600)	($3,600)	($3,600)
Capital Input	$0	$0	$0	$0	$0	$0	$0	$0	$0	$0	$0	$0	$0	$0	$0
Subtotal	$1,390	$1,382	$2,773	$2,227	$2,229	$2,231	$3,008	$2,791	$2,793	$3,018	$1,823	$2,798	$28,462	$39,500	$46,095
Less:															
Change in Accounts Receivable	$0	$0	$0	$0	$0	$0	$0	$0	$0	$0	$0	$0	$0	$0	$0
Change in Inventory	($438)	$282	$281	$0	$0	$0	$113	$0	$0	$0	$0	$0	$238	$279	$152
Change in Other ST Assets	$0	$0	$0	$0	$0	$0	$0	$0	$0	$0	$0	$0	$0	$0	$0
Capital Expenditure	$0	$0	$0	$0	$0	$0	$0	$0	$0	$0	$0	$0	$0	$0	$0
Dividends	$0	$0	$0	$0	$0	$0	$0	$0	$0	$0	$0	$0	$0	$0	$0
Subtotal	($438)	$282	$281	$0	$0	$0	$113	$0	$0	$0	$0	$0	$238	$279	$152
Net Cash Flow	$1,827	$1,100	$2,492	$2,227	$2,229	$2,231	$2,895	$2,791	$2,793	$3,018	$1,823	$2,798	$28,225	$39,221	$45,943
Cash Balance	$6,827	$7,928	$10,419	$12,647	$14,876	$17,107	$20,002	$22,793	$25,586	$28,603	$30,426	$33,225	$33,225	$72,446	$118,389

Personnel Plan

Job Title	Jul-02	Aug-02	Sep-02	Oct-02	Nov-02	Dec-02	Jan-03	Feb-03	Mar-03	Apr-03	May-03	Jun-03	FY2003	FY2004	FY2005
Emma Hart	$1,700	$1,700	$1,700	$1,700	$1,700	$1,700	$1,700	$1,700	$1,700	$1,700	$1,700	$1,700	$20,400	$21,420	$22,491
Person 2	$600	$600	$600	$600	$600	$600	$600	$600	$600	$600	$600	$600	$7,200	$7,560	$7,938
Person 3	$480	$480	$480	$480	$480	$480	$480	$480	$480	$480	$480	$480	$5,760	$6,048	$6,350
Other													$0	$0	$0
Subtotal	$2,780	$2,780	$2,780	$2,780	$2,780	$2,780	$2,780	$2,780	$2,780	$2,780	$2,780	$2,780	$33,360	$35,028	$36,779

Sales Forecast

Sales	Jul-02	Aug-02	Sep-02	Oct-02	Nov-02	Dec-02	Jan-03	Feb-03	Mar-03	Apr-03	May-03	Jun-03	FY2003	FY2004	FY2005
Beverages	$4,200	$6,300	$8,400	$8,400	$8,400	$8,400	$9,240	$9,240	$9,240	$9,240	$9,240	$9,240	$99,540	$121,968	$134,165
Food	$630	$945	$1,260	$1,260	$1,260	$1,260	$1,386	$1,386	$1,386	$1,386	$1,386	$1,386	$14,931	$18,295	$20,124
Other	$0	$0	$0	$0	$0	$0	$0	$0	$0	$0	$0	$0	$0	$0	$0
Total Sales	$4,830	$7,245	$9,660	$9,660	$9,660	$9,660	$10,626	$10,626	$10,626	$10,626	$10,626	$10,626	$114,471	$140,263	$154,289

Cost of sales	Jul-02	Aug-02	Sep-02	Oct-02	Nov-02	Dec-02	Jan-03	Feb-03	Mar-03	Apr-03	May-03	Jun-03	FY2003	FY2004	FY2005
Beverages	$900	$1,350	$1,800	$1,800	$1,800	$1,800	$1,980	$1,980	$1,980	$1,980	$1,980	$1,980	$21,330	$26,136	$28,750
Food	$225	$338	$450	$450	$450	$450	$495	$495	$495	$495	$495	$495	$5,333	$6,534	$7,188
Other	$0	$0	$0	$0	$0	$0	$0	$0	$0	$0	$0	$0	$0	$0	$0
Subtotal Cost of Sales	$1,125	$1,688	$2,250	$2,250	$2,250	$2,250	$2,475	$2,475	$2,475	$2,475	$2,475	$2,475	$26,663	$32,670	$35,938

Pro-Forma Income Statement

Category	Jul-02	Aug-02	Sep-02	Oct-02	Nov-02	Dec-02	Jan-03	Feb-03	Mar-03	Apr-03	May-03	Jun-03	FY2003	FY2004	FY2005
Sales	$4,830	$7,245	$9,660	$9,660	$9,660	$9,660	$10,626	$10,626	$10,626	$10,626	$10,626	$10,626	$114,471	$140,263	$154,289
Direct Cost of Sales	$1,125	$1,668	$2,250	$2,250	$2,250	$2,250	$2,475	$2,475	$2,475	$2,475	$2,475	$2,475	$26,663	$32,670	$35,938
Other	$0	$0	$0	$0	$0	$0	$0	$0	$0	$0	$0	$0	$0	$0	$0
Total Cost of Sales	$1,125	$1,668	$2,250	$2,250	$2,250	$2,250	$2,475	$2,475	$2,475	$2,475	$2,475	$2,475	$26,663	$32,670	$35,938
Gross Margin	$3,705	$5,557	$7,410	$7,410	$7,410	$7,410	$8,151	$8,151	$8,151	$8,151	$8,151	$8,151	$87,808	$107,593	$118,351
Gross Margin Percent	76.71%	76.70%	76.71%	76.71%	76.71%	76.71%	76.71%	76.71%	76.71%	76.71%	76.71%	76.71%	76.71%	76.71%	76.71%
Operating Expenses:															
Advertising/Promotion	$100	$100	$100	$100	$100	$100	$100	$100	$100	$100	$100	$100	$1,200	$1,100	$1,210
Accounting/Legal	$40	$40	$40	$40	$40	$40	$40	$40	$40	$40	$40	$40	$480	$480	$480
Payroll Expense	$2,780	$2,780	$2,780	$2,780	$2,780	$2,780	$2,780	$2,780	$2,780	$2,780	$2,780	$2,780	$33,360	$35,028	$36,779
Leased Equipment	$645	$645	$645	$645	$645	$645	$645	$645	$645	$645	$645	$645	$7,740	$7,744	$7,744
Utilities	$0	$0	$0	$0	$0	$0	$0	$0	$0	$0	$0	$0	$0	$0	$0
Insurance	$50	$50	$50	$50	$50	$50	$50	$50	$50	$50	$50	$50	$600	$600	$600
Rent	$0	$0	$0	$0	$0	$0	$0	$0	$0	$0	$0	$0	$0	$0	$0
Depreciation	$0	$0	$0	$0	$0	$0	$0	$0	$0	$0	$0	$0	$0	$0	$0
Payroll Burden	$278	$278	$278	$278	$278	$278	$278	$278	$278	$278	$278	$278	$3,336	$3,503	$3,678
Licenses, etc. (SCAA, Health Bd.)	$40	$40	$40	$40	$40	$40	$40	$40	$40	$40	$40	$40	$480	$480	$480
Contract/Consultants	$0	$0	$0	$0	$0	$0	$0	$0	$0	$0	$0	$0	$0	$0	$0
SCAA Convention	$0	$0	$0	$0	$0	$0	$0	$0	$0	$1,000	$0	$0	$1,000	$1,000	$1,000
Total Operating Expenses	$3,933	$3,933	$3,933	$3,933	$3,933	$3,933	$3,933	$3,933	$3,933	$4,933	$3,933	$3,933	$48,196	$49,935	$51,971
Profit Before Interest and Taxes	($228)	$1,624	$3,477	$3,477	$3,477	$3,477	$4,218	$4,218	$4,218	$3,218	$4,218	$4,218	$39,612	$57,658	$66,380
Interest Expense ST	$0	$0	$0	$0	$0	$0	$0	$0	$0	$0	$0	$0	$0	$0	$0
Interest Expense LT	$115	$112	$110	$107	$105	$102	$100	$97	$95	$92	$90	$87	$1,210	$865	$505
Taxes Incurred	($86)	$373	$842	$842	$843	$844	$1,030	$1,030	$1,031	$781	$1,032	$1,033	$9,601	$14,198	$16,469
Net Profit	($257)	$1,134	$2,526	$2,527	$2,529	$2,531	$3,089	$3,091	$3,093	$2,344	$3,096	$3,098	$28,802	$42,595	$49,406
Net Profit/Sales	-5.32%	15.65%	26.14%	26.16%	26.18%	26.20%	29.07%	29.09%	29.10%	22.06%	29.14%	29.16%	25.16%	30.37%	32.02%

A Final Word

If you need any more convincing of the value of writing a business plan for the success of your business, Steve Crow, our planning expert, offers the following words of advice.

The Bottom Line

As I look back at the five plans used as examples in this book, I think of the hours invested in each one of them. Hard hours of research, thinking, talking, evaluating, testing ideas, writing and rewriting. I try to put myself in your shoes: a new or hopeful entrepreneur, a reader of this book. What are the questions you're asking yourself right now? What will it take to convince you and enable you and encourage you to create a solid business plan for your new venture? My answers always come back to one central issue: You've got to be truly convinced that the process and product of business planning will add to your bottom line.

Everyone in "the business world" seems to be interested in the bottom line—the real value of a business, or an expansion, or a new product. The bottom line is sometimes easy to predict and simple to measure. But what about the "bottom line" when it comes to the value of a carefully developed, well-written business plan? How is that value to be measured? Do business owners who plan well really have a better bottom line than those who don't? Not easy questions. But there must be an answer, and there is an answer.

In January of 1995, the Journal of Small Business Management *published a paper entitled "A Nonfinancial Business Success Versus Failure Model for Young Firms." The purpose of the study was to develop and test a nonfinancial model that will predict a young business's success or failure.*

Fifteen variables that may have predictive value were isolated and measured to determine how each variable does or does not affect a young business's success. The 15 variables studied were drawn from 20 previous articles on the same subject, and included those variables one might expect: having or not having adequate capital, having or not having previous management experience, etc.

Two matched sets of companies were examined. Set one included 108 companies which had failed (Chapter 11 bankruptcy), while set two included 108 viable companies. Importantly, for each failed company included, the researchers included a matching successful company that was similar with regard to size, age, location, and industry.

Of the 15 variables tested, only four had a statistically significant impact on these firms' success:

1. *Businesses that used <u>professional advisors</u> were more successful than those that did not.*

2. *Businesses that developed <u>specific business plans</u> were more successful than those that did not.*

3. *Businesses that had <u>more difficulty filling staff positions</u> were more successful than those that had less difficulty.*

4. *Businesses with <u>owners with less formal education</u> were more successful than those with more education.*

What's the bottom line on business planning? If you're serious about succeeding in your new venture, I think you already know the answer. Accept what you already instinctively know is true: Businesses that start without a written plan are statistically more likely to fail. Period. End of debate. So, grit your teeth, square your shoulders, and just do it.

As you work, remember:

- *This is not rocket science; it's words and numbers.*

- *By the mile it's a trial, but by the inch it's a cinch. Little steps are OK, but start walking!*

- *Start with the industry, then the target market, then your competition. Then decide what the market needs that you can provide better than your competition does.*

- *Determine the four or five key issues that you must successfully address in order to win.*

- *Think and plan as if your success depends on it — because it does.*

Here are four concrete suggestions that might help you get started. Try the one that matches your talent, time, and money. You may want to combine two or more of these to get the job done.

1. *Use this book as a guide to organize and guide your thoughts. If you aren't a good typist, write your ideas, then hire someone else to do the typing for you.*

2. *If your computer skills are decent, some basic business planning, accounting, or spreadsheet software can help you to format the plan and generate the financial statements.*

3. *Visit your local Small Business Development Center/SBA office. You'll find free help and advice.*

4. *If you still need more assistance, there are probably consultants in your area that can work with you, for a fee, to help you design and complete your plan. Don't let them tell you how you should run your business. Instead, they should help guide you through the important questions and issues, allowing you to build your answers carefully at your own pace. Check in your yellow pages under "Business Consultants."*

Finally, let me simply say that I wish you the best as you embark on the journey to plan your business. Seeing a new business planned, launched, and succeeding is one of the greatest pleasures of my profession. If you need to talk with me, call me anytime. I'll do my best to help.

Steve Crow
719-535-2992

Index

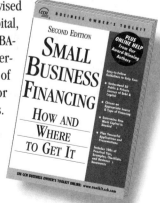

the amounts you earned. Since 1951, Social Security taxes have also been paid on reported self-employment income.

Social Security keeps a record of your earnings over your working lifetime and pays benefits based upon the average amount you earned. However, the only income considered is that on which Social Security tax was paid. Income such as interest or dividends, or income from the sale of a business or investments, and unreported income is not counted in calculating Social Security benefits.

Four basic categories of Social Security benefits are paid based upon this record of your earnings: retirement, disability, dependents, and survivors benefits.

Retirement Benefits

You may choose to begin receiving Social Security retirement benefits as early as age 62. But the amount of your benefits permanently increases for each year you wait, until age 70. The amount of your retirement benefits will be between 20% of your average income (if your income is high) and 50% (if your income is low). For a 66-year-old single person first claiming retirement benefits in 2015, the average monthly benefit is about $1,330; $2,175 for a couple. The highest earners first claiming their benefits in 2015 would receive about $2,660 per month; $4,000 for a couple (receiving benefits on one spouse's earnings record). These benefits usually increase yearly with the cost of living. (See Chapter 2 for a full description of retirement benefits.)

Disability Benefits

If you are younger than full retirement age but have met the work requirements and are considered disabled under the Social Security program's medical guidelines, you can receive disability benefits. The amount of these benefits will be roughly equal to what your retirement benefits would be. (See Chapter 3 for a full discussion of disability benefits.)

Dependents Benefits

If you are married to a retired or disabled worker who qualifies for Social Security retirement or disability benefits, you and your minor or disabled children may be entitled to benefits based on your spouse's earning record. This is true whether or not you actually depend on your spouse for your support.

Married recipients should determine whether they will receive a greater sum from the combination of one Social Security benefit and one dependent benefit or from two Social Security retirement benefits (assuming both partners are entitled to one). A spouse may be awarded retirement or dependent benefits, but not both. (See Chapter 4 for a full discussion of dependents benefits.)

Survivors Benefits

If you are the surviving spouse of a worker who qualified for Social Security retirement or disability benefits, you and your minor or disabled children may be entitled to benefits based on your deceased spouse's earnings record. (See Chapter 5 for a full discussion of survivors benefits.)

 TIP
You can choose the program from which to claim benefits.
You may meet the eligibility rules for more than one type of Social Security benefit. For example, you might be technically eligible for both retirement and disability, or you might be entitled to benefits based on your own retirement as well as on that of your retired spouse. You can collect which-ever one of these benefits is higher, but not both.

Eligibility for Benefits

The specific requirements vary for qualifying to receive retirement, disability, dependents, and survivors benefits. The requirements also vary depending on the age of the person filing the claim and, if you are claiming as a dependent or survivor, on the age of the worker.

However, there is a general requirement that everyone must meet to receive one of these Social Security benefits. The worker on whose earnings record the benefit is to be paid must have worked in "covered employment" for a sufficient number of years by the time he or she claims retirement benefits, becomes disabled, or dies.

Earning Work Credits

All work on which Social Security taxes are reported is considered covered employment. About 95% of all American workers—around 170 million people—work in covered employment. For each year you work in covered employment, you receive up to four Social Security work credits, depending on the amount of money you have earned. Once you have accumulated enough work credits over your lifetime, you, your spouse, and your minor or disabled children can qualify for Social Security benefits.

The amount of work credits you need in order to qualify for specific programs is discussed in Chapter 2 (retirement benefits), Chapter 3 (disability benefits), Chapter 4 (dependents benefits), and Chapter 5 (survivors benefits).

The Social Security Administration keeps track of your work record through the Social Security taxes paid by your employer and by you through FICA taxes.

The self-employed—that is, people who take a draw from a self-owned or partnership business, or who receive pay from others without taxes being withheld—earn Social Security credits by reporting income and paying tax for the net profit from that income on IRS Schedule SE. Income that is not reported will not be recorded on your earnings record. Although many people fail to report income to avoid paying taxes, a long-term consequence is that the unreported income will not count toward qualifying for Social Security retirement or other benefits, and will reduce the amount of benefits for those who do qualify.

The Importance of Names and Numbers

The Social Security system does everything—records your earnings, credits your taxes, determines and pays your benefits—according to your Social Security number. On every form you fill out or correspondence you have with the Social Security Administration, you must include your Social Security number. You should also use your name exactly as it appears on your Social Security card. This will make it easier for Social Security to track the correct records.

If you have used more than one name on work documents, indicate all names you have used on correspondence with the Social Security Administration. As long as you have used the same Social Security number, your records should reflect all of your earnings.

If you have changed your name and want to ensure that all your future earnings will be properly credited to your Social Security record, you can protect yourself by filling out an *Application for Social Security Card*. This form allows you to register your new name and match it with your existing Social Security number. You will be sent a new Social Security card with your new name, but the same number.

To complete this form, you must bring to your local Social Security office the originals or certified copies of documents that reflect both your old and new names. If your name has changed because you married or remarried, bring your marriage certificate.

If your name change is due to divorce, bring the final order of divorce, which includes reference to the return of your former name.

If you have any questions, particularly concerning the type of documents you may bring to show your old and new names, call Social Security at 800-772-1213.

Coverage for Specific Workers

There are special Social Security rules for coverage of some workers in certain sorts of employment.

Federal Government Workers

If you were hired as an employee of the federal government on or after January 1, 1984, all your work for the government since then has been covered by Social Security.

If you worked for the federal government before 1984, your work both before and after January 1, 1984 has been covered by the separate federal Civil Service Retirement System. (See Chapter 10 for a full description of civil service retirement benefits.)

State and Local Government Workers

Many state and local government workers are not covered by Social Security. State government employees are usually covered by their own pension or retirement systems, and local government employees have their own public agency retirement system, or PARS.

However, some state and local government employees are covered by Social Security instead of—or in addition to—a state or PARS pension system. If so, these governments and their workers pay at least some Social Security taxes. And workers under these plans are entitled to Social Security benefits if they meet the other regular requirements.

If you are a government employee and aren't sure whether you are covered by Social Security, check with the personnel office at your workplace. And remember, even if your employment at a state or local agency does not entitle you to Social Security benefits, any other work you have done during your lifetime may qualify you, if you paid Social Security taxes.

Workers for Nonprofit Organizations

Since 1984, all employment for charitable, educational, or other nonprofit organizations is covered by Social Security. (Some churches and religious organizations, however, are exempt from this rule.) Before that time, nonprofit organizations were permitted to remain outside the Social Security system, and many chose to do so. Because people who worked for such organizations were left out of any retirement plan, the Social Security system now permits some of them to qualify for benefits with about half of the normal number of years of work credit. If you reached age 55 before January 1, 1984, and you worked for such a nonprofit organization, you and your family can qualify for Social Security benefits with a reduced number of work credits.

Members of the Military

Whether your military service was considered by Social Security to be "covered employment" depends on when you served and whether you were on active or inactive duty. From 1957 on, all service personnel on active duty have paid Social Security taxes, and so all active service from that date is covered employment. Since 1988, periods of active service, such as reserve training, while on inactive duty have also been covered.

Household Workers

Household work—cleaning, cooking, gardening, child care, minor home repair work—has been covered by Social Security since 1951; work before that date is not credited on a worker's earnings record.

A major problem for household workers is that most employers do not report their employees' earnings to the Internal Revenue Service (IRS) and do not pay Social Security taxes on those earnings. Of course, a lot of domestic workers do not want their earnings reported. They are paid so little that they prefer to receive the full amount, often in cash, without any taxes withheld.

One result of this nonreporting, however, is that the earnings do not get credited to the worker's Social Security record. So when the worker or worker's family later seeks Social Security benefits, they may have trouble qualifying and, if qualified, may have lower benefit amounts.

If you want your earnings from household work reported to Social Security, you have several options. If you work for different employers and make less than $1,000 per year from any one of them, you can report that income yourself as self-employment income and pay 15.3% self-employment tax on it in addition to income tax. Paying self-employment tax, on federal income tax Form 1040, Schedule SE, credits the earnings to your Social Security earnings record.

If you work for any one employer who pays you a total of $1,700 or more over the course of a year, you can ask that employer to withhold Social Security taxes from your pay, report your income to Social Security, and pay the employer's share of the Social Security tax on that income, as the law requires. (See "Employer's Duty to Report Earnings of Household Workers," below.)

Farmworkers

Farm and ranch work is covered by the Social Security system. If you do crop or animal farmwork, your employer must report your earnings and pay Social Security taxes on them. The employer must also withhold your share of Social Security taxes from your paycheck if you earn $150 or more from that employer in one year, or if the employer pays $2,500 or more to all farm laborers, regardless of how much you earn individually. Any amounts you are paid in housing or food do not have to be reported by the employer.

Farmworkers have long faced problems with employers who do not pay their share of the Social Security tax. To make sure your farmwork is counted toward your Social Security record, check your pay stub to see if Social Security taxes—labeled FICA—are being withheld. Also ask the person who handles payroll to give you paperwork indicating that Social Security taxes are being paid on your earnings. If your employer is not paying Social Security taxes on your earnings, or you get the runaround and you are unsure what the employer is doing, ask your local Social Security office to find out for you.

If you are worried about your employer's finding out that you are checking on this, ask the Social Security field representative to make a confidential inquiry. Social Security can request all the employer's wage records without letting the employer know which employee in particular has brought the matter to its attention.

Employer's Duty to Report Earnings of Household Workers

If an employer hires a household worker—cleaner, cook, gardener, child sitter, home care aide—who is not employed by and paid through an agency, and the employer pays that worker a total of $1,700 or more during the year, the employer is required by law to report those payments and pay Social Security taxes on them. This rule exempts any worker who was younger than 18 during any part of the year.

An individual employer can report these taxes on his or her own federal income tax return Form 1040, and pay the Social Security tax obligation along with the personal income taxes. To file and pay these taxes, the employer will need the name of the employee as it appears on his or her Social Security card, the employee's Social Security number, and the amount of wages paid.

Earning Work Credits

To receive any kind of Social Security benefit—retirement, disability, dependents, or survivors—the person on whose work record the benefit is to be calculated must have accumulated enough work credits. The number of work credits you need to reach the qualifying mark—what Social Security calls insured status—varies depending on the particular benefit you are claiming and the age at which you claim it.

You can earn up to four work credits each year, but no more than four, regardless of how much you earn. Before 1978, work credits were measured in quarter-year periods: January through March, April through June, July through September, and October through December. You had to earn a specific minimum amount of income to gain a work credit for that quarter:

- Before 1978, you received one credit for each quarter in which you were paid $50 or more in wages in covered employment, or each quarter in which you earned and reported $100 or more from self-employment.

- Beginning in 1978, the rules were changed to make it easier to earn credits. From 1978 on, you receive one credit, up to four credits per year, if you earn at least a certain amount in covered employment, regardless of the quarter in which you earn it. That means that if you earn all your money during one part of the year and nothing during other parts of the year, you can still accumulate the full four credits. The amount needed to earn one credit increases yearly. In 1978, when the new system was started, it was $250; in 2015, it is $1,220.

EXAMPLE 1: In 1975, Ulis was paid $580 between January and March, nothing between April and July when he could not work because of a back injury, $340 in August, and $600 in cash from self-employment in October and November. For the year 1975, Ulis earned three credits: one credit for the first quarter, in which he was paid more than the $50 minimum; nothing in the second quarter, so he got no credit; one credit in the third quarter, because he earned well over the $50 minimum even though he worked only one month; and one credit for the last quarter, because in 1975 self-employment income was covered by Social Security.

EXAMPLE 2: Eve was paid $800 in January 1978, but did not earn anything the rest of the year. Based on the earnings test in effect in 1978, she got three credits for the year—one for each $250 in earnings—based on her earnings for January alone.

EXAMPLE 3: Rebecca was paid $500 a month in 2015 at her part-time job, for total earnings for the year of $6,000. Because her earnings of $6,000 divided by $1,220 (the amount needed to earn one credit in 2015) is more than 4, she received the maximum four credits for 2015.

Determining Your Benefit Amount

If you are eligible for a Social Security benefit, the amount of that benefit is determined by a formula based on the average of your yearly reported earnings in covered employment since you began working. Social Security adjusts your earnings records every year that you have Social Security-taxed earnings. This is true even after you begin collecting benefits.

How Your Earnings Average Is Computed

Social Security computes the average of your yearly earnings, but places a yearly limit on the amount you can be credited with, no matter how much you actually earned that year. These yearly income credit limits are shown in the following table, "Yearly Dollar Limit on Earnings Credits."

> CAUTION
> **Only employment-related income counts, and you must have paid Social Security taxes on that income.** Other income that you may have earned, such as interest, dividends, capital gains, rents, and royalties, will not be considered in calculating your Social Security benefits.

Benefit Formula

Based on a worker's earnings record, the Social Security Administration computes what is called the worker's Primary Insurance Amount, or PIA. This is the amount a worker will receive if he or she claims retirement benefits at full retirement age, which is 66 for everyone born in 1943 through 1954. The full retirement age is 67 for those born in 1960 or later. The exact formula applied to each worker's earnings record depends on the year the worker was born.

Yearly Dollar Limit on Earnings Credits

1951–1954	$ 3,600	1991	$ 53,400
1955–1958	4,200	1992	55,500
1959–1965	4,800	1993	57,600
1966–1967	6,600	1994	60,600
1968–1971	7,800	1995	61,200
1972	9,000	1996	62,700
1973	10,800	1997	65,400
1974	13,200	1998	68,400
1975	14,100	1999	72,600
1976	15,300	2000	76,200
1977	16,500	2001	80,400
1978	17,700	2002	84,900
1979	22,900	2003	87,000
1980	25,900	2004	87,900
1981	29,700	2005	90,000
1982	32,400	2006	94,200
1983	35,700	2007	97,500
1984	37,800	2008	102,000
1985	39,600	2009–2011	106,800
1986	42,000	2012	110,100
1987	43,000	2013	113,700
1988	45,000	2014	117,000
1989	48,000	2015	118,500
1990	50,400		

CAUTION

There is no "minimum" Social Security benefit amount. If your average earnings were quite low, your check will also be low.

Social Security benefits for a disabled worker (as described in Chapter 3), or for a worker's dependents (as described in Chapter 4) or survivors (as described in Chapter 5), are based on a percentage of the worker's PIA. Social Security will give you an estimate of your future retirement or disability benefits, or those of a worker on whose earnings record you will receive dependents or survivors benefits.

Veterans May Receive Extra Earnings Credit

If you're a veteran of the U.S. Armed Forces, you may be eligible for extra earnings credit, including:

- an extra $300 per quarter for active duty from 1957 through 1977, and
- $100 of credit for each $300 of active duty basic pay, up to a maximum credit of $1,200 per year for active duty from 1978 through 2001. No extra credit is given if you enlisted after September 7, 1980 and did not complete at least 24 months' active duty or your full tour.
  Notice that no extra credit is given for active duty after 2001.
  Don't be alarmed if you don't see your extra credits reflected on your Social Security Statement. These will be added to your record when you actually apply for benefits, at which time you'll have to provide proof of your military service. Active duty earnings from 1968 on should be included in the benefit estimates on your statement, although the extra credit amounts will not show up in the statement's year-to-year list of your earnings.

Taxes on Your Benefits

A certain amount of Social Security benefits may be taxable, depending on your total income. In determining whether you owe any income tax on your benefits, the Internal Revenue Service looks at what it calls your combined income. This consists of your adjusted gross income, as reported in your tax return, plus any nontaxable interest income, plus one-half of your Social Security benefits. If your combined income as an individual is between $25,000 and $34,000 (or, for a couple filing jointly, between $32,000 and $44,000), you may have to pay income taxes on 50% of your Social Security benefits. If your combined income is more than $34,000 ($44,000 for a couple filing jointly), you may owe income taxes on up to 85% of your benefits.

The way to calculate any income taxes you may owe on your Social Security benefits is explained in the instruction booklet that accompanies the Form 1040 federal tax return. The IRS also publishes a free information booklet explaining numerous tax rules pertaining to older people. It is called *Tax Guide for Seniors*, Publication 554. To get the booklet, call the IRS at 800-829-3676 or download it from the website www.irs.gov.

Taxes paid on Social Security benefits go back into the Social Security Trust Fund, not the general fund.

Your Social Security Earnings Record

The Social Security Administration keeps a running account of your earnings record and the work credits it reflects. (It tracks these by use of your Social Security number.) Based on those figures, Social Security can give you an estimate of what your retirement benefits would be if you took them at age 62, full retirement age, or age 70. It can also estimate benefits for your dependents or survivors, or your disability benefits, should you need them.

It makes good sense to find out what your Social Security retirement benefits will be several years before you actually consider claiming them. You're probably curious, and finding out can help you plan for the future. And because so much is riding on your official earnings record, it is important to check the accuracy of that record every few years. You want to make sure that all your covered earnings are credited to you.

To check your earnings record and estimate of benefits, go to the Social Security Administration's website at http://ssa.gov/mystatement.

A Social Security Statement is supposed to be mailed yearly to everyone age 60 and older who is not currently receiving Social Security benefits. In addition, Social Security sends out statements every five years for people between the ages of 25 and 60. If you have not received a Social Security Statement, or if you have a question about your earnings record, call Social Security at 800-772-1213.

U.S. Citizens' Rights to Receive Benefits While Living Abroad

If you are a U.S. citizen living in another country, you are entitled to the same Social Security benefits—to the extent you have earned them through work in the United States—as if you lived in the United States. However, if you are married to someone who is not a U.S. citizen, and you both live outside the United States, your spouse is not entitled to Social Security dependents or survivors benefits based on your work record. (Your spouse might still be entitled to Social Security retirement benefits based on his or her own work performed while living in the United States; see the following section, "Receiving Benefits as a Noncitizen.")

If you live in one of a few particular countries, there are restrictions on the sending of your Social Security benefits. If you live in Cuba or North Korea, a law passed during the days of Cold War anti-Communist policy forbids the Social Security system from sending your benefits there. Instead, you would have to have the benefits sent to a bank in the United States or in some third country, and then transfer the money on your own. If you live in Vietnam or Cambodia, or in one of the Central Asia former Soviet republics, you may be able to receive Social Security payments there, but only if you make special arrangements with Social Security and the U.S. embassy in that country.

Receiving Benefits as a Noncitizen

It is increasingly common for people who are not U.S. citizens to live and work here for long periods of time. This section explains your rights to collect Social Security benefits if you are not a U.S. citizen, whether you're living in the United States now or have since left to live in another country.

Noncitizens Living in the United States

Noncitizens living in the United States are entitled to all the Social Security benefits that they or their spouse or parents have earned—under the same rules as U.S. citizens—if they are lawfully in the United States. For example, you might benefit from this if you:

- were not a U.S. citizen during some or all of the time you or your family member worked in the United States, but have since become a U.S. citizen, or
- are not a U.S. citizen, but are a lawful permanent U.S. resident or have another immigration status permitting you to be lawfully present in the United States.

Non-U.S. Citizens Living Abroad

Many non-U.S. citizens live and work for a time in the United States, paying Social Security taxes and earning enough work credits to qualify for benefits for themselves and their families. However, many of these people ultimately leave the United States. Their ability to collect earned Social Security benefits after departing depends in large part on whether the United States has entered into agreements with their home countries. If you've formerly worked in the United States, you need to look at three things to figure out your eligibility for benefits, including:

- your country of citizenship
- the country where you're living when you request Social Security benefits, and
- the type of benefit you're requesting.

To find out what your rights are to collect Social Security benefits based on your country of citizenship, your country of residence, and the type of Social Security benefit you're entitled to receive, see the Social Security Administration's official online publication "Your Payments While You Are Outside the United States," available at www.socialsecurity.gov/pubs/10137.html.

Social Security Retirement Benefits

Many people look forward to retirement as a time of contentedness and quiet, a new time for old friendships, a period of calm sufficiency. They imagine they will be able to do things they always wanted to do but never had time for. While this may prove to be a true picture for some people, others find a far different reality. Reduced financial resources make it tough to cope with a high-priced world. In a society that has forgotten how to revere and support its elders, retirement often becomes another difficult siege in the old battle for survival.

The reality for many Americans is that after what they had hoped would be retirement age—usually anticipated as age 65—they must continue working to make ends meet. Often, they end up doing so at lower-paying work than they had before retiring.

The Social Security retirement benefit program, as well as private pension and other retirement plans, helps with some of the financial strain of retirement years. But Social Security retirement benefits alone are not sufficient for most people to live at anything near the standard of living they had during their working years.

These problems bring into question both the age at which you retire and whether you'll continue to work after beginning to collect Social Security. Under Social Security rules, retirement does not necessarily mean you have reached a specific age, or that you have stopped working altogether. It merely refers to the time you claim and start collecting Social Security retirement benefits. If you claim benefits before you reach your full retirement age, but continue to work, the amount of your benefits will be reduced if you earn more than a specific amount of income. (See "Timing Your Retirement Benefits Claim," below.) Once you reach your full retirement age, however, you will collect the full amount of your retirement benefits no matter how much you continue to earn.

This chapter explains how Social Security figures your eligibility for retirement benefits, when you may and when you should claim the benefits, and what the rules are regarding earnings after you have begun to claim your retirement benefits.

Work Credits Required

To be eligible for Social Security retirement benefits, officially referred to by Social Security as being "fully insured," you must have earned at least 40 work credits over all your working years. See Chapter 1 to review how work credits are earned.

Checking Your Earnings Record

Even if you have not worked for many years, and you did not make much money in the few years you did work, check your earnings record. You may be surprised to find that you have quite a few credits from years gone by, since the rules for getting work credits were pretty easy to comply with before 1978.

To check your earnings record, go to the Social Security Administration Web page called "Get Your Social Security Statement Online" at http://ssa.gov/mystatement.

If you find that you do not have enough work credits to be eligible for retirement benefits now, you may be able to work part time for a while and earn enough new credits to become eligible. You've got a high incentive for doing this, because once you qualify for retirement benefits, you are eligible to receive them for the rest of your life. That could mean a lot of money over the years to come.

> EXAMPLE: After graduating from college in 1970, Millie immediately got a good-paying job at a large insurance company. After several years there, she married and stopped working outside the home. Her husband was quite a bit older and had earlier made money in business for himself, and he supported them both on his investments. After his death in 1980, Millie was able to live carefully on these investments. By the time she was in her 50s, however, Millie found that her assets were dwindling and the monthly income they produced no longer went very far.
>
> When Millie turned 60, she asked Social Security whether she was eligible for survivors benefits (see Chapter 5) based on her husband's work record. But because he had made almost all his

money from his investments rather than from work, Millie found that she was not entitled to any survivors benefits based on her husband's work record.

But Millie also checked her own Social Security work record and found that she had 36 work credits from her time at the insurance company many years before. With 36 credits, she needed only four more to be eligible for her own retirement benefits (born in 1949, she needed a total of 40 credits). She was able to get a part-time job at a local restaurant—the pay was low, but the work allowed her to earn her four additional work credits within a year, qualifying her for Social Security retirement benefits. Even though these benefits were not that much, when added to her income from savings and investments, they made Millie's life much more comfortable.

Benefits for Employees of Nonprofits

Before January 1, 1984, nonprofit organizations did not have to participate in Social Security. Some organizations did participate, and their employees' work was covered by Social Security, earning the employees credits just as if they worked for private profit-making employers.

Nonprofit organizations that did not participate, however, paid no Social Security taxes on behalf of their employees, and the employees paid no Social Security taxes out of their wages. As a result, during all their work years before 1984, employees of these nonprofit organizations did not earn any Social Security work credits for their labors.

To help make up for these lost years of work, the Social Security laws permit certain employees of nonprofit organizations to qualify for Social Security benefits with less than the standard number of work credits. If you were at least 55 years old on January 1, 1984, and on that date were employed by a nonprofit organization that had not been participating in Social Security, you can qualify for retirement benefits with the amounts of work credits, earned after January 1, 1984, listed in the "Workers in Nonprofits" chart, below.

These special rules do not apply to you if the nonprofit organization gave you the opportunity to participate in Social Security before 1984 but you declined.

Workers in Nonprofits: Work Credits Required for Social Security Retirement Eligibility	
Your Age on January 1, 1984	Work Credits Required
55 or 56	20
57	16
58	12
59	8
60 or older	6

Timing Your Retirement Benefits Claim

Two factors determine the amount of your retirement benefits. The first is your earnings record: How much you have earned over your working life. The higher your earnings, the higher your benefits.

The second is the age at which you claim your retirement benefits. You are allowed to claim benefits as early as age 62 up to age 70, but the earlier you claim them, the lower the benefits will permanently be. This section explains how the timing of your claim affects the amount of your retirement benefits.

If You Claim Benefits Before Full Retirement Age

You're allowed to claim retirement benefits as soon as you turn 62, but if you claim benefits before your "full retirement age," your monthly payment will forever be considerably less than if you wait until full retirement age. Nonetheless, out of financial need or other calculation, about 60% of all people eligible for retirement benefits claim them before they reach full retirement age. Also, if you claim benefits before your full retirement age but continue to work, your benefits may be significantly reduced if your earnings are over certain yearly limits. (See "Working After Claiming Early Retirement Benefits," below, for these limits.)

The amount by which your benefits would be permanently reduced if you claimed them early depends on the year of your birth and the time between when you claim benefits and when you reach your full retirement age. If you were born in 1937 or earlier, the reduction is about 0.555% per month, or 6.7% per year, up to a total reduction of 20% if you claim benefits three years early. And, remember, the reduction in monthly benefits is permanent. Benefits do not increase to the full amount when you reach your full retirement age.

Full retirement age is going up gradually, from 65 to 67, for people born after 1937. For these people, early (and reduced) retirement benefits will still be available at exactly age 62. As you'll notice on the "Benefit Reductions for Early Retirement" table below, those born in 1960 or later who retire at 62 will see their benefits shrink by as much as 30%.

Your Break-Even Point

Of course, claiming retirement benefits at less than full retirement age means you will collect benefits for a longer time. But the permanent reduction in the amount of your monthly benefits means that if you live past a certain age—in your early 80s, depending on whether you are a man or a woman and when you were born—you will wind up collecting less in total lifetime benefits than if you had waited until full retirement age. This point in life is referred to by Social Security as the "break-even age." See Chapter 6 to learn more about the break-even point.

The following two tables, "Benefit Reductions for Early Retirement" and "Retirement Benefits at Age 62," illustrate the effect of claiming early benefits. The first table shows how much a monthly retirement benefit is reduced for each month it is claimed before full retirement age. The second table assumes a retirement benefit for the worker at full retirement age of $1,000; this table shows exactly how much claiming benefits at age 62 would reduce the retired worker's monthly amounts, plus the overall percentage reduction in benefits.

Benefit Reductions for Early Retirement

Year Born	Full Retirement Age	Monthly Reduction
1938	65 + 2 months	0.548%
1939	65 + 4 months	0.541%
1940	65 + 6 months	0.535%
1941	65 + 8 months	0.530%
1942	65 + 10 months	0.525%
1943–54	66	0.520%
1955	66 + 2 months	0.516%
1956	66 + 4 months	0.512%
1957	66 + 6 months	0.509%
1958	66 + 8 months	0.505%
1959	66 + 10 months	0.502%
1960	67 and later	0.500%

Retirement Benefits at Age 62

(based on a $1,000 retirement benefit at full retirement age)

Year of Birth*	Normal (or full) retirement age	Retirement Benefit	
		Amount	Percent Reduction
1937 or earlier	65	$800	20.00%
1938	65 + 2 months	790	20.83%
1939	65 + 4 months	783	21.67%
1940	65 + 6 months	775	22.50%
1941	65 + 8 months	766	23.33%
1942	65 + 10 months	758	24.17%
1943–54	66	750	25.00%
1955	66 + 2 months	741	25.83%
1956	66 + 4 months	733	26.67%
1957	66 + 6 months	725	27.50%
1958	66 + 8 months	716	28.33%
1959	66 + 10 months	708	29.17%
1960 and later	67	700	30.00%

* If you are born on January 1, use the prior year of birth.

TIP

What if you must retire for health reasons? Some people are forced to stop working before full retirement age because of ill health. If you are under full retirement age and in that position, consider applying for Social Security disability benefits rather than early retirement. The reason is that disability benefits are calculated by the same formula as full retirement benefits, but the amount does not depend solely on the age at which you qualify for them. And the "disability freeze," a benefit calculation rule by which Social Security ignores your low-earning years that were caused by your disabling condition, can actually increase your disability and retirement benefits. Be warned, however, that proving you're incapable of doing any sort of work can be a long and difficult process. .

TIP

Widows and widowers can switch from retirement to survivors benefits. Financial straits force many widow(er)s to claim their retirement benefits at or before full retirement age, even though they would become eligible for a higher monthly retirement amount if they waited longer. Although claiming early retirement benefits permanently reduces their retirement benefits based on their own earnings record, Social Security rules permit widow(er)s who have previously claimed early retirement to switch to survivors benefits at full retirement age. And, for many people, these full survivors benefits are higher than their own reduced retirement benefits. (See Chapter 5 for a full description of survivors benefits.)

The same rules apply to widows as to widowers, although the disparity in earnings between men and women means this ability to switch benefits is used mostly by women.

Full Retirement Age

For a long time, Social Security considered 65 to be full or normal retirement age. Benefit amounts were calculated on the assumption that most workers would stop working full time and would claim retirement benefits upon reaching age 65.

Now that people are generally living longer, the Social Security rules for what is considered full retirement age are changing. Age 65 is still considered full retirement age for anyone born before 1938. However, full retirement age gradually increases from age 65 to 67 for people born in 1938 or later. For people born between 1943 and 1954, full retirement age is 66.

In addition, to give incentive for people to delay making their retirement claims, Social Security offers higher benefits for people who wait to make their claims until after reaching full retirement age.

Full Retirement Age for Those Born After 1937	
Year Born	**Full Retirement Age**
1938	65 years + 2 months
1939	65 years + 4 months
1940	65 years + 6 months
1941	65 years + 8 months
1942	65 years + 10 months
1943–1954	66 years
1955	66 years + 2 months
1956	66 years + 4 months
1957	66 years + 6 months
1958	66 years + 8 months
1959	66 years + 10 months
1960 or later	67 years

If You Claim Benefits After Full Retirement Age

If you wait until after your full retirement age to claim Social Security retirement benefits, your benefit amounts will be permanently higher. Your benefit amount is increased by a certain percentage each year you wait up to age 70. Also, if you increase your retirement benefits by delaying your benefits claim until after full retirement age, after you die, your spouse's survivors benefits (see Chapter 5) will also be correspondingly higher. This is a particularly good strategy if, financially, you do not need your retirement benefits at full retirement age and you are in good health, expecting to live well past age 70, which means you are likely to collect your higher benefits for many years.

After age 70, there is no longer any increase and no reason to delay claiming benefits. This is true even if you keep working after you reach full retirement age, because reductions in Social Security benefits due to earned income end when you reach full retirement age. The amount of the yearly percentage increase in benefits depends on when you were born.

TIP

If you want to delay retirement benefits, claim them at full retirement age but "suspend" collecting them. To delay receiving retirement benefits to increase your benefits as shown on the chart below, technically you don't have to do anything when you reach full retirement age—you can just wait and claim your benefits whenever you decide to (up to age 70, after which there's no point in delaying). But because of two special Social Security rules described below, instead of waiting silently it is better if you contact Social Security when you reach full retirement age and claim your retirement benefits but "suspend" collecting them. This claim-and-suspend procedure allows your family to immediately collect dependents benefits, if any one of them is eligible. It also might allow you to collect back benefits if your circumstances change (we'll discuss this below).

Increase per Year in Benefits for Delayed Retirement

Year Born	Percentage Increase
1927–1928	4.0
1929–1930	4.5
1931–1932	5.0
1933–1934	5.5
1935–1936	6.0
1937–1938	6.5
1939–1940	7.0
1941–1942	7.5
1943 or later	8.0

 TIP

Everyone should claim some or all Medicare coverage at age 65.
Even if you do not claim Social Security retirement benefits when you turn
65, you are eligible for Medicare benefits and may want to sign up for some
or all of them. (Enrolling in Medicare does not affect your current or future
retirement benefits.) (See Chapter 12 for more information.)

"Suspending" Benefits Procedure for Delaying Retirement

You may be one of the many people who want to delay your retirement
claim until after you reach full retirement age because your benefits
will be permanently higher for each year you wait, up to age 70.
But what if you have a spouse, or a minor child, who qualifies for
dependents benefits? (A spouse can qualify as early as age 62, a child
can qualify up to age 18; see Chapter 4 for more information.)

Social Security rules do not allow an eligible dependent spouse or
child to collect dependents benefits until you actually claim your retirement benefits. Fortunately, a special rule allows you to claim your
retirement benefits at full retirement age, then immediately "suspend"
collecting those benefits. This allows your qualifying spouse or child
to claim his or her dependents benefits immediately (because officially

you have "claimed" your benefits), while you delay collecting your retirement benefits, which allows your ultimate retirement benefit amount to grow.

If you claim but suspend your own retirement benefit payments when you reach full retirement age, you can later choose to begin collecting them at any time simply by notifying Social Security. And once you reach age 70, there is no longer any reason to delay.

Reversing Suspension of Benefits and Collecting a Lump Sum

What happens if you delayed collecting retirement benefits until after full retirement age, but at some point before age 70, your finances suddenly change for the worse, or you become seriously ill and your life expectancy suddenly greatly shrinks? In such a situation, a special Social Security rule would allow you to "undo" your earlier decision to delay collecting benefits *if, and only if, you had claimed benefits at full retirement age but suspended collecting them.*

If you undo your decision to delay, the amount of your monthly benefit would permanently return to the amount it would have been at full retirement age, but you can then collect a lump sum equal to all the payments you would have received if you had actually begun collecting benefits at full retirement age.

For example, assume that your retirement benefits at full retirement age would have been $2,000 per month. And let's say you delayed collecting those benefits, intending to wait until age 70 to claim them, when they'd be around $2,700 per month. But then unexpectedly your other income drops sharply and your savings are eaten up (maybe by large medical bills), or perhaps your life expectancy is greatly reduced by an illness. In such a situation, you could contact Social Security, undo your suspended claim, and collect all your Social Security payments from the time you suspended them. You would be repaid at the monthly rate you would have collected at full retirement age (in our example, $2,000 per month). So, if you are age 68 when you undo your suspended benefits, and your full retirement age was 66, then you could collect a lump sum of $48,000 ($2,000 per month multiplied by 24 months). From that time on, your monthly benefits permanently would be $2,000 (plus increases for inflation).

The Amount of Your Retirement Check

Your Social Security retirement benefits depend on how much you earned in covered employment over all your working years. Social Security calculates your benefits based on the amounts in your highest-earning 35 years. Then it applies a set of formulas to these earnings; the exact figures depend on the year you were born.

Spouse's Benefits Do Not Affect Your Retirement Account

The amount of your retirement benefits is not affected by the fact that your spouse, or ex-spouse, is also collecting benefits. This is true whether your spouse collects his or her own retirement benefits or collects dependents benefits based on your work record. There is a limit on how much all your dependents may collect based on your work record (see Chapter 4), but this does not affect the amount you personally receive in retirement benefits.

Social Security's calculations are complex and the results are less than bountiful. For example, the average retirement benefit for someone who reaches full retirement age in 2015 is about $1,330 per month. The maximum retirement benefit for someone first claiming benefits in 2015 is about $2,660 per month. Once you claim your benefits, there is a small cost-of-living increase each year.

Under Social Security's benefit calculation system, the lower your average lifetime earnings, the higher a percentage of those earnings you'll receive in benefits. If your earnings have averaged in the middle range—the equivalent of around $30,000 to $40,000 in today's dollars—you can expect full retirement benefits of about 40% of your average earnings for the last few years before you reach full retirement age.

If your average earnings have been on the low side—under $30,000 a year in current dollars—then your benefits will be about 50% of your earnings in the years just before you claim retirement benefits.

If your earnings have always been at or near the maximum credited earnings for each year (see Chapter 1), then your retirement benefits will be about 20% of the maximum amount for the year in which you retire.

But these figures are just rough averages. To get a much more accurate estimate of what your retirement benefits will be, you can either phone Social Security at 800-772-1213 or use the online benefits estimator on the Social Security Administration website, at www.ssa. gov/estimator. This tool will provide you with an estimate of what your monthly retirement benefits would be if you claim benefits at age 62, at full retirement age, or at age 70. The actual amount you will receive in retirement benefits will depend on what your actual earnings are in the years between getting this estimate and claiming those benefits. So, the closer you are to actually claiming your retirement benefits, the more accurate this estimate will be.

Increases for Cost of Living

Whatever the amount of your Social Security retirement benefit, you will usually receive an automatic cost-of-living increase on January 1 of each year. This increase is tied to the rise in the Consumer Price Index: the cost of basic goods and services. In the late 1970s, this Consumer Price Index rose more than 10% each year, causing Social Security benefits to rise more than 10% per year. In the 1980s, however, the yearly cost-of-living increase began to drop. In some years, there is no cost of living increase at all. For 2015, the cost-of-living increase is 1.7%.

Increases If You Keep Working After Claiming Retirement Benefits

As explained above, the amount of your Social Security retirement benefits depends on your average qualifying income over your highest 35 years of lifetime earnings. But can your benefit amount go up if you continue to earn and pay Social Security taxes after you claim retirement benefits? The answer is yes. If, after you claim benefits, your earnings in any year raise your earnings average over your highest 35 years, Social Security will raise your retirement benefit amount accordingly. This is true whether you claimed benefits early, at full retirement age, or after full retirement age.

Reductions for Government Pensions

Many people have worked both at government agency jobs and at jobs covered by Social Security. And some have worked long enough in each that they have earned the right not only to Social Security retirement benefits, but also to a public employee retirement system pension.

Social Security calculates its benefits based on an average of earnings over 35 years. However, if you had many years in employment with low wages, Social Security will artificially adjust your benefits upward. Also, if you spent years in public employment, Social Security used to consider these as nonincome years, which made you eligible for the artificially raised retirement benefits.

Social Security has now decided that if you earned a government pension during those years, your artificially raised benefit amount was an unfair windfall to you. And so your benefits have been reduced.

Those Affected

If your age and work history fit certain categories, your Social Security check will be reduced by 10% to 35% because of this windfall. You may be affected by this reduction if you:

- were born in 1924 or later
- first became eligible for a government pension in 1986 or later, and
- worked fewer than 30 years at jobs covered by Social Security.

Those Not Affected

The windfall reduction does not affect you if you:

- only worked for an employer not covered by Social Security before 1957
- only earned a government pension based solely on work for the railroad, or
- were a federal government employee hired on January 1, 1984 or after.

> **CAUTION**
>
> **Government pensioners seeking spouse's benefits may face limits.** Another rule limits benefits to people who collect both Social Security benefits as the spouses of retired or deceased workers and public employment pensions based on their own work records. (See "Government Pension Offset" in Chapters 4 and 5 for details.)

Working After Claiming Early Retirement Benefits

Because Social Security retirement benefits plus savings and other investments are often not enough to live on comfortably, many people keep working for at least a few years after they claim Social Security retirement benefits. Other people keep their jobs or take new ones to stay active and involved in the world of work. If you keep working at a high enough salary, you may increase your lifetime earnings average, thereby slightly increasing your benefits for the years to come.

If you claim early retirement benefits and continue to work, be aware that the money you earn over a certain amount each year may reduce your Social Security retirement benefits (until you reach full retirement age). Such a reduction in benefits applies only to that year. It has no permanent effect on the amount of benefits you'll receive in future years.

Limits on Earned Income If Claiming Early Benefits

Until you reach full retirement age, Social Security will subtract money from your retirement check if you exceed a certain amount of earned income for the year. For the year 2015, this limit on earned income is $15,720 ($1,310 per month). The amount goes up each year. If you are collecting Social Security retirement benefits before full retirement age, your benefits are reduced by $1 for every $2 in any month you earn over the limit. Once you reach full retirement age, there is no limit on the amount of money you may earn and still receive your full Social Security retirement benefit.

EXAMPLE: Henry is considering claiming early retirement benefits this year, at age 64. Social Security calculates that if he does so, he'll receive $866 a month (which is about 13% less than if he waited until his full retirement age of 66). But Henry also intends to continue working part time, with an income that will be about $5,000 over the yearly limit on earned income. If he does claim the early benefits and makes that part-time income, Henry would lose one dollar out of two from the $5,000 he earns over the limit, which means $2,500 for the year, or $208 per month. Therefore, his $866 per month retirement benefit amount would be reduced to $658. So, by claiming early retirement and continuing to earn over the limit, Henry incurs a double penalty: His retirement benefits are permanently reduced by 13%, and he loses an additional amount every month (until he reaches full retirement age) to the extent he earns over the income limit.

The amounts of early retirement benefits you lose as a setoff against your earnings are not necessarily all gone forever. When you reach full retirement age, Social Security will recalculate upward the amount of your benefits to take into account the amounts you lost because of the earned income rule. The lost amounts will be made up only partially, however, a little bit each year. It will take up to 15 years to completely recoup your lost benefits. And remember, none of this readjustment will change the permanent percentage reduction in your benefits that was calculated when you claimed early retirement benefits (look again at the chart "Benefit Reductions for Early Retirement" earlier in this chapter).

TIP

You can collect retirement benefits plus unemployment benefits. As this chapter explains, you may continue to work even after you begin claiming your Social Security retirement benefits. If you are working and you lose your job, you may collect unemployment benefits (assuming you otherwise qualify for them) even though you are also collecting your Social Security retirement benefits.

Special Rule as You Approach Full Retirement Age

If you are already receiving your retirement benefits, a special higher earnings limit applies in the 12 months while you're approaching full retirement age. If you will reach full retirement age in 2015, you may earn up to $3,490 per month without losing any of your benefits. For every $3 you earn over that amount in any month, you will lose $1 in Social Security benefits. Beginning in the month you reach full retirement age, you become eligible to earn any amount without penalty.

Change in How You Report Earnings

The Social Security Administration bases its benefit calculations on earnings reported on W-2 forms and self-employment tax payments. Most individual benefit recipients are not required to send in an estimate of earnings

But the Social Security Administration does request earnings estimates from some beneficiaries: those with substantial self-employment income or whose reported earnings have varied widely from month to month, including people who work on commission. Toward the end of each year, Social Security sends those people a form asking for an earnings estimate for the following year. The agency uses the information to calculate benefits for the first months of the following year. It will then adjust the amounts, if necessary, after it receives actual W-2 or self-employment tax information in the current year.

Once a beneficiary reaches full retirement age, his or her income will no longer be checked. Because there is no Social Security limit on how much a person can earn after reaching full retirement age, there is nothing to report.

If you are self-employed, you may receive full benefits for any month during this first year in which you did not perform what Social Security considers substantial services. The usual test for substantial services is whether you worked in your business more than 45 hours during the month (or between 15 and 45 hours in a highly skilled occupation).

Only "Earned Income" Affects Your Benefits

The rule that reduces your early retirement benefits based on income over a certain yearly amount applies only to what Social Security considers "earned income." Basically, earned income means money you receive during the year for work you currently do. This rule favors the well-to-do who have significant income from sources other than current work.

Earned income does *not* include:

- interest on savings or investments
- capital gains (profits from the sale of stock, property, or other assets)
- IRA or 401(k) withdrawals
- insurance cash-ins
- rental income, or
- private pensions.

Also, money you receive from certain types of sources based on work you performed before you claimed retirement benefits—known as "special sources"—is not counted as earned income. These exempted amounts include:

- bonuses
- accumulated vacation pay or sick leave compensation
- private retirement fund payments
- deferred compensation
- accumulated commissions, and
- payments to the self-employed, for work performed before claiming retirement benefits, received more than one year after claiming benefits.

Social Security Disability Benefits

O ver eight million disabled workers and their families receive Social Security disability benefits. Many of these people developed their severe injuries or illnesses when they were not old enough to collect retirement benefits. Social Security disability benefits provided an answer.

If you find it very difficult to work because of a physical or emotional condition that is not likely to resolve itself within a year—and you are short of retirement age—read this chapter carefully. If you have enough work credits for your age, you may be eligible for monthly disability benefits. And if you are eligible to receive disability benefits, your spouse and minor or disabled children may also be eligible to collect benefits. (See Chapter 4 for more information about dependents benefits.)

Who Is Eligible

Social Security disability benefits are paid to workers and their families only when workers have enough work credits to qualify. Work credits for disability benefits are calculated in the same way as for retirement benefits, although the number of credits required to qualify for the disability program depends on a person's age. A person can earn up to four work credits per year, and anyone who works part time, even at a very low-paying job, easily accumulates them. (See Chapter 1 for a discussion of how work credits are earned.)

 RESOURCE

This chapter will introduce you to Social Security disability benefits. To learn more about disability benefits, including how to convince the Social Security Administration that a particular disability makes you unable to work, read *Nolo's Guide to Social Security Disability: Getting & Keeping Your Benefits*, by David A. Morton III, M.D. (Nolo). It includes details on whether you might qualify for benefits, how to apply, how to keep existing benefits, and how to work while you're still receiving benefits.

Work Credits Required

The number of work credits you'll need to qualify for disability benefits depends on your age when you become disabled.

The "Work Credits Required to Qualify for Disability Benefits" chart below provides a quick reference to see how many work credits you need to qualify for disability benefits.

There are also rules that make it easier for younger workers and people who become blind to qualify for disability benefits. (See "Young Workers" and "Blind Workers," below.)

Work Credits Required to Qualify for Disability Benefits	
If you became disabled at age:	You need this many work credits:
21 to 24	6
24 to 31	6-18
31 to 42	20
44	22
46	24
48	26
50	28
52	30
54	32
56	34
58	36
60	38
62 or older	40

Help From the Americans with Disabilities Act

A federal law, the Americans with Disabilities Act, or ADA, prohibits employment discrimination on the basis of a worker's disability. The ADA is intended to help people with disabilities who want to work but are frustrated by noncooperative employers.

In general, the ADA prohibits employers from discriminating against disabled people when hiring, promoting, and making other job decisions. It also requires employers to maintain a workplace that doesn't have substantial physical barriers to people with disabilities. Under the ADA, employers must make reasonable accommodations for qualified workers with disabilities, unless that would cause the employers undue hardship.

Unfortunately, the ADA is full of vague language. Disability rights advocates, lawyers, employers, and courts are still wrangling over precisely what terms like "reasonable accommodations" and "undue hardship" mean. And given the current antiregulation climate in government, it is not clear how strenuously the government or the courts will enforce the law. All in all, it is difficult to say how effective the law will be in the coming years in assisting people to keep working despite their disabilities.

For information about how the ADA is being enforced and where you can go for help in seeking its protection, contact the Office on the Americans with Disabilities Act in the Civil Rights Division of the U.S. Department of Justice at 800-514-0301 (voice) or 800-514-0383 (TDD). The Justice Department also has an ADA website at www.ada.gov. For help and referrals from an activist disabled citizens action group, contact the Center for Independent Living in Berkeley, California, at 510-841-4776 or 510-848-3101 (TTY), or see its website at www.cilberkeley.org.

Requirement of Recent Work

You must have earned at least 20 of the required work credits within the ten years just before you became disabled, unless you qualify under one of the special rules for young or blind disabled workers.

EXAMPLE: Monica worked for ten years before she had children, earning 40 work credits during that time. After her children were in high school, she went back to work. That was in 2010, and, at the end of 2014, she became disabled with a back injury.

Although she had more than the 40 total credits required for disability benefits, she could not collect them because she had only worked four years—earning 16 credits—within the ten previous years (2005 through 2015). She would need to work long enough to earn four more credits before she could qualify for disability benefits. In 2015, that means she would need to earn $4,880 during the year (four credits at $1,220 per credit) before she could qualify.

Young Workers

If you were disabled between the ages of 24 and 31, you need only half of the work credits you could have earned between age 21 and the time you became disabled. And if you were disabled before age 24, you would need only six credits in the three-year period immediately before you became disabled. These special rules exist because workers who become disabled at a young age obviously do not have the opportunity to acquire many work credits.

EXAMPLE: Boris became disabled at age 29. There were eight years between when he was age 21 and the time he became disabled. During those years he could have earned 32 work credits: four per year. Under the special rule for young workers, however, Boris needs only half, or 16 credits, to qualify for disability benefits.

Blind Workers

If you are disabled by blindness, you must have the same number of work credits as anyone else your age. However, you need not have earned your work credits within the years immediately preceding your disability, as required for other workers. Your work credits can be from any time.

For purposes of Social Security disability benefits, being blind generally means having no better than 20/200 vision in your better eye with glasses or other corrective lenses, or having a visual field of 20 degrees or less (or a combination of the two). (See "What Is a Disability?" below, for more information on blindness as a disability.)

Disabled Widows and Widowers

If you are a widow or widower age 50 or older and disabled, you may receive disability benefits even though you do not have enough work credits to qualify. The amount of these benefits depends entirely upon your deceased spouse's average earnings and work record. Because they are based on your spouse's work record, these benefits will end if you remarry before age 50.

You must meet a number of qualifications:
- You must be disabled as defined by Social Security rules. (See "What Is a Disability?" below, for more on these rules.)
- Your spouse, at death, must have been fully insured—meaning he or she had enough work credits to qualify for disability benefits based on his or her age.
- Your disability must have started no later than seven years after your spouse's death.
- If you already receive Social Security benefits as a surviving widow or widower with children, your disability must have begun no later than seven years after your child or children became adults, causing those benefits to end. (See Chapter 5.)
- If you divorced before your former spouse died, you will be eligible for these benefits only if the two of you were married for ten years or more.

What Is a Disability?

To receive Social Security disability benefits, you must have a physical or mental disability that both:

- is expected to last (or has lasted) at least one year, or to result in death, and
- prevents you from doing any "substantial gainful work."

Of course, several of the terms within these definitions are subject to different interpretations. This section explains some guidelines developed by Social Security and the courts regarding qualifications for disability.

Conditions That May Qualify

Social Security keeps a list of common conditions it considers disabling. (See "Listed Impairments," below.) And the medical community has a tendency to treat more seriously the things it can easily name. But every person's physical and mental state is different, and the human mind and body can be very complex. So you may well have a condition that prevents you from working but is difficult to get doctors to name and describe. Don't let that discourage you from filing for disability benefits.

The only absolute rule regarding disability is that your condition must be "medical," meaning that it can be discovered and verified by doctors. It does not have to be a simple condition that can be immediately given a name.

If you are considering making a claim for disability benefits, examine the requirement that the disability must prevent you from performing substantial gainful work, as described below. Discuss the matter thoroughly with your doctor or doctors.

If the people who have treated you for your condition do a good job of describing it, with the substantial gainful employment rule in mind, any physical or mental medical condition can qualify you for benefits if it is truly disabling. (How to organize and present your disability application is discussed in Chapter 8.)

Listed Impairments

To simplify the process of determining whether a disability makes a person eligible for benefits, Social Security has developed a list of common serious conditions that it considers disabling if your condition meets the criteria in the listing. If you prove, through medical records and doctors' reports, that you have one of the listed conditions—paralysis of both an arm and a leg, for example—Social Security will likely consider you eligible for benefits without making you prove that you cannot perform substantial gainful work. If you have one of the listed conditions, Social Security will simply assume that you are eligible.

The more common serious conditions that Social Security normally considers disabling are listed below. Every person's disability claim is considered individually, however, and having a condition on this list does not automatically qualify you for disability benefits. You must have medical verification—from a doctor or hospital that has treated you—of the condition that appears on the list and evidence that it meets the requirements of the "listing." If you do, your application for disability benefits is likely to be approved unless you have been working since you became disabled. If you have been working, Social Security will determine whether this work disqualifies you from getting disability or whether it can be considered an "unsuccessful work attempt."

A select few of the conditions Social Security lists as being disabilities include the following, simplified for our discussion:

- a disease of the heart, lung, or blood vessels resulting in a serious loss of heart or lung reserves as shown by X-ray, electrocardiogram, or other tests—and, in spite of medical treatment, causing breathlessness, pain, or fatigue
- severe arthritis causing recurrent inflammation, pain, stiffness, and deformity in major joints so that the ability to get about or use the hands is severely limited
- mental illness resulting in marked limiting of activities and interests, deterioration in personal habits, and seriously impaired ability to get along with other people, such that it prevents substantial gainful employment

- damage to the brain, or brain abnormality resulting in severe loss of judgment, intellect, orientation, or memory
- cancer that is progressive and has not been controlled or cured (though some cancers qualify at any stage)
- Acquired Immune Deficiency Syndrome (AIDS) or its related secondary diseases, causing an inability to perform substantial gainful employment
- a disease of the digestive system that results in severe malnutrition, weakness, and anemia
- loss of major function of both arms, both legs, or a leg and an arm
- serious loss of function of the kidneys, and
- total inability to speak.

The full listings are found in the Code of Federal Regulations (C.F.R.) Title 20, Part 404, Subpart P, Appendix 1. You can also find the listings on the Social Security website at www.ssa.gov.

Must Be Expected to Last One Year

No matter how seriously disabling a condition or an injury is, it will not make you eligible for disability benefits unless it has lasted, or is expected to last, one year. The disability will also qualify if it is expected to cause death within a year.

TIP

Apply for benefits upon diagnosis. Even though the disability must be expected to last at least a year, you do not have to wait for a year to apply for benefits. As soon as the condition is disabling and a doctor can predict that it is expected to last a year, you may qualify. (The application process is described in Chapter 8.)

EXAMPLE: Ladonna fell down some stairs and dislocated her hip. She was placed in a body cast and was told by her doctor to stay in bed for three to four weeks. The cast would stay on for four months. After that, Ladonna would need a cane for another two or three months. In six to nine months, she would be walking normally again, although a little bit more cautiously. She would be off work for a total of seven or eight months.

Despite the seriousness of her injury and her total inability to work while she recovered, Ladonna will probably not qualify for Social Security disability benefits. The reason is that her disability is not expected to last for a year. However, she might qualify for her company's disability benefits, if the company provides them, or for unemployment or state disability compensation through her state's employment or disability office.

If, after you begin receiving benefits, it turns out that your disability does not actually last a year, Social Security cannot ask for its money back. You are not penalized for recovering sooner than expected, as long as the original expectation that the disability would last a year was expressed in writing by your doctor and accepted by the Social Security review process (and there was no fraud involved).

EXAMPLE: Ravi had a stroke, leaving most of his left side paralyzed. He was unable to walk on his own, was unable to speak clearly, and needed help with most simple daily life tasks. He began physical and speech therapy, but his doctors predicted that he was unlikely to recover full use of his left arm and leg. He applied for disability benefits, and after waiting three months to see if Ravi's condition was likely to improve, Ravi was found eligible for disability benefits because his condition was totally disabling and it was not expected that within a year he would recover sufficiently to return to work. However, through hard work, Ravi recovered both his speech and enough of the use of his arm and leg to return to work in ten months.

Although his disability did not last the required year, Ravi was able to keep the disability payments he had already received because the doctors had expected that his condition would be totally disabling for at least a year and the Social Security disability review process had accepted that prognosis.

No Substantial Gainful Activity

To be eligible for Social Security disability benefits, you must be unable to perform any substantial gainful activity—generally considered to be any work from which you earn $1,090 (in 2015) per month or more.

In determining whether your condition prevents you from doing substantial gainful activity, Social Security will first consider whether it prevents you from doing the job you had when you became disabled, or the last job you had before becoming disabled. If your disability prevents you from performing your usual job, Social Security will next decide whether you are able to do any other kind of substantial gainful work—that is, any job in which you could earn $1,090 per month or more.

As part of this determination, Social Security considers your education, training, and work experience (vocational factors). For example, a highly trained professional, whose work does not require any physical exertion but which is highly compensated, may still be able to earn $1,090 a month despite a certain physical disability. However, someone whose entire working life has been in lower-skilled, lower-paying work that requires considerable physical labor might have a harder time earning $1,090 per month with exactly the same physical disability.

Age is also taken into consideration. Social Security realizes that it won't be committing to as great an outlay of money when it grants disability benefits to people nearing retirement age as it does to younger workers (older workers were on the brink of collecting retirement benefits anyway). For this reason, and because it is more difficult for older workers to find new employment or to retrain for other kinds of work, Social Security approves the disability claims of those over 50 more readily than those of younger workers.

In determining whether you can switch to a less demanding job, Social Security will assess whether you are able to perform any kind of work for pay existing anywhere in the economy, whether or not there are actually any such jobs available in the area in which you live. However, it is up to Social Security to prove that there is gainful employment you can perform, unless you fit into its grid of medical-vocational guidelines that specify when you are disabled.

Special Rules for Blindness

If your vision in your better eye is no better than 20/200 with correction, or if your peripheral field of vision is limited to 20 degrees or less, you are considered blind under Social Security disability rules. (There are a few other ways to qualify for disability for blindness as well.) Assuming that your work credits add up to the required amount for your age, you (and your family) can receive disability benefits.

Some blind persons are able to continue working, at least part time, while simultaneously collecting benefits. If you are blind you can earn up to $1,820 per month—the amount increases from year to year—before your job is considered substantial gainful work that would disqualify you from benefits.

Applying Protects Your Retirement Benefits

If you are legally blind and earning too much money to qualify for disability benefits, but also earning significantly less than before your blindness, you may want to apply for disability benefits. Even though you won't receive cash benefits, Social Security can put what is called a "disability freeze" on your earnings record to protect your overall average.

The amount of your retirement benefits, or of your disability benefits if you later qualify, is determined by your average income over the years. (See "Determining Your Benefit Amount" in Chapter 1 for further explanation.) If, because of your disability, you are now making considerably less than you were before, these lower earnings will pull your lifetime average income lower, resulting in a lower ultimate Social Security payment. This special disability freeze provision for blindness permits you to work without having your lower income figured into your lifetime average earnings.

If you are over 55 and blind, you can qualify for disability benefits even if you're still doing substantially gainful work. The key is to show that you are unable to perform work requiring skills or abilities comparable to those required by the work you did before you turned 55 or before you became blind, whichever was later. This level of performance is measured by whether you work at the kind of job you previously had and you earn more than $1,820 every month. If you earn that much occasionally but not every month, you can still qualify for benefits. Disability checks will be withheld, however, for any month in which you do perform substantial gainful work—that is, earn over $1,820.

Examples of Disability Determinations

The following examples help illustrate Social Security's reasoning in applying its guidelines and making disability determinations.

Unsuitability for Other Work

EXAMPLE: Arnold has been a longshoreman for most of his life. At age 58, his back has been getting progressively worse. His doctor told him that he could no longer do longshore work. The doctor also said that sitting for any length of time will aggravate the condition. Arnold applies for disability.

Because there is no question that Arnold's condition will last more than a year, Social Security will next ask whether it prevents Arnold from performing substantial gainful activity. Arnold's back prevents him not only from doing his regular job or other physical labor, but also from sitting for long periods of time. Unless Social Security can describe a job that requires neither heavy physical labor nor sitting, Arnold would probably get disability payments. Because Arnold has done physical labor all his life, he may not have the training, work experience, or education to do many other jobs. Considering his age and the difficulty finding any type of work for which he could be retrained, it is likely that Social Security would find him eligible for disability benefits.

Two Conditions Combined

EXAMPLE: Ernestine has been a music teacher for many years. She is now 60 years old and is losing her hearing. She has also developed phlebitis, which makes it difficult for her to walk very far or to stand for long periods of time. She has to elevate her legs for a while every few hours. When her hearing loss makes it impossible for her to continue teaching music, she applies for disability benefits.

The combination of her two conditions may make her unable to maintain any gainful employment. She would have to find a job that required neither good hearing nor standing, and permitted her to put her legs up for a half hour several times a day. Because such jobs are scarce, Social Security would very likely find Ernestine eligible for disability, particularly in light of her age.

Mild Disability

EXAMPLE: Rebecca is 52 and has an aortic aneurysm. Despite medication, she has intermittent fatigue and shortness of breath, especially at her job as a waitress. Her doctor says that her work is too physically demanding and stressful for her heart. Rebecca applies for disability benefits.

Although Rebecca's condition—aortic aneurysm—is on Social Security's listing of impairments, she is not automatically eligible for disability benefits. Her condition has to meet the criteria in the cardiovascular listing; in this case, an aneurysm must be dissecting (that is, separating from the wall of the artery).

If Rebecca's aneurysm is not dissecting, Social Security would assess her limitations to see if she could do some type of less demanding work. Even if Social Security found she could only do sedentary work, Social Security would probably find that she has job skills, such as dealing with the public and taking orders, that could be used at a desk job (called "transferable skills"). She would probably not be found disabled.

Amount of Disability Benefit Payments

Like other Social Security benefits, the amount of your actual disability check is determined by your age and your personal earnings record: your average earnings for all the years you have been working, not just the salary you were making most recently.

Disability benefits are also available for disabled workers' families (spouses and minor or disabled children). The maximum amount for worker and family combined is either 85% of what the disabled worker was earning before becoming disabled, or 150% of what the worker's individual benefit is, whichever is lower.

> EXAMPLE: Manu was making $3,200 a month when he became disabled at age 56. At that time, Manu's Social Security earnings record gives him an individual disability benefit of $900 a month. Manu's wife and teenage daughter are also eligible to collect dependents benefits. Their benefits would be the lower of 85% of Manu's $3,200 monthly salary, which comes out to $2,720, or 150% of what Manu's individual disability benefit ($900) would be, which comes out to $1,350. Manu's wife and daughter together would receive $1,350 a month, the lower of the two amounts.

Estimating Benefit Amounts

There is no simple formula for what your actual disability payments will be. Although some books and magazines print tidy charts matching age and income with disability benefit amounts, more often than not these charts mislead people, causing them to overestimate their benefits. The charts all base their figures on your current earnings and assume that you have had a consistent earning pattern during your entire working life. Most people, however, do not have such a perfect curve of earnings, so the estimates the charts give you are bound to be wrong.

You can get a general idea of disability benefits amounts by considering average payment and maximum amounts for 2015:

- Overall average monthly payment for disabled individual: $1,165
- Overall average monthly payment for disabled individual plus spouse and children: $1,976, and
- Maximum monthly payment for disabled individual: $2,663.

In addition, it can be helpful to look at averages based on income levels.

Estimated Disability Benefits for 2015

Average Annual Lifetime Income in Current Dollars	Monthly Benefits
$10,000 to $20,000	$550 to $825 (individual)
	$935 to $1,150 (couple or parent and child)
$20,000 to $30,000	$770 to $1,100 (individual)
	$1,210 to $1,650 (couple or parent and child)
$30,000 to $40,000	$1,100 to $1,980 (individual)
	$1,350 to $2,530 (couple or parent and child)
$40,000 and up	$1,500 to $2,600 (individual)
	$1,800 to $3,000 (couple or parent and child)

TIP

Check your eligibility for supplemental benefits. If you receive only a small disability benefit, and you have savings or other cash assets of less than $2,000 ($3,000 for couples), you may be eligible for Supplemental Security Income benefits (SSI) in addition to your Social Security disability benefits. (See Chapter 7 regarding SSI.)

Relying on general estimates of disability benefits makes little sense, however, because you can get a very accurate estimate, based on your exact earnings record, directly from Social Security. You can get this estimate when you apply for benefits or by going to http://ssa.gov/mystatement.

Cost-of-Living Increases

Monthly disability benefit amounts are based entirely on your personal earnings record, with no consideration given to the minimum amount you need to survive. Whatever your monthly amount, however, there is usually a yearly cost-of-living increase based on the rise in the Consumer Price Index; in recent years, the increase has been only 1% to 4%, and in some years, there is no cost-of-living increase at all.

CAUTION

Don't expect to start receiving disability benefits right away.
Applying for disability benefits and proving your disability can be a slow, sometimes difficult business. You need to organize your paperwork, have the cooperation of your doctors, and be patient and persistent. What to expect in the application process and how best to prepare for it are discussed in Chapter 8.

Collecting Additional Benefits

Because disability payments are often not enough to live on, it is important for you to collect all the other benefits to which you may be entitled. You may even want to try to supplement your income by working to the extent you can.

Disability and Earned Income

Your benefit check will not be reduced if you earn a small amount of income while collecting Social Security disability benefits. However, if you regularly earn enough income for your work to qualify as gainful employment, you might not be considered disabled any longer and your benefits could be cut off entirely.

Social Security usually permits you to earn up to about $1,090 a month—$1,820 if you are blind—before you will be considered to be performing substantial gainful work. Also, in deciding how much you are earning, Social Security is supposed to deduct from your income the amounts of any disability-related work expenses, including medical devices or equipment such as a wheelchair, attendant care, drugs, or services required for you to be able to work. It will be up to you to prove such expenses.

The $1,090 per month amount is not fixed. You cannot simply keep your income just below this level and expect that your disability benefits will automatically continue. Both your physical condition and the amount of your work will be reviewed periodically. (See "Continuing Eligibility Review," below, regarding periodic reviews.) This review will take into account the amount and regularity of your income, your work duties, the number of hours you work, and, if you are self-employed, the extent to which you run or manage your own business.

If you are working long hours or have significant work responsibility, particularly if you are in business for yourself, Social Security will look hard, during its review of your disability status, at whether the $1,090 income limit is a true measure of your work. If, for example, family members are suddenly earning quite a bit more than they used to from the business, Social Security may suspect that you are doing the work and simply paying them instead. Or, if you are not getting paid much but you are working long hours for a business in which you have an ownership interest, they may look more closely at whether you are still disabled.

Other Social Security Benefits

You are not permitted to collect more than one Social Security benefit—retirement, dependents, survivors, or disability—at a time. If you are eligible for more than one monthly benefit based either on your own work record or on that of a spouse or parent, you will receive the higher of the two benefit amounts to which you are entitled, but not both. Supplemental Security Income (SSI) is an exception; you may collect SSI in addition to any other Social Security benefit. (See Chapter 7 for more on SSI.)

Other Disability Benefits

You are permitted to collect Social Security disability benefits and, at the same time, private disability payments from an insurance policy or coverage from your employer. You may also receive veterans (VA) disability coverage at the same time as Social Security disability benefits. (See Chapter 11 for a full discussion of VA benefits.)

Workers' Compensation

You may collect workers' compensation benefits—payments for injuries suffered during the course of employment—at the same time as Social Security disability benefits. Workers' compensation benefits are paid only until you recover, or until your injuries are determined to be permanent, at which time you receive a lump sum compensation payment.

While you are receiving monthly workers' compensation payments, the total of your disability and workers' compensation payments cannot be greater than 80% of what your average wages were before you became disabled. If they are, your disability benefits or workers' comp benefits will be reduced so that the total of both benefits is 80% of your earnings before you became disabled. If you are still receiving Social Security disability benefits when your workers' compensation coverage runs out, you can again start receiving the full amount of your Social Security benefits.

> EXAMPLE: Maxine became disabled with a back condition while working as a gardener and earning $1,400 a month. Her Social Security disability benefits were $560 a month, and, because her disability was related to her job, she also received workers' compensation benefits of $625 a month. The total of the two benefits was more than 80% of her prior salary (the combined benefits of $560 and $625

total $1,185, and 80% of $1,400 is $1,120), so her disability benefits were reduced by the extra $65, down to $495 a month.

If Maxine was still disabled when her workers' compensation benefits ended, her Social Security disability benefits would go back up to $560 a month (plus whatever cost-of-living increases had been granted in the meantime).

Medicare

After you have been entitled to disability benefits for 24 months—and those months need not be consecutive—you become eligible for Medicare coverage. This is true even if you are not age 65, which is otherwise the standard age to qualify for Medicare. Medicare hospitalization coverage (Part A) is free. However, you must pay a monthly premium if you want to be covered by Medicare Part B medical insurance or by Part D for prescription drug costs. (See Chapter 12 for a full discussion of Medicare.)

Medicaid and SSI

If you have few or no assets—or your disability and the resulting medical costs deplete your assets and hamper your ability to earn income—you may qualify for Medicaid coverage. Medicaid is a program of government medical coverage available to people based on their low income and assets, excluding their home. You may be eligible for Medicaid coverage as soon as you qualify under its rules, without the 24-month wait Medicare requires. And even when you do qualify for Medicare, Medicaid can continue to pay medical bills that Medicare won't. (See Chapter 16 for a full discussion of Medicaid.)

If you qualify for Medicaid assistance, you may also qualify for cash payments from the SSI program, on top of your Social Security disability benefits. Like Medicaid, SSI is intended to assist people with low income and assets. (See Chapter 7 for more on SSI.)

Protecting Your Medicaid Eligibility

If your disability was caused by an accident that was someone else's fault, you may have a chunk of money coming to you as the result of an insurance claim or a lawsuit. Receiving that money, however, might disqualify you from Medicaid and eligibility for other benefits, which would mean you'd have to spend it all on future medical bills, with nothing left for other living expenses.

Federal law and the laws of many states address this problem by allowing you to set up a "special needs trust." This permits you to accept accident compensation without losing your Medicaid and other benefit eligibility. With such a trust, instead of the accident compensation going to you in a lump sum, it is held for you by a bank or similar institution and is used to pay only certain types of bills—usually medical and basic living expenses. If your situation requires a special needs trust, consult an experienced estate planning lawyer for help.

Continuing Eligibility Review

Eligibility for disability benefits is not necessarily permanent. Depending on the nature and severity of your condition, and on whether doctors expect it to improve, Social Security will periodically review your condition to determine whether you still qualify for benefits.

When Your Eligibility Will Be Reviewed

If, when you apply for disability benefits, your doctors and Social Security's medical experts expect that your condition will improve, your medical eligibility will be reviewed six to 18 months after you are approved for benefits. If improvement in your condition is theoretically possible but not predicted by the doctors, Social Security will review your eligibility approximately every three years. If your condition is not expected to improve after you apply, Social Security will review your case every five to seven years.

If at any point after you are receiving disability benefits, you earn a steady or frequent monthly income of close to $1,090 (in 2015) a month, Social Security may also call you in for a work review. The agency will determine whether you are actually able to perform substantial gainful employment for more than $1,090 per month. Social Security will also check to see whether you are arranging to be paid less than $1,090 per month by having someone close to you receive money for your work, or whether you are being paid in some way other than cash wages or salary.

If you are in a trial work period, however, your benefits will not be terminated if you are doing work over the limit (see below).

The Review Process

The first step in a review of your eligibility for disability benefits is a letter from Social Security. The notice will either include forms for you to fill out, instruct you to call Social Security, or will summon you to a local office for an interview. The subject of the interview will be your medical condition and any work you are doing. You should bring with you the names and addresses of the doctors, hospitals, and other medical providers you have seen since your original eligibility was established, or since your last review. You should also bring with you information about any income you are currently earning, if any—including where you work, how much you earn, and the person to contact at your place of employment.

The local Social Security office service worker will ask you about your condition and work, and will then refer your file to Disability Determination Services (DDS), the state agency that reviews all disability claims.

The DDS will obtain your current medical and employment records and may ask that you undergo a medical consultation or examination. The DDS will make a determination about your continued eligibility based on the medical records and reports and on your earned income. Unless your condition has substantially improved, or you have regularly been earning more than $1,090 per month, or you are found to be doing substantial gainful employment despite being paid less than $1,090 a month, your benefits will continue.

If your eligibility is terminated, you have a right to appeal that decision. (See Chapter 9 for a full discussion of the appeal process.) And if you lose your eligibility, benefits can continue for an adjustment period of up to three months while you look for work and wait for a paycheck.

Returning to Work

Most disabled people would rather work than not, and many try to find ways of working despite their disabling conditions. Social Security provides various forms of encouragement for people to return to work. For example, it ensures that people will continue to receive their disability benefits during time they spend testing the workday waters. And if, after returning to work, a person later finds that his or her disability makes the work too difficult, the person's disability benefits can be restarted quickly and easily.

Trial Work Period

Within any five-year period, you may try out some kind of work— and keep any income you earn—for up to nine months while still receiving full disability benefits. (Your medical condition must still qualify you as disabled during this trial period.) You may try one job for a month or two and, if it doesn't work out, attempt the same or another job sometime later—up to a total of nine months within any five-year period. These nine months do not have to be consecutive.

Any month in which you make more than $780 is considered one of the nine trial work months (so you could be doing trial work without even knowing it). If you are self-employed, any month in which you work 80 hours or more is considered a trial work month.

After you have worked for nine trial work months, your trial work period is over, and Social Security will assess whether you've been doing substantial gainful activity during this time. Generally, if you made over $1,090 on average, your disability benefits will be discontinued.

Extended Eligibility for Benefits

After you have worked for nine months—the trial work period—during a five-year span, Social Security gives you another 36-month period of eligibility during which you can continue to work without necessarily losing your eligibility for benefits. During this time, you will receive your full disability benefits for any month you do not have "substantial" earnings. Again, earnings of $1,090 per month are considered "substantial"; the amount is $1,820 if you are blind. You do not need to file a new application for benefits or go through any eligibility review.

The first time that you make substantial earnings during this "extended period of eligibility" (EPE), a grace period starts, during which you can receive your full benefits and keep the income you make from work. The grace period lasts three months.

Quick Restart of Benefits

What if you've finished your trial work period and EPE, your benefits have been stopped because you're working enough to bring in "substantial" earnings, but you again find yourself unable to work? In such a situation, Social Security makes it easy to restart your benefits. For five years after your disability benefits stop, called the "expedited reinstatement" period, you may get an immediate restart of benefits if you again are unable to work, so long as your inability to work is caused by the same disabling condition as before.

You need not file a new application for benefits, although you do need to file a simple form requesting the resumption of benefits. Social Security will again review your condition to determine whether you are disabled. However, your benefits should be restarted on the first of the month following your request, without waiting for the review to be completed.

> EXAMPLE: Roberta qualified for Social Security disability benefits because of a congenital back condition that worsened so much in her 30s that she could no longer work. After several years, however, a new surgical technique was developed that greatly improved Roberta's condition. Roberta returned to work part time and soon earned a "substantial" income. That meant she no longer qualified for disability benefits. Her back remained strong enough for her to work for two years, but then it began to deteriorate again. Within another six months, she found she could no longer work. Because Roberta's original disability was the same disability that caused her to stop working again within 60 months after she had returned to work, she regained her disability benefits within a month, simply by applying for reinstatement.

Continuing Medicare Coverage

If you became eligible for Medicare coverage because you qualified for disability benefits, you do not immediately lose that Medicare coverage once you return to work. After you return to "substantial" work for more than nine months, and therefore your disability benefits stop, your Medicare coverage continues for another 93 months. This is the period between the end of your grace period and the end of your expedited reinstatement period. During that time, your Medicare Part A coverage is free; you must pay the same premium for Medicare Part B as other Medicare beneficiaries.

Social Security Dependents Benefits

A retired or disabled worker with a family obviously needs more money than someone living alone—especially given that Social Security benefits currently average only about $1,300 per month. The situation is particularly acute when the retired or disabled worker was the family's primary breadwinner. Congress woke up to this reality in 1939, four years after it passed the original Social Security retirement law. It began providing dependents benefits to the spouse and minor children of a retired or disabled worker.

Who Is Eligible

Certain family members of a retired or disabled worker are eligible for monthly dependents benefits if the worker has enough work credits to qualify for, and has actually claimed, his or her own retirement or disability benefits. A qualifying divorced spouse need not wait until the ex-spouse worker actually claims retirement benefits (see "Effect of Marriage and Divorce," below).

What if a worker wants to delay collecting retirement benefits until after full retirement age (up to age 70), in order to increase the benefit amount? Do the dependents also have to wait before they can begin collecting their benefits? Fortunately, no. While a spouse and/or minor child who is eligible for dependents benefits cannot collect those dependents benefits unless the worker formally claims retirement benefits, a special Social Security rule allows them to claim their dependents benefits as soon as the worker reaches full retirement age, regardless of whether the worker actually collects retirement benefits then. However, to take advantage of this rule, the worker must formally claim retirement benefits at full retirement age but then "suspend" collecting those benefits (see Chapter 2). This claim-and-suspend procedure allows the worker's eligible dependents—spouse and/or minor child(ren)—to immediately collect dependents benefits.

The amount of benefits paid to dependents is determined by the worker's earnings record and, for a spouse, the age at which the dependent claims the benefit.

You don't have to actually depend on the worker for support in order to claim dependents benefits.

Individuals Who Qualify

To be entitled to benefits, you need to fit one of the following categories:

- a spouse age 62 or older
- a divorced spouse age 62 or older, with certain conditions (see "Effect of Marriage and Divorce," below)
- a spouse younger than 62 who is caring for the worker's child who is younger than 16 or became disabled before age 22
- unmarried children younger than 18 (although the mother's or father's benefit ends when the child turns 16, the child continues to receive benefits until age 18)
- unmarried children up to age 19 and still in high school
- unmarried children of any age if they were severely disabled before they reached age 22, for as long as they remain disabled (disability is defined by Social Security in the same way as for Supplementary Security Income benefits; see Chapter 7)
- unmarried stepchildren up to age 18 (19 if still in high school) if living with and under the care of the retired or disabled worker, or
- grandchildren of the worker, if they live with and are under the actual care of the worker and the parents are deceased or disabled, or if the grandparent has adopted them.

Effect of Marriage and Divorce

Couples come in many forms: companions who are not married; couples who are divorced; people who were divorced but have married again. Each status has some ramifications regarding dependents benefits.

Divorced Spouses

You are eligible for dependents benefits if both you and your former spouse have reached age 62 and your marriage lasted ten years, and you have been divorced two years. This two-year waiting period does not apply if your former spouse was already entitled to retirement benefits before the divorce.

You can collect benefits as soon as your former spouse is eligible for retirement benefits at age 62. He or she does not actually have to be collecting those benefits for you to collect your dependents benefits.

Remarried

If you are collecting dependents benefits on your former spouse's work record and then marry someone else, you lose your right to continue those benefits. However, you may be eligible to collect dependents benefits based on your new spouse's work record.

Try to Stretch the Marriage to Ten Years

If you are in the process of getting a divorce and you have been married almost ten years, try to have your spouse agree—or stall the legal paperwork long enough—that the divorce will not become final until after ten years. This is the amount of time you must have been married to get dependents benefits.

Under Social Security rules, the marriage is considered in effect until the divorce legally becomes final, even if you and your spouse have already been living apart, you have separated your property, and one of you has begun paying spousal or child support.

If you anticipate that your spouse might object to the delay, you might remind him or her that your dependents benefits have no effect on the amount he or she may collect in retirement benefits. Nor would your benefits affect the amount of dependents benefits a new spouse could collect in addition to yours.

If you divorce again, you can collect benefits again on your first former spouse's record, or on your second spouse's record if you were married for ten years the second time as well.

Whether your former spouse remarries does not affect your eligibility. Nor does your collecting dependents benefits through your former spouse affect his or her new spouse's right to collect benefits. And there is no reduction in either of your benefits because two spouses are collecting them.

Same-Sex Married Couples

A recent United States Supreme Court ruling overturned part of the federal Defense of Marriage Act, which had previously denied Social Security and other federal spousal benefits to same-sex spouses. The Social Security Administration (SSA) has yet to determine exactly how the court's ruling will apply to Social Security benefits for same-sex married couples. But it is most likely that if a same-sex married couple lives in a state that recognizes the couple's marriage as valid, then either spouse is eligible for Social Security dependents benefits based on the other spouse's earnings record. It may also be—though this has yet to be finally determined by SSA—that if the marriage was valid in the state where it was performed, benefits are available regardless of the state the spouse now resides in. Even if you have doubt about your status, SSA encourages you to apply for benefits.

Unmarried

For the most part, Social Security laws do not recognize the relationship between two adults who are not officially married. There are two exceptions.

First, if one person in an unmarried couple adopts the minor child of the other person, that child becomes eligible for dependents benefits based on the adoptive parent's work record. The other person in the couple does not, however, become eligible for Social Security benefits.

Second, if you live in a state that recognizes common law marriage and you qualify under that state's rules for such marriages, you may also qualify for dependents benefits. The states that recognize common law marriages are Alabama, Colorado, the District of Columbia, Iowa, Kansas, Montana, Oklahoma, Pennsylvania, Rhode Island, South Carolina, Texas, and Utah. Georgia, Idaho, and Pennsylvania recognize common law marriages that were formed before certain dates.

The qualifying rules for a common law marriage vary somewhat from state to state, but all require that you have lived together and have represented yourselves as married by such things as using the same name and owning property together.

Calculating Dependents Benefits

The amount of benefits available to a retired or disabled worker and his or her dependents is calculated based on the total number of people in the immediate family. Social Security figures that the economies of scale permit two to live more cheaply than one, three to live more cheaply than two, and so on. Therefore, the amount by which benefits increase with each additional dependent is smaller and smaller for each person added. (But don't worry, claiming dependents benefits won't reduce the primary worker's retirement or disability benefits.)

One Dependent

The basic Social Security benefit for one dependent, whether the dependent is a spouse, divorced spouse, or qualifying child, is 50% of the worker's retirement or disability benefit amount. If a divorced spouse and a new spouse both receive dependents benefits, each receives 50%.

The actual amount of your dependents benefit is based on the earnings record and timing of the retirement benefit claim of the worker on whom you are a dependent. Even if the worker has claimed retirement benefits at less than his or her full retirement age, dependents benefits will be based upon what the worker would have received at full retirement age.

Some workers delay claiming retirement benefits until after full retirement age, up to age 70, in order to receive higher benefits. If so, the worker's retirement benefits will be higher, but the dependent's benefits will not. Dependents benefits are based on what the worker would have received if he or she had claimed retirement benefits at full retirement age, not on the worker's higher delayed benefit amount. However, if you are the worker's spouse, the amount of your dependents benefits depends on your age when you first claim the benefits. The amount of a spouse's dependents benefits is permanently lower if he or she claims them between age 62 and his or her full retirement age. At each of the ages listed below, a dependent whose full retirement age is 66 receives a benefit as follows:

Dependent Spouse's Age	Percent of Worker's Benefit
62	35.0%
63	37.5%
64	41.7%
65	45.8%
Full Retirement Age	50.0%

The best way to find out the amount of retirement or disability benefits that you and your dependents are likely to receive is to review your official Social Security Statement (discussed in Chapter 1).

TIP

Dependent eligible for Medicare at age 65. At age 65, a spouse may be eligible for Medicare coverage based on the worker's earnings record, even if he or she does not have enough Medicare earnings to qualify on his or her own. In order for a spouse to qualify for Medicare on the worker's record, the worker must be at least age 62 and personally have sufficient work credits to qualify for Social Security benefits.

Family Benefits

If your family includes more than one dependent—a spouse and one or more children, or no spouse but two or more children—the benefits paid to the worker and the dependents will be calculated according to the "family benefit amount." This amount is less than the total would be if the worker's benefits and individual dependents benefits were paid separately without a family limit.

The maximum family benefit is 150% to 180% of the retired worker's benefits—the precise amount depends on a complicated Social Security formula—or 150% of a disabled worker's benefits. The retired or disabled worker collects 100% of his or her benefits, and the remaining 50% to 80% is divided equally among the dependents. This maximum family benefit does not apply to spouses when the spouse is collecting retirement benefits based on his and her own work record.

> EXAMPLE: Chiang-Fa is retired. Alone, he would be entitled to $900 per month in retirement benefits. He and his wife Yoka have a 17-year-old daughter. With no daughter, Yoka would be entitled to a $450-per-month dependents benefit—50% of Chiang-Fa's $900 retirement benefit.
>
> However, because his daughter is also eligible, the three of them together are limited to a maximum family benefit of 180% of Chiang-Fa's benefit, or $1,620. That amount would be divided as follows: Chiang-Fa, $900; Yoka and the daughter, each $360. Once the daughter reaches age 18, however, she is no longer eligible for dependents benefits, and Yoka would begin to get a full 50% dependents benefit of $450 per month.
>
> If Yoka is entitled to her own benefit (on her own work record), that could lower the portion of Yoka's benefit that counts toward the family maximum and raise the daughter's amount.

Eligibility for More Than One Benefit

Many people are not only eligible for their own Social Security retirement or disability benefits, but also for dependents benefits based on their spouses' work records. As with other Social Security benefits, you are not permitted to double up and collect both at the same time.

But do the math before you choose. If your own earnings record is low and your spouse's earnings record high, you may be entitled to higher benefits as a dependent than you would be by collecting your own retirement or disability benefits. You can choose either to wait to claim dependents benefits when your spouse claims retirement or disability, or to claim your own retirement benefits and then switch to higher dependents benefits when your spouse later claims retirement or becomes eligible for disability benefits. Options for claiming one benefit and later switching to another, and the best time to do so, are explained in Chapter 6.

Working While Receiving Benefits

Before full retirement age, a dependent's benefit will be reduced by $1 for every $2 of income earned over the yearly maximum. Once a dependent reaches full retirement age, benefits are not reduced, regardless of how much the dependent is earning. (See Chapter 2 for a full explanation of benefit reductions.)

If several dependents are receiving a combined family benefit amount, one dependent's earnings do not affect the amount the other family members receive.

> EXAMPLE: Grace and Omar and their teenage son receive a combined family retirement and dependents benefit of $1,650 a month. Grace and the son's portions of the family benefit are $350 each. Grace is offered a job for a year as a substitute teacher at a salary that is $6,000 over the yearly earnings limit for her age of 63 years old.
>
> Since Grace's benefit amount is reduced $1 for every $2 she earns over the limit, her benefit would be reduced by half ($1 out

of $2) of $6,000. That means a reduction of $3,000, or $250 per month. Since her own part of the family benefit is $350, that benefit would be reduced to $100 per month. The rest of the family's benefits—Omar's $950 per month and the son's $350—would not be affected.

Possible Perils of Claiming Early: Reduced Benefits

If you claim retirement benefits at less than full retirement age, your retirement benefits are reduced by between 0.5% and 0.55% per month before full retirement age, depending on the year you were born. (See Chapter 2 for details.) And if you later switch to dependents benefits, those benefits, too, will be reduced by the same amount as your retirement benefits were reduced.

EXAMPLE: Clare became eligible for retirement benefits of $500 per month at age 65. She decided to claim early retirement benefits at age 62—her full retirement amount of $500 less 20%, for a monthly sum of $400. When her husband turned 65, he applied for retirement benefits and received $1,200 per month. Clare switched from her own retirement claim to dependents benefits, which ordinarily would have been $600, or 50% of her husband's monthly amount. But because Clare had already taken 20% reduced retirement benefits at age 62, her dependents benefits were now reduced by 20%. She ended up getting $480 per month, instead of the $600 per month she would have received had she waited.

Government Pension Offset

Most people who work for a federal, state, or local government or for a public agency are now fully covered by the Social Security system, and are also eligible to receive benefits under their agency's public retirement system. But millions of people of retirement age worked for a branch of government—federal, state, or local—or for a public agency such as a school district, and earned a retirement pension under the Civil Service Retirement System (CSRS) or a similar pension system that paid no Social Security taxes. (See Chapter 10 for more information about the CSRS.) These people may be subject to a reduction in Social Security dependents benefits called the "government pension offset."

The government pension offset applies if you receive Social Security dependents or survivors benefits and also receive a retirement pension based on your own work record from the CSRS or another Civil Service pension system that did not contribute to Social Security. If you receive this type of pension, your Social Security dependents or survivors benefits are reduced dollar for dollar by two-thirds of the amount of your Civil Service pension.

The government pension offset does not apply, however, to people who are eligible to receive retirement benefits under the Federal Employees Retirement System (FERS), state or local Public Employees Retirement System (PERS), or any other public employment retirement system that does pay Social Security taxes.

In particular, the government pension offset does not apply to:

- federal employees who pay Social Security taxes on their earnings
- federal Civil Service Offset employees (employees who had at least five years of federal employment under the CSRS, then left federal employment but were rehired after December 31, 1983 following a break of a year or more)
- federal employees who switched from the CSRS to the FERS before July 1, 1988
- federal employees who switched from the CSRS to the FERS after June 30, 1988 and worked for at least five years under FERS
- people whose retirement benefit is based on work for a state or local government or public agency whose pension system paid Social Security taxes at the time they retired (and who retired before July 1, 2004), or
- people who retired on or after July 1, 2004, and whose retirement benefit is based on work for a state or local government or public agency whose pension system paid Social Security taxes during the last five years of employment.

If you are entitled to benefits under any CSRS pension, you should consider this government pension offset when calculating the amount of your combined CSRS retirement pension and Social Security dependents or survivors benefits. This rule may also affect which pension benefit you choose to collect.

EXAMPLE: Gina and her husband both worked for the government under the Civil Service Retirement System (CSRS). Her husband also worked in the private sector, paying Social Security taxes on his earnings. Gina is entitled to $500 per month in Social Security dependents benefits, based on her husband's private sector work record. She is also entitled to a CSRS pension of $400 per month (her own retirement pension) and a $250 per month CSRS dependents benefit based on her husband's work under the CSRS.

If Gina claims her own CSRS retirement pension, her Social Security dependents benefits would be reduced by two-thirds of her $400 pension (meaning the amount deducted from her Social Security benefit would be $266). If, instead, she claims her CSRS pension dependents benefits but not her own CSRS retirement pension, her Social Security dependents benefits are not affected. So, she is better off collecting her smaller CSRS dependents benefits ($250) plus her full Social Security dependents benefits ($500), for a total of $750 per month, than she would be collecting her own larger CSRS retirement benefit ($400) with her reduced Social Security dependents benefit amount ($500 – $266 offset = $234), for a total of only $634 a month.

TIP

Private employer pensions are not affected. The pension offset rule does not apply to pensions paid by private, as opposed to Civil Service Retirement System, employers. As far as Social Security is concerned, you are entitled to your full Social Security dependents benefits as well as your private pension benefits. However, your private pension plan may require that your pension benefits be reduced by the amount you receive from Social Security.

Social Security Survivors Benefits

The Social Security laws recognize that a worker's family may need financial support after the worker dies. Even if the surviving spouse has always worked, the loss of the deceased spouse's income will almost surely be an economic blow to the family. And if the surviving spouse did not work, or earned much less than the deceased spouse, the loss of the deceased worker's income can be financially devastating. Recognizing the family financial burden brought on by the loss of the primary earner, Social Security provides for what are called survivors benefits to be paid to the spouse and children of an eligible worker who has died.

Work Credits Required for Eligibility

Surviving family members of a deceased worker are entitled to survivors benefits only if the worker earned enough work credits before dying. Work credits are accumulated based on earnings from employment covered by Social Security. The required number of work credits depends on the worker's age at death. (See Chapter 1 for more on work credits.)

Number of Work Credits Required

The number of work credits on the worker's Social Security record needed for survivors to collect benefits is listed in the "Credits Required From Deceased's Work Record" chart, below.

Credits Earned Just Before Death

Even if the deceased worker did not have enough work credits according to the chart below, benefits may still be paid to the surviving spouse and children if the worker had at least one and one-half years of work in covered employment in the three years immediately before dying.

Credits Required From Deceased's Work Record	
If the worker died or became disabled at age:	Work credits needed:
28 or younger	6
30	8
32	10
34	12
36	14
38	16
40	18
42	20
44	22
46	24
48	26
50	28
52	30
54	32
56	34
58	36
60	38
62	40

Who Is Eligible

Provided the deceased worker had enough work credits, here's who can claim survivors benefits:

- a surviving spouse age 60 or older
- a divorced surviving spouse age 60 or older, if the marriage lasted at least ten years
- a surviving spouse younger than 60, if he or she is caring for the worker's child who is younger than 16 or disabled; this benefit, sometimes called the mother's benefit or father's benefit, may also be paid to a surviving divorced spouse

- a surviving spouse age 50 or older who becomes disabled within seven years of the worker's death or within seven years after mother's benefits or father's benefits end; if you were divorced, you can collect these disabled survivors benefits only if your marriage lasted at least ten years

Same-Sex Surviving Spouse

A recent Supreme Court ruling overturned part of the federal Defense of Marriage Act, which had denied Social Security and other federal spousal benefits to same-sex spouses. The Social Security Administration (SSA) has yet to determine exactly how this ruling will apply to Social Security survivors benefits for same-sex married couples. But it is most likely that if the surviving spouse of a same-sex married couple lives in a state that recognizes the couple's marriage as valid, that spouse is eligible for Social Security survivors benefits based on the deceased spouse's earnings record. It may also be—though this has yet to be finally determined by the SSA—that if the marriage was valid in the state where it was performed, benefits are available regardless of the state where the spouse now resides. Even if you have doubt about your status, the SSA encourages you to apply for benefits.

- unmarried children younger than 18; benefits may continue to age 19 if the child is still a full-time high school student
- unmarried children of any age who were severely disabled before age 22 and are still disabled, or
- one or both parents of the worker who are at least age 62 and who were dependent on the worker for at least one-half of their financial support. If an unmarried dependent parent remarries after the worker's death, the parent loses the survivors benefits.

Length of Marriage Rule

To collect benefits as a surviving spouse, you must have been married for at least the nine months before the worker's death. However, there are some exceptions to this rule. If you are the biological parent of a child with the worker, or you adopted the worker's child or adopted a child with the worker before the child was 18, the nine-month rule does not apply.

The rule is also waived if you were previously married to the same person and your first marriage lasted more than nine months. And the nine-month rule does not apply if the worker's death was the result of an accident, as opposed to illness, or occurred while he or she was on active military duty. There are a few other, rare exceptions as well.

Effect of Remarrying

One of the assumptions behind survivors benefits for spouses is that the majority of surviving spouses are women and that women are financially dependent on their husbands. Although things are changing, the fact that there are still fewer women than men in the workforce and that women still make less than 80 cents for every dollar men earn in wages in comparable jobs means this assumption isn't entirely out of date.

Another assumption is that if a surviving spouse—usually a woman—remarries, her need for survivors benefits will end, because there is a new spouse upon whom to depend financially. So a series of qualifying Social Security rules apply to collecting survivors benefits after remarriage:

- A widow or widower who remarries before age 60 loses the right to collect survivors benefits through the deceased spouse, even if he or she still cares for the former spouse's children. The children, however, remain eligible for benefits. (At age 62, the remarried spouse may be eligible for dependents benefits based on the new spouse's record.)

- If the widow or widower is over the age of 50 and disabled, getting remarried won't affect his or her benefits.
- A widow or widower who remarries after reaching age 60 does not lose survivors benefits from the deceased former spouse. However, he or she may want to transfer—at age 62 or later—to dependents benefits based on the new spouse's earnings record if that benefit would be higher than the survivors benefits.
- If you were divorced from your now-deceased former spouse, and the two of you had been married for at least ten years, you are eligible for survivors benefits even if you remarried before age 60 but are again widowed or divorced. After age 60, you may remarry without losing your survivors benefits.
- If you were divorced from your now-deceased spouse, you are over the age of 50, and you are disabled, getting remarried won't affect your benefits.

EXAMPLE: Akiko and Yosh were divorced ten years ago, after being married for 25 years. Three years ago, Yosh died. Akiko has a new sweetheart, Ben. They have been together for the past year and are now considering marriage. But Akiko is concerned about the effect their marriage would have on her right to collect Social Security survivors benefits. Akiko is 59, and next year she would be eligible for survivors benefits based on Yosh's work record because their marriage had lasted more than the required ten years.

If Akiko waits one more year, she and Ben can marry and she will still be able to collect survivors benefits based on Yosh's record. If she marries before reaching age 60, she will lose those benefits.

Amount of Survivors Benefits

Like all other Social Security benefits, the dollar amounts of survivors benefits are determined by the deceased worker's earnings record. In addition, the amount of the survivors benefit depends on whether and when the worker had claimed retirement benefits. If the worker had claimed Social Security retirement benefits before death, the amount of survivors benefits is equivalent to what the deceased worker was receiving. That is, if the worker claimed reduced retirement benefits before full retirement age, survivors benefits will be similarly reduced. On the other hand, if the worker waited until after full retirement age to claim benefits, and therefore got a higher benefit amount, the survivors benefits will be similarly higher. If the worker died before claiming retirement benefits, Social Security determines what the worker's retirement benefit would have been and bases the survivors benefits on that amount.

Percentage of Benefits Awarded

Exactly what percentage of the deceased worker's retirement benefit will be awarded to a survivor depends on whether you are the spouse or child of the deceased worker. Also, if you're a surviving spouse, the amount goes up or down depending on the age between 60 and "full benefits age" at which you first claim benefits. Full benefits age is set by Social Security based on the year of your birth; it parallels the full retirement age set for workers.

As with retirement benefits, the full benefits age will be going up in the coming years. The changes are shown on the following chart.

Surviving Spouse at Full Benefits Age

A surviving spouse who waits until the age at which he or she becomes eligible for full benefits to claim benefits will receive 100% of what the deceased worker's full retirement benefit would have been if the deceased worker died before claiming those benefits or if the worker claimed the benefits at full retirement age. If the deceased worker had claimed retirement benefits early or deferred payments until after full retirement age, the amount of the survivors benefits will be based on the level of benefits the worker was actually receiving (reduced for an early claim, increased for a delayed claim).

As with retirement benefits, the age at which a person may collect full survivors benefits is currently 66—but this will change for some people. For people born in 1940 or after, the survivors full benefits age is gradually rising, finally reaching age 67 for those who were born in 1962 or after.

Full Benefits Age for Widow(er)s

Birth Date	Full Benefits Age
1/1/40 or earlier	65 years
1/2/40–1/1/41	65 + 2 months
1/2/41–1/1/42	65 + 4 months
1/2/42–1/1/43	65 + 6 months
1/2/43–1/1/44	65 + 8 months
1/2/44–1/1/45	65 + 10 months
1/2/45–1/1/57	66 years
1/2/57–1/1/58	66 + 2 months
1/2/58–1/1/59	66 + 4 months
1/2/59–1/1/60	66 + 6 months
1/2/60–1/1/61	66 + 8 months
1/2/61–1/1/62	66 + 10 months
1/2/62 and later	67 years

Surviving Spouse Under Full Benefits Age

A surviving spouse at age 60 will receive 71.5% of what the worker would have been receiving (reduced if the worker claimed early benefits, enhanced if the worker delayed the claim until after full retirement age). Each year a surviving spouse delays claiming benefits after age 60, those benefits will rise 4.1% to 5.7% per year, depending on the year of birth, until the survivor reaches full benefits age. (See the "Full Benefits Age for Widow(er)s" chart, above.)

Delaying benefits may be a good idea for survivors who are under full retirement age and who are still working. (See "Working While Receiving Benefits," below, for more information.)

Surviving Spouse Caring for Child

A surviving spouse who is caring for the worker's child, if that child is younger than 16 or disabled, is eligible for benefits regardless of the surviving spouse's age. The amount of benefits will be 75% of what the worker's retirement benefits would have been.

Minor or Disabled Child

A surviving minor or disabled child receives 75% of what the worker's retirement benefits would have been. This is over and above what the parent receives. This amount is, however, subject to the per-family maximum discussed in "Surviving Spouse and Children Together," below.

Dependent Parent

A surviving parent who was dependent on his or her deceased son or daughter for at least half of his or her financial support may be eligible for 82.5% of what the deceased worker's retirement benefit would have been. If there are two surviving dependent parents, they each get 75%.

Surviving Spouse and Children Together

A surviving spouse and children together are not entitled to the full amount each would get alone. A maximum is placed on the total amount that one family can receive.

The family benefit limit is 150% to 180% of what the deceased worker's retirement benefits would have been. The benefits are divided equally among the surviving spouse and children.

Estimating Benefit Amounts

You can get a general idea of survivors benefit amounts by looking at these recent average figures:

- overall average monthly benefit for surviving spouse: $1,275, and
- overall average monthly benefit for surviving spouse with two children: $2,680.

In addition, it can be helpful to look at averages based on income levels.

Low Income

The survivor of a worker who had relatively low income most of his or her working life—less than $30,000 per year in current dollars—

will receive monthly benefits between $600 and $1,000. If both a surviving spouse and a minor child will be receiving benefits, the total for the two would be between about $1,000 and $1,500.

Moderate Income

The survivor of a worker who had a moderate annual income— around $30,000 to $40,000 in current terms—will receive between $1,000 and $1,500 per month. A surviving spouse and child would receive a total between about $1,500 and $2,000.

High Income

The survivor of a worker who averaged relatively high earnings— $40,000 per year or more in current dollars—can expect between $1,400 and $2,600 per month. The high earner's surviving spouse and child together would receive between $1,600 and $3,900.

Getting an Official Estimate

While a worker is alive, he or she can get a very accurate personal estimate of what his family members' survivors benefits are likely to be, directly from Social Security.

Eligibility for More Than One Benefit

Many surviving spouses are eligible for their own Social Security retirement or disability benefits, and also for benefits based on their spouses' work records. However, you are permitted to collect only one type of benefit. If your own earnings record is low and your deceased spouse's earnings record was high, you may be entitled to higher benefits as a surviving spouse than as a retired or disabled worker.

Even if you will ultimately be eligible for a higher retirement benefit after you turn age 62, you can claim survivors benefits as soon as you are eligible at age 60, and then switch to your own retirement benefits whenever they become higher than your survivors benefits. Claiming survivors benefits before you reach full retirement age does not reduce your own retirement benefit.

It also works in reverse: You can claim reduced early retirement benefits—between age 62 and full retirement age—on your own work record, and then switch to full survivors benefits at any later age if those benefits would be higher. Options for claiming one benefit and later switching to another, and the best time to do so, are explained in Chapter 6.

EXAMPLE: Francesca would be eligible for full retirement benefits of $600 per month at age 65, based on her own work record; at age 62, she is eligible for reduced retirement benefits of $480 per month. At age 65, she would also be eligible for a full survivors benefit of $800 per month based on her deceased husband's work record; at age 62, she is eligible for a reduced survivors benefit of $660 per month.

Francesca has two choices at age 62: She can claim her early retirement amount of $480 per month and then switch to full survivors benefits of $800 per month at age 65. Or she can claim her reduced survivors benefits of $660 per month at age 62 and collect that amount, plus cost-of-living increases, for the rest of her life. (She would not want to switch to full retirement benefits at age 65, because in her case they would be only $600 per month, less than her reduced survivors benefits.)

Francesca has to decide whether she can get along well enough with the $480-per-month retirement benefits she would receive for three years until she switched to her $800 survivors benefits. If she can manage, then waiting would be better in the long run. Waiting makes particularly good sense if she will also be working during those three years, because her benefits might be reduced because of her earnings.

One-Time Payment for Funeral or Burial Expenses

In addition to the monthly survivors benefits to which family members may be entitled, a family may also receive a one-time-only payment—currently $255—intended to defray funeral or burial expenses. A surviving spouse can claim the money if the couple was not divorced or legally separated at the time of death.

A divorced widow or widower can still collect the $255 if there is no surviving spouse and if he or she qualifies for the regular survivors benefits. Also, if there is no qualifying spouse, the sum may be paid to the surviving minor children, divided equally among them. You must file a claim for the death benefit at your local Social Security office within two years of the worker's death.

Working While Receiving Benefits

Many surviving spouses find that despite their survivors benefits, they also have to work to make ends meet. How much a surviving spouse earns, however, can affect the amount of benefits he or she receives.

The benefit for a surviving spouse who is less than full retirement age will be reduced by $1 for every $2 of income earned over the yearly maximum. Once a surviving spouse reaches full retirement age, there is no reduction in benefits, regardless of how much is earned. (See Chapter 2 for details.)

If a widow or widower and children are receiving a combined family benefit amount, the parent's earnings do not affect or lower the amount the children receive.

EXAMPLE: Manjusha and her teenage son receive a combined family survivors benefit of $1,500 a month, or $750 each. Manjusha is taking a job at a salary that is $6,000 over the yearly earnings limit.

Since Manjusha is 62, her benefit amount is reduced $1 for every $2 she earns over the limit. Her benefits would be reduced by half of $6,000, for a total reduction of $3,000, or $250 per month. Since Manjusha's part of the family benefit is $750, that benefit would be reduced to $500 per month. Her son's $750 would not be affected.

Government Pension Offset

If you worked enough years for a local, state, or federal government or public agency, you may be entitled to retirement benefits from that agency's pension system. You may also be entitled to Social Security survivors benefits based on your deceased spouse's work record. Most people don't have any problem collecting the full amount of both benefits. But people whose government agency work was more than 20 years ago may find themselves subject to a reduction in their survivors benefits. If your government agency work was under the Civil Service Retirement System (CSRS) or another pension system that did not pay into the Social Security system, collecting your own retirement pension may cause you to lose a substantial portion of your Social Security survivors benefits.

This government pension offset rule for Social Security survivors benefits is the same as for Social Security dependents benefits. For more information, see "Government Pension Offset" in Chapter 4.

This rule will not only affect how much your combined government pension and dependents benefits are, but it may also cause you to choose to collect your own Social Security retirement benefits, if you are eligible for them, rather than Social Security survivors benefits. The combination of your CSRS pension and your own Social Security retirement benefits may total a higher amount than your survivors benefits reduced by two-thirds of the amount of your pension.

EXAMPLE 1: Marta worked for a state government for a number of years, earning a CSRS pension of $690 per month. She is also entitled to a Social Security survivors benefit of $1,400 per month based on her late husband's work in the private sector, for which he and his employers paid Social Security taxes. Because of the public pension offset rule, however, Marta may not collect the full amount of both benefits. Her Social Security survivors benefit will be reduced by two thirds of the amount of her CSRS pension. So, she collects her $690 per month retirement benefit plus a $940 per month survivors benefit ($1,400 − $460 offset [which is two thirds of $690] = $940).

EXAMPLE 2: Alice is entitled to $500 per month in Social Security survivors benefits based on her deceased husband's nongovernment work record, for which he and his employer paid Social Security taxes. She is also entitled to both a CSRS pension of $400 per month and a $250 per month benefit as a widow based on her husband's public employee retirement record. Ordinarily, she would choose to claim her own CSRS pension rather than the lower public employee widow's benefit.

But her Social Security survivors benefits would be reduced by two-thirds of her CSRS pension ($400); if she claims CSRS pension dependents benefits, her Social Security amounts will not be reduced at all. She is better off collecting both her smaller CSRS pension dependents benefits ($250) and her full Social Security dependents benefits ($500) rather than her larger CSRS pension retirement benefit ($400) and the reduced Social Security amount which would result ($500 − $267 offset = $233).

The pension offset rule does not apply to pensions paid by private, nongovernmental employers. However, the rules of a few private pension plans provide that your pension benefits will be reduced by what you receive from Social Security. ●

When to Claim Social Security Benefits, and Which One to Claim

A s explained in Chapters 1 through 5, the age at which you claim Social Security retirement, dependents, or survivors benefits affects the monthly amount you receive—earlier claims (up to age 70) mean lower monthly benefits. In some situations, an early claim will also reduce how much you will receive if you later switch to a different benefit. Also, when you claim your benefits can affect how much your survivors collect. Altogether, the difference between filing a claim before or after full retirement age can be many thousands of dollars over your and your family's lifetime.

So, how do you choose the best time to claim a Social Security benefit? And which benefit should it be? There is no simple answer, but several factors may help you make a decision that best fits your personal situation. This chapter discusses the factors that apply to everyone, and then explains how specific situations—which depend on your family situation and work history—may present you with certain options.

Considerations for All Beneficiaries

You may claim your Social Security retirement or dependents benefits as early as age 62, or survivors benefits as early as age 60 (and sooner if you are disabled or caring for the deceased worker's child who is under age 16 or disabled; see Chapter 5). But the monthly amount you receive—for your lifetime—is reduced for every month before you reach full retirement age (66, for people born 1943–1954) that you claim these benefits. (See Chapter 2 to learn about full retirement age.) On the other hand, you can increase your retirement benefit amount for every year past full retirement age (up to age 70) that you wait to claim benefits. Also, by delaying retirement benefits, you increase the amount your surviving spouse can collect.

Your Lifetime Total: The Break-Even Point

Based on the way the Social Security system calculates benefits, if you claim benefits early but you live past a certain age—called your "break-even point"—you will wind up collecting less in total lifetime benefits than if you had waited to claim them at full retirement age. Similarly, if you wait until full retirement age to claim benefits, or delay them further, but do not live past your break-even point, you will have collected less in total lifetime benefits than if you had claimed benefits early.

Here's how these break-even points work.

Early claim break-even point. For people who claim benefits at age 62, their break-even point is between 75 and 76 years old (the exact point depends on your earnings record and the year you were born). That means, if you claim early benefits but live past that age, your total lifetime benefits will be less than if you had waited until full retirement age to claim them. The longer you live past the break-even point, the more you lose by having claimed early benefits. (Remember, though, that you might want to claim early benefits despite this, for other reasons discussed in this chapter.) Because average life expectancy for people age 62 is about 18 years for men and 21 years for women, most people will lose money over their lifetime if they claim benefits at age 62.

Delayed claim break-even point. For most people who delay claiming retirement benefits until age 70, their break-even point is about age 79. For people who live past that age and delayed benefits until age 70, total lifetime benefits will be more than if they had claimed them at full retirement age.

Your personal break-even point. Your personal break-even point may differ slightly from the figures above. Your actual break-even point will depend on a combination of factors, including your earnings record and when you were born. However, the figures above will give you a very close estimate. To get more specific information about your personal break-even point, you can call Social Security at 800-772-1213 and ask them to do the calculations for you, or go to the Social Security website's page "When To Start Receiving Retirement Benefits" at www.ssa.gov/pubs/EN-05-10147.html.

Factors to Consider

Many people jump at the chance to begin collecting benefits as early as possible, regardless of their break-even point. For some, claiming early benefits is a necessary, or at least sensible, financial choice. But for others, it may be a poor decision that can cost them many thousands of dollars over a lifetime. Before you decide whether to claim early benefits or to delay your claim, consider the following factors.

You Can Undo an Early Claim

Some people claim early benefits because they need the money immediately, but then their work situation changes. If, after claiming early benefits, you find new work, switch jobs, or get a pay raise, your new income could reduce your need for early benefits, or even wipe out those benefits entirely because of the earned income offset rule. (For more about this rule see "Continuing to Earn Before Full Retirement Age," below.)

If you find yourself in this situation, you're not stuck with the decision you made to claim early benefits. You have the following two options.

Suspend benefits. You can ask Social Security to suspend your benefits. This means your benefits will stop until you notify Social Security that you want your benefits to resume. While your benefits are suspended, your lifetime benefits will not suffer the monthly percentage reductions that would have occurred if you had continued to collect early benefits. When you resume collecting your benefits, Social Security will recalculate them, with a reduction based only on those months you actually collected early benefits.

Withdraw claim, repay benefits. Another option is to withdraw your benefit claim entirely, which allows you to start from scratch. This removes all early claim reductions from Social Security's calculation of your benefit amounts, meaning you will be able to claim your full benefit at full retirement age, or a greater amount if you delay your claim even further. The catch is that in order to start from scratch you have to repay Social Security the full amount of all benefits you have collected to date. To learn more about how to withdraw a claim, and what you will have to repay, see Social Security's online information "If You Change Your Mind" at www.socialsecurity.gov/retire2/withdrawal.htm.

Immediate Financial Need

You may be in a financial situation that leaves you no real choice—you need your Social Security benefits now, even though your monthly benefits will be lower than if you wait, and your total lifetime benefits will probably be lower. For many people in these difficult economic times, the extra income of even a substantially reduced Social Security benefit is what allows them to afford the bare essentials of daily life.

Even if you do not need your Social Security benefit to meet essential daily expenses, you may want to collect a reduced benefit early in order to have a little extra money to make yourself or your family more comfortable. Having the extra money to use now—to do things you might not otherwise be able to afford—may be worth the chance that you will collect less in benefits over your entire lifetime. For example, you might want to use the extra money to do some traveling that you could not otherwise afford or might not be physically able to do later. Or, you might want to use the money to offer financial help to your children or grandchildren at a time when they could really use it. If there is any reason why you feel that using the money now is important to you, you may want to claim benefits early even though in a purely financial sense it may not be the best decision. (If you are going to continue to work and earn, however, this might be a bad decision in any event—see "Continuing to Earn Before Full Retirement Age," below.)

Continuing to Earn Before Full Retirement Age

Even if you could really use your retirement benefits before you reach full retirement age, it may not make sense to claim them now if you are going to keep working and earning more than a very small income. As explained in Chapters 2, 4, and 5, a Social Security penalty takes $1 from your retirement, dependents, or survivors benefits for every $2 in income you earn (until you reach full retirement age) over a low, yearly limit. If you will be earning only a slight amount over the yearly limit, it may still make sense to claim early benefits if you immediately need the amount that would be left over after this offset deduction. But if you will be working and earning a substantial amount over the yearly limit, claiming your benefits early would be a double mistake: Your immediate benefits would be substantially reduced if not wiped out altogether by the $1-out-of-$2 earnings offset rule; and your lifetime benefits would be permanently lower because you claimed them early.

Life Expectancy

If a health condition makes it likely you will not have a long life (meaning not live past your mid-70s), then claiming early retirement benefits makes sense. You will get to use or save the money, even though it's a reduced amount, for however many years you live. If, instead, you wait until full retirement age to claim benefits, but die within a few years of receiving them, you will have received less in total lifetime benefits even though your monthly benefit amount will have been greater than if you had claimed early benefits.

If, on the other hand, you have no life-threatening medical conditions, your health is generally good, and you have a family history of relatively long life, you may want to delay claiming retirement benefits at least until, and perhaps even later than, full retirement age. With a long life expectancy (likely to live past your mid-70s), you are more likely to collect greater total lifetime benefits by delaying your benefits claim.

Availability of Other Benefits

Your eligibility for Social Security dependents (see Chapter 4) or survivors (see Chapter 5) benefits may allow you to delay claiming your own retirement benefits past full retirement age, making those retirement benefits higher than if you claim them earlier. Claiming early survivors benefits may be a good idea even if those benefit amounts are lower than your early retirement benefits. That's because in the long run, the yearly increase in your unclaimed retirement benefits can make up the difference between lower dependents or survivors benefits you claim now and what your present retirement benefits would be. The scenarios for claiming one benefit while delaying another are discussed in the following sections.

Considerations for Specific Situations

In addition to the factors that apply to everyone (discussed above), if you qualify for more than one type of Social Security benefit, you may want to delay claiming one benefit while you collect another type instead. How this works depends on your prior and current marital status and the benefit amounts available to you.

Dependent Children Can Change the Equation

Any decision about when to claim retirement benefits might be a bit different if you have a minor or disabled child who is eligible for dependents benefits (which would pay the child an additional 50% of your retirement benefits). Dependents benefits payable to a minor child last only until the child turns 18, so if your child is already close to that age, the extra benefits wouldn't last long and probably won't affect your decision one way or the other. If, on the other hand, you have a much younger child, the total benefits your child could collect until age 18 might make it worth claiming your retirement benefits earlier than you otherwise would.

Another possibility for a worker who reaches full retirement age and who has a minor child is to claim but suspend his or her retirement benefits. This allows the child to collect dependents benefits immediately while the worker's retirement benefit amount rises until he or she actually begins to collect it (see the section "Worker With Minor Child" at the end of this chapter).

Unmarried, Divorced, or Widowed

If you have never been married, or if you were married but are now divorced or widowed, the best time to claim benefits depends on which benefits you are eligible for, and whether you have dependents yourself.

With No Benefits From Anyone Else's Work Record

If you are not eligible for dependents or survivors benefits based on the work record of a prior spouse, you probably only need to consider the factors discussed in the previous sections—your immediate financial need, continuing work, and life expectancy—in deciding when to claim your retirement benefits.

With Other Benefits From a Former Spouse's Work Record

If you were married previously, you may be eligible for dependents or survivors benefits based on your former spouse's work record. (Remember, though, that if you are divorced, you must have been married for at least ten years to be eligible for dependents or survivors benefits. A divorced spouse can claim dependents benefits as soon as the former spouse reaches full retirement age, whether or not he or she actually claims retirement benefits then; see Chapter 4.) If either your dependents or survivors benefits are higher than your own retirement benefits, you can claim those instead of your own benefits. Whether and when to consider such benefit claims also depend on the following rules.

Dependents benefits. If you claim reduced dependents benefits before you reach full retirement age and then switch to your own retirement benefits later, the early dependents claim will also cause your retirement benefits to be reduced by the same percentage.

Survivors benefits. A wrinkle in the Social Security laws allows you to claim early retirement or survivors benefits and then switch to the other of these two benefits without the early claim reducing the new benefit amount. It can work in either of two ways:

- You can claim survivors benefits as early as age 60 (or earlier if you're disabled or caring for the deceased worker's child who is under age 16 or disabled; see Chapter 5). If you claim survivors benefits before full retirement age, your early claim reduces those survivors benefits but does not affect your own retirement benefits. Your retirement benefit will continue to grow (until you reach age 70) while you are collecting survivors benefits. At any point, you can switch to your own retirement benefits. Given this rule, even if your survivors benefits are slightly smaller than your retirement benefits, you might want to claim those smaller benefits for several years while your retirement amount grows.

- You can claim your own retirement benefits before you reach full retirement age even if your survivors benefits would be larger. Why? Because your early retirement benefits claim will not affect your later survivors benefits, which can grow if you delay claiming them. So, you can first take your reduced retirement benefits without affecting your survivors benefits. When you switch to the survivors benefits later, they will be higher for the rest of your life.

Married Couples

The rules for married couples allow for some manipulations that can mean higher lifetime benefits for one or both spouses.

If Only One Spouse Is Eligible for Retirement Benefits

Although their numbers are shrinking rapidly, there are still many married women who did not do enough paid work outside the home during their lifetime to have earned Social Security retirement benefits. (This happens with men, too, of course; but the number of men in this situation is so small that the discussion here will assume a no-retirement-benefit wife/retirement-benefit husband example.)

The wife in this circumstance is eligible for dependents benefits only when her husband claims retirement benefits, and survivors benefits when the husband dies. If she claims dependents or survivors benefits before her full retirement age, she gets a reduced benefit.

The husband, in this case, is eligible only for his own retirement benefits. He would have no dependents benefits based on his wife's work record, and no survivors benefits if she died before him.

"Claim and suspend" is a Social Security strategy that can mean higher benefits. In addition to reductions in benefits if they make early claims, a married couple with only one retirement benefit is faced with two Social Security rules that together might seem to make a difficult choice for the couple:

- If the husband delays his retirement benefits claim until after full retirement age (up to age 70), both his retirement benefits and the wife's survivors benefits (if she outlives him) will go up.
- The wife cannot claim dependents benefits (the spousal benefit) until the husband claims his retirement benefits.

What would be a tough choice between these two approaches has been eliminated by a special claim-and-suspend rule enacted by Congress in 2000. Now, the husband can claim his retirement benefits at full retirement age, which allows the wife to begin collecting dependents benefits (if she's at least age 62 or caring for their minor or disabled child). The husband can then immediately "suspend" his retirement benefits, meaning that he does not actually collect them. In return, his benefits will continue to grow (up to age 70) until he "unsuspends" and actually begins collecting them. Also, for the entire time his retirement benefits are suspended and growing, his wife's potential survivors benefits are also growing.

Both Spouses Eligible for Their Own Retirement Benefits

In most couples now reaching retirement age, both husband and wife have earned Social Security retirement benefits. That means that each one is also entitled to dependents (and, eventually, survivors) benefits based on the other spouse's work record. At any time after each one reaches age 62, he or she can claim retirement benefits. As soon as one claims retirement benefits, the other (once reaching age 62) can claim dependents benefits (the spousal benefit). And when one spouse dies, the other can claim survivors benefits, as early as age 60 (or earlier if disabled, or if caring for the deceased spouse's minor or disabled child).

All this operates, though, under one basic principle: You can claim only one benefit at a time. Most people simply claim the highest benefit currently available to them. But that's not always the best way to maximize benefits. Following is a look at the rules at work in this situation, along with some options that might allow you to get higher joint lifetime benefits:

- **Claim and suspend retirement benefits.** One spouse's dependents benefits are up to 50% of the other spouse's full retirement benefits. For many people, dependents benefits are higher than their own retirement benefits. This is most often the case for women, who may have worked less outside the home and tend to be paid less than men even for similar work.

If a spouse who was a higher earner waits until after full retirement age to claim retirement benefits, those benefits will increase up to age 70. But the lower-earner spouse cannot claim dependents benefits until the other spouse claims retirement benefits; and dependents benefits can climb no higher than 50% of the retirement spouse's benefits at full retirement age. In other words, there is no increase in dependents benefits if the high-earner spouse delays claiming retirement benefits past full retirement age.

A special Social Security regulation, called claim and suspend, gives people a way around these two counteracting rules. It lets the higher-earning spouse claim retirement benefits at full retirement age—which allows the other spouse to claim dependents benefits—and then permits the higher-earning spouse to "suspend" the retirement benefits claim. While the retirement benefits are suspended, the other spouse can collect dependents benefits; at the same time, the higher-earning spouse's retirement benefits continue to grow (up to age 70) until he "unsuspends" and actually collects them. This also has the benefit of increasing survivors benefits if the higher-earning spouse dies first.

- **Claim lower dependents benefits at full retirement age, allowing retirement benefits to grow.** At full retirement age, a spouse can claim either full retirement or full dependents benefits (if the other spouse has claimed retirement benefits). Usually, people simply claim the higher of the two. But that's not always the best decision. If the amount of your dependents benefits (spousal benefit) is not too much lower than your retirement benefits would be, it might make good financial sense for you to file what's sometimes called a "restricted application" that claims only dependents benefits, which allows your retirement benefits to grow. You can later switch to your own retirement benefits, which will be 8% higher—and will remain so for the rest of your life— for each year you delayed past full retirement age (up to age 70).

- **Claim early retirement or dependents benefits, then switch to survivors benefits.** At age 62, a spouse may be reluctant to claim reduced retirement or dependents benefits because those reductions are permanent. Plus, an early claim of either of those benefits permanently reduces the other one, too. But the same is not true for survivors benefits; claiming your own early retirement or dependents benefits does not affect the amount of your survivors benefits (based on your spouse's record). (Though if your spouse claims early retirement benefits, your eventual survivors benefit will be reduced.) So, if you have a considerably older spouse who has a higher earnings record, or your higher-earning spouse is in poor health, you might want to claim your early retirement or dependents benefits (whichever is higher), relying on the fact that you will be able to switch to full survivors benefits in the not-too-distant future.

Reminder: Early Retirement or Dependents Claim Means the Other Benefit Is Reduced, Too

You are eligible for a reduced retirement benefit at age 62. If you claim retirement benefits at any time before you reach full retirement age, that early claim permanently reduces those benefits by 0.52% per month (up to full retirement age). The same is true for dependents benefits: if you claim dependents benefits between age 62 and full retirement age, those benefits are permanently reduced by 0.52% per month.

Many people don't realize, though, that claiming either early retirement or early dependents benefits also permanently reduces that other benefit for you. You cannot claim early retirement benefits and then switch to full dependents benefits, or claim early dependents benefits and then switch to full retirement benefits. As soon as you claim one early, the other one is also reduced by the same percentage. Note, however, that your claiming early retirement benefits does not reduce the amount of your spouse's or child's dependents benefit amount. Nor does your early retirement benefits claim affect the amount of your survivors benefits based on your spouse's work record.

Worker With Minor Child

A worker approaching full retirement age may want to delay claiming his or her retirement benefits for a year or more, up to age 70, to get the benefit of a permanently higher retirement benefit amount, and also a higher amount for his or her surviving spouse. But if the worker has a minor child, the child would be eligible for dependents benefits as soon as the worker claims retirement benefits. This seems to present a conflict: either wait to claim and therefore get higher delayed retirement benefits but no dependents benefits for the child, or get dependents benefits now for the minor child but lose out on the higher delayed retirement benefits. Fortunately, the "keep your cake and eat it too" solution of claim and suspend allows the worker who has reached full retirement age to claim his or her retirement benefits but suspend collecting those benefits. The claim allows the minor child to begin collecting dependents benefits immediately, while suspending collection of the worker's own benefits allows those benefits to increase for every year the worker waits to claim them, up to age 70. ●

Supplemental Security Income

Over eight million people receive some Supplemental Security Income, or SSI, benefits. SSI is a program jointly operated by the federal and state governments and administered by the Social Security Administration. SSI is intended to guarantee a minimum level of income to financially hard-pressed older, blind, and disabled people.

SSI eligibility is based on your age or disability and on financial need as determined by both your income and your assets. SSI benefits do not depend on how long you have worked, or on how much you have paid into the Social Security system.

You must be quite financially needy to qualify for SSI payments. Indeed, your income and assets must be so low that many people with no income other than their Social Security retirement benefits are not eligible for SSI. Others whose Social Security retirement benefit is very low may receive a small SSI payment.

Nevertheless, if after reviewing the rules explained in this chapter, you think you may be close to meeting the requirements for SSI eligibility, it will be worth your while to apply for it. If you qualify for SSI, you may also be eligible for Medicaid (discussed in Chapter 16) and food stamps, as well as free rehabilitation and home care programs, should you need them.

Who Is Eligible

You must meet four basic requirements to be eligible for SSI cash benefits:

- You must be 65 or older, or blind or disabled.
- If you're a new applicant for SSI benefits, you must be a citizen of the United States, or meet strict requirements for longtime residency, military service, or political asylum or refugee status.
- Some legal permanent residents of the United States may be eligible for SSI benefits if they are blind or disabled.
- Your monthly income must be less than a certain minimum amount established by the state in which you live.
- Your assets must be worth less than $2,000, or $3,000 for a couple, although certain items are exempted from this amount, including your car and home.

TIP

The rules for each of these requirements are more complicated than they first appear. But the complications almost always make it easier for you to qualify for SSI benefits than you might first imagine. Generally speaking, you are permitted to have more income and assets than the initial figures indicate.

Blind or Disabled

If you are younger than 65, you can qualify for SSI payments if you are blind or disabled.

Basically, you are considered blind if your vision is no better than 20/200, or your field of vision is limited to 20 degrees or less, even with corrective lenses.

You are considered disabled if you have a physical or mental impairment that prevents you from doing any substantial work and that is expected to last at least 12 months, or to result in death. This definition of disabled is the same as the test used for Social Security disability benefits. But unlike the Social Security disability program, which looks only at the income you currently earn in order to determine whether you are doing substantial work, SSI looks at income from all sources, and measures that income in a more complicated way.

Citizens or Longtime Residents

SSI benefits are generally available only to U.S. citizens and longtime legal residents. Noncitizens must fall within one of the narrow categories described below.

The restrictions hit some of the country's neediest people the hardest. These are people, often elderly, who have lawfully immigrated to this country to join their children or siblings, only to be met here by joblessness and poverty.

As a noncitizen of the United States, you qualify for federal SSI benefits only if one of the following applies:

- You have a legal right to live in the United States and you were already receiving SSI benefits on August 22, 1996.

- You were legally living in the United States on August 22, 1996, and you are now blind or disabled.
- You are a lawful permanent resident of the United States (a green card holder) and you or your spouse have worked for at least ten years in this country, having paid at least the minimum Social Security taxes to qualify for 40 quarters of work credits (see Chapter 1 for more information about work credits).
- You are a veteran (honorably discharged) or active duty member of the U.S. Armed Forces, or the spouse or child of one.
- You have been granted political asylum or refugee status; however, your benefits in this situation will last for only seven years after you have been admitted to the country.

RESOURCE

For a more detailed discussion of immigrants' eligibility for SSI: See the National Immigration Law Center website at www.nilc.org or contact their Los Angeles office at 213-639-3900.

State Benefits May Be Available

Nondisabled noncitizens who were in the United States but not receiving SSI benefits as of August 22, 1996 are generally not eligible for federal SSI benefits. However, if you fall into this category but you have now reached age 65, your state might provide you with state supplement benefits as well as food stamps. You may also be eligible if you arrived in the United States after August 22, 1996 but your immigration sponsor has since died or become disabled. If you are in one of these categories, apply for both federal and state SSI assistance; you may be entitled to state benefits even if you are denied federal SSI.

Income Limits

To figure out whether your income is low enough to qualify for SSI, you first need to understand that there are actually two SSI payments:

- the basic federal SSI payment, and
- a supplemental SSI payment in some states. Most states pay an additional amount over and above the federal benefit, and some of these states pay it alone if you qualify for it, even if you do not qualify for the federal payment.

Not all your income is counted when deciding whether you qualify for SSI. In fact, more than half of your earned income— wages and self-employment income—is not counted. And even though you may have income over the allowable maximum for federal SSI payments, you might still qualify for your state's supplemental payment. A few states set a higher income limit than the federal SSI program does, making it easier to qualify for those states' supplemental payment than for the federal one. (See "Benefit Amounts," below.)

The federal SSI limit on counted income is about $735 per month for an individual, or about $1,100 per month for a couple. The exact figure varies from state to state. In many states, however, you might qualify for the state's SSI supplemental payment—as well as Medicaid, food stamps, and other assistance—even if your counted income was too high to qualify for federal SSI.

Income That Is Counted

In general, half of any income you earn in wages or self-employment plus any money you receive from investments, pensions, annuities, royalties, gifts, rents, or interest on savings is counted toward the SSI limits. Social Security benefits are also considered counted income. In addition, if you receive free housing from friends or relatives, SSI may attribute some value to that housing. (See "Reductions to Benefits," below, regarding these limits on outside support.)

Income That Is Not Counted

Some specific amounts of money and support are not counted in determining whether you need SSI benefits.

SSI will not count:

- the first $20 per month you receive from any source—except other public assistance based on need, such as General Assistance

- the first $65 per month of your earned income—wages or self-employment
- one-half of all your earned income over $65 a month
- irregular or infrequent earned income—such as from a one-time-only job—if such income is not more than $10 a month
- irregular or infrequent unearned income—such as a gift or dividend on an investment—up to $20 per month
- food stamps, energy assistance, or housing assistance from a federal housing program run by a state or local government agency
- some work-related expenses for blind or disabled people that are paid for through public assistance, or
- some other types of one-time payments, such as tax refunds, reimbursement for financial losses such as insurance payments for medical bills, or compensation for injury to you or your property.

Differences in Local Rules

Keeping in mind that different income limits apply in various states, one general suggestion applies to everyone: If you are age 65, blind, or disabled, and you are living on a small fixed income, and you have relatively few assets, apply for SSI benefits. The local Social Security or social welfare office may consider certain income differently than you do, and you may be pleasantly surprised to gain some help from SSI.

EXAMPLE: Carmela receives Social Security survivors benefits of $310 a month and a $40-per-month private pension payment, for a total of $350 in regular unearned income. She also receives a quarterly dividend check; the most recent was $15.

The dividend check would not be counted at all, because it is infrequent income less than $20. The first $20 of income from any source is not counted, so the $350 total of unearned income would be reduced to $330 of countable income.

Carmela also earns $210 a month doing part-time work. Since the first $65 a month of earned income is not counted, her earned income amount would be reduced to $145; and since one-half of all earned income over $65 a month is not counted, half of $80 ($145 – $65) would not be considered for SSI purposes.

This leaves Carmela with $105 countable earned income to be added to the $330 countable unearned income for the month, for a total of $435 countable income. Since this amount is under the basic SSI qualifying limit of $721 per month, Carmela would be eligible for the basic federal SSI payment. Because Carmela lives in New York where there is a state supplemental benefit, she may be eligible for that amount as well. (See "States With Federally Administered Supplements," below.)

Asset Limits

In addition to the limits on your income, SSI rules limit the amount of assets and other resources you may have and still qualify. The general limit is $2,000 in assets for an individual, $3,000 for a married couple living together. But as with the rules regarding income, people are actually allowed more assets than these figures seem to indicate.

Assets That Are Counted

The assets or resources that are counted by SSI include money in the bank, investments of any kind, real estate other than a primary residence, and personal property and household goods over certain limits.

SSI also counts any money or property in which you have an interest, even if you are not the sole owner. If you have a joint bank account with someone, or hold any property in joint tenancy with someone else, SSI will consider that you own the entire account or property, because you have access to all of it. If you have only a partial interest in some property—for example, an ownership interest in a family home along with other family members—SSI will determine how much your individual ownership portion is worth and count that as an asset.

Assets That Are Not Counted

You are allowed to have more property of value than the $2,000 and $3,000 limits first seem to indicate. Several important categories of assets are not counted in determining your eligibility for SSI benefits. They include:

- your home and the land it sits on, regardless of value, as long as you live in it
- one automobile, regardless of market value
- your personal property and household goods—such as clothing, furniture, appliances, tools, sporting goods, and hobby or craft material—up to a total current value of $2,000; the value is not judged by what the articles cost new, but by what you could sell them for now, less the amounts you still owe on them
- wedding and engagement rings, regardless of value
- property needed for medical reasons, such as wheelchairs, hospital beds, and prosthetics
- property essential to "self-support"—such as tools and machines used in your trade—up to a value of $6,000
- life insurance policies with a total face value of $1,500 or less per person, and term life insurance policies with no cash surrender value, and
- burial spaces for you and your spouse, plus a specially earmarked fund of up to $1,500 for funeral and burial expenses.

EXAMPLE: Rose and Peter are living on Peter's Social Security retirement benefits and on Rose's pension. They qualify under SSI income limits, and have the following assets: their home; a five-year-old car; $1,500 in savings; stocks worth $500; kitchen appliances worth about $300; a TV worth about $100; a stereo worth perhaps $150; Peter's carpentry tools, worth about $500; and Rose's jewelry, which, aside from her wedding band, is worth about $200.

Despite the fact Rose and Peter's house is now worth $120,000, it is not counted as an asset. The value of their car is not counted at all. Their personal property and household goods add up to about $1,350, but none of it will be counted because this is within the permissible amounts for personal property.

Their total counted assets would be their savings and stocks worth about $2,000. Since the SSI limit on resources is $3,000 for a couple, Rose and Peter would qualify for SSI benefits.

Selling or Spending Assets

Even if your countable assets appear to be over the limit, it may still be possible for you to qualify to receive some SSI benefits. You may begin to receive SSI payments if you sell or spend enough property to come under the limits within a certain time period. That time period begins when you apply for benefits and runs six months for real estate and three months for personal property and liquid assets.

However, the sale or transfer must be a real one. Simply transferring title on the property to someone else while you keep control or use of it is not enough; neither is selling something for a small token amount.

EXAMPLE: Mariana applies for SSI benefits when she has more than $5,000 in the bank. She is told that she will not be immediately eligible for benefits unless that amount is reduced to $2,000 within the next three months. Mariana had always planned to be buried near her deceased husband, but never got around to making the arrangements. She now buys a burial space for $2,000 in the same cemetery as her husband. Then she puts $1,000 in a special account to cover her funeral expenses. Since funeral and burial amounts are not counted as assets under SSI rules, and her assets are now down to $2,000 (within three months of her application for SSI), she will begin receiving benefits as of the date she applied.

Periodic Review of SSI Eligibility

Social Security periodically reviews your SSI eligibility and the amount of SSI you receive. These reviews take place at least once every three years, although there may be a brief review of your finances annually. When you receive a notice of review, you will have to produce the same kinds of information as you did for the original application: your income, assets, living arrangements, and, if claiming based on a disability, updated medical information. Often, most of this process can be handled by mail or telephone, although you may have to make a trip to the Social Security office for an interview.

Benefit Amounts

Because supplement payments vary from state to state, the amount of your SSI check will vary depending on where you live, as well as on the amount of your countable income. The basic federal SSI payment for 2015 is $735 a month for an individual and $1,100 a month for a couple. These figures usually go up on January 1 each year; the amount of increase depends on the rise in the federal Consumer Price Index.

States With Federally Administered Supplements

A number of states pay supplements to the basic federal SSI amount. In some of these states, the supplement is added on directly to the federal SSI payment. This means that a person needs to apply only once, to Social Security, to receive both the basic amount and the supplement. Both amounts are included in one payment, which is administered by Social Security.

The supplement amount differs for a single individual, a couple, or a person who is blind. Also, the amount may be affected if the person receiving SSI lives in the home of a family friend, in congregate living arrangements, or in a nursing facility.

States in which SSI recipients receive a federally administered supplement include:

California	Michigan	Pennsylvania
District of Columbia	Nevada	Rhode Island
Hawaii	New Jersey	Utah
Iowa	New York	Vermont

In addition, Delaware and Montana have federally administered supplements that are available only to people who live in protective care arrangements. Social Security administers the supplement for some SSI recipients in Iowa.

SSI May Get You Medicaid

If you are found eligible for SSI benefits, most states will also give you free health coverage through the Medicaid program (called Medi-Cal in California). You don't need to qualify for Medicare to get Medicaid. For an explanation of what Medicaid offers, see Chapter 16.

Your enrollment is automatic in many states, including Alabama, Arizona, Arkansas, California, Colorado, Delaware, District of Columbia, Florida, Georgia, Iowa, Kentucky, Louisiana, Maine, Maryland, Massachusetts, Michigan, Mississippi, Montana, New Jersey, New Mexico, New York, North Carolina, Pennsylvania, Rhode Island, South Carolina, South Dakota, Tennessee, Texas, Vermont, Washington, West Virginia, Wisconsin, and Wyoming.

In other states, you must separately apply for Medicaid after being granted SSI. This usually involves submitting an application to a state social services or welfare office. Some states will automatically enroll you based on your SSI grant. Others have slightly more restrictive eligibility standards and will separately evaluate your Medicaid application.

The states that automatically enroll you after you apply for Medicaid are Alaska, Kansas, Idaho, Nebraska, Nevada, Oregon, and Utah. The states that make an independent decision about whether you are eligible for Medicaid are Connecticut, Hawaii, Illinois, Indiana, Minnesota, Missouri, New Hampshire, North Dakota, Ohio, Oklahoma, and Virginia.

States With Their Own Supplements

Most other states provide some kind of supplement to the basic federal SSI payment, but the kinds of supplements and rules for qualifying are administered entirely by the states. You must apply for these state supplements separately, at the social welfare agency in the county where you live.

Amount of state supplements. Your supplement payments might range from a few dollars to a few hundred dollars above the basic federal SSI payment, or include noncash assistance with food, housing, transportation, and/or medical care. The amounts change frequently, based on the willingness of state legislatures to provide for SSI recipients in their state budgets.

Reductions to Benefits

Your maximum SSI benefit amount will be reduced by income you make over allowable countable limits, as dictated by a number of specific rules.

Limit on Earned Income

Your benefits are reduced by one dollar for every two dollars more than $65 per month that you earn in wages or self-employment.

EXAMPLE: Ronda has a part-time job at which she earns $280 a month. She is entitled to the basic federal SSI benefit of $721 per month, but that amount is reduced by $107.50 because of her earnings. (The total of $107.50 is arrived at by taking the amount of her earned income over $65 ($215) and dividing it in half—$1 out of every $2 over the limit.) Her monthly income would then be her earnings of $280 plus her SSI benefit of $602.50, for a total of $882.50.

Limit on Unearned Income

Your benefits are reduced dollar for dollar by the amount of any *unearned* income you receive over $20 a month. This unearned income includes Social Security benefits, pensions, annuities, interest on savings, dividends, or any money from investments or property you own.

EXAMPLE: Carl lives alone in a home he owns. His only income is his Social Security retirement check of $330 per month. From Carl's $330 Social Security check, $20 is excluded, making his total countable unearned income $310. Since he has no earned income, his total countable income would be the same: $310. In the state in which Carl lives, the basic SSI payment is $800 per month. From this, Carl's total countable income of $310 is subtracted, leaving $490 as Carl's monthly SSI payment.

Limit on Outside Support

Your basic SSI payment may be reduced up to one third if you live in a relative's or friend's home without paying rent and/or you receive regular, substantial support in the form of food, clothing, and personal items.

EXAMPLE: Adam lives in his daughter's house without paying rent. His daughter also provides Adam all of his meals. Adam's only income is his $370 per month Social Security check. The basic monthly SSI benefit of $750 in Adam's state would be reduced by one third because Adam receives both regular food and free lodging from his daughter. This would leave an SSI amount of $500. In determining Adam's countable income, SSI does not count $20 of his $370 Social Security check, leaving a total countable amount of $350. This $350 is subtracted from his reduced SSI benefit, leaving an actual monthly SSI payment to Adam of $150, in addition to his Social Security benefit.

Limit on Working Couples

A final example shows how SSI amounts are figured for a couple, and how SSI payments change when one person takes a job.

> EXAMPLE: Beverly marries Carl and together they collect a monthly Social Security check of $455. In figuring Carl and Beverly's SSI payment, $20 would be exempted from the $455 Social Security check, for a total countable income of $435 a month. That $435 would be subtracted from the basic SSI benefit for a couple, which in Carl and Beverly's state is $937, leaving a monthly SSI payment of $502.
>
> When Beverly takes a part-time job paying $100 a month, their SSI payment changes. Beverly and Carl's countable unearned income is still the same, $435 a month—their Social Security check minus $20. But now they have an earned income of $100 a month. The first $65 of this $100 is not counted under SSI rules. Of the remaining $35 of earned income, only one half of it, or $17.50, is considered counted income. Only $17.50 is added to the $435 of counted unearned income, making a total countable income of $452.50 a month.
>
> The basic SSI benefit for a couple in Carl and Beverly's state is $937 a month. The $452.50 countable income would be subtracted from this amount, leaving a monthly SSI payment to Carl and Beverly of $484.50. Their monthly income would be their Social Security check of $455, plus their part-time income of $100, plus their SSI check of $484.50, for a total of $1,039.50. ●

Applying for Benefits

Once you get an accurate estimate of how much your Social Security benefits will be and decide when it is best to begin receiving them, applying for those benefits is usually fairly simple. Most people will already have all the documents needed and can complete their application in one or two trips to a local Social Security office. This chapter discusses the application process and explains how to organize the required documents relating to your income and assets.

Retirement, Dependents, and Survivors Benefits

The application processes for retirement benefits, dependents benefits, and survivors benefits all involve the same basic documents and procedures. The hardest part is figuring out the best time to claim benefits. For this, you must understand the relationship between your age and the amount you will receive.

When to Claim Benefits

You may be eligible for different types of benefits at different times in your life—for example, survivors benefits at age 60, based on your deceased spouse's work record, and retirement benefits at age 62, based on your own work record. And you are eligible for increased benefits for every month you wait to claim them up to age 70.

As a result, your decision about which benefits to claim and when to claim them should be based on how much each benefit would be, measured against the earnings limit for your age, if you intend to continue working. (For earnings limits and reductions, see Chapter 2; for reductions for working dependents, see Chapter 4; for reductions for working survivors, see Chapter 5; and for options about choosing between benefits and deciding when to claim them, see Chapter 6.)

To see what each type of benefit would be at different ages, take a look at your Social Security Statement. Social Security used to send it to you each year, but you can now view it online (see Chapter 1 for details). You should examine your statement about six months before you might claim any benefit. This will give you plenty of time to decide what's best for you, and to get the process started if you choose to file soon for a benefit.

How and Where to File Your Claim

All Social Security claims for benefits can be filed at local Social Security offices. In addition, retirement, dependents, survivors, and disability benefits may be initiated by phone or through the Internet (see "Begin your application process online," below.) Even online applications usually require a visit to a local office to complete, however.

Most sizable cities have at least one local Social Security office, and in major urban areas there are usually several. To find the address and telephone number of the nearest office, check your telephone directory under the listing for U.S. Government, Social Security Administration, or sometimes under U.S. Government, Department of Health and Human Services, Social Security Administration. The SSA website also has listings of local offices, at www.ssa.gov. Look for the link "Locate a Social Security office." If you're still having trouble finding a local office, call the SSA at 800-772-1213.

The following subsections describe how to get personal assistance with and local information about filing your claim.

Help on the Internet

The Social Security Administration now offers a good deal of information and some of its application processes online at www.ssa.gov. Some of the information can be hard to locate, but Social Security is making good progress in helping people to apply for many Social Security benefits online.

You can also find a lot of information to help you with a disability claim on www.disabilitysecrets.com.

COMPUTER

Begin your application process online. Social Security allows people to use its website to file many types of claims for benefits, which may save one or more trips to a Social Security office.

You may file an online application—or at least begin the process—for:

- retirement benefits
- survivors benefits
- disability benefits
- spouse's (dependents) benefits
- Supplemental Security Income (SSI)
- Medicare Part A and Part B, and
- extra help with Medicare Part D.

To learn more about what Social Security permits you to do over the Internet, see its Web page "What You Can Do Online" at www.ssa.gov/onlineservices.

Help in Person

A Social Security worker in your local office is usually the best source of information and assistance for filing your claim. Face-to-face conversation is almost always more productive than discussions over the phone or via email messaging. And when you're ready to file your application, handing it to a real person is more secure than sending it by mail.

Most offices permit you to phone in advance and make an appointment to speak to someone personally—a good idea, because you may face long lines if you show up unannounced.

Whenever you consult with someone in a Social Security office, write down the person's name and keep it with your other Social Security papers. That way, when you next contact the office, you can ask to speak with the same person, or you can refer to that person if a question arises about what occurred during your previous visit.

When filing papers, make sure the office gives you some proof that you filed—for example, bring along your personal copy and ask them to stamp it "received" with the date, as they would for their daily mail.

Help Over the Telephone

Social Security offers advice and help over its toll-free phone line at 800-772-1213. The phone lines are open between 7 a.m. and 7 p.m. Eastern time Monday through Friday. It's busiest at the beginning of the month and early in each week, so choose your time to call accordingly.

You can accomplish a great deal over the phone. The Social Security workers can answer your general questions about benefits and rules and tell you how to fill out or submit a particular form. They may also be able to start your claim process for retirement and dependents benefits. However, that process cannot be completed over the phone. Before your claim can actually be processed, you'll have to sign a written application and bring certain original documents to Social Security (see "Documents You'll Need," below).

Sign Up Three Months Before Your Birthday

If you will need to actually receive a benefit payment as soon as you reach the youngest eligibility age, file your claim three months before the birthday on which you will become eligible. This will give Social Security time to process your claim so that you will receive benefits as soon as you become eligible. If you file a claim later, you cannot get benefits retroactively for the months during which you were eligible but before you applied.

Anyone eligible for Social Security benefits is also eligible for Medicare coverage at age 65 (explained in Chapter 13). Even if you are not going to claim Social Security benefits at age 65—because your benefit amount will be higher if you wait—you should sign up for Medicare coverage three months before your 65th birthday. There is no reason to delay signing up for Medicare, and waiting until after your 65th birthday will delay coverage.

Getting the Best Results: Preparation, Patience, Perseverance

Social Security offices are usually understaffed. Although individual Social Security workers are often helpful, polite, and well versed in the various regulations that govern Social Security programs, the maze of rules, when added to normal human fallibility, inevitably makes for delays, misunderstandings, and mistakes.

It's up to you to help yourself. The best way to begin the Social Security application process is to use this book to understand the workings of whichever benefit program you will apply for.

The next most important thing is to keep your papers organized. During the benefit application process, you may mail papers and forms to your local Social Security office. However, it is best to deliver important papers—any original document or certified copy—in person. That way, the papers not only will be sure to get to the local office but also will go directly into your file. This will cut some time off the process and will help to avoid the adventures that sometimes befall papers that go into Social Security's incoming mail stacks.

Keep copies of any form or document you submit to Social Security. If the local Social Security office asks to see the original or a certified copy, it will usually make a copy on the spot and return the original to you. It's best to keep a copy in your files in case the original gets lost.

Documents You'll Need

Whether you file for a Social Security benefit in person at a local Social Security office or do all or some of it online through the Social Security website, you'll need to have certain personal papers or information. What you need will depend upon the type of benefit you're applying for, as explained below.

Most documents required by Social Security must be originals or certified copies. However, if you want to apply for benefits right away but do not yet have all your documents together, file your claim anyway—either by phone, on the Internet, or by going to your local Social Security office. The Social Security workers will advise you about how to get the documents you need, and, in the meantime, the application process can begin.

CAUTION
Make sure all your papers can be traced to you. On any copy of a document you bring or send to Social Security, write your name as it appears on your benefit application and your Social Security number. Also include the name and Social Security number of the person on whose work record you are claiming benefits. If you bring or send an original document, clip a piece of paper to it with those names and numbers.

When you apply for any type of benefit, bring with you the number of your account at a bank, a credit union, or another financial institution. Social Security will arrange to have your monthly benefit payment sent directly to your account—a process called direct deposit. Direct deposit is now used for all Social Security and SSI beneficiaries. It saves money for the Social Security Administration and also avoids the problem of lost or stolen checks.

Retirement Benefits

You may need some or all of the following documents or information to apply for retirement benefits:

- your Social Security number. You do not need your actual Social Security card.
- your birth certificate. If you do not have a birth certificate, bring any other evidence of the date of your birth: baptism record, military papers, immigration papers, driver's license, or passport.
- your military discharge papers, if you served in the military, and
- your most recent W-2 tax form or federal self-employment tax return.

Dependents Benefits

You may need some or all of the following documents or information to apply for dependents benefits:

- marriage certificate, if you are applying for benefits based on your spouse's work record, and
- birth certificate of any children claiming benefits. If you do not have a birth certificate, bring any other evidence of the date of your child's birth: baptism record, immigration papers, or passport.

Survivors Benefits

You may need some or all of the following documents or information to apply for survivors benefits:

- Social Security number of the deceased person on whose work record you are claiming benefits, and your own Social Security number
- divorce papers, if you are applying as a divorced spouse
- death certificate of your deceased spouse
- your birth certificate and those of your children who are claiming benefits. If a birth certificate is not available, bring any other evidence of date of birth: baptism record, military papers, immigration papers, or passport.
- if your spouse died within the past two years, the most recent W-2 tax form or federal self-employment tax return of your deceased spouse, and
- if applying as a surviving dependent parent who was receiving support from your son or daughter who died, a recent tax return from your deceased child showing you as a dependent, or proof of expenditures by your deceased child showing how much support was given to you, as well as your own most recent tax returns.

If You Retire From Your Own Business

If you are self-employed and are claiming retirement benefits before your full retirement age, Social Security may require some extra information from you. They'll want to see evidence that you are really giving up full-time work and not merely shifting your pay (in name only) to someone else.

The reason for this concern is the rule that retirement benefits will be reduced if you are less than full retirement age and earn income over certain limits for your age. (See Chapter 2 for these limits.) Some people with their own businesses try to get around this rule by continuing to work and paying a relative instead of themselves, or by continuing to run the business but being paid only for reduced work time.

Social Security is likely to ask for information regarding your continuing involvement with your own business if any of the following are true:

- You maintain ownership of the business.
- Other family members are involved in the business and a relative is assuming most of your previous duties.
- You continue to work for the business at lower pay.
- You control the amount you work and how much you are paid, such that you could manipulate either one.
- Your relatives now receive the salary you previously earned.

Social Security may ask for such documents as the business's pay and personnel records, personal and business tax returns, stock transfer agreements, and business expense records. Try to contact your local Social Security office several months in advance, so that you'll learn what documents Social Security wants and have time to gather the documents.

If Social Security determines that you provide services to the business that exceed the amount you are paid—based on the time you spend, the level of your responsibility, and the value of services you provide—the agency may attach a dollar value to those services. If this dollar value exceeds the amount of earned income permitted for your age, your benefits may be reduced.

At the Social Security Office

When submitting your application at your local Social Security office, you will be interviewed by a case worker. If you haven't already submitted your claim application form online or over the telephone, the worker will help you fill out the form. The worker will open a file for you, which from then on will contain all of the documents pertaining to your application.

Write down the name of the worker who talks with you, and his or her direct telephone line if available, so that you can speak with the same person if you need to call in to provide or receive further information. The Social Security worker will make copies of the documents you have brought and will explain what other information is needed to process your application.

If additional documents are needed, ask whether you may mail in copies instead of bringing originals in person.

When you first apply, do not expect to be told precisely how much your benefits will be. Exact benefit amounts are based upon the computerized records kept at the Social Security Administration's national records center. Your precise benefit amount will be calculated there.

Applications take six to eight weeks to be processed, but when you receive your first payment, it will include benefits back to the date you first applied, or to the date on which you are first eligible, whichever is later (except in the case of disability benefits).

Withdrawing a Benefits Application

It may happen that after you have turned in your application for retirement, dependents, or survivors benefits, your work situation changes, altering significantly the amount of benefits to which you are entitled. This might, for example, occur if you are offered a new position, a new job, or an increased salary, or you are not laid off from a job you expected to lose, or you are called back to work after a temporary job loss, or you simply change your mind and decide to continue working full time.

In any of these situations, if the income you earn at your continued work significantly exceeds the earnings limit for your age, it may eat up your benefits. If so, your decision to claim benefits may prove to be a bad one, because you will receive little or no benefit payments while you continue to work, and your benefit amount will be permanently lower than if you had waited to file your claim at a later age.

You may withdraw your application within 12 months after first becoming eligible for benefits, if you repay all the benefits you have received so far. To do so, you may go to Social Security's official online publication "If You Change Your Mind" at www. socialsecurity.gov/retire2/withdrawal.htm, which explains the procedure and also the amounts you will have to repay. You can also make an appointment at a local Social Security office to discuss with a Social Security worker the process and consequences of withdrawing your application.

Disability Benefits

Eligibility for disability benefits depends upon your physical or mental condition, and your inability to work because of that condi-tion. (See Chapter 3 for a more detailed account of the eligibility requirements.) Because it involves these qualifying standards, the application requires much more time and effort than other Social Security benefit applications do. You must get and keep your papers organized, and be thorough and persistent in your contacts both with doctors and with Social Security personnel.

RESOURCE

Proving that your particular medical condition renders you unable to work may not be easy. This book provides an introduction, but for more information and specialized advice concerning particular physical and mental conditions, see *Nolo's Guide to Social Security Disability: Getting & Keeping Your Benefits*, by David A. Morton III, M.D. (Nolo).

When to File Your Claim

You will not be paid any disability benefits until you have been disabled for five full months. This waiting period begins with the first full month after the date your disability began. That date is usually the date you stopped working because of your physical or mental condition.

However, disability claims take between two and six months to be decided. Do not wait for six months of disability to elapse before filing your claim. Don't even wait to gather all the necessary information and doctors' reports. File the claim as soon as your medical condition forces you off work and the doctors expect that it will prevent you from working for a year or more. You can complete the gathering of necessary documents while the claim is being processed, with the help of your local Social Security office.

Fast Claims for Severe Medical Conditions

The Social Security Administration has created a streamlined disability benefits claims process for people with certain severe medical conditions. For these people, the Social Security Administration will process benefit claims within a few days of completing the application. There are over 200 conditions for which this fast application process, called "Compassionate Allowance," applies. To see the list of conditions and to get more information, go to the Social Security website: www.socialsecurity.gov/compassionateallowances.

Documents You'll Need

When you file an application for Social Security disability benefits, whether online or in person at a local Social Security office, you may need some or all of the following documents or information:

- your Social Security number and proof of age (such as a birth certificate) for yourself and any person eligible for dependents benefits

- names, addresses, and phone numbers of doctors, hospitals, clinics, and other health service institutions that have diagnosed your medical condition and have given estimates of the length of time it is expected to keep you disabled, plus the approximate dates of your treatment. Although you are not required to produce medical records of your disability—Social Security can request them directly from doctors and hospitals—you might speed up the process if you bring copies of medical records you already have.
- a list of where you have worked in the past 15 years and a description of the kinds of work you did
- a copy of the past year's W-2 forms, or your last federal income tax return if you are self-employed
- the dates of any military service
- information concerning any other type of disability payment you are receiving
- if your spouse is applying based on your work record, the dates of any prior marriages. A certified copy of the divorce papers will provide this information.
- if you are applying as a disabled widow or widower, your spouse's Social Security number and a copy of the death certificate, and
- if you are applying as a disabled surviving divorced husband or wife, proof that your marriage lasted ten years. Marriage and divorce papers will serve this purpose.

If you are physically unable to get to a Social Security office in person, or you are unable to complete the forms or meet other filing requirements, your application can be completed by your spouse, a parent, another relative, a friend, or your legal guardian. And once the initial claim has been filed, a service worker in the local Social Security office can assist you by having the Social Security office directly request necessary documents.

How Your Eligibility Is Determined

Applications for disability benefits go through several stages. Initially, you will fill out an application at a local Social Security office and provide documents regarding your age and employment. After that, however, the process becomes more complicated, as Social Security determines whether your physical condition is actually disabling according to its standards.

Disability Determination Services

When your claim has been completed and the local Social Security office has checked to see that you meet all the general requirements regarding work credits for your age (see Chapter 3 for the work credit requirements), it will forward your claim to a Disability Determination Services (DDS) office in your state. The DDS office will use your medical records and employment history to decide whether you are disabled under the rules of the Social Security law.

The decision at DDS is made by a doctor and a disability evaluation specialist. They examine all medical records you have provided with your application and may request more information from you, your doctors, and your employers.

Based on these records, the doctor and the specialist determine whether your disability is expected to last more than one year and whether it is severe enough to interfere with your ability to perform any work you have done over the past 15 years. If so, they then determine whether it is also so severe that you cannot perform any substantial gainful work. (See "No Substantial Gainful Activity" in Chapter 3 for more on how Social Security determines this.)

If your medical records show your condition limits you from performing substantial gainful work, you will be found eligible for benefits. If not, those evaluating you may request further medical records and you may be referred for a consultative physical examination.

Enlisting the Help of Your Doctor

Your medical records will be the biggest factor in the state DDS office's determination of your eligibility for disability benefits. Therefore, what your doctor puts in your records can be all-important.

If possible, discuss the matter with your doctor before you file your application for disability benefits. Inform your doctor that you intend to apply, and ask him or her to make specific notations in your medical records of how your physical activities—particularly work-related activities, such as walking, sitting, lifting, carrying—are limited or how your emotional condition affects your ability to regularly perform work. Ask also for your doctor to make a note of when your disability reached a point that it interfered with your ability to work.

Do not ask the doctor to give an opinion about whether you are disabled according to Social Security guidelines. Doctors will readily describe a specific medical condition, but many are unwilling to give an opinion about your ability to do any work at all. And, in any event, the DDS evaluation team would not accept your doctor's opinion on this ultimate question of eligibility. Instead, it will base its determination on its own evaluation of your symptoms and limitations that appear in your medical records.

In determining the nature and extent of your disability, the DDS will rely almost exclusively on the diagnoses of medical doctors, as opposed to physical therapists, chiropractors, and other nonphysician healers. This reflects an institutional bias against nontraditional medical treatment. But it also reflects the fact that the decision about eligibility depends on diagnosis of your condition, not on the best way to treat it, and that physicians have diagnostic tools—such as laboratory tests, X-rays, and other technological and intrusive procedures—that are not available to nonphysician healers.

Medical Examinations

In some cases, the DDS evaluators may not feel that they can come to a conclusion about your disability based on your existing medical records. They may request further reports from doctors who have examined or treated you. And they may request that you undergo a medical evaluation or test, called a consultative examination.

Social Security pays the cost of the additional reports, examinations, or tests. If you must travel outside your immediate area to get to this examination, Social Security can pay for the cost of that travel, if you request it.

Fortunately, this extra examination or testing is often done by a physician who has already examined or treated you. This is particularly true if one of your doctors is a specialist in the area of medicine that deals directly with your disability. In other words, if you have seen an orthopedic surgeon for your back problem, Social Security is likely to have that same doctor perform the consultative examination. However, if you have not been treated by a specialist in the field—for example, if only your internist or general practitioner has treated you for a particular medical problem—Social Security may send you to another doctor for this examination.

Consultative examinations are limited to specific issues the DDS needs to clarify regarding your ability to work. The exam often involves certain kinds of tests—a range of motion test, for example, if your disability involves restricted movement—that your doctor has not recently performed and that give DDS specific information on the extent of your disability.

The DDS will set up the examination and send the doctor a written request for the information needed and any specific tests it wants performed. The doctor will not conduct a general examination and will not prescribe any treatment for you. On occasion, a representative from DDS will attend the examination to record specific test results. The doctor will send a report to DDS describing the results of the examination, but he or she will not take part in the final decision about whether you are eligible for disability benefits.

Even though you may not like the idea of going through another medical examination, especially if it is by a doctor you do not know, you must cooperate with the DDS to successfully process your disability claim.

Vocational Rehabilitative Services

When you apply for disability benefits, you may be referred to your state's vocational rehabilitation agency for a determination of whether any of its services might be of help to you. These free services can include job counseling, job retraining and placement, and specialized medical assistance. The services can also train you to use devices—such as a modified computer keyboard—that may enable you to work despite your disability.

Supplemental Security Income (SSI)

You may file a claim for SSI benefits either online or at your local Social Security office at the same time you file for retirement, disability, dependents, or survivors benefits. (See Chapter 7 for a full discussion of the SSI program.) However, SSI is not automatically included in these other applications, so you must tell the Social Security worker that you wish to file for SSI benefits as well.

If you believe you might be close to the qualifying income and asset limits for SSI benefits, go ahead and apply. If your state offers a separate state-administered supplementary payment in addition to the basic federal SSI payment, you will have to apply for that supplement at your local county social welfare office.

The process of applying for SSI benefits is very similar to applying for Social Security benefits. You will need to provide the same general documents. (See "Retirement, Dependents, and Survivors Benefits," above, for instructions.) However, unlike Social Security benefit applications, SSI benefit applications also require that you show records of your income and assets.

Proof of Income and Assets

Regardless of whether you are applying for SSI payments as disabled or over age 65, you must also bring information regarding your income and assets. This includes:

- information about where you live: for homeowners, a copy of your mortgage papers or tax bill; for renters, a copy of your rental agreement or lease and the name and address of the landlord
- documents indicating your current earned income, such as pay stubs and income tax returns
- papers showing all your financial assets, such as bankbooks, insurance policies, stock certificates, car registration, burial fund records, and
- information about your spouse's income and assets, if the two of you live together.

Even if you do not have all these papers available, go to your local Social Security office and file your application for SSI as soon as you think you may qualify for assistance. The Social Security workers can tell you how to get whatever papers and records are necessary, and in some instances will get copies of the required records for you.

Proof of Age If 65 or Older

If you are age 65 or older, bring your Social Security number and proof of your age, such as a birth certificate. If you do not have a birth certificate, bring any other evidence of the date of your birth: baptism record, military papers, immigration papers, driver's license, or passport. If you are already receiving any kind of Social Security benefit, you do not have to bring proof of your age.

Proof of Blindness or Disability

The process for proving that you are blind or disabled for purposes of SSI benefits is the same as the disability determination process when qualifying for Social Security disability benefits. (See Chapter 3 for the medical eligibility requirements.) The information you need to gather and the process of applying for disability benefits is discussed in "Disability Benefits," above.

Proof of Citizenship or Qualifying Legal Residence

For a reminder of what immigration status you must hold in order to qualify for SSI, see Chapter 7.

If you are a U.S. citizen, you'll need to prove your citizenship by showing copies of your birth certificate, baptismal records, U.S. passport, or naturalization papers.

If you are a noncitizen, bring proof of your qualifications under one of the categories listed in Chapter 7.

For proof of work for ten years, bring your legal resident alien card ("green card") and Social Security numbers for yourself and your spouse. The Social Security or local welfare office will use the numbers to check your reported Social Security taxes.

If you seek to qualify as a veteran of the U.S. Armed Forces, bring evidence of honorable discharge from the military. You will also need a copy of your marriage certificate if you are seeking SSI as the spouse of a veteran.

Finding Out What Happens to Your Claim

You will not find out from your local Social Security office whether your claim for benefits has been approved; that word has to come from the Social Security Administration in Washington, DC.

Notification of Eligibility

Social Security will notify you in writing whether your claim has been approved, how much your benefits will be, and when you will get your first check.

From the time the application is filed, a retirement, dependents, or survivors claim usually takes from four to eight weeks. A disability claim can take up to six months. For all retirement, dependents, or survivors claims, you will receive benefits dating back to the date you first applied, or first became eligible if you applied before you reached an age of eligibility. Social Security disability payments are discussed below.

SSI benefits usually begin four to eight weeks after you complete the necessary paperwork. If your claim is based on a disability that has not already been established for Social Security disability payments, it may take three to six months. When you do finally get your money, however, it will cover the period from the month after you filed your claim.

If you were unable to work for more than five months before applying for Social Security disability benefits, you might be eligible for back benefits. If Social Security determines that your disability actually began more than five months before your application, based on when you actually stopped work, it can grant up to 12 months of back benefits.

If your claim for any Social Security or SSI benefit is denied, the written notice of denial will state the reasons why. You have a right to appeal a denial of your claim. Your appeal must be submitted within 60 days from the date you receive written notice of the denial or other decision. (See Chapter 9 for appeal procedures.)

When You Need Money in a Hurry

It is possible to get some SSI payments even before your claim is finally approved. If you appear to be eligible for SSI and you need immediate cash to meet a financial emergency, the Social Security office can issue you an advance payment. The amount of this emergency payment will be deducted from your first regular SSI check.

Similarly, if you have already qualified for Social Security disability benefits and you appear financially eligible for SSI, you may be approved for and begin receiving SSI benefits immediately, without medical review.

If you are financially eligible and appear to meet the disability requirements, but your disability application has not yet been approved by Social Security, you can receive SSI payments while your claim is being reviewed by the disability office. These are called presumptive disability payments, and they don't need to be repaid.

Methods of Receiving Payment

All new beneficiaries are expected to receive their Social Security and SSI benefits by direct deposit into their bank accounts. It is possible, however, for a representative payee to receive payments on your behalf. You must indicate on the application if you want these options. You may change your method of payment after you begin to receive benefits.

Direct Deposit

Direct deposit has a number of advantages: You do not have to wait for your check to arrive in the mail, nor do you have to travel to your bank to make the deposit. And you do not have to worry about your check's being lost or stolen.

When you first sign up for benefits at your local Social Security office, workers there will ask for the name and address of your bank branch and the number of the account where you want the funds deposited. The bank where you have your account can help you fill out the form to request direct deposit.

If you change banks—or want to close one account and open another—you must fill out a new direct deposit form. The bank where you open your new account will assist you with the form. But do not close your old account until you see that your benefit has appeared in your new one. If your benefit continues to be deposited in the old account, contact your local Social Security office.

Debit Card

Social Security now requires all new applicants to use direct deposit. But you may not want to receive your payment this way, either temporarily or for the long term. For example, you may not want to pay the bank charge to maintain an account. Or, you may be moving and temporarily will not have a local bank account. If, for any reason, you do not want to receive your benefit payment by direct deposit, you may arrange with your local Social Security office to receive your payments via a Direct Express debit card.

Substitute Payee

If you are unable to handle your own banking and check writing, you may have a family member, close friend, or legal representative receive the benefit payments on your behalf. That person should spend the money according to your wishes or directions. This may be done informally, by simply adding the other person as a joint account holder on the bank account where Social Security deposits your check. The bank can make this arrangement for you.

If you feel more comfortable with some oversight on how that person spends your benefits, you can have this other person officially appointed by Social Security as a substitute, or representative, payee. That person would then personally receive the benefit payments on your behalf.

Anyone proposing to be your representative payee must bring to the local Social Security office medical proof—for example, a letter from your doctor—that you are unable to care for yourself. The representative payee must sign a sworn affidavit at the Social Security office stating that he or she will use the Social Security check for your benefit. The Social Security office will then verify your medical condition and the identity of the representative payee.

If a person has already been appointed by a court to serve as legal guardian or conservator, proof of that court appointment is all that is required to be appointed representative payee. But people who are named to act in powers of attorney do not automatically qualify as representative payees; they must still apply for representative payee status at the local Social Security office.

The rules require that a representative payee deposit and keep the money belonging to the person entitled to Social Security in a separate bank account and periodically file an accounting with Social Security to show how the money has been spent to care for the beneficiary. The representative payee should keep all bills and receipts in a systematic and organized way so they can be produced easily. ●

Appealing a Social Security Decision

N
o matter how certain you feel that you deserve Social Security benefits, the agency may have other ideas and deny your claim. Sometimes this is a mere mistake and can be corrected. More often, the decision was a matter of judgment, as with disability claims, where questions about medical conditions, ability to work, or income levels (in SSI cases) are subjective and susceptible to different interpretations.

But if your application for benefits is initially denied, or is granted but you are awarded less than you had hoped, that need not be the end of the matter. Virtually all decisions of the Social Security Administration may be appealed, and many appeals are successful. If a new benefit has been denied or an existing benefit reduced or ended, you may appeal the decision as long as you follow some fairly simple rules and are willing to think creatively about how to present your case in a more convincing way. You'll need to put yourself into the shoes of the Social Security workers who first denied your claim, try to understand their reasoning, and then provide convincing evidence so that the next person who sees your file won't view your claim in exactly the same way.

This chapter explains the four possible levels of appeal following any Social Security decision. In most states, the first level is called reconsideration; it is an informal review that takes place in the local Social Security or Disability Determination Services (DDS) office where your claim was filed. (Technically, this isn't really an "appeal," because it doesn't go to a higher authority—but it's a step that you must take, nonetheless.)

The second level is a hearing before an administrative law judge (an ALJ); this is an independent review of what the local Social Security office has decided, made by someone outside the local office. The third level is an appeal to Social Security's national Appeals Council in Falls Church, Virginia. And the final level is filing a lawsuit in federal court.

RESOURCE

Get extra advice regarding disability appeals. More than 90% of all Social Security appeals involve claims for disability benefits (including SSI). Most of these appeals revolve around whether the claimant's physical or mental condition actually prevents gainful employment. Proving this requires careful presentation of medical information as well as completing certain special forms. This book will give you an introduction to this process, but for more information and specialized advice for various physical and mental conditions, see *Nolo's Guide to Social Security Disability: Getting & Keeping Your Benefits*, by David A. Morton III, M.D. (Nolo), and www.disabilitysecrets.com.

CAUTION

Beware of the time limit for filing appeals. The same time limit applies to each step of the appeals process. From the date on the written notice of Social Security's decision—whether denying or granting a benefit—you have 60 days within which to file a written notice that you are appealing that decision to the next stage in the process. If you receive the notice by mail, you have an additional five days within which to file your notice of appeal.

Reconsideration of Decision

When a claim for any type of Social Security benefit—retirement, disability, dependents, or survivors—is denied, or an existing benefit is ended, or you receive an amount you feel is less than that to which you are entitled, in most states, the first step to appeal that decision is to request reconsideration.

As part of an experiment to streamline appeals, some states have eliminated the reconsideration review for disability appeals; in these states, when you appeal a disability denial, the first level of appeal is a hearing in front of an ALJ. Social Security may end this experiment in the future, but at the time of printing, the states without a reconsideration step for disability appeals were:

Alabama	Colorado	New Hampshire
Alaska	Louisiana	New York
California (L.A. North and	Michigan	Pennsylvania
L.A. West Branches only)	Missouri	

If the negative decision involved a denial of Social Security benefits, follow the procedures discussed below. Some special procedures to follow when appealing denial of an SSI claim are discussed in "Requesting Reconsideration of SSI Decision," below.

Is an Appeal Worth the Effort?

The first question that may occur to you when considering an appeal is whether it is worth the effort.

Let's start with some encouraging numbers: A substantial percentage of decisions are changed on appeal. Almost half of all disability appeals, which are by far the most common, are favorably changed in the appeal process.

And appealing a Social Security claim need not be terribly difficult. If you properly organized and prepared your original claim, most of your work for the appeal has already been done. In many situations, the appeal will require little more from you than explaining once more why the information you already presented should qualify you for a benefit. In other cases, it will simply involve presenting one or two additional pieces of information that better explain your situation to Social Security personnel.

A negative Social Security decision may affect your rights for many years. Because it is so important, and because the appeal process is relatively simple, it is almost always worth the effort to appeal.

Requesting Reconsideration of Decision on Initial Benefits Claim

To start the appeal process, you file a written request for review of the decision, called a *Request for Reconsideration* (SSA-561-U2). The form is available online from Social Security's website at www.socialsecurity. gov/online/ssa-561.pdf. You can also obtain a copy at your local Social Security office or by calling Social Security at 800-772-1213.

This is also the step you take if you are allotted benefits less than the amount to which you believe you are entitled. A sample of the form follows.

The form comes in duplicate: a top copy for the Claims Folder (the Social Security office's copy) and a bottom Claimant's Copy (for you). You fill in only the top part of the form. The information requested is straightforward: name, address, Social Security number, and type of claim—retirement, disability, dependents, or survivors.

The appeals process is explained in the sections below. Social Security also provides information about the appeals process on its website at www.socialsecurity.gov/pubs/EN-05-10041.html. More specific information about filing an appeal of the denial of a claim for disability benefits is also available online from Social Security at www.socialsecurity.gov/disability/appeal. If you were denied Social Security or SSI disability benefits for medical reasons, you can file a request for reconsideration online.

Completing the Request for Reconsideration Form

The first few lines of the *Request for Reconsideration* form are fairly simple. On the top left, fill in your own name, exactly as it appears on your Social Security card.

Use the box on the top right only if you are claiming dependents or survivors benefits; if so, put the name of your spouse or parent on whose work record you are claiming benefits.

On the second line to the left is the box for the Social Security claim number. Copy that number from the written denial of your claim that you received from Social Security.

SOCIAL SECURITY ADMINISTRATION   TOE 710   Form Approved
                                                                                 OMB No. 0960-0622

REQUEST FOR RECONSIDERATION

(Do not write in this space)

NAME OF CLAIMANT	NAME OF WAGE EARNER OR SELF-EMPLOYED PERSON *(If different from claimant.)*

CLAIMANT SSN _ _ _	CLAIMANT CLAIM NUMBER *(if different from SSN)* _ _ _	SUPPLEMENTAL SECURITY INCOME (SSI) OR SPECIAL VETERANS BENEFITS (SVB) CLAIM NUMBER

SPOUSE'S NAME *(Complete ONLY in SSI cases)*	SPOUSE'S SOCIAL SECURITY NUMBER *(Complete ONLY in SSI cases)* _ _ _

CLAIM FOR *(Specify type, e.g., retirement, disability, hospital /medical, SSI, SVB, etc.)*

I do not agree with the determination made on the above claim and request reconsideration. My reasons are:

SUPPLEMENTAL SECURITY INCOME OR SPECIAL VETERANS BENEFITS RECONSIDERATION ONLY
(See the three ways to appeal in the How To Appeal Your Supplemental Security Income (SSI) Or Special Veterans Benefit (SVB) Decision instructions.)
"I want to appeal your decision about my claim for Supplemental Security Income (SSI) or Special Veterans Benefits (SVB). I've read about the three ways to appeal. I've checked the box below."

☐ Case Review   ☐ Informal Conference   ☐ Formal Conference

ENTER ADDRESSES FOR THE CLAIMANT AND THE REPRESENTATIVE

CLAIMANT SIGNATURE- OPTIONAL	NAME OF CLAIMANT'S REPRESENTATIVE ☐ NON-ATTORNEY ☐ ATTORNEY
MAILING ADDRESS	MAILING ADDRESS

CITY	STATE	ZIP CODE _	CITY	STATE	ZIP CODE _
TELEPHONE NUMBER *(Include area code)* ( ) _		DATE	TELEPHONE NUMBER *(Include area code)* ( ) _		DATE

TO BE COMPLETED BY SOCIAL SECURITY ADMINISTRATION

See list of initial determinations

1. HAS INITIAL DETERMINATION BEEN MADE? ☐ YES ☐ NO	2. CLAIMANT INSISTS ON FILING ☐ YES ☐ NO

3. IS THIS REQUEST FILED TIMELY?   ☐ YES ☐ NO
(If "NO", attach claimant's explanation for delay and attach any pertinent letter, material, or information in Social Security office.)

RETIREMENT AND SURVIVORS RECONSIDERATIONS ONLY (CHECK ONE) REFER TO (GN 03102.125)   SOCIAL SECURITY OFFICE ADDRESS

☐ NO FURTHER DEVELOPMENT REQUIRED   (GN 03102.300)

☐ REQUIRED DEVELOPMENT ATTACHED

☐ REQUIRED DEVELOPMENT PENDING, WILL FORWARD OR ADVISE STATUS WITHIN 30 DAYS

ROUTING INSTRUCTIONS (CHECK ONE)	☐ DISABILITY DETERMINATION SERVICES *(ROUTE WITH DISABILITY FOLDER)* ☐ ODO, BALTIMORE	☐ PROGRAM SERVICE CENTER ☐ OIO, BALTIMORE ☐ OEO, BALTIMORE	☐ DISTRICT OFFICE RECONSIDERATION ☐ CENTRAL PROCESSING SITE (SVB)

NOTE: Take or mail the **completed original** to your local Social Security office, the Veterans Affairs Regional Office in Manila or any U.S. Foreign Service post and keep a copy for your records.

Form **SSA-561-U2** (6-2012) ef (06-2012)   Prior Edition May Be Used Until Exhausted   **Claims Folder**

The remaining boxes on the top three lines apply only if you are appealing the denial of SSI benefits. If so, you must fill in your spouse's name and Social Security number so that the agency can check his or her earnings. And on the middle line to the right, you must note your SSI claim number, which you will find on the written denial of your SSI claim.

The most important part of the form comes on the lines following the words: "I do not agree with the determination made on the above claim and request reconsideration. My reasons are: ...." On those lines, state briefly and simply why you think you were unfairly denied your benefits.

You need not go into great detail, because your entire file will be examined—including any additional materials you want to submit. Your statement should simply identify the problem, such as: "The decision that I am not disabled was based on insufficient evidence about my condition. I am submitting an additional letter from my doctor about my condition." Or: "The DDS evaluation of my disability did not take into account my inability to sit for prolonged periods."

Along with your completed *Request for Reconsideration* form, you may submit a form called a *Disability Report—Appeal* (SSA-3441-BK) to explain any changes in your condition since you filed your original claim for benefits. Instructions for completing this form can be found in *Nolo's Guide to Social Security Disability: Getting & Keeping Your Benefits*, by David A. Morton III, M.D. (Nolo). In addition, you can submit a letter describing in more detail why you think Social Security's decision was incorrect.

You should also submit any other relevant materials to your file, such as recent medical records or a letter from a doctor or an employer about your ability to work. Such new material may be crucial to winning your reconsideration request—government workers have a tendency to believe that their agency was right the first time, unless you give them something new and different to change their minds.

This additional information does not have to be submitted by the 65th day after the written decision. But if you are planning to submit it after your *Request for Reconsideration*, indicate this on the form. (Use the space where you explain your disagreement with the decisions.)

Be sure to include your Social Security number and your claim number, in addition to your full name and the date, on all material you send in. And keep a copy for your records.

The Importance of Reviewing Your File

Sometimes a Social Security or SSI claim is denied because a document or another piece of information that should be in your file is not there. Or perhaps some misinformation has gotten into your file without your knowledge. This happens most often on the question of medical condition, where an incomplete medical record is in your file, or the report from the DDS examination includes a mistake based on a misunderstanding with the doctor who did the examination.

The only way for you to find out if such mistakes exist is to look at your file, which should contain all documents related to your claim. After you file your *Request for Reconsideration*, call your local Social Security office to set up an appointment to see your file.

If you find a mistake in the file, write a letter to Social Security explaining the situation. Send the letter to your local Social Security office, asking that it be made part of your file for reconsideration. And, as always, keep a copy of the letter.

The Reconsideration Process

Your claim will be reconsidered by someone in the Social Security or DDS office other than the person who made the decision on it the first time around. He or she will consider everything that was in your file when the decision was made, plus anything you have submitted to the office since the original decision.

Generally, you do not appear in person at this review; you do not have the right to speak face to face with the person making the decision, although you can request a chance to do so. The person doing the review may request more information and may ask you to come in for an informal interview.

You will receive a written notice of the decision made on your request for reconsideration—usually within 30 days. If 30 days go by with no word, contact the local Social Security office and ask about the delay. Reconsideration of a disability claim often takes two to three months, particularly if new medical information has been provided during the course of the appeal.

Once you receive your written decision, you can, if the decision is negative, file a request for an administrative hearing if you want one. (See the discussion of administrative hearings, below, for more information.) You must file your request within 65 days of the date on the written decision.

Continuing Your Benefits During an Appeal

In some circumstances, you can continue to receive Social Security disability benefits and SSI benefits while Social Security is deciding your appeal. You can request this in either of the following situations:

- You have been collecting Social Security disability benefits and you are now appealing Social Security's decision to end your benefits because it has determined that your condition has improved.
- You have been collecting SSI benefits and Social Security has decided that you are no longer eligible, or that you are eligible for lower benefits.

If you want your benefits to continue during the appeal process, you must make the request to your local Social Security office within ten days of the date you receive a written notice ending or reducing your benefits.

CAUTION

Continued benefits may not be for keeps. If you continue to collect benefits while appealing Social Security's decision to end those benefits, and Social Security denies your appeal, you may have to pay back the benefits you received during the appeal process.

Requesting Reconsideration of SSI Decision

If you request a reconsideration of a decision regarding a claim for SSI benefits, you'll be asked to choose among three possible procedures listed on the *Request for Reconsideration* form. Which one you choose depends upon how and why you were denied:

- If Social Security denied your claim for SSI because it says that you are not disabled, you are entitled only to what is called a "case review." This means that you can add more documentation to your file, which will then be reviewed again. You will not, however, be permitted to meet face to face with the Social Security representatives deciding your claim.

- If your claim for SSI benefits was denied for nonmedical reasons—such as your immigration status, or your income and asset levels—you may request a case review or an "informal conference." This permits you to speak with the person reviewing your claim and to show additional documents. You can also bring along anyone you want to help support your argument.

- If you have been receiving SSI benefits but Social Security decides to end or reduce them, you can request a "formal conference." This is actually an informal meeting at which you can present whatever written materials you want, have people come to the meeting and give information, and also explain your situation in your own words. It is only formal in the sense that the Social Security office can issue a legal summons for people to show up and answer questions if they refuse to come voluntarily. If you want Social Security to force someone to appear, you must notify your local office several weeks before the hearing date.

Informal Hearings at Social Security

You might have an opportunity to meet with the Social Security representative who is reviewing your file during the initial reconsideration of your retirement, disability, dependents, or survivors claim. Or, you might meet with him or her during the informal or formal conference regarding an SSI claim. These meetings are very informal. You will be given the chance to explain, in your own words and in person, why you believe the decision denying or ending your benefits was wrong.

There are several things to bear in mind during one of these meetings:

- Focus on addressing whatever reason Social Security gave (in the notice denying or ending your benefits) to justify its decision. Perhaps it was your physical condition, changes in your condition, your income, or your work hours. Be strong and direct in explaining why its reasoning was wrong. Don't dilute your argument by telling your whole life story or explaining your whole medical history.

- If, along with your appeal, you submitted material that was not in your original file, ask whether the representative has had a chance to read it. If so, explain how the new material shows that the original decision was incorrect. If not, give the representative copies of these new materials and ask that he or she read them before you continue with the meeting.

- There is no need to go over all the documents in your file except to point out what you believe are errors, or to focus on something in a document that you believe is important but that seemed to have been ignored in the original decision.

- The Social Security representative will ask you questions to focus in on what Social Security considers important. Do not dismiss or ignore any question. Try to answer all questions clearly and directly. If there is other information—from your doctor or employer, for example—that you believe might help answer the question, tell the representative and either direct the representative to an existing document in your file, or ask that you be allowed to provide the information before the representative makes a decision.

Informal Hearings at Social Security (cont'd)

- Be calm and polite. Social Security representatives understand that the denying or ending of benefits is an emotional matter for you, but they are not the person who made the initial decision, and they are human, so you will not do yourself any good by taking out your frustration on them.

Administrative Hearing

If Social Security denies your claim again after reconsidering it, you may request a formal administrative hearing. The hearing will be held in front of an administrative law judge. The people in the office that denied your claim won't take part in the judge's decision. That means you have a good chance of having the denial of your claim reversed at this hearing, even if you have no new information to present.

Requesting a Hearing

As with other steps in the appeal process, you must file a request for this hearing with your local Social Security office within 65 days of the date on the written notice of the decision after reconsideration.

Your request must be filed on a form called *Request for Hearing by Administrative Law Judge* (HA-501-U5), reproduced below.

Along with your completed *Request for Hearing* form, you will need to submit a form called a *Disability Report—Appeal* (SSA-3441-BK) to update your disability information. This is the same form you may have used in filing for reconsideration of your original claim. Complete instructions for completing this form can be found in *Nolo's Guide to Social Security Disability: Getting & Keeping Your Benefits*, by David A. Morton III, M.D. (Nolo).

SEE AN EXPERT

Consider getting assistance with hearing preparation from an outside professional, such as a lawyer or another counselor specializing in Social Security matters. This is particularly true if the issue is whether your physical or emotional condition qualifies you as disabled, because you'll need to gather and present evidence that's convincing enough to sway a judge's subjective determination. Your best chance of reversing Social Security's decision comes at the administrative hearing, and so you will want to be as well prepared as possible at this stage.

Completing the Request for Hearing by Administrative Law Judge Form

The first four sections of the form are straightforward. If you are seeking a spouse's dependents benefits, make sure to enter the spouse's name and Social Security number in Section 4.

Section 5 of the *Request for Hearing by Administrative Law Judge* form asks for you to state the reasons you disagree with the determination made on your claim. State your reasons here simply and briefly, for example: "The decision that I am not disabled was based on incorrect statements about the number of hours I regularly work. I am submitting letters from my coworkers explaining that I actually work fewer hours than stated in the decision ending my benefits." Or: "The DDS evaluation of my disability did not take into account my inability to travel to and from work without assistance."

Section 6 includes two boxes to indicate whether you have additional evidence to submit. You should always check the first box—the one that says you do have additional evidence. This will allow you to submit a new written statement to the judge, as well as any letters or documents that were not already in your file. If it turns out that you do not have any additional letters or documents to submit, at the hearing you can inform the judge that you have no new written materials but would like an opportunity to speak.

After you and your representative have organized your papers and spoken with your doctor, your employer, or another person who can provide additional or clarifying information about your claim, you, or you and your representative, should write a detailed statement summarizing and arguing your claim. Send that statement to your local Social Security office to be placed in your file, and also send it directly to the administrative law judge who will hear your claim. Do this at least two weeks before your hearing date so that the administrative law judge will have a chance to read the statement before the hearing. If you do not prepare it in advance, bring it with you to the hearing and present it there.

In Section 7 on the hearing request form, you must indicate whether you want to attend the hearing in person. If you don't, the judge will make a decision based on the papers in your file. It is almost always to your advantage to be present at the hearing. Your presence puts a human face on your claim and shows the judge that you are truly concerned about the outcome. It also allows the judge to ask you questions that might not get answered if you were not there.

If you check "I wish to appear at a hearing" in Section 7 but later decide not to attend the hearing, you must notify the hearing judge's office beforehand. If, on the other hand, you checked the box saying that you do not want to attend the hearing but later decide you do, contact the hearing judge's office as soon as you can. The hearing will probably have to be rescheduled to a later date. That is because hearings with the claimant present are usually scheduled at different times and places than a hearing consisting solely of a review of the file.

Section 9 asks for your representative's name and address. If you do not have a representative by the time limit for filing your request for hearing, file the request without naming anyone. If later you obtain a representative, you can supply that information then.

CAUTION

Timing may be important. To make sure that all your evidence gets in your file and to the administrative law judge in time for your hearing, you must submit all new evidence—letters, documents, records that were not previously given to Social Security—within ten days of filing your request for a hearing. So, even if you are ready to file a request for an administrative hearing immediately after you receive written notice of the reconsideration decision, it is a good idea to wait until you have gathered whatever additional information you want the hearing judge to see. This may delay slightly the date of your hearing, but it will allow you to make sure all your evidence will be considered there.

Preparing for the Hearing

During the time between filing your request for a hearing and the hearing date, you should take several steps.

First, discuss your claim with the attorney or representative who will assist or represent you at the hearing. (See "Lawyers and Other Assistance," below, for suggestions on obtaining legal representation.) It is particularly important to make sure that your representative understands what you believe to be the most important part of your claim and that he or she has thoroughly reviewed any documents that you believe support your position.

Second, examine your file, either at your local Social Security office or at the hearing office. This allows you to see that all the papers you have given to Social Security have found their way into your file. It also allows you to review all of the positive and negative information that Social Security has collected, such as a report on your disability from a DDS examination. Call your local Social Security office to see when and where you can examine your file, or if a CD containing your file can be sent to you.

Finally, ask for letters or records from your medical providers or employers establishing your claim and responding to the reasons expressed by the Social Security office or DDS examiners for rejecting your claim. Submit copies to your local Social Security office and directly to the administrative law judge, while keeping the original and at least one more copy.

SOCIAL SECURITY ADMINISTRATION
OFFICE OF DISABILITY ADJUDICATION AND REVIEW

Form Approved
OMB No. 0960-0269

REQUEST FOR HEARING BY ADMINISTRATIVE LAW JUDGE

*(Take or mail the **completed original** to your local Social Security office, the Veterans Affairs Regional Office in Manila or any U.S. Foreign Service post and keep a copy for your records)*

See
Privacy Act Notice

1. CLAIMANT NAME	CLAIMANT SSN	2. WAGE EARNER NAME, IF DIFFERENT

3. CLAIMANT CLAIM NUMBER, IF DIFFERENT	4. SPOUSE'S NAME, IF NOT WAGE EARNER	SPOUSE'S CLAIM NUMBER OR SSN

5. I REQUEST A HEARING BEFORE AN ADMINISTRATIVE LAW JUDGE. I disagree with the determination made on my claim because:

An Administrative Law Judge of the Social Security Administration's Office of Disability Adjudication and Review or the Health and Human Services will be appointed to conduct the hearing or other proceedings in your case. You will receive notice of the time and place of a hearing at least 20 days before the date set for a hearing.

6. I have additional evidence to submit. ☐ Yes ☐ No	7. Do not complete if the appeal is a Medicare issue.
Name and address of source of additional evidence: _____ _____ (Please submit it to the hearing office within 10 days. Your servicing Social Security Office will provide the address. Attach an additional sheet if you need more space.)	Check one of the blocks: ☐ I wish to appear at a hearing. ☐ I do not wish to appear at a hearing and I request that a decision be made based on the evidence in my case. (Complete Waiver Form HA-4608)

You have a right to be represented at the hearing. If you are not represented but would like to be, your Social Security office will give you a list of legal referral and service organizations. If you are represented and have not done so previously, complete and submit form SSA-1696 (Appointment of Representative) unless you are appealing a Medicare issue.

Regardless of the issue you are appealing, you should complete No. 8 and your representative (if any) should complete No. 9. If you are represented and your representative is not available to complete this form, you should also print his or her name, address, etc., in No. 9.

8. CLAIMANT'S SIGNATURE- Optional	DATE	9. REPRESENTATIVE'S NAME	DATE
RESIDENCE ADDRESS		ADDRESS ☐ ATTORNEY ☐ NON-ATTORNEY	
CITY	STATE	ZIP CODE	CITY	STATE	ZIP CODE
TELEPHONE NUMBER	FAX NUMBER	TELEPHONE NUMBER	FAX NUMBER

TO BE COMPLETED BY SOCIAL SECURITY ADMINISTRATION- ACKNOWLEDGMENT OF REQUEST FOR HEARING

10. Request received for the Social Security Administration on _____ by: _____
_____(Date)_____ _____(Print Name)_____

_____(Title)_____ _____(Address)_____ _____(Servicing FO Code)_____ _____(PC Code)_____

11. Was the request for hearing received within 65 days of the reconsidered determination?   ☐ YES   ☐ NO
If no is checked, attach claimant's explanation for delay; and attach copy of appointment notice, letter, or other pertinent material or information in the Social Security office.

12. Claimant is represented ☐ Yes ☐ No ☐ List of legal referral and service organizations provided	15. Check all claim types that apply:	
13. Interpreter needed ☐ Yes ☐ No Language (including sign language): _____	☐ RSI only	(RSI)
14. Check one: ☐ Initial Entitlement Case ☐ Disability Cessation Case ☐ Other Postentitlement Case	☐ Title II Disability-worker or child only	(DIWC)
	☐ Title II Disability-Widow(er) only	(DIWW)
	☐ SSI Aged only	(SSIA)
	☐ SSI Blind only	(SSIB)
16. HO COPY SENT TO: _____ HO on _____	☐ SSI Disability only	(SSID)
☐ CF Attached: ☐ Title II; ☐ Title XVI; ☐ Title VIII; ☐ T XVIII; ☐ Title II CF held in FO ☐ Electronic Folder ☐ CF requested ☐ Title II; ☐ Title XVI; ☐ Title VIII; ☐ T XVIII (Copy of email or phone report attached)	☐ SSI Aged/Title II	(SSAC)
	☐ SSI Blind/Title II	(SSBC)
	☐ SSI Disability/Title II	(SSDC)
	☐ Title XVIII	(HI/SMI)
17. CF COPY SENT TO: _____ HO on _____	☐ Title VIII Only	(SVB)
☐ CF Attached: ☐ Title II; ☐ Title XVI; ☐ Title XVIII ☐ Other Attached: _____	☐ Title VIII/Title XVI	(SVB/SSI)
	☐ Other - Specify: _____	

Form HA-501-U5 (08-2012) ef (08-2012)   **TAKE OR SEND ORIGINAL TO SSA AND RETAIN A COPY FOR YOUR RECORDS**
Use 02-2011 Edition Until Stock is Exhausted

The Hearing

After you file the request for hearing, you will be notified by mail of the hearing date and place. You'll receive this notice at least three or four weeks before the hearing.

If you cannot attend on that date, contact the office of the administrative law judge and arrange for a new date. Act quickly: Most offices of administrative law judges are reasonable about rescheduling, but if you wait until the last week to request a change, and you do not have a medical or another valid emergency, the judge could refuse to postpone your hearing. In that case, the judge would hold the hearing without you.

The hearing itself is conducted in a style less rigid than in a traditional courtroom but a bit more formal than a hearing at the local Social Security office. An administrative law judge presides, and everything said or done is recorded. You may be represented or assisted at the hearing by a friend or relative or by a lawyer or another advocate. (See "Lawyers and Other Assistance," below, for more information about getting legal or other help.)

You may present any evidence you would like the judge to consider—including documents, reports, and letters. And you may present the testimony of any witnesses you would like to have help prove your claim. This testimony is also informal. The person simply gives information regarding your employment or medical condition to the judge and answers any questions from the judge. The judge will give you an opportunity to explain your claim in your own words, and may also ask you some questions.

The administrative law judge who presides at your hearing is a lawyer who works for the Social Security Administration. He or she must not have taken part in the original claim decision or in reconsidering your claim. The judge will follow certain rules of procedure and may ask you questions about your claim that are not easy to answer. In general, however, the judges try to be as helpful as possible. If you are not sure how to present certain information to the judge, explain the problem and the judge should help you get the information into the official record of the case.

The judge will issue a written decision on your appeal, usually within four to six weeks of the hearing. You will receive a copy of this decision in the mail. If your claim has been denied, you will have 65 days from the date on the written notice of the denial to file a further appeal. If your claim has been approved, you may be entitled to receive benefits dating all the way back to the time you filed your original claim or even earlier.

Appeal to the National Appeals Council

If your appeal has been denied after an administrative hearing, your next step is to file a written appeal with the Social Security Administration Appeals Council. You must file this within 65 days from the date on the written notice of the administrative law judge's decision.

Completing the Form

The form you'll need at this stage of the appeals process is called *Request for Review of Hearing Decision/Order* (HA-520-U5).

The form is fairly straightforward, asking only that you give a brief explanation of why you think the administrative law judge's decision was wrong. If there's more to say than will fit onto this form, attach a separate piece of paper with the explanation. Also submit any documents that the judge did not consider but that you believe are important to your claim.

On Question 10 of the form, you'll be asked to check either "Initial Entitlement" or "Termination or other." Initial Entitlement means you were denied after your first attempt to obtain a particular benefit. Termination or other refers to when you were already receiving a benefit but Social Security decided to end it or to reduce the amount you receive.

Also notice the explanation in the middle of the form under the heading Additional Evidence. Any documents you wish to submit to the Appeals Council that are not already in your file must be either

SOCIAL SECURITY ADMINISTRATION/OFFICE OF DISABILITY ADJUDICATION AND REVIEW

Form Approved
OMB No. 0960-0277

REQUEST FOR REVIEW OF HEARING DECISION/ORDER

(Do not use this form for objecting to a recommended ALJ decision.)

(Either mail the signed original form to the Appeals Council at the address shown below, or take or mail the signed original to your local Social Security office, the Department of Veterans Affairs Regional Office in Manila, or any U.S. Foreign Service Post and keep a copy for your records.)

See Privacy Act Notice

1. CLAIMANT NAME	CLAIMANT SSN - -
2. WAGE EARNER NAME, IF DIFFERENT	3. CLAIMANT CLAIM NUMBER, IF DIFFERENT - -

4. I request that the Appeals Council review the Administrative Law Judge's action on the above claim because:

_____

_____

_____

ADDITIONAL EVIDENCE

If you have additional evidence submit it with this request for review. If you need additional time to submit evidence or legal argument, you must request an extension of time in writing now. This will ensure that the Appeals Council has the opportunity to consider the additional evidence before taking its action. If you request an extension of time, you should explain the reason(s) you are unable to submit the evidence or legal argument now. If you neither submit evidence or legal argument now nor within any extension of time the Appeals Council grants, the Appeals Council will take its action based on the evidence of record.

IMPORTANT: WRITE YOUR SOCIAL SECURITY NUMBER ON ANY LETTER OR MATERIAL YOU SEND US. IF YOU RECEIVED A BARCODE FROM US, THE BARCODE SHOULD ACCOMPANY THIS DOCUMENT AND ANY OTHER MATERIAL YOU SUBMIT TO US.

SIGNATURE BLOCKS: You should complete No. 5 and your representative (if any) should complete No. 6. If you are represented and your representative is not available to complete this form, you should also print his or her name, address, etc. in No. 6.

I declare under penalty of perjury that I have examined all the information on this form, and on any accompanying statements or forms, and it is true and correct to the best of my knowledge.

5. CLAIMANT'S SIGNATURE	DATE	6. REPRESENTATIVE'S SIGNATURE	DATE
PRINT NAME		PRINT NAME ☐ ATTORNEY ☐ NON-ATTORNEY	
ADDRESS		ADDRESS	
(CITY, STATE, ZIP CODE)		(CITY, STATE, ZIP CODE)	
TELEPHONE NUMBER ( ) -	FAX NUMBER ( ) -	TELEPHONE NUMBER ( ) -	FAX NUMBER ( ) -

THE SOCIAL SECURITY ADMINISTRATION STAFF WILL COMPLETE THIS PART

7. Request received for the Social Security Administration on _____ by: _____

                (Date)   (Print Name)

(Title)	(Address)	(Servicing FO Code)	(PC Code)

8. Is the request for review received within 65 days of the ALJ's Decision/Dismissal?   ☐ Yes   ☐ No

9. If "No" checked: (1) attach claimant's explanation for delay; and
                (2) attach copy of appointment notice, letter or other pertinent material or information in the Social Security Office.

10. Check one:
     ☐ Initial Entitlement
     ☐ Termination or other

APPEALS COUNCIL
OFFICE OF DISABILITY ADJUDICATION AND REVIEW, SSA
5107 Leesburg Pike
FALLS CHURCH, VA 22041 - 3255

11. Check all claim types that apply :
   ☐ Retirement or survivors   (RSI)
   ☐ Disability-Worker   (DIWC)
   ☐ Disability-Widow(er)   (DIWW)
   ☐ Disability-Child   (DIWC)
   ☐ SSI Aged   (SSIA)
   ☐ SSI Blind   (SSIB)
   ☐ SSI Disability   (SSID)
   ☐ Title VIII Only   (SVB)
   ☐ Title VIII/Title XVI   (SVB/SSI)
   ☐ Other - Specify: _____

Form **HA-520-U5** (07-2011) ef (07-2011)
Destroy Prior Editions

TAKE OR SEND ORIGINAL TO SSA AND RETAIN A COPY FOR YOUR RECORDS attached to the form or sent directly to the Appeals Council within 15 days after filing your request for review.

SEE AN EXPERT

If you are not yet represented by a lawyer who specializes in Social Security matters, hire one now. The Appeals Council usually reverses an administrative law judge's decision only when a technical argument can be made as to why the administrative law judge made a legal mistake. Simply arguing to the Appeals Council that the judge was wrong in deciding your case will not be enough.

Appeal Procedure

Unfortunately, your appeal to the Appeals Council is not likely to meet with much success. The Appeals Council usually reviews a case based on the written documents in your file only. It very rarely accepts a case for a hearing, and when it does, the Council meets only in Falls Church, Virginia. If you want to appear at the hearing, you have to go or send a representative to the hearing.

More often, if the Appeals Council believes there is some merit to the appeal, it sends the case back to the administrative law judge with the direction that the judge hold a new hearing and reconsider something the Appeals Council points out in its written decision.

Although the success rate of having claims denials overturned by the Appeals Council is very low, filing an appeal may be important. You are required to file this appeal before you can move on to the next step, which is filing a lawsuit in federal court.

Lawsuit in Federal Court

If your claim has been denied and you have unsuccessfully exhausted all the Social Security Administration appeals procedures, you are entitled to bring a lawsuit against the Social Security Administration in federal district court. You must file the initial papers of this lawsuit within 60 days after the Appeals Council's decision is mailed.

A federal court lawsuit is a complicated, time-consuming, and expensive procedure. However, it may be worth it. When you add up the total amount of benefits you might receive in your lifetime if your claim is approved, there may be a lot of money at stake. If the amount seems worth the time and effort to you, then you should at least investigate the possibility of filing a lawsuit. Consult with attorneys who specialize in Social Security appeals.

Whether or not you had legal assistance at some earlier stage of the appeal process, you certainly need expert legal assistance to file a lawsuit in federal court. Your odds of winning there depend almost entirely on convincing a court that the administrative law judge who heard your appeal made a mistake in interpreting the Social Security law. Simply asking a court to take another look at the facts of your case is almost never enough to win a federal lawsuit.

The main things to weigh in deciding whether to file a lawsuit are your chances of winning (as explained to you by an attorney specializing in such cases), the money it will cost you to fight the legal battle, and the amount of money in benefits that you stand to gain. If you balance all these things and it still seems like a good idea to go ahead with the lawsuit, then consider hiring an attorney to help you proceed.

Lawyers and Other Assistance

Under Social Security rules, you have a right to be represented at every stage of the appeal process by someone who understands the Social Security rules. This person may be a lawyer who specializes in Social Security matters, a nonlawyer from one of the many organizations that help people with Social Security claims, or a family member or friend who may be better than you are at organizing documents, writing letters, or speaking.

Deciding Whether You Need Assistance

It is not usually necessary to get assistance in preparing or presenting your appeal at the reconsideration stage. After reconsideration, however, and particularly if your appeal involves medical issues, it is often wise to seek assistance. This assistance can take several forms: talking over your appeal with a knowledgeable friend or relative; having a person who specializes in Social Security problems go over your papers with you, make suggestions, and assist you at hearings; or having a lawyer or another specialist prepare and present the appeal on your behalf.

What a Representative Can Do to Help

If you decide to have someone represent you during the course of your appeal—either a lawyer or another specialist—he or she can handle as much or as little of the process as you want. A representative can:

- look at and copy information from your Social Security file
- file a request for reconsideration, hearing, or Appeals Council review, and schedule or reschedule hearings
- provide Social Security with information on your behalf
- accompany you, or appear instead of you, and speak on your behalf at any interview, conference, or hearing, and
- receive copies of any written decisions or other notices sent by Social Security.

Deciding whether to hire a lawyer or to seek an experienced nonlawyer representative depends on several things, such as:

- the complexities of your case. The more complicated the issues—particularly those involving a physical or emotional condition as it relates to qualification for disability benefits—the more likely that you need expert help.
- how much money is at stake. For example, if your appeal is only about whether your disability began in March or April, it is probably not worth hiring an attorney to represent you. On the other hand, if your benefits have been reduced significantly or denied entirely, it may well be worth it to hire an attorney.

- how comfortable you feel handling the matter yourself. Particularly in the reconsideration stage of the appeal process, many people feel confident obtaining their own records and documents and discussing their claim with a local Social Security office worker. However, many other people are uncomfortable about explaining things convincingly, and so would like assistance even at this early stage. And most people become uncomfortable at the prospect of an administrative hearing, because they have never been through such a procedure before. If so, it is a good idea at least to get some advice, and perhaps representation, before this stage of the appeal process.

Where to Find Assistance

Whether you should seek assistance from a lawyer or another specialist depends on whether one or the other is easily available to you, and with whom you are most comfortable. If you reach the stage of considering going to federal court, however, you should consult with an attorney who is experienced in similar cases.

CAUTION

Appointment of a representative must be in writing. Once a person has agreed to become your representative for the appeal, you must provide his or her name to Social Security on a form entitled *Appointment of Representative* (SSA-1696). If the representative is not a lawyer, he or she also has to sign the form, agreeing to serve as your representative. If your representative is a lawyer, he or she needs only to be named on the form. The form is available online (www.ssa.gov) or at your local Social Security office, which is also where the completed form is to be filed.

Hiring Specialists Other Than Lawyers

The first place to inquire about assistance with your Social Security appeal may be Social Security itself. Every written notice denying a claim is accompanied by a written list of local community groups and legal services organizations—such as disability rights groups, legal aid offices, and senior counseling services—that either assist with appeals or refer claimants to appeal representatives.

The fact that you find someone through one of these groups or organizations does not guarantee that you will want that person to represent you; that will depend on how well you and the person communicate and whether you feel confident in his or her advice. But finding someone to assist or represent you through one of these organizations at least assures you that the person has experience in Social Security appeals and has backing from a legitimate organization.

Senior centers are good resources, too. Many have regularly scheduled sessions during which trained advocates offer advice on Social Security problems. Whether or not a particular senior center has such a program, it can usually refer you to a Social Security advocacy group whose members are trained to assist in Social Security matters. You can usually make use of these referrals if you have a disability claim, even if you are not a senior citizen.

Each state has its own agency or department handling problems of older people, including Social Security disputes. They are referred to, variously, as the office, department, bureau, division, agency, commission, council, administration, or center on aging. In most cases, this state agency will be able to refer you to some place near your home that offers assistance in preparing and presenting Social Security appeals. Call your state's agency and explain what you are looking for.

Other sources of assistance with Social Security matters are religious and social groups, business and fraternal associations, and unions. If you belong to such a group, it may have a referral service that can put you in touch with Social Security advocates.

Although many nonlawyer assistants and representatives provide free services, most charge a fee (although the amount is limited by Social Security rules—see below). The time to ask about fees is before you hire someone to assist or represent you. Get any fee agreement in writing.

Hiring Lawyers

If your income is low, a lawyer may be available to assist or represent you through a "legal services" organization that has specialists in Social Security appeals. These are nonprofit organizations that seek funding from outside sources in order to serve low-income people. The first place to look for legal services offices is on the list of references provided by Social Security along with its notice denying your claim. You can also find legal services offices—sometimes listed as Legal Aid—online or in the white pages of your telephone directory.

Beware, however, that in the steady campaign by the federal government over the past 20 years to slash public services for low-income people, many legal services offices have suffered staff cutbacks or have been eliminated altogether. So, it may not be easy to find a legal aid lawyer who can help you with your appeal.

You may also find an attorney in private practice. Be aware, though, that most private lawyers know very little about Social Security; you need to find one who specializes in Social Security claims. The Social Security referral list will either give you the names of local attorneys who specialize in Social Security appeals or give you the name of an organization that gives referrals to such private attorneys.

For directories of lawyers who specialize in Social Security issues, see www.disabilitylawyers.com and www.disabilitysecrets.com.

Your local county bar association will also have a reference list of lawyers who specialize in Social Security appeals. And while, in general, these bar association referral lists do not always include the best lawyers, in Social Security appeal matters, they usually do have the best people. That is because very few lawyers specialize in Social Security appeals, and the few who are expert in the field usually list themselves with the bar association.

Normally, lawyers cost a lot of money. However, Social Security rules strictly limit the amount of money a lawyer or anyone else can charge for a Social Security appeal, which may explain why so few lawyers specialize in the field.

Legal Limits on Lawyers' Fees

Whether your representative is a lawyer or another specialist, Social Security rules limit the fees your representative may charge. And not only are fees limited, but they must be approved by Social Security in each individual case.

Fee Agreements

Most lawyers and some nonlawyers can charge a fee only if, with their help, you win your appeal. If you win your appeal at any stage of the process, you will be entitled to benefits from the date you first applied for them (or for Social Security disability, the date you became disabled)—referred to as past-due benefits. The lawyers take their fees as a percentage of your past-due benefits. Social Security rules say that a lawyer or another representative can take as a fee 25% of your past-due benefits, or $6,000—whichever is less. If the lawyer pursues a lawsuit for you in federal court, these limits do not apply.

Fee Petitions

In some situations, lawyers are allowed to ask Social Security if they can charge more than the $6,000 cap. Social Security has the power to limit how much you are made to pay, however. If you agree to hire a lawyer under such a fee-for-service arrangement, the lawyer can't collect from you until after he or she has submitted a kind of bill called a "fee petition" to Social Security for approval.

The petition is filed when the appeal is finished, and lists in detail each service the lawyer provided for your appeal and the amount of time the lawyer spent on each such service. The lawyer must provide you with a copy of the petition. If you disagree with any of the information on the petition, you must notify your local Social Security office within 20 days of the date you receive it.

Social Security will examine the petition and determine a reasonable fee for the lawyer's services. Social Security will send you a written notice of the amount it has approved under the fee petition. The lawyer or other representative cannot charge you any more than the fee Social Security decides on, except for out-of-pocket expenses incurred during your appeal (such as costs for photocopying, phone calls, postage, and transportation to and from your hearings).

Get It in Writing

If you come to a fee arrangement with your lawyer or other representative, the representative must put it in writing, you both must sign it, and the representative must submit it to Social Security for approval. This can be done at any time before your claim is approved.

Federal Civil Service Retirement Benefits

M ore than three million people are employed by federal government agencies and departments; millions more have previously been employed there. And although the salaries of these government jobs are not always as high as those in the private sector, a comprehensive retirement system is one of the benefits that makes federal government employment attractive.

This chapter discusses the two different federal retirement systems—the Civil Service Retirement System and the Federal Employees Retirement System—and explains the benefits available under each.

Employees of State and Local Governments

Each state and many local governments have their own retirement systems for their employees. It isn't possible here to discuss the rules of all these plans, but most of them work very much like the federal government's Civil Service Retirement System (CSRS), described in this chapter.

The amount of pension funds to which an employee may be entitled is not based on total payroll contributions, as with the Social Security system, but on the highest average salary the employee reached and the number of years of employment. The age at which the employee can claim retirement benefits also depends on the number of years of employment.

As of July 1, 1991, employees of state or local governments who are not covered by an employer pension plan are covered by Social Security. These are usually part-time, temporary, or probationary workers.

To find out what retirement plan covers your work, contact your personnel or retirement plan office, or the pension office of your public employees' union, if you belong to one.

On request, the pension office should provide you with an estimate of how much your pension benefits would be if you claimed those benefits at the various retirement ages permitted by the plan.

RESOURCE

For information about nongovernment, personal retirement plans. See *IRAs, 401(k)s & Other Retirement Plans: Taking Your Money Out,* by Twila Slesnick and John Suttle (Nolo).

Federal Retirement Benefits for Same-Sex Married Couples

A recent Supreme Court ruling overturned part of the federal Defense of Marriage Act, which had denied federal retirement spousal benefits to same-sex spouses. The Office of Personnel Management (OPM), which operates the federal civil service retirement system, has yet to formally determine exactly how this ruling will apply to federal retirement benefits for same-sex married couples. But OPM states that it will extend benefits to the spouse of a same-sex marriage that was valid in the state where the marriage was performed, regardless of what state the applicant for benefits lived in at the time of the marriage or now lives in. Even if you have doubt about your status for receiving federal retirement benefits, you should apply for them.

Two Retirement Systems: CSRS and FERS

There are two entirely separate retirement systems for federal workers, depending on the date the worker was first hired. Until 1984, all federal government workers were part of the Civil Service Retirement System, or CSRS. Workers covered by the CSRS do not receive Social Security benefits for their government employment; the CSRS provides the only benefits those workers will receive for their years of federal government employment.

All federal workers hired on or after January 1, 1984 were made part of a different plan called the Federal Employees Retirement System, or FERS. Workers hired by the federal government on or after January 1, 1984 are also covered by Social Security, which means that work for the government simultaneously builds toward both FERS and Social Security benefits.

Employees who were already working for the federal government on January 1, 1984 were given a choice. They could either remain in the CSRS or switch over to the FERS. For those who switched, their years of employment under the CSRS were credited to the FERS.

The rules for both systems are quite similar, and both are administered by the federal government's Office of Personnel Management (OPM). Both the CSRS and the FERS are funded by a combination of automatic payroll deductions from federal employees and by contributions made by the employing agencies.

Under both systems, an employee can receive benefits if disabled, take early retirement, provide for a survivor, take a lump sum retirement amount instead of monthly benefits, and participate in a special savings program called the Thrift Savings Plan.

However, eligibility and benefit amounts are determined in a very different way than under the Social Security system. In particular, benefits are based on the highest average salary for any three years of employment, but do not depend on the total amount contributed in payroll deductions. And although benefits may be paid to retirees and to survivors, they are not increased if the retiree has dependents.

CSRS Retirees May Face Pension Offset

People who earned a retirement pension under the Civil Service Retirement System (CSRS) or a similar pension system that paid no Social Security taxes may be subject to a reduction in certain Social Security dependents benefits called the "government pension offset." This applies if you receive Social Security dependents or survivors benefits and also receive a retirement pension based on your own work record from the CSRS. The government pension offset does not apply to people whose own retirement benefit is under the Federal Employees Retirement System (FERS). For a full explanation of the government pension offset, see Chapter 4.

Retirement Benefits

Both CSRS and FERS retirement benefits are easy to qualify for and can be paid out in any one of several ways. Both programs also permit retirement benefits to be structured to provide for a survivor after the retired worker has died. And both offer a special savings plan that provides tax benefits and, in the case of the FERS, includes contributions by the government.

If You've Left Federal Work, Then Returned

Some people worked for the federal government before 1984—when the CSRS was their only option for retirement benefits—then left their jobs and rejoined the federal government after 1984. Those people may be entitled to retirement benefits under both systems.

If you worked for the federal government for at least five years but left that job before 1984, you may return to the CSRS if you started a new job with the federal government after January 1, 1984. If you do not choose to reenter the CSRS, you will work under the FERS, and you may qualify for retirement benefits under both the CSRS and the FERS once you have more than five years of employment under each system.

If you were out of federal employment for at least a year and you choose to reenter CSRS, you will also be covered by the Social Security system, as are FERS employees. However, once you collect both Social Security benefits and a CSRS retirement annuity, your CSRS payment will be reduced by the amount of your Social Security benefits attributable to your federal government employment.

This prevents double payment, since most CSRS recipients do not receive Social Security benefits from their federal employment, and the amount of CSRS benefits is calculated as if there were no additional retirement money from Social Security.

Who Is Eligible

If you have worked at least five years for the federal government as a civilian employee, you can qualify for a pension, referred to as a retirement annuity. In addition, you can get retirement credit for any years of military service after 1956 if you pay a premium based on the amount of your military pay. However, you cannot get credit for military service if you are collecting a military retirement pension. You can also get credit, after paying a small premium, for time you spent in the Peace Corps.

There are two types of retirement annuities under the CSRS and FERS: an immediate annuity and a deferred annuity.

Minimum Retirement Age (MRA) by Year of Birth	
The following chart tells you when you reach your MRA, depending on the year you were born.	
Birth Year	MRA
Before 1948	55
1948	55 + 2 months
1949	55 + 4 months
1950	55 + 6 months
1951	55 + 8 months
1952	55 + 10 months
1953–64	56
1965	56 + 2 months
1966	56 + 4 months
1967	56 + 6 months
1968	56 + 8 months
1969	56 + 10 months
1970 and after	57

Immediate Annuity

You can retire at age 62 and immediately begin receiving an annuity if you worked for the federal government a total of five years. The years do not have to be consecutive, nor do they have to be for the same federal agency or department. Any combination of jobs totaling five years of work will qualify you.

If you have 20 years of service with the federal government, you can claim your immediate annuity at age 60.

With 30 years of service, a CSRS-covered worker can retire with a pension at age 55. A worker covered by FERS with 30 years of service can retire with a pension at what is called the minimum retirement age (MRA). Your MRA depends on the year you were born. For people born before 1948, it is 55. For those born in 1948 and after, see the chart above.

If You Are Laid Off Before Becoming Eligible for Your Pension

CSRS and FERS rules allow some long-term workers to collect an immediate annuity if they are laid off from their jobs before reaching the normal eligibility age.

Under CSRS, a worker who has been employed for at least one year in the two years immediately before being laid off, and who is age 50 with 20 years of service or any age with 25 years of service, may be eligible for an immediate annuity.

Under FERS, the eligibility for this immediate annuity is the same, except that you need not have been employed within the past two years.

The amount of the immediate annuity is reduced from its full amount by 2% per year for every year you are under age 55 when claiming this immediate annuity.

There are two circumstances in which you may not be entitled to an immediate annuity after losing your job. The first is if you have been fired for cause: misconduct, delinquency, or poor job performance. The second is if you have been offered another job in the same agency, in the same geographic area, which is not more than two grades or pay levels below the current job, but you refuse to take it.

TIP

Special rules apply to law enforcement personnel, firefighters, and air traffic controllers. Recognizing the high stress of these jobs, the CSRS system has set early retirement years and lower requirements for years of service for these jobs. If you have been a law enforcement officer or fire fighter under the CSRS, you can claim retirement benefits at age 50 with 20 years of service. If you have been an air traffic controller, you may be able to retire at age 50 with 20 years of employment, or at any age once you have 25 years of service.

Deferred Annuity

If you end your federal employment before retirement age, you have a choice of leaving your payroll contributions in the CSRS or FERS, or withdrawing them in a lump sum when you leave employment. If you leave the contributions in the system when you end your federal job, you can claim a retirement annuity at age 62. If you leave the money in the retirement system but later decide you want it without waiting for retirement, you can collect it in a lump sum at any time before you reach age 62.

If you switch jobs, then depending on the amount of your salary and your years of service with the government, it may be to your benefit to leave your money in the retirement system. The amount of your federal retirement annuity would be based on your length of service and the highest levels of pay you received. (See "Calculating Benefits," below, for more information.)

If you have worked for a long time and have reached a relatively high salary, you will be eligible for a large pension when you reach age 62. That pension will probably amount to much more money than the lump sum you could withdraw when leaving your federal job.

EXAMPLE 1: Kazuo worked for the federal government from 1965 through 1992. In 1984, he decided to remain in the CSRS rather than switch to the FERS. By the time he left his government job, he had contributed over $10,000 to the CSRS retirement fund. Kazuo moved to another job outside the government, and did not immediately need the money in his retirement fund, so he left his contributions in the CSRS.

When Kazuo turns 62, he could collect a deferred annuity, which would then add to his monthly income from his job, or to Social Security retirement benefits if he had qualified for them by working long enough in the private sector both before and after his government job.

EXAMPLE 2: Angela worked for the federal government from 1980 through 2000. In 1984, she switched her pension coverage from the CSRS to the FERS. By the time she left her job, she had contributed almost $28,000 to the retirement fund. When Angela left the federal government, she did not immediately need the money in her retirement fund, so she left her contributions in the FERS.

When she turns 62, she can collect her FERS deferred annuity, in addition to whatever she is making on a nonfederal job, or to Social Security retirement benefits that she also earned from her years of FERS-covered government employment.

Before deciding which course of action to take, find out from the OPM exactly how much your lump sum withdrawal would be, and get an estimate of what your annuity would be at age 62. Of course, your decision will also depend on how badly you need the cash immediately upon leaving your federal job.

Calculating Benefits

Two factors are used to figure the amount of your federal CSRS or FERS retirement annuity.

The first factor is the number of years you have been employed by the federal government and contributing to the retirement fund. This can include years of military service if you also have at least five years of civilian service (unless you are receiving a military retirement pension).

The second factor is your "high-three average salary"—meaning your average salary for the three consecutive years in which you had your highest earnings. For example, if in three successive years you reached $55,000, $55,000, and $58,000, you would add these together and divide the total by three. (The total would be $168,000, which divided by three equals a high-three average of $56,000.)

Both CSRS and FERS base the retirement annuity on the high-three average, but each computes the resulting benefit differently.

TIP

You'll get a cost-of-living increase. Both CSRS and FERS benefits are increased annually to keep pace with the rising cost-of-living. As with Social Security benefits, these cost-of-living increases are tied to the rise in the Consumer Price Index, a yearly indicator of the cost of goods and services. In some years, however, there will be no cost-of-living increase if there is no increase in the Consumer Price Index.

COMPUTER

You can get benefit estimates online. The Office of Personnel Management (OPM), which operates the CSRS and FERS systems, now offers a website with a calculator that will estimate your federal civil service retirement benefits. Go to www.seniors.gov and click "Federal Employees Retirement Calculators" (under "Retirement"). The calculator can estimate what your normal, early, or disability retirement benefits are likely to be. However, the accuracy of the estimate depends greatly on how near you are to claiming your benefits—the nearer you are, the more accurate the estimate.

CSRS Benefits

Once your high-three average is calculated, CSRS computes your pension benefits by adding:

- 1.5% of your high-three average pay, multiplied by your first five years of service, plus
- 1.75% of your high-three average pay, multiplied by the number of your years of employment over five, up to ten, plus
- 2% of your high-three average pay, multiplied by the number of years of service over ten.

EXAMPLE: John put in 25 years working for a federal government agency. His highest three consecutive years of pay were $28,000, $30,000, and $32,000. That makes his high-three average pay $30,000. After 25 years, John's retirement pension would be figured like this:

- 1.5% of the $30,000 average is $450; that $450 is multiplied by the first five years of service, for a total for the first five years of service of $2,250; plus
- 1.75% of the $30,000 average is $525; that $525 is multiplied by the second five years of service, for a total for the second five years of $2,625; plus
- 2% of the $30,000 is $600; that $600 is multiplied by the remaining 15 years of service, for a total for the last 15 years of service of $9,000.

Together, the three parts of John's pension would add up to a yearly benefit of $13,875.

CSRS Benefits and Social Security

If your federal employment is covered by CSRS, it is not also covered by the Social Security system. However, most people who worked for the federal government under CSRS have also worked, or will work, at some other jobs during their lifetimes. If that other work is covered by Social Security and you have enough work credits to qualify for Social Security retirement benefits, you can collect both your retirement benefits and your CSRS annuity.

If you receive a CSRS pension and also Social Security dependents or survivors benefits based on your spouse's work record—rather than Social Security retirement benefits based on your own work record—those benefits will be severely reduced. This is known as the pension offset rule. (See Chapters 4 and 5 for further discussion of the offset rule.) If you are receiving a CSRS annuity as the survivor of a CSRS worker, this rule does not apply.

CAUTION

Some workers will receive separate CSRS and FERS benefits.
If you had years of service under the CSRS, left that job, and later returned
to work for the federal government under the FERS, you will receive two
separate annuities, one using your high-three earnings under CSRS and
the other your high-three earnings under FERS.

FERS Benefits

FERS has several different types of retirement benefits: full benefits,
reduced early retirement benefits, deferred benefits for people who
left their federal jobs before retiring, and a supplement for longtime
employees.

Full retirement annuity. Full FERS pension benefits are figured
by taking 1% of the high-three average and multiplying it by the
number of your years of service.

> EXAMPLE: Elvira worked 25 years for the federal government,
> switching to FERS in 1984. Her highest three consecutive years
> of pay were $38,000, $40,000, and $42,000. That makes her
> high-three average pay $40,000. Elvira's retirement pension
> would be figured like this: 1% of $40,000 = $400; $400 x 25
> (years of service) = $10,000, which would be her yearly pension
> annuity. And under FERS, Elvira would also collect Social
> Security retirement benefits as soon as she reaches an eligible age.

Reduced benefits for early retirement. If you have accumulated
enough years of service under the FERS, you can take early retirement with lower benefits. With ten years of service, you can take
early retirement at the minimum retirement age (MRA). (See chart
above.) Your benefits will be reduced from the full retirement amount
by 5% for each year under age 62 at which you claim retirement.

Deferred benefits if you leave. If you leave your federal job after at
least five years of service but before reaching retirement status, you
can claim retirement benefits when you reach a certain retirement
age, which depends on your years of service. With five years of

service, you can claim retirement benefits at age 62. With ten years or more, you can claim retirement at the minimum retirement age, currently 55, but the benefit will be reduced by 5% per year for every year earlier than age 62 at which you claim benefits.

 TIP

Reduced benefits may make financial sense. Although your deferred retirement benefits will be reduced 5% for every year under age 62 at which you claim them, it may still be to your advantage to claim as early as age 55. Since you are not adding any more years of service and your high-three salary remains the same, the base amount of your benefit will be the same whenever you take it.

Annuity supplement for long-term employees. A special supplement to the retirement annuity is available at age 55 to people with 30 years' service and at age 60 with 20 years' service. The supplemental amount is based on total earnings and years of service and is figured using a complex set of calculations. To determine how much your annuity supplement would be, contact the OPM office at the agency where you work.

CAUTION

Your supplement may be reduced by your earnings. Unlike the standard FERS annuity, if you are under age 62, your annuity supplement is reduced by $1 for every $2 over a certain yearly amount in earnings from other employment after you retire from federal government work. This earnings limit rule works the same as the earnings limit for Social Security benefits. (For more information, see "Working After Claiming Early Retirement Benefits" in Chapter 2.)

Survivors Benefits

Unlike Social Security retirement benefits, the surviving spouse or another survivor of a federal CSRS retiree does not necessarily receive survivors benefits after the retiree dies. To plan ahead for this, the federal worker is given several choices at retirement.

The retiring worker can choose to:

- take a full retirement annuity—if so, no benefits will be paid to any survivors after the retiree dies
- elect a full survivor benefit for a current spouse, in which case the retiree's own annuity will be less
- elect to have survivor benefits paid to someone other than a current spouse (which would also reduce the retiree's own annuity), or
- choose to provide a reduced survivor benefit, which means his or her own annuity will be lower than a full retirement annuity but higher than if a full survivor annuity were provided.

Annuity Without Survivor Benefits

At retirement, a CSRS or FERS employee can choose to take full retirement benefits without any provision for survivors. This makes particular sense if the retiree is unmarried and has no one else depending on him or her for financial support. It also makes good sense if the retiree, or retiree and spouse, have extremely limited income and immediately need the full retirement annuity to get by. Finally, it is a wise choice if the retired worker is married but his or her spouse is not likely to outlive the worker.

A worker who is married at retirement must specifically choose this no-survivor-benefit option by filing a form with the Office of Personnel Management (OPM). The worker's spouse must sign and notarize this form, which acknowledges that the retiree has given up the right to a survivor annuity. If the spouse's whereabouts are unknown, or the spouse is unable to understand the waiver and knowingly sign the form, a petition can be filed with the OPM to waive the requirement of a written consent form.

Annuity With Full Spousal Survivor Benefits

If you are married when you retire from federal employment, and you and your spouse do not waive your right to a survivor annuity, your retirement annuity will be reduced slightly to provide a lifetime annuity for your spouse if you die first.

This full survivor annuity can also be provided for a former spouse, although if the worker has remarried, the current spouse must consent. A survivor benefit ends when the surviving spouse dies, or when the surviving spouse remarries before age 55. After age 55, the surviving spouse is free to remarry without losing the survivor annuity.

The amount of full survivor annuity is slightly different for CSRS and FERS employees.

CSRS full survivor benefits. A CSRS retirement annuity is reduced, to provide full survivor benefits, by 2.5% of the first $3,600 per year, plus 10% of any amount over $3,600. The surviving spouse's annuity will be 55% of the full retirement annuity—that is, 55% of the amount before the 2.5% and 10% reductions are taken. And the 55% will include any yearly cost-of-living raises the retiree has received since the pension began.

> EXAMPLE: Ethel is eligible to receive a pension of $9,250 a year. She provides a full survivor benefit for Dante, her husband, so her own retirement annuity is reduced.
>
> The first $3,600 is reduced by 2.5%, which means Ethel receives $3,510 of that first $3,600. The remaining $5,650 is reduced by 10%, leaving $5,085. Ethel's total pension is $8,595 a year instead of $9,250, a reduction of $655 a year. For that reduction, Dante is entitled (if Ethel dies) to a surviving spouse's pension of 55% of the original $9,250, which works out to $5,087.50 a year.

FERS full survivor benefits. A FERS full retirement pension is reduced by 10% to provide an annuity for the surviving spouse. The surviving spouse's annuity will be 50% of the retiree's full pension amount—that is, 50% of the amount before the 10% reduction.

A retiring FERS worker can also choose a 5% reduction in his or her annuity, which will provide for a 25% annuity for a survivor. The survivor annuity will include any yearly cost-of-living raises the retiree receives after the pension begins.

EXAMPLE: Rigoberto is eligible to receive a pension of $12,000 a year. He provides for a full survivor benefit for Doris, his wife, reducing his own retirement annuity by 10%, or $1,200. So instead of $12,000 per year, Rigoberto receives $10,800—$12,000 minus the $1,200 reduction. In exchange for that reduction, Doris will be entitled, upon Rigoberto's death, to receive a surviving spouse's pension of 50% of the original $12,000, which works out to $6,000 a year.

Survivor Annuity to Other Than Spouse

Both the CSRS and FERS provide for a 55% survivor annuity that can be paid to a person other than a current spouse. The amount your own retirement annuity is reduced to pay for this annuity depends on the difference in age between you and the named beneficiary.

If the beneficiary you name is older than you or no more than five years younger than you, your annuity will be reduced by 10%. Your annuity is reduced 5% for every additional five years the beneficiary is younger than you—reduced 15% if five to ten years younger, 20% if ten to 15 years younger, and so on.

If the person you name as beneficiary dies before you do, you can have your own annuity restored to the full amount for the rest of your life by simply notifying the OPM. Once you have chosen to name a beneficiary, however, you cannot change your mind and restore yourself to a full pension as long as that person lives.

Reduced Survivor Benefits

Both CSRS and FERS rules allow a retiring employee to divide up his or her annuity, taking the full amount of one part and using the rest to set up a survivor annuity. You can split up your annuity into survivor and nonsurvivor parts in any proportions you want.

For example, if you are entitled to a $10,000-per-year annuity, you can choose to keep $5,000 as fully your own and direct that the other $5,000 be allotted to and reduced for a survivor benefit. That second $5,000 would be reduced by the normal survivor percentages—2.5% of the first $3,600, and 10% of the remaining $1,400—leaving you $4,770 plus the untouched $5,000. This arrangement would provide a survivor with 55% of the $5,000 you assigned to the survivor annuity, which amounts to a yearly benefit of $2,750 after your death.

Deciding Whether to Reduce Your Annuity

No obvious answer exists regarding whether to take a reduced pension to provide for another person. Each retiree and spouse, or other person who would be named as beneficiary, must decide for him or herself. It will help to consider:

Age. If your spouse or other potential beneficiary is considerably younger than you are and likely to outlive you by many years, taking a reduced pension now probably makes good sense. The 55% pension could go for many years to your beneficiary. On the other hand, if your beneficiary is considerably older than you are, there may be little advantage to reducing your own immediate pension.

Health. If you are in poor health and may not survive for many years, then it is probably more important to provide a survivor annuity. Conversely, if your beneficiary is in poor health and not likely to survive you, it is probably better to take your full pension.

Income. If your spouse or other beneficiary has or will have a substantial retirement pension or other income of his or her own, there is less need to reduce your own pension to protect your beneficiary. On the other hand, if your beneficiary is working now and earning a salary that will enable you to afford taking a reduced pension, that will permit your beneficiary to count on a survivor annuity after you are gone.

Thrift Savings Plan

In addition to the annuity pension plan to which both the employee and the employer contribute, the federal employee has the opportunity to build up tax-deferred retirement savings through the Thrift Savings Plan (TSP). The TSP is similar to 401(k) savings plans made available to some employees in the private sector.

Contributions to TSP Account

The TSP for a CSRS worker is funded solely by the worker; it is a savings account of the worker's own money, which defers tax liability until retirement. For FERS employees, the government also contributes to TSP accounts, so that the TSP is both a tax-deferring savings plan and an additional pension.

CSRS contributions. CSRS-covered workers may put up to 5% of their before-tax wages into a TSP savings account. They pay no income tax on the income, or on interest earned, if they leave the money in the account until retiring from federal service with a CSRS annuity.

FERS contributions. The government automatically contributes an amount equal to 1% of an employee's pay into a TSP account for the employee. A worker who is covered by FERS may also put up to 10% of his or her pretax wages into the TSP savings account. If so, the government will match some of the amounts an employee puts in, in addition to its automatic 1% contribution.

The government matches dollar for dollar the first 3% of wages that an employee puts in the TSP account, and matches 50 cents per dollar for the next 2% of pay the employee puts in the TSP account. If the employee leaves the money in the account until retiring from federal service, he or she won't owe any tax on the money put into the account or on the interest earned until the money is withdrawn at retirement.

Withdrawal From TSP Account

When an employee retires from federal service with either a deferred or immediate annuity, the employee may take out his or her TSP money in a lump sum or in payments of equal amounts over time. The employee will owe income tax when the amounts are withdrawn. But a person who is no longer working full time is likely to be in a lower individual income tax bracket and so will owe less in taxes.

The retiring employee also has the option to transfer the money to an Individual Retirement Account (IRA), which continues the money's tax-deferred status. The retiring employee may also use the TSP account funds to purchase an annuity, which is a plan that pays a set amount for life to the retired worker. Some annuities also permit additional payments to the spouse of a retired worker after the worker dies.

An employee who leaves federal service and withdraws the TSP money before being eligible for a retirement annuity will owe a 10% penalty tax on the money in the account. However, the employee has the option of transferring, or rolling over, the money in the TSP account to a nongovernment Individual Retirement Account (IRA), which will maintain the same tax-exempt status and avoids the tax penalty. The normal limit on yearly contributions to an IRA account does not apply to this one-time transfer of TSP funds.

 CAUTION
There is a time limit for withdrawing your funds from your TSP Account. If you leave your retirement money in your TSP account after you stop working for the federal government, you are required to start withdrawing your money by April 1 of the year following either:

- the year you turn age 70½, if you are at that time no longer employed by the federal government, or
- if you continue in federal employment after age 70½, whatever year you end that employment.

Disability Benefits to Federal Workers

Both the CSRS and FERS provide benefits for employees who become disabled while working for the government.

Who Is Eligible

If you have worked for the federal government for five years or more under CSRS, you may be eligible for benefits if you become disabled before you reach retirement age. If you are covered by FERS, you need to have been employed for only 18 months.

Definition of Disability

Under both CSRS and FERS rules, you are considered disabled if, because of disease or injury, you are unable to perform your job. In deciding whether a worker is disabled, the OPM determines if all of the following are true:

- The employee can perform useful and efficient service in the specific job.
- Every reasonable effort to preserve the person's employment, such as making physical modifications to the jobsite, has failed.
- There is no other vacant position in the same government agency and geographic area and at the same civil service grade or class as the current job that the employee could perform.

It is somewhat easier to qualify for federal civil service disability than for Social Security disability benefits. Under federal civil service rules, you don't have to be so disabled that you are unable to do any sort of paid work. Instead, you can qualify for disability benefits merely because you are unable to work in the same government agency where you already work, doing a vacant job there, at the level you had attained when you became disabled. It doesn't matter that you might be able to work at some other job at a different level or outside the government agency.

Proof of disability depends on information from two separate but equally important sources. First, your physician must write a letter to the OPM fully describing your disability and the date it began, and explain why he or she believes you are unable to perform your job effectively. You can assist your doctor by carefully explaining what your job entails and why your disability prevents you from performing it.

The second source of information is your supervisor at work. He or she must give the OPM a written statement explaining your duties at work, how your disability impairs your job performance, and whether any other job of comparable rank and pay is available to you. You can help yourself and your supervisor by pointing out the specific ways in which your disability interferes with your job and by noting when your disability began to make efficient work impossible.

Review of Disability Status

Your disability does not have to be permanent for you to receive federal employees' disability benefits. But the government, at its expense, will periodically require that you be examined by a physician to determine whether or not you continue to be disabled.

As with your original claim for disability benefits, it will be helpful if your own physician can write a letter detailing the specific ways in which your condition continues to be disabling. The letter will assist the government's doctor—who will probably only see you once, for a brief examination—in understanding why you are still disabled. The best approach is to have your own doctor write to the government doctor directly, so that the explanation of your condition and its limitations will already be in his or her file when you undergo your examination.

If your disability is found to be permanent, or if you reach age 60 without recovering from the disability, you will receive permanent disability retirement benefits. You will not be subjected to any further government examinations, and you will receive your disability benefits for life unless you are later considered to have recovered.

You are officially considered recovered if:

- You voluntarily take any new job with the federal government.
- Your yearly earnings at jobs or self-employment outside the federal government reach 80% of the current pay for your previous government job.
- A medical examination determines you are physically able to perform your job.

If any of these types of recovery occur, your disability payments will end either:

- on the date you begin reemployment with the government

- six months from the end of the year in which you earn 80% of your prior salary, or
- one year from the date of the medical exam that determined you had physically recovered.

Amount of Benefits

The amount of disability benefits is figured differently by the CSRS and the FERS.

CSRS Disability Benefit Amounts

CSRS disability benefits are the lower of either:

- 40% of your high-three average pay (defined in "Calculating Benefits," above), or
- a portion of the regular pension you would have received if you had worked until age 60. This pension figure is computed by adding together your years of service plus the number of years remaining until you reach age 60. Depending on this total, your high-three average salary is multiplied by a certain percentage—slightly more than 16% for ten years total; slightly over 26% for 15 years; slightly over 36% for 20 years; 40% for 22 years or more—to arrive at the disability benefits figure.

EXAMPLE 1: Henry went on disability at age 55, after ten years of employment during which he had reached a high-three average pay of $34,000; 40% of his high-three pay would be $14,400. Using the alternate method of computation, the number of years remaining until he reached age 60 is five, which would be added to his number of years of employment for a total of 15 years. At 15 years, the high-three average salary is multiplied by just over 26%, for a total of $8,925. Since Henry is entitled only to the lower of the two computations, he would receive $8,925 per year in benefits.

EXAMPLE 2: Alice went on disability at age 50, with 15 years of service. Her high-three average salary was $38,000. She had ten years until she reached age 60, which were added to her 15 years of service for a total of 25 years. Because this is more than 22 years, her yearly disability benefit would be 40% of her high-three average salary—which is the same figure as the alternate method of computing benefits—amounting to $15,200.

FERS Disability Benefit Amounts

Benefit amounts under FERS change over time. In the first year after disability, the disabled worker receives 60% of the high-three average pay, reduced by any Social Security disability benefits he or she may be receiving.

From the second year of FERS disability until age 62, the worker receives 40% of the high-three salary, minus 60% of any Social Security disability benefits. These benefits are increased yearly, based on a cost-of-living formula that is 1% lower than the rise in the Consumer Price Index.

At age 62, FERS computes what the disabled worker's retirement annuity would have been had he or she worked until reaching age 62. A benefit figure is determined by taking 1% of the total number of years of employment plus the number of years on disability up to age 62, and multiplying that by the worker's high-three average salary plus all cost-of-living increases since going on disability. That figure will be the yearly disability benefits for the remainder of the worker's lifetime.

Payments to Surviving Family Members

In addition to their retirement pension programs, the CSRS and FERS provide some financial support for the family of a federal worker who dies while still employed by the government.

Who Is Eligible

If a federal worker covered by either CSRS or FERS dies while still employed by the government, the surviving spouse and minor children can receive survivor benefits if the worker had been employed by the government for at least 18 months.

Benefits for Spouse

For the surviving spouse to collect benefits, either the couple must have been married at least a year when the worker died, or the surviving spouse must be the parent of the worker's child. The survivor benefit is paid to the surviving spouse regardless of the spouse's age.

A surviving spouse who also works for the federal government can collect both survivor benefits and his or her own retirement pension.

Benefits for Children

The children of a deceased federal worker also receive benefits until each reaches 18 years of age or gets married. If the child is a full-time high school or college student, benefits can continue until age 22. If a child becomes disabled before reaching age 18, the survivor benefits may continue for as long as the child is incapable of full self-support.

A child of an unmarried deceased worker also qualifies for a survivor annuity. If the unmarried worker was the father, the worker must have acknowledged the child or a court must have established paternity. A stepchild may also qualify for benefits if he or she lived with the worker in a parent-child relationship.

Amount of Benefits

The amount of survivor benefits depends on whether the deceased employee was covered by CSRS or FERS.

CSRS Benefits

If a CSRS-covered worker dies while still employed by the government, his or her surviving spouse and qualifying children will each receive an annuity.

Spouse. The surviving spouse's CSRS annuity is 55% of the retirement annuity that the worker earned before dying. The survivor is guaranteed a minimum benefit of 55% of whichever is less, either:

- 40% of the worker's high-three average pay, or
- the amount the worker's retirement annuity would have been at age 60.

A surviving spouse loses the annuity if he or she remarries before age 55; after age 55, the annuity continues regardless of remarriage. If the second marriage ends before the surviving spouse turns 55, he or she can have the survivor annuity reinstated.

Children. The amount payable to the surviving children of a CSRS-covered worker depends on whether the other parent is still alive. Each qualifying child receives an annuity based on the following computations:

- if there is a surviving parent who was the spouse of the deceased employee, 60% of the worker's high-three average pay, divided by the number of qualified children, or approximately $350 per month (the figure goes up slightly most years, adjusted for inflation), whichever is less, or
- if there is no surviving parent, 75% of the high-three average pay, divided by the number of qualified children, or approximately $400 per month, whichever is less.

FERS Benefits

FERS benefits payable to a qualified surviving child are the same as for CSRS-covered employees, discussed just above. However, they are reduced by any Social Security survivors benefits the child receives. (See Chapter 5 regarding survivors benefits.)

The amount of FERS benefits a surviving spouse may receive depends on the number of years the deceased worker was employed.

If the worker was employed for more than 18 months but less than ten years, the surviving spouse is entitled to a lump sum payment. That payment is approximately $22,000 (the figure goes up most years, adjusted for inflation), plus either 50% of the worker's yearly pay at the time of death, or 50% of the worker's high-three average, whichever is higher.

If the worker was employed for more than ten years, the surviving spouse also gets an annuity equal to 50% of what the employee's retirement annuity would have been.

These spouse's survivor benefits are not reduced by any Social Security survivor benefits.

Applying for CSRS or FERS Benefits

Decisions about both CSRS and FERS benefit claims are made by the federal government's Office of Personnel Management (OPM). You must file a written application for specific benefits. You may apply at the personnel office within the agency at which you work. If you no longer work for the agency, you may file your application at any OPM office.

You can get general information about benefits, application forms, the application process, and appeals from decisions of the OPM by telephone from the OPM's Retirement Information Office. Recorded information is available 24 hours a day at 202-606-0400. For additional help, call 888-767-6738 (toll-free) or visit www.opm.gov/retirement-services.

To obtain information about the benefits available to you based on your personal employment record, go in person to your agency's personnel office or put your request in writing and send it to:

U.S. Office of Personnel Management
Employee Services and Records Center
Boyers, PA 16017

This is the office where employee records are maintained, and most questions can be answered by the staff there. If there is some complicated question they cannot answer, they will forward your inquiry to the Washington office of the OPM, which will respond. ●

Veterans Benefits

I n addition to the pensions and benefits that arise from both public and private civilian employment, many older Americans may be eligible for certain benefits based on their military service.

The Department of Veterans Affairs (VA) operates a number of programs providing financial, medical, and other assistance to veterans. Eligibility may depend on financial need or time of service.

For older veterans, three major benefit programs are of particular value: disability compensation, veterans pensions, and, perhaps most significant, free or low-cost medical care through VA hospitals and medical facilities. This chapter explains some of these benefits.

Types of Military Service Required

Veterans benefits are available only to people who performed active service in a uniformed branch of the military: Army, Navy, Marine Corps, Air Force, Coast Guard, Women's Army Auxiliary Corps (WAAC), or Women's Air Service Pilots (WASP).

Active service is defined as either active duty or active duty for training.

Active Duty

Active duty means full-time service in one of the uniformed branches of the military forces mentioned above. It also includes full-time duty in the Commissioned Officer Corps of the Public Health Service or National Oceanic and Atmospheric Administration (NOAA), formerly Coast and Geodetic Survey. And, under some circumstances, full-time members of the Merchant Marine who served during wartime and wartime members of the Flying Tigers may also qualify.

Any length of active duty can qualify a veteran for benefits, with the exception of pensions for financially needy veterans, which require at least 90 days of active duty service. (See "Pension Benefits for Financially Needy Disabled Veterans," below, for more on need-based pensions.)

Active Duty for Training

Generally, membership in the National Guard or Reserve Corps does not qualify a person for veterans benefits. However, if a person in the Guard or Reserves is called up for full-time duty in the Armed Forces, this period of service is called active duty for training. A person who is injured or becomes ill during that period of active duty for training may be eligible for veterans disability benefits if the injury or illness leads to a disability.

Compensation for Service-Connected Disability

The VA administers a system of benefits for veterans who have a disability that can be connected in any way to a period of service. More lenient than civil disability benefit programs, a veteran can receive assistance even if he or she is only partially disabled, and almost regardless of the cause, as long as it occurred while performing some duty related to service. And if your injury or illness first arose during a period of wartime, the rules for compensation are even easier to meet.

Who Is Eligible

Compensation is available for veterans who have a "service-connected disability." Service connected means that they were wounded, injured, or became ill—or aggravated an existing condition—while on active duty, or training for active duty, in the Armed Forces.

If your condition arose while you were on active duty during peacetime, your disability must have resulted directly from military duties. In reality, though, this requirement rules out only injuries sustained while on leave, for example, or while AWOL or committing some militarily punishable offense. Virtually all other activities—including playing for the base softball team, eating in the mess, traveling to and from training, and going on authorized leave—are considered part of military duties.

The rules are even more lenient if the condition or injury occurred during time of war or national emergency, as officially designated and listed below. In such cases, you can be compensated even though the injury or illness was completely unrelated to military duties, such as while on furlough or leave. These official periods of war or national emergency include:

- **World War II.** December 7, 1941 through December 31, 1946
- **Korean War.** June 27, 1950 through January 31, 1955
- **Vietnam War.** August 5, 1964 through May 7, 1975, and
- **Persian Gulf War.** August 2, 1990 through a date yet to be set by Congress or Presidential Proclamation.

Note that the periods of time considered part of the Second World War and the Korean War are longer than the time spans normally attributed to those conflicts.

Amount of Benefits

The amount of disability compensation to which you are entitled depends on the seriousness of the disability. When you apply for disability compensation, your medical records are reviewed and VA personnel will examine you to assess your disability.

Your disability is given a rating, based on the extent to which it interferes with the average person's ability to earn a living. This rating is expressed in percent of disability—0% to 100% disabled, in increments of 10%.

Unfortunately, this rating system does not normally take into account the real effect of your disability on the work you do. Rather, it applies arbitrary percentages—20% or 30% for the loss of a finger or toe, for example—to the theoretical average person's ability to earn a living. Obviously, the loss of a finger affects a piano player much more than it affects an opera singer. But the VA usually applies its fixed schedule of disabilities to common injuries and diseases.

Disabilities From Agent Orange, Radiation, and Gulf War Syndrome

Because of the military use of chemicals and radioactive materials, many veterans have fallen ill with serious, disabling diseases years after their service ended. These veterans used to have no way to prove their disease was caused by exposure during military service. After sustained pressure from veterans groups, the VA has finally admitted that certain exposure does indeed cause specific diseases. As a result, if a veteran was exposed to Agent Orange or radiation and later is disabled by certain diseases, the disability is *presumed* to be service connected. To a limited extent, the same can be said of "Gulf War Syndrome."

Vietnam and Agent Orange: If you served in Vietnam and have become disabled by one of the following diseases, you are presumed to have contracted the disease through exposure to Agent Orange and may be eligible for service-connected disability benefits. Diseases include prostate cancer, Hodgkin's disease, multiple myeloma, respiratory cancers (lung, bronchus, larynx, trachea), non-Hodgkin's lymphoma, chloracne, porphyria cutanea tarda, soft-tissue sarcoma, and acute/subacute peripheral neuropathy.

Radiation exposure: If your work in the military exposed you extensively to ionizing radiation, you may be eligible for service-connected disability benefits if you have become disabled by most types of leukemia or lymphoma, most types of cancer, brain or central nervous system tumors, thyroid disease, or multiple myeloma.

Gulf War Syndrome: Almost immediately after serving in the Gulf War, many veterans complained about illnesses—joint pain, rash, fatigue, memory loss, intestinal problems—that they did not have before service in the Gulf. The cause(s) of these illnesses have not been definitively diagnosed, and the government initially went to great lengths to deny that they were caused by military service—even suggesting that they were not really illnesses at all. Slowly and grudgingly, the government changed its tune. If a veteran has a chronic qualifying disability, that illness may now be presumed to

> ### Disabilities From Agent Orange, Radiation, and Gulf War Syndrome (cont'd)
>
> be connected to Gulf service. And if the illness results in a persistent disability, the veteran may be eligible for service-connected disability compensation. For information about Gulf War-related illness and compensation, a veteran may call a special Gulf War Veterans Information Hotline at 800-PGW-VETS.

However, if your disability does not match any of the simple descriptions in the VA's rating system, when rating your individual disability, the VA may consider the effect of your condition on the work you are able to do.

Benefits range from about $130 per month for a 10% disability to about $2,900 per month for total or 100% disability. If you have at least a 30% disability rating, your dependents are also eligible for some minimal benefits.

Eligible dependents include your spouse and your children up to age 18, or age 22 if a full-time student, or of any age if disabled. The total amount received depends on the number of dependents and on your disability rating—the higher the rating, the higher the benefits. The additional amounts for dependents range from $45 to $160 per month for a spouse and $30 to $100 per month for each child.

Changes to Your Rating

Although most service-connected disabilities show up during or soon after military service, some conditions may not appear, or not become disabling, until years after you get out of the service. Regardless of when a condition actually becomes disabling, if it can be traced to injury or illness that occurred while you were in the service, it can be compensated.

EXAMPLE: Claudio's knee was bashed while serving as a cook at a training camp during the Vietnam War. The knee healed well and Claudio had no serious trouble with it during the war or the years immediately following it. However, as he got older, his knee got steadily worse. His doctor diagnosed Claudio with a serious arthritic condition in the knee, a result of the wartime injury.

Because Claudio's knee condition resulted from his wartime service, he was entitled to claim disability benefits when the knee began to interfere with his normal activities, even though he made no such claim before he was discharged from the service.

Sometimes, a disability that rated low when it first appeared will grow progressively worse in later years. In such a case, a veteran can claim disability benefits even if he or she was previously rated by the VA as not disabled. Or the veteran can apply for an upgrading of an already-existing disability rating if the condition has worsened over time.

EXAMPLE: Ernie was an M.P. in Kuwait during the Persian Gulf War. While on leave, Ernie picked up a lung infection. The scarring from it, over the years, occasionally gave him minor respiratory difficulty. A few years after his discharge, Ernie applied for a service-connected disability. Although he picked up his illness while on leave, he was eligible for benefits because he had been on active duty during wartime. He was given a 10% disability rating for his labored breathing.

As he got older, Ernie experienced more breathing difficulties, to the point that even mild exertion made his breathing painful and dangerously difficult. His doctor said that poorer circulation with age was making Ernie's lung condition worse. Since his doctor verified that his condition had worsened, Ernie could apply for an upgrading of his disability rating. The new disability rating was 40%, which meant not only that Ernie's own benefits would be higher, but that his wife was also eligible for some benefits as a qualifying dependent. (See "Amount of Benefits," above, regarding dependents benefits.)

Pension Benefits for Financially Needy Disabled Veterans

A small monthly cash benefit is available to a financially needy wartime veteran who is 100% disabled from causes that are not service-connected. Unfortunately, the amount is usually extremely low, only enough to bring the veteran's total income from all sources to just above the poverty line.

To qualify for this small cash benefit, the veteran must have had 90 days or more of active duty, with at least one day during a period of war. (See "Compensation for Service-Connected Disability," above, for the list of recognized periods of war.) However, there is no requirement of service in or near actual combat.

A totally disabled veteran who meets the service requirements is granted an amount that will bring his or her total annual income—including income from private pensions, Social Security, and SSI—up to minimum levels established by Congress. Those minimum levels, however, are extremely low: about $1,000 per month from all sources for a veteran with no dependents, about $1,350 per month for a veteran with one dependent—a spouse, or a child under age 18, or disabled—and slightly higher for each additional dependent.

Some veterans are entitled to a larger benefit if they live in nursing homes, are unable to leave their houses, or are in regular need of aid and attendance. Veterans with out-of-pocket medical expenses are also entitled to a larger benefit.

Limits on Assets

The pension described in this section is not for veterans with savings or other assets that could be used or cashed in for living expenses. (Fortunately, these potential living expense assets exclude the value of a home the veteran lives in.) Even disabled veterans with little or no income will not qualify for the pension benefits if they have assets over $80,000, depending on the cost of living where the veteran lives and the amount of ongoing medical expenses that the veteran pays out of pocket.

Survivors Benefits

Several VA programs provide benefits to a veteran's surviving spouse, and in some instances to surviving children.

The VA's Definition of Eligible Marriage

To collect benefits as the surviving spouse of a veteran, you must have been married to the veteran for at least one year and be married at the time of his or her death.

If you were divorced from the veteran, you cannot claim survivors benefits. Even if you were still married when the veteran died, you lose survivors benefits if you later marry someone else.

If you remarried after the veteran's death but that later marriage has ended, you may again be eligible for survivors benefits through your first spouse's record.

VA Benefits for Same-Sex Spouses

A recent United States Supreme court decision now allows the same-sex married spouse of a veteran to collect VA benefits. Whether the same-sex spouse of a veteran can collect a VA benefit, under the same terms as an opposite-sex spouse, depends on whether the spouse lives in a state that recognizes the validity of same-sex marriage. Here are the situations where the VA, for purposes of paying any VA spousal benefit discussed in this chapter, will recognize your same-sex marriage as valid:

- You legally resided in a state that recognized same-sex marriage at the time you got married, regardless of whether the state you now live in recognizes same-sex marriage.
- When you married, you lived in a state that did not recognize same-sex marriage, but you travelled to marry in another state that did recognize same-sex marriage. You later moved to another state that recognizes same-sex marriage, and while living there you became eligible for VA benefits.

Dependency and Indemnity Compensation

A benefit known as Dependency and Indemnity Compensation (DIC) is paid to the surviving spouse of an armed forces member who died either while in service or from a service-connected disability after discharge. However, if the veteran was dishonorably discharged, no benefits will be paid to the survivor.

The amount of the DIC benefit depends on when the veteran died, and on whether he or she had a service-connected disability at the time of death:

- For the surviving spouses of veterans who died on or after January 1, 1993, the basic monthly DIC benefit is $1,233; an additional $262 per month is paid if the veteran had a 100% disability rating from a service-connected disability during the eight years immediately before his or her death. Additional amounts can be paid if the veteran has a minor child or the surviving spouse is in a care facility or housebound.
- For the surviving spouses of veterans who died before 1993, the benefit amounts depend on the veteran's military rank.

For a complete listing of DIC benefit amounts, see the Department of Veterans Affairs website at www.benefits.va.gov/compensation.

Wartime Service Pension

The surviving spouse of a veteran may claim a monthly pension, regardless of whether death was connected to service, if that veteran would have been eligible for a wartime service pension. This survivor pension, like the veteran's wartime pension, requires that the survivor have a low income, taking into account money from any other pensions or Social Security benefits the surviving spouse receives.

A veteran's surviving children may also collect a survivors wartime pension after the veteran's death.

The amount of a survivor's pension depends on the survivor's income and whether or not the survivor also has dependent children, is housebound, or requires "aid and attendance" (see below). Maximum pensions are between about $700 and $1,300 per month, but these amounts are usually reduced based on the survivor's income.

Aid and Attendance

The Aid and Attendance (A&A) benefit is a special additional program to assist veterans and survivors who are eligible for DIC benefits and who are either living in a nursing facility or are housebound. If a survivor is in a nursing facility, an A&A benefit can add about $300 per month to whatever DIC benefit he or she is already receiving; for a housebound survivor, the benefit is usually slightly less. The amount of the benefit depends on whether the survivor has additional sources of income, and on the survivor's medical expenses.

TRICARE Medical Coverage for Military Retirees and Dependents

A comprehensive and generous system of medical coverage, completely separate from veterans benefits, is available for retired military service members, their spouses, and their children younger than 21. This system is known as TRICARE and is administered by the Department of Defense. People with TRICARE coverage who become eligible for Medicare must be enrolled in both programs. For details on TRICARE eligibility, benefits, and the coordination of TRICARE and Medicare, visit the TRICARE website at www.tricare.mil.

Medical Treatment

One of the most important benefits available to veterans is free or low-cost medical care. The VA operates more than 150 hospitals throughout the country. In addition, a great number of outpatient clinics provide health care for veterans. Also, specialized care may be available at no charge through a VA hospital, while the same care might be unavailable or beyond a veteran's means in the world of private medicine.

Medicare and VA Medical Treatment

Many veterans who are eligible for VA medical treatment are also covered by Medicare. The general rule is that for any specific medical treatment, you can choose either of the benefits, but not both. This means that if you are charged copayments for treatment at a VA facility, Medicare cannot pay for them. However, if you are treated by a private doctor or facility and the VA pays most but not all of the cost, Medicare may be able to pay some of the unpaid amount. If you are treated by a private doctor or facility and Medicare covers the bills, you cannot submit any unpaid portion to the VA.

There is a significant exception to this rule, which kicks in where the VA covers services that Medicare doesn't. For example, if the VA authorizes you to receive treatment at a private facility but does not cover all the services you receive, Medicare can pay for any of those services if Medicare does cover them.

Additional Veterans Programs Are Available

This chapter explains the major programs for which older veterans are usually eligible. However, the VA administers many more programs that a veteran may find useful.

The VA also provides financial support for education and vocational training, life insurance, home loans and other housing assistance, and a National Cemetery burial program.

Eligibility requirements vary for each of these programs, but either active duty or active duty for training are usual requirements. (See "Types of Military Service Required," above, for definitions.) For information about other services the VA offers veterans and their families, visit the VA's website at www.va.gov.

If you had active duty in the military and were discharged under conditions other than dishonorable, you may be eligible for VA health care benefits. If you enlisted after September 7, 1980 or entered active duty after October 16, 1981, you must have served for 24 uninterrupted months to be eligible for health care. This minimum service time may not apply if you were discharged due to a service-connected disability or for hardship. In a few pilot programs at VA medical centers, dependents and survivors of a veteran may also receive some care if they are unable to afford care in the private sector. (But this kind of care for dependents and survivors is rare in a VA medical system heavily stressed by Vietnam, Iraq, and Afghanistan war veterans.) The VA may also pay for long-term care in certain private facilities for some veterans with serious service-connected disabilities, if there is no space in a local VA facility.

Even if you qualify for treatment at a VA medical facility, however, you may not always be able to get the care when you need it, or the treatment may be available only at a VA facility far from your home. The reason for these limits, even for eligible patients, is that while there are close to 100,000 beds in VA hospitals, many more than 100,000 veterans and dependents need medical care.

To meet the demand for medical care, and particularly for the limited number of hospital beds, the VA has established a priority system for deciding who gets treatment directly from VA hospitals, clinics, and doctors:

- **Priority Group 1:** Veterans with service-connected disabilities rated 50% or more disabling
- **Priority Group 2:** Veterans with service-connected disabilities rated 30% or 40% disabling
- **Priority Group 3:** Veterans who are former POWs, were discharged for a disability incurred or aggravated in the line of duty, have service-connected disabilities rated 10% or 20% disabling, or were disabled by treatment
- **Priority Group 4:** Veterans who are receiving aid and attendance or housebound benefits (see "Aid and Attendance," above)
- **Priority Group 5:** Veterans with a 0% disability rating whose income and assets are below certain dollar limits

- **Priority Group 6:** Gulf War veterans receiving care solely for Gulf War-related disorders not amounting to compensable disabilities, veterans with compensable 0% service-connected disabilities, and World War I veterans, and
- **Priority Group 7:** All other veterans. If accepted for treatment, this group must pay a copayment for services.

Getting Information and Applying for Benefits

The Veterans Administration maintains a website (www.va.gov) with much useful information about the programs discussed in this chapter. The website can be a little overwhelming, but if you're comfortable navigating on the Internet, you may find the site very useful. You might find it easiest to use the site's search engine (in the upper right-hand corner of the home page) by filling in just the specific subject you are interested in, such as disability benefits or Aid & Attendance.

The VA maintains large regional offices in major cities, and many smaller offices known as Vet Centers in cities both large and small. Although applications are processed and decisions made at the regional offices, the Vet Centers provide information about benefits and claims. The Vet Centers can also provide you with application forms for various benefits, assist you in filling them out, and help you with any appeal if you are denied a benefit.

To find either the regional office or the Vet Center nearest you, look in the government pages in your telephone directory under United States Government, Veterans Affairs Department. Or, call the VA's national benefits information line at 800-827-1000, or their health benefits line at 877-222-8387. Also check the VA website at www.va.gov.

When appearing in person at a Vet Center, the veteran should bring discharge papers, medical records if applying for disability benefits, and wage or tax records indicating current income if considering an application for wartime service pension benefits.

A surviving spouse should bring the veteran's discharge or other military papers, marriage certificate, recent wage or tax records, and birth certificates for any minor children, or for a surviving child up to age 22 who is disabled or a full-time student, plus evidence of their disability or student status.

Requests for medical treatment or admission to a VA medical facility, or VA coverage of medical treatment by a private facility, are usually handled at the admitting office of the VA medical facility or clinic itself. A veteran seeking medical attention at a VA hospital should (after calling to find out its appointment procedures) bring discharge papers, documents indicating that the veteran is receiving VA disability benefits and whether or not any medical condition is service connected, and documents indicating whether the veteran is receiving a VA pension. ●

Medicare

The high cost of medical care and medical insurance, coupled with the lack of a comprehensive health plan available to all, is not a credit to the United States. Yet whenever discussion of this monumental failure makes its way into the political arena, proposals for creating a decent health care system run into dual roadblocks. The first is mounted by heavily bankrolled corporate interests—pharmaceutical, medical technology, and hospital companies; the insurance industry; and most doctors' groups—who fight any limits on their profit making. The second is set up by politicians who refuse to take any steps that might be seen as opposing the interests of the moneyed portion of the population.

In 1965, however, over howls of protest by many in corporate boardrooms and government, the Medicare national health insurance system was introduced as a way of providing a certain amount of guaranteed coverage for older citizens. And for over 40 years now, Medicare has been carving an inroad into the mountain of consumer health care costs.

Medicare pays for most of the cost of hospitalization and much other medical care for older Americans (though for some, it still leaves almost half of all medical costs unpaid). Medicare now provides this coverage for over 50 million people, most of them age 65 and older.

Despite its broad reach, Medicare does not pay for many types of medical services, and it pays only a portion of most services it does cover. Although Medicare expanded its coverage in 2006 to include some of the cost of prescription drugs, it has done nothing to address the overall spiraling costs of those drugs.

And while the 2010 federal health care reform act expanded Medicare coverage of certain preventive screenings and examinations, and slightly improved prescription drug coverage, it did not otherwise broaden Medicare.

This chapter discusses the Medicare system, what it covers, and how much it pays. Chapter 13 shows you how to apply for Medicare and take full advantage of its benefits.

The chapters that follow present detailed information about how to fill the gaps in Medicare coverage. Medigap supplemental insurance is discussed in Chapter 14, and the various Medicare Advantage plans are sorted out in Chapter 15. If you have a low income and few assets, Chapter 16 explains the government Medicaid program, which provides free coverage in place of buying private insurance or a managed care plan.

If You Will Turn 65 Soon

If you are turning 65 soon (and are not already enrolled in Medicare through disability benefits eligibility), there are several things you need to do to prepare for Medicare.

Find out if your current health insurance will continue when you hit 65 and, if so, how it works in conjunction with Medicare.

See what Medicare supplement ("medigap") insurance policies (Chapter 14) and Medicare Advantage plans (Chapter 15) are available where you live.

Decide whether to enroll in traditional fee-for-service Medicare (this chapter), and whether to add a medigap policy (Chapter 14) to this, or instead to enroll in a Medicare Advantage plan (Chapter 15).

Look into whether you may be eligible for Medicaid (Medi-Cal in California) coverage, or for state assistance with your Medicare costs (Chapter 16).

Learn about Medicare prescription drug coverage and the insurance plans available in your state to deliver that coverage (this chapter).

Speak to your physician about scheduling an initial Medicare physical examination (within six months after first enrolling) and about preventive services covered by Medicare that are appropriate to your physical condition and health history.

The Medicare Maze

There are two different ways that someone eligible for Medicare can receive the program's benefits. The first way is called "traditional Medicare" or "original Medicare." With this type of Medicare coverage, a beneficiary can receive care from any doctor, hospital, clinic, or other provider who accepts Medicare patients. Medicare pays the provider a fee for each specific service. For services for which Medicare does not fully pay, the patient has several choices. The patient can choose to:

- pay out of pocket
- buy a private supplemental insurance policy—commonly known as "medigap" insurance—that pays much of what Medicare does not (see Chapter 14)
- buy a separate Medicare Part D prescription drug coverage insurance plan, or
- apply for Medicaid coverage (Medi-Cal in California), which is a federal program for low-income people that pays almost all of the health care costs that Medicare does not pay. Even if you do not qualify for Medicaid, you can apply for subsidized coverage of prescription drugs through Medicare Part D.

The second way that people can receive Medicare benefits is through a Medicare Advantage plan, offered by private insurance companies. These plans cover everything that traditional Medicare does, plus some services Medicare doesn't cover at all. Some Medicare Advantage plans also include outpatient prescription drug coverage. And, they eliminate some of the copayments and deductibles required by traditional Medicare.

Medicare Advantage plans are managed care plans similar to an HMO. They are generally a bit less expensive than a combination of traditional Medicare with a medigap supplemental insurance policy. However, Medicare Advantage plans limit the doctors and other health care providers a patient may use, control referrals to specialists, and otherwise sometimes place restrictions on care. Medicare Advantage plans also annually change the copayment amounts they charge enrollees and sometimes limit or eliminate specific coverage, and sometimes even eliminate coverage entirely in a particular geographic area. (For more information, see Chapter 15, Medicare Part C: Medicare Advantage Plans.)

Because of these limitations, only about 28% of Medicare beneficiaries are enrolled in Medicare Advantage plans, and many of those are required to enroll because of their dual status as enrollees in both Medicare and Medicaid (see Chapter 16).

Medicare Prescription Drug Coverage

At the end of 2003, Congress passed the Medicare Modernization Act—a large-scale change to the Medicare laws. As a result, Medicare now includes Part D, which provides some coverage for outpatient prescription drug costs. And in 2010, the new federal health care reform law improved that coverage for people with high drug costs.

Unfortunately, Medicare Part D prescription drug coverage leaves many drug costs uncovered. And it does nothing about the soaring overall costs of prescription drugs. In fact, the law specifically bars the Medicare program from negotiating with drug companies for lower prices on behalf of Medicare patients. This restriction, which received almost no media attention, is a staggering giveaway to the pharmaceutical industry. It ensures that in the years to come, drug prices will continue to increase at rates far above the cost of living, which will, in turn, place enormous economic pressure on seniors and the Medicare program alike. Also, the law enacting the new program handed the drug plans over to private insurance companies—whose inefficient overhead and enormous profits will likely add to the cost of prescription drugs under the new program.

Nonetheless, the Medicare Part D program does provide some prescription drug coverage not previously available to many Medicare beneficiaries. (Medicare Part D's coverage is explained at the end of this chapter.)

> ⚠ CAUTION
>
> **Once you're Medicare eligible, your retirement health coverage may be cut off.** About 12 million Medicare beneficiaries receive some kind of retirement health benefits from their former employers. These benefits often dovetail with Medicare coverage, paying its deductibles and copayments, and covering services Medicare does not, including prescription drugs. However, under a rule issued by the federal Equal Employment Opportunity Commission, employers are free to reduce that health coverage or eliminate it entirely for retirees age 65 or older—even if they maintain the coverage for younger retirees. If this happens to you, you'll have to fill in the gaps in Medicare coverage some other way, as described in Chapters 14 through 16.

Medicare: The Basics

Medicare is a federal government program that assists older and some disabled people with paying their medical costs. Part A is called hospital insurance, and covers most of the costs of a stay in the hospital, as well as some follow-up costs afterward. Part B, medical insurance, pays some of the costs of doctors and outpatient medical care. And Part D pays some prescription drug costs. Medicare Part C refers to separate Medicare Advantage plans, which can replace Parts A and B (see Chapter 15).

Medicare is operated by the Centers for Medicare & Medicaid Services (CMS), part of the Department of Health and Human Services, in cooperation with the Social Security Administration. The Medicare program's daily business, however, is run by private companies, called carriers or intermediaries, operating under contract with the federal government.

Most of a patient's direct contact with Medicare happens with the company—Blue Cross, Blue Shield, or another large insurance company—that administers Medicare in his or her state or that runs the patient's Medicare Part D prescription drug plan.

One of the outrages of the current Medicare political storm is that giving Medicare administrative monopolies to these private insurance companies drives up the cost to the public.

Health Coverage If You Stop Working Before Age 65

Medicare and Medicare supplemental insurance and Medicare Advantage plans are available to most people age 65 and older. But what if you stop working before age 65—either because you choose to retire, are laid off, or lose your business? Chances are you'll lose your health insurance at the same time. Then the issue becomes finding affordable medical coverage, and a plan that will cover preexisting conditions, to fill the gap until you turn 65.

Here are some ways to try to stretch your medical coverage without turning to the open market for an individual health insurance policy:

- **Take advantage of continued health insurance from your employer.** If you are entitled to retirement benefits from your employer, these may include continued health care coverage. Be aware, however, that your employer is permitted to drop that retiree health coverage once you turn 65 and are eligible for Medicare. If you aren't automatically eligible for retiree health coverage, you may be able to negotiate continued health coverage with your employer as part of your severance package, or with the purchaser of your business as part of its sale price.

- **Convert to individual coverage under an employer-sponsored plan.** Some employer-sponsored insurance plans permit employees to convert their group coverage to individual coverage upon leaving their employment. If your plan allows this, you will probably have to pay all the premiums—and they may well be higher than when you were part of a group policy. Even if such individual coverage is available to you through your employer, you may want to compare its coverage and cost with individual insurance available through the new federal or state health insurance exchanges (see below).

- **Continue coverage under COBRA.** The U.S. Congress passed the Consolidated Budget Reconciliation Act (COBRA) in 1985. It mandates a period of continued health coverage for people who

Health Coverage If You Stop Working Before Age 65 (cont'd)

lose or leave their jobs (unless they're fired for gross misconduct) and their spouses and children. It also applies to employees whose hours are reduced below the number that qualifies them for health benefits. If you qualify, you are entitled to buy 18 months of health insurance from the same company following the end of your employer-sponsored coverage. However, the extent of your coverage may be reduced, and you'll have to pay the full premiums—which will probably be higher than what your employer paid for you. For more information, see *The Essential Guide to Federal Employment Laws*, by Amy DelPo and Lisa Guerin (Nolo), or search "COBRA" on the Department of Labor website at www.dol.gov. Also, check with the agency in your state dealing with labor and employment—most states have passed their own laws expanding on COBRA's coverage.

- **Find individual health insurance through your state's insurance exchange or the federal insurance marketplace.** Any individual can buy a health insurance policy regardless of his or her prior medical history. These policies are sold through what is called a health insurance exchange, or marketplace, established by the Affordable Care Act (also known as Obamacare). The cost of the health insurance policies depend on your age, the level of coverage you seek, and your income. Twenty-three states and the District of Columbia have established their own state health insurance exchanges, while residents of the other states are eligible to use the federal marketplace. To find out what's available where you live, go online to the government site www.healthcare.gov.

- **Claim early Medicare based on disability.** If you stop working because of a disability and you qualify for Social Security disability benefits, you will qualify for full Medicare coverage once you have been entitled to disability benefits for 24 months. (See Chapter 3 for a full discussion of Social Security disability benefits.)

Medicare and Medicaid: A Comparison

People are sometimes confused about the differences between Medicare and Medicaid. Medicare was created to deal with the high medical costs that older citizens face relative to the rest of the population—especially troublesome given their reduced earning power. However, eligibility for Medicare is not tied to individual need. Rather, it is an entitlement program; you are entitled to it because you or your spouse paid for it through Social Security and Medicare taxes.

Medicaid, on the other hand, is for low-income, financially needy people, set up by the federal government, and administered differently in each state.

Although you may qualify for and receive coverage from both Medicare and Medicaid, you must meet separate eligibility requirements for each program; being eligible for one program does not necessarily mean you are eligible for the other. If you qualify for both, Medicaid will pay for most Medicare Part A and B premiums, deductibles, and copayments or will offer you enrollment in a managed care plan that provides a combination of Medicare and Medicaid coverage.

Chapter 16 explains Medicaid and the chart below describes the basic differences between the two programs.

Part A Hospital Insurance

Medicare is divided into several parts. Hospital insurance, referred to as Part A, covers most of the cost of care when you are at a hospital as an inpatient. Your remaining medical costs are covered, at least in part, by Medicare Part B. And Medicare Part D covers part of your prescription drug costs. If you are enrolled in a Medicare Part C Medicare Advantage plan (see Chapter 15), your hospital insurance is provided by that plan rather than by Medicare Part A.

A Comparison of Medicare and Medicaid

Medicare	Medicaid
Who Is Eligible	
Medicare is for almost everyone 65 or older, rich or poor; people on Social Security disability; and for some people with permanent kidney failure.	Medicaid is for low-income and financially needy people, including those older than 65 who are also on Medicare.
Medicare is an entitlement program; people are entitled to Medicare based on their own or their spouse's Social Security contributions, and on payment of premiums.	Medicaid is an assistance program only for the needy.
Who Administers the Program	
Medicare is a federal program. Medicare rules are the same all over the country.	Medicaid rules differ in each state.
Medicare information is available at your Social Security office or through the Centers for Medicare & Medicaid Services.	Medicaid information is available at your local county social services, welfare, or department of human services office.
Coverage Provided	
Medicare hospital insurance (Part A) provides basic coverage for hospital stays and posthospital nursing facility and home health care.	Medicaid provides comprehensive inpatient and outpatient health care coverage, including many services and costs Medicare does not cover, most notably, prescription drugs, some diagnostic and preventive care, and eyeglasses. The amount of coverage, however, varies from state to state.
Medicare medical insurance (Part B) pays most of basic doctor and laboratory costs, and some other outpatient medical services, including medical equipment and supplies, home health care, and physical therapy. It covers some of the cost of prescription drugs for those who sign up for supplemental drug coverage (Part D).	Medicaid can pay Medicare deductibles and the 20% portion of charges not paid by Medicare. Medicaid can also pay the Medicare premium.

A Comparison of Medicare and Medicaid (cont'd)	
Medicare	Medicaid
Costs to Consumer	
You must pay a yearly deductible for both Medicare Part A and Part B. You must also pay hefty copayments for extended hospital stays.	In some states, Medicaid charges consumers small amounts for certain services.
Under Part B, you must pay the 20% of doctors' bills Medicare does not pay, and sometimes up to 15% more. Part B also charges a monthly premium. Under Part D, you must pay a monthly premium, a deductible, copayments, and all of your prescription drug costs over a certain yearly amount and up to a ceiling amount, unless you qualify for a low-income subsidy.	

Who Is Eligible

There are two types of eligibility for Medicare Part A hospital insurance: free and paid. Most people age 65 and older are eligible for free coverage, based on their work records or on their spouse's work records. People older than 65 who are not eligible for free Medicare Part A coverage can nevertheless enroll in it and pay a monthly fee. (See Chapter 13 for enrollment procedures.)

Free Coverage

Most people age 65 and older are automatically eligible for Medicare Part A hospital insurance. They do not have to pay any monthly premium for it; the coverage is free.

The two largest categories of people automatically eligible are:

- people age 65 or older who are eligible for Social Security retirement benefits, or have civil service retirement work credits equal to an amount that would make them eligible for Social Security retirement. (See Chapters 2 and 10 regarding eligibility for these two programs.) You are automatically eligible for Medicare coverage even if you do not actually begin collecting your retirement benefits at 65, as long as you could have started collecting them. If you wait to claim retirement benefits until after 65, you may still begin Medicare coverage at 65. However, if you begin collecting retirement benefits before age 65, you must wait until age 65 to get Medicare coverage.

- people age 65 or older who are eligible for Social Security dependents or survivors benefits. Note that people who are age 65 or older and eligible for dependents benefits when a spouse turns 62 are entitled to Medicare coverage whether or not the spouse actually claims retirement benefits.

Some additional categories of people who may also be eligible for free coverage include:

- people of any age who have been entitled to Social Security disability benefits for 24 months
- people with amyotrophic lateral sclerosis (ALS) who have been approved for Social Security disability benefits (no waiting period), and
- anyone who has permanent kidney failure requiring either a kidney transplant or maintenance dialysis, if the person or spouse has worked a certain amount at jobs covered by Social Security. For details of this coverage, check with your local Social Security office. If you have any trouble qualifying for Medicare based on kidney failure, contact the National Kidney Foundation, 30 East 33rd Street, New York, NY 10016; 800-622-9010, www.kidney.org.

Paid Coverage

If you are age 65 or older but not automatically eligible for free Part A hospital insurance coverage, you can still enroll in the Medicare hospital insurance program by paying a monthly premium. The amount of your premium depends on how many Social Security work credits you or your spouse have earned, and on how long after your 65th birthday you apply for coverage.

If you or your spouse has 30 to 39 work credits, the monthly premium is lower: $204 per month in 2015. If neither you nor your spouse has 30 work credits, the monthly premium is higher: $407 per month in 2015. Also, if you enroll in Part A coverage more than a year after you turn 65, your premium will be 10% higher than these monthly figures (unless you fit under an exception, such as having health coverage through an employer).

> CAUTION
>
> **Make sure to compare costs.** If you are considering enrolling in and paying for Medicare Part A hospital insurance, it may be cheaper for you to do so through an HMO or a health plan. The cost of such coverage will be part of the broader coverage and cost for full participation in the HMO or health plan, which will vary among different plans. Before purchasing Medicare Part A coverage as an individual, compare premiums and benefits of various group plans.

If you enroll in paid Part A hospital insurance, you must also enroll in Part B medical insurance, for which you pay an additional monthly premium. However, you may enroll in Part B without Part A.

Types of Care Covered

Part A hospital insurance pays much of the cost you incur directly from a hospital as part of inpatient care. Under some circumstances, it also covers some of the cost of inpatient treatment in a skilled nursing facility and by a home health care agency. Doctors' bills are not included in Part A coverage; they are covered under Medicare Part B.

A few basic rules apply to all claims under Part A hospital insurance coverage, whether for inpatient care at a hospital or nursing facility or for home health care.

Doctor-Prescribed Care

The care and treatment you receive must be prescribed by a licensed physician.

Reasonable and Necessary Care

The inpatient care you receive must be medically reasonable and necessary—that is, the type of care that can be provided only at a hospital or nursing facility. If you could receive the particular treatment just as well and safely as a hospital outpatient, at the doctor's office, or at your home, Part A will not cover you if you receive that treatment as an inpatient. Also, Part A will not normally cover the cost of hospitalization for elective or cosmetic surgery—except for reconstructive surgery after an accident or a disfiguring illness—because these are not considered medically necessary.

 CAUTION

"Held for observation" is not the same as "admitted." Medicare Part A hospital insurance covers someone only if and when he or she is actually admitted to the hospital as an inpatient. Many times a patient is held and treated at the hospital—in a bed, in a room for as much as 48 hours—but not formally admitted to the hospital. This is known as being "held for observation" and does not trigger coverage by Medicare Part A. Instead, Medicare Part B medical insurance (see later in this chapter) would be available to cover the care provided by the hospital and the doctors, and Medicare Part D prescription drug coverage could cover any medications provided.

The problem is that the copayments and deductibles a patient has to pay under Medicare Part B and Part D are generally much higher than under Part A. Also, being held for observation—rather than being actually admitted to the hospital—does not trigger eligibility for Part A coverage of follow-up skilled nursing facility or rehabilitation care (see the following section), which is quite common after hospital treatment. This can mean the entire very expensive cost of the nursing or rehab facility care must be paid out of the patient's pocket.

If you or a loved one are taken to the hospital and treated there for more than 24 hours, ask your doctor to have you or the loved one formally admitted to the hospital, rather than merely being held for observation, so that Medicare Part A coverage will be available to cover the stay and any following skilled nursing or rehabilitation facility inpatient care.

> ! CAUTION
> **Custodial care isn't covered.** Part A hospital insurance covers only skilled medical treatment of an illness or injury. It does not pay for a stay in a hospital or nursing facility, or for care from a home health agency, when the services you receive are primarily to make life more comfortable—to help with dressing, eating, bathing, or moving around. In reality, distinctions between medical treatment and custodial care sometimes blur, which can result in disputes between Medicare administration and patients.

Medicare-Approved Facility or Agency

Medicare issues licenses to hospitals, nursing facilities, and health care agencies certifying that they meet its standards for quality of care and staffing. Medicare will cover only care that is provided by facilities it approves.

Find out in advance if the facility to which you plan to be admitted, or the home health care agency you intend to hire, is approved by Medicare and accepts Medicare payment. Check with the facility's admissions services or administrator's office, or with the administrator of the home health care agency.

Nowadays it is rare to find a hospital or skilled nursing facility that is not Medicare approved. Some home health care agencies, however, are not Medicare approved. That does not necessarily mean that the agency is not reputable. Under most circumstances, Medicare Part A pays for very little home care, anyway. So if Medicare is not going to cover much of your costs, you may want to switch to an agency that is good and less expensive, but not Medicare approved, as soon as your Medicare coverage ends.

Facility Review Panel Approval

Each hospital and nursing facility has a panel of doctors and administrators that reviews your doctor's decision to treat you as a hospital inpatient or at a nursing facility. The panel usually agrees with your doctor's initial decision. And the panel and your doctor usually agree on how long you should remain in the facility. Sometimes, though, the panel decides you do not need to be an inpatient to receive certain treatment. Or it decides that you could be discharged from the facility earlier than your doctor recommended. The panel and your doctor will then consult with one another. Usually, they reach an agreement.

If, however, your doctor and the review panel do not agree that you require inpatient care, or they differ as to your discharge date, the question of whether Medicare Part A will pay for your inpatient care will be referred to a Peer Review Organization (PRO). (See Chapter 13 for more on the review process.)

CAUTION
Psychiatric stays are limited. Medicare Part A covers inpatient psychiatric hospital care, but the total number of days covered is limited. (See the "Psychiatric Hospitals" section, below, for details.)

Foreign Hospital Stays

In almost all situations, Medicare does not cover hospital stays outside the United States, Puerto Rico, the Virgin Islands, Guam, and American Samoa, even in an emergency. There are, however, three exceptions to this rule:

- If you are in the United States when an emergency occurs and a Canadian or Mexican hospital is closer than any U.S. hospital with emergency services, Medicare will help pay for your emergency care at that foreign hospital.
- If you live in the United States and a Mexican or Canadian hospital is closer to your home than the nearest U.S. hospital, Medicare can cover your care there even if there is no emergency.
- If you are in Canada while traveling directly to Alaska from one of the other states, or from Alaska to one of the other states, and an emergency arises, you may be covered for your care at a Canadian hospital. However, Medicare will not cover you if you are vacationing in Canada.

CAUTION

Consider buying travel insurance. Because there is no Medicare protection for you while you are traveling outside the United States, and if you have no other medical insurance that would cover you while traveling, it might be wise to look into traveler's insurance. These short-term policies are available for a one-time-only premium. A travel agent should be able to give you details. Many medigap supplemental insurance policies and Medicare Advantage plans provide coverage for foreign travel emergencies. If you have such coverage, you may not need extra travel insurance.

Skilled Nursing Facilities

A growing number of patients recovering from surgery or a major illness are referred by their doctors to skilled nursing facilities (sometimes also called rehabilitative care centers). These provide an important, less expensive alternative to hospitalization. Medicare may cover some of your costs of staying in a skilled nursing facility, but strictly limits how much it will pay. (See "How Much Medicare Part A Pays," below, for details.)

You'll need to make sure your stay will be covered at all. You must meet two requirements before Medicare will pay for any nursing facility care. You must have recently stayed in a hospital, and your doctor must verify that you require daily skilled nursing care.

Prior Hospital Stay

Your stay in a skilled nursing facility must begin after you have spent at least three consecutive days, not counting the day of discharge, in the hospital as a formally admitted inpatient—and within 30 days of being discharged. If you leave the nursing facility after coverage begins, but are readmitted within 30 days, that second period in the nursing facility will also be covered by Medicare. For details, see "Benefit Period or Spell of Illness," below.

Inpatient Care Generally Covered by Part A

The following list gives you an idea of what Medicare Part A does, and does not, pay for during your stay in a participating hospital or skilled nursing facility. Remember, though, even when Part A covers a cost, there are significant financial limitations on its coverage. (See "How Much Medicare Part A Pays," below, for the dollar figures.)

Medicare Part A hospital insurance covers:

- a semiprivate room (two to four beds per room); a private room if medically necessary
- all meals, including special, medically required diets
- regular nursing services
- special care units, such as intensive care and coronary care
- drugs, medical supplies, and appliances furnished by the facility, such as casts, splints, wheelchair; also, outpatient drugs and medical supplies if they permit you to leave the hospital or nursing facility sooner
- hospital lab tests, X-rays, and radiation treatment billed by the hospital
- operating and recovery room costs
- blood transfusions; you pay for the first three pints of blood, unless you arrange to have them replaced by an outside donation of blood to the hospital, and
- rehabilitation services, such as physical therapy, occupational therapy, and speech language pathology services (speech therapy) provided while you are in the hospital or nursing facility.

Medicare Part A hospital insurance does not cover:

- personal convenience items such as television, radio, or telephone
- private duty nurses, or
- a private room, when not medically necessary.

Requiring Daily Skilled Nursing Care

Your doctor must certify that you require daily skilled nursing care or skilled rehabilitative services. This care includes rehabilitative services by professional therapists and skilled nursing treatment, such as giving injections, changing dressings, monitoring vital signs, or administering medicines or treatments, which cannot be performed by untrained personnel. This daily care must be related to the condition for which you were hospitalized.

If you are in a nursing facility only because you are unable to feed, clothe, bathe, or move yourself, even though these restrictions are the result of your medical condition, this will not be covered by Part A.

Levels of Nursing Facility Care

Most nursing facilities provide what is called custodial care—primarily personal, nonmedical care for people who are no longer able to fully care for themselves. Custodial care often lasts months or years, and is not covered at all by Medicare. For the most part, custodial care amounts to assistance with the tasks of daily life: eating, dressing, bathing, moving around, and some recreation. It usually involves some health-related matters: monitoring and assisting with medication and providing some exercise or physical therapy. But it is ordinarily provided mostly by personnel who are not highly trained health professionals, and does not involve any significant treatment for illness or physical condition.

A different, short-term kind of care known as skilled nursing facility care is covered by Medicare, although there are severe limits. (See "How Much Medicare Part A Pays," below, regarding these limits.) Skilled nursing facility care, which takes place in a hospital's extended care wing or in a separate nursing facility, provides high levels of medical and nursing care, 24-hour monitoring, and intensive rehabilitation. It is intended to follow acute hospital care due to serious illness, injury, or surgery—and usually lasts only a matter of days or weeks.

This is because you do not require skilled nursing care as defined by Medicare rules. However, if you require occasional part-time nursing care, you may be eligible for home health care coverage (described below) through Part A.

The nursing facility care and services covered by Medicare are similar to what is covered for hospital care. They include:

- a semiprivate room (two to four beds per room); a private room if medically necessary
- all meals, including special, medically required diets
- regular nursing services
- special care units, such as coronary care
- drugs, medical supplies, treatments, and appliances provided by the facility, such as casts, splints, wheelchair, and
- rehabilitation services, such as physical therapy, occupational therapy, and speech therapy, provided while you are in the nursing facility.

Medicare coverage for a skilled nursing facility does not include:

- personal convenience items such as television, radio, or telephone
- private duty nurses, or
- a private room when not medically necessary.

Home Health Care

Progressive health care professionals often encourage people to get out of hospitals and nursing facilities and into their own or family members' homes while recovering from injury or illness. With less honorable motives, insurance companies also pressure hospitals to release patients earlier so that if they continue to receive care, it will be a less costly variety at home.

In response to both these movements, the use of home health care (including part-time nursing care and physical and other therapies), and home health care agencies to provide the care, has increased enormously over the past two decades. The following sections explain Medicare's substantial coverage of home health care. You can also read Medicare's online publication "Medicare and Home Health Care" at www.medicare.gov/publications/pubs/pdf/10969.pdf.

RESOURCE

Learn more about home health care. For a complete discussion of long-term care, particularly for older people, and how to finance it, see *Long-Term Care: How to Plan & Pay for It*, by Joseph Matthews (Nolo). For ordering information, visit www.nolo.com.

Skilled Nursing Home and Home Health Care Even If No "Improvement"

Medicare Part A coverage for inpatient skilled nursing facility care or for home health care is intended for a period of recovery following a hospital stay for an illness, an injury, or surgery. But there is some dispute as to whether Medicare coverage ends when patients reach a "plateau" of recovery and their condition is stable with no likelihood of improving. Medicare takes the position that once there is no more improvement, Part A coverage ends. Several federal courts, though, have said that coverage should continue if only skilled care can help keep the patient's condition from deteriorating.

The question of whether a person's condition continues to require Medicare Part A-covered skilled nursing care, either in a nursing facility or at home, or instead only requires nonskilled custodial care, which Medicare Part A does not cover, is tricky. If you or a loved one are in a situation in which Medicare is threatening to cut off skilled nursing care, your best allies in keeping coverage are your doctor and the facility or agency providing the care. They need to make it clear to Medicare that skilled nursing care is still needed in order to maintain the patient at a functioning level, even if the patient's underlying condition is not likely to improve.

Coverage Provided

Part A home health care coverage requires a prior three-day hospital stay. Home care without a prior hospital stay may be covered by Part B. If you qualify for home care coverage, Medicare pays for the following services provided by a participating home health care agency:

- part-time skilled nursing care—usually two to three visits per week as part of a plan certified by a physician, and
- physical therapy, occupational therapy, and speech therapy.

If you are receiving part-time skilled nursing care, physical therapy, occupational therapy, or speech therapy, Medicare can also pay for:

- part-time home health aides
- medical social services, and
- medical supplies and equipment provided by the agency, such as a hospital bed, a walker, or respiratory equipment.

However, Medicare will not pay for a number of services sometimes provided as part of home health care, including:

- full-time nursing care
- drugs and biologicals administered at home
- meals delivered to your home, or
- housekeeping services.

Restrictions on Coverage

Despite the obvious financial as well as recovery advantages of home health care, Medicare coverage for it is severely restricted to the following:

- The agency providing the care must participate in Medicare—meaning it must be approved by Medicare and must accept Medicare payment. Many agencies do not participate in Medicare, so find out before making arrangements.
- You must be confined to your home by an injury, illness, or other medical condition. If you need nursing care or other medical services but you are physically able to leave home to receive it, you might not be eligible for Medicare home health care coverage.
- You must initially require part-time skilled nursing care or physical or speech therapy. After your home health care coverage begins, Medicare can continue to cover your home care even if you need only occupational therapy—which helps you regain physical skills needed for daily living that you may have lost because of the illness or injury. Occupational therapy alone, however, cannot justify home health care coverage in the first place.

- Your doctor must determine that you need home health care and must help set up a care plan in cooperation with the home health care agency. If your doctor has not mentioned home care to you but you feel it would be a good idea, make your wishes known. Most doctors will prescribe home care, can give you a referral to a Medicare-approved agency, and will cooperate with the home health care agency.

Hospice Care

Hospice care is home health care provided to a terminally ill patient who is in the last six months or so of life (as certified by his or her physician). Hospice care focuses not on treating the illness or fostering recovery, but on making the patient as comfortable as possible. Good hospice care may combine the efforts of family, doctors, nurses, social workers, dietitians, and clergy, as well as physical therapists and other trained caregivers.

Medicare does not provide 24-hour hospice care, but it does cover visits by health care workers to the patient's home on a regular basis—daily if necessary—including a hospice nurse on 24-hour call. Significantly, and unlike other nonhospital Medicare coverage, Medicare also pays for any medication prescribed by a physician for symptom management and hospice patient comfort.

Medicare may also cover up to five days of inpatient care in a hospital or skilled nursing facility to give the family or other primary caregivers a respite from their duties. If approved by the hospice, this five-day respite care period may be repeated during a patient's care.

The following sections explain how Medicare coverage of hospice works. Medicare's website also provides information about its hospice coverage in the booklet *Medicare Hospice Benefits*, which you can find at www.medicare.gov/Publications/Pubs/pdf/02154.pdf.

Coverage Provided

Medicare Part A can cover nearly the full cost of hospice care. Hospice care covered by Medicare includes:

- physician services provided by a physician connected with the hospice—Medicare Part B will continue to cover services provided by the patient's personal doctor
- nursing care
- medical supplies and appliances
- drugs for management of pain and other symptoms
- health aide and homemaker services
- physical and speech therapy, and
- medical social services, counseling, and dietary assistance.

Restrictions on Coverage

Care must be provided by a Medicare-approved hospice, under a plan developed by the hospice and the patient's attending physician. The patient's doctor and the hospice's medical director must certify that the patient is terminally ill, with a life expectancy of six months or less. And the patient must sign a statement choosing hospice care instead of standard Medicare Part A benefits.

Right to Return to Regular Medicare Coverage

Some people do not take advantage of hospice care, out of a misunderstanding about how it impacts their Medicare coverage. They may mistakenly fear that they'll permanently lose their regular Medicare coverage, won't be covered by Medicare for hospitalizations, or will outlive their six-month diagnosis and be stuck without Medicare coverage. The fact is, however, that a Medicare patient may disenroll from hospice care and return to regular Medicare coverage at any time. If the patient's doctor certifies that the six-month life expectancy no longer applies, the patient can "graduate" from hospice and return to regular Medicare.

This sometimes occurs with degenerative diseases, such as congestive heart failure or emphysema; the physician's best time estimate may be off by years. Most people who disenroll do so after the first or second 90-day evaluation period (discussed further in the next section).

How Much Medicare Part A Pays

To understand any Medicare decision about how much of your hospital, nursing facility, or home care bill it will pay, you have to know the basics of Part A payments. Those basics include benefit periods and deductible and coinsurance amounts.

Benefit Period or Spell of Illness

How much Medicare Part A pays depends on how many days of inpatient care you have during what is called a benefit period or spell of illness.

A benefit period or spell of illness refers to the time you are treated in a hospital or skilled nursing facility, or some combination of the two. The benefit period begins the day you enter the hospital or skilled nursing facility as an inpatient—and continues until you have been out for 60 consecutive days. If you are in and out of the hospital or nursing facility several times but have not stayed out completely for 60 consecutive days, all your inpatient bills for that time will be figured as part of the same benefit period (even if you are readmitted for a different illness or injury).

There is no limit to the number of benefit periods you can have over your lifetime, except for stays in psychiatric hospitals (see below).

Hospital Bills

Medicare Part A pays only certain amounts of a hospital bill for any one benefit period.

The Deductible Amount

For each benefit period, you must pay an initial amount before Medicare will pay anything. This is called the hospital insurance deductible. The deductible is increased every January 1. In 2015, the amount is $1,260.

First 60 Days Hospitalized

For the first 60 days you are an inpatient in a hospital during one benefit period, Part A hospital insurance pays all of the cost of covered services.

You pay only your hospital insurance deductible. If you are in more than one hospital, you still pay only one deductible per benefit period—and Part A covers 100% of all your covered costs for each hospital. However, nonessentials, such as televisions and telephones, are not covered.

61 Through 90 Days

After your 60th day in the hospital during one spell of illness, and through your 90th day, each day you must pay what is called a "coinsurance amount" toward your covered hospital costs. Part A of Medicare pays the rest of covered costs. In 2015, this daily coinsurance amount is $315; it goes up every year.

Two Benefit Spells May Be Better Than One

You can get more total days of full Medicare coverage during two spells of illness than in just one. As a result, it can be in your financial interest to stretch your hospital or nursing facility stays into two benefit periods, if possible. For example, using home health care may help you stay out of the hospital or nursing facility for 60 days before you must return as an inpatient for further treatment. If the timing of your inpatient treatment could be somewhat flexible, discuss that timing and its effect on Medicare coverage with your doctor.

EXAMPLE: Oscar is in the hospital with circulatory problems, being treated with medication. His doctor recommends surgery, operating on one leg at a time, monitoring the first leg before attending to the second. Oscar and his doctor plan the dates of surgery so that he will be released from the hospital and will convalesce at home, with the help of home health care services, for more than 60 days before he returns to have the second operation.

This way, Medicare will consider the time Oscar spends in the hospital after the second surgery to be part of a new spell of illness, even though it results from the same condition that made the first operation necessary. If there had not been a 60-day break between hospitalizations, Oscar would have been in the hospital a total of more than 60 days and would have had to pay a hefty coinsurance amount for every day after his 60th day in the hospital—up to his 90th day.

Reserve Days

Reserve days are a last-resort coverage. They can help pay for your hospital bills if you are in the hospital more than 90 days in one benefit period. But the payment is quite limited. If you are in the hospital for more than 90 days in any one spell of illness, you can use up to 60 additional reserve days of coverage. During those days, you are responsible for a daily coinsurance payment. For 2015, the reserve days coinsurance amount is $630 per day. Medicare pays the rest of covered costs.

You do not have to use your reserve days in one spell of illness; you can split them up and use them over several benefit periods. But you have a total of only 60 reserve days in your lifetime. Whatever reserve days you use during one spell of illness are gone for good. In the next benefit period, you would have available only the number of reserve days you didn't use in previous spells of illness.

TIP

Try to save up your reserve days. Even if you are in the hospital for more than 90 days, you may want to save your reserve days for an even rainier day. For example, you may not want to use your reserve days if you currently have some private insurance, such as from an employer, that can help cover the costs of those extra days of hospitalization, but you may not have that insurance later in life.

EXAMPLE: Bert had a serious stroke, followed by several complications involving kidney failure and pneumonia. For six months, he was in and out of both a hospital and a skilled nursing facility (SNF), for a total of 130 days. Because Bert never spent 60 consecutive days out of the hospital or SNF, all his inpatient treatment was considered part of the same "benefit period." So when his time in the hospital reached 91 days, he had no choice but to begin using up his "reserve days" coverage. He used 20 reserve days during this benefit period, leaving him with only 40 reserve days for the remainder of his lifetime.

If Bert had remained out of the hospital and SNF for 60 consecutive days during any part of this stretch of treatment, he would not have had to use up any reserve days. Or, if his condition had permitted it, he might have been able to receive some care in an intermediate-level or custodial care nursing facility instead of in an SNF. However, this would have been a practical alternative only if he had some supplemental health coverage that would have paid for some or all of this level of care (Medicare doesn't cover it at all).

Or, if Bert's condition had permitted, he might have received some care at home from a Medicare-approved home health care agency. Medicare would have paid the full amount of this care. And it would not have affected his right to receive coverage when he needed to return to the hospital or SNF.

If you want to use your reserve days, you don't have to make a formal request or fill out any form. Medicare will automatically apply them to cover your hospital bills—minus the daily coinsurance you have to pay.

But if you do not want to use those reserve days, or want to use some but not all of them, you must notify the hospital administrator or billing office. Plan ahead: You must submit your notification before the reserve days come up.

Psychiatric Hospitals

Medicare Part A hospital insurance covers a total of 190 days in a lifetime for inpatient care in a specialty psychiatric hospital (meaning one that accepts patients only for mental health care, not just a general hospital).

If you are already an inpatient in a specialty psychiatric hospital when your Medicare coverage goes into effect, Medicare may retroactively cover you for up to 150 days of hospitalization before your coverage began. In all other ways, inpatient psychiatric care is governed by the same rules regarding coverage and copayments as regular hospital care.

There is no lifetime limit on coverage for inpatient mental health care in a general hospital. Medicare will pay for mental health care in a general hospital to the same extent as it will pay for other inpatient care.

EXAMPLE: During the five months before his 65th birthday, Horace spent 60 days in a psychiatric hospital. Those 60 days are subtracted from Horace's lifetime total of 190 days of Medicare coverage in a psychiatric hospital. It leaves him with only 130 days more coverage under Part A for psychiatric hospitalization.

Skilled Nursing Facilities

Despite the common misconception that nursing homes are covered by Medicare, the truth is that it covers only a limited amount of inpatient skilled nursing care.

For each benefit period, Medicare will cover only a total of 100 days of inpatient care in a skilled nursing facility. For the first 20 of these 100 days, Medicare will pay for all covered costs, which include all basic services but not television, telephone, or private room charges. For the next 80 days, the patient is personally responsible for a daily copayment; Medicare pays the rest of covered costs. In 2015, the copayment amount is $157.50; the amount goes up each year.

Reserve days, available for hospital coverage, do not apply to a stay in a nursing facility. After 100 days in any benefit period, you are on your own as far as Part A hospital insurance is concerned. However, if you later begin a new benefit period, your first 100 days in a skilled nursing facility will again be covered.

EXAMPLE: Bettina was hospitalized for several weeks with a broken hip. Upon leaving the hospital, she was moved to a Medicare-approved SNF for rehabilitation and recovery. She remained in the SNF for 18 days, then went home. However, some setbacks in Bettina's healing forced her to return to the SNF a week later, where she stayed for another 12 days.

Because Bettina's stays in the SNF were not separated by 60 days, they were considered to be within the same "benefit period." Therefore, of her total 30 days in the SNF, Medicare will pay the entire amount of her bills (minus Bettina's phone calls to her brother in New Zealand) for only the first 20 days. For the remaining ten days, Bettina will be responsible for a copayment of $157.50 per day, for a total of $1,575.

If Bettina had had a medigap supplemental insurance policy (see Chapter 14) or a Medicare managed care plan (see Chapter 15) that covered Medicare nursing facility copayments, or had she been eligible for Medicaid (see Chapter 16), that insurance, care plan, or government program would have paid all or part of the $1,575. Having no such extra coverage, Bettina will have to pay out of her own pocket.

Home Health Care

Medicare Part A pays 100% of the cost of your covered home health care when provided by a Medicare-approved agency—and there is no limit on the number of visits to your home for which Medicare will pay.

Medicare will also pay for the initial evaluation by a home care agency, if prescribed by your physician, to determine whether you are a good candidate for home care.

However, if you require durable medical equipment, such as a special bed or wheelchair, as part of your home care, Medicare will pay only 80%.

Hospice Care

Medicare pays 100% of the charges for hospice care, with two exceptions. First, the hospice can charge the patient up to $5 for each prescription of outpatient drugs the hospice supplies for pain and other symptomatic relief. Second, the hospice can charge the patient 5% of the amount Medicare pays for inpatient care in a hospice, nursing facility, or the like every time a patient receives respite care.

How Part A Payments Are Figured

To get a picture of how the overall Part A payment scheme works, an example of one person's hospital stay may be useful.

Annika was hospitalized for three weeks for a serious intestinal disorder, went home for a week, came back to the hospital for another ten days, was released again, and then had to return to the hospital for surgery. Annika spent two more weeks in the hospital recovering from the operation. Annika's hospital bill for all this treatment includes:

Semiprivate room, 45 days at $604 per day	$27,200
Surgery surcharge	1,675
Intensive care, 2 days at $1,820 per day	3,640
Laboratory	980
Medication	465
Whole blood (6 pints at $32 per pint)	192
Telephone	94
Television (6 weeks at $70 per week)	420
TOTAL DUE	$34,666

Medicare will pay all covered costs less the $1,260 deductible:

- 45 days in a semiprivate room ($27,200)
- surgery surcharge ($1,675)
- intensive care costs for two days ($3,640)
- the second three pints of blood ($96)
- laboratory work ($980), and
- medication ($465).

Medicare will not pay for:

- television or telephone costs ($514 must be paid by Annika), or
- the first three pints of blood; Annika must pay the $96.

So Medicare covers $34,056, minus the $1,260 deductible, which Annika must pay. Annika also remains responsible for the $610 in uncovered costs (phone, TV, and blood).

Remember, though, that Annika will still have to face her doctors' bills, whose coverage depends on her Medicare Part B medical insurance. (See "Part B Medical Insurance," below, for a discussion of Part B coverage.)

There is no limit on the amount of hospice care you can receive. At the end of the first 90-day period of hospice care, your doctor will evaluate you to determine whether you still qualify for hospice— meaning your disease is still considered fatal and you are still estimated to have less than six months to live. A similar evaluation is made after the next 90-day period, and again every 60 days thereafter. If your doctor certifies that you are eligible for hospice care, Medicare will continue to pay for it even if it exceeds the original six-month diagnosis. And if your condition improves and you switch from hospice care back to regular Medicare coverage, you may return to hospice care whenever your condition warrants it.

> EXAMPLE: Ted is suffering from cancer. His doctors say it will be fatal within six months. Ted chooses to stop his chemotherapy treatment, stay at home, and receive hospice care there. After 90 days, however, Ted has not gotten any worse. His doctors determine that Ted's cancer has not progressed much and that Ted may live for another year or two. So Ted returns to traditional Medicare coverage.
>
> After another nine months, however, Ted's cancer becomes much more aggressive. After Ted undergoes a short course of chemotherapy, his doctor estimates that Ted now has less than six months to live. Ted can now return to hospice care and stay on it for as long as his doctor still believes the cancer will be fatal within six months.

Part B Medical Insurance

The second part of Medicare coverage, Part B, is medical insurance. It is intended to help pay doctor bills for treatment either in or out of the hospital, as well as many of the other medical expenses you incur when you are not in the hospital.

Eligibility and Premiums

The rules of eligibility for Part B medical insurance are much simpler than for Part A: If you are age 65 or older and are either a U.S. citizen or a resident of the United States who has been here lawfully for five consecutive years, you are eligible to enroll in Medicare Part B medical insurance. This is true whether or not you are eligible for Part A hospital insurance.

Anyone who wants Part B medical insurance must enroll in the program. (See Chapter 13 for details on enrollment procedures.) Everyone enrolled must pay a monthly premium. The premium is raised each year on January 1.

For 2015, the basic monthly Part B premium for most people is $104.90. This includes everyone:

- who is already enrolled in Medicare Part B
- who has their Part B premium deducted from their monthly Social Security benefit check, and
- whose adjusted gross income is less than $85,000 ($170,000 for a couple filing jointly), based on a 2013 tax return.

However, if your adjusted gross income is at least $85,000 ($170,000 for a couple), the monthly premium is higher, as shown on the following chart.

Yearly Income	Monthly Premium
Single $85,000–$107,000	$146.90
Married $170,001–$214,000	
Single $107,001–$160,000	$209.80
Married $214,001–$320,000	
Single $160,001–$213,000	$272.70
Married $320,001–$426,000	
Single more than $213,000	$335.70
Married more than $426,000	

If in the prior two years (since your 2013 tax return) you have become widowed or divorced, or had a significant drop in income because of retirement or reduced work, you may contact Medicare and request an adjustment of the surcharge on your premium.

Medicare Medical Insurance Is Never Enough

Part B Medicare medical insurance is intended to pay for a portion of doctor bills, outpatient hospital and clinic charges, laboratory work, some home health care, physical and speech therapy, and a very few drugs and medical supplies. But there are heavy restrictions on what is covered and on how much is paid.

Private Medicare supplement insurance—referred to as medigap insurance—may help you make up the difference. Instead, many people fill in the gaps in Medicare by joining a Medicare Part C Medicare Advantage health plan, often in the form of a managed care plan, that combines basic Medicare-level coverage with supplemental benefits. (See Chapter 14 for a discussion of medigap insurance, and Chapter 15 to learn more about Medicare Advantage plans.) If you cannot afford private supplement insurance, you may be eligible for Medicaid—a public program for people with low income and few assets. (See Chapter 16 regarding the Medicaid program.)

Types of Services Covered

Part B medical insurance is intended to cover basic medical services provided by doctors, clinics, and laboratories. However, the lists of services specifically covered and not covered are long, and do not always make a lot of common sense.

Making the effort to learn what is and is not covered can be important, because you may get the most benefits by fitting your medical treatments into the covered categories whenever possible.

Doctor Bills

Part B medical insurance covers medically necessary doctors' services, including surgery, whether the services are provided at the hospital, at a doctor's office, or—if you can find such a doctor—at home. Part B also covers outpatient medical services provided by hospital and doctors' office staff who assist in providing care, such as nurses, nurse practitioners, surgical assistants, and laboratory or X-ray technicians.

> **TIP**
> **Medicare pays for a second opinion before surgery.** Before undergoing surgery, it is usually medically wise to get a second opinion from another doctor. Second opinions often lead to the decision not to have surgery. Recognizing this, and the savings involved, Medicare will cover your obtaining a second doctor's opinion before undergoing any kind of surgery. And if the second doctor's opinion conflicts with the original doctor's recommendation for surgery, Medicare will pay for an opinion by yet a third doctor.

Outpatient Care and Laboratory Testing

Medicare medical insurance covers outpatient hospital treatment, such as emergency room or clinic charges, X-rays, injections that are not self-administered, and laboratory work and diagnostic tests. Lab work and tests can be done at the hospital lab or at an independent laboratory facility, so long as that lab is approved by Medicare.

> **CAUTION**
> **Beware of outpatient hospital charges.** Medicare pays only a limited amount of outpatient hospital and clinic bills. And unlike most other kinds of outpatient services, Medicare places no limits on how much the hospital or clinic can charge over and above what Medicare pays. (See "Different Payment Structure for Hospital Outpatient Charges," below, for details.)

Ambulances

Part B medical insurance will cover the cost of transporting a patient by ambulance, if transport by any other means would not have been medically advisable. This may include not only emergencies, but also nonemergency trips following discharge from a hospital—for example, to the patient's home or to a nursing facility. Transporting residents of nursing facilities to see their doctors may also be covered. However, Medicare does not cover ambulance transport for regular visits from a person's home to a doctor's office, if the trip was arranged simply because the person needed some assistance.

If your doctor prescribes an ambulance for you for a trip from home to the doctor's office, Medicare may cover it but is not required to. Medicare will cover the ambulance trip only if the doctor's communication with Medicare convinces Medicare that the ambulance was medically necessary.

If Medicare covers an ambulance trip, the ambulance company must accept the Medicare-approved amount as full payment for its services. Medicare will pay 80% of the Medicare-approved amount. You, or your medigap insurer or managed care plan (see Chapters 14 and 15 for descriptions of these plans), are responsible for paying the remaining 20%. The ambulance company may not bill you for any amount over that 20%.

If you need help getting to and from doctor visits, but an ambulance is not considered medically necessary, look into free transportation for seniors in your community. Call your local senior center or the senior information line or elder care locator listed in the white pages of your telephone directory or look online for these kinds of resources.

Administered Drugs

Drugs or other medicines administered to you at the hospital or a doctor's office are covered by medical insurance. Medicare Part B does not cover drugs you take by yourself at home, including self-administered injections, even if they are prescribed by your doctor. Exceptions to this rule are self-administered oral cancer medication, antigens, and immunosuppressive drugs, which are covered by Medicare. Also, flu shots and pneumonia vaccines are covered by Medicare, even though other vaccinations are not; the flu shot you can obtain on your own, but the pneumonia vaccination requires a doctor's prescription.

Medical Equipment and Supplies

Splints, casts, prosthetic devices, body braces, heart pacemakers, corrective lenses after a cataract operation, therapeutic shoes for diabetics, and medical equipment such as ventilators, wheelchairs, and hospital beds—if prescribed by a doctor—are all covered by Part B medical insurance. This includes glucose monitoring equipment for people who have diabetes.

To learn more about the many types of medical equipment and supplies Medicare Part B covers, and how different equipment may be rented or purchased, see Medicare's online publication *Medicare Coverage of Durable Medical Equipment and Other Devices* at www.medicare.gov/publications/pubs/pdf/11045.pdf. To find a Medicare-certified supplier of medical equipment near you, go to the Medicare website home page at www.medicare.gov, and under the Help and Resources tab, click "Where to get covered medical items." This will take you to the "Medicare Supplier Directory."

Oral Surgery

Some types of surgery on the jaw or facial bones, or on the related nerves or blood vessels, can be covered by Part B medical insurance. However, surgery on teeth or gums, even when related to an injury or a disease that did not originate with the teeth, is usually considered to be dental work, and so is not covered by Medicare.

This is one of Medicare's somewhat nonsensical bureaucratic distinctions. Although normal dental care is not covered by Medicare, damage to teeth or gums connected to an injury or disease is a medical as much as a dental problem. However, there is one route to coverage: Even if the work is done by an oral surgeon rather than by a physician, Medicare may cover it if it is the kind of treatment that physicians also provide and if Medicare would have covered it if a physician had performed it. This may be determined by whether the treatment involves just the teeth and gums (not covered) or also the bones, inside mouth, blood vessels, or tongue (covered). If Medicare is to cover work performed by a nonphysician oral surgeon, that surgeon must participate in—that is, be certified by—Medicare. You should have your oral surgeon's office check with Medicare about coverage before undergoing any procedure.

Outpatient Physical Therapy and Speech Therapy

Part B of Medicare will cover some of the cost of outpatient physical and speech therapy—if it is prescribed and regularly reviewed by a doctor and provided by a Medicare-approved facility or therapist. However, there are limits on how much Medicare will pay for these therapies. And the amount Medicare pays will be partially determined by who provides you with the services. These limits are explained in "Payments for Outpatient Therapies," below.

Home Health Care

The same home health care coverage is available under Part B medical insurance as is provided by Part A hospital insurance. (See "How Much Medicare Part A Pays," above, for information about home health care coverage under Part A.)

If you have both Part A and Part B, Part A will cover your home health care following a hospital stay of at least three days; otherwise, Part B will cover it. There is no limit on the number of home health care visits that are covered, and you are not responsible for paying your Part B deductible for home health care. Only skilled nursing care or therapy while you are confined to your home is covered, however, and such care must be ordered by your doctor and provided by a Medicare-approved home health care agency.

Part B medical insurance, like Part A coverage, will pay 100% of the approved charges of a participating home health care agency.

Chiropractors

Part B may cover some care by a Medicare-certified chiropractor. Generally, Medicare will cover a limited number of visits to a chiropractor for manipulation of neck or back vertebrae that are out of place.

Medicare will not, however, cover general health maintenance visits to a chiropractor, nor will it usually cover therapeutic manipulation other than that of the vertebrae. And Medicare generally will not cover

X-rays or other diagnostic tests done by the chiropractor. Instead, your physician normally must order these tests.

If you go to a chiropractor and hope to have Medicare pay its share of the bill, have the chiropractor's office check with Medicare ahead of time about the treatment being proposed. And even if Medicare initially covers the treatment, it may not do so indefinitely. So, if you continue with the treatments, have the chiropractor's office regularly check with Medicare to find out how long it will keep paying.

Preventive Screening Exams

Medicare covers the following examinations to screen for a number of serious illnesses:

- a one-time routine physical exam (sometimes called an "initial wellness exam") within six months of the date a person first enrolls in Part B coverage
- an annual physical exam that includes a comprehensive risk assessment, which may lead to further Medicare-covered testing
- a Pap smear and pelvic exam every three years; every year for women at high risk of cervical or pelvic disease; Medicare covers this exam even if you have not yet met your annual Part B deductible
- colorectal cancer screening, as your physician deems necessary (sometimes without meeting your deductible)
- bone density tests for women at high risk of developing osteoporosis or for anyone receiving long-term steroid therapy, who has primary hyperparathyroidism, or who has certain vertebrate abnormalities
- blood glucose testing supplies—if prescribed by a physician—for patients with diabetes
- annual prostate cancer screenings for men over 55
- annual flu shot, with no deductible and no coinsurance amount
- positron emission tomography (PET) scans, a diagnostic test for certain cancers
- annual eye screening for glaucoma

- blood screening for early detection of cardiovascular disease, if your doctor says you have risk factors
- screening test for diabetes, if your doctor says you're at risk for the disease, and
- PET brain scans for patients with unusual Alzheimer's-like symptoms, if your doctor believes the source may be a different type of brain disease known as "frontotemporal dementia."

Mammography

Part B covers a yearly mammogram, even if you have not yet met your annual deductible. The mammogram must be performed by a doctor or facility certified by Medicare to perform mammograms.

Podiatrists

Medicare covers podiatrist services only when they consist of treatment for injuries or diseases of the foot. This does not include routine foot care or treatment of corns or calluses.

Eye Care and Eyeglasses

Medicare does not cover routine eye examinations, glasses, or contact lenses. The only exception is for people who have undergone cataract or other eye surgery. For them, Medicare covers glasses, contact lenses, or intraocular lenses, as well as the cost of an examination by a Medicare-certified optometrist. Medicare Part B does cover medical care from an ophthalmologist (an eye doctor with an M.D., not an optometrist) or other medical doctor for illness or injury to your eyes.

Clinical Psychologists or Social Workers

When a doctor or hospital prescribes it in conjunction with medical treatment, Medicare Part B can cover limited counseling by a clinical psychologist or clinical social worker. The practitioner must be Medicare-approved. If your doctor suggests a clinical psychologist or social worker to help in your recovery from surgery, injury, or illness, contact the practitioner in advance to find out whether the services will be approved by Medicare.

Day Care Mental Health Treatment

Medicare Part B can, in some cases, cover mental health care, in the form of day treatment—also called partial hospitalization—at a hospital outpatient department or community mental health center. The facility must be Medicare-approved and the particular day program certified for Part B coverage by Medicare.

Alzheimer's-Related Treatments

Until recently, Medicare did not cover various kinds of physical, speech, and occupational therapy, or psychotherapy and other mental health services, for people who had been diagnosed with Alzheimer's disease. Medicare's reasoning was that patients with Alzheimer's were incapable of medically improving, and that the treatment was therefore not "medically necessary."

Medicare has now reversed its backward stance. A patient can no longer be denied Medicare coverage for physician-prescribed therapies or treatments solely because the patient has been diagnosed with Alzheimer's. So, if you or a loved one has Alzheimer's and a physician prescribes a form of therapy or other treatment to counter the effects of the disease, make sure the treatment provider submits its bills to Medicare for payment.

Obesity

Medicare will cover various scientifically proven and medically approved weight-loss therapies and treatments for obesity, if properly prescribed by a physician. These range from stomach surgeries to diet programs to psychological and behavior-modification counseling.

Not all treatments are covered, and not all patients will be eligible for all covered treatments. But if you are undergoing care from a physician for obesity, the physician can recommend a specific treatment for you and submit it to Medicare for coverage approval.

Services Not Covered by Medicare Part B

When you look at the list of what Medicare medical insurance does not cover, it's easy to understand why people with traditional

Medicare still wind up personally responsible for half of their medical bills. It also underlines the need for you to consider additional medical insurance, either through private supplemental plans, an HMO or other Medicare Advantage plan, or Medicaid or Qualified Medicare Beneficiary coverage. (See Chapters 14, 15, and 16 for more on these alternatives.)

The categories of medical treatment and services listed below are not covered by Medicare.

However, the noncovered services listed below do not necessarily apply to HMO or other Medicare Advantage plan coverage. Many Medicare Advantage plans include some coverage for these medical services even though Medicare itself does not cover them.

Treatment That Is Not Medically Necessary

Medicare will not pay for medical care that it does not consider medically necessary. This includes some elective and most cosmetic surgery, plus virtually all alternative forms of medical care such as acupuncture, acupressure, and homeopathy—with the one exception of limited use of chiropractors. This is despite the fact that many people find these therapies more beneficial than traditional forms of medical care.

Vaccinations and Immunizations

Medicare Part B covers a yearly flu shot and pneumonia vaccination. Otherwise, it does not cover vaccinations and immunizations, such as those taken for travel abroad. An exception is for emergencies in which a vaccination is required because of risk of infection or exposure to communicable disease. Medicare Part B does not cover the shingles vaccine, though a Part D prescription drug plan might (see "Part D Prescription Drug Coverage" later in this chapter).

Prescription Drugs You Take at Home

Medicare Part A covers drugs administered while you are in the hospital or in a skilled nursing facility. Part B medical insurance covers drugs that cannot be self-administered and that you receive as an outpatient at a hospital, a clinic, or at the doctor's office. There are a few exceptions for self-administered drugs; see "Types of Care Covered," above. Potential coverage for all other prescription drugs falls under Medicare Part D, which you must enroll in and pay for separately from Parts A and B. (See "Part D Prescription Drug Coverage," below.)

Nonprescription Drugs

Medicare Part B does not cover any of the cost of nonprescription ("over-the-counter") medicines, vitamins, or supplements, regardless of whether they provide help with a medical condition, even if they have been recommended by a doctor.

Hearing Exams and Hearing Aids

Medicare Part B does not cover routine hearing examinations or hearing aids. However, if your ears or hearing is affected by a specific illness or injury, examination and treatment by a physician is covered.

General Dental Work

Medicare does not cover work performed by a dentist or an oral surgeon, unless the same work would be covered if performed by a physician. In other words, if the treatment is considered medical rather than dental, Medicare may cover it. Generally, Medicare will not cover treatment unless the problem is unrelated to normal tooth decay or gum disease, and involves either the blood vessels, nerves, or interior of the mouth, or the bones of the mouth or jaw.

Long-Term Care

Medicare Part B covers some home health care, as described in the previous section. But that care is always relatively short-term, limited to a period of recovery from an acute illness, injury, or condition. Medicare does not provide the kind of long-term care, either at home or in a facility, that many older people need because of frailty or other inability to perform, without help, the activities of daily life. Medicaid and long-term care insurance does cover certain nursing home costs. For a complete discussion of coverage for nursing home costs, see *Long-Term Care: How to Plan & Pay for It*, by Joseph Matthews (Nolo).

How Much Medicare Part B Pays

When all your medical bills are added up, you'll see that Medicare generally pays for only about half the total. Medicare gets away with this in three major ways.

First, Medicare does not cover all major medical expenses—for example, it doesn't cover routine physical examinations, some medication, glasses, hearing aids, dentures, and some other costly medical services.

Second, Medicare pays only a portion of what it decides is the proper amount—called the approved charges—for medical services. In addition, when Medicare decides that a particular service is covered and determines the approved charges for it, Part B medical insurance usually pays only 80% of those approved charges; you are responsible for the remaining 20%.

Third, the approved amount may seem reasonable to Medicare, but it is often considerably less than what the doctor actually charges. If your doctor or other medical provider does not accept assignment of the Medicare charges, you are personally responsible for the difference.

Now that you know the worst, you can deal with the details of how much Medicare Part B pays. The rules are not hard to understand—just hard to swallow.

Deductible Amounts

Before Medicare pays anything under Part B medical insurance, you must pay a deductible amount of your covered medical bills for the year. The Part B deductible amount is currently $147 per year.

Medicare keeps track of how much of the deductible you have paid in a given year. It generally does a good job of keeping track, but it is always a good idea to keep your own records and double-check the accounting.

80% of Approved Charges

Part B medical insurance pays only 80% of what Medicare decides is the approved charge for a particular service or treatment. You are responsible for paying the other 20% of the approved charge, called your coinsurance amount. And unless your doctor or other medical provider accepts assignment (see "Assignment of Medicare-Approved Amount," below), you are also responsible for the difference between the Medicare-approved charge and the amount the doctor or another provider actually charges.

> TIP
> **Low-income seniors may receive state help.** Under programs known as Qualified Medicare Beneficiary (QMB), Specified Low-Income Medicare Beneficiary (SLMB), and Qualifying Individual (QI), Medicare recipients who have low incomes and few assets can receive considerable help with their basic Medicare expenses.
> If you qualify as a QMB, your state will pay all Medicare premiums, deductibles, and coinsurance amounts. If you qualify as an SLMB, your state will pay the monthly Medicare Part B premiums, though not deductibles or coinsurance amounts. If you meet the standards as a QI, your state will pay all or part of your monthly Medicare Part B premium, but not any deductible or coinsurance. (See Chapter 16 for a full discussion of options for low-income persons.)

100% of Approved Charges for Some Services

There are several types of treatments and medical providers for which Medicare Part B pays 100% of the approved charges rather than the usual 80%, and to which the yearly deductible does not apply. In these categories, you are not required to pay the regular

20% coinsurance amount. In most of them, the provider accepts assignment of the approved charges as the full amount, so you actually pay nothing at all.

Home Health Care

Whether you receive home health care under Part A or Part B, Medicare pays 100% of the charges, and you are not responsible for your yearly deductible. However, if you receive medical equipment—a wheelchair, chair lift, or special bed—from the home health care agency, you must pay the 20% coinsurance amount.

Clinical Laboratory Services

Medicare pays 100% of its approved amount for such laboratory services as blood tests, urinalyses, and biopsies. And the laboratory must accept assignment, except in Maryland where a hospital lab can bill you, as an outpatient, for a 20% coinsurance amount.

Preventive Care Screenings

Medicare Part B will pay 100% of the Medicare-approved amount for any covered preventive screening examination appropriately prescribed by a physician (see "Types of Care Covered," above).

Flu and Pneumonia Vaccines

Medicare pays the full 100% of its approved charges for these vaccinations, and the yearly deductible does not apply. However, the provider is not required to accept assignment, so there may be up to an additional 15% charge on top of the amount Medicare approves.

Payments for Outpatient Therapies

How much Medicare pays for outpatient physical therapy (PT), speech-language pathology (SLP), and occupational therapy (OT) depends on where you receive the therapy.

Therapy received in a doctor's or therapist's office, a rehabilitation facility, or a skilled nursing facility while you're an inpatient. Medicare will pay 80% of the Medicare-approved amount. You or your supplemental insurance or managed care plan remain responsible for the other 20%. There is a cap on the total amount Medicare will pay for therapy in these settings. Medicare will pay up to $1,920 per year for outpatient physical therapy and speech-language pathology (combined). There is a separate cap of $1,920 for occupational therapy. These amounts may be increased if your therapist tells Medicare that more care is medically necessary and Medicare approves.

Therapy received at home. If you receive therapy at home from a Medicare-certified home health care agency as part of a comprehensive Medicare-covered home health care program, Medicare will pay 100% of the cost. If you receive therapy at home that is not part of a Medicare-covered comprehensive home health care plan, Medicare will pay 80% of approved charges up to the yearly cap of $1,920 described immediately above.

Therapy received at a hospital outpatient department. There are financial advantages and disadvantages to receiving Medicare-covered therapy at a hospital outpatient department instead of in a doctor's or therapist's office, or at home. One advantage is that Medicare Part B pays the full Medicare-approved amount for the therapy, except for a patient copayment for each visit. This copayment is usually less than the 20% of the Medicare-approved amount a patient would be responsible for if therapy were provided in a doctor's or therapist's office, or at home.

The disadvantage is that a hospital outpatient department may charge an unlimited amount above the Medicare-approved amount for the therapy—an amount you would be personally responsible for. Before you begin therapy at a hospital outpatient department, find out whether they will accept "assignment" of the Medicare-approved amount as the total amount of the bill. (For a full explanation see "Legal Limit on Amounts Charged" and "Assignment of Medicare-Approved Amount," below.) If not, find out in advance how much more than the Medicare-approved amount they will charge. If it is more than you can comfortably afford, you might want to consider getting your therapy somewhere else.

Outpatient mental health treatment. For mental health services provided on an outpatient basis, Part B pays only 80% of approved charges. This is true whether the services are provided by a physician, clinical psychologist, or clinical social worker at a hospital, nursing facility, mental health center, or rehabilitation facility. The patient is responsible for the yearly deductible, for the unpaid 20% of the Medicare-approved amount, and, if the provider does not accept assignment, for the rest of the bill above the regular Medicare-approved amount, up to an additional 15%.

Legal Limit on Amounts Charged

By law, a doctor or another medical provider can bill you no more than what is called the "limiting charge," even if he or she doesn't accept assignment from Medicare. The limiting charge is set at 15% more than the amount Medicare decides is the approved charge for a treatment or service. That means you may be personally responsible—either out of pocket or through supplemental insurance—for the 20% of the approved charges Medicare does not pay, plus any amount the doctor charges up to the 15% limiting charge. Regardless of how much the doctor or other medical provider charges non-Medicare patients for the same service, you can be charged no more than 15% over the amount Medicare approves.

Assignment of Medicare-Approved Amount

In most instances, Medicare pays 80% of the approved amount of doctor bills; you or your private insurance pay the remaining 20%. However, you can avoid having to pay anything above the Medicare-approved amount if your doctor accepts assignment of that amount as the full amount of your bill.

Over 99% of all doctors who treat Medicare patients accept assignment of the Medicare-approved amount. That is because almost all doctors have signed up with Medicare in advance, agreeing to accept assignment, and so have become what are called "participating doctors." They do this because they get paid by Medicare at a slightly higher rate.

There are still a few doctors, mostly specialists, who do not accept assignment. When deciding whether to see a new doctor you have been referred to, check to see whether the doctor accepts Medicare assignment.

 TIP

Treating doctors must accept assignment for Medicaid and QMB patients. If you receive Medicaid assistance (called Medi-Cal in California) as well as Medicare, or are a Qualified Medicare Beneficiary (QMB), federal law requires that a doctor who agrees to treat you must also accept assignment. (See Chapter 16 for more on the Medicaid and QMB programs.)

Different Payment Structure for Hospital Outpatient Charges

Medicare pays hospital outpatient departments differently from how it pays doctors and other providers. Sometimes, the difference can mean savings for you, but other times it can leave you with a large unpaid bill. Unlike charges for doctors or other providers, Medicare Part B pays 100% of the Medicare-approved amount for services provided by a hospital outpatient department, except that for each service the patient may be responsible for a copayment that varies with the type of service provided. These copayments are usually smaller than the 20% coinsurance amount you would pay if you received the same service at a doctor's office or clinic. (Note, however, that if a doctor who is not employed by the hospital outpatient department provides services to you at the hospital, that doctor will bill you separately and Medicare will pay only 80% of the Medicare-approved amount for that bill.)

But there is also some payment risk if you receive care from a hospital outpatient department. As with individual doctors, the hospital does not have to accept "assignment" of the Medicare-approved amount as the full charge for a particular service. Unlike doctors who don't accept Medicare assignment, however, a hospital outpatient department is not restricted to charging only 9.25%

more than the Medicare-approved amount. Their charges can go as high as they want, and you would be personally responsible for everything above the Medicare-approved amount.

Beware of Huge Outpatient Hospital Bills

There is no limit to the amount a hospital outpatient department can charge a Medicare enrollee above the Medicare-approved amount for a particular service. Because of this loophole in Medicare rules, Medicare patients wind up paying on average almost 40% of the total charges for hospital outpatient department charges. For outpatient surgery, and for outpatient radiology and other diagnostic services, patients end up paying about 50% of total hospital charges. Because of these high costs, you should be wary of receiving medical care at a hospital outpatient department. Be sure to find out the charges *before* beginning treatment.

COMPUTER

The Medicare website at www.medicare.gov has two helpful links for information on keeping down your medical costs. The first, called the Health Care Provider Directory, will tell you which doctors and other health care providers in your area will accept assignment on Medicare-covered services. You'll find this directory at www.medicare. gov/find-a-doctor/provider-search.aspx.

The Medicare website also offers a list, sorted by geography, of Medicare-certified suppliers of medical equipment and supplies. These suppliers accept Medicare's approved amount as the limit of what they can charge. To use this directory, go to the Medicare website home page at www. medicare.gov, and under the Help and Resources tab, click "Where to get covered medical items." This will take you to the "Medicare Supplier Directory."

There are several ways to respond to the high prices charged by hospital outpatient departments. First, before you receive any care at a hospital outpatient department, ask their financial office whether they accept assignment of the Medicare-approved amount as payment in full (except for your copayment). If so, find out what the copayment is. You'll then know the total amount—that is, the per-service copayment—that you'll have to pay each time you receive the service.

Private Fee-for-Service Plans Outside Medicare

Some businesses, unions, and other organizations offer general health insurance plans—either during employment or after retirement—that accept people eligible for Medicare. A private health insurance plan that accepts Medicare enrollees must offer at least as much coverage as basic Medicare would provide, and most of these plans provide more than that.

If you choose to join or remain with such a health plan once you become eligible for Medicare, the plan—and not Medicare—will make all decisions about coverage for specific services and the amount of payment.

You may be responsible for plan premiums and copayments, as well as the difference between what the plan pays the provider and what the provider actually charges. Unlike regular Medicare, there is no legal limit on the amount a provider may charge you above what the insurance pays.

If the hospital outpatient department does not accept assignment of the Medicare-approved amount, find out how much more than that amount they will charge. If it's just a little bit higher, you might want to receive your treatment there anyway, if the care is recommended by your doctor and the facility is convenient for you.

If the hospital's charges will be considerably higher than the Medicare-approved amount, explain the situation to your doctor and ask whether the service could be performed just as well in a doctor's office or at an independent clinic or laboratory. If not, ask whether there is another hospital outpatient department where the service could be performed. If so, find out what that hospital's charges would be.

Part D Prescription Drug Coverage

In 2006, Medicare began covering some of the costs of prescription medications you take at home. This Medicare Part D benefit is administered through private insurance companies that offer Medicare-approved prescription drug plans (PDPs), and through Medicare Advantage managed care plans that include a Part D drug benefit (MA-PDs). The federal health care reform act of 2010 began a gradual expansion of the Medicare Part D coverage for people with high annual drug costs.

The Part D program replaces drug coverage that was offered through medigap plans (see Chapter 14), many Medicare Advantage plans (see Chapter 15), Medicare drug discount cards, and most Medicaid coverage (see Chapter 16). It does not replace employer-sponsored prescription drug coverage for Medicare beneficiaries if that coverage is at least equal to the coverage offered by a basic Medicare Part D plan. And, some state-sponsored pharmacy assistance programs continue to help fill some of the drug coverage gaps in the Medicare program.

For many people, Medicare Part D reduces their out-of-pocket costs for prescription drugs. And people with very high annual drug expenses can see a substantial reduction in their out-of-pocket costs. For some people with low incomes, however, the new Medicare program may cost them *more* than they previously paid under state Medicaid programs.

Eligibility

Anyone who is entitled to Medicare Part A coverage (whether actually enrolled in it or not) or who is currently enrolled in Medicare Part B may join a Medicare Part D plan. This is true regardless of whether a person's Medicare eligibility is based on age or disability. Except for people who also receive benefits from the Medicaid program (Medi-Cal in California), enrollment in Part D is voluntary. (The enrollment process is explained in Chapter 13.)

Medicare Part D Drug Coverage: The Basics

Medicare Part D provides some coverage for the cost of prescription drugs for people enrolled in Medicare. Before you plunge into the details offered in this section, you may want to familiarize yourself with the overall operation of the program by reading through this summary.

Who is eligible? If you are entitled to Medicare Part A or are enrolled in Medicare Part B, you may join a Medicare Part D prescription drug plan. Participation is voluntary for most people. But, if you receive benefits through Medicaid (Medi-Cal in California) you are automatically enrolled in a Part D plan in order to continue receiving drug coverage.

Who runs the program? Medicare operates the overall program, but you must choose one of the specific Part D prescription drug plans offered by private insurance companies in your state. You enroll directly with that insurance company.

What does it cost to participate? Most people pay a monthly premium to the insurance company. The premium can range from $0 to $50 per month—the cost varies depending on the plans available in your town, and on the particular plan you choose.

What does it cover? All plans cover some, but not all, prescription drugs in every category of medication. Each plan has a list, known as a formulary, of the specific drugs it covers. The plan will pay its share only for drugs listed on its formulary and purchased from a pharmacy or another distributor that participates in that plan.

How much does the plan pay? For basic Part D coverage, there are four payment stages (these figures are for 2015):

- **Deductible.** You pay for the first $320 per year of the total cost of your drugs. Some plans waive or reduce this deductible.

- **Partial coverage.** Once your total yearly drug expense reaches $320 (and before it reaches $2,960), the plan pays roughly 75% and you pay 25% of your drug costs. Your portion comes in the form of a copayment for each prescription. Your copayment may be higher for brand-name drugs and less for generics, depending on your plan.

Medicare Part D Drug Coverage: The Basics (cont'd)

- **Coverage gap (the "doughnut hole").** Once your total yearly drug expense reaches $2,960 (and until your total out-of-pocket costs reach $4,700), you must pay the entire amount of your drug costs. Your plan generally pays no part of your prescription drug costs within this doughnut hole, although a few high-premium plans may pay some portion of your costs. However, in 2015, brand-name prescription drugs must be sold at a 55% discount to anyone who reaches the coverage gap and generic drugs are sold at a 35% discount.

- **Catastrophic coverage.** If your total out-of-pocket costs for drugs in one year reach $4,700, the Part D plan plus Medicare will pay 95% of all further costs; you pay the remaining 5% or up to $2.65 for a generic multisource drug and up to $6.60 for all other drugs.

How do I choose the right plan? Not all plans are alike, and choosing the best plan for you involves several steps. You must get the widest possible coverage of the drugs you take, with the fewest restrictions on the drugs' availability to you. And you must do so with the lowest overall out-of-pocket cost to you. That doesn't necessarily mean the lowest premium, but instead takes into account premium, deductible, copayments, availability of generic drugs, and coverage in the "doughnut hole" coverage gap. (See "Deciding on a Part D Plan," below, for a step-by-step discussion of choosing the right plan.)

Can I switch plans if I'm not happy with my plan? Anyone can switch Part D plans. People who receive both Medicaid and Medicare benefits, and people who live in long-term care facilities, can switch at any time. Most people, however, can switch only during an open enrollment period from October 15 to December 7 of each year. The rules and procedures for switching plans are explained in Chapter 13.

People With VA, TRICARE, or FEHB Medical Coverage Need Not Join a Part D Drug Plan

If you receive medical coverage through the Department of Veterans Affairs (VA), the Defense Department's TRICARE program, or the Federal Employee Health Benefits Program (FEHB), you do *not* need to join a Medicare Part D plan when you become eligible for it at age 65. You will continue to receive prescription drugs through your existing program (which provides essentially the same coverage as Part D, but at less cost to you). If for any reason you lose coverage under any of these programs, you have 63 days to join a Medicare Part D plan without a penalty for late enrollment.

The Politics of Part D Administration

Even for people who save money in the short run under Part D, those savings will likely be swallowed up in the long run by the program's little-discussed giveaway to two of the country's biggest industries: insurance and pharmaceuticals.

The enormous Medicare hospital and medical programs (Parts A and B) are operated by Medicare's own extremely low-overhead bureaucracy, with only certain administrative tasks run by insurers. Nonetheless, in enacting Part D, Congress handed over almost the entire prescription drug program to private insurance companies. That means the program has to support their notoriously inefficient overhead, plus their profits.

Also, a provision in the Part D law actually prohibits Medicare from negotiating with pharmaceutical companies for lower drug prices for Medicare beneficiaries. As a huge market, Medicare could utilize its buying power to get price reductions; the Veterans Administration, for example, has done this for many years and its drug prices are half as much as those through most Part D plans. The law's prohibition on such negotiations amounts to a massive pork barrel for the pharmaceutical industry, ensuring that overall drug costs for everyone on Medicare will climb steeply in the years to come.

If you qualify for Medicaid (see Chapter 16) as well as Medicare, you must enroll in a Medicare Part D plan in order to receive any prescription drug coverage. Medicaid no longer covers any drugs for people who are also eligible for Medicare if those drugs are covered by an available Part D plan. In some states, however, Medicaid continues to cover a few drugs that are not available under Part D. If you receive Medicaid benefits as well as Medicare, you may enroll in certain, but not all, Medicare Part D plans—but if you do not enroll yourself, Medicare will automatically enroll you in a plan.

Part D May Not Be Right for Everyone

If you have prescription drug coverage through a Medicare Advantage plan (see Chapter 15) or through employer-based coverage from your or your spouse's current work, you do not also need a Medicare Part D plan. Even if you're not otherwise covered for prescription drugs, enrollment in a Part D plan is voluntary. But program rules (for instance, a penalty on the premium you eventually pay if you later enroll in a plan after not enrolling when you turn 65) puts some pressure on you to enroll even if you don't yet need the coverage. To decide whether enrolling is a good idea for you, and when, see "Deciding on a Part D Plan," below.

Premiums, Deductibles, Copayments, and Coverage Gaps

The cost structure of Medicare Part D is complicated. Except for those who qualify for a low-income subsidy, most beneficiaries pay monthly premiums, a yearly deductible, and a copayment for each prescription filled. And there is a coverage gap that affects most beneficiaries, making them personally responsible for all drug costs that are above a certain amount but below a "catastrophic" level. For those who qualify for the low-income subsidy, Part D costs are significantly less.

Premiums

Premiums are the monthly amounts you pay directly to your prescription drug plan or managed care plan to enroll you in Part D coverage. These amounts cover only your membership in the plan and do not pay the cost of any drugs, nor do they count toward your deductible or other cost-sharing amounts.

Standard enrollment. Most people must pay a monthly premium for Part D coverage, either for a stand-alone prescription drug plan or as part of the larger premium they pay if they are enrolled in a managed care plan. Monthly premium amounts for basic benefits vary from plan to plan and by geographic region.

> CAUTION
>
> **Lowest premiums are not always the best.** Finding a plan with a low monthly premium is important, but it is not the only factor to consider in choosing a plan. A low premium does you little good if the plan doesn't cover some of your medications, or if it covers them but requires much higher copayments than other plans. Also, you may want to pay a higher premium for a plan that offers you first-dollar coverage (no deductible) or some payments within the "doughnut hole" coverage gap. See "Deciding on a Part D Plan," below, for more information.

Medicare's "Extra Help" low-income subsidy. People with low incomes who enroll in Part D and qualify for Extra Help Categories One, Two, or Three (discussed below) pay no premium at all if they join a plan that charges below the average premium for their state. Unfortunately, plans with these lower premiums tend to have the most coverage restrictions. Beneficiaries who qualify for Category Four pay between 25% and 75% of a plan's full premium, depending on their actual income.

Deductibles

The deductible is the amount you must pay out of pocket for covered medications before your Part D plan begins paying your covered prescription drug costs.

Apply for Medicare Part D's Extra Help Program Before, and Separately From, Enrolling in a Part D Plan

If you think you are anywhere close to qualifying for a Part D Extra Help low-income subsidy (discussed immediately below), you should apply for it. You apply for an Extra Help low-income subsidy separately from applying for Part D coverage, and applying for an Extra Help low-income subsidy does not commit you to join any Medicare Part D plan. If you are accepted for an Extra Help low-income subsidy, your Part D plan premium will be much less expensive regardless of which plan you choose. To learn about applying for an Extra Help low-income subsidy, see Chapter 13.

Standard enrollment. With most plans, a Part D enrollee must pay out of pocket for the first $320 (in 2015) of costs each year for prescription drugs that are covered by the enrollee's particular plan. But some plans offer "first dollar" (no-deductible) coverage, meaning they begin paying their share of covered drugs for an enrollee's first prescription of the year (see below).

With low-income subsidy. Part D beneficiaries in LIS Categories One, Two, and Three do not pay any deductible amount. Beneficiaries in Category Four pay a deductible amount of $66 per year.

Waiver of deductible. Some plans offer what is called "first dollar" coverage, which means you do not pay any deductible and the plan begins paying its share of drug costs with your first prescription. These no-deductible plans tend to have higher premiums. The amount you save, if any, will depend on the plan's premium and other cost features. (See "Deciding on a Part D Plan," below, for more information.)

Initial Copayments

After you have reached your deductible amount in out-of-pocket costs for covered prescription drugs, your plan pays most of the cost of a covered drug and you are personally responsible for the remainder, known as a copayment. This arrangement continues until you and your Part D plan combined reach a specific yearly total of expenditures—the beginning of the "coverage gap"—on drugs covered by your Part D plan.

Medicare's Extra Help Program to Lower the Cost of Part D

There are four categories of people who qualify for an Extra Help low-income subsidy (LIS) to help pay costs associated with a Part D prescription drug plan. (Signing up for an Extra Help assistance is explained in Chapter 13.)

The categories are defined by the beneficiary's income in relation to the Federal Poverty Guideline (FPG). In 2014, the FPG for a single person was an annual income of less than $11,670 ($13,420 in Hawaii, $14,580 in Alaska). For larger family units (people related by blood, marriage, or adoption and living together), the figure goes up by about $4,000 per person (about $5,000 per person in Hawaii, about $5,000 per person in Alaska). FPG amounts go up slightly each year.

The amount of Part D low-income subsidy a beneficiary receives varies with the category:

- **Category One.** This category includes individuals eligible for Medicaid (see Chapter 16) whose incomes are under the FPG. They pay no premium or deductible, have no gap in coverage, and have reduced per-prescription copayments.

- **Category Two.** This category includes individuals eligible for Medicaid but with incomes above the FPG. They pay no premium or deductible and have no coverage gaps, but pay a higher per-prescription copayment than other Medicaid recipients.

- **Category Three.** This category includes individuals not eligible for Medicaid but with incomes less than 135% of the FPG and assets (not including their homes) of less than about $10,000 (about $15,000 for married couples living together). They pay no premium or deductible, have no gap in coverage, and have reduced per-prescription copayments.

- **Category Four.** This category includes individuals with incomes of 136% to 149% of the FPG and assets less than about $15,000 (about $30,000 for married couples). They pay a reduced premium and deductible and have reduced per-prescription copayments.

Medicare's Extra Help Program to Lower the Cost of Part D (cont'd)

Throughout this section, explanations of Part D payments and coverage for people eligible for Medicare's Extra Help program will refer to the above category numbers. These category numbers are only for the convenience of readers of this book; official Medicare publications do not usually assign any reference numbers to the categories.

Standard enrollment. After you pay your $320 deductible for covered drugs, your Part D plan pays 75% of the cost for covered drugs (and you pay the remaining 25% out of pocket) until your total covered expenditures have reached the beginning of the year's coverage gap. For 2015, the coverage gap begins at $2,960 in total costs for covered drugs.

What Counts as an Out-of-Pocket Cost?

Many of the rules concerning deductibles, copayments, and catastrophic limits revolve around the amount you pay out of pocket for your medications. In calculating these amounts, Medicare considers only what it determines to be a "true out-of-pocket" cost, or "TrOOP."

In order for a prescription drug payment to qualify as a TrOOP, the prescription drug must be:

- a drug prescribed by a physician and covered by the specific plan's formulary, or covered for a particular enrollee through an exception to the formulary, and

- paid for by the beneficiary, a relative, a charity, church, or service organization, or the like, but not by another insurance plan.

It's important to remember that what you pay for your premium is *not* considered an out-of-pocket cost.

With low-income subsidy. Category One beneficiaries pay $1.20 per prescription for generic covered drugs and $3.60 per prescription for brand-name covered drugs—the Part D plan pays the rest. Categories Two and Three beneficiaries pay $2.65 per prescription for generic covered drugs and $6.60 for brand-name covered drugs. Category Four enrollees pay 15% of the cost of drugs, after paying their $66 deductibles.

You Pay the Full Cost of Any Drugs That Your Particular Plan Doesn't Cover

It is important to understand that your plan will pay its portion of the costs only for those drugs specifically included on its "formulary" (a list of the drugs your plan covers), unless you obtain an "exception" from the plan. Similarly, amounts you personally pay for drugs count toward your deductible and the coverage gap limits only if the drugs are specifically covered by your plan's formulary, or are covered by your plan after you obtain an exception for that drug from your plan. See "Restrictions on Coverage," below, for a discussion of plan formularies and other plan payment restrictions.

Actual copayments may vary. Your actual copayments for each prescription can vary:

- The total cost of a drug can vary from plan to plan. This is because each plan individually negotiates prices with pharmaceutical companies. So, if your copayment is a percentage of the drug's total cost, what you pay will also vary. For example, if 30 doses of a medicine cost a total of $80 with Plan 1 and $100 with Plan 2, a 25% copayment would be $20 per prescription with Plan 1, but $25 with Plan 2.
- A plan is permitted to set up a different copayment system—such as tiered copayments for generic drugs and brand-name drugs, or higher copayments for certain drugs but none at all for other drugs—from the standard copayments described above. Plans may change their copayment structure as long as the average copayments for all covered drugs work out to be

the same as with the standard copayment schedule. For this reason, before choosing a plan you must find out in advance what the actual copayment is for your specific drugs.

Coverage Gap (the "Doughnut Hole")

One of the notorious parts of the Part D program is the gap in coverage, or "doughnut hole," within which most Medicare beneficiaries must personally pay all of the cost of their prescription drugs. And if they want to keep their Part D coverage, they must continue to pay their plan's monthly premium even though the plan is not paying for any drugs because the gap has been reached.

Under Obamacare, Drugs Cost Less in the Coverage Gap

As a result of the federal health care reform act of 2010, the coverage gap will shrink over time until it is completely eliminated by 2020. In addition, during those years there are restrictions on the price pharmaceutical companies may charge to Medicare Part D enrollees. In 2015, brand-name drugs must be sold at a 55% discount, and generic drugs at a 35% discount, to anyone with a Medicare Part D plan whose annual covered drug costs have reached the coverage gap.

Finding a Plan That Offers Coverage in the Gap

If you have high drug costs, you may find a plan with some coverage in the doughnut hole coverage gap. A few plans pay some of a patient's drug costs within the gap—some of these plans pay a smaller than normal share within the gap while others reduce the extent of the gap (meaning they pay their share for a larger portion of a patient's total drug costs than a standard plan does). The premiums for these plans tend to be quite a bit higher than for more standard plans. But the higher premium may be worth it if you expect that your yearly drug costs will extend well into the coverage gap. About 5% of Medicare beneficiaries signed up with such plans in Part D's first year of operation.

Standard enrollment. Once you and your plan together have paid for a certain amount of prescription drugs that are covered by your Part D plan, your plan will pay nothing more that year until you reach what is called a "catastrophic coverage" level of spending. In 2015, your Part D plan will stop paying its portion of your covered medications when your total covered drug costs reach $2,960. Your premiums do not count toward this amount. The plan will begin to pay again when total expenditures for covered drugs reach the catastrophic coverage amount (see below). A few plans continue to pay for drugs during the gap; many plans that provide gap coverage do so only for generics. These plans are considerably more expensive than plans that have no gap coverage. (See "Finding a Plan That Offers Coverage in the Gap," above.)

With low-income subsidy. There is no coverage gap for those qualifying for any category of low-income subsidy.

Reducing costs within the doughnut hole. You may reach the coverage gap but still have months to go before getting to either the catastrophic coverage limit or the end of the year. If so, you may want to consider using one or more of these seven strategies for lowering the total cost of your medications, and thus the amount you pay out of pocket, within the gap. For more on finding the programs that might work for you, see "Finding discount programs," below.

The seven strategies are:

- **State and community assistance programs.** Some states have programs to help older patients pay for prescription medicines that are not otherwise covered by Medicare or Medicaid. Some of these programs offer across-the-board discounts on all drugs while others provide only limited discounts on certain drugs. Some programs offer special tax credits for prescription drug costs and others limit their prescription drug assistance to lower-income seniors. Local community-based programs also sometimes provide free or discounted drugs to seniors. To find out about state and community-based prescription drug assistance programs near you, call the Eldercare Locator at 800-677-1116 or go to the official Medicare website listing of state pharmaceutical assistance programs at www.medicare.

gov/pharmaceutical-assistance-program/state-programs.aspx. You can also contact the local office of your State Health Insurance Assistance Program (SHIP), discussed at the end of Chapter 13.

Some Discount Drug Purchases May Not Count as Out-of-Pocket Costs

If your out-of-pocket cost for prescription drugs reaches more than $4,700 for the year (in 2015), you will probably pass the coverage gap and reach Part D's catastrophic coverage. Once you reach that coverage, your Part D plan will begin to pay 95% of your drug costs until the end of the year.

But not all of the money you spend out of your own pocket for prescription drugs during the coverage gap will necessarily "count" toward reaching the catastrophic coverage threshold. If you buy discounted prescription drugs through a state or local government-assisted drug program, the amounts you spend out-of-pocket for those drugs might not count. That's because government funding is already supporting the purchase of these low-cost drugs. If you use one of these programs, check with the program staff about whether your out-of-pocket costs for drugs they supply will count toward reaching catastrophic coverage under Plan D.

- **Veterans benefits.** If you are a veteran, you may be eligible for free or low-cost medical treatment by Veterans Affairs health providers. If so, this can include free (for disabled or low-income veterans) or low-cost prescription drugs, if prescribed by a VA doctor. Even if you normally see a civilian doctor and use Medicare to cover your care, you might want to see a VA doctor to get a prescription for long-term medication that would be expensive if you had to pay for it out of pocket. For a discussion of medical benefits for veterans, see Chapter 11.
- **Physician samples.** In an effort to push their particular brands of drugs, pharmaceutical companies give free samples to

doctors. The doctors, in turn, distribute those drugs free to patients. Doctors do not normally have enough samples to fill a long-term need for a medication. But your doctor may have enough free samples of your drugs to help lower your out-of-pocket costs while you are within the Part D coverage gap.

- **Switching to generic.** If you have been taking a brand-name medication, you may find that you can obtain the same results at a lower price with its generic equivalent, if one is available, or with a lower-cost drug that treats the same condition. (In 2015, however, under new rules provided by the health care reform act, you can buy brand-name drugs at a 55% discount once you have reached the coverage gap. In some cases that may make the brand-name drugs cheaper than the generic equivalent.) Check with your doctor to see if a generic or another drug is available and whether the doctor believes that it would provide you with the same results. If so, you might want to try it. If you are satisfied with the less-expensive drug, you might save considerable money by continuing to use it. And you may even want to continue using it year-round, particularly if your drug plan offers it at a lower copayment than with the brand-name equivalent you originally used.

- **Pharmaceutical company discount programs.** Under pressure from consumer groups, some pharmaceutical companies have created programs to provide certain specific medicines at reduced prices for Medicare patients. Most of these programs are available only for seniors with limited incomes. The programs do not necessarily include every drug manufactured by the company. And the discounts are not usually very generous. Nonetheless, even a small discount on an expensive drug can amount to significant savings over time. In order to participate in one of these programs, you have to register with the pharmaceutical company. The doctor who prescribes the medication for you may have to fill out enrollment papers for you, too. Some of these programs provide free or discounted drugs only to doctors, who then distribute them to patients. To learn about specific pharmaceutical company programs that might help with the costs of drugs you take, see the official Medicare website's Pharmaceutical Assistance Programs page at www.medicare. gov/pharmaceutical-assistance-program/Index.aspx.

- **Nonprofit and retail discount programs.** Several nonprofit and retail organizations, including large chain pharmacies, have set up programs—some through the use of discount "cards"—to provide discounted prescription drug medications, particularly for seniors. These organizations use their large membership's purchasing power to leverage drug companies into offering discounts on certain drugs, passing those savings on to their members. There is usually a membership fee and a copayment or processing fee for each medicine you order. Savings from these programs average less than 10%. For an expensive drug, however, that can still amount to a substantial amount.

- **Medications from Canada.** The exact same prescription drugs for which we pay exorbitant prices in the United States are available for far less—often 50% to 80% less—in Canada. That is because the Canadian public health system limits what pharmaceutical companies can charge for drugs there. (Even at these much-reduced prices, the drug companies profitably continue to sell their wares in Canada.) Because of the huge price differences, many people in this country have been taking the trouble to buy their prescription medications from Canadian pharmacies.

  The U.S. Federal Drug Administration, acting to protect American pharmaceutical companies at the expense of consumers, has made it illegal to import American-made drugs from Canada. But individuals have not been prosecuted for importing legitimate drugs from Canada. And the U.S. Customs service does not seize any mail-order drugs imported from Canada. As a result, many people use mail-order and online prescription drug outlets to buy drugs from Canada, while others physically travel across the border to obtain their drugs at Canadian health clinics.

  If you choose to explore this option, you may be able to find services providing medicines from Canadian pharmacies by searching on the Internet under "prescription drugs Canada."

But before using any mail-order or online Canadian drug outlet, ask people you know, or your local senior center, or a SHIP counselor (see Chapter 13) if they know anything about the particular program and the reliability of its services.

Waiver or Reduction of Copayments

Under certain circumstances, you may not have to pay the normal copayment for a covered drug. For example:

- If you reside for more than 90 days in a long-term care nursing facility and are enrolled in both Medicare Part D and Medicaid, you do not have to make any copayments for covered drugs.

- Some plans waive or reduce copayments for certain drugs, particularly generic versions, mostly to coax people to join their particular plans. Waiving or reducing the copayment for a particular drug during a period of time, however, does not obligate the plan to continue doing so, nor must it continue to waive or reduce copayments on any comparable drug. The plan can change its copayment rules at any time.

- Pharmacies may waive copayments for any enrollee with a low-income subsidy, for any drug. There are no Medicare rules about when pharmacies may do this, except that they are not supposed to advertise a policy of waivers. So, you may not know in advance whether your pharmacy will waive a copayment for you. If you are a Part D enrollee who receives a low-income subsidy, you should always ask the pharmacy to waive your copayment. You may be pleased to find out that the pharmacy is willing to do so.

Finding discount programs. There are several ways to find out about government, pharmaceutical company, and nonprofit organization discount drug programs available where you live—starting with the four options below. Once you locate a program for which you might be eligible, you or your doctor must contact the program directly in order to enroll.

- **Information from Medicare.** Medicare itself can direct you both to your state assistance program and to pharmaceutical company programs for a particular drug. It can also alert you to local programs in your area, and can refer you to nonprofit and retail organizations that offer drug discount cards and other plans.

  Medicare's information is on its website at www.medicare.gov. Under the Help and Resources tab, click "Find health & drug plans." This will take you to a page called "Medicare Plan Finder." This link asks you for some personal information—which is strictly confidential—in order to determine which programs you might be eligible for. It then directs you to your state's prescription drug assistance program and to any community-based programs in your area. And it directs you to some pharmaceutical company discounts that may be available for that drug. Finally, the Medicare website lists contact information for some of the nonprofit and retail organizations that offer drug discount cards and similar plans, and explains their basic benefits and eligibility rules.

  You may also get this same information by calling Medicare's toll-free telephone line at 800-MEDICARE and asking about prescription drug assistance programs.

- **State Health Insurance Assistance Program (SHIP) and Health Insurance Counseling and Advocacy Program (HICAP).** Every state has a program to provide free counseling and assistance regarding Medicare, Medicaid, health insurance, and related problems. This program is called the State Health Insurance Assistance Program (SHIP) or the Health Insurance Counseling and Advocacy Program (HICAP). The program maintains local offices with trained counselors who can help you learn about your state's prescription drug assistance program and other drug discount programs that may be available to you. They can also help you with the enrollment process. For more about SHIP and HICAP, see Chapter 13.

- **Area Agency on Aging.** The Area Agency on Aging is a federal government clearinghouse for information about issues relating to seniors. Your agency can provide you with information about your state's assistance program and about community-based drug assistance programs. To find the Area Agency on Aging office nearest you, call their toll-free line at 800-677-1116 or visit www.eldercare.gov.

- **Drug discount information clearinghouses.** Through several clearing-houses, most of which provide their information on the Internet, you can find out about numerous drug assistance and drug discount card and similar programs. Here are some of these clearinghouses and the information they offer:

  - Partnership for Prescription Assistance (www.pparx.org; 888-477-2669) helps patients identify programs that can provide them with free or low-cost medications.

  - The Medicine Program (www.themedicineprogram.com; 573-996-7300) identifies the programs for which a patient might be eligible, and provides information to help patients apply for free medication.

  - RxAssist Patient Assistance Program Center (www.rxassist.org) maintains a website that provides both a direct link to pharmaceutical company drug assistance programs and information about other sites and organizations that can help you apply for assistance, as well as links to nonprofit and retail drug discount cards and similar programs.

Catastrophic Coverage

Once your total expenditures for medications covered by your plan reach a certain level, the plan will provide "catastrophic coverage" that pays almost the entire cost of covered drugs. Your total expenditures are amounts paid by you and your plan combined during any year.

Standard enrollment. After the catastrophic limit for the year is reached, you pay 5% of the cost, or $2.65 per prescription for generic drugs and $6.60 per prescription for brand-name medications, whichever is greater. Your plan pays the rest, with no limit on the total amount. In 2015, catastrophic coverage begins at $4,700 in your out-of-pocket costs.

With low-income subsidy. After the catastrophic limit for the year is reached, Categories One, Two, and Three beneficiaries have no copayments for medications covered by their plans. Category Four beneficiaries pay $2.55 per prescription for generic drugs and $6.35 per prescription for brand-name drugs.

Restrictions on Coverage

Medicare gives the private insurance and Medicare Advantage companies that operate Part D plans a lot of leeway in imposing limits on the coverage they offer. There are a number of different ways the plans may limit coverage, including restricting the specific drugs covered, providing different levels of payment for different drugs, requiring drug regimens such as step therapy, or requiring prior approval before covering certain drugs.

Certain Drugs Excluded by Law

The Medicare program specifically prohibits Part D plans from covering most medications within certain categories of drugs, even if these medications were lawfully prescribed by your physician. These categories include:

- barbiturates (certain sedatives and sleeping pills)
- benzodiazepines (certain tranquilizers)
- drugs used for weight loss or weight gain, and
- over-the-counter medications.

Many of these drugs, which the Part D plans are required to exclude, would have been covered by Medicaid (Medi-Cal in California) for those people who qualify for that program. But "dual eligible" beneficiaries—those who are eligible for both Medicare Part D and Medicaid (including many nursing facility residents)—are required to get their drug coverage through a Part D plan. Dual eligible beneficiaries in some states, however, may still get coverage for some of these drugs if the Medicaid programs in their states will allow it. Certain state Medicaid programs continue to allow coverage for these excluded drugs for those individuals who are also enrolled in a Medicare Part D plan. (See Chapter 16 for more information on Medicaid.)

Formularies

Every Part D plan issues a list, called a formulary, of the specific drugs it covers. Medicare requires each plan to include in its formulary at least two drugs in each "therapeutic class"—meaning a group of drugs used to treat a specific illness or condition. Some plans offer more than two drugs in certain categories. But the availability of coverage for these "extra" drugs may depend on plan member's paying a higher premium or copayment, or having to get prior authorization or another exception from the plan before using the drug.

Formulary Changes May Force You to Change Plans

A Part D plan may also change its formulary whenever it wants, by providing 60 days' notice to Medicare and plan members. Such changes may include dropping a drug entirely from its formulary, dropping the coverage of a brand-name drug and substituting its generic equivalent, or increasing a patient's copayment for a drug. If your plan changes coverage for one of your drugs, you have some protection, as follows:

- If the plan entirely drops a drug it has been covering for you, it must continue to cover it for you until the end of the calendar year.
- If the plan raises the copayment it charges for a drug, the plan must continue providing it to you at the former copayment level until the end of the calendar year.

However, if the plan switches from covering a brand-name drug to a generic equivalent, it may immediately require you to use the generic or else lose all coverage for that drug.

If you don't want to continue with a plan after it changes its coverage, you can explore switching to a different plan. If you are eligible for both Medicare and Medicaid, or are a resident of a long-term care facility, you may switch plans at any time. If not, you may switch plans only during the annual open enrollment period (starting October each year).

If you do not want to change plans, or can't find a plan with better coverage, consider asking your physician to switch you from your previous drug to a different, equivalent drug that your plan covers.

Under Part D rules, if a drug is not on your plan's formulary, the plan will not pay any portion of the cost of that drug, even if a physician has lawfully prescribed it for you (unless you ask for and receive an exception, discussed below). Also, the money you spend on that nonformulary drug will not count toward your Part D deductible or the coverage gap and catastrophic coverage limits.

Tiered Copayments

Medicare allows the insurance companies that operate Part D plans to charge different copayment amounts for different drugs within the same class, even if the drugs are "therapeutically equivalent" (meaning they are used in a similar way to treat the same illness or condition). Part D plans may structure their copayments in a number of ways: They may have lower copayments for generic drugs than for brand-name equivalents; there may be no copayments at all for certain generic drugs; or there may be different copayments for different brands within the same class.

Exceptions to Drug Restrictions

Plan formularies and other cost containment restrictions are not necessarily the last word on coverage for a drug you use or want to use. Every plan is required to have two systems in place to allow you to challenge that plan's listing or decision regarding coverage of your drug.

The first system allows you to file a request for an "exception" to the plan's listing or decision. This means that you ask the plan to provide coverage that differs from its standard formulary. This type of exception usually requires that you and your doctor show some kind of "medical necessity," meaning that the particular drug you want works better for you or has fewer or milder side effects than other drugs in the class.

The second system permits you to appeal a plan's decision. Each plan has its own appeal process, but every plan allows you to ask for an internal review by the plan itself. If an internal review is unsuccessful, you may seek independent review and ultimately take the plan to court, if necessary.

Plans' exceptions and appeals processes are discussed in Chapter 13.

Drug Substitution

The Medicare Part D program allows plans to substitute a generic or another therapeutically equivalent drug instead of the drug you request. That means that although your doctor prescribes a specific drug for you, the plan can have the pharmacy dispense to you a different but equivalent drug. Of course, "equivalence" does not mean "exactly the same." You may have better results or fewer side effects with the drug your physician prescribes you. But under these drug substitution rules, a plan may overrule you and your physician and pay only for the substituted drug. In order to overcome such a drug substitution, you must request an exception to the plan's substitution policy. (See Chapter 13 for more information about exceptions and appeals.)

Prior Authorization

A Part D plan may place certain drugs on a restricted list that requires the plan's prior authorization before it will cover the drug. This means that if you and your physician decide you should take any drugs on this restricted list, you must obtain the plan's approval or else the plan will not cover it. The plan may offer less expensive drugs that it considers to be "equivalent," in which case your doctor may need to give a medical reason why you need this particular drug. Or, perhaps the drug you want to use is prescribed only in special situations, in which case your doctor may need to show the plan that yours is such a special case.

Step Therapy

Step therapy refers to a treatment structure in which a patient must try a certain drug—one that is less expensive for the insurance company—before the plan will cover a different drug in the same class. If a Medicare Part D plan offers more than two drugs within a drug class, the plan may impose a step therapy requirement for certain drugs in that class. If that happens to you, your doctor must certify that you have tried the lower-tier drug and that it did not work well for you. Then, the plan will allow you to "step" up your therapy to the next-higher-tier drug.

Broader Coverage, But Difficult Access, for Certain Drugs

Medicare requires each Part D plan to cover at least two drugs for each therapeutic category. And for the following six specific categories of drugs, Medicare plans must provide coverage for "all or substantially all" available drugs:

- antidepressants
- antipsychotics
- anticonvulsants (treatment of seizures)
- antiretrovirals (treatment of certain viruses, including HIV)
- immunosuppressants (cancer treatment), and
- antineoplastics (chemotherapy).

Although Part D plans must extend coverage to all drugs in these categories, the plans may restrict access to these drugs (except antiretrovirals) in other ways. Plans are permitted to make obtaining these drugs more difficult or expensive through "management" devices, such as tiered copayments, prior authorization, and step therapy requirements.

Supply Limits

You will pay a copayment for each prescription you fill. So, one way to keep copayment costs down might be to have the doctor prescribe a large supply of a certain medicine so that it will take fewer prescriptions to get the same number of doses. Plans may block this tactic by imposing a supply limit that restricts the number of doses of a drug that may be filled per prescription.

Pharmacy Restrictions

Each Part D plan contracts with certain pharmacies to deliver prescription medications. To receive full coverage from your plan, you must get your drugs from a participating pharmacy, which includes large chains, independent drugstores, HMO pharmacies, or mail-order pharmacies. If you fill your prescription at a pharmacy that does not contract with your plan (an "out-of-network" pharmacy), you may have a larger copayment, or you might not receive any coverage at all (depending on the drug and on your plan's rules).

Deciding on a Part D Plan

If you are eligible for Medicare and are also enrolled in the Medicaid program (Medi-Cal in California), Medicare will automatically sign you up for a Part D drug plan. If you are not enrolled in Medicaid, your participation in Medicare Part D is voluntary. Deciding whether to join a Part D plan, and if so what plan to choose, depends on several factors:

- whether you have other health insurance coverage (through your or your spouse's employer or union) that includes drug coverage
- whether you enroll in a Medicare Advantage (Medicare Part C) managed care plan that includes prescription drug coverage
- whether you are eligible for a low-income subsidy
- your age and health
- the total cost of the drugs you use
- whether your drugs are covered by a particular plan
- how much the plan charges in premiums and copayments, and
- the plan's restrictions on access to drugs.

Should You Participate in Part D?

Medicare Part D is mandatory for people who are also enrolled in Medicaid. For those who qualify for a low-income subsidy, Part D is an attractive low-cost option. And for most other people, Part D is still better than no coverage at all. But for a few people, deciding whether to join a Part D plan is a bit more complicated.

In an effort to encourage everyone to join a Part D plan as soon as they are eligible, Medicare has created a financial penalty for those who delay enrolling. The penalty takes the form of a rise in premiums of 1% per month—if and when you do eventually enroll in a plan— for every month you delay enrolling after you first become eligible.

And that rise is permanent. So, for example, if you wait to join a Part D plan for two years after you are first eligible for Part D coverage, you will always pay 24% (1% per month for 24 months) more in premiums for any plan you join.

This penalty for late enrollment offers a strong incentive for most people to join a Part D plan as soon as they are eligible. This is true even if you do not presently have many out-of-pocket prescription drug costs and:

- do not regularly take any prescription drugs, or
- take only one relatively low-cost drug.

If you are not enrolled in an employer-sponsored insurance plan with drug coverage or a Medicare Advantage plan with drug coverage, and you have no or very low regular prescription drug costs, you have the following two options.

Option 1: Not enrolling. You can choose not to enroll in any drug plan for as long as you do not have any significant out-of-pocket drug costs. This means you will incur the 1% per month penalty on the premium cost of any plan in which you eventually enroll. But that penalty will be partially or fully offset by the fact that you will not be paying any monthly premium for the years you are not enrolled.

The risk with this approach is that after a few years your drug needs may change and you may then want to enroll in a particular plan that has a high monthly premium. If so, the 1% per month of delay penalty might add up to more than you have saved by not enrolling early. For example, if you delay 36 months before enrolling, then enroll in a plan that has an initial premium of $50 per month, you will be penalized $18 per month in premiums. And these monthly premium amounts go up each year.

Option 2: Enrolling in a low-premium plan. For many people in the categories above, a better option than not enrolling at all in a plan is to enroll as soon as eligible in a low-premium plan. Several insurance companies offer plans with no monthly premium, or a premium under $10. These plans tend to have poorer coverage than plans with higher premiums. But if such a plan is available where you live, it may allow you to enroll in Part D for little or no money as soon as you are eligible, thus avoiding the late enrollment penalty. If and when your drug costs go up and you need better coverage, you can then switch to a more comprehensive plan with a higher premium. For an explanation of switching plans, see Chapter 13.

No Penalty for Delayed Enrollment If Covered by Equivalent Employer-Sponsored Health Insurance

As explained above, Medicare imposes a financial penalty on people who delay enrolling in Part D coverage. But this penalty does *not* apply if you are covered by an employer- or union-sponsored health plan (for either current employees or retirees) that provides what is called "creditable prescription drug coverage," meaning coverage that is as extensive as a basic Part D plan. When you first become eligible for Medicare, your employer- or union-sponsored plan will notify you whether that plan qualifies as creditable coverage. If your employer-sponsored plan does offer creditable coverage, you may remain in that plan as long as you can and want to, and incur no penalty if you later join a Medicare Part D plan.

If you subsequently lose coverage by a creditable plan, or the plan's drug coverage falls below what qualifies as creditable, then you may enroll without penalty in a Part D plan. You will pay no higher premium than a person who is first eligible for Medicare as long as you enroll in a Part D plan within 63 days from the date you lose creditable coverage.

If your health plan does not qualify as providing creditable coverage, you must join a Part D plan when you first become eligible or else pay the 1% per month premium penalty when you do finally enroll. Even if you join a separate Part D plan, you may want to keep your employer-sponsored coverage instead of relying entirely on Medicare coverage. If your employer-sponsored coverage provides less expensive and/or more complete general health coverage than Medicare Parts A and B do, you may want to retain that coverage even though you also join a Part D plan.

Stand-Alone Drug Plan or Managed Care Plan

Part D drug coverage is available either through a separate, stand-alone prescription drug plan (PDP) or as the prescription drug component (MA-PD) of full health coverage under a Medicare Advantage plan (see Chapter 15). Each type of plan offers a generally equivalent range of available coverage, though each specific plan is slightly different and costs vary.

If you belong to a Medicare Advantage plan that does not offer MA-PD drug coverage and you want drug coverage, you must leave your plan and enroll in a stand-alone PDP, which also means returning to regular Medicare coverage (also referred to as Medicare fee-for-service) as described in earlier sections of this chapter. Or, you may join a Medicare Advantage plan that offers MA-PD drug coverage. Making this choice is discussed in Chapter 15.

Finding Out About Available Part D Plans

You may enroll only in a plan that operates in the state where you live. There are several ways to find out about the specific Part D plans available to you.

Medicare. The Centers for Medicare & Medicaid Services (CMS) is the federal agency that administers the Medicare program, including Part D prescription drug coverage. It provides personalized help in locating Part D plans. CMS can tell you not only what plans are available where you live, but can also narrow your choice for you according to the medications you regularly take. You can contact CMS by phone at 800-MEDICARE (800-633-4227). Or, you can visit its website at www.medicare.gov and find information tailored to your specific geographic location and medication regimen.

SHIP or HICAP. Every state has a certified program that provides free advice to consumers about Medicare, Medicaid, and other health insurance matters. It's called the State Health Insurance Assistance Program (SHIP), or sometimes the Health Insurance Counseling and Advocacy Program (HICAP). These programs maintain local offices in most urban areas as well as some central rural locations.

Trained counselors in these offices can tell you about all the Part D plans available in your state, and can identify the plans that cover the drugs you regularly use. Once you have investigated several plans, the counselors can meet with you in person to help you make a final decision. To find your SHIP or HICAP office, see the contact information at the end of Chapter 13.

Have Your Information Handy When You Contact Part D Assistance

In figuring out which Part D plan is best for you, you'll want to consider the medications you regularly use and the pharmacy where you prefer to get your drugs. Before you contact any agency or counselor for assistance in choosing a plan, have the following information handy:

- a list of the specific drugs you regularly use, including the brand (or generic) name, the dose size and frequency, and the current monthly cost
- the name and address of your pharmacy
- whether you currently receive Medicaid benefits, and
- whether you are, or think you might be, eligible for a Part D low-income subsidy.

State department of insurance. Every state has a government agency that oversees insurance matters. You can contact your state department of insurance for the names, addresses, and phone numbers of every company offering a Part D plan in your state. See the end of Chapter 14 for a website that lists all of the state departments of insurance.

CAUTION

Get complete information from the plan itself. You can get very helpful information about Part D plans from several sources. But the most thorough information about a specific plan comes from the plan itself. So, before you make a final choice, contact any plan that interests you and ask them to send you a complete description of the plan, including all the matters discussed in this section. You can get the phone number and address of any plan from Medicare itself, or from the other sources discussed above. Make sure to get any important information from the plan in writing. Unfortunately, the insurance companies' telephone information centers tend to be somewhat unreliable. Also, you have no way of forcing the insurance company to abide by what someone tells you on the phone.

Choosing a Part D Drug Plan

Once you decide to enroll in Part D and you find out what plans are available where you live, you must consider several factors in deciding which plan to choose. (When you're ready to join a particular plan, you enroll directly with that plan. The mechanics of enrollment are discussed in Chapter 13.) Here is a step-by-step guide to choosing the plan that's right for you (you can also use the Medicare Plan Finder at Medicare.gov):

Step 1: List your regular medications and their costs. The first step in deciding on a specific plan is to list the medicines you regularly take, including:

- the brand name and generic name (if there is one) of each drug; (if you take the generic version and don't know the brand name, ask your doctor what it's called)
- the dosage you take
- how many doses are in each prescription you fill, and
- how often you fill the prescription.

Step 2: See which plans include your medications in their formularies. The single most important thing to consider in choosing a plan is whether all the drugs you regularly take are included in the plan's formulary. Eliminate from consideration any plan that does not include either the brand-name or the generic version of your drugs. Some plans may cover only the generic version of a drug you take, while others may cover both the brand-name and the generic versions. Under any plan that covers a brand-name drug, copayments for the brand-name will be higher than for the generic version.

Free One-on-One Help in Choosing a Part D Plan

If you have any doubts or questions about choosing a Part D plan, it may be a very good idea to get free personal advice from an expert counselor with SHIP or HICAP near you. These trained counselors are familiar with all the plans offered in your geographic area. They will sit down with you and help you match your needs, preferences, and finances with the available plans. To find your local SHIP or HICAP office, see the contact information at the end of Chapter 13.

Step 3: Check with the different plans to see what the total monthly cost of your drugs would be, as well as your initial copayments. For each plan that includes all your drugs on its formulary, ask the sponsoring company to provide you with an estimate (in writing) of the total monthly cost of each of your prescriptions—taking into account your normal dosage and number of doses. (Total costs differ among insurance companies because each one negotiates different drug prices with the pharmaceutical companies.) Also ask the plans to tell you what your copayments would be for each prescription during the initial coverage period (prior to the "doughnut hole" coverage gap).

Step 4: See whether the plan provides "first dollar" coverage. The standard Part D benefit requires each person to pay out of pocket a $310 (in 2014) per year deductible before the plan begins providing any coverage. Some plans, however, provide what is called "first dollar" coverage, meaning that they waive this deductible and begin paying their share from the first dollar you spend on covered medicines. These plans are generally more expensive, but may be worth it if your prescription costs are high.

Step 5: Ask whether the plan offers any coverage within the "doughnut hole" coverage gap. A few plans offer some coverage within each year's "doughnut hole" coverage gap, during which most people must pay the entire amount of the cost of their drugs. If the total cost of your drugs will put you into the coverage gap, this added coverage may be very important. You can determine whether the cost of your drugs will enter into the coverage gap by calculating the total monthly cost of each of your drugs under each plan, multiplying each by 12 (months), then adding them all together.

Step 6: Total the various costs, including the monthly premium. Eliminate those plans that don't cover your particular medications on their formulary. For the remaining plans, use the information you've gathered to determine how much money you would spend each year under each plan you are considering. For each plan, add up:

- the plan's yearly premiums
- your yearly deductible amount (if the plan does not provide "first dollar" coverage)
- your copayments for all your drugs during the initial coverage period, and
- how much you would pay out of pocket during the coverage gap (this requires you to figure out how quickly—meaning, with how many monthly prescriptions—you would reach the coverage gap; you do this by adding up the total monthly cost of your drugs under each plan).

Once you've added up all of these items for each plan, you'll be able to compare the annual cost of each plan side-by-side. Before you make your final decision, though, there's one more step.

Step 7: Look into access restrictions. Though the cost of drugs is important, you should also consider ease of access to your drugs when choosing among plans. This is particularly true if your costs would be nearly the same for two or more plans. Plans restrict access in two different ways. They may place restrictions on coverage—for example, they may require or have drug substitution, prior authorization, step therapy, and supply limits—and they may require you to purchase your drugs from selected pharmacies and other sources. If a plan places a difficult or cumbersome restriction on your access to the drugs you need, you may want to consider a different plan with fewer restrictions at a somewhat higher cost.

TIP

Switching from one plan to another. Enrolling in a particular Part D plan is not necessarily forever. If you pick a plan that doesn't suit your needs and you can find a better one, you may switch plans. When and how often you may switch plans depends upon whether you are also eligible for Medicaid, you receive a Part D low-income subsidy, or you reside in a long-term care facility. The options for switching plans are explained in Chapter 13.

Medicare Procedures:
Enrollment, Claims, and Appeals

C hapter 12 described the eligibility rules for Medicare. As you'll remember, most people are eligible for Part A hospital insurance free of charge; if you are not, you may enroll by paying a monthly premium. Part B medical insurance coverage is available to most people age 65 and older, and everyone covered pays a monthly premium for it. And Part D—which covers some of the cost of prescription drugs you take at home—is available to everyone who is eligible for Part A or B. Everyone who enrolls in Part D pays a monthly premium for prescription drug coverage except those who are also eligible for Medicaid or who receive a special Part D low-income subsidy.

This chapter explains:

- how to enroll in Medicare Part A and Part B
- how to get Medicare to pay its share of your medical bills once you are enrolled
- what portion of the bill you must pay yourself
- how to read the notice Medicare sends you
- how to appeal a Medicare decision regarding your claim, and
- the separate procedures for enrolling in a Part D plan, switching Part D plans, requesting an exception to a Part D plan's formulary or another access restriction, and appealing a Part D plan's decision.

Enrolling in Part A Hospital Insurance

Medicare Part A, also called hospital insurance, covers most of the cost of inpatient care in a hospital or skilled nursing facility, and also the costs of home health care. Most people age 65 or older are eligible for Part A coverage. Some will receive it automatically and free of charge, along with their Social Security benefits. Others will need to enroll and possibly pay a monthly fee.

Those Who Receive Social Security Benefits

If you are under age 65 and already receive Social Security retirement, dependents, or survivors benefits or Railroad Retirement benefits, you don't need to do any paperwork to enroll in Medicare Part A hospital insurance. Social Security will automatically enroll you, and coverage will take effect on your 65th birthday. About three months before your 65th birthday, Medicare will mail you a Medicare card and information sheet.

If you receive Social Security disability benefits for two years, regardless of your age, you will be automatically enrolled in Medicare Part A, effective 24 months from the date Social Security declared that your disability began. The Medicare card you receive in the mail will indicate that you are enrolled in both Part A and Part B. If you do not want to be enrolled in, and pay the monthly premium for, Part B, there is a form for you to sign and return to Medicare. If you do want to be enrolled in both Parts A and B, you don't have to do anything. Just sign your card and keep it handy.

Managed Care Plans Handle Medicare Paperwork

Many people who are about to qualify for Medicare have an HMO or another managed care insurance plan that they intend to keep when they become eligible for Medicare. Other people decide to join an HMO or another managed care plan when they first become eligible for Medicare.

If you intend to remain with your current insurance plan when you become eligible, it can sign you up for Medicare and switch you to the plan's Medicare coverage. Begin this process two to three months before you become eligible for Medicare.

Similarly, if you decide to join a managed care plan for the first time when you become eligible for Medicare, you can sign up for Medicare at the same time you sign up for the plan. Try to get the paperwork started at least two months before your Medicare eligibility begins. Medicare managed care plans are discussed in Chapter 15.

If you are receiving Social Security benefits but do not receive your Medicare card in the mail within a month of your 65th birthday, or within a month of your 24th month of disability benefits, contact your local Social Security office or call the national Social Security office at 800-772-1213.

Your Medicare Card

When you are enrolled in Medicare, you will be sent a Medicare card that states:

- your name
- whether you have both Part A and Part B coverage or just Part A
- the effective date of your Medicare coverage, and
- your health insurance claim number—also called your Medicare number—which consists of your Social Security number and one or two letters.

Always carry your Medicare card with you. You will be asked to present it when you seek medical treatment at a hospital, a doctor's office, or another health care provider.

Also, you must include your Medicare number on all payments of Medicare premiums or correspondence about Medicare.

If you lose your Medicare card, you can have it replaced by applying in person at your local Social Security office or by calling the toll-free information line at 800-MEDICARE, or Social Security's main office at 800-772-1213. Alternatively, you can apply for a new card online at www.medicare.gov.

Those Who Do Not Receive Social Security Benefits

If you are soon to turn 65 but you are not receiving Social Security retirement, dependents, or survivors benefits, Railroad Retirement benefits, or federal civil service retirement benefits, you must apply either online on the official Social Security Administration website at www.ssa.gov/medicareonly, or at your local Social Security office, to enroll in Medicare Part A. If you are going to apply for retirement or other Social Security benefits to begin on your 65th birthday, you can apply for Medicare at the same time, at your local Social Security office.

Who Is Eligible

If you are eligible for Social Security benefits, you can receive free Medicare Part A coverage at age 65 whether or not you actually claim your Social Security benefits.

For example, many people who continue working after reaching age 65 do not claim retirement benefits until later. Still, they can receive free Part A Medicare coverage by applying for it at their local Social Security office.

Also, if you are not automatically eligible for free Part A coverage, you may be able to purchase it for a monthly premium. The amount of the premium depends on how many work credits you or your spouse have earned. (See "Part A Hospital Insurance" in Chapter 12 for details.)

When to Apply

Whether you wish to claim Social Security benefits and Medicare, or just Medicare, apply well before you turn 65. You can apply as early as three months before your 65th birthday.

Signing up early is important for two reasons: First, it will ensure that your coverage begins as soon as you are eligible, on your 65th birthday. Second, if you wait more than three months after your 65th birthday to enroll, you will not be allowed to enroll in Part B until the following January 1, and your eligibility will not begin until July 1 of that year. (See "Enrolling in Part B Medical Insurance," below, regarding delayed enrollment.)

CAUTION

Avoid delays in Part B coverage. If you do not enroll in both Parts A and B during your initial enrollment period, your enrollment in Part B will not only be delayed, but you will also have to pay a higher monthly premium for it. (See "Enrolling in Part B Medical Insurance," below, for details.)

When Benefits Begin

If you apply for Part A of Medicare within six months after you turn 65, your coverage will date back to your 65th birthday. But if you apply after that, your coverage will date back only up to six months before the month in which you applied. If your Medicare eligibility is based on disability, however, your coverage will date back up to one year before the date on which you apply.

Appealing Denial of Coverage

Eligibility for coverage by Part A of Medicare depends solely on your age and on the number of Social Security work credits you or your spouse have acquired. (See "Part A Hospital Insurance" in Chapter 12 for a review of the eligibility requirements.) You can be denied coverage by Medicare Part A only if there is a dispute about whether you have reached 65, about the number of your or your spouse's work credits, or about the validity of your marriage.

Decisions about these matters are handled not by Medicare but by Social Security. And, like any other decision of the Social Security Administration, a decision denying eligibility for Medicare Part A hospital insurance coverage can be appealed. The appeal process is discussed later in this chapter.

Enrolling in Part B Medical Insurance

Medicare Part B, referred to as medical insurance, covers doctors' services plus laboratory, clinic, home therapy, and other medical services you receive other than when you are a patient in a hospital or skilled nursing facility. Most people age 65 are eligible for Part B.

Everyone must pay a monthly premium to enroll, although some people may pay for Part B fees in the premiums they pay to HMOs or other Medicare Advantage plans (see Chapter 15).

This section explains who is automatically enrolled in Part B, who must take steps to enroll, and when to do so.

Those Who Receive Social Security Benefits

If you are younger than 65 and already receiving Social Security retirement, Railroad Retirement, dependents, or survivors benefits, you will be automatically enrolled in both Medicare Part A and Part B within three months of turning 65. Your coverage will become effective on your 65th birthday. Near that time, you will be sent your Medicare card through the mail, along with an information packet. The monthly premium for Part B coverage will be deducted automatically from your Social Security check, beginning with the first month after your 65th birthday.

If you do not want Medicare Part B coverage—perhaps because you are still working and are covered by an employment-related health plan—notify Social Security of that fact on the form that comes with your Medicare card. If you reject Part B coverage when you are first eligible for it, you can enroll in Part B later on, although only during the first three months of any year. And if you enroll later, your premiums may be higher.

Those Who Do Not Receive Social Security Benefits

If you are turning 65 but are not eligible for Social Security benefits, or are not yet going to claim benefits to which you are entitled, you may still enroll in Part B medical insurance either online on the official Social Security website at www.ssa.gov/medicareonly, or at your local Social Security office.

You can enroll during an initial period of seven months, which begins three months before the month you turn 65 and ends three months after the end of the month you turn 65. For example, if you turn 65 in July, your initial enrollment period starts April 1 and ends October 31. However, the earlier you enroll during this initial period, the better. If you enroll during the three months before you turn 65, your coverage will begin on your 65th birthday. If you enroll during the remaining four months of your initial enrollment period, your coverage may be delayed from one to three months after you sign up, depending on how long it takes to process your application.

Delayed Enrollment

If you do not enroll in Part B medical insurance during the seven-month period just before and after you turn 65, but later decide you want the coverage, you can sign up during any general enrollment period. These are held January 1 through March 31 every year. If you sign up any time during one of these general enrollment periods, your coverage will begin on July 1 of the year you enroll.

Your monthly premium will be higher if you wait to enroll during one of the general enrollment periods instead of when you turn 65. For each year you were eligible for Part B coverage but did not enroll, your premium will be 10% higher than the basic premium.

Free Late Enrollment If Covered by Current Employment Health Plan

If you are covered by a group health plan based on your own or your spouse's current employment, you can enroll in Part B coverage after your 65th birthday without having to wait for the open enrollment period and without any penalty. This exception refers only to a group health plan based on current employment, not to one based on retirement benefits from employment.

If you have delayed signing up for Medicare Part B because you have been covered by a health plan based on current employment, you can sign up for Part B coverage at any time while you are still covered, or within seven months of the date you or your spouse end that employment, or the date the health coverage ends, whichever comes first.

Medicare's Payment of Your Medical Bills

Medicare does not handle day-to-day paperwork and payments with patients and doctors or other health care providers. It contracts out this work to what are called Medicare carriers or intermediaries. These are huge private corporations, such as Blue Cross or other large insurance companies, each of which handles claims for an entire state, and sometimes for more than one state.

The Medicare intermediary in your state receives, reviews, and pays claims. It sends notices that tell you and the medical provider of the amount of benefits paid, the amount of your medical bill that has not been paid, and the amount the health care provider is legally permitted to charge. (See "How to Read a Medicare Summary Notice," below, for more on these notices.) And it is with the intermediary that you will initially correspond if you want to appeal a decision about Medicare coverage of health care charges. (See "Appealing the Denial of a Claim," below, for appeal procedures.)

Medicare intermediaries handle billing for inpatient charges covered under Part A differently from outpatient charges covered under Part B. This section explains the differences in the billing process.

Inpatient and Home Care Bills

Medicare Part A covers inpatient care in a hospital or skilled nursing facility, as well as some home health care. (See "How Much Medicare Part A Pays" in Chapter 12 for a review of Medicare Part A coverage.)

Medicare Billed Directly by Facility

When you first check into a hospital or skilled nursing facility, you present your Medicare card to the admissions office and it takes care of the rest. Similarly, when you and your doctor make arrangements for a Medicare-approved home care agency to provide your care, you give the agency your Medicare number and it takes care of all the paperwork. The provider—the hospital, skilled nursing facility, or home health care agency—sends its bills directly to Medicare. The patient should not have to do a thing to get Medicare to pay its part of the bill.

The hospital, nursing facility, or home care agency accepts as payment in full the amount the Medicare intermediary decides is the approved charge for those of your inpatient services that are covered by Medicare (but see Chapter 12 for a reminder of what costs are covered). Unlike doctors' bills—in which you may be personally responsible for the difference between Medicare's approved charges and the actual amount of a bill—a hospital, nursing facility, or home care agency is not permitted to bill you for any covered inpatient charges over the amounts paid by Medicare.

The Medicare carrier will also send you a copy of the bills so that you will know how much has been paid and how much you must cover on your own.

Patient Billed for Some Charges

The hospital, nursing facility, or home care agency will bill you, and your private Medicare supplement insurance company (if you have such insurance), for:

- any unpaid portion of your deductible
- any coinsurance payments—for example, for hospital inpatient stays of more than 60 days, and
- charges not covered at all by Medicare, such as for a private room you requested that was not medically necessary, or for television and telephone charges.

The Medicare carrier will send you a form called a Medicare Summary Notice that will show what hospital services were paid for and the portion of your deductible for which you are responsible. The hospital or other facility will bill you directly for the unpaid portion of your deductible and for those amounts not covered by Medicare or by Medicare supplemental insurance. (See Chapter 14 regarding supplemental insurance.)

Outpatient and Doctor Bills

How much of your covered doctor and outpatient medical bills Medicare Part B will pay depends on whether your doctor or other medical provider accepts assignment of the Medicare-approved amount as the full amount of the bill. (For more information, see "How Much Medicare Part B Pays" in Chapter 12.)

Catching Overbilling

Medicare has been doing a better job in recent years of cracking down on billing errors and fraud by health care providers. But you must still check your bill carefully to determine whether the facility or other provider has billed you for services you did not receive or services that Medicare has paid, or has charged more than once for the same service.

The Medicare intermediary may look closely at the portion of the bill Medicare is supposed to pay, and if you have medigap supplemental insurance, the insurance company will also check the bill. But neither one will carefully examine the amounts for which you are personally responsible.

Check all medical bills to make sure there are no charges for services you did not receive. Then, place the bill from the facility or other provider next to the statement from the Medicare carrier and from your medigap insurance company. Compare them to see whether any amount the facility or other provider has billed you directly has been paid by Medicare or by your medigap insurer.

If so, you must contact the billing office at the facility or other provider, sending a copy of your statement from the Medicare carrier or medigap insurer which shows that the charges have been paid. If the problem is billing for a service you do not believe you received, ask the facility's or provider's billing office to send you a copy of your medical record where the service was recorded.

For more information about how to deal with what you believe are billing errors, go to the Medicare website at www.medicare.gov and look under the tab "Claims and Appeals," then click on "Filing a Complaint."

If the doctor accepts assignment, you—perhaps assisted by private medigap insurance or Medicaid—are responsible only for your yearly Part B deductible, plus the 20% of the approved charges Medicare does not pay.

If the doctor or other provider does not accept assignment, then you and your additional insurance may also be responsible for all amounts of the bill up to 15% more than the Medicare-approved amount.

 TIP

HMOs and Medicare Advantage plans do their own paperwork. If you belong to an HMO or another Medicare Advantage plan, the billing office there handles all the Medicare-related paperwork. In fact, Medicare pays Medicare Advantage plans a flat amount for each enrolled patient, rather than a separate payment for each treatment. All you have to do is pay your plan's own monthly premiums and copayments and deal with its paperwork. You don't have to directly handle any Medicare forms.

Assignment Method of Payment

If your doctor or other health care provider accepts assignment of your Medicare claim, you are personally responsible for your yearly medical insurance deductible, and then only the 20% of the Medicare-approved amount of the bill that Medicare does not pay. By accepting assignment, the doctor or other provider agrees not to charge you a higher amount than what Medicare approves for the treatment or other covered service you have received.

After you and the health care provider are informed by a Medicare Summary Notice form from Medicare how much the Medicare-approved charges are, the provider's office will either bill you directly for the remaining 20% of approved charges or bill your medigap supplemental insurance carrier if you have one.

EXAMPLE: Franco was examined for a painful knee by his regular doctor, who then decided to refer him to an orthopedist. Franco asked his doctor to refer him to someone who accepted Medicare assignment. The orthopedist examined Franco, took X-rays, and prescribed exercises and some medication. Franco's own doctor charged $100 for Franco's original examination. The orthopedist charged $150. Both doctors accepted assignment.

Medicare's approved amount for Franco's regular doctor was $75 and, for the orthopedist, $120. Because Franco had already paid his yearly deductible for Part B, Medicare paid 80% of the approved amount of each doctor's bill: $60 to Franco's regular doctor (80% of $75 = $60) and $96 to the orthopedist (80% of $120 = $96). Medicare sent these amounts directly to the doctors. Franco had to pay only the remaining 20% of the approved amounts.

The following chart shows who paid what amount of Franco's bills in this example.

Payment of Doctor Bills—Assignment Accepted

	Initial exam	Orthopedic exam	Total
Doctor normally charges	$100	$150	$250
Amount approved by Medicare	$75	$120	$195
Amount paid by Medicare (80%)	$60	$96	$156
Amount patient paid (20%)	$15	$24	$39

Payment When No Assignment

If your doctor or other health care provider does not accept assignment of the Medicare-approved charges as the full amount of the bill, you —or you and your medigap supplemental insurance—will owe the difference between what Medicare pays and the full amount of the doctor's bill, up to 15% more than the Medicare-approved amount. But Medicare pays a bit less than 80% of the approved amount on these claims. And you end up having to pay one third (33.25%) of the Medicare-approved amount, rather than one fifth (20%) of the approved amount.

Medicare has a complicated way of calculating this. For nonparticipating doctors, Medicare lowers the approved fee to 95% of what it would be for participating doctors. But it allows nonparticipating doctors to charge 15% of this lowered fee to patients, in addition to their 20% copayment.

EXAMPLE: In the example above, Franco's own doctor normally charged $100 for an examination and the orthopedist charged $150. If neither doctor accepted assignment, but stuck to their normal fees, the payment amounts would be as follows.

Medicare's approved amount for Franco's regular doctor was $75 and, for the orthopedist, $120. But Medicare will allow only 95% of this fee as the approved fee since the doctor doesn't accept assignment. The doctor can charge 115% of this lowered fee (which works out to an additional 9.25% of the regular approved fee). Medicare will pay 80% of the lowered fee.

The following chart summarizes who paid what amount of Franco's bills in this example. You'll see your payment is one third of the regular approved amount.

Payment of Doctor Bills—Assignment Accepted			
	Initial exam	Orthopedic exam	Total
Doctor normally charges	$100.00	$150.00	$250.00
Amount approved for nonparticipating doctors (95% of approved fee)	$71.25	$114.00	$185.25
Total amount doctor allowed to charge (115% of lowered fee)	$81.94	$131.10	$213.04
Amount paid by Medicare (80% of lowered fee)	$57.00	$91.20	$148.20
Amount paid by patient (20% of lowered fee)	$14.25	$22.80	$37.05
Additional amount doctor can charge (15% of lowered fee)	$10.69	$17.10	$27.79
Total amount paid by patient (20% of lowered fee + additional amount)	$24.94	$39.90	$64.84

TIP

Handling Medicare billing paperwork is free. Even a doctor or another health care provider who does not accept assignment must fill in the Medicare paperwork and send it to Medicare for payment—and you cannot be charged for processing this Medicare paperwork.

Paying Your Share of the Bill

Doctors and other health care providers must wait to find out how much the Medicare-approved charges are before asking you to pay your share. Until they know what the Medicare-approved amount is, they cannot know the legal limit—15% over those approved charges—on how much they can require you to pay.

Following your treatment or other service, the doctor's or other provider's office will submit their bills for payment to Medicare. You do not have to submit the paperwork yourself.

If you have private medigap supplemental insurance that pays your deductible and the 20% coinsurance amount that Medicare does not pay, the doctor's office will send its paperwork to the insurance company as well as to Medicare. The doctor will receive payment directly from both Medicare and the supplemental insurance, after Medicare has determined the approved amount for the care you received.

Every three months you will receive a form called a Medicare Summary Notice, or MSN, that includes the following information about every Medicare-billed service you received during the previous three-month period:
- how much of each bill is Medicare approved
- how much Medicare will pay the provider
- how much of your deductible has been met, and
- how much must be paid by you or your private medigap insurance.

How to Read a Medicare Summary Notice

The Medicare Summary Notice (MSN) shows how your claims were settled. The MSN is not a bill. It is a tally of procedures and payments for your information. Every time you get an MSN form, you should check several important pieces of information. (See "Sample Forms," below, for examples of MSN forms, along with notes pointing out important information.)

Date of the Notice

You have six months from the date printed in the top right corner of the first page to appeal any decision that your Medicare carrier makes. (See "Appealing the Denial of a Claim," below, for appeal procedures.) The deadline for filing an appeal is listed on the second page of the MSN.

Medicare Intermediary

The name, address, and phone number of your Medicare intermediary is listed in a box in the upper right corner of the MSN. Contact the intermediary if you have questions about the notice or disagree with the way a payment was made and want to appeal. For medical services, this will be the Medicare intermediary in your state that handles almost all Part B claims. For durable medical equipment, however, this will be a regional intermediary, which may be located in another state.

Type of Claim

In the middle of the first page, in large, bold capital letters, is a line that reads "Part B Medical Insurance." The box under this heading describes the type of claims included in the notice.

For example, an MSN might be for Outpatient Facility Claims, referring to laboratory, diagnostic, or surgical procedures you received as an outpatient at a hospital or clinic; another notice might be for Assigned Claims, referring to visits to doctors who accepted assignment of the Medicare-approved amount.

Services Provided

In the box beneath the heading "Part B Medical Insurance," you'll find the name and address of the doctor or provider of services, the dates of the services you received, and a description of the specific services. The Medicare code for each service will be included in parentheses after the description of the service.

Contact the billing office of the health care provider immediately if you believe that the description of the service is incorrect, or if it is correct and you believe it should be a covered service. Ask workers there to check the description of the service and the code number. If there has been a clerical error, it can be changed in informal contact between the doctor's office or other provider and the Medicare intermediary.

Coverage may have been denied because the medical service you received was wrongly described as something Medicare does not cover—as a routine physical exam, for example, when you really went in for back pain. Or the description may be correct but the Medicare service code may be wrong. Codes can be jumbled by the doctor's office. In that case, the rejected coverage should have been approved.

Division of the Bills

The Part B Medical Insurance box contains columns that show the cost of each procedure or service and how those costs will be divided among those paying:

- **Amount Charged.** The first figure is the amount the doctor or other provider would bill a non-Medicare patient. This usually means nothing to you; a doctor may charge you this full fee only if Medicare does not cover the service at all.
- **Medicare Approved.** Next comes the amount Medicare sets as its approved charges for the service provided. This is often considerably less than what the doctor or other provider would charge a non-Medicare patient. If the doctor has accepted assignment, this amount will be the total the doctor may collect from Medicare and you or your supplemental insurance. If the doctor or other provider did not accept assignment, the total may be only as much as 15% more than these Medicare-approved charges. (See "How Much Medicare Part B Pays" in Chapter 12 for more information on doctors' acceptance of Medicare-assigned charges.)

- **Medicare Paid Provider.** The third figure is usually the amount Medicare paid to the provider. In the case of unassigned claims, however, this may be titled "Medicare Paid You" and will list the amount Medicare paid you directly.
- **You May Be Billed.** The most important figure is the amount you may be billed. This is the amount Medicare approved (plus 15%, if assignment was not accepted) minus the amount Medicare actually paid. If you have medigap supplemental insurance, this is the amount that will be billed to it for payment. If you have no supplemental insurance, this is the amount you will have to pay out of your own pocket.

  The amount you may be billed can include:

  - the unpaid portion of your annual deductible
  - the 20% coinsurance amount Medicare Part B does not pay for most covered services
  - up to 15% over the Medicare-approved amount for doctors who did not accept assignment, and
  - any amount for services Medicare does not cover at all.

Sample Forms

The next two pages show a sample Medicare Summary Notice. Along the side are our notations indicating key points of information in the notice.

MSN Form Example #1

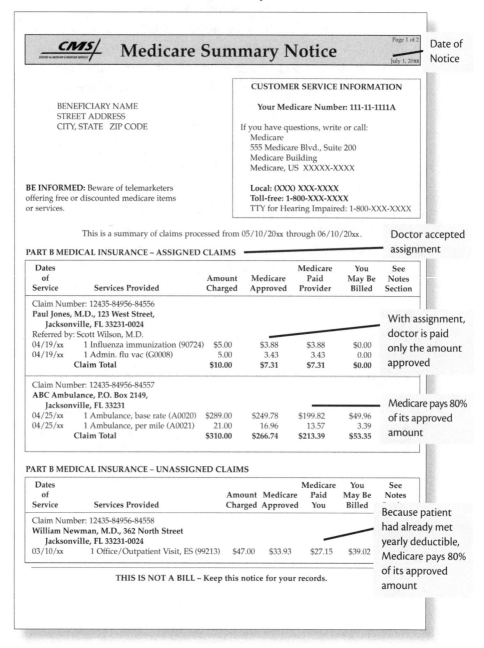

CMS Medicare Summary Notice

Page 1 of 2

July 1, 20xx

Date of Notice

CUSTOMER SERVICE INFORMATION

BENEFICIARY NAME
STREET ADDRESS
CITY, STATE   ZIP CODE

Your Medicare Number: 111-11-1111A

If you have questions, write or call:
Medicare
555 Medicare Blvd., Suite 200
Medicare Building
Medicare, US XXXXX-XXXX

BE INFORMED: Beware of telemarketers offering free or discounted medicare items or services.

Local: (XXX) XXX-XXXX
Toll-free: 1-800-XXX-XXXX
TTY for Hearing Impaired: 1-800-XXX-XXXX

This is a summary of claims processed from 05/10/20xx through 06/10/20xx.

Doctor accepted assignment

PART B MEDICAL INSURANCE – ASSIGNED CLAIMS

Dates of Service	Services Provided	Amount Charged	Medicare Approved	Medicare Paid Provider	You May Be Billed	See Notes Section
Claim Number: 12435-84956-84556						
Paul Jones, M.D., 123 West Street, Jacksonville, FL 33231-0024						
Referred by: Scott Wilson, M.D.						
04/19/xx	1 Influenza immunization (90724)	$5.00	$3.88	$3.88	$0.00	
04/19/xx	1 Admin. flu vac (G0008)	5.00	3.43	3.43	0.00	
	Claim Total	$10.00	$7.31	$7.31	$0.00	

With assignment, doctor is paid only the amount approved

Claim Number: 12435-84956-84557						
ABC Ambulance, P.O. Box 2149, Jacksonville, FL 33231						
04/25/xx	1 Ambulance, base rate (A0020)	$289.00	$249.78	$199.82	$49.96	
04/25/xx	1 Ambulance, per mile (A0021)	21.00	16.96	13.57	3.39	
	Claim Total	$310.00	$266.74	$213.39	$53.35	

Medicare pays 80% of its approved amount

PART B MEDICAL INSURANCE – UNASSIGNED CLAIMS

Dates of Service	Services Provided	Amount Charged	Medicare Approved	Medicare Paid You	You May Be Billed	See Notes
Claim Number: 12435-84956-84558						
William Newman, M.D., 362 North Street Jacksonville, FL 33231-0024						
03/10/xx	1 Office/Outpatient Visit, ES (99213)	$47.00	$33.93	$27.15	$39.02	

Because patient had already met yearly deductible, Medicare pays 80% of its approved amount

THIS IS NOT A BILL – Keep this notice for your records.

MSN Form Example #1, page 2

Your Medicare Number: 111-11-1111A

Notes Section:

a This information is being sent to your private insurer. They will review it to see if additional benefits can be paid. Send any questions regarding your supplemental benefits to them.

b This service is paid at 100% of the Medicare approved amount.

c Your doctor did not accept assignment for this service. Under Federal law, your doctor cannot charge more than $39.02. If you have already paid more than this amount, you are entitled to a refund from the provider.

Deductible Information:

You have met the Part B deductible for 20xx.

General Information:

You have the right to make a request in writing for an itemized statement which details each Medicare item or service which you have received from your physician, hospital, or any other health supplier or health professional. Please contact them directly, in writing, if you would like an itemized statement.

Compare the services you receive with those that appear on your Medicare Summary Notice. If you have questions, call your doctor or provider. If you feel further investigation is needed due to possible fraud and abuse, call the phone number in the Customer Service Information Box.

Appeals Information – Part B

If you disagree with any claims decision on this notice, you can request an appeal by **November 1, 20xx**. Follow the instructions below:

1) Circle the item(s) you disagree with and explain why you disagree.

2) Send this notice, or a copy, to the address in the "Customer Service Information" box on Page 1. (You may also send any additional information you may have about your appeal.)

3) Sign here _____ Phone number _____

Revised 02/04

Don't Let a Doctor Take More Than the Law Allows

Medicare rules are clear—and every doctor and other health care provider knows them. You can be charged only an extra 9.25% above what Medicare decides is the approved amount for a specific medical service (which is actually an extra 15% of the approved amount for unassigned claims). And the Medicare Summary Notice form does the arithmetic for you, stating the amount of the maximum charge.

If a doctor or another provider does not accept assignment and bills you more than the allowable amount, send the doctor's office a copy of your Medicare Summary Notice form, underlining the spot where the maximum bill is stated—and keep a copy for yourself. If you already paid the bill, and the amount you paid was more than the allowable Medicare-approved amount plus 15%, you are entitled to a refund.

Again, contact the doctor's or other provider's billing office and request your refund, letting them know the date you paid the bill, the amount you paid, and the Medicare-approved amount. If they will not refund the overpayment, contact the Medicare carrier, which will then contact the doctor or other health care provider directly.

Appealing the Denial of a Claim

Unfortunately, not every request for Medicare payment runs a smooth course. Occasionally, a Medicare hospital or nursing facility review committee may decide your inpatient stay need not last as long as you and your doctor think, and will recommend ending Medicare Part A coverage. Or, more commonly, the Medicare carrier will deny Part B coverage for what you believe is a covered medical service. Or sometimes it will cover only some but not all of a treatment that you believe should be covered.

You may appeal any of these decisions. This section explains the procedures you must follow.

Help From the State Health Insurance Assistance Program (SHIP) and Medicare Rights Center

Every state has a program to provide free assistance to any person with questions or problems regarding Medicare, medigap supplemental insurance, Medicare managed care, Medicaid, and long-term care. For example, people often have questions about enrollment, paying bills, and filing appeals. The overall program is called the State Health Insurance Assistance Program (SHIP), though in your state the program may go by one of several different names—Health Insurance Counseling and Advocacy Program (HICAP), Senior Health Insurance Benefits Advisors (SHIBA), or something similar. Whatever the name, the program provides free counseling by professional staff plus trained volunteers. The offices are often connected to legal service agencies that can provide free or low-cost legal advice if the matter involves an interpretation of a law or rule, or a legal battle.

SHIP offices are staffed by dedicated people who are not only knowledgeable and trained to give helpful advice but are also willing to fight for your rights. They sit down with you in person, review your story and papers until they understand your situation, and help you handle the paperwork and telephoning sometimes necessary to make your enrollment or appeal work.

To find the SHIP office nearest you, see the contact information at the end of this chapter.

Help with all sorts of Medicare questions and problems is also available from the nonprofit Medicare Rights Center. Its website, www. medicarerights.org, provides the answers to many common questions about Medicare. And you can call the center toll free at 800-333-4114 to speak, at no cost to you, with a knowledgeable counselor.

Decisions About Inpatient Care (Medicare Part A)

Occasionally, disputes arise about whether treatment as an inpatient in a hospital or skilled nursing facility continues to be medically necessary. These disputes often pit the patient and doctor on one side, and the facility's Medicare review committee on the other. The review committee may believe that the patient can be moved from the hospital to home or to a nursing facility sooner than the doctor advises, or moved from the skilled nursing facility to a nonskilled facility or to home care. If this happens to you, there are several steps you can take to convince Medicare to pay for your continued inpatient care.

Coverage Decisions

Initial Medicare approval of whether your treatment must be as an inpatient is made by the facility's Utilization Review Committee (URC), a group of doctors and hospital administrators. The committee makes this determination before you are admitted, or within one day of your emergency admission. The URC also periodically reviews your condition and progress in the facility, and can decide—after checking your medical records and consulting with your doctor—that you no longer require inpatient care at that facility.

Such a decision does not mean that you will be kicked out of the facility, but it may mean that the URC will recommend to Medicare that your inpatient stay at the facility no longer be covered by Part A insurance. If you and your doctor believe you should remain in the hospital, there are procedures to follow that may reverse the URC's decision. And even if the decision is not reversed, the process of appealing can give you a bit more time in the facility without being personally responsible for the huge inpatient bills.

Notice of Noncoverage. If the URC decides that your condition no longer requires inpatient care, it will consult with your doctor. If your doctor agrees, the URC will give you a written Notice of Noncoverage stating that your Medicare hospitalization coverage will end on a certain day. If you do not feel that you should be discharged from the hospital at that point, first express your wishes to your doctor. Ask that the doctor request from the URC that a longer period of inpatient care be approved.

If your doctor is unavailable, ask to speak with the hospital ombudsman. Many hospitals have an ombudsman who is an independent volunteer whose job is to help mediate disputes between the patient and the hospital.

Your Doctor Can Be Your Best Ally

The most important element in winning an appeal, particularly for coverage of inpatient care, is gaining your doctor's cooperation. The decision on a Medicare appeal often depends on what the doctor notes in your medical records about your condition and the treatment involved—and on how much assistance you can get from the doctor in providing clarification to the people doing your Medicare review.

The problem is that many doctors view their responsibility to the patient as including only the technical treatment of a medical condition: your body and how it works. Many doctors are not particularly concerned with how you pay the bill, as long as you pay it. And if it's someone else's bill—the hospital's, for example—the doctor may not care if it's paid at all.

If you are fortunate, your doctor will give some attention to your Medicare needs, calling the Medicare appeal personnel and writing a letter, if necessary. If so, you'll find the Medicare appeal process fairly simple. But if your doctor won't take the time to listen to your Medicare problem and help you with the appeal, you may have a frustrating time, which cannot help your recovery process. It may also prompt you to consider changing doctors.

If the doctor or ombudsman cannot change or delay the URC's decision, or your doctor will not oppose the decision, but you still feel that you should not be discharged, you will have to file an appeal to protect your right to have Medicare Part A cover your inpatient care.

If your doctor disagrees with the URC opinion that you should be discharged, the URC will either back off its decision and not contest your Medicare coverage—in which case you will hear nothing about it—or it will ask for an opinion from the state's Peer Review Organization (PRO). The PRO is a group of doctors who are paid by Medicare to review the medical necessity and appropriateness of inpatient care. This is a bit like the foxes guarding the chickens, but the PROs are also medical professionals who respect the opinions of treating physicians. The PRO will review your medical records, the URC's recommendation, and your doctor's position.

If the PRO agrees that your continued stay at the hospital is medically necessary, you will hear nothing more about the matter and Medicare will continue to cover your inpatient care. However, if the PRO decides that your inpatient care is no longer medically necessary, you will receive a Notice of Noncoverage stating that your coverage for hospitalization will end as of a certain day.

Immediate Review

If you receive a Notice of Noncoverage, it will contain important information, including when the URC intends to end your Medicare coverage and whether your doctor or the state PRO has agreed with the decision. How you'll obtain immediate review—the first step in appealing the decision—differs slightly depending on whether your doctor agreed with the URC or the decision was made by the PRO over your doctor's objection.

Immediate review of joint URC and doctor decision. If the Notice of Noncoverage states that your doctor agreed with the URC that coverage for your inpatient care should end, you must take some action to get the process moving.

If you are in the hospital, chances are you may have physical difficulty making phone calls and having conversations to get your immediate review started. You may have a friend or relative act on your behalf by making the necessary call requesting review of your case. You may also ask your doctor to initiate the review, even though he or she initially agreed with the URC's recommendation that Medicare inpatient coverage should end on the specified date. You can ask to speak with the hospital ombudsman, who can then make your request for immediate review.

Once the PRO has been notified that you are requesting immediate review, it will contact you in order to discuss the matter.

Request an immediate review by the PRO by noon of the first work day after you receive the Notice of Noncoverage. Contact may be made by phone or in writing at the number and address of the PRO given on the notice.

A representative of the PRO will speak with you directly about why you believe you still require inpatient care—and with the doctor who had you admitted to the hospital, or with the physician overseeing your care.

> TIP
>
> **Try again with your doctor.** Help from your doctor is the best hope you have of convincing the PRO to approve your continued coverage. Speak with the doctor again and try to change his or her mind. Sometimes a doctor agrees with the URC decision on care without consulting the patient, or based on an expectation of the patient's improvement that has not occurred. Also, there may be more than one doctor treating you. If so, try to enlist the help of your other doctors. Ask them to speak with your admitting physician to convince him or her that you need more inpatient care.

The PRO will review your case and, within a matter of days, inform you directly of its decision—either by phone or in writing. If the PRO agrees with the facility that your coverage should end, coverage will continue only until noon of the day after you receive notice of the PRO's decision. After that, the facility will bill you for all inpatient costs.

> TIP
>
> **Your coverage will continue during the review.** If you have requested an immediate review of a joint URC and doctor decision, Medicare will continue to cover your inpatient care until the PRO makes a decision.

Immediate review of a URC decision your doctor opposes. If your doctor believes that you need to remain in the hospital but the URC disagrees, the URC will have taken your case to the PRO before you receive a Notice of Noncoverage. And the notice will tell you that the PRO has already agreed with the URC.

You must still ask the PRO for immediate review. But unless you and your doctor can present some strong reasons why the decision should be changed, it will likely remain in effect.

The review process should then proceed as follows:

- Contact the PRO at once by phone or in writing to explain why you believe your continued inpatient care is necessary.
- Ask your doctor—or several doctors if more than one is treating you—to immediately call the PRO to give reasons why your inpatient care continues to be medically necessary. If doctors who are treating you have not previously been in contact with the PRO regarding your case, they can help immensely now by backing up what your admitting physician has said about your continuing need for inpatient care.
- Within three working days of your request for review, the PRO will notify you in writing of its decision.
- Medicare Part A coverage will end the third day after you receive the Notice of Noncoverage, even if the PRO has not yet decided. If the PRO takes the full three days to decide on your coverage and then agrees with the Notice of Noncoverage, you will be personally responsible for the full cost of one full day of hospital costs—the day after coverage stops but on which the PRO has not yet decided.

If the PRO upholds the decision that your inpatient coverage should end, that is not the last word on your Medicare coverage. Similarly, if you did not request immediate review, you can still appeal the decision of noncoverage. Several stages of appeal are open to you, as described below.

Have Your Bill Submitted to Medicare

Whether or not you asked for immediate review, you must ask that the hospital or other facility billing office submit the bill to the Medicare intermediary for payment. If you can get strong backing from your doctors, the intermediary might reverse the decision of the URC. Without such support, however, the intermediary will probably uphold the decision of the URC. Either way, if you want to pursue an appeal of the decision, you must have the hospital submit the bill to Medicare. Only by getting a Medicare carrier's decision can you move your appeal to the next stage.

Unfortunately, while the intermediary is deciding on your claim, the hospital or nursing facility may bill you for the uncovered part of your inpatient stay. If you pay the bill and later win your appeal, Medicare will reimburse you.

Reconsideration of Carrier's Decision

If the Medicare intermediary denies the claim for payment of part of your inpatient bill, you have 60 days from the date you receive the denial notice to submit a request for reconsideration. You'll find the address for sending this request on the notice denying your claim.

This reconsideration will be made by what Medicare calls a Qualified Independent Contractor (QIC). The QIC was not involved in the original determination of your appeal.

This request for reconsideration can be made by filing a special Medicare Reconsideration Request form. You can find this form online on Medicare's official website at www.cms.gov/Medicare/CMS-Forms/CMS-Forms/downloads/cms20033.pdf. Or, this request can be made in the form of a simple letter explaining why your stay in the facility continues to be necessary. Once again, however, it is not so much what you say in your letter as whether you have the support of one or more of your doctors. Ask every doctor who supports your position to send a letter to the intermediary stating his or her medical opinion, and also to give you a copy. Attach a copy of each doctor's letter to your request for reconsideration, and always keep an extra copy for yourself.

It is sometimes difficult to get a doctor to write a letter on your behalf, even if the doctor supports your position. Sometimes it is simply a matter of the doctor being too busy, or not concerned enough with your financial problem, to speak with you in person before you must send in your request for reconsideration. Other doctors charge a fee for writing any letter that does not involve consultation about treatment—as opposed to payment of bills—and the fee may be too high for you.

If you have not obtained a letter from a doctor who supports your position, at least list his or her name and phone number in your request to the QIC. Ask that the QIC contact the doctor before completing its reconsideration.

The QIC will give you a written decision on its reconsideration. If it again denies coverage, you have 60 days to begin the next step in the appeal process.

TIP

Put everything in writing and keep copies. Keep copies of all correspondence and other papers concerning Medicare claims and appeals. Also, keep notes on all conversations you have with your doctor, representatives from the hospital, the PRO, and the intermediary. Write down the date of the conversation, the name of the person with whom you talked, and what information was given or taken.

Request an Administrative Hearing

If, upon reconsideration, your appeal is denied by the QIC, you have 60 days from the date on the QIC's written decision to request a hearing by an administrative law judge (ALJ). The hearing is held before an ALJ who is attached to a local office of the Office of Medicare Hearings and Appeals (OMHA). You may ask that an actual hearing be held, which the ALJ will conduct either in person or by telephone. Or you may ask that the ALJ decide your appeal without a hearing, just by reviewing written materials. You can request a decision by an ALJ only if the amount you're contesting is $140 or more.

The form for requesting this administrative hearing is provided online by Medicare at www.cms.gov/Medicare/CMS-Forms/CMS-Forms/downloads/cms20034ab.pdf. For more information about how the hearing process works, you can go directly to the website of the Office of Medicare Hearings and Appeals at www.hhs.gov/omha.

As with every other stage of a Medicare appeal, your doctors' cooperation is the single most important element. Your doctor could appear personally at the hearing and testify on your behalf in front of the judge, but most doctors would charge an arm and a leg to do this. Instead, ask your doctor—or several of your doctors, if possible—to write an explanation of why your medical condition required inpatient treatment. You can then present the written explanation to the judge. Be aware that many doctors charge for writing such a letter, and Medicare laws permit them to do so.

Appeals Council and Federal Lawsuit

If the decision of the administrative law judge goes against you, you can file an appeal to the Social Security Appeals Council. And if that appeal goes against you, you can file an action in federal court challenging the Medicare decision. (See Chapter 9 for more information.)

You can file such a lawsuit only if the amount you are contesting is $1,400 or more. Because of the time and expense involved, it is likely you would file such a lawsuit only if the amount is quite a bit higher than that anyway. If you are considering such a lawsuit at this stage, consult with an experienced attorney. You may be able to get a referral to such an attorney from a SHIP office (see contact information at the end of this chapter).

Payment of Doctor and Other Medical Bills (Part B)

During the course of one or more of your Medicare Part B medical insurance claims, you may disagree with the carrier's decision about whether a particular treatment or service is covered by Medicare. If you find that the Medicare carrier has denied coverage for a certain bill, you have a right to appeal. However, the Medicare Part B appeal process is quite limited, and most people have more success informally contacting the carrier than they do with formal appeals.

Read the Medicare Summary Notice

The place to start with a question or complaint about your Medicare Part B coverage of a particular treatment or service is the Medicare Summary Notice (MSN) you receive from the carrier. (See "How to

Read a Medicare Summary Notice," above, for a discussion of the MSN.) It not only shows whether a health care service is covered but also gives a description of the service, a Medicare code number—called a procedure code—for the service, and an explanation of why a particular service was not covered.

Certain services are covered if they are described one way by your doctor's office in the Medicare forms they submit, but not covered if described differently. These problems are sometimes caused simply by a wrongly placed checkmark—for example, indicating a routine physical exam (not covered) instead of indicating physical examination for a particular patient complaint (covered). Such a mistake could be made by any number of people involved in handling your claim: your doctor, someone in your doctor's office, or someone in the Medicare carrier's vast paperwork machinery.

The MSN may also indicate that you were denied coverage for a particular service because you had the service performed too frequently during a given time. For example, you may have had two mammograms in one year when Medicare normally only covers one per year. However, if the treatment was determined to be medically necessary by your doctor—because, for example, you have a family history of breast cancer, or prior exams have disclosed potential problems—Medicare can and should cover the second mammogram.

In either situation, the next step is to contact your doctor's office to get a letter supporting the medical necessity for the treatment provided.

Check With Your Doctor's Office

If you believe that the MSN incorrectly describes the service or treatment you had, call your doctor's office and ask whether the claim form sent to Medicare had the same information as shown on your MSN. If either the claim form or the MSN had incorrect information, ask that the doctor's office contact the carrier with the correct information.

If coverage was denied because Medicare claims the treatment was not medically necessary or that you received the treatment too often, ask the doctor to write a letter explaining why the treatment was medically necessary. Also, ask that doctor to make a copy of any of your medical records that support this conclusion—and to send the letter and records to you so that you can then deal with the Medicare carrier.

Contact the Medicare Carrier

Most mistakes in billing and coverage are corrected informally, by phone and letter. The Medicare carriers know that mistakes are often made, and they would rather correct them quickly and inexpensively than go through a lengthy and more costly appeal process.

The number to call to reach your carrier is printed in the "Customer Service Information" box in the upper right-hand corner of the first page of your MSN. When you reach your Medicare carrier, give your name, your Medicare number, and the date of the MSN, explaining that you want to discuss coverage of a particular item. Then explain why you believe a mistake was made and describe your doctor's response to the problem. If you have a letter or any medical records from the doctor that explain matters, tell the Medicare carrier what you have. The carrier will either contact your doctor's office or ask you to send in a copy of your doctor's letter, or both.

If this informal contact results in a change in decision by the Medicare carrier, it will send you a revised MSN explaining what the new Medicare payments are and how much you owe. If it does not change the coverage decision based on this informal contact, your next step would be to push on to a more formal written appeal.

Write a Request for Redetermination

If you have not been able to resolve the coverage question informally, you have 120 days from the date you receive the MSN within which to file a written request for redetermination of the carrier's decision—also called a request for review. The bottom of the second page of your MSN provides information and a short form to help you appeal the decision.

Make a copy of the MSN, circle the items you want to challenge, sign the back of the copy, and send it to the carrier listed on the front of the form. Although the MSN says you may write your appeal on the form itself, it is better to send along a separate, signed letter with the MSN, stating your reasons for appealing. There is very little space allowed for your statement on the appeal form, usually not enough to explain your reasoning adequately. Or, you can file your request for redetermination on a form provided by Medicare online at www.cms.gov/cmsforms/downloads/CMS20027. pdf, but this form, too, has only limited space to explain your reasons for requesting a change in Medicare's decision.

The letter should include your full name as it appears on the MSN, your Medicare number, the date of the MSN, the date of the disputed medical service, and a brief explanation of why you believe the treatment or other service should be covered. Include any letter or other records from your doctor that support your position.

TIP
Hold on to the documents. Keep copies of all letters and documents you send to or receive from the Medicare carrier and from your doctor. Also, keep notes of every conversation you have with anyone at the Medicare carrier, including the date of conversation, the name of the person with whom you spoke, and any action decided upon in the phone call—such as, you will send them a letter, they will contact your doctor, or they will call you back within a week.

Time to Seek Assistance

If you are considering a request for a review of your medical bills, or you have completed the written review and are considering a request for a hearing, it may be time for you to get some assistance from a local State Health Insurance Assistance Program (SHIP) office (see contact information at the end of this chapter). This is particularly true if the amount you are contesting would put a sizable hole in your budget.

If you are considering an appeal to an administrative law judge for a hearing, you may want to consider not only help from SHIP but also the assistance of an experienced Medicare lawyer. (See Chapter 9 for tips on finding legal help.) SHIP can also help refer you to such lawyers.

On the following pages are samples of request for redetermination letters to a Medicare carrier. There are no magic words you must include in such a letter, but these examples demonstrate the kind of simple information required. A letter should include several key points, each of which should be described as briefly and clearly as possible. Keep in mind that the letter is meant merely to point out how and where the error was made and where proof of the error can be found, not to serve as proof itself. Only your medical records and the opinion of your doctors can actually prove anything.

First, you should briefly describe the treatment you received.

Second, you should point out the specific reasons why the intermediary's decision not to cover the treatment was incorrect—for example, you did not have merely a routine physical exam but an exam to determine the cause of a specific problem, or you did not have a dental exam but an examination by an oral surgeon of the nerves in your jaw.

Third, refer to the doctor's letter or other medical records that support your claim.

Notice that at the bottom left of each letter is the notation "cc:" and next to it the name of the doctor. This indicates to the Medicare carrier that you have sent a copy of this letter to your doctor—an action you should take so that the letter goes into your medical file. Sending a copy of the letter to the doctor will help prepare the doctor if the Medicare carrier contacts him or her, and it may remind the doctor to do a better job of explaining the medical necessity of your care the next time you have treatment.

When the carrier reconsiders your claim, it will review your file, check the documents on which the original decision was made, and investigate any new information you have presented or the carrier has obtained by contacting your doctor. You do not have an opportunity at this stage to appear in person and explain things.

If a mistake was made because incorrect or incomplete information had originally been provided to the carrier or someone made a simple clerical error, the carrier is likely to reverse its decision and provide you with coverage. You will then receive a written notice of its review determination and a new MSN.

Request for Redetermination Letter: Sample # 1

Betty Patient
222 Public Street
Consumer, USA 12345
Telephone: 123-123-1234

March 1, 20xx

Transprofit Insurance Company
P.O. Box 123
Moneyville, USA 12345

Re: Request for Review and Redetermination
Medicare Part B
Medicare Number xx-xxx-xxxxA
MSN Notice dated January 2, 20xx

To Whom It Concerns:

This letter is a request for review and redetermination of a decision made by Transprofit denying coverage of medical treatment I received on November 1, 20xx. A copy of the MSN notice of January 2, 20xx, denying coverage, is enclosed.

I believe that Transprofit denied coverage of the mammogram I received on November 1, 20xx, from Dr. Alice Well because I had previously had a mammogram in January 20xx, which Medicare covered, and Medicare does not normally cover more than one mammogram per year. However, this second mammogram was medically necessary because I have a family history of breast cancer and because my previous mammogram in January showed some spots of potentially cancerous tissue.

Apparently the original Medicare claim from my doctor's office did not include this background information. However, I am enclosing a copy of a letter from Dr. Well and a copy of the medical records from my January mammogram to indicate why the second mammogram was medically necessary.

Based on this information, please reconsider the original decision denying Medicare coverage of the November 1, 20xx treatment.

Yours truly,

Betty Patient

cc: Dr. Alice Well

Request for Redetermination Letter: Sample #2

Andy Q. Everyone
18B Main Street
Anytown, USA 12345
Telephone: 222-222-2222

June 1, 20xx

Ourworld Insurance Inc.
P.O. Box 567
Big Money, USA 12345

Re: Request for Review and Redetermination
Medicare Part B
Medicare Number xx-xxx-xxxxB
MSN Notice dated March 1, 20xx

To Whom It Concerns:

This letter is a request for review and redetermination of a decision made by Ourworld Insurance denying coverage of medical treatment I received on January 10, 20xx. A copy of the MSN notice of March 1, 20xx, denying coverage, is enclosed.

I believe that Ourworld Insurance denied coverage of the eye exam I received on January 10, 20xx, from Dr. Barry Eyesore, because Dr. Eyesore's office mistakenly noted on the Medicare claim form that I underwent a routine eye examination refraction on that date, marking on the form Procedure Code 92015.

This was a mistake. In fact, I had a specific examination and treatment for blurred vision and eye pain that I had been suffering. Dr. Eyesore's records indicate that this was a medically necessary examination for a medical condition, for which he prescribed medication, rather than a routine eye examination. Enclosed is a copy of my medical record from Dr. Eyesore indicating the nature of the exam on that date.

Based on this additional information, please reconsider the original decision denying Medicare coverage of the January 10, 20xx examination and treatment of my eyes.

Yours truly,

Andy Q. Everyone

cc: Dr. Barry Eyesore

If there is a dispute about whether a certain treatment truly was medically necessary, the carrier may well reverse itself at this stage, but it does so less often than in cases of simple clerical errors or missing documentation from the doctor.

Once the Medicare carrier has received your request for redetermination and your supporting documents, someone within the company who was not involved in making the original decision will decide on your request. You will receive a written response from the carrier, called a Medicare Redetermination Notice, about 60 days after you file your request and supporting papers. It will contain information about a further appeal if you are not satisfied with the decision.

Request for Reconsideration by Qualified Independent Contractor (QIC)

If the carrier reviews your file and still refuses to cover your treatment, you can continue your appeal by requesting a reconsideration.

You have 180 days from the date you receive the written notice of determination to request a reconsideration by what's called a Qualified Independent Contractor (QIC). A QIC is a company separate from the Medicare carrier itself. The address to which to send your request is printed on the carrier's written notice of determination.

You can file your Request for Reconsideration on a form provided by Medicare online at www.cms.gov/cmsforms/downloads/CMS20033.pdf. However, space on the form is limited, and you may prefer to write a letter request instead, an example of which is shown below (see "Letter Requesting Reconsideration by QIC"). The letter requesting a reconsideration is similar to the letter requesting redetermination, except that you should refer to the date of the carrier's written notice of determination following your request for redetermination in addition to the original MSN.

In separate paragraphs, make the following points:

- Describe the treatment you received and the dates on which you received it. This description should be brief, since the carrier will get its full explanation from your medical records.
- State the specific reasons why the intermediary's initial decision not to cover the treatment was incorrect.

Letter Requesting Reconsideration by QIC

Rosa Albertez
3456 Broadway Anytown, USA 45678
Telephone: 333-333-3333

June 1, 20xx

Your Money Insurance Co.
P.O. Box 1234
Greentown, USA 12345

Re: Request for Reconsideration by QIC, Medicare Part B
Medicare Number xx-xxx-xxxxC
Notice of Determination After Review Dated May 1, 20xx

To Whom It Concerns:

This letter is a request for a reconsideration by QIC following a determination made on May 1, 20xx. That determination upheld a decision made by Your Money denying coverage of a medical service I received on February 1, 20xx, and laboratory work performed on February 5, 20xx. A copy of the MSN notice of March 15, 20xx, denying coverage, is enclosed. Also enclosed is a copy of the written determination after review, dated May 1, 20xx.

I believe that Your Money denied coverage of the physical examination I received from Dr. Walter Thorough and of laboratory work ordered by Dr. Thorough because Dr. Thorough failed to give certain information to the carrier. The physical and the laboratory tests were not routine examinations but were a response to severe muscle fasciculation and cramping that I had been suffering over the previous several weeks. Dr. Thorough's records indicate that the examination and laboratory tests were medically necessary to diagnose and treat my condition.

I have enclosed a copy of my medical records from Dr. Thorough, as well as a letter from Dr. Thorough, both of which make clear that the examination and laboratory tests were medically necessary and should be covered by Medicare.

Yours truly,

Rosa Albertez

cc: Dr. Walter Thorough

- Refer, by name and date, to your doctor's letter and to the specific medical records that support your claim.

Attach to your request for a reconsideration copies of letters from your doctors and of your medical records, if you have them. Also, call your doctors' offices to request that they send copies of your records to the address you have been given on the notice.

You will get a written decision, called a Medicare Reconsideration Notice, from the QIC within about 60 days after you file your request for reconsideration. If you are not satisfied with this decision, you have 60 days from the date you receive the notice to request a hearing before an administrative law judge.

Hearing Before Administrative Law Judge

If your claim for doctor bill coverage is once again denied after the reconsideration by the QIC, you can request a hearing before an administrative law judge if the amount you are contesting is $140 or more. If the amount in dispute is less than $140, the hearing before the carrier's hearing officer is the end of the line.

You must request a hearing before an administrative law judge within 60 days of the date you receive written notice of the decision by the carrier's hearing officer. (See Chapter 9 for a full discussion of the administrative hearing process.) Medicare provides an online form to request this hearing at www.cms.gov/cmsforms/downloads/CMS20034AB.pdf.

Medicare Appeals Council Review

If you do not receive a favorable ruling from the administrative law judge, you may appeal the decision to the Medicare Appeals Council. In Medicare Part B claims, the written appeal must be filed within 60 days of the date of the administrative law judge's written decision.

Federal Court Case

It is highly unlikely that a Medicare Part B decision will involve enough money that it would be economically sensible for you, and a lawyer representing you, to file a lawsuit in federal court to challenge a negative decision by the Medicare Appeals Council. However, if your claim is for $1,400 or more, you do have such a right. You must file the lawsuit within 60 days of the written decision by the Appeals Council.

Medicare Part D: Enrollment, Exceptions, and Appeals

How you enroll in a Part D plan will depend on several factors, including whether you:
- receive Medicaid benefits
- live in a long-term care facility
- have had employer-sponsored health coverage that included drug coverage, and
- qualify for a Part D low-income subsidy.

Note that if you believe you might be eligible for the Part D low-income subsidy, you must file two separate applications—one for Part D coverage, and one for the low-income subsidy.

Once you are enrolled in a Part D plan, your plan's decisions about coverage and costs are not necessarily final. The plan may exclude one of your drugs from coverage, may require you to jump through hoops to get coverage for a particular drug, or may charge you a higher copayment for your drug than for a generic equivalent. In any of these situations, you have the right to request an exception. And you have the right to appeal the plan's decision.

Enrollment

How and when you enroll in a Part D plan depends on whether you are a Medicaid beneficiary or have been accepted for a Part D low-income subsidy. Regardless of the plan you enroll in or how you are enrolled, your coverage will not begin until the first of the month following the completion of your enrollment.

Applying for Extra Help Paying for Medicare Part D

Medicare's Extra Help program offers different levels of assistance (also called a low-income subsidy) to help pay for the cost of prescription drugs above and beyond what a standard Part D plan pays. (See Chapter 12.) But you apply for Extra Help by sending an application to the Social Security Administration (SSA) rather than to Medicare or to a Part D plan. Contact the SSA to get an Extra Help application and instructions. You can reach the SSA toll free at 800-772-1213, or visit the special Social Security website page called "Extra Help with Medicare Prescription Drug Plan Costs," at https://secure.ssa.gov/i1020/start, to file an application online. In person, you can apply at a Social Security office near you. Or, you can also apply for Extra Help at a local county Social Services office or another local government office in your state that processes Medicaid applications.

Free one-on-one help is available at your local SHIP or HICAP office. These programs have trained counselors on staff to help you with your application. To find the office nearest you, contact the SHIP or HICAP program in your state (for details, see the end of this chapter).

If your application for Extra Help is approved, the benefits will be retroactive to the date you first applied. Once approved, your participation in Extra Help will remain in effect for one year. Within the first year of your Extra Help, the Social Security Administration will review your finances to see if you remain eligible. If so, your participation in Extra Help will be automatically renewed. After the first year, SSA will periodically review your Extra Help eligibility.

Enrolling in a Part D Plan

Most people will follow the standard enrollment procedures described below. If you are a Medicaid beneficiary or are qualified for a Part D low-income subsidy, your enrollment procedures will differ slightly (see below).

Standard enrollment. If you are not a Medicaid beneficiary and have not qualified for a Part D low-income subsidy, you enroll in Part D by signing up directly with the plan you want to join. Private insurance companies administer each Part D plan using their own enrollment forms and procedures. Some plans may permit you to enroll online, while others may require written forms. You must contact the plan directly to find out the details of their coverage and costs, and to enroll in the plan.

Your Part D plan will cover the cost of your medications only after you have completed enrollment in the plan and your Medicare Part A or B coverage has begun. This means that any drugs you buy while your application is pending will not be covered. It is therefore a good idea to decide on a plan and submit an application in the months before you become eligible for Medicare, so that coverage will begin as soon as you are eligible.

If you do not enroll in a Part D plan when you are first eligible for it, your premiums will be higher when you do finally enroll. Medicare charges an additional 1% for each month you delay enrolling. So, if you intend to enroll in a Part D plan as soon as you are eligible for Medicare, you should do the paperwork ahead of time. This will ensure not only that your coverage begins immediately, but also that you will not have to pay a higher premium because of a simple paperwork delay.

Medicaid beneficiary. If you are a Medicare beneficiary who is also eligible for Medicaid assistance (Medi-Cal in California), you may enroll in any Part D plan. But in order to get the full benefit of your low-income subsidy, you must enroll in a plan whose premium is at or below your state's average. If you enroll in a plan with a premium higher than the state average, you will be responsible for the extra premium cost out of your own pocket.

If you don't enroll in a Part D plan on your own, the Medicare program will automatically enroll you in a plan with a premium below the state's average. And if that plan doesn't fit your needs for drug coverage, you may switch plans at any time (see "Switching Part D Plans," below).

Low-income subsidized enrollment. If you are eligible for one of the Part D low-income subsidies but are not a Medicaid beneficiary, you may enroll in a Part D plan at any time, directly with the plan of your choice. If at any later time your plan no longer offers you the best coverage, you may switch to another plan (see "Switching Part D Plans," below).

Exceptions

Part D plans use a variety of methods to restrict or control the use of medications by their enrollees, thereby reducing their own costs. (See "Part D Prescription Drug Coverage" in Chapter 12.) These restrictions include excluding drugs from coverage, setting higher costs for certain drugs within the same class, substituting one drug for another, imposing a drug supply limit, and requiring you to try a series of other drugs before the plan will cover the one you want.

Medicare gives plans very broad discretion to create and change coverage restrictions. This means that you may begin coverage with a plan whose restrictions do not seriously affect you, only to find the plan changes its rules later on. You may then find yourself with a restriction on one of your drugs that is financially burdensome, physically discomfiting, or even medically dangerous. For example, your plan may drop one of your drugs from its formulary and replace it with a drug that the plan considers "equivalent," but this drug may not provide you with the same quality of relief or may have more side effects. Or, your plan may increase the copayment for your drug, costing you more money per prescription.

Eventually, you may be able to switch to a plan with fewer restrictions on your drugs. But until you are able to do so, or if there is no other plan available at the same cost with fewer restrictions, you have a chance to get your plan to lift its restriction in your individual case. You do this by requesting an "exception" from your plan's rules, based on "medical necessity." You make this request to the plan itself, not to Medicare. Each plan has its own rules for handling exception requests, and Medicare requires only that a plan have a formal procedure and make a decision, called a "Coverage Determination," within 72 hours after you file an exception request.

Medical necessity. Your doctor's support is the key to success with any exception request. To convince your plan that you need easier access to your drug, you must show that you have a medical necessity to take that particular drug rather than another drug that the plan considers equivalent. Medical necessity does not necessarily mean that you will have very serious or dangerous medical consequences if you take the equivalent drug. But it does mean that there will be some change in your physical condition—for example, less effective treatment or more severe side effects—if you take the so-called equivalent drug instead of the one you usually take.

Help With Exceptions and Appeals

As discussed in these sections about exceptions and appeals, it's crucial to have your doctor's help in explaining the medical necessity of a particular drug. But your doctor can only do so much—he or she is not going to help you fill out request and appeal forms, or write your letters to the insurance company explaining your situation. To get help with the exception or appeal process itself, you may want to contact the counselors at your local SHIP or HICAP office, whose expert advice is free. You can find the local office of these counseling organizations by calling the central office for your state; for contact information, see the end of this chapter.

You can also get free expert counseling from the Medicare Rights Center; contact them through www.medicarerights.org.

If your appeal reaches the later stages, and particularly if you intend to take it to federal court, you will likely need the assistance of a lawyer experienced in Medicare appeals. For a discussion of when a lawyer may be needed, and how to find one, see Chapter 9.

Your chance of convincing the plan of your medical need for a particular drug almost certainly requires an explanation from your doctor. The plan may request a letter from your doctor, or a copy of your medical records demonstrating your complaints to the doctor about the substituted medicine, or simply a phone conversation with your doctor. Whatever form the contact will take, it is important that you prepare your doctor to explain your problem. Meet with or talk to your doctor by phone about the problem and about your exception request. This will allow you to make certain that the doctor understands the full extent of your difficulty with the substituted drug, and gives the doctor advance warning that the plan will be requesting information.

If the plan denies your request for an exception, you may file an appeal. Appeals are discussed below. And if your appeal is denied, or if you simply do not want to bother going through the appeal process, you can switch to another plan that offers better coverage of your drug (if you can find one) as soon as you are permitted to switch by Part D enrollment rules (see "Switching Part D Plans," below).

Appeals

Part D plans regularly make decisions and change rules about their drug coverage. But these decisions and rules are not necessarily the final word about coverage. You can appeal a plan's rule or decision if you find that it forces you to give up, or pay a higher copay for, a drug you and your doctor believe is medically necessary. Appeals initially go to the plan itself. At later stages, an appeal may be considered by independent reviewers outside the plan.

If at any stage of the process an enrollee wins a change in the plan's decision, its effect will be retroactive back to the time the enrollee first challenged the plan's coverage decision. This retroactivity works well when the issue is the amount of money an enrollee has to pay out of pocket. Retroactivity is only cold comfort, however, if the enrollee has been forced to make do with a substitute drug during the time spent on the appeal.

In almost every case, success with an appeal depends on your doctor's presenting a convincing argument that the drug in question is "medically necessary" to you (see "Exceptions," above).

Types of Decisions That Can Be Appealed

Part D enrollees may appeal several types of plan decisions, including a plan's:

- denial of an exception request
- decision not to cover a drug, or to cover it only at a higher copay because it is not on the plan's formulary or because

of some other access restriction (such as step therapy or therapeutic substitution)

- decision not to cover a drug for a particular enrollee because it is not "medically necessary"
- decision not to cover a drug because it is excluded from the Medicare Part D program, and
- decision not to cover a drug, or to cover it at a higher copay, because it was provided by a pharmacy that did not have a contract with the plan (called an out-of-network pharmacy).

Appeal Procedure

Each plan determines the details of its appeal procedure. But all plans must follow certain basic rules.

Coverage determination. When a plan makes a decision about coverage or an exception request, it issues a written letter called a "coverage determination." The plan must issue the coverage determination within 72 hours of the enrollee's filling of a prescription, denial of a prescription, or request for an exception.

Redetermination. Once an enrollee receives an unfavorable written coverage determination from the plan, the enrollee has 60 days to request what is called a "redetermination." This second-round decision will also be made by the plan itself, though it may be made by someone within the plan bureaucracy other than the person who made the original coverage determination. From the date the plan receives a written request for redetermination, it has seven days within which to issue its redetermination decision.

Reconsideration. If an enrollee's request for redetermination still does not result in a favorable decision, the enrollee may file a written request for reconsideration by an Independent Review Entity (IRE). This is where an independent arbitrator reviews and considers both the enrollee's request and the plan's reasons for denying the request. An enrollee must file a request for reconsideration by an IRE within 60 days following receipt of the redetermination decision. Your plan will provide contact information for the IRE that will hear your request. Once the IRE receives your written request for reconsideration, it has seven days to make a decision.

Administrative hearing. If the IRE turns down the enrollee's request, the enrollee has 60 days within which to file a request for a hearing before an administrative law judge (ALJ). To have an administrative hearing with an ALJ, the amount in controversy must be at least $140. But unless the drug coverage question for an enrollee involves only a one-time prescription, the ongoing cost of the drug to the enrollee will almost always exceed $140. The ALJ must issue a decision within 90 days from the date of receiving the request.

Medicare Appeals Council. If the enrollee gets a negative decision from the ALJ, the enrollee has 60 days to file an appeal to the next highest level, called the Medicare Appeals Council (MAC). The MAC has 90 days to issue its decision.

Federal court. If the MAC denies an enrollee's appeal, and the amount in controversy concerning the drug is at least $1,400, the enrollee may file a claim in federal court. The enrollee has 60 days from the MAC's decision to file the claim in federal court. If your coverage issue involves continuing expensive medication and you believe that appealing your decision to federal court may be worth the time and expense, you almost certainly will want to consult with an attorney who specializes in Medicare appeals. For more information on hiring an attorney, see Chapter 9.

Switching Part D Plans

The fact that you have enrolled in a particular Part D prescription drug plan does not mean that you are forever stuck with that plan, or with the insurance company that issued the plan. There are several good reasons why you might want to switch from one plan to another. You may want to switch plans in the following cases:

- you begin taking a new medication, and your old plan does not cover that drug or covers it at a higher copayment than offered by another plan.
- Your current plan drops one of your drugs from its list of covered medications.
- Your current plan raises its premiums, or changes its terms of coverage, making a different plan a better fit for you.

- A new plan is offered, or you learn about another plan, which would give you better coverage or lower costs than your current plan.

Whatever your reason, you may switch plans—to a different plan offered by the same insurance company or to a plan with a different company—at least once every year. And some people may switch as often as every month.

When You May Switch Plans

Monthly switch. People in two different categories may switch from one Part D plan to another as often as every month, with the new plan's coverage beginning on the first of the month following enrollment. Dual eligibles—people enrolled in both Medicare and Medicaid (Medi-Cal in California)—may switch plans as often as monthly. And a person who lives in a long-term care nursing facility (if the facility is certified by Medicare or Medicaid) may also switch plans monthly.

Once-yearly switch. Low-income subsidy beneficiaries and standard enrollees (people who do not receive Medicaid coverage and who do not reside in a long-term care facility) may switch plans once a year, but the switch must happen during an open enrollment period (from October 15 to December 7 each year).

Plans You May Switch To

If you want to switch from one Part D drug plan to another, you may switch to any Medicare-approved plan currently offered in your state by any company. If you are switching during the open enrollment period from October 15 to December 7 of each year, you may enroll in any plan being offered for the following calendar year, to begin coverage on January 1.

If you are a dual-eligible beneficiary (Medicare and Medicaid or Medi-Cal), the full cost of your Part D premium is paid by Medicare, as long as your plan's premium is less than your state's average for all Part D plans. If you want to continue receiving that full premium payment, you may only switch to a new plan with a premium lower than your state's average premium. If you switch to a plan with a premium above your state average, you must pay the difference between the new premium and the state average

How to Switch From One Plan to Another

Switching from one plan to another is not difficult, but it does involve several steps.

Step 1: Find a plan in your area. Find out what plans are offered in your geographic area and select a plan that's right for you, using the selection methods explained in "Part D Prescription Drug Coverage" in Chapter 12.

Step 2: Enroll in the new plan. Once you've found a plan you like, contact the insurance company directly to make sure you are eligible for the plan. If you are eligible, follow the insurance company's directions to enroll in the plan.

Step 3: Cancel your old plan. Once you receive written confirmation from your new insurance company that you are enrolled in your new plan, it's time to cancel your old plan. Notify your old plan—in writing —that you are canceling your policy. Do this even if the new insurance company has told you that it will notify the old company. Make sure that your cancellation is effective after your new plan is in effect.

CAUTION

Don't cancel your old plan too soon. You may be signing up for a new plan to begin the following month, or changing plans during the yearly open enrollment period to begin coverage on January 1. In either case, do not cancel enrollment in your current plan until you have written notification of enrollment in your new plan. And make sure you check the date that the new coverage begins, so that you do not cancel your old plan before the new one goes into effect. As with any bureaucratic institution, delays and mistakes do occur. You want to avoid having any gaps in your insurance coverage.

Step 4: Don't double-pay. Make sure your old and new insurance policies don't overlap. If you pay for your Part D plan by sending the insurance company a check, this is easy—you simply do not send in any payment to the old company once your new coverage begins. But many people have their Part D premium amount automatically paid (for example, withheld from their Social Security benefit or transferred directly from their bank). If you pay your old Part D plan automatically, you must stop the automatic payment as of whatever date you begin your new plan.

Step 5: Notify your pharmacist. After you receive confirmation of enrollment in the new plan, notify the pharmacists you use about your new plan. This will make things go more smoothly when you fill your prescriptions.

State Health Insurance Assistance Programs (SHIPs)

Every state has a nonprofit organization for consumer counseling about Medicare, medigap, Medicare Advantage plans, and related matters. The organization operates under the general name State Health Insurance Assistance Program (SHIP) or Health Insurance Counseling and Advocacy Program (HICAP), though in some states it has a similar but slightly different name. These central offices can direct you to a local counseling office near you. You can find the phone number and website for your state's SHIP/HICAP office on the SHIP-Talk organization website at https://shipnpr.shiptalk.org. You can also find the website for your state's SHIP/HICAP office by going to Medicare's website at www.medicare.gov/Contacts.

Medigap Insurance

Even for people who have coverage from both Medicare Part A and Part B, a serious illness or injury can cause financial havoc because of the bills Medicare leaves unpaid. Well over half of all Medicare recipients age 65 and older respond to this risk by buying a private supplemental health insurance policy known as medigap or med-sup insurance.

The term medigap comes from the fact that these insurance policies are designed to cover the gaps in Medicare payments. Unfortunately, most medigap coverage is not nearly as complete as its advertising would lead you to believe.

The alternatives, managed care and other Medicare Advantage plans, typically provide broader coverage at slightly lower cost than most medigap insurance policies. However, Medicare Advantage plans restrict the doctors and other providers available to you. And in recent years, some Medicare Advantage plans have been raising enrollee costs, reducing coverage, and dropping coverage entirely in many areas, adding an element of risk to the Medicare Advantage option.

Before choosing one type of coverage or another, compare benefits and approaches and measure your preferences against the price you would have to pay for each.

This chapter gives you guidance about the gaps in Medicare that need to be filled, and the types of medigap insurance policies that exist to partially fill them. Chapter 15 covers the various types of Medicare Advantage plans available as alternatives to medigap supplements. Before selecting either a medigap policy or a Medicare Advantage plan, review the advantages and disadvantages discussed in Chapter 15, and use the charts at the end of that chapter to compare the costs of and coverage provided by individual policies and plans.

As with other decisions about Medicare and related insurance coverage, you can get excellent, free counseling regarding medigap insurance from your local office of the State Health Insurance Assistance Program (SHIP), also known in some states as the Health Insurance Counseling and Advocacy Program (HICAP).

Insurance From Continuing or Former Employment

Many people who become eligible for Medicare at age 65 continue to work and have health insurance through their employers. Many others have health insurance through a spouse's employer.

And many other people keep their job-related health insurance after they retire, as part of their retirement benefits packages, although they usually have to pay much more than current employees.

Most employment-based health plans require you to sign up for Medicare Part A when you turn 65, but cover your hospitalization in conjunction with Medicare. Most plans based on current employment do not, however, require you to sign up (and pay for) Medicare Part B, but many retiree plans do require you to enroll in Medicare Part B. The health benefits or human resources office at your work or union can explain the details of coordinating coverage.

The fact that you are eligible for a work-related health plan, however, does not mean that you have to continue with it. Work-related health insurance has become more expensive and less comprehensive for employees—particularly retired employees. You may find that Medicare plus a medigap policy, or Medicare through a Medicare Advantage managed care plan, provides you with as good or better coverage at a better price than your employer-based medical insurance does.

Even if you decide not to participate in the regular health plan offered in your workplace, your employer's insurance company may offer you a different policy with limited coverage for some services Medicare does not cover at all, such as prescription drugs, dental care, or hearing aids. Compare such a policy with the medigap policies and managed care plans discussed in this chapter to see which one offers you the best coverage for your money.

Gaps in Medicare

When considering the kinds of supplemental coverage available, keep in mind the specific gaps in Medicare payments that you are trying to fill. Medicare coverage is explained in detail in Chapter 12, but some of the most significant things it does not cover, or covers but only partially pays for, are listed below.

Gaps in Part A Hospital Insurance

Medicare Part A covers almost all the cost of most hospital stays. Its most common gap is the deductible, which everyone must pay before Medicare pays any part of a hospital bill. A much less frequent but much more frightening gap is the daily coinsurance amount for hospital stays of more than 60 days. All of the gaps are listed below.

Hospital Bills

Medicare Part A hospital insurance does not pay the following costs during a hospital stay:
- a deductible for each benefit period—$1,260 in 2015
- a daily coinsurance amount ($315 in 2015) for each day you are hospitalized more than 60 days and up to 90 days for any one benefit period
- a daily coinsurance amount ($630 in 2015) for each day you are hospitalized more than 90 days and up to 150 days for any one benefit period
- anything past a hospitalization of 150 days
- first three pints of blood, unless replaced, or
- anything during foreign travel.

Skilled Nursing Facility Bills

Medicare Part A does not pay the following costs during a stay in a skilled nursing facility:
- a coinsurance amount of $157.50 per day for each day you are in the facility more than 20 days and up to 100 days for any one benefit period, and
- anything for a stay of more than 100 days.

Home Health Care

Medicare Part A does not pay the following costs for home health care:

- 20% of the approved cost of durable medical equipment or approved nonskilled care, and
- anything for nonmedical personal care services.

Gaps in Part B Medical Insurance

Medicare Part B leaves some very large gaps in the amounts it pays doctors, depending on whether the doctors accept assignment. Everyone faces the 20% of the Medicare-approved amount that Medicare does not pay. And if your doctor does not accept assignment, you are also responsible for up to 15% more than the amount Medicare approves.

Medicare Part B does not pay the following costs for doctors, clinics, laboratories, therapies, medical supplies, or equipment:

- a yearly deductible ($147 in 2015)

- 20% of the Medicare-approved amount

- 15% above the Medicare-approved amount if the provider does not accept assignment, or

- 20% of the total charges for some outpatient hospital services.

Standard Medigap Benefit Plans

The federal government regulates Medicare supplement (medigap) insurance policies—and insurance companies may not offer medigap policies that duplicate Medicare's own coverage. You may choose among the nine currently available standard medigap plans. The standard policies are specifically tailored to Medicare coverage, each one filling a certain number of Medicare's gaps.

Important Changing Landscape for Medigap Policies

First, in 2006, the Medicare Part D prescription drug program went into effect. The Part D program replaced the drug coverage that had been provided in medigap policies under standard plans H, I, and J.

On June 1, 2010, the medigap landscape changed again. New medigap policies in plans E, H, I, and J are no longer sold, though people with existing policies under those plans may continue them. People who continue with these policies should be aware, though, that their premiums are likely to rise more steeply over the coming years because there will be increasingly fewer people enrolled in these plans.

Beginning June 1, 2010, policies began to be issued under two new plans, M and N. Also, the little-used at-home recovery benefit is no longer part of any new policies, and a hospice copayment benefit has been added to new policies under all plans.

For more information on these changes and the coverage provided under each plan type, see "Descriptions of the Standard Medigap Plans," below.

CAUTION

Delay may limit your choices. Insurance companies would be happiest if they could sell coverage only to healthy people. When you're shopping for a medigap policy, you may find it hard to buy a policy if you're already ill. (The Affordable Care Act eliminated preexisting condition limitations for regular private insurance, but not medigap.)

The federal government has, however, established some protections for people buying medigap policies. Being able to take advantage of these protections depends on when and under what circumstances you apply. You'll receive the most coverage options if you apply within the first six months after you begin your Medicare Part B coverage. In a few other circumstances, you may also have options to purchase some, though not all, medigap policies without fear of being turned down because of your preexisting condition. If you wait too long to apply for a policy, however, the insurance companies are allowed to review your medical records and reject you if they consider you a bad profit risk. To understand the rules regarding your right to purchase a medigap policy, see "Terms and Conditions of Medigap Policies," below.

Medigap Does Not Cover Long-Term Care

Many older people fear the possibility of living out the final years of life in a nursing home. The prospect of nursing home life itself provokes distress for many, as does the financial ruin that can be brought about by the cost of long-term care. Unfortunately, neither Medicare nor medigap supplemental insurance nor managed care health plans protect against this potentially enormous cost. Medicare covers only a limited period of skilled nursing facility care and covers nothing of long-term custodial, or nonmedical, care in a nursing home. Medigap policies and HMOs similarly fail to cover long-term nursing home care.

Long-term care at home is increasingly an option for people who in years past would have been forced to enter a nursing home. More services are available at home, and more agencies and providers offer home care. However, neither Medicare nor medigap policies cover long-term home health care.

There is a type of private insurance that can cover some of the cost of long-term nursing home or at-home care. Referred to as long-term care insurance, it is available in a variety of benefit packages but comes with numerous restrictions and exclusions. The cost of these policies varies greatly, depending on the extent of coverage and the age of the person covered. Medicaid also covers long-term care costs.

For a complete discussion of these policies, the kinds of care they cover, and Medicaid coverage for nursing homes, see *Long-Term Care: How to Plan & Pay for It,* by Joseph Matthews (Nolo). See Nolo's website at www.nolo.com for ordering information.

Not every company offers every plan. And only the benefits included in the plans are standardized. Other important aspects— premium increases and preexisting illness exclusions—vary from policy to policy and require careful comparison shopping.

When you consider medigap policies, your task is to see how many of the gaps in Medicare payments you can fill within the constraints of your budget. The broader the coverage in a medigap policy, the higher the cost.

And although the benefits are standardized, the cost of a standard policy varies widely from company to company. So you must determine not only which benefit plan best suits your needs, but which company offers which plan at the best price. Then examine the other elements of each policy, such as premium increases and preexisting illness exclusions, before making your choice.

Basic Benefits Included in All Medigap Plans

The benefits included in the standard medigap plans and a chart comparing their coverage follow.

All standard medigap policies begin by offering the same basic benefits, including coverage of:

- hospital coinsurance amounts under Medicare Part A (but not necessarily the deductible)
- 365 days of hospital coverage after Medicare coverage ends
- some or all of the cost of covered blood transfusions
- some or all of the Medicare Part B coinsurance amount (the 20% of Medicare-approved amounts that Medicare Part B does not pay), and
- some or all of the out-of-pocket cost for hospice care (for all policies issued on or after June 1, 2010).

Notice that these basic benefits really are meant to close gaps in Medicare coverage, not to provide separate medical insurance. If a hospitalization or medical treatment is not covered at all by Medicare, a medigap policy will not cover any of it, either. The exception to this is those medigap policies that cover foreign travel.

Inpatient Hospital Costs

For every benefit period, every medigap plan pays all your Medicare Part A coinsurance amounts through your first 90 days as an inpatient, plus your coinsurance amount for any reserve days. After your reserve days are used up, every plan pays for the entire Medicare-approved amount of hospital charges for an additional 365 days. All plans pay some amount for the first three pints of blood you receive (Plans A through J pay the full amount; K pays 50%; L pays 75%). All plans except Plan A pay the yearly Part A hospital inpatient deductible (but Plans K and M pay only 50%, Plan L pays only 75%).

Medigap: It Pays to Shop Around

The federal government decides what benefits must be included in standard medigap policies. But it does not control prices, which vary widely. Prices vary for different ages and change from state to state, reflecting regional health care costs and level of competition for customers.

But the price for the same policy may vary tremendously even within the same state. Even the most basic Plan A policy can vary in cost by hundreds or even thousands of dollars per year in some states. And the more extensive the plan, the greater the cost disparity among policies from different insurance companies.

Most of the time, there is no basis for the price disparities other than "name" recognition. Don't fall for the first policy that comes along. Even when you've decided what standard policy you want, comparison shop for the best price from several different insurance companies.

Medical Expenses

Every plan pays some of the 20% coinsurance amount that Medicare Part B does not pay (except for preventive care copayments, which are covered separately). Plans A through J and Plan M pay the full Part B coinsurance amounts; Plan K pays 50% and Plan L 75% of the Plan B coinsurance amounts (up to those plans' yearly caps, after which they pay 100%). And Plan N pays the full Part B coinsurance amount except for a $20 copayment for office visits and a $50 copayment for emergency room visits (which the patient must pay out of pocket).

Only Plans C, F, and J pay the yearly Medicare Part B deductible. And only Plans F, G, I, and J pay the 15% "excess charges" above the Medicare-approved amount that a doctor is allowed to charge a patient if the doctor does not accept "assignment." (See "How Much Medicare Part B Pays" in Chapter 12 for more on Part B payments.)

> CAUTION
> **Make sure there are limits on premium raises.** It is always important to check the terms under which an insurance company may raise the amount of your premium. But it is particularly important when the initial premium already stretches your budget. Pay particular heed to the rules regarding hikes in medigap insurance premiums. (See "Terms and Conditions of Medigap Policies," below.)

Descriptions of the Standard Medigap Plans

Medigap policies are standardized. That means every policy in each lettered plan category must offer the same minimum coverage regardless of which insurance company offers it (though extra coverage may be added, and premiums vary). These standard plans changed as of June 1, 2010. After that date, no new policies are sold in Plans E, H, I, and J. People who are already enrolled in one of those plans' policies will be allowed to continue with it. Also, two new policy categories—Plans M and N—became available as of June 1, 2010.

Special Rules for Massachusetts, Minnesota, and Wisconsin

If you live in Massachusetts, Minnesota, or Wisconsin, the standard medigap policies are somewhat different from the standard policies offered elsewhere. Each of these three states has a basic plan plus options. You pay extra for any of the options you choose. The basic benefits in Massachusetts and Wisconsin include some things that the ten standard medigap policies do not. For information on the details of medigap policies in any of these states, call your state's department of insurance. You'll find its phone number and contact information for its website at the end of this chapter.

Standard Medigap Insurance Policies

All plans include these basic benefits:

- Hospitalization: Medicare Part A coinsurance plus 365 days of coverage after Medicare ends.
- Medical costs for outpatients: Some or all of the Medicare Part B coinsurance (the 20% of Medicare approved costs that Medicare Part B does not pay).
- Blood transfusions: All plans cover some or all of the first three pints of blood each year.
- Hospice: All plans issued June 1, 2010 or later cover hospice copayments (Plan K 50%, Plan L 75%); for policies issued before June 1, 2010, only Plans K and L provided this coverage.

A bullet below means that the plan covers the item 100%.

	Plan													
	A	B	C	D	E¹	F⁶	G	H¹	I¹	J¹	K	L	M⁴	N⁴
Medicare Part A Deductible		•	•	•	•	•	•	•	•	•	50%	75%	50%	•
Medicare Part B Deductible			•			•				•				
Part B Coinsurance	•	•	•	•	•	•	•	•	•	•	50%	75%	•	$20
Skilled Nursing Coinsurance			•	•	•	•	•	•	•	•	50%	75%	•	•
At-Home Recovery ²				•			•		•	•				
Blood Transfusion Coinsurance (first three pints of blood)	•	•	•	•	•	•	•	•	•	•	50% of first 3 pints	75% of first 3 pints	•	•
Foreign Travel			•	•	•	•	•	•	•	•			•	•
Preventive Care Coinsurance ²	•	•	•	•	•	•	•	•	•	•	•	•	•	•
Medicare Part B Excess Charges						•	•⁵		•	•				
Prescription Medicine	No plan offers prescription drug coverage—you'll need to sign up for Medicare Part D to cover your medications (see "Part D Prescription Drug Coverage" in Chapter 12).													
Cap on out-of-pocket expenses³											$4,940 per year (in 2015)	$2,470 per year (in 2015)		

¹ As of June 1, 2010, no new Plan E, H, I, or J policies will be sold. Existing policies may be continued.

² Coverage for preventive care (that is not covered by Medicare Part B) continues for Plans E and J issued before June 1, 2010.

³ After the cap on out-of-pocket expenses is reached, the policy will pay 100% of all covered Part A and Part B costs.

⁴ Available as of June 1, 2010.

⁵ 80% for policies issued before June 1, 2010; 100% for all Plan G policies issued June 1, 2010 or later.

⁶ There are also high-deductible Plan F policies in which the insured pays the first $2,000 out of pocket before the policy pays anything.

The standard plans are summarized in the "Standard Medigap Insurance Policies" chart, above, and are discussed more fully in the subsections that follow, with separate sections on rules for policies issued before and after June 1, 2010.

Medigap Plan A

Policies Issued Pre-June 2010

Plan A medigap policies include only the basic benefits discussed earlier. (See "Basic Benefits Included in All Medigap Plans," above.) Because of their limited benefits, Plan A policies are the least expensive.

Plan A policies are most useful if the doctors who regularly treat you accept assignment of Medicare-approved amounts, and you can afford to pay for the uncovered costs of doctors who do not accept assignment but by whom you might have to be treated. (See "How Much Medicare Part B Pays" in Chapter 12 regarding assignment practices.) Also, you must be able to afford the Part A hospital insurance deductible, bearing in mind that because there is a separate deductible for each separate hospital stay, you may have to pay it more than once in a year. (See "How Much Medicare Part A Pays" in Chapter 12 regarding Part A coverage.)

If these potential expenses plus the cost of a Plan A policy would put a severe strain on your finances, consider the alternative of an HMO, which may provide broader coverage for less money. (See Chapter 15 for a full discussion of the HMO option.)

Policies Issued June 1, 2010 or Later

Plan A policies issued June 1, 2010 or later also include coverage for hospice copayments.

Medigap Plan B

Policies Issued Pre-June 1, 2010

In addition to the basic benefits, a Plan B policy also pays your Medicare Part A deductible.

If your doctors all accept assignment but your budget would be severely strained by paying more than one hospital deductible in a year, Plan B may be marginally better for you than Plan A.

However, if you have to pay more than a few dollars a month more for Plan B than for Plan A, it may be a bad bargain.

Measure the yearly cost of a Plan B against the cost of a Plan A policy. If you are reasonably healthy—meaning you do not expect frequent hospitalizations—and the difference in premiums is more than 25% of the Part A Medicare deductible ($1,260 in 2015), it is probably not worth the extra premium, and you should stick to a Plan A policy.

Policies Issued June 1, 2010 or Later

Plan B policies issued June 1, 2010 or later also include coverage for hospice copayments.

Medigap Plan C

Policies Issued Pre-June 1, 2010

Plan C adds three benefits beyond the basic and other benefits offered in Plan B. First, it pays your yearly Medicare Part B deductible of $147. (But because this policy will probably cost you more than $147 per year over Plan A or B, that alone isn't a good reason to purchase it.)

Second, Plan C policies cover the Medicare coinsurance amount for skilled nursing care. Remember that under Medicare skilled nursing coverage, you are personally responsible for a coinsurance amount ($157.50 per day in 2015) for stays of 21 to 90 days in a skilled nursing facility. This can add up to a considerable amount of money, but it applies only if you are covered by Medicare for short-term skilled nursing care in a nursing facility. (See "Part A Hospital Insurance" in Chapter 12 regarding Medicare skilled nursing coverage.) If you have a medical condition that puts you in and out of the hospital, this can be a valuable addition to your policy. But the odds are low that most people will be in a skilled nursing facility for more than 20 days more than once or twice in a lifetime.

Finally, Plan C offers some coverage for medical care while traveling outside the United States. For people who travel abroad frequently, this can be a valuable benefit. After you pay a $250 deductible, Plan C pays for 80% of emergency medical costs you incur abroad. For purposes of these policies, emergency means any unplanned medical costs; it is not restricted to "emergency room" treatment (as it's called in the United States).

However, there are some restrictions on the coverage. Your emergency medical care must begin within the first 60 days of each trip abroad; if you take long trips, this policy will not protect you after the first two months. And there is a $50,000 lifetime maximum on these foreign travel medical benefits. If you spend a good portion of each year abroad, you may need a separate—that is, nonmedigap—health insurance policy to cover you fully for treatment received outside the United States.

Remember that your overseas medical care must be emergency care; if you regularly spend time abroad and simply want to be able to see a doctor for ongoing medical problems, this policy will not cover such visits.

The cost for Plan C policies is considerably higher than for Plan A or B but runs about the same as for Plans D and E.

Policies Issued June 1, 2010 or Later
Plan C policies issued June 1, 2010 or later also include coverage for hospice copayments.

Medicare SELECT Medigap Policies

In addition to regular fee-for-service medigap policies, there is a category of supplemental insurance that is partly fee-for-service and partly managed care. It is called Medicare SELECT. A SELECT policy must provide the same benefits as any of the standard medigap policies, but it has a two-tiered payment system.

If you use hospitals—and under some policies, doctors—who are members of the policy's network, the policy pays full benefits. If you use a provider outside the network, the policy pays reduced benefits. In this way, a Medicare SELECT medigap policy works like a preferred provider organization or an HMO with a point-of-service option, except that those managed care plans usually cover more services than most medigap policies. Because of the provider restrictions, Medicare SELECT policies are somewhat less expensive than regular medigap policies.

Medigap Plan D

Policies Issued Pre-June 1, 2010

Plan D is the same as Plan C, except it does not pay the yearly Medicare Part B deductible and it does pay for at-home recovery (home health aide services).

Policies Issued June 1, 2010 or Later

Plan D policies issued June 1, 2010 or later also include coverage for hospice copayments, but do not include at-home recovery.

Medigap Plan E

CAUTION

Plan E has been discontinued. No new Plan E policies have been sold since May 31, 2010. If you already had a Plan E policy as of that date, you may continue it.

Plan E adds minimal coverage of some preventive care but eliminates Plan D's coverage of at-home recovery. Plan E pays for only $120 per year of such preventive health care and screening, so it's not much of a benefit.

Medigap Plan F

Policies Issued Pre-June 1, 2010

Plan F offers the most significant added benefit beyond Plans B, C, D, and E: payment of 100% of what a doctor actually charges you above the Medicare-approved amount. (Remember, doctors who do not accept assignment are permitted to charge a patient up to 15% more than the Medicare-approved amount for any covered service, as discussed in "How Much Medicare Part B Pays" in Chapter 12.) If you receive extensive medical care from doctors who do not accept assignment, that extra 15% mounts up quickly.

Because the extra 15% of medical bills can amount to a lot of money, insurance companies charge higher premiums for Plan F than for the plans discussed previously. If you are in generally good health and the few doctors you see all accept assignment, this higher premium may not be worth the extra coverage. If, on the other hand, you require frequent or extensive medical care and you receive it from doctors who do not all accept assignment, Plan F may be worth the higher premiums.

If you like the coverage offered by Plan F but find the higher premiums too much for your budget, many companies that offer Plan F also offer a high-deductible version of this plan for a much lower premium. These high-deductible plans provide coverage only when your out-of-pocket costs for covered services exceed a certain amount for the year.

Policies Issued June 1, 2010 or Later

Plan F policies issued June 1, 2010 or later also include coverage for hospice copayments.

Medigap Plan G

Policies Issued Pre-June 1, 2010

Plan G is similar to Plan F. However, unlike Plan F, Plan G does not cover the Medicare medical insurance deductible. Plan G policies issued before June 1, 2010 cover only 80% of the excess charges some doctors and other providers charge under Medicare Part B.

Policies Issued June 1, 2010 or Later

Plan G policies issued June 1, 2010 or later provide 100% coverage for doctors' excess charges under Medicare Part B, and also include coverage for hospice copayments.

Medigap Plan H

CAUTION

Plan H has been discontinued. No new Plan H policies have been sold since May 31, 2010. If you already had a Plan H policy as of that date, you may continue it.

Plan H policies (without the drug coverage provided before January 1, 2006) cover the Part A deductible, Part A skilled nursing facility coinsurance amounts, and some coverage for emergency care while traveling outside the United States. Without their previous drug coverage, Plan H policies provide the same coverage as a Plan C policy except for the yearly Part B deductible that a Plan C policy covers. If you are considering keeping a Plan H policy, comparison shop with available Plan C policies.

Medigap Plan I

CAUTION

Plan I has been discontinued. No new Plan I policies have been sold since May 31, 2010. If you already had a Plan I policy as of that date, you may continue it.

Plan I policies (without the drug coverage provided before January 1, 2006) cover 100% of doctors' excess charges under Part B, which can be a significant amount if you regularly see a number of doctors or have major treatment in any particular year. It also includes coverage of at-home recovery, in addition to more commonly covered Part A deductible, skilled nursing facility coinsurance amounts, and emergency care during foreign travel. It is comparable to a Plan F policy, except that Plan F pays the Part B deductible instead of covering at-home recovery. If you can find a Part F policy for a considerably lower premium than your Plan I policy, it may be worth it to switch.

Medigap Plan J

CAUTION

Plan J has been discontinued. No new Plan J policies have been sold since May 31, 2010. If you already had a Plan J policy as of that date, you may continue it.

Plan J policies (without the drug coverage provided before January 1, 2006) are the luxury model of medigap policies, and also the most expensive. They cover 100% of doctors' excess charges and the Part B deductible, as well as all the other costs covered by any other plan policy.

Medigap Plan K

Policies Issued Pre-June 1, 2010

Plan K policies cover many Medicare gaps but pay only 50% of certain covered costs. Plan K compensates for this partial coverage by providing a cap on an insured person's out-of-pocket expenses. In addition to the standard Part A hospital coinsurance and extra lifetime hospital inpatient coverage offered under all medigap plans, Plan K policies cover 100% of the coinsurance amounts for Part B preventive care, and 50% of the Part A inpatient deductible, Part A coinsurance amounts for blood transfusions, skilled nursing facility stays and hospice care, and Part B coinsurance amounts. Plan K policies also place a $4,940 per year limit (in 2015) on a policyholder's out-of-pocket costs for covered medical expenses. After the policyholder reaches that amount, the policy pays 100% of all covered Part A and B costs.

Policies Issued June 1, 2010 or Later

There are no changes to Plan K policies issued June 1, 2010 or later.

Medigap Plan L

Policies Issued Pre-June 1, 2010

Plan L policies provide the same coverage as Plan K policies, and have the same kind of yearly cap on a policyholder's out-of-pocket expenses. But Plan L policies cover 75% of the Part A inpatient deductible, Part A coinsurance amounts for blood transfusions, skilled nursing facility stays and hospice care, and Part B coinsurance amounts. And Plan L's yearly cap on out-of-pocket expenses is $2,470 (in 2015). Because of this better coverage, Plan L policies are more expensive than Plan K policies.

Policies Issued June 1, 2010 or Later

There are no changes to Plan L policies issued June 1, 2010 or later.

Medigap Plan M

Beginning June 1, 2010, this new type of medigap policy is being sold. Plan M policies offer the same coverage as Plan D, but pay only 50% of the Medicare Part A deductible.

Medigap Plan N

Beginning June 1, 2010, this new type of medigap policy is being sold. Plan N policies offer the same coverage as Plan D, but you must pay a $20 copayment for each health care provider visit under Medicare Part B and a $50 copayment for an emergency room visit.

Terms and Conditions of Medigap Policies

In addition to comparing the services covered, the amount of benefits, and the monthly cost of different medigap insurance policies, there are several other things to consider before making a final decision.

Look first at how high the company says it may raise its premiums in the years to come—and therefore whether you will still be able to afford the policy when you may need it most. Also important are policy terms that determine whether you are covered for a particular illness during a certain time period after you purchase the policy.

Premium Increases

It is one thing to find insurance coverage you can afford today. It may be quite another to find a policy that you can continue to pay for in the future when your income and assets have decreased and the policy premium has increased. In choosing a medigap policy, consider what the contract says about how much the policy premiums will rise over time. If the current premium will already be a significant strain on your financial resources, consider a less expensive policy, because any policy is sure to get more expensive in the future.

There are several ways insurance companies set up premium increases in medigap policies. Choosing the best premium increase terms—what the insurance companies call "rating" methods—is something for you to consider along with other terms of the policy.

Level Premiums

The best method for the consumer is one called "level premiums." This means that premiums do not go up on your policy as you reach a certain age, but only when the insurance company raises premiums on all medigap policies of the type you have. Of course, the premiums will go up regularly, but the amount they go up will be at least partially controlled by market forces and by your state's insurance commission.

Attained Age

"Attained age" policies base your premium entirely upon your age. The company charges the same premium to everyone of the same age who has the same policy. As you get older, the premiums rise in lockstep, by a set amount. Some policies mandate that your premiums go up yearly, others hike the premiums when you reach a certain age plateau, such as 70, 75, or 80. Attained age policies tend to be cheaper at age 65 than comparable policies. However, once you reach 70 or 75, attained age policies tend to become, and stay, more expensive than other types.

When considering a policy with attained age premium rises, ask to see not only how much it would cost you at your present age, but also the current premium costs at each of the next age levels. That will give you a sense of how high the rates jump for that policy. Figure that your premiums will rise by at least the same percentages, and calculate how much your policy is likely to cost at your next two age levels. Only then will you have a realistic picture of how much this policy will cost.

COMPUTER
Medigap information from Medicare's website. Medicare's official website at www.medicare.gov offers a link that can provide you with the names and contact information of insurance companies that offer specific medigap policies available where you live. On the medicare.gov home page, click the "Supplements & Other Insurance" tab, then click "Find a Medigap Policy." Enter the requested information about your location. It will then provide you with information about specific medigap policies being sold where you live, including what the policies cover and which companies offer each type of policy, with contact information for those companies.

Issue Age

The initial premium for an "issue age" policy is determined by your age when you first purchase it. From then on, as long as you keep the same policy, you pay the same premium as someone else who buys the policy at the same age at which you bought it.

For example, if you buy an issue age medigap policy at age 65, in five years you will pay the same as a person who first buys the policy at that time at age 65. Your premium will steadily rise, but the increases may be controlled by the insurance company's need to keep the premium competitive to continue signing up new policyholders.

No Age Rating

A few insurance companies sell policies that charge the same amount regardless of age. They base their premiums entirely on the cost of medical care in the geographic area in which you live. (For this reason, these are sometimes referred to as "community-rated policies.") These policies tend to be a bit more expensive than others for people ages 65 to 75 and a bit less expensive for people age 75 and older.

Eligibility and Enrollment

Your ability to purchase the medigap policy of your choice depends on when and under what circumstances you apply for it. We discuss applying during open enrollment periods, applying during limited guaranteed enrollment periods, and applying outside these enrollment periods on your own, below.

Applying During Open Enrollment

You are guaranteed the right to buy any medigap policy sold in your state, without any medical screening or limits on coverage, if you:
- are within your first six months of Medicare Part B, or
- leave a Medicare Advantage plan within a year of age 65.

Your First Six Months With Medicare Part B

During the six months after you first enroll in Medicare Part B (see "Enrolling in Part B Medical Insurance" in Chapter 13 for enrollment procedures), you may buy any medigap insurance policy sold in the state where you live. During this initial enrollment period, federal law prohibits an insurance company from requiring medical underwriting—that is, prior screening of your health condition—before issuing a policy. Nor may the insurance company delay coverage because of preexisting health conditions. Companies are also prohibited from charging higher premiums based solely on your age or area of residence.

Most people enroll in Medicare Part B as soon as they turn 65. Your six-month open enrollment period for medigap begins on the first of the month during which you reach age 65 and are enrolled in Part B.

If you did not enroll for Medicare Part B on your 65th birthday but enroll during a yearly Medicare general enrollment period (January through March), your six-month open enrollment period for any medigap policy begins on July 1 of the same year. If you did not enroll in Medicare Part B on your 65th birthday because you were still covered by an employer-sponsored health plan, you have a six-month open enrollment period for any medigap policy beginning whenever you enroll in Medicare Part B.

You Leave a Medicare Advantage Plan Within a Year of Age 65

If you joined a Medicare Advantage plan (see Chapter 15) at age 65 when you first became eligible for Medicare, but you leave the plan within a year, you have a guaranteed right to buy any medigap plan sold in your state. This is true whether your Medicare Advantage plan dropped you—perhaps because it stopped doing business in your county of residence, or because you moved out of its business area—or because you left the plan voluntarily.

However, to protect this guaranteed right, you must apply for a medigap policy within 63 days of the date your Medicare Advantage plan coverage ends. If you are still in the six-month period immediately following your enrollment in Medicare Part B, you have whatever is left of that six-month period within which to apply for a medigap policy, or 63 days from the end of your Medicare Advantage coverage, whichever is greater.

Medigap Coverage If You Move

What happens if you buy a medigap policy while living in one place, then move elsewhere? Because all medigap policies are "guaranteed renewable," your insurance company can't cancel your policy. This is true even if you move to an area where the company doesn't normally sell similar policies. However, the insurance company has a right to increase your premium if you've moved to an area where the costs of medical care are higher. The rates must be approved by the department of insurance in the state to which you have moved.

Applying With Limited Guaranteed Enrollment

You have the guaranteed right to buy a medigap policy if, under certain circumstances, you:

- lose your Medicare coverage, or
- drop medigap, join a Medicare Advantage plan, then leave the Medicare Advantage plan.

You can use this right for any of several standard medigap plans, though not for all plans (see below). For those plans to which you have no guaranteed right, however, you may still purchase a policy if the issuing insurance company approves your application.

You Lose Coverage by a Medicare Advantage Plan or an Employer-Sponsored Policy

With alarming frequency, insurance companies all over the United States are dropping their Medicare Advantage plans in counties in which the companies are unhappy with their profit margins. (See Chapter 15 for details.)

If you have been dropped from a Medicare Advantage plan because the plan is leaving Medicare altogether, or is leaving the county in which you live, you have a guaranteed right to purchase any standard medigap Plan A, B, C, or F policy sold in your state. (In Massachusetts, Minnesota, and Wisconsin, you have a right to purchase a medigap policy with provisions similar to these four standard medigap plans.) You have the same guarantee if you are losing your Medicare Advantage coverage because you are moving out of the plan's service area.

These rules also apply if you lose employer-sponsored insurance which had operated like a medigap policy, meaning that it paid for some costs your Medicare coverage did not.

If you had a medigap Plan D, E, or G before dropping it to join a Medicare Advantage plan that has now dropped you, you also have a guaranteed right to again purchase that same plan from the same insurance company, if the company still sells the plan in your state.

To take advantage of any of these guaranteed rights, you must apply for a medigap plan within 63 days from the end of your Medicare Advantage or employer-sponsored coverage.

Some States Offer Extra Protection

Some states' laws offer even more protection around your right to purchase a medigap policy than the federal guarantee described in this chapter. These state laws typically give you more medigap plans from which to choose. To find out what extra protection your state might offer, call your state's department of insurance (see contact information at the end of this chapter) or your local SHIP office (see contact information at the end of Chapter 13).

You Dropped a Medigap Policy to Join a Medicare Advantage Plan or a Medicare SELECT Policy, Then Left the New Plan Within a Year

If you once had a medigap policy but dropped it to join a Medicare Advantage plan or to purchase a Medicare SELECT policy (see "Medicare SELECT Medigap Policies," above), you may have a guaranteed right to drop the Medicare plan and repurchase a medigap plan. However, you must meet two conditions:

- The Medicare Advantage plan or Medicare SELECT policy you drop must be the only one in which you have been enrolled.
- You must leave the Medicare Advantage plan or drop the Medicare SELECT policy within a year of when you joined.

If you meet these two conditions, you may either buy your original medigap policy from the same company (if it is still sold in your state), or buy any medigap Plan A, B, C, or F sold in your state. There is a time limit on applying for the new medigap policy, however. Your guaranteed right to purchase lasts only 63 days from the end of your previous coverage.

Applying Without Guaranteed Enrollment

If you want to buy a medigap policy but have none of the guaranteed rights described above, an insurance company can freely choose whether or not to sell you a policy. Even if the company does offer you coverage, it may attach whatever terms, conditions, and premiums it chooses, as long as the coverage matches one of the standard plans.

In such circumstances, the insurance company is likely to demand that you undergo medical underwriting (screening)—particularly before they'll sell you one of their more desirable policies. The screening will involve a detailed examination of your medical history.

If your history shows a likelihood of extensive or expensive medical treatment in the foreseeable future, the company might refuse to sell you the policy. Or, they might offer to sell it to you at a high premium, perhaps also with limitations on when coverage begins.

Preexisting Illness Exclusion

Most medigap policies contain a provision excluding coverage, for a set time immediately after you purchase a policy, of any illness or medical conditions for which you received treatment within a given period before your coverage began. Six months is a typical exclusion period. Many policies provide no coverage for six months after you buy the policy for illnesses you were treated for within six months before the policy started. Usually, the shorter the exclusion period, the higher the premium.

If you have a serious medical condition that may require costly medical treatment at any time, and you have been treated for that condition within the recent past, consider a policy with a short exclusion period or none at all.

Discounts for the "Healthy"

Some insurance companies offer extra discounts on medigap policies for people they consider to be better risks than others. For example, women may be offered lower premiums than men because women tend to remain healthier longer, meaning the insurance company collects more premiums before having to pay out on claims. For the same reason, nonsmokers are also frequently offered discounts.

You may also be able to reduce your premiums if you have been free of any serious illness or condition and are willing to prove it by undergoing what is called medical underwriting—a screening process during which the insurance company examines your medical history to see whether you are likely to cost them a lot of money in the near future. If the screening shows that you have had no serious illnesses or medical conditions over the previous ten years, you may be able to purchase the policy at a significantly lower premium than if you had bought it without first being medically screened. Ask the insurance company whether they offer this sort of discount.

Finding the Best Medicare Supplement

Shopping for a medigap policy can be difficult, not only because of the differences in policy terms among the ten standard policies, but because of the wide spectrum of prices among insurance companies. Near the end of Chapter 15 is a chart to help you do a side-by-side comparison among different medigap and Medicare Advantage plans.

Fortunately, your first step, namely finding out what medigap insurance policies are available in your state, is fairly simple. Your state department of insurance can give you a complete list of available policies (see the contact information at the end of this chapter). Be warned, however, that their lists are often a bit stale, so you'll need to follow up with the insurance companies or insurance agents for the latest facts and figures. Many people also use insurance agents to find policies, although you should first read the cautions in "Using an Insurance Agent," below. In addition, some seniors' organizations offer discounts on certain medigap policies.

Medicare.gov also has a useful medigap policy finder that lists and compares policies in your area.

Using an Insurance Agent

If you use an insurance agent to present you with a choice of medigap policies, make sure the agent is experienced with the provisions of several different policies. Insurance agents tend to work with policies from certain companies and may not know of less expensive or less restrictive policies from other companies. So you may want to consult more than one agent.

Even if you arrange to get your insurance through an agent, keep your own ears and eyes open for policies that might fit your needs. Friends, relatives, and organizations to which you belong may all be resources to find out about available plans. And senior organizations can be a good source of information. A good insurance agent should be willing to find out the details of a policy you have located yourself. If the agent cannot or will not check on such a policy, it is probably time to find a new agent. Likewise, if an insurance agent is unwilling to sit down with you and compare the coverage and costs of different policies, then you ought to comparison shop for a new insurance agent.

Senior Associations

A number of organizations of seniors or retired people advertise medigap policies. These organizations do not actually act as insurers. Instead, they negotiate deals with insurance companies to offer medigap policies to their members, sometimes at reduced rates.

But some senior organizations act almost as fronts for insurance companies. These organizations may appear to exist for the benefit of older people, offering a number of programs or services for seniors. But many of these alleged benefits are nearly worthless. In truth, these organizations exist to sell themselves through membership dues and products (including overpriced insurance) behind a facade of supposedly protecting senior citizens.

Help With Decisions About Medigap and Medicare Advantage Plans

Each state has a program to assist people with Medicare, medigap supplemental insurance, and Medicare Advantage plans. It is called the State Health Insurance Assistance Program (SHIP), although in some states it may have another, similar name.

SHIP has professional staff and volunteers who are knowledgeable not only about the rules pertaining to Medicare and medigap insurance but also about what policies are available in your state and what HMOs and other Medicare Advantage plans are available in your local area. SHIP staff can look over particular insurance policies and managed care plans and help you see the strengths and weaknesses of each.

In larger states there are many SHIP offices, and you can reach the office nearest you by calling the state's general toll-free number. In smaller states there may be fewer offices, and you will be referred to a SHIP program at a local senior center or another nonprofit organization. (See the end of Chapter 13 for contact information.)

The best way to tell whether the policies a particular organization offers are good or bad is to compare their specific terms and prices with those of other policies offered by different insurance companies or health plans. In the final analysis, it is the terms of the policy, not an organization's good intentions or friendly advertising, that determine the quality of your coverage. The insurance company, not the senior organization, determines your coverage and pays your claims.

Beware of Mail-Order and Limited-Offer Policies

Beware of medigap policy offers you receive unsolicited in the mail. Their flashy promises often far outstrip their coverage. If you do become aware of a policy through the mail, and its provisions seem good to you after comparing it with other policies, check the reputation of the company offering the policy. You can get information on the company from your state's insurance department or commission, or from your state or local consumer protection agency.

Also be wary of policies that are offered with short-time enrollment periods. You have likely heard or seen advertisements for insurance that holler: "Limited offer! One month only! Buy now, the greatest offer in years! Once the offer is over, you'll never get another chance at an opportunity like this again! Once-in-a-lifetime offer!"

This is nonsense.

If it's a reputable company with a legitimate policy to offer you, the same or similar terms will be available any time—although you must keep in mind your own six-month open enrollment period after you sign up for Medicare Part B. These advertising slogans are just another way insurance companies have of pressuring you into buying a policy without first carefully considering and comparing its terms.

Most companies permit you to look over your policy and carefully examine its terms for ten days before you are obligated to keep it. If you decide you don't want the policy—for any reason—you can return it within ten days to the company or to the insurance agent you bought it from. You'll be owed a refund of all the money you have paid up to that point. And if you are buying a new medigap policy to replace one you already have, you are legally entitled to 30 days to review the new policy to decide whether you want to keep it. You can cancel it without penalty at any time during those 30 days.

Only One Medigap Policy Required

You need only one policy to supplement your Medicare coverage— and it is illegal for an insurance company to sell you a health insurance policy that duplicates coverage you already have with a medigap policy.

When you apply for a medigap policy, you will be asked to provide information concerning any health insurance policies you have. This gives written notice to the seller of your policy—insurance agent, broker, or company representative—about your existing insurance so that you will not be held responsible for paying for duplicate coverage if the insurer mistakenly sells it to you.

If you already have medigap insurance but want to replace it with a new policy, some rules help protect you while you make the change.

Replacement Policies

If you are considering replacing your existing policy with a new one, there are a number of things to keep in mind.

First, even if your new policy would ultimately provide better coverage, it may have a preexisting condition exclusion that would deny you coverage for up to six months after you switched policies. If you have been treated in the previous six months for any serious medical condition that might require further treatment in the near future, don't cancel a basically good policy for one that is only slightly better.

Second, unless you are signing up within the first six months following your enrollment in Medicare Part B, the new insurance company from which you applied for coverage might reject you if you have had serious medical problems in the recent past. Don't cancel your old policy until you have been given written notice from the new insurance company—not just from the agent or broker who sold you the policy—that your new policy is in effect.

When you apply for a replacement policy, you must sign a statement agreeing that you will drop your old policy when the new one takes effect. The law gives you a review period within which to decide between the old and new policies. Once you have received written notice of your acceptance in the new insurance plan, and you have been given a written copy of the new policy, you have 30 days to cancel either the new policy or the old one.

Dread Disease Policies: A Dreadful Idea

A few insurance companies offer policies that do not provide medigap supplemental coverage but provide particularized health coverage that may overlap some with medigap policies and even Medicare coverage itself. Most of these policies cover treatment for a specific disease and are known as indemnity or "dread disease" policies. They are often solicited over the phone or by direct mail and are offered at low monthly premiums.

One of these policies may initially sound promising if it covers a particular disease—for example, a specific type of cancer—for which you have a high risk. However, close examination of these policies usually shows them to be a waste of money. They pay only a small, set amount of money for each day you are hospitalized or for each medical treatment for the specific disease, usually far less than the Medicare deductible or coinsurance that a medigap policy would pay.

And because they pay only when you are treated for the specific disease, you wind up needing to carry a medigap policy anyway to cover all medical bills not related to this particular disease. Or if you don't carry a medigap policy, you will be responsible for paying out of pocket for all medical bills not covered by this specific-disease policy. Either way, these policies are a bad investment.

Department of Insurance

You can contact your state's department of insurance to ask for information about medigap insurance policies being sold in your state. To find contact information for your state, see the official Medicare website listing of state departments of insurance at www.medicare.gov/Contacts.

Medicare Part C:
Medicare Advantage Plans

Medicare Part C health plans, referred to as Medicare Advantage plans, fill gaps in basic Medicare, as do medigap policies. But the two systems operate differently. As explained in Chapter 14, medigap policies work alongside Medicare: Medical bills are sent both to Medicare and to a medigap insurer, and each pays a portion of the approved charges. With a Medicare Advantage plan, on the other hand, an enrollee no longer deals with Medicare directly. A Medicare Advantage plan provides all basic Medicare coverage and often offers some extended coverage in addition to basic Medicare. The extent of coverage beyond basic Medicare, the size of premiums and copayments, and decisions about whether a particular treatment should be covered, are all controlled by the Medicare Advantage plan, not by Medicare. (See "Comparing Medigap and Medicare Advantage Plans," toward the end of this chapter, to help compare specific policies.)

Medicare Advantage plans come in two basic forms: managed care plans and fee-for-service plans.

- **Managed care plans.** In return for coverage beyond basic Medicare, Medicare Advantage managed care plans charge a low monthly premium—or none at all—and small copayments. But they limit the doctors and other providers from which you can receive care. They restrict doctors as well—placing limits on treatments and the length of hospital stays for managed care patients.

- **Fee-for-service plans.** With these plans, you may receive care from any doctor or other provider who participates in Medicare. But for each service or treatment, the doctor or other provider must accept the Medicare Advantage plan's restrictions and amount of payment. If a doctor or another provider will not accept the plan's restrictions or payment level for a particular medical service, the plan will not cover the patient's care by that provider. In that case, the patient must either personally pay the provider or seek care from a different provider who will accept the plan's terms.

Medicare Part D Means New Decisions About Medicare Advantage Plans

Deciding whether to remain in or join a Medicare Advantage plan has become trickier since the introduction of prescription drug coverage under the Medicare Part D program. Before Part D, many Medicare Advantage plans offered some prescription drug coverage. Now, some Medicare Advantage plans offer drug coverage, but others have none.

If a Medicare Advantage plan includes drug coverage, enrolling in that plan means that you do not also enroll in a Part D plan. But enrolling in a plan with drug coverage is a good idea only if that plan covers the drugs you regularly take, and offers them at a reasonable copayment without serious access restrictions. (Coverage restrictions are discussed in more detail in Chapter 12. See "Part D Prescription Drug Coverage.")

If a Medicare Advantage plan does not offer Plan D coverage, you may still want to keep or join that plan if you like its other coverage features and costs. But if you also want prescription drug coverage, you will have to enroll in a separate, stand-alone Part D prescription drug plan.

If your current Medicare Advantage plan offers Plan D drug coverage but does not cover your drugs, or does so with high copayments or access restrictions, consider joining a different Medicare Advantage plan that better meets your needs. Or, leave the managed care system altogether and return to original Medicare coverage under Parts A and B, and separately enroll in a stand-alone Part D prescription drug plan that does a good job of covering your drugs. (See Chapter 12.) If you leave Medicare Advantage altogether, you may also want to take out a medigap supplemental insurance policy to fill some of the gaps in Medicare coverage that your Medicare Advantage plan used to cover. (See Chapter 14.)

If you are considering a Medicare Advantage plan, you must decide whether any of the plans available in your area offer adequate care at an affordable cost. You should evaluate not only the cost of premiums and copayments but also how the plan limits the particular doctors and other providers you can get care from. Despite the lower monthly cost for Medicare Advantage plans, their limitations have resulted in only about 30% of Medicare beneficiaries enrolling in these plans.

When considering a Medicare Advantage plan, you'll also need to assess the risks of yearly changes—including the chance that a particular plan may drop out of an entire geographic region— associated with these types of plans. Just because many of them are sponsored by big insurance companies does not make them stable. In the past several years, the number of plans people have to choose from has steadily declined. Many seniors have been dropped from Medicare Advantage plans that stopped serving the areas where they lived and been forced to find another plan or return to original Medicare coverage. And millions of people have found their premiums shooting up, copayments rising, and coverage shrinking for those services not legally required by Medicare.

Not only do you risk your plan's disappearing or becoming far more expensive, but if you choose to return to regular Medicare, your chance to buy a medigap insurance policy (as discussed in Chapter 14) may be much more limited.

To learn what Medicare Advantage plans are available in the area where you live, you can visit the Medicare website at www. medicare.gov. To find out the recent history of a particular Medicare Advantage plan—whether it has dropped patients or hiked costs, for example—call your local SHIP or HICAP counseling office (see the end of Chapter 13 for contact information) or your state department of insurance (see Chapter 14 for contact information). If you are dropped from a Medicare Advantage plan, your alternatives and when you must exercise them are explained in "Your Rights When Joining, Leaving, or Losing a Medicare Advantage Plan," below.

Joining a Medicare Advantage Plan Means Leaving Direct Medicare Protection

If you join a Medicare Advantage plan, in effect you leave the Medicare program. The insurance company that runs the Medicare Advantage plan gets a monthly payment from Medicare on your behalf, but the plan itself then decides what health care providers you can use, and approves or denies medical coverage for all of your specific medical care. (When the plan denies coverage, the plan itself handles the first level of your request for reconsideration. But if your request for reconsideration is still denied, then you are entitled to independent review, just as in an appeal under original Medicare (covered in Chapter 13). For more information, see Nolo's website article on Appealing a Denial of Medicare Part C.)

If you leave a Medicare Advantage plan, you are permitted to rejoin traditional Medicare. But if you return to Medicare after the first year following your initial Medicare eligibility, you may find that not all medigap supplemental insurance policies will accept you. And you may be able to join another Medicare Advantage plan only during open enrollment.

Medicare Advantage Managed Care Plans

Many Medicare Advantage plans are structured as managed care plans. In these plans, a patient's care is managed by the insurance company that issues the plan. The basic premise of managed care is that the member-patient agrees to receive care only from specific doctors, hospitals, and others—called a network—in exchange for reduced overall health care costs. The patient also agrees that the plan, rather than Medicare itself, will decide whether a particular medical service is covered.

There are several varieties of Medicare Advantage managed care plans. Some have severe restrictions on consulting with specialists or seeing providers from outside the network. Others give members more freedom to choose when they see doctors and which doctors they may consult for treatment. Generally, more choice translates into higher cost.

Health Maintenance Organization (HMO)

The HMO is the least expensive and most restrictive Medicare Advantage managed care plan. It is also the most common type of Medicare managed care plan. There are four main restrictions.

Care Within the Network Only

Each HMO maintains a list—called a network—of doctors and other health care providers. The HMO member must receive care only from a provider in the network, except in emergencies.

If the plan member uses a provider from outside the network, the plan pays nothing toward the bill. And because a Medicare Advantage plan member has withdrawn from traditional Medicare coverage, Medicare itself picks up none of the tab, either. The plan member must pay the entire bill out of pocket.

Because of this restriction, it is very important to find out whether the doctors and other providers you use are included in the HMO's network. This is particularly true for your primary care physician, who will not only handle routine medical problems but will also decide whether you should be referred for treatment or to a specialist. It is also important to make sure that the hospital in your vicinity, or a hospital you and your doctor prefer to use, is in the network. If all of your doctors and your preferred hospital are in the HMO's network, the restriction may not be as important to you.

However, most HMOs and other managed care plans (except for integrated HMOs like Kaiser Permanente) do sometimes drop doctors and hospitals. And doctors' groups and hospitals leave HMOs that become too stingy in reimbursing for medical care or authorizing services for their patients. If the plan or one of your providers decides to cut ties, you won't be able to continue seeing that provider. So, even if you begin a managed care plan with all the right doctors and hospital, you may later find yourself traveling long distances to get to a new hospital and searching for new doctors, or searching for a new managed care plan or medigap policy.

This instability of many managed care plans makes it important for you to discuss with your doctors any particular HMO you are considering. Ask whether your doctor has experienced problems with the plan, particularly with approval of treatments, referrals to specialists, or early release from inpatient hospital care.

Some doctors are uncomfortable speaking with patients about insurance companies. But responsible physicians will at least tell you if their offices have had regular, serious problems getting a plan's coverage for their patients, and certainly should tell you if they are considering dropping their contract with a particular plan.

Emergency and Urgent Care Anywhere

Federal law requires that all Medicare Advantage plans cover emergency services nationwide, regardless of restrictions they place on the use of doctors and hospitals for routine care. The law also requires that these plans pay for covered services you receive from a nonplan provider if the treatment was urgently needed while you were temporarily outside the plan's geographic service area. Urgently needed care means care for an unforeseen illness or injury for which a reasonable person would not wait until they could return home to seek medical help.

This required emergency coverage does not apply to most foreign travel. However, some plans offer such coverage on their own. If you travel or live any part of the year outside the United States but are not covered while abroad, it may be a good idea to buy a temporary travel medical policy covering you for the time you are out of the country.

All Care Through Primary Care Physician

An HMO member must select a primary care physician from the plan's network. This is the doctor the member must usually see first for medical needs. In most HMOs, a member may not see other doctors or providers—even from within the plan's network—or obtain other medical services without a referral by the primary care physician. Even if you regularly see a variety of specialists, your primary care physician must refer you to those doctors. You may not usually make an appointment to see them on your own.

This system encourages the primary care physician—who is paid less than a specialist by the plan—to take care of medical problems that don't absolutely require a specialist. Because of the hassle of the extra step, it also discourages the plan member from seeking specialist care.

This restriction is a significant reason that managed care is cheaper for insurance companies than traditional fee-for-service policies. Since many seniors require specialist care, this restriction is also a reason that many of them reject HMO coverage in favor of medigap insurance or less restrictive types of managed care.

Prior HMO Approval of Some Services

HMOs require that your primary care physician or other network physician obtain prior approval from the plan for certain medical services the doctor may want to prescribe. If plan administrators do not believe a service is medically necessary, or believe service from a nonspecialist or other less expensive treatment would do just as well, they may deny coverage for that prescribed service.

HMO With Point-of-Service (POS) Option

A few Medicare Advantage HMOs have a significant wrinkle that makes them more attractive—and more expensive—than standard HMO plans. These plans offer what is called a point-of-service option. This option allows a member to see physicians and other providers who are not in the HMO's network, and to receive services from specialists without first going through a primary care physician.

However, if a member does go outside the network or sees a specialist directly, the plan pays a smaller part of the bill than if the member had followed regular HMO procedures. The member pays a higher premium for this option than for a standard HMO plan, and a higher copayment each time the option is used.

Special Needs Plans for Certain Chronic Conditions

In some states, a particular kind of Medicare Advantage plan, called a Special Needs Plan, may be offered to people with a specific serious chronic or disabling medical condition. Like all other Medicare Advantage plans, these C-SNPs (meaning Chronic-Special Needs Plans) offer both inpatient and outpatient care at least as broad as Medicare Part A and Part B, plus prescription drugs. Unlike other Medicare Advantage plans, though, a C-SNP is tailored to a specific condition, providing a network of doctors and other providers who specialize in the treatment of that condition, a broad selection of the drugs used to treat that condition, and usually a "care coordinator" who monitors a patient's health status and helps ensure that the patient follows proper care procedures at home.

C-SNPs are offered in only about half of all states, with a total enrollment of only about 0.5% of all Medicare beneficiaries. And almost all C-SNPs (more than 95% of all C-SNPs offered) cover one or more of only three sets of conditions. If your doctor certifies that you have one of these three sets of conditions, you might qualify for a C-SNP that specifically covers your condition and actually find such a policy offered where you live:

- cardiovascular disorders, including chronic or congestive heart failure
- diabetes mellitus, or
- chronic lung failure.

If you have one of the following conditions, technically you might also qualify for a C-SNP, but insurance companies have offered such C-SNPs in only a very few places in the country:

- cancer
- stroke
- alcohol/drug dependence
- Alzheimer's or dementia
- disabling mental health disease
- neurological disorders
- HIV/AIDS
- autoimmune disorders
- end-stage liver or kidney disease, or
- severe hematological disorders.

Special Needs Plans for Certain Chronic Conditions (cont'd)

In addition to the difficulty of finding a C-SNP for your condition where you live, there is the issue of whether the plan would actually be better for you than other Medicare Advantage plans. In theory, concentrating providers around a single condition and coordinating care should improve care. However, the government's own Medicare Payment Advisory Committee has found that on average C-SNPs do not perform as well as regular Medicare Advantage plans do, as judged by certain "quality measures." Of course, that's on average, and specific plans might do quite well on those measures.

If you are interested in exploring whether a C-SNP might be right for you, you can find out what plans are available in your area by going online to the government's Medicare Plan Finder, www.medicare.gov/find-a-plan/questions/home.aspx. If you find a plan that interests you, be sure to compare it to what's offered by other Medicare Advantage plans in your area, including asking the insurance company what the plan's "quality measures" ratings are. For help in choosing a plan, you can get free counseling from a local office of the State Health Insurance Assistance Program (SHIP). See information about SHIP at the end of Chapter 13. More information is also available from Medicare's online pamphlet "Medicare Special Needs Plans" at www.medicare.gov/Pubs/pdf/11302.pdf.

If you decide that you want to try a C-SNP offered where you live, you may enroll (with your doctor's certification that you have a qualifying condition) or disenroll under the same terms as you could with any Medicare Advantage plan (see "Your Rights When Joining, Leaving, or Losing a Medicare Advantage Plan," below). In addition, you can enroll in a C-SNP anytime you are newly diagnosed with the condition that qualifies you for the plan.

Preferred Provider Organization (PPO)

Although it has a different name, the PPO works the same as an HMO with a point-of-service (POS) option (discussed above). If a member receives a service from the PPO's network of providers, the cost to the member is lower than if the member sees a provider outside the network.

PPOs tend to be more expensive than standard HMOs, charging both a monthly premium and a higher copayment for nonnetwork services. However, many people find that the extra flexibility in choosing doctors is an important comfort to them, and therefore worth the extra money.

Provider Sponsored Organization (PSO)

The PSO is a group of medical providers—doctors, clinics, and a hospital—that skips the insurance company middleman and contracts directly with patients. As with an HMO, the member pays a premium, as well as a copayment each time a service is used.

PSOs are rare, and you're unlikely to find one where you live. However, if a PSO operates in your area, you may want to consider it as an alternative to other types of Medicare Advantage Plans.

Medicare Advantage Fee-for-Service Plans

In recent years, insurance companies have been offering a new type of Medicare Advantage plan, called "private fee-for-service," that they tout as offering greater enrollee "freedom" in choice of doctors and other providers. Unfortunately, for reasons described below, many people discover that this freedom is an illusion. Nonetheless, in some places—particularly in rural areas—these fee-for-service plans are a viable alternative if there are few or no other Medicare Advantage plans available.

How Most Medicare Advantage Fee-for-Service Plans Work

Unlike managed care plans, most Medicare Advantage private fee-for-service plans do not maintain a membership network of doctors, hospitals, and other health care providers from which a plan enrollee must receive health care services. Instead, a private fee-for-service plan may cover care provided by any health care provider that accepts Medicare patients. Also, many of these plans have a cap on the total out-of-pocket payments an enrollee will pay each year for care that is covered by the plan.

Fee-for-Service Plans With Tiered Payment

A few fee-for-service plans maintain provider networks, just like a managed care plan. With these plans, you may receive medical services from any doctor or other provider who accepts the terms of the plan. But if you receive medical services from a provider within the plan's network, your out-of-pocket costs are lower than if you receive services from a provider who is not in the plan's network.

Disadvantages of Medicare Advantage Fee-for-Service Plans

Fee-for-service plans impose several significant restrictions that may severely limit a patient's choice of doctors and other providers, making such a plan a poor option if other types of Medicare Advantage plans are available. These restrictions are:

- **Strict rules for providers.** For any specific medical treatment or service, a doctor or another provider must accept the terms offered by the fee-for-service plan. These terms include the nature and extent of care the insurance company will approve and what the provider will be paid. If the doctor or other provider is not willing to accept the plan's terms, the plan will not cover the particular care with that provider. In that case, the patient must either personally pay for the care or seek treatment from a different provider.

- **Lack of predictable care.** The fact that a doctor or another provider previously accepted a plan's terms does not mean the provider will accept the terms the next time the patient wants care, either for the same or a different medical service. In other words, if you enroll in one of these plans, you won't know whether care from a particular doctor or other provider will be covered by the plan until the time comes when you need it.
- **Few additional services.** Fee-for-service plans usually don't cover as many extra services (meaning services not covered by original Medicare Part A and Part B) as do other types of Medicare Advantage plans.
- **Extra costs.** In some plans, you may have to pay the doctor or other provider out of your pocket—up to 15% more than the amount the plan pays the provider.

If you are considering a private fee-for-service plan, be sure to carefully evaluate your choices by following the suggestions offered in the rest of this chapter.

Choosing a Medicare Advantage Plan

To evaluate a Medicare Advantage plan of any type, it is important to get a complete written explanation of its coverage, costs, and procedures. These are usually contained in a printed brochure called a summary of benefits, available from each plan. Also, ask each plan for a chart showing premiums and copayments. Compare that written information with each important category discussed in this chapter.

If you do not understand exactly what the coverage, costs, and procedures are, ask a plan representative to tell you where they are explained in the written information. If you can't get an important piece of information in writing, don't join the plan.

Choice of Doctors and Other Providers

For many people, the most important factor in choosing a Medicare Advantage plan is whether the doctors, hospitals, and other providers they already use and trust are in the plan's network of providers or, in the case of fee-for-service plans, whether those providers regularly accept the plan's terms.

Tracking Membership Satisfaction

Your state department of insurance or department of corporations is charged with monitoring Medicare Advantage plans. And it pays to see whether many members complain about crucial services. Most complaints are based on a plan's having:

- rejected referrals to specialists
- ordered early discharge for hospital inpatients
- dropped coverage in certain geographic areas
- dropped doctors and hospitals from its network
- raised copayments
- switched drugs on the plan's formulary, or
- dropped extra coverage.

An excellent and free source of information about Medicare Advantage plans is the State Health Insurance Assistance Program (SHIP), in some places called the Health Insurance Counseling and Advocacy Program (HICAP). To find your local office, contact the SHIP or HICAP office in your state; for contact information, see the end of Chapter 13.

Managed care plans. If the people and places you prefer for care are in a managed care plan's network, the tight restrictions of HMOs may not have much effect on you, at least for the foreseeable future. But if they're not, you will have to find new doctors, which is rarely an easy or comfortable process. And you might have to use a hospital that is more distant from your home, leaving you a little less secure.

The problem is not quite as great with PPOs or HMOs with a point-of-service option. These plans permit you to use providers who are not in a plan's network. So, if you want to continue with a particular doctor or provider who is not in the network, you may do so, but with a higher copayment each time you use the nonnetwork provider. If you are frequently treated by nonnetwork doctors, the extra payments may cancel out the cost advantage of managed care.

Private fee-for-service plans. With Medicare Advantage private fee-for-service plans, the decision is more difficult. With most of these plans, there is no network, so there is no simple, automatic way to know that the doctors and other providers you use will accept the plan for any particular treatment or service. Before joining one of these plans, it is important to talk directly with your primary care doctor and any other doctor or other provider you regularly receive care from. Ask them whether they have experience with the plan you are considering and if so, whether they often refuse to accept the plan's terms. If your regular providers have little experience with the plan, or regularly refuse the plan's offered terms, joining that plan is probably not a good idea if you want to continue being treated by the same providers.

Help With Medicare Advantage Choices

People finding their way through the Medicare Advantage maze can get help from the State Health Insurance Assistance Program (SHIP), also frequently called the Health Insurance Counseling and Advocacy Program (HICAP). SHIP is funded by a combination of government grants and private donations and has no connection to the health care or insurance industries. SHIP provides free counseling about Medicare Advantage plans and medigap policies. Local staff can help you compare plans and policies. They can also tell you about other people's recent experiences with specific plans and policies.

To find the SHIP or HICAP office nearest you, contact your state's central SHIP or HICAP office (see the end of Chapter 13 for contact information).

COMPUTER

Compare plans on Medicare's website. Medicare's official website at www.medicare.gov offers a link that can give you the names and contact information for insurance companies offering Medicare Advantage plans available where you live. On the medicare.gov home page is a box titled "Find Health & Drug Plans"; clicking on that box takes you to a page called the "Medicare Plan Finder," which asks for your zip code and some personal information (optional). This page can then take you to information about specific Medicare Advantage plans being sold where you live, including basic information about what the policies cover and how to contact the insurance companies offering those plans.

In addition, it offers patient satisfaction ratings and statistics on how many people left each plan. Be aware, though, that the information on this page is only intended to give you basic information about these health plans. To get the detailed information you need—about costs, networks, and coverage—and to make a decision, you must contact the plans themselves. Also, you should always double-check such information with your local SHIP or HICAP office, because some of it may be out of date, and it may not include how many people have been dropped by the plan.

Access to Specialists and Preventive Care

The requirement that you must visit your primary care physician to obtain most specialist referrals is one of the main customer objections to managed care plans. If you are considering a Medicare Advantage managed care plan, try to learn how difficult it is to get referrals to specialists, using the suggestions in this section.

Coverage for Referrals

Your primary care physician refers you for testing, laboratory work, and treatment by most specialists. Speak with your primary care doctor and other providers you see regularly about their experiences with a particular plan. Does the plan often overrule the doctor's recommendation? Has the plan set guidelines for the doctors that might affect their ability to send you for treatment?

Access to Specialists

Medicare rules require managed care plans to develop a specific treatment plan for patients with a complex or serious condition, such as heart disease, cancer, or kidney failure. The treatment plan must outline what specialists you require, and it must allow you to see them without a referral from your primary care doctor. If you have a condition that requires care by specialists, find out from the plan whether your condition is considered sufficiently serious or complex to permit direct access to your specialists.

Preventive Care Options

Under Medicare rules, a managed care plan must permit members to obtain routine preventive women's health care screening from a gynecologist without first seeing a primary care physician. It must also permit a member to obtain Medicare-mandated mammograms without a referral. Find out from a managed care plan what other preventive care services—such as annual physical exam, prostate screening for men, cholesterol testing, or hearing exams—the plan permits members to schedule on their own.

Now You Get Coverage, Now You Don't

The government does not regulate Medicare Advantage plan coverage except to insist that the plans offer at least basic Medicare benefits. Nor is there any regulation of premiums and copayments. What this means is that Medicare Advantage plans are free to change coverage and charges at any time.

To compete with other insurance plans, your plan might expand coverage. In recent years, for example, short-term custodial care and overseas travel coverage have been added to many plans, although most charge an added premium for these "extras."

But plans will just as often cut back on coverage. In some plans, benefits are shifted from no-premium plans to deluxe plans with a premium. Raising copayments for specific services—particularly prescription drugs—is also common, as is restricting access to certain medications.

Prescription Drug Coverage

Since January 1, 2006, Medicare has offered prescription drug coverage through its Part D program. Many people enroll in Part D coverage through separate, stand-alone prescription drug plans. But many other people get prescription drug coverage through their Medicare Advantage plan, putting all their Medicare and supplemental coverage under one umbrella.

If you are thinking about joining a Medicare Advantage plan with prescription drug coverage, it's very important that you examine that coverage closely. When you are considering plans that include drug coverage, be sure to review that coverage just as you would when considering a stand-alone prescription drug plan. (See "Part D Prescription Drug Coverage" in Chapter 12.) In particular, you must determine whether the plan:

- includes on its formulary (its list of covered drugs) the drugs you regularly take
- charges reasonably low copayments for those drugs, and
- imposes no significant access restrictions to those drugs.

Once you have determined how well various Medicare Advantage plans cover the particular prescription drugs you take, you must weigh that information along with the other aspects of the plans discussed in this chapter. If you use many costly prescription drugs, how well a particular plan covers your drugs should be a major part of your decision. If you use few prescription drugs, then the other aspects of a plan may influence your decision more strongly.

Before you choose any Medicare Advantage plan, be sure to investigate the stand-alone Part D prescription drug plans that are available to you. Then, add the costs of the Part D stand-alone drug plan that best covers your drugs to the costs of a Medicare Advantage plan without drug coverage. It is this combination of costs and stand-alone Part D drug coverage benefits that you should consider when comparing these plans to other Medicare Advantage plans that include drug coverage.

Consider Total Costs, Not Just Premiums

Many Medicare Advantage plans, particularly managed care plans, charge relatively small premiums, often much lower than the combined premiums of a medigap policy plus a Part D drug plan. But premiums do not tell the whole story of what your supplemental Medicare coverage will actually cost you. This is because a Medicare Advantage plan's medical coverage and its prescription drug coverage will both require you to make copayments.

Most Medicare Advantage managed care plans charge a copayment for doctor visits (usually $5 to $20), and many older people frequently consult several doctors. Drug coverage is offered only for drugs on a plan's formulary (see "Part D Prescription Drug Coverage" in Chapter 12), and copayments vary depending on the type of medication and whether it is a brand name or generic drug. Within these parameters, Medicare Advantage drug copayments can run up to 25% of the drug's actual retail cost.

Only by comparing the copayments and premiums of various plans can you fully understand how much each plan is likely to cost you.

Extent of Service Area

Consider the extent of a plan's service area, particularly if you live in a rural or spread-out suburban area. If the service area is not broad enough to include a good selection of specialists, you may find your future care choices limited.

Also, find out whether the plan has what are called extended service areas. Some plans permit you to arrange medical care far from your home if you travel frequently or spend a regular part of the year away from its primary service area. This allows you to take care of nonurgent medical needs even if you are not at your primary residence.

Appealing a Plan's Decision About Your Care

About 30% of Medicare Advantage plan patients report having been denied coverage for medical care or services their plan deemed to be medically unnecessary or otherwise not covered. This phenomenon of having an insurance company overruling your doctor can be upsetting, and if it involves a serious condition, the plan's rejection can be devastating.

There is a standard process for you to appeal such a denial of coverage. Unfortunately, the first step in the review process is handled by the plan's insurance company itself. The plan will provide you with a written decision denying the coverage, which will also include instructions for filing the initial step in your appeal. This first step is a written request for reconsideration of their decision; you must do so within 60 days of receiving the notice from the plan denying coverage. The plan must then make a reconsideration decision within a set time limit: 30 days for a decision regarding coverage of a service you want to have performed; 60 days regarding payment for a service you've already had.

If the plan does not provide the coverage you want after this initial reconsideration, your next step is to appeal to an independent review entity (IRE), that does not work for the plan insurance company. At this point, your appeal will follow the same procedures as if you were in traditional Medicare, as explained in Chapter 13.

Other Plan Features

In addition to the key features of Medicare Advantage plans, many plans offer a variety of other features beyond basic Medicare coverage. The following extra benefits are either minor services some plans provide or major medical expenses for which some plans pay a small portion. If you are likely to use any of these benefits, a plan that offers them may be more attractive to you.

Short-Term Custodial Care

Following an injury, surgery, or a serious illness, you may not be strong enough to take care of yourself, but may not require skilled nursing care. Instead, you might need custodial care—help with dressing, bathing, eating, and other regular activities of daily living.

Custodial care is not covered at all by Medicare, unless you are already receiving skilled nursing care or therapy. But some Medicare Advantage plans do offer coverage for short-term custodial care, either at home from a certified home health care agency or in a certified nursing facility.

Such plans usually limit the number of home care visits or days you can spend in a nursing facility and charge copayments as well as a separate premium for the coverage. Despite these limitations, this can be valuable added coverage, because almost every senior can use this kind of care at some point.

Medical Equipment

By way of reminder, Medicare pays 80% of the amount it approves for most doctor-prescribed medical equipment, such as wheelchairs, hospital beds, ventilators, and prosthetic devices. But the recipient is responsible for 20% of the approved amount, plus anything above that amount if the equipment company does not accept Medicare assignment. Some Medicare Advantage plans pay the full cost of prescribed medical equipment, although it must be purchased or rented from a provider in the plan's network or, if you choose a private fee-for-service plan, from one that accepts the plan's term and payment level.

Chiropractic Care, Acupuncture, and Acupressure

Medicare pays for a very limited amount of chiropractic care and pays nothing at all for acupuncture or acupressure treatment. Some Medicare Advantage plans cover a greater amount of chiropractic care. And a few recognize the value of acupuncture and acupressure and pay for some of the cost.

Treatments must be received from providers in the plan's network or those who accept the plan's terms, and a copayment is almost always charged for each visit. However, if you regularly use one of these treatments and your practitioner happens to be in the plan's network or regularly accepts your fee-for-service plan's terms, this coverage can be a good money saver.

Foreign Travel Coverage

Many people travel abroad to visit family; others hope to do some foreign traveling during retirement. Medicare provides no coverage for medical costs incurred outside the United States, nor do most Medicare Advantage plans. But a few Medicare Advantage plans offer coverage for emergency care while abroad. And some also offer free or low-cost immunizations for foreign travel. If you plan on traveling abroad frequently or for long stays, this coverage can be valuable.

Eye Examinations and Glasses

Medicare covers only eye examinations and optometry services that are necessary because of an eye disease or other medical conditions. It does not pay for any part of regular vision testing or for eyeglasses or contact lenses, except after cataract surgery. A number of Medicare Advantage plans offer some kind of bonus vision coverage, although none of them pays the full cost of glasses.

Some plans cover an eye examination every two years and offer a set annual amount—usually $50 to $100—toward prescription lenses. Instead of a set amount, other plans offer discount examinations, lenses, frames, and contacts. The managed care plans include only network optometrists; they often simply hook you up to an existing chain of optometry clinics and provide you with a discount.

Hearing Tests and Hearing Aids

Some Medicare Advantage plans offer a free regular hearing exam, plus discounts on hearing aids. As with other Medicare Advantage coverage, the care must be obtained from a hearing center that is connected to the plan's network or that accepts the plan's terms and payment amounts.

Dental Work

A few Medicare Advantage plans offer discounts on dental work. The discounts usually include a low copayment for cleaning and examination and up to a 35% reduction in the cost of other services. The networks of dentists are usually quite limited, however. Finding a dentist who participates in the plan, and with whom you are comfortable, is the key to making this extra coverage worthwhile.

After-Hours Advice and Treatment

People don't always become ill during regular office hours. But visiting an emergency room can be a miserable—and often unnecessary—experience. Some Medicare Advantage managed care plans maintain 24-hour phone lines staffed by experienced nurses who can help you stay out of the ER. Other plans—usually provider-sponsored organizations or individual groups of doctors within larger HMOs—maintain evening and weekend clinics. There, you can consult a doctor for a lower copayment and less stress than a visit to an emergency room.

Chronic Disease Management and Wellness Programs

The managed care industry does better than original Medicare in recognizing how much money it saves by monitoring and managing chronic conditions and offering programs to improve general health. As a result, many managed care plans offer free or low-cost educational and monitoring programs to help people with chronic illness keep their conditions under control. Some programs include blood pressure and cholesterol education for heart patients, diabetic classes to control blood sugar levels, and classes for Parkinson's patients to reduce their risk of falls. Some plans offer programs to help people lead healthier lives, such as nutrition and exercise programs to improve flexibility and cardiac health, to help lose weight, and to quit smoking.

Comparing Medigap and Medicare Advantage Plans

After you've found several medigap (see Chapter 14) and Medicare Advantage plans that seem to fit your needs and budget, the best way to compare them is to view their costs and coverage side by side. Refer to the "Comparing Medigap to Managed Care" chart below for a comparison of the major benefits of medigap and Medicare Advantage plans. Then, use the next chart to help you compare the actual plans you are considering.

Your Rights When Joining, Leaving, or Losing a Medicare Advantage Plan

Insurance companies offering Medicare Advantage plans are free to charge whatever they want in premiums and copayments. They alone decide what types of medical care to cover, although they must provide at least the same basic services that Medicare does. Moreover, they may offer a Medicare Advantage plan one year and withdraw it the next—leaving its beneficiaries without coverage. Some Medicare Advantage plans do this region by region around the nation, deciding which spots are profitable enough for them and dropping plans—and the people in them—in places that don't measure up.

Despite this general corporate freedom for Medicare Advantage insurance companies, they must follow a few rules concerning people's rights to join or to leave their plans.

Joining in the First Six Months After Enrolling in Medicare

Within the first six months of enrolling in both Part A and Part B of Medicare, you have an unqualified right to join any Medicare Advantage plan that operates in the county of your primary residence. This means that the plan must accept you without any medical screening and on the same terms and conditions as anyone else of your age, regardless of your medical history or physical condition.

Comparing Medigap to Managed Care

	Medigap Plans	Managed Care Plans
Choice of Doctor and Providers	As long as doctor or other provider accepts Medicare, a medigap policy will cover whatever Medicare does.	Choice restricted to doctors and providers in the network. PPO and some HMO options allow nonnetwork providers at higher cost. Fee-for-service plans cover care only from providers who accept a plan's terms.
Access to Specialists	As long as specialist accepts Medicare, a medigap policy will cover whatever Medicare does.	Must get referral from primary care doctor to specialist also in plan's network. Limited direct access available for some serious conditions. In fee-for-service plans, specialist must accept plan's terms.
Premiums	Varies widely, with higher cost for plans with more services. Plan A: $50–$400/month. Plans B–G: $100–$400/month. Plans H–J: $75–$500/month ($150–$500/month for continuing Plans with drug coverage). Plan K: $50–$150/month. Plan L: $75–$200/month.	Usually no or low premium for basic HMO that only provides coverage equal to traditional Medicare Part A and Part B. Member must pay Medicare Part B premium. Broader coverage or more provider choices may cost between $25–$200/month.
Copayments	No copayments for services except under Plan N policies, which charge a $20 copayment for each doctor's office visit and $50 for each emergency room visit.	Require copayment for most services, $5–$25 per visit. In fee-for-service plans, may be responsible for up to 15% more than what plan pays.
Treatment Approval	Automatic if service is covered by Medicare.	Coverage denied if plan decides that treatment is medically unnecessary (perhaps if a different, cheaper treatment is available) or experimental.
Geographic Mobility	Most plans may be used wherever you obtain Medicare-covered services in the United States.	With managed care plans, non-emergency coverage limited to specific geographical area. Some plans offer care away from home. All plans must cover emergency care anywhere in the U.S.

Comparing Medigap to Managed Care (cont'd)

	Medigap Plans	Managed Care Plans
Emergency Care Overseas	Covered by Plans C–J, M, and N.	Some plans cover, but for a higher premium.
At-Home Recovery	Covered by Plans D, G, I, and J, but only if also receiving skilled nursing care at home (only if issued before June 1, 2010).	Some plans cover, but for a higher premium and copayment.
Eye Exams and Glasses	No, unless connected to illness or injury.	Most offer limited discounts on exams and lenses
Hearing Exams and Aids	No, unless connected to illness or injury.	Most offer limited discounts on exams and hearing aids.
Dental Discounts	No.	Some offer limited discounts.
Wellness Programs	No.	Many offer a variety of low-cost or free wellness programs, including heart-healthy education, weight loss, quitting smoking, and cholesterol management.
Chiropractic Care	Only if covered by Medicare.	Some offer broader coverage than Medicare.
Prescription Drugs	No coverage (except for some people who had a Plan H, I, or J prior to January 1, 2006 and who keep that plan). Requires purchase of a separate stand-alone Medicare prescription drug plan. Must add the premium cost of the Medicare drug plan to the cost of the medigap policy when comparing costs with a managed care plan. Must also compare the drug copayments of the drug plan against the copayments of the managed care plan.	Some plans offer coverage, with copayments of $5–$25 per prescription. Amount of copay depends on whether you use generic or brand-name medication and your specific plan's formulary list (which may have separate copayment levels for different medications).

Comparing Medigap Policies and Managed Care Plans

		Plan Name	Plan Name	Plan Name	Plan Name	Plan Name
Cost (monthly premium)						
Copayments (amount I must pay per visit)						
Other Medicare gaps left unfilled						
Is there coverage outside the plan?	Yes					
	No					
Cost of care outside the plan						
Dental care covered	Yes					
	No					
Choice of dentists	Yes					
	No					
Short-term custodial care	Yes					
	No					
Eyeglasses	Copayments					
	Visits per year					
Other services:						
Hearing exam	Yes					
	No					
Chiropractic	Yes					
	No					
Foreign travel	Yes					
	No					
Exercise program	Yes					
	No					
Other	Yes					
	No					
Prescription drug coverage (compare Part D drug plans and managed care plans)	Copayments					
	Annual limit					

Joining During a Plan's Open Enrollment Period

Every Medicare Advantage plan must have at least one month every year of what is called "open enrollment"—meaning that during that time anyone eligible for Medicare may join the plan regardless of their medical history or condition. Open enrollment is October 15 to December 7 each year, with coverage to begin the following January 1. But some plans also have more open enrollment during other months of the year.

Leaving the Plan

To leave a Medicare Advantage plan, you must give 30 days' written notice between January 1 and February 15.

Joining When Dropped From Another Medicare Advantage Plan

If you have been enrolled in a Medicare Advantage plan and that plan notifies you—by October 1—that at the end of the year it is dropping the plan in the county where you live, you have several options. You may return to original Medicare Part A and Part B coverage, and you are guaranteed the right to supplement that coverage by purchasing one of several medigap insurance policies. (See "Finding the Best Medicare Supplement" in Chapter 14 for a discussion of choosing a medigap policy.)

Or, you may enroll in any other Medicare Advantage plan being sold in your county, if the plan has not reached its membership limit for the year. You have this right to join any Medicare Advantage plan during a "Special Election Period" from October 1 through December 31. You may have your coverage begin on November 1, December 1, or January 1, as long as you apply before the date you choose.

Joining When Moving to a New Geographic Area

Each Medicare Advantage plan serves only a specific geographic area, often a single county. If you move from the plan's service area, you lose the right to continued coverage with that Medicare Advantage plan.

If you move out of a plan's service area and want a Medicare Advantage plan, you must apply to a plan that serves your new community. You have a guaranteed right—meaning that no medical screening is necessary—to join a Medicare Advantage plan there during that plan's open enrollment period. There's an exception if you enrolled in Medicare within the last six months: In that case, you may join any plan in the area at any time. ●

Medicaid and State Supplements to Medicare

When all types of medical expenses for older Americans are added up, Medicare pays for only about half of them. This leaves most people with considerable worry about how they will cover the rest. One approach is to buy private Medicare supplement insurance; another is to enroll in a Medicare Advantage plan. But many people cannot afford such insurance or health plans. For a number of low-income people, fortunately, there are some alternatives.

If you have a low income and few assets other than your home, you may qualify for assistance from your state's Medicaid program. Medicaid pays not only Medicare premiums, deductibles, and copayments, it also covers some services Medicare does not.

If you have too high an income or too many assets to be eligible for Medicaid, you may still qualify for one of several Medicaid-administered programs to help you meet medical costs: Qualified Medicare Beneficiary (QMB), Specified Low-Income Medicare Beneficiary (SLMB), or Qualifying Individual (QI). (For a discussion of these programs, see "Other State Assistance," below.)

Medicaid Defined

Medicaid's purpose is to help pay medical costs for financially needy people. The program was established by the federal government and is administered by the individual states. Medicaid operates in addition to Medicare to pay for some of the medical costs Medicare doesn't cover.

The basic difference between Medicare and Medicaid is simple: Medicare is available to most everyone age 65 or older, regardless of income or assets, while Medicaid is available to people over 65 or disabled, and to families with minor children, and in some states, to individuals of any age, who are financially needy. Just how "needy" you must be in order to get Medicaid is up to the state in which you live.

There are currently more than 30 million adults who receive some form of Medicaid assistance; about one-fourth of them are also on Medicare. (For a fuller comparison of the programs, see "Medicare: The Basics" in Chapter 12.)

There are federal guidelines for Medicaid, but they are fairly broad. Each state is permitted to make its own rules regarding eligibility, coverage, and benefits. This chapter explains the basic eligibility and coverage rules of Medicaid, and indicates where eligibility standards may be higher or lower than the basic levels.

Who Is Eligible

Generally, states use one of two ways to determine who is eligible for Medicaid. One way is to base eligibility on income and assets alone ("categorically needy"). The other is to base eligibility on income and assets plus medical costs ("medically needy").

Medicaid Eligibility Expanded to People Under 65 in Some States

Under Medicaid rules that have been in effect since the program's beginnings, eligibility has been limited to people age 65 or older, disabled, or with minor children, if they also met the financial standards discussed in the following sections. However, under the health care reform law passed in 2010, individual states may expand Medicaid eligibility to financially needy people of any age. Under a Supreme Court ruling upholding the law, states were given the option to expand the age of eligibility or not. As of early 2014, about half of the states had decided to expand Medicaid under the Affordable Care Act.

Categorically Needy

To qualify for Medicaid as categorically needy, your income and assets must be at or below certain dollar amounts. Some states use the same income and asset limits set by the federal Supplemental Security Income, or SSI, program. Other states establish their own Medicaid limits.

SSI-Based Standards

In most states you can automatically receive Medicaid if you are eligible for SSI assistance. To be eligible for SSI, you can't earn more than $700 to $1,400 per month, or $1,100 to $2,200 for a couple, depending on your state. Also, you can't possess cash and other assets of more than $2,000 for an individual and $3,000 for a couple.

Fortunately, a number of important assets are not counted in the SSI eligibility calculation. You may own your own home of any value; a car in some states only up to a certain market value; engagement and wedding rings; household goods; life insurance; and a burial fund. (For details of SSI eligibility rules, see Chapter 7.)

State Standards

States have gone in all directions when establishing their own Medicaid standards. In a few states, the standards are slightly less difficult to meet than SSI standards. In some others, the standards are stricter, including a dollar limit on the value of your home and lower limits on the values of your automobile and other property.

To find out your state's standards, contact your local county department of social services or department of welfare. You can also find the basic Medicaid eligibility requirements in your state by visiting the website of your state's Medicaid program. To find that website, go to medicaid.gov and click on the Medicaid tab, and then "By State."

If you are anywhere close to the eligibility limits in your state, consider applying for Medicaid or a state Medicare supplement (described in "Other State Assistance," below) as well.

Medically Needy

What if your income and assets are higher than your state Medicaid limit under categorically needy, but your medical expenses cancel much of this out? You may be what's called "medically needy," and eligible for Medicaid coverage in some states. Medically needy means your income and assets are over the Medicaid eligibility levels for your state but your current or expected medical expenses will reduce your income or assets to eligible levels.

This process of subtracting actual medical bills from income and assets is called "spending down," in Medicaid slang. This is because medical bills would force you to spend your extra money down to the point that you would meet eligibility levels.

The following states offer Medicaid coverage to medically needy people:

Arizona	Minnesota
Arkansas	Montana
California	Nebraska
Connecticut	New Hampshire
District of Columbia	New Jersey
Florida	New York
Georgia	North Carolina
Hawaii	North Dakota
Illinois	Pennsylvania
Iowa	Rhode Island
Kansas	Tennessee
Kentucky	Utah
Louisiana	Vermont
Maine	Virginia
Maryland	Washington
Massachusetts	West Virginia
Michigan	Wisconsin

EXAMPLE: Roberta's income is low, but her savings are $2,000 more than what is allowed to qualify for Medicaid as categorically needy by the rules in her state. However, surgery, home nursing care, physical therapy, and medication have left Roberta with medical bills of almost $3,000 (not paid for by Medicare). Roberta's state offers Medicaid coverage to the medically needy. If she paid her $3,000 medical bills, she would be spending her savings down to a level that would meet the Medicaid standards.

Instead of forcing her to spend that money and be reduced to Medicaid savings levels, Roberta qualifies immediately for Medicaid, which will pay the bills.

Medicaid When One Spouse Is in a Nursing Home

The Medicaid rules get a bit tricky when one spouse is in a nursing home while the other spouse remains at home. Most states look only at income in the nursing home resident's name, but some states consider the joint income of both. A monthly allowance is permitted for at-home spouses, who are also allowed to keep their homes and to retain between about $23,000 and $117,000 in other assets, depending on the state. These figures go up periodically, usually on July 1 of each year.

However, Medicaid may also place a lien on the home or on other assets in an amount equal to the entire amount Medicaid spends on nursing home care for the spouse. When the at-home spouse dies or sells the house, Medicaid will enforce the lien, taking money that the at-home spouse would otherwise be able to spend or leave to survivors.

To take best advantage of Medicaid coverage for long-term care, it is important to understand these rules and also the alternatives to nursing homes that can serve your needs while preserving as much of your savings as possible.

Long-term care and how it is paid for, including a comprehensive discussion of Medicaid nursing home rules, is covered fully in *Long-Term Care: How to Plan & Pay for It*, by Joseph Matthews (Nolo).

TIP

If your income and assets are a little too high for Medicaid, the government may help through other programs. If your income and assets are low but slightly too high for you to be eligible for Medicaid in your state, you may still be eligible for state Qualified Medicare Beneficiary (QMB), Specified Low-Income Medicare Beneficiary (SLMB), or Qualifying Individual (QI) benefits. These programs help meet medical costs not paid for by Medicare. You may also qualify for a low-income subsidy to help pay the costs that come with Medicare Part D prescription drug coverage. (See "Other State Assistance," below, for details.)

Determining Couples' Income and Assets

In determining your eligibility, Medicaid generally considers your income and assets plus those of your spouse, if you live together. If you are divorced or separated and living apart, your spouse's income and assets are not counted, except to the extent that your spouse is actually contributing to your support.

This rule of considering a spouse's income in determining Medicaid eligibility has had the unfortunate effect of keeping many older couples from marrying. They fear that if they marry, a serious illness could bankrupt both of them before they would become eligible for Medicaid assistance.

If both become eligible for Medicare, however, this loss of Medicaid may not be as serious. And if they marry, each becomes eligible at age 62 for Social Security dependents benefits based on the other's work record. If one person has earned considerably higher Social Security or civil service benefits than the other, this ability to get dependents benefits may make a considerable difference. (See Chapter 4 regarding dependents and Chapter 10 regarding civil service benefits.) The same is true of Social Security or civil service survivors benefits. Marriage would allow one spouse to claim these benefits when the other dies, and to collect them for life (see Chapters 5 and 10 for details).

Financial Help From Friends or Family

The income or assets of your children, other relatives, or friends, even if you live with them, are not considered in deciding your Medicaid eligibility. However, if you receive regular financial support from a relative or friend—cash or help with rent—Medicaid can consider that assistance as part of your income.

Also, if you are living rent free with children or other relatives and they give you all of your food and clothing, Medicaid could figure out a dollar amount for that support and count it as part of your income. This does not happen frequently. But it is possible that during the application process, the person reviewing your eligibility could visit your home and determine whether you are receiving substantial, regular income in the form of noncash support.

Medical Costs Covered by Medicaid

Medicaid covers the same kinds of services as Medicare and, in most states, also covers a number of medical services Medicare does not. One of its best features is that it covers most long-term care, both at home and in nursing facilities. This includes not only long-term skilled nursing care, but also nonmedical personal care—such as adult day care and at-home assistance with the activities of daily living (ADLs). These are the very needs that force many people into nursing homes and keep them there for years.

Medicaid also pays many of the amounts Medicare does not pay in hospital and doctor bills. Specifically, this means Medicaid pays:

- the inpatient hospital insurance deductible and coinsurance amounts that Medicare does not pay
- the Medicare Part B medical insurance deductible
- the 20% of the Medicare-approved doctors' fees that Medicare medical insurance does not pay, and
- the monthly premium charged for Medicare Part B medical insurance.

Services Covered in Every State

In every state, Medicaid completely covers certain medical services, paying whatever Medicare does not. It has to do so—it's a matter of federal law.

These services include:
- inpatient hospital or skilled nursing facility care
- nursing home care in approved facilities
- outpatient hospital or clinic treatment
- laboratory and X-ray services
- physicians' services
- home health care, and
- transportation—by ambulance, if necessary—to and from the place you receive medical services.

Most Prescription Drug Coverage Comes From a Separate Drug Plan Under Medicare Part D

For people who are eligible for both Medicare and Medicaid (known as "dual eligibles"), Medicaid does not provide much prescription drug coverage. Instead, a dually eligible person must receive most drug coverage through a Medicare Part D prescription drug plan. This may be with a Medicaid/Medicare managed care plan, or through a separate stand-alone Part D prescription plan.

People who become dually eligible will be automatically signed up for a Part D prescription drug plan. But a dual eligible who does not like the coverage or access to drugs offered by the automatic-enrollment plan may switch plans at any time. Automatic enrollment for dual eligibles and their right to switch plans is explained in the sections that discuss Part D prescription drug coverage in Chapters 12 and 13.

Medicare Part D provides coverage for most categories of drugs but not all. To fill these gaps, many state Medicaid programs cover some of the drugs, both prescription and over the counter, that Medicare Part D plans do not.

Optional Services

In all states, Medicaid also covers many other types of medical services (over 30 types, if you add them up). However, state Medicaid programs are not required to cover these optional services, and in some states they may charge a nominal fee for them. (See "Cost of Medicaid Coverage," below.)

Most states provide the following optional medical services commonly used by older people:

- **Prescription drugs.** All states provide Medicaid coverage for prescription drugs, though there may be a small copayment for each prescription filled. For people eligible for Medicare as well as Medicaid (known as "dual eligibles"), however, Medicaid no longer covers most drugs. Instead, dual eligibles receive their drug coverage through a separate Medicare Part D plan. In some states, though, Medicaid covers the cost of some prescription and over-the-counter drugs for dual eligibles that Medicare Part D plans do not cover.

- **Eye care.** Standard eyesight exams (every one to two years), plus the cost of eyeglasses.

- **Dental care.** Routine dental care, though the list of dentists whom you're allowed to see may be quite limited; most states also cover the cost of dentures.

- **Transportation.** Nonemergency transport to and from medical care, usually with some sort of van service under contract to the county.

- **Physical therapy.** Most states provide some amount of physical therapy beyond the very limited amount covered by Medicare.

- **Prosthetic devices.** All states cover the costs of medically necessary prosthetics beyond what is paid for by Medicare.

The types and amount of coverage for other optional services vary widely from state to state. However, these other optional services often include chiropractic care, podiatry, speech and occupational therapy, private-duty nursing, personal care services, personal care and case management services as part of home care, adult day care, hospice care, various preventive, screening, and rehabilitative services, and inpatient psychiatric care for those 65 and older.

Medicaid Through Managed Care

People who qualify for both Medicaid and Medicare are known as "dual eligibles." Increasingly, Medicaid and Medicare coverage is offered to dual eligibles through managed care (an HMO or similar plan). In some cases, these managed care plans are optional—a dual eligible can choose to receive traditional Medicare Part A and Part B and enroll in a Medicare Part D prescription drug plan, with Medicaid paying for the Medicare premiums and also providing some additional coverage (which varies from state to state). In many geographic regions, though, dual eligibles who want Medicaid coverage are required to enroll in a Medicaid managed care plan.

These Medicaid managed care plans operate like Medicare Advantage plans, explained in Chapter 15. Their advantage for the patient is that all medical care—inpatient and outpatient, and usually prescription drugs—is handled by a single program, instead of the patient having to negotiate both Medicare and Medicaid, and perhaps a private insurance company for drug coverage. However, these plans require that medical care be received only from certain doctors, hospitals, clinics, and other providers, and they control a patient's ability to see specialists.

Some of these managed care plans for dual eligibles are called "Special Needs Plans" (SNPs). This means that the plan is specially designed for older people, particularly those with chronic conditions. The major difference between an SNP for dual eligibles and other Medicaid managed care plans is that an SNP has what's called a "care coordinator" or "interdisciplinary care team" that helps the patient deal with the several different medical providers that older people often see, and tries to help the patient follow all medical instructions and properly take medications. If you are interested in an SNP for dual eligibles, you may enroll in it at any time of the year.

Each participating Medicaid/Medicare managed care plan for dual eligibles operates differently. Your county department of social services (or other department that administers Medicaid in your state) can explain what Medicaid managed care options are available to you. To help compare such a managed care plan with standard Medicare and Medicaid coverage—if your Medicaid program gives you the choice— contact the SHIP office nearest you for free counseling (see contact information at the end of Chapter 13).

⚠ CAUTION

Coverage changes frequently. Medicaid coverage for optional services changes frequently, with states adding some services and dropping others. Check with your local social services or social welfare office for the latest. You must also find out the terms on which such optional services are offered. Sometimes you can obtain such services only if the care is provided by county or other local health clinics, rather than from a private doctor or clinic of your choice.

Requirements for Coverage

Even if a particular medical service or treatment—such as a prosthetic device—is generally covered by Medicaid, you must make sure that the care was prescribed by a doctor, administered by a provider who participates in Medicaid, and determined to be medically necessary.

Care Must Be Prescribed by Doctor

The medical service you receive must be prescribed by a doctor. For example, Medicaid will not pay for chiropractic services or physical therapy you seek on your own. And if it pays for certain prescription medications not covered by Medicare, it might not pay for an equivalent medicine you could buy over-the-counter.

For services in which a medical doctor is generally not involved— such as regular eye exams or dental care—Medicaid may place restrictions on how often you can obtain the service and who can authorize it. And Medicaid will cover some services for those who qualify as medically needy only if the care is provided by certain public health hospitals, clinics, or agencies.

Provider Must Be Participating in Medicaid

You must receive your treatment or other care from a doctor, a facility, or another medical provider participating in Medicaid.

The provider must accept Medicaid payment—or Medicare plus Medicaid—as full payment. And if you see a nonphysician such as a physical therapist or chiropractor, or are visited by a home care agency, that provider must be approved by Medicaid.

Not all doctors and clinics accept Medicaid patients. You can get referrals from your local social welfare office. And before you sign up with any doctor or other provider, ask whether they accept Medicaid payment.

Treatment Must Be Medically Necessary

All care must be approved by Medicaid as medically necessary. For inpatient care, the approval process is similar to the one used for Medicare coverage. By requesting your admission to a hospital or another facility, your doctor sets the approval process in motion. You won't need to be involved. In fact, you won't even hear about it unless the facility decides you should be discharged before your doctor thinks you should. (See "What to Do If You Are Denied Coverage," below.)

You must get prior approval from a Medicaid consultant before you obtain certain medical services. The rules vary from state to state, requiring prior approval for such services as elective surgery, some major dental care, leasing of medical equipment, and nonemergency inpatient hospital or nursing facility care.

If a particular medical service requires prior Medicaid approval, your doctor or the facility will contact Medicaid directly. You may be asked to get an examination by another doctor before Medicaid will approve the care, but this does not happen often.

If you have questions about the approval process, discuss it with both your doctor and a Medicaid worker at your local social service or welfare office. Ask what Medicaid considers most important in making the decision about the medical care you are seeking. Relay that information to your doctor, so that the doctor can provide the necessary information to Medicaid.

Cost of Medicaid Coverage

Almost all Medicaid-covered care is free. And Medicaid also pays your Medicare premium, deductibles, and copayments if you are a dual eligible. However, there are a few circumstances in which you might have to pay small amounts for Medicaid-covered care.

No Payments to Medical Providers

Hospitals, doctors, and other medical care providers who accept Medicaid patients must accept Medicare's approved charges—or the amount approved directly by Medicaid if it is not covered by Medicare—as the total allowable charges. They must accept as payment in full the combination of payments from Medicare and Medicaid, or Medicaid alone; they cannot bill you for the 15% more than the Medicare-approved amount (which they could do if you were not on Medicaid).

Fees to State Medicaid Agency for Services

Federal law permits states to charge some small fees to people who qualify for Medicaid as medically needy. (See "Who Is Eligible," above, for the definition.) If you qualify as categorically needy, however, states can charge you a fee only for optional covered services. (See "Optional Services," above, for a description of these services.) State Medicaid charges will take one of three forms: an enrollment fee, a monthly premium, or copayments.

Enrollment Fee

Some states charge a small, one-time-only fee when medically needy people first enroll in Medicaid. This fee cannot be charged to people who are considered categorically needy.

Monthly Premium

States are permitted to charge a small monthly fee to people who qualify for Medicaid as medically needy. The premium may be charged whether or not Medicaid services are actually used that month. The amounts vary with income and assets, but usually come to no more than a few dollars.

Copayments

State Medicaid programs are permitted to charge a copayment for each Medicaid-covered service you receive. A copayment can be charged to the medically needy for any service, and to the categorically needy for optional services only. (See "Optional Services," above, for a description of these services.)

Medicaid and Private Health Insurance

Insurance companies are not permitted to sell you a medigap insurance policy if you are on Medicaid. However, you are permitted to have other private health insurance—such as that provided by a retirement program or a policy you purchase to protect against a specific illness—and still qualify for Medicaid.

Medicaid will deduct the amount of your private health insurance premiums from the calculation of your income when determining whether you are under the allowable income levels to qualify.

However, if you do have private health insurance, and a medical service is covered by both your insurance and by Medicaid, Medicaid will pay only the amount your insurance doesn't. If you receive a payment directly from your insurance company after Medicaid has paid that bill, you must return that insurance money to Medicaid.

Other State Assistance

Many people with low income and assets have trouble paying the portion of medical bills left unpaid by Medicare and cannot afford private medigap insurance, but do not qualify for Medicaid. If this is your situation, you may still get help paying Medicare premiums and portions of Medicare-covered costs that Medicare does not pay.

Three cost-reduction programs—called Qualified Medicare Beneficiary (QMB), Specified Low-Income Medicare Beneficiary (SLMB), and Qualifying Individual (QI)—are administered by each state's Medicaid program. They do not offer the extensive coverage beyond Medicare that Medicaid does, but the savings to you in Medicare-related medical costs can be substantial.

You Also Qualify for Medicare Part D Prescription Drug Program Extra Help

If you qualify for any of the state assistance programs described in this section, you also qualify for a low-income subsidy called Extra Help to help pay the personal out-of-pocket costs that come with Medicare's Part D prescription drug coverage. The Medicare Part D program and Extra Help are explained in Chapter 12. You can apply for the Part D low-income subsidy when you apply for other state assistance programs (discussed below).

Qualified Medicare Beneficiary (QMB)

If you are eligible for Medicare and meet the income and asset eligibility requirements for the QMB program, your state will pay all of your Medicare Part A and Part B premiums, deductibles, and coinsurance. Depending on how much you use Medicare-covered services in a year, this could mean a savings of up to several thousand dollars.

Income Limits

To be eligible as a QMB, your income must be no more than slightly above the Federal Poverty Guidelines (FPG). This figure is established each year by the federal government; in 2015, the income level is about $12,000 per year for an individual; about $16,000 per year for a married couple. These figures are slightly higher in Alaska and Hawaii. Some states, however, allow residents to have higher income and still qualify as QMBs.

It's important to know, however, that certain amounts of income are not counted in determining QMB eligibility. Particularly if you are still working and most of your income comes from your earnings, you may be able to qualify as a QMB even if your total income is almost twice the FPG. QMB follows the SSI guidelines for countable income, described in Chapter 7. If, after applying these rules, the figure you arrive at is anywhere close to the QMB qualifying limits, it is worth applying for it.

Asset Limits

There is a limit on the value of the assets you can own and still qualify as a QMB—generally, no more than about $7,000 for an individual and about $10,000 for a married couple. However, many assets, such as your house, your car, and certain personal and household goods, are not part of the resources that are counted. (See "Who Is Eligible" in Chapter 7 for how SSI counts assets.)

Specified Low-Income Medicare Beneficiary (SLMB) and Qualifying Individual (QI)

If your income is slightly too high for you to qualify for QMB benefits, you may still be eligible for one of two other state medical assistance programs: Specified Low-Income Medicare Beneficiary (SLMB) or Qualifying Individual (QI). The resource limits for eligibility are the same as for a QMB, but the income limits are 20% to 80% higher, depending on the program.

If your counted monthly income—after the same adjustments made in calculating income for SSI purposes (see Chapter 7 for these calculations)—is under $1,400 for an individual, or $1,800 for a couple, you are likely to qualify for SLMB or QI support. (These figures go up slightly each year.)

Because the SLMB and QI programs are for people with higher incomes, they have fewer benefits than the QMB program. The SLMB and QI programs pay all or part of the Medicare Part B monthly premium, but do not pay any Medicare deductibles or coinsurance amounts. Nonetheless, this means potential savings of more than $500 per year.

Applying for Medicaid, QMB, SLMB, or QI

Before you can get coverage by the Medicaid, QMB, SLMB, or QI programs, you must file a written application separate from your Medicare application. An application for Medicaid also serves as an application for QMB, SLMB, or QI. If you are found ineligible for one program, you may still be found eligible for one of the others.

This section explains some of the things you will need to do and documents you will need to gather to file an application for Medicaid, QMB, SLMB, or QI.

Where to File

To qualify for Medicaid or the QMB, SLMB, or QI programs, you must file a written application with the agency that handles Medicaid in your state—usually your county's department of social services or social welfare department.

In many states, if you are applying for SSI benefits at your local Social Security office, that application will also serve as a Medicaid application. You will be notified of Medicaid eligibility at the same time as you receive notice regarding SSI. (See Chapter 7 for a full discussion of the SSI program.)

If you or your spouse is hospitalized when you apply for Medicaid, ask to see a medical social worker in the hospital. He or she will help you fill out the application.

Required Documents and Other Information

Because eligibility for Medicaid and the QMB, SLMB, or QI programs depends on your financial situation, many of the documents you must bring to the Medicaid office are those that will verify your income and assets.

Although a Medicaid eligibility worker might require additional specific information from you, you will at least be able to get the application process started if you bring:

- pay stubs, income tax returns, Social Security benefits information, and other evidence of your current income

- papers showing all your savings and other financial assets, such as bankbooks, insurance policies, and stock certificates
- automobile registration papers if you own a car
- your Social Security card or number
- information about your spouse's income and separate assets, if the two of you live together, and
- medical bills from the previous three months, as well as medical records or reports to confirm any medical condition that will require treatment in the near future. If you don't have copies of these bills, records, or reports, bring the names and addresses of the doctors, hospitals, or other medical providers who are treating you.

Even if you don't have all these papers, go to your local social services or social welfare department office and file your application for Medicaid as soon as you think you may qualify. The Medicaid eligibility workers will tell you what other documents you need—and sometimes can explain how to get necessary papers you don't have, or help get them for you.

Application Procedure

A Medicaid eligibility worker—or an SSI eligibility worker if you apply for SSI at a local Social Security office—will interview you and assist you in filling out your application. There may be lots of forms to fill out, and you may have to return to the office for several different interviews.

TIP

Don't get discouraged. Delays, repeated forms, and interviews do not mean you will not be approved. The state has created procedures that make it difficult for people to get through the qualification process, driving some people to give up on benefits to which they are entitled. Patience is not only a virtue, it is an absolute necessity.

Normally, you will receive a decision on your Medicaid application within a couple of weeks after you complete the forms and provide the necessary information. The law requires that a decision be made within 45 days. If you don't hear from Medicaid within a month after you apply, call the eligibility worker who interviewed you. Sometimes it takes a little polite pushing to get a decision out of an overworked social services agency.

Retroactive Benefits

If you are found to be eligible and have already incurred medical bills, Medicaid may cover some of them. This retroactive eligibility can go back to the beginning of the third month before the date you filed your application. Make sure to show your Medicaid eligibility worker any medical bills you have from this period.

If you are denied eligibility for Medicaid, QMB, SLMB, or QI, you have a right to appeal.

Review of Eligibility

How long your Medicaid coverage will last depends on your finances and your medical costs. Medicaid eligibility is reviewed periodically, usually every six months and at least once a year.

If, upon review, the Medicaid agency finds that your financial situation has changed to put you over the eligibility limits for your state's Medicaid program, your coverage may be discontinued. Until then, you will be continued on Medicaid or QMB, SLMB, or QI coverage, even if your income or assets put you over the limits some months before.

Likewise, if you became eligible for Medicaid as medically needy because of high medical costs, but those medical costs have ended, you may be dropped from Medicaid when your review is completed. Until the review, however, you will remain on Medicaid regardless.

If new medical costs arise after your coverage has been ended, you may apply again for Medicaid coverage.

What to Do If You Are Denied Coverage

If you are denied Medicaid, QMB, SLMB, or QI coverage for which you believe you are eligible, go immediately to the office where you applied. Ask about the procedure in your state for getting a hearing to appeal that decision. In some states, if you request a hearing in writing within ten days after receiving the notice saying that your coverage is going to end, your coverage can stay in effect until after the hearing officer makes a decision.

At an appeal hearing, you will be able to present any documents or other papers—proof of income, assets, medical bills—that you think support your claim. You will also be allowed to explain why the Medicaid decision was wrong. If expected medical bills, which you claim will qualify you as medically needy, are the main question concerning your eligibility, then a letter from your doctor explaining your condition and the expected cost of treatment would be important.

The hearing itself is usually held at or near the welfare or social service office. You are permitted to have a friend, relative, social worker, or lawyer, or another representative appear with you to help at the hearing.

Getting Assistance With Your Appeal

If you are denied Medicaid, QMB, SLMB, or QI, you may want to consult with someone experienced in the subject to help you prepare your appeal. The best place to find quality free assistance with these matters is the nearest office of the State Health Insurance Assistance Program (SHIP) (see the end of Chapter 13 for contact information).

If there is no SHIP office near you, you may be able to find other assistance through your local senior center or by calling the senior information line listed in the white pages of your telephone directory.

You can also hire a Medicaid lawyer or health care lawyer to help.

Although the exact procedure for obtaining this hearing, and the hearing itself, may be slightly different from state to state, they all resemble very closely the hearings given to applicants for Social Security benefits (covered in Chapter 9).

You should be notified of the decision on your appeal within 90 days after the hearing.

For more information, see Nolo's series of articles on Medicaid appeals at www.nolo.com/legal-encyclopedia/medicaid-law. ●

Index

⚖ NOLO *Online Legal Forms*

Nolo offers a large library of legal solutions and forms, created by Nolo's in-house legal staff. These reliable documents can be prepared in minutes.

Create a Document

- **Incorporation.** Incorporate your business in any state.
- **LLC Formations.** Gain asset protection and pass-through tax status in any state.
- **Wills.** Nolo has helped people make over 2 million wills. Is it time to make or revise yours?
- **Living Trust (avoid probate).** Plan now to save your family the cost, delays, and hassle of probate.
- **Trademark.** Protect the name of your business or product.
- **Provisional Patent.** Preserve your rights under patent law and claim "patent pending" status.

Download a Legal Form

Nolo.com has hundreds of top quality legal forms available for download—bills of sale, promissory notes, nondisclosure agreements, LLC operating agreements, corporate minutes, commercial lease and sublease, motor vehicle bill of sale, consignment agreements and many, many more.

Review Your Documents

Many lawyers in Nolo's consumer-friendly lawyer directory will review Nolo documents for a very reasonable fee. Check their detailed profiles at **Nolo.com/lawyers**.

DISCARD

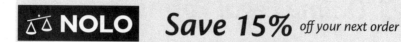
On Nolo.com you'll also find:

Books & Software

Nolo publishes hundreds of great books and software programs for consumers and
business owners. Order a copy, or download an ebook version instantly, at Nolo.com.

Online Legal Documents

You can quickly and easily make a will or living trust, form an LLC or corporation, apply
for a trademark or provisional patent, or make hundreds of other forms—online.

Free Legal Information

Thousands of articles answer common questions about everyday legal issues
including wills, bankruptcy, small business formation, divorce, patents,
employment, and much more.

Plain-English Legal Dictionary

Stumped by jargon? Look it up in America's most up-to-date source for
definitions of legal terms, free at nolo.com.

Lawyer Directory

Nolo's consumer-friendly lawyer directory provides in-depth profiles of lawyers all
over America. You'll find all the information you need to choose the right lawyer.

SOA20

"The inside scoop on how to get the most out of the current system..."
ACCOUNTING TODAY

Your complete guide to Social Security retirement and medical benefits

Everyone wants the highest possible retirement and pension income, not to mention the best medical coverage. Find out what you're entitled to with *Social Security, Medicare & Government Pensions*—completely updated for 2015.

Social Security benefits. Figure out how to get retirement, disability, dependents and survivors benefits, or Supplemental Security Income (SSI). Decide whether it's best to claim benefits early, at full retirement age, or not until you turn 70—and how to time your claims so you and your spouse get the best benefits.

Medicare & Medicaid. Learn how to qualify for and enroll in both programs, including Medicare Part D drug coverage.

Medigap insurance & Medicare Advantage plans. Understand what new Medigap policies are available (and old ones that aren't), compare Medigap and Medicare Advantage plans, and choose what's best for you.

Government pensions & veterans benefits. Discover when and how to claim the benefits you have earned.

Whether you're looking for yourself or helping a parent, you'll find valuable information here, including how to file many essential forms online.

Joseph Matthews, an attorney since 1971, has written several Nolo titles, including *How to Win Your Personal Injury Claim* and *Long-Term Care*.

This book comes with a **website**

With this book you get access to a unique web page on nolo.com where you can:

- Stay current with legal updates to this book
- Access podcasts and blogs

And in nolo.com's Social Security & Retirement center, you'll find even more help from the experts at Nolo:

- Hundreds of valuable articles and FAQs
- Useful legal forms
- In-depth profiles of elder law attorneys in your area

www.nolo.com

LAW for ALL

Nolo is passionate about making the law accessible to everyone. Our high-quality books, software, legal forms, and online lawyer directory have helped millions of people find answers to their everyday legal and business questions.

ISBN: 978-1-4133-2104-3

$29.99

SUPPLEMENT IX
Nelson Algren to David Wagoner

American Writers
A Collection of Literary Biographies

JAY PARINI
Editor in Chief

SUPPLEMENT IX
Nelson Algren to David Wagoner

Charles Scribner's Sons
an imprint of the Gale Group
New York • Detroit • San Francisco • London • Boston • Woodbridge, CT

Copyright © 2002 by Charles Scribner's Sons, an imprint of the Gale Group

Charles Scribner's Sons
1633 Broadway
New York, New York 10019

1 3 5 7 9 11 13 15 17 19 20 18 16 14 12 10 8 6 4 2

Library of Congress Cataloging-in-Publication Data

American writers; a collection of literary biographies.

Leonard Unger, editor in chief. p. cm.

The 4-vol. main set consists of 97 of the pamphlets originally published
as the University of Minnesota pamphlets on American writers; some have been
rev. and updated. The supplements cover writers not included in the original series.
Supplement 2, has editor in chief, A. Walton Litz; Retrospective suppl. 1, c1998, was edited by A. Walton Litz & Molly Weigel; Suppl. 5 has editor-in-chief, Jay Parini. Includes bibliographies and index.
Contents: v. 1. Henry Adams to T. S. Eliot - v. 2. Ralph Waldo Emerson to Carson McCullers - v. 3. Archibald MacLeish to George Santayana - v. 4. Isaac Bashevis Singer to Richard Wright - Supplement: 1, pt. 1. Jane Addams to Sidney Lanier. 1, pt. 2. Vachel Lindsay to Elinor Wylie. 2, pt.1. W.H. Auden to O. Henry. 2, pt. 2. Robison Jeffers to Yvor Winters. - 4, pt. 1. Maya Angelou to Linda Hogan. 4, pt. 2. Susan Howe to Gore Vidal. 5. Russell Banks to Charles Wright.
ISBN 0-684-19785-5 (set) - ISBN 0-684-13662-7 1.
American literature-History and criticism. 2. American literature-Bio-bibliography. 3. Authors, American-Biography. I. Unger, Leonard. II. Litz, A. Walton. III Weigel, Molly. IV. University of Minnesota pamphlets on American writers.

PS129 .A55 810'.9 73-001759

ISBN 0-684-80648-7

Acknowledgment is gratefully made to those publishers and individuals who have permitted the use of the following material in copyright.

Rachel Carson
Excerpts from *The Edge of the Sea.* Houghton Mifflin Company, 1955. Copyright © 1955 by Rachel L. Carson, renewed 1983 by Roger Christie. All rights reserved. Reprinted by permission of Houghton Mifflin Company and Frances Collins, Trustee. Excerpts from *Silent Spring.* Houghton Mifflin Company, 1980. Copyright © 1962 by Rachel L. Carson, renewed 1990 by Roger Christie. All rights reserved. Reprinted by permission of Houghton Mifflin Company and Frances Collins, Trustee.

Amy Clampitt
Excerpts from "A Baroque Sunburst," "A Hedge of Rubber Trees," "A Hermit Thrush," "A Procession at Candlemas," "A Silence," "Amherst," "The August Darks," "Black Buttercups," "Fireweed," "Iola, Kansas," "Losing Track of Language," "Man Feeding Pigeons," "Margaret Fuller, 1847," "Marine Surface, Low Overcast," "Meridian," "The Olive Groves of Thasos," "The Prairie," "Salvage," "The Spruce Has No Taproot," "Syrinx," "Thermopylae," "Townhouse Interior with Cat," "The Waterfall," "Witness," in *The Collected Poems of Amy Clampitt.* Alfred A. Knopf, Inc., 1997. Copyright © 1997 by the Estate of Amy Clampitt. Used by permission of Alfred A. Knopf, a division of Random House, Inc.

Zelda Fitzgerald

Excerpts from the dedication in *The Collected Writings.* Edited by Matthew J. Bruccoli. Charles Scribner's Sons, 1991. Copyright © 1991 by The Trustees under agreement dated July 3, 1975, created by Frances Scott Fitzgerald Smith. All rights reserved. Reprinted with permission of Scribner, a division of Simon & Schuster. In the UK by permission of Harold Ober Associates, Inc. Excerpts from a letter to F. Scott Fitzgerald in February 1920; a letter to F. Scott Fitzgerald in March 1932; a letter to F. Scott Fitzgerald in June 1933; a letter to F. Scott Fitzgerald in March 1934, in *The Collected Writings.* Edited by Matthew J. Bruccoli. Introduction by Mary Gordon. Charles Scribner's Sons, 1991. Copyright © 1991 by The Trustees under agreement dated July 3, 1975, created by Frances Scott Fitzgerald Smith. All rights reserved. Reprinted with permission of Scribner, a division of Simon & Schuster. In the UK by permission of Harold Ober

Associates, Inc. Excerpts from "Scandelabra," in *The Collected Writings*. Edited by Matthew J. Bruccoli. Introduction by Mary Gordon. Charles Scribner's Sons, 1991. Copyright © 1991 by The Trustees under agreement dated July 3, 1975, created by Frances Scott Fitzgerald Smith. All rights reserved. Reprinted with permission of Scribner, a division of Simon & Schuster. In the UK by permission of Harold Ober Associates, Inc. Excerpts from *Save Me the Waltz*. Southern Illinois University Press, 1967. Copyright 1932 by Charles Scribner's Sons. Copyright renewed 1960 by Frances Scott Fitzgerald Lanahan. Copyright © 1967 by Southern Illinois University Press. All rights reserved. Reprinted with permission of Scribner, a division of Simon & Schuster. In the UK by permission of Harold Ober Associates, Inc. Gordon, Mary. Excerpts from the introduction to *The Collected Writings by Zelda Fitzgerald*. Edited by Matthew J. Bruccoli. Charles Scribner's Sons, 1991. Copyright © 1991 by The Trustees under agreement dated July 3, 1975, created by Frances Scott Fitzgerald Smith. All rights reserved. Reprinted with permission of Scribner, a division of Simon & Schuster. Fitzgerald, F. Scott. Excerpts from a letter to Edmund Wilson in January 1922; a letter to Maxwell Perkins on August 12, 1922; a letter to Maxwell Perkins on August 27, 1924; a letter to Zelda Fitzgerald in 1930; a letter to Dr. Squires on March 14, 1932; a letter to Adolf Meyer on April 10, 1933; a letter to Zelda Fitzgerald in 1935; a letter to Sara Murphy on March 30, 1936, in *F. Scott Fitzgerald: A Life in Letters*. Edited by Matthew J. Bruccoli. Scribner, 1994. Copyright © 1994 by the Trustees under agreement dated July 3, 1975, created by Frances Scott Fitzgerald Smith. Reprinted with permission of Scribner, a Division of Simon & Schuster. In the UK by permission of Harold Ober Associates, Inc.

Robert Francis
Excerpts from "Biography," "The Black Hood," "Bronze," "By Night," "City," "Fall," "Glass," "The Goldfish Bowl," "Juniper," "Come Out into the Sun," "Old Man Feeding Hens," "Sheep," "The Sound I Listened For," "The Spy," "Two Words," "Willow Woman," in *Collected Poems: 1936–1976*. University of Massachusetts Press, 1976. Copyright © 1976 by Robert Francis. All rights reserved. Reproduced by permission. Excerpts from "The Brass Candlestick," "Gray Squirrel," "Play Ball," in *Late Fire, Late Snow: New and Uncollected Poems*. University of Massachusetts Press, 1992. Text copyright © 1992 by the Trustees for the Estate of Robert Francis. Reproduced by permission. Excerpts from "Blood Stains" and "Silent Poem," in *Like Ghosts of Eagles: Poems, 1966–1974*. University of Massachusetts Press, 1974. Copyright © 1953, 1967, 1968, 1969, 1970, 1971, 1972, 1973, 1974 by Robert Francis. All rights reserved. Reproduced by permission.

Tony Kushner.
Excerpts from *Theater Week,* no. 1, January 14–21, 1991, for "Look Back-and Forward-in Anger," by Tom Szentgyorgyi. Cohen, Rabbi Norman J. Excerpts from "Wrestling with Angels." Minnie Petrie Synagogue, Hebrew- Union College-Jewish Institute of Religion. Excerpts from "Characters," "Production Notes," in *A Bright Room Called Day*. Theatre Communications Group, 1994. Copyright © 1987, 1992, 1994 by Tony Kushner. Excerpts from *Angels in America: A Gay Fantasia on National Themes, Part Two; Perestroika*. Theatre Communications Group, 1995. Copyright © 1992, 1994 by Tony Kushner. All rights reserved. Reproduced by permission. Excerpts from *Thinking About the Longstanding Problems of Virtue and Happiness: Essays, a Play, Two Poems, and a Prayer*. Theatre Communications Group, 1995. Copyright © 1995 by Tony Kushner. All rights reserved. Reproduced by permission. Vorlicky, Robert. Excerpts from "Introduction: "'Two Not One'" and "Afterword," in *Tony Kushner in Conversation*. Edited by Robert Vorlicky. The University of Michigan Press, 1998. Copyright © by the University of Michigan, 1998. All rights reserved. Reproduced by permission.

William Matthews
Excerpts from *Antaeus,* v. 47, 1982 for "The Interpretation of Dreams," by William Matthews/ autumn, 1991 for "Mingus in Diaspora," by William Matthews. Both reproduced by permission. Excerpts from *The Georgia Review,* v. XLVI, winter, 1992 for "Jazz and Poetry: A Conversation," by Yusef Komunyakaa and William Matthews. Copyright, 1992, by the University of Georgia. Excerpts from *Missouri Review,* v. 6, 1982 for "We Shall All Be Born Again but We Shall Not All Be Saved," by William Matthews. Reproduced by permission. Excerpts from *Moose,* for "Masterful," by William Matthews. Reproduced by permission. Excerpts from *New England Review,* v. IV, no. 1, autumn 1981 for "Rosewood, Ohio," by William Matthews. Reproduced by permission. Excerpts from *Ohio Review,* v. 44, 1989 for "It Don't Mean a Thing If It Ain't Got That Swing," by William Matthews/ v. 13, spring, 1972. Copyright © 1972 by the Editors of the *Ohio Review.* Both reproduced by permission. Excerpts from *Poetry,* v. 136, June, 1980 for "That We Keep Them Alive," by Marvin Bell/ v. 161, February 1993 for "Looking Toward the Fin de Siecle," by Alfred Corn/ v. 162, June, 1993 for "Time," by William Matthews/ v. 174, May, 1999 for "Late Night Music," by Bill Christophersen. Copyright 1980, 1993, 1999 Modern Poetry Association. Reproduced by permission of the publisher and the authors. Excerpts from *Quarterly West,* v. 49, autumn, 1999. © 1999 by Quarterly West. Reproduced by permission. Excerpts from *Seattle Review,* for "Pissing off the Back of the Boat into the Nevernais Canal," by William Matthews. Reproduced by permission. Excerpts from "A Happy Childhood," in *A Happy Childhood*. Little, Brown and Company, 1984. Copyright © 1984 by William Matthews. All rights reserved. Reproduced by permission. Excerpts from "The Bar at the Andover Inn," "Euphemisms," "Mingus in Shadow," in *After All: Last Poems*. Houghton Mifflin Company, 1998. Copyright © 1998 by the Estate of William Matthews. Reprinted by permission of Houghton Mifflin Company. All rights reserved. Excerpts from "Blue Notes," "Hope," in *Foreseeable Futures*. Houghton Mifflin, 1987. Copyright © 1987 by William Matthews. All rights reserved. Reprinted by permission of Houghton Mifflin Company. Excerpts from "Spring Snow," in *Rising and Falling*. Little, Brown and Company, 1979. Copyright © 1973, 1974, 1975, 1976, 1977, 1978, 1979 by William Matthews. All rights reserved. Reproduced by permission. Excerpts from "Blues for John Coltrane, Dead at 41," "The Search Party," in *Ruining the New Road*. Random House, 1970. Copyright © 1967, 1968, 1969, 1970 by William Matthews. All rights reserved. Reproduced by permission. Excerpts from "Another Beer," "The Cat," in *Sleek for the Long Flight*. Random House, 1972. © 1972, 1988 William Matthews. Reproduced by permission. Excerpts from "The Waste Carpet," in *Sticks & Stones*. Pentagram Press,

Editorial and Production Staff

Managing Editor
ANNA SHEETS NESBITT

Copyeditors
BARBARA C. BIGELOW
MELISSA A. DOBSON
JESSICA HORNIK EVANS
GRETCHEN GORDON
ROBERT JONES
JEAN KAPLAN
MICHAEL L. LEVINE
MARCIA MERRYMAN MEANS

Proofreaders
BARBARA C. BIGELOW
UMA KUKATHAS

Permission Researcher
SARAH TOMASEK

Indexer
KATHARYN DUNHAM

Associate Publisher
TIMOTHY DeWERFF

Publisher
FRANK MENCHACA

List of Subjects

Introduction

In a book on Charles Dickens, G. K. Chesterton wrote: "There is a great deal of difference between the eager man who wants to read a book, and the tired man who wants a book to read." This volume of articles on American writers is for eager readers who want a book to read. That is, it is for those with enough energy to pursue a book, to read it critically, and to examine its context as well as its content. My hope is that the eighteen articles included here will aid and abet serious readers in the work of interpretation and evaluation.

This series had its origin in a remarkable series of critical and biographical monographs that appeared between 1959 and 1972. The Minnesota Pamphlets on American Writers were incisively written and informative, treating ninety-seven American writers in a format and style that attracted a devoted following of readers. The series proved invaluable to a generation of students and teachers, who could depend on these reliable and interesting critiques of major figures. The idea of reprinting these essays occurred to Charles Scribner, Jr. (1921–1995). The series appeared in four volumes entitled *American Writers: A Collection of Literary Biographies* (1974).

Since then, eight supplements have appeared, treating well over two hundred American writers: poets, novelists, playwrights, essayists, and autobiographers. The idea has been consistent with the original series: to provide clear, informative essays aimed at the general reader and intelligent student. These essays often rise to a high level of craft and critical vision, but they are meant to introduce a writer of some importance in the history of American literature, and to provide a sense of the scope and nature of the career under review. A certain amount of biographical and historical context is also offered, giving a context for the work itself.

The authors of these critical articles are mostly teachers, scholars, and writers. Most have published books and articles in their field, and several are well-known writers of poetry or fiction as well as critics. As anyone glancing through this volume will see, they are held to the highest standards of good writing and sound scholarship. The essays each conclude with a select bibliography intended to direct the reading of those who want to pursue the subject further.

Supplement IX is mostly about contemporary writers, many of whom have received little sustained attention from critics. For example, William Humphrey, Shirley Jackson, Tony Kushner, Richard Powers, and James Salter have been written about in the review pages of newspapers and magazines, and their fiction has acquired a substantial following, but their work has yet to attract significant scholarship. That will certainly follow, but the essays included here constitute a beginning.

Some of the important writers from the past, such as John Muir, Zelda Fitzgerald, Dorothy Parker, Jean Toomer, Nelson Algren, Henry Roth, and Rachel Carson, have already attracted a good deal of sustained attention, and their work is often taught in college courses, but for various reasons their careers have not yet been discussed in *American Writers*. It is time they were added to the series.

The poets included here—from Robert Francis (a contemporary of Robert Frost) to Amy Clampitt, William Matthews, Louis Simpson, Gerald Stern, and David Wagoner—are well known in the poetry world, and their work has in each case been honored with major literary prizes. These poets have been widely anthologized as well. Nevertheless, the real work of assimilation, of discovering the true place of each poet in the larger traditions of American poetry, has only begun. In each case, these poets are written about by critics who are themselves poets, and the depth and eloquence of their essays should be obvious even to casual readers.

The critics who contributed to this collection represent a catholic range of backgrounds and critical approaches, although the baseline for inclusion was that each essay should be accessible to the non-specialist reader or beginning student. The creation of culture involves the continuous reassessment of major texts produced by its writers, and my belief is that this supplement performs a useful service here, providing substantial introductions to American writers who matter, and it will assist readers in the difficult but rewarding work of eager reading.

—JAY PARINI

Contributors

Carolyn Alessio. Prose editor of *Crab Orchard Review,* and teacher of English at Cristo Rey High School, a dual-language school in Chicago. Her work has appeared in the *Chicago Tribune, TriQuarterly, Boulevard,* and elsewhere. SHIRLEY JACKSON

Bert Almon. Professor of English, University of Alberta. Author of eight collections of poetry and a critical biography, *William Humphrey: Destroyer of Myths.* WILLIAM HUMPHREY

Charles R. Baker. Poet, essayist, and short story writer. Author of the short stories "What Miss Johnson Taught," "Christmas Frost," and "A Peacock in a Pecan Tree." JAMES SALTER

Jonathan N. Barron. Associate Professor of English, University of Southern Mississippi. Editor (with Eric Murphy Selinger) of *Jewish American Poetry: Poems, Commentary, and Reflections,* and forthcoming collections on the poetic movement New Formalism, and on the poetry of Robert Frost. Editor in chief of *The Robert Frost Review.* GERALD STERN

Cornelius Browne. Professor of English, Ohio University. He has published essays on John Steinbeck, Barry Lopez, and American-Canadian literary relations. He is currently at work on a book about Pragmatism, John Dewey, and American environmental writing. RACHEL CARSON, JOHN MUIR

Joseph Dewey. Associate Professor of Contemporary American Literature, University of Pittsburgh. Author of *In a Dark Time: The Apocalyptic Temper in the American Novel of the Nuclear Age, Novels from Reagan's America: A New Realism,* and a forthcoming volume on Richard Powers. RICHARD POWERS

Tracie Church Guzzio. Assistant Professor of English, State University of New York at Plattsburgh. Author of essays on Charles Chesnutt, Clarence Major, and John Edgar Wideman, and a forthcoming book on John Edgar Wideman's work. JEAN TOOMER

Steven G. Kellman. Professor of Comparative Literature, University of Texas at San Antonio. Author of *Loving Reading: Erotics of the Text, The Plague: Fiction and Resistance, The Self-Begetting Novel,* and *The Translingual Imagination.* Editor of *Perspectives on Raging Bull,* and coeditor of *Into the Tunnel: Readings of Gass's Novel, Leslie Fielder and American Culture,* and *Torpid Smoke: The Stories of Vladimir Nabokov.* HENRY ROTH

Melissa Knox. Author of *Oscar Wilde: A Long and Lovely Suicide* and *Oscar Wilde in the 1990s: The Critic as Creator.* She has published articles about Henry James, Thomas De Quincey, William Butler Yeats, and Anaïs Nin. DOROTHY PARKER, TONY KUSHNER

James A. Lewin. Associate Professor of English, Shepherd College. He has published essays about Shakespeare's political ghosts and Nelson Algren. NELSON ALGREN

Alexander Long. Graduate of the Writing Seminars at the Johns Hopkins University. His poetry, essays, and book reviews have appeared in such journals as *Quarterly West, The Connecticut Review, Solo, Third Coast, The Prose Poem: An International Journal,* and *Montserrat Review.* WILLIAM MATTHEWS

Josef Raab. Associate Professor of American Studies, University of Bielefeld, Germany. Author of *Elizabeth Bishop's Hemisphere,* editor of *Das 20. Jahrhundert: Nachkriegszeit* and *Klassische Menschenbilder,* and coeditor of *Negotiations of America's National Identity.* His other publications concern Mexican American literature, inter-American relations, popular culture, Benjamin Franklin, Emily Dickinson, Walt Whitman, José Martí, and twentieth-century American poetry. TONY KUSHNER

Steven P. Schneider. Professor of English, University of Texas, Pan American. Author of *A. R. Ammons and the Poetics of Widening Scope* and editor of *Complexities in Motion: New Essays on A. R. Ammons's Long Poems.* His poetry has appeared in such journals as *Critical Quarterly, Prairie Schooner,* and *The Literary Review.* LOUIS SIMPSON

Robert B. Shaw. Professor of English, Mount Holyoke College. Author of *Below the Surface* and other collections of poetry, as well as numerous articles on modern poetry. ROBERT FRANCIS

Sylvia Shurbutt. Professor of English, Shepherd College. Author of articles published in such journals as *Essays in Literature, Women's Studies, Southern Humanities Review, The Southern Literary Journal, Women and Language,* and *Victorian Poetry.* ZELDA FITZGERALD

Willard Spiegelman. Hughes Professor of English, Southern Methodist University. Editor of *Southwest Review,* and author of *Wordsworth's Heroes, The Didactic Muse: Scenes of Instruction in Contemporary American Poetry,* and *Majestic Indolence: English Romantic Poetry and the Work of Art.* He is a frequent contributor to the *Wall Street Journal.* AMY CLAMPITT

Richard Wakefield. Professor of American literature at The Evergreen State College, Tacoma Community College, and the University of Washington at Tacoma. He is the poetry critic for the *Seattle Times.* DAVID WAGONER

SUPPLEMENT IX
Nelson Algren to David Wagoner

Nelson Algren

1909–1981

*L*IKE THE BIBLICAL prophet and the Shakespearean fool, Nelson Algren stood up to privilege and power even as he confirmed the foundation on which civilized culture is based. Challenging the authority of judges, officials, pundits, and promoters, he made enemies in the literary as well as the political establishment, and he paid for his defiance. With very few exceptions, academic critics have ignored Algren. Best known for *The Man with the Golden Arm* (1949), which received the National Book Award in 1950, Algren identified with the literary realism and radical politics of Stephen Crane, Jack London, Theodore Dreiser, Carl Sandburg, and Eugene V. Debs. Building on the Chicago school of literary realism, Algren represented slum dwellers, vagrants, and petty criminals as a reflection of the repressed soul of shallow materialism. In *Chicago: City on the Make* (1951), he defined literature as "a challenge . . . to the legal apparatus by conscience in touch with humanity." In outcasts of respectable society he found the humanism that an established legal and literary elite hypocritically espoused.

For having created a literature based on compassion for misfits and rejects, individuals who live forever on the dark side of the American Dream, Algren has never been forgiven by his critics. But neither did Algren ever forgive those guardians of respectability who made such a studied effort to ignore him. Precisely because he wrote about outcasts, Algren was able to express the values lacking among the gatekeepers of literary officialdom. He defined the cultural establishment's limitations. The author's ideology is summed up in the confession made by an ex-priest, arrested on suspicion of passing phony checks, under the glare of a police line-up in *The Man with the Golden Arm.* Asked why he was defrocked, the anonymous ex-priest explains to Saloon Street District Captain "Record Head" Bednar: "Because I believe we are members of one another."

ALGREN'S LIFE

Born in Detroit, Michigan, on March 28, 1909, Nelson Algren wrote about East Texas, New Orleans, the Far East, and other exotic locales. But he spent most of his life singing in poetic prose of Chicago. His relationship with his hometown was bittersweet, often cynical, but never condescending or blasé. He called it, in *Chicago: City on the Make,* "the place built out of Man's ceaseless failure to overcome himself." A song of unrequited love by a writer for his source of inspiration, this essay in the form of a prose poem argues that Chicago does not belong to the big shots in the high-class offices, fancy restaurants, and exclusive clubs so much as to all the anonymous and homeless urban wanderers and lost souls on the street. He likens loving Chicago to "loving a woman with a broken nose," noting "you may well find lovelier lovelies. But never a lovely so real."

According to Algren's unofficial history, the city's founding fathers "were all of a single breed. They all had hustler's blood." Reformers of the city, Algren writes, found themselves playing catch-up in a rigged ball game. "Do-Gooders" like Jane Addams "get only two outs an inning," while Hustlers like Hinky Dink and

Bathouse John "are taking four." The fight for the eight-hour day was won by workers, he suggests, only at the cost of living in a city ruled by a stifling spirit of corporate mediocrity. Thus, Chicago "is a drafty hustler's junction in which to hustle a while and move on out of the draft." But Chicago's "rusty heart," he admits, holds on to its own "for keeps and a single day."

The author's paternal grandfather, Nels Ahlgren converted to Judaism in Stockholm and changed his name to Isaac Ben Abraham in the 1850s. Finding life difficult for a Jew in Sweden, he came to America. As a fur trader in Minnesota, however, Algren's grandfather found life could also be difficult in his new country. In *Nelson Algren: A Life on the Wild Side* (1989), Bettina Drew notes that his trading post "was burned out in the last Indian raid east of the Mississippi." After marrying a Jewish woman in Chicago, he tried running a store in Black Oak, Indiana. Failing as a storekeeper, his next stop was San Francisco, where the author's father was born before the family sailed to the Holy Land around 1870. The earliest memories of Algren's father, who later worked as a mechanic in the Yellow Cab Company in Chicago, were of Arabs on camels in Palestine.

But life proved difficult in Jerusalem as well. As a self-proclaimed prophet, Algren's grandfather gathered a group of like-minded wise men around him and lived on a higher spiritual level while his wife kept house. Algren's grandmother decided, with monetary assistance from the American consulate, to return to America. At the last minute, her husband joined her. Once on board, Algren's grandfather decided that the consulate's money represented idol worship and made a show of throwing the graven images overboard. Other passengers raised a collection among themselves so the family could complete its journey back to the United States. The grandfather later became a socialist and simultaneously a convert to all religions and to none. However embellished, the often-told tale of Algren's grandfather represented the author's own combination of iconoclastic faith and innocent skepticism. Proud of his namesake, whom he never met, Algren wondered aloud in an interview with Martha Heasley Cox and Wayne Chatterton: "Can pseudo-intellectualism be inherited?"

Algren hid his Jewishness. He has never been included in a list of Jewish-American writers. But his itinerant grandfather left a trace of the wandering Jew. Born Nelson Algren Abraham, he dropped the family name of his second-generation immigrant parents because, as he said in an interview with H. E. F. Donohue, he did not think it "could get on a theater marquee." He described his parents as "neither Gentiles nor Jews." As a child, Algren went to a Congregationalist Sunday school on the South Side of Chicago because his mother "didn't like the Irish" who dominated the neighborhood.

After the family moved to the North Side, Algren graduated from high school near the bottom of his class. With his sister's encouragement, however, he received a bachelor of science degree in journalism from the University of Illinois at Urbana-Champaign in 1931. He worked odd jobs and hoboed his way to Texas and back, collecting experiences he used as the basis of his short story, "So Help Me," published in *Story* magazine in 1933. Soon after, he received a letter from Vanguard Press asking if he was working on a novel. Algren hitchhiked to New York City and met James Henle, president of Vanguard, who offered him an advance. Both writer and publisher believed they had driven a fantastic bargain when Algren asked for, and received, $100 to be paid over a period of three months.

Traveling by freight train and hitchhiking, Algren returned to Texas to gather material for his book. On the campus of Sul Russ State Teacher's College in Alpine, he discovered a roomful of typewriters. Nobody seemed to mind when Algren began working on "an old upright

Royal" to which he became attached, so, he told Donohue, he "simply picked it up and walked . . . to the hardware dealer and got a box, packed it . . . and mailed it" to himself in Chicago. Algren then got on a boxcar, intending to catch up with the typewriter, still thinking he had made a "shrewd move" until the sheriff arrested him and took him to be locked up.

Unable to pay for bail, Algren remained in the Brewster County Jail until the circuit-riding judge came to Alpine. On advice of his public defender, Algren pled not guilty, although he had signed a confession. Algren's lawyer appealed for mercy. Using an argument based on English common law, he compared the young writer trying to obtain the tools of his craft to Jean Valjean in Victor Hugo's *Les Miserables.* Sentenced to two years on the pea farm in Huntsville, Algren was freed on condition that he leave Texas within twenty-four hours. His experience behind bars became the basis for Algren's lifelong fascination with the world of prisoners.

Back in Chicago, Algren finished his first novel, *Somebody in Boots,* published in 1935. He worked for the Works Progress Administration Illinois Writers' Project and the Venereal Disease Control Program of the Chicago Board of Health. His second novel, *Never Come Morning,* was published in 1942. In the U.S. Army during World War II, he served in Wales, Germany, and France, never rising above the rank of private.

The Neon Wilderness, a collection of short stories published in 1947, included five stories that had appeared in O. Henry Memorial Collections or *Best American Short Stories,* two of which, "A Bottle of Milk for Mother" (which encapsulates the saga of Lefty Bicek, the protagonist of Algren's *Never Come Morning*) and "How the Devil Came Down Division Street," were widely anthologized.

In 1947 Algren received grants from the American Academy of Arts and Letters and the Newberry Library to assist him in writing his masterpiece, *The Man with the Golden Arm.* Algren was disappointed, however, in the cinematic version, which he considered a mockery of his novel. The producer Otto Preminger made millions on the film, starring Frank Sinatra, while Algren received a total of $15,000 in royalties. Preminger claimed all the credit for breaking the taboo against portraying drug addiction, and Sinatra saved his acting career. But Algren felt betrayed by a Hollywood movie that sensationalized his distinctive vision of the struggle for survival on Chicago's Near Northwest Side. The year 1951 saw the publication of his *Chicago: City on the Make,* which began as a magazine article.

His *A Walk on the Wild Side* (1956) was slashed by establishment critics. First, Alfred Kazin, writing for the *New York Times Book Review,* sniffed at Algren's "surrealist predilection" for the grotesque, dismissing the novel as an exercise in "puerile sentimentality." Then, in an article published in *The New Yorker* with the mocking title "The Man with the Golden Beef," Norman Podhoretz took offence because Algren seemed to find "bums and tramps" more worthy of attention than "preachers and politicians and the otherwise respectable." Finally, in a review printed in *The Reporter,* Leslie Fiedler skewered Algren with the sneering sobriquet "bard of the stumblebum." Algren, according to Fiedler, had become "almost a museum piece" because he refused to develop beyond the social protest novel.

In rebuttal, Lawrence Lipton accused Algren's critics of betraying themselves. By renouncing the political activism of the 1930s as a sort of youthful indiscretion, Fiedler and company bowed to the idols of Cold War ideology, Lipton charged. By refusing to take Algren's writing seriously, they conformed to the commercialism of a shallow, materialistic culture— while using Algren as a whipping boy to emphasize their own smug superiority. Lipton, however, published his scathing riposte in a little-noted edition of the *Chicago Review,* while the attacks on Algren's work appeared in periodicals influential among the intellectual elite. As a result, Algren was branded as a writer who had fallen out of step with mainstream readers.

After the 1950s, when many professors were required to sign loyalty oaths, and New Critics espoused literary formalism to the exclusion of historical context and social critique, Algren was dropped from reading lists. As Carla Cappetti observed in *Writing Chicago: Modernism, Ethnography, and the Novel* (1993), Algren fell victim to a campaign that "exiled the whole urban sociological tradition from the hall of fame of American letters." Before his fall from favor, Algren's short fiction appeared in *Short Story Masterpieces, Seventy-Five Short Masterpieces, Stories From World Literature, The Best American Short-Stories, 1915–1950, Stories of Modern America, Big City Stories of Modern American Writers* and other anthologies. Nonetheless, in the current literary canon, he is nonexistent. *The Norton Anthology of Short Fiction* leaves Algren out. Standard textbooks such as *The American Tradition in Literature* omit him. Even *The Heath Anthology of American Literature,* which extends traditional limits to include more women, Native Americans, African Americans, and experimentalists can not find a place for Algren.

For his part, Algren struck back at the formalist assumptions of New Criticism. In his introduction to the 1960 edition of *The Neon Wilderness,* he noted that the "new owners" of literature had arrived "from their respective campuses armed with blueprints to which the novel and short story would have to conform," abolishing "prewar mottoes" of the humanistic tradition. "Until that moment," he continued, "I hadn't known that sympathy for perverts and savages had gone out of style, yet the point was clear: compassion was just too good for some

people." Bettina Drew has noted that, for Algren, the artist's mission was to take risks by which if one fails, one fails alone, but "if one succeeds, one succeeds for all." This open-ended inclusion was in direct opposition to the notion that literature served as a buffer protecting the privileges of class. As Martha Cox and Wayne Chatterton have observed, Algren insisted that "the role of the writer is to stand against the culture he is in."

The most celebrated love of his life, Simone de Beauvoir, the French writer and philosopher, also brought Algren heartbreak and humiliation. Beauvoir used her relationship with Algren to put her lifelong partnership with the philosopher Jean-Paul Sartre in perspective. She found passion with Algren yet remained devoted to her intellectual companionship with Sartre. It took Algren a long time to realize that he would never be her first priority, despite her avowals of love. The long-distance literary love affair depended on Beauvoir's finding time to visit Algren in Chicago. After his outspoken support of protests against the execution of Julius and Ethel Rosenberg, convicted of spying for the Soviet Union, Algren could not get a visa from the State Department to leave the country. Finally, in 1960, when the travel ban against him was lifted and he managed to go to Paris, Beauvoir gave Algren the keys to her apartment and announced that she had to accompany Sartre on a trip to Cuba.

Algren remained loyal until Beauvoir expounded her theory of "contingent loves," specifically referring to her affair with Algren to rationalize her willingness to experiment despite her commitment to Sartre. Beauvoir published "A Question of Fidelity" and "An American Rendezvous" in the November and December 1964 issues of *Harper's.* In response, Algren published "The Question of Simone de Beauvoir" in the May 1965 issue of the same magazine. "Anybody who can experience love contingently has a mind that has recently snapped," he wrote, concluding that: "Procurers are more honest than philosophers."

Increasingly disillusioned, Algren wrote journalism and travel books and indulged his weakness for betting on horse races and poker games. A few months before his death of a heart attack on May 9, 1981, in Sag Harbor, New York, Algren was inducted into the American Academy and Institute of Arts and Letters, which in 1974 had presented him with its prestigious Award of Merit for the novel, given only to a select handful of authors. This belated recognition confirmed the merit of Algren's work but did not prevent his books from going out of print. *The Devil's Stocking,* a novel based on the case of boxer Rubin "Hurricane" Carter, was published posthumously in 1983.

SOMEBODY IN BOOTS

Algren began his first book with the projected title "Native Son," but when his publisher suggested a change, Algren let Richard Wright use it for his own work. When published in 1935, Algren's book was titled *Somebody in Boots.* In his preface to the 1965 reprint edition, the author called it "an uneven novel written by an uneven man in the most uneven of American times." Filled with images of cruelty, grisly scenes of horror and bottomless depths of alienation, the novel reads as an apprentice's effort to capture the lives of the dispossessed legions of the American Southwest during the 1930s.

The book's protagonist, Cass McKay, is the ultimate underdog. Cowardly, selfish, and ignorant, he maintains a romantic yearning for impossible purity through every misadventure. Despite all the odds, Cass maintains his humanity in a world ruled by man's inhumanity to man: "Cass never became hardened to fighting. . . . He was to see men fight with guns and knives, with bare fists and with their teeth. . . . Yet not once in his young manhood was he to see the shadow of pain cross a human face without being touched to the heart."

Son of Stub McKay, a man who "felt he had been cheated with every breath he had ever drawn," Cass inherits a secret pain with no name other than "The Damned Feeling." Age fifteen in 1926, Cass is described as "lank . . . red-haired . . . somewhat cave-chested" and barely literate. Cass's brother Byron is a World War I veteran who has never recovered from having "been gassed at St. Mihiel." With no recollection of their mother, Cass looks to his sister Nancy as the only maternal figure and sole friend of his brutal childhood. He and his sister, however, grow apart as they calculate their different strategies for survival. When their father kills the man who has taken his job on the railroad, an angry mob surrounds the house.

Cass escapes. Before he goes, however, he flippantly tells his sister to "go down valley-way like you said wunst, to get yo'self a job in a spik whorehouse in La Feria," and never forgives himself when his offhand curse comes true. For Cass, the shame his father brings the family as a murderer is insignificant compared to the embarrassment of his sister's becoming a whore, partly because of his repressed incestuous desire for her and also because she is the only gentle soul he has ever known.

As a hobo riding the rails, Cass learns that for him, "there was no escape from brutality. The world was a cruel place, all men went alone in it. Each man went alone, no two went together. . . . There were only two kinds of men wherever you went—the men who wore boots, and the men who ran." Algren describes the "dark human tide" of anonymous masses of superfluous humanity, refugees in their own country, swept up by the waves of economic depression swirling them into the depths of the 1930s inferno:

There was no standing still and there was no turning back. No place to go, and no place to rest. No time to be idling and nothing to do. He moved,

moved, everything moved; men either kept moving or went to jail. Faces like fence-posts seen from trains, passed swiftly or slowly and were no more. . . . From day to day faces appeared and passed, from hour to hour dimmed and died. . . . In a sullen circle they stared for an hour, neither hostile nor friendly nor kind. They too were of the hunted. They moved aside to make place for him or silently turned away; he stood among them in silence, he then too stared unhostile in his turn. Then it was *move, move—Don't come here any more*—and the faces were gone again.

Sentenced to ninety days in the El Paso County Jail, Cass finds that his punishment is to be administered by a kangaroo court of convicts, presided over by Judge Nubby O'Neill, who espouses "a highly-feigned hatred of everything not white and American." The one-handed barn boss threatens Cass with the greatest number of "swangs" he can imagine from the belts of all the prisoners in the tank, applied with force on the naked buttocks of the defendant, for the offense of relating to a black person as an equal. The court has mercy when Cass denounces his past and swears loyalty to all whites, granting Cass a suspended sentence of "ten thousernd swangs on his left butt an' five thousernd swangs on his right."

The purpose of the jail is to support the jailers. Most of the inmates are not guilty of any crime. They had been "pulled out of box-cars for the sake of the feed-bill" that provide sixty cents per day per prisoner, allowing a larger profit margin when the cells are filled. The sheriff feeds them an oatmeal and turnip-green diet on both weekdays and Sundays. When one convict has the courage to protest, he is led out for a visit to the commissioner so he can officially register his complaint. But as soon as he steps out of the cell, the sheriff beats him with his ring of keys until the terrified and badly injured convict crawls back in meek submission. Before a grand jury comes to investigate conditions, the prisoners receive meat, milk, and potatoes three times a day and know better

than to utter a peep when the foreman asks if they have any complaints. Cass drifts to Chicago where he meets Norah Egan, a "haybag whore" who specializes in rolling drunks and trying to avoid extortion by the cops. They rob a drug-store together and make a haul of $500 that transforms the summer of 1932 into the only season of idyllic bliss in Cass McKay's life. Inevitably, Cass winds up in Cook County Jail and loses track of Norah. Cass takes a job as barker in the burlesque house where Norah had worked before they met. There he meets an intellectual black man, Dill Doak, a fellow worker who takes Cass to left-wing rallies in Washington Park and gives Cass a transient glimpse of radical ideology. But the search for the lost love of Norah leads to heartbreak. Cass hooks up again with Judge Nubby O'Neill who takes the role of surrogate father and spiritual guide, promising to turn Cass into "a *real* white man."

Conventionally read as a proletarian protest novel, *Somebody in Boots* is not about the proletariat. Algren, instead, writes about what *The Communist Manifesto* calls the "'dangerous class,'" the lumpen proletariat, which is less likely to join a working-class revolution than to become criminals and tools of "reactionary intrigue." A born follower, Cass seems to need somebody stronger to lead him through the wilderness of American society. The dominant characters of the book, always "somebody in boots," either with a gun or a badge or both, represent a jungle world where survival is the only law. Lost in a wasteland of American capitalism, Cass seems destined to a life of petty crime and brokenhearted dreams of love. The book is especially effective in conveying a sense of individual isolation in the fragmented fraternity of the dispossessed that survives below the surface of America. Whether he develops as an individual seems doubtful, but Cass is definitely changed by the end of the novel, if only from an innocent victim of society to a guilty one, forced by circumstances into the criminal underworld that is the only place he feels at home.

The novel received mixed reviews. In the *New York Times Book Review,* H. W. Boynton declared: "There is a creative impulse at work here which declines to be subdued to the uses of mere realism or propaganda." But in the *The New Republic,* Otis Ferguson suggested that *Somebody in Boots* "would make a fair book only if its author had thrown it out and used what he has apparently learned to write another." Perhaps taking this advice seriously, it took Algren seven years to produce his second novel.

NEVER COME MORNING

Algren's long-neglected *Never Come Morning* unveils the author's tragic "central vision," defined by George Bluestone as based on "the impulse to destroy love," leading to the living death of self-destruction. The flawed protagonist, a child of the slums named Bruno "Lefty" Bicek, can knock out an opponent in a boxing ring, but is unable to overcome his own moral weakness. Caught between inchoate feelings for Steffi Rostenkowski and the peer pressures of his fellow hoodlums, Bruno betrays his love in one of the most disturbing scenes of gang rape ever written. Unable to forgive himself, Lefty struggles to free himself of his past.

Like other second-generation Polish immigrants in his neighborhood, Lefty lives in a shadow world under the supervision of an immigrant barber. An evil monster of insatiable greed and paranoid fear, the barber has ties to the interlocking criminal underworld and network of police protection that rules West Division Street. The barber arranges fixed boxing matches and controls a variety of criminal enterprises, including a neighborhood brothel. Under his influence, the "Twenny-six Ward Warriors Social 'n Athletic Club" members have their heads shaved by the barber and change their name to the "Baldhead True-American S.A.C."

Confined to a small ethnic enclave in a huge and impersonal metropolis, the world of *Never Come Morning* provides Algren with a canvas to etch miniature portraits of the juvenile delinquents in the story. The toothless, noseless, washed-out Casey Benkowski is Lefty's partner in crime and his manager in the boxing ring. "Finger" Idzikowski is Lefty's trainer; he puts his patented hex on Lefty's opponents in the ring or on the baseball field. Sly, insidious "Catfoot" Nowogrodoski walks and even laughs "noiselessly," "his face sallow and aquiline, with red dice hanging for luck from his belt and his hatbrim turned up in front."

There is also the dangerous and demented "Fireball" Kodadek, who carries a spring-blade knife and is desperate enough to use it without warning. Fireball cannot forgive Lefty for replacing him as starting pitcher on the gang's baseball team, and gets his revenge by forcing the rape of Steffi. Intimidated by the threat of Fireball's switchblade, Lefty allows Catfoot to insinuate himself into a tryst between him and Steffi in the gang's hangout. As the rape proceeds, word spreads and everyone in the neighborhood lines up for their turn. When an unknown Greek tries to join the line, Lefty takes out his rage on the interloper and leaves him dead in the alley.

While the police do not yet suspect him of killing the Greek, Lefty serves time in jail for a different crime. To cover up for his friend Casey, he takes the rap for mugging an elderly Polish man and stealing his welfare check. Lefty realizes, however, that his real guilt is for having "killed Steffi in his heart." Buried in his "muffled conscience" is the knowledge he "would pay all the rest of his life" for his abandonment of her and "the conviction that no punishment was too great for such a betrayal":

Yet there was no way of paying for Steffi. . . . So he could not, even to himself, see his guilt clearly toward her. According to his code he had done no more for Catfoot and the others than Catfoot and the others had at times done for him. He had been straight with the boys, he had been regular. And to be regular was all he had ever been schooled to accomplish. Beyond being regular there was nothing expected of a man. To give more wasn't regular. To give less wasn't straight.

In this novel, Algren also makes the first of his memorable depictions of the inside of a brothel, without either mawkish sentimentality or moralizing condescension. Stigmatized by the rape, Steffi finds herself with no other option than to go to work for the barber as a prostitute: "The enormity of being accessible to any man in the whole endless city came to her like a familiar nightmare. It was true. It was really true. It was true of herself, truly true; it was to herself this had happened and to none other. It was true."

With Steffi trapped in the endless night of the Milwaukee Avenue brothel, Lefty defies the barber's stranglehold on him and tries to win enough money in the boxing ring to allow him to begin a new life with Steffi. In a finely described prizefight, Lefty, cast as the Polish White Hope, defeats "Honeyboy" Tucker, a black contender for the championship. But before he can leave the arena, the police arrest him and take him to the prison that has always awaited him as his fate.

The novel transforms the Triangle between Chicago Avenue and Division Street, transected by the slanting Milwaukee Avenue running from Ashland Avenue to Damen Avenue, into a dreamscape city of the damned. In this book, says Carla Cappetti in *Writing Chicago*, Algren goes beyond sociological observation to represent the inner city as the repressed subconsciousness of capitalist psychology, revealing the contradictions that "make the slum and the criminal both *margin* and *center* of the city."

The barber's favorite Polish saying is "When the thunder kills a devil, . . . then a devil kills a Jew." Two minor characters in the book are Jew-

ish: the doctor who checks the prostitutes for disease and Snipes, a survivor of shell shock from World War I who runs errands for Mama Tomek and listens to her endless litany of hard times in the big city. But metaphorically the Jew is Lefty, who is doomed by the consciousness of his own guilt for betraying his love to the peer pressures of the gang. Lefty's last words are the epitaph for all the lost children of the city of night who never have the chance to grow up: "'Knew I'd never get t' be twenty-one anyhow,' he said."

In Lefty's tale Algren sums up the despair of all young people, of whatever ethnic or racial origin, who are trapped in the violence of doomed neighborhoods from which they cannot hope to escape. Algren's description of the dynamics of street gangs has lost none of its shocking truth and is even more relevant in the contemporary world than when the book was first published.

As an epigraph, used to emphasize the universality he wishes to express, Algren cites Walt Whitman:

I feel I am one of them—
I belong to those convicts and prostitutes myself—
And henceforth I will not deny them—
For how can I deny myself?

After it was published in 1942, *Never Come Morning* received enthusiastic praise in the *New York Times* and *The Saturday Review of Literature*. The critics Philip Rahv and Clifton Fadiman gave the book glowing reviews. But the editors of Chicago's Polish daily newspaper, *Zgoda,* denounced the book as "Nazi propaganda" designed to discredit all people of Polish descent and accused Algren of being a paid agent of "Herr Goebbels." The furor raised by the Polish community resulted in the removal of Algren's book from the Chicago Public Library. In typically acerbic fashion, Algren not only refuted his critics but went on the offensive against them. In the author's preface to the 1962 reprint of the book, he again cited Whitman as his authority, challenging all the guardians of respectability as one: "The source of the criminal act, I believed twenty years ago and believe yet, is not in the criminal but in the righteous man: the man too complacent ever to feel that he—even *he*—belongs to those convicts and prostitutes himself." As if in anticipation of the argument that he was defending the criminals against their victims, Algren accused his critics of a "failure of feeling":

> Nor all your piety nor all your preaching, nor all your crusades nor all your threats can stop one girl from going on the turf, can stop one mugging, can keep one promising youth from becoming a drug addict, so long as the force that drives the owners of our civilization is *away* from those who own nothing at all.

THE MAN WITH THE GOLDEN ARM

Poet laureate of the urban underworld, Algren broke new ground with the first serious literary treatment of drug addiction in the inner city. Yet *The Man with the Golden Arm* was never exclusively about illegal drugs. Conceived as a novel about a backroom card shark in the Division Street neighborhood of Chicago, the theme of heroin addiction entered the book as an afterthought. Algren was outraged when the movie version missed the point by concentrating on the agonies of an addict in withdrawal without taking the novel's characters seriously as people. Hollywood advertised the film as "Otto Preminger's *Man with the Golden Arm*" while cutting Algren out of both the credits and the profits.

Rereading Algren's masterpiece confirms that the novel is about addiction as metaphor. Algren may have been the first to inscribe the phrase "monkey on his back" to signify the burden of addiction. Yet Algren also observed in the novel that "'the monkey never dies. When you kick him off he just hops onto somebody else's back.'" The monkey on Frankie Machine's back becomes a symbol for the unfulfilled yearnings of men and women caught on an endless treadmill of poverty and ignorance. The novel takes a snapshot of a predominantly Polish neighborhood in Chicago just after World War II. Love, friendship, alienation, and betrayal are Algren's central themes.

Frankie cannot kick his addiction because he cannot stop blaming himself for the car accident that has left his wife Sophie in a wheelchair. Having drunk too many of Owner Antek's "A-Bomb Special, made simply by pouring triple shots instead of doubles" in celebration of "what a single bomb had done on the other side of the world," Frankie had impulsively climbed behind the wheel of a car and "crashed into the light standard of the safety island." At first, Frankie's problems seem to be solved easily enough by Zygmunt the Prospector, a debarred lawyer who specializes in processing fraudulent insurance claims. Zygmunt can fix anything from a traffic ticket to a manslaughter rap. He sees himself as an idealist who dreams of making Chicago "the personal injury capital of the United States of America." Some weeks later, however, Sophie wakes up with paralysis in her legs. For Sophie, whose illness is psychosomatic, the accident "had truly married them at last. For where her love and the Church's ritual had failed to bind, guilt had now drawn the irrevocable knot so fiercely that she felt he could never be free of her again."

Trapped by his guilt for Sophie's condition, Frankie stumbles on the hope of redemption in the arms of dark-haired Molly Novotny. Molly, herself a refugee from the abusive Drunkie John, offers Frankie refuge from the sickness of withdrawal and the loneliness of his guilt. But only in the "iron sanctuary" of County Jail is Frankie able to remove "the thirty-five pound monkey on his back." And by the time he is released, Molly has drifted away from him into the endless labyrinth of the city.

Algren describes a world of dim half-lights where the blaze of the sun is lost in the glare of the lineup in the back room at the precinct station. Under the omnipresent elevated train or locked behind bars, Algren's characters live in the shadow of "a dull calamitous light like a madhouse light" that comes "filtering down from somewhere far above . . . down the disinfected corridors . . . down many a narrow long-worn wrought-iron way . . . into the dangers of the unfingered, unprinted, unbetrayed and unbefriended Chicago night." Daylight reveals the abject betrayal, the truth of corruption, and the ultimate horror, as expressed in the epigram taken from Alexandre Kuprin, "that all the horror is in just this—that there is no horror!" Mercy can be found, Algren suggests, only in the shadows out of which the darkness comes. And the only hint of redemption is in the furtive embrace of love, the privacy of anonymity, and the oblivion of drug or drink.

From this dimly lit background emerges Nifty Louie Fomorowski with "amber eyes and two-tone shoes, his sea-green tie and soft green fedora with the bright red feather in its band above the pale asthenic face touched faintly with violet talc." Louie, "the one junkie in ten thousand who'd kicked it and kicked it for keeps," knows the lies an addict lives by: "When I hear a junkie tell me he wants to kick the habit but he just can't I know he lies even if *he* don't know he does. He *wants* to carry the monkey, he's punishin' hisself for somethin' 'n don't even know it."

Nifty Louie sends "God's medicine" via the sightless Blind Pig, who cannot see where he is going or how he is being used. Blind Pig never washes himself in order to be as disgusting to others as possible, exuding "an odor of faintly rancid mutton, moldering laundry, long dead perch and formaldehyde." Behind his "creamy, dreamy smirk" he harbors "veiled malice" for everyone who has sight—and repeats over and over his mantra of greed: "I take *all* I can get."

Frankie deals cards in a backroom poker game run by Zero Schwiefka, who is described as "a paunch draped in a candy-striped shirt and a greasy black mortician's suit" with slackened jowls and a huge bulbous nose. When Frankie is arrested because the police have not been paid off in time, Zero rushes to bail him out, "rubbing his hands together breathlessly, clear to the elbows, like a great bluebottle fly preening its front legs." Regulars in the all-night card game include Umbrella Man, "who walked about the streets smiling gently, day after day, tinkling an old-fashioned school bell and bearing a battered umbrella strapped to his back." The others indulge Umbrellas because he is the brother to the "smartest cop on the street," Cousin Kvorka, "the captain's man," who is everybody's cousin "for a double saw"—twenty dollars. Another regular, Meter Reader, "once played sandlot baseball and now coached his employers' team, the Endless Belt & Leather Invincibles, an aggregation that hadn't won a game since Meter Reader had taken it over." In Algren's world there can be no winners: "'I hope I break even tonight' was the sucker's philosophy. 'I need the money so bad.'"

Frankie and his sidekick Solly "Sparrow" Saltskin, who consider themselves "about as sharp as the next pair of hustlers," are defined by their function in the game. "Flat-nosed, buffalo-eyed" Frankie Machine is known simply as Dealer. "It's all in the wrist 'n I got the touch," Frankie was fond of boasting of his nerveless hands and steady eye. Sparrow, who guards the door and runs errands, earns the title of Steerer:

"I'm a little offbalanced," Sparrow would tip the wink in that rasping whisper you could hear for half a city block, "but oney on one side. So don't try offsteerrin' me, you might be tryin' my good-balanced side. In which case I'd have to have the ward super deport you wit' your top teet' kicked out."

Before teaming up with Frankie, Sparrow had been "a lost dog finder" who stole pets from neighborhood backyards and either sold them or returned them for a reward. Through "tortoise-shell glasses separating the outthrust ears" of his pointed head, Sparrow goggles in admiration at Frankie's car tricks, no matter how often repeated. "Half-Hebe 'n half crazy," as Frankie call him, Sparrow is willing to follow him through jail cells, barrooms, and back alleys, but does not know the secret guilt of Frankie's addiction until it is too late.

Other faces in the crowd include the sadistic Drunkie John, "a man who didn't know what to do with himself, for he didn't yet know who he was" except as "a mouth at the end of a whisky glass"; the secretly good-hearted Landlord Schwabatski, known to the tenants of 1860 West Division Street as Jailer; Old Husband, who lives only for the joys of buying day-old bread at bargain rates and tearing the date off the calendar; his wife, Violet, who takes Sparrow as her lover, leading to the hilarious Great Sandwich Battle, when a sausage slips down the old man's pajama legs leading to a wild chain of events; and Antek "the Owner" Witwicki, proprietor of the Tug & Maul Tavern, where the neighborhood drunks congregate, who proudly displays a sign above the cash register that reads: "I'VE BEEN PUNCHED, KICKED, SCREWED, DEFRAUDED, KNOCKED DOWN, HELD UP, HELD DOWN, LIED ABOUT, CHEATED, DECEIVED, CONNED, LAUGHED AT, INSULTED, HIT ON THE HEAD AND MARRIED. SO GO AHEAD AND ASK FOR CREDIT I DON'T MIND SAYING NO."

In *Confronting the Horror: The Novels of Nelson Algren* (1989), the sole book-length study of Algren published since his death, James R. Giles construes *The Man with the Golden Arm* as an existentialist novel: "Frankie's dream of playing drums in a jazz band . . . represents the 'authentic' 'Self' that he might create." Frankie Machine has the talent to "go on the legit" as a drummer, but the reason salvation through respectability remains beyond his reach may go back farther than a philosophy of Being-for-itself, back to the Fall of Man. Frankie's failure is deeper than his fantasy of becoming a jazz drummer. Frankie's guilt is shrouded in indeterminacy; his mask of nonchalant indifference may be his original sin. In a momentary flash of anger, he kills Nifty Louie and cannot escape the consequences. The novel ends with the coroner's terse report on his apparent suicide.

The characters in *The Man with the Golden Arm* inhabit an underworld of petty crime controlled by an invisible upper world of big-time crime. Antek informs Frankie that because the alderman is up for reelection, the latter needs somebody to blame for the murder of Nifty Louie. So the alderman is putting pressure on the ward super and "the super is going to lose his job if Record Head don't clear the books on Louie." With Sparrow in the vise of police entrapment, it is a matter of time before he squeals on his pal. Algren's Chicago is a system of loyalty to corruption. Its legal apparatus depends on the betrayal of those you love.

Algren revealed that the roots of Frankie's heroin habit cannot be separated from a society that blights trust with the confidence artist's wary suspicion and persecutes intimacy with the scourge of guilt. To cure the addict, Algren implied, it is necessary to heal the human relationships of a sick society. Francis Majcinek—known as Automatic Majcinek and then simply as Frankie Machine—cannot be cured of his addiction, Algren suggested, until society is cured of deceit, greed, and indifference.

A WALK ON THE WILD SIDE

When Doubleday decided to capitalize on the success of *A Man with the Golden Arm,* the author was known as the Division Street Dostoevsky. But in *Nelson Algren* (1975), Martha Heasley Cox and Wayne Chatterton observed that critics "had forgotten that Algren had begun as a chronicler of the South rather than as a Chicago novelist." Asked to edit his first novel for republication, the author instead made a complete revision.

Somebody in Boots was politically and artistically crude, stringing together one atrocity after another with poetic and reportorial credibility but without more than a loosely picaresque plot and shallow character development. *A Walk on the Wild Side* emerged as an "accidental novel" that modulates outrage and subtlety beneath a surface of raunchy humor and exaggerated irony in the American tradition of the tall tale.

In the reimagined 1930s of *A Walk on the Wild Side,* the world has turned topsy-turvy: "The Ladder of Success had been inverted, the top was the bottom and the bottom was the top." From this perspective, Dove is so far down in the hierarchy of respectability that he can claim to be the true prince of America. Dove is the last descendant of a long line of free spirits. Exiled from "some colder country," the first free Linkhorn landed on the "old Dominion shore" with a bad reputation: "Watch out for a wild boy of no particular clan, ready for anything, always armed. Prefers fighting to toil, drink to fighting, chasing women to booze or battle: may attempt all three concurrently." Dedicated to the solemn avoidance of manual labor, Dove's ancestors wished neither to own slaves nor to slave for others either as sharecroppers or mill workers. "Saying A Plague on both Your Houses," they renounced "Mr. Linkhorn's war" as concerning no "kin of our'n" and migrated westward from the Ozarks until—some sixty years after Appomattox—Dove's father Fitz "showed up in the orange-scented noon of the Rio Grande Valley."

Saturday nights, with the help of a "little brown bottle he called his 'Kill-Devil,'" Fitz preaches from the courthouse steps against the evils of "modern dancing, modern dress, swearing, gambling, cigarettes and sin." To pro-test the hiring of a Catholic principal, Fitz keeps Dove home from school. "But no one had protested his protest," and Dove remains illiterate.

The only education Dove receives, apart from his father's sermons, comes from the hoboes in the train yard:

> Dove learned that Beaumont was tough. That Greensboro, in some place called Nawth Klina, was a right mean little town to get through. That Boykin, right below it, was even harder. That toughest of any was any town anywhere in Georgia. If you were caught ridin there your heard the long chain rattling. . . .
>
> Look out for Lima—that's in Ohio. And look out for Springfield, the one in Missouri. Look out for Denver and Denver Jack Duncan. Look out for Chicago. Look out for Ft. Wayne—look out for St. Paul—look out for St. Joe—look out—look out—look out—.

Yet looking is not the same as seeing, and *A Walk on the Wild Side* is a journey into the country of the blind. Dove finds success in a New Orleans brothel, located fittingly enough on Perdido Street, where "sometimes once a day, sometimes twice" the respectable customers pay ten dollars each "to achieve vicariously that ancestral lust: the deflowering of a virgin."

Each "buyer puts his eye to the peep-hole for which he had paid" to see a "pale, demented girl, blonde braids bound tightly about her head, wearing a simple cotton frock" who is sexually violated, despite her protests, by "some kind of redheaded hayseed in a sheriff's hat with a flashy cord and boots that were all but spurred." As the male lead in this sordid ritual, Dove fulfills his innate certainty of being "a born world-shaker."

After the performance itself, everyone returns to the downstairs parlor which is where "the fun really began. The sight of the fellow combing his hair or playing the juke, seemingly innocent that he had performed publicly, sent such glances of cold glee back and forth that soon every one had their money's worth." Had the suckers understood "that the dunce in the stetson was not only aware that he was watched, but was secretly proud to display his powers," they could have started a riot and torn Dove to pieces. Paid to be seen in the nakedness of his lust by citizens clothed in respectability, Dove seems all but blind to both the guilt and shame that gnaw within him. By the novel's end, however, Dove suffers literal blindness, being beaten to a sightless pulp in a gruesome barroom brawl, to finally achieve the insight of his own inviolable innocence.

The "do-right daddies" who keep the sex show in business parallel the middle-class readers who vicariously walk on the wild side with Algren's lowlife characters. Compounding the irony, the acquisition of literacy is, for Dove, the hardest-won achievement of his unblinded days. The inversion of blindness and insight—where the sighted pay to look through peepholes at a projection of their own blindness—parallels the novel's treatment of an illiterate who could not read the book he inhabits.

In a "seersucker suit and sea-green tie," Dove moves "as fast as his butter-colored shoes could make steps," choosing—when given a choice—the "nowhere road," because "that was the only place, in his heart of hearts, that he really wanted to go." Dove refuses to feign blindness to beg on the street. Nor is he slow at calculating sums up to and including the one-hundred-dollar bill, conned off the diminutive pimp and master con artist who initiates Dove in the mysteries of his chosen profession. But whatever Dove's sexual prowess, only with the literary help of two women can he overcome the inferiority complex based on his inability to put letters together on a page.

Terasina Vidarria, proprietress of the Hotel Davy Crocket in Dove's hometown of Arroyo, is the first person in his life "to try to see could I live up to the alphabet." But Terasina teaches Dove only the first two letters and a tale of a one-legged tin soldier from a children's picture-book of fairy tales. Another copy of the same book with the same one-legged soldier turns up again on Perdido Street; it belongs to the former schoolteacher Hallie Breedlove, who not only teaches Dove to make letters into words but even initiates him into the joys of literature. Escaping the brothel together, they see a riverboat performance of *Othello*. Dove becomes intoxicated with the language of Shakespeare. At last, for one brief golden season, "all the anguish he had felt for his ignorance was gone."

Dove's final tragic transcendence ends with him feeling his way, sightless and scarred—disfigured by the revenge of Achilles Schmidt, the double-amputee on wheels, his nemesis and rival for Hallie's affections—back to Terasina, to seek her forgiveness for seducing and abandoning her. Yet the issue at the novel's end is not whether Terasina will forgive Dove but the fact that he asks for forgiveness. Like the biblical harbinger of peace, Dove returns from a deluged world with an implicit hope for humanity despite all curses of destruction. In the end, he learns there are

> two kinds of people. Them that would rather live on the loser's side of the street with the other losers than to win off by theirselves; and them who want to be one of the winners even though the only way left for them to win was over them who have already been whipped.

In *A Walk on the Wild Side,* Dove transcends all levels of degradation, transforming revenge into a plea for mercy and progressing from the blindness of lust and ignorance to the insights of comic poetry.

ALGREN'S NATURALISM

Algren crashed the banquet of American literature with two uninvited guests: the Shakespearean Fool and the Hebrew Prophet. Throughout his career, Algren remained faithful to the naturalism that reaches back to Stephen Crane, Frank Norris, Jack London, and Theodore Dreiser, and that extends forward to Sherwood Anderson. But his protest against injustice derived from our oldest traditions of outspoken satire and our basic texts of guilt and redemption. Even though his heroes are neither idealists nor ideologues, Algren took seriously the struggle of the individual against the forces of social determinism. He anticipated the insight that both determinism and reformism exist in dynamic tension within the genre of naturalistic fiction, creating a historical dialectic between human fate and human hope.

In *The Man with the Golden Arm,* Solly "Sparrow" Saltskin is the latter-day disadvantaged much younger brother to Feste in *Twelfth Night* and the Fool in *King Lear,* prototypes of Algren's street-wise clown. Sparrow learns to use his demented simplicity to create his own protective camouflage like the motley of the court Fool. In *A Walk on the Wild Side,* Algren created Dove Linkhorn as a worthy companion to Shakespeare's Falstaff with a pedigree in the literary tradition of Mark Twain. Algren's outcasts prove their noble patrons to be the real fools. And Algren the author calls down the high-and-mighty to the street level of the lowest of the low. Before passing judgment, Algren maintained, the judge should see things from the perspective of the accused. Algren's fooling is anything but harmless. He takes a stand against the repression of the individual, no matter how degenerate, by the crowd, no matter how respectable.

Furthermore, Algren is just the kind of jester to joke darkly on the theme of impending doom. As spokesperson for the minority of one within the anonymous masses swallowed up by the darkness of the Chicago night, Algren's vision is related to the biblical man of truth who warns, in Amos 5:20: "Shall not the day of the Lord be darkness and not light? Even very dark and no brightness in it?" For Algren, the artificial light of the city at night provides the harsh illumination for a terrible and hidden mortality. Yet on Algren's West Division Street, even the deity plays by Chicago rules:

> For here God and the ward super work hand in hand and neither moves without the other's assent. God loans the super cunning and the super forwards a percentage of the grift on Sunday mornings. The super puts in the fix for all right-thinking hustlers and the Lord, in turn, puts in the fix for the super. For the super's God is a hustler's God; and as wise, in his way, as the God of the priests and the businessmen.
>
> (*The Man with the Golden Arm*)

The Almighty is the Chief Hustler and heroin is ironically referred to as "God's medicine." In such an environment there can be no trust. Survival depends on hustling somebody before somebody can hustle you.

Algren wrote about the need for redemption in a world without hope. He drew inspiration from the prophetic tradition of the Hebrew Bible and the Sermon on the Mount and took seriously the notion that the outcast and poor in spirit are blessed with the kingdom of heaven. But he himself could never believe in the blessing. In Algren's world the deity is distant, indifferent, and incompetent. For Algren, only spiritual salvation could transform the corruption of modern society. But that salvation never comes.

In the endless parade of freaks and geeks in the routine police lineup, Algren sketched miniature portraits of Judgment Day. Emerging from the same shadows to which they return, naked souls step into the blinding light to stand before the wisecracking police captain. "Record Head" Bednar, like "the recording Angel of all men," knows the secret of all who are guilty with "the great, secret and special American guilt of owning nothing, nothing at all, in the one land where ownership and virtue are one." With a tone reminiscent of the Gravedigger in *Hamlet,* the narrator observes: "Indeed your query room is your only house of true worship, for it is here that men are brought to their deepest confessions."

Only the captain is denied the purification of what Maxwell Geismar, in *American Moderns: From Rebellion to Conformity* (1958), called the "iron sanctuary," where victims of the system "rest their fevered and distorted hopes." Despite his facade of hard-boiled pessimism, the captain is finally forced to emerge from the safety of anonymous darkness and face the merciless glare of the light. In *The Man with the Golden Arm,* Algren makes the irony of the captain's dilemma explicit: "'Come down off that cross yourself,' he [the captain] counseled himself sternly, like warning another. But the captain couldn't come down. The captain was impaled."

In an early evaluation of his work, Chester E. Eisinger describes Algren as a "naturalist who cares about style." Writing from a more complete perspective, Bluestone insists that "to read him in the naturalist tradition is to misread him." For Bluestone, Algren "is concerned with the living death that follows love's destruction." In *Confronting the Horror* (1989), James R. Giles argued persuasively that Algren advanced the dialectic of environmental determinism and social protest characteristic of earlier naturalist writers. Algren no longer looked at the urban lower depths as an internal colony, as had Frank Norris and Theodore Dreiser, who regarded their subjects with curious detachment as sociological specimens. Removing the distance between the narrator and the narrative, Algren not only identified with the shared humanity of the urban lower classes. According to Giles, Algren became so intimately involved with his fictional characters that the assumption of a secure self-identity in the middle-class readers is put into doubt.

Algren explicitly rejected literary naturalism as social documentary for its own sake. In a book-length essay he wrote in the early 1950s

about the role of the writer in society—published in 1996 under the title *Nonconformity*—Algren identifies his approach with that of F. Scott Fitzgerald, who may seem an unlikely role model for an author who devoted himself to writing about the lowest classes. Yet, Algren writes: "What Fitzgerald risked"—as distinguished from writers of merely stenographic realism—was "an emotional sharing of the lives he recorded." Furthermore, like Fitzgerald, Algren also found himself becoming increasingly and inexorably "identified with the objects of my horror or compassion."

Algren did not write about the dispossessed of American society as "those people" but as "We, the People." He held a funhouse mirror up to American society, showing us the inner souls of our high-profile trendsetters and power brokers through the negative light of our pariahs and panhandlers, deviants and backroom deal makers. Algren defined in his own terms a literary tradition associated with Abraham Lincoln, Walt Whitman, Carl Sandburg, and Eugene V. Debs, appreciated by those who can read him without condescension or squeamishness. As Algren remarked in a conversation with Donohue:

American literature is the woman in the courtroom who, finding herself undefended on a charge, asked "isn't anybody on my side?" It's also the phrase I used that was once used in court of a kid who, on being sentenced to death, said, "I knew I'd never get to be twenty-one anyhow. . . ." I think American literature consists of these people.

ALGREN'S NONFICTION

In *Who Lost an American?* (1963), the author identifies himself with all the "fighters who came up fast and couldn't be beat" but "then went down slow and finally didn't fight anymore." In this volume Algren, at the height of his powers, reveals the tensions and conflicts that tore his soul. Published in 1963, the book is the self-deposition of an author who has given up creative literature and settled on the life of a "free-lance journalist," a label Algren used to describe himself in his later years. For the proud novelist, it was as if an honest boxer and contender for the world championship had become sideshow strongman in a traveling carnival. On the evidence of *Who Lost an American?* the tragic failure of Nelson Algren was that, at a certain point, he chose to withdraw from the ego-obsessed competition of the world of letters, much as a prizefighter who has taken too many punches retires from the ring.

Yet Algren's decision to give up writing novels and retreat to occasional journalism and satirical essays was an act not only of resignation but of subversive rebellion against the literary marketplace, consistent with the radical stance of his fiction. In 1965 he published *Notes from a Sea Diary: Hemingway All the Way,* based on a tour of Korea, Bombay, Calcutta, and the Philippines, and interwoven with an exaltation of Ernest Hemingway as an antidote to the literary world that had rejected Algren and that he condemned. *The Last Carousel,* an assortment of fiction and nonfiction, published in 1973, includes revisions of short pieces that had appeared previously in various books and periodicals. Published posthumously in 1983, Algren's last novel, *The Devil's Stocking,* still shows his distinctive power to challenge the smug assumptions of a complacent establishment. Based on the Rubin "Hurricane" Carter murder trials, it relates the rise and fall of an African-American prizefighter in terms of the cultural, legal, and personal dynamics of racism and sexism in a winner-take-all society.

Because he was defiantly neither this-kind-of-American nor that-kind-of-American but simply an American writer, Algren has been condemned to a strange kind of literary limbo. Algren's fictional world was never based on plodding social realism as much as on an upside-down reflection of a grotesque social order. In his work there is the implicit sense that, even if individuals are doomed by forces of social determinism, still there is some chance that as a collective consciousness we might yet raise our cultural level by including the exceptions at both the bottom and the top of the spectrum. Whether Algren's work can be redeemed as a coherent alternative to mainstream values defined exclusively in terms of materialistic success depends on readers sympathetic to the underlying concerns he expounded.

In an article in *Rolling Stone* titled "Perspectives: Is It Out of Control?" Ralph J. Gleason was the first to point out the debt that writers and musicians of the 1960s owed to "the fantasy/reality, inside/outside paradoxical view of the inversion of the American Dream" as

> first laid out by Algren in *A Walk on the Wild Side*: Up until Algren, no American writer had really combined a poetic gift for words and a vision of the truth about the textbook democracy. He saw it . . . and he put it down in the one novel which blew the minds of hundreds of other writers.

What Algren and the 1960s had in common might be called the principle of inclusion. In the 1960s this meant inclusion of the excluded. For Algren it meant that the exception determines the rule; the outsider defines the values on which society is based.

Despite progressive trends of multiculturalism, Algren at the turn of the twenty-first century is more of an outsider than when he lived and wrote. To explain why he did not fit any subcategory of American literature, Algren told Donohue of a sign he had seen on a door in Greenwich Village: "Non-Conformist Meeting at 8:30—Be On Time." His midwestern nonconformity does not belong in any of the preconceived categories of the literary canon. Because he insisted on recognizing the humanity of the anonymous bum on the street, Algren's work remains a litmus test for readers who seek to redeem the outcasts of established culture.

He did not simply talk the talk about universality of the spirit and the dignity of the individual. Algren walked the walk. Never did he merely mouth platitudes about the universality of the spirit and the dignity of humanity; Algren meant it.

Selected Bibliography

WORKS OF NELSON ALGREN

NOVELS

Somebody in Boots. New York: Farrar, Straus & Giroux, 1935. Reprint with a new preface by the author, New York: Berkeley Publishing Corporation, 1965. Reprint, New York: Thunder's Mouth Press, 1987.

Never Come Morning. New York: Harper and Brothers, 1942. Reprint, New York: Four Walls Eight Windows, 1987.

The Man with the Golden Arm. New York: Doubleday, 1949.

A Walk on the Wild Side. New York: Farrar, Straus and Cudahy, 1956.

The Devil's Stocking. New York: Arbor House, 1983.

SHORT STORIES

The Neon Wilderness. Garden City, N.Y.: Doubleday, 1947. Reprint, New York: Hill and Wang, 1960.

The Texas Stories of Nelson Algren. Edited by Bettina Drew. Austin: University of Texas, 1995.

NONFICTION

Chicago: City on the Make. Garden City, N.Y.: 1951. Reprint, Chicago: University of Chicago Press, 1987.

Introduction to *The Neon Wilderness.* Reprint, New York: Hill and Wang, 1960.

Who Lost an American? New York: Macmillan, 1963.

Notes from a Sea Diary: Hemingway All the Way. New York: Putnam, 1965.

"The Question of Simone de Beauvoir." *Harper's,* May 1965, p. 134.

The Last Carousel. New York: Putnam, 1973. (Includes some short fiction.)

Nonconformity: Writing on Writing. New York: Seven Stories Press, 1996.

MANUSCRIPTS

Algren's papers are located at the Algren Archive at the Ohio State University Library.

BIBLIOGRAPHY

Bruccoli, Matthew J. *Nelson Algren: A Descriptive Bibliography.* Pittsburgh: University of Pittsburgh Press, 1985.

CRITICAL AND BIOGRAPHICAL STUDIES

Anania, Michael. *"Nelson Algren and the City," Writing in the First Person: Nelson Algren, 1980–81.* Grand Army of the Republic Museum/The Chicago Public Library Cultural Center Catalog, 1988. Pp. 17–25.

Bluestone, George. "Nelson Algren." *Western Review* 22:27–44 (autumn 1957).

Boynton, H. W. "Somebody in Boots and Other Recent Works." *New York Times Book Review,* April 7, 1935, p. 6.

Cappetti, Carla. *Writing Chicago: Modernism, Ethnography, and the Novel.* New York: Columbia University Press, 1993.

Chicorel, Marietta, ed. *Chicorel Index to Short Stories in Anthologies and Collections.* New York: Chicorel Library Publications, 1974.

Cox, Martha Heasley, and Wayne Chatterton. *Nelson Algren.* New York: Twayne, 1975.

Drew, Bettina. *Nelson Algren: A Life on the Wild Side.* New York: Putnam, 1989.

Eisinger, Chester E. *Fiction of the Forties.* Chicago: University of Chicago Press, 1963.

Ferguson, Otis. "Somebody in Boots." *The New Republic,* July 17, 1935, pp. 286–287.

Fiedler, Leslie. "The Noble Savages of Skid Row." *The Reporter,* July 12, 1956, pp. 43–44.

Geismar, Maxwell. *American Moderns: From Rebellion to Conformity.* New York: Hill and Wang, 1958.

Giles, James R. *Confronting the Horror: The Novels of Nelson Algren.* Kent, Oh.: Kent State University Press, 1989.

Gleason, Ralph J. "Perspectives: Is It Out of Control?" *Rolling Stone,* August 6, 1970, p. 9.

Howard, June. *Form and History in American Literary Naturalism.* Chapel Hill: University of North Carolina Press, 1985. (Does not mention Algren.)

Kazin, Alfred. "Some People Passing By." *New York Times Book Review,* May 1956, pp. 4, 24.

Lipton, Lawrence. "A Voyeur's View of the Wild Side: Nelson Algren and His Reviewers." *Chicago Review Anthology,* winter 1957, pp. 4–14.

Podhoretz, Norman. "The Man with the Golden Beef." *The New Yorker,* June 2, 1956, pp. 132, 133–139.

Rotella, Carlo. *October Cities: The Redevelopment of Urban Literature.* Berkeley: University of California Press, 1998.

INTERVIEWS

Anderson, Alston, and Terry Southern. "Nelson Algren." *Paris Review* 11:37–58 (winter 1955).

Corrington, John William. "Nelson Algren Talks with NOR's Editor-at-Large." *New Orleans Review* 1:130–132 (winter 1969).

Donohue, H. E. F. *Conversations with Nelson Algren.* New York: Hill and Wang, 1964. (A book-length series of extended interviews.)

Pintauro, Joe. "Algren in Exile." *Chicago,* February 1988, pp. 93–101, 156–163.

Ray, David. "Talk on the Wild Side: A Bowl of Coffee with Nelson Algren." *The Reporter,* June 11, 1959, pp. 31–33.

FILMS BASED ON THE WORKS OF NELSON ALGREN

The Man with the Golden Arm. Screenplay by Walter Newman. Directed by Otto Preminger. United Artists, 1955.

Walk on the Wild Side. Screenplay by John Fante and Edmund Morris. Directed by Edward Dmtryk. Columbia, 1962.

—*JAMES A. LEWIN*

Rachel Carson

1907–1964

*I*N THE MODERN Library's list of the one hundred best nonfiction books written in English during the twentieth century, Rachel Carson's *Silent Spring* (1962) ranks fifth, following Henry Adams's *The Education of Henry Adams*, William James's *The Varieties of Religious Experience*, Booker T. Washington's *Up from Slavery*, and Virginia Woolf's *A Room of One's Own*, thus locating Carson's book among the most respected and influential texts of the last century. With its searing indictment of corporate- and government-sanctioned pesticide use in the United States, *Silent Spring* is considered by many to have ushered in the modern environmental movement.

In 1963, during Senate hearings on pesticide use initiated by public response to its publication, *Silent Spring* was compared with the most influential American book of the nineteenth century, Harriet Beecher Stowe's *Uncle Tom's Cabin*. *Silent Spring* not only condemned pesticide use but challenged the anthropocentric attitudes with which Western culture rationalizes its often destructive relationships to the natural environment. Like *Uncle Tom's Cabin* and *A Room of One's Own*, *Silent Spring* calls into question the basic underpinnings of a culture, in this case not racist or sexist cultural structures but those that allow human beings to use up and degrade natural systems as they deem fit. In all her work, Carson attempts to give the natural world a voice of its own, and argues for the extension of ethical consideration to all life-forms. In this, as Donald Worster wrote in *Nature's Economy: A History of Ecological Ideas* (1977), "the scientific conscience she symbolized became the central creed of the ecology movement: a vision of the unity of life, as taught by science, and a moral ideal of living cooperatively with all members of the natural community."

Carson, who was named by *Life* magazine in September 1990 as among the one hundred most important Americans of the twentieth century, attained her status as an advocate for the environment through a lifelong love of nature first imbued in her as a child, and through a life committed to studying and writing about the natural world, a progression evidenced in particular by her three acclaimed books about the sea: *Under the Sea-Wind: A Naturalist's Picture of Ocean Life* (1941), *The Sea around Us* (1951), and *The Edge of the Sea* (1955). Carson claimed that she felt the powerful pull of the ocean before she ever traveled to the shore, after reading these lines from Alfred, Lord Tennyson's "Locksley Hall" as a young student:

> Cramming all the blast before it, in its breast a thunderbolt.
> Let it fall on Locksley Hall, with rain or hail or fire or snow;
> For the mighty wind arises, roaring seaward, and I go.

As she later wrote in an autobiographical statement, quoted in Linda Lear's 1997 biography *Rachel Carson: Witness for Nature,* "That line spoke to something within me, seeming to tell me that my own path led to the sea—which then I had never seen—and that my own destiny was somehow linked with the sea."

BACKGROUND

Rachel Louise Carson was born in Springdale, Pennsylvania, on May 27, 1907, to Robert Warden Carson, an insurance salesman and part-time employee of West Penn Power Company, and Maria (MacLean) Carson. She had two older siblings, a sister, Marian, and a brother, Robert. At the time of her birth, Springdale was situated in a rural, wooded area in the lower Allegheny valley, and the Carson home was on sixty-four acres outside of town. Its orchards and the surrounding woods and hills proved a seminal influence on Carson, whose early love for the natural world was consistently fostered by her mother, who according to Carson held all life in reverence. Her mother's influence was deeply felt and long lasting. In fact, Carson cared for her aged and often ailing mother until her mother's death at nearly ninety years of age. Carson's upbringing in and around Springdale probably had an added effect on her that contributed to the critical edge found in all of her writing. Like that of so many small towns at the beginning of the century, Springdale's rural character succumbed to the mass industrialization and development of the times. Springdale was eventually sandwiched between two huge, sooty power plants, one belonging to West Penn Power Company and the other to Duquesne Light Company. Ultimately, the degradation of the place embarrassed Carson greatly. A critique of industrial culture's destruction of the natural world and its creatures is at least implicit through all of her writing.

Encouraged by her mother, Carson began composing stories at an early age. Her first published work came when she was ten, in *St. Nicholas* magazine. A popular children's magazine of the time that featured the work of young authors, *St. Nicholas* also published such well-known literary talents as William Faulkner, F. Scott Fitzgerald, Edna St. Vincent Millay, E. E. Cummings, and E. B. White. With her eye soon set on a writing career, Carson continued publishing her juvenile work in *St. Nicholas*. After finishing high school she received a one-hundred-dollar scholarship to attend Pennsylvania College for Women (now Chatham College) with firm plans to study English. Though lonely for much of her time at this institution, she proved a gifted student, publishing in the college's literary magazine and winning the admiration of both teachers and peers.

Carson's commitment to English as a subject of study was shaken in 1926 when she came under the influence of Mary Scott Skinker, a brilliant science teacher at the college. Once Carson enrolled in Skinker's biology seminar, her enthusiasm for the subject quickly caught fire under Skinker's tutelage, and the trajectory of Carson's career was initiated. The course of her career from this point on roughly coincides with the development of the science of ecology. However, at the time, science writing for general audiences was not widely practiced, and Carson agonized over her decision to change her major to biology. Looking back on her choice, in an address delivered in 1954 ("The Real World around Us," included in the 1998 collection *Lost Woods: The Discovered Writing of Rachel Carson,* edited by Linda Lear), Carson wrote, "I had given up writing forever, I thought. It never occurred to me that I was merely getting something to write about." Carson graduated from the Pennsylvania College for Women magna cum laude in 1929. She then went on to earn her master's degree at Johns Hopkins in marine zoology with a thesis titled "The Development of the Pronephros during the Embryonic and Early Larval Life of the Catfish (*Ictalurus punctatus*)." At periods during her graduate study, Carson worked at the Marine Biological Laboratory, in Woods Hole, Massachusetts, which furthered her interest in the ocean and provided rich source material for her later books about the sea.

Carson graduated from Johns Hopkins in 1932, entering the job market as a prospective female scientist in the thick of the Great Depression. During this difficult time she supported both her parents. Then her father died in 1935, and in 1937 her sister died, leaving two daughters whom Carson and her mother agreed to raise. After piecing together a living, Carson finally landed a job in Washington, D.C., with the Bureau of Fisheries (which became the Fish and Wildlife Service) in 1935 as a technical writer and often wrote scripts for bureau radio broadcasts. She was one of the few women hired by the bureau in a professional capacity, and she worked for the federal government for sixteen years, eventually rising to editor in chief of Fish and Wildlife Service publications. In fact, her first literary success stemmed from her government work.

Carson's article "Undersea" was originally written as the introduction to a Bureau of Fisheries publication, but Carson's supervisor, Elmer Higgins, declared the work too literary for a government publication. He suggested that Carson submit it to the *Atlantic Monthly,* which she did, and it was published in the magazine's September 1937 issue. Carson stated in "The Real World around Us" that from "Undersea," "everything else followed." "Undersea" took up only four pages of the *Atlantic Monthly,* but most of Carson's concerns are clearly evident in this early piece. Primary among these concerns is the literary presentation of complex scientific information to a general reading public, indeed the rendering of scientific material into poetry, as much of Carson's writing about the sea attains the status of an extended prose poem.

"Undersea" (also reprinted in *Lost Woods*) opens with the rhetorical question "Who has known the ocean?" Of course, no human being can know the ocean as its inhabitants do, and Carson employs in this piece the strategy she would hone in writing her first book, the attempt to narrate from an underwater perspective. "Undersea" is a poetic submarine grand tour in which Carson evokes the strangeness of

ocean life: "Dropping downward a scant hundred feet to the white sand beneath, an undersea traveler would discover a land where the noonday sun is swathed in twilight blues and purples, and where the blackness of midnight is eerily aglow with the cold phosphorescence of living things." While Carson's prose brings the undersea world vividly before the reader, she is careful to metaphorically link the sea world to the more familiar land world of her readers. The ocean is likened to pastures, and the shifting tides to night and day. Although she insists that "to sense this world of waters known to the creatures of the sea we must shed our human perceptions of length and breadth and time and place," the references to familiar phenomena such as "night," "day," and tides that "abandon pursuit" and "fall back" establish a connection between a habitat so strange as to be beyond the imagination and the quotidian experience of her readers. Further, she conveys scientific information in a way that sparks the imagination: "The sea performs a vital alchemy that utilizes the sterile chemical elements dissolved in the water and welds them with the torch of sunlight into the stuff of life." Carson's prose itself performs a "vital alchemy" by relaying to her land-dwelling readers the wonder of the sea, the "slow swells of mid-ocean," and its processes, in lines such as, "One by one, brilliant-hued flowers blossom in the shallow water as tube worms extend cautious tentacles."

Carson's prose is exact, careful, and lyrical, and without overtly calling attention to the science of ecology, she nonetheless constructs a picture of a world in which "individual elements are lost to view, only to reappear again and again in different incarnations in a kind of material immortality." This is the great cycle of life that so fascinated Carson and that she so loved. This unmitigated love of the world and its creatures—from fish to insects to human beings (this last despite her belief that "chief, perhaps, among the plunderers is man, probing the soft mud flats and dipping his nets into the shallow waters")—drives all Carson's work. Coupled with that love was Carson's unswerving belief that the human and the nonhuman worlds are part of the same system and that both warrant ethical consideration. Before her time, perhaps, she strove to see beyond the human.

UNDER THE SEA-WIND

Picking up where "Undersea" left off, Carson's first book, *Under the Sea-Wind,* peers out beyond the human, and this book remained Carson's favorite throughout her life. It appeared in 1941, approximately one month before the Japanese attack on Pearl Harbor, and though well reviewed by top naturalists, *Under the Sea-Wind* sold only modestly. The three sections of the text narrate the life cycles of shore birds, mackerel, and eels from the animals' perspectives. The chief characters in the first section are a black skimmer named Rynchops, a couple of sanderlings named Blackfoot and Silverbar, a snowy owl called Ookpik, Pandion the osprey, and White Tip, a bald eagle. Section two traces the life of Scomber the mackerel, and the third section follows the destiny of Anguilla the eel. According to Lear, Carson believed that "taken together, the three narratives would weave a tapestry in which the ecology of the ocean and the interdependence of all its creatures would emerge." *Under the Sea-Wind* presents an interdependence of narratives. Tapestry is a traditional metaphor for text, and Carson extends the metaphor to include ecological ideas. In weaving her narratives, Carson is careful to avoid claiming human motivation, consciousness, and emotions for her nonhuman characters. Although she provides her fish and bird characters with human names, she struggles to see from their nonhuman perspective. Her narrative strategy is to provoke in her audience an emotional response to these creatures, in an effort to establish a context that joins reader, text, and sea life.

In the foreword to the 1941 edition of *Under the Sea-Wind,* interestingly omitted in reissues of the book, Carson writes:

> I have spoken of a fish "fearing" his enemies . . . not because I suppose a fish experiences fear in the same way that we do, but because I think he *behaves as though he were frightened.* With the fish, the response is primarily physical; with us, primarily psychological. Yet if the behavior of the fish is to be understandable to us, we must describe it in the words that most properly belong to human psychological states.

Carson employs literary strategies to help her readers identify with her animal characters and remains attentive to the scientific facts available to her. Not only her subject matter but her writing itself can be described as ecological. Her writing works to present the life-forms of the sea as honestly as possible. This is not to say that her presentation is photographic, but that she attempts to illustrate the life cycles of sea creatures with the skills that she has at hand, both literary and scientific. An excerpt from the chapter "Birth of a Mackerel" is a good example:

> The next three days of life brought startling transformations. As the processes of development forged onward, the mouth and gill structures were completed and the finlets sprouting from back and sides and underparts grew and found strength and certainty of movement. The eyes became deep blue with pigment, and now it may be that they sent to the tiny brain the first messages of things seen.

Carson selects accurate biological details of the physical development of a hatchling, and the sprouting of fins and gills is decidedly nonhuman. But Carson then sharpens her focus, concentrating on the deep blue eyes of the baby mackerel, zooming in on the most human-like characteristic of the profoundly other-than-human fish and leaving the reader with the suggestion that this tiny creature has an awakening perception distinctly its own. It is a perception beyond human knowledge, but no less important for that fact. Perhaps because of the subtle link Carson creates through her description of the fish's eyes, we find it at least plausible that the mackerel has some sort of consciousness. Yet the fish, with its dawning awareness, remains most fascinating precisely because it is something other than human. The nonhuman fish glances back at the human reader.

Human beings appear in *Under the Sea-Wind* infrequently, usually taking on the role of predators. The book also has a minimum of authorial intrusions, and when they do occur, they function to emphasize the importance of the animals' context. For example, Carson has this to say about fish migrating from the sea back into the rivers: "By the younger shad the river was only dimly remembered, if by the word 'memory' we may call the heightened response of the senses as the delicate gills and the sensitive lateral lines perceived the lessening saltiness of the water and the changing rhythms and vibrations of the inshore waters." She again suggests an alignment of human "memory" and perception with the physical sense organs of the fish. Their world is one dominated by instinct, but just the same, that instinct is valued on a plane with human memory and perception. In this narrative of instinct and interconnections, often with fish in the subject position, the near universal privileging of human structures gives way to an aesthetic that values a realm of reality beyond full human understanding.

This realm of reality, the sea, is an astonishing interface of ecosystems:

> There could be scarcely a stranger place in the world in which to begin life than this universe of sky and water, peopled by strange creatures and governed by wind and sun and ocean currents. It was a place of silence, except when the wind went whispering or blustering over the vast sheet of water, or when sea gulls came down the wind with their high, wild mewing, or when whales broke the surface, expelled the long-held breath, and rolled again into the sea.

A world wholly governed by air, water, and light and inhabited by birds, fish, and mammals, the sea is a vast sheet from which human influence is absent or minimal, although the verbs "peopled" and "governed" function to create a verbal link between the human sphere and the "stranger" spaces of the nonhuman. The surface of the water serves as a metaphor for the interaction of wind and water, of flying and swimming creatures that, in breaking the surface of the sea, signify interdependence. Carson attempts to bring the creatures of the sea and their environment into common human experience. This happens in *Under the Sea-Wind* partly through a presentation of nonhuman subjectivity, and Carson's interwoven narratives about sea creatures introduce her readers to an experience of the sea itself. The sea becomes a universe—an experiential space—teeming with ecological and aesthetic meaning. For Carson, at least in 1941, these spaces of the sea—brimming with evolutionary and creative potential—seemed impervious to lasting human damage.

THE SEA AROUND US

When Carson began to think about her next book, she envisioned a more comprehensive work, still clinging to the belief, as she stated early in *The Sea around Us,* that humans "cannot control or change the ocean as, in his brief tenancy of earth, he has subdued and plundered the continents." Although prematurely optimistic, perhaps, *The Sea around Us* is an attempt to grasp the whole of the ocean, and Carson is more inclusive than she was in her previous book. The text is divided into three sections: "Mother Sea," "The Restless Sea," and "Man and the Sea about Him." *The Sea around Us,* with chapters within the sections such as "The Pattern of the Surface" and "Wind, Sun, and the Spinning of the Earth," is more objective in point of view than *Under the Sea-Wind*. Carson used thousands of sources during her research for the book, and *The Sea around Us*, parts of which were first serialized in *The New Yorker*, includes the most up-to-date science of her time as well as allusions to the literature and mythology of the sea. Moving beyond *Under the Sea-Wind*, the ecology of *The Sea around Us* involves not only landforms and inhabitants of the oceans but also human perceptions and representations of them. In fact, humans have much in common with the creatures of the sea: "Each of us begins his individual life in a miniature ocean within his mother's womb, and in the stages of his embryonic development repeats the steps by which his race evolved, from gill-breathing inhabitants of a water world to creatures able to live on land." Whereas in *Under the Sea-Wind* Carson sought an emotional connection, in *The Sea around Us* she insists also on a biological one. *The Sea around Us* functions as an integration of text, observer, natural phenomena, and reader—a mixture of fact and lore, of doubt and inquiry that weakens the subject-object barrier and envisions all entities in ecosystemic relationships.

Though her prose most often celebrates these relationships, in this book Carson has become, nonetheless, more critical of the human destruction of ecosystems that goes hand in hand with our unexamined faith in science and reason. In "Heroines of Nature: Four Women Respond to the American Landscape" (in *The Ecocriticism Reader: Landmarks in Literary Ecology,* 1996), Vera Norwood writes, "Throughout *The Sea Around Us* Carson points out humankind's inability to live in terms of the grand natural cycles science has enabled us intellectually, at least, to know." A good example is the chapter "The Birth of an Island," in which Carson describes the process of island building and

comments on the human-induced tragedy of some Pacific Islands. When ships first visited these isolated places, Europeans introduced goats and cattle and exotic plants that decimated unique island ecologies. Even rats swimming ashore from a ship could by themselves destroy an ecosystem, as had happened as late as 1943.

Writing about an Australian island where shipwrecked rats made land, altering the environment, Carson quotes an islander in an eerie echo of *Silent Spring*: "This paradise of birds has become a wilderness, and the quietness of death reigns where all was melody." Carson goes on to say:

> The tragedy of the oceanic islands lies in the uniqueness, the irreplaceability of the species they have developed by the slow processes of the ages. In a reasonable world men would have treated these islands as precious possessions, as natural museums filled with beautiful and curious works of creation, valuable beyond price because nowhere in the world are they duplicated.

Here she inverts what might be considered the dominant understanding of "reason" and "a reasonable world." It is, of course, reason that leads people to "improve" islands by introducing agricultural methods, animals, and plants. Carson would revise our conception of reason so that it recognizes the value of ecological relationships and the sanctity of all life-forms. To her mind, we should treasure these things as we treasure great art, and recognize their aesthetic value.

In another echo of *Silent Spring*, Carson retains some hope for the inviolability of the sea—"There is the promise of a new spring in the very iciness of the winter sea"—and she remains on some levels caught up in the postwar optimism of America, praising advances in technology and oceanography spurred on by the war effort: "We seem on the edge of exciting new discoveries. Now oceanographers and geologists have better instruments than ever before to probe the depths of the sea, to sample its rocks and deeply layered sediments, and to read with greater clarity the dim pages of past history."

Carson was never opposed to technology per se. She was, however, critical of an unexamined faith in technology: "Most of man's habitual tampering with nature's balance . . . has been done in ignorance of the fatal chain of events that would follow." She was deeply concerned about the consequences for the rest of creation as faith in science remained inviolable, as technology became powerful beyond all expectations, as rational knowledge and aesthetic perception became even more compartmentalized.

Its blending of science and art in a style accessible to a wide readership constitutes much of the appeal of *The Sea around Us*. This book cemented Carson's fame and enabled her to leave her job with the Fish and Wildlife Service and to devote her time entirely to writing. It won the John Burroughs Medal for excellence in nature writing, as well as the National Book Award, and the 1952 documentary film version of the book (produced by RKO Radio Pictures) won an Oscar. *The Sea around Us* proved a key text in the development of Carson's ecological aesthetic, and its fame gave her ample opportunity to reflect on her creative process. On the occasion of accepting the National Book Award on January 27, 1952 (the speech is collected in *Lost Woods*), Carson had much to say about both her aesthetic and the ethical valence of her writing practice. Concerning the poetic nature of her book, she claimed:

> The winds, the sea, and the moving tides are what they are. If there is wonder and beauty and majesty in them, science will discover these qualities. If they are not there, science cannot create them. If there is poetry in my book about the sea, it is not because I deliberately put it there, but because no one could write truthfully about the sea and leave out the poetry.

Like Henry David Thoreau, who wrote, "Let us not underestimate the value of a fact, it will one day flower in a truth," Carson felt that there was beauty in scientific information about the natural world. An accurate description of physical phenomena need not be mundane. Her poetry, she insisted, is manifest in her subject, in the fact that, for example, humans carry the chemical structure of seawater in their very blood: "Fish, amphibian, and reptile, warm-blooded bird and mammal—each of us carries in our veins a salty stream in which the elements sodium, potassium, and calcium are combined in almost the same proportions as in sea water." The structure and rhythm of the sea must, then, be both in our veins and in our poetry. Carson was, of course, a highly skilled writer and a tireless reviser. She insisted upon hearing her work read aloud to her. It would be incorrect to think that she was unaware of her own poetic skill. But she makes no effort to impose an imaginative order upon the sea, in the style of the Romantic poets. On the contrary, her writing reveals the juncture at which literary harmony and natural harmony meet and interpenetrate. As Linda Lear so succinctly puts it, "Accuracy and beauty were never antithetical qualities in her writing."

THE EDGE OF THE SEA

Writing about Carson in 1996 in *American Nature Writers,* edited by John Elder, Cheryll Glotfelty asserted that, after *The Sea around Us,* Carson "had become an authority whose opinions were quoted, rather than an unknown writer who quoted authorities." Carson's next book, *The Edge of the Sea,* is in some ways a companion piece to *The Sea around Us.* Where the earlier book attempts to grasp the entire sea, *The Edge of the Sea* engages the United States Atlantic shore and the three broad littoral habitats it provides, a rocky shoreline from Cape Cod north, a sandy one from Cape Cod south, and the coral reefs of the Florida Keys, and she writes, according to Lear, "about each geological area as a living ecological community rather than about individual organisms." Each place is a life zone in itself, and each life zone contains a myriad of smaller divisions, each a world unto itself, yet influenced by and influencing all the others.

Edges are places long known to ecologists, bird-watchers, and field biologists. The places where field and forest merge, riparian areas, and the littoral zones between tide lines are places of genetic exchange, places of extraordinary evolutionary potential. *The Edge of the Sea* was first proposed to her as a field guide to the shorelines, but Carson took the concept of a field guide and radicalized it. A field guide typically features photographs of birds or fish or trees followed by simple descriptions and tips toward field identification. Carson dismisses this format as inadequate. Things can be identified only in the context of their relationships to other animals and habitats. Her outlook is ecosystemic: early in the book she writes, "Nowhere on the shore is the relation of a creature to its surroundings a matter of single cause and effect; each living thing is bound to its world by many threads, weaving the intricate design of the fabric of life." In this book even more than in her previous one, her aesthetic depends upon ecological principles of interrelation.

Further, Carson's ecosystemic view seems to have important ethical ramifications. In *The Edge of the Sea* Carson asks a series of questions:

> What is the message signaled by the hordes of diatoms, flashing their microscopic lights in the night sea? What truth is expressed by the legions of the barnacles, whitening the rocks with their habitations, each small creature within finding the necessities of its existence in the sweep of the surf? And what is the meaning of so tiny a being as the transparent wisp of protoplasm that is a sea lace, existing for some reason inscrutable to us—a reason that demands its presence by the trillion amid the rocks and weeds of the shore?

While these creatures in their own world have no "message," no "truth," and no "meaning" as we conceive of these terms, they exist in a relationship that possibly does have an ethical message, truth, or meaning. Carson does not answer her rhetorical questions because there are no answers, only a continuity of questions—the questions are open-ended and intended to contribute to ongoing experience. The meaning inherent in these creatures is the unreachable meaning of life, and each creature contributes to the integrity of life in an interrelational, ecological community. Meaning is in relationships.

Many passages in *The Edge of the Sea* are perceptions of these centrally important connections and relationships. Carson's prose gears these perceptions to the physical environment and engages the reader with the ecology of facts and ideas contained in the book. Paul Brooks, in *The House of Life: Rachel Carson at Work* (1972), insists that "as a writer she used words to reveal the poetry—which is to say the essential truth and meaning—at the core of any scientific fact. She sought the knowledge that is essential to appreciate the extent of the unknown." *The Edge of the Sea* is a text in which the mental, physical, known, and unknown worlds interrelate. At the beginning of the book, Carson looks out over a cove on the western coast of Florida, and senses the following:

> The sequence and meaning of the drift of time were quietly summarized in the existence of hundreds of small snails—the mangrove periwinkles—browsing on the branches and roots of the trees. Once their ancestors had been sea dwellers, bound to the salt waters by every tie of their life processes. Little by little over the thousands and millions of years the ties had been broken, the snails had adjusted themselves to life out of water, and now today they were living many feet above the tide to which they only occasionally returned. And perhaps, who could say how many ages hence, there would be in their descendants not even this gesture of remembrance for the sea.

For many people, perhaps, the snails on the mangrove roots would qualify as a curiosity. But Carson is able to translate their silent experience into a general experience of time and evolution, making it available to her readers. Carson insisted that the physical human being still retains some elements of the sea in her or his body, and through this subtle link, the relationship of human evolution and the evolution of the snails is established. We share a similar pattern of evolution and adjustment.

We are linked, and through Carson's prose that link is clarified and concentrated. And Carson perceives further relationships. Her experience does not stop with her thoughts on the snails in isolation—it has continuity. She notices other shells on the beach, horn shells, and wishes that

> I might see what Audubon saw, a century and more ago. For such little horn shells were the food of the flamingo, once so numerous on this coast, and when I half closed my eyes I could almost imagine a flock of these magnificent flame birds feeding in that cove, filling it with their color. It was a mere yesterday in the life of the earth that they were there; in nature, time and space are relative matters, perhaps most truly perceived subjectively in occasional flashes of insight, sparked by such a magical hour and place.

In a flash of insight spurred by small shells in the sand, Carson imagines the beach as a swash of living color. Her vision is rendered even more compelling by the juxtaposition of the evolutionary scale of millions of years enjoyed by the periwinkles, animals that human beings have left alone, with the tragic fate of the flamingos, creatures that human beings have killed in large numbers. One feels a deep sense of loss, and the birds are raised to almost Homeric status through the epithet "flame birds." Her use of phrases such as "might see," "half closed my eyes," and "could almost imagine" lend a special poignancy to the sense of loss, as if the birds and the beauty they brought with them

were just out of reach. Carson also makes an interesting connection between the particular and the general by juxtaposing "time" and "space" with "hour" and "place." To be able to undergo a profound experience in a particular hour and place—to experience the local—is, paradoxically, to experience the world in its largest categories—those of time and space. Carson perceives relationships here in an ecological web that connects abstract and concrete, ocean and shore, present and vanished creatures, and past and present writers and painters of the natural world. In fact, the distinctions between these pairs begin to vanish, and dualistic thinking begins to drop away. To figure oneself—whether artist, critic, scientist, or philosopher—primarily as a subject gazing onto an objectified world elides the possibility of meaningful experience. It denies the subject's intimate and intricate relationship to the object-world.

The *Edge of the Sea,* more than the two books preceding it, draws Carson's personal experience into its discourse. The book is framed by Carson's personal observations and thoughts about the sea. This adds another layer to the texture of the book. But more importantly, it takes the human observer out of the background and foregrounds the human author in a position relative to her environment as both subject and object. She attempts to see objectively, but her own response to the world is a subject of the book. This integrates the human response into the ecosystem of the shoreline. For example, reflecting upon the book she has just written, Carson takes us both to the sea and to the site of writing: "Now I hear the sea sounds about me; the night high tide is rising, swirling with a confused rush of waters against the rocks below my study window." The writing subject and the subject of her writing are one. The sounds of the sea, the tides and water and rocks, find their way into Carson's study and onto the page—they are literally there with her. She is implicated in a web of relationships that include the physical and the textual. The seashores are perhaps the most productive edges on earth, and Carson's book becomes a part of this rich, relational zone.

The Edge of the Sea opens with an introductory section called "The Marginal World," in which Carson reveals herself to her readers. She tells us:

> Once, exploring the night beach, I surprised a small ghost crab in the searching beam of my torch. He was lying in a pit he had dug just above the surf, as though watching the sea and waiting. The blackness of the night possessed water, air, and beach. It was the darkness of an older world, before Man. There was no sound but the all-enveloping, primeval sounds of wind blowing over water and sand, and of waves crashing on the beach. There was no other visible life—just one small crab near the sea. I have seen hundreds of ghost crabs in other settings, but suddenly I was filled with the odd sensation that for the first time I knew the creature in its own world—that I understood, as never before, the essence of its being. In that moment time was suspended; the world to which I belonged did not exist and I might have been an onlooker from outer space.

Alone with the crab on the night beach on the Georgia coast, Carson has an epiphany of sorts. She shares an eloquent awareness that although humans are related to all things, they remain emphatically different. This awareness surfaces periodically in her writing, but this time Carson draws readers into her own, very real, discomfort—into "the darkness of an older world"— where she is suddenly filled with the wonder of new discovery in a scene she had encountered hundreds of times before. She perceives a renewed relationship in experience, feels that she has seen into the essence of the crab, yet remains qualitatively different from it. This does not remove the crab to a transhistorical or transcendental realm, but rather, it momentarily privileges the crab's experience over that of the perceiving human. Carson undergoes a shiver of realization that she somehow knows the world of the crab, and this in turn throws her world into question. Finding herself in a realm of intersubjectivity, she experiences a dissolution of ego. Carson insists that any ecological aesthetic or ethical structure must incorporate respect for other life-forms with whom we share this world, and that this respect entails relinquishing the belief that humans stand separate from the physical environment. We are among a myriad of subjectivities. From an environmental perspective, as we diminish these others, we deny other beings the right to evolve in their own ways, and we degrade the texture of the world for ourselves and for all living things. A purely human world would be profoundly void of the edges where both life and art are generated.

As mentioned earlier, in Carson's work the surface of the sea suggests interrelationship, and in *The Edge of the Sea,* this idea becomes far more complex. Carson writes:

> For it is now clear that in the sea nothing lives to itself. The very water is altered, in its chemical nature and in its capacity for influencing life processes, by the fact that certain forms have lived within it and have passed on to it new substances capable of inducing far-reaching effects. So the present is linked with past and future, and each living thing with all that surrounds it.

The seawater drives life itself, and all forms of living things contribute to the power of the water to support life. The sea provides an interface not only of creatures and habitats, but of time. It contains the past, present, and future; indeed, in the cycle of things, the distinctions between these humanly defined temporal categories become blurred. Time does not seem linear—if anything it is cyclical, linked with the processes of living, dying, and decomposing of various life-forms.

To take this cycle one step further, the creatures of the coral reefs blur distinctions between biology and geology, between living and nonliving things:

All are important in the economy of the marine world—as links in the living chains by which materials are taken from the sea, passed from one to another, returned to the sea, borrowed again. Some are important also in the geologic processes of earth building and earth destruction—the processes by which rock is worn away and ground to sand, by which the sediments that carpet the sea floor are accumulated, shifted, sorted, and distributed. And at death their hard skeletons contribute calcium for the needs of other animals or for the building of the reefs.

The actual building of the earth happens within the sea, and the importance of these little creatures begins to rival the efforts of human beings. For all our massive construction projects, the tiny creatures of the sea are essential to building the world itself, and they contain the potential for its future. Carson's assertions here are admittedly subtle, but we begin to sense that we destroy these other worlds only at dire risk to ourselves. Along with the pleasure derived from and the beauty perceived in Carson's writing comes an ethical imperative that human beings handle themselves with renewed respect for and restraint toward the natural world.

There are, of course, many reasons why people should behave in this respectful way toward the natural world. Many of them are practical—we may run out of wood and water. But Carson makes other reasons clear too. Part of her project seems to be the reconstitution of our sense of pleasure in our world. Simply, we are lucky to be living in a world that remains beautiful. We are participants in an ongoing process of life on earth about which we have no final knowledge. Carson takes this concept of interrelationship out of the laboratory, where, as Lawrence Buell comments in *The Environmental Imagination,* "These arenas of biological interdependence can . . . be talked about in wholly clinical ways devoid of political or affective content." She casts the scientific fact of interrelationship in "affective," aesthetically pleasing prose. An aesthetic appreciation of anything usually entails an enjoyment of that thing, and in renewing readers' capacity for joy and wonder in their interdependence with the biosphere, Carson takes an aesthetic and ethical position toward both human and other-than-human environments.

Revising the dominant, bureaucratic scientific discourse of her time, Carson charts scientific facts and concepts in literary language. For example, she explains in the book's preface that *The Edge of the Sea* includes an appendix "for the convenience of those who like to pigeonhole their findings neatly in the classification schemes the human mind has devised." Carson's language is clearly dismissive of neat classification. She insists that "to understand the shore, it is not enough to catalogue its life. Understanding comes only when, standing on a beach, we can sense the long rhythms of earth and sea that sculptured its land forms." Carson tries to create an aesthetic experience that binds science and art. Aesthetic experience implies for her an interrelationship between reader, text, and world.

She hopes to encourage a perception of the relationships between earth and sea, between the human and the environment. Looking into a tidepool "paved" with mussels, Carson sees the following: "The water in which they lived was so clear as to be invisible to my eyes; I could detect the interface between air and water only by the sense of coldness on my fingertips. The crystal water was filled with sunshine—an infusion and distillation of light that reached down and surrounded each of these small but resplendent shellfish with its glowing radiance." The edge here between air and water is invisible, yet cool to the touch, and in this passage Carson does not insist that we see this permeable boundary, but that we look at it not only with our eyes but with all our senses and our imaginations. She posits an ethical commitment of the human organism to looking at the world beyond itself.

This commitment does not release her from the bonds of language and culture. Carson employs metaphors deeply ingrained in the Western cultural tradition to evoke a sense of wonder at the world she looks into. The water is like a crystal chalice, full to the brim, in which light is infused and distilled, and the light "reached down" to the mussels in an image packed with religious overtones. The light is like the hand of a god, and the mussels are "resplendent" in its "radiance," haloed if you will. Further, the mussels provide a site of connection, and Carson, with her metaphor, sets the reader up to perceive what she seems to insist is a quality of sacredness in ecological interconnection: "The mussels provided a place of attachment for the only other visible life of the pool. Fine as the finest threads, the basal stems of colonies of hydroids traced their almost invisible lines across the mussel shells." Carson extends the metaphor of the "crystal water" to the description of the hydroids, whose "branches are enclosed within transparent sheaths, like a tree in winter wearing a sheath of ice," linking the ecosystem of the tide pool to the ecosystem of the land. She continues, "From the basal stems erect branches arose, each branch the bearer of a double row of crystal cups," and the metaphor is extended further with the connection to the cup-bearer, one who holds a profoundly important place in religious and heroic lore.

Of course, the hydroids are predators, and because Carson cannot see any other life-forms in the water does not mean that they are not there. In fact, they must be there:

Somewhere in the crystal clarity of the pool my eye—or so it seemed—could detect a fine mist of infinitely small particles, like dust motes in a ray of sunshine. Then as I looked more closely the motes had disappeared and there seemed to be once more only that perfect clarity, and the sense that there had been an optical illusion. Yet I knew it was only the human imperfection of my vision that prevented me from seeing those microscopic hordes that were the prey of the groping, searching tentacles I could barely see.

Carson, one could say, is "groping" and "searching" too. The "crystal" metaphor is carried through, yet in spite of the limpid environment, Carson can "barely see." With this construction, "barely see," Carson sets the human being in relationship to the small ecosystem she has perceived in the tide pool. She realizes that she is not (or is only barely) a part of this little world, yet by casting it in affective prose, she draws herself and her readers into the life of the tide pools. However, we can read here a note of caution. This world is something we can barely see; for Carson, it is sacred in that it is an example of the ecological intricacy of life itself, yet the human apparatus can barely perceive it, cannot, certainly, understand it in its full complexity. In the face of such beauty and complexity, any approach should be one of restraint. Damage to these places and creatures damages life itself.

Her aesthetic and ethical practice are distilled when she recalls her first sighting of a West Indian basket star: "For many minutes I stood beside it, lost to all but its extraordinary and somehow fragile beauty. I had no wish to 'collect' it; to disturb such a being would have seemed a desecration." Carson's experience with the starfish provides a marker for an ecological stance toward the entire biosphere. The star is not something for humans to "collect," though we have the right to enjoy it as long as we leave it as undisturbed as possible. Its beauty is wonderful, and we know theoretically that it and its habitat are extremely fragile, yet we cannot seem to put our theoretical knowledge to practical use. Alone, theory is little help. Again, the allusion to religion with the term "desecration" suggests that the degradation of the natural world is, for Carson, akin to the desecration of a temple. At its most radical sense—at its root—Carson's call is for respect and restraint concerning the natural world.

Her ethical call, in large part grounded in aesthetic appreciation, still has an unpalatable ring in our dominant culture. In *Speaking for Nature: How Literary Naturalists from Henry Thoreau to Rachel Carson Have Shaped America* (1980), Paul Brooks describes how Carson's ethical and aesthetic position challenged the status quo. He writes that in her stance toward the scientific establishment, she declared "the basic responsibility of an industrialized, technological society toward the natural world. This was her heresy. In eloquent and specific terms she set forth the philosophy of life that has given rise to today's environmental movement[s]." Carson's philosophy is grounded in the interrelatedness of all things, in an ecology of values. At the close of *The Edge of the Sea,* she writes:

> Once this rocky coast beneath me was a plain of sand; then the sea rose and found a new shore line. And again in some shadowy future the surf will have ground these rocks to sand and will have returned the coast to its earlier state. And so in my mind's eye these coastal forms merge and blend in a shifting, kaleidoscopic pattern in which there is no finality, no ultimate and fixed reality—earth becoming fluid as the sea itself.

The state of the world is fluid, cyclical, and contingent.

SILENT SPRING

Silent Spring grew in part from Carson's grudging awareness that the cycles of life had perhaps become all too contingent upon human behavior. In a revealing letter that she wrote to her friend Dorothy Freeman in February 1958, Carson acknowledged her concern that the natural world may not outlast human onslaught:

> I suppose my thinking began to be affected soon after atomic science was firmly established. Some of the thoughts that came were so unattractive to me that I rejected them completely, for the old ideas die hard, especially when they are emotionally as well as intellectually dear to one. It was pleasant to believe, for example, that much of Nature was forever beyond the tampering reach of man—he might level the forests and dam the streams, but the clouds and the rain and the wind were God's. . . .
>
> It was comforting to suppose that the stream of life would flow on through time in whatever course that God had appointed for it—without interference by one of the drops of the stream—man. And to suppose that however the physical environment might mold Life, that Life could never assume the power to change drastically—or even destroy—the physical world.

Silent Spring is set against this stage of awareness, and coupled to the threat of nuclear devastation was the profound increase in the use of chlorinated hydrocarbon pesticides such as DDT and organic phosphorous compounds such as malathion, which Carson had noticed years before were taking a toll on the physical environment. As early as 1945, Carson had proposed an article on the toxic effects of DDT, but could find no venue. DDT was developed during World War II and was acclaimed as a wonder chemical. Its discoverer was awarded a Nobel Prize. Carson, then, found herself in a position not only challenging the purveyors of pesticides but confronting a cold war mentality that valued technological advance over environmental concerns.

At the same time, she faced personal hardship. In 1957, following the death of her niece, she adopted her grandnephew, Roger Christie. Her mother died in 1958. Carson herself suffered from a number of physical problems, including an ulcer, debilitating arthritis, a painful eye infection, and chief among them, breast cancer, for which she had been initially misdiagnosed and inadequately treated. She underwent a mastectomy and radiation treatments while she was researching and writing *Silent Spring.* The book is a testimony to her mental and physical courage.

Carson's final decision to write *Silent Spring* was spurred on by a letter written to the *Boston Herald* by a local writer and editor, Olga Huckins. Aerial spraying of pesticides had been taking place on a large scale around the Boston area in the late 1950s, and concerned citizens had written to the newspaper to complain about loss to wildlife. In response to these letters and to a group who called themselves the Committee against Mass Poisoning, several letters appeared—one from R. C. Coleman, who was involved in the spraying—denying that wildlife had been harmed, and deriding the people who claimed that their backyards were full of dead and dying birds as "hysterical." After the publication of *Silent Spring,* Carson herself was widely attacked as a "hysterical" woman. Huckins, who had favorably reviewed *The Sea around Us* years before, wrote a scathing letter to the *Herald* in response to the denials of wildlife poisoning. She sent Carson a copy of the letter, which helped solidify Carson's commitment to producing an article on the use of DDT. Eventually Carson contacted E. B. White at *The New Yorker,* who showed interest, and Carson was on her way toward engaging a task she had no idea would grow to such enormity. On the acknowledgments page of *Silent Spring,* Huckins is the first person mentioned: "In a letter written in January 1958, Olga Owens Huckins told me of her own bitter experience of a small world made lifeless, and so brought my attention sharply back to a problem with which I had long been concerned. I then realized I must write this book."

Silent Spring, like *The Sea around Us,* was initially serialized in *The New Yorker.* After two sections appeared in the magazine, several chemical producers tried to stop the third installment, and ultimately the publication of the book itself, with lawsuits and threats, but *The New Yorker* and Carson's publisher at Houghton Mifflin, Paul Brooks, were unshakable in their support for Carson. In classic cold war bombast, the spokesman for Velsicol, maker of chlordane and heptachlor, in a letter to Houghton Mifflin, pinned Carson as part of a conspiracy with intent "to create the false impression that all business is grasping and immoral, and to reduce the use of agricultural chemicals in this country and the countries of western Europe, so that our supply of food will be reduced to east-curtain parity." Carson herself makes masterful use of cold war rhetoric, turning it ingeniously to her own use. Just as *The Edge of the Sea* begins with a personal anecdote of a small person in a large world, Carson begins *Silent Spring* with a fable about a small town in a big country. She uses this rhetoric to appeal to her largely suburban readership—to instill an awareness of and awaken a fear for the dangers posed to suburban communities by pesticide use. After describing an idyllic landscape—"There was once a town in the heart of America where all life seemed to live in harmony with its surroundings . . ."—she introduces silence and poison:

> There was a strange stillness. The birds, for example—where had they gone? Many people spoke of them, puzzled and disturbed. The feeding stations in the backyards were deserted. The few birds seen anywhere were moribund; they trembled violently and could not fly. It was a spring without voices. On the mornings that had once throbbed with the dawn chorus of robins, catbirds, doves, jays, wrens, and scores of other bird voices there was now no sound; only silence lay over the fields and woods and marsh. . . .
>
> In the gutters under the eaves and between the shingles of the roofs, a white granular powder still showed a few patches; some weeks before it had fallen like snow upon the roofs and the lawns, the fields and streams.

Carson brings the stark recognition of risk directly into the lives of average Americans, and she makes apparent the threat to that most cherished American symbol, the home.

Having successfully set her readers on edge, Carson moves on in the next chapter to explain in general terms the environmental dangers of pesticide use, and to focus on the fact that employment of pesticides goes on without full public knowledge and often with disdain for public concern. In this, she takes her place among writers such as Harriet Beecher Stowe, John Muir, and John Steinbeck, whose calling has been to contribute to the public good. As mentioned earlier, a characteristic of the aesthetic Carson developed in her writing is the poetic presentation of scientific ideas to the general public. Although *Silent Spring* contains passages that are indeed lyrical, the emphasis of this book is far different from that of the other three. Although the earlier books too have a political underpinning, *Silent Spring* is a profoundly political book. In writing it Carson wanted something to happen, and it did.

Silent Spring describes in detail the various types of chemicals used, their effects on the lives of all creatures, their misuse by uninformed or uncaring technicians and farmers. She investigates entanglements among the U.S government, large research units at state-supported universities, and chemical-producing industries. The work marks an interesting shift in her thought, one that still bears on ecological perception. In her earlier writing, Carson celebrated ideas of ecological interdependence, interrelationship, food chains, and webs. But now she reveals a dark side of interrelationship: the cycles of life that she so celebrated now undeniably contain billions of tons of man-made poisons.

Carson is angry about this. And the ecology of the problem includes a whole linkage of characters. Suburbanites, in order to eliminate crabgrass according to neighborhood mores, administer astounding amounts of poison to their lawns:

Marketed under trade names which give no hint of their nature, many of these preparations contain such poisons as mercury, arsenic, and chlordane. Application at the recommended rates leaves tremendous amounts of these chemicals on the lawn. Users of one product, for example, apply 60 pounds of technical chlordane to the acre if they follow directions. If they use another of the many available products, they are applying 175 pounds of metallic arsenic to the acre. The toll of dead birds . . . is distressing. How lethal these lawns may be for human beings is unknown.

Such passages have a powerful rhetorical effect, given that "lawns" conjure images of the ground upon which one rolls and frolics with the children and the family dog.

Carson goes on to morally question the marketing strategies used to sell chemicals. For instance, if one buys poison at the drugstore, one must sign a register, but one can buy any number of lethal poisons in the supermarket and hardware store without ever realizing the potency of what one buys. The poison is shelved next to the dishwasher soap and the lawn mower. The questions that Carson asks in this book force the American public into recognizing crucial links among scientific knowledge, commercial freedom, and morality. The needs of commerce and science seem always to take precedence, and Carson seeks to redress this myopia in *Silent Spring*. Her central inquiry remains pertinent: "The question is whether any civilization can wage relentless war on life without destroying itself, and without losing the right to be called civilized."

The relationship of modern industrial culture to the natural world demands revision. Carson began with an aesthetic that grew from love of the natural world, and though she never lost the intensity of that love, environmental degradation caused her to demand answers to questions she would rather not have asked. "Who has decided—who has the *right* to decide—for the countless legions of people who were not consulted that the supreme value is a world without insects, even though it be also a sterile world ungraced by the curving wing of a bird in flight?" She insists that "beauty and the ordered world of nature still have a meaning that is deep and imperative."

Carson was heard by many, and following the public outrage incited by *Silent Spring,* attitudes in the United States and around the world began to change. Despite the attacks against her, Carson was steadfast in her defense of her book, even to the point of concealing the fact as best she could that she was dying from cancer, because she feared her opponents would use that information against her. In 1963 Carson testified before a special Senate subcommittee convened to look into pesticide use and headed by Abraham Ribicoff. Within a year, forty states had passed pesticide bills. The Clean Air Act followed in 1963, the Water Quality Act in 1965, and many others were introduced directly or indirectly as a result of Carson's work. DDT was banned in 1972 in the United States, although U.S. companies continued to produce and export staggering amounts.

On April 14, 1964, at her home in Silver Spring, Maryland, Carson died of heart failure after her long battle with cancer. She had worked right through to the end of her life on projects, left unfinished, that championed the integrity of the environment. Her life is a testament to life itself, and for this she was posthumously awarded, in 1980, the Presidential Medal of Freedom. Three decades earlier, during her acceptance of the John Burroughs Medal, Carson spoke these words, which at the beginning of the twenty-first century continue to offer both warning and hope:

> I myself am convinced that there has never been a greater need than there is today for the reporter and interpreter of the natural world. Mankind has gone very far into an artificial world of his own creation. He has sought to insulate himself, in his cities of steel and concrete, from the realities of earth and water and the growing seed. Intoxicated

with a sense of his own power, he seems to be going farther and farther into more experiments for the destruction of himself and the world.

> There is certainly no single remedy for this condition and I am offering no panacea. But it seems reasonable to believe—and I do believe—that the more clearly we can focus our attention on the wonders and realities of the universe about us the less taste we shall have for the destruction of our race. Wonder and humanity are wholesome emotions, and they do not exist side by side with a lust for destruction.

Selected Bibliography

WORKS OF RACHEL CARSON

BOOKS

Under the Sea-Wind: A Naturalist's Picture of Ocean Life. New York: Simon and Schuster, 1941. Reprint, New York: Penguin, 1996.

The Sea around Us. New York: Oxford University Press, 1951. Reprint, New York: Oxford, 1991.

The Edge of the Sea. Boston: Houghton Mifflin, 1955. Reprint, Boston: Houghton Mifflin, 1998.

Silent Spring. Boston: Houghton Mifflin, 1962.

The Sense of Wonder. New York: Harper & Row, 1965. (Book version of Carson's 1956 article "Help Your Child to Wonder.")

The Rocky Coast. New York: McCall, 1971. (Reprint of section three of *The Edge of the Sea.*)

Lost Woods: The Discovered Writing of Rachel Carson. Edited by Linda Lear. Boston: Beacon, 1998.

ARTICLES AND GOVERNMENT PUBLICATIONS

"A Battle in the Clouds." *St. Nicholas Magazine* 45:1048 (September 1918).

"Undersea." *Atlantic Monthly* 160:322–325 (September 1937). Reprinted in Paul Brooks, *The House of Life: Rachel Carson at Work,* 1972, and in *Lost Woods.*

Food from the Sea: Fish and Shellfish of New England, U.S. Department of the Interior, Office of the Coordinator of Fisheries, Fish and Wildlife Service, Conservation Bulletin 33. Washington, D.C.: Government Printing Office, 1943.

Food from the Sea: Fishes of the Middle West, U.S. Department of the Interior, Office of the Coordinator of Fisheries, Fish and Wildlife Service, Conservation Bulletin 34. Washington, D.C.: Government Printing Office, 1943.

Food from the Sea: Fish and Shellfish of the South Atlantic and Gulf Coasts, U.S. Department of the Interior, Office of the Coordinator of Fisheries, Fish and Wildlife Service, Conservation Bulletin 37. Washington, D.C.: Government Printing Office, 1944.

"Ocean Wonderland." *Transatlantic,* March 1944, pp. 35–40.

Food from the Sea: Fish and Shellfish of the Middle Atlantic Coast, U.S. Department of the Interior, Office of the Coordinator of Fisheries, Fish and Wildlife Service, Conservation Bulletin 38. Washington, D.C.: Government Printing Office, 1945.

Chincoteague: A National Wildlife Refuge. Conservation in Action #1. Illustrated by Shirley A. Briggs and Katherine L. Howe. Washington, D.C.: U.S. Fish and Wildlife Service, Government Printing Office, 1947.

Parker River: A National Wildlife Refuge. Conservation in Action #2. Photos and drawings by Katherine L. Howe. Washington, D.C.: U.S. Fish and Wildlife Service, Government Printing Office, 1947.

Mattamuskeet: A National Wildlife Refuge. Conservation in Action #4. Illustrated by Katherine L. Howe. Washington, D.C.: U.S. Fish and Wildlife Service, Government Printing Office, 1947. (Reprinted in *Lost Woods.*)

Guarding Our Wildlife Resources. Conservation in Action #5. Washington, D.C.: U.S. Fish and Wildlife Service, Government Printing Office, 1948.

"The Great Red Tide Mystery." *Field and Stream,* February 1948, pp. 15–18.

"Lost Worlds: The Challenge of the Islands." *The Wood Thrush* 4, no. 5:179–187 (May–June 1949). (Reprinted in *Lost Woods.*)

Bear River: A National Wildlife Refuge. Conservation in Action #8. Coauthored by Vanez T. Wilson.

Illustrated by Bob Hines. Washington, D.C.: U.S. Fish and Wildlife Service, Government Printing Office, 1950.

"The Birth of an Island." *Yale Review* 40, no. 1:112–126 (September 1950).

"The Sea" in "Profiles," *The New Yorker,* June 2–16, 1950.

"Help Your Child to Wonder." *Woman's Home Companion,* July 1956, pp. 25–27, 46–48.

"Our Ever-Changing Shore." *Holiday* 24:71–120 (July 1958). (Reprinted in *Lost Woods.*)

"Vanishing Americans." *Washington Post,* April 10, 1959, p. 26. (Reprinted in *Lost Woods.*)

"To Understand Biology." *Humane Biology Projects.* Washington, D.C.: Animal Welfare Institute, 1960. (Reprinted in *Lost Woods.*)

"The Sea." *Johns Hopkins Magazine* 12, no. 8:6–20 (May–June 1961).

"Of Man and the Stream of Time." Public address, Scripps College, Claremont, Calif., June 12, 1962. Printed in *Scripps College Bulletin* 36, no. 4 (1962).

"Rachel Carson Answers Her Critics." *Audubon* 65:262–265, 313–315 (September–October 1963).

Foreword to Ruth Harrison, *Animal Machines: The New Factory Farming Industry.* London: Vincent Stuart, 1964.

MANUSCRIPTS, PAPERS, AND LETTERS

Rachel Carson Papers, Yale Collection of American Literature, Beinecke Rare Book and Manuscript Library, Yale University, New Haven, Conn.

Rachel Carson History Project, Rachel Carson Council, Chevy Chase, Md.

Always, Rachel: The Letters of Rachel Carson and Dorothy Freeman, 1952–1964. Edited by Martha Freeman. Boston: Beacon, 1995.

CRITICAL AND BIOGRAPHICAL STUDIES

Bonta, Marcia Myers, *Women in the Field: America's Pioneering Women Naturalists.* College Station: Texas A&M University Press, 1991.

Briggs, Shirley A. "Remembering Rachel Carson." *American Forests* 76:8–11 (July 1970).

———. "A Decade after *Silent Spring.*" *Friends Journal,* March 1, 1972, pp. 148–149.

———. "Twenty Years After *Silent Spring.*" *Garden,* May 1982, pp. 10–15.

———. *Silent Spring: The View from 1987.* Chevy Chase, Md.: Rachel Carson Council, 1987.

———. "The Rachel Carson Legacy." *Pesticides News* 1:7 (September 1992).

Brooks, Paul. *The House of Life: Rachel Carson at Work.* Boston: Houghton Mifflin, 1972.

———. *Speaking for Nature: How Literary Naturalists from Henry Thoreau to Rachel Carson Have Shaped America.* Boston: Houghton Mifflin, 1980.

Buell, Lawrence. *The Environmental Imagination: Thoreau, Nature Writing, and the Formation of American Culture.* Cambridge, Mass.: Harvard University Press, 1995.

"Courage of Rachel Carson." *Audubon,* January 1987, pp. 12–15.

Fox, Stephen. *The American Conservation Movement: John Muir and His Legacy.* Madison: University of Wisconsin Press, 1985.

Gartner, Carol B. *Rachel Carson.* New York: Frederick Ungar, 1983.

Glotfelty, Cheryll. "Rachel Carson." In vol. 1 of *American Nature Writers.* Edited by John Elder. New York: Scribners, 1996. Pp. 151–171.

Graham, Frank, Jr. *Since Silent Spring.* Boston: Houghton Mifflin, 1970.

Hanley, Wayne. *Natural History in America: From Mark Catesby to Rachel Carson.* New York: Quadrangle, 1977.

Hynes, Patricia H. *The Recurring Silent Spring.* New York: Pergamon, 1989.

Kass-Simon, G., and Patricia Farnes, eds. *Women of Science: Righting the Record.* Bloomington: Indiana University Press, 1990.

Lear, Linda. *Rachel Carson: Witness for Nature.* New York: Henry Holt, 1997.

Lyon, Thomas J., ed. *This Incomperable Lande: A Book of American Nature Writing.* Boston: Houghton Mifflin, 1989.

Marco, Gino J., Robert M. Hollingworth, and William Durham, eds. *Silent Spring Revisited.* Washington, D.C.: American Chemical Society, 1987.

McCay, Mary. *Rachel Carson.* New York: Twayne, 1993.

Nash, Roderick Frazier. *The Rights of Nature: A History of Environmental Ethics.* Madison: University of Wisconsin Press, 1989.

Norwood, Vera L. "The Nature of Knowing: Rachel Carson and the American Environment." *Signs* 12, no. 4:740–760 (1987).

———. *Made From This Earth: American Women and Nature.* Chapel Hill: University of North Carolina Press, 1993.

———. "Rachel Carson." In *The American Radical.* Edited by Mari Jo Buhle, Paul Buhle, and Harvey J. Kaye. New York: Routledge, 1994, pp. 313–318.

———. "Heroines of Nature: Four Women Respond to the American Landscape." In *The Ecocriticism Reader: Landmarks in Literary Ecology.* Edited by Cheryll Glotfelty and Harold Fromm. Athens: University of Georgia Press, 1996. Pp. 323–350.

Sterling, Philip. *Sea and Earth: The Life of Rachel Carson.* New York: Crowell, 1970.

Stewart, Frank. *A Natural History of Nature Writing.* Washington D.C.: Island Press, 1995.

Waddell, Craig, ed. *And No Birds Sing: Rhetorical Analyses of Rachel Carson's Silent Spring.* Carbondale: Southern Illinois University Press, 2000.

White, Fred D. "Rachel Carson: Encounters with the Primal Mother." *North Dakota Quarterly* 59, no. 2:184–197 (spring 1991).

Worster, Donald. *Nature's Economy: A History of Ecological Ideas.* San Francisco: Sierra Club, 1977.

—CORNELIUS BROWNE

Amy Clampitt

1920–1994

AMY KATHLEEN CLAMPITT occupies a unique position in American poetry. In the scant years between her late and enormously successful arrival on the poetry scene in the late 1970s and her death from ovarian cancer on September 10, 1994, Clampitt was both praised and condemned. Interestingly her admirers and detractors often agree in their characterization of her work. Everyone acknowledges its old-fashioned lushness; its frank interest in the lives and writing of the British Romantic poets; its indebtedness to such early American precursors as Emily Dickinson and Margaret Fuller; its flaunting of scholarly and scientific knowledge; its playful elegance; and its unashamed reveling in language at once arcane and precise. Readers tend to differ only in their evaluation of these characteristics. Some love the rich accretion of detail; others, suspicious of ornament, belittle Clampitt's elaborate style that seems to them a throwback to the late nineteenth century. Bemused by the constantly enthusiastic, often gushing quality of Clampitt's ready interest in almost all aspects of the world around us, what these readers seem to ignore is the method, as well as the spirit, of her vision.

It is appropriate to take the measure of America's oldest young poet, whose five books of poetry, published between 1983 and 1994, were handsomely re-issued in 1997 in a single volume sympathetically introduced by her younger friend, the poet Mary Jo Salter. (All of Clampitt's poems quoted hereafter can be found in that volume, *The Collected Poems of Amy Clampitt,* published by Alfred A. Knopf in 1997.)

Clampitt's individual books are different from one another, as any constantly producing writer's works should be, but in part because of her sensibility and in part because she was over sixty when her first book was published, it seems easier and more effective to consider her work nonchronologically. There are few signs of growth or progress from one volume to the next, although her last book, published posthumously, contains poems written when the poet knew she was dying from cancer. These have in them unmistakable signs of mortality and of urgency to have a final say. The present essay will treat poems from throughout Clampitt's brief career without reference to their chronology.

The effect of reading *The Collected Poems of Amy Clampitt* is one of inundation, and the poetry certainly will not suit everyone's taste. Aspects of Clampitt's poetry that were under attack at the end of the 1990s were her heavy syntax and decoration, her poetry's baroque and ornamental qualities, and her dramatic use of description. Clampitt habitually employs difficult diction—sometimes scientific, sometimes obscure.

In an autobiographical essay, the title piece of her collected prose, *Predecessors, Et Cetera* (1991), Clampitt tells how new and unknown words, "tortfeasor" for instance, excite her. As other critics have observed, reading Clampitt's poetry requires having a good dictionary at hand. She is wonderfully allusive, though detractors call her pretentious or maddening.

An attentive reader will come away from Clampitt's work knowing much about botanical nomenclature and such English and American writers as William and Dorothy Wordsworth, Samuel Taylor Coleridge, John Keats, George Eliot, and Emily Dickinson, who served as a constant source of inspiration for her. Like many well educated writers Clampitt makes little distinction between the lived life of her own outward experience and her richly imaginative inner life as a person committed to books and their authors. (Ironically, the beautiful sequence "Three Voyages: A Homage to John Keats" must be counted a poetic failure since only a reader with a grasp of the details of Keats's life and works can respond fully to these deeply referential poems.)

Compared to the ornateness of Hart Crane and the plainness of William Carlos Williams roughly three-quarters of a century earlier, Clampitt's delicately powerful mingling of high and low, big and small, fancy and fact, the extravagant and the mundane, seems like a revolutionary stance for a late-twentieth-century American poet. Clampitt's readers must work hard, but the poems repay the effort.

Ralph Waldo Emerson once wrote that nature "cannot be surprised in undress. Beauty breaks in everywhere." Few of her contemporaries are as attuned to beauty or reproduce it as lovingly as Clampitt does. And in an age much concerned with issues of gender, Clampitt is unique as a female poet who unashamedly tackles subjects and techniques ordinarily associated with the poet who was rightfully and peculiarly her truest precursor: not her beloved Keats, Wordsworth, or Hopkins, but Walt Whitman. Among women poets in the latter half of the twentieth century, only the younger and more flamboyantly abstruse Jorie Graham has anything approaching Clampitt's ambition.

Amy Clampitt's intellectual and cultural appetite is easy to miss amid the sheer gorgeousness of her sounds, streaming off the page as though released after years of captivity. Clampitt had several unpublished novels stashed away in a drawer when her first volume of poetry, *The Kingfisher,* appeared in 1983. Its publication was heralded as though it and its author had sprung full-blown like Athena from the head of Zeus—or from nowhere. Actually, of course, she had been writing poems for most of her life and for years had been appearing in little magazines before finally breaking into wider view in *The New Yorker* in the late 1970s.

From the start Amy Clampitt sounds linguistically inebriated, as in her early poem "Losing Track of Language" when she moves eagerly from tongue to tongue, landscape to landscape, on a train into Italy from France:

> The train leaps toward Italy, the French Riviera
> falls away in the dark, the rails sing dimeter
> shifting to trimeter, a galopade to a galliard.
> We sit wedged among strangers; whatever
> we once knew (it was never much) of each other
> falls away with the landscape. Words
> fall away, we trade instead in flirting
> and cigarettes; we're all rapport with strangers.

Loss and losing, like all other processes of diminishment, are the original causes of accumulation in whatever form. As with this signature piece, Clampitt often builds her poems insouciantly from an anecdotal opening that broaches major themes (language, history, and culture) in the most offhand way. The delights of experience not only balance, but also depend upon, the losses we have suffered.

And Clampitt is a poet well aware of loss. The details of her life—which she treats in thoughtful but unsentimental ways throughout her work—are significant because they demonstrate where, quite literally, she came from. Her parents, Roy and Pauline Clampitt, were farmers of pioneer stock who owned three hundred acres in New Providence, Iowa, a town of roughly two hundred people. The family was Quaker. Late in her life Clampitt could still recall details of the natural surroundings from her third year. In childhood she developed an interest in bird watching, which remained with her for the rest of her life. And she wrote her first poems when she was nine years old.

Because of the Great Depression the Clampitts lost their ancestral farm and moved to a smaller hardscrabble place, three miles away. For little Amy, age ten, the move felt like expulsion from Eden. For this reason, among others, the adult Clampitt could announce proudly, "I am a poet of place," by which she meant that because of early displacement she yearned for a stable center. As a watcher and a poet she always attended to details of landscape and to the lives of the people resident there.

As intellectuals often do, Clampitt felt like something of a misfit. She said that England became important for her because, in the early 1950s when she first went there, she felt herself more at home among people in a country that prides itself on a populace of eccentrics. A bookish child growing up as the eldest of five in a Quaker household, Amy Clampitt, born June 15, 1920, had an independent streak, always knowing that she could not live a life of midwestern conformity.

Essentially a religious nonbeliever, she retained throughout her life an interest in spirituality culled from her exposure to Society of Friends meetings, Methodist hymns, Episcopal (or Anglican) ritual, and, as a first poetic influence, the deeply religious and lushly lyrical poetry of Gerard Manly Hopkins. Everyone who knew her commented on the serious intellect and almost girlish glee that made her cheerful, earnest, astute, and thoughtful, often in quirky combinations.

Clampitt was educated at Iowa's Grinnell College. After she was graduated in 1941 with honors in English and was inducted into Phi Beta Kappa, she headed for New York City where she began graduate studies at Columbia University. But soon she laid aside that pursuit in exchange for a quiet life working at Oxford University Press (1943–1951) as a secretary and then promotions director of the college textbook division. Following her trip to Europe in 1951 she returned to New York and took up a job first as a reference librarian at the National Audubon Society (1952–1959) and then as a freelance writer (1960–1977).

During this time she tried without success to write novels but eventually concentrated her attention on poetry. Clampitt was finally "discovered" as a literary figure—after the publication of her poetry chapbook *Multitudes, Multitudes,* in 1974—primarily by the late Howard Moss, himself a distinguished poet and longtime poetry editor of *The New Yorker.* From that time onward Moss published Clampitt's poetry regularly in *The New Yorker.*

Although Amy Clampitt lived in Manhattan for her entire adult life, with extensive travels in Europe and the United States, she had an essentially midwestern consciousness, preferring to move through the country by bus (she hated planes) in order to experience the terrain. Jobs in publishing and in libraries, political work, and writing kept her occupied throughout the late 1960s. While campaigning for Eugene McCarthy's bid for the presidency in 1968 she met Harold Korn, a Columbia Law School professor, with whom she lived for the rest of her life. They spent summers in Maine, along a rocky coast that Clampitt loved and often wrote about. Several months before her death, she and Korn married at a home they had bought in the Berkshire Hills of Massachusetts. It was the only real estate she ever owned. She always kept her little flat in Greenwich Village as a means both symbolic and practical of maintaining her independence. Poems of place and poems of uprooting exist in equal measure within her pages and both types derive from the circumstances of the life she lived.

The richness of diction, tone, syntax, and sentiment informing Clampitt's work from the start, like her love of Keats and the other Romantics, can be traced to her upbringing in the Midwest. Just as her passions stemmed from early losses, so Clampitt as a richly decorative poet harbored a chilly persona beneath the exterior. Although she did not have a heart or mind of winter—like Wallace Stevens's "Snow Man"—she had been quite literally cold for a long time. In conversation she once said that no one who has never known viscerally what it is like to be cold to the bone can understand Keats's "The Eve of St. Agnes" with its ravishing, compensatory dreams of sensuous fulfillment, warmth, and escape to the southern moors.

Amy Clampitt arrived at lushness from the chill of her childhood farmstead and from political and religious austerity bred into her by her Quaker forebears and developed through years of political awareness and activity. (Strangely, her detractors tend to ignore the serious poems of political protest in her work, and treat her poetry as if it were mere decoration.) The same distinction obtains with regard to style. She is a poet of the plain as well as the fancy. For every synesthetic embellishment and every hothouse bloom—take for example, "Mirrored among jungle blooms' curled crimson / and chartreuse, above the mantel, diva-throated / tuberoses, opening all the stops, deliver / Wagnerian arias of perfume" ("Townhouse Interior with Cat")— she gives us simple declarative sentences, aphoristic nuggets of wisdom, and moral principles from which some poems proceed and to which others often lead. "A Hermit Thrush," for instance, begins with a two-word sentence: "Nothing's certain." The stark certainty of this opening prepares us for her investigation of tenuousness and tenacity, focusing upon a "gust-beleaguered single spruce tree," the uncertainty of everything except "the tide that / circumscribes us," and the title figure, which serves as Clampitt's homage to the various race of Romantic birds, especially Thomas Hardy's "Darkling Thrush." The poem ends:

> Watching
> the longest day take cover under
> a monk's-cowl overcast,

with thunder, rain and wind, then waiting,
we drop everything to listen as a
hermit thrush distills its fragmentary,
hesitant, in the end

unbroken music. From what source (beyond us, or
the wells within?) such links perceived arrive—
diminished sequences so uninsistingly
not even human—there's

hardly a vocabulary left to wonder, uncertain
as we are of so much in this existence, this
botched, cumbersome, much-mended,
not unsatisfactory thing.

All of the hallmarks of Clampitt's poetry are here: the parenthetical questions that sidetrack and amplify (a lesson learned from her predecessor Elizabeth Bishop); the long sentences; the personification of "the longest day" (with a reminder of its connection to her human observers, themselves taking separate but parallel cover); the skepticism in the face of happiness and wonder, tellingly arrived at in the extended adjectives of the last two lines; and the characteristic British understatement ("not unsatisfactory"), which articulates the sudden happiness that Clampitt is always surprised to encounter. In a world where nothing is certain except the tide that circumscribes all human and natural activity, Clampitt appropriately writes *around* her subject (a disgruntled reader might even call her poems periphrastic) and embodies her vision of the world within sentences that home in on, attack, retreat from, and then re-approach their main objects. For her a "thing in itself" cannot exist; it will always invite another look, another "take," or it will require a supplemental effort to describe and present it.

For all the richness in her poetry Clampitt is, like her contemporary James Merrill (who died five months after she did), an elegiac poet of loss and dislocation. "Losing Track of Language" examines one kind of loss and compensatory gain. "Midsummer in the Blueberry Barrens" begins with a nod in the direction of

Wordsworth, Bishop, and Frost ("Tintern Abbey," "Cape Breton," and "Directive," respectively) by conveying a pattern of disappearance within a landscape: "Away from the shore, the roads dwindle and lose themselves / among the blueberry barrens." Clampitt is sensitive to natural erosion and encroachment for more than merely ecological or aesthetic reasons. All evidence of change echoes personal instability. As early as "On the Disadvantages of Central Heating," which appears in the first section of *The Kingfisher*, she remarks "the farmhouse long sold, old friends / dead or lost track of." Later in that volume, in her first great long poem, "A Procession at Candlemas," Clampitt alludes to Native Americans as merely one of many migratory groups:

> The westward-trekking
> transhumance, once only, of a people who,
>
> in losing everything they had, lost even
> the names they went by, stumbling past
> like caribou, perhaps camped here.

Such renderings of loss, forgetting, unwrapping, returning, and unpeeling are the essential cause of all those accumulations—in imagery, metaphor, rhythm, and syntax—that annoy or fatigue Clampitt's thoughtless or lazy readers.

Amy Clampitt always puts the weight of her style at the service of her sense of diminishment. She is, in fact, as likely to dismiss as to welcome ornament for its own sake; she disdains the merely cute, once referring condescendingly, in "The Nereids of Seriphos," to "Guido Reni, master / of those who prettify." Her Americanness reveals itself in those moments when she adheres to a Yankee's, or a farmer's, sense of value: she loves "all that / utilitarian muck down underfoot" ("The Local Genius"), or *objets trouvés* that are dear for their fragility *and* their usefulness, like the straw ricks in "Stacking the Straw" that exemplify the biblical ephemerality of all flesh. Yet these "beveled loaves" also amount to "the nearest thing the region had / to

monumental sculpture." Like Walt Whitman ("This Compost"), Wallace Stevens ("The Man on the Dump"), and A. R. Ammons (*Garbage*), she bears witness to the beauty of accumulated masses of compost, as in "The Reedbeds of the Hackensack," a bravura sestina (itself a classic form of recycling) with overtones of John Milton's pastoral elegy "Lycidas," in which she meditates on "a poetry of the incorrigibly ugly." Or she contemplates "the pleasures of the ruined" in "Salvage":

> I find esthetic
> satisfaction in these
> ceremonial removals
>
> from the category of
> received ideas
> to regions where pigeons'
> svelte smoke-velvet
> limousines, taxiing
>
> in whirligigs, reclaim
> a parking lot. . . .

She abhors wastefulness, admiring the Darwinian elegance of destruction on the Serengeti plains where first lions, then "down-ruffed vultures," then "feasting maggots / hone the flayed wildebeest's ribcage / clean as a crucifix" ("Good Friday"). Of such natural selection does Clampitt build her own idiosyncratic theology. The study of biology, of all the forces of life, stimulates in Clampitt an almost religious reverence.

One typical misunderstanding of ornament resents it for manufacturing false, unwarranted hullabaloo and for confusing mere excess with depth. In fact Clampitt proves everywhere that "Depth isn't everything," as she aphoristically announces in "The Spruce Has No Taproot." We can take this arboreal example as one of Clampitt's own talismans. Like all the weeds, seedlings, easily displaced persons, tribes, and species with which she identifies, it roots itself shallowly in order to adapt and to form a subtle community:

                    the spruce
has no taproot, but to hold on
spreads its underpinnings thin—

a gathering in one continuous,
meshing intimacy, the interlace
of unrelated fibers
joining hands like last survivors
who, though not even neighbors

hitherto, know in their predicament
security at best is shallow.

Such shallowness makes freedom the reward for truancy. Thus the "pokeweed, sprung from seed / dropped by some vagrant" ("Vacant Lot with Pokeweed") seizes a temporary foothold; or, in the same group of poems, a set of bamboo curtains, "going up where / the waterstained old ones had been, and where the seedlings— / O gray veils, gray veils—had risen and gone down" in the apartment of a Greenwich Village eccentric ("A Hedge of Rubber Trees"). "Nothing stays put," she announces in a poem of that title in this series that celebrates as well as laments eternal impermanence: "All that we know, that we're / made of, is motion." No other contemporary poet except A. R. Ammons has such a grasp on the fact—dangerous and attractive at once—of entropy as a force operating microscopically, historically, and cosmically.

Motion has political—as well as psychological—causes and effects. Clampitt cites the words of an Omaha Indian in her signature piece "The Prairie": "*The white man does not understand America, / a red man wrote: the roots of the tree of his life / have yet to grasp it.*" Any good poet always strives to create a proper form and style for her vision, her subjects. The essence of motion has syntactic consequences, as will be discussed in greater detail later in this essay. What Clampitt calls the "interlace" of her spruce tree also applies to the meshings by which she—here and elsewhere—duplicates and represents other familial, cultural, and historical interlacings, the elaborately constructed networks that enable individual lives to flourish. Where uprooting and exile—even when tempo-

rarily denied or held at bay—pose a constant threat, the only home a poet might finally claim for herself is a strongly built, deeply involuted poetic structure. (A bit less compulsively than Merrill and the younger Mark Doty, Clampitt has a fondness for compact stanzaic "rooms" that offer one kind of refuge.)

The early poem "Black Buttercups" exemplifies the wariness Clampitt learned as a child in the face of unhousing and exile. Although she never suffered, as Merrill did, from a home broken by divorce, her loss of the Edenic farmstead repeats a standard American pattern: families are always on the move. Disruption and exile were the lot of her ancestors. Nothing is permanent. Even the original farmstead gave onto a symbol of final menace:

        the terrain began to drop (the creek
down there had for a while powered a sawmill,
but now ran free, unencumbered, useless)—
that not-to-be-avoided plot whose honed stones'
fixed stare, fanned in the night
by passing headlights, struck back
the rueful semaphore:
There is no safety.

Like Gerard Manley Hopkins, Robert Frost, and Seamus Heaney, other masters of rural pleasure and rural coldness, Amy Clampitt knows how to brace her Latinate syntax and vocabulary with a harsh, grim monosyllabic string ("plot whose honed stones' / fixed stare, fanned in the night . . .") for a maximally chilling effect.

Once readers look closely at the relationship between levels of diction, or at kinds of syntax, they necessarily become aware of the consequences of Clampitt's stylistic choices. Her so-called "literariness" unites the political and aesthetic dimensions of her poetry: it proves that words, phrases, and even allusions are, like human beings, intricately enmeshed in greater units. Any reader, especially a younger one, who has not been trained in either Milton or Latin will have difficulty following the syntax of even a short poem such as "Witness," a single-sentence bus-ride poem (discussed below), or understanding the use of "depends from" in its literal sense of "hanging" ("Savannah"), or being sensitive to the combination of the laconic and ascetic with the extensive and embellished at the end of "Thermopylae":

> we ponder a funneled-down inscription: Tell
> them for whom we came to kill and were killed,
>   stranger,
>
> how brute beauty, valor, act, air, pride, plume here
> buckling, guttered: closed in from behind, our
>   spears
> smashed, as, the last defenders of the pass, we
>   fell,
> we charged like tusked brutes and gnawed like
>   bears.

It is daring enough to make the grim epitaph of Leonidas move directly into the thrilling nouns of Hopkins's "The Windhover," but to move his falcon's "buckle" into the Spartans' "buckling, guttered," and to urge a reminder of beauty's brutality in the "tusked brutes" of carnage makes an even grander—and more resourceful—literary leap. And who else these days employs the Latin construction known as the ablative absolute, Clampitt's own learning having become a naturalized part of her, with as much ease, as this "old-fashioned" poet? "Our spears smashed" pushes us back into high-school memories not of Leonidas and his Spartans but of Caesar and Cicero.

Far from being a merely ornamental poet, in other words, Clampitt has the artistry necessary to weigh, sometimes precariously, the trivial against the extraordinary. When thinking of the inevitable brevity of human life, she adjusts her syntax by relying on appropriate phrases instead of clauses, as at the end of her homage, "Margaret Fuller, 1847":

> What did she *do*?
> it would be asked (as though that mattered).
> Gave birth. Lived through a revolution.

Nursed its wounded. Saw it run aground.
Published a book or two.
And drowned.

Verbs with only an implicit subject, and a glaring rhyme ("aground / drowned") heighten the catastrophe of Fuller's early death. Clampitt snips her normally lengthy sentences to match her heroine's brief, thin-spun life. She knows, as did William Butler Yeats, that sometimes "there's more enterprise in going naked" but only because she knows the feeling of going clothed.

It is no distortion to call her a religious poet, not just in her allegiance to a native Quaker spirit but also in her acknowledgment of many kinds of horror that threaten to undo the inner light and inner voice altogether except in rare moments of privilege, chance, or intuition. In "The August Darks" she cites a phrase from *Middlemarch* by George Eliot—another of her spiritual and cultural heroes—which probably represents her own belief better than any other passage alluded to by this most allusive of contemporary poets: "If we had a keen vision and feeling of all ordinary human life, it would be like hearing the grass grow and the squirrel's heart beat, and we should die of that roar which lies on the other side of silence." Always aware of "the dolor of the particular" ("High Noon"), from which she never shies away, Clampitt is also a sufficiently political poet to know a fundamental truth about Eliot's "roar," which she announces matter-of-factly at the end of "The August Darks": "Many / have already died of it." Even in poems not explicitly concerned with history or politics, Clampitt demonstrates her awareness of our common human destiny.

Clampitt has restored ornament to poetry and has also relied on ambitious use of civilized scholarship, scientific learning, and bookish references. What is most important about her poetic work stylistically is the interplay between two seemingly antithetical aspects: their Keatsian lusciousness and Quaker austerity. We can see this combination most clearly within a genre that Clampitt has made peculiarly her own—the one-sentence poem—of which she has written probably a larger number than any other contemporary poet adhering to conventional punctuation and sentence formation. Of the 193 poems in *The Collected Poems,* thirty-seven are one sentence long. In at least two others, one of which is discussed below, one extremely long sentence is followed by a clipped phrase or a short sentence or two; and there are countless poems with several *very long* sentences in them or several equal stanzas all comprised of a single sentence.

The whole issue becomes more complicated when one takes into account the matter of punctuation. For example, "Or Consider Prometheus" consists of two sections, each of five quatrains. Each section has two sentences, both questions, divided by a question mark and a capital letter to signify the beginning of sentence two. Elsewhere in Clampitt the same rhetorical structure is delineated not by full stops but by colons or semicolons. This choice of punctuation is, of course, not logical or natural, but neither is it merely arbitrary or conventional. A reader with a feeling for Clampitt's syntax might *hear* each of the parts of this poem as a single sentence composed of equal parts. Likewise in "The Waterfall" two initial questioning sentences are succeeded by a longer declarative one that ends without firm closure ("everywhere, existences / hang by a hair"). Even the determination of sentence is not so easy as one might think.

The issue of sentence formation links Clampitt to Whitman, that other Quaker Romantic, whom she resembles in more than her tendency to fuse lushness with a stern moral vision and her American commitment to the inhabitants' relationship to their land. Like Whitman's, Clampitt's sentences tend to welcome us and then set us loose us amid their elaborate extensions. From Whitman, the grand seigneur of

poems-as-lists, Clampitt has learned to construct entire poems, or large portions of them, by relying more on nouns and nominal constructions than on predicates and verbal ones. And as he does she often resorts to a poetic structure dominated by apposition or anaphora (the beginning of successive phrases, clauses, or lines with the same sound or word) rather than subordination. The full effect of a sometimes exhaustive (or exhausting) encyclopedic list depends not only on the nature of its items but also on its syntactic arrangements. Clampitt's syntax, far from self-indulgent display of intricacy, possesses a powerful dramatic force.

More than her diction, her learning, or her subjects, poetic syntax—the sheer ordering of words—is the field in which Clampitt stakes her claims and makes her discoveries, while forcing her readers to make theirs. The drama of her syntax exposes and enacts a central pair of American obsessions: the need to stay put and the need to move on. These are mentioned obliquely and in a British context in a note appended to the one-sentence lyric "Fireweed." Clampitt quotes from John Donne's last sermon at St. Paul's Cathedral in London: "Whatsoever moved Saint Jerome to call the journies of the Israelites, in the wilderness, Mansions, the word . . . signifies but a journey, but a peregrination. Even the Israel of God hath no mansions; but journies, pilgrimages in this life." The passage is attached to a poem that defines a fast-spreading weed:

A single seedling, camp-follower
of arson—frothing bombed-out
rubble with rose-purple lotfuls

unwittingly as water overbrims,
tarn-dark or sun-ignited, down
churnmilk rockfalls—aspiring

from the foothold of a London
roof-ledge, taken wistful note of
by an uprooted prairie-dweller. . . .

Clampitt locates the fireweed within the detritus of urban blight, planting it in her poem, so to speak, everywhere but really nowhere at all. Like the prairie-born poet, the weed is uprooted and easy-to-root at the same time. To understand the poem we must supply the missing verb "is" several times throughout its course. Thus "[Fireweed is] a single seedling"; "[it is] unwitting / of past devastation as of what / remains"; and so forth. The poem is itself like a journey, a continuous act of definition, and also like a mansion or a cluster of single items. The ubiquitous title plant appears, at least linguistically, in the seven tercets as an object of appositional phrasing, a sequence of present participles but with no main verb. Journeys and mansions, centrifugal and centripetal forces, exist in a delicate balance within Clampitt's ornate descriptions.

Why would a poet write a one-sentence poem, one that is longer than, for example, a sonnet? And what are the effects of such a choice? A reader inevitably and automatically reduces a complex, lengthy unit into shorter experiential ones in order to take it all in. Among Clampitt's one-sentence poems, two kinds stand out. The first of these is visually conspicuous: the unpunctuated or sparsely punctuated poem, or the poem arranged with spatial designs on the page. Take for example "Easter Morning," which omits capital letters and a period, or "Let the Air Circulate," which lacks a real beginning and ending but which imagines "spaces between / things looked at" and within the air as blanks within its own typographical structure.

Another sort of one-sentence poem may be identified not by its physical appearance but by its subject. This is what we might call the journey poem, Clampitt's homage to Elizabeth Bishop. Poems like Bishop's "The Moose"— whose first sentence is thirty-six lines long— consist of a long string of phrases and clauses that replicate the poet's movement through a shifting landscape. These poems-of-process originate not only in Bishop but also in Clampitt's imitation of the Romantic poets in

general, and of Keats in particular. Examples include "Witness," in which the mind, mirroring the landscape, actually tells the landscape how it looks, as the landscape itself becomes an abstraction; and "Dallas–Fort Worth: Redbud and Mistletoe," "Iola, Kansas," and "The Subway Singer," the first about an airplane descent, the second about a bus ride, the third about a moving subway train.

In "Iola, Kansas" and "The Subway Singer" Clampitt dramatizes the same sense of community that Bishop's passengers acquire on their long move from Nova Scotia to Boston when stopped and confronted by that famous towering, antlerless, female moose. Like a bus or subway compartment, a sentence contains its own community of phrases, clauses, parts of speech instead of people, although (as explained below) this meeting place can harbor either equals or a hierarchy of members, some subordinate to others. The idea of a sentence as a community corresponds to the twin aspects of Clampitt's character and style. As a Romantic she responds to hierarchy and to highlights, whereas the Quaker in her notices the inner light shining equally through various parts of a sentence, as through a human populace.

Our most famous poet-orphan, Elizabeth Bishop was deeply skeptical of happiness and wisdom in equal measure. "Iola, Kansas" is an implicit homage to the Bishop of such poems as "Arrival at Santos" and "Cape Breton," in addition to "The Moose," which square the fear of the unknown with the thrill of adventure (even that of tourism), and which measure the satisfactions of a seldom achieved community of feeling against the relative unlikelihood that we will ever experience—let alone deserve—happiness, pleasure, and personal identity.

"Iola, Kansas," a one-sentence tour de force that reports an all-night bus ride through the heart of the country, begins by echoing "Arrival at Santos," which ends with the ominous flat statement, "We are driving to the interior," after thirty-seven lines of wittily observed details. Clampitt's journey is more industrialized and more noun heavy:

> Riding all night, the bus half empty, toward the
> interior,
> among refineries, trellised and turreted illusory
> cities,
> the crass, the indispensable wastefulness of oil
> rigs
> offshore, of homunculi swigging at the gut of a
> continent. . . .

Having proceeded from Texas, through Oklahoma, and into Kansas, the bus pauses at a rest stop in the godforsaken town of the title, where the narrator "with something akin to reverence" eats a piece of home-baked boysenberry pie before piling back onto the bus with her fellow travelers:

>   . . . then back to our seats,
> the loud suction of air brakes like a thing alive,
> and
> the voices, the sleeping assembly raised, as by an
> agency
>
> out of the mystery of the interior, to a com-
> munity—
> and through some duct in the rock I feel my heart
> go out,
> out here in the middle of nowhere (the scheme is
> a mess)
> to the waste, to the not knowing who or why, and
> am happy.

Like the bus riders in "The Moose," stopped by a giant creature in the middle of the road, and then united by a "sweet / sensation of joy" before resuming their journey, Clampitt and her companions join together in one of those rare moments of what can only be called grace. Spiritual longing and an awareness of "the strangeness of all there is" inspire her, in spite of her religious, political, and emotional wariness, to be ready to relish such moments when they do—however infrequently—come. Rejoicing often takes place within a context of sharing that is within a community of other people whose very presence assures greater pleasure— and it takes place as well within the syntactic equivalent of community: a long sentence.

"Witness" (the title has overtones of both religion and various kinds of "looking") exemplifies the difficulty of understanding punctuation and its symbolic effects in Clampitt's work. Typically we might assume that a colon suggests both identity of the elements on either side of it and of linear progression. (A. R. Ammons, the contemporary poet most enamored of the colon, comes immediately to mind.) This poem, however, is somewhat more complicated. Its three parts, divided by colons, treat what the speaker in her bus sees first within and then outside a small town. In the third section she finally suggests what it all means. The three sections are part of "an ordinary evening in Wisconsin," somehow equivalent to one another. But the first two sections are more than merely balanced by the third; they are offset by it. Here are the last two-thirds:

>   . . . outside town
>
> the barns, their red gone dark with sundown,
> withhold the shudder of a warped terrain—
> the castle rocks above, tree-clogged ravines
> already submarine with nightfall, flocks
>
> (like dark sheep) of toehold junipers,
> the lucent arms of birches : purity
> without a mirror, other than a mind bound
> elsewhere, to tell it how it looks.

Everything in the first two parts of the poem suggests that single details add up to an abstraction ("purity"). At the same time, the three parts of the poem are distinct, and nothing derives from or mirrors anything else, except the mind moving elsewhere, which reflects (in two senses: it mirrors and it considers) and "tells." In the world of these poems things often seem disjointed, superfluous, offhand, because randomly noticed or fitfully connected, as by the metaphorical associations of ravines with water ("submarine"), junipers with sheep, and birches with human arms.

The more difficult of the single-sentence poems can be defined rhetorically rather than thematically. They rely on the triple modes of apposition, enumeration, and subordination to make their points. The first two are overlapping but different. As a trope of definition, apposition moves by discerning deeper versions of the same thing. Its form follows a version of the paradigm: "X is equally A, which resembles B, which reminds me of C" and so on. Enumeration, the trope of democratic equality, makes Whitmanian lists of separate items. The whole is the sum of its parts. It may work, paradoxically, by accretion and subtraction simultaneously. In the early one-sentence poem "On the Disadvantages of Central Heating"—all phrasal, with no capital letters—Clampitt refers to "the perishing residue / of pure sensation," a residue clarified at last by a verb that supplies a definition: "what's salvaged / is this vivid diminuendo." A list poem works by accumulation. The title "On the Disadvantages of Central Heating" suggests the list that follows, but the poem works at the same time to reduce its enumerated objects to a stripped-down version of reality, since many of its details refer to a past "now quite forgotten" or "lost track of." As forms of listing, apposition and enumeration constitute what we might label Clampitt's poetry of "sensations," whereas subordination—a sentence composed of dependent and interrelated parts—produces her poetry of "thought," to revert to Keats's famous distinction between immediate effects and rational processes.

Clampitt relies on apposition as invocation ("Athena") or on enumeration in the form of a list ("Kudzu Dormant") to suggest spiritual equality. This reliance may explain why so many of her poems lack simple independent verbs, developing instead through a gathering of nouns, noun phrases, *objets trouvés,* and their equivalents. Like Bishop, whose astute line

"Everything only connected by 'and' and 'and'" ("Over 2,000 Illustrations and a Complete Concordance") could stand as her own borrowed motto, Clampitt often culminates her lists by articulating gratitude for simple gifts and truths. Romantic and baroque effects, rich imagery and syntactic complications (especially in the heavily subordinating poems that are discussed below) are reduced, distilled to their essences.

A typical appositive poem is "Marine Surface, Low Overcast." Its seven seven-line stanzas risk losing the reader in a nonstop welter of revisions, some merely a phrase, others more elaborate. The opening demands an elliptical verb:

> Out of churned aureoles
> [comes?] this buttermilk, this
> herringbone of albatross,
> floss of mercury,
> déshabille of spun
> aluminum, furred with a velouté
> of looking-glass. . . .

All the images are equivalent ways of troping a specific scene. It is as though Clampitt has taken Wallace Stevens's "Thirteen Ways of Looking at a Blackbird," eliminated the numbers for the separate sections, and run together all of her figurations.

The first three stanzas proceed with such metaphoric elaborations, and in the fourth the poem expands in two different ways:

> laminae of living tissue,
> mysteries of flex,
> affinities of texture,
> subtleties of touch, of pressure
> and release, the suppleness
> of long and intimate
> association. . . .

Clampitt continues with her "x of y" constructions, but they have now become largely plural and grow from sensuous specificity to abstraction.

By the end of the fifth stanza the poem's first enjambment spills over into the sixth, impulsively heightening a steady progress. And between the sixth and seventh stanzas an even more dramatic syntactic breach appears in order to move the poem out of apposition and into implicit subordination. Here is the beginning of the poem's last concerted image:

> cathedral domes that seem to hover
> overturned and shaken like a basin
> to the noise of voices,
> from a rustle to the jostle
> of such rush-hour
> conglomerations
>
> no loom, no spinneret, no forge, no factor,
> no process whatsoever, patent
> applied or not applied for,
> no five-year formula, no fabric
> for which pure imagining,
> except thus prompted,
> can invent the equal.

For all Clampitt's sensuousness—here evident in the accumulation of details, the reliance on Keatsian double-barreled adjectives, the insistent rhymes and half rhymes—there is something ascetic about the end of the poem. As Merrill does, Clampitt sometimes omits relative pronouns and conjunctions, thereby forcing us to make sense of the missed connections: "of such . . . conglomerations [that there is] no loom. . . for which pure imagining . . . can invent the equal." Whatever else could be said about the experimental nature of this sort of poem of definition, it is clear that Clampitt expects the structure of her sentence, as well as the substance of her images and the truthfulness of her thoughts, to carry the weight of the discovery she challenges us to make along with her. From single noun phrases, through extended varieties of plurals and abstractions, to an increasingly elaborate syntax, this poem deepens, becoming more mysterious than any simple experiment in imagism or listmaking. Having forayed into the fog, she comes to realize the partiality of all attempts of "pure" or even impure imagining. Her poem's breathless, strung-together quality has its own expansiveness.

The second type of single-sentence poems, poems of enumeration, also pays implicit homage to Bishop's and Whitman's habitual anaphora and polysyndeton (the accumulation of phrases or clauses divided by "and" and "and"), although Clampitt works less obviously and more deviously in her accumulations. An early enumerative poem, "Meridian," reflects the complexities of punctuation, verblessness, and the duplicity of equality and process mentioned above. Here it is complete:

> First daylight on the bittersweet-hung
> sleeping porch at high summer : dew
> all over the lawn, sowing diamond-
> point-highlighted shadows :
> the hired man's shadow revolving
> along the walk, a flash of milkpails
> passing : no threat in sight, no hint
> anywhere in the universe, of that
>
> apathy at the meridian, the noon
> of absolute boredom : flies
> crooning black lullabies in the kitchen,
> milk-soured crocks, cream separator
> still unwashed : what is there to life
> but chores and more chores, dishwater,
> fatigue, unwanted children : nothing
> to stir the longueur of afternoon
>
> except possibly thunderheads :
> climbing, livid, turreted alabaster
> lit up from within by splendor and terror
> —forked lightning's
>   split-second disaster.

Here enumeration is equivalent to process. Although such process often involves physical travel, it need not. In fact the most beautiful of these process-poems is the one-sentence "A Winter Burial" which chillingly charts birth, growth, death, and burial in twenty-seven haunting lines.

It is tempting to call "Meridian" a description of a summer day, moving as it does from early morning, through noon, to late afternoon, but it really has the quality of a conjuror's trick. The title announces a potential climax (noon as the day's high point), but this is undermined by the negation at the poem's heart—"no threat in sight"—which may well mean that noon and then afternoon never arrive in the poem but are merely inferred by the poet's reflecting mind that fills in absences. In other words, the poem seems to march through the day, but it also potentially never gets beyond the morning, in spite of its title. There is a hanging back in all those hung phrases: when does "the noon of absolute boredom" *occur* as something other than a part of an unclear sequence ("that apathy")? As often happens in her work, Clampitt's natural timidity or reluctance to specify (in this case the precise time at which noon strikes, or fails to, in the poem's rendering of time) coincides with her richly inventive descriptions. A haunting absence permeates the accumulations of the sentence-as-list.

Where "Meridian" represents the peculiar poise of absence and presence within a natural process, "A Baroque Sunburst" plays with participles to skew our sense of action. Verbs, minimal in some of Clampitt's poems, are here of the essence. The title functions as the subject of the sentence and moves uninterruptedly into the first line:

> struck through such a dome
> as might await a groaning Michelangelo,
> finding only alders and barnacles
> and herring gulls at their usual squabbles,
> sheds on the cove's voluted
> silver the aloof skin tones
> of a Crivelli angel. . . .

What initially appears to be a simple preterite verb ("struck") turns out to be a past participle ("[having] struck through such a dome") that leads through an intervening present participle ("finding") to the simple present-tense "sheds": Clampitt's ingeniously deceptive verbal sequence replicates a natural temporal process.

Clampitt wants us to see reality *in* process and things *as* process: it's the old light-as-wave-and-particle syndrome. Like any work of literature, an Amy Clampitt poem progresses through time; additionally, it often treats time as a subject composed of stark, successive, and often nominal moments. Abidance and movement go hand in hand. In this matter Clampitt's syntax becomes, along with the luxuriousness of her sounds and images praised by partisans and condemned by critics, her sharpest tool, especially in the more complicated poems, which weave their way in and out of a final shape. Just as "Meridian" presents and also withholds the climax of noon, so "Man Feeding Pigeons" gives, though more complexly, with one hand and takes with the other. A twenty-one-line description devolves from an opening generalization: "It was the form of the thing, the unmanaged / symmetry of it." The configuration of pigeons feeding in a circle reminds the poet of angels in a Ravenna mosaic, of colorful sculpted Della Robbia fruit, of a "dance of freewheeling dervishes." After a colon the poem resumes but with a qualification: "it was the form / of the thing, if a thing is what it was, / and not the merest wisp of a part of / a process." And what we might have initially mistaken for artifacts, however rapidly transformed and transforming they are, is now reimagined not only as an unending sequence of events but also as a symbolic representation of spiritual conditions unrealizable except through bodily states:

> this unraveling inkling
> of the envisioned, of states of being
>
> past alteration, of all that we've
> never quite imagined except by way of
> the body: the winged proclamations,
> the wheelings, the stairways, the
> vast, concentric, paradisal rose.

Clampitt deploys the colon more conventionally here. It does not stand naked, between two equal spaces, but snug against the word it follows and opening into that which comes after a polite, normal break. And she makes ingenious use of her participles, present as well as past, and gerunds (with the implicit uncertainty of "being," both participle *and* gerund) to present movement without time. These pseudoverbal words impel us into heavenly realms, those "states of being" in which we become *beings,* beyond alteration ourselves, and resembling the figures from the paradisal inner circle, "a l'alta fantasia qui mancò possa," as Dante has it at the end of the *Paradiso.*

"Man Feeding Pigeons" embodies what John Hollander has described as the truth-giving fiction of any poem's form. We witness two takes on the same phenomenon, as though the poet wants us to feel the relative value of both but finally the superiority of the latter, in which process and spirituality transcend but simultaneously depend upon—quite literally—"the form of things." Like the spirals of incoming and outgoing flocks of pigeons making their ambiguous undulations, Clampitt's sentence pushes us in and speeds us out. Centripetal and centrifugal motions suggest mansions and then journeys to our true spiritual home.

Justifying his own overfondness for parentheses, Samuel Taylor Coleridge once referred in a letter to the "drama of reason" contained within a style that could "present the thought growing, instead of a mere Hortus siccus." What parentheses enabled him to do, syntactic ramification does for Clampitt. Syntax (and not just in a single-sentence poem) serves a dramatic, indeed a mimetic, function. For this reason, a complex poem like "The August Darks" deserves to be included among any list of Clampitt's one-sentence works. Thirty-four lines, one sentence, move to a conclusion, following which a six-word declarative sentence makes a chilling coda, climaxing and undermining the sinuous description of herring boats that set out in darkness before daylight appears.

Although I have called the bulk of this poem a sentence, precisely speaking it is not. Once again Clampitt relies on the fiction of a completed utterance, but the combination of apposition, enumeration, and subordination weaves her readers through strung-out phrasing, and never leaves them in possession of anything more than glittering parts. Like Keats's "To Autumn," Clampitt's poetry of misconceived termination carries us along until we either forget our grammatical progress or mistakenly think that we have encompassed a series of discrete clauses.

Like those other poems that take as their subject almost imperceptible temporal change, "The August Darks" works by slowly transforming its scope and focus. It does so by eliminating natural connectives—not just explicit verbs but also prepositions or conjunctions that might put things in perspective for us—and by replacing them with metaphors that subtly shift attention from one item in a sequence to the next. Here are the first six lines:

> Stealth of the flood tide, the moon dark
> but still at work, the herring shoals
> somewhere offshore, looked for
> but not infallible, as the tide is,
> as the August darks are—
>
> stealth of the seep of daylight. . . .

Even before the second stanza essentially restarts it, we are aware that the poem hangs upon missing statements. We must translate in order to fill the lacunae. Here is an expanded prose paraphrase:

> Here we have the stealth of the flood tide, in which the moon
> is dark but still at work, and the herring shoals, even when looked for,
> can't be found because they and we are not infallible,
> whereas the tide and the darks are always infallible. And at the same
> moment that the flood tide and darkness are stealthy, the light is
> with equal stealth seeping into the scene.

In this depiction of first light Clampitt's figuration complements her syntax. Just as the scene and the syntax move imperceptibly from darkness to daybreak, a central metaphor invades the poem, leaving us uncertain as to what represents what or, in an older critical vocabulary, what term is tenor and what is vehicle. The first fishing boat, ahead of the light, slips out

> into the opening aorta, that heaving
> reckoning whose flux informs the heart-
> beat of the fisherman—poor,
> dark, fallible-infallible
> handful of a marvel
>
> murmuring unasked inside the ribcage,
> workplace covert as the August darks are,
> as is the moon's work, masked within
> the blazing atrium of daylight,
> the margin of its dwindling
>
> sanguine as with labor, but effortless. . . .

"Aorta" initially looks like a rhetorical catachresis (a term misapplied, borrowed, or wrested from one thing in order to name something else that lacks its own). But it then merges with the actual vascular system within the fisherman ("informing" it in several senses). The invisible circulation of the blood within the ribcage parallels the external marine scene and the darkness of the moon, which is replaced by daylight in the shape of the sun, itself a bloody ("sanguine") ornament rising in the skies. Clampitt seems to have absorbed those poems of Percy Bysshe Shelley ("To a Skylark," "The Sensitive Plant") which revolve around the figure of a known but invisible lunar presence that is dimmed by the sun's light. The application of "fallible-infallible" to the human heart recapitulates, of course, the opening of the poem, and it also mimics the systole-diastole sequence of a heartbeat.

The paradox of an "effortless labor," as well as the vast hematological circulatory system within and between external and internal spaces, prepares us for the poem's conclusion, after an intervening description of a cruise ship on the horizon, on which a performance of Tchaikovsky's *Swan Lake* might be taking place:

> . . . the heartbeat's prodigies of strain
> unseen, the tendons' ache, the blood-
> stained toe shoes, the tulle
> sweat-stained, contained
>
> out where the herring wait, beyond
> the surf-roar on the other side of silence
> we should die of (George Eliot
> declared) were we to hear it.

From the aorta of the ocean, to the fisherman's ribcage, to a stage set for dancers with bloodied feet, Clampitt ends her poem with the herring shoals with which she started. She brings it home and moves it out by reminding us of the revelations available through what George Eliot termed "a keen vision and feeling of all ordinary human life." This poem, whose theme is imperceptible borders (between darkness and light, outside and inside, work and pleasure, silence and sound), tests our own sense of borders by its leisurely pacing. The interlacing of image, diction, and syntax buoys and propels the poem until it reaches its philosophical conclusion.

As often happens in Clampitt's expanded poems, however, this one retreats at its end to a statement of simple truth in the form of an anticlimactic sotto voce aside that balances the preceding thirty-four lines: "Many / have already died of it." After the expansion comes the reining in; after the artful spinning-out of detail comes the grim simplicity of a short declarative sentence. The rhythm of opening and closing belongs to rhetoric as well as to the human heart.

Another intricate poem that deserves attention takes a stylistic cue from its subject, "The Olive Groves of Thasos," and depicts, within a deeply convoluted sentence, a gnarled, entwined landscape. It too is both a poem of process (harvesting the olive crop) and a stationing, an attempt to convert a scene into an object, constantly transforming itself before our eyes. Syntax here dramatically replicates the shape of the trees and the depth of the landscape. A progressive subordination submerges us within the sentence that we never know quite where we are until, at the twenty-first line, a human action begins a human action but, as so often in Clampitt's poems, one without a main verb: this sentence, too, turns out to be a fragment. Beginning with a participle in the first line ("Thronging the warped treadmill / of antiquity"), twenty lines of apposition and enumeration capture the image of the trees, "these wards of turbulence" in their "burled stupor." A procession of harvesters appears, but within a subordinate clause so far removed from the poem's opening that we have forgotten that there has been no independent one:

> when from the villages along
> the shore, where in the evenings
> we watched the fishing
> boats go out in strings
>
> of three, in trinities. . . .

From line 21 to line 46, Clampitt begins to notice the various termini ("villages," "hill villages," "middle villages") from which, we are relieved to learn, "the whole populace / turns out, with tarpaulins and / poles, to bring in the harvest / of these trees." And the poem ends, rounding back to its beginning with a series of appositives concerning the trees, but now also with a backward glance at the previous human element in the poem:

>   . . . this time-gnarled
> community of elders—so many-
> shaped, so warped, so densely
> frugal, so graceful a company,
>
> what more can we say, we who have
> seen the summer boats go out,
> tasted the dark honey, and savored
> the oil-steeped, black, half-bitter fruit?

In these lines that sound like a coda the humanized trees remain the genuine, permanent figures of wisdom and authority, whereas people, whether native workers or American tourists, are merely transient passersby. As the poem began with the trees, so it ends with their fruit.

Clampitt seldom uses so rapid a sequence of verbs ("say," "seen," "tasted," "savored") and rarely puts questions in terminal positions. I take the last line as an homage to a whole series of earlier poems that end inquisitively, such as Keats's "Ode to a Nightingale," Shelley's "Mont Blanc" and "Ode to the West Wind," and Yeats's "Among School Children" and "Leda and the Swan." "Frugal" might not be among the first adjectives one would apply to Clampitt's art, but at this point the relatively simple syntax, the clarity of construction, and the modest evasion of moralizing ("what more can we say?") conclude her poem economically as well as gracefully. These gestures have an effect comparable to that of the short declarative sentence at the end of "The August Darks," or the abstraction of "Man Feeding Pigeons," or the clarified residue of "On the Disadvantages of Central Heating." And one might also infer that, just as there is no legitimate independent clause in this sprawling one-sentence poem, neither is there any genuine independent universe, scene, community, or observation that is not organically, logically, or even partially dependent for its existence on a larger commonwealth of relationships. The truth at the heart of Clampitt's poetry is her updating of what Coleridge called the "one life within us and abroad" ("The Aeolian Harp").

Clampitt's poems challenge us to perform readerly gymnastics. Instead of feeling frustration readers must recognize the fact that more than any other contemporary poet—more than Merrill with his quicksilver delicacy, or John Ashbery with his perplexingly seamless transitions from one register of diction to another, or Jorie Graham with her abstruse metaphysical thinking—Clampitt *uses* her syntax to represent the entire spectrum of processes that engage us within the world.

Throughout her work Clampitt masterfully mingles the elegiac and the celebratory, the laconic and the baroque, the clipped and the expansive. Her finely honed style must ultimately be understood as her adjustment of technique to purpose. Her sensuous, deliciously embellished renditions of the natural, the artistic, and the human worlds come in many states of dress and undress. Her poetry gives more than decorative pleasures. It proves that we can appreciate richness without embarrassment.

Such appreciation should become still greater because of Clampitt's turn away from syntax, indeed from language, from all sound but music, at the end. Her last volume, *A Silence Opens,* appeared just after her death in 1994. She knew she was dying as she composed much of it. For that reason as well as others, the book celebrates silence, paucity, lacunae, and diminishments as her earlier ones sometimes giddily celebrate accumulation and richness. Its opening and closing poems listen to the complexities of silence, before language adds its meaning to pure sound and after language disappears from hearing. "Syrinx"—neither the nymph chased by Pan nor the pipe into which she was transformed but "that reed / in the throat of a bird"—reminds us that significance is really an inconsequential, fortuitous part of sound, and that "syntax comes last." This "higher form of expression . . . / is, in extremity, first to / be jettisoned." Sheer breath comes first and is last to go. At the end Amy Clampitt, this poet of vast subordinating syntax, makes a symbolic gesture. "A Silence" abjures punctuation, sentence structure, and all capital letters except those in personal names— God, Joseph Smith, God, and George Fox. Clampitt writes with a refined wildness, delaying the independent clause with its main verb until the end of twenty lines of phrasal units that locate the place "past parentage or gender / beyond sung vocables / . . . beyond the woven / unicorn . . . past the earthlit / unearthly masquer-

ade" at which "a silence opens." Grace, nirvana, syncope, call it what you will: the complex religious impulse that drives poets, saints, and mountebanks alike encourages one's best efforts to define it but always at last thwarts them. The poem leaves us hanging:

> a cavernous
> compunction driving
> founder-charlatans
> who saw in it
> the infinite
> love of God
> and had
> (George Fox
> was one)
> great openings

The Collected Poems closes with this opening. The rest of course is silence. Such a final utterance testifies to Clampitt's place in American poetry in a religious as well as secular sense. More than anyone else she combines the legacy and the example of the symbolic father and mother of modern American poetry, Walt Whitman and Emily Dickinson. It is clear that Clampitt's quirky and heterodox religious sense puts her in league with Dickinson, a more austere eccentric, whose "breathless, hushed excess . . . stoppered prodigies, compressions and / devastations within the atom" ("Amherst"). Clampitt has studied, absorbed, and reinvented, although she never resorts to Dickinson's prim syncopations of hymn meter. To have combined so dramatically the models of our national poetic forebears gives Clampitt another claim on our attention. She has secured a place in America's literary history that is, quite simply, unlike that of any of her contemporaries.

Selected Bibliography

WORKS OF AMY CLAMPITT

POETRY
Multitudes, Multitudes. Limited edition. New York: Washington Street Press, 1974.

The Kingfisher. New York: Knopf, 1983.

A Homage to John Keats. New York: Sarabande Press, 1984.

What the Light Was Like. New York: Knopf, 1985.

Archaic Figure. New York: Knopf, 1987.

Westward: Poems. New York: Knopf, 1990.

Manhattan: An Elegy, and Other Poems. Iowa City: University of Iowa Center for the Book, 1990.

Predecessors, Et Cetera: Essays. Ann Arbor: University of Michigan Press, 1991.

A Silence Opens. New York: Knopf, 1994.

The Collected Poems of Amy Clampitt. New York: Knopf, 1997.

CRITICAL AND BIOGRAPHICAL STUDIES

Costello, Bonnie. "Amy Clampitt: Nomad Exquisite." *Verse* 10, no. 3:34–46 (1993).

Goodrich, Celeste. "Reimagining 'Empire's Westward Course': Amy Clampitt's *A Silence Opens.*" In *Poets of the Americas: Toward a Pan-American Gathering.* Edited by Jacqueline Vaught Brogan and Cordelia Chavez Candelaria. Notre Dame: University of Notre Dame Press, 1999. Pp. 159–175.

O'Neill, Michael. "'The Knowledge of Contrast, Feeling for Light and Shade': Amy Clampitt's 'Voyages: A Homage to John Keats.'" *Keats-Shelley Review,* no. 3:47–61 (1988).

Ramazani, Jahan. "'Nucleus of Fire': Amy Clampitt's Elegies for her Parents." *Verse* 10, no. 3:47–55 (1993).

Snively, Susan. "Amy Clampitt's Elegiac Witnessing." *Verse* 10, no. 3:56–62 (1993).

Weisman, Karen A. "Starving before the Actual: Amy Clampitt's 'Voyages': A Homage to John Keats." *Criticism* 36:119–123 (1994).

INTERVIEWS

Huesgen, Jan, and Robert W. Lewis. "An Interview with Amy Clampitt." *North Dakota Quarterly* 58:119–128 (1990).

Paschen, Elise. "An Interview." In *Predecessors, Et Cetera.* Pp. 158–64.

—WILLARD SPIEGELMAN

Zelda Fitzgerald

1900–1948

"THE MOST ENORMOUS influence on me in the four 1 1/2 yrs since I met her," wrote F. Scott Fitzgerald in a January 1922 letter to the American critic Edmund Wilson, "has been the complete fine and full hearted selfishness and chill-mindedness of Zelda." (Scott Fitzgerald's letters cited herein are collected in the 1994 text *F. Scott Fitzgerald: A Life in Letters,* edited by Matthew J. Bruccoli.) That this extraordinarily candid remark unlocks a door to Scott Fitzgerald's prose is certain; it is the key as well to comprehending the rich and complex art of his wife, Zelda. Zelda Fitzgerald became the heroine of her husband's novels—she became his objet d'art, the text that allowed him to define the Jazz Age, a "lost generation," in the words of Gertrude Stein, of expatriated young Americans who would rescript the world of their Victorian parents with both raw cynicism and exquisite style. Zelda Fitzgerald's work was in large part an attempt to reclaim herself—from "work of art" to artist, from novel to novelist— and in the process to write and paint her life according to her own vision, a vision complex, troubled, yet honest and fine. In the work of Zelda Fitzgerald, there are two overriding considerations: first, that she re-create herself as an artist; and second, that she tell her own story, write her own version of her life. Thus, the life and art of Zelda Fitzgerald are inseparable.

LIFE AS ART

Born on July 24, 1900, to Anthony Dickinson Sayre, a lawyer who in 1909 became an Alabama Supreme Court judge, and Minnie Machen Sayre, Zelda, last of their six children, was given free reign in a household and family that ruled the quiet southern town of Montgomery, Alabama, a place steeped in traditions and manners of a bygone age. While Judge Sayre was distant and disconnected from Zelda and her siblings, Mrs. Sayre, with literary and artistic inclinations, encouraged a refined iconoclasm in each of her children; Zelda, particularly, was instilled with a spirit of adventure and demonstrated a proclivity to "go beyond the bourne." That the Sayres were socially prominent and politically important acted to shield Zelda from overt societal criticism. However, the tendency toward what would today be diagnosed as clinical depression in Judge Sayre and in Zelda's older sister Marjorie and brother Anthony, who as an adult committed suicide, was evidence of a family predisposition to bipolar disorder, or manic depression. A beautiful and impetuous child, fond of swimming and ballet, Zelda Sayre grew from a tomboyish daredevil to belle of every ball and relentless slayer of young men's hearts.

By the summer of 1918 there had been an explosion in the population of Montgomery, due principally to the expansion of Camp Sheridan, where young recruits were brought for training before being shipped overseas to fight on the European front in World War I. Among these recruits was a young Irish Catholic from the Midwest, F. Scott Fitzgerald. Fitzgerald had already distinguished himself at Princeton, if not academically then artistically, writing skits and musicals for the Triangle Club, and when he arrived at Camp Sheridan, he joined the crew of other callow hopefuls who ensconced themselves on the Sayre front porch each evening, vying for the attention of Zelda Sayre. For Scott, Zelda was completely different from any girl he had known—totally fearless, shamelessly confident, and absolutely free from the Victorian prudery of most of her female contemporaries. By the time Scott received his orders to prepare for shipment overseas, he had won a place on the porch swing beside Zelda and most of the spots on her dance card.

The war taking him only as far as Camp Mills, New York, before Armistice, Fitzgerald returned to Montgomery to be with Zelda and await his discharge. Their courtship and the style and manner of Zelda provided material for the novel that he was writing, and when Scott left to secure a literary place for himself in New York and win Zelda for his wife, he carried with him not only the image of Zelda for his prose but her letters and her extraordinary diary, all of which were incorporated into the story that became his first novel, *This Side of Paradise*. Two years later, while writing a mock review for the *New York Tribune* of Scott's 1922 novel *The Beautiful and Damned* ("Friend Husband's Latest" in Zelda Fitzgerald, *The Collected Writings* [1991], edited by Bruccoli), Zelda playfully commented on Scott's habit of using her words in his stories: "It seems to me that on one page I recognized a portion of an old diary of mine which mysteriously disappeared shortly after my marriage, and also scraps of letters which, though considerably edited, sound to me vaguely familiar. In fact, Mr. Fitzgerald—I believe that is how he spells his name—seems to believe that plagiarism begins at home."

This Side of Paradise published on March 26, 1920, and Zelda and Scott were married several days later, on April 3. Scott had pursued Zelda shamelessly, having written to her on February 22, 1919, that with her love "everything [was] possible" for him. Zelda at first had balked at marriage, but in a letter to Scott dated February 1920 (included in *The Collected Writings*) she admitted, "I do want to marry you—even if you

do think I 'dread' it. . . . I'm not afraid of anything—To be afraid a person has either to be a coward or very great and big. I am neither." In the same letter, she expressed her belief that they would be happy, though she lamented their propensity toward "debates"; still, she liked being "very calm and masterful," while Scott was "emotional and sulky." Zelda was uncomfortably aware, even at this early stage of their relationship, of Scott's sense of proprietorship of her, and it rankled, particularly when he alluded to her as a princess he wished to keep locked in a tower.

Although Zelda was aware of her own talent and even occasionally exhibited interest in pursuing some kind of artistic expression, she was schooled in an age that lent full acceptance to her functioning only as a muse, as a decoration, but not having a separate identity and artistic life apart from her husband. Years later, her daughter, Frances Scott "Scottie" Fitzgerald, wrote in an introduction to a catalog that accompanied a 1974 exhibition of Zelda's paintings in the Montgomery Museum of Fine Arts (reprinted in the dedication of *The Collected Writings*) that Zelda was "the classic 'put down' wife, whose efforts to express her artistic nature were thwarted by a typically male chauvinist husband (except that authors are the worst kind, since they spend so much time around the house)." In the next years, as Zelda and Scott traveled and gathered material for Scott's books and suffered a succession of knocks and bruises to their joint fame, Zelda was often put on display and expected to perform for an ever increasing and demanding audience, and she was not an unwilling actress on the stage that she and Scott had made for themselves.

For three months after their marriage, the Fitzgeralds lived in Westport, Connecticut, where Scott was able to finish his collection of short stories *Flappers and Philosophers* (1920) and commence work on a new novel. It was during their stay in Connecticut that George

Nathan, who had published a number of Scott's stories in *The Smart Set,* discovered Zelda's diaries while visiting the Fitzgeralds in their Westport home. In a 1958 article in *Esquire,* Nathan recalled, "[The diaries] interested me so greatly that in my capacity as a magazine editor I later made her an offer for them. When I informed her husband, he said that he could not permit me to publish them since he had gained a lot of inspiration from them and wanted to use parts of them in his own novels and short stories." There is no record that Zelda objected to Scott's decision against publishing the diaries or his use of them. Shortly after Nathan's offer, the Fitzgeralds took an apartment in New York, at 38 West Fifty-ninth Street, where they were assured superb maid service, since Zelda, like the title character of her 1931 short story "Miss Ella," "was not a kitchen sort of person." In May 1921, with Zelda pregnant, they made their first trip to Europe.

During this time, their friends, most of whom were primarily Scott's friends, began to note a pattern in Zelda and Scott's relationship that would color the rest of their lives together. Zelda, the heroine of his books, was acquiring a fictional life, whereas in real life, there were fantastic brawls marked by periods of extraordinary affection—all the while, Scott was becoming absorbed in Zelda's personality and increasingly given to heavy drinking. Scott freely admitted that Zelda was, at this point, the stronger of the two, that she was always new to him, and that she provided him with all of his copy for his women characters. And this "heroine" with whom he had fallen in love was ever persuaded by Scott to perform, to play the role that he was scripting for her. For Zelda's part, while she frankly enjoyed "starring" in his stories, the limitations of such a role, and the limitations inherent in simply being a woman in the early decades of the twentieth century, began to weigh heavily. When her only child, Scottie, was born, Zelda expressed frank disappointment that the baby was a girl.

After Zelda and Scott returned from Europe, they spent a brief period in Scott's hometown of Saint Paul, Minnesota, to await the birth of Scottie on October 26, 1921. By September 1922, both had grown tired of the Midwest and longed to go East. After the publication of *The Beautiful and Damned* and another collection of short stories, *Tales of the Jazz Age* (1922), Zelda and Scott found a house to rent in Great Neck, Long Island. There they remained while Scott had a brief fling writing for the theater, but after the failure of his play *The Vegetable,* they sailed again for France in April 1924, to live as expatriates for the next several years and to cultivate friendships and acquaintances with Ernest Hemingway, Gertrude Stein, Edith Wharton, and a host of other intellectuals and artists disenchanted with American culture and society after the war. It was in Europe that the fragile glue binding together these two remarkable individuals began to disintegrate. It was also in Europe that Zelda consciously began to long for something more meaningful to do with her life and to see herself, if only tentatively, as an artist, experimenting with both writing and painting. Also during this time, Scott began to be threatened by Zelda's creative transformation.

Scott had come to think of himself and Zelda as almost a single entity, yet at the same time he acknowledged this fusion of identities as a threat to his artistic integrity. Writing to Maxwell Perkins (in a letter dated "c. August 12, 1922") concerning the proofs of *The Jazz Age,* he links his own aesthetic judgment with that of Zelda's; referring to a story that Perkins wished cut from the collection, Scott writes: "If you insist I will cut it out though very much against my better judgement and Zelda's." In another letter to Perkins (dated "c. August 27, 1924"), commenting on the progress of *The Great Gatsby* (1925), Scott alludes to the nature of his and Zelda's collaboration: "The novel will be done next week. That doesn't mean however that it'll reach America before October

1st, as Zelda + I are contemplating a careful revision after a weeks complete rest." Again and again Scott's letters reveal his dependence on Zelda, as well as the personal discomfort to him that such a partnership induced: writing to Perkins (in a letter dated "c. April 10, 1924"), he included among his "terrible" habits that he was determined to break his "referring everything to Zelda."

Increasingly, Zelda found their continental wanderings and her own incipient existence hollow. She and Scott seemed to be endlessly waiting for something to happen, as if, in the words of David Knight, a character from her autobiographical novel *Save the Waltz* (1932), "somebody would come along to remind us about how we felt." More and more Zelda felt herself a mere appendage to Scott's fame, a character in someone else's play, a footnote in a novel. She mused through the protagonist of *Save Me the Waltz,* Alabama Knight, "Men . . . never seem to become the things they do, like women, but belong to their own philosophic interpretations of their actions."

In June 1924 Scott and Zelda found themselves on the French Riviera. To occupy herself while Scott finished revising *The Great Gatsby,* she played in the sun and swam in the afternoons with a young French aviator, Edouard Jozan, whom she had met on the beach. Their relationship, whether sexual or not, caused Scott grief and precipitated a tangible crisis in their marriage; for Zelda, the event was directly connected with an attempted suicide. Three years later, Scott reciprocated with an extramarital relationship of his own.

The following spring, 1925, found them in Capri, where Zelda began seriously to paint. That year, they moved to Paris, Antibes, and back to the Riviera by March 1926, where Scott cultivated his friendship with Ernest Hemingway, whom Zelda did not like and who did not care for Zelda. If nothing else, the Fitzgeralds lived with a certain style, cataloged in Scott's

fiction, in Zelda's so-called girl stories, in "A Couple of Nuts," published in *Scribner's Magazine* in 1932, and in *Save Me the Waltz.* While their glamorous lifestyle was outwardly devil-may-care, while it carried them through the capitals of Europe in the decadent and lively period following the Great War, it also took a toll on their relationship and on their physical and mental health. During these years, Scott descended deeper into alcoholism, and Zelda began her own slow descent within herself, eventually to experience serious depression and finally schizophrenia.

Scott and Zelda returned to the United States at the end of 1926 to live little more than a year near Wilmington, Delaware, with Scott resorting to a stint scriptwriting in Hollywood in order to pay the mounting bills. There he pursued a romantic relationship with a seventeen-year-old actress, Lois Moran, much to Zelda's chagrin and discomfort. During this period, in part as a response to the Moran incident, Zelda began to write in earnest and to study ballet, first in Philadelphia with Catherine Littlefield and then, after they returned to Paris in April 1928, with Lubov Egorova, a teacher with the Diaghilev ballet company. Zelda threw herself into ballet with uncharacteristic seriousness and absorption. For months she seemed to live and breathe dance, fearful that she had begun serious study far too late in life to achieve a career. As she looked back on her life from the vantage point of her late twenties, she saw only wasted time, spent effort, and few tangible accomplishments for herself. Her obsession with dance was painful for her friends to watch and more than a little irritating for Scott to endure, yet she was determined.

Later in her life, Zelda produced sketches and oils of ballet figures presented as ponderous, heavy-limbed creatures with muscles tight and tortured from the endless physical labor required by the art of dance. She writes in *Save Me the Waltz* of her heroine's attempt to make herself, at twenty-eight, into a first-rate ballerina: "Alabama's work grew more and more difficult. In the mazes of the masterful fouetté her legs felt like dangling hams; in the swift elevation of the entrechat cinq she thought her breasts hung like old English dugs. It did not show in the mirror. She was nothing but sinew. To succeed had become an obsession. She worked till she felt like a gored horse in the bullring, dragging its entrails."

The more Scott drank, the more Zelda danced, and the two, rarely apart since their marriage, gradually saw each other less and less in a day. Evidence of her talent, however, is found in the fact that Zelda was invited in September 1929 to join the San Carlo Opera Ballet Company in Naples and was scheduled to perform a solo in Aïda, with other solo performances to follow. It was an extraordinary opportunity, which she declined to take. A few days later, as she and Scott drove along the Grande Corniche, on a dangerous road winding along precipitous and picturesque escarpments, Zelda attempted to grab the steering wheel and force the car off the cliff. There is no record of the disappointment she felt at not taking the San Carlo offer, but her work must have meant a great deal by this point in her life. Shortly after this event, Zelda and Scott, following a script they would write for themselves again and again, tried to escape their unhappiness and themselves by taking a trip, in this case to North Africa. Their travels did not have the desired effect. On returning to Paris, Zelda was clearly no longer able to function, thus beginning a series of hospital and asylum visits until she entered Les Rives de Prangins, a clinic near Geneva. She wrote later of her journey to the asylum June 4, 1930:

> Our ride to Switzerland was very sad. It seemed to me that we did not have each other or anything else and it half killed me to give up all the work I had done. I was completely insane and had made a decision: to abandon the ballet and live quietly with my husband. . . . If I couldn't be great, it wasn't worth going on with though I loved my work to the point of obsession. It was all I had in the world at the time.

Scott's version of Zelda's breakdown is found in *Tender Is the Night* (1934), while Zelda tells her story in *Save Me the Waltz* (at Scott's insistence, she limited her heroine to a physical breakdown so that his own book might deal exclusively with the mental). Their letters outline the raw details of what would become the final chapter in Zelda's story. Scott wrote to her in 1930, looking back on this difficult period: "You were going crazy and calling it genius—I was going to ruin and calling it anything that came to hand." He surmised, in a letter to one of her physicians in October 1932, that Zelda's illness was the result of "a rather clear-cut struggle of egos." "We ruined ourselves," he concluded. "I have never honestly thought that we ruined each other."

Zelda remained in Prangins, battling depression, acute eczema, and asthma, and undergoing what Scott referred to as her "re-education," until September 15, 1931, after which she, Scott, and Scottie returned to the United States—Zelda to stay at a rented house on Felder Avenue in Montgomery while Scott went on alone to Hollywood, once more to work for Metro-Goldwyn-Mayer. For a few months Zelda fared well in the quiet southern setting that supplied the backdrop for her childhood memories. During this period she painted, wrote, and renewed her relationship with her daughter, but the chasm between her and Scott continued to grow. In December 1931, one of her finest short stories, "Miss Ella," appeared in *Scribner's Magazine.* Just a few weeks before, her father died, and by the following February she had her second breakdown, entering the Phipps Clinic at Johns Hopkins in Baltimore. There, in a virtual paroxysm of creative energy, she wrote *Save Me the Waltz* in just six weeks, finishing the book in March 1932.

The manuscript was sent to Maxwell Perkins at Scribners and dedicated to her physician at Phipps, Dr. Mildred Squires. When Scott received word about the novel, he was livid, in large part because of her use of what he considered his "material." Writing to Dr. Squires in a letter dated March 14, 1932, Scott protested that he was not consulted about Zelda's book: "This mixture of fact and fiction is simply calculated to ruin us both, or what is left of us, and I can't let it stand. . . . My God, my books made her a legend and her single intention in this somewhat thin portrait is to make me a nonentity." For her part, Zelda wrote back to Scott in March 1932, apologizing for not sending the book first to him and explaining her intention:

> Purposely I didn't—knowing that you were working on your own and honestly feeling that I had no right to interrupt you to ask for a [perilous] opinion. . . .
>
> Scott, I love you more than anything on earth and if you were offended I am miserable. We have always shared everything but it seems to me I no longer have the right to inflict every desire and necessity of mine on you. *I was also afraid we might have touched the same material.* Also, feeling it to be a dubious production due to my own instability I did not want a scathing criticism such as you have mercilessly—if for my own good given my last stories, poor things.

In her letters that followed in April, Zelda again apologized to Scott and agreed to submit to the cuts and revisions he had requested—most of which dealt with her portrayal of David Knight, the Scott Fitzgerald character—adding, however, in an effort to maintain some small degree of artistic control over her work, that any revisions be "made on an aesthetic basis." Later, Scott would admit to Maxwell Perkins (in a letter dated "c. May 14, 1932") his feeling that *Save Me the Waltz* was a "good novel . . . perhaps a very good novel."

Despite her mental breakdowns, Zelda was remarkably lucid and touchingly candid in her understanding and assessment of her skills and relationship to Scott. "I have often told you," she wrote to him in a letter in March 1932, shortly after checking in to the Phipps Clinic, "that I am that little fish who swims about under a shark and, I believe, lives indelicately on its offal. . . . Life moves over me in a vast black shadow and I swallow whatever it drops with relish, having learned in a very hard school that one cannot be both a parasite and enjoy self-nourishment without moving in worlds too fantastic for even my disordered imagination to people with meaning."

In June 1932, after a little more than four months at the Phipps Clinic in Baltimore, Zelda was released and went to live with Scott in a house in Towson, Maryland, called La Paix. There she worked on the proofs of *Save Me the Waltz* and went to Phipps weekly. Scott and Dr. Thomas Rennie, Zelda's new physician, put her on a rigid schedule of exercise and painting, hoping that this structure would be beneficial to her state of mind. During this time Scott worked to complete *Tender Is the Night,* and Zelda began a play, *Scandalabra*; however, the industrious and artistic household of La Paix masked the unhealthy competition between the two that Scott's letters clearly reveal. Scott's letters also suggest his own need to control Zelda's life and her art and to manage her illness.

In May 1933 Zelda and Scott underwent counseling sessions with Dr. Rennie at La Paix, which were transcribed by a stenographer. In the course of these discussions, excerpts of which are quoted in Nancy Milford's *Zelda: A Biography* (1970), Scott complained that he had not published for more than eight years, and he frankly blamed Zelda. Zelda reminded him of his propensity for drinking, whereupon Scott countered: "It is a perfectly lonely struggle that I am making against other writers who are finely gifted and talented. You are a third rate writer and a third rate ballet dancer." Zelda responded that he had told her that before. Ignoring her words, Scott complained again: "I am a professional writer, with a huge following. I am the highest paid short story writer in the world. I have at various times dominated—" at which point Zelda broke in with, "It seems to me you are making a rather violent attack on a third rate talent then." Scott was clearly angered that Zelda had absconded with what he considered "his" material. Finally, the exchange came to an end when Zelda asked Scott simply to tell her what it was he wanted of her. "I want you to stop writing fiction," he declared.

Zelda's words throughout the session revealed her to be remarkably calm, while Scott's statements seemed almost at times hysterical. Shortly afterward, there was a fire in La Paix, probably started by Zelda, which burned the roof of the house. Scott was able to rescue his manuscripts and most of his books, as well as an assortment of expensive items that Zelda cataloged in her autobiographical essay "Auction—Model 1934," which appeared in *Esquire* that year and later in *The Crack-Up* (1956). This was Zelda's second episode with fire; in 1927, she had burned some clothes in a bathtub after learning of Scott's liaison with the starlet Lois Moran.

On June 25, 1933, a few weeks after the fire, Zelda's play *Scandalabra* premiered in Baltimore, performed by the Vagabond Junior Players at a theater on Read Street. Zelda designed the sets for the production, and Scott helped with rehearsals and did a last-minute rewrite to trim the four-hour satire. The play went badly and closed after a week. A few weeks later, in July 1933, Zelda heard from her mother that her brother Anthony had suffered a breakdown. After a short hospitalization, he committed suicide.

In January of the following year, Zelda entered the Sheppard-Pratt Hospital outside Baltimore. Her third breakdown roughly coincided with the serialization of Scott's *Tender Is the Night* in *Scribner's Magazine*. If Scott had felt incensed that Zelda had used events from her life in *Save Me the Waltz,* Zelda must have felt equally betrayed that he would expose her mental breakdown to the world in *Tender Is the Night.* He had used her life and her letters for the novel, and his April 26, 1934, letter indicates his concern as to how Zelda might react to his book; yet her response to Scott that same month, after having read the book, was confined to a short paragraph, in which she merely complimented Scott as a writer· "The book is grand. . . . and the prose is beautiful."

During this period of Zelda's hospitalization, Scott wrote reams to her various doctors in an attempt to explain her illness, to justify his actions, and to recommend treatment. He was hard-pressed, however, to come up with the money to keep Zelda in good institutions, as well as Scottie in expensive finishing schools and later at Vassar. Zelda's letters to him indicate that she was painfully aware of the financial strain of her illness on him and that she was doing her best to cope with her situation and her crumbling life. Writing to Scott in March 1934, she attempted to assuage his discomfort with her beginning another novel:

> Dear: I am not trying to make myself into a great artist or a great anything. Though you persist in thinking that an exaggerated ambition is the fundamental cause of my collapse. . . . I do the things I can do and that interest me and if you'd like me to give up everything I like to do I will do so willingly if it will advance matters any. . . .
>
> As you know, my work is mostly a pleasure for me, but if it is better for me to take up something quite foreign to my temperament, I will—Though I can't see what good it does to knit bags when you want to paint pansies, maybe it is necessary at times to do what you don't like.

Zelda's letters at this time are filled with encouragement about the critical reception of *Tender Is the Night* and support for Scott, such as she could offer. Her admiration of his talent was sincere. Writing to him a year later, in June 1935, she sums up what he meant to her: "You have been so good to me—and all I can say is that there was always that deeper current running through my heart: my life—you." Zelda, however, had no illusions that their happiness was anything but forever gone. In the same letter, she goes on to write: "Now that there isn't any more happiness and home is gone and there isn't even any past and no emotions . . . it is a shame that we should have met in harshness and coldness where there was once so much tenderness and so many dreams." For his part, Scott would write during these years that Zelda's "will to power must be broken without that—the only alternative would be to break me and I am forewarned & forearmed against that." Earlier, in a letter dated April 10, 1933, to one of Zelda's doctors, Adolf Meyer, Scott seemed acutely aware that posterity might see Zelda in a more sympathetic light than it would see him: "The picture of Zelda painting things that show a distinct talent, of Zelda trying faithfully to learn how to write is much more sympathetic . . . than the vision of me making myself iller with drink." In this same letter he candidly admitted: "Possibly she would have been a genius if we had never met."

From March 29 through April 30, 1934, twenty-eight of Zelda's paintings and drawings were exhibited at the Ross Gallery on East Eighty-sixth Street in New York. Zelda's paintings, many finished while she was confined in psychiatric hospitals, exhibit extraordinary talent and creative imagination. Their surreal quality also reflected, to many of her contemporary reviewers, the troubled mind that produced them; thus reviews were generally unfavorable and negatively affected sales. Most of the paintings were sold to friends of Zelda and Scott. One of the buyers was Dorothy Parker, with whom Scott had a brief affair that spring in New York. Another was Gertrude Stein, who bought two paintings and told Scott that she thought Zelda's talent remarkable. Zelda traveled from Craig House clinic in Beacon, New York (where she had been staying since the beginning of March), to see the show. She also took the opportunity to see the work of Georgia O'Keeffe while in New York: O'Keeffe's paintings moved Zelda in their grand and awesome simplicity, and the surety of O'Keeffe's immense talent characteristically made her doubt her own.

After her short stint in Craig House, Zelda returned, in May 1934, to Sheppard-Pratt. During this time, she again attempted suicide. The incident occurred during Scott's visit, when the conversation took the usual combative turn as they walked about the grounds of the series of gothic buildings that made up the Pratt Institute. Zelda ran from Scott toward the sound of an oncoming train; Scott chased after her and grabbed her just before she would have flung herself before the train. Her life at this time seemed to her hopeless. Her acute manic depression could easily be exacerbated by Scott, who admitted to Dr. Forel in December 1932 that he could cause Zelda to become psychotic within a few minutes of a "well-planned conversation." Scott, on the other hand, turned to drink and to other women for consolation, yet he always kept Zelda between himself and any real relationship that he might form.

By 1936, Zelda seemed to have climbed far into herself and pulled down the shades; no longer was she suicidal but neither were there many lucid moments. Scott, who had occasionally stayed in Ashville, North Carolina, and had thought the setting both quiet and more economical than Sheppard-Pratt, decided to bring Zelda down to the Highland Hospital nearby. Writing to his old family friend Sara Murphy, he describes, in words that reveal more about him than about Zelda, how he had long viewed his wife. "In an odd way," he wrote to Murphy on March 30, 1936, "perhaps incredible to you, she was always my child . . . my child in a sense that Scottie isn't. . . . I was her great reality, often the only liaison agent who could make the world tangible to her."

Dr. Robert Carroll ran Highland in strict accordance with his philosophy of treatment, which was a combination of rigorous if mindless exercise, wholesome diet, and intellectual stimulation. Scott moved from his Baltimore apartment to Ashville. Zelda, whose mental condition showed signs of some improvement by 1937, thrived physically, even as Scott deteriorated. His alcoholism and the financial burdens associated with Zelda's treatment and Scottie's Connecticut boarding school were by now beyond his ability to cope, so it was with relief that he accepted MGM's offer of $1,000 a week for a six-month contract. Almost immediately after arriving in Hollywood in July 1937, Scott met Sheilah Graham, a gossip columnist and transplanted Englishwoman. Graham offered Scott a reprieve from the emptiness of his life, and the following year, when Scottie entered Vassar, he undertook to outline for both Graham and his daughter courses of study that would constitute, in his mind, the ideal college education.

As Scott negotiated a new contract with MGM, this time for $1,250 a week, Zelda was continuing to make steady improvement. She had been institutionalized now for almost four years. Though her painting offered some relief from the monotony of Highland's regimen, she longed to be free from what she considered little better than prison. What is more, Zelda's family in Montgomery was also pressuring Scott for her release. While there were occasional trips and holidays away from Highland—one notable adventure to Cuba found Scott drunk much of the time and Zelda returning to the hospital alone—Zelda's life for the most part was dreary and dull. The regimented routine of Highland was broken, however, in February 1939, when she was allowed to study painting for a month at the Ringling School of Art in Sarasota, Florida.

In October 1939 Scott began work on *The Last Tycoon* (1941). Frances Kroll Ring gives us an interesting and poignant account of Scott's last two years and an indirect portrait of Zelda in her 1987 memoir *Against the Current: As I Remember F. Scott Fitzgerald.* Kroll went to work for Scott as his secretary in April 1939, when she was twenty. Scott was then living in a cottage on the estate of Edward Everett Horton. Scott's health was already in marked decline, and he was feverishly trying to make headway on his new novel. Kroll's memories of Scott were that he was ill, living under stressful conditions, drinking too much, but usually a gentleman and always curious about her family and experiences. When Scottie came to visit for a summer, Kroll remembered that Zelda and Scott's only child seemed surprisingly levelheaded and well adjusted for having been parented primarily by means of Zelda and Scott's letters for the past decade or more. She noted Scottie's reminiscing about a life that was sprinkled with many good memories of both her parents. "I can remember nothing but happiness and delight in his company," Scottie said of her father, "until the world began to be too much for him when I was about twelve." She recalled that even the sad times were tempered for her by the love that both parents gave her. "Daddy never let me feel the tragedy of mother's illness," she told Frances, "and I never had a sense of being unloved." As for Zelda, Scottie remembered a wonderfully creative, natural, if sometimes nervous, mother, who cataloged her young life in paintings and paper dolls.

By the end of 1940 Scott was experiencing recurrent episodes of dizziness and shortness of breath, and he moved in with Graham, who had a ground-floor apartment and spare bedroom. On the Saturday before Christmas, December 21, Kroll dropped by to deliver Scott's mail, including a letter from Scottie and one from Zelda. Kroll performed a few tasks for Scott, whose mood was good, then drove home. When she arrived, she received a message asking her to return to Graham's immediately. There she found two hospital attendants standing next to Scott, who lay on the floor, dead. Graham told Kroll that Scott had dressed for lunch and was rising from a chair when he reached for the mantle and fell over. Some days later, Kroll received a phone call from Zelda, to whom she had never before spoken. Kroll writes, "She said she needed to talk to someone who had been with him at the end so that she could believe he was gone." The last time that Zelda had seen Scott was during their disastrous trip to Cuba. After the phone call, Kroll received a letter from Zelda, thanking the young woman for her service to Scott and promising her "some little testimonial" of her kindness when she had "access to any money." Kroll was touched by Zelda's graciousness.

Writing a tribute to Scott for a 1941 posthumous collection of personal recollections that the editors of *The New Republic* wished to assemble, Zelda called him a "prophet destined to elucidate and catalogue" his times. "His poignancy," she wrote, "was the perishing of lovely things and people on the jagged edges of truncate spiritual purpose. . . . [His work] presented in poetic harmonies the tragically gallant stoicism so indispensable to traversing that troubled and turbulent epoch between world wars." Despite their difficult personal history, Zelda had retained an understanding of and appreciation for her husband and his work; the magazine, however, chose not to include her tribute in the collection.

The April before Scott's death, Zelda had left Highland to go to Montgomery to live with her mother at 322 Sayre Street. There she lived quietly, if agitatedly, for eight more years—punctuated by recurring trips to Highland, where she would commit herself. Zelda spent these last years painting and working on a novel titled "Caesar's Things," finishing 135 pages of the manuscript. She eventually made a studio in her mother's garage, and Minnie Sayre was very protective of her daughter's health and well-being. In May 1942 Zelda's paintings were exhibited at the Museum of Fine Arts in Montgomery and again the following December at the Montgomery Woman's Club. Zelda would give away many of her paintings over the years, and during World War II she donated many of her canvasses to be reused by wounded soldiers for art therapy. (After her death, her sister Rosalind had a yardman burn many of her paintings.) In February 1943, Scottie married a young naval lieutenant, Samuel Jackson Lanahan, in New York. Zelda did not attend the wedding but commemorated the event in a gouache on paper painting called "Scottie and Jack Grand Central Time." Three years later, Scottie's first child was born, and Zelda found another artistic outlet, constructing a series of paper dolls for her grandchildren, just as she had done for Scottie.

On November 2, 1947, Zelda returned to Highland for the last time. Around midnight on March 10, 1948, a fire began in the kitchen of the main building and quickly spread through a dumbwaiter shaft to the top floor, where Zelda and several other women were staying. There were no fire alarms and no sprinkler system. Six of the women on the top floor were trapped, and nine women in all died in the incident. Zelda's body was identified by means of a charred slipper found beneath it. She was buried on Saint Patrick's Day beside Scott in the Fitzgerald family plot in Rockville, Maryland. The house at 819 Felder Avenue in Montgomery, where Zelda and Scott lived for a short time in 1931–1932, was turned into the Fitzgerald Museum. Twenty-six years after her death, the first large retrospective of her visual art was shown at the Montgomery Museum of Fine Arts, made possible in large part by Scottie's move to Montgomery with more than one hundred of her mother's paintings and paper dolls. In June 1980, the National Portrait Gallery in Washington paid tribute to the Jazz Age with a series of portraits of the Fitzgeralds and their friends: "Zelda and Scott: The Beautiful and Damned." Again, in the summer of 1996, another retrospective of Zelda's painting was shown at the Montgomery Museum. Interest in Zelda's fiction prompted Scribners to publish *The Collected Writings* in 1991. The collection contains many of Zelda's letters to Scott, as well as her creative and nonfiction writing.

A MATTER OF STYLE

If Scott were prone to criticize her prose somewhat zealously, one can understand the dissatisfaction, from his point of view, he may have found with Zelda's writing—dissatisfaction, that is, beyond his natural inclination to keep her life and its material solely for his own fictional purposes. Scott's classical linear style stands in stark contrast to Zelda's circular narrative approach, with its stream-of-consciousness technique and use of language yielding a profusion of color and imagery. Hers is a sensory rich, often surreal style that also characterizes her painting. Sara Mayfield, in *Exiles from Paradise: Zelda and Scott Fitzgerald* (1971), called Zelda's *Save Me the Waltz* "one of the best of the expressionistic novels," indicating that "its style was a generation ahead of its time." Zelda's is a style completely her own, in no way, as Dan Piper asserts in *F. Scott Fitzgerald: A Critical Portrait* (1966), imitative of Scott's. When Alabama Knight, Zelda's fictional heroine in *Save Me the Waltz,* lies prostrate as a result of blood poisoning, Fitzgerald captures, in her prose, a Freudian, surreal twilight between the conscious and unconscious:

> Sometimes her foot hurt her so terribly that she closed her eyes and floated off on the waves of the afternoon. Invariably she went to the same delirious place. There was a lake there so clear that she could not tell the bottom from the top. . . .

Phallic poplars and bursts of pink geranium and a forest of white-trunked trees whose foliage flowed out of the sky covered the land. Nebulous weeds swung on the current. . . . Crows cawed from one deep mist to another. The word "sick" effaced itself against the poisonous air and jittered lamely. . . . "Sick" turned and twisted about the narrow ribbon of the highway like a roasting pig on a spit, and woke Alabama gouging at her eyeballs with the prongs of its letters.

Edmund Wilson, Scott's Princeton classmate and a close family friend of the Fitzgeralds, gave a clear description of Zelda's writing style when he described her habit of conversation (quoted in the introduction to *The Collected Writings*): "She talked with so spontaneous a color and wit—almost exactly in the way she wrote—that I very soon ceased to be troubled by the fact that the conversation was in the nature of free association of ideas and one could never follow up anything. I have rarely known a woman who expressed herself so delightfully and so freshly."

Zelda Fitzgerald's sparse literary canon consists of one completed novel, *Save Me the Waltz,* unquestionably her masterwork and worthy of study with the best prose of her era; a dozen or so short stories, most published under Scott's byline or their joint authorship; a handful of articles and reviews, published in such magazines and newspapers as the *New York Tribune, McCall's,* and *College Humor*; a manners play, *Scandalabra,* after the wit and satiric style of Oscar Wilde; and an unfinished novel, "Caesar's Things," which Bruccoli, editor of *The Collected Writings,* calls fundamentally "incoherent."

The similarities between Zelda's visual and literary art are apparent in both tone and style: the same intensity of color, lushness of imagery, fragmented, disjointed composition, and propensity toward the surreal. Fitzgerald's aesthetic embraces those modernist tendencies apparent in the art and literary worlds at the beginning of the twentieth century through World War II, specifically her interest in the subconscious and the irrational and her stream-of-consciousness, fractious narrative style, with its lack of syntactic connectives and reliance on associative, vivid images. Thus the literary works informing Fitzgerald's prose are the texts of such modernist writers as Virginia Woolf and Gertrude Stein, while the visual techniques informing her painting belong to nineteenth- and twentieth-century French illustrational art, surrealism, set and theater design as found in the work of Natalya Goncharova and Léon Bakst, and the varied modernist work of Georgia O'Keeffe and such European painters as Picasso, Georges Braque, and Matisse, all of whom she either personally knew or with whose work she was intimately familiar.

In addition to the colorful palette and fragmentation of design and composition that Fitzgerald employs in her writing and painting, her idea about the function of art is akin to that of Walter Pater, Wilde, and the proponents of fin de siècle aestheticism. She writes in a letter to Scott (dated "after 13 June 1934" in *The Collected Writings*), that the impetus for art is "all emotions and all experience" and that "the transposition of these into form [is] individual and art." She questions whether the "cerebral" is a more compelling approach to art than the "emotional," and she likewise asserts that one cannot rate "the purpose" of art over "the shape of the edifice." Fitzgerald believes that the business of the artist is "to take a willing mind and guide it to hope or despair" but without the intrusion of the artist's own interpretation. She writes: "I am still adamant against the interpretive school. Nobody but educators can show people how to think—but to open some new facet of the stark emotions or to preserve some old one in the grace of a phrase seem nearer the artistic end." The most the artist should do, according to Fitzgerald, is to present one story in time that may have happened to one isolated person, but without any incipient "judgment."

In other words, style and emotion, for Zelda Fitzgerald, precede essence or substance. These ideas are particularly prescient in Fitzgerald's *Save Me the Waltz.*

SAVE ME THE WALTZ

Save Me the Waltz, Zelda's literary declaration of independence and equality (and her attempt to repossess both her life and her story from Scott) is a touching *Künstlerroman*—a narrative of an artist's "becoming." The book details a young woman's struggle to find an identity and meaningful work separate from that of her famous artist husband. Alabama Knight, a Southern flower but, after her marriage at any rate, decidedly not a steel magnolia, is on a personal journey into the world of art as she attempts to make herself into a dancer. The book records Alabama's effort to create her own story, to write or "play" her life according to a script of her making rather than follow the one written for her by her father or her husband. To a friend who remarks to Alabama that she is as "good as a book," she replies, "I am a book. Pure fiction." The friend answers Alabama's cryptic assertion by asking, "Then who invented you?" Alabama's blithe response belies the fact that it has now become her painful task to create or script herself. In this respect then, *Save Me the Waltz* is almost a half-century ahead of such groundbreaking studies as Sandra M. Gilbert and Susan Gubar's *The Madwoman in the Attic: The Woman Writer and the Nineteenth-Century Literary Imagination* (1979) and Carolyn G. Heilbrun's *Writing a Woman's Life* (1988). Zelda clearly saw the need for women to "write," as Heilbrun has asserted, their own stories and not "live their lives isolated in the houses and [in] the stories of men."

The narrative that Alabama constructs as she and David wend their way through a series of adventures, from Birmingham to Paris, from the Riviera to the ruins of Rome, is a portrait of marital dysfunction. It is clear that David adores Alabama as an appendage, a beautiful decoration or accoutrement, more than he admires and respects her for the complex person that she is. He displays her to friends and acquaintances "as if she were one of his pictures," and he insists that "a woman's place is with the wine," the perennial still life. Fitzgerald makes clear that Alabama has been objectified by her artist husband and that he considers her the "work of art" rather than the artist. David has no interest or advantage in encouraging Alabama's discovery of a sense of self apart from him or of her "artist" within; she is at one moment his "illusive possession" and at another "an aesthetic theory—a chemistry formula for the decorative." David tells her at one point, "my dear, you are my princess and I'd like to keep you shut forever in an ivory tower for my private delectation." Yet David is not blind to the emptiness of the still life he has sketched for Alabama. On a night he returns from an unchaste interlude, the night Alabama tells him that she wants to become a dancer, it is David who articulates the shallow dimensions of her life with him: "Poor girl," he says with candid compassion, "I understand. It must be awful just waiting around eternally."

Alabama begins to compose a different script for herself when she comes to the realization that her "dance" with David is quite out of step. The two are waltzing at the Ritz, when David tries to bring her back in tow—both with his step to the music and with his life: "Listen, Alabama," he insists, "you're not keeping time." No, she shoots back and demands, "David, for God's sake will you try to keep off of my feet?" They cease to dance, and David sulks, acknowledging that he "never could waltz anyway." Later, in a less metaphoric and more direct moment, Alabama asserts that "no individual can force other people forever to sustain their own versions of that individual's character—that sooner or later they will stumble across the person's own conception of themselves"—an important idea Fitzgerald will echo in her play, *Scandalabra.*

Only in her work does Alabama find a sense of her own autonomous self. As she feverishly dedicates herself to dance, she becomes "gladly, savagely proud of the strength of her Negroid hips, convex as boats in a wood carving. The complete control of her body freed her from all fetid consciousness of it." When she dances, she understands clearly, for the first time, the limitations and meaninglessness of her life with David. "Work," she says, "is the only pretty thing . . . at least, I have forgotten the rest." Work begins to fill the emptiness in Alabama's life, replacing the mindless materialism that had pervaded her time with David: "Spending money," muses the narrator, "had played a big part in Alabama's life before she had lost, in her work, the necessity for material possessions."

Very few in Alabama's life understand her need for work. A friend questions her new dedication to dance, and cannot comprehend, since Alabama already has a husband, why she should inflict such physical pain on herself and anger David as well; Alabama attempts to explain: "To sit this way, expectant of my lesson, and feel that if I had not come the hour that I own would have stood vacant and waiting. . . . Yes. He is so angry that I must be away even more to avoid rows about it." Later another woman friend laments Alabama's obsession for perfecting her art: "I think it's ridiculous to work like that. She can't be getting any fun out of it, foaming at the mouth that way!" And still another adds, "It's abominable! She'll never be able to get up in a drawing room and do *that!* What's the good of it?" Eventually, Alabama ceases trying to explain herself; what others think doesn't matter, because she "had never felt so close to a purpose" as when she dances. David's reaction to her work is at first grudgingly tolerant, then outright condescending. "I hope that you realize that the biggest difference in the world is between the amateur and the professional in the arts," he snobbishly asserts. Alabama understands the full measure of his remark, replying: "You might mean yourself and me."

In its portrayal of an individual's attempt to find the artist within, achieved as it was from the female perspective, *Save Me the Waltz* is a unique *Künstlerroman* for its day. Alabama's joy in her work and new sense of autonomy are accompanied by profound feelings of guilt, particularly regarding her neglect of Bonnie, her young daughter. Brought to her mother's studio, Bonnie is asked by her nanny whether she too will become a dancer when she grows up. The child replies emphatically, "No, it is too 'sérieuse' to be the way Mummy is. She was nicer before." At one point in the story, Bonnie lies ill for a week in Naples, where Alabama is rehearsing. The pressure of Bonnie's illness and the imminent performance make Alabama question herself both as a dancer and as a mother: "[Bonnie] was ghastly pale. . . . Alabama forgot to get the emetic [the doctor had] prescribed . . . and Bonnie lay in bed for a week, living on limewater and mutton broth while her mother rehearsed the waltz."

Though Alabama, as did Zelda, comes admirably close to achieving success with dance, the family battles, exhaustion, illness, and guilt—not to mention David's endless "appropriation" of her—win the war. At the end of the story, after a physical breakdown and blood poisoning, she must give up dancing forever, while David commences a new series of paintings depicting the ballet, a series that becomes his most highly acclaimed work: "Nobody has ever handled the ballet with [such] vitality," an adoring critic declares. Alabama Knight forgoes the last waltz and with it ceases to write her own story, once again becoming the work of art rather than the artist.

SATIRE AND SURREALISM

Scandalabra, written when the Fitzgeralds were living at La Paix near Baltimore and performed six nights in June and July 1933 by the Baltimore Junior Vagabonds, exists in two three-act versions—a sprawling, ninety-one page script, probably the version used for the original production which Scott spent the night before opening cutting down to a playable length, and an edited sixty-one page version found among Zelda's papers at Princeton and included in Scribner's *Collected Writings.* Utilizing a motif found in *Save Me the Waltz* that portrays our perceptions of others as distorted or misleading and truth as nebulous and relative, Zelda develops her play as a surrealistic deconstruction of morality and marriage of the flapper fast set. In this zany satire, art imitates life, which imitates art, and it is clear that it is often difficult to discern the real from the surreal.

In tone and style, *Scandalabra* follows the tradition of Restoration comedy, as it filters up to the works of Wilde and George Bernard Shaw. In particular, *Scandalabra* resembles John Dryden's *Marriage A-la-Mode* (1672), in which a happily married couple feigns an affair in order to be consistent with the connubial mode of the day. Most of the satiric conventions of the comedy of manners are present in Fitzgerald's play: the traditional battle of the sexes with a modern, flapper twist; ironic character names (Baffles the butler possesses a droll, epigrammatic wit and displays a propensity for making sense of the absurd); character types and tags (the sassy maid; the controlling Uncle Messogony, who works his will through his will; his country-come-to-town nephew Andrew; the foppish Peter Consequential; and Consequential's bored wife, Connie, who regales us with empty-headed malapropisms). There are also present in the play the witty repartee and the traditional "mask" motif, as characters attempt to get their way through insincerity and machination. The objects of

Zelda's satire include gossipmongering newspapers, the legal and medical professions, Zelda's notion of the frivolous French, and modern marriage. Set within the conventional framework of satire and manners plays, *Scandalabra* is a fairly successful script and an excellent vehicle for two of Fitzgerald's most important criteria for art: style and wit.

Fitzgerald begins the play with a traditional prologue, which sets up the complex plot and presents the figure of the "leprechaun," a symbol for the mischievous genie Gossip. Uncle Andrew Messogony is about to pass on to his reward, but not before he has located his only heir, his nephew Andrew, described as "weak, but good," —"[which is] enough," says Uncle Messogony, "to incapacitate him for living." To assure that his control of the situation extends beyond the grave, the patriarchal uncle has written a will which stipulates that Andrew must cultivate every vice of life before he can "assume control of the money." Act 1 opens with Andrew, who is happily married to an ex-Follies girl, Flower. Both, however, are forced to pretend "dissolution" to satisfy the doctors and the lawyers overseeing implementation of Uncle Messogony's will. So Flower must lay down her knitting in the evenings and pretend "to be gay and frivolous" by paying court to the string of nightclubs that Baffles has listed for her, while Andrew must cultivate a taste for liquor and convince the lawyer he is a libertine. Flower laments: "Life's hardly worth living. Nothing but orchids and a Rolls-Royce," while Baffles tells his master, who prefers beer to champagne, that "in this world we have to consider the labels, Mr. Andrew."

When doctor and lawyer arrive to check on the prescribed "devolution" of Andrew, he earnestly shows them his latest reading material—*Treatise on Preserving the Disgraces of Life*—while Baffles suggests helpfully, "Morals, sir, are the result of experience." The doctor diagnoses "character" as the culprit, declaring,

"Character is what people tell us about ourselves." This conversation takes us to the play's satiric point, as the doctor advises Andrew to simply play his part, since essentially "All life is a play"—to which Baffles answers that it is likely "Mr. Andrew will confuse life with reality." The lawyer warns Andrew, "If you want to keep your money and your wife we'll have to get down to [Uncle Messogony's version of] the truth [reality]." Andrew then responds, by referencing the motif of the mask or appearances: "I hate the truth when it's a lie! Flower's just out masking her virtue the best she could," and Andrew knows that he must follow suit if the money is to be theirs.

When Flower returns from her unenthusiastic night on the town, she laments the fact that she must "pretend" to be what she is not, while Baffles answers, "Life without pretensions leaves us facing the basic principles, which are usually a good deal worse and harder to unravel." Act 1 closes with Flower resorting to the phone book to locate a posh address from which she can conjure a lover. A phone call to the Morning Incubator informs the newspaper that Mrs. Andrew Messogony is involved in a scandalous affair with Mr. Peter Consequential of 1066 Park Avenue.

As act 2 opens, we meet the foppish Peter Consequential, who lives in less than matrimonial bliss with his wife, Connie, their relationship having suffered from the moment the bored and frivolous Connie uttered the words "I do." Peter lives in mortal fear that his wife is having an affair, while the maid assures him, "The great thing that love affairs all have in common, sir, is that they come out wrong." Nonetheless, Connie's attitude toward Peter miraculously alters when she reads the *Morning Incubator,* detailing, with photographs, the particulars of his "affair" with Flower Messogony. Connie becomes consumed with interest in a photograph of Flower and whether the "other" woman's profile is better than her own: "Is that a good likeness, Peter? If it is, her nose is too alkaline"—Peter, by now, happily accustomed to his wife's unwitting malapropisms. A short scene with curious reporters bent on getting wrong the details of the "affair" closes the act.

Scene 2 of the second act takes place ten days later on the French Riviera, where the two couples have fled to escape the press. Two French gendarmes follow Flower and Andrew on the beach, demanding that they not picnic in the area—until they learn that both are involved in a lascivious scandal, whereupon the city keys are handed them. Andrew is now under the impression that the affair is a reality, and he is jealously going through the papers for details. Flower coos to him, "Oh, I think jealousy sometimes keeps a marriage from going bad," whereupon Baffles adds with typical ironic clarity that jealousy certainly "acts as a sort of spiritual cellophane." As soon as Flower promises not to see Peter again, the Consequentials appear on the beach, and the thoroughly modern Messogonys invite them to join their picnic. After Peter shares the fact that Connie has been more congenial since his "affair" with Flower, Flower announces that she does indeed feel quite "creative" to have brought about such marital reform. Then Andrew flies off, "Creative! I s'pose you mean, Flower, you'd like us to *believe* what looks so like lies." "Whether you believe it or not," says Zelda's center of intelligence Baffles, "makes the only difference between fiction and reality." The surreal picnic progresses to a discussion of marital faithlessness—"Connie thinks monogamy is what the parlor chairs were made of in the Nineties," Peter deadpans—and Baffles cynically delivers what Zelda finds is the peculiar foundation for understanding between the sexes: "Sex, Madam, and climate. Our only real basis of communication!" At this point Flower maneuvers Peter into taking a walk, and the two "spurned" spouses, Connie and Andrew, are left alone to get to know each other. The act closes with the return of the two gendarmes, who arrest Connie and

Andrew when they ignore an order to leave the beach.

Act 3 finds Peter and Flower on a completely blackened stage, having broken into Peter's villa in an attempt to discover whether Andrew and Connie, who were nowhere to be found when Peter and Flower returned from their walk, are having an affair themselves as retribution. They turn on the lights to find Baffles, who explains his presence by asserting cryptically, "There was the milkweed to milk . . . and there's dust on the parlor sky." Peter and Flower now regret their feigned affair: "We'll never set this thing to rights," says Peter; to which Flower responds, "Not till it's sold to the moving pictures." Peter hopes that his wife is not "living up to [his] reputation"; then he adds, "Maybe I was too quiet. Maybe other people's ideas of us are truer than our own"; Baffles clarifies, "Other People's ideas of us are dependent largely on what they've hoped for."

The denouement occurs after Andrew and Connie appear from the balcony, and Andrew announces that he and Flower are "going back to the farm." "A man's got to choose sometimes between other people's ideas of himself and his own," asserts Andrew, giving up his claim on his inheritance. With that confession, Baffles announces that indeed all the money is now Andrew's, free from any restrictions by lawyers or doctors. "The will was drawn up as it was, sir, to ensure you the experiences of life before allowing you the full responsibilities. Now that you've profited so wisely . . . [the money] passes unprovisionally to Mr. Andrew." And so, with toasts to the phone book and a genial look to that mischievous leprechaun, now escaped from the stage into the audience, Baffles assures them all: "You never know what will turn out all right in the end."

FICTION AND NONFICTION

Zelda Fitzgerald's literary canon includes a series of stories and sketches, seven of which are known as the "girl stories" and a number of newspaper and magazine articles for the *New York Tribune, Metropolitan Magazine, McCall's, Harper's Bazaar, Esquire,* and *College Humor.* Some of these were published under Scott's byline, others jointly (with Scott giving Zelda credit in the meticulous ledger he kept), and a few under Zelda's own name. All exhibit the stylistic qualities consistent with Zelda's work: vivid description, ironic humor and sarcastic wit, original turns of phrases and a style that is essentially epigrammatic, and skillful use of parallelism, and occasional use of both zeugma (yoking the literal with the metaphoric) and chiasmus (inverting the relationship between the elements of parallel phrases). In "Eulogy on the Flapper," Zelda describes her subject as follows: "She flirted because it was fun to flirt and wore a one-piece bathing suit because she had a good figure; she covered her face with powder and paint because she didn't need it and she refused to be bored chiefly because she wasn't boring. . . . Mothers disapproved of their sons taking the Flapper to dances, to teas, to swim, and most of all to heart." In articles such as "What Became of the Flappers?" and "Paint and Powder" Zelda defends the outrageous acts of flappers and their flaunting of Victorian conventions, because, as she writes in the latter piece, their very rebellion empowered young women who "wanted to choose their destinies" for themselves.

The sketches known as the girl stories have a common theme: how to be a full and complete person in a world no longer certain about the place of women. Whether the "girl" protagonists are hometown, slightly crass beauties like Gracie Axelrod in "Our Own Movie Queen," the ill-fated Gay in "The Original Follies Girl," Harriet in "Southern Girl," Helena in "The Girl the Prince Liked," Eloise Everette Elkins in "Poor Working Girl," or Lou the dancer driven to succeed in "The Girl with Talent," they all represent a "type" of the time, spanning regional

and economic statuses during the period between the two world wars: young women bored with traditional values, ambitious, pulled between the will for work or fame and a longing for home and family. The stories are often rendered in Jamesian first-person narratives, with an observer speaker painting for the reader a portrait he discerns by means of glimpses at young women, pulling at the bit, "sick with spiritual boredom," and driven by a desire for success in a public world that often demanded, in the words of "The Original Follies Girl," "physical perfection" and stereotypical behavior. If Zelda's flappers and Southern belles seem shallow and overly absorbed in the material and the superficial, if they too often feel incomplete unless married to the "right" man, they have, nonetheless, followed the road to fame and power in about the only way society afforded them.

Two of the best of Zelda's short fiction pieces are "Miss Ella" and "A Couple of Nuts," both published in *Scribner's Magazine* in 1931 and 1932, respectively. "Miss Ella" is the story of a Southern woman's quiet rebellion. The writing has a particularly rich lyrical quality, with prose awash in the smells and sights of Southern flowers. The narrator is a young child, enamored by the enigmatic persona of Miss Ella and her romantic past. At the beginning of the story, Miss Ella's life has settled into an acceptable and quiet Victorian sameness that belies the passion that once and perhaps still runs through her veins. The narrator recalls how she "twitter[ed] about on our hearth after supper, dodging the popping bits of blue flame from our bituminous coal," her elegance testimony to the fact that Miss Ella, like her creator, "was not a kitchen sort of person." There was about her a sense of rigid control, of barely contained energy, of imminent explosion. The narrator remembers Miss Ella sitting in the hammock, "holding tightly to the strings at one end and desperately straining her foot against the worn patch of clay in the grass underneath"—just managing "to preserve a more or less static position" as she opened letters and held her book with her free hand, "and scratched the itchings that always commence when stillness is imperative."

Particularly fascinating to the children is the wooden playhouse in the garden, a "relic of Miss Ella's youth." Here, "buried in a tangle of jonquils and hyacinths dried brown from the summer heat, its roof strewn with the bruised purple bells of a hibiscus overhanging its tiny gables, the house stood like a forgotten sarcophagus, guarding with the reticent dignity that lies in all abandoned things." It was an "oasis apart from the rest of the orderly garden," and the playhouse holds the mystery of Miss Ella's story, one that "like all women's stories," writes Fitzgerald, "was a love story and like most love stories took place in the past."

As the reader comes to learn, Miss Ella had once been engaged to her steady and staid suitor, Mr. Hendrix—that is, until the church social that brought young Andy Bronson to rescue her from the "fire" ignited by a firecracker that he threw, which set her dress aflame. Andy's attempts to make amends—the gifts brought from his travels, especially the star sapphire "which she tied about her neck in a chamois bag lest Mr. Hendrix should know"—work their will, and one night, he kisses her "far into the pink behind her ears and she folded herself in his arms, a flag without a breeze about its staff." On the afternoon Miss Ella and Andy are to be married, Mr. Hendrix commits suicide, calmly shooting himself in the head on the playhouse steps, his will intrusive and lasting in the end. The years pass, Miss Ella's beauty fades, the rims of her eyes grow "redder and redder, like those of a person leaning over a hot fire"—yet it is clear, as the narrator repeats, "she was not a kitchen sort of person." Thus the ending is cleverly ambiguous in terms of whether Miss Ella is mistress of her fate or mastered by the events of her life.

In "A Couple of Nuts" Lola and Larry's story is told by another first-person narrator, a fellow expatriate who encounters the American couple now and again as they travel across Europe, from the Champs-Elysées, Cannes, Monte Carlo, Paris, and finally to New York. Lola and Larry are musicians, troubadours, who hook up with a playboy whose affair with Lola brings the first rift in their marriage, only to be matched later by Larry's affair with the narrator's ex-wife, a wealthy socialite on whose yacht they encounter a storm that swallows them "like gulls pouncing on the refuse from an ocean liner." Theirs is the story of Jazz Age fallen angels, a lyrical portrait of the beautiful and damned, who could no more forgo their tragedy than could Zelda and Scott, whose story they reflect. Thus does Zelda Fitzgerald's art imitate her life, as her life was tragically shaped by fiction.

Selected Bibliography

WORKS OF ZELDA FITZGERALD

FICTION, DRAMA, AND COLLECTIONS
Save Me the Waltz. New York: Scribners, 1932.

Bits of Paradise: Twenty-one Uncollected Stories by F. Scott and Zelda Fitzgerald. Edited by Matthew J. Bruccoli. New York: Scribners, 1973.

Scandalabra: A Farce Fantasy in a Prologue and Three Acts. Bloomfield Hills, Mich.: Bruccoli Clark, 1980.

The Collected Writings. Edited by Matthew J. Bruccoli. New York: Scribners, 1991. (Includes *Save Me the Waltz, Scandalabra,* the short stories and articles, and Zelda's letters to F. Scott Fitzgerald.)

Zelda, An Illustrated Life: The Private World of Zelda Fitzgerald. Edited by Eleanor Lanahan. New York: Harry N. Abrams, 1996.

CRITICAL AND BIOGRAPHICAL STUDIES

Anderson, W. R. "Rivalry and Partnership: the Short Fiction of Zelda Sayre Fitzgerald." *Fitzgerald/ Hemingway Annual,* 1977, pp. 19–42.

Bruccoli, Matthew J., ed. *F. Scott Fitzgerald: A Life in Letters.* New York: Simon and Schuster, 1994.

Davis, Simone Weil. "'The Burden of Reflecting': Effort and Desire in Zelda Fitzgerald's *Save Me the Waltz.*" *Modern Language Quarterly* 56, no. 3:327–361(September 1995).

Cary, Meredith. "*Save Me the Waltz as a Novel.*" *Fitzgerald/Hemingway Annual,* 1976, pp. 65–78.

Castillo, Susan. "(Im)Possible Lives: Zelda Fitzgerald's *Save Me the Waltz* as Surrealist Autobiography." In *Writing Lives: American Biography and Autobiography.* Edited by Hans Bak. Amsterdam: VU University Press, 1998. Pp. 55–62.

Fetterley, Judith. "Who Killed Dick Diver? The Sexual Politics of *Tender Is the Night.*" *Mosaic* 17:111–128 (1984).

Fitzgerald, F. Scott. *The Crack-Up.* Edited by Edmund Wilson. New York: J. Laughlin, 1956.

Fryer, Sarah Beebe. "Nicole Warren Diver and Alabama Beggs Knight: Women on the Threshold of Freedom." *Modern Fiction Studies* 31:318–326 (summer 1985).

Mayfield, Sara. *Exiles from Paradise: Zelda and Scott Fitzgerald.* New York: Delacorte, 1971.

Mellow, James R. *Invented Lives: F. Scott and Zelda Fitzgerald.* Boston: Houghton Mifflin, 1984.

Meyers, Jeffrey. *Scott Fitzgerald: A Biography.* New York: HarperCollins, 1994.

Milford, Nancy. *Zelda: A Biography.* New York: Harper & Row, 1970.

Nanney, Lisa. "Zelda Fitzgerald's *Save Me the Waltz* as Southern Novel and Künstlerroman." In *The Female Tradition in Southern Literature.* Edited by Carol S. Manning. Urbana: University of Illinois Press, 1993.

Nathan, George Jean. "Memories of Fitzgerald, Lewis and Dreiser." *Esquire,* October 1958, pp. 148–149.

Petry, Alice Hall. "Women's Work: the Case of Zelda Fitzgerald." In *Literature, Interpretation, Theory.* New York: Gordon and Breach, 1989.

Piper, Henry Dan. *F. Scott Fitzgerald: A Critical Portrait.* New York: Holt, Rinehart, and Winston, 1966.

Ring, Frances Kroll. *Against the Current: As I Remember F. Scott Fitzgerald.* San Francisco: Donald S. Ellis, 1985.

Robertson, Elizabeth "Speaking from the Place of the Other: Identity and Narrative Form in the Life and Art of Zelda Fitzgerald." *Denver Quarterly* 19:130–139 (summer 1984).

Shurbutt, Sylvia Bailey. "Creating a Woman's Life through Words: A Language of Their Own." *Women and Language* 7:38–42 (spring 1994).

———. "Writing Lives and Telling Tales: Visions and Revisions." In *Untying the Tongue: Gender, Power, and the Word.* Edited by Linda Longmire and Lisa Merrill. Westport, Conn.: Greenwood Press, 1998.

Tavernier-Courbin, Jacqueline. "Art as Woman's Response and Search: Zelda Fitzgerald's *Save Me the Waltz.*" *Southern Literary Journal* 11:22–42 (spring 1979).

Wagner, Linda W. "*Save Me the Waltz*: An Assessment in Craft." *Journal of Narrative Technique* 12:201–209 (fall 1982).

White, Ray Lewis. "Zelda Fitzgerald's *Save Me the Waltz*: A Collection of Reviews from 1932–1933." *Fitzgerald/Hemingway Annual,* 1979, pp. 163–168.

—SYLVIA SHURBUTT

Robert Francis

1901–1987

SLOW IN STARTING but ultimately long and prolific, the writing career of Robert Francis is marked by many durable achievements and a number of quiet surprises. Often thought of as a quintessentially New England poet, Robert Churchill Francis was born in Upland, Pennsylvania, on August 12, 1901, to Ida May (Allen) Francis and her husband, Ebenezer Fisher Francis, who was then completing his studies at a Baptist seminary. Robert had a half-sister, Ruth, seven years older, from his father's first marriage. After the elder Francis was ordained, the family moved with him from pastorate to pastorate. In 1910 they arrived in Massachusetts, where Ebenezer Francis served congregations in a number of towns until his death in 1940, and where his son received most of his education. The younger Francis attended high school in Medford and went on to Harvard College, from which he graduated in 1923.

By his own account, Francis was a timid, hypersensitive child who was unathletic and who found it hard to make friends. His social awkwardness and isolation persisted through high school. As a teen his favorite recreational reading was books on self-improvement with titles like *Power of Will*. A good student, he had little sense of what he might do with his life. At Harvard Francis was not particularly drawn to poetry, although later he enjoyed recalling encounters with the poet Robert Hillyer, who instructed him in English composition. Francis's father urged him to enter the ministry. Gently resisting, he taught for a year at the prep school of the American University in Beirut, then returned to Harvard to earn a degree from the Graduate School of Education. With this credential in hand, he arrived in 1926 in the town of Amherst, Massachusetts, where he would live except for a few brief intervals for the rest of his life.

His experience of high school teaching proved a disaster. Francis failed to win the attention or the respect of his students. He quit after a year and for the rest of his life made do without the security of regular employment. His mother had died a short time earlier, and his father, remarried, had settled in South Amherst. For the next few years Francis remained in the family home, earning money by giving violin lessons. As most of his students lived near the center of Amherst, he became a boarder in town with a series of elderly women, covering his rent by tending the coal furnace and doing yard work and other chores.

Francis had by this time discovered that he wanted to be a writer. Shutting his door against the current landlady, or cloistering himself in a quiet corner of the Jones Library, he devoted his time seriously to both prose and poetry and began to have some modest success in placing his work in periodicals. For many years payments for short personal and literary essays in the *Christian Science Monitor* and *Forum* provided the most predictable part of his small income.

THE INFLUENCE OF ROBERT FROST

One of Francis's landladies, Mrs. Hopkins, introduced him to Robert Frost—an event Francis always viewed as a milestone. Not surprisingly, since at this stage Francis's poems had a definite Frostian cast, the older poet was largely encouraging in his response. His negative comments on certain poems were welcomed by Francis as constructive. Francis noted candidly in his journal *Frost: A Time to Talk* (1972) that Frost "defined my greatest danger as preciousness." Besides offering sympathetic criticism, Frost showed Francis's poems to Louis Untermeyer and other editors. It was, however, another poet connected with Amherst College, David Morton, whose recommendation led Macmillan to publish Francis's first collection, *Stand with Me Here,* in 1936 after it had been rejected by several other publishers.

Although Francis was later to extend his thematic and stylistic range, his first book illustrates several persistent aspects of his work. His almost exclusive use of rural New England settings and his preference for plainspokenness naturally led his first readers to connect his work with Frost's. In a few of these early pieces, the effect is almost one of ventriloquism, as the first lines of "Fall" show:

Leave the bars lying in the grass.
Let all wanderers freely pass
Into the pasture now.

Gone are the fawn-shy heifers, gone
The little calf almost a fawn
And the black two-year cow.

Still, differences between the poets are observable, both in style and outlook. Francis's better poems here are more terse and epigrammatic than most of Frost's pastoral lyrics. Often they develop a single image or metaphor. They sometimes sacrifice suggestiveness in their bid for declarative finality. Closure is enhanced by dutiful adherence to traditional verse forms, whether blank verse or tidily rhyming stanzas. Lacking some of the lordly ease of Frost's manner, these early pieces also view their subjects differently. This is especially noticeable in poems about people, who are typically contemplated from a distance. The poet's engagement is more esthetic than psychological, more

confined and picturesque than Frost's is in poems on rural work or leisure. At this stage there often was more charm than power in Francis's vignettes. Two very short poems forecast stronger and subtler tactics. "By Night" is memorably unsettling:

After midnight I heard a scream.
I was awake. It was no dream.
But whether it was bird of prey
Or prey of bird I could not say.
I never heard that sound by day.

"Bronze," daringly unrhymed, infuses an erotic tinge into its descriptive delicacy:

Boy over water,
Boy waiting to plunge
Into still water
Among white clouds
That will shatter
Into bright foam—
I could wish you
Forever bronze
And the blue water
Never broken.

In *The Trouble with Francis: An Autobiography* (1971), Francis recalls that in 1937 he took leave of "the last in my series of old ladies" and rented a dilapidated house without electricity in the Cushman section of Amherst for ten dollars a month. The solitude informing so many of his poems became a primary condition of his life. He was no hermit; unlike many people he widened his circle of friends as he grew older. Yet he valued the independence of living on his own and came to view it as indispensable to his writing. His career as a poet was actively proceeding. When Macmillan published his second book, *Valhalla and Other Poems* (1938), Frost wrote him a letter (reprinted in *The Trouble with Francis*) expressing unalloyed praise: "I am swept off my feet by the goodness of your poems this time. Ten or a dozen of them are my idea of perfection." Frost does not specify titles, but one can imagine he would have appreciated "Sheep," a commandingly clear view of the animals at rest on a stony hillside:

Two mingled flocks—
The sheep, the rocks.

And still no sheep stirs from its place
Or lifts its Babylonian face.

Here the wit and strange accuracy of the exotic epithet fit effortlessly into the poem's homespun setting. Other pieces render the New England rural scene affectionately ("Mountain Blueberries," "The Stile," "Blue Winter") or with traces of bleakness or foreboding ("The Plodder," "Return," "Two Women"). "Biography," a twelve-line self-portrait, acknowledges that the poet has been "Slow to outgrow / A backward youth," but ends by asserting, "Yet being slow / Has recompense: / The present tense. / Say that I grow."

The most conspicuous sign in this volume that Francis was ambitious to grow as a poet is the title poem. "Valhalla," a narrative in blank verse, is the longest poem he ever published, filling seventy-two pages when reprinted in his *Collected Poems, 1936–1976* (1976). Francis spent almost three years writing it and never published anything similar in content afterward. He may well have decided, as most readers have, that his gifts were far more inclined toward lyric pieces than toward narrative ones. Much longer than any of Frost's narrative poems, "Valhalla" can be compared with works produced in the 1920s and 1930s by poets such as E. A. Robinson and Robinson Jeffers—short novels in verse, essentially, often with a strong regional interest.

Francis chronicles the lives of a family whose remote upland farm is the Valhalla of the title. As the name suggests, the farm is a paradise removed from the turmoil and sorrow of the lower world; here parents, children, and servants work the land in blissful self-sufficiency. Over the course of the poem this charmed existence

is revealed to be, in fact, all too humanly fragile. The parents age and die; the elder daughter becomes pregnant, marries the man responsible, and moves away; the son goes to sea and drowns; and finally the younger daughter, diagnosed with cancer, commits suicide. This dolor carries little emotional impact. Characters remain opaque, the dialogue stiff. The sketchy symbolic connections with Norse mythology do little to add depth. "Valhalla" adds nothing to Francis's reputation, but it retains some fascination for being so profoundly anomalous. His poetic efforts from this point on were concentrated on shorter forms.

Whatever the artistic shortcomings of "Valhalla," Francis was soon to realize the poem's ideal of self-sufficiency more fully in his own life. When his father died in 1940, he used the $1,000 insurance payment to buy a half-acre lot near the house he was renting and to build on the parcel a three-room cottage. Unlike his former residence, the new building had electricity and running water. Francis moved into the new home on Market Hill Road on December 5, 1940; for the rest of his life the place was as central to his imaginative efforts as it was serviceable in providing shelter. Thoreau's Walden experiment was an obvious model upon which Francis elaborated freely and resourcefully. Hearing of the fall of Singapore in 1942 and musing on the juniper shrubs surrounding his house, sturdy evergreens no wind could uproot, he christened his home "Fort Juniper." It was, he wrote in *The Trouble with Francis,* "the base of my defense not so much against distant Germans and Japanese as against the war [World War II] itself with all its looming involvements and disruptions."

The disruptions in Francis's case were considerable. Within a few months of naming his house, he was drafted. A conscientious objector, he served for a short time as a noncombatant at Camp Breckenridge, Kentucky. For someone as shy and retiring as he was, the coarseness and lack of privacy in army life proved an ordeal. Discharged on account of age, he was required to do government-approved work for the duration of the war. He worked on chicken and apple farms, then taught at a prep school and, for the 1944–1945 academic year, at Mount Holyoke College. With the end of the war Francis returned to Fort Juniper and to a renewed commitment to living on his writing.

The years following the publication of *Valhalla and Other Poems* offered their share of accomplishment, despite the global distractions posed by World War II. Francis received the Shelley Memorial Award in 1939 and held the Golden Rose of the New England Poetry Club in 1942–1943. While Macmillan initially turned down his third collection, leading him to publish it privately in 1943 in a paper edition of 300 copies, in 1944 the publisher reversed course and brought out the book, with some additional poems included, under the same title: *The Sound I Listened For.*

THE SOUND I LISTENED FOR

In this book the poet's mastery of his material is fully established; and a resulting confidence, perhaps, allows for more subtlety of tone, less constriction of form. These are differences of degree: the verse is still trim and traditional. Something deeper, though—a response, maybe, to his father's death as well as his own lengthening life experience—makes this volume as a whole more resonant than its predecessors. When Francis writes about people in these poems he does so with feelings that are complicated and intense, however compactly expressed. Two poems ("That Dark Other Mountain" and "The Laugher") are brief but affecting reactions to Ebenezer Francis's death. Several other poems offer vignettes of human adversity. In "Old Man Feeding Hens," the title character is a rustic image of loneliness and mortality, "The oldest-looking man, the slowest-moving, /

I ever saw." The speaker forecasts the day of the old man's death with a grim metonymy as "that day the hens may not be fed / Till noon or evening or the second morning." In "Willow Woman," a poem that recalls Thomas Hardy, the speaker asks the unsuccessful vendor of pussy willows, "don't you know / It's only winter in the marketplace / However springlike where the willows grow?" Still more intensely troubled, "If We Had Known" ponders a suicide, vainly imagining how it might been prevented: "He never would have reached the river / If we had guessed his going. Never."

Less intimate but tinged with similar emotions are several poems touching on World War II: "Perspective," "I Am Not Flattered," "Where Is the Island?," and perhaps the most memorable, "The Goldfish Bowl." In this last poem Francis uses a numbed, documentary tone to survey a college swimming pool against a sinister backdrop of winter and war:

> The time is winter night, but in the swimming
>   pool
> Is summer noontime, noon by the electric sun.
> The young men dive, emerge, and float a while,
>   and fool,
> And dive again. The year is nineteen forty-one.

The last stanza effectively harks back to the title:

> The time is ten o'clock in nineteen forty-one.
> Somewhere a bell upon a tower begins to toll,
> While hour by hour the moon, its fat face warm
>   with sun,
> Gloats like a patient cat above a goldfish bowl.

This is very different from what we tend to think of as war poetry of its period; its homefront setting and pacifist convictions set it apart. Its avoidance of any easy lapse into propaganda distinguishes it as well.

Not all the poems in *The Sound I Listened For* are studies in dejection. The book includes a generous quantity of Francis's typical, finely etched pastoral lyrics. And some of its more ambitious poems exude a Wordsworthian sense of communion—both with nature and with the poet's fellow human beings. In the title poem the speaker overhears his neighbor plowing a nearby field; the farmer's voice recurrently telling the horses to turn becomes an image of the link between the two men, no less genuine for being known only to one of them. "The Reading of the Psalm" balances a sympathetic view of old age with elemental awe as it describes an old woman raptly following the progress of a thunderstorm. A more personal poem, which may be taken as a modest manifesto, is "Juniper." Here Francis celebrates the tough evergreens that gave his recently built house, Fort Juniper, its name. Their tenacity and ground-hugging habit make them an emblem for the poet's own self-reliant and earth-loving life:

> Here is my faith, my vision, my burning bush.
> It will burn on and never be consumed.
> It will be here long after I have gone,
> Long after the last farmer sleeps. And since
> I speak for it, its silence speaks for me.

"Juniper" implies what Francis openly attested to in his prose: the vital importance of his home as the center of his life and writing.

If Francis's poetry in this volume and henceforth was fueled by his ongoing adventure in homesteading, his only novel, published in 1948, looks back to the days before he won that independence. *We Fly Away,* from everything we know of Francis's life and by his own acknowledgment, is almost purely autobiographical. The character supplying the point of view throughout is a young, thus far unsuccessful writer named Robert. The novel chronicles his several months spent living, as his creator and alter ego sometimes did, as a resident chore man for an elderly woman. The landlady's character, Mrs. Bemis, is modeled in precise detail on Mrs. Boynton, with whom Francis

boarded from September 1935 to June 1936. Mrs. Boynton had a slightly less elderly housekeeper, Mrs. Kellogg, who is rendered with similar accuracy in the novel as Mrs. Teal. The only purely fictional character in the book is Henry, the other boarder, a carefree, heavy-drinking college student fifteen years younger than Robert.

We Fly Away is punctilious in description, sparing in action. By restricting himself to such a small corner of life and loading it with so much palpable detail, Francis adjusts the reader's gauge of significance. He immerses us in the rituals of domesticity: beating rugs, wrestling with storm windows, stoking a coal furnace. In this microscopically observed ambience, small triumphs and tragedies loom unexpectedly large. One is reminded of the narrative method of a novel like Elizabeth Gaskell's *Cranford,* or of regional vignettes by New England predecessors like Sarah Orne Jewett or Mary E. Wilkins Freeman. Francis, in pursuing this mode, differentiates himself by his more modern avoidance of sentimentality. The story is not without feeling, but it typically emerges through implication or understatement.

Subsisting uncomfortably in Mrs. Bemis's white elephant of a house, Robert observes her well-worn routine with mingled amusement, admiration, and horror. Her courage and self-reliance in confronting old age are constantly being weighed in his mental balance against her less amiable traits: pettiness, parsimony, small-minded complacency. Her principal foil is Mrs. Teal, who easily matches her in self-absorption and lack of imagination. The two women's skirmishes end when Mrs. Teal leaves to accept a more comfortable position—a disruption that in the pared-down world of the novel exerts the force of an earthquake. The other two major turns in the action also concern departures. The first is that of Henry, the likable reprobate whom the older, sober, cautious Robert views with troubled fascination and envy. After some awkward interaction that never becomes real friendship, Henry leaves in midwinter for Florida, having flunked out of college. A few months later Robert sees a newspaper story reporting the young man's death in a motorcycle accident. His regret and his decision not to pass the news along to Mrs. Bemis provide an emotional climax to the story. This is followed, however, by an equally important turning point, when Robert himself decides to move out and live on his own in a moldering old house, much as the author did after leaving his Amherst landladies behind. The protagonist's thoughts at this point express the central theme of the work: "Freedom—that was the word. . . . Freedom was walking out a road into the country, choosing your own direction, your own gait, your own time of going, and not having to think about coming back."

For all its comic touches, the novel is moving in depicting the human yearning for independence, and discerning in its view of the widely varying ways people achieve it. It is charming as a record of a now-vanished way of life in New England small towns, and interesting for its autobiographical content. Out of print for decades, it deserves to be better known.

Except for the publication of his novel, Francis's career for many years after World War II was marked with disappointment. "Lean years for a writer," he later called this period in his autobiography. Unable to find a publisher for his fourth collection of poems, *The Face against the Glass,* he finally published it himself in 1950. He put a great deal of effort into a nonfiction book describing his way of life at Fort Juniper. This manuscript, with a title taken from Thoreau, *Travelling in Concord,* was never published.

When *Forum* (a magazine to which he had regularly contributed essays) ceased publication, Francis found his already meager income painfully reduced. Demoralized, he became despondent and reclusive for a time. Aside from his financial plight, it can be assumed that he must have suffered from a sense of critical neglect. The years after the war were a time in which the modernist revolution in poetry became fully entrenched in both the academic and the literary realms; formalist poets dealing with rural subject matter were regarded as quaint, old-fashioned, inconsequential. Even a much better-known poet like Frost received his share of condescension during this period; Francis's profile being so much lower, he was all the more easily ignored.

Perhaps reflecting its author's beleaguered state, *The Face against the Glass* seems muted in spirit and restless in technique. It is a brief collection, and is even briefer as it appears in Francis's *Collected Poems, 1936–1976.* (Having reprinted some pieces in a later volume, he chose in 1976 not to return them to their original position.) No poem in the book is longer than a page. Although still conservative in style, the book experiments more freely with form than previous collections. More than half of the poems do not rhyme; in others Francis uses widely separated occasional rhymes or slant rhymes. A poem like "Glass" indicates that issues of poetic style had come to be much on his mind:

> Words of a poem should be glass
> But glass so simple-subtle its shape
> Is nothing but the shape of what it holds.
> . . . .
> If the impossible were not,
> And if the glass, only the glass,
> Could be removed, the poem would remain.

Perhaps Francis's experiments with unrhymed forms were an effort to bring language closer to the sort of transparency he imagines here. Always inclined toward a plain style, he seems at this time to have grown more self-conscious in examining the esthetic preferences underlying his art.

Glass is a recurrent image in the book, beginning with its appearance in the title. The title is taken from "The Spy," in which a solitary man peers in through the windows of his own empty house at night. Eerily trancelike, the piece seems to split the man's identity in two, into an inner and an outer self: ". . . the prowler peers in deeper / Spying upon the empty chair, spying / Upon the man who is and is not there." The touch of alarm here is intriguing in a poet so frequently prone to write in praise of solitude. The dark mood of "The Spy" surfaces in "The Amanita," about a poison mushroom; in "The Hawk," a Darwinian view of the raptor; in "Hide-and Seek," about children playing in a graveyard; and in a number of other pieces brooding on mortality. There are a few not very successful attempts at social and political satire ("The Heiress," "The Big Tent"). Most readers will prefer lyrics in his more typical pastoral mode, whether nature vignettes or oblique self-portraits, such as "Squash in Blossom," "Thistle Seed in the Wind," or "Two Words," which plays with both landscape and language to achieve its chords:

> Two words are with me noon and night
> Like echoes of the solitude
> That is my home—half field, half wood,
> Feldeinsamkeit, Waldeinsamkeit.

> In words as quiet as the Psalms
> I hear, I overhear the tone
> Of Concord and of Emerson,
> And all the autumn mood of Brahms.

The Face against the Glass received almost no critical attention, though Francis attempted to provoke some by publishing a playfully negative review of it himself under a pseudonym. Throughout the 1950s he was unable to publish another book, and his ability to make a living was tenuous. There were a few bright spots, though. Francis was engaged to teach at the Chautauqua Writers Workshop for a once-a-year session from 1954 to 1958. In 1955 he was Phi Beta Kappa poet at Tufts University, and he took the same position at Harvard University in 1960. Most strikingly for a poet who had rarely traveled, in 1957–1958 he lived in Rome as a recipient of the Prix de Rome Fellowship, awarded by the American Academy of Arts and Letters. (He would return more briefly to Italy, and tour ancestral sites in Ireland, in the spring of 1961.) In 1960 Francis's long publishing drought came to an end when Wesleyan University Press brought out a new collection of poems, *The Orb Weaver.*

THE ORB WEAVER

This collection, Francis's fifth, projects a more confident air than its predecessor. Knowing the trials Francis had faced for the last decade leaves a reader impressed with his capacity for self-renewal. His choice of "The Orb Weaver" as a title poem is intriguing. The spider, "Devised of jet, embossed with sulphur, / Hanging among the fruits of summer," is seen as part and parcel of the beauty of nature. But the sight of a grasshopper entrapped in the web's "winding-sheet" leads to this reflection:

> The art, the craftsmanship, the cunning,
> The patience, the self-control, the waiting,
> The sudden dart and the needled poison.

> I have no quarrel with the spider
> But with the mind or mood that made her
> To thrive in nature and in man's nature.

Here Francis's troubled recognition of the presence of evil in creation is effectively concentrated in a single image. Both in imagery and theme the poem bears comparison with Frost's "Design." Though Francis had dealt with such material earlier, this was his first such piece to receive the emphasis carried by a title poem. It is as if, while his own misfortunes were receding, he did not wish his darker vision of the world to drop too far into the background.

Even so, and even allowing for the presence of certain other darker poems, the overall mood of *The Orb Weaver* is far from bleak. Many pieces feature a sunny, buoyant, celebratory tone. As Francis himself later put it in *The Trouble with Francis*:

These poems, unlike my earlier ones which had been for the most part quiet, brooding, even melancholy, the month seemingly November, the color gray, had color, energy, action. Growing older I wanted to call up, like a magician, the vitality and exuberance of youth. More and more I craved the heat and brilliance of the noonday sun.

Certainly this description fits "Come Out into the Sun," a chant that honors the first bright days of spring and invites the reader to share the poet's rapture:

Come shed, shed now, your winter-varnished shell
In the deep diathermy of high noon.
The sun, the sun, come out into the sun,
Into the sun, come out, come in.

Equally celebratory are such lyrics as "Gold," "Tomatoes," "Waxwings," and "The Seed Eaters," stressing nature's beauty and plenitude.

Several poems focus on the human figure with a particular care for capturing physical action in words. Usually in these pieces the point is an implied or explicit metaphor. In "Swimmer," the relation of swimmer to sea is compared to that of a lover to love, which can either drown or uphold him. In "Apple Peeler," one of Francis's most often anthologized poems, the analogy seems to be with artistic creation: the "Virtuoso" produces a single "unbroken spiral" that is "like a trick sonnet in one long, versatile sentence." In "Catch," the metaphor is announced in the first line—"Two boys uncoached are tossing a poem together"—and developed with remarkable rhythmic inventiveness:

Fast, let him sting from it, now, now fool him
  slowly,
Anything, everything tricky, risky, nonchalant,
Anything under the sun to outwit the prosy,
Over the tree and the long sweet cadence down,
Over the head, make him scramble to pick up the
  meaning,

And now, like a posy, a pretty one plump in his
  hands.

Two other baseball poems, "Pitcher" and "The Base Stealer," similarly play daringly with kinetic effects. Others, too, are alert to motion, even if somewhat more reserved in style: "High Diver," "Boy Riding Forward Backward," and "The Rock Climbers" fit into this category.

Perhaps the most ceremonious of Francis's celebratory poems is his tribute to his father, "Hallelujah: A Sestina." There was something of a vogue for this exacting verse form in the late twentieth century; this sestina of Francis's predates the trend by a few decades. Francis handles the repeated six end-words of his stanzas with wit, resourcefulness, and feeling through their permutations. The result is praise that seems both powerfully incantatory and winningly personal:

A wind's word, the Hebrew Hallelujah.
I wonder they never give it to a boy
(Hal for short) boy with wind-wild hair.
It means Praise God, as well it should since praise
Is what God's for. Why didn't they call my father
Hallelujah instead of Ebenezer?

Francis controls the complicated chiming patterns of this traditional form as deftly as he handles stanzas of his own devising. *The Orb Weaver* may well strike out in new emotional directions, as Francis observed, but it also displays an impressive versatility in stylistic strategies.

Francis's career, at this point out of the doldrums, continued to flourish. He began to be invited more frequently to read at colleges, and this exposure increased the audience for his poems. He also was able, in the 1960s, to say farewell to his years of bad luck with publishers. The University of Massachusetts Press in Amherst took an ongoing interest in his work beginning in 1965, with the publication of his *Come Out into the Sun: Poems New and Se-*

lected. Thereafter the university press published three more books of his poetry and three of his prose. In 1975 the publishing house established the Juniper Prize in his honor, an award to a poetry manuscript submitted to an annual open competition. For this Amherst poet to have found at last a supportive relationship with a publisher right in his own hometown seems a rare instance of poetic justice.

Come Out into the Sun offers a generous selection from previous volumes while opening with a section of new poems. Of these, "The Black Hood," Francis's Phi Beta Kappa poem for Harvard, is an exquisitely balanced mixture of lightness and profundity. The poem muses on how artists and thinkers attempt to reconcile beauty and truth, the ideal and the real, in ways that when strictly judged are deceptive or self-deceiving. Yet the poet goes on to confess his own involvement with "the dark mysteries of Paradox":

> I marry freedom to fastidious form.
> I trust the spirit in the arms of sense.
> I can contrive a calm from any storm.
> My art, my business is ambivalence.
> In every poem by me on my shelf
> Confidentially yours I hide myself.

This subtle, extended argument marks an interesting change from Francis's usual short image-centered poems. There are, to be sure, many of these as well, including a few derived from his travels abroad.

Several of the new poems in this volume are written in a form Francis originated, a versification system he called word-count. Rather than adhering to a regular number of syllables or metrical feet in a line, the poet counts whole words and maintains the same number of words per line throughout. Although this regular count is often unobtrusive to a reader, Francis thought its arbitrary demands could lead a poet to concentrate more intensely on choices of diction and control of rhythm. The form is highly flexible in the effects it allows: "Dolphins," "Stellaria," "Museum Vase," and "Icicles" are all word-count poems, and each has its own distinctive sound. Word-count represents the sort of artistic paradox celebrated in "The Black Hood." It is indeed a marriage of "freedom to fastidious form."

In 1967–1968 Francis was awarded the Amy Lowell Traveling Scholarship and visited Italy a third time. He spent most of his time living and writing in Florence. Shortly before his return to Amherst, his new publishers brought out a collection of critical prose, *The Satirical Rogue on Poetry* (1968). This book was reissued in a considerably expanded form by the University of Michigan Press in 1980 as *Pot Shots at Poetry.* As the latter title suggests, these prose pieces are short—often less than a page—and narrowly focused (or, one might say, targeted). Francis takes aim at the peculiarities, puzzles, and pretensions of the poetry world. Sometimes he is humorously cranky, as in "Lounge":

> God forbid I ever have to give a poetry reading in a lounge, a lounge where the listener sinks out of sight and sound in some deep-bosomed overstuffed divan.
>
> If anyone ever drops a pin during my reading, for God's sake let me be where I can hear it!

Sometimes he is bitter, as at the close of "No Poem So Fine":

> No poem is fine enough to be safe. A critic can always maul it or pooh-pooh it if he has a mind to. Poems have not learned jujitsu or karate. They go naked and trusting.
>
> On the other hand, no poem is too wretched for some critic (if he has a mind to) to hail as a gem.

And sometimes, as at the end of "Defense of Poetry," he is memorably shrewd:

> I would say that a poem worth defending needs no defense and a poem needing defense is not worth defending. I would say it is not our busi-

ness to defend poetry but the business of poetry to defend us.

Throughout, however the tone may vary, the perspective is that of a bemused outsider. The book received little notice. Looking back on it a few years after it appeared, he wrote ruefully in *The Trouble with Francis*:

> My hidden motive in writing *The Satirical Rogue* was to get even with the world of poetry which had caused me so much suffering over the years. To get even with it by pin-pricking and deflating it. Unknown to the reader and only partly known to myself, I was expressing my hostility in socially acceptable terms.

Francis was soon able to present himself to the reading public in two more substantial works of prose: his autobiography and a memoir of Robert Frost.

A REVEALING AUTOBIOGRAPHY

The Trouble with Francis: An Autobiography (1971) is the indispensable source for information on the poet's life. Generous in circumstantial detail, it is, like Francis's poetry, somewhat guarded in its approach to the poet's emotional development. The dearly valued privacy of Fort Juniper is in some respects firmly maintained. Yet in the end it proves a revealing document. Its organization is quirky. Francis begins his life story at the point where his fictional treatment of it in *We Fly Away* ended—in 1937, when he left the last of his Amherst landladies to move into "the old house by the brook." He then proceeds chronologically to the present, filling eleven chapters. In Chapter 12 he circles back to his birth and brings us in the next several chapters from his childhood on through his early years in Amherst.

This segmented approach to reminiscence tends to emphasize certain areas of the writer's experience. The initial emphasis is on maturity: we witness Francis's struggle for personal autonomy, through the whole saga of the building of Fort Juniper and the literary career he pursued while leading a spartan, self-sufficient life. It is only after the image of his hard-won success has been placed before us that Francis turns to show us the timidity and awkwardness of his earlier self. It is like a before-and-after pair of pictures, viewed in reverse order. This structure, by impressing us with the great gap dividing the finished man from the uncertain youth, stresses Francis's ability, discovered over the years, to make himself into a stronger, more creative person. It presents his life, as much as any writing of his, as an esthetic work (and, at the time he was writing *The Trouble with Francis,* as a work in progress). In this regard it seems very much a poet's consciously shaped approach to autobiography.

As one would expect from his poetry, Francis's descriptions are enlivened with telling detail. Whether writing of Amherst or of Italy, he shows an intuitive grasp of the texture of life in the place. We see his power of observation in his vignettes of his family and his Amherst neighbors, and his Thoreauvian way of life loses its air of quaintness as he exhibits it confidently and candidly to the reader. Some parts of the book smack of the manifesto, as Francis explains his extraordinary economies and also enthusiasms like his vegetarianism, which had an ethical as well as an economic basis. In an extended passage he sings the praises of the soybean.

At the end of the book, with some signs of reluctance, he makes two disclosures. The first concerns sexual orientation. "Ever since adolescence," he writes, "I had been drawn erotically to members of my own sex and to them only." For most of his life, he tells us, his timidity and awareness of the possible social consequences kept him from expressing these feelings overtly. In 1958, however, he began a love affair with an Italian whom he had met on shipboard on his way back from his Rome fellowship year. This relationship continued over the next few years through occasional meetings and was renewed during Francis's second residence in Italy. Francis's discussion of his sexual preference and of this affair is reticent by present-day standards. He never reveals his lover's name, and he does not describe intimacies. This was apparently the only such relationship he engaged in over the course of his life.

How much, a reader may wonder, should Francis's sexual nature figure in interpreting his poems? Sexuality seems more a significant absence than a major presence in his work. The self-control he exercised in life extended to his writing, in which erotic feelings are rarely expressed directly. When such feelings are hinted at, as in some poems describing young males engaged in athletic or other physical activity, the elegance of the language and the detachment of the observing speaker make the effect predominantly esthetic. Francis himself took this view of such poems. In 1976 he reprinted several of his poems about young males together with prose sketches in the same vein in a chapbook, *A Certain Distance.* In his foreword to this collection he wrote:

> Many an artist over the centuries has concentrated on the female form, using it sometimes as a finality and other times as a point of departure for all sorts of elaborations, abstractions, and speculations. The erotic impulse that stimulated the artist at the outset may at times be so far transcended as to be quite lost sight of. These pictures of the young male can be accounted for, I suppose, by the same psychology.

The second revelation at the close of Francis's autobiography concerns his religious outlook. In the book's final chapter he describes himself as an atheist, but his emphasis is not on particular problematic church doctrines. More sweepingly, he expounds his view of a world in which what he calls evil (or E, for much of the chapter) is a chronic and inescapable reality. By E he means "all that is hostile to human life and its fulfillment," and believing such a malignant power to be pervasive, he finds it impossible to believe in a merciful God. Most of the chapter is devoted to his vision of the ubiquity of evil; in the end he is forced into a somewhat paradoxical vein when discussing how this worldview has affected his own life. He writes, "Though my view of the human situation is dark, in my own life I embrace all available brightness. Having faced intellectually the full force of evil, I want to face imaginatively the full possibility of good." And he ends by professing a system of values that, he argues, may be independent of religious belief: "truthfulness, justice, courage, mercy, and that most difficult of virtues: the putting of the interest of another person above the interest of oneself."

Considering the full range of Francis's poetry, one would have to say that these ideas on evil are touched on numerous times but come to the forefront in a relatively small number of poems, "The Orb Weaver" being a prime example. It is no doubt because his poetry is so grounded in the particulars of a daily life he found happy and rewarding that Francis's pessimism is kept within bounds in his work. His bleak philosophical position, however sincerely held, does not mark his writing as deeply as a similar view does, for example, the work of Thomas Hardy. Francis remained bemused by this apparent contradiction, labeling himself "a happy pessimist."

The Trouble with Francis was soon followed by a brief but absorbing memoir, *Frost: A Time to Talk.* We learn much about Francis as well as about Frost from this respectful but not uncritical portrait. In his autobiography Francis had written briefly of his friendship with the older poet and of his attraction to Frost's "power." "He was a poet and he had power; the combination was striking. . . . As for me, power, any kind of power, was notably what I didn't have."

Given this disparity, and the ease with which admiration can sour into envy, it is remarkable that Francis's memoir is not more barbed than it is. By the time he wrote it, he must have been thoroughly weary of seeing his work compared (usually to its disadvantage) with that of Frost.

In *Frost: A Time to Talk* Francis for the most part transcribes from his journal the records he kept of his conversations with Frost. He usually refrains from retrospective judgmental comment, letting dialogue speak for itself. It is clear that, like others, he was at times repelled by Frost's egotism. Yet his view both of the man and the poet is balanced and without apparent prejudice. At the end of the memoir he declares his favorites among Frost's poems, in a list that shows much critical acuity. In an interesting passage he offers his opinion that Frost was at his best as a lyric poet. The very best of Frost's lyrics, he writes, are "cut and shining gems." While he admires some of the longer poems, he finds fault with Frost's blank verse: "the problem of sustaining the underlying iambic beat and doing it without monotony was sometimes too much for him." One may wonder if these comments reflect something of Francis's own earlier disaffection with the meter: after "Valhalla" blank verse was a form he returned to infrequently.

The 1970s proved an active and fruitful decade for Francis. As his publication rate increased, he was more in demand for poetry readings and stints at writers' conferences. He had developed a winning platform manner, often reciting from memory rather than reading. An honorary degree from the University of Massachusetts (1970), a Creative Arts Award in Poetry from Brandeis University (1974), and the establishment of the Juniper Prize honored him and increased his visibility. He was at the same time active as a citizen in opposing the Vietnam War. From 1966 to 1973 he took part in a weekly vigil on Amherst Common to protest American involvement in the conflict.

In 1974 he brought out another collection, *Like Ghosts of Eagles*. Here his experiments with form branch out in new directions. Some poems consist of a single sentence or of sentences flowing into each other without punctuation. Others make use of a technique Francis called "fragmented surface." Such pieces are constructed of single words or brief phrases juxtaposed without conventional grammar, syntax, or punctuation. Francis thought the technique yielded "greater emotional impact." Some lines from "Blood Stains"—the beginning and the end—are representative:

blood stains   how to remove   from cotton
silk   from all fine fabrics   blood stains . . .

headlines   dispatches   communiqués   history
white leaves   green leaves   from grass growing
or dead   from trees   from flowers   from sky
from standing from running water   blood stains

Like some of the other more jagged and agitated pieces, this one reflects Francis's outrage at the Vietnam War.

Surprisingly, the fragmented surface poem from this volume that has proved most memorable is anything but agitated. "Silent Poem" is a work of daring minimalism and amazing purity. Its twelve lines, each made up of four compound nouns, are arranged in six distichs. With this unadorned inventory Francis evokes an entire landscape—that of rural New England—and the life led in it. He begins, "backroad leafmold stonewall chipmunk / underbrush grapevine woodchuck shadblow"—and he ends with a more haunting sequence: "gravestone groundpine windbreak bedrock / weathercock snowfall starlight cockcrow." Few poems of the twentieth century display such simultaneous control of rhythm, assonance, and imagery as this one does. It reminds us in a startling way that a poem can be made in only one way: by placing one word after another.

In this book and in his later work Francis shows a heightened sensitivity to single words;

in certain pieces metaphor merges with word-play of various kinds. "City" begins, "In the scare / city / no scarcity / of fear." "The Bulldozer," Francis tells us, "Bulls by day / And dozes by night." Some of these pieces settle for cleverness rather than depth. They are, however, outweighed by more substantial lyrics: "Three Old Ladies and Three Spring Bulbs," "The Half Twist," and "When I Come." "His Running My Running" achieves an imaginative identification similar to that in "The Sound I Listened For":

> Out of leaves falling
> Over leaves fallen
> A runner comes running
>
> Aware of no watcher
> His loneness my loneness
> His running my running.

Francis's impressive publishing record of the 1960s and 1970s was capped by the appearance of his *Collected Poems, 1936–1976.* This attractively designed volume includes all of his collections through *Like Ghosts of Eagles* and adds a brief section of "New Poems." Francis did not rewrite his earlier poems, but he frequently made changes in the order in which they had appeared in their separate volumes. It is clear from these reconfigurations that Francis saw artistic opportunities in the presence of certain recurring themes in his work. Setting poems side by side with new neighbors, he enlivened their conversation with each other. Except for a chapbook published in the mid-1980s and one posthumous volume, *Collected Poems, 1936–1976* provides the standard text of the writer's lifework in poetry.

The new poems provide more examples of formal experimentation. Unusual in Francis's work is a dramatic poem, "Two Ghosts," in which the two specters in dialogue are his two revered predecessors as poets of Amherst, Robert Frost and Emily Dickinson. Another new formal strategy appears in "Fire Chaconne," a sequence of twenty tiny poems all centered on the image of fire. (Wallace Stevens's "Thirteen Ways of Looking at a Blackbird" may have provided a model.) "Poppycock" is one of the more entertaining of his poems that dwell on a single word. "Spell" and "Pedal Point" are delicate lyrics of a more traditional sort.

Francis furnished *Collected Poems, 1936–1976* with a short preface in which he highlights what he sees as evidence of progress in his work. He describes his early poems as having been written by "a serious young man whose most constant pleasure was a silent dialogue carried on with himself, a prolonged solitary brooding." Continuing in the third person, he asserts that "as he grew older his poems grew younger until, toward the end of this collection, some poems are positively frisky." It is true that Francis grew more inclined toward satire and light verse as he grew older. To judge from his comments, he prized such poems as an advance beyond the naïve solemnity he saw in his younger self. A reader may accept his lighter pieces as a mark of emotional flexibility while still not ranking them on a par with his best work. Some of his humorous poems manage to be mildly amusing; but too many are strained bits of whimsy or self-indulgent triviality.

Around this time Francis briefly attempted a change in his living arrangements. Now in his mid-seventies, he took an apartment in the center of Amherst, planning to stay there through the winters and return to Fort Juniper for the pleasanter parts of the year. After a few months he decided he had made a mistake and went home to Fort Juniper before his apartment lease expired. There he continued to live until the end of his life, regardless of the health problems that in his late seventies began to accumulate. He was occasionally afflicted by an irregular heartbeat and also suffered a series of small strokes. Both conditions were controlled by medication, though his speech was slightly affected by the strokes. In the 1980s Francis became legally blind from deterioration of the retina. His last poems were not written down by him but dictated to friends.

Throughout his last years Francis enjoyed a degree of celebrity, though he still treasured his solitude. The town of Amherst honored him with a Robert Francis Day and named a foot-bridge over a creek for him. He took pleasure in the visits of old friends and new, serving them his homemade dandelion wine while pursuing conversation on literature and much else. By now frequently anthologized and with a substantial body of work before the public, he felt fulfilled as a poet. His friends recall that he often spoke of his poems as his children and that he claimed to have no favorites among them.

The Academy of American Poets named him a fellow in 1984. In the same year a chapbook, *Butter Hill and Other Poems,* was published. (Part of its contents were reprinted in the posthumous volume *Late Fire, Late Snow: New and Uncollected Poems,* 1992.) The last books of his to appear in his lifetime were two widely different works of prose: *The Trouble with God* (1984) and *Travelling in Amherst: A Poet's Journal, 1931–1954* (1986).

The Trouble with God, a short book published in an edition of a hundred copies, is a work of religious controversy. It goes over much the same ground as the chapter on religion in the author's autobiography but lodges many more detailed objections to theistic religion and to Christianity in particular. Compared with the argument in *The Trouble with Francis,* this one seems weary and rambling. Francis does not show much awareness of the historical development of the doctrines he attacks, or of the sometimes varying interpretations of them by communities of believers. As with all theological disputations, his is unlikely to convince anyone who is not already inclined to agree. The most puzzling and disheartening thing in the book is Francis's reaction to religious language. With a sort of cheerless sportiveness,

he takes a rationalistic ax to the symbolic language of the Bible. For example, he comments on the famous metaphor of separating the sheep from the goats at the Last Judgment:

> What an unfortunate simile! The shepherd does not separate his sheep from his goats to save the sheep and destroy the goats, but only for the convenience of counting them and taking care of them. Sheep and goats are presumably of equal value to him, with the goats having the advantage of being able to subsist on sparser diet than the sheep.

Many readers, whatever their religious opinions, will find something odd and ironic in the spectacle of a master of metaphor assailing metaphorical uses of language. In a final chapter, perhaps to forestall psychoanalytic speculations, Francis assures us that he did not by any means come to his views out of rebellion against his minister father.

Travelling in Amherst makes pleasanter reading. These selections from his journals, with their spontaneous reactions to contemporary events, offer a confirming supplement to the retrospective account of his early life in *The Trouble with Francis* and in his Frost memoir. Most of the entries are brief and there are few surprises; yet the story gains some immediacy in this telling of it. One is impressed by how constant some of his preoccupations were. In 1931, years before the building of Fort Juniper, we find him musing on Thoreau:

> Thoreau went to Walden to escape the village, but not to escape himself. He went to find himself, to find life. Whenever a man cuts himself off partially or wholly from his fellows and simplifies his mode of life in order to have more of life and to become better acquainted with himself, he is following Thoreau.

Almost as far back, in 1933, he is pondering the problem of evil:

> I see all the evil of the world as a black tapestry against which and within which man is to weave

the golden threads of his life. He can never blot out the black. He can only weave a more and more beautiful pattern. If he could blot out the black, where would his pattern be?

Throughout, there is a profound commitment to his artistic discipline. He writes, "I want form to be the perfect expression of the content. I want form to fit feeling as skin fits flesh." And elsewhere, wittily: "Writing poetry is like playing the harp: it often takes as long to get in tune as it does to play." Like Francis's other autobiographical works, this book suggests how enriching an embrace of simplicity can be, whether in life or in art.

Although increasingly infirm and hindered by poor eyesight, Francis continued to compose poems and, with the help of his friend Henry Lyman, set about compiling a new volume of lyrics. Before he could complete this work, in the summer of 1987, he fell and broke a hip. Although the operation to repair it was a success, it left him too weak to go home. After lingering a few weeks, Francis died of pneumonia in the hospital in Northampton on July 14, 1987. He was a little less than a month short of his eighty-sixth birthday. In accordance with his wish, the trustees of his estate have since maintained Fort Juniper as a residence for writers, with tenancy customarily of a year.

The year following Francis's death saw the publication of a brief prose work, *Gusto, Thy Name Was Mrs. Hopkins: A Prose Rhapsody.* Perhaps because of its brevity or the highly local nature of its material, Francis had trouble finding a publisher for this memoir, although he continued to hope for one. He mentions it as a completed work in 1971 in his autobiography. Finally, a young Canadian admirer and small press proprietor, Gordon Lawson McLennan, took it on with Francis's blessing, although the poet did not live to see the finished book. This tribute to the first of Francis's landladies, Margaret Sutton Briscoe Hopkins, is written in some of his most delightful prose. The redoubt-able Mrs. Hopkins, an Amherst College professor's wife, was the woman who introduced Francis to Frost. Francis offers an amusing and affectionate description of her commanding ways and eccentricities, and he makes clear the appreciation he felt for the impetus she gave him at the outset of his career. It is a pity that this book, published in a small edition in Canada, has been almost unobtainable in the United States.

Francis's late poetry is easier to come by. Lyman, his literary executor, edited the posthumous volume *Late Fire, Late Snow.* Starting with the manuscript Francis had been compiling with his assistance, Lyman augmented it with a number of uncollected poems, some retrieved from correspondence. Some poems from the chapbook *Butter Hill* are included. The result is a substantial collection of fifty-six poems.

Both the chapbook and this final volume show that Francis maintained a remarkable vitality as an aging poet. His writing may have slowed, but its virtues did not fade. The poems are not dated, so it is not always certain which are early and which are late. In his later years Francis moved easily between more traditional and more innovative verse forms. As might be expected in a final volume, several pieces contemplate mortality, at times impersonally, at other times quite personally. He makes a grim nursery rhyme on the theme in "Play Ball!":

Ball we were born on
Ball that keeps turning

Ball we will die on
When life stops burning.

In "The Brass Candlestick," death is the ultimate separation, impervious to any human wish or ritual. The poet depicts a private rite of memory for his dead father. Time after time he has lit a single candle,

And seen the flame in the still room shiver
As in a ghost of wind, or moveless like

The tear-drop evening star, and with the black
Iron box-snuffers trimmed the charred wick
And in the candle's light have lived and breathed

And still the old man would not come.

Other meditations of this sort, ranging widely in tone, include "The Old Peppermint Ladies," "Cadence," and "Columbarium."

Equally typical and equally adept are poems focusing on vital energy, whether viewed in nature or in humanity. "Bravura," "Late Fire Late Snow," "The Far Northern Birch," "The Whippoorwill," "The Long Shower," and others explore the brighter end of the emotional spectrum. An extraordinarily vigorous feat of rhythm, "Gray Squirrel" begins, "Flighty as birds, fluid as fishes / He flies, he floats through boughs, he flashes," and ends, "How could I catch him, how can I match him / Except with a fast eye and my best wishes?" One finishes this book persuaded that the poet's eye was often fast enough and his sympathies large enough to capture fleeting perceptions and preserve them, through years of writing, in the permanence of art.

By the end of his life Francis occupied an honored position in American letters. But although his readership has increased greatly, his work has yet to receive much close critical attention. Almost all the critical response to his poetry has come in the form of usually brief reviews of individual volumes. The exceptions to this, for the most part, have been articles in special issues of literary magazines devoted to his work, and many such pieces have offered more appreciation than interpretation, or have been confined in space and scope. That said, there are helpful comments on his work to be found in the issue of *Field* honoring his eightieth birthday (fall 1981) and the memorial issue of the *Painted Bride Quarterly* (1988).

As of 2001, there was not yet a complete edition of Francis's poems in print, and a small amount of his verse remains uncollected in any volume. A large number of his prose pieces have yet to be reprinted from periodicals. A book-length critical treatise, *Francis on Poetry,* remains in manuscript. He has thus left work to be done by editors as well as critics. The major gatherings of his papers are deposited in the Special Collections of three libraries: at Syracuse University, at the University of Massachusetts, and at the Jones Library in Amherst, where as a young man Francis labored over his poems every day at an upstairs desk.

Francis's reputation is likely to increase with the scholarly and critical scrutiny time will bring. His appeal as a writer is not to one specialized audience but to a number of overlapping ones. Readers who ordinarily find modern poetry difficult appreciate the accessibility of his style. At the same time, his mastery of conventional verse forms and his creation of new ones draw the attention of those concerned with poetic techniques. At present, when formalist strategies in poetry are being reexamined and reinvigorated by younger poets, Francis provides many salient examples of what his mentor Frost called "the old way to be new."

Other responses to the author are likely to be invited by content rather than by style. Francis was unapologetically a New England writer; his descriptive fidelity preserves an image of the place in a time now rapidly disappearing from living memory. His connections with earlier important writers of the region—Frost, Dickinson, Emerson, and Thoreau—are complex, and they stem not only from shared locality but from a wealth of ideas, some of which Francis embraced, others of which he debated. All this makes his writing of signal interest to students of New England's intellectual and literary history. Finally, Francis has attracted, and will no doubt continue to attract, certain readers with the compelling story of his pursuit of a life of simplicity and self-sufficiency. Thoreau occupied his cabin at Walden Pond for two years; Francis made Fort Juniper his home for close to half a century. Although he would have been most uncomfortable in the role of a guru, he was and remains an exemplary figure for many who dissent from conventional mores. Late in his life, without any calculation on his part, his antiwar views and his unencumbered lifestyle struck a chord with the counterculture. There is much in his work that speaks to the condition of those who are repulsed by the effects of militarism and consumerism upon society.

Brief as the critical discussions of Francis tend to be, many of them sooner or later get around to a comparison of Francis with Frost. The consensus, unlikely to be changed, is that Frost is a major poet, Francis a minor one. Francis himself accepted the designation with good humor. "I am a poet, minor. Or I try," he wrote in "The Black Hood." Without disputing the label, one might note that Francis, unlike many minor poets, was not only keenly aware of his limitations but was eventually able, to the degree that it was possible, to turn them into strengths. The individualism of his outlook, the clarity of his perceptions, and the consistently high quality of his unshowy craftsmanship have few parallels in modern American poetry. His poems continue to remind his readers that the pleasures afforded by some minor poetry are anything but minor.

Selected Bibliography

WORKS OF ROBERT FRANCIS

POETRY

Stand with Me Here. New York: Macmillan, 1936.

Valhalla and Other Poems. New York: Macmillan, 1938.

The Sound I Listened For. Self-published, 1943. (Edition of 300 copies.) Reprint, New York: Macmillan, 1944. (Reprint contains additional poems.)

The Face against the Glass. Self-published, 1950. (Edition of 300 copies.)

The Orb Weaver. Middletown, Conn.: Wesleyan University Press, 1960.

Come Out into the Sun: Poems New and Selected. Amherst: University of Massachusetts Press, 1965.

Like Ghosts of Eagles: Poems, 1966–1974. Drawings by Jack Coughlin. Amherst: University of Massachusetts Press, 1974.

Collected Poems, 1936–1976. Amherst: University of Massachusetts Press, 1976.

Butter Hill and Other Poems. n.p.: Paul W. Carman, 1984. (Chapbook; edition of 400 copies.)

Late Fire, Late Snow: New and Uncollected Poems. Amherst: University of Massachusetts Press, 1992. (Includes some of the contents of Butter Hill. A fine press edition, published in the same year, is available from the Estate of Robert Francis in Northampton, Massachusetts.)

AUTOBIOGRAPHY AND MEMOIRS

The Trouble with Francis: An Autobiography. Amherst: University of Massachusetts Press, 1971.

Frost: A Time to Talk. Amherst: University of Massachusetts Press, 1972. British ed. published under title Robert Frost: A Time to Talk—Conversations and Indiscretions Recorded by Robert Francis.

Travelling in Amherst: A Poet's Journal, 1931–1954. Boston: Rowan Tree Press, 1986.

Gusto, Thy Name Was Mrs. Hopkins: A Prose Rhapsody. Toronto: Chartres Books, 1988. (Virtually undistributed in the United States. Copies are available from the Estate of Robert Francis in Northampton, Massachusetts.)

CRITICISM AND SATIRICAL COMMENTARY

The Satirical Rogue on Poetry. Amherst: University of Massachusetts Press, 1968.

Pot Shots at Poetry. Ann Arbor: University of Michigan Press, 1980. (Reprints The Satirical Rogue on Poetry with many additional pieces.)

The Satirical Rogue on All Fronts. n.p.: Paul W. Carman, 1984. (Chapbook; satirical miscellany.)

UNCOLLECTED PROSE PIECES

Rome without Camera. Amherst: Jones Library, 1958. (Travel essay.)

"Emily for Everybody." New England Review 1, no. 4:505–511 (summer 1979). (Comparison of the real Emily Dickinson with the portrayal of her in the play *The Belle of Amherst.*)

OTHER WORKS

We Fly Away. New York: Swallow Press and William Morrow, 1948. (Fiction.)

A Certain Distance. Woods Hole, Mass.: Pourboire Press, 1976. (Chapbook; combines prose sketches and selected poems.)

Francis on the Spot: An Interview with Robert Francis. Interview conducted by Philip Tetreault and Kathy Sewalk-Karcher. Woonsocket, RI: Tunnel Press, 1976. (Later included in *Pot Shots at Poetry.*)

The Trouble with God. West Hatfield, Mass.: Pennyroyal Press, 1984. (Religious controversy; edition of 100 copies.)

Clarification of God. n.p., n.d. (Ten-page tract.)

MANUSCRIPT ARCHIVES

The Robert Francis Collection, Jones Library, Amherst, Massachusetts; The Robert Francis Collection in the Library Archives, University of Massachusetts; The Robert Francis Papers, George Arents Research Library, Syracuse University; and Archive of the Canadian Friends of Robert Francis, Toronto.

CRITICAL AND BIOGRAPHICAL STUDIES

Field 25 (fall 1981). (Special issue containing brief articles by David Young, Donald Hall, Robert Wallace, Alberta Turner, Richard Wilbur, and David Walker on individual Francis poems.)

Gillman, Richard. "The Man Robert Frost Called 'The Best Neglected Poet.'" *New York Times Book Review,* March 10, 1985, p. 32.

———. Introduction to *Travelling in Amherst,* by Robert Francis. Boston: Rowan Tree Press, 1986. Pp. vii–xviii.

———. "Color, Energy, Action." *Sewanee Review* CII, no. 1:xi–xii (winter 1994).

Holmes, John. "Constants Carried Forward: Naturalness in Robert Francis's Poems." *Massachusetts Review* 1, no. 4:765–774 (summer 1960).

McLennan, Gordon Lawson. Afterword to *Gusto, Thy Name Was Mrs. Hopkins,* by Robert Francis. Toronto: Chartres Books, 1988. Pp. 43–49.

McNair, Wesley. "The Triumph of Robert Francis." *Harvard Review* 11:81–90 (fall 1996).

Nelson, Howard. "Moving Unnoticed: Notes on Robert Francis's Poetry." *The Hollins Critic* 14, no. 4:1–12 (October 1977).

Painted Bride Quarterly 35 (1988). (This "Robert Francis Issue" contains many poems later included in *Late Fire, Late Snow,* followed by essays by Joseph Langland, Mary Fell, Richard Bradley, David Graham, Jonathan Blunk, Robert Bly, and Wang Hui-Ming.)

Phillips, Robert. "'Even Here . . .': Notes on Robert Francis." *American Poet: The Journal of the Academy of American Poets,* fall 1998, pp. 9–11.

Shaw, Robert B. "Outside of Amherst." *Poetry* 121, no. 2:102–105 (November 1972).

———. "Coming Out into the Sun." *Poetry* 131, no. 2:106–110 (November 1977).

———. "Seers and Skeptics." *Poetry* 163, no. 1:39–42 (October 1993).

Veenendaal, Cornelia. Afterword to *Travelling in Amherst,* by Robert Francis. Boston: Rowan Tree Press, 1986. Pp. 97–101.

Wilbur, Richard. Introduction to *Butter Hill and Other Poems,* by Robert Francis. n.p.: Paul W. Carman, 1984. Unpaginated.

—ROBERT B. SHAW

William Humphrey

1924–1997

WILLIAM HUMPHREY'S PLACE of birth and social origins had a profound effect on his writing. An obituary by Mel Gussow in the *New York Times* (August 21, 1997) was titled "William Humphrey, 73, Writer of Novels about Rural Texas." His finest work came out of northeast Texas, but he would not have appreciated any suggestion of his being a narrow regionalist. Humphrey was more a small-town writer than a rural one. His town was Clarksville, in Red River County, Texas. It was a market town where, as in the opening of his most successful novel, *Home from the Hill* (1958), the first bale of cotton, wrapped in red bunting, would sit on a platform after the harvest. The area was culturally southern rather than western. Clarksville's population was around three thousand when he left it. He was born there on June 18, 1924, to Clarence and Nell Humphrey. His father was a mechanic who owned his own business, and his mother was a housewife. His grandparents on both sides were sharecroppers, and Humphrey would carry the fear of being considered "poor white trash" into his old age. He would go very far from Clarksville, living in Italy and New York's Hudson River valley, but a loving ambivalence about the South with its racism and its cult of the hunter would help shape his writing.

Humphrey was an obsessively secretive man who never went on promotional tours. He took jobs as a writer-in-residence only when he needed money and turned down permanent jobs teaching creative writing, preferring to work in relative solitude. Until his death in 1997, the major source of information about his life was his own memoir, the brilliant *Farther Off from Heaven* (1977), which takes his life only as far as his departure from Clarksville at thirteen, the day after his father's funeral in July 1937. The book makes Clarksville and the Humphrey family extraordinarily vivid. A year after the author's death, a critical biography appeared. *William Humphrey, Destroyer of Myths,* by Bert Almon, was based on Humphrey's archives at the University of Texas and letters to his friends, Katherine Anne Porter and F. W. Dupee, and to Annie Laurie Williams, his film agent.

Humphrey's memoir, which is considered in depth later in this study, is as much a family history as a self-portrait. His parents were upwardly mobile until the Depression undermined the father's business. Conflicts between his parents, brought about by financial difficulties and the father's increasing problems with alcohol, were left unresolved at the time of Clarence Humphrey's death in an automobile crash. Humphrey and his mother then left Clarksville for Dallas. The son did not return to Clarksville for thirty-two years, but his traumatic departure seemed to fix the town in his memory forever with a Joycean richness of detail. In Dallas, almost immediately, he won a scholarship to the Dallas Institute of Art and planned to become a painter. Only when he tried to join the army did he learn that he was in fact color blind. He attended Southern Methodist University in Dallas in 1940, then spent a year at the University of Texas, where he joined the Young Communists. Radical politics soon dropped away, but he remained a strong liberal and civil rights supporter all his life. After a year, he returned to Southern Methodist University and majored in German. He translated works by Freud, whose views on family dynamics influenced him; his own oedipal currents run through the memoir and all of the novels except *No Resting Place* (1989). During the writing of his third novel, *Proud Flesh* (1973), he reshaped the work to fit the pattern of the Electra complex.

In his teens Humphrey found a used copy of *Don Quixote* at a bookstall. The edition was in the Harvard Classics series, edited by Charles W. Eliot. Humphrey's notebooks make it clear that the inspiration for his literary career came from Norton's introduction to this work, in which he suggests that writers can achieve immortality and that a novel can achieve universality through the local. Cervantes wrote about a parochial part of Spain and created a timeless classic. Humphrey would try to do the same for Clarksville. His serious pursuit of a writing career began when he walked out of a German class—and Southern Methodist University—in 1944. He never lived in Texas again. Humphrey first went to Chicago, where he worked for the Chicago Screw Company, then to New York City, where he met W. H. Auden and Randall Jarrell, who gave him literary advice. While working as a shepherd on an estate near Woodstock, New York, he met Dorothy Feinman, a dancer and painter from Brooklyn who was also the married daughter of his employer. They decamped on his twenty-first birthday, hoping to make it to Mexico on seventy-five dollars. They wound up broke in Dallas and had to be rescued by his relatives. The couple eventually married, and remained so until Humphrey's death. Like Humphrey, she had been a Young Communist in her university days.

Humphrey's literary career followed a familiar pattern for the period. He published stories that got him a job at Bard College in the Hudson River valley, an area where he spent much of his life. His first collection, *The Last Husband, and Other Stories,* appeared in 1953. The stories led to inquiries by publishers looking for new novelists, a traditional route for the start of a career. As James Ward Lee points out in the *Dictionary of Literary Biography,* some of the stories, especially the title work, appear to be attempts to write fiction in *The New Yorker* style. The title story, for example, deals with the cocktail parties and erotic intrigues of commuters who live in the suburbs and work in Manhattan. It is overcomplicated and unconvincing. Ironically, the one story by Humphrey that did appear in *The New Yorker* is the one which most clearly manifests his typical subject matter and attitudes. In "Quail for Mr. Forester," a southern family invites the last representative of a glamorous old lineage to dinner. As it turns out, he is interested in making a living; the past glories of the South and the Civil War mean little to him. The story is perhaps too Faulknerian in theme, but it foreshadows Humphrey's later interest in demolishing the aura of the Old South and the Lost Cause. Another story, "The Shell," echoes Ernest Hemingway but is still one of Humphrey's best, a touching treatment of his favorite father-son theme. The boy in the story suffers from grief over the death of his father. He keeps one shotgun shell belonging to the father, afraid of losing his link to the past. When he finally forces himself to use it, the shell turns out to be a dud: he has kept it for too long. The experience allows him to mature. In the remaining stories of *The Last Husband,* Humphrey is still an apprentice. Two of them, "In Sickness and in Health" and "Man with a Family," are heavily derivative of works by Katherine Anne Porter, one of the two American writers he most admired—and the only one he liked to acknowledge as an influence.

In 1950 Humphrey invited Porter to the college for a reading. Porter, a fellow Texan who was born in Indian Creek and grew up in Kyle, towns even smaller than Clarksville, showed what could be done with people and places like those in his hometown. Her clear and precise style was a major influence on his own. She had a long correspondence with Humphrey, and they met often. Their mentor-disciple relationship, however, was sometimes stormy.

Humphrey's other major influence, the one he often tried to deny, was William Faulkner, the greatest of southern novelists. The influence in this case was on subject matter: Humphrey's view of race relations and country life owed much to Faulkner. Humphrey, unlike his model, did not remain in the South. The novelist Joan Williams, who was Humphrey's student at Bard and later was mentored by Faulkner, has said that the young Texas writer was so vehement about repudiating Faulkner's influence that he refused to attend a reading by the Mississippian at Bard. Early in his correspondence with Katherine Anne Porter, Humphrey told her that he had an aversion to Faulkner's work, which astonished her, but later he admitted that the boar hunt in *Home from the Hill* owed much to Faulkner's "The Bear" in *Go Down, Moses.*

Humphrey's first novel, *Home from the Hill,* was published by Alfred A. Knopf in 1958. Favorable reviews appeared in *Life, Time,* and the *New York Times*; the novel became a Book-of-the-Month Club selection and a best-seller, and was nominated for the National Book Award. The Gallimard firm issued a French translation, and interest in Humphrey's work in France persisted throughout his career. MGM bought the movie rights and made a film starring Robert Mitchum. Humphrey turned down an offer to be a technical adviser for the film, which was made in Clarksville. In fact, he refused to attend the premiere and always claimed never to have seen the movie. He and his wife sailed to Europe instead.

In England the new novelist met his British publisher, Ian Parsons, who introduced him to Leonard Woolf and other famous writers. The Humphreys spent most of the years from 1958 to 1961 in Italy, where he worked on his second novel, *The Ordways,* published in 1965, and on a collection of stories, *A Time and a Place*

(1968). He also began a novel about a larger-than-life Texas family, the Renshaws. Over the years Humphrey occasionally took jobs as a writer-in-residence: at Washington and Lee University (1963–1964), MIT (1965–1966), and Princeton (1981–1982). He would spend most of his time at High Meadow, a house near Hudson, New York, built in 1795, which he and his wife filled with antiques.

The Ordways was not as successful as his first novel; Humphrey was disappointed not to be nominated for major prizes, but it had respectable sales. Humphrey spent much of his time from 1961 to 1972 struggling to write *Proud Flesh* (1973), the Renshaw novel, eventually descending into alcoholism and drug abuse before finishing it. This third novel was a failure. The review by Christopher Lehmann-Haupt in the *New York Times* (April 4, 1973) was crushing. Lehmann-Haupt referred to Humphrey's "inexhaustible stock of clichés," compared his writing to a dust storm, and used the title of the novel—which refers to rotting flesh as well as family pride—as a way to ridicule the book as one that stinks. Other hostile reviews included D. B. Swope's in *Best Seller* (July 15, 1972), which suggested that the novel was "one of those books that will end up in great numbers on the bookstore discount tables where it should still be shunned by the discriminating purchaser." It did indeed end up on discount tables.

Humphrey's subsequent career was devoted to recovering from the failure of this work. Much of his income came from his excellent essays about hunting and fishing, which appeared in magazines like *Esquire* and *Sports Illustrated.* Two of these, the amusing fishing tales, "The Spawning Run" and "My Moby Dick," were long enough to be issued subsequently as short books. They were also published, along with shorter pieces, in the collection *Open Season: Sporting Adventures* (1986). Humphrey still had major books to come, namely *Farther Off from Heaven* (1977) and the fine *Hostages to Fortune* (1984), but his career as a famous American writer was over. Aside from an award from the National Institute of Arts and Letters in 1963, he received prizes only from the Texas Institute of Letters: the Carr P. Collins Award for nonfiction in 1977 for *Farther Off from Heaven* and the Lon Tinkle Prize for lifetime achievement in 1996.

Humphrey's life took an even darker turn after the harsh reviews of *Proud Flesh.* Before *Proud Flesh,* Humphrey had a good circle of friends, including F. W. Dupee, Mary Lee Settle, Gore Vidal, and Theodore Weiss, the poet he had known since his Bard days. But in a moving tribute to Humphrey, the novelist Hilary Masters wrote that after the *New York Times* review of the novel appeared, Humphrey dropped all of his friends except Weiss and became a recluse. Certainly he dropped most of his literary friends. His isolation became more acute because of his growing deafness. Humphrey's late notebooks are certainly disturbing in their bitterness and melancholy. In one of them, Humphrey reflects that when he bought a new address book, he found that almost every person in the old book was dead or had ceased to be a friend. His wife, who was eight years older than he, was ill and went to live with her daughter. Humphrey was left alone as he died of cancer, cared for, according to Masters, by a hospice team.

HOME FROM THE HILL

Humphrey's career as a major writer began with *Home from the Hill,* published in 1958. His first novel defines, to put it in Faulknerian terms, his postage stamp of soil: a town like Clarksville and the farming country around it. The body of the novel takes place in 1939, the year that war began in Europe, with a prologue set in 1954, the year that school segregation was overturned by the U.S. Supreme Court. The novel exists in the last era of the traditional southern way of life. The town is typically southern, with a statue of a Confederate soldier on the town square. Under the shadow of the monument passes a hearse. Humphrey has an intricate story to tell, and he leaves the reader in doubt about many things until the end. Even in the prologue, pages pass before the body in the hearse is identified as that of Hannah Hunnicutt, who has died in an asylum and is to be buried in a grave between the headstones of her son, Theron, and her husband, both of whom died on May 28, 1939, according to their epitaphs. But the narrator says that there is no one buried in Theron's grave. The oddity is that Hannah has a headstone which says that she too died on May 28, 1939. These peculiar circumstances will be explained by the end of the novel.

The early narration is collective, using the first-person plural, "we," to tell much of the story. The "we" is a kind of representation of the conservative community that has witnessed the fall of the Hunnicutts. This point of view is clearly modeled on Faulkner's "A Rose for Emily," which also deals with madness and the fall of a leading family. More particularly, the collective narrator seems to represent the men who whittle and talk on the town square, the males of a traditional, patriarchal society. Fairly early, however, the storytelling slides into the unobtrusive norm of third-person narration.

Humphrey liked to describe his novel as a modern tragedy. His central character, Wade Hunnicutt, is presented as socially superior to everyone in the community, fulfilling the Aristotelian requirement that the tragic hero be better than other men. But he is deeply flawed, unable to leave other men's wives alone, a trait that leads to his downfall. His wife is flawed as well, an intelligent woman who deplores her husband but stays with him in a loveless marriage to raise her child; she undoes herself by blurting out the truth about the father to the son. Theron, the product of this blighted marriage, hardly understands the oedipal undercurrents in his family. He becomes a priggish idealist who marries for one of the worst possible reasons, to make an honest woman of someone he thinks his father has seduced; the oedipal aura is unmistakable. He has acquired his father's rigidity and his mother's Puritanism.

The work moves in a leisurely way, indelibly portraying life in an East Texas town. The southern pastime of hunting for coons at night is brilliantly described; the traditional prank of a "snipe hunt" is used to develop Theron's character; and archaic customs like Graveyard Decoration Day, when the whole community turns out to clean and tend the community's graves, are skillfully depicted. Black-white relations are traditional, which is to say racist. The servants, Chauncey and Melba, are rather antebellum in their deference, but their speech is beautifully rendered, as is the scene in which Melba tells Theron's fortune using apple seeds and a hot shovel. After Theron proves his manhood (as his father had before him) by killing a marauding boar, they host a barbecue on a Homeric scale. The son has become a man, and a great hunter like his father. The killing of the rampaging boar is the apex for father and son both, yet it marks the beginning of their downfall.

When Theron goes to pick up his date, Libby, her father, Albert Halstead, turns Theron away at the door because of Wade's reputation as a Don Juan. Theron and Libby eventually find their way into each other's arms, and the scenes depicting their affair are tender and marked by convincing symbolic details, such as the moment when Libby screws an earring too tightly into her flesh in Theron's presence. But Captain Wade, as Wade Hunnicutt is styled (although not quite a king, he has a kingly aura), in turn sends Halstead away when he comes to ask for Theron to take Libby after all. Hunnicutt suspects that Libby is no longer a virgin, and

the sexual politics of a traditional southern town emerge when he says that his family does not want any damaged goods. When Hannah learns that Theron has been rejected by Halstead, she blurts out to her son that Wade is a lecher: "Like father, like son," she says. The son not only turns against his father, but rejects his mother for telling him. Theron is not aware that Libby is pregnant by him, and in a classic Freudian way, he turns from the idealized love object, Libby, to a degraded one. He marries the pregnant Opal Luttrell, the daughter of a sharecropper, though he refuses to consummate the union. He believes that Wade is the father of her child and he wishes to make reparations and, of course, to punish his father by marrying downward on the social scale. Wade's downfall is almost complete, for he loves his son deeply and has been scorned by him; worse, the justice of the rejection is clear even to him.

In their short works on Humphrey, James Ward Lee and Mark Royden Winchell have both criticized the complications and contrivances that accumulate as the plot accelerates. Libby marries a man in order to have a father for her baby, and the snickering, misogynist comments at the christening lead poor Albert Halstead to think that the real father of his grandchild is Wade Hunnicutt. The timid Albert kills Wade with a blast from his own shotgun at the moment that Wade has reached full tragic recognition of the isolation he has brought upon himself. Albert Halstead is not a hunter, which makes Hunnicutt's fall especially heavy. Albert is pursued into the legendary wilderness of Sulphur Bottom by Theron, who kills him a moment too late to recognize that he is shooting the father of the woman he loves. He has no choice but to disappear forever into the uncharted wilderness to die. We can imagine Libby's grief and hopelessness, and we know from the prologue that Hannah goes mad. None of the characters can transcend the patriarchal code of their society, a code that seems to benefit Wade (who has fathered half the children of the town) but leads him to destroy the heir he loves and the wife that he does not love but admires for her devotion to the son.

Critics have misunderstood Humphrey's portrait of Wade Hunnicutt. He is a confident and commanding presence, and it is often assumed (by Gary Davenport and Mark Royden Winchell, for example) that Humphrey admires him and wants readers to hold him in awe as well. Katherine Anne Porter recognized immediately that all three of the Hunnicutts were in fact suffering from neurosis and indeed were marred by a tragic flaw. A passage from Humphrey's notebooks written in 1965 comments bitterly on the assumption that he endorsed certain myths and mystiques of his region that he wished to destroy: the masculine myth of the hunter; the Glorious Lost Cause myths of the Civil War; the myth of oil; the myth of Texas; and the myths of the cowboy and the outlaw. By the myth of the hunter, he had in mind not so much actual hunting, which he himself loved, but the macho attitudes of a man like Wade Hunnicutt, for whom women are game to be bagged. Hunting functions as a symbol of a patriarchal society. As the collective narrator of *Home from the Hill* says, "it must certainly be owned that even those of us who have gone to college, lived in the East, and ought perhaps to know better, never quite get over admiring a man who is a mighty hunter—and who, for the two things go together, takes many trophies poaching in the preserves of love." The same narrator admits that women suffer from the mystique of the hunter, "in a place where even the womenfolks felt that no man was a man who was not a hunter."

The demolition of myths is pervasive in Humphrey's work. The cowboy is a figure deep in American popular culture, as is the outlaw. In *The Ordways,* he takes on both figures through Sam Ordway, whose quest for his lost son is a parody of the Wild West, and he satirizes the

glorification of the Civil War in the figure of Thomas Ordway. In *A Time and a Place,* he ridicules the folk mindset of respect for the bank robbers of the Texas-Oklahoma border. The mystique of oil, which includes tales of flamboyant oil drillers and stories about great wealth bestowed on ordinary people, is particularly strong in Texas. The folklore of striking oil is not relevant merely to Texas; the strike-it-rich mentality has been part of American life since the California Gold Rush of 1849. The myth of Texas refers to the ideology of the Texas Revolution centered around San Jacinto and the Alamo. Humphrey was aware that the revolution—which was triggered by the adoption of an antislavery provision in the Mexican constitution—fostered chauvinism in Texas life. His suspicion of Texas chauvinism and expansionism applied to similar tendencies in American life in general, hence his profound antagonism toward Richard Nixon and the Vietnam War, an obsession that actually wrecked his unfinished novel of the late 1970s, "Horse Latitudes."

THE ORDWAYS

Life-denying codes are transcended in Humphrey's second novel, *The Ordways.* The myths chosen for deconstruction are the glorification of the Civil War and the revenge code of the Old West. The novel puzzled Harding Lemay, Humphrey's editor at Knopf, who had difficulty with its loose structure, and critics have also questioned the unity of the work. In the picaresque tradition, which permits digressions and the mixture of comic and tragic, the novel deals with the wanderings and hard times of a protagonist who is on the road. But readers were not then familiar with the form; the novel's escapes from realism in the portions about Sam Ordway in fact seem to anticipate postmodernist fiction.

Sam's wanderings enable Humphrey to cover a wide landscape and juxtapose two ways of life. As Craig Clifford has astutely observed, Texas itself brings together South and West, regions of the United States with distinct life patterns. On the first page of the novel, we are told that the Clarksville area is "where the South draws up to a stop." Humphrey enjoys creating a contrast between the South of the Thomas Ordway section of his novel (cotton farming, towns with squares) and the West, where Sam Ordway goes on a quixotic quest for his lost son (ranch country where the towns have one street, as in Western movies).

The opening section of the novel, "In a Country Churchyard," uses the frame of a Graveyard Cleaning Day in Mabry, near Clarksville, to introduce the Ordway family and to tell the story of the first Thomas Ordway. The narrator is his great-grandson, also named Thomas. What better place to narrate the origins and history of a family than among the graves of the American Ordways? The graves are all in East Texas because the older Thomas Ordway took them with him when he left Tennessee at the end of the Civil War. Blinded at Shiloh, with shredded legs described as looking like "boiled soup shanks," he journeyed with his pregnant wife and their son and daughter to Texas in a wagon laden with the bones and gravestones of his ancestors. Southern piety toward the family is mocked by such an absurdity.

Humphrey is trying here to purge himself of his Faulknerian influences by parodying *As I Lay Dying*. In Faulkner's novel, the Bundren family piously drag their mother's rotting corpse around Mississippi to carry out an absurd pledge to bury her with her family in Jefferson. Humphrey's characters take the graveyard with them, and the father of the family is the rotting corpse. Like the Bundrens, the Ordways struggle against flood and fire and have to cross a raging torrent, the Red River in the Ordways' case. They lose their son Dexter in the struggle, but the ancestral bones survive, so to speak, and a

new son, Sam Ordway, is born in Texas. He will be the subject of most of the novel.

The myth of the glorious southern cause is mocked by the presence of Thomas Ordway in every Confederate Memorial Day celebration in Clarksville, for Ordway's wounded legs never heal and the blind and mutilated man is a disquieting presence among the Civil War pieties. The erection of a Civil War monument, a statue of a soldier, is followed by the death of Ordway; the elegant statue replaces the terrible reminder of the carnage and waste of the war. One of the pleasures of the description of Memorial Day celebrations is Humphrey's evocation of the lavish potluck dinner associated with the holiday. This feast will be balanced by the family barbecue at the end of the novel, a feast which celebrates life rather than death.

The saga of the Ordway migration to Texas mixes pathos and satire, tragedy and farce. The remainder of the book, the quest of Sam Ordway for his stolen son, is heavily comic, making Sam a burlesque figure in a picaresque plot. After Sam, the son of the Civil War victim, loses his wife to death and remarries, he loses his son Ned to his neighbors, Will Vinson and his wife, who had come to love the child. Sam pursues the Vinsons all over Texas, leaving his wife behind. The quest for a missing family member is the stuff of Western novels and films, and Sam dutifully tries to play the role of powerful avenger as he goes westward to track down the kidnappers. John Wayne would have found them and taken immediate revenge. Ordway takes an ancient pistol with him, and rides away not on a fine horse but in a farm wagon pulled by a mare and a mule. His adventures are often hilarious and approach magic realism in their extravagance. After Sam is overheard rehearsing to kill Will Vinson, he is put on trial for attempted murder. He is acquitted, not because he is innocent, but because his lawyer quotes a famous jurist who said that "in a Texas murder trial the first thing to be established is whether or not the deceased ought to have departed." Ordway turns out not to be a ruthless killer in spite of the great loss he wants to avenge; his bravado is imaginary.

As Sam's adventures take him throughout Texas, he holds various absurd jobs, such as working in an orphanage worthy of *Oliver Twist* and a turn in a circus. He learns that Vinson has taken the name of Sam Ordway, and in turn adopts the persona of Will. He wanders through the Edward Plateau and into West Texas, where he visits the ghost town of Fort Griffin, which had been one of the wildest towns in the Old West, a haunt of Wyatt Earp and Bat Masterson, but had quickly become a pitiful ruin. The history of the town was one of extermination, of Indians, of the buffalo. Nothing about it seems admirable. In the barren windswept plains of far western Texas, he meets a pioneer woman so crazed by loneliness that she survives only by inventing an imaginary friend, Mrs. Blainey. Sam's understanding of women (which has never been very good) is enhanced, and he misses his second wife deeply. He finally reaches the Balcones escarpment at a point overlooking the Rio Grande valley. He gives up the quest at that point, realizing that Will Vinson must have loved his son more than he did. The old adage about walking in another man's moccasins leads him to human sympathies he had never before experienced.

The ultimate blow to the mystique of the cowboy-gunfighter comes years later with the return of Ned, grown up and in need of his real father, like Telemachus coming to find Odysseus. But Ned does not return as an impressive cowboy, as the narrator of the novel, his cousin Tom, expected. Rather, he has become a goatherd down on the Mexican border, not a Western hero. Herding sheep is bad by cowboy standards, but goats rank even lower as pastoral charges. It is possible to go West and not become a cowboy. But the novel ends with family harmony and one of the feasts, in this case a barbecue, that Humphrey describes so well.

A TIME AND A PLACE

Although *The Ordways* was successful (a Literary Guild selection, with six printings), it did not have the impact of Humphrey's first novel. Columbia Pictures bought the movie rights but scriptwriters found it lacking in drama. Humphrey's novel about another family, the Renshaws, gave him enormous trouble. But meanwhile he had written short stories that were collected in *A Time and a Place* (1968), a work begun in Italy in the early 1960s and his best in the genre. The stories deal with greed, popular delusions about crime, and the devastating effects of sudden oil wealth. The stories, as the title of the collection implies, have a specific setting: the Red River valley in Texas and Oklahoma during the 1930s, the era of the Dust Bowl, which brought poverty to most, and the oil boom, which brought riches to a few.

One of Humphrey's finest stories is "The Ballad of Jesse Neighbours," which deals in a comic way with the oil boom and the cult of the outlaw. The impoverished young Oklahoman of the title has the misfortune to see his sweetheart's family strike oil. The Childress clan indulges itself with luxuries, including a trip to the Neiman-Marcus department store, a Texas institution for the ostentatious rich. Humphrey enjoys presenting it as a place of Arabian Nights luxury to spoof the image of the rich Texan. After the strike, Jesse is no longer fit company for Naomi Childress. The 1930s fostered another myth that Humphrey deplored: the notion that outlaws like Pretty Boy Floyd and Bonnie and Clyde were noble Robin Hoods. Jesse in desperation turns to bank robbery, but his attempt to stick up a bank in Clarksville over the state line is a comic failure. It leads to the death penalty for armed robbery and Jesse, like a mournful outlaw in a ballad, goes to the electric chair. Humphrey was surprised that the story was nominated for an Edgar Award from the Mystery Writers' Association of America.

Humphrey's other story about outlaws, "A Voice from the Woods," deals with an actual bank robbery in Blossom Prairie, near Clarksville. It was based on a story told to Humphrey by his mother, who was courted briefly by one of the outlaws. Although Bonnie and Clyde and Pretty Boy Floyd are mentioned in the story, the robbers do not enjoy the long careers of their models. They are betrayed by one of their number and killed with ease as they leave the bank. Humphrey skillfully has the mother in the story narrate it in the presence of her son and daughter-in-law. The daughter-in-law has no conception of the supposed glamour of figures like Bonnie and Clyde. She has never even heard of them; outside of a particular time and place, such figures may not seem important. In his memoir, *Farther Off from Heaven,* Humphrey discusses the wish fulfillment represented by the outlaw among the have-nots of the Depression and Dust Bowl, people who had no fondness for banks. His own father became fascinated with these figures as he became poorer.

Stories of the oil industry in *A Time and a Place* include "A Home Away from Home," the account of a farmer whose daughter runs off on a motorcycle with one of the supposedly glamorous figures of the trade, an explosives expert. He looks like a bug in his motorcycling gear and has been deprived of his hair, beard, and eyebrows by explosions. The unsuccessful oil drilling on the farm leaves the family poorer than when they started, with only a dry hole to show for their experiences, the kind of story that rarely makes it into folklore. On the other hand, in "The Pump" an old farmer, Jordan Terry, becomes rich when oil is struck on his land but is destroyed by envy and suspicion when oil is also found on the neighboring farm of his friend Clarence Bywaters. The pumps on each farm draw from the same pool, and Terry finds sharing the riches unendurable. He sits on his porch in his rocker (which is a parody of a

pump, a sterile motion going nowhere), listening to the sound of pumping and fretting until he finally dies of bad feelings. His grave is fittingly described as a "dry hole."

One of the best stories is "A Job of the Plains," which reverses the biblical story. A farmer named Chester Dobbs survives the privations and natural disasters of the Dust Bowl but is driven into despair after oil is struck on his land and his friends and family are corrupted by wealth. The story, like others in the collection, reflects a deepening tone of cynicism and despair in Humphrey's work, a tone that would reach its height in his last book, *September Song* (1992). The most effective story about the devastating drought of the Dust Bowl period is "The Rainmaker," a hilarious tale of a con man, Professor Orville Simms, who disastrously brings too much rain to his Red River valley clients.

Race is an important subject in several stories. Two works with young protagonists, "Mouth of Brass" and "The Last of the Caddoes," are among Humphrey's best. "Mouth of Brass" is a story about the friendship between a black man and a white boy in Clarksville, in which the black man is murdered in the town square by a white racist. The story is Humphrey's most sensitive look at race relations in the segregated Texas of his youth. "The Last of the Caddoes" grows out of the author's craving to understand his own Native American background: his great-grandfather was part Indian, but the name of the tribe was suppressed or forgotten by the family. In the story, a boy becomes obsessed with Native artifacts and finally recasts his identity as the last of the vanished Texas Caddo tribe. The story is not about Native Americans as such but about race as a symbolic focus for dysfunctional family life, a kind of fantasy escape from one's own identity. The work was made into a short film by Ken Harrison in 1981. Another work about Native Americans is "The Only Good Indian," narrated by a cynical automobile dealer who loves to sell expensive cars to oil-rich Indians. One of his customers, a man named John who does not know how to drive, buys and wrecks two cars in one day, killing himself in the second wreck, to the amusement of the dealer. The story is the weakest in a fine volume, foreshadowing the cynicism of Humphrey's last collection, *September Song*.

PROUD FLESH

After approximately twelve years of struggle, Humphrey finally finished *Proud Flesh* (1973), his novel about the Renshaw clan, the members of which live on a farm near a town similar to Clarksville. The work started as a short novel about the death of the clan matriarch, Edwina, and its impact on her children. The family is larger than life, made up of violent and emotional people who intimidate the inhabitants in their area. Humphrey found a symbolic structure to shape his material when he read the Oresteia trilogy of Aeschylus. It occurred to him that the family conflicts in his novel could be accounted for by the oedipal and Electra complexes of Freud, and that the plot of his book could be given a structure derived from Aeschylus, just as James Joyce's *Ulysses* was built on an armature of Homer's *Odyssey*. He also found some of his inspiration in Sophocles' *Electra* and in one of his favorite novelists, Fyodor Dostoyevsky, whose *Brothers Karamazov* deals with family enmities and parricide. He was particularly interested in Sigmund Freud's commentaries on Dostoyevsky's book.

The six sons and four daughters of Edwina are competitors for her love. Unfortunately, there are too many of them to permit the novelist to define each as an individual. Edwina is the Clytemnestra of the novel; her husband is not literally killed like Agamemnon but simply reduced to a cipher in the family. One daughter, Amy, appears (as her name implies) to be the most loving child, but like Electra, she secretly hates her mother. Northrop Frye has suggested that literature is displaced mythology, and Humphrey displaces the myth by rearranging the structure and altering details. The other child who hates the mother is the absent Kyle, who is not in literal exile like Orestes but in self-exile, possibly in New York City—the most distant place imaginatively from the provincial world of northeast Texas. His refusal to return as his mother lies dying is the rather weak basis of the plot of Humphrey's long novel. A hateful look from the ostensibly loving Amy triggers Edwina's final collapse. The family seeks Kyle's whereabouts to get him to the funeral; it is an attempt to compel him to honor her at least in death. Amy in remorse locks herself in the cellar and smears her breasts and fills her mouth with cow dung. The cellar locale is derived from the *Electra* of Sophocles, in which the title character in the end is in a dungeon. Amy's refusal to emerge makes the national news and she turns into a scapegoat figure-confessor for people all over the country. Humphrey was prescient about the confessional obsessions of television in contemporary America.

The Electra pattern is never made explicit in the novel, and it has gone mostly unnoticed by critics. In theory the pattern could work subliminally, but it certainly did not save the novel. The book is loosely organized and the plot is full of contrivances. Its view of race relations in Texas is distorted by Humphrey's failure to reacquaint himself with his native state. The novel is set during the time of the civil rights movement (which Humphrey personally supported), but the black characters seem to be drawn from antebellum times, if not from sleazy novels like *Mandingo*. Humphrey no longer had a strong grasp of the Texas setting. One of the Renshaw children, Clyde, carries on an affair with a black woman named Shug and suffers deep guilt for being, as he says, a "Nigger-lover." He even tries to castrate himself out of guilt and grief for his mother, an act that Christopher Lehmann-Haupt in his review thought absurd and hilarious. Shug is a flat character, as is her husband, Jug (a stereotyped shuffling drunk), and her brother, Archie. The black characters are meant to be choral figures (as are the black characters in *The Sound and the Fury*) who observe and comment on the action. They correspond to the chorus for whom the second play of the *Oresteia, The Libation Bearers,* is named.

The book is also painfully Faulknerian. Humphrey's notebooks for the novel contain an entry reminding himself not to sound too much like Faulkner, especially in the portrait of Eulalie, the family's black housekeeper. But she comes across as a weak version of Dilsey in *The Sound and the Fury.* The key outsider in the book, Doctor Metcalf, who functions as a horrified observer, is similar to Faulkner's Doc Peabody. Faulkner's familiar device of transfixing observers in astonishment is used constantly in the novel. The story of the collision of Hugo Mattox's borrowed truck full of cotton with Mrs. Shumlin's cow could come out of *The Hamlet* (1940) or any number of stories by Faulkner. The most obvious derivation for Humphrey's novel is from *As I Lay Dying* (1930). The Bundrens, dominated by their mother after her death, take her rotten body with them wherever they go. The Renshaws are also overpowered by their mother's death, although they at least keep her body in the town icehouse to preserve it for the return of the prodigal Kyle. The absent Kyle keeps the wounds of the family open and festering. He does not return for the funeral, and at the end of the novel, two of his brothers are improbably searching for him from door to door in New York City.

FARTHER OFF FROM HEAVEN

Humphrey's instincts and experience as a novelist seemed to have deserted him in the writing of *Proud Flesh.* His next book renewed his imaginative contact with his native earth. Humphrey received an honorary doctorate from Southern Methodist University in 1969, and on that occasion he finally made a visit to Clarksville after an absence of thirty-two years. In *Farther Off from Heaven* (1977), he reached back into his past and recreated it in one of the finest American memoirs. The details are preternaturally vivid, the structure a marvel of elegant simplicity.

The death of his father in a car crash was the overwhelming event of Humphrey's childhood, and the book is built around the accident and its aftermath: a death watch at the Paris, Texas, hospital and the funeral, which young Humphrey refused to attend. The book begins with the boy being awakened by his mother, Nell, on the night of July 5, 1937, so that he could accompany her and the injured father, Clarence, on the ambulance ride to Paris. Every chapter follows a stage of development in the days that followed, and each opens up in a skillfully articulated way to reveal the history of the extended family—his grandparents and their children—and of the nuclear family—with a focus on the intense and increasingly dysfunctional marriage of Clarence and Nell. A major protagonist of the work is Clarksville itself, with its social geography (Silk Stocking Street, "Niggertown," the town square, the "white trash" area near the cemetery) and its great landmark, Old Red, the clock on the courthouse. The chimes of Old Red run through the novel not only as a reminder of time passing but also as the profound symbol of home and belonging for the boy whose life was measured by them.

Farther Off from Heaven creates and solves several mysteries and reveals some family secrets. The reader is told that the home where Humphrey first lived had mysteriously vanished and that the author had died in childhood. The "death" is a minor but intriguing mystery and involves a swimming accident and a drunken medical examiner who filled out a death certificate before young Humphrey was revived. An important secret was that Humphrey was born with a deformed foot, something he only learned about years afterward. His mother felt she was somehow to blame for the defect and sought help for the infant from a specialist in Dallas (a bold step for an impoverished small-town woman). She kept the episode a secret from her son until he discovered it by chance. The vanished house of his birth and infancy was another mystery, one concealing a family secret: the low social status of the parents when they first married. On his visit to Clarksville, Humphrey learned that the house had not vanished: it still stood, in the poor white trash section of town. In the early days, the family had seemed upwardly mobile, and the mother had had great hopes for her son. Parents who began life as the children of sharecroppers would be reluctant to admit to their son that their marriage started in a poor white district. Young Humphrey was the only boy in town not permitted to hang around his father's garage, as if being there would lower him. Humphrey's notebooks reveal that he himself was marked by the white trash label; standard southern snobbery has always maintained that white trash rank below blacks on the social scale. The belittling or comic portraits of poor whites in some of his fiction are probably ways of creating distance from them. Opal Luttrell in *Home from the Hill* is a good example, as is the Hugo Mattox family in *Proud Flesh*. *Farther Off from Heaven* deftly portrays the relationship between Clarence Humphrey and his black employee, Wylie. The two men looked like black and white versions of each other and would have been friends had the social system not dictated a paternalistic relationship rather than an equal one.

The memoir has scenes of comedy and pathos. Its tone is overwhelmingly elegiac and manages to be nostalgic without sentimentality, a rare achievement. The title is drawn from a poem by the nineteenth-century Irish poet Thomas Moore, which describes a child's vision of the trees touching the sky. That vision has to be corrected by memory, but the correction leaves the adult "farther off from heaven." Humphrey's Clarksville was a kind of heaven for him before his parents sank into despair and conflict. Few towns have been so lovingly portrayed. The book was not actively promoted by Knopf, however, and Humphrey soon saw it on the remainder tables in New York bookstores, which undermined his confidence in his writing.

From 1977 to 1979 Humphrey worked on a novel that turned out to be unpublishable, an extravagant picaresque satire sometimes called "The Last Refuge," sometimes "Horse Latitudes." It features a redneck protagonist, Cecil Smoot, who aims to corner the market in horses as a way to get rich when automotive civilization breaks down. The book, which betrays an obsession with satirizing Richard Nixon, failed to attain a fictional poise. His other work of the period, *Ah, Wilderness!: The Frontier in American Literature* (1977), is a pamphlet reprinting a minor lecture on American literature that he gave while a visiting writer at Washington and Lee University in 1963 and 1964.

HOSTAGES TO FORTUNE

In 1984 Humphrey published *Hostages to Fortune,* his first novel set outside of Texas. It is a deeply moving book that received little attention; Humphrey's career was past its prime. He had ceased to be one of the writers who counted with reviewers and book clubs.

In *Hostages to Fortune,* its title drawn from Francis Bacon's saying, "He that hath wife and children hath given hostages to fortune," Humphrey explores the impact of a son's suicide on a marriage. Fortune treats the protagonist, Ben Curtis, with great cruelty. Curtis is a novelist who lives in the Hudson River valley in an old house filled, like Humphrey's, with antiques.

His son, Anthony, a seemingly happy young student at Princeton, commits suicide. Curtis's wife leaves him, unable to continue her old life, and he descends into alcoholism and near psychosis. The writing of *Farther Off from Heaven,* with its tremendous concentration, seems to have revived and honed Humphrey's technique. In the new novel he focuses on the return of Ben Curtis to his fishing club a year after his devastating plunge into despair. The action of the novel is conveyed in flashbacks as Ben resumes his place in the clubhouse and goes trout fishing.

A great deal of research went into the novel, work that served Humphrey better than the study of Aeschylus, Dostoyevsky, and Freud in the writing of *Proud Flesh.* He looked into the causes of suicide among the young, and after the publication of the book, he received a number of letters from parents who had lost children. He also wished to make the breakdown of Ben Curtis a true foray into the pathologies of the inner life, and he read works on the doppelgänger figure in literature and psychology, including Otto Rank's *The Double* (1925) and Ralph Tymms's *Doubles in Literary Psychology* (1949). Other influences were such classics of the double theme as Dostoyevsky's *The Double* (1846), Edgar Allan Poe's "William Wilson" (1839), Joseph Conrad's "The Secret Sharer" (1912), and Oscar Wilde's *The Picture of Dorian Gray* (1890). The double was a way to project self-alienation in a character. It could be argued that Humphrey's near-collapse in the late 1960s, when he sank into alcoholism and drug use during the struggle with *Proud Flesh,* served as another resource for him; he liked to tell people that Ben Curtis was himself. Humphrey also made use of what he knew about adolescent suicides in the families of two of his closest friends.

The portrait of Anthony Curtis presents him from outside, through his father's eyes. We see him as a person who strives to achieve mastery (specifically in hawking, another focus of Humphrey's research), the sort of perfectionist whose desire for control might take the form of choosing his own death over some frustration or psychic injury. Humphrey recognized that the portrait of Anthony was a more sophisticated version of Theron Hunnicutt. There are two other suicides offstage in the novel: the daughter of Ben's confidante, Tony Thayer, kills herself, and Thayer himself falls into despair and dies in a supposed ice-sailing accident on the Hudson.

After his son's death and his wife's departure, Curtis sinks into lonely alcohol and drug abuse in his country home and tries to understand his son's motive for self-destruction, his search tinged by the Oedipus story along with its Freudian interpretations. Like Oedipus, Curtis is trying to solve a murder in the family. He is not sure if, like Oedipus, he himself is somehow the murderer; parents typically feel responsible for the suicides of children. He also thinks there may have been some oedipal neurosis in his son's relationship with the mother. Curtis himself comes close to suicide. He sees visions of his mocking son inviting him to die. And as his crisis reaches its height of tension, the ghost he sees is not Anthony but himself; he attempts suicide by a drug overdose. Saved by medical intervention, he feels that he is leading a posthumous existence. Those who see him at the fishing club are shocked by his transformation; he is a ghost of the man he was a year before.

The depiction of the club is one of Humphrey's triumphs. Some of Curtis's most important experiences, like his courtship and wedding, are associated with it, but it is an institution that insists on the surfaces of life: good humor and no talk about controversial or painful subjects. The club has one of those life-destroying mystiques that Humphrey deplores; it is not quite a myth, but a commitment to a sportsman's code of reticence and dignity. This code is often identified with Ernest Hemingway, especially as it was formulated in the 1938 story "The Short Happy Life of Francis Macomber." Curtis wants the kind of emotional healing through fishing sought by Nick Adams after World War I, in Hemingway's "Big Two-Hearted River," a story in *In Our Time.* Curtis has already made tentative progress toward renewal, but his real step forward comes when a fellow fisherman breaks the club's taboo on serious talk and insists on discussing Anthony's suicide. The man's own father killed himself. Curtis finds this contact a liberation; he had until then found himself in the position of someone who never had a son because no one has dared to mention Anthony. By the end of the novel he has gingerly moved toward rejoining the human race by abandoning the narrow code of the fishing club.

The novel contains some of the author's best writing, with set pieces on herring fishing, ice sailing, and falconry, scenes as rich as the genre painting in *Home from the Hill.* It also has a deep measure of wisdom. The dark night of Curtis's soul is convincingly rendered. It works as felt life, not as theory turned into fiction. The myth satirized in the work, the stiff-upper-lip fisherman's code of the club, is more universal than the southern myths dealt with in the early work. Yet despite some respectful reviews, the novel had no great success in the market.

In 1985, the year after *Hostages to Fortune* appeared, *The Collected Stories of William Humphrey* was published. It contains two new stories, neither of which has a Texas setting. "Dolce Far' Niente" compresses the life of an Italian immigrant couple into a short span through flashbacks from the husband's retirement dinner. Especially successful is "The Patience of a Saint," a tale of a handyman and gardener in the Hudson River valley who dedicated his life to taking care of his mother. Finally, as he discloses to the narrator, he killed her so that he could resume activities like card playing. The matricide reminds the narrator of two of Humphrey's favorite classical myths, the story of Oedipus and the killing of Clytemnestra by Orestes.

NO RESTING PLACE

William Humphrey's next project was to have been a book about a murder trial in his area, the Wyley Gates case. In 1986 the seventeen-year-old Gates and a friend murdered Gates's father and three other family members, events that call to mind one of Humphrey's favorite novels, Dostoyevsky's *The Brothers Karamazov.* Humphrey wanted to write an account of the murders and trial, but he found that his hearing was so bad that he could not follow the court proceedings. He then reverted to a plan he had made in 1979 to write a novel inspired by his Indian ancestry. The result was an account of the Trail of Tears of 1838 and 1839, the infamous removals of the Five Civilized Tribes from the South to the Indian Territory later known as Oklahoma. The trail followed by the Choctaws ended not far from Clarksville, as Humphrey knew from childhood. His focus, however, was on the much-better-known Cherokee Removal, with a Georgia family as central characters. He found a Texas connection for his story, *No Resting Place* (1989).

Some of the Cherokees subject to the Removal went to Texas to join the loose federation of tribes led by Chief Diwali (also known as Colonel Bowles, Bold Hunter, Duwali, or the Bowl). Mirabeau Buonaparte Lamar, a hero of the Texas Revolution of 1836, drove them out by force in the Battle of the Neches in 1839. The incident is no credit to Texas or to Lamar, and Humphrey found it an opportunity to attack another myth, the image of the gallant Texans in the battles of the Alamo and San Jacinto. He had already dealt with the romance of the oil fields and the life of the cowboy; now he was ready to take on the early history of his state, in which every schoolchild in Texas used to be immersed.

The novel is framed by fictional events set in 1936, the centennial of the Texas Revolution and two years before the centennial of the Cherokee removals. The Texas centennial generated a great deal of rhetoric about the glories of the revolution. Humphrey's narrator, Amos Smith IV, aged twelve, is to play Lamar in a school pageant marking the Battle of San Jacinto on April 21, 1836, the clash that secured Texas its independence from Mexico. His father, Amos Smith III, is outraged and takes him down to the Red River to explain why Lamar was an evil man. They sit among blooming Cherokee roses, flowers said to have been brought to Texas by the Cherokees. One symbolic contrivance of the novel is the improbable early blooming of the roses, on which even the narrator remarks. The father reveals to his son that the first Amos Smith was a Cherokee who was driven out of Georgia at thirteen and who witnessed the Battle of the Neches on July 16, 1839. The story has been handed down through the generations and is told again for the benefit of the latest Amos.

As if the abundance of "Amos Smiths" were not confusing enough, the first Amos Smith has a number of names and nicknames, beginning with Noquisi. The name "Smith" is given to him at the end of the novel by one of the men who killed Noquisi's father as the two tried to escape across the Red River near Clarksville. The man assumes that Noquisi, who like many Cherokees was part white, is a captive of the Indians in need of rescue. At the start of the novel the boy has three names in Georgia: Amos Ferguson for the public world, Noquisi (Bright Star) at home, and Ajudagwasgi (Stays-Up-All-Night), his initiation name. The multiple names convey the complexity of Cherokee life, but they are a cumbersome device. Later Noquisi-Amos is called in succession Tad, Cap, and Doc,

with each nickname conveying a new role for him in the story.

The Civilized Tribes are rightly called civilized: they had quickly devised an alphabet, constitutions, newspapers, schools, and industries. They were well on the way to assimilation. Indeed, their success in emulating white ways may have provoked their expulsion as much as the desire of white settlers for their lands. In the novel, Cherokees who approximate whites are considered sinister by their neighbors, more dangerous than the stereotypical "redskins." They very readily accepted whites into their own communities; Noquisi's maternal ancestors are mainly white in origin. Humphrey's extensive readings in Native ethnography enabled him to present such customs as the initiation ceremony and to deal with the role of the paranormal in Cherokee life; Noquisi experiences telepathy on several occasions. These touches suggest that the Cherokees fused the best of Native culture with white civilization.

The book suffers from an overabundance of detail. Humphrey's publisher, Seymour Lawrence, who had awaited it eagerly, thought that it should be marketed as nonfiction. This disturbed Humphrey, who had to defend the novelistic character of his work in a long letter. But the history is relatively undigested. Humphrey devotes part of his story to describing the legal maneuvers to save the lands of the Civilized Tribes. There were conferences and lawsuits before the U.S. Supreme Court, which ruled in favor of the tribes. But Andrew Jackson replied with his famous statement that "Chief Justice Marshall has made his decision, let him enforce it." Much attention is given to the men who might have helped the Cherokees but did not: Jackson, who won a major battle against the British with their help, and Sam Houston, the hero of San Jacinto, who had lived among them. This background often obscures the narrative.

The story is as tragic as the term "Trail of Tears" implies. The Cherokees described by Humphrey were deprived of their property by the state of Georgia and sent off with scant preparations. The state militia often committed violence against them. The U.S. forces that escorted them to the Indian Territory were less brutal, but promised supplies were either substandard or nonexistent, and many people died on the trip. The author seems to have created his characters to illustrate the sufferings on the journey, and most of them fail to achieve individuality. He relies on one major white character, the Reverend Malcolm Mackenzie, to offer an outsider's outraged view of events. More device than character, Mackenzie loses faith in the goodness of God after his wife dies on the journey with the Cherokees. The grandfather of Noquisi represents the old ways, and the presentation of Cherokee religious customs is stronger than that of the character. Noquisi's mother functions primarily to arouse pathos when Noquisi finds her grave on the trail; she is as shadowy a figure as Noquisi's grandmother. The father of Noquisi is absent through much of the story—he goes to Oklahoma before the rest of the family—and therefore has little chance to emerge.

When Noquisi arrives in the Indian Territory, he and his father are the only members of the family still alive. They decide to join Chief Diwali in Texas. Diwali's branch of the Cherokees had come to Texas in 1819. Their presence in Texas was guaranteed by a treaty of 1836 when the Texan forces sought their neutrality in the war with Mexico. It appears that the Fergusons have reached safety until Mirabeau Buonaparte Lamar, the newly elected president of Texas, decides that the East Texas tribes led by Diwali must go and reneges on the treaty. Diwali, who is portrayed in keeping with contemporary sources as a man of dignity and peace, is forced to fight a hopeless battle; he is killed, and Noquisi and his father have to flee. The reader soon learns how Niquisi became Amos Smith. In accepting his adoption by one of his father's killers, the weary boy gives up his heritage and receives the most generic surname in English. The novel ends with Amos IV's words: "And that is how I, Amos IV, of the clan of Smiths, author of this book, got my name there on the bank of that red river which gives its name to my home county in the northeast corner of Texas where the trail of Cherokee roses begins and ends."

The good intentions of the novel are apparent: it is meant to bring the Cherokees back into the American consciousness, to reinscribe their names. But it is weak as fiction and shows a real decline from *Hostages to Fortune.* Humphrey's notebooks and letters from the period of its writing reveal a man who was deeply discouraged and exhausted.

SEPTEMBER SONG

Humphrey's last book, *September Song,* is a collection of stories. He and his wife were ill and he had quarreled with his old friend, Nick Lyons; a sense of isolation and despair fills his notebooks. The tone of the stories is gloomy, marked by old age, sickness, and death (including three suicides). Great art can be made from despair, but in his last book he seems to jeer at his characters, to put them into hopeless situations as if to prove a proposition about life. In "An Eye for an Eye," he rewrites Edith Wharton's *Ethan Frome* (1911), making the plight of the trapped characters even worse than in his model. A blind wife regains her sight briefly and realizes that her husband is having an affair with her caregiver. She pours sulfuric acid in her rival's face, blinding her in turn; the husband is left to spend the rest of his wretched life taking care of them. Humphrey admired Thomas Hardy, and he seems to follow Hardy's example in contriving fates for his characters. The denouement, too, often seems imposed rather than an outcome arising plausibly from situation. In her excellent 1989 essay, "Irony as Art: The Short Fiction of William Humphrey," Elizabeth Tebeaux pointed to the mixture of irony and sympathy for trapped characters as a strength in Humphrey's stories, but *September Song* increases the irony while losing most of the sympathy.

The longest effort in the book is "The Apple of Discord," a work in which an apple farmer, desperate to perpetuate the family business, uses King Lear–like tactics in an effort to force his daughters to accept his plans. When he fails, he sells his beloved apple trees to a developer out of spite. He then tries to kill himself, but failing pathetically, he loses all tragic dignity. Humphrey overdoes the symbolism of the apple and the fall from Eden.

More effective are two stories about old hunters, "Mortal Enemies" and "Buck Fever," less ambitious stories in which mortality is accepted. The tone of the stories suggests that Humphrey was facing his own mortality. Two other stories clearly reflect on Humphrey's life: "A Portrait of the Artist as an Old Man," in which a reporter comes to interview a novelist in order to write his obituary for files, and "The Dead Languages," a story based on Humphrey's inability to follow the Wyley Gates trial because of his deafness.

ASSESSMENTS

William Humphrey's strength lay in his depiction of rural and small-town Texas. He did not, however, aspire to be merely a local colorist but a great novelist. In *Hostages to Fortune* he demonstrated that he could write powerful fiction without mentioning his home state. He was interested in family and the influence of place, which are universal subjects, even if southern writers sometimes seem to have proprietorship of them in American fiction. His concern for the ways that glamorous myths delude and damage was a constant in his career: every novel presents his critique of at least one myth or mystique. Texas was rich in examples for him, and the myths he deplored—the reverence for its past and its part in the Civil War, its storied wealth and the dangerous opportunity to strike it rich, and its admiration for outlaws—are versions of subjects common in American literature. He was never hypnotized by the glamour of these images.

The first full treatment of Humphrey, a 1967 pamphlet in the Steck-Vaughn *Southwestern Series* by James W. Lee, concentrated on his qualities as a regionalist, with high but judicious praise given to *Home from the Hill* and with misgivings about the disunity of *The Ordways*. Lee expressed admiration for Humphrey's verisimilitude in his portraits of East Texas characters. In a 1980 essay for the *Dictionary of Literary Biography,* Lee called *Proud Flesh* a "failure" with a good style "but . . . little else to recommend it." But in the same essay he ranks *Farther Off from Heaven* with memoirs by James Agee and Virginia Woolf. Mark Royden Winchell's 1992 pamphlet in the *Western Writers Series* took a harsh view of most of Humphrey's fiction, with the exception of *Hostages to Fortune,* which Winchell praised for transcending the Texas setting. In contrast to Lee, he saw Humphrey's local color as a weakness, although voicing praise for *Farther Off from Heaven.* His Humphrey canon was very small.

The work most deserving a revival is *Farther Off from Heaven,* which never received the attention given to the early novels. The popularity of the memoir genre in American publishing offers some hope that Humphrey's remarkably elegant and moving account of Clarksville and his family may find its proper readership. Humphrey's best work is contained in that book and in three novels—*Home from the Hill, The Ordways,* and *Hostages to Fortune*—along with several fine stories. Most of Humphrey's work is set in the landscape of East Texas, but all of it is set in the landscapes of the human heart.

Selected Bibliography

WORKS OF WILLIAM HUMPHREY

NOVELS

Home from the Hill. New York: Knopf, 1958.

The Ordways. New York: Knopf, 1965.

Proud Flesh. New York: Knopf, 1973.

Hostages to Fortune. New York: Delacorte/Seymour Lawrence, 1984.

No Resting Place. New York: Delacorte/Seymour Lawrence, 1989.

SHORT STORIES

The Last Husband, and Other Stories. New York: Morrow, 1953.

A Time and a Place: Stories. New York: Knopf, 1968.

The Collected Stories of William Humphrey. New York: Delacorte/Seymour Lawrence, 1985.

September Song. Boston: Houghton Mifflin/Seymour Lawrence, 1992.

SPORTING STORIES

The Spawning Run: A Fable. New York: Knopf, 1970.

My Moby Dick. Garden City, N.Y.: Doubleday, 1978.

Open Season: Sporting Adventures. New York: Delacorte/Seymour Lawrence, 1986.

NONFICTION

Ah, Wilderness!: The Frontier in American Literature. El Paso: Texas Western Press, 1977.

Farther Off from Heaven. New York: Knopf, 1977.

"Why Do I Write Fiction?" In *Writing in the Southern Tradition: Interviews with Five Contemporary Authors.* Edited by A. B. Crowder. Atlanta, Ga.: Rodopi, 1990. Pp. 183–189.

MANUSCRIPTS AND PAPERS

The Harry Ransom Humanities Research Center at the University of Texas has William Humphrey's extensive personal archives, consisting of letters, journals, and drafts. His correspondence with Katherine Anne Porter is held by the McKeldin Library, University of Maryland. The Rare Book and Manuscript Collection at Columbia University has his letters to his agent, Annie Laurie Williams, and his letters to F. W. and Barbara ("Andy") Dupee. The University of Mississippi Library has the letters of Humphrey to Seymour Lawrence.

BIBLIOGRAPHY

Kich, Martin. *Western American Novelists,* vol. 1. New York: Garland, 1995. Pp. 707–802. (Annotated entries.)

CRITICAL AND BIOGRAPHICAL STUDIES

Almon, Bert. "William Humphrey's Blue Heaven." *Southwest Review* 63:84–86 (winter 1978).

———. "William Humphrey's 'Broken-Backed Novel': Parody in *The Ordways.*" *Southern Quarterly* 32:107–116 (summer 1994).

———. *William Humphrey: Destroyer of Myths.* Denton, Tex.: University of North Texas Press, 1998.

———. "William Humphrey and Katherine Anne Porter: A Mentorship Reconsidered." In *From Texas to the World and Back: Essays on the Journeys of Katherine Anne Porter.* Edited by Mark Busby and Dick Heaberlin. Fort Worth: Texas Christian University Press, 2001. Pp. 164–177.

Bowden, Larry R. "A Lament for the Vanishing." *Cross Currents* 41:107–115 (spring 1991).

Bowen, Elizabeth. "Texas beyond the Oil Wells." *The Tatler,* March 12, 1958, p. 506.

Chaney, L. Dwight. "William Humphrey, Regionalist: Southern or Southwestern?" *Journal of the American Studies Association of Texas* 19:91–98 (October 1988).

Clifford, Craig Edward. *In the Deep Heart's Core: Reflections on Life, Letters, and Texas.* College Station: Texas A&M University Press, 1985.

Clute, John. "Mooning over Genocide." *The Times Literary Supplement,* December 1, 1989, p. 1338.

Cooper, Stephen. "William Humphrey." In *Contemporary Fiction Writers of the South: A Bio-*

Bibliographical Sourcebook. Edited by Joseph M. Flora and Robert Bain. Westport, Conn.: Greenwood, 1993. Pp. 234–243.

Davenport, Gary. "The Desertion of William Humphrey's Circus Animals." *Southern Review* 23:494–503 (April 1987).

Giles, Molly. "The Insults of Old Age." *New York Times Book Review,* August 23, 1992, p. 18.

Grammer, John M. "Where the South Draws Up to a Stop: The Fiction of William Humphrey." *Mississippi Quarterly* 44:5–21 (winter 1990–1991).

Grider, Sylvia, and Elizabeth Tebeaux. "Blessings into Curses: Sardonic Humor and Irony in 'A Job of the Plains.'" *Studies in Short Fiction* 23:297–306 (summer 1986).

Gussow, Mel. "William Humphrey, 73, Writer of Novels about Rural Texas." *New York Times,* August 21, 1997, p. D19.

Havighurst, Walter. "Prelude to Violence." *Saturday Review,* January 11, 1958, p. 15.

Hiers, John T. "The Graveyard Epiphany in Modern Southern Fiction: Transcendence of Selfhood." *Southern Humanities Review* 9:389–403 (fall 1975).

Hudziak, Craig. "William Humphrey." In *Contemporary Novelists.* 4th ed. Edited by D. L. Kirkpatrick. London: St. Martin's Press, 1986. Pp. 447–448.

Janeway, Elizabeth. "Journey through Time." *New York Times Book Review,* January 31, 1965, pp. 1, 40.

Kappler, Frank. "Texas with Another Accent." *Life,* February 5, 1965, p. 17.

Kilgo, James P. "Book Briefs." *Georgia Review* 40:1051–1052 (winter 1986).

Lee, James W. *William Humphrey. Southwest Writers Series,* vol. 7. Austin, Tex.: Steck-Vaughn, 1967.

———. "William Humphrey." In *Dictionary of Literary Biography.* Vol. 6, *American Novelists since World War II.* Second series. Edited by James E. Kibler. Detroit, Mich.: Gale Research, 1980. Pp. 148–153.

———. *Classics of Texas Fiction.* Dallas, Tex.: E–Heart, 1987.

Lehmann-Haupt, Christopher. "More Meat for the Boycott." *New York Times,* April 4, 1973, p. 41.

Maddocks, Melvin. "Ten-Gallon Gothic." *Time,* April 30, 1973, p. 74.

Masters, Hilary. "Proud Flesh: William Humphrey Remembered." *Sewanee Review* 108:254–258 (spring 2000).

Morsberger, Robert E. "Reviews." *Western American Literature* 24:391–392 (winter 1990).

Mullen, Patrick B. "Myth and Folklore in *The Ordways.*" In *Hunters and Healers: Folklore Types and Topics.* Publications of the Texas Folklore Society, vol. 35. Edited by Wilson M. Hudson. Austin, Tex.: Encino Press, 1971. Pp. 133–145.

Rubin, Louis D., Jr. *The Curious Death of the Novel: Essays in American Literature.* Baton Rouge, La.: Louisiana State University Press, 1967.

Stevenson, David L. "Ceremony of Prose." *Nation,* February 22, 1958, pp. 172–174.

Sullenger, Lee. "The Book Review." *Library Journal,* April 1, 1973, p. 1192.

Sullivan, Walter. "The Continuing Renascence: Southern Fiction in the Fifties." In *South: Modern Southern Literature in Its Cultural Setting.* Edited by Louis D. Rubin Jr. and Robert Jacobs. Garden City, N.Y.: Dolphin/Doubleday, 1961. Pp. 376–391.

Swope, D. B. "Review of Proud Flesh." *Best Seller,* July 15, 1972, p. 86.

Tebeaux, Elizabeth. "Irony as Art: The Short Fiction of William Humphrey." *Studies in Short Fiction* 26:323–334 (summer 1989).

Williams, Joan. "Review of William Humphrey, Destroyer of Myths," by Bert Almon. *Southern Quarterly* 37:183–184 (winter 1999).

Winchell, Mark Royden. "Beyond Regionalism: The Growth of William Humphrey." *Sewanee Review* 96:287–292 (spring 1988).

———. *William Humphrey. Boise State University Western Writers Series,* no. 105. Boise, Idaho: Boise State University, 1992.

INTERVIEWS

Crowder, A. B., ed. *Writing in the Southern Tradition: Interviews with Five Contemporary Authors.* Atlanta, Ga.: Rodopi, 1990. (Collects "William Humphrey: Defining Southern Literature," *Mississippi Quarterly* 41:529–540 [fall 1988], and "History, Family, and William Humphrey," *Southern Review* 24:825–839 [autumn 1988].)

Yglesias, José. "William Humphrey." *Publishers Weekly,* June 2, 1989, pp. 64–65.

FILMS BASED ON THE WORKS OF WILLIAM HUMPHREY

Home from the Hill. Screenplay by Irving Ravetch and Harriet Frank. Directed by Vincente Minnelli. MGM, 1960.

The Last of the Caddoes. Screenplay by Ken Harrison. Directed by Ken Harrison. Phoenix Films, 1981.

—BERT ALMON

Shirley Jackson

1919–1965

SHIRLEY JACKSON EXPLORED the intersection between the domestic and the demonic. She conjured the idea for one of the most unsettling short stories in American literature in June 1948, while pushing a stroller up a hill in the small Vermont town in which she and her family lived. Twelve years later, in "Biography of a Story" (included in the 1968 collection *Come Along with Me: Part of a Novel, Sixteen Stories, and Three Lectures*), Jackson reflected on the genesis of "The Lottery" (1948), her celebrated and controversial work, with these words: "It was . . . a warm morning, and the hill was steep, and beside my daughter the stroller held the day's groceries—and perhaps the effort of that last fifty yards up the hill put an edge to the story."

To say that "The Lottery" had edge was a staggering understatement. Known as a classic of gothic fiction and an exploration of man's innate savagery, the story concerns one town's annual ritual of selecting and brutally killing one of its members. Critics have described it variously as a grim fairy tale, a biblical parable, and an anthropological demonstration of ritual and sacrifice. As the novelist Patrick McGrath stated in the introduction to the Modern Library edition of *The Lottery* (2000), its "capacity to shock is as potent today as when the story first appeared more than fifty years ago." Its first publication, in *The New Yorker,* prompted more than four hundred letters from readers ranging from the outraged (some of whom canceled their subscriptions) to the curious (some readers wanted to know where the story took place so that they could witness the ritual). The story's impact extended far beyond the United States—

the apartheid government of South Africa banned it, a fact that made the author proud.

Although Jackson tended to dissociate herself from overly academic—and especially dark—interpretations of her work, she did admit to a *San Francisco Chronicle* columnist at the time of the story's publication, "I suppose I hoped, by setting a particularly brutal rite in the present and in my own village, to shock the readers with a graphic dramatization of the pointless violence and general inhumanity of their own lives." Asked about reader response, she stated dryly, "The number of people who expected Mrs. Hutchinson to win a Bendix washer at the end would amaze you" (quoted in *Private Demons: The Life of Shirley Jackson,* by Judy Oppenheimer, 1988).

Until her death in 1965, Jackson remained closely linked with her 1948 story, which was the title story of her first collection, *The Lottery; or, The Adventures of James Harris* (1949). "The Lottery" was widely anthologized and pored over by critics, high school teachers and students, as well as the general reader. Jackson's obituaries testified to her close association with this tale: the *New York Times* headline referred to her as "Shirley Jackson, Author of Horror Classic." In an essay following Jackson's death, her husband, the literary critic Stanley Edgar Hyman, lamented such narrow assessments of her achievement, alluding to one death notice that dubbed Jackson the "Virginia Werewolf of séance-fiction writers."

Taken in the context of her prolific career, Jackson's association with a single story is both understandable and misleading. The themes she touched upon in "The Lottery" resurface again and again in her writing—the concept of the scapegoat, prejudice, and the human capacity for everyday savagery. But she wrote more than one hundred other short stories, six novels, two humorous memoirs, three children's books (including a nonfiction account of the Salem witch trials), a play, and numerous nonfiction articles. In light of Jackson's relatively short life, her output was especially impressive. She published stories and essays in an array of publications with extremely different audiences, from *The New Republic* to *Playboy* to *Ladies Home Journal.*

Reviews of Jackson's work were primarily positive. Four of her short stories were selected for the annual *Best American Short Stories,* "The Lottery" won an O. Henry Award, and several of her novels were listed as among the best fiction of the year by the *New York Times Book Review.* But some saw the recognition she received as incommensurate with her impact. Hyman wrote in the *Saturday Evening Post* shortly after her death in 1965, "For all her popularity, Shirley Jackson won surprisingly little recognition. She received no grants or fellowships; her name was often omitted from lists on which it clearly belonged, or which it should have led."

Jackson's range of admirers attests to her work's deep and widespread appeal. Writers such as Bernard Malamud, Isaac Bashevis Singer, Dorothy Parker, and Dylan Thomas praised Jackson's work. Roald Dahl expressed the desire to collaborate on a project with her. The dedication of Stephen King's novel *Firestarter* reads, "to Shirley Jackson, who never had to raise her voice." Jackson's social circle was equally impressive: Ralph Ellison and Howard Nemerov were close friends and frequent guests in her home. Among literary critics, Jackson was compared with authors as diverse as Nathaniel Hawthorne and John Cheever for her insight into societal ills and persecution.

As the variety of Jackson's fans and publishing venues suggest, her work resists classification. While critics have attempted to label her a genre writer (her fiction was typically marketed as "horror," and even her husband referred to her family stories as "potboilers"), Jackson refused to be limited by labels. To her, writing was a job she engaged in every day, despite the demands of motherhood.

Though she remained prolific during most of her professional life, Jackson struggled with emotional and physical problems. She suffered from anxiety, claustrophobia, and agoraphobia. She was morbidly obese, a condition that probably contributed to her death, of heart failure, on August 8, 1965. During times in her life, she also relied on liquor and prescription drugs.

Jackson's personal demons found a place in her art. However disruptive her obsessions and fears were in her everyday life, they translated vividly into her writing. Many of her stories and most of her novels feature wounded female characters who feel threatened and displaced. Persecutors sometimes come in the form of family and lovers, even ghosts, but most often they are neighbors—native village people, smug suburbanites, college dorm-mates, or the members of academic families like the one Jackson created with her husband.

BACKGROUND

According to her biographers, Shirley Hardie Jackson seemed fated to develop an outsider status almost from the start. She was born on December 14, 1919, in San Francisco, to upper-middle-class, socially conscious parents. Her father, Leslie Hardie Jackson, was a British-born lithograph company executive, and her mother, Geraldine Bugbee Jackson, descended from a family of notable San Francisco architects (an interesting lineage, considering that Shirley Jackson would come to demonstrate a fascination for old houses in her fiction).

According to Oppenheimer, Geraldine, twenty-one when Shirley was born, "was far from domestic, and child-rearing held small interest for her." Jackson's mother found her young daughter willful and perplexing, and made little secret of her feelings.

When Shirley was six and her brother, Barry, was four, the Jacksons moved from the Ashbury Park area of San Francisco to Burlingame, a white up-and-coming suburb about sixteen miles from the city. Burlingame was, as Jackson describes it in a memoir piece published in *Life Among the Savages* (1953), "far enough away from San Francisco to have palm trees in the gardens," but near enough to allow her and her mother to shop in the city. Jackson's first novel, the semiautobiographical *The Road through the Wall* (1948), is set in a similar California town the author calls Cabrillo. Pepper Street, where the novel's action takes place, is cordoned off from less desirable neighborhoods by a wall and gates: "The sun shone cleverly on Pepper Street, but it shone more bravely still beyond the gates; when it rained on Pepper Street the people beyond the gates never got their feet wet . . . all the houses were marked 'No Trespassing.'" The inhabitants are self-satisfied and hypocritical.

As a child, Shirley struggled with her circumscribed surroundings and her mother's emphasis on decorum and gender-appropriate activities. She balked at her mother's efforts to groom and prettify her, an attitude she carried into adulthood by rarely combing her hair and paying little attention to dress and weight. Throughout Jackson's life, her mother criticized what she saw as Shirley's tendency toward slovenliness; Geraldine Jackson once wrote her daughter a harsh letter after having seen an unflattering photo of Shirley published in *Time* (alongside a positive review of one of Shirley's novels). Shirley's relationship with her parents, especially her mother, was frequently strained, but Jackson wrote Geraldine and Leslie regular, long letters and they, for their part, occasionally assisted their daughter's family financially. Jackson revealed her ambivalence about the relationship by dedicating her searing collection *The Lottery* to her mother and father.

As a child Jackson learned to assert herself through her imagination and demonstrated a love for literature at a young age. Her grandmother, who lived with the family, sometimes read Edgar Allan Poe stories to her, and Jackson began to use the library often. At age twelve, she won a prize for a poem from *Junior Home Magazine*. In junior high, she began to keep a diary, and she found that regularly recording her thoughts offered solace from everyday woes. She wrote about her daily activities, including time spent playing the piano and with her best friend, Dorothy, as well as her desire to be thinner and kinder to others. She also recorded her earliest thoughts on superstition and the supernatural.

Jackson may have questioned the values of the grown-ups she encountered in her native state, but she did grow to love the California climate, and her family's move from the area when she was sixteen was difficult for her. Her father was promoted to a position in Rochester, New York, a shift that affected his daughter profoundly. In Jackson's essay about that year, "All I Can Remember" (included in the 1997 collection *Just an Ordinary Day*), she writes: "Sixteen . . . was a particularly agonizing age; our family was in the process of moving East from California, and I settled down into a new high school and new manners and ways, all things that I believe produce a great uneasiness in a sixteen-year-old." The displacement did have some benefits, however; as she points out, it was after the move that she embarked upon writing her first full-length book. The result was an ill-fated mystery, mocked by her family (she never again pursued the genre), but the project offered a demonstration of her ability to create art under challenging conditions.

Jackson was an inquisitive teen who challenged conventional mores. Her youthful persona is perhaps reflected in the short story "The Intoxicated" (collected in *The Lottery*), in the figure of a high school senior who contemplates a grim future for the world while her parents throw a raucous party. The narrator is a friend of the girl's parents, who, though drunk, quickly realizes that she is unlike other teens. As the two talk in the kitchen over coffee, the narrator repeatedly tries to change the subject, but the girl persists with her apocalyptic visions: "Somehow I think of the churches as going first, before even the Empire State building. . . . The office buildings will be just piles of broken stones." The girl revels in her morbid precocity, yet surprises the man by giggling at the end of the conversation and assuring him that she still does her homework every night.

At Brighton High School in Rochester, Jackson struggled between individual expression and social acceptance. She was rejected from membership in a sorority, an experience that stung, but she moved on to find a crowd of friends, eccentrics like herself. Her grades were unremarkable, but she wrote regularly and even completed some stories.

After graduation in 1934, Jackson had hoped to attend college away from home, but her parents insisted that she enroll at the nearby University of Rochester. She spent two unhappy years there, feeling uninspired academically and socially bored—the classes were gender segregated. In later years, despite her proximity to academic life, she retained an uneasy attitude toward higher education and conveyed doubts about the academic environment in her work. The character Natalie in her second novel, *Hangsaman* (1951), is harassed by the female students at her liberal university and disappointed by her professors. The theme is echoed in several short stories and in one of Jackson's lighter pieces, "The Smoking Room" (collected in *Just an Ordinary Day*), in which the devil

appears to a coed as she types a paper. The two end up struggling to purchase each other's souls.

At the University of Rochester, Jackson did make an important friend, a radical French exchange student who exposed her to the works of François Villon and commedia dell'arte. This student also introduced Jackson to a young Russian pianist, with whom she fell briefly in love. Jackson began to develop imaginary characters around this time based on the figures of Pan and Harlequin. According to friends, she spoke of them as real.

During Jackson's time at Rochester, she dealt with bouts of melancholy. She may even have tried to commit suicide; she refers in passing to a suicide attempt in an unpublished essay. Oppenheimer concluded in her biography of Jackson that she was probably not very serious in her intent; Jackson's parents may not even have known about the incident.

Jackson ultimately left the University of Rochester in 1936 without a degree. Accounts vary, but it is likely that her poor grades forced her expulsion. In the year that followed, she experienced a nervous breakdown. She was treated by a psychiatrist and lived at home with her parents. Despite—or perhaps because of—Jackson's psychiatric problems, she wrote more than ever, setting as a goal one thousand words a day. At the end of the year, she informed her parents that she would be attending Syracuse University in the fall.

Syracuse was geographically close to Rochester, but it offered Jackson a far more invigorating, less conventional environment. Socially, she became a member of an intellectual, politically radical group. Jackson also showed more interest in her studies. She enrolled in creative writing courses, where she wrote about mythical figures. One, based on an old Scottish ballad about a seaman, was to surface years later in her writing. "The Daemon Lover" (1949) appeared in *The Lottery* and focused on one James Harris, a shadowy figure. He proposes marriage to a lonely woman in her thirties, then disappears. Throughout the story, it is never quite clear if Harris is an actual character or a figment of the woman's imagination. To underscore the effect of unnerving ambiguity, Jackson used the name James Harris in several other stories in the collection, always attached to unreliable and mysterious men.

In 1938 Jackson published her first story, "Janice," in *Threshold,* the anthology of her creative writing class. A short piece told mostly in dialogue, "Janice" centers on a college student, the title character, who nonchalantly informs her friends that she tried to kill herself earlier in the day; the narrator of the story describes Janice's tone as "almost whimsical, indifferent." Her friends respond with shock, but Janice brushes off their concern. She provides only a few details, about how she had locked herself in the garage and turned on a motor, but then returns to normal social chatter, repeatedly silencing herself by changing the subject. The story is scant, but Janice emerges as a young woman caught between the conflicting desires of her mother, her friends, and the disquieting region of the self. Ironically, this story of thwarted selfhood led to Jackson's meeting of her future husband. Hyman, who nearly thirty years later included the story in the posthumous collection of Jackson's work *Come Along with Me,* was only a freshman when he read the story. Jackson's prose so impressed him that he declared he was going to marry the author. He arranged to meet her immediately.

Hyman and Jackson were a good match intellectually. Hyman, who was born and raised in Brooklyn, came from a Jewish family of modest means. He was a literary autodidact. His family was not particularly intellectual, but by the time Hyman was in high school, he was writing and coproducing the senior play and telling classmates he intended to become a drama critic for *The New Yorker* (he eventually did become a staff writer for the magazine). By

the time he became a student at Syracuse and read Jackson's story, Hyman already considered himself a literary critic. When they met, they became a couple almost immediately.

Jackson and Hyman shared two important traits: a passion for literature and an early seriousness about their professional and artistic goals. They also believed strongly in social justice. Together, they became a formidable duo. In 1939 Jackson and Hyman founded and edited *The Spectre,* a campus literary magazine that became controversial for its provocative artwork and editorials on the race issue at the university. Hyman later referred to it as a "wild mimeographed literary magazine." Jackson was the author of some of the journal's most strident editorials. The magazine's mentor was professor Leonard Brown, and Jackson and Hyman found his encouragement indispensable. Jackson dedicated her penultimate novel, *The Haunting of Hill House,* to Brown in 1959, and upon Brown's death in 1960, Jackson wrote a eulogy that asserted her own creative values: "He taught us that the aim of reading and criticizing was to know and understand, not to like or dislike, and the aim of writing was to get down what you wanted to say, not to gesticulate or impress" (quoted in *Shirley Jackson,* by Lenemaja Friedman, 1975).

When Jackson and Hyman announced their intention to marry after graduation in 1940, their parents were not pleased. The couple proceeded with their plans, though they also underwent personal turmoil due to Hyman's notorious flirtatiousness. The early relationship between Jackson and Hyman was as passionate and tumultuous as later periods of their twenty-five-year marriage. In many ways, Hyman was Jackson's literary champion; he encouraged her in her art and instilled in her the confidence that her family had often undermined. Until Hyman's death—at age fifty-one, five years after Jackson's—he continued to promote his wife's prose. Though he considered her family stories of less serious quality, he recognized her wit in such pieces as "The Night We All Had Grippe" (published in *Life Among the Savages*), which in the preface to *Come Along with Me,* he likened to the work of James Thurber.

Most important, Hyman recognized his wife's masterpieces immediately. In 1948, upon reading Jackson's newly written story, "The Lottery," he wrote to a friend, "Shirley has written a story that just astounds me. . . . She's written a real masterpiece, and I don't know where it came from." According to Oppenheimer, Hyman had contributed to the story its chilling maxim, "Lottery in June, corn be heavy soon." But Hyman was also a relentless evaluator of his wife's work and it is clear that Jackson recognized this. Her dedication of *The Road through the Wall* reads, "For Stanley, a critic."

Hyman began his career with *The New Republic* and later moved on to *The New Yorker,* but he spent the majority of his professional career teaching at Bennington College in Vermont. Jackson did not always take well to life in a small town, or to her husband's position at the then all-girls school. In later years, according to Oppenheimer, he became known for carrying on affairs with former students. Jackson, meanwhile, had competing concerns: she performed the bulk of the household chores and served as primary caretaker of their four children—Laurence Jackson, born in 1942; Joanne Leslie, born in 1945; Sarah Geraldine, born in 1948, and Barry Edgar, born in 1951.

LITERARY THEMES

Jackson's most familiar characters are women on a quest. Often, they seek solace in an unjust world or relief from their own inner terrors. They also negotiate chaos and injustice with humor; Jackson's first nationally published story, "My Life with R. H. Macy" (collected in *The Lottery*), is a witty critique of bureaucracy. The piece begins with a humorous but loaded line: "And the first thing they did was segregate me." The short, ironic story, which reads more like an essay or memoir, focuses on the layers of paperwork and procedure involved in working at an immense department store. Jackson, who did work briefly for Macy's, describes how she sold books, though not those that she might have chosen herself—the popular title for the Christmas season is *The Stage-Struck Seal.* Jackson's essay, which brought her $25, appeared in 1941 in *The New Republic,* where Hyman was working as an editorial assistant.

The harried but humorous tone Jackson uses in "My Life with R. H. Macy" characterized her autobiographical prose. One piece, "My Recollections of S. B. Fairchild" (published in *Just an Ordinary Day*), mirrored the format and approach of the former. In this essay, Jackson describes how she and her husband celebrated their fifteenth wedding anniversary by buying a used tape recorder from a large New York department store. The tape recorder, with which they had hoped to record the voices of their children, soon breaks, and when Jackson brings it to the music store in their small town for repair, she is admonished for not buying it from there and told that the machine could not be fixed. Over a year passes, and despite having returned the faulty recorder to the original store and written numerous letters of complaint, Jackson and her husband receive neither a new instrument nor reimbursement. They end up buying a tape recorder from the music store in town, which functions beautifully but costs quite a bit more.

Both essays are witty disparagements of administrative red tape, but as in much of Jackson's autobiographical work, they possess a more serious undercurrent. In "My Life with R. H. Macy," Jackson describes being isolated and anonymous, even when surrounded by books. In "My Recollections of S. B. Fairchild," she learns that she cannot circumvent the watch of her small-town neighbors by appealing to the city. The incident with the tape recorder reminds her that she is beholden to her small town. Not even her formidable resources—her wit and writing skills—can mitigate the connection. This uneasy relationship between small-town obligations and big-city bureaucracy recurred in Jackson's work.

Jackson's second national publication, "After You, My Dear Alphonse," ran in *The New Yorker* in 1943 and was the first of twelve of her stories to be published in the prestigious magazine. By that time, she had given birth to her first child, Laurence, and her husband was working at *The New Yorker* as a staff writer. "After You, My Dear Alphonse," examines the pernicious effects of subtle prejudice. As in several of her strongest short stories written during the 1940s, "After You, My Dear Alphonse," shows that Jackson's true subject is everyday cruelty.

The story is about Mrs. Wilson, a Caucasian woman in a small town, who is surprised when her young son brings home a black playmate. She serves the child lunch and quizzes him about his family, making it clear that she assumes his father is a laborer in a factory (he is a foreman) and that he has many brothers and sisters (he has only one). Finally, Mrs. Wilson offers the black child a bundle of old clothes to take home to his family. When the child politely declines the offer, Mrs. Wilson responds with a rebuke: "There are many little boys like you, Boyd, who would be very grateful for the clothes someone was kind enough to give them." The bewildered child apologizes.

Jackson returned to the theme of false charity in her next published story, "Come Dance with Me in Ireland" (collected in *The Lottery*). The story, which first appeared in *The New Yorker* in 1943, was selected for *The Best American Short Stories of 1944*. The tone is much the same as in "After You, My Dear Alphonse," and the story also examines issues of class and culture. Three well-off women are startled when a beggar rings the door of an apartment where they are gathered. The beggar purportedly is

selling shoelaces, but when he comes in, he collapses drunkenly. The women hesitate, confer, then decide to offer him a meal; after all, they won't have to go to too much trouble, given the man's station. (One of the women suggests that they feed him eggs and potatoes—"He won't care if they're half-raw," she says. "These people eat things like heaps of fried potatoes and eggs.") The man begins to eat, stops, then gets up to leave. When they question him, he quotes from the Irish poet W. B. Yeats (one of the women has inferred that the beggar is from Ireland) and offers a stinging blow: "I may have imbibed somewhat freely . . . but I never served bad sherry to my guests." The matrons in this story do not comprehend their clumsy and condescending offers of assistance. They remain concerned about their domestic responsibilities and routines, their duties to prepare supper for the men and watch the baby. They are vigilant, but, as Jackson seems to suggest, about the wrong things.

Prejudice continued to figure heavily in Jackson's work, particularly in her short fiction published during the 1940s. In "Flower Garden" (in *The Lottery*) a widow and her son learn a shattering lesson about prejudice and ignorance when they move into a small New England town. At first, the neighbors are friendly—one woman, Mrs. Winning, finds the widow a refreshing addition to the stodgy town and seeks her out. Even the shopkeepers seem impressed by the new resident; the grocer speaks of her as a "lady." But the villagers are soon dismayed when the widow hires a black man to work as her gardener and allows her son to play with the gardener's son (whose mother is a local white woman). The villagers are so xenophobic, they fail to comprehend the injustice of their actions. In the end, both the widow and the friend who withdrew find themselves alone again, frightened and without reassurance.

Jackson did not confine her social critiques to race-related issues. Through her relationship with Hyman, she became acutely aware of anti-Semitism. Some critics, including Oppenheimer, have said that "The Lottery" enacted the anti-Semitism that Jackson and her family felt in Bennington. Jackson also addresses the topic through the Perlmans, a marginalized family in *The Road Through the Wall,* and in the chillingly underhanded story "A Fine Old Firm" (in *The Lottery*). The latter tells of a meeting between the mothers of two young men from the same hometown who become good friends in the army. One of the young men is Jewish; the other Christian, and the Christian mother, Mrs. Concord, treats the Jewish mother, Mrs. Friedman, with wariness. When Mrs. Friedman mentions that Mrs. Concord's son might be interested in joining her husband's law firm, Mrs. Concord recoils and says that her son will work for a firm with a highly Anglo name; "a fine old firm," as the Christian woman puts it.

Jackson's most effective novels and stories feature women displaced both by their own troubled minds and the troubling society that surrounds them. Yet despite the recurrent themes of discontent and quest, her protagonists, rather than becoming types, are distinct, fully developed characters. The root sources of their dissatisfaction may be similar, but their individual arcs of discovery offer as many diversions and complications as Quixote's or Candide's. In this sense, Jackson was a pioneer in writing the women's adventure story, one in which the psychological complications are just as potent and convincing as the literal. As the critic Carol Cleveland points out, "from the beginning to the end of her writing career, Shirley Jackson was at work mixing genres, confounding the expectations of the self-righteous and the placid, examining the lot of women, and exploring the differences between crime and evil."

As ironic as it might seem, the supposedly sentimental realms of motherhood and marriage were crucial to Jackson's insight into societal ills. Several of her short-fiction narrators are mothers and wives who learn through criticism

from neighbors that they must suppress their desires for individuality and passion. One such character, Mrs. Walpole in "The Renegade" (collected in *The Lottery*), is a housewife having a frustrating morning as she prepares her children for school and completes the chores. She performs these tasks efficiently, until the phone rings. A neighbor woman is on the line to deliver the chilling message that Lady, Mrs. Walpole's beloved family dog, has been killing her chickens. The dog will have to be put to sleep, the woman all but commands. Mrs. Walpole responds with horror—until then she had thought of her dog as a gentle member of the family. Her dismay deepens when her children return home, speaking blithely of a method to kill the dog by making it wear a spiked collar. As the children speak of punishment and gore, Mrs. Walpole reflects on "the murderous brutality a pretty dog like Lady could keep so well hidden in their home." In 1997 Laura Shapiro of *Newsweek* described the way Jackson mined the primal through the domestic in her review of Jackson's posthumous collection, *Just an Ordinary Day*: "[Jackson's] disquieting take on home life will still resonate when Martha Stewart is a memory."

Home life, for Jackson, often meant tension between the natives of small communities and newcomers. Her interloper characters are often more wealthy and educated than the indigenous, but they lack a most crucial quality: the self-assurance that comes with having been born and raised in a particular area. In the short story "The Summer People" (collected in *Come Along with Me*), a city couple who have vacationed in a small eastern town each summer decide to extend their stay past Labor Day. They are retired, and enamored of the parochial village. But their country neighbors balk at the plan: local merchants and gas suppliers refuse to serve the out-of-towners; their phone line is severed and mail comes late. The locals' hostility reaches a climax when the tires on the couple's car are slashed.

Jackson often disparages village natives and their wariness of strangers and new customs, but she also displays a certain grudging respect for these characters. In an essay on writing titled "Experience and Fiction" (in *Come Along with Me*), she explained what she meant by the phrase "village women": "I do not mean by that that they are primitive, or uneducated, or unsophisticated; I think of them only as a tightly knit group, interested in their own concerns, and as resentful of outsiders as any of us."

Though Jackson's characters often pervert and upend social customs, she herself was known for her hospitality. This quality is ironic, considering her lifelong obsession with social ostracization. Jackson's biographers often mention her skill as a hostess and how she served as a one-woman support system for other parents. Sometimes this impulse led to genuine connection with others and sometimes to self-destructive behavior. Hospitality, to Jackson, could mean everything from making batches of brownies for neighbors to gorging herself. Food was a potent, loaded tool, involving both social and antisocial action.

After publication of "The Lottery," readers and critics speculated about Jackson's interest in witchcraft. The tradition of mistrusting neighbors in the story seemed suspiciously close to practices in Salem, Massachusetts, in the late 1600s. It is true that Jackson nurtured a long-term interest in witchcraft and magic, though it is unlikely that she practiced either seriously. Jackson's interest in the working of the occult began when she was a teen and continued into adulthood. She owned a private library of books on the subject and in 1956, she published a nonfiction book for young adults, *The Witchcraft of Salem Village*. In a 1947 biographical sketch ("Notes on Shirley Jackson," in *Shirley Jackson: A Study of the Short Fiction*, by Joan Wylie Hall), Hyman wrote of his wife and her unusual hobby: "She . . . is perhaps the only contemporary writer who is a practicing amateur witch,

specializing in small-scale black magic and fortune-telling with a Tarot deck."

Much has been made of Jackson's interest in the supernatural, particularly in her novel *The Haunting of Hill House*, yet the subject never became a facile plot device or narrative crutch. It is unclear how serious Jackson was in her efforts as an "amateur witch." Rumors circulated in the publishing world about the author's casting spells and using voodoo dolls. In her art, ghosts and mental maladies frequently converge in her characters. The supernatural elements in Jackson's writing rarely remain abstract—as the *Times Literary Supplement* said of *The Haunting of Hill House*, "Nowhere is there any whiff of pointless eerie-weerie detectable." Jackson addressed the matter in a 1962 lecture about writing ("Notes for a Young Writer," in *Come Along with Me*): "Suppose you want to write a story about what you might vaguely think of as 'magic.' You will be hopelessly lost, wandering around formlessly in notions of magic and incantations; you will never make any forward progress at all until you turn your idea, 'magic,' into a person, someone who wants to do or make or change or act in some way."

Considering Jackson's seriousness as an artist, the author probably was drawn to the ways in which witchcraft and magic focused on revealing the terrors of the human psyche. For Jackson, as for Henry James, the supernatural and the subconscious worked in tandem; Jackson matter-of-factly included elements of both in her writing, even in her lighter-toned family memoirs. When explored together in darker works, such as *We Have Always Lived in the Castle* (1962), Jackson used the workings of the supernatural and subconscious to serve as the terrain of the ostracized. "To all the classic paraphernalia of the spook story she adds a touch of Freud to make the whole world kin," one writer observed in the *New York Times Book Review* in 1959. Stacey D'Erasmo, writing in *The Nation*, also remarked on Jackson's authentic use of the terrifying: "In the strongest Jackson . . . strange calls to stranger in the guise of ghost stories: apparitions, bogymen, things that go bump in the night. They are cliches, really, that somehow add up to art, a consciousness not easily apprehended, written in a genre we think we know."

From Jackson herself to the hounded Tessie Hutchinson in "The Lottery," the women in Jackson's work often grapple with the seeming injustice of their situations. Most conventional women protagonists in Jackson's short fiction attempt to escape their fates by taking journeys. Soon they become unrecognizable, both in body and demeanor. In "The Tooth" (in *The Lottery*) a woman deadened by the routines of marriage and motherhood becomes so disoriented while away from her family (and under the influence of pain medication) that when she looks in the mirror in a public bathroom, she cannot pick out her own face. In the 1961 story "Louisa, Please Come Home" (collected in *Come Along with Me*), winner of the Edgar Allan Poe Award, a young woman who ran away from her home years before changes so much in attitude that when she reunites with her family, they fail to recognize her and consider her a fortune-hunting imposter. *Come Along with Me,* Jackson's unfinished novel at the time of her death, focuses on a middle-aged woman who begins her life afresh after the death of her irksome husband. The woman, who adopts a new name—Angela Motorman—is almost giddy with relief at her freedom. The unfinished novel takes on a light, comic air absent from much of Jackson's later fiction.

THE ROAD THROUGH THE WALL AND THE LOTTERY

In 1945 Jackson and her husband moved to North Bennington, Vermont, where Hyman had accepted a teaching position at Bennington College. The town was to become a perverse muse for Jackson, a contrast to the urban life she was accustomed to living, and a source of social isolation and vulnerability. The critic Jonathan Lethem, who grew up in Bennington, writes, "It was Jackson's fate, as a faculty wife and an eccentric newcomer in a staid, insular village, to absorb the reflexive antisemitism and anti-intellectualism felt by the townspeople toward the college. She and her children were accessible in a way that her husband and his colleagues and students, who spent their days on the campus, were not."

In short order, Bennington became the setting for Jackson's most famous story. "The Lottery" opens innocuously, in Jackson's typically concise style. The June morning is "clear and sunny, with the fresh warmth of a full-summer day; the flowers were blossoming profusely and the grass was richly green." Jackson quickly pans across the village, population 300, introducing the rhythms of small-town life and an air of congenial expectancy such as might precede a civic parade. Selecting stones and setting them into a pile seems a harmless practice for young boys. Depicted early in the story, by the end this image has become shockingly horrific, with Davy Hutchinson, Tessie Hutchinson's youngest son, receiving pebbles from the other villagers as they gear up to chase and pummel Davy's mother to death.

The critic Helen Nebeker, who calls "The Lottery" a "symbolic tour de force," discusses the importance of the wooden box from which the slips of paper are drawn and the lottery conducted. Black, old, likely constructed by the village's first settlers, the box "suggests the body of tradition—once oral but now written—which the dead hand of the past codified in religion, mores, government, and the rest of culture, and passed from generation to generation, letting it grow ever more cumbersome, meaningless, and indefensible."

Notably, the box is handled only by the men of the village. As in much of Jackson's writing, men make most of the decisions in "The Lottery." Mr. Graves and Mr. Summers, a matter-of-fact civic leader, are in charge. We learn that Mr. Summers, who oversees the ominous black box, was given his position because he had no children and his wife was "a scold." Old Man Warner acts as the town archivist, judgmental and unreceptive to change. The men, the "heads of households," draw from the box; sons fill in for deceased fathers. Women are allowed to draw for their families only as a last resort. The women arrive wearing faded housedresses and sweaters, and remain physically removed from "the menfolk." Tessie Hutchinson arrives late; she appears both avoidant and flighty. She jokes with the other women and even makes a quip at the expense of her husband. The crowd laughs, but soon, when her name is drawn, her neighbors and allies turn on her. The women she had been chatting with earlier urge her to be a "good sport."

Many critics view "The Lottery" as an enactment of the ideas from James Frazer's *The Golden Bough,* a text on anthropology and mythology, which examines the sacrificial killings of god-figures to ensure fecund harvests. Jackson certainly knew the book well—she read it in a college course on folklore and even alluded to it in her novel *Hangsaman.* Other critics have compared the story to a biblical parable, a parallel to the Salem witch trials, or merely a lesson about creating pariahs in communities. Still others suggest that the story is merely one town's archaic system of dealing with overpopulation.

Regardless of the story's symbolic meanings, Tessie Hutchinson is an example of the kind of woman Shirley Jackson feared in life, and feared for in her writing. In many ways she was one of the "village women" Jackson derided as narrow-minded and hostile to outsiders, but in other ways, she represented the futility and danger of questioning tradition. Tessie's neighbors betray her, and then her family follows

suit. Two of her children even jump around in glee when they realize that *they* are not going to be killed. Worse, Tessie's reluctance to accept her sentence ensures that she will not be afforded martyr status. As critic Fritz Oehlschlaeger writes, "Tessie fails to be a heroine, and the way that she does so testifies to the success with which the male-dominated order has imposed itself upon her." The theme of women being controlled and even sacrificed by males would recur frequently in Jackson's work.

In many ways, it is fitting that Tessie is Jackson's most famous character. She attempts to question the order of all that surrounds her—first with wit and flippancy, then anger and indignation. Soon she realizes that, even as an insider, she never was truly assured of her place. Her final line of dialogue might even be a mini ars poetica for Jackson and her concerns: "It isn't fair, it isn't right."

The publication of "The Lottery" might have been enough to distinguish most authors' reputations for years, but it was only one event in an extremely productive year for Jackson. In 1948 she also published her first novel, several autobiographical essays, and gave birth to her first daughter. *The Road Through the Wall,* her first novel, both lampoons the suburbs and examines the parallel, isolated lives of the characters living in a well-appointed, conservative town. Lonely but imaginative, Harriet Merriam and Marilyn Perlman are the heroines of the novel, adolescent misfits who disappoint their mothers and seek solace at the library. Harriet is ostracized because she is overweight and bookish; Marilyn because she is from the only Jewish family in the neighborhood. Both girls read widely and write about their lives. Harriet labels her notebooks "Poems," "Moods," "Me," and "Daydreams." Marilyn reads Thackeray and copies vocabulary words into her journal, juxtaposing terms that might well describe her conflicting emotions, such as "adorable," "fearsome," "storied," and "grisly." The suburb, meanwhile, experiences a crisis when a little girl disappears; her body is then found. She probably has been murdered, possibly by a loner adolescent boy in the suburb. The boy then kills himself. Both the boy and the girl become symbolic sacrifices for a group of adults who cannot see past their own hypocrisy.

Reviewers generally praised *The Road Through the Wall. The New Yorker* extolled "the author's style, a supple and resourceful instrument that makes her shopworn material appear much fresher than it is." But the critical response to the novel hardly compared to the torrent of publicity and praise Jackson received the next year, in 1949, for the publication of her story collection, *The Lottery.* Almost immediately, the collection went into additional printings and delighted the publisher, Farrar, Straus & Giroux. One thing about the publicity campaign irked Jackson, however: her publisher sensationalized her and her writing, labeling it "terrifying" and including a blurb by Christopher Morley that warned readers about feeling "the tweak of ulcers."

PSYCHOLOGICAL NOVELS

Jackson's second and third novels deal with the horrors of the subconscious, and the pernicious effects of mental and emotional illness. *Hangsaman,* published in 1951, and *The Bird's Nest,* which followed three years later, featured protagonists driven to distraction by their vivid and sometimes even psychotic imaginary cohorts. Natalie Waite, in *Hangsaman,* is a precocious young woman beginning college. A writer, she has a strong and even visceral imagination. The reader first encounters Natalie trying to tune out her ill-matched parents by conducting full conversations in her head with imaginary characters. One such made-up person, a detective, prods Natalie about a murder mystery. The juxtaposition between the suburban domestic scene and an interior monologue centering on a

murder is disquieting: "Will you talk now? . . . Do you think that you alone can stand against the force of the police, the might and weight of duly constituted authority, against *me?*" Some of the imagined dialogues are humorous and bear elements of an inquisitive young woman's fantasies, but they also have an alarming undertone.

Away at college, Natalie struggles to combat loneliness. At one point, she even considers jumping from a bridge to her death. She becomes best friends with Tony, a character who may or may not be real. Jackson keeps the reader guessing throughout; Tony is a shadowy character. The two young women become close friends, and Tony introduces Natalie to new, mysterious realms of knowledge—for example, she loves Tarot cards. In one pivotal scene, Natalie, who is confused by Tony's ardent desire to be her friend, follows Tony into the woods armed for a confrontation.

Reviewers' opinions differed about Tony's status as a character or figment of Natalie's imagination, but most commented on the disturbing possibilities of Natalie's inner realm. The *New York Herald Tribune* noted that "Miss Jackson writes with grace and precision of this tenuous borderland country of the emotionally disturbed."

The Bird's Nest (1954) also centers around a troubled young woman, but she is more deeply ill than Natalie. Elizabeth Richmond is a timid, twenty-three-year-old woman who works in an uninspiring job in a museum. Her mother is dead, and she lives with her aunt. At first Elizabeth seems merely depressed, but then the reader begins to glimpse her other personalities. Soon she is sent to a doctor who specializes in hypnosis.

To write this novel, Jackson researched multiple personalities extensively. She also worked with a psychologist at Bennington who provided her with case histories and advice. The resulting novel dips into alternate perspectives to provide insights into the woman's psychological puzzle. Sometimes, through hypnosis, the personalities even confront each other. In one unsettling scene with the doctor, Bess and Betsy write each other acrimonious notes that reveal information about Elizabeth's relationship to her aunt.

The book's title (and epigraph) is a variation on an old riddle that begins: "Elizabeth, Lizzie, Betsy and Bess / All went together to see a bird's nest." It becomes clear in the riddle that the four names, all variations of "Elizabeth," belong to one person. Each of Elizabeth's selves has her own trademark style: Beth is pleasant and social; Betsy mocks both Elizabeth and the doctor (she calls Dr. Wright "Dr. Wrong"); and Bess is calculating and stubborn. Through the alternating narration of the four selves and the doctor, we learn about different aspects of Elizabeth's past including her fear of her mother's boyfriend, her mother's death, and the fact that she soon would inherit money from her mother's will.

The Bird's Nest was made into a film called *Lizzie* by Metro-Goldwyn-Mayer in 1957, but it dismayed the author. Several of Jackson's works were adapted for film and television, but the only one that pleased her, or in her opinion stayed true to the script, was the 1963 film *The Haunting,* which starred Julie Harris and Claire Bloom.

FAMILY MEMOIRS

During the 1950s, Jackson published two memoirs, *Life Among the Savages* (1953) and *Raising Demons* (1957). The accounts, comprised largely of autobiographical pieces first published in magazines, portray a zany household of imaginative individuals. These pieces poignantly reveal that, in contrast to her own mother, Jackson was accepting of her children's individual eccentricities. She writes vividly about her children's diverse interests and desires. Her oldest child, Laurie, for example,

desperately lobbies to play the trumpet (and does so with élan); Laurie and his father collect coins and become amateur numismatists. Her daughter Jannie convinces Jackson, against her will, to host a chaotic slumber party, and her younger daughter Sally speaks openly of magic. Jackson keeps the tone light and comic even when the situation is serious, but it is clear that she and her husband were fascinated by their children's various leanings and talents.

These memoirs also reveal that Jackson's domestic responsibilities could be daunting, especially during difficult periods in her marriage with Hyman and bouts of emotional illness. The critic Carol Cleveland observed that Jackson's memoirs are "early and admirable examples of an American literary subgenre: the diary of the mad housewife. Jackson was among the first to admit publicly that, while motherhood might be a useful institution for children, it was not conducive to serenity in the mother."

Despite this assessment, Jackson shows herself to be a mainly unflappable mother and wife who finds herself in funny and chaotic situations. "Charles," one of the most famous episodes from the memoirs, was first published in *Mademoiselle* and reprinted in *The Lottery.* It appears as a passage in Chapter 1 of *Life Among the Savages,* and describes the first year of kindergarten for Jackson's oldest son, Laurie. In this witty piece, Laurie comes home from school with reports of a hellion classmate, Charles. Soon Jackson's family looks forward to the scandalous stories of how Charles infuriated and sabotaged his teacher and classmates. The climax of the story occurs when Jackson attends a teacher-parent conference and realizes that there is no Charles in her son's class, and that Laurie probably was telling the story of his own difficult adjustment to school.

Another, less humorous strain runs through Jackson's memoirs, particularly in *Raising Demons.* In this later memoir volume, Jackson allows the occasional painful episode to slip into the jocular accounts. "Notes of a Faculty Wife," a piece included in *Raising Demons,* conveys Jackson's uneasy feelings about her husband's position as a professor. "A faculty wife is a person who is married to a faculty," she writes; "She has frequently read at least one good book lately, she has one 'nice' black dress to wear to student parties, and she is always just the teensiest bit in the way, particularly at a girls' college such as the one where my husband taught."

Another episode in the same memoir demonstrates Jackson's feelings of displacement and jealousy. When Hyman is asked to serve as a judge for the Miss Vermont contest, Jackson writes that the community and his own family are surprised. "Daddy likes to look at girls," Jackson quotes one of their young children as saying. The episode maintains a humorous tone, but the undercurrent of pain remains.

Jackson's writing shows evidence that she probably registered her feelings of jealousy. According to Oppenheimer, she suffered from her strong suspicions of her husband's infidelity. Yet with characteristic insight, Jackson's work also shows a sophisticated understanding of jealousy and betrayal, and a recognition of the fact that all affairs are not a simple story of villain and victim. In this sense, the memoirs can shed light on the fiction, and vice versa. One story in particular, "The Very Hot Sun in Bermuda" (published in *Just an Ordinary Day*), demonstrates pity for an errant husband. In the story, an attractive young coed walks through campus imagining how lovely she will look tanned and wearing a swimsuit. Meanwhile, her married lover, a professor and artist, waits for her in his studio, nervous and desperate. From the young woman's general self-absorption, though, it is clear to the reader that she considers her lover a passing fancy. Yet the professor agonizes over his situation, caught between his lust and sense of duty to his wife and children. By emphasizing the young woman's diffidence,

Jackson manages to strike a chord of sympathy for the anguished professor.

LATER FICTION

Several of the more memorable protagonists in Jackson's novels are women seeking refuge in ancient, imposing houses. This is the conceit for Jackson's last three novels, *The Sundial* (1958); *The Haunting of Hill House*; and *We Have Always Lived in the Castle* (1962). In each, the protagonists take literal refuge in eerie old homes to stave off further trauma, but find that the ornate gates and walls will not insulate them against their own mental and emotional demons.

The Sundial, Jackson's only novel to receive lukewarm reviews, is a combination farce and apocalyptic parable. The Hallorans are a wealthy family who live in a bizarre house built by the now-infirm father of the family. The peculiar sundial, which Mr. Halloran had had built with the house, bears an ominous slogan: "WHEN SHALL WE LIVE IF NOT NOW?"

Early on in the novel, several of the characters experience visions and harbingers. Aunt Fanny, for example, insists that her dead father is warning her about a coming apocalypse, through which only the family and their house will survive. Aunt Fanny and the matriarch of the house, Mrs. Halloran, struggle for control of the home and family throughout the preparations for this catastrophe. Jackson examines two power struggles in the novel: the first is among the inhabitants of the house, and the second is between the inhabitants and the future. Jackson seems to suggest that both are naive and could even have fatal consequences.

Much of the novel, written during the bomb-shelter craze of the 1950s, is spent preparing for the end of the world. The family stockpiles basic provisions, and even go so far as to burn books in order to provide more space in the mansion for essentials. The survivalist tale *Robinson Crusoe* is alluded to throughout;

Mr. Halloran, the elderly patriarch, listens to his nursemaid reading it aloud. Jackson also makes references to religion in the novel, especially to Catholicism and its promise of redemption.

Critics expressed confusion about the novel, particularly its genre. Reviewers considered the book everything from a serious allegory to a high-spirited satire. "Miss Jackson mixes Gothic horror and suburban fun," wrote a reviewer in *Commonweal.* The *New York Times* took Jackson to task for the "preposterous" characters and predictable dialogue. Perhaps the book's real challenge is the weight of the ideas and traditions, specifically those of Catholics and apocalypse-oriented believers, that Jackson takes on. In this sense, the message presses too heavily on its characters.

A Gothic mansion once again provides refuge in *The Haunting of Hill House.* Eleanor Vance, the protagonist, attempts to erase years of a servile existence in her family by moving into a menacing mansion to take part in a study of the occult. Eleanor was selected by Dr. Montague, the director of the study, because of an experience with an alleged poltergeist when she was young. Dr. Montague is a self-assured philosopher who studies the supernatural. While the inhabitants' experience chaos in the house, Montague entertains himself by speaking of poltergeists and ghosts and reading novels by Samuel Richardson (also a favorite of Jackson's). Soon, though, even Dr. Montague's preoccupations cannot keep the house's forces (and the residents' own demons) at bay.

At Hill House, Eleanor feels liberated and valued for her mind. She meets and becomes infatuated with more worldly characters, including Theodora, an artist with psychic abilities, and Luke, the rich nephew of the house's owner. But soon even Theo and Luke cannot satisfy Eleanor's need for affirmation. The novel climaxes in a scene in which Eleanor walks into a tower, where the residents had been forbidden to go, and climbs a precarious iron staircase.

She scales it quickly, and soon ends up far above the stone floor. When the other residents discover her, they realize that the house and experiment has meant much more to Eleanor than to them. The moment foreshadows the distraught woman's suicide—when the group disbands and she is forced to return home, she kills herself by driving into a tree.

Throughout the novel, as in *The Sundial,* the house reflects both the disquieting spirits of the past and the psychological terrors of the current inhabitants. Jackson imbues the architecture with texture and emotion. Chapter 2 of *The Haunting of Hill House* begins with the following passage:

> No human eye can isolate the unhappy coincidence of line and place which suggests evil in the face of a house, and yet somehow a maniac juxtaposition, a badly turned angle, some chance meeting of roof and sky, turned Hill House into a place of despair, more frightening because the face of Hill House seemed awake, with a watchfulness from the blank windows and a touch of glee in the eyebrow of a cornice.

In *We Have Always Lived in the Castle,* two sisters, Merricat and Constance, live sequestered in the family mansion. The neighbors, the village people, scorn them, both for their family's wealth and another, more troubling, reason: Constance served time for allegedly murdering most of her family with arsenic. Since the murders, the villagers have exhibited acrimony toward the young women, taunting them with cruel rhymes. At the beginning of the book, the story's narrator, Merricat, the more eccentric sister, describes doing errands in town, where she is subjected to jeers. But she remains firm in her belief that her home is true refuge. She adores her sister Constance, and generally treats her invalid Uncle Julian, who nearly died from arsenic poisoning, with deference. Yet she shows no sorrow over the gruesome deaths of her parents, brother, and aunt. It soon becomes clear that Merricat is the likely murderer. Her fantasy is to live "on the moon" with Constance, where none of her hateful memories of the family can haunt her. When their cousin Charles shows up, however, and Constance begins to show signs of wanting to reenter society, Merricat suspects that he is seeking the family fortune and sets out to dissuade him from remaining.

One of the pivotal scenes of the novel occurs when the house catches fire and the neighbors, after helping to put it out, smash the windows and wreck the remaining rooms. The young women return to their badly damaged home, however, and board up the windows and secure the doors around them. They remain there, living in greatly reduced circumstances. Merricat is mollified; she finally has her sister all to herself.

CONCLUSION

One way that Jackson nurtured her creative life was by reading widely. Her formal education ended with graduation from Syracuse, but she continued to study the art of her literary ancestors. In addition to reading about witchcraft, she devoured the work of authors such as Samuel Richardson, Henry Fielding, Jane Austen, the Brontës, E. M. Forster, and Louisa May Alcott. She used work by the latter as a palliative after writing *The Haunting of Hill House*. Reading *Little Women* before bed, she said, helped ease the onslaught of disturbing, otherworldly thoughts. She also admired the contemporary writers Katherine Anne Porter and Elizabeth Bowen.

Her favorite writer remained Richardson. Jackson's ardor for this eighteenth-century author might seem illogical, considering Richardson's arguably florid, long-winded style, so in contrast with Jackson's sparse, understated prose. But in an unpublished essay, "Notes on an Unfashionable Novelist," she answered her own question, "Why read Richardson, who was certainly very moral and extremely long, and, not to put too fine a point on it, dull?"

Jackson isolates three attributes that Richardson possessed, but which, she says, are lacking in modern, "distempered" times: "Peace, principle, kindness." Peace she identifies as the characters' leisure to think, to write letters, and to reflect on and consider their lives. Jackson praises the slow pace of Richardson's prose, and what she knew of him as a man—that he liked food and was overweight, that he had many concerns but still was able to gossip with friends and write. Principle, Jackson says, is the dignity and respect Richardson's heroes exhibit; how they honor their commitments regardless of temptations. Finally, kindness lies in Richardson's obvious sympathy for his characters, for all human beings. Jackson admits that kindness is an "outlandish word to use about a writer, or about writing, or about anything except people and the way they feel." Yet Richardson had it, she writes; his words reveal not that "'we are all from the same mind, Richardson's,'" but "'we are all from the same people, the mortal.'"

The distinction is important in Jackson's work, as well. Though critics have often sought to emphasize the dark or Kafkaesque in her creative vision, hopeful elements exist in her writing. Even at their most misguided and desperate, characters such as Merricat reach out to others for solace. Some of Jackson's characters demonstrate through their obsession with the future a genuine concern for the future of humanity. In a sense, Jackson's narrative messages are warnings rather than indictments. Hyman articulated this idea in his posthumous article about his wife: "[Jackson's] fierce visions of dissociation and madness, of alienation and withdrawal, have been taken to be personal, even neurotic, fantasies. Quite the reverse: they are a sensitive and faithful anatomy of our times, fitting symbols for our distressing world of the concentration camp and the Bomb."

Selected Bibliography

WORKS OF SHIRLEY JACKSON

NOVELS AND SHORT STORIES

The Road Through the Wall. New York: Farrar, Straus, 1948.

The Lottery; or, The Adventures of James Harris. New York: Farrar, Straus & Giroux, 1949. Reprinted as *The Lottery and Other Stories.* New York: Farrar, Straus & Giroux, 1982. Reprinted as *The Lottery and Other Stories,* with a preface by Patrick McGrath. New York: Modern Library, 2000.

Hangsaman. New York: Farrar, Straus and Young, 1951.

The Bird's Nest. New York: Farrar, Straus and Young, 1954.

The Sundial. New York: Farrar, Straus and Cudahy, 1958.

The Haunting of Hill House. New York: Viking, 1959.

We Have Always Lived in the Castle. New York: Viking, 1962.

COLLECTIONS

Come Along with Me: Part of a Novel, Sixteen Stories, and Three Lectures. Edited with a preface by Stanley Edgar Hyman. New York: Viking, 1968.

The Magic of Shirley Jackson. Edited with a preface by Stanley Edgar Hyman. New York: Farrar, Straus & Giroux, 1969.

Just an Ordinary Day. Edited with a preface by Laurence Jackson Hyman and Sarah Hyman Stewart. New York: Bantam Books, 1997.

NONFICTION

Life Among the Savages. New York: Farrar, Straus and Young, 1953.

Raising Demons. New York: Farrar, Straus and Cudahy, 1957.

JUVENILE BOOKS

The Witchcraft of Salem Village. New York: Landmark Books/Random House, 1956.

The Bad Children: A Musical in One Act for Bad Children. Chicago: Dramatic Publishing, 1959.

Nine Magic Wishes. New York: Crowell-Collier, 1963.

Famous Sally. New York: Harlin Quist, 1966.

MANUSCRIPT PAPERS

A collection of Jackson's manuscripts and correspondence is at the Library of Congress.

BIBLIOGRAPHIES

Hall, Joan Wylie. "Shirley Jackson." In vol. 1 of *Facts on File Bibliography of American Fiction: 1919–1988.* Edited by Matthew Bruccoli et al. New York: Facts on File, 1991. Pp. 266–267.

Herrick, Casey. "Shirley Jackson's 'The Lottery.'" *Bulletin of Bibliography* 46, no. 2:120–121 (June 1989).

Phillips, Robert S. "Shirley Jackson: A Checklist." *Papers of the Bibliographical Society of America* 56, no. 1:110–113 (January–March 1962), pp. 110–113.

CRITICAL AND BIOGRAPHICAL STUDIES

Allen, Barbara. "A Folkloristic Look at Shirley Jackson's 'The Lottery.'" *Tennessee Folklore Society Bulletin* 46:119–124 (December 1980).

Breit, Harvey. "Talk with Miss Jackson." *New York Times Book Review,* June 26, 1949, p. 15.

Brooks, Cleanth, and Robert Penn Warren. "'The Lottery': Interpretation." In their *Understanding Fiction.* New York: Appleton-Century-Crofts, 1959. Pp. 72–76.

Carpenter, Lynette. "Domestic Comedy, Black Comedy, and Real Life: Shirley Jackson, a Woman Writer." In *Faith of a (Woman) Writer.* Edited by Alice Kessler-Harris and William McBrien. Westport, Conn.: Greenwood Press, 1988. Pp. 143–148.

Cleveland, Carol S. "Shirley Jackson." In *And Then There Were Nine . . . More Women of Mystery.* Edited by Jane S. Bakerman. Bowling Green, Ohio: Bowling Green State University Popular Press, 1985. Pp. 199–219.

Davenport, Guy. "Dark Psychological Weather." *New York Times Book Review,* September 15, 1968, p. 4.

D'Erasmo, Stacey. Review of *Just An Ordinary Day. The Nation,* December 23, 1996, p. 25.

Frank, Elizabeth. "The Sorceress of Bennington." *New York Times,* August 7, 1988, pp. 6–7.

Friedman, Lenemaja. *Shirley Jackson.* Boston: Twayne, 1975.

Gates, David. "Hard Lives, Lasting Prose." *Newsweek,* August 22, 1988, pp. 66–67.

Hall, Joan Wylie. *Shirley Jackson: A Study of the Short Fiction.* New York: Twayne, 1993.

Hicks, Granville. "The Nightmare in Reality." *Saturday Review* XLIX, no. 38:31–32 (September 17, 1966).

Hyman, Stanley Edgar. "Shirley Jackson: 1919–1965," *Saturday Evening Post,* December 18, 1965, p. 63.

Janeway, Elizabeth. "The Grotesque around Us." *New York Times Book Review,* October 9, 1966, p. 58.

Kittredge, Mary. "The Other Side of Magic: A Few Remarks about Shirley Jackson." In *Discovering Modern Horror Fiction.* Edited by Darrell Schweitzer. Mercer Island, Wash.: Starmont House, 1985. Pp. 3–12.

Kosenko, Peter. "A Marxist/Feminist Reading of Shirley Jackson's 'The Lottery.'" *New Orleans Review* 12:27–32 (spring 1985).

Lainoff, Seymour. "Jackson's 'The Lottery.'" *Explicator* 12, item 34 (March 1954).

Lethem, Jonathan. "Monstrous Acts and Little Murders." *Salon* (www.salon.com), January 1997.

Mukamel, Eran. "The Irrepressible Individual in the Works of Shirley Jackson" (http://www.bcsd.org/BHS/ENGLISH/mag97/papers/jackson.htm), May 1999.

Nebeker, Helen E. "'The Lottery': Symbolic Tour de Force." *American Literature* 46:100–107 (March 1974).

Oehlschlaeger, Fritz. "The Stoning of Mistress Hutchinson: Meaning and Context in 'The Lottery.'" *Essays in Literature* 15:259–265 (fall 1988).

Oppenheimer, Judy. *Private Demons: The Life of Shirley Jackson.* New York: Putnam, 1988.

Parks, John G. "The Possibility of Evil: A Key to Shirley Jackson's Fiction." *Studies in Short Fiction* 15:320–323 (summer 1978).

———. "Waiting for the End: Shirley Jackson's *The Sundial.*" *Critique* 19, no. 3:74–88 (summer 1978).

———. "Chambers of Yearning: Shirley Jackson's Use of the Gothic." *Twentieth Century Literature* 30:15–29 (spring 1984).

Pascal, Richard. "'Farther than Samarkand': The Escape Theme in Shirley Jackson's 'The Tooth.'" *Studies in Short Fiction* 19:133–139 (spring 1982).

Shapiro, Laura. Review of *Just an Ordinary Day. Newsweek,* January 1997, p. 70.

Warnock, Kathleen. "Meet the Author: Shirley Jackson." *Literary Cavalcade* 10 (February 1997).

Woodruff, Stuart C. "The Real Horror Elsewhere: Shirley Jackson's Last Novel." *Southwest Review* 52:152–162 (spring 1967).

—CAROLYN ALESSIO

Tony Kushner

1956–

S INCE THE EARLY 1990s and especially since he was awarded a Pulitzer Prize for drama, a New York Drama Critics Circle Award for best new play, and a Tony Award for best play, all in 1993, Tony Kushner has been considered one of America's foremost playwrights. His breakthrough came with *Angels in America: A Gay Fantasia on National Themes* (1992, 1995), a seven-hour play in two parts that seems reminiscent of Walt Whitman's desire to embrace all aspects of America. In the essay "With a Little Help from My Friends," in his *Thinking about the Longstanding Problems of Virtue and Happiness: Essays, a Play, Two Poems, and a Prayer* (1995), Kushner explains:

> When I started to write these plays, I wanted to attempt something of ambition and size even if that meant I might be accused of straying too close to ambition's ugly twin, pretentiousness. . . . Melville, my favorite American writer, strikes inflated, even hysterical, chords on occasion. It's the sound of the Individual ballooning, overreaching. We are all children of "Song of Myself."

Kushner refers to Walt Whitman's masterpiece "Song of Myself" (1855), a long poem celebrating the American gay poet's self and sexuality that in the nineteenth century was shocking in its openness. Kushner credits his own openness about himself and his sexuality partly to Whitman's verbal intimacy. Whitmanesque in his expansive reflections on his own and others' humanity, Kushner brings onto the American stage explorations of the human condition and of national issues, and he presents them through an innovative mixture of genres, reality levels, and themes, a dramatic technique that wavers between the realistic and the surreal, the comic and the tragic. His wide-reaching interests are also reflected in his numerous adaptations of plays by an international range of authors, including Johann Wolfgang von Goethe, Pierre Corneille, Ariel Dorfman, Shloime Ansky, and Bertolt Brecht. The wide scope of his concerns and the passion with which he conveys them have won Kushner the applause of large, diverse audiences at his plays and public appearances.

This author delights in a multiplicity of themes and forms. In his original dramatic work as well as in his adaptations, diverse elements appear side by side, sometimes merging, sometimes enlightening each other through their degrees of difference. He therefore has compared the desired outcome of his literary efforts to the "opulence" of lasagna, a dish he describes in "On Pretentiousness," an essay in *Thinking about the Longstanding Problems of Virtue and Happiness,* as "garlicky garrulous, excessively, even suspiciously generous, promiscuous, flirtatious, insistent, persistent overwhelming exhaustive and exhausting." To Kushner the perfect lasagna

> effects a balance between fluidity and solidity, between architecture and melting. It is something between a pie and a mélange, there are membranes but they are permeable, the layers must maintain their integrity and yet exist in an exciting dialectic tension to the molten oozy cheesy oily juices which they separate, the goo must almost but not completely successfully threaten the always-discernible-yet-imperiled imposed order.

Baking lasagna has long been my own personal paradigm for writing a play. A good play I think should always feel as though it's only barely been rescued from the brink of chaos, as though all the yummy nutritious ingredients you've thrown into it have almost-but-not-quite succeeded in overwhelming the design. . . . A good play, like a good lasagna, should be overstuffed: It has a pomposity, and an overreach: Its ambitions extend in the direction of not-missing-a-trick, it has a bursting omnipotence up its sleeve, or rather, under its noodles: It is pretentious food.

Pretentiousness, overstatement, rhetoric and histrionics, grandiosity and portentousness are, as much as they are also the tropes of fascists and demagogues everywhere, American tropes, gestures of habitual florid overstep common among those practitioners of American culture to whom I have always been most instantly attracted. It is an aspect of American history and culture we have developed that I am keen to possess, to transform for my own purposes.

Such a celebration of diversity, in which the real tends to give way to the magical and in which even the most problematic characters are given some redeeming qualities, is Kushner's trademark. While he traces its roots to the pretentiousness and grandiosity of American history and culture, a more autobiographical basis for valuing diversity—and for dealing with center and margin, empathizing with both power mongers and outsiders—becomes apparent considering the diverse experiences that have characterized this author's life as well as his self-avowed attraction to public display.

A gay man, a Jew, a writer of extreme political awareness, Kushner recognizes and articulates the fears of those who, like himself, feel marginalized by a larger culture and by a homophobic religious right wing. Yet an earmark of this cosmopolitan writer, who like most New York intellectuals feels deep affinities with psychoanalysis, has been to recognize his own ambivalence toward his sexuality as well as toward his personal, political, and religious feelings about Judaism. He has the courage to admit feeling infected by the idea of the Jew and the homosexual as deviants deserving punishment

and equally infected by the willingness to voice this ambivalence. In an interview with Rabbi Norman J. Cohen, published in Robert Vorlicky's interview collection *Tony Kushner in Conversation* (1998), Kushner remarks:

> Being gay, I can't help but have a deep ambivalence, because there is a fantastically powerful homophobic tradition within Judaism. When I was at the Wailing Wall with a gay journalist from Tel Aviv . . . I was looking at these varieties of orthodox and Hasidic Jews who were praying at the Wall. And I said, "You know, it hurts me that these people . . . it hurts me that they don't think of me as a Jew." And he said, "Oh, well, they think of you as a Jew. They think of you as a Jew who should be killed."

Kushner wrote that he went into psychoanalysis to change his sexuality, even though the analyst made it clear from the beginning that the treatment would not do so. In the brief play *Terminating, or Sonnet LXXV, or "Lass Meine Schmerzen nicht verloren sein," or Ambivalence* (2000), dedicated to his analyst, he presents her as a lesbian who is a soul mate in the sense of feeling as filled with despair as he is. At one point the character Hendryk—clearly based upon Kushner himself—remarks: "Ambivalence expands our options. It increases our freedom to, to . . . tattoo. Our selves . . . makes us more ambivalent and more free. Which drives us crazy." In an afterword to Vorlicky's collection Kushner expands on this theme: "I often wish I was a Stoic, some sort of Roman who knew the virtue and value of suffering silently. But I'm not and I don't. I'm a modern man and I like to share—feelings, at any rate. Here, have some more, I have puh-lenty!" Sorrow and laughter hang in the balance in all of Kushner's work, and his recurrent sense of despair is woven into a recurrent fantasy of salvation and resurrection, namely the idea that death, decay, and corruption, literally as well as metaphorically or politically, can and do produce new life.

LIFE AND VIEWS

Antony Robin Jeremy Kushner was born to Jewish American parents, Sylvia Deutscher and Bill Kushner, in New York City on July 16, 1956, and shortly thereafter the family moved to Lake Charles, Louisiana. Since both parents were classical musicians and Kushner's mother worked as an actress, it is not surprising that literature and the arts played an important role in the early lives of Tony and his siblings. As Kushner told Susan Cheever of the *New York Times*, he saw his mother on stage when he was four or five years old, a threshold experience that resulted in vivid dreams as well as a lifelong passion for the theater.

Kushner also locates the discovery of his sexual preference in his childhood years. In an interview with Richard Stayton of the *Los Angeles Times* he confesses that around the age of six he discovered he was gay, a realization that had become a certainty by age eleven. However, he did not reveal his sexual identity then or during his adolescence. After finishing high school in Louisiana, Kushner returned to New York City to attend Columbia University. As an undergraduate he sought psychotherapy, which led to a gradual acceptance of his sexual identity, but not until his early twenties did he finally come out openly.

In 1978 Kushner graduated from Columbia University with a bachelor's degree in medieval history. He then worked as a switchboard operator at the United Nations Plaza Hotel in New York City, a job he held for six years. Deciding to pursue a career in the theater, Kushner enrolled at New York University (NYU) and graduated with an M.F.A. in directing in 1984. By then he also was writing plays. As he later recalled, this was a difficult time in his life. His great-aunt died unexpectedly; a good friend was in a serious taxi accident; the theater collective he had cofounded fell apart; and his mentor at NYU, Carl Weber, left New York City for a position at Stanford University. In addition, the reelection of Ronald Reagan to the U.S. presidency in 1984 depressed Kushner. "The desolate political sphere mirrored in an exact and ugly way an equally desolate personal sphere," he observes in retrospect in *A Bright Room Called Day* (1994).

In 1985 Kushner left New York to become assistant director at the St. Louis Repertory Theatre for one season. There his first play, *Yes, Yes, No, No* (1987), was produced in 1985. His next play, *Stella,* an adaptation of Goethe's *Stella* (1776), was produced in New York two years later; it has not been published. Also in 1987 two more original plays by Kushner were staged, *A Bright Room Called Day* in San Francisco, following its 1985 workshop production in New York, and *Hydriotaphia; or, The Death of Dr. Browne: An Epic Farce about Death and Primitive Capital Accumulation* (2000) in New York City. Kushner was artistic director of the New York Theatre Workshop from 1987 to 1988, and he was director of literary services for the Theatre Communications Group from 1990 to 1991. Appointments as playwright-in-residence and as guest artist took Kushner to the Juilliard School of Drama in New York City, the New York University Graduate Theatre Program, Yale University, and Princeton University.

Kushner, who settled in Brooklyn, New York, has used drama as one venue through which to plead for a more humane society and for communal values. Other venues include his appearances as a public intellectual at readings, at lectures, at protest rallies, or on talk shows. He considers drama and politics closely connected, and in interviews he has acknowledged the influences of William Shakespeare, Karl Marx, Bertolt Brecht, Walter Benjamin, and Tennessee Williams. While Kushner wants to reinvigorate language, storytelling, and the imagination, he sees his work in the theater primarily as an ethical responsibility, as a thought-provoking effort to contribute to social change.

Kushner's breakthrough as a playwright came in the early 1990s with the overwhelming success of *Angels in America.* His later plays did not recreate the audience appeal of that masterpiece, however. Kushner used the national and international reputation he gained with *Angels* to promote an awareness of AIDS and of how American culture deals with the disease. An active member of the AIDS Coalition to Unleash Power (ACT UP), Kushner has spoken out in many interviews, lectures, and essays on AIDS-related issues. Above all he has asked for an unprejudiced approach to AIDS victims and for the compassion and support of those in power. In "A Prayer," written for the Episcopalian National Day of Prayer for AIDS, delivered at the Cathedral Church of St. John the Divine in New York City in 1994, and published in *Thinking about the Longstanding Problems of Virtue and Happiness,* Kushner asks God to

Enlighten the unenlightened: The Pope, the cardinals, archbishops and priests, even John O'Connor, teach him how Christ's kindness worked: Remind him he's forgotten, make them all remember, replace the ice water in their veins with the blood of Christ, let it pound in their temples: The insurance executive as well as the priest, the congressional representative, the Justice and the judge, the pharmaceutical profiteer, the doctor, the cop, the anchorwoman and the televangelist, make their heads throb with memory, make them see with new eyes Christ's wounds as K.S. lesions. Christ's thin body AIDS-thin, his shrunken chest pneumonia-deflated, his broken limbs, his pierced hands: stigmata of this unholy plague. Let the spilled blood which angels gathered, Christ's blood be understood: It is shared and infected blood. Even John O'Connor, even Bob Dole, Giuliani and Gingrich, Jesse Helms and Pat Robertson—tear open their hearts, let them burn with compassion, stun them with understanding, ravish their violent, politick, cynical souls, make them wiser, better, braver people.

The passage illustrates Kushner's characteristic crossing of boundaries, for example, between Judaism and Christianity or between religion and politics. It also demonstrates his wide-ranging critique of those who define public opinion in America, of those in positions that could exert a certain power over AIDS victims and public perceptions of the disease. Moreover, Kushner makes daring associations, for example, between Christ's blood and HIV-infected blood. Criticizing the irresponsible, inhumane exertion of political, economic, financial, religious, or media power is a key element of Kushner's life and work. This critique is substantiated through a reminder of the principles on which individual figures or institutions allegedly base their power, a reminder that usually reveals hypocrisy.

In "A Prayer," Kushner includes God in the ranks of those in power, and he challenges God to act according to his principles, to be unlike "the monstrously indifferent, no better than a Washington politician." Kushner prays for an even distribution of God's grace and especially for an inclusion of AIDS victims in that grace. But he does not stop there, appealing for more equality and compassion in all areas:

So a cure for AIDS. For racism too. For homophobia and sexism, and an end to war, to nationalism and capitalism, to work as such and to hatred of the flesh. Restore the despoiled world, end the pandemic of breast cancer too. . . . At least guarantee that loss is not irrecoverable, so that life can be endured.

As this passage infers, Kushner has Marxist leanings. He blames capitalism and profiteers for much of what he sees as wrong with contemporary American culture, especially for its pernicious hierarchies.

Kushner's work suggests, however, that a large part of his version of socialism derives less from Marx than from Oscar Wilde's essay-dialogue of 1891, *The Soul of Man under Socialism,* which opens with Wilde's observation, "The chief advantage that would result from the establishment of Socialism is, undoubtedly, the fact that Socialism would relieve us from that sordid necessity of living for others which, in the present condition of things, presses so hardly upon almost everybody." Wilde, a brilliant Irish playwright and a martyr and revolutionary for the rights of gay men, was sent to prison in 1895 ostensibly for breaking a law prohibiting so-called "indecent acts" between men. Actually he went to prison for parading his homosexual activities and lovers. Closeted gay men as a rule were not prosecuted.

In his essay "A Socialism of the Skin (Liberation, Honey!)" in *Thinking about the Longstanding Problems of Virtue and Happiness,* Kushner quotes Wilde's *Soul of Man* as a means of taking to task two prominent conservative (or "neo-con") gay writers, Andrew Sullivan and Bruce Bawer. "A map of the world that does not include Utopia is not worth even glancing at, for it leaves out the one country at which Humanity is always landing," Wilde writes. Had these neo-cons been Wilde's contemporaries, Kushner speculates, "Lord knows how they would have tut-tutted at his scandalous carryings-on." Kushner contends that Sullivan and Bawer disapprove of the flamboyant personal styles of some gay men, which they feel increases violence against homosexuals and gives homosexuals a bad image.

Disgust with their views leads Kushner to Wilde's idea that Utopia is possible and thence to connections between a utopia for homosexuals and Wilde's vision of socialism. Quoting John Cowper Powys's remark that Wilde's complaint against capitalism and industrialism is "'the irritation of an extremely sensitive *skin* . . . combined with a pleasure-lover's annoyance at seeing other people so miserably wretched,'" Kushner pounces. "If there is a relationship between socialism and homosexual liberation," he asserts, "perhaps this is it: an irritation of the skin." He then returns to Wilde's views about the benefits socialism holds for society: "'One's regret,' Oscar tells us, 'is that society should be constructed on such a basis

that man is forced into a groove in which he cannot freely develop what is wonderful and fascinating and delightful in him—in which . . . he misses the true pleasure and joy of living.'" "Socialism," Kushner concludes, "as an alternative to individualism politically and capitalism economically, must surely have as its ultimate objective the restitution of the joy of living we may have lost when we first picked up a tool."

Morality and human values all too often give way to materialistic and egotistic interests in contemporary America, Kushner believes. In an interview with Tom Szentgyorgyi during the Gulf War (later included in Vorlicky's collection) Kushner said:

> Leaders like Reagan and Bush are essentially as morally debased as the people who followed Hitler. . . . Whether or not they sound as crazy or have the same mustache, these are people who fundamentally place all sorts of ideological agendas and personal success above human rights. I think one of the things pushing Bush toward his holocaust in the Gulf is a slip in his popularity.
>
> It may be the case that because of the media, and the pressures of public life, most of the people that we elect to public office are not morally fit to be in a position of leadership. That's terrifying.

Kushner also uses public lectures and appearances at demonstrations to voice his stance. For example, he participated in the ARTNOW demo-celebration in Washington, D.C., in April 1997 in favor of continued federal funding for the arts in the United States. As a public and literary figure Kushner is passionately outspoken about what he believes is the basis of the cultural malaise he has diagnosed. This gives him, as Vorlicky states, "a kind of 'poet laureate' position for many of the disenfranchised—for those who experience their lives as voiceless or marginalized—a position that Kushner fills (involuntarily but nonetheless graciously and knowingly) within the American media, if not the American psyche."

The themes of the disenfranchised, the powerful, hierarchies, and constructions of center versus margins figure prominently in Kushner's drama. They are combined with his recognition of America's diversity, in which, as a left-leaning homosexual Jew with a mixed southern and New York heritage, he occupies various outsider positions. He deals with his multiple marginalizations in his work as a playwright, director, essayist, artistic collaborator, and public speaker but also in his roles of son, brother, uncle, and lover. "I contain multitudes," said Whitman in "Song of Myself," and Kushner writes in the same spirit. Vorlicky concurs:

Any single identification of Kushner fails to capture the breadth and depth of who he is and the value of his public presence. He is among the very few living Americans under the age of fifty who have been able to carve out a public space in contemporary American life for the many who otherwise feel unaddressed and unheard—a space in which he candidly speaks out for the marginalized communities from which he derives a sense of being and strength of purpose. Kushner names his otherness boldly, actively, and proudly. He affirms our potential as a people to recommit ourselves to the ideals of living dynamically and democratically on a global scale. . . . Kushner believes in and offers in his work a "hope" for humans to locate the space within, the soul without, to live and work beside one another cooperatively and peacefully, always mindful of both our differences and sameness. He is also aware of the ambiguities of life that constantly challenge this vision and the crises of experience that make one wary of utopianism while wholly embodying its hope.

Both Kushner's personal identity and that of his culture are characterized by a complex diversity, the intersection of areas, and the crossing of boundaries. For him the personal and the social converge with the political. And since in all these spheres the Other is inextricably connected to the Self, he shows that most facets of the contemporary America he represents, including those of which he is most critical, have a certain justification and dignity. Rather than claiming any definitive truth for his own position, he values discussion and argument, preferring dialectics to dogmatism. Exclusion—whatever its basis—is what Kushner rejects for himself as an individual and for the nation at large. As he once remarked to Szentgyorgyi:

Anyone who thinks that completely self-interested politics is going to get you anywhere in America is making a terrible mistake. Which is why I object to Louis Farrakhan. Which is why I object to gays and lesbians in ACT UP who say "I hate straights." Or to Jews who think that the only thing that matters is Israel and defense against anti-Semitism. People who don't recognize common cause are going to fail politically in this country. Movements that capture the imagination of people are movements that deny racism and exclusion. The country is too mongrel to do otherwise.

KUSHNER'S WORK: *HYDRIOTAPHIA*

"Though I didn't realize it at the time," Kushner says in the introduction, "I think I wrote *Hydriotaphia* as a crash course in learning how to write jokes." This confession underscores the importance of humor as a weapon against despair in Kushner's work, dominated as it is by concern with discrimination against gays, the horrors of an early and often painful death from AIDS, as well as the social instability and revolution—especially revolutions in art, culture, and politics—spurred by the impact of such a disease.

Kushner's title comes from an essay, "Hydriotaphia; or, Urne-Buriall" (1658), by a seventeenth-century English physician, Sir Thomas Browne, who is considered one of the great prose stylists of his age and who was by inclination a metaphysical theologian. While Browne's *Hydriotaphia* is an exploration of ancient burial rites, it also questions the nature of death and immortality, meditating on the contrasts between pagan and Christian attitudes toward death and weaving through a variety of reflections about friendship, death, and uncertainty. Browne asserts:

> But who knows the fate of his bones, or how often he is to be buried? who hath the Oracle of his ashes, or whether they are to be scattered? The Reliques of many lie like the ruins of *Pompeys,* in all parts of the earth; And when they arrive at your hands, these may seem to have wandred far, who in a direct and *Meridian* Travell, have but few miles of known Earth between your self and the Pole.

Christopher Bigsby notes that Kushner has remarked, "I firmly believe in using the Holocaust model, promiscuously" and "we should be very liberal with likening people to Nazis." As a gay Jewish man, Kushner's concern about the ultimate fate of his bones and his knowledge that human beings have no control over the disposal of their bodies after death or frequently during the dying process led to an overpowering despair. The result, a play filled with a humor that reveals the dark side of the human soul, is meant to highlight affinities between the social upheavals of Browne's day and our own. Everyone in Kushner's *Hydriotaphia* is driven by personal greed. "The play is semi-historical and semi-biographical," Kushner remarked in an online interview published on the Alley Theatre's website in conjunction with the production of his play, adding:

> *Hydriotaphia* chronicles a period of revolution in England on all sorts of levels, from the political to the social to the religious. . . . The moments in history that interest me the most are of transition. . . . *Hydriotaphia* is set after a revolution has occurred, in the Restoration. I am interested in periods in history that seem to be transitional, when an old social order is on its way out and new social orders are on their way in. These are very much representative of the period that I was born into—that we live in now—a period of

instability where we're turning some kind of a corner. The possibilities range from a vastly improved world to no world at all. The big question right now I think is up for grabs, and I think that's been true for most of this century. And so I think I'm drawn to other periods in history where that was the case.

The play opens on the day of Sir Thomas Browne's death, and the drama concerns his struggle between his will to live and his will to die. The real Browne died on his birthday, like a number of well-known Renaissance figures, among them, Shakespeare and the poet Andrew Marvell. Perhaps the orderliness of this exit, the apparent control of one's own extinction, appeals to Kushner, who sets the entire play in Browne's sickroom.

In the first scene two of the "bumpkin" characters (as Kushner dubs them), Babbo and Maccabbee, are copulating on the floor beside the sickbed. They strike the play's keynote, later articulated by a Gothic character, Dr. Schadenfreude, who announces, "There is a vitality in putrefaction, a life in death." His German name, which has no exact translation in English, might be rendered "Harm-joy" and refers to the rush of delight felt when one's enemies suffer, an obviously pagan concept. If one message of the original *Hydriotaphia* is to accept life and death with the equanimity of the believing Christian surrendering himself or herself to God, Kushner's message is just the reverse. "NOT YET, GODDAMNIT!" Sir Thomas yells in the first act. No one in Kushner's world goes gently into that good night. Browne's dying, Kushner said in the online interview, is

> a very athletic process, and the other characters comment on it all the time. It's as Schadenfreude says: it was very much a notion of the period as well that death is not the end but the beginning—a new form of life basically. Existence was really coming into view rather than the cessation of existence.

Essentially all that follows extrapolates from this idea—at times in the form of a philosophy, at times the wish fulfillment of the generation afflicted with AIDS—of life arising out of decay and death. The play ends with the bursting of a maggot-filled rotting chicken that magically produces honey. The maggots turn into flies then into bees, and honey and clover run all over the floor. To drive the wish fulfillment home, the bronze nose of one of the bumpkins, whose real nose has been lost to "the clap," as he says, is miraculously replaced. The wheel comes full circle with the last scene echoing the first. Babbo and Maccabbee begin copulating as the lights fade.

The struggle with AIDS, the desire to see a life rising out of death in the wake of this terrible plague, influences much if not all of Kushner's work. In *Reverse Transcription* (2000), a play produced in 1996, six playwrights secretly bury a seventh, who has died of AIDS, at the Abel's Hill cemetery on Martha's Vineyard. A character dubbed Happy, described by Kushner as "a little bored, but very happy," who possibly echoes the unhappy Happy of Arthur Miller's *Death of a Salesman* (1949), makes an unexpected connection:

> I remember being impressed when I learned that the HIV virus . . . reads and writes its genetic alphabets backwards, RNA transcribing DNA transcribing RNA, hence, *retro*virus. I'm not gay but I am a Jew and so of course I, too, "read backwards, write backwards"; I think of Hebrew. . . .
>
> HIV, reverse transcribing, dust to dust, writing backwards, Hebrew. . . . Perhaps, maybe, this backwards-writing viral nightmare is keeping some secret, subterraneanly affianced to a principle of . . . Reversals: good reversals and also very bad, where good meets bad.

Other characters say he is equating Hebrew with AIDS. The implication that a persecuted people—the Jew seems equated with the homosexual here—have a plague inscribed in their culture and in their being is dismissed ultimately by Happy, who claims that he never meant to equate Hebrew with AIDS: "It's just the words: reverse transcription. *Thinking* about it. Something I can't help doing." Kushner here expresses the sad truth that those who are infected with AIDS feel irrational guilt.

A BRIGHT ROOM CALLED DAY

At New York University, Kushner was a student of the German émigré Carl Weber, a director and translator. Kushner wrote in *A Bright Room Called Day* that from Weber he "learned much of what I know about the theatre." Weber also may have been in part responsible for Kushner's interest in translating drama. Kushner's early adaptations of Goethe's *Stella* and Corneille's *L'Illusion comique* (1635) as well as his joint adaptation with Ariel Dorfman of Dorfman's *Viudas* (1981) all were produced between 1987 and 1991. Kushner has not allowed the original text to restrict his options as a playwright. About his second adaptation, *The Illusion* (1992), he wrote in its acknowledgments: "This version of Corneille's *L'Illusion comique* contains several scenes and many speeches which do not appear in the French original. There are virtually no lines directly translated from the French." Kushner continued to adapt texts of world literature for the American stage. For example, he created *A Dybbuk, or Between Two Worlds: Dramatic Legend in Four Acts* (1997), set in late nineteenth-century Poland and adapted from Joachim Neugroschel's translation of Ansky's Yiddish text, and he translated Bertolt Brecht's *Der gute Mensch von Sezuan* (produced 1943; published 1953).

When Weber departed New York, Kushner felt a need to write his play *A Bright Room Called Day*. He notes in *A Bright Room Called Day* that when Weber left, "I felt abandoned, and I compensated for Carl's departure by acquiring a huge appetite for histories, novels and plays about German refugees in the 1930s." At the same time he felt depressed about national and international developments in the mid-1980s. He continues:

> With a grim relentlessness that now seems almost magical, every day brought news of either global failure or some intimate loss. The literature about Germany I was voraciously consuming began to savor nastily of the prophetic. Brecht's description of his era, "When there was injustice only / And no rebellion," seemed frighteningly applicable to the present.

Through *A Bright Room Called Day*, Kushner tried to transform his disappointment into a raising of political awareness in the Reagan era. As he explains in his afterword, he considers it a task of the theater to oppose totalitarian power:

> Those who govern us, in whose hands power is most concentrated, have as their objective, if we can judge by their actions, to bring time to an end, to abolish past and future. That this is so, that these people are who they are, that we have permitted them to wield such power and may permit worse yet, is so fundamentally threatening that we reject immediate knowledge of it. In the grip of that knowledge, every human action, including the making of theatre, would have to be directed toward the abolition of such power and of the systems that maintain it. The brightest hope for the future would be any event, theatrical and otherwise, that presses this knowledge closer to home.

These political considerations and personal experiences are the background for the play, which is set in an apartment in Berlin in 1933. Kushner makes clear in his directions that he wants not a realistic set but one that is "wonderfully warm and inviting . . . verging on the fantastical," suggesting that, rather than giving a historical account, he is trying to convey emotional responses to external events. Those events are illustrated or announced through

slides. Fittingly the first series of slides shows a woman at a rally for Hitler. Unlike everyone around her, the woman is not giving the Nazi salute. This gesture announces the main tension explored in *A Bright Room Called Day*, principles and individual freedom versus compliance with dictates and norms. By concentrating on a group of outsiders, including two actresses, a homosexual man, an émigré cinematographer, and two functionaries of the Communist Party, in the Germany of 1932–1933, Kushner expresses his conviction that choices are possible even in the face of a seemingly unstoppable catastrophe. As he explains in his afterword:

> I concentrated on the history of the last phase of the collapse of the Weimar Republic, rather than on the crimes of the Third Reich, intending to rescue the play from hopelessness by showing a period of choices, when things might have turned out very differently if only. . . . The play's story ends before the worst nightmare begins, but its ending looks to the camps, the bombings, and even to the Bomb. . . . The play is intended as a warning signal, not a prediction, but I often ask myself: Is it politically effective? Will it galvanize an audience to action or, less ambitiously, will it make an audience think, argue, examine the present through the example of the past?

To stress that he sees parallels between Nazi Germany and Reagan-era America, Kushner introduces the figure of Zillah Katz, a nonconformist "contemporary American Jewish woman. . . . with Anarcho-Punk tendencies" who links the play's German past with the American present. Kushner's production notes specify, "There should be a continual updating of the specifics of Zillah's politics of paranoia, in the form of references to whatever evildoing is prevalent at the time of production." The present, Kushner believes, must be seen in the light of the past, which is why he prefaces the play with a historical note on the Weimar Republic. He has Zillah point out:

Ask yourselves this: it's 1942; the Goerings are having an intimate soiree; if he got an invitation, would Pat Buchanan feel out of place? Out of place? Are you *kidding?* Pig *heaven,* dust off the old tuxedo, kisses to Eva and Adolf. I mean just because a certain ex-actor-turned-President who shall go nameless sat *idly* by and watched tens of thousands die of a plague and he couldn't even bother to say he felt *bad* about it, much less try to *help,* does this mean he merits comparison to a certain fascist-dictator anti-Semitic mass-murdering psychopath who shall also remain nameless? OF COURSE NOT! I mean I ask you— how come the only people who ever say "Evil" anymore are southern cracker televangelists with radioactive blue eyeshadow? None of these bastards *look* like Hitler, they never will, not exactly, but I say as long as they look like they're playing in Mr. Hitler's Neighborhood we got no reason to relax. . . .

I hit the streets at three a.m. with my can of spray paint: REAGAN EQUALS HITLER! RESIST! DON'T FORGET, WEIMAR HAD A CONSTITUTION TOO!

Such sweeping judgments that do not explore the American present at all but simply use passing references are, Bigsby feels, in part responsible for the play's unenthusiastic critical reception. However, Kushner stressed to Szentgyorgyi that Zillah is "not me getting up on stage."

In the 1991 New York Shakespeare Festival version of *A Bright Room Called Day,* Kushner had Zillah move to Berlin in 1990 and live in the same apartment in which the play's main action takes place in 1932 and 1933. In that version Zillah is with the young East German man named Roland, who speaks no English and whose German is, unintentionally on Kushner's part, unidiomatic and sometimes ungrammatical.

A Bright Room Called Day offers little in terms of action. The play rests on conversations that analyze the course of historical events and the individuals' responses to them. The main characters struggle with the choices they have to make: sleeping with the Nazi enemy versus active opposition; hiding from the world versus giving temporary refuge to persecuted communists; saving a friend from Nazi brutality versus accepting employment in the Nazi film industry; emigrating to Chicago, Moscow, or Switzerland versus staying in Berlin. That four members of this circle of artists, nonconformists, and political activists leave illustrates that resistance is failing.

As seen in Agnes, the protagonist and the only character who stays in Berlin, choosing moral commitment creates a sense of disorientation and angst:

> I fear the end
> I fear the way
> I fear the wind
> Will make me stray
> Much farther than
> I want to stray
> Far from my home
> Bright room called day;
> past where deliverance or hope
> can find me.

The play offers no clear antidote to the main figures' sense of loss. As Bigsby notes:

> Not the least of the ironies of the play . . . lies in the fact that the characters . . . themselves inhabit fantasies. . . . Even while inhabiting an historical moment that demands action, they respond to it with political theories, sexual paradigms, adolescent ideas that have no bearing on the brute reality which confronts them. . . . [They are] blind to the fact that they inhabit an altogether more sinister world, which their own confusions . . . and those of the culture that they reflect, have conspired in creating.

Kushner reinforces the disorientation of individual dramatis personae through his dramatic techniques. From Brecht and to a lesser degree from Thornton Wilder, he takes over a *Verfremdungseffekt* (alienation). Kushner discussed Brecht's *Mother Courage* (1941), a play Kushner directed at the University of New

Hampshire, with Carl Weber in an interview later published in Vorlicky's collection, noting "I loved the multifocal, the multiple perspective of it . . . the complexity of signs." It is not mimetic depiction that Kushner is after but an illustration of the conflict's multiplicity. The division of *A Bright Room Called Day* into twenty-five scenes, a prologue, and an epilogue, the interruption of the plot through slides, and particularly the various intrusions of Zillah create a sense of alienation. But Kushner especially departs from realism by introducing the devil in a scene reminiscent of Goethe's *Faust*. The asthmatic, clubfooted prince of darkness, who has "taken up temporary residence in this country," is summoned and appears disguised as Herr Swetts, an Aryan "importer of Spanish novelties." Kushner also introduces Die Alte, a surreal figure reminiscent of Brecht's Mother Courage. Die Alte is "a woman, very old but hard to tell how old—somewhere between 70 and dead-for-20-years. White face and rotten teeth. Dressed in a nightgown, once white but now soiled and food-stained." She appears repeatedly in Agnes's apartment, asking for food and drink, challenging Agnes, and undermining Agnes's sense of reality. On a metaphoric level she is "a bad dream" and Agnes's alter ego. In their culminating standoff

> *Agnes grabs the old woman and begins to drag her towards the door. Die Alte suddenly becomes very strong, and the two women begin to struggle. . . .*
>
> *Die Alte wraps Agnes in a fierce embrace, which transforms as Agnes stops struggling into a tender, enveloping hug. Die Alte rocks Agnes in her arms.*

Symbolically, opposites merge in this scene, just as elsewhere in the play the contrasting choices that the characters can make are depicted as inextricably linked. This is also a common feature of Kushner's work in general. The road taken and the road not taken, the apparently good and the apparently evil, the ho-mophobic and the humane are usually presented not as absolutes but in a dialectical tension.

ANGELS IN AMERICA: A GAY FANTASIA ON NATIONAL THEMES

Kushner's claim to literary fame rests primarily on his seven-hour play *Angels in America*. The two parts of this epic drama, *Millennium Approaches* (1992) and *Perestroika* (1995), have been produced and published both separately and jointly, and debate continues on whether to think of *Angels in America* as one play or as two. This murkiness of boundaries is integral to the play as a whole, including its thematic and technical aspects.

As the subtitle announces, this is *A Gay Fantasia on National Themes*. "Gay" is to be taken here in the double sense of "joyful" and "homosexual." The play is filled with (black) humor, and a central thematic concern is Americans' reactions to homosexuality. However, the play goes well beyond the topics of homosexuality and AIDS. It explores a multiplicity of "national themes," ranging from conservative politics and political corruption via religion, especially the attitudes of Jews and Mormons toward homosexuality, to homelessness to behavioral matters, like love, faithfulness, escapism, and hypocrisy. At the center of this masterpiece in American theater are human relationships. Exploring their complexities, the playwright appeals for replacement of hierarchies and hypocrisy with compassion and commitment.

Kushner worked on *Angels in America* for about three and a half years before a first version was produced in San Francisco in May 1991. About six months before opening night he told Szentgyorgyi that this epic is

> about people being trapped in systems that they didn't participate in creating. The point being we're now in a new world in so many ways, we have to reinvent ourselves. It's the reverse of

Bright Room; the characters need to create their own myths to empower themselves. I think that's the whole point of liberation politics: to try to create new systems.

The titles of both parts, *Millennium Approaches* and *Perestroika,* Mikhail Gorbachev's term for the political changes initiated in the former Soviet Union in the early 1990s, underscore Kushner's conviction that massive transformations on a global scale are under way, and his play is a contribution to discussions shaping those transformations. In *Angels,* as in *A Bright Room Called Day,* he emphasizes that events and systems are not predetermined or inevitable but can be influenced by the choices an individual makes. In this way *Angles in America* is a utopian play.

In another, formal parallel to *A Bright Room Called Day, Angels* is divided into Brechtean scenes with several surreal characters from different times or spheres. While the production notes of *A Bright Room* ask for "something verging on the fantastical," *Angels* goes even further: "The moments of magic . . . are to be fully realized, as bits of wonderful *theatrical* illusion—which means it's OK if the wires show, and maybe it's good that they do, but the magic should at the same time be thoroughly amazing." Kushner creates Brechtean alienation through "a pared-down style of presentation, with minimal scenery and scene shifts done rapidly (no blackouts!), employing the cast as well as stagehands."

The main technical device through which Kushner illustrates the blurring of boundaries is his frequent use of split scenes. On different parts of the stage two separate conversations occur simultaneously, thereby commenting on each other and illustrating the interconnection of seemingly separate issues or relationships. In his preface to *Roderick Hudson* (1876), Henry James states that "relations stop nowhere."

The following scene from *Angels in America* part one illustrates how parallel and intertwined

the situations of different people in different locations can be. Louis has decided to leave his lover Prior, who is dying of AIDS, and Joe has decided to leave his wife Harper because he is starting to come to terms with his homosexuality. An added connection is that Joe and Louis have developed a romantic interest in each other. In the simultaneous conversations of the two couples on the verge of breaking up, many phrases are interchangeable.

The following morning, early. Split scene: Harper and Joe at home; Louis and Prior in Prior's hospital room. Joe and Louis have just entered. This should be fast and obviously furious; overlapping is fine; the proceedings may be a little confusing but not the final results.

HARPER: Oh God. Home. The moment of truth has arrived.

JOE: Harper.

LOUIS: I'm going to move out.

PRIOR: The fuck you are.

JOE: Harper. Please listen. I still love you very much. You're still my best buddy; I'm not going to leave you.

HARPER: No, I don't like the sound of this. I'm leaving.

LOUIS: I'm leaving. I already have.

JOE: Please listen. Stay. This is really hard. We have to talk.

HARPER: We are talking. Aren't we. Now please shut up. OK?

PRIOR: Bastard. Sneaking off while I'm flat out here, that's low. If I could get up now I'd beat the holy shit out of you.

JOE: Did you take pills? How many?

HARPER: No pills. Bad for the . . . (*Pats stomach*)

JOE: You aren't pregnant. I called your gynecologist.

HARPER: I'm seeing a new gynecologist.

PRIOR: You have no right to do this.

LOUIS: Oh, that's ridiculous.

PRIOR: No right. It's criminal.

JOE: Forget about that. Just listen. You want the truth. This is the truth. I knew this when I married you. I've known this I guess for as long as I've known anything, but . . . I don't know, I thought maybe that with enough effort and will I could change myself . . . but I can't . . .

PRIOR: Criminal.

LOUIS: There oughta be a law.

PRIOR: There is a law. You'll see.

Apart from recalling Kushner's own earlier ambivalence about his homosexuality, the passage illustrates the pressures that conventionality places on those whom it labels "deviant." As the parallel situations show, such pressures affect a wide range of relationships, and any course of action is double-edged. Offering no prescribed or generally applicable ideal way of managing such pressures and systems, Kushner's utopianism asks for compassion, tolerance, openness, and the empowerment of individuals to make choices. The dramatic technique of the split scene suggests that issues have complex interrelations, that the boundaries people put up are artificial, and that to make the world a better place requires a diverse range of improvements. Kushner also transcends boundaries by specifically asking the same actor to play a variety of roles. In part one, for example, the twenty-one figures are played by eight actors, who also transcend gender boundaries. The same actor or actress, for instance, plays the widowed older Mormon woman Hannah, a male rabbi, a male doctor, and Ethel Rosenberg.

In terms of narrative technique, Kushner uses the simultaneity of interrelated plot lines. Robert Altman, the director for whom Kushner wrote a screenplay version of *Angels in America,* employed this technique, for example, in the film *Short Cuts* (1993). Although Altman abandoned the idea of filming *Angels,* Kushner pointed out that Altman's *Nashville* (1975) was a narrative model for his play. The multiplicity of Kushner's plots, scenes, times, and realities corresponds to the play's themes. Kushner does not concentrate exclusively on how American society confronts AIDS but addresses a whole range of "national themes." As he recalled in the interview with Cohen, *Angels in America* "was going to be a play about AIDS, gay men, Reagan, and Roy Cohn, and Mormons, and angels." The play's national issues are not discussed abstractly but are always shown in their impacts on individuals. In their complex diversity made personal, Kushner and *Angels in America* recall Whitman, another gay New Yorker concerned with national themes who presented himself in "Song of Myself," section 24, as follows:

> Walt Whitman, a kosmos, of Manhattan the son,
> Turbulent, fleshy, sensual, eating, drinking and
>   breeding,
> No sentimentalist, no stander above men and
>   women or apart from them,
> No more modest than immodest.

For both Whitman and Kushner the political is also the personal, and the one is always inextricably linked to the many, the individual to the community.

Most of the characters in *Angels in America* deviate from what is conventionally deemed the WASP norm in America, or they have traits that contradict their performed identity. Joe is a Republican chief clerk at a federal court, a Mormon who moved from Salt Lake City to New York City, a closeted homosexual. He is married to Harper, "an agoraphobic with a mild Valium addiction" who has imaginary pregnancies and who escapes into media images of Antarctica with the help of an imaginary travel agent based on the man who sold them the airline tickets to come to New York City. Joe's mother Hannah, a Mormon living in Salt Lake City, decides to sell her house and move to New York City when she gets a 4:00 a.m. phone call from her son informing her that he is gay. She is conservative and compassionate, but her religion deviates from the American norm.

These are the main characters in one plot line concerned with Joe becoming more forthcoming about his sexual orientation.

Joe is also a factor in two other plot lines, both of which concern AIDS and dying as well as Jewish identity. The first of these narrative strands revolves around Louis and Prior, who are a couple at the beginning of the play. They split up when Prior is hospitalized for AIDS and Louis develops an interest in Joe. Kushner told Cohen that Louis is "the closest character to myself that I've ever written." Louis struggles with his lover's imminent death and his own inability to deal with it. The relationship between Louis and Prior is further complicated when Belize, a former drag queen and an ex-boyfriend of Louis, becomes Prior's nurse. Kushner has Prior and Harper appear in each other's hallucinations to highlight the similarities in their victim statuses.

The final plot line centers around Roy M. Cohn, a Jewish American New York lawyer and power broker based on a historical figure of that name who was instrumental in bringing about the controversial death sentences and executions of Julius and Ethel Rosenberg on espionage charges in 1953. On the one hand Roy is staunchly conservative and intolerant, and on the other he is a homosexual infected with AIDS. Having misappropriated a client's funds, Roy faces disbarment and therefore pulls all legal and illegal strings available to him.

Both Roy and Louis are homosexual Jewish men struggling to find an adequate response to AIDS, but they are otherwise diametrically opposed, for example, with regard to their political leanings or their humanistic values. Consequently *Angels in America* is also about Jewish identity. In Vorlicky's collection Kushner admits this was not his original intention, but

in the sort of thematic struggle . . . that was going on between Louis and Roy in the two plays, I think I guaranteed that the thing was going to be to a certain extent about being Jewish. And I'm

sort of mystified by that, because I didn't come from a religious family, and I grew up in a Jewish community in the South, but most of my friends were not Jewish. In fact, until I came to New York I had not had any Jewish friends.

As he does in other works, Kushner links Jewishness with unjust suffering and dying.

But Kushner does not limit the outsider, victim status to a Jewish identity or to the present. For example, he introduces two characters named Prior Walter, which is also the name of one of the figures dying from AIDS in *Angels*. The first Prior is the ghost of a thirteenth-century Yorkshire farmer; the second is the ghost of a sophisticated seventeenth-century Londoner. Both are ancestors of the contemporary Prior Walter in the play, and both ancestors died from pestilence, highlighting the "mortal affinities" among the family members.

Much of the play's dynamics—the construction of outsider versus insider, of margin versus center, of deviant versus mainstream—rests on power relations and hierarchies, which are in turn upheld by labels. This becomes apparent when the doctor Henry diagnoses that Roy has AIDS. Henry hesitates to call Roy "homosexual" because this label would designate Roy as deviant, which would contradict and undermine the power Roy wields.

ROY: So say it.

HENRY: Roy Cohn, you are . . . You have had sex with men, many many times, Roy, and one of them, or any number of them, has made you very sick. You have AIDS.

ROY: AIDS. Your problem, Henry, is that you are hung up on words, on labels, that you believe they mean what they seem to mean. AIDS. Homosexual. Gay. Lesbian. You think these are names that tell you who someone sleeps with, but they don't tell you that.

HENRY: No?

ROY: No. Like all labels they tell you one thing and one thing only: where does an individual so identified fit in the food chain, in the pecking order? Not ideology, or sexual taste, but something much simpler: clout. Not who I fuck or who fucks me, but who will pick up the phone when I call, who owes me favors. This is what a label refers to. Now to someone who does not understand this, homosexual is what I am because I have sex with men. But really this is wrong. Homosexuals are not men who sleep with other men. Homosexuals are men who in fifteen years of trying cannot get a pissant antidiscrimination bill through City Council. Homosexuals are men who know nobody and who nobody knows. Who have zero clout. Does this sound like me, Henry? . . .

I have sex with men. But unlike nearly every other man of whom this is true, I bring the guy I'm screwing to the White House and President Reagan smiles at us and shakes his hand. Because *what* I am is defined entirely by *who* I am. Roy Cohn is not a homosexual. Roy Cohn is a heterosexual man, Henry, who fucks around with guys.

HENRY: OK, Roy.

ROY: And what is my diagnosis, Henry?

HENRY: You have AIDS, Roy.

ROY: No, Henry, no. AIDS is what homosexuals have. I have liver cancer.

Kushner criticizes American society for being too wrapped up with labels and for using these labels hypocritically as instruments of power and exclusion. Kushner has a "flackman" of the Reagan administration proclaim the antithesis of the playwright's own political leanings: "It's really the end of Liberalism. The end of New Deal Socialism. The end of ipso facto secular humanism. The dawning of a genuinely American political personality. Modeled on Ronald Wilson Reagan." Kushner's humanism militates against the boundaries that labels reinforce.

The playwright's response stresses the importance of connection and solidarity. As he told David Savran in *Speaking on Stage,* "I realized that the key is the solidarity of the oppressed for the oppressed—being able to see connecting lines—which is one of the things that AIDS has done, because it's made disenfranchisement incredibly clear across color lines and gender

lines." Kushner's theatrical construction of a less-divided world, however, remains tenuous and theoretical. An epitome of this utopia is the play's angel, an ambivalent image of both death and salvation. Continuing in his conversation with Savran, Kushner said the image of an angel crashing through a bedroom ceiling was his point of departure for the play, and this image concludes part one. The directions describe the angel as *"four divine emanations, Fluor, Phosphor, Lumen and Candle; manifest in One: the Continental Principality of America."* After its triumphal entrance, the angel ends *Millennium Approaches* stating, "The Great Work begins: / The Messenger has arrived," thus stressing that an era of new beginnings and potential utopias is opening.

This idea continues in part two, *Perestroika.* Although both Prior and Roy die, the play celebrates the life force. Roy comes back to dominate with his demonic energy. Prior goes to heaven, where he rejects the role of prophet and the valorization of stasis. Instead, he asks for more life. The epilogue, dated February 1990, shows him at the Bethesda angel's fountain in New York City's Central Park, having lived with AIDS for five years. Prior, Louis, Belize, and Hannah are gathered around the fountain, having bridged the differences of gay and straight, victim and victimizer, progressive and conservative. They invoke a new era in which humanism and solidarity replace repressive hierarchies: "The Berlin Wall has fallen. The Ceausescus are out. He's building democratic socialism. The New Internationalism. Gorbachev is the greatest political thinker since Lenin. . . . Perestroika! The Thaw! It's the end of the Cold War! The whole world is changing!" The group shares a vision in which those suffering from AIDS are not ostracized; the healing waters of the fountain of life will flow again.

The concluding vision makes *Angels in America* a celebration of the life force, an exuberant utopia, a plea for humanism and connection, an indictment of exclusionary hierarchies. Comedy and tragedy as well as realism and magic exist in a dialectical tension throughout both parts of the play, and the life-affirming principle gains the upper hand in the end.

Angels in America has received much critical and scholarly attention, including two essay collections and a sizable number of individual articles. Literary scholarship, queer theory, cultural studies, and other approaches have explored aspects of performance and dramaturgy; literary and non-literary models and inspirations; Kushner's uses of history and politics; his concern with identities and boundaries; and the millennial, utopian, and apocalyptic dimensions of *Angels*. Harold Bloom included the play in his *Western Canon: The Books and Schools of the Ages* (1994), and many have praised *Angels in America* as a milestone not only in gay theater but in the history of American drama. The diversity of critical approaches testifies to the complexity of Kushner's play. The overwhelmingly positive reception of *Angels in America* indicates the extent to which Kushner's optimism, outspokenness, and humanistic values appeal to audiences.

SLAVS! THINKING ABOUT THE LONGSTANDING PROBLEMS OF VIRTUE AND HAPPINESS

In 1995 Kushner wrote and produced *Slavs! Thinking about the Longstanding Problems of Virtue and Happiness,* which he described as a "coda" to *Angels in America*. Set in a bleak post-perestroika Soviet world of snow, empty vodka bottles, and carcinogenic industrial and nuclear wastes, the play resembles *Angels in America* because, as Kushner related in an interview with Andrea Bernstein of *Mother Jones,* it reflects that, if you do not know where you are heading, it is difficult to move or to make choices. Inspired by Raymond Williams's statement in "Walking Backwards into the

Future," an essay from his collection *Resources of Hope* (1989), which provided an epigraph and the subtitle, the play attempts to put the "social" back into socialism. "The idea of socialism," Williams writes, "is based on the idea and the practice *of a society.*" In the selection quoted by Kushner, Williams writes, "The very idea of a society—that is, a definite form of human relationships in certain specific conditions at a particular moment in history—is itself comparatively modern." This explains why people thinking about "virtue and happiness" did not "immediately refer the problems to a general human nature or to inevitable conditions of existence; they looked first at the precise forms of the society in which they were living, and at how these might, where necessary, be changed." Following Williams, Kushner gave nearly every highly individualized character a name revealing the "definite form of human relationships in certain specific conditions at a particular moment in history," such that the character's name defines while satirizing his or her role and function in the decaying Soviet society. First Babushka and Second Babushka, described by Kushner as snow sweeps of indeterminate age, seem to represent Mother Russia, depressed by the loss of her children. Alexsii Antedilluvianovich Prelapsarianov is, as his name suggests, both *the world's oldest living Bolshevik, considerably older than ninety,* in Kushner's words, and a man representing a time before the fall of communism, when faith in its virtues propelled the social changes leading to the defeated society of the characters. The play's comedy and tragedy stem from the inability of all characters to function apart from their socially defined roles.

ABOVE AND BEYOND

Kushner's work continues with an autobiographical fiction tentatively titled "The Intelligent Homosexual's Guide to Socialism and Capitalism, with a Key to the Scriptures." A chapter from the unfinished manuscript was published in 1998; it emphasizes that life and work remain inseparable for this author, that his personal concerns are also those of his writing. In this fiction Kushner writes with his characteristic self-irony and sweeping Whitmanesque grandeur. In the afterword of Vorlicky's collection Kushner describes the work:

> The Intelligent Homosexual is midway through his fortieth year. I have been observing him all my life. He is busy with his life's work, a massive book running to many volumes entitled *The Intelligent Homosexual's Guide to Socialism and Capitalism, with a Key to the Scriptures.* He has been writing this book, day after day, for forty years; since parturition he's been writing it, he knows he is working himself to death—though he does not want to die.
>
> Every book he reads is fed into this book, which is insatiable. . . . If it reaches his ears it goes into his book: every droplet of conversation he overhears . . . every idea filched from friends, his lovers' chance observations about anything (in bed or out of it, an elegant British friend's shocking deficiencies in personal hygiene, the tricks he uses to catch the attentions of very young children, his nightmares, the death throes of his dearly beloved, newspaper accounts of calumny and torture, his weight, his bowels, his bibliomania, betrayals, loyalties, losses, generational shifts, night sweats, lapses in judgment and ethics and taste and kindness, films and television, wasted irretrievable hours, missed and misspent opportunities, laziness, cowardice, the lyrics to a thousand Tin Pan Alley tunes . . . , the panic over a face remembered and a name forgotten. . . . Well, you get the idea. . . .)

Selected Bibliography

WORKS OF TONY KUSHNER

PLAYS

Yes, Yes, No, No. In *Three Plays for Young Audiences.* Plays in Process, vol. 7, no. 11. New York: Theatre Communications Group, 1987.

Angels in America: A Gay Fantasia on National Themes. Part 1, *Millennium Approaches.* Toronto: Nick Hern, 1992.

The Illusion. In *Plays.* New York: Broadway Play Publishing, 1992. New ed., New York: Theatre Communications Group, 1994. (An adaptation of Pierre Corneille's *L'Illusion comique.*)

A Bright Room Called Day. New York: Theatre Communications Group, 1994.

Angels in America: A Gay Fantasia on National Themes. Part 1, *Millennium Approaches,* Part 2, *Perestroika.* New York: Theatre Communications Group, 1995.

Slavs! Thinking about the Longstanding Problems of Virtue and Happiness. New York: Theatre Communications Group, 1996.

A Dybbuk, or Between Two Worlds. New York: Theatre Communications Group, 1997. (Adapted from Joachim Neugroschel's translation of S. Ansky's *Dybbuk.*)

Widows. With Ariel Dorfman. London: Nick Hern Books, 1997. (Adapted with Dorfman from Dorfman's *Viudas.*)

Love's Fire: Seven New Plays Inspired by Seven Shakespearean Sonnets: Original Works. With Eric Bogosian et al. New York: Quill, 1998.

Death & Taxes: Hydriotaphia & Other Plays. New York: Theatre Communications Group, 2000. (Contains *Reverse Transcription: Six Playwrights Bury a Seventh*; *Hydriotaphia; or, The Death of Dr. Browne*; *G. David Schine in Hell*; *Notes on Akiba*; *Terminating, or Sonnet LXXV, or "Lass Meine Schmerzen nicht verloren sein," or Ambivalence*; and *East Coast Ode to Howard Jarvis: A Little Teleplay in Tiny Monologues.*)

PLAYS PRODUCED (FIRST PRODUCTION)

Yes, Yes, No, No. St. Louis, Mo., 1985.

A Bright Room Called Day. San Francisco, 1987.

Hydriotaphia; or, The Death of Dr. Browne. New York City, 1987.

Stella. New York City, 1987. (Adapted from Johann Wolfgang von Goethe's *Stella.*)

The Illusion. New York City, 1988. (Adapted from Pierre Corneille's *L'Illusion comique.*)

Angels in America: A Gay Fantasia on National Themes. Part 1, *Millennium Approaches.* San Francisco, 1991.

Widows. With Ariel Dorfman. Los Angeles, Calif., 1991. (Adapted from Ariel Dorfman's *Viudas.*)

Angels in America: A Gay Fantasia on National Themes. Part 2, *Perestroika.* New York City, 1992.

Slavs! Thinking about the Longstanding Problems of Virtue and Happiness. Louisville, Ky., 1995.

A Dybbuk, or Between Two Worlds. New York City, 1997. (Adapted from Joachim Neugroschel's translation of S. Ansky's *Dybbuk.*)

Henry Box Brown, or the Mirror of Slavery. London, 1998.

OTHER WRITINGS

A Meditation from "Angels in America." San Francisco: HarperSan Francisco, 1994.

Thinking about the Longstanding Problems of Virtue and Happiness: Essays, a Play, Two Poems, and a Prayer. New York: Theatre Communications Group, 1995.

CRITICAL AND BIOGRAPHICAL STUDIES

Bigsby, Christopher. "Tony Kushner." In his *Contemporary American Playwrights.* Cambridge: Cambridge University Press, 1999. Pp. 86–131. (Occasionally inaccurate but an adequate overview.)

Bottoms, Stephen J. "Re-Staging Roy: Citizen Cohn and the Search for Xanadu." *Theatre Journal* 48, no. 2:157–184 (1996).

Brask, Per, ed. *Essays on Kushner's "Angels."* Winnipeg, Canada: Blizzard, 1995. (Somewhat mistitled since the collection is almost exclusively concerned with productions of the play in different countries.)

Cohen, Peter F. *Love and Anger: Essays on AIDS, Activism, and Politics.* New York: Haworth, 1998.

Fisher, James. "On the Front Lines of a Skirmish in the Culture Wars: *Angels in America* Goes to College." *On-Stage Studies* 21:6–30 (1998).

———. *The Theatre of Tony Kushner: Living Past Hope.* New York: Routledge, 2001.

Frantzen, Allen J. *Before the Closet: Same-Sex Love from "Beowulf" to "Angels in America."* Chicago: University of Chicago Press, 1998.

Freedman, Jonathan. "Angels, Monsters, and Jews: Intersections of Queer and Jewish Identity in Kushner's *Angels in America.*" *PMLA* 113, no. 1:90–102 (January 1998).

Geis, Deborah R., and Steven F. Kruger, eds. *Approaching the Millennium: Essays on "Angels in America."* Ann Arbor: University of Michigan Press, 1997. (The most comprehensive scholarly appraisal of Kushner's best-known play.)

Kekke, Lasse. "Gay Male Identities in Tony Kushner's Play *Angels in America.*" In *After Consensus: Critical Challenge and Social Change in America.* Edited by Hans Löfgren and Alan Shima. Göteborg, Sweden: Acta Universitatis Gothoburgensis, 1998.

McNulty, Charles. "*Angels in America*: Tony Kushner's Theses on the Philosophy of History." *Modern Drama* 39, no. 1:84–96 (spring 1996).

Montgomery, Benilde. "*Angels in America* as Medieval Mystery." *Modern Drama* 41, no. 1:596–607 (winter 1998).

Muller, Ulrich. "Modern Morality Plays on Broadway: *Jelly's Last Jam* and *Angels in America.*" In *Trends in English and American Studies: Literature and the Imagination—Essays in Honor of James Lester Hogg.* Edited by Sabine Coelsch-Foisner, Wolfgang Görtschacher, and Holger M. Klein. Lewiston, N.Y.: Edwin Mellon Press, 1996.

Quinn, John R. "*Corpus Juris Tertium*: Redemptive Jurisprudence in *Angels in America.*" *Theatre Journal* 48, no. 1:79–90 (1996).

Remschardt, Ralf Erik. "'*History Is about the Crack Wide Open*': Kushner, Parks und die Geschichte im amerikanischen Theater der neunziger Jahre." In *Transformationen: Theater der neunziger Jahre.* Edited by Erika Fischer-Lichte, Doris Kolesch, and Christel Weiler. Berlin: Kothen, 1999.

Savran, David. "Tony Kushner Considers the Longstanding Problems of Virtue and Happiness." *American Theatre* 11, no. 8:20–27 (October 1994).

Tuss, Alex J. "Resurrecting Masculine Spirituality in Tony Kushner's *Angels in America.*" *Journal of Men's Studies: A Scholarly Journal about Men and Masculinities* 5, no. 1:49–63 (August 1996).

INTERVIEWS

Arons, Wendy. "Preaching to the Converted? You Couldn't Possibly Do Any Better!: An Interview with Tony Kushner on September 19, 1994." *Com-*

munications from the International Brecht Society 23, no. 2:51–59 (fall 1994).

Bernstein, Andrea. "Tony Kushner: The Award-Winning Author of *Angels in America* Advises You to Trust Neither Art nor Artists." *Mother Jones,* July–August 1995, p. 59.

Hayes, Jarrod, Lauren Kozol, and Wayne Marat Van-Sertima. "'Stonewall: A Gift to the World': An Interview with Tony Kushner and Joan Nestle." *Found Object* 4:97–107 (fall 1994).

Savran, David. "Tony Kushner." In *Speaking on Stage: Interviews with Contemporary American Playwrights.* Edited by Philip C. Kolin and Colby H. Kullman. Tuscaloosa, Ala.: University of Alabama Press, 1996.

Vorlicky, Robert, ed. *Tony Kushner in Conversation.* Ann Arbor, Mich.: University of Michigan Press, 1998. (The most comprehensive collection of Kushner's own comments on his life and work.)

—JOSEF RAAB AND MELISSA KNOX

William Matthews

1942–1997

For nearly thirty years readers of contemporary American poetry have come to recognize the poems of William Matthews for their wit and wisdom, attraction to paradox, liminal devotion to form, and diversity of subjects and interests. The Matthews signature consists of a terse line steered by precise diction that is equal parts colloquial, intellectual, and playful. His penchant for the epigram often riffs on idiomatic phrases or cliché, which in turn afford his work its swiftness, humor, and pathos. Matthews's poetry has been praised not only for its intellect and technical agility but also for its ability to reconcile and celebrate differences. "To see oneself as struggling," Matthews said in an interview with Molly McQuade collected in *Stealing Glimpses,* "and funny at the same time is the richer and more complicated view." More often than not, Matthews's poetry moves seamlessly from the tragic to the comic, from benign vulgarity to tender irony, from the sardonic to the romantic. Honestly and poignantly, his works offer a complex but accessible confrontation and subsequent revelation of the self that relishes pleasure as much as it laments loss.

A reliable word on Matthews's poetry may come from the poet himself. Here are the closing words from his short essay "Merida, 1969," from his collection of essays, *Curiosities,* in which he recalls both the details and processes that shaped the poem, a sonnet, of the same name:

> My friend [the novelist Russell Banks], an able writer of stories, was coming to visit, and one of the things I was mulling was how stories work.

Fourteen lines was no accident. I've written a number of pale sonnets, unrhymed and in a trimeter or tetrameter line that hovers somewhere between so-called free verse and metrically regular verse. It's a territory I've been attracted to by noticing how the two modes, so often poised against each other in neat and false opposition, want to be each other. . . . [This] satisfied both my need for familiarity and my need for surprise. With luck, then, the poem had a form to become, and I had both the comforts and challenges of an apt form. . . .

> What else should I say about the form? Content is often unsettling or painful in poems, but form is play, a residue of the fun the poet had while working. Of course, like form and content, pain and fun want to be each other. . . .

Matthews's poems are nothing if not ironic and democratic; they layer a collage of diverse obsessions and concerns rendered in a voice balancing casual and comic language with lyricism, eloquence, and intelligence. It should come as no surprise, then, that his poems contain his heroes and influences (Charles Mingus, Babe Ruth, Thelonious Monk, Bud Powell, Oscar Robertson, Vladimir Nabokov) as well as his sources of heartache and grief (his father's death, divorce, a spouse's cancer). The stories of his poems are often stories culled from his life, but they also serve as a representative biography, a cross-sectioning of a common humanity.

Matthews's passions consistently bring to light what it means to grieve and celebrate the world of experience within the realm of poetic language. At first glance, his body of work might seem like a set of loosely connected ideas. A short list of Matthews's subjects and obsessions may draw attention to themselves for their illusion of unlikeness: music and language, play and work, Mingus and Freud (among others), idiom and eloquence, Nabokov and Bob Marley, melody and improvisation, humor and melancholy, opera and jazz, imagination and intellect. What unifies these themes are Matthews's diplomatic handling of them, his impeccable sense of rhythm, perfect timing, and mastery of simile and imagery. Moreover, in Matthews's treatment of his subjects one senses the thoroughness of his thought processes, which demonstrate a genuine concern for his readers.

The Matthews poem basks in its contradictory nature, exhibiting an uncanny ability to fuse, refute, or merely point out the disparate nature of his world. At the same time, his incorporation of vernacular language into conditions that are equal parts comedic, serious, painful, and glorious places Matthews, as the critic Peter Stitt has noted, among the wisest and wittiest poets of his generation. The poet and critic Marvin Bell wrote:

> Matthews is from my generation, which is separating itself into those poets who try to recreate the mystery and depth of the inner life through lush and sometimes hermetic images, or through sophisticated talk about it, and those who try to locate it in the outer world. Because of all the loose talk about the inner life, my generation has had to rediscover the outer life—which is still the shape the psyche makes, out there. . . . When the exact and the unknown show up together, there is the chance to articulate an important quality of life and perhaps the mysterious basis for our certain yet indefinable emotional lives.

Indeed, Matthews's vision is rooted in the outer world (particularly New York City, where he lived the last fifteen years of his life) of modern life and all the anxieties and pleasures that come with it. This world for Matthews is often replete with irony. The mind at work in the poems never loses its composure and ear for the musicality of language, always draws its conclusions from circumstance, individuals, and specific events. His intelligence in poems, frequently mitigated by self-effacement pointing toward our common frailties rather than self-pity, is sincerely human. And while critics have been unable to place him into one poetic "school" or style, his early work sometimes pays homage through imitation to middle-late James Wright, as well as Robert Bly, and W. S. Merwin. Matthews's later work has been compared to that of John Berryman for its wit and idiomatic speech, as well as for its love of jazz.

By the time of his death from a heart attack at the age of fifty-five (he died the day after his fifty-fifth birthday), Matthews's oeuvre consisted of eleven books of original verse; various translations, including the French prose poems of Jean Follain (on which he collaborated with Mary Feeney) and works by the Latin poets Martial and Horace and the Bulgarian poets Ussin Kerim and Vasil Sotirov; and *Curiosities,* a collection of prose on poetry.

LIFE AND CAREER

William Procter Matthews was born November 11, 1942, in Cincinnati, Ohio. At that time his father was in the U.S. Navy, and his parents traveled between bases, among them those in Bremerton, Washington, and Norman, Oklahoma. Matthews spent his first months of life with his father's parents in Cincinnati. In his essay "Durations," the poet recalls his first memory:

> There's a sandbox, a tiny swatch of grainy sidewalk, and—there! it's moving—a ladybug. I have tried again and again to construct a tiny narrative from these bright pops, but they won't connect. They lie there and gleam with promise but won't connect.

Here we can see the initial stimuli of Matthews's vision, the roots of his ironic organizing of contrasts, which blossom as wit and pathos.

At the end of World War II, Matthews's father took a job with the Soil Conservation Service in Ohio. The poet's sister Susan was born soon after, and the family moved to Rosewood, Ohio. The next year they moved to Troy, Ohio. During these early years Matthews was taught to read by his mother. It was an activity he loved for the rest of his life; he was particularly fond of the Sunday comics. He attended local sporting events with his father. Matthews's fondness for baseball and basketball—two subjects that appear frequently in his poems—most likely stemmed from this early exposure. With characteristic honesty Matthews addresses the indelibility of childhood remembrances in "Durations":

> A child's world is small. . . . I don't remember it myself. In 1945 I remember I suddenly had a sister. I saw in the kitchen those puzzling afternoons how the cruelty of the official world, the world history records and by whose accounts I knew to write above that "the war ended," could come into the house and linger, itself a sort of odor. . . . There was a basket over the garage door and the solitude I didn't share with a dog or a pile of books from the library I spent with a basketball. These are, I now think, the imaginary friends a boy has when he is too old to admit to himself he wants an imaginary friend.

In 1954 Matthews traveled to Göteborg, Sweden, as part of the Children's International Summer Villages (CISV), a peace organization whose primary objective was to bring children from different countries together for one month during the summer. Matthews was one of four children selected from Miami County, Ohio. He spent time with children from seven other countries, "playing games I'd never heard of before. And singing, always a hallmark of CISV gatherings, I've learned since." To raise money for the trip, Matthews spoke to local community organizations such as the Lions Club, the Kiwanis, and others. "My presentation," Matthews said in his essay "Durations," "once I'd polished it a little, explained the CISV program, studded

the program with a few boyish jokes, and gave thumbnail sketches of the various delegates pictured in the slides. I taught myself, without ever quite naming the project, to become an effective public speaker." This eagerness to apply himself energetically to a given task would carry over into Matthews's adult and professional life, garnering him a stellar reputation as an instructor and administrator.

In 1955 the Matthews family moved to Cincinnati, where Matthews's father accepted the head post with the U.S. branch of the CISV, a position he earned through volunteer work. This new position required the Matthews family to travel extensively, and by 1965 his parents had settled in England, where his father ran the CISV international office for the next twenty years.

The young Matthews proved to be very bright and finished his high school education at the Berkshire School, near Great Barrington, Massachusetts. He served as the editor of the high school paper and literary magazine. Matthews played basketball while maintaining his commitment to academic excellence. Admitted to Yale in 1961, he studied literature with Cleanth Brooks and John Hollander. In his sophomore year he published poems in *The Sewanee Review*. "It now began to seem possible," Matthews said, "that my dreaminess, obsession, and love of words pointed toward writing or editing or teaching or some combination of the three."

At Yale, Matthews met the poet Marie Harris. They married at the end of his sophomore year, and on December 8, 1963, they had their first child, William. In 1965 Matthews graduated from Yale, and he and his family moved to Chapel Hill, North Carolina. On August 25 of that year, their second son, Sebastian, was born. In 1966 Matthews completed his master's degree at the University of North Carolina. While at North Carolina, he founded, with Russell Banks, the literary magazine and press *Lillabulero,* which he ran and operated until 1974. It was at North Carolina that Matthews had what he called "a crisis of faith." Here are the author's own words on the matter from "Durations":

I was trying to balance family life and my literary ambitions, and uneasy about it because my work—and I could barely call it work, for I was a student—came first, and my family next. Also it seemed clear to me that my work—my studies—was not what I really wanted to do. I could "do scholarship," as the idiom had it, but not with excellence or passion. What seemed to my fellow graduate students the path (*la via diretta*) to the Ph.D. seemed to me a dark wood (*una selva oscura*). . . . My wife resented—how could she not?—the way I could name an obligation and leave the house to meet it. And so I scarcely relished telling her, and so I didn't, how little that obligation truly engaged me, day by day.

And like anyone caught in a mess of his own making, I was angry. And so I began to write poems seriously. I had written and even published a few poems when I was in college. I cared about them furiously while I was writing them and then I was done. Now I wrote and the poems weren't good enough and I thought about them all the time. I was never done. It wasn't that I wrote poems because I knew that was what I really wanted to do. Indeed, I wrote poems to escape thinking about what I really wanted to do. But I wrote them as if some essential honesty in me were at stake—and I think now, as I did then, that it was—and as if writing them so seriously led me to understand that what I really wanted to do was to write poems.

Matthews's road to poetry, then, circumvented what has now become the standard graduate-program-in-writing regimen.

In 1970 *Ruining the New Road* was published by Random House, and Matthews began teaching at Wells College in Aurora, New York. The next year he moved to Ithaca, New York, as he began the first of four years at Cornell University. His second book, *Sleek for the Long Flight,* was written during that time and published in 1972, also by Random House. Matthews was

the writer-in-residence at Emerson College for the 1973–1974 academic year. Also during this time he served as a member of the editorial board for poetry with the Wesleyan University Press (1969–1974) and as an advisory editor for *Tennessee Poetry Journal* (1970–1972). By then, in Matthews's words, his eleven-year-long marriage to Harris had "exhausted itself and collapsed. The boys were brave but hurt."

Matthews then moved to Colorado, where he taught at the University of Colorado at Boulder; his sons lived with him during the school year. In 1974 he was awarded the first of two grants from the National Endowment for the Arts. His third book, *Sticks & Stones,* was published in 1975 by Pentagram Press. For the next ten years Matthews would live on and off with the poet Sharon Bryan. In 1976 he was a visiting lecturer at the Iowa Writers Workshop and served as the poetry editor of the *Iowa Review.* From 1978 to 1983 he was a professor of English at the University of Washington in Seattle, where he ran the creative writing program. His first book of translations, *Removed from Time* (1977), on which he collaborated with Mary Feeney, translated the prose poems of French poet and jurist Jean Follain. In the early 1980s Matthews served on the panel for the National Endowment for the Arts, spent two years as a visiting professor at the University of Houston, and became a member of the board of directors for the Associated Writing Programs, for which he later served as president. In addition, Matthews was awarded fellowships from the Guggenheim Foundation, the National Endowment for the Arts, and the Ingram-Merrill Foundation. Two books, *Rising and Falling* (1979) and *Flood* (1982), were published while he was living in Seattle.

When his son Sebastian left Seattle for college, Matthews moved to New York City. Or as Matthews put it:

I could almost write "came back," for New York had been the preferred weekend destination from boarding school and then from college. . . . The large world, which had beckoned to me first from reading and then from the international outlook CISV and my parents fostered in me, had one of its major crossroads in New York. . . . The rich linguistic pool excited me—all those languages overheard on the streets, and all the dialects of English! . . . All those books, and I might read any of them.

His first year in New York he taught at Brooklyn College and the next at the City University of New York. He also taught at Sarah Lawrence College, Columbia University, and New York University and was a visiting writer at the University of Iowa, the Bread Loaf Writer's Conference, and the University of Michigan. At NYU and Columbia, Matthews taught the works of Dante, Freud, Nabokov, Horace, and Virgil, as well as classes on prosody. From 1984 to 1988 he served as president of the Poetry Society of America.

The poet's mature style blossomed in these years. Matthews's affinity with Freud, in particular, informed *A Happy Childhood* (1984). The remaining collections—*Foreseeable Futures* (1987), *Blues If You Want* (1989), *Time & Money* (which won the National Book Critics Circle Award in 1995), and the posthumously released *After All: Last Poems* (1998), all from Houghton Mifflin—contain the poems for which Matthews is best known. During these years he received a grant from the Lila Wallace-Reader's Digest Fund, and in April 1997 he was awarded the Ruth Lilly Prize from the Modern Poetry Association, one of the United States' most prestigious awards for a poet. His work for organizations such as the Associated Writing Programs, the Poetry Society of America, and the National Endowment for the Arts; his devotedness to his writing peers and—as many pointed out at his memorial service on March 5, 1998—to his friends; and his generosity to students and young writers shed a favored light on the man as well as on his poetry.

RUINING THE NEW ROAD, SLEEK FOR THE LONG FLIGHT, AND STICKS & STONES

Matthews's first three collections—*Ruining the New Road, Sleek for the Long Flight,* and *Sticks & Stones*—work in a primarily neosurrealist mode that was prevalent during the 1960s and 1970s. Many of these poems explore the psyche's interior in what Robert Pinsky, writing in *Poetry,* called "gobbets of poetic diction . . . doing the wildly unexpected." Compressed and cerebral, these early poems move with a tentative self-possession; the casual speaking voice is immersed in immense subjects such as psychoanalysis and national identity. Wit and pathos, the trademarks of Matthews's mature style, are hard to come by in the early books. (The poems from these volumes were reassembled in *Selected Poems and Translations: 1969–1991.*) The poet himself wrote in "Moving Around" (1976, from *American Poets in 1976*) that these poems "were as opaque to the few who read them as they were transparent to me."

Ruining the New Road exhibits elements of the contemporaneous popular style whose dominant figures were Bly, Wright, Merwin, and Mark Strand, among others. There are frequent attempts at deep imagery and by extension a heavy reliance on simile and metaphor. The unconscious is at the root of the poems' diversity of subjects (elegies for jazz masters, the Vietnam War, domestic and family experience). This neosurrealist mode for Matthews was a departure from the British and American canons he had been studying at Yale with Brooks and Hollander. Matthews explained in a 1973 interview in *Ironwood*:

> I didn't write at all for three and half years and I was in graduate school prepared to become a career academic when I started to thumb some copies of *The Sixties,* a magazine which convinced me that poetry could do other things, could be about things that were "interior" or "underground," to use Bly's vocabulary.

Ruining the New Road is comprised largely of tight, well-developed poems. Many of them confront and celebrate the natural world, human nature, and the relationship between the two. One such poem is "The Search Party," which opens the collection and displays Matthews's wit supported by an elaborate metaphorical structure. The poem's narrative details the speaker's fears and hopes as he and his community look for a lost child. In the second stanza we get to the heart of the poem:

> Reader, by now you must be sure
> you know just where we are,
> deep in symbolic woods.
> Irony, self-accusation,
> someone else's suffering.
> The search is that of art.

Through authorial intrusion, Matthews makes explicit the not-always-clear subtext one encounters when reading any poem, experiencing any art. In so doing, he has not only contrasted the "real" narrative on the page with the metanarrative in the minds of the readers; he has also widened the "interior" arena of discussion to include dialogues concerning his stance on the function of art. By the third stanza Matthews broadens this contrast by validating his initial conceit in writing the poem:

> You're wrong, though it's
> an intelligent mistake.
> There was a real lost child.
> I don't want to swaddle it
> in metaphor.
> I'm just a journalist
> who can't believe in objectivity.
> I'm in these poems
> because I'm in my life.

This volley between these two "stories" and how they mirror each other is one of the primary concerns and achievements of Matthews's poetry. The poet also focuses a fair amount of his attention on the reader, without whom, he acknowledges, there would be no poem. The poem concludes:

> You've read this far, you might as well
> have been there too. Your eyes accuse
> me of false chase. Come off it,
> you're the one who thought it wouldn't
> matter what we found.
> Though we came with lights
> and tongues thick in our heads,
> the issue was a human life.
> The child was still
> alive. Admit you're glad.

Whether the story is "true" is, finally, immaterial; the poem's authenticity rests in the search and the processes by which we look for whatever truth exists. In an article for *Poetry,* Alfred Corn commented on "The Search Party":

> Matthews knows his disavowal of metaphor can't finally be accepted; the reader will concede that the event actually happened but will then see it in a context of wider possibilities as well. Neither reality nor interpretation is *necessarily* diminished by this Siamese connection. That's the way the author wants it, finally. . . . Matthews never again so nakedly spells out the problem of poet-reader relations, but almost every one of his poems is an implied dialogue with a future audience, and the courteous touch . . . where we are told our mistake was "intelligent," is reproduced in a thousand other forms.

As Corn points out, "The Search Party" serves as a sort of user's manual not only for *Ruining the New Road* but for Matthews's entire body of work. Matthews's ability to telegraph his audience's reaction—guided by metaphor—breaks open the interior landscape of the poem and transforms it into a social dialogue. This social, or communal, aspect in the poet's work, which more often than not explores the conditions of language and, to a large extent, the human condition, gives rise to such poems as "Bystanders" (from *Flood*), "Familial" (from *A Happy Childhood*), "Fellow Oddballs" (from

Foreseeable Futures), "107th & Amsterdam" (from *Blues If You Want*), "Self Help" and "President Reagan's Visit to New York, 1984" (both from *Time & Money*), and "Morningside Heights, July," "Oxymorons," and "Euphemisms" (all from *After All*).

Some poems in *Ruining the New Road* are less ambitious in conceit but nevertheless carve a distilled image and evoke an emotional texture that is congruent with later poems. "Blues for John Coltrane, Dead at 41" is one such poem.

Although my house floats on a lawn
as plush as a starlet's body
and my sons sleep easily,
I think of death's salmon breath
leaping back up the saxophone
with its wet kiss.

Hearing him dead,
I feel it in my feet
as if the house were rocked
by waves from a soundless speedboat
planing by, full throttle.

The poem aspires to convey emotion—and nothing more. The continuity of imagery—largely that of seascapes, the oceanic unconscious—gives the poem a singular, honed focus. The image of the soundless speedboat is typical of Matthews's early poems: the encroachment of modern life upon nature is addressed imagistically and emotionally rather than didactically. The soundless speedboat rumbles rather than roars and is suggestive of the now-silenced jazz master. Almost cinematic, the concluding lines have a touch of surrealism, but because they are mitigated by simile, the poem avoids slipping into a strictly interior realm. Matthews's poetry always has at least one foot in the daylight world, and with each successive book his poetry climbs out of the deep image into social and public discourse.

What this elegiac vignette lacks, however, is perhaps the aspect of poetry Matthews loved the most: space in which one can move around.

Here are his words from the 1973 *Ironwood* interview:

I like poems with certain holes in them and you go inside the poems first. Secondly you have the experience of knowing what it would be like to be that poem just for that period of time. I find this very important and so I dislike poems which have a resistant surface. I like poems which are more like a—well if they were like a ball they would be more like a lattice-work ball, or a ball made of wrought iron, so that you could move in and out of the thing and there would be enough holes in it. A way that you could swim into it and around.

The epigram—suffused with wit, brevity its primary objective—would supply Matthews the space he sought.

The poems in *Sleek for the Long Flight* are more discursive, less celebratory of change than those in *Sticks & Stones*. The majority of them refer to sleep, night, and dreams; they explore various forms in an attempt to generate energy and fluidity. Matthews works in prose forms, one-line poems, odes, a letter, and a prayer. "The Cat" and "The Snake" pay homage to Pablo Neruda's odes. In these poems Matthews's own voice begins to take shape precisely because of this mimetic project. As in Neruda's odes, Matthews supplies a depiction of the cat that begins with physical detail and seamlessly moves into a metaphysical glow. What Matthews seems to have learned from Neruda is the ability to look long and hard at other beings in order to make psychic sense of their actions in reference to our own. Matthews creates an archetypal cat. What separates Matthews from Neruda is the voice that supplies these observations. The opening lines are characteristic of Matthews's maturing voice:

While you read
the sleepmoth begins
to circle your eyes
and then—
a hail of claws
lands the cat
in your lap.

The little motor
in his throat
is how a cat says
Me. He rasps the soft
file of his tongue
along the inside
of your wrist.
He licks himself.
He's building
a pebble of fur
in his stomach.
And now he pulls
his body in a circle
around the fire of sleep.

The short lines move quickly down the page, but the specificity of detail and freshness of imagination slow us down, encourage us to go back for rereadings. This tension of energy is a primary characteristic of Matthews's voice. Another is the precise diction that contains only traces now of the neosurrealist mode: the sleepmoth, a hail of claws, the fire of sleep. Matthews's phrasing is rooted in the exterior world of physical experience as well as within the unconscious. This is a crucial achievement in Matthews's style, for the later books involve themselves more and more with the social aspect of language, exhibiting a chatty casualness alongside a tightened syntax and experimentation with traditional forms.

Pinsky argued that the language in *Sleek for the Long Flight* is mannered in places, symptomatic of what he called "a new orthodoxy" of "poetic diction of the Silence-Eating School." "Another Beer" possesses some of this language, but it also contains the first glimpses of Matthews's sense of humor and wit. The sixth stanza reads:

Then a beer for the juke box.
I wish it had a recording
of a Marcel Marceau mime performance:
28 minutes of silence,
2 of applause.

The absurdity of listening to a mime performance is humorous enough, but Matthews delivers the necessary punch line, which puns off the expected connotations "silence" brought to poetry at that time, precisely the sort of connotations Pinsky argues against. The context of "silence" here is very much in the public realm—in a bar. The poem's reliance on "silence" shifts from the mysteriousness of the deep image, as it did in other poems, to serving as the setup line. The payoff is laughter and pleasure rather than a reverberation of something mystical inside the unconscious.

In "The Waste Carpet," from *Sticks & Stones,* we see Matthews extending his tonal and conceptual range. With T. S. Eliot's "The Waste Land" (1922) as a backdrop, Matthews's voice immediately strikes the reader as one that is tongue-in-cheek. Again, this is due in large part to the details of the poem:

No day is right for the apocalypse,
if you ask a housewife in Talking
Rock, Georgia, or maybe Hop River,
Connecticut. She is opening a plastic bag.
A grotesque parody of the primeval muck
starts oozing out. And behold,
the plastic bag is magic;
there is no closing it. Soap
in unsoftened water, sewage, asbestos
coiled like vermicelli, Masonite shavings,
a liquefied lifetime subscription
to *The New York Times* delivered all at once.
Empty body stockings, limp, forlorn,
like collapsed lungs. A blithering slur
of face creams, an army of photocopies
travelling on its stomach of acronyms,
tooth paste tubes wrung rigid and dry.
Also, two hundred and one tons
of crumpled bumpers wrapped in insurance
claims, slag, coal dust, plastic trimmings,
industrial excrementa. Lake Erie is returning
our gifts.

Matthews himself is opening up a "grotesque parody." But he does not invoke "The Waste Land" for purely self-serving reasons. Rather, he does so tonally to juxtapose one larger theme of poetry, the crumbling of civilization. The lightness with which the poem begins, told in a voice that we might hear in a television advertisement or read on the covers of supermarket tabloids; the seemingly trivial nature of the contents of the "primeval muck," which grow more and more absurd and damaging; the bastardized Latin neologism "excrementa"—all of these show Matthews purposely riffing on Eliot. The begged comparison to the great master supports the humor, and the humor in turn relaxes us so we more easily accept the hyperbolic litany of which the waste carpet is comprised. As of 1975 this was Matthews at his wittiest.

At nearly 140 lines, this is also the longest poem Matthews had published. He discussed longer poems in a 1972 interview in the *Ohio Review*:

> The short poem is like a flashbulb; it pokes a hole in time. It's like the opening of a lens—something is caught. While in the longer poem the relationship to time is like—I've never done it, but it's what I imagine it to be like on a surfboard. You sort of climb on a little ripple of time, and go as long as you can stay on it.

This is precisely how Matthews moves the waste carpet through the poem. The waste carpet sheds its literal muck, acquiring a mythic dimension in the second stanza, as it "took / the shape of the landscape / it rippled across." It travels west in the third stanza, which opens with echoes of James Wright, circa *The Branch Will Not Break*:

> Outside Ravenswood, West Virginia,
> abandoned cars shine in the sun
> like beetlebacks. The ore it took
> to make the iron it took to make the steel
> it took to make the cars, that ore
> would remember glaciers if it could.
> Now comes another grinding, but not—
> thanks to our new techniques—so slow.

The humor that introduced the poem is replaced with disdain for technology, how it abuses and abandons that which it has produced. Matthews describes a cemetery for junked cars:

> The amiable cars wait still in their pasture.
> Three Edsels forage in the southeast corner
> like bishops of a ruined church.
> There are Fords and Dodges, a Mercury
> on blocks, four Darts and a Pierce-Arrow,
> a choir of silenced Chevrolets.
> And, showing their lapsed trademarks
> and proud grilles to a new westward
> expansion, two Hudsons, a LaSalle
> and a DeSoto.

If the landscape is James Wright's, the rhetoric is unmistakably Matthews's. The anthropomorphisms are surprising and specific, and the particular model names are purposely hung out across three lines so their meanings accrue and resonate musically and ironically. Eventually, the waste carpet engulfs the entire nation, and the telling of the final stages of the apocalypse comes from a voice that, if not calm, then at least is indifferently melancholic:

> While the rivers thickened and fish
> rose like vomit, the students of water
> stamped each fish with its death date.
> Don't let a chance like this go by,
> they thought, though it went by
> as everything went by—towers
> of water flecked by a confetti
> of topsoil, clucked tongues, smug
> prayers. What we paid too much for
> and too little attention to,
> our very lives, all jumbled
> now and far too big in aggregate
> to understand or mourn, goes by,
> and all our eloquence places its
> weight on the spare word *goodbye*.

For Matthews, the world strips itself down to language. What begins as a tongue-in-cheek parody evolves into a quasi-sermon and concludes with ironic pathos. As Bill Christophersen noted, "[Matthews's] refusal to play to expectations [in his later works] would outlast the shaman's penchant for summoning up mind-scapes [found in his earlier works]."

RISING AND FALLING AND *FLOOD*

In *Rising and Falling* and *Flood,* poems on subjects such as child support, jazz legends, and professional athletes are next to those exploring and meditating on memory, language, life, and death. The language shows an authoritative control not previously seen in Matthews's work. Critics and reviewers noted the illusion of spontaneity that distinguishes the work in these volumes, and a tact Matthews acquired from his love of reading and teaching the classical Greeks and listening to jazz.

Jazz's influence on Matthews is evident in *Rising and Falling.* The poems improvise imagistically, whereas poems in his earlier books would conjure one or two neosurrealist deep images. In these poems Matthews riffs on a central image, object, word, or phrase, supplying multiple but emotionally linked interpretations of that subject. "Spring Snow" is one such poem. In it, Matthews bridges childhood and death through a series of images that originate in falling snow:

Here comes the powdered milk I drank
as a child, and the money it saved.
Here come the papers I delivered,
the spotted dog in heat that followed me home

and the dogs that followed her.
Here comes a load of white laundry
from basketball practice, and sheets
with their watermarks of semen.

And here comes snow, a language
in which no word is ever repeated,
love is impossible, and remorse. . . .
Yet childhood doesn't end,

but accumulates, each memory
knit to the next, and the fields
become one field. If to die is to lose
all detail, then death is not

so distinguished, but a profusion
of detail, a last gossip, character
passed wholly into fate and fate
in flecks, like dust, like flour, like snow.

The metamorphoses are quick, but not so quick that they pass by underdeveloped. The continuity of imagery is logically traceable through the voice, which is at once chatty and lyrical. The powdered milk, the newspapers, and the laundry are all coefficients for snow, which is finally a metaphor for language. And it is language that offers the signifiers for what is contained in memory. Like a jazz tune, snow serves as the head or melody, and the imagery and ruminations that follow are the solos borne from that opening. Finally, "Spring Snow" desires and searches not only for new ways of speaking and seeing but ultimately for a reclamation of childhood. Perhaps it is of particular interest because it also can be seen as a precursor to the larger conceit found in *A Happy Childhood.*

In *Flood,* Matthews shifts his unit of measure from the image to the phrase. The poems begin in the outer world of observation and stay there most of the time; only occasionally do they move inward toward self-interrogation. "By-standers" and "Good Company," for example, examine awkward social exchanges and the subsequent divided attention of social gatherings. Likewise, the language makes use of idiom and cliché and renders it fresh, as in "Rose-wood, Ohio":

But soon it's June
usually rainy here, then summer
arrives in earnest, as we say,
with its long, flat light pulling
like an anchor against the sun.

It is the aside, "as we say," embedded between images, that surprises the reader and reinforces the frustrating yet communal nature of language. Other times, Matthews deliberately inserts inelegance for comic effect, as he does in "Pissing off the Back of the Boat into the Nevernais Canal":

It's so cold my cock is furled
like a nutmeat and cold,
for all its warm aspirations
and traffic of urine. 37
years old and it takes me a second
to find it, the poor pink slug,
so far from the brash volunteer
of the boudoir. I arc a few
finishing stutters into the water.

For all its humor and crudeness, however, the poem is ultimately concerned with the schism between body and imagination and how the two mutually destroy and recover themselves:

How much damage to themselves
the body and imagination
can absorb, I think as I drizzle
to sleep, and how much
the imagination makes
of its body of work
a place to recover itself.

The ending is anything but humorous, but without the humor and wordplay the poem would lose its complexity, the dimension of pleasure to be found in self-mockery. This seriousness of purpose at one end and sheer laughter at the other would define Matthews's vision.

A HAPPY CHILDHOOD

A Happy Childhood, published in 1984, was Matthews's watershed book. Drawing upon Freud, Matthews embraces a more discursive and conversational mode as he investigates the psychological aspects of everyday life. David Lehman commented in a review that Matthews "emulates the poet in Freud, fastening on our errors and dreams and accidental patterns as badges of enchantment." David Wojahn wrote that "what saves his work from the stultifying prosiness that afflicts most poets who work in [this] mode is the agility of Matthews's mind and the pointedly didactic intentions of his poems." The poems' tone is relaxed, the syntax supple, while at the same time the diction is precise and the attention to structure rigorous; at no point do the poems devolve into psycho-babble. The elliptical sequence that contains the poems "Good," "Bad," "Right," and "Wrong" anchor and pace the collection's weighty subjects. Other poems have larger conceptual titles, borrowed from Freud as well, such as "Civilization and Its Discontents," "The Interpretation of Dreams," "The Psychopathology of Everyday Life," "Manic," and "Depressive."

Still other poems in *A Happy Childhood* are Matthews's strongest lyrical poems, "Loyal," "Whiplash," and "We Shall All Be Born Again But We Shall Not All Be Saved" among them. Others contain compressed rage. "Masterful," quoted here in full, is one such poem:

They say you can't think and hit at the same time,
but they're wrong: you think with your body, and
    the whole

wave of impact surges patiently through you
into your wrists, into your bat, and meets the ball

as if this exact and violent tryst had been a fevered
secret for a week. The wrists "break," as the bat-
    ting

coaches like to say, but what they do is give away
their power, spend themselves, and the ball
    benefits.

When Ted Williams took—we should say
    "gave"—
batting practice, he'd stand in and chant to himself

"My name is Ted Fucking Ballgame and I'm the
    best
fucking hitter in baseball," and he was, jubilantly

grim, lining them out pitch after pitch, crouching
and uncoiling from the sweet ferocity of excellence.

This is vintage mature Matthews. The loose six-beat line is set up to create room so the poem can meditate—or think, to use the poem's language—on its given subject. That subject begins as baseball, specifically hitting, and more specifically, about arguably the best hitter the game has had, Ted Williams. As the poem moves from couplet to couplet, the focus shifts ever so slightly from what is observed to what that observation represents. Matthews maps the road to excellence, and it is a trip not easily or frequently traveled. Paradox permeates the poem—thinking with the body, patient surges of that body transferred into an inanimate bat, the jubilantly grim Williams, the sweet ferocity of excellence—so strongly that irony becomes not the exception to experience's rule but rather the larger experience itself. An observation of such a world generates frustration in both Williams and Matthews. Both are engrossed in their given work—in the zone, as the sports idiom has it. Williams chants curses and hits long ball after long ball. Singing even as it communicates, the poem slides from sound to sound, the alliteration ("ballgame," "best," "baseball"; "crouch" and "uncoiling"), internal off-rhymes ("wrists" and "tryst"), and assonance ("stand" and "chant") making the poem hiss like a line drive. While the poem desires to amble, and it does, its force surfaces from this type of linguistic control. Finally, Matthews, in his method and message alike, uses baseball as a metaphor for writing.

For all the serious subjects and elaborate conceits at work in Matthews's poetry up to this period, perhaps his most notable trait is his ability to find the good in the world he observes. Matthews's poetic territory contains as much light as it does darkness. In a section from "A Happy Childhood," the poet expounds upon the Wordsworthian theme of childhood commemorated in "Ode (Intimations of Immortality)" and its umbilical connection to the afterlife:

It turns out you are the story of your childhood
and you're under constant revision,
like a lonely folktale whose invisible folks

are all the selves you've been, lifelong,
shadows in fog, grey glimmers at dusk.
And each of these selves had a childhood

it traded for love and grudged to give away,
now lost irretrievably, in storage
like a set of dishes from which no food,

no Cream of Wheat, no rabbit in mustard
sauce, nor even a single raspberry,
can be eaten until the afterlife,

which is only childhood in its last
disguise, all radiance or all humiliation,
and so it is forfeit a final time.

While the subject is not a new one, Matthews elegantly observes and interprets how childhood and the afterlife are at once different and the same, "all radiance or all humiliation." The poet is keenly aware of the paradoxical condition of experience; while we may desire the fusion of certain polarities, they simply cannot be coupled practically and comfortably. Nevertheless, Matthews tries. Here are the concluding lines from "We Shall All Be Born Again But We Shall Not All Be Saved," in which the speaker describes his recuperation from a heart attack:

In this one I'm untethered from my
machines, my mild, green-faced flock,

and can walk around weakly on my own,
can pack my bags and pills and go out
into Boston safe to die some other day.
"How will this change your life?"
My heart will push me along like a good
rhythm section. I plan to notice everything.

Matthews's awareness of the destructive and fertile codependency of the body and the imagination lends much of his work its irony and pathos. One of *A Happy Childhood*'s strongest achievements is Matthews's ability to carry such complex ideas in the most poignant and resonant of images, as he does in "The Interpretation of Dreams":

. . . "Let's go to Gubbio
tonight and eat tortellini."
How long it takes to make them right,

and how they flare up
in the mouth like sunspots,
both dense and evanescent.

Matthews is talking not only about pasta but about the activity of the mind, whether it is dreaming, fantasizing, or, in Matthews's case, writing poems. The tonal range of *A Happy Childhood*—lyrical, intellectual, controlled rage, humorous—led Stitt to write in 1984 in the *Georgia Review* that the volume "cleared the decks of this Freudian version of the past," allowing readers to "look forward to the truly significant work that may lie ahead."

FORESEEABLE FUTURES AND BLUES IF YOU WANT

Foreseeable Futures and *Blues If You Want* are informed by the conversational modes initiated in *A Happy Childhood*. In *Foreseeable Futures*, Matthews employs a stringent approach to form, primarily five three-line stanzas. This book's achievement is that he maintains the loosely conversational tone within his assigned parameters. The wit and apparent lightness of many of the poems yield no easy laughs, but rather relax the readers' minds so we might think with a greater clarity, so we are properly prepared to receive Matthews's understanding of experience. "Wit should be an instrument of poise," Matthews said in an interview with Molly McQuade (published in *Stealing Glimpses,* 1999). "What's humorous should be discovered, rather than sought." Such is the case in the poem "Hope." Here is the poem in its entirety:

Beautiful floors and a lively
daughter were all he'd wanted, and then—
that the dear piñata of her head

not loose its bounty, the girl's
father scored the soles of her new shoes
with a pocketknife, that she not slide

nor skid nor turn finally upside-
down on the oak floors he'd sanded
and buffed slick long before she first

gurgled from her crib. Now he's dead
and she's eighty. That's how time
works: it's a tough nut to crack

and then a sapling, then a tree, and
then somebody else's floor long
after we ourselves are planted.

Matthews's ironic vision relies not only on the specificity of details but also on the anonymous nature of his characters, which are at once intimate and distanced. To describe one's head not only as a piñata, but as a "dear piñata," forges a voice that is simultaneously wise, idiosyncratic, and endearing. If "Hope" is a fable, then as readers we should not only enjoy the poem for its artistic merits—dexterity, levity, pathos, wit, imagery, rhythm—but we should also take heed of what Matthews is "saying": be wary of trivolous ambition, and be aware of the fact that time simultaneously cuts us down and lulls us along toward our most benevolent desires. All in fifteen lines, a testament to Matthews's nimble and sharp mind.

The poem's enjambments and inverted syntax give it its leisurely energy, its illusion of calm spontaneity. In this and many other poems in the book, the loose tetrameter line paces the flourish of the sentences. The poems' economy, their epigrammatic quality, prevents them from slipping into something that could be dismissed as sentimental or histrionic. Behind a façade of simplicity and nonchalance is a precision of craftsmanship that supports wit and irony.

Blues If You Want, despite some of its clever titles—"Every Dog Has a Silver Lining," "Every Cloud Has Its Day"—is also essentially serious. Judith Kitchen commented that "humor is merely the medium through which Matthews can make his observations. It allows him to sidle up to the serious." Jazz surfaces as both the subject for some of his poems and the method in which he wrote the poems. In a 1992 interview Matthews discussed the parallel between jazz and poetry:

It's a sense of procedure rather than subject matter that is the deep link between jazz and poetry. I happen to write frequently about jazz because I write about what I love, but it's the procedural link that interests me the most. . . . Jazz gave me permission to begin composing a poetic language based on the rhythms of the speaking voice: the voice rationalizing to itself, jiving other people, trying to seduce a comparative stranger, explaining why a paper is not ready on time, doing puns and jokes and imitations—in sum, doing the real emotional business of daily life, full of weird quirks and odd lilts.

"It Don't Mean a Thing If It Ain't Got That Swing" is as much about language as it is about jazz, as its borrowed title from Duke Ellington implies. The very structure of the poem is arranged like a jazz tune: intro (including melody, chord structure, and, if sung, lyrics), solos, and outro (which is a repeated version of the intro). Matthews begins and ends the poem with a twenty-two-lined stanza, and in between are nineteen quatrains. Staying true to the jazz form, but in verse, he begins the poem with a straightforward narrative about lovers on the cusp of consummating their relationship. After a little scene setting the details—details that carry Matthews's signature acute observations and turns of phrasing—he begins his first "solo":

> From what follows we turn away,
> for we have manners
> and our lovers need privacy to love
> and talk and talk, for love is woven
>
> from language
> itself, from jokes, pet names and puns,
> from anecdote, from double entendre
> (already invaded by *tendre*), until
>
> our lovers are a kind of literature
> and sole mad scholiasts of it.
> *Inventors at Work,* a sign on the bedroom
> door might say.

The first riff leaps from love and modulates to language, the language of fun, love, laughter—in short, the language of pleasure, the pleasure of language. The self-conscious move found in the parenthetical subtly reinforces the poem's larger concern, a meditation on the birth and function of language.

The shift in the fourth quatrain is a jarring one:

> It wasn't from the gods fire was stolen,
> but from matter
> (decay burning so steadily who'd think to speed
> it up? . . .)

Searching for the origin of language, Matthews begins with the elemental (fire) and recreates the Prometheus myth. In this version Prometheus steals language from heaven, and with tongue in cheek Matthews speculates:

> . . . If I remember
> the story right, he sailed
> to the island of Lemnos, where Hephaestus
>
> kept his forge, stole a brand of fire
> and carried it back in a hollow stalk,
> like smuggling music in a clarinet.
> Who'd think to look
>
> for it there? . . .

In writing the poem—in its structure and subject—Matthews implicitly answers his own question. It's Matthews who looks for language in music, and like any good jazz tune, the language, too, has to swing, to use the idiom. Here "swing" pertains not only to the rhythm of the poetic line—the syncopated rhythms of casual conversation, everyday speech—but also to the swinging from one subject to the next and how each successive subject is part and parcel of the one that precedes it.

Matthews concedes the poem is a fable, and in this one he makes language a "she." By anthropomorphizing language, the poet allows himself to riff a little further on the function of language, how it is used by and how it uses humans:

> . . . She could
> implore and charm, she could convince and scathe,
> pick laughter's lock,
> she could almost glow with her own powers,
>
> but she was the wind's,
> like jazz before recordings. . . .

Like any good poem, this one serves as its own commentary. The attributes Matthews assigns to his female lead, Language, are the same characteristics of his oeuvre. Finally, Language becomes memorable by making a deal with the devil, but in doing so:

> . . . she gave up
> pout, toss, crinkle,
> stamp and shrug, shiver, flout and pucker,
>
> the long, cunning lexicon of the body,
> and thus what we lazily call "form"
> in poetry,
> let's say, is Language's desperate
>
> attempt to wrench from print
> the voluble body it gave away
> in order to be read.

Rarely does Matthews so explicitly state his source of irony in a poem. In the concluding stanza he returns to the lovers who opened the poem, and from there he ruminates on his own condition:

> A snowflake sizzles against the window of my
> hotel room. Ann Arbor, late at night. My bonnie
> lies not over the ocean but over a Great Lake
> or two. Now I lay me down to sleep, I used
> to say, the first great poem I knew by heart.
> Could I but find the words and lilt, there's some
> thing I'd tell you, sweetie. I don't know what
> it is, but I'm on the case, let me tell you,
> the way convicts can tell you all about the law.

Matthews locates the poem in the "real" world, a place separate from fable. The references to nursery rhymes are suggestive of his own introduction to language, and to "find the words and lilt" is the assignment of every poet and every jazz musician. The concluding comparison to convicts is one last modulation; the obsessive and desperate nature in which criminals study the law in order to attain freedom, if not absolution, despite their largely irreversible convictions speaks to Matthews's vision of humanity's relationship with language. We know not what to say, Matthews says, but we keep talking, and at our best, we keep singing. This is the source

of the blues according to Matthews, full of irony, pathos, and provisional joy when we hit the notes we meant to hit.

TIME & MONEY

Time & Money (1995), Matthews's tenth collection, won the National Book Critics Circle Award for Poetry. The poet Richard Jackson wrote that "the book moves from poems about isolation, depersonalization, dissatisfaction, malaise to an incredible sense of healing at the end. This is a book that faces squarely all our fears, frustrations, failures, and makes of them a triumph that is indeed rare." In this book the choices of language are the choices of life. The obsessions and subjects that readers of Matthews have come to recognize surface once more: a trio of Mingus poems, elegies for his father, and poems for his sons. We also see Matthews at the opera and in cheap seats at the old Cincinnati Gardens for a professional basketball game. In others Matthews tells an apocryphal story, serving as a ventriloquist of sorts in poems such as "Old Folsom Prison" and "New Folsom Prison." Most reviewers and critics of this book deemed it Matthews's strongest, citing a refined tightness of the line as well as a clarity and consistency of vision.

This vision is a braver one that stares time directly in the eye, as the poet does in "Time":

> . . . You can't "save time"
> this way or any. Nor, since it can't be
> owned, can it be stolen, though afternoon
>
> adulterers add to the tryst's fevers—
> the codes and lies, the sunlight sieved by blinds,
> the blank sheets and the ink at the brim—the
>   pleased
> guilt of having stolen time. What might they
> do for time, those from whom it got stolen?

As we might have come to expect, Matthews ruminates on the language we assign to time and how it surfaces in everyday life. For him it is an exploration into the language of the condition, first and foremost:

> They bowl, they shop, they masturbate before
> a nap (a spot of body work at O'
> Nan's Auto Service), they finish their day's
> work. To begin thinking about time, we might
> take all the verbs we like to think we do
>
> to time, and turn those verbs on us, and say
> that time wastes us, and time saves and buys us,
> that time spends us, and time marks and kills us.
> We live as direct object of verbs
> we hoped we could command. . . .

Desire for control, however, is a waste of time because, "we must remember this: / dire time hectors us along with it, and so / we might consider thanks." Not all of the poems conclude with such optimism, however. Matthews writes in "Money":

> What's wrong with money is what's wrong with
> love:
>
> it spurns those who need it more for someone
> already rolling in it. . . .
> Money's not an abstraction; it's math
> with consequences, and it's a kind
> of poetry, it's another inexact way,
> like time, to measure some sorrow we can't
> name. The longer you think about
> either, the stupider you get,
>
> while dinner grows tepid and stale.
> The dogs have come in like a draft
> to beg for scraps and nobody's
> at the table. The father works on tax forms.
> The mother folds laundry and hums
> something old and sweetly melancholy.
> The children drift glumly towards fracas.
> None of these usual doldrums will lift
> for long if they sit down to dinner, but
> there's hunger to mollify, and the dogs.

Matthews taps into the universal anxiety over money by focusing on the archetypal, albeit dysfunctional, American family. This family,

representing us all at one time or another, is in short supply, and aren't we all, Matthews implies. And the poem would not be Matthews's without a reference to language and the art of poetry.

The Mingus poems also work on multiple levels. While they are elegies and homages to the great jazz bassist and composer, they are also self-portraits and *ars poeticas*. "Mingus in Diaspora" begins by riffing, or euphemizing, on how to phrase the demise of Mingus:

> You could say, I suppose, that he ate his way out,
> like a prisoner who starts a tunnel with a spoon,
> or you could say he was one in whom nothing
> was lost,
> who took it all in, or that he was big as a bus.

The level of imagination is engaged in something serious—death—but Matthews's witty linguistic agility makes it palatable. Humor here softens the inevitable blow time strikes not just on Mingus, but also on himself, on all of us. We'd better laugh, Matthews implies, because the joke, too, is on us. The words Matthews puts into Mingus's voice are more direct:

> "I just ruined my body." And there, Exhibit A,
> it stood, that Parthenon of fat, the tenant voice
> lifted, as we say, since words are a weight, and
> music.

Matthews teases yet more meaning out of the poem by talking about poetry itself. Again, jazz becomes a vehicle for Matthews to examine his craft and himself:

> You have to pick up The Bass, as Mingus called
> his, with audible capitals, and think of the slow
> years
> the wood spent as a tree, which might well have
> been
>
> enough for wood, and think of the skill the bass-
> maker
> carried without great thought of it from home
> to the shop and back for decades, and know
> what bassists before you have played, and know

how much of this is stored in The Bass like energy
in a spring and know how much you must coax
out.

Replace "Bass" with "poem" and Matthews
could well be describing himself. The parallel between jazz and poetry, between Mingus
and Matthews, is "coaxed" out at the poem's
conclusion:

> . . . Religious stories are rich
> in symmetry. You must release as much of this
>   hoard
> as you can, little by little, in perfect time,
> as the work of the body becomes a body of work.

The control of language is masterful in that it
does what it says. The mimesis is not just to
dazzle, though. The poem finally takes us to the
point in time when what we do becomes who
we are. The symmetry here, too, is rich, as the
last line shows. This is hard-won beauty borne
from the knowledge of experience. Matthews
may not call it beauty, however, as he says in
Time & Money's concluding poem, "A Night at
the Opera":

> . . . They have to hit the note
> and the emotion, both, with the one poor
> arrow of the voice. Beauty's for amateurs.

Whatever he dubs this soul-taxing, soul-making
work—perhaps ". . . hope for accuracy / and
passion, both . . . ," also from "A Night at the
Opera"—Matthews's vision is one that stares at
the thorniest issues of being human and refuses
to be overtaken by them.

AFTER ALL

Matthews's posthumous collection, *After All*
(1998), contains poems centered largely on
death. Christophersen wrote in *Poetry*:

> Throughout these poems, nature is nothing if not
> Darwinian. . . . The spectacle of life being eroded
> by disease or shattered by sudden violence is the
> recurring nightmare of this collection. . . . *After
> All* registers in particular specters of urban
> paranoia and mortality. The book presents a world
> in which rage—the rage not only of jazz legends
> but of cabbies and bicycle messengers, jilted lov-
> ers, bereaved spouses, overwrought patients—is
> rampant and death is a slow burn or a hair trigger.

In characteristic Matthews style, however, the
book is not one-dimensional. Love poems suffused with candidness, humor, and tenderness
balance the book's darker poems. Others lean
more toward the love of language, its capacity
to communicate and please simultaneously.
"Euphemisms" is a poem that jives on the
language of, among other things, death:

> Let's skip those undertakers love, like *pass
> away* and *join the majority.*
> Likewise let's spurn the tittery genteel,
> like *make water* or *ladies of the night.*
> Why *make water* and not *tinkle*?

Under the humor is a desire not to sugarcoat
one of the harshest realities we have: mortality.
Then Matthews quickly reverts back to more
mundane activities and inserts some cute, albeit
sophomoric, humor before he takes on a headier
subject:

> I like the uric whiff of Genesis,
>
> the combination of false modesty
> and grandeur. Instead, let's think how class
> works, and deference, on the British
> woman who spoke mildly to the police
> of "the gentleman who raped me." Is that
> what language is for, to bring us to our knees?

Such interrogation is anything but humorous,
and the quick turn in subject, in true Sopho-
clean fashion, moves from levity (to relax and
entertain) to seriousness (to evoke pathos and
irony). There is nothing glib or trite about the
conceit of this poem . . . anymore. The shift to

serious considerations, such as religious interpretation, social hierarchy, and violence, emphasizes Matthews's point: a matter of consequence is a matter involving language, and vice versa. But the poet does not allow himself, or us, to ruminate too long on such dire subjects and consequences:

> How about phrases without opposites,
> like *legal ethics* or *natural world*?
> Also, surely, *the right to bear arms.*
> What fun it is to scorn those who'd rather
> sound right than think. I count among the charms
> of feeling superior to them that
>
> it makes us the same fools we think they are:
> one touch of smugness makes the whole world
> kin.

Again, humor is the vehicle that allows Matthews to set up his audience. Once more we are prepped to receive something serious, this time an invective on how we abuse language. Matthews is concerned about "language the tool of delight" as well as "language the carrier of information." If the poem is didactic, Matthews is certainly aware of it, as he attempts to defer responsibility by the conclusion:

> We need to unlearn what we think we know
> lest we spool on like answering machines
> until we choke on chatter. Who says so?
> Not I. English itself murmured this prayer.

The second reference to organized religion is no coincidence. Language is a religion of sorts for Matthews. And he is a master theologian. This fresh and painful realization typifies the brilliance of Matthews's later poems.

The vacillation of emotion in "Euphemisms" is microcosmic of the book's larger movement. There are a number of sonnets—"The Place on the Corner," "Rocas del Caribe, Isla Mujeres, 1967," "Prescience," "Vermin," and "Le Quatre Saisons, Montreal, 1979" among them—whose intelligence and wordplay not only demonstrate his skill but also point toward a common suffer-

ing and pleasure. (See also "A Poetry Reading at West Point" and "Inspiration.") Others such as "Dire Cure" and "Defenestrations in Prague" are rooted only in suffering. Hope can be found in the sonnet "The Bar at the Andover Inn," in which Matthews refuses to brood over his marital mishaps and wishes his newly married son well. The right words and exact thoughts escape him, but that does little to deter him:

> The rueful pluck we take with us to bars
> or church, the morbid fellowship of woe—
> I've had my fill of it. I wouldn't mope
> through my son's happiness or further fear
> my own. Well, what instead? Well, something else.

Such tenacity of will allows Matthews to take on the harder subjects and render them with clarity and compassion. "Mingus in Shadow," the final installment of what was started in *Time & Money,* is a fine example:

> What you see in his face in the last
> photograph, when ALS had whittled
> his body to fit a wheelchair, is how much
> stark work it took to fend death off, and fail.
> The famous rage got eaten cell by cell.
>
> His eyes are drawn to slits against the glare
> of the blanched landscape. The day he died,
> the story goes, a swash of dead whales
> washed up on the Baja beach. Great nature grieved
> for him, the story means, but it was great
>
> nature that skewed his cells and siphoned
> his force and melted his fat like tallow
> and beached him in a wheelchair under
> a sombrero. It was human nature,
> tiny nature, to take the photograph,
>
> to fuss with the aperture and speed, to let
> in the right blare of light just long enough
> to etch pale Mingus to the negative.
> In the small, memorial world of that
> negative, he's all the light there is.

This is not about Mingus, the jazz genius, but rather Mingus, the man. And so Mingus becomes a symbol for the human struggle against nature. One master is paying homage to another as only a master can do; the language is precise and jazzy, the alliteration and assonance of "swash" and "washed" almost function onomatopoetically for the waves themselves. But it's also what Matthews says about human nature. The poet Christopher Buckley commented in *Quarterly West*:

Our petty and mercenary ambitions make us small—that we would want to photograph someone in the final stages of his illness, that someone would want to get the setting right in that darkness, is what we come to understand by "tiny nature." And it's the memory, the "shadow" of his talent, which, despite the deteriorating exterior, shows us that the genius inside is the only light left shining through. The best tenors and sopranos sing of such tragic courage, the best jazz too embodies such final flickering of the spirit—the best lives sometimes come to that.

"Mingus in Shadow," then, serves as one of Matthews's last great turns of irony. The poet, too, died too young, whittled by time, nature, and the spending of the body that creates good art. It's a poignant poem above all else, and poignancy is the thread that runs through *After All*; it is what unites the perceived dualities throughout Matthews's entire body of work, as he says in "Blue Notes," from *Foreseeable Futures*:

. . . Each emotion lusts for its opposite—

which is to say, for itself. Our water music every morning rains death's old sweet song, but relentless joy infests the blues all day.

Selected Bibliography

WORKS OF WILLIAM MATTHEWS

POETRY

Ruining the New Road. New York: Random House, 1970.

Sleek for the Long Flight. New York: Random House, 1972.

Sticks & Stones. Drawings by Ray Kass. Milwaukee: Pentagram Press, 1975.

Rising and Falling. Boston: Atlantic-Little, Brown, 1979.

Flood. Boston: Atlantic-Little, Brown, 1982.

A Happy Childhood. Boston: Atlantic-Little, Brown, 1984.

Foreseeable Futures. Boston: Houghton Mifflin, 1987.

Blues If You Want. Boston: Houghton Mifflin, 1989.

Selected Poems and Translations: 1969–1991. Boston: Houghton Mifflin, 1992.

Time & Money. Boston: Houghton Mifflin, 1995.

After All: Last Poems. Boston: Houghton Mifflin, 1998.

OTHER WORKS

"Moving Around." In *American Poets in 1976*. Edited by William Heyen. Indianapolis: Bobbs-Merrill, 1976. (Matthews's contribution to a collection of essays.)

Removed from Time. Translation from the French with Mary Feeney of prose poems by Jean Follain. Tannersville, NY: Tideline Press, 1977. (Pamphlet.)

A World Rich in Anniversaries. Translation from the French with Mary Feeney of prose poems by Jean Follain. Iowa City: Grilled Flowers Press, 1979.

Curiosities. Ann Arbor: University of Michigan Press, 1989. (Essays on poetry.)

The Poetry Blues: Essays and Interviews. Selected by Sebastian Matthews and Stanley Plumly. Ann Arbor: University of Michigan Press, 2001.

CRITICAL AND BIOGRAPHICAL STUDIES

Bell, Marvin. "That We Keep Them Alive." *Poetry* 136:164–170 (summer 1980).

Buckley, Christopher. "Ave Atque Vale." *Quarterly West* 49:238–248 (autumn 1999/winter 2000).

Christophersen, Bill. "Late Night Music." *Poetry* 174, no. 2:99–107 (May 1999).

Corn, Alfred. "Looking toward the Fin de Siècle." *Poetry* 161:286–291 (fall 1993).

Costello, Bonnie. "Orders of Magnitude." *Poetry* 142:106–113 (May 1983).

Foy, John. "Jiving toward the Heart of Speech." *Parnassus* 21:257–272 (1996).

Hicks, Jack. "William Matthews's *Ruining the New Road.*" *Carolina Quarterly* 23:99–101 (spring 1971).

Jackson, Richard. "William Matthews's *Flood.*" *American Book Review* 6:16 (March–April 1984).

———. "A Reverie on What I Love: William Matthews and the Question of Style." *Poetry Miscellany* 26:1–4 (1998).

Kalstone, David. "Lives in a Rearview Mirror." *New York Times Book Review,* July 1, 1984, p. 14.

Kitchen, Judith. "William Matthews's *Blues If You Want.*" *Georgia Review* 46:154–157 (September 1992).

Lehman, David. "William Matthews's *A Happy Childhood.*" *Washington Post Book World,* September 2, 1984.

McQuade, Molly. "The Wit of William Matthews." In her *Stealing Glimpses.* Louisville, KY: Sarabande Books, 1999. Pp. 15–22.

Pinsky, Robert. "Far from Prose." *Poetry* 123:241–247 (January 1974).

Reeve, F. D. "Forces at the Bottom." *Poetry* 118:237–238 (July 1971).

Seidman, Hugh. "William Matthews's *Rising and Falling: Poems.*" *New York Times Book Review,* October 21, 1979.

Shaw, Robert B. "Short Reviews." *Poetry* 150:234–237 (July 1987).

Smith, Dave. "The Second Self: Some Recent American Poetry." *American Poetry Review* 8:33–37 (November–December 1979).

Stitt, Peter. "Resemblances and Transformations." *Georgia Review* 34:428–430 (summer 1980).

———. "Poems in Open Forms." *Georgia Review* 36:675–685 (fall 1982).

———. "Wisdom and Being in Contemporary Poetry." *Georgia Review* 38:859–861 (winter 1984).

West, Paul. "Four Poets." *Washington Post Book World,* May 31, 1970.

Wojahn, David. "Short Review." *Poetry* 146:178–180 (June 1985).

INTERVIEWS

"Talking about Poetry with William Matthews." *Ohio Review* 13:32–51 (spring 1972).

"Interview with William Matthews." *Ironwood* 3:58–69 (1973).

"An Interview with William Matthews." *Words* 2:6–11 (winter 1974).

"A Conversation with William Matthews." *Black Warrior Review* 1:57–77 (spring 1975).

"Interview with William Matthews." *Aegis* 3:50–58 (fall 1975).

"Jazz and Poetry: A Conversation." *Georgia Review* 46:645–661 (winter 1992).

"The Experience of Pleasure, the Pleasure of Experience: An Interview with William Matthews." *Atlantic Monthly Unbound Poetry Pages* (http://www.theatlantic.com/unbound/poetry/antholog/matthews/wmint/htm), October 29, 1997.

—ALEXANDER LONG

John Muir

1838–1914

Just as Henry David Thoreau is seen as inseparable from Walden Pond, Mark Twain from the Mississippi River, and John Steinbeck from the Dust Bowl of the 1930s, John Muir is inextricably linked with the Sierra Nevada of California. From the initial settlement of North America, the vexed relationship between European peoples and a continent they variably wished to exploit and worship has been a dominant theme in American writing and thinking. The theme persists to this day—public conflicts over the use of natural lands and books of nature writing surface at about the same rate. From among the canonized writers who celebrate the natural world—William Bartram, John James Audubon, Thoreau, and John Burroughs, to name a few—John Muir stands out as exerting the most lasting influence on American culture.

Muir, for instance, presided over the political fight to carve a national park out of the region surrounding the Yosemite Valley in California, and in doing so he helped open the first nationwide public discussion in the United States about the protection of wilderness for its own sake. Whereas the world's first national park, Yellowstone, had been created primarily for recreational use, the justification for setting Yosemite aside was its wild nature. Muir took Thoreau's well-known cry, "In wildness is the preservation of the world," and put it into practice, often wielding his own writing as a tool or weapon in the fight for preservation of wild lands. He also cofounded the Sierra Club, which became the most powerful environmental advocacy group in the United States. His words can be found on calendars and greeting cards, and a national monument (Muir Woods) and an Alaskan glacier are named for him.

Muir is a fascinating figure in a related way. His life and work can be seen as interlocking grids charting a more ecological way of living in the world. Muir, as well as he was able, wrote what he lived and vice versa. He claimed that he was a hiker first and a writer second, and writing did not come easily to him. In 1872 he noted in his journal, "No amount of word making will ever make a single soul to know these mountains" (*John of the Mountains: The Unpublished Journals of John Muir,* 1938). Nevertheless, he attempted in his prose to instill in his readers an appreciation for wilderness, and his writing is informed by his scientific understanding, his advocacy, and especially his wonder at the natural world. His scientific acumen and the genuine sense of awe with which he beheld all of nature combine to make Muir and his work compelling among a wide readership of mountaineers, the general public, ecologists, geologists, historians, and literary critics. His words have inspired many to try to know the natural world. And in a world of specialization, Muir provides an example of competence in many fields, of a "naturalist" in the truest sense of the word. Straddling the nineteenth and twentieth centuries, he is a nexus of many different intellectual, emotional, and material influences.

As these influences coalesced, Muir was able to perceive the interrelation of all things. To his way of thinking, the ability to perceive the beauty of interrelationships allowed human beings to participate in them. Beauty was to Muir evidence that God, or some kind of deity, as Muir came to abandon the Calvinist God of his father, exists in the world. In his work, Douglas squirrels, water ouzels, dogs, glaciers, and bristlecone pines all participate in the abundance of life of which the human drama is but a small part. He weights human participation optimistically, and even when he condemns the abuses he saw heaped upon the natural world by the rapidly industrializing culture of his time, he always came back to celebrating the interrelatedness of the human and the nonhuman. Many commentators have seen Muir's coming to this ecological outlook as the result of a kind of conversion experience he underwent as he walked up into the Sierra Nevada for the first time in the summer of 1869 (the same year that Ernst Haeckel, a biologist at Friedrich Schiller University in Jena, Germany, coined the term *ökologie,* or ecology). But a view of the world such as the one Muir came to possess is rarely, if ever, achieved in a burst of insight. It develops over a lifetime of experience.

SCOTTISH BOYHOOD

John Muir was born in Dunbar, Scotland, to Daniel Muir and Ann Gilrye Muir. Daniel Muir was orphaned as a child and raised by relatives, and during his teens he underwent an intense religious experience. He eventually became a Campbellite, whose adherents later evolved into the Disciples of Christ. A strident fundamentalist, he subscribed, among other tenets, to a literal belief in the Bible. This deep belief in the sacredness of a text was passed down to Daniel's son John, although not always in a biblical context. Nature as book or palimpsest surfaces as a prominent metaphor in John Muir's work; in *My First Summer in the Sierra* (1911) he described his surroundings as "a grand page of mountain manuscript that I would gladly give my life to be able to read."

In 1829 Daniel Muir was sent to Dunbar as a recruiting agent for the British army. He married shortly thereafter, bought his release from the army, and upon the death of his first wife, he inherited a substantial amount of property and moved his feed and grain store to a prime business location on High Street. Across the street from his store lived the Gilrye family, and Daniel Muir courted one of the daughters, Ann. Her father had reservations about the marriage because of Daniel's religious zeal, but Ann prevailed and they were married in 1833. A daughter, Margaret, was born in 1834; Sarah followed in 1836; and John Muir was born on April 21, 1838, the first son. In 1840 his brother David was born and three years after that Daniel junior arrived in the world. Finally, in 1846, Ann Muir gave birth to twins, Mary and Annie.

Muir offers his version of his early life in *The Story of My Boyhood and Youth* (1913). This book has been mined for clues as to how Muir developed his ecological worldview, and some interpreters have taken the book on its face value. It is essential to the understanding of both Muir and his work to keep in mind that many of the texts that contain seminal information about Muir's early life were actually written toward the end of his life or published posthumously. In the course of this essay, Muir's books will be discussed as their subject matter becomes relevant to the period under discussion, rather than chronologically by publication date. While there is little argument about the basic facts and time frame of a book like *The Story of My Boyhood and Youth,* students of Muir must remain alert to the fact that the mature ecological insights found in these books may well have been read back into the incidents Muir retells. To keep this in mind, as environmental biographer Steven J. Holmes insists that we do, is to acknowledge that Muir underwent a long development before he came to his most profound insights. Such acknowledgement enhances Muir's cultural status rather than diminishes it, because beneath the myth of ecological prophet that developed around Muir, useful as that myth may at times be, is the story of a complex individual attaining over time an extraordinary awareness of the world around him.

In *The Story of My Boyhood and Youth,* Muir recalls his childhood in and around Dunbar. From the opening paragraph we are told that, "When I was a boy in Scotland I was fond of everything that was wild, and all my life I've been growing fonder and fonder of wild places and wild creatures." In Scotland, Muir and his friends wandered the surrounding hills, roamed the stormy beaches, and played among the ruins of Dunbar Castle. But Daniel Muir worried that too much experience of the world would expose his children to evil, and Muir writes that he was "solemnly warned that I must play at home in the garden and back yard, lest I should learn to think bad thoughts and say bad words. All in vain. In spite of the sure sore punishments that followed like shadows, the natural inherited wildness in our blood ran true on its glorious course as invincible and unstoppable as stars."

The "sure sore punishments" were intense. Muir's father dealt violently with any intransigence, and although it is clear that Muir loved and, to varying degrees, needed his father throughout his life, his father's incessant repression of his son's selfhood profoundly affected Muir and contributed to his eventual movement away from a rigid conception of human beings as sinful creatures inhabiting an evil world. In Muir's later years, his ecological perspective was to some extent achieved by setting his own views in opposition to what he remembered of his father's beliefs and behaviors, which followed Muir like shadows for most of his life.

One of the more positive images that stuck with Muir throughout his lifetime was that of the garden in his Dunbar backyard. This garden seems to be one of the few things that Ann and Daniel Muir openly delighted in. His aunt too had a plot there, where she grew marvelous lilies; Muir, who as a boy was fascinated by flowers, became as an adult an avid botanist. In *My*

First Summer in the Sierra, he writes: "Columbine and larkspur grow on the dryer edges of the meadows, with a tall handsome lupine standing waist-deep in long grasses and sedges. Castilleias, too, of several species make a bright show with beds of violets at their feet. But the glory of these forest meadows is a lily (*L. parvum*)." The lilies stand tall in Muir's memory, and some of the most pleasant times of his life seem to have been shared in the garden of his youth and among the Yosemite lilies. Elsewhere in *My First Summer in the Sierra* he describes "saunter[ing] along the river bank to my lily gardens. The perfection of beauty in these lilies of the wilderness is a never-ending source of admiration and wonder."

Muir's maternal grandparents lived across the street from their Dunbar home, and Muir developed a close relationship with his nurturing grandfather, who read with him and took him for long walks in the country. In *The Story of My Boyhood and Youth* Muir recalls that during one such walk, he and his grandfather sat down to rest on a haystack. Muir "heard a sharp, prickly, stinging cry, and, jumping up eagerly, called grandfather's attention to it. He said he heard only the wind, but I insisted on digging into the hay and turning it over until we discovered the source of the strange exciting sound,—a mother field mouse with half a dozen naked young hanging to her teats."

This passage identifies a few predominant themes and influences in Muir's writing. First, the experience takes place out of doors and involves animals. Muir claims that his discovery was "wonderful" to him, and central to the young child's wonder as presented in this image is his perception of the cycle of life suggested by the young mice clinging to their mother. Also, there can be little doubt that the Scottish poet Robert Burns's influence is felt in this recollection, and the echoes of Burns's poem "To a Mouse" underline Muir's identity as a Scot and suggest his debt to Romantic poetry;

at the same time, the poem hints at Muir's mature worldview in the lines "man's dominion / Has broken nature's social union," and with its insight that the poet is the mouse's "fellow mortal." Referring to the dog Stickeen in the 1909 book of the same name, Muir uses this very wording in writing about an expedition in southeastern Alaska: "Our storm-battle for life brought him to light, and through him as through a window I have ever since been looking with deeper sympathy into all my fellow mortals."

But Muir's relationship to Scotland and to his extended family was to change abruptly. Muir writes in *The Story of My Boyhood and Youth* that one night in 1849 as he and his brother studied by their grandfather's fire, his father entered the room and told them, "You needna learn your lessons the nicht, for we're gan to America the morn!" and, good to his word, the next morning Daniel took three of his children—Sarah, who was thirteen, John, who was eleven, and David, nine years old—to Glasgow, and from there the four sailed to North America. They eventually traveled to Wisconsin, where Daniel established a farm near the town of Montello. Though thrilled by the move, John was sad to have left his elderly grandparents, and he could not have understood that the bulk of the farm work would fall to him at a very young age. In fact, the experience nearly killed him.

WISCONSIN FARM LIFE

The family's first farm was called Fountain Lake, and although his father worked him mercilessly, Muir came to love the area to such an extent that in later life he tried unsuccessfully to purchase part of it from his brother-in-law, with an eye toward preserving it. In one of the most distressing tales of his time on the frontier, Muir tells of an incident after the family had moved nearby to their second farm, Hickory Hill. When they struck sandstone while digging a well, his father ordered Muir to continue the work with masonry tools. Muir describes the many days he spent working alone in the well:

> I had to sit cramped in a space about three feet in diameter, and wearily chip, chip, with heavy hammer and chisels from early morning until dark, day after day, for weeks and months. In the morning, father and David lowered me in a wooden bucket by a windlass, hauled up what chips were left from the night before, then went away to the farm work and left me until noon, when they hoisted me out for dinner. After dinner I was promptly lowered again, the forenoon's accumulation of chips hoisted out of the way, and I was left until night.

One morning he was lowered into the eighty-foot-deep hole and nearly suffocated from the carbonic acid gas, or "choke damp," that had settled in the well bottom. He claims that he held on to awareness through "glimpse of a branch of a bur-oak tree which leaned out over the mouth of the shaft." His father allowed him two days' recovery time and then lowered him down again until he finally struck water at ninety feet. Despite the fact that his "father never spent an hour in that well," the family drank from it "for many a day." It seems probable that on some level, this experience predisposed Muir to his ecstatic responses to the wide vistas of mountains, glaciers, and vast storms at sea.

Muir's father devoted more and more time to Bible study and less and less time to the farm, and the family members performed most of the work—the rest of the family had long since joined Daniel, John, Sarah, and David in Wisconsin. For all his faults, however, Muir's father seemed at times attentive to the natural beauty of the world; he made sure that the family witnessed the aurora borealis, explaining to them in vivid language that the colors in the sky were God's clothing, and he marveled at the intricacy of God's work in the plumage of a bird. At the same time, he was capable of riding his son's favorite horse to death in order to get to a prayer meeting on time. Throughout this confusing and troublesome time on the Wisconsin frontier, Muir also found time to wonder at the beauty around him, and his appreciation of the natural world led him to sense the foolishness of human attempts to subdue nature through endless, life-shortening toil, although he never lost a tendency toward hard work.

While on the farm, Muir took to rising from bed at one o'clock in the morning in order to work on inventions that he thought about during the day as he plowed the fields. His father had forbidden him to sit up nights reading, but he had nothing against his son rising early, although he begrudged John the firewood he needed to read by. Tinkering in the basement in the early morning hours, Muir carved pendulum clocks out of wood, fashioned a bed that would automatically eject him in the morning, and contrived a combined thermometer, hygrometer, barometer, and pyrometer. He wanted to mount one of his clocks on the roof of the barn, but his father would not allow it because he was afraid of drawing a crowd—or unwilling to let Muir assert himself through his craft. One of Muir's inventions, a study desk that automatically placed books from a stack in front of the reader after a designated time, is on permanent display at the Wisconsin State Historical Society.

EDUCATION AND EARLY WRITINGS

In the late 1850s the area around Hickory Hill became more populous, and Muir began to participate in a growing community. Of particular help to him was William Duncan, who lent him books, Sir Walter Scott's novels in particular, and Philip Gray, who set up a lending library in his home, giving Muir access to the classics of literature. His neighbors also began to take notice of him and his inventions, readily acknowledging Muir as a brilliant young man. Muir had thoughts of apprenticing in a machine shop, and in late summer 1860 William Duncan suggested that to get exposure Muir exhibit his inventions at the state fair in Madison. Muir asked his father for monetary and, implicitly, moral support; both were refused, and Muir's brother David drove him part of the way to Madison.

Met with praise at the fair, Muir and his inventions were so well received that he was persuaded to enroll at the new Wisconsin State University in Madison. Intellectually, Muir began to come into his own at the university. One of the primary influences on his life was Professor Ezra Carr, who taught classes in chemistry and geology. Muir became close to the professor, and he also came under the influence of Carr's wife, Jeanne, who was a friend of Ralph Waldo Emerson's. Muir and Jeanne Carr exchanged letters for years, and she appears to have been for a time both his mentor and his muse. His writing developed under the guidance of James D. Butler, whom Muir would encounter by chance in the Yosemite years later. During his studies, Muir was introduced to current scientific ideas about the creation of the earth and the depth of geological time; he was taken with the formal study of botany and was introduced to the thinking of Emerson and perhaps to Thoreau. As Thomas Lyon suggests, the transcendentalist thought of the time drew Muir away from his father's dark Puritanism, and introduced him to a philosophy of light and seeing in which all things are conceived as part of a larger reality. God is both in the world and in human beings. Muir's excitement at such a new latitude of thought must have been intense, and even if in later years Muir came to oppose much of Emerson's anthropocentric thought, Emerson's influence lingered.

At this crucial time in his development, Muir's sense of wonder at the natural world, whether innate, acquired, or both, was underpinned by scientific theory and fact. The interrelatedness he had sensed among the things of the world was now given scientific credence. Muir was to expand upon this nexus of emotional wonder, aesthetic perception, and scientific understanding for the rest of his life. This juncture of feeling, seeing, and fact led him also into the realm of ethics, and his corpus remains one of the clearest statements of an environmental ethic in Western literature.

It took him some time to arrive at this ethical stance, but its underpinnings were certainly set in place at the University of Wisconsin. His thoughts on leaving the university are contained in a famous passage at the end of *The Story of My Boyhood and Youth*: "There with streaming eyes I bade my blessed Alma Mater farewell. But I was only leaving one University for another, the Wisconsin University for the University of the Wilderness." Of course, the situation was far more complex than that. At the time that Muir was at college, South Carolina seceded from the union, initiating the formal hostilities of the Civil War. Muir was opposed to war on all fronts, and he refused to volunteer for the army. By 1863, the draft had been instated, and anti-draft riots were breaking out in cities around the country. Muir was never drafted, but he left the United States for Canada in 1863. There he wandered the forests and worked for a time at a broom factory. He is reticent in his writing about his reasons for going to Canada, but, significantly, his first publication originates from this time. The article—"For the Boston Recorder. THE CALYPSO BOREALIS. Botanical Enthusiasm. From Prof. J. D. Butler"—was taken from a letter Muir wrote to Jeanne Carr, which was sent by Butler to the *Boston Recorder* and published on December 21, 1866. The letter details Muir's discovery of the rare orchid Calypso borealis, or "hider of the north," and Muir later claimed that the two great moments of his life were finding this flower and meeting Emerson in Yose-

mite. In the letter to Mrs. Carr, Muir reveals the ethical position he was then forming:

> How good is our Heavenly Father in granting us such friends as these plant-creatures, filling us wherever we go with pleasure so deep, so pure, so endless. I cannot understand the nature of the curse, "Thorns and thistles shall bring forth thee." Is our world indeed worse for this "thisly curse?" Are not all plants beautiful? Or in some way useful? Would not the world suffer by the banishment of a single weed?

Plants are afforded the ethical consideration normally reserved to humans, and Muir senses that "the curse" he refers to "must be within ourselves." The final question of the quoted passage is one Muir put directly or implied in all of his subsequent work. In the context of the war just ended in the United States, this passage is poignant. If the world is impoverished by the loss of one weed, what can organized mass carnage mean for the world?

After the war, Muir left the Canadian woods. In 1866 he went to work at a manufacturing plant in Indianapolis, where he prospered and was a highly valued employee. He also underwent one of the most traumatic experiences of his life. While he worked on a machine in March 1867, the sharpened end of a file he was using caught in a belt and pierced his right eye, damaging the aqueous humor and temporarily blinding him. On the initial diagnosis, Muir was told that he would never see from the right eye again. However, after remaining in a darkened room for four weeks he regained imperfect sight in his right eye and full sight in the left. During this time he began to think about his love of wild places and to weigh his future options. Having almost lost the use of his eyes, he naturally wanted to see things. He considered traveling to the Amazon in the footsteps of Alexander von Humboldt, and according to his biographer Linnie Wolfe, "someone had given him an illustrated folder about the Yosemite

Valley." Upon his recovery, Muir took a trip botanizing on the Wisconsin River and spent some time with his family. Then, on September 1, 1867, Muir took the train to Jeffersonville, Indiana, and the next morning he crossed the Ohio to Louisville, Kentucky, from where he set out for the Gulf of Mexico.

A THOUSAND-MILE WALK TO THE GULF

A Thousand-Mile Walk to the Gulf (1916) narrates the story of Muir's journey through the South, still largely ravaged by the war. *A Thousand-Mile Walk to the Gulf* was published posthumously from the journal Muir kept during his trip, and once again caution must be exercised when reading the published text. There is ample evidence that the journals are revised, and that the book we have is, at least in part, a retelling of actual events inflected with Muir's later perspective. (Steven J. Holmes discusses the journals that provide the basis for *A Thousand-Mile Walk to the Gulf* and *My First Summer in the Sierra* in his *The Young John Muir* [1999]). Muir's route south took him through Kentucky, Tennessee, the western corner of North Carolina, Georgia, by steamer from Savannah to Fernandina, Florida, and then across Florida to Cedar Keys on the Gulf Coast. During this trip, Muir is consistently disturbed by the condition of the land and the people due to the war, and he is also dismayed by what he perceives as the backwardness of the population. It was in the South that, for the first time in his life, Muir encountered significant numbers of African Americans, and his sometimes racist comments are difficult to come to terms with—it is disappointing, at the very least, that someone who viewed the world in an ecological way would avail himself of contemporary cultural stereotypes of African Americans. Though his perceptions are often ambiguous—he sees a black family around a fire in the Florida woods and perceives them as both Edenic and Sa-

tanic—there is no way to explain his early racism away. Although he certainly opposed slavery, and although late in life he revised his early views on both African Americans and Native Americans, his comments in this book detract from its appeal.

A Thousand-Mile Walk to the Gulf must be read as Muir's search for himself, and perhaps, as Holmes suggests, his reliance on racial stereotypes served as a foil in his own attempts at self-definition. Muir also came to a more immediate understanding of the cyclic nature of life when he camped for a few days in the Bonaventura cemetery outside of Savannah, awaiting money to be wired him and living off crackers. The beauty of the cemetery, with its live oaks draped with Spanish moss, caused Muir to reflect on mortality:

> But let children walk with Nature, let them see the beautiful blendings and communions of death and life, their joyous inseparable unity, as taught in woods and meadows, plains and mountains and streams of our blessed star, and they will learn that death is stingless indeed, and as beautiful as life, and that the grave has no victory, for it never fights. All is divine harmony.

Muir's focus on death is natural considering where he was, but it also seems either prescient or achieved through hindsight, because by the time he reached Cedar Keys he fell deathly ill with malaria. Perhaps his illness and near death caused him once again to see that "the universe would be incomplete without man; but it would also be incomplete without the smallest trans-microscopic creature that dwells beyond our conceitful eyes and knowledge." To Muir, he and the sporozoan parasites (*Plasmodium*) that caused his malaria exist on a level. A family in Cedar Keys nursed him back to health, and then in January 1868 he took a steamer to Cuba. He then returned to New York, boarded another ship for Panama, crossed the isthmus, and sailed for San Francisco.

There is a gap between the time frame of the journal that is the basis for *A Thousand-Mile Walk to the Gulf* and *My First Summer in the Sierra,* which corresponds to the time between Muir's arrival in California and his first hike into the mountains; the editor William Frederic Badè sought to bridge the gap by appending Muir's essay "Twenty Hill Hollow" to the end of *A Thousand-Mile Walk to the Gulf.* The essay describes the area where Muir spent the summer of 1868 and the spring of 1869 and was first published in the July 1872 issue of the *Overland Monthly.* One of the most interesting aspects of the essay is that it allows us to track Muir in two passages as he works through the influence of Thoreau and Emerson. The essay as it appears in *A Thousand-Mile Walk to the Gulf* is edited, and one of the passages expunged is an almost verbatim echo of the opening to Thoreau's famous essay "Walking." As quoted by William F. Kimes and Maymie B. Kimes in *John Muir: A Reading Bibliography* (1986), Muir originally wrote, "I wish to say a word for the great central plain of California," whereas Thoreau in "Walking" wished "to say a word for Nature." Muir, following more closely the Thoreau of *Walden,* wished to say a word for a particular landscape, this time the landscape of California. The second passage, near the end of the essay, is an inversion of Emerson. Emerson wrote in *Nature* that "the currents of the Universal Being circulate through me; I am part or parcel of God." At the end of his essay, Muir writes, "Presently you lose consciousness of your own separate existence: you blend with the landscape, and become part and parcel of nature." Notice that in Emerson's version, the Universal Being is focused in the individual human being. Not so in Muir; he has reversed the relationship—the individual dissolves into the landscape; thus the emphasis shifts from an egocentric understanding of the Universal to an ecocentric understanding of a particular landscape. In Muir's essay, God becomes nature, perceivable in the California landscape.

MY FIRST SUMMER IN THE SIERRA

Muir left Twenty Hill Hollow in the spring of 1869. That summer, Muir, then thirty-one years old, a shepherd named Billy, a Chinese and a Native American helper, and a Saint Bernard dog named Carlo helped drive a flock of two thousand sheep owned by the rancher Patrick Delaney to high pasture in the Sierra Nevada. This was Muir's first summer among the peaks of California, and over forty years later, in 1911, *My First Summer in the Sierra* appeared, drawn mostly from Muir's journals and notebooks and written when Muir was seventy-three. The original journals of the trip are lost, and *My First Summer in the Sierra* was drawn mostly from three notebooks dated 1887 that are either a revised, reworked, or totally rewritten version of Muir's entries from the summer of 1869. If not a faithful recording of an actual conversion experience, it may well be that with this text Muir attempted to create a conversion experience for the benefit of his readers. *My First Summer in the Sierra* is considered by many if not most commentators to be Muir's outstanding book, and in it can be traced most of Muir's characteristic prose strategies: a focus on process, an unbridled enthusiasm, a presentation of the natural world as flowing, an almost microscopic attention to natural detail, and a consistent use of personification. Muir celebrates a process enacted between human beings and the natural world, as in the following passage:

> We are now in the mountains and they are in us, kindling enthusiasm, making every nerve quiver, filling every pore and cell of us. Our flesh-and-bone tabernacle seems transparent as glass to the beauty about us, as if truly an inseparable part of it, thrilling with the air and trees, streams and rocks, in the waves of the sun,—a part of all

nature, neither old nor young, sick nor well, but immortal.

The ability to participate in the beauty of the natural world was, for Muir, humankind's redeeming characteristic. This perception of beauty situated the human being in an ecological relationship with the physical environment. When writing about this ability to interrelate, most often conveyed through the example of his own person, Muir's stance is unabashedly joyous, and his prose functions to convince the reader of the possibility of engaging in an elevated process of interrelation.

The American philosopher John Dewey said in a noted quote that the mountains are not separate from the earth—not *on* the earth—but rather, they "are the earth in one of its manifest operations"; similarly Muir, when looking out over the Sierra peaks, exclaimed, "How near they seem and how clear their outlines on the blue air, or rather *in* the blue air." Correcting himself in midstatement, Muir revised his observation, preferring to see the mountains not as a picture on a blue canvas, against a static background, but as they exist in a world process. To Muir, humans participate in a process that is philosophical, aesthetic, and ecological, and all expression is a form of interaction between an agent and its environment.

This interaction is often imagined as dynamic and fluid. *My First Summer in the Sierra* retains the journal structure, and the entry for July 19 epitomizes both Muir's writing and his relationship to the world. Beginning the entry with a lyrical description of the dawn, Muir proceeds to describe one of his favorite natural occurrences, a mountain storm: "Now comes the rain, with corresponding extravagant grandeur, covering the ground high and low with a sheet of flowing water, a transparent film fitted like a skin upon the rugged anatomy of the landscape, making the rocks glitter and glow, gathering in the ravines, flooding the streams, and making

them shout and boom in reply to the thunder." The rain runs off the surface of the ground as if that surface were a giant skin, and the weight of the description focuses on the sheet of water in motion. The landscape is described metaphorically as having an anatomy—as a living body—but not necessarily a human one. Muir does not privilege the human body so much as he sees the landscape as a living thing in itself, a glittering, glowing, and gathering organism. Our bodies are our way of having a world, and by endowing the mineral world in this passage with a body, Muir creates a world with a medium for having *us,* if you will, a world with creative sentience.

As the focus shifts from the water running over the ground to the water falling from the sky, Muir begins a marvelous meditation on raindrops:

> Some, descending through the spires of the woods, sift spray through the shining needles, whispering peace and good cheer to each one of them. Some drops with happy aim glint on the sides of crystals,—quartz, hornblende, garnet, zircon, tourmaline, feldspar,—patter on grains of gold and heavy way-worn nuggets; some, with blunt plap-plap and low bass drumming, fall on the broad leaves of veratrum, saxifrage, cypripedium. Some happy drops fall straight into the cups of flowers, kissing the lips of lilies. How far they have to go, how many cups to fill, great and small, cells too small to be seen, cups holding half a drop as well as lake basins between the hills, each replenished with equal care, every drop in all the blessed throng a silvery newborn star with lake and river, garden and grove, valley and mountain, all that the landscape holds reflected in its crystal depths, God's messenger, angel of love sent on its way with majesty and pomp and display of power that make man's greatest shows ridiculous.

What is it about the rain that inspires such ebullience in Muir? These raindrops, and Muir and his readers through them, experience the world intimately, which leads to a sense of harmony and well-being. In Muir's almost microscopic perception of rock crystals, the naming of the minerals becomes incantatory in itself. The raindrops know the cups of flowers, kiss the lips of lilies, and enter into an erotic, celebratory relation with the flora. They land in cells too small to be seen and in enormous lake basins, and the landscape itself binds this whole process together. Finally, the hydrologic cycle is transformed by Muir's imagination into an enormous living entity, and, ultimately, it is the natural, climatic function that gives and sustains life—if and when it ceases to function, so must life on the planet.

Joy and beauty result from an ecological perception of the world. The hydrologic cycle—flow in the largest sense—becomes a messenger of God, something far greater than "man's greatest show." Muir attempts to create a living world of words that opens a new field of experience. At the very heart of this text exist Muir's words as an interface among the writer, the reader, the text, and the natural world upon which the first three depend. Facts and ideas are brought to life in an ecological relationship. The basic fact—the hydrologic cycle—is constellated with the idea—the angel of love—and both have equal value. The culture-based figure of the angel does not take precedence over the life-giving cycle of water. The nonhuman world and the world of the imagination create experience. Both are essential.

It is important to pause here and examine Muir's use of personification. Throughout *My First Summer in the Sierra* and most of his work, Muir refers to plants, insects, and animals as people, insisting upon their integrity as living things in a community of living beings. As opposed to a sentimental, appropriative use of personification to induce an emotional response in the reader, Muir's use of personification seeks to be accountable to both the natural world and to literary expression. When Muir refers to "plant people," for instance, he often lists the plants' scientific names, which are usually coupled to a detailed and ecologically correct description of the plants and their environment. Consistent with his view that human beings are participants in ecological processes, when Muir personifies flowers and bees and squirrels, he insists upon a horizontal relationship between humans and the rest of creation, avoiding a hierarchical perception of the world.

Whether or not *My First Summer in the Sierra* is a faithful rendering of Muir's actual experience in the Sierra, it is certainly a most powerful evocation of the human potential to flourish in an informed, ecological relationship with the natural world. While Muir lived in the Yosemite he began to assemble scientific evidence that the Yosemite Valley was formed by glacial forces. One of the most widely held geological theories up to Muir's time was catastrophism, and the accepted explanation of the origin of the valley—voiced most prominently by Josiah Whitney, the head of the California State Geological Society—was that it was formed in one catastrophic event as the valley floor fell out after the Sierra fault block was tilted to the west. But Muir was familiar with more up-to-date science. During his studies at the University of Wisconsin, he would have heard of the American naturalist Louis Agassiz's work on glaciation in the Alps through Professor Carr. Catastrophism had become dated after the Scottish geologist James Hutton and later the British geologist Charles Lyell advocated uniformitarianism, which holds that geological processes and natural laws now operating to modify the earth's crust have acted in much the same way and with essentially the same intensity throughout geologic time. By observation of geological events today, one can surmise what happened in the past. The past is apparent in the present. This view advocates a far deeper range of geological time, and it implies a continuity in the development of the physical structure of the earth. Charles Darwin read Lyell on his southern expeditions aboard the *Beagle,* and Darwin's theories of evolution are part of the same shift in scientific understanding. Of course, these theories held great appeal to Muir, although he was put off by the idea of competition among species. He intuitively affirmed the continuity of the world, the cyclical nature of life.

Also, this idea of process was amenable to the way Muir did his science. He had joined in the scientific discussion about the formation of the Yosemite by 1871 with his second publication, "Yosemite Glaciers: Ice Streams of the Great Valley," which appeared in the *New York Daily Tribune.* As he explained in this piece, "Two years ago when picking flowers in the mountains back of Yosemite I found a book. It was blotted and storm beaten; all its pages were mealy and crumbly." This "book" was a living glacier that Muir had discovered, which helped him cement his argument that the valley was formed by glacial excavation. His language makes evident his method of fusing scientific analysis with his characteristic literary flair. In an essay titled "Exploration in the Great Tuolumne Cañon," published in August 1873 in the *Overland Monthly,* Muir had more to say about his research methods, and surely he must have infuriated conventional geologists like Josiah Whitney:

> This was my "method of study." I drifted about from rock to rock, from stream to stream, from grove to grove. Where night found me, there I camped. When I discovered a new plant, I sat down beside it for a minute or a day, to make its acquaintance and hear what it had to tell. . . . I asked the bowlders I met, whence they came and whither they were going.

Even though his main intent here seems to be in offering a challenge—Whitney would dismiss him as a "sheepherder" when it became apparent that Muir was correct about the origin of the valley—much of what Muir wrote here held true for him. He came to know the Yosemite Valley more intimately than any living person at the time, and the evidence supporting long glacial excavation in the region was obvious to him. His findings grew out of sustained, intense attention to a local landscape. Muir continued the debate, writing seven articles in 1874–1875 on the glacial history of the Sierra, and his theory is still accepted today, although geologists now maintain that there was a succession of glaciations, not one massive glacial winter, as Muir believed. These essays have been reprinted as *John Muir's Studies in the Sierra* (1960).

ENVIRONMENTAL ADVOCACY

By the middle of the 1870s, Muir had become a fixture around Yosemite Valley, and he was becoming well-known nationally for his writing. In 1872 the British author Theresa Yelverton published a novel, *Zanita: A Tale of the Yosemite,* whose much romanticized main character—Kenmuir—is obviously modeled after Muir. Also during this time, Emerson came to visit, spending time with Muir in his room above a sawmill, where Muir showed him his plant collections. Muir was disappointed when Emerson's entourage would not let the old philosopher camp out under the trees with him, but Muir still felt Emerson to be, as he noted toward the end of his life in his journal, "the most serene majestic, sequoia-like soul I ever met." Although he continued to correspond with Emerson for years (there are eight letters from Muir to Emerson extant), Muir makes clear in *Our National Parks* (1901) that he remained deeply disappointed in Emerson's refusal to camp: "The house habit was not to be overcome, nor the strange dread of pure night air, though it is only cooled day air with a little dew in it. So the carpet dust and unknowable reeks were preferred. And to think of this being a Boston choice! Sad commentary on culture and the glorious transcendentalism." By this time Muir had developed a philosophy that was a mixture of science and emotional and spiritual nearness to the natural world. He had clearly built on, yet moved beyond, Emerson's transcendentalism.

After almost six years, Muir reluctantly came down out of the mountains to live in Oakland and San Francisco, and he committed himself to his writing. He made extended jaunts into the mountains, but never again lived in them except in spirit. By 1875, Muir had published over fifty articles in magazines, scientific journals, and newspapers. By 1879, he was nationally known and an established advocate of the natural world. In that year, Muir became engaged to Louie Strenzel, and they were married in 1880. They had two daughters, Annie Wanda, born in 1881, and Helen, born in 1886. His wife was the daughter of a successful fruit farmer from Martinez, California, and she and Muir settled down on the Strenzel farm, where by all accounts the extended family was close knit and happy. Between his engagement and marriage, Muir made a trip to Alaska, where he met his longtime friend S. Hall Young, a missionary who shared many of Muir's adventures in Alaska. Muir made seven trips to Alaska in all, and his famous dog story *Stickeen* originates in a near-death experience Muir and the dog shared on the Taylor glacier in 1880. The manuscript pages of *Travels in Alaska* (1915), taken from the journals of this trip, were at Muir's bedside when he died. Muir cruised back to Alaska aboard the *Corwin* in 1881, but for the larger part of ten years, he settled down to the life of a hardworking farmer, father, and husband. He was successful, having ample experience working a farm, and he proved as well to be a shrewd businessman.

However, Muir's health and spirit had suffered from the years of hard farm work, and on a trip to the Northwest in July 1888, he received a letter from his wife that urged him to again take up his writing and advocacy. Within the next several years they sold or leased sections of the farm, and Muir turned back to his pen. In 1889 Robert Underwood Johnson, associate editor of the *Century,* formerly *Scribner's Monthly,* was in San Francisco looking for a story on the gold rush. He made contact with Muir, and the two men began talking about the Yosemite and eventually decided to take a trip up to the valley. The Yosemite was not what it had been when Muir first experienced it twenty years earlier. The land had been ceded to the state of California by the federal government in 1864, but the state had not looked after it, and it was heavily logged. Underwood was disappointed when he failed to see the wildflowers for which Yosemite was famous—many of its meadows and lily gardens were trampled by sheep, which Muir called "hoofed locusts." As the two men sat around their campfire they discussed the idea of petitioning the federal government to create a national park out of the Yosemite Valley and the surrounding areas. Muir agreed to write two articles in support of the idea for the *Century,* both of which appeared in 1890, and to draw up a set of proposed boundaries for the park. Johnson, for his part, lobbied in Washington, D.C. Both men were effective. On September 30, 1890, following Muir's specifications almost exactly, Congress passed the bill to create Yosemite National Park, and President Benjamin Harrison signed the bill the next day. The Yosemite Valley itself, however, remained adjacent to the park and under the control of the state of California. Even though the legislation had passed, Muir knew that simply giving Yosemite national park status would not necessarily protect it from utilitarian interests. Johnson came up with an idea for a preservation society, the Yosemite and Yellowstone Defense Association. At the same time, a group of professors from Berkeley and Stanford were attempting to form an alpine club. Muir immediately saw the possibility of merging the two ideas, and on June 4, 1892, the Sierra Club came into legal being. Muir was elected the first president of the club, and he remained in office until his death twenty-two years later.

Shortly after this time, Muir's first book, *The Mountains of California* (1894), appeared. *The Mountains of California* is a collection of previously published essays, and when it was published Muir was fifty-six. One of his most widely read essays, "A Near View of the High Sierra," remains one of the best-known mountaineering essays of all time, and it is a classic example of the nature essay. The title of the essay could just as well indicate Muir's life goal—to see nature as nearly as possible. In a famous passage, Muir describes being paralyzed with fear on the face of Mount Ritter. He recalls that at around 12,800 feet above sea level, about halfway up the cliff face, "I was suddenly brought to a dead stop, with arms outspread, clinging close to the face of the rock, unable to move hand or foot either up or down. My doom appeared fixed. I *must* fall. There would be a moment of bewilderment, and then a lifeless rumble down the one general precipice to the glacier below." Face-to-face with the mountain, Muir is plastered to rock, and this radical nearness initiates a shift in his consciousness.

This shift occurs in the face of the seeming necessity marked by the emphasis on the word "must." Life asserts itself in the face of fear, but in this experience such assertion seems beyond will:

When this final danger flashed upon me, I became nerve-shaken for the first time since setting foot on the mountains, and my mind seemed to fill with a stifling smoke. But this terrible eclipse lasted only a moment, when life blazed forth again with preternatural clearness. I seemed suddenly to become possessed of a new sense. The other self, bygone experiences, Instinct, or Guardian Angel,—call it what you will,—came forward and assumed control. Then my trembling muscles became firm again, every rift and flaw in the rock was seen as through a microscope, and my limbs moved with a positiveness and precision with which I seemed to have nothing at all to do. Had I been borne aloft upon wings, my deliverance could not have been more complete.

In this passage the relationship between "Guardian Angel" and the close observation that is key to Muir's entire canon surfaces again, recalling the image from *My First Summer in the Sierra* where Muir conceives the hydrologic cycle as a messenger from God. Muir is of course a first-class observer of the natural world, and in this passage he is also an accomplished observer of his own process of coming into awareness of his relationship to the natural world. Part of what makes his literary revisions of these intense outdoor experiences so compelling is his close attention to detail—his shift from "Guardian Angel" to "every rift and flaw in the rock." On Mount Ritter he saw into the rock and described the texture of the crystals themselves. It is as if he looks at the world through a microscope, and through his focus on the rock, the self recedes and something else surfaces, crystallizes, guiding Muir upward toward safety. Muir is reticent in identifying exactly what this something is, but it leads him to safe haven and at the same time allows him to see into the structure of the rock; instead of "conquering" the rock face, Muir comes to identify with it. The experience on Mount Ritter might also be seen as a figure for Muir's method of writing generally. This radically close attention gears Muir onto a particular landscape, and the recasting of the experience attempts to gear his readers onto a world as well, a world of words that he hopes will lead people to the actual world. It is in this close contact that Muir finds deliverance, salvation, and it is because of the vital importance of this interface that the natural world, in his view, must be preserved.

In 1891 Congress passed the Forest Reserve Act, allowing the president to create forest reserves now known as national forests, but the protection of public timberlands remained on paper only. Over this issue the split between preservationists and conservationists became and remains a deep cleft. Pressure from many sides was brought to bear on the Cleveland administration to settle the question of forest use, and in 1896 Secretary of the Interior Hoke Smith responded by forming a commission to study the state of U.S. forests. Muir was an adjunct to the commission, whose most powerful voice was Gifford Pinchot. Pinchot would become head of the Interior Department's Division of Forestry in 1898 and was still chief when that agency became the U.S. Forest Service in 1905. While Muir believed in the preservation of wild lands for their own sake, Pinchot's loyalty was to progress and civilization. At first there was a warm friendship between the two men, but their differences came to a head when Pinchot publicly stated his view that grazing sheep did no harm to wild lands and should be allowed in the new forest reserves. These comments made Muir rancorous, and finally he broke off his association with Pinchot. In 1897 the Forest Management Act was passed, which granted timber, mining, and grazing interests access to the national forests.

While the voices of preservation had suffered a setback, Muir did not remain silent on the issues of national parks and national forest lands. In 1901 he collected ten *Atlantic Monthly* articles and published them as *Our National Parks.* The opening of the first essay states Muir's position concisely: "The tendency nowadays to wander in wilderness is delightful to see. Thousands of tired, nerve-shaken, over-civilized people are beginning to find out that going to the mountains is going home; that wildness is a necessity; and that mountain parks and reservations are useful not only as fountains of timber and irrigating rivers, but as fountains of life." His voice was widely recognized, and on a trip to Yosemite in 1903, President Theodore Roosevelt requested that John Muir accompany him. Muir, of course, took the opportunity to bend Roosevelt's ear to his views on the negative effects of timbering and grazing on the forests. Muir also advocated federal protection

of the Grand Canyon and the Yosemite Valley. The battle to recede Yosemite Valley to the federal government was vitriolic, and some of the arguments over the rights of western states to control their own land free from federal regulations are strikingly similar to states' rights debates of the twenty-first century. State Senator John Curtin of California, an attorney for Yosemite concessionaires and a stockman who desired to graze cattle in the region, took his argument to a pitch that rings familiar to present-day Americans; because firearms are not permitted in national parks, he declared: "I would not live under a government that would not let me carry a gun." According to Robert Underwood Johnson in *Remembered Yesterdays,* during their camping trip in the Yosemite, Muir finally asked President Roosevelt about his avid participation in hunting: "Mr. Roosevelt, when are you going to get beyond the boyishness of killing things? . . . Are you not getting far enough along to leave that off?"

Largely because of Muir's influence, Yosemite Valley was returned to federal control in 1906, and part of the Grand Canyon was declared a national monument in 1908. But Muir's success was eclipsed by his wife's death in 1905 and by his daughter Helen's worsening respiratory illness. Muir also entered into the last heartbreaking public battle of his life. Hetch Hetchy Valley is a neighboring valley to the Yosemite, and, according to Muir, nearly as marvelous. Hetch Hetchy was not included within the new national park borders, though it was a designated wilderness preserve. As early as 1882, the valley had been eyed as a site for a possible dam to provide hydroelectric power and drinking water for San Francisco. San Francisco had once before applied for and been denied permission to turn the valley into a reservoir. However, in 1906 the city suffered a great earthquake and fire, and public opinion on the matter shifted. The application was granted in 1908, and Robert

Underwood Johnson and Muir led a national campaign to save Hetch Hetchy Valley. Though Hetch Hetchy is not a name familiar to Americans today, the issues raised in this debate remained part of the political climate. As Roderick Nash wrote, "for the first time in the American Experience the competing claims of wilderness and civilization to a specific area received a thorough hearing before a national audience."

In the heat of this fight, Muir published both *My First Summer in the Sierra* and *The Yosemite* (1912). The final essay in *The Yosemite* is titled "Hetch Hetchy Valley," and in the opening passage, Muir is careful to point out that although places like Hetch Hetchy and Yosemite are beautiful and unique in their own right, they are not exclusive in their need for protection: "Yosemite is so wonderful that we are apt to regard it as an exceptional creation, the only valley of its kind in the world; but Nature is not so poor as to have only one of anything." The implication is that people might benefit from paying more attention to their surroundings— there might be a Yosemite in one's backyard. As he moves along in this essay, as in all his work, Muir calls for a heightened awareness in human beings toward the world in which they live. For him, nothing in the natural world was to be taken for granted, and there is still something to be learned from Muir's stance. We have grown accustomed and resigned to seeing strip malls and parking lots where once were fields, impounded water where once rivers flowed. He praises the beauty of the national parks, whose mandate, according to the Act to Create a National Park Service (1916), is "to conserve the scenery and the natural and historic objects and the wild life therein and to provide for the enjoyment of the same in such manner and by such means as will leave them unimpaired for the enjoyment of future generations." He notes, however, that

like anything else worth while, from the very beginning, however well guarded, [the parks] have always been subject to attack by despoiling gain-seekers and mischief-makers of every degree from Satan to Senators, eagerly trying to make everything immediately and selfishly commercial, with schemes disguised in smug-smiling philanthropy, industriously, shampiously crying, "Conservation, conservation, panutilization," that man and beast may be fed and the dear Nation made great.

Muir ends with a metaphor linking the natural world to religion: "Dam Hetch Hetchy! As well dam for water-tanks the people's cathedrals and churches, for no holier temple has ever been consecrated by the heart of man." However, as Muir was fond of saying, the money-changers were in the temple, and in 1913 President Woodrow Wilson signed the Hetch Hetchy over to the city of San Francisco, and it remains submerged to this day.

Muir was by this time an old man, and he was exhausted from the long fight over the Hetch Hetchy. On a trip to the Mojave Desert to visit his daughter Helen in 1914, he caught a cold that developed into pneumonia, and he died quietly in a Los Angeles hospital on Christmas Eve, December 24, 1914. Muir's work and his life are on one level a testimony to one individual's powerful love of the world. On another, his writing calls for a heightened level of human existence, one that respects and honors a natural world that Muir perceived as almost unbearably beautiful, not only in the majesty of its mountains but in the connections it manifests—between things, people, rocks, trees, animals, and snowstorms alike. His ecological understanding led him to appreciate these connections; as he writes in *My First Summer in the Sierra*, "When we try to pick out anything by itself, we find it hitched to everything else in the universe." As Muir sensed the importance of these connections, his perception shifted. He wrote in *Travels in Alaska*, "Every thing, even the commonest, was seen in new light and was looked at with new interest as if never seen before."

At the turn of the twenty-first century the writings of John Muir continued to be read in a new light, by readers who, in a technological age, felt more and more removed from wilderness. The awe with which Muir wrote about the natural world continued to resonate in readers whose exposure to wild places was increasingly limited to the natural parks that Muir helped create. And Muir's environmental ethic remained politically relevant: Muir inspired the passage in 1906 of the Lacey Antiquities Act, which allows the president to set aside land that is culturally or historically significant. In 1980 President Jimmy Carter used this act to set aside millions of acres of wilderness in Alaska. In 2001 President George W. Bush endorsed opening hitherto protected lands on the coastal plain of Alaska for oil exploration. The Sierra Club joined other environmental groups and activists in its opposition to drilling for oil in the Arctic National Wildlife Refuge.

Selected Bibliography

WORKS OF JOHN MUIR

BOOKS

The Mountains of California. New York: Century, 1894. Reprint, Garden City, N.Y.: American Museum of Natural History, 1961.

Our National Parks. Boston and New York: Houghton Mifflin, 1901.

Stickeen: The Story of a Dog. Boston and New York: Houghton Mifflin, 1909. Reprint, Berkeley, Calif.: Heyday Books, 1981.

My First Summer in the Sierra. Boston: Houghton Mifflin, 1911. Reprint, New York: Penguin, 1997.

The Yosemite. New York: Century, 1912.

Edward Henry Harriman. New York: Doubleday, Page, 1912.

The Story of My Boyhood and Youth. Boston: Houghton Mifflin, 1913.

Travels in Alaska. Boston: Houghton Mifflin, 1915. Reprint, San Francisco: Sierra Club, 1988.

A Thousand-Mile Walk to the Gulf. Edited by William Frederic Badè. Boston: Houghton Mifflin, 1916.

The Cruise of the Corwin. Edited by William Frederic Badè. Boston: Houghton Mifflin, 1917.

Steep Trails. Edited by William Frederic Badè. Boston: Houghton Mifflin, 1918.

COLLECTED WORKS

The Writings of John Muir: Manuscript Edition. 10 vols. Edited by William Frederic Badè. Boston: Houghton Mifflin, 1916–1924.

The Wilderness World of John Muir. Edited by Edwin Way Teale. Boston: Houghton Mifflin, 1954.

John Muir's Studies in the Sierra. Edited by William E. Colby. San Francisco: Sierra Club, 1960.

South of Yosemite: Selected Writings of John Muir. Edited by Frederic R. Gunsky. Garden City, N.Y.: American Museum of Natural History, 1968.

To Yosemite and Beyond: Writings from the Years 1863 to 1875. Edited by Robert Engberg and Donald Wesling. Madison: University of Wisconsin Press, 1980.

John Muir Summering in the Sierra. Edited by Robert Engberg. Madison: University of Wisconsin Press, 1984.

Muir among the Animals: The Wildlife Writings of John Muir. Edited by Lisa Mighetto. San Francisco: Sierra Club, 1986.

Northwest Passages: From the Pen of John Muir in California, Oregon, Washington, and Alaska. Palo Alto, Calif.: Tioga, 1988.

The Eight Wilderness Discovery Books. Seattle, Wash.: Mountaineers, 1992.

John Muir: His Life and Letters and Other Writings. Edited by Terry Gifford. Seattle: Mountaineers, 1996.

CORRESPONDENCE AND JOURNALS

Letters to a Friend: Written to Mrs. Ezra S. Carr, 1866–1879, by John Muir. Boston: Houghton Mifflin, 1915.

The Life and Letters of John Muir. 2 vols. Edited by William Frederic Badè. New York: Houghton Mifflin, 1924.

John of the Mountains: The Unpublished Journals of John Muir. Edited by Linnie Marsh Wolfe. Boston: Houghton Mifflin, 1938.

Dear Papa: Letters between John Muir and His Daughter Wanda. Edited by Jean Hanna Clark and Shirley Sargent. Fresno, Calif.: Panorama West, 1985.

Letters from Alaska. Edited by Robert Engberg and Bruce Merrell. Madison: University of Wisconsin Press, 1993.

MANUSCRIPTS AND PAPERS

The primary archive of Muir's papers is housed at the University of the Pacific, Stockton, California. See also *The Guide and Index to the Microform Edition of the John Muir Papers, 1858–1957,* edited by Ronald H. Limbaugh and Kirsten E. Lewis. Alexandria, Va.: Chadwyck–Healy, 1986, in collaboration with the University of the Pacific.

BIBLIOGRAPHIES

Kimes, William F., and Maymie B. Kimes. *John Muir: A Reading Bibliography.* Second ed., Fresno, Calif.: Panorama West, 1986.

Lynch, Ann T. "Bibliography of Works by and about John Muir, 1869–1978." *Bulletin of Bibliography* 36:71–80, 84 (1979).

CRITICAL AND BIOGRAPHICAL STUDIES

Badè, William Frederic. *The Life and Letters of John Muir.* 2 vols. New York and Boston: Houghton Mifflin, 1924.

Branch, Michael. "'Angel Guiding Gently': The Yosemite Meeting of Ralph Waldo Emerson and John Muir, 1871." *Western American Literature* 32, no. 2:126–149 (1997).

Clarke, James Mitchell. *The Life and Adventures of John Muir.* San Francisco: Sierra Club, 1979.

Cohen, Michael P. *The Pathless Way: John Muir and American Wilderness.* Madison: University of Wisconsin Press, 1984.

Elder, John. "John Muir and the Literature of Wilderness." *Massachusetts Review* 22, no. 2:375–386 (1981).

Fleck, Richard F. *Henry Thoreau and John Muir among the Indians.* Hamden, Conn.: Archon, 1985.

Fox, Stephen. *John Muir and His Legacy: The American Conservation Movement.* Boston: Little, Brown, 1981.

Hansen, Arlen J. "Right Men in the Right Places: The Meeting of Ralph Waldo Emerson and John Muir." *Western Humanities Review* 39, no. 2:165–172 (1985).

Holmes, Steven J. *The Young John Muir: An Environmental Biography.* Madison: University of Wisconsin Press, 1999.

Johnson, Robert Underwood. *Remembered Yesterdays.* Boston: Little, Brown, 1923.

Jones, Holway R. *John Muir and the Sierra Club: The Battle for Yosemite.* San Francisco: Sierra Club, 1965.

Limbaugh, Ronald H. "Stickeen and the Moral Education of John Muir." *Environmental History Review* 15, no. 1:24–45 (1991).

Lyon, Thomas J. *This Incomperable Lande: A Book of American Nature Writing.* Boston: Houghton Mifflin, 1989.

———. "John Muir." In vol. 2 of *American Nature Writers.* Edited by John Elder. New York: Scribners, 1996, pp. 651–669.

McKusick, James. "From Coleridge to John Muir: The Romantic Origins of Environmentalism." *Wordsworth Circle* 26, no. 1:36–40 (1995).

Miller, Sally M, ed. *John Muir in Historical Perspective.* New York: Peter Lang, 1999.

Nash, Roderick. *Wilderness and the American Mind.* New Haven, Conn.: Yale University Press, 1967.

O'Grady, John P. *Pilgrims to the Wild: Everett Ruess, Henry David Thoreau, John Muir, Clarence King, Mary Austin.* Salt Lake City: University of Utah Press, 1992.

Smith, Herbert F. *John Muir.* New York: Twayne, 1965.

Stanley, Millie. *The Heart of John Muir's World: Wisconsin, Family, and Wilderness Discovery.* Madison, Wis.: Prairie Oak, 1995.

Tallmadge, John. "John Muir and the Poetics of Natural Conversion." *North Dakota Quarterly* 59, no. 2:62–79 (1991).

Turner, Frederick. *Rediscovering America: John Muir in His Time and Ours.* New York: Viking, 1985.

Wesling, Donald. "The Poetics of Description: John Muir and Ruskinian Descriptive Prose." *Prose Studies 1800–1900* 1, no. 1:37–44 (1977).

Wilkins, Thurman. *John Muir: Apostle of Nature.* Norman: University of Oklahoma Press, 1995.

Wolfe, Linnie Marsh. *Son of the Wilderness: The Life of John Muir.* New York: Knopf, 1945.

Young, Samuel Hall. *Alaska Days with John Muir.* New York: Fleming Revell, 1915.

—CORNELIUS BROWNE

Dorothy Parker

1893–1967

WITH ITS DARKLY comic view of the human condition, "Résumé," one of Dorothy Parker's most famous poems, evokes the period in the United States between the Allied Powers' bitter victory in World War I and the stock market crash of 1929:

> Razors pain you;
> Rivers are damp;
> Acids stain you;
> And drugs cause cramp.
> Guns aren't lawful;
> Nooses give;
> Gas smells awful;
> You might as well live.

The book of poems in which "Résumé" appeared, *Enough Rope,* became a national best-seller in 1926, the year of its release, running to eight printings. Many of the poems have the spontaneity of Parker's memorable off-the-cuff remarks, although in reality she labored over them, writing with painstaking slowness.

Like Oscar Wilde, Dorothy Parker's fame as a personality overshadows her fame as a writer; like Wilde, she seemed to spout bons mots and epigrams whenever she opened her mouth. She became an icon of popular as well as highbrow culture, so well known that the American composer and lyricist Cole Porter devoted a line of one of his songs to her: "As Dorothy Parker once said to her boyfriend: Fare thee well." Her wit and humor helped to establish the magazines *Vanity Fair* and *The New Yorker,* epitomizing an urbanely ironic perspective that came to characterize these publications. New York remained her spiritual and literary home all her life: the attitude of Hazel Morse, the main character of her short story "Big Blonde," was undoubtedly Parker's own: "There was always something immensely comic to her in the thought of living elsewhere than New York." Hazel turns down marriage proposals from men because they live in Des Moines and Houston and Chicago and, to her, "even funnier places."

Parker's reputation as the voice of the 1920s and the wittiest muse of Manhattan rests on a small but potent output: three slim volumes of poems and two volumes of short stories during her lifetime, and a series of irreverent book and theater reviews. A great strength of her work as a critic lies in her disdain for sentiment. Under her nom de plume Constant Reader she panned A. A. Milne's 1928 children's book *The House at Pooh Corner,* revealing her disgust with this summation: "Tonstant Weader Fwowed up." Tweaking Katharine Hepburn's performance in the 1933 play *The Lake,* Parker wrote that Hepburn "ran the whole gamut of emotions, from A to B." Parker also wrote plays and collaborated on screenplays, but these seldom showcased her originality and mordant humor.

Her life and her remarks became a favorite topic of conversation among the urban smart set; a rhyme she wrote about Oscar Wilde (included in her 1928 book of poems, *Sunset Gun*) caught precisely the attitude of the public toward Parker herself:

> If, with the literate, I am
> Impelled to try an epigram,
> I never seek to take the credit;
> We all assume that Oscar said it.

An entire generation of college students assumed that Dorothy Parker said it, worshipping her as a figure who created new directions for art and life in the late 1920s and early 1930s. Newspaper columnists recorded her remarks, practically every witticism of the day was attributed to her, two Broadway plays were written about her, and a third boasted a character based upon her. Her wit remained dry, self-deprecating, original, the titles of her poems funny in themselves. In "News Item" (in *Enough Rope*), for example, she observes: "Men seldom make passes / At girls who wear glasses." To Parker's chagrin in later years, this poem seemed more remembered than what she considered to be her serious, and more accomplished, verse. The irony of the title, the piquant portrayal of men's and women's traditional roles, ensured that this light verse would be recited ad nauseum at cocktail parties.

Parker, who was nearsighted and wore glasses herself, achieved notoriety for her tempestuously unhappy love life. According to John Keats in *You Might As Well Live: The Life and Times of Dorothy Parker* (1970), after a boyfriend left her, she affirmed that "she would give love another chance . . . but this time on her own terms. 'I require only three things of a man,' she said. 'He must be handsome, ruthless, and stupid.'" Her poetry bears out her lifelong sense of doom about love. In "Unfortunate Coincidence" (in *Enough Rope*), for example, she writes:

> By the time you swear you're his,
>   Shivering and sighing,
> And he vows his passion is
>   Infinite, undying—
> Lady, make a note of this:
>   One of you is lying.

Her cynical humor both expressed and defined the experiences of the increasingly urban, increasingly cosmopolitan post–World War I generation.

A rising star of the literary world in the 1920s, she honed her rapier wit as a member of the famed Algonquin Round Table, a group of otherwise male writers to whom the American critic Edmund Wilson referred as an "all-star literary vaudeville." The historian James R. Gaines, in *Wit's End: Days and Nights of the Algonquin Round Table* (1977), remarked that the group was more than a clique of writers who enjoyed lunching together, having begun to "take shape as a public institution, one defined by the careers of its members and the cravings of a new public taste, of which all of them . . . were becoming public retailers." Situated in the Algonquin Hotel on New York City's West Forty-fourth Street, a short walk from Parker's office at *Vanity Fair,* the Round Table had evolved into a meeting place for some of the best-known journalists and writers of the day, including Alexander Woollcott, Heywood Broun, Franklin P. Adams, John Peter Toohey, Robert Benchley, George S. Kaufman, Marc Connelly, Robert Sherwood, and Harold Ross.

In such society, Parker held court, queen of the repartée. "Wasn't the Yale prom wonderful?" she asked. "If all the girls in attendance were laid end to end, I wouldn't be at all surprised." Hearing that a friend had injured her leg in London, Parker is said to have voiced the suspicion that the woman had been injured while "sliding down a barrister." When a boyfriend ended their relationship after she became pregnant, she was quoted as saying that it served her right "for putting all my eggs in one bastard." Her quips, endlessly repeated, made her a household name. Over many a boozy lunch, Parker delighted literary companions and dropped lines that have been quoted ever since. Asked to use the word "horticulture" in a sentence, she said, "You may lead a horticulture but you can't make her think." As a young professional bored with writing fashion blurbs, she offered the following caption for a photograph of women's underwear in *Vogue*: "Brevity is the soul of lingerie."

In later years she downplayed the Round Table in her career, implying that its importance had been greatly exaggerated: "It was no Mermaid Tavern, I can tell you. Just a bunch of loudmouths showing off, saving their gags for days, waiting to spring them. The whole thing was made up by people who'd never been there. And may I say they're still making it up?"

Although she is particularly known for depicting the disappointing love experiences of women, she excels at portraying the miscommunications between the sexes as well as the devil-may-care, ain't-we-got-fun drinking parties of the years of Prohibition. In the 1928 short story "Just a Little One," for example, a woman sits with her date in a smoky speakeasy. The story is styled as a monologue, and the reader experiences the scene through the comments of the woman speaker. Referring to the bar's atmosphere, for example, the woman quips, "They got the idea from the Mammoth cave." She goes on to praise the "real Scotch" in a highball: "Well, that will be a new experience for me. You ought to see the Scotch I've got home in my cupboard; at least it was in the cupboard this morning—it's probably eaten its way out by now."

Parker joked about alcohol the same way she joked about everything that seriously concerned her: On one occasion, when a bartender asked what she was having, she remarked, "Not much fun." Another time, she cracked, "One more drink and I'd be under the host." In fact, her abuse of alcohol steadily eroded her ability to write. But since heavy drinking was in style throughout the 1920s as a socially acceptable challenge to Prohibition, for a time her alcoholism was not difficult to conceal.

BACKGROUND

Parker is an autobiographical writer whose chief subjects—drinking, women who have been jilted, suicidal despair, and death—reveal her lifelong battle with depression, a condition that she may have first experienced following the unexpected death of her mother when Parker was five years old. Born Dorothy Rothschild (no relation to the banking family) on August 22, 1893, in West End, New Jersey, Parker lived much of her life in New York City, which would have been her place of birth had she not been two months premature. Her mother, Eliza Marston, of Scottish Presbyterian descent, and her father, J. Henry Rothschild, endured for over ten years the Marston family's opposition to Eliza marrying a German Jew; they were finally wed in 1880. Dorothy was their fourth and last child, born when her mother was forty-two. Her brothers Harold and Bertram were twelve and nine, respectively; her sister, Helen, was six.

On July 20, 1898 (some biographers give 1897), Dorothy's mother died after an illness lasting about five days. The five-year-old Dorothy "screamed her head off," according to her biographer Marion Meade, and consoled herself with the thought of her mother listening to the rain as she died. Parker reflected on the experience in the poem "Condolence" (collected in *Enough Rope*), in which the speaker remembers relatives hastening to tell her "of that Other Side," and how "even then, you waited there for me." In the poem she describes the speaker as smiling, which causes the relatives to tell her how brave she is, prompting the following explanation:

> But I had smiled to think how you, the dead,
> So curiously preoccupied and grave,
> Would laugh, could you have heard the things
>   they said.

Parker laughed much of her life to cheer herself up, but the howl of despair can be heard through every chuckle. "A girl's best friend is her mutter," she would one day say, perhaps realizing that her sotto voce sense of humor functioned as a best friend, protecting her from desolation of the kind she had experienced in childhood.

"Laughter and hope and a sock in the eye," were, she admitted in the poem "Inventory" (also in *Enough Rope*), the three things she would have until she died. It might have felt to her like a sock in the eye when her father married again, on January 3, 1900; his new wife, Eleanor Frances Lewis, was forty-eight, about the same age as Parker's mother at her death; both women were Scottish Presbyterian; and, like Parker's mother before her marriage, Eleanor was a Christian spinster schoolteacher. Like Parker's maternal grandparents, Lewis had a decidedly anti-Semitic attitude. Demanding love from the Rothschild children, who addressed her as "Mrs. Rothschild" by way of retaliation for their father's hasty marriage, she won only their scorn. Parker bore the brunt of her stepmother's religious zeal and stern ways, since the other children were by that time eighteen, sixteen, and thirteen years old, and would soon be away from her influence.

The titles of Parker's three major collections of poems—*Enough Rope, Sunset Gun,* and *Death and Taxes* (1931)—all refer to death. The title of her collected poems, *Not So Deep as a Well* (1936), glumly begins with a negation, and titles she selected for collections of her stories proved funereal: *Laments for the Living* (1930) and *Here Lies* (1939). She attempted suicide at least four times: in 1923, after her first abortion; in 1925; in 1930, one year after winning the O. Henry Award for the year's best short story, "Big Blonde," the story of an alcoholic woman unhappy with her many lovers, congenitally depressed, and driven to a suicide attempt; and in 1932, a year after the publication of *Death and Taxes.* Parker finally died in 1967—some felt she had long outlived herself—of a heart attack in her room at the Hotel Volney in New York City. She had become by then a lonely, half-forgotten old woman, too often in her cups, whose fame had steadily dwindled since her heyday in the 1920s and 1930s. By then she rarely wrote, and her writing remained out of tune with the times.

The central theme of all her work, obsessively repeated, is the experience of being abandoned, or jilted. In "A Fairly Sad Tale" (from *Sunset Gun*), she observes, "A heart in half is chaste, archaic; / But mine resembles a mosaic—" In "Coda" (also from *Sunset Gun*) she remarks,

This living, this living, this living
    Was never a project of mine . . .
For art is a form of catharsis,
    And love is a permanent flop . . .

The poem ends with a question: "Would you kindly direct me to hell?" Hell was where she tragicomically conceived herself as living most of her life. In "Ballade at Thirty-five" she confesses her need to create situations in which she would be rejected by whomever she loved:

Always knew I the consequence;
Always saw what the end would be.
    We're as Nature has made us—hence
I loved them until they loved me.

This final line embodies the crisis of her life: she could not bear to return love when love was offered. Her world-weary self-contempt, twinned with a girlish gaiety piping through nursery-rhyme rhythms, rendered her a complex figure, always admired yet illusory. "I don't care what they write about me as long as it isn't true," she remarked once, echoing Oscar Wilde's confession that he lived in terror of not being misunderstood. She, too, had her secrets, mostly sad secrets that she kept from herself, although her private life was always an open book.

In the poem "A Portrait" (in *Enough Rope*)—which might as well have been titled "A Self-Portrait"—the experience of love inevitably leads to feelings of loss. In her poetry Parker's seeming compulsion to bring about rejection by the loved one is perhaps an attempt to relive symbolically the trauma of her mother's death, in hopes of changing the sad outcome. Parker seemed driven to throw herself into doomed relationships, as she writes in these lines:

> You do not know how heavy a heart it is
> That hangs about my neck—a clumsy stone
> Cut with a birth, a death, a bridal-day.
> Each time I love, I find it still my own.

The birth (her own), the death (her mother's) and the bridal day (her disastrous marriage to the shell-shocked alcoholic and morphine-addicted Eddie Parker) proved to be the tragedies of Parker's life; the poem asserts that her birth "cut" her, initiating her many injuries of the heart.

If her poems are filled with broken hearts, her short stories are replete with mothers who ignore their children or treat them badly. Marion Meade has observed that Hazel Morse's mother in "Big Blonde," described as a "hazy" woman who had died, resembled Parker's own. Female friends often play the role of bad mother, like the unnamed narrator of "Lady with a Lamp." The title alludes to Florence Nightingale, the great maternal nurse to soldiers during the Crimean War; Parker's narrator is ironically designated. Visiting a friend who has had, it is hinted, an illegal abortion, she torments her by disclosing the romantic infidelities of the man who impregnated her, and patronizingly criticizes her under the guise of offering comfort.

Other bad mothers include Camilla in "Horsie," who says "Goodnight, useless," to her newborn daughter; Fan Durant, who lets her overbearing husband get rid of the children's puppy one night, after he has reassured them that they can keep it; Mrs. Ewing in "Lolita," who patronizes her plain daughter, expresses disbelief when the daughter marries a handsome, wealthy man, and assures her that when he rejects her she can always return to Mama; and Mrs. Matson in "Little Curtis," who adopts a four-year-old boy, beats him and harangues him in the manner of the proverbial wicked stepmother—much the same way that Dorothy's stepmother treated her. Mrs. Matson is depicted as an extremely controlled, controlling woman, who enters every expenditure down to a few cents neatly in a little book, glares at beggars, whom she believes all have hefty bankrolls, and whose anger volcanically erupts at the drop of a hat.

According to Meade, Parker hated her stepmother, who sent her to a strict Catholic school, the Blessed Sacrament Academy, and would ask upon Dorothy's return each day, "Did you love Jesus today?"—as if that could eradicate Dorothy's Jewishness. Meanwhile, she insisted that Dorothy was Jewish by virtue of her lineage, and voiced her disapproval of Jews. She lectured her stepdaughter about regular bowel movements, and made her say prayers. Dorothy defended herself, referring to the Immaculate Conception as "spontaneous combustion," and, if one can believe her, getting "fired" from that school. She later attended, but never graduated from, the academically demanding and socially exclusive Miss Dana's School in Morristown, New Jersey. She stopped attending at age fourteen, but by then had studied algebra, Greek, American history, French, Latin, physiology, and advanced English. "Because of circumstances, I didn't finish high school," she told a newspaper reporter when she was a visiting professor at California State College, "But, by God, I read." The circumstances she alludes to probably included the rapid decline of her father after his brother drowned in the sinking of the *Titanic*. When Parker was twenty, her father, who was about sixty, died of a heart attack. Her stepmother had died ten years before of a cerebral brain hemorrhage.

CAREER

In an interview with Marion Capron in 1959, Parker claimed, possibly exaggeratedly, that after her father's death she was practically destitute:

There wasn't any money. I had to work, you see, and Mr. Crowninshield [the editor of *Vanity Fair*], God rest his soul, paid twelve dollars for a small verse of mine and gave me a job at ten dollars a week. Well, I thought I was Edith Sitwell. I lived in a boarding house at 103rd and Broadway, paying eight dollars a week for my room and two meals, breakfast and dinner. Thorne Smith was there, and another man. We used to sit around in the evening and talk. There was no money, but Jesus we had fun.

Thorne Smith would later achieve fame as the author of *Topper*. At twenty, Parker had begun supporting herself by playing the piano at a dance school. The latest fad in the New York of 1914 was dancing; everywhere people were doing the tango, the Castlewalk, and the turkey trot. Purchasing quantities of sheet music, Parker practiced "The Floradora Glide" and "Everybody's Doin' It (Doin' What, Turkey Trot)." While memorizing song hits, she began to write light verse; as she later said, she had "fallen" into writing.

She submitted some of her work to *Vanity Fair,* and one morning a check for twelve dollars and a letter of acceptance arrived. Seizing the opportunity, Parker put on her best suit and hat, sprayed herself with cologne, and, according to Meade, presented herself at Frank Crowninshield's office, where she claimed that the poem he had accepted, "Any Porch," was the first thing she had ever written, that she was an orphan whose father had recently died, that she was working at a dance school although she hadn't the slightest idea how to teach. Might Mr. Crowninshield have a job for her, since "the literary life" would suit her better?

Crowninshield told her that he would keep her in mind, and she went back to the dance school. A few months later, when a position opened on the staff of *Vogue, Vanity Fair*'s sister magazine, Parker was offered the job at a salary of ten dollars a week. Her assignment was to write captions for art and photographs. She gave up trying to sound literary and vented her ef-

forts in pieces such as the following, which, as explained by Meade, very nearly got published before an editor expunged it at the last moment. In it, Parker had dared to hint that *Vogue* readers were sexually active, an idea then considered too provocative for the magazine's readership:

> There was a little girl who had a little curl, right in the middle of her forehead. When she was good she was very very good, and when she was bad she wore this divine nightdress of rose-colored mousseline de soie, trimmed with frothy Valenciennes lace.

No wonder Alexander Woollcott (at the Algonquin Round Table) had referred to Parker as a combination of Little Nell and Lady Macbeth.

During the summer of 1916 Dorothy met Edwin Pond Parker II, but their marriage in June 1917 posed no interruption to her career. Like her father, she chose a non-Jewish partner whose family disliked the idea of their child marrying a Jew. Eddie's family on both sides had been in the ministry for generations, and his grandfather had been Connecticut's leading Protestant clergyman. According to Meade, when Eddie brought Dorothy home, his grandfather called the family in for prayers, and then asked the Lord to "grant to the unbeliever in our midst the light to see the error of her ways." He went so far as to refer to Dorothy as "a stranger within our gates." Eddie himself was an atheist, but his family's attitude must have stung. To some extent Dorothy had internalized her stepmother's anti-Semitism; years later, according to Meade, she told friends that she had wanted to marry Eddie because he had a "nice clean name." She was never to use her family name, Rothschild, again. Long after her divorce from Parker, she made it clear that she wished to be addressed as "Mrs. Parker." Whenever people asked about her name, she airily assured them that there had indeed once been a Mr. Parker.

Almost as soon as they were married— and both their families were barred from the wedding—Eddie joined the Thirty-third Ambulance Corps, Fourth Division, and departed for Summit, New Jersey. World War I was raging, and like most able-bodied men, he rushed to the defense of his country. Dorothy, bereft, felt that she had been married "about five minutes" before he left. She wrote to him frequently, but he was often unable to reply. He eventually endured heavy combat in France. Driving his ambulance under intense bombardments to pick up the wounded, he risked his life to save men who sometimes died on the way back to the field hospital. A drinker before the war, Eddie resorted to morphine to calm his nerves under fire, because alcohol was not available. By the time he returned to the States he was a broken man, unable to resist either drink or morphine. The marriage was to end in much the same way the marriage ends in Parker's masterpiece, "Big Blonde." After a number of fights and reconciliations, Parker came home one day to find Eddie packing his bags In "Big Blonde," she paints a grim portrait of the way in which her own marriage may have fallen apart:

He became annoyed by her misty melancholies. At first, when he came home to find her softly tired and moody, he kissed her neck and patted her shoulder and begged her to tell her Herbie what was wrong. She loved that. But time slid by. . . .

She was completely bewildered by what happened to their marriage. First they were lovers; and then, it seemed without transition, they were enemies. She never understood it. . . .

Each time he left the place in a rage, he threatened never to come back. She did not believe him. . . .

One afternoon she came home . . . to find Herbie in the bedroom. . . . On the bed were two old suitcases, packed high. Only her photograph remained on his bureau, and the wide doors of his closet disclosed nothing but coat-hangers.

By the time Eddie had left for the front, Dorothy had joined the staff of *Vanity Fair*, as she had longed to do for some time. When P. G. Wodehouse took a leave of absence from the magazine, Crowninshield made Parker New York's first female drama critic. She began her column with the April 1918 issue.

In 1919 Robert Benchley, at twenty-nine an undistinguished newspaperman, publicist, freelance writer, and former editor of the *Harvard Lampoon,* was hired as managing editor of *Vanity Fair.* He shared an office with Parker and became one of her most loyal, trusted friends. Never romantic partners, Parker and Benchley enjoyed a close camaraderie grounded in their unspoken knowledge of the ways in which the depths of despair can produce scintillating laughter. According to Meade, they shared the experience of feeling abandoned by their mothers, and both battled depression and alcoholism. As a hobby, both read funeral industry trade magazines, a practice that inspired Parker to wear tuberose perfume, used by undertakers to mask the odor of corpses. Adopting the carpe diem philosophy of the Roaring Twenties, they frittered away time drinking and philandering, and in the process their verbal sparring helped create a new American sense of humor.

Each must have sensed the other's secret, that the wisecracks the world perceived as the effusions of happy people sprang from a longing to cheer themselves up. After Parker's first suicide attempt, when she slashed her wrists with her husband's razor blade, Benchley reportedly advised her to "cut deeper" next time. After her second, when she swallowed a bottle of Veronal, a barbiturate, he visited her in the hospital. According to her biographer Keats, Parker asked the doctor, "May I have a flag for my [oxygen] tent?" Benchley could not resist a quip: "If you don't stop this sort of thing, you'll make yourself sick." Then he grew serious, describing what she had looked like when he found her lying comatose on the floor of her apartment. He lingered on the graphic details, perhaps in hopes of shaming her—if not frightening her—into changing her behavior. "If you realized how repulsive you looked, you'd never try this again. You were a mess. You were lying there drooling, and if you had any consideration for your friends, you'd shoot yourself—but don't be this messy." Parker used these images—the ones Benchley had relayed to her—in writing, a few years later, in the scene in "Big Blonde" in which Hazel Morse tries to kill herself with Veronal and is saved by the chance arrival of the maid.

Writing about Parker in *An Unfinished Woman* (1969), Parker's friend and confidante, Lillian Hellman, summed up the reasons for the artistic success of "Big Blonde" over some of Parker's other work: "The good short stories, like 'Big Blonde,' are her imaginative projections of what she knew or feared for herself, and have nothing to do with vengeance on the rich. Her put-them-in-their-place stories are often undigested, the conclusions there on the first page." Although the buxom, uneducated Hazel Morse differs outwardly from Parker, who was short, slim, dark-eyed, and intellectual, emotionally the resemblance is close. In portraying a woman who was physically and mentally her opposite, Parker may have reassured herself that her fictional character's emotions might not be so easily recognized as her own. But Parker's associates knew that she, like Hazel Morse, "could weep at anything in a play—tiny garments, love both unrequited and mutual, seduction, purity, faithful servitors, wedlock, the triangle." Wearing Hazel as a mask, it is assuredly Parker who confesses: "To her who had laughed so much, crying was delicious."

Parker, like Hazel, was happy to be married, and bewildered, forlorn, and increasingly alcoholic as her marriage unraveled. Like Hazel, she drifted from man to man, "never noticeably drunk and seldom nearly sober. It required a larger daily allowance to keep her misty-minded. Too little, and she was achingly melancholy." Unlike Hazel, Parker was technically more capable of making a living, well-known writer and wit that she was. But actually, her affairs remained in chaos unless friends, and eventually her second husband, Alan Campbell, took charge of them. Emotionally, she derived the same sense of security as Hazel from being told what to do and where to live, and from being handed presents as a trade-off for sex. If Hazel does so by virtue of necessity, Parker did so as part of a pattern of seeking relationships in which she could be exploited, or exploit her partner. Hellman observed that for Parker, respect seemed to cancel out romantic love.

Like Hazel, the thought of death "came and stayed" with Parker "and lent her a sort of drowsy cheer." For both, death seemed to offer rest: "There was no settled, shocked moment when she first thought of killing herself; it seemed to her as if the idea had always been with her." The accident of being rescued drives Hazel to tears, bitter laughter, and the request for a drink; Parker, awakening in the hospital after her overdose, cursed her doctor for reviving her. Writing "Big Blonde" had seemed an exorcism of sorts, but the demons returned almost immediately, and the fame and financial success garnered by the story never seemed to bring Parker any measure of happiness.

EMOTIONAL IMPACT OF PARKER'S FAMILY LIFE

From age fourteen until twenty Parker had remained at home as the sole caretaker of her increasingly weak and demanding father; her sister was married with a family of her own, and her brothers no longer lived at home. Accounts differ about Parker's relationship with her father. One biographer depicts him as an ogre who, when Parker was a child, hammered her wrists with a spoon if she were a moment late to dinner. Another claims that he showed her considerable affection, and cites poems that he wrote to her. Whatever the reality, it seems likely that her father suffered after losing both wives and a loved brother, and having sole responsibility for his care must have weighed heavily on Parker's spirits. In the ironically titled story "The Wonderful Old Gentleman" (which first appeared in *Pictorial Review,* in January 1926), Parker revealed many resentments she bore her father, making it clear that being his nurse had created an enormous strain for her. The "old gentleman" in the story, an invalid dependent on his children to care for him, exhibits controlling ways resembling those of Dorothy's stepmother: he interrogates them constantly, asking how much they spend on eggs, why they go to a butcher he thinks is too expensive, and whom they spend so much time with on the telephone. If we understand the story to be autobiographical, her father left most of his money to Dorothy's sister, who had not cared for him in his last days. Parker was so concerned that her family might recognize themselves in "The Wonderful Old Gentleman" that she took pains to disguise them, aging her father twenty years, for example. She had wanted to develop the story to into a novel, but fear of family reprisal inhibited her.

Apart from the care of her father, Parker was forced to contend with the remarkably similar losses of her mother and stepmother. Both women had died unexpectedly, and both had functioned partially as a means of social climbing for their German Jewish husband, eager to assimilate himself into the anti-Semitic American upper classes, self-consciously ambivalent about his Jewishness, and contemptuous of the hordes of impoverished Jewish immigrants living a mile or two away on New York's Lower East Side, even though their cheap labor had enabled his considerable success as a cloak manufacturer.

The pernicious effects of her father's attitudes toward his ancestry, combined with the shock of unexpected deaths in the family, cannot be exaggerated in their influence on Parker's life and career, and on the ways in which she exploited her deeply torn sense of self in her life and writings. Two mothers, remarkably alike, both non-Jewish, had died when she was young, and the second one had denigrated Dorothy's Jewishness, undermining the young girl's self-esteem. Summing herself up late in life, Parker carped, "I was just a little Jewish girl trying to be cute." She once said that she would title her autobiography—which was never written—Mongrel.

Her sense of herself as a mutt, inferior to her pedigreed admirers, many of whom were listed in the *Social Register,* vied with her public image as a liberated sophisticate, the only woman in the man's world of journalism and the Algonquin Round Table. Her love of New York City, whose streets and hangouts she alludes to in her stories, perhaps grew also out of her identification with Manhattan as a mongrel in the best sense. Manhattan included *Vogue,* where the fashionable world she had glimpsed at the Episcopalian Miss Dana's School became something she could now help to create; she may not have been born into the privileged class, but as an adult she exemplified the "smart set," defining their clothes and their world with her breezy, wisecracking captions, and she could afford clothing that made her look like one of them.

At the same time, racially and ethnically diverse Manhattan of the 1920s had become a mecca for black jazz composers, musicians, and poets. The dazzling era of the Harlem Renaissance was in full swing. No other American city of the 1920s encouraged black talent the way New York did. All-inclusive Manhattan, then as now, attracted writers, artists, and musicians from all walks of life. Profiling New Jersey–born Alexander Woollcott for *Vanity Fair* in 1934, Parker paused dramatically to remark: "Then he came to New York. Don't we all?" A racially mixed social scene was emerging, and

Parker wrote a story about it: "Arrangement in Black and White" exposes the racial prejudice of a white socialite invited to a party in honor of a black pianist. The socialite embarrasses the host with a barrage of remarks that reveal her bigotry. She congratulates herself for not having "any feeling at all because he's a colored man. I felt just as natural as I would with anybody," and exults over being able to tell her husband that she addressed the black musician as "mister." Parker's stories are filled with gimlet-eyed critiques of such social hypocrisies.

In 1934 Parker married Alan Campbell, like her a "mongrel" of mixed Scottish and Jewish descent. His mother was the daughter of a kosher butcher; his father was rumored to be a "Virginia tobacco man." Parker was forty, and her marriage to Eddie Parker had been over since 1928, when her divorce was granted. Campbell's sexual preference allegedly was for men, and that added to his appeal; Parker had often socialized with gay men, saying that she needed the protection of "good fairies." Campbell enjoyed cooking and interior decorating and Parker appreciated this, and she liked the ways in which he organized her life, curtailed her drinking, cleaned up after her dogs, and in general took care of her. Marrying Parker boosted Campbell's career; he knew that in Hollywood her name would command a large salary for the screenplays he wanted the two of them to write together, and he was right.

Eleven years her junior, Campbell was an actor and a writer, and the two of them made each other laugh. The couple became a Hollywood screenwriting team whose credits included the original *A Star Is Born* (1937), which was nominated for an Academy Award. They worked together on a number of screenplays, between 1933 and 1938 receiving screen credits for fifteen films, including *Sweethearts, Here Is My Heart, One Hour Late, The Big Broadcast of 1936, Mary Burns, Fugitive, Hands across the Table, Paris in the Spring, Three Married Men,* *Lady Be Careful, The Moon's Our Home, Suzy, Crime Takes a Holiday,* and *Flight into Nowhere.*

Liking the generous paychecks, Parker loathed her work in Hollywood and felt (as she did about reviewing) that screenwriting wasted energies that should have been invested in serious literary writing. She wrote stories and poems only occasionally in the 1930s and later years, and never reached the level of productivity to which she aspired nor wrote the novel she had always dreamed of writing. Parker and Campbell's relationship was complicated by economic woes as well as alcoholism, from which Campbell also suffered, and Parker's eventual need to provoke and insult him. In one account, Parker remarked at a dinner party, "What am I doing with him? He's queer as a goat," and asked her mother-in-law, "Where's my homo husband?" Ambivalent as always, Parker had swung from viewing Campbell's homosexuality as pleasantly unconventional to affecting or adopting a traditional disgust. They divorced in 1947 and remarried in 1950; about that wedding, according to Hellman, Parker observed that "the room was filled with people who hadn't talked to each other in years, including the bride and groom." The two separated in 1953, reconciled again in 1956, and remained together until Campbell's apparent suicide from an overdose of sleeping pills in 1963—incidentally, the same way Eddie Parker had died.

In Dorothy Parker a constant duel waged between her strong sense of social justice for persons who were discriminated against because of their race, nationality, social class, or religion, and her longing to be just the sort of aristocrat lording it over those unfortunates whom she chose in other moods to defend. A good example of this mixed sense of self occurs in one of her best stories, "The Standard of Living," concerning two young, uneducated office workers, whom Parker sneers at, simultaneously envying them: "Annabel and Midge came out of the tea room with the arrogant slow gait of the leisured," the story begins, immediately making it clear that these are not members of the leisured classes, but rather working girls:

> They had lunched, as was their wont, on sugar, starches, oils, and butter-fats. Usually they ate sandwiches of spongy new white bread greased with butter and mayonnaise; they ate thick wedges of cake lying wetly beneath ice cream and whipped cream and melted chocolate gritty with nuts. As alternates, they ate patties, sweating beads of inferior oil, containing bits of bland meat bogged in pale, stiffening sauce; they ate pastries, limber under rigid icing, filled with an indeterminate yellow sweet stuff, not still solid, not yet liquid, like salve that has been left in the sun.

Underscoring her aristocratically vast disapproval, Parker writes, "They chose no other sort of food, nor did they consider it." What ignoramuses! Then her envy breaks through: "And their skin was like the petals of wood anemones, and their bellies were as flat, and their flanks as lean as those of young Indian braves." So the girls are aristocrats after all. But quickly Parker downgrades them again. Describing their "thin, bright dresses," their use of makeup and "scent," Parker writes, "They looked conspicuous and cheap and charming." But within a few sentences the girls become aristocrats yet again: Ignoring the young men blowing wolf whistles at them as they walk down Fifth Avenue "with their skirts swirled by the hot wind," Annabel and Midge "held their heads higher and set their feet with exquisite precision, as if they stepped over the necks of peasants."

In her depiction of Annabel and Midge, Parker has an almost Jeffersonian sense of the American ideal of an aristocracy of talent and genius, not birth and wealth. Just as Annabel and Midge are, at least in their own eyes, self-made aristocrats, Parker strove for the assured, arrogant sense of belonging of America's wealthiest classes, the sort about whom F. Scott Fitzgerald remarked: "The rich are different from you and me. They have more money." Parker socialized with the rich and famous frequently, especially after Hollywood successes bloated her bank account, although she often abruptly ended relationships with such associates. She loved and hated them. Wanting to belong, she nevertheless identified with the "mongrel" servants and the lower classes exploited by the wealth she cherished. The result, a constant maneuvering between conflicting values, made it possible for her to bequeath nearly all of her money to the National Association for the Advancement of Colored People (NAACP), to write two stories explicitly criticizing racial injustice ("Arrangement in Black and White," "Clothe the Naked,") several stories descrying the isolation and poor treatment of women and adopted children ("Horsie," "Little Curtis"), and numerous stories that rage against social snobbery, but then also to produce rhymes such as this:

> Higgledy Piggledy, my white hen;
> She lays eggs for gentlemen.
> You cannot persuade her with gun or lariat
> To come across for the proletariat.

Although she enjoyed the identification with the white hen who lays eggs only for gentlemen, Parker did in fact come across for the proletariat, and for those she deemed mongrels or underlings. She demonstrated for the fair treatment of Nicola Sacco and Bartolomeo Vanzetti, Italian-American anarchists, a fish-peddler and a shoemaker, who had been accused of the 1920 murders of a paymaster and a guard in South Braintree, Massachusetts. Executed despite considerable public outcry, they may well have been guilty, but antianarchist sentiment, not hard evidence, led to their conviction. She joined committees in support of, and gave a dinner to raise money for the defense of, the Scottsboro boys, nine black youths who in 1931 were accused of raping two white girls on a train, one of whom later recanted her testimony. She helped found the Hollywood Anti-Nazi League to propagandize against Hitler. She spoke out against Francisco Franco and fascism, giving speeches recounting her trips to war-torn Spain, where the sight of hungry, frightened children had greatly moved her. The FBI investigated her during the McCarthy years, and she denied then belonging to or having donated money to the Communist Party, although in fact she had had great sympathy with that movement because of her belief that it would help the poor. She felt traumatized by the effects of McCarthyism upon friends and writers she knew who were blacklisted and whose lives were destroyed, or who, like Ring Lardner and Dashiell Hammett, served prison terms.

Parker's internal divisions remained so great, however, that her friends considered her politics mere theatrics, and were in part justified in doing so. When she started dressing as a proletariat—peasant blouse, babushka, baggy dirndl skirt, flat shoes—they laughed. She played proletariat in Hollywood after her income had ballooned into the thousands per week; when she had really been a proletariat in the financial sense, flat broke, she somehow managed to dress in designer outfits by Valentino and Hattie Carnegie. She became a heartfelt sympathizer with the proletariat at the point when she could consider herself an aristocrat as a self-made wealthy woman. Her impulses remained more those of a would-be Lady Bountiful than those of the Communist she declared herself to be in 1934. According to Keats, Parker's friend Beatrice Ames Stewart commented that once Parker had decided the party wanted to help suffering humanity, she could not criticize it. Ames Stewart remarked, "She didn't get it, you know, but she was not a personal friend of the multitudes. She was a very, very grande dame, and contrariness was the wellspring of her Communism. She was anti. She was anti the Establishment."

THE QUESTION OF PARKER'S FEMINISM

A young man announced that he could not bear fools. "That's funny," Parker is said to have mused, "Your mother could." Fending off a man she found unappealing, she reportedly snapped, "With the crown of thorns I wear, why should I worry about a little prick like you?"

These remarks could be read as challenging male authority, and in that sense feminist, but Parker was equally capable of making sexist remarks about women (as in the often-quoted statement: "You know, that woman speaks eighteen languages? And she can't say 'No' in any of them.") What the remarks highlight is less an anti-male or a pro-feminist stance than a personal ambition of Parker's, discussed above, to be an aristocrat, and her intuition that her wit propelled her into the aristocracy. As a young woman she claimed to be in favor of women's rights, equal pay for equal work. She expressed her commitment to the cause by smoking—which was then a man's prerogative—renting her own apartment, writing verses about love, announcing her own opinions, and getting a job.

Going about this apparent show of creating herself as a feminist, she had since she was "a woman of eleven," as she once said, idealized Becky Sharp, the heroine of William Makepeace Thackeray's 1848 novel, *Vanity Fair.* Subtitled "A Novel without a Hero," it had a heroine for Parker in the figure of the penniless orphan Becky, who manipulates her way into high society, even being presented to King George IV, flirting, cheating, lying, and, the text intimates, committing murder along the way. Becky is a courtesan par excellence. Late in life, Parker read and reread *Vanity Fair,* claiming, in her sixties, that she still found comfort in the novel, in particular in the slaying of the cad and bounder George Osborne; Parker relished the line in which he is found "lying on his face, dead, with a bullet through his heart." Lillian Hellman, in *An Unfinished Woman,* remembered that Parker had, "even in her best days, clung to the idea that she was poor." She did not manage money well, giving generous gifts to friends and mislaying checks for large sums. More often, Hellman writes, Parker's demeanor regarding money came from an insistence on a world where the artist was the "put-upon outsider, the épaté rebel who ate caviar from rare china with a Balzac shrug for when you paid."

Using Becky as a blueprint, Parker revealed again her identification with her father, who was, like Becky, a social climber trying to worm his way into high society. The goal of becoming an aristocrat proved to be worth anything: prostituting herself, Becky uses others but is constantly being used herself. This seems to have been Parker's sad vision of her life, and of the only possibilities for life. The happenstance of the magazine she admired and wanted to write for being named *Vanity Fair* must have given her a frisson of confirmation that she had chosen the correct path. Breezing into Frank Crowninshield's office as an ambitious twenty-year-old eager to be admired but also pitied as an attractive orphan in a cloud of perfume, Parker had become Becky Sharp qua woman of the world, a subversive, a rebel, but hardly a feminist.

By the time Parker had established herself as her own woman, independent and self-sufficient, she became eager to affect the life of the ladies of leisure she loved to lampoon in stories like "The Custard Heart" and "From the Diary of a New York Lady." For instance, after she moved out to Hollywood with Alan Campbell and was making $5,200 a week—during the depression—she was asked what more she could possibly want. "Presents!" she answered. She loved to be pampered and to appear helpless and doe-eyed; when she was pregnant with Campbell's child, which she miscarried, she had herself photographed knitting baby clothes.

Dorothy Parker's style of wit has a long and illustrious tradition; it is that of the social satirist exposing a fool. It has—as the well-read Parker knew—particularly shining predecessors in ancient Roman times (Martial, Horace, Catullus) and in the eighteenth century (Jonathan Swift) and it assumes an anti-egalitarian stance: it slashes, pokes, and exposes for the purpose of asserting the primacy of one person or one group or one point of view over another. The fool Parker exposes in her work is frequently herself, coolly assessed from the standpoint of her author self, determined to digest a bad experience by writing about it. As her friend and fellow Algonquin Round Tabler Frank Sullivan remarked after her death, "All the digs she took at people, friend and foe alike, were really digs at herself." Hypocrisy was her enemy, and she was as ruthless in exposing her own as she was in exposing that of others.

From Parker's point of view, women were often fools, as her poem "On Being a Woman" (in *Sunset Gun*) suggests:

Why is it, when I am in Rome,
I'd give an eye to be at home,
But when on native earth I be,
My soul is sick for Italy?

And why with you, my love, my lord,
Am I spectacularly bored,
Yet do you up and leave me—then
I scream to have you back again?

This attempt at self-analysis is also an indictment of her lifelong ambivalence, and what she views as the ambivalence of women in general. (In her memoir Hellman called Parker "a tangled fishnet of contradictions"). The man in the poem is addressed as "my love, my lord," which suggests a traditional—that is, nonfeminist because nonegalitarian—erotic enjoyment of the man as a being more powerful, to whom the woman thrillingly subjugates herself.

The problem with finding a feminist ideology in Parker's work—as some studies do—is that she vehemently rejects, with the fervor of the would-be aristocrat, the egalitarianism of the sexes and the classes that the more democratically inclined feminism endorses and occasionally credits her with. It is not unusual to find a feminist study of one of Parker's best and most frequently anthologized stories, "A Telephone Call," that portrays the tale as an indictment of patriarchy, a critique of gender stereotypes, a diatribe against the subjugation of women. Some critics have gone so far as to say that Parker wanted to transform thinking about gender. This last is perhaps true, in the sense that Parker wanted what she regarded as the inner turmoil of womanhood to be exposed and understood.

She took it for granted that, in the language of a popular self-help book of the 1990s, men are from Mars and women are from Venus, and she wondered why other people had not perceived the fact as thoroughly as she had. Praising, in a 1927 review, Ernest Hemingway's collection of short stories *Men without Women,* she remarked as an aside that among what she considered to be the four greatest American stories is Ring Lardner's "Some Like Them Cold," a story, she confesses, "which seems to me as shrewd a picture of every woman at some time as is Chekhov's 'The Darling.'" This remark, like much of her poetry, announces that she saw men and women as entirely different creatures.

Both of these stories may be read as reinforcing sexual stereotypes of women that feminism has long striven to demolish. In "Some Like Them Cold," a young woman sparks a conversation with a young man at a railway station just as he is leaving Chicago for New York. Charmed, he writes to her, but the letters are laced with frequent allusions to the fact that she attempted to pick him up, and that in the same situation other men might think her "trying to make them." By the end of the story, he is engaged to a different woman who attracted him by being "cold," and who doesn't object to his making only sixty dollars a week. In revenge, the jilted girl writes a letter making it clear that

he wasn't making enough money to suit her ambitions for a husband anyway. In "The Darling," Chekhov portrays a woman devoid of self-interest, whose sole longing in life is to devote herself to a man. Thrice married, she interests herself exclusively in the profession of the husband of the moment; when the last man dies she dreams only of her empty backyard, until the opportunity to lavish maternal love on a young boy again fills her life with meaning.

In a 1928 review of a popular advice book, *The Technique of the Love Affair,* Parker wrote, "Despite its abominable style and its frequent sandy stretches, *The Technique of the Love Affair* makes, I am bitterly afraid, considerable sense. If only it had been written and placed in my hands years ago, maybe I could have been successful, instead of just successive." In the review, she sums up the advice given as follows: "You know how you ought to be with men? You should always be aloof, you should never let them know you like them, you must on no account let them feel that they are of any importance to you, you must be wrapped up in your own concerns, you may never let them lose sight of the fact that you are superior, you must be, in short, a regular stuffed chemise." In short, she subscribes to the status quo. She is not trying to alter what she regards as an essential condition.

"A Telephone Call" is technically an interior monologue, but in effect it is an interior dialogue between two conflicting tendencies. In the story, a woman struggles with her urge to telephone a man who has promised to call her. As the story opens, Parker writes in the voice of the forlorn and abandoned child, helplessly dependent and pleading with the paternal deity for intervention.

> Please, God, let him telephone me now. Dear God, let him call me now. I won't ask anything else of You, truly I won't. It isn't very much to ask. It would be so little to You, God, such a little, little thing. Only let him telephone now. . . .

Please let me see him again, God. Please, I want him so much. I want him so much. I'll be good, God. I will try to be better. . . .

Are You punishing me, God, because I've been bad?

The narrator then counts to five hundred by fives, makes desperate deals with God, threatens to pull the phone out by the roots, appeals to her own sense of pride, and then throws pride to the winds, reverting, in the last lines, to the ploy of counting to five hundred by fives as a means of fending off her urge to give in and telephone the man she well knows has no intention of bothering to phone her. Along the way, she mutters to herself lines that feminist critics have read as an expression of her ambivalence about being a woman:

> I know you shouldn't keep telephoning them—I know they don't like that. When you do that, they know you are thinking about them and wanting them, and that makes them hate you. But I hadn't talked to him in three days—not in three days. And all I did was ask him how he was; it was just the way anybody might have called him up.

The character has internalized a gender role that prevents her from taking positive action, from asserting her will. It is not inaccurate to say that Parker was ambivalent about being a woman, but it is incomplete. She was ambivalent about literally everything: the condition of feeling ambivalent overwhelms all aspects of her life and art. She loves; she hates. She wants to phone; she doesn't. It is this general free-floating ambivalence that captures her imagination. That is why she excels at monologues that are in actuality dialogues between two opposing internal voices; the dialogue form helped to give artistic expression to her personal chaos. Projecting her own extreme ambivalence onto all women, she captured enough of reality to provide glimpses of the complications wrought by human ambivalence.

Some feminist critics have asserted that Parker's portrait of the woman in the story is intended to be ironic, not realistic; one commented that no real woman could possibly talk the way the woman in "A Telephone Call" talks, that Parker is exaggerating for the purpose of attacking a gender stereotype, that the story is dedicated to producing language that masquerades as authentic, all for the political purpose of restoring gender equity.

On the contrary, Parker might say, every woman talks like this: it is so exact a portrait of a distressed woman waiting for a man to call that it deserves to be canonized as wit. It is worth quoting here one of Parker's remarks about wit. Interviewed by the *Paris Review* in 1956, she said, "Wit has truth in it; wisecracking is simply calisthenics with words." Parker's truths are sometimes just what go unrecognized by feminist critics; when she is serious in her depiction of a woman longing for a man to call, they want to believe she must be being ironic, because they do not accept her acceptance of the idea that women are fundamentally, psychologically, essentially different from men.

"The Telephone Call," Parker's wicked send-up of herself, is sometimes—like "Big Blonde," "The Waltz," and "Mr. Durant"—read as propaganda rather than as literature and autobiography. In the push to portray Parker as a feminist fighting the subjugation of women, other subjugated groups are occasionally enlisted. One study, for example, "foregrounds" the African American presence in "Big Blonde," asserting that it "discloses the real source of the story's power to disturb," the idea being that the black characters in the story, like the white female characters, are exploited by a white male hierarchy. However, since the story concerns a suicide attempt, it is questionable that one needs to look further for the "real" power to disturb. The African American figures in the text are there for realistic, one might say anthropological, reasons: Parker had a black maid who thwarted one suicide attempt by happening to arrive in time to save her from the effects of the overdose she had taken. One of the few professions open to African Americans at the time of the writing of the story was that of domestic servant, so Parker's inclusion of a black maid seems entirely consistent with the world of her characters.

Feminist critics often cast Parker in the role of victim, a role neither she nor Becky Sharp would find congenial. Reading her stories about women as revelations of female victimization by a male-dominated society, feminist critics interpret "The Waltz," for example, Parker's tale of a woman dancing with an undesirable partner, as an indictment of conventional gender roles that condemned women to speech that is deferential, tentative, qualified, apologetic.

However, in the story, told as an interior monologue interrupted by the woman's actual responses to her dance partner's conversation, the narrator's unspoken objections to her partner focus almost exclusively on his social class, not his gender; when she wants to insult him, as she frequently does, she thinks to herself, "Get off my instep, you hulking peasant!" When she wants to make excuses for his poor dancing, she muses, "After all, the poor boy's doing the best he can. Probably he grew up in the hill country, and never had no larnin'."

The story therefore concerns a self-styled aristocrat forced to dance with a man she considers her social and intellectual inferior. Her own failure is a matter of discretion, not gender; she has made the mistake of following the crowd instead of setting her own standard: "Everyone else at the table had got up to dance, except him and me. There was I, trapped. Trapped like a trap in a trap." Self-entrapped, as Parker well knew. Only one line in the story conforms to feminist interpretations of it as a tale of female victimization, but even that one is problematic: the narrator, accidentally kicked by her bumbling partner, casts herself as "Outraged Womanhood," but it is clear that at the same time she envisions herself as the queen sending the hapless offender to the gallows:

"Die he must, and die he shall, for what he did to me." Toward the end of the story, she philosophizes that she is better off stuck dancing than talking with this man whose extremely low intellectual capacity she is at pains to delineate: "Look at him—what could you say to a thing like that! Did you go to the circus this year, what's your favorite kind of ice cream, how do you spell cat?"

CONCLUSION

Parker lived out her last years as her own worst nightmare: Robert Benchley had once warned her that people become the thing they despise the most, and she loathed alcoholism and dependency. Relying on friends to feed her, get her through the day without drinking too much, and entertain her, she looked forward to death, but with her customary good humor. To her friend Lillian Hellman she said, "Lilly, promise me that my gravestone will carry only these words: 'If you can read this you've come too close,'" words that Hellman quoted at her funeral. To Robert Benchley, Parker suggested that her tombstone should read, "Excuse my dust." Her wit, Hellman remembered, "was so wonderful that neither age nor illness ever dried up the spring from which it came fresh each day. No remembrance of her can exclude it."

Selected Bibliography

WORKS OF DOROTHY PARKER

POETRY
Enough Rope. New York: Boni and Liveright, 1926.
Sunset Gun. New York: Boni and Liveright, 1928.
Death and Taxes. New York: Viking, 1931.

FICTION
Laments for the Living. New York: Viking, 1930.
After Such Pleasures. New York: Viking, 1933.

EDITED WORK AND CRITICISM

Short Story: A Thematic Anthology. Edited by Parker and Frederick B. Shroyer. New York: Scribners, 1965.

Constant Reader. New York: Viking, 1970.

DRAMA

Close Harmony. With Elmer L. Rice. New York: Samuel French, 1929.

The Ladies of the Corridor: A Play. With Arnaud D'Usseau. New York: Viking, 1954.

The Coast of Illyria: A Play in Three Acts. With Ross Evans. Iowa City: University of Iowa Press, 1990.

COLLECTED WORKS

Not So Deep as a Well. New York: Viking, 1936.

Here Lies: The Collected Stories of Dorothy Parker. New York: Viking, 1939.

The Collected Stories of Dorothy Parker. New York: Modern Library, 1942.

The Collected Poetry of Dorothy Parker. New York: Modern Library, 1944.

The Portable Dorothy Parker. New York: Viking, 1944.

The Best of Dorothy Parker. London: Methuen, 1952.

Complete Stories. Edited by Colleen Breese. New York: Penguin, 1995.

Not Much Fun: The Lost Poems of Dorothy Parker. Edited by Stuart Y. Silverstein. New York: Scribners, 1996.

RECORDINGS

Dorothy Parker: Poems and "Horsie." Spoken Arts 726, n.d.

The World of Dorothy Parker. Verve V-15029, n.d.

CRITICAL AND BIOGRAPHICAL STUDIES

Barreca, Regina. *Introduction to Dorothy Parker, Complete Stories.* Edited by Colleen Breese. New York: Penguin, 1995.

Capron, Marion. "Dorothy Parker." In *Writers at Work.* Edited by Malcolm Cowley. New York: Viking, 1959.

Craig, Andrea Ivanov. "Being and Dying as a Woman in the Short Fiction of Dorothy Parker." In *Per-forming Gender and Comedy: Theories, Texts, and Contexts.* Edited by Shannon Hengen. Amsterdam: Gordon and Breach, 1998.

"Dorothy Parker, Compassionate Liberal." *The American Enterprise,* May/June 1995, p. 93.

Douglas, Ann. *Terrible Honesty: Mongrel Manhattan in the 1920s.* New York: Farrar, Straus & Giroux, 1995.

Ephron, Nora. "Dorothy Parker." In her *Crazy Salad: Some Things about Women.* New York: Knopf, 1975. Pp. 133–136.

Frewin, Leslie. *The Late Mrs. Dorothy Parker.* New York: Macmillan, 1986.

Gaines, James R. *Wit's End: Days and Nights of the Algonquin Round Table.* New York: Harcourt, Brace, Jovanovich, 1977.

Gill, Brendan. Introduction to *The Portable Dorothy Parker.* New York: Viking, 1973, 1977.

Hellman, Lillian. "Dorothy Parker." In her *An Unfinished Woman: A Memoir.* Boston: Little, Brown, 1969. Pp. 212–228.

Hollander, John. "Poetry in Review." *Yale Review* 85, no. 1 (January 1997).

Horder, Mervyn. Introduction to *The Best of Dorothy Parker.* London: Folio Society, 1995.

Johnson, Ken. "Dorothy Parker's Perpetual Motion." In *American Women Short Story Writers: A Collection of Critical Essays.* Edited by Julie Brown. New York: Garland Publishing, 1995. Pp. 251–265.

Keats, John. *You Might As Well Live: The Life and Times of Dorothy Parker.* New York: Simon and Schuster, 1970.

Kinney, Arthur F. *Dorothy Parker, Revised.* New York: Twayne, 1998.

Lansky, Ellen. "Female Trouble: Dorothy Parker, Katherine Anne Porter, and Alcoholism." *Literature and Medicine* 17, no. 2:212–230 (fall 1998).

Meade, Marion. *Dorothy Parker: What Fresh Hell Is This?* New York: Villard, 1988.

Melzer, Sondra. *The Rhetoric of Rage: Women in Dorothy Parker.* New York: Peter Lang, 1997.

Miller, Nina. *Making Love Modern: The Intimate Public Worlds of New York's Literary Women.* New York: Oxford University Press, 1999.

Pollack, Ellen. "Premium Swift: Dorothy Parker's Iron Mask of Femininity." In *Pope, Swift, and*

Women Writers. Edited by Donald C. Mell. Newark: University of Delaware Press, 1996. Pp. 203–221.

Simpson, Amelia R. "Black on Blonde: The Africanist Presence in Dorothy Parker's 'Big Blonde.'" *College Literature* 23, no. 3:105–116 (October 1996).

Treichler, Paula A. "Verbal Subversions in Dorothy Parker: 'Trapped Like a Trap in a Trap.'" *Language and Style* 13, no. 4:46–61 (fall 1980).

Walker, Nancy A. "The Remarkably Constant Reader: Dorothy Parker as Book Reviewer." *Studies in American Humor* 3 (New Series), no. 4:1–14 (1997).

FILM BASED ON THE LIFE OF DOROTHY PARKER

Mrs. Parker and the Vicious Circle. Directed by Alan Rudolph. Turner Entertainment Company, 1994.

—*MELISSA KNOX*

Richard Powers

1957–

IT IS AN enchanting tale that since its publication in 1963 has become a classic of children's literature. In Maurice Sendak's *Where the Wild Things Are,* Max, a rambunctious child smarting from a disastrous brush with the real world (he has played too boisterously), is sent to his bedroom without supper. Thus exiled, he gleefully escapes into a magical environment, self-fashioned and self-sustaining, wherein he cavorts with wild-eyed creatures of his own making. Empowered by the generous play amid his own shadow show, he is proclaimed king and thus touches an omnipotence denied him in the brutish world beyond his bedroom door. Yet even as he celebrates this resplendent position, he wearies of playing among shadows, feels the keen cut of loneliness, and understands that such retreat is given its wonder only because it is temporary. The child then "departs" his fanciful creatures and "returns" to his bedroom. At narrative's end, Max prepares to feast on the still-hot dinner waiting on his bedside table, the simple gift of someone who loves him "best of all."

It may seem odd to use a children's tale as entrance to the novels of Richard Powers. After all, since 1985 Powers has produced fiction of considerable scope, architectural nerve, and linguistic daring, novels of ideas, or more specifically, novels about characters unafraid to tangle with ideas and to articulate that enterprise with wit and erudition, cerebral novels that have generated excitement among academics searching for the first major literary voice since Thomas Pynchon. Powers's novels have received sophisticated analysis in academic forums in both the humanities and the sciences;

he has given nuanced interviews on the state of contemporary fiction. His narratives are layered with dense informational passages on a wide range of specialized subjects, including genetic recombination, saponification, oncology, photographic reproduction, pediatric medicine, artificial intelligence, polyphonic music, corporate economic theory, medieval architecture, and tropical botany.

Yet despite the breadth and complexity of his works, Powers has frequently centered his novels on stories of compelling simplicity, on fairy tales, among them Jack and the Beanstalk, Snow White, Sleeping Beauty, Peter Pan, Rapunzel, Pinocchio, the Pied Piper, and lesser known tales drawn from Far Eastern and Middle Eastern cultures. But Max from *Where the Wild Things Are* (which figures in Powers's fifth novel) suggests the theme critical to Powers's fictions: the seductive pull (and considerable risk) of the imagination. Powers celebrates the imagination, its expansive energy all but forgotten in an era of budget-busting Hollywood spectacles, garish audio-animatronic theme parks, and enclosing cyberscapes. Powers's characters discover that the imagination is a potent connecting force at once intensely private—at unexpected moments, characters are stunned into deep response by a chance encounter with a suggestive artifact—and yet splendidly communal, as, having been altered by their individual response, they assume their place within the larger interpretive community. Although Powers's characters negotiate the awkward ad-lib of relationships, they connect most passionately with objects of the creative imagination—with lines from an obscure poem, a work hanging forgotten in a museum, a movement from an esoteric musical composition, a fairy tale heard long ago, a stylishly sentimental classic movie. Or they themselves fashion such remarkably affective constructs—they are irrepressible storytellers, amateur painters, weekend poets, avant-garde composers—enthralled by the detonating impact of art and by the marvelous reach of the imagination, able to forge an impromptu community with an unnamable but nevertheless real audience, a wonderfully accidental cooperation that defies the apparent limits of time and space.

Given his career-long investigation into the mechanics of the imagination, Powers would seem to fit within the postmodern tradition that began in the mid-twentieth century. The works associated with this tradition are carnival texts of lexical daring that investigated with relentless self-awareness the interior worlds fashioned by the imagination. They foregrounded the process of encoding experience into language, often at the expense of developing character, theme, and plot. Such baroque texts dismissed as irrelevant—even unknowable—the environment outside the imagined; their fiercely introspective characters retreated from an irrational world where the individual had been brutalized into irrelevance, where death had become random and generic, and where we were left each to ourselves in a universe that two centuries of scientific probing had found vaster and emptier than any ever conceived. These structurally intricate texts—executed most notably by Pynchon, William Gaddis, William Gass, and John Barth—deliberately denied validity to the mimetic premise of the fiction of midcentury writers such as John Updike, John Cheever, William Styron, and John O'Hara, who probed the anxieties of the complicated business of living in such a difficult world. Not surprisingly, those fictions were decidedly descendant, revealing an oppressive sense of limitations and exhausted options; the real world was a distressing text-site where even the noblest characters had whatever tender idealism they could sustain rudely shattered as the rich experiences of love and death, the traditional plotlines of realistic fiction, were exposed as disappointingly banal.

Serious fiction at midcentury then either celebrated retreat into elaborate private worlds designed by the heated imagination (King Max amid his "monsters") or engaged the world in sobering endgames in which that stark environment crushed whatever slender aspirations characters dared harbor (the boy Max sentenced to bedroom exile). Powers, however, rejects as melodramatic this retreat-or-engage dilemma. He consciously occupies a refulgent middle ground and brings to contemporary fiction a disarmingly ascendant premise appropriate for the flush of a new millennium. Schooled in the late 1970s, he has acknowledged postmodernism's influence. His novels evidence elements of postmodern experiments: a fluid narrative structure, a delight in scale, a love of the elaborate sentence, an autodidactic command of arcane knowledge, a combination of fascination and dread regarding the metaphors of science, a resistance to narrative closure, a broad use of referents drawn from both high and low culture, and a keen interest in language and the bothersome distance between experience and the stories we tell. Yet few writers of his generation have demonstrated as well a command of the defining elements of traditional realism: rich storytelling; a robustness of theme; recognizable characters who struggle with familiar frustrations and aspirations; and especially, an abiding compassion for such pedestrian struggles. Powers sees the two camps as ultimately cooperative: we have only language to create purpose, direction, dignity.

What emerges as the critical agency for this reconciliation is the imagination itself. Consider Sendak's tale of retreat and return. In Powers's novels, characters—damaged by love or unsettled by mortality—seek the refuge of the imagination. Like Max, such characters—wounded and in recoil—forsake even the urge to embrace the roiling give-and-take of the immediate and retreat into the secured, supple sanctuary of, say, a novel, a piece of music, a movie, a museum, a computer. But Powers insists that such withdrawal must be temporary, that the world outside such constructs—museums, movie houses, TV rooms, libraries, computer screens—can enrich us moment to moment with its unsuspected complexity, its engrossing spectacle, and its staggering density. Powers's fictions, grounded in the argument of the life sciences that he relished growing up, trigger a new alertness; reading becomes a strategy for recovering—rather than rejecting—the world, a defiant affirmation that we cannot afford to allow our fragile moment of living to expire without taking full measure of the world's depth and nuance, its complex dignity. Powers cautions that contemporary serious fiction, locked within academia and absorbed in propounding impenetrable theories about its own importance, has killed awe and no longer speaks to what it means to be alive.

This is not to say that Powers is a sentimentalist. His novels have investigated the twentieth century's signature dilemmas—the arms race; civil strife; terrorism; environmental mismanagement; cancer. They have dealt with computer technologies that, despite the premise of World Wide Webbing, have left us more alone than we have ever been; the wrenching rhythm of economic booms and busts; the unsettling implications of the midcentury social revolution that left us free to deconstruct love into sexual indulgence. His characters engage that world with unflinching determination. Inevitably overwhelmed, they retreat to the pleasure cells fashioned by the imagination. It is a strategy, of course, necessarily shared by any reader. Beleaguered, overtired of engagement, we do not simply read texts (or watch movies or listen to symphonies); rather, we visit them. It is a

logic familiar to any child who has needed the calmative of a bedtime story. Rekindled within the generous space apart that the imagination provides, reassured by the premise of order and the possibility of clean lines, readers nevertheless understand that, like children come morning, they must reengage the freewheeling chaos of the world.

It is, finally, the twin pulls of escape and engagement that define the imagination—and us. If the imagination is the energy that refurbishes the interior world and benevolently structures safe harbor, it is as well that infixed capacity for wonder that disturbs our complacency, wills us to violate our isolation, and insists on wonder, even reverence, for the real world. It is, then, necessarily centripetal and centrifugal. To deny either impulse is to diminish our fullest capacities. Powers is fond of relating a Dutch fairy tale in which an innkeeper's wife in Zeeland, a country town, dreams that she finds a fortune outside a bank in Amsterdam. When she wakes, she is so taken by the vividness of the dream that she spends her savings to travel to the city. Once at the bank, however, she despairs when she finds no fortune. A broker coming out of the bank stops to ask why she is weeping. When she tells him, he laughs, saying, "You must never believe such things. I dreamed that I found treasure under the bed of a little inn in Zeeland where I dreamed I was staying." The woman rushes home, tears up the floorboards of her inn, and indeed finds the treasure. One dream needed the other to complete it. The urgent need to escape makes sense only with the equally urgent need to return.

Typically in Powers's novels, two central characters are juxtaposed: one who engages the world and one who retreats from it. One character is compelled to attempt the trick of trust with a needful other, to accept the implications of vulnerability amid the unfolding of chance, to tap the reassuring animation of the living earth, and ultimately to accept the irresistible pull of mortality; another devises a strategy of wholesale retreat, and amid protective isolation and uncontested self-sufficiency is empowered by the satisfying order of the symbolic transcriptions of the real world. Deliberately, Powers alternates privileging as the heroic center those who retreat and those who engage, careful not to endorse entirely either strategy but rather to point out that, like Max (like the innkeeper's wife), we find the treasure only through their cooperation. To appreciate his take on the imagination, then, Powers's novels must be read as a single unit that moves as a twin-piston engine. He is fascinated not so much by withdrawal or engagement but rather by the necessary movement between these strategies. Each of his books interrogates loopholes raised by the previous work—thus, Powers's novels form an unbroken dialogue on the complex engine of the imagination.

That respect for complexity extends to the novels themselves. Powers's daunting fictions do not inspire immediate affection. The novels are formidable constructs. Restless with the notion of specialization and deeply committed to the widest range of intellectual play, Powers's narratives deftly coordinate their plots with meditations on a range of topics, an interplay that can quickly frustrate readers more compelled by action and character. In *The Gold Bug Variations* (1991), for instance, the reader is quickly drawn from characters passionately stealing a kiss to a lengthy aside on the mechanics of DNA recombination complete with genetic tables. For some readers, the frequent intrusions of such static passages of arid specialized information—intended to inspire the reader with the same cerebral excitation as the author and to give unsuspected depth to the characters' actions—can prove bewildering, even infuriating.

Powers's prose can be equally frustrating. His evident fondness for language contributes to a razzle-dazzle style that can astonish with its rich verbal play and its complex system of allusions but can also become the focal point of the reading experience. Powers's passionate concern with the sound and suasion of language, his commanding gift for verbal rifts compelled by an immensely rich vocabulary and a sure-hand for elegantly terraced sentences, can upstage the unfolding action. For some, Powers tries too hard to dazzle. Novels like Powers's, the argument runs, are admired but not loved, for they are considered too cerebral and overly written to allow for character sympathy and plot involvement. Even so, as novels of ideas, Powers's fictions do involve, intrigue, even astound with their ambitious investigations into the infinite capacities of the mind. And because, as Powers is fond of reminding his readers, there is nothing the mind cannot master, patient readers ultimately come to glimpse a provocative conception of the contemporary technological world that is both complex and engaging.

BIOGRAPHY

Powers has lived—like his characters (like all of us)—between the complex responsibility to engage and the sweet impulse to escape. Born June 18, 1957, in Evanston, Illinois, he was the fourth of five children (two older sisters and two brothers, one younger and one older). In the mid-1960s, his father, Richard, a high school principal with a working-class background, moved the family to the North Chicago suburb of Lincolnwood. In an unpublished interview with Joseph Dewey, Powers described Lincolnwood as an older neighborhood that was heavily Jewish. "My sisters and brothers and I would be about the only kids in school for the high holy days. I always had the sense that we weren't quite native." This sense of dislocation was compounded when, in 1968, Powers's father accepted an appointment with the International School of Bangkok and Powers commenced five eye-opening years in Thailand during the height of the American military presence in Southeast Asia.

Amid such a dramatic relocation, the young Powers discovered the aesthetic sanctuary: he tapped into both a sustaining love of music (an accomplished student of vocal music, he trained in the cello but also plays guitar, clarinet, and saxophone) and a curiosity fed by voracious reading. He recounts the impact of both the *Iliad* and the *Odyssey* (testimony again to a position between engagement and retreat: on the one hand, the historian's meticulous transcription; on the other, the poet's fanciful license). His earliest reading passion, however, was for nonfiction, specifically biographies and science (he has cited particularly Charles Darwin's *Voyage of the Beagle,* a text that combines exotic escapism with exploratory science). He recalls the assumption, largely because of the panicked surge of interest in science following the Soviet Union's launch of *Sputnik,* the first artificial satellite, that he was somehow destined to be a scientist. Thus, after returning with his family to De Kalb, Illinois, to finish high school, he weighed careers in paleontology, oceanography, and archaeology before ultimately selecting physics.

During his formal studies, however, Powers found himself pulled between science and the arts. In 1975 he enrolled as a physics major at the University of Illinois at Urbana-Champaign. Increasingly frustrated over the specialization demanded by the sciences and more interested in a broader view, Powers changed his major to English and rhetoric (with a minor in math and physics). Complicating the decision to switch disciplines was Powers's father, who valued literature but argued for the social usefulness of the sciences. Powers has expressed regret about never being able to put one of his books in his father's hands—his father died from cancer during the first year of Powers's graduate work.

Powers's mother, Donna, went to work as a secretary to support the family.

In his university literature studies, Powers was drawn to the first-generation European modernists (particularly the intricate narrative structurings of Marcel Proust, Thomas Mann, and James Joyce) and to the churning (melo)dramas of Thomas Hardy—again positioned in between, drawn to both experimental modernism with its strident conception of the novel as a self-justifying architectural form and to the compelling tradition of narrative realism. Powers completed his master's degree in late 1979 but elected not to pursue his doctorate, as he feared literary study, like the sciences, would prove too specialized.

Powers moved to Boston in January 1980 and worked as a computer programmer and freelance data processor, utilizing skills he had developed during off-hours spent learning the massive computer systems at Illinois. By night he continued his eclectic reading program, ingesting volumes of history, sociology, political science, aesthetics, and science theory, as well as a wide range of European novels and poetry, with an emerging emphasis on the era of World War I. He lived near the Museum of Fine Arts, where he would spend Saturdays (admission was free before noon), and where, one week, he viewed an exhibit that included a 1914 black-and-white photograph by August Sander that depicted three Westerwald farmboys heading, according to the title, to a dance. The image inexplicably enthralled Powers. It seemed that his year's random reading suddenly coalesced in that single photographic image. Within days, he quit his job to devote himself to producing his first (and what he assumed would be his only) novel, which took more than two years to write. That book, *Three Farmers on Their Way to a Dance* (1985), explores the obsessions triggered by an accidental encounter with Sander's haunting photograph among characters across the twentieth century. The novel met with significant critical success. Hailed as a dazzlingly inventive debut, it was named a National Book Critics Circle Award finalist and won the American Academy and Institute of Arts and Letters, award as well as a special citation from the PEN/Hemingway competition.

Distracted by the implications of finding himself suddenly a writer, Powers (Max-like) retreated and moved to southern Holland—in part because of a romantic entanglement he would later use as the subject of his fifth novel but more to immerse himself in that region's rich play of multiple languages. He also secured the distance necessary to finish the draft of his second novel, *Prisoner's Dilemma* (1988), his most American work, which audaciously linked Disney and nuclear warfare. The critical response to this second novel compared Powers, at thirty-one, to the elite voices in American fiction—to Pynchon, Vladimir Nabokov, Saul Bellow, Don DeLillo. In 1989 Powers became one of the youngest recipients ever of the MacArthur Foundation "genius" Fellowship, a five-year award whose generous annuity provided Powers sufficient freedom to pursue work on what would become his most ambitious and influential work to date. Still in the Netherlands, Powers completed *The Gold Bug Variations,* a dense and luminous story of two disastrous love affairs separated by more than twenty-five years, a work that intricately braided the metaphor systems of genetics, computer science, and polyphonic music.

Two years after *The Gold Bug Variations,* a Circle Award finalist as well as *Time* magazine's outstanding novel of 1991, Powers released *Operation Wandering Soul,* which chronicled the slow-motion meltdown of a young resident-doctor confronting the nightmarish realities of a pediatric ward in an East Los Angeles public hospital. Although critics found the novel unrelentingly bleak, the work was short-listed for the National Book Award. Work on that manuscript was done during a yearlong stay in

Cambridge and then completed when Powers returned stateside in 1992 to accept a position as artist-in-residence at Illinois. Powers would use this academic experience to fashion *Galatea 2.2* (1995), an ingenious retelling of the Pygmalion story in which an eccentric neurologist (assisted by a young, successful novelist named Richard Powers) attempts to teach a computer network to respond to literature.

Galatea 2.2's theorizing on the implications of the reader/writer contract, as well as its confident deployment of the metaphors of artificial intelligence, garnered renewed critical respect for Powers. In a pattern that has come to define Powers's work—in the odd-numbered books, characters tap into expansive confidence; in the even-numbered books, they struggle with chilling anxieties—his follow-up effort, in 1998, was a disturbing look at a twentieth-century pandemic. In *Gain* Laura Bodey, engaged full-tilt in the unexamined busyness of being a divorced mother, must come to terms at midlife with ovarian cancer, caused by the environmental carelessness of a nearby chemical corporation, whose absorbing two-hundred-year economic history Powers relates in alternating chapters. Largely on the strength of that fabricated chronicle, *Gain* received the James Fenimore Cooper Prize from the Society of American Historians as the outstanding American work of historical fiction. That same year, Powers was named a Fellow of the American Academy of Arts and Sciences for his significant explorations of knowledge and culture. In 1999, just after his forty-second birthday, Powers received one of the prestigious Lannan Literary Awards that annually honor "writers of exceptional quality." Past winners have included John Hawkes, Grace Paley, and Alice Munro.

As he has indicated in interviews, Powers conceives of *Plowing the Dark* (2000) as a summary text that closes off the first phase of his evolving career. The work chronicles in contrapuntal fashion the emotional devastation of Adie

Klarpol—a former artist who joins the efforts of a Seattle-based computer research company to produce the first self-contained virtual reality environment—and the emotional revival of Taimur Martin, an Iranian-American English teacher held hostage in Beirut for four years, who is left to the stunning devices of his imagination. Like Sendak's tale, *Plowing the Dark* is both a celebration of the splendid realms that, back to the cave paintings at Lascaux, have been constructed by the inexhaustible imagination (and given new possibilities by the commanding muscle of virtual technologies) as well as a sobering meditation on the loneliness at the heart of the aesthetic enterprise.

In 1996 Powers was named to the Swanlund Chair in English at the University of Illinois, and at the beginning of the new millennium he continued to write (he was at work on a novel with the characteristically ambitious themes of time, music, and race), to teach (a graduate seminar in multimedia authoring as well as an undergraduate course in the mechanics of narrative), and to travel and give interviews (a change from a time, after his early success, when his resistance to engaging the public drew comparisons with the notoriously reclusive Pynchon). After a lifetime of shifting between exotic neighborhoods and diverse cultures, at midlife he had found, appropriately, a home in the university—a traditionally protected preserve between engagement and withdrawal.

THREE FARMERS ON THEIR WAY TO A DANCE AND PRISONER'S DILEMMA

Powers's novels are accomplished exercises in contrapuntal narration. To this author, form is visceral; how the story is shaped reveals character and theme. Drawn by the elegant solidity of architecture and the exuberant mathematics of music, Powers executes each novel with a design he hopes will hover about the reader's awareness. Two (and sometimes three) narrative braids are offered polyphonically, told side by side, creating a narrative harmony that is as much vertical as horizontal (like the staggered chorus of "Row, Row, Row Your Boat"). The narrative lines often do not touch or are only lightly linked—indeed, to the unprepared reader they may initially appear to be incompatible. Yet they come to complement, even deepen, each other.

Powers's first novel is perhaps best approached as an invitation to the reader to participate in the exuberant work/play of creating narratives. *Three Farmers on Their Way to a Dance* is comprised of three narratives, each centering on the Sander photograph, which is reproduced in the novel's frontispiece. In one, and of the three the only first-person account, a nameless stockbroker is inexplicably moved, while passing time in a Detroit museum, when he sees the Sander photograph. Unable to shake the image, he begins researching the era. Frustrated in his attempts to learn about the photo, he meets an elderly immigrant cleaning woman from his office who eventually reveals her ties to one of the men in the photograph (a copy of which she has enshrined in her bedroom), ties the narrator suspects may be the woman's imaginings. Since her lover's death in the Great War, she has been comforted by the photo, which she apparently purchased from Sander himself before she left for America; if she squints, one of the farmers resembles her lost lover. The narrator is rejuvenated by the revelation of the power of the imagination and departs eager to pore anew over the photograph and to cull from that haunting image his own stories about its characters.

In the second narrative braid, Peter Mays, a technical writer for a Boston computer magazine, is captivated by an actress he glimpses in a Veterans' Day parade. He tracks her to a theater where she is playing a succession of influential women from history in a one-woman mixed-media show. During the show, Mays is surprised when he sees projected above the stage a photograph of Henry Ford with a man who resembles himself. Curious, he returns to his family's Chicago home and there discovers that he is related to one of the men in the Sander photo, a copy of which Peter finds in the attic. Along with the photograph is a signed letter from Ford, bequeathing Peter's family a trust fund derived from the Model T. The gesture was based on Ford's immense respect for Peter's relative (the middle figure in the photo), a journalist Ford met during his quixotic Peace Ship mission to end World War I. Although Mays discovers that the trust fund is worthless, along the way he becomes involved with a waitress, who is unexpectedly left an inheritance by an eccentric restaurant patron whose dead wife the waitress happens to resemble. At novel's end, the two embark on their own relationship.

Yet a third narrative tracks each of the three farmers in the Sander photograph. In effect we step into the photograph. Presumably, these are the narrator's speculations, a convincing virtual reality unlicensed by historic sanction. Two die in absurd circumstances, appropriate to a war sustained by horrific pointlessness; the third survives the war, but his family is given a rich array of possible narrative outcomes. Clearly the reader is invited to exercise creative authority, to spin their own take, Powers willingly sharing the empowerment that comes from the engaged imagination (Powers glosses Jack and the Beanstalk throughout to suggest the magic brought forth from unpromising sources).

In what would become a pattern in Powers's novels, then, we are given two characters—in this case, the nameless narrator and Peter Mays. While the narrator discovers the exhilarating rush of the ignited imagination, and withdraws from the narrative to fashion the engaging stories presented to the reader (King Max amid his shadows), Peter Mays abandons his early position of aloofness and cynicism, responds to the pull of the heart; rediscovers his neglected family history; engages the absurdities of the immediate; and prepares to discover his fullest self in shared territory, with the one who, to paraphrase Sendak, loves him best. We are given then a character who is *apart* and a character who is *a part,* a dichotomy of withdrawal and engagement reflected in the cooperative enterprise of Powers and his reader. While rooting about in his attic, Peter Mays finds a stereoscopic camera and a box of old photos. With the handheld viewer, two-dimensional photos, placed side by side, are coaxed into the living magic of a third dimension, suggesting the cooperative enterprise of the writer and reader in bringing to its fullest life an otherwise lifeless artifact. We participate in the narrative, renew it, keep it viable. And once released from its tender trap, once we close up the book, we reengage the immediate, impressed by what Powers has revealed—the unsuspected architecture of chance, the grace of the heart stumbling toward its desire, the dignity of the individual as part of the unfolding complex of history.

Powers's second novel, however, tempers both the narrator's celebration of disengagement and Peter's embrace of engagement. *Prisoner's Dilemma* centers on a charismatic high school history teacher, Eddie Hobson, who is dying from the effects of radiation poisoning suffered thirty years earlier when he witnessed the first blast of the atomic age at Trinity Test Site. As the novel opens, Eddie's condition is worsening: fainting spells, weight loss, bleeding gums, purplish lesions. Pressured by his family, he agrees to check in to a hospital. As the family struggles to help the ailing father, Powers offers in counterpoint a fantastic mock-historic narrative in which the American film producer Walt Disney, eager to help the propaganda effort during World War II, conceives of an experimental cinematic project, combining live action and animation, designed to inspire the home front. A cross between *It's a Wonderful*

Life and *Fantasia,* it would follow a young boy guided by Mickey Mouse through personal setbacks and brutal encounters with the twentieth century but would ultimately affirm that his life—and, by extension, ours—mattered. Such unearned optimism underscores the strategy of disengagement that dominates Eddie Hobson's life. Powers provides the necessary counterargument to the tonic vision of his first novel: the imagination, for all its energy, can isolate us from a complex reality that we too easily abandon, forgetting how much the imperfect world justifies wonder.

Although the center of the family's emotional dynamic, Eddie has never been comfortable with affection. Overwhelmed by the implications of the nuclear arms race, by the slow creep of his own death, and by the death of an older brother in a fluke wartime training accident, Eddie has retreated. Such isolation is only heightened by his eccentric thirty-year obsession: inhumed in a back room, he has dictated into an old tape recorder the details of a private world, Hobstown, an imaginary community that draws its fantastic premise from Eddie's fascination with the 1939 World's Fair. The novel, with its generous use of Hollywood feel-good productions both real and imagined, explores the tension between the horrors of our history and the parallel growth in our entertainments. Eddie Hobson, the Great Dictator with his boxful of tapes, and Disney, with his complex of inviting theme parks, both endorse the therapy of escape. Not surprisingly, when he feels death near, Eddie runs. He checks himself out of the hospital and heads back to the New Mexico wastes. When his youngest son goes in search of him, he understands that his tormented father has made peace with his difficult century in the only way he could: by disappearing. No body is ever found. To emphasize the absurdity of such strategic disengagement, Powers resurrects Eddie in the closing pages, a specter who casually joins his family for a card game, as he was in life, a haunted absence accepted as a presence.

It is that youngest son who offers the balancing testimony to the pull of engagement. Eddie Hobson Jr. is a misfit among the Hobsons. Much younger than his siblings, he does not have their intellectual prowess, but he displays a remarkable capacity for generosity and sympathy. We follow his first date with Sarah, a sweet evening in which the youngest Hobson revels in the unrehearsed immediacy of the heart's attraction; his family members are by contrast unimpressed by their experiences with love. But in addition to love, this Hobson has a scientist's enthusiasm for the world about him. He speaks glowingly of fungi and nourishing spring rain; he turns over rocks to watch the fury of the exposed insect life. He is dumbfounded by the elegant drama of the earth itself, its architecture of chance, the inevitable stroke of death (which so terrifies his father).

Driven to connect with others and with his world, the young Eddie provides *Prisoner's Dilemma* its slender centrifugal impulse. Otherwise the book is relentlessly centripetal, nested narratives that explore the impulse that drives us to fashion insular protective spaces. The dominant gloss here is to Boccaccio's *Decameron,* where storytellers escape a poisoned world to fashion an enticing place apart. Against that comforting impulse, Powers sets the tale of Snow White, who, invaded by life-threatening forces, must learn the reassurance that alone comes from others. That need is exemplified by the game-theory problem from which Powers draws his title: two prisoners separated in a threatening environment and exposed to harsh interrogation must learn to trust each other if they are both to survive, must reject the logic of self-interest that dominated the Cold War. But engagement is the descant narrative line here. The dominant impulse is withdrawal. As Disney ironically speculates during World War II, "The side that comes through this final fight still loving this exhausted, ruined world, the side with more delight, will be the winning side." Save for the slender presence of young Eddie, delight here is too cheaply confected from pixie dust, love too appallingly fragile, death too unnervingly thick.

THE GOLD BUG VARIATIONS AND *OPERATION WANDERING SOUL*

In his third novel, *The Gold Bug Variations,* Powers locates another character at the epicenter of a scientific revolution. If Eddie Hobson is deconstructed after witnessing the experiment in quantum physics conducted at Trinity, Stuart Ressler, a promising molecular biologist unraveling the mysteries of genetic coding in the aftermath of Francis Crick and James Watson's discovery of DNA, is energized by the midcentury revolution in genetics that confirmed how, generation to generation, relentless continuity defies the melodrama of apocalypse culled too easily from the metaphors of physics.

But as we may suspect, such delight can prove difficult to sustain. In one narrative thread set in 1957, Ressler, part of a university project working on genetic coding, conducts a brief, incendiary affair with a married colleague, who introduces him to Bach's *Goldberg Variations* by making a gift of the pianist Glenn Gould's classic 1955 recording. When she decides to forsake Ressler for the banality of her conventionally doting husband, a devastated Ressler abandons his career, even as he is on the brink of cracking the genetic coding sequence, and in effect disappears. Twenty-five years later, Jan O'Deigh, a Manhattan librarian, is approached (in a second narrative thread) by a stranger, Franklin Todd, who is seeking information about an eccentric coworker. This coworker is Ressler, now an anonymous graveyard-shift computer programmer for a vast New York financial-data-retrieval system, where each night, surrounded by glowing consoles, he hums along to a tape of Bach's *Variations.* Todd, a perpetual graduate student contentedly toiling away on an unfinishable dissertation on an obscure Renaissance artist, is curious about the lonesome figure, certain only that he was nearly famous once, and enlists the librarian's assistance in unearthing information on him. In the process, Jan, drifting through a stale relationship of her own, falls disastrously in love with Franklin and, along the way, comes under the mesmerizing spell of the brilliant Ressler.

In a third narrative thread, nearly a year after Franklin and Jan's relationship ends due to Franklin's infidelity, Franklin contacts Jan by postcard to tell her that Ressler has died. Her emotions unexpectedly churned, Jan quits her job to live off her savings and devote her time to studying genetics, a subject not only vast enough to justify such an undertaking but one that would offer a closeness to the lonely, charismatic figure now lost to her. Yet Jan's notebooks record as well her lingering desire for Franklin Todd, a nagging pull outward toward the one she loves best of all. She begins to track him down, using only the postmarks of his few correspondences. Ultimately her savings dwindle and, as she prepares after nearly a year to reenter the job market, she affects a charged reunion with Franklin himself.

Powers uses the revolution in life sciences not only to counter the human compulsion to withdraw from a doomed world, which Eddie Hobson succumbed to, but also to explore the implosive force of desire, the dicey struggle to bond that articulates the most powerful force in the universe—the mysterious will of the natural world to continue itself. Genetics here is an expression of wonder, a reverence for the natural world. When Franklin Todd queries Ressler about genetic engineering and its promise of "fixing" nature, Ressler dismisses it:

> It's not science. Science is not about control. It is about cultivating a perpetual condition of wonder in the face of something that forever grows one step richer and subtler than our latest theory about it. It is about reverence, not mastery. It might, from time to time, spin off an occasional miracle

cure of the kind you dream about. The world we would know, the living, interlocked world, is a lot more complex than any market. . . . The human marketplace has about as much chance of improving on the work of natural selection as a *per diem* typist has of improving Bartlett's *Familiar Quotations*.

Yet when the experience of desire leaves them cold, both Ressler and Jan exile themselves to long stretches of denied life, like Eddie—or Max—locked in his room. But here we track their return. Something in the maddeningly indirect courtship of Jan and Franklin stirs Ressler into thinking happiness might be attainable this time. He encourages them but must watch helplessly, as he did twenty-five years earlier, the rich possibility of desire self-destruct. It will be Ressler, dead more than a year, who will revive that connection. Before he leaves Manhattan to check into a Midwestern cancer facility, Ressler will program into the financial network a message keyed to Jan's bank card. At the close of her sabbatical, more than a year after Ressler's death, when she finally uses her card (she has husbanded her savings), to her amazement on the ATM screen appears a message telling her, "He is a man. Take him for all in all." Even as it advises her, "Please enter your transaction," Jan suddenly intuits that Franklin is near and rushes back to her apartment to find him waiting for her—and, indeed, enters her transaction.

The energy here is relentlessly centrifugal. Whether reviewing in ecstatic set pieces the excesses of the natural world or following the excruciating negotiation of human hearts, Powers limns the benediction of engagement. The imaginative impulse cannot sustain the same wonder. (Similar to Eddie Hobson in his back room, dictating into a tape recorder, Ressler has spent much of his monastic antilife composing experimental musical scores that no one ever hears; Jan composes cryptic poetry; Franklin prowls art museums.) The most dramatic exercise of the imagination here is defiantly connec-

tive. Jan and Franklin—unable to have children because long ago Jan, fearing the blind roulette of birth defects, had a tubal ligation—have cooperated, it turns out, to produce the text we have been reading, a braiding of heryearlong notes on genetics and his dissertation, refashioned into a speculative biography on Ressler based on lengthy talks they had shared before Ressler died. And, ultimately, even the reader is invited in. The closing round, the next variation as it were, is ours—we are given the possibilities of the closing reunion and asked, in effect, to add to the round, to speculate over the outcome of this iteration of love.

Not surprisingly, given this celebration of animation and (re)generation, Powers turns in his follow-up work to the paradox central to the natural world that so enthralls Ressler: that nature's bold drama of animation is achieved only because its every individual bit dies. Powers shifts from the wide-open eyes of a scientist to the bloodshot eyes of an ER doctor. In *Operation Wandering Soul* Powers presents a case study of an overwhelmed heart. As a surgical resident in the pediatric ward of a public hospital in East Los Angeles, Richard Kraft, sensitive and openhearted, must sift through the appalling evidence of human disregard, the children left to die unloved, some victims of violence, others of genetic mishaps. Thus engaged in the world (he abandons a career playing the French horn after he witnesses a vicious mugging), he wallows in its irreparable chaos and in his helplessness, delivering lengthy screeds against a junk culture whose end he greedily anticipates. When at a discount store, he contemplates a bank of "demonic" televisions, each set on a different station. Kraft seethes with hyperprophetic rage as he absorbs this "shock-wave assault of images":

This brief cross-sectional spin through the dial's mandala suffices to remind Kraft of what incontestable research continuously discovers and covers back up: the species is clinically psychotic.

Pathetic, deranged, intrinsically, irreversibly mercury-poisoned by nature, by birth. And what more could one expect of a cobbled-up bastard platypus, a creature whose spirit is epoxied to its somatic foundation? Mental thalidomide cases, every last mother's son, as far back as accounts take things.

In the narrative present Kraft turns to a ward psychotherapist, Linda Espera, herself molested as a child but who has recovered sufficiently to respond to the impulse to heal. With the ward children, she practices recovery therapy, centered on sharing songs and stories. She undertakes a similar reclamation effort with Kraft, but her tender ministrations, asserted against Kraft's resistance to emotional attachment, remain stubbornly physical. Yet Kraft does find that, despite the necessity of closing his heart against the sadness of his ward, he is profoundly moved by a young Laotian refugee, a fragile girl named Joy. As he monitors the bone cancer that gnaws through her system (including conducting amputations of both her legs), he struggles to introduce the shy, studious girl to the soft shimmer-worlds of children's books (*The Secret Garden, Peter Pan,* the Alice books, *The Wizard of Oz*) that speak of fantastic magic kingdoms, certain that escape is what the dying child needs. Ironically, Joy resists retreat. She wants only to share her anxious helplessness; she struggles to understand how exactly she is to go about this business of dying. Eventually, she tires of Kraft's campaign to ignore the obvious, both through his persistent (and futile) surgeries and his sunny fairy tales. She hungers only for the comfort of company, to complete the self at its most vulnerable moment by sharing it. (She writes a poignant love letter to another child in the ward, and during a ward field trip she and Kraft share a halting dance.)

Her death devastates Kraft. During a particularly grueling ER shift (repairing school children shot by a sniper armed with an assault rifle) Kraft's mind quietly implodes. He looks up to the observation seats that overlook the operating theater and there sees Joy, alive and fully limbed, preparing to depart with a legion of ghost-children for a splendid kingdom far away. Kraft determines that he will be their guide. We last see Kraft on the hospital roof in full mental collapse, confirming what we have suspected since our engagement with Eddie Hobson and his tape recorder: that the imagination, torn free of its responsibility to engage the imperfect world, leads to madness.

Coming hard upon the resplendent affirmation of *The Gold Bug Variations,* we need Kraft's story; his misanthropic vision of the species as damaged beyond repair reminds us what we risk when we abandon the willingness to engage with the immediate. Structurally, Powers suggests such jarring disjunction by abandoning the easy shifting of contrapuntal narration. Here the disintegration of Kraft is cut into by narratives that recount tales—historic and fictional—of exploited children, tales Joy evidently is reading in her hospital bed, each tale moving toward a happy ending in which the children escape to some sweet other-place. This rude shifting from engagement to escapism is executed with violence. Not surprisingly, at narrative's close, we are summarily pulled out of the engaging cell of the novel itself. Powers himself steps into the narrative. Fretting that his novel had become too heavy, he has sent the manuscript to his brother, a doctor who did residency in Watts. He hopes the brother might offer a happier ending. The brother tells him that a cancer patient Joy's age has, in fact, responded to treatment and suggests that, even if Joy must die, she might donate her organs and thus participate in nature's sprawling recycling system. It is a far more balanced sense of the real world than any offered by the poisoned Kraft.

In a final narrative gambit, Powers closes with a set piece about a young father just beginning to appreciate the "killing responsibility" of caring for his children. Our last glimpse is of his daughter, long dispatched to bed, who comes downstairs, clutching a blanket, her wide eyes wet with excitement, having just finished a gripping read. Kraft's is just such a gripping tale, told, like the grimmest children's story (the young father's son had begged for a scary story before lights out), to reenchant the world we temporarily departed. If *The Gold Bug Variations* celebrates the delight of engagement, *Operation Wandering Soul* reminds us that such engagement can easily break even the most resilient heart—but that this fact cannot justify abandoning the world for our invented places apart.

GALATEA 2.2 AND *GAIN*

If in *Operation Wandering Soul* Powers suggests that the retreat encouraged by the imagination leads to madness, appropriately, in his next work, he once again defends the strategic disengagement of the imaginative enterprise. In *Galatea 2.2* we trace the reclamation of a writer via two tightly braided contrapuntal narratives. Richard Powers, a successful novelist who at midlife finds himself suddenly out of stories, accepts a yearlong appointment as humanist-in-residence at the Center for the Study of Advanced Sciences at his midwestern alma mater. Even as he struggles to reignite his narrative powers, he spends his days assessing the calamitous experiences of his heart (particularly his uneven relationship with his dead father, an alcoholic, and a long affair with a former student, a relationship that had only recently ended).

But while he is remembering things past (colleagues at the center nickname him "Little Marcel," a reference to Proust, author of *In Search of Lost Time*), he is drawn into a bizarre research project that starts as a bar wager: to construct within ten months a computer program able to mimic the response tactics of a reader, specifically to produce a graduate-level commentary on a randomly selected passage of canonical literature. The project is patently absurd, like some science-fiction premise, but Richard becomes caught up in the endeavor and eventually becomes the chief programmer for the neural net that the project team assembles. As the computer program, which he names Helen, learns the fundamentals of language and literature and begins to respond to literary passages in cryptic ways, suggesting to Richard a depth that we resist attributing to software, she also develops a sense of her own identity. But, like Pinocchio, Helen comes most to understand her limits, how she can never fully appreciate the breadth of literature because she cannot engage the world that it interprets. Although Helen falls short of the goal laid out in the wager, Richard reclaims his enthusiasm for narration and departs this narrative pursuing with infectious joy the same protective hibernation that had damned Eddie Hobson, Stuart Ressler, and Richard Kraft.

But there is a difference. Like each of those characters, Richard has lived an antilife. At midlife, he has no wife, no ties to his family, no friends, no lover, no children. Like Max delighted within his bedroom exile, Richard has since childhood drawn his emotional sustenance from imaginings, from books, those he reads and now those he writes. The long affair with the woman he identifies only as C. eventually collapses when the woman suggests, after six years, that they marry and have children, an invitation to engagement that Richard (who has already begun to explore narrative worlds of his own making) coolly rejects. Ink-fed and book fat, Richard has been empowered by the imagination, a lifelong self-sustaining act of calculated withdrawal uncomplicated by the intrusion of love. Thus, in middle age, suddenly stripped of the heavy insulation of his imagination, he feels at odds with his own life and with a world that has never justified wonder. He struggles to establish the slimmest sort of connection, first with a single-mother colleague and then with a beautiful graduate student (both efforts fail) but finds himself most taken by Helen. But we see what Richard does not—that, like Gepetto, Victor Frankenstein, Prospero, Pygmalion (each of whom Powers introduces), Richard is a closet misanthrope unavailable to the simplest pull of the heart, who exerts control over a helpless object in a ghastly parody of love.

It is Helen who comes to tire of artifacts. She asks Richard about the world not encoded in the books that she ingests nightly. Reluctantly, he programs into her five years' worth of news articles. Overwhelmed by the evidence of the violent world outside the neat sanctuary of her reading list, she simply shuts down. Richard revives her only by telling her that it is no trick to celebrate the soul fastened to the dying animal but rather the trick is to celebrate the animal, its "miraculous banality." Richard, who has spent a life in careful retreat, argues here that the artist must engage the imperfect world. Such stark confession convinces Helen to return, but she understands now that she can never be a reader, not in the fullest sense. In her painfully brief commentary to lines spoken by Shakespeare's monster Caliban, Helen writes, "I never felt at home here. This is an awful place to be dropped down halfway." Then, like Eddie in his back room, Stuart Ressler amid his computer consoles, and Kraft on the hospital rooftop, Helen shuts herself down, committing a sort of virtual suicide.

For his part, Richard has discovered that the story he most needs to tell is his own—his previous novels had drawn their exotic narrative lines from others' lives or had been entirely invented. We are, as Richard decides, the stories we tell. And thus he relates his own emotional life, its dreary ordinariness elevated to art simply by the act of telling it. He has learned what Max intuits cavorting among his own monsters—such escape is meaningless without the premise of return. Thus Richard Powers does what no previous Powers character has

done: savaged by experience, he recovers its complicated density to make from it the deeply affective stuff of the aesthetic enterprise.

But what happens to a character similarly savaged by experience but who does not have the requisite faith to seek out the protective sanctuary of the imagination? *Gain*'s Laura Bodey is deeply involved with the busy life of a single mother, raising two conventionally (un)happy teenagers and pursuing significant professional satisfaction as a realtor, the very business suggesting her investment in the immediate. She has little interest in the arts; she cannot even help her son puzzle through Walt Whitman's "Crossing Brooklyn Ferry" for an English assignment. We will watch Laura confront, at forty-two, the unscripted invasion of mortality—within fifty pages of the opening, she is diagnosed with ovarian cancer, caused, she comes to suspect, by the careless dumpings of the Clare International, a chemical conglomerate headquartered in her Illinois town. Given such an unpromising story line—one offering as plot only the stage-by-stage ordeal of chemotherapy—Powers nevertheless fashions a difficult affirmation (keyed to Whitman's poem): the press of dying alone justifies a greedy embrace of every morning for exactly what it is, a reprieve.

Laura, and by extension the chemical corporation that poisons her, suffers under a damning illusion: that somehow we can cheat death, ironically the only thing that gives living its sweet urgency. Powers affirms Laura's fragile presence by means of a vital natural context, the resiliency of which gives depth to her fast-approaching absence. Hard on the heels of *Galatea*'s celebration of the vitality of disengagement, *Gain* provides Powers's fiction its most dramatic celebration of engagement. Thus, Laura's agonizing movement toward inevitability is not the final word, nor is the record of the amorality of capitalism as recorded in Powers's recreation of the growth of Clare. *Gain* is more about the natural envelope and its logic of incessant change. Within that logic, Laura's death is part of an organized system of perpetual replenishment that, like her beloved backyard garden, is driven by the muscle of a natural world. Although that world may lack the poetry of Christianity, it does furnish reassuring patternings and the evidence of resilience. That world, Powers shows, is pure process; it will not recognize diminishment, nor permit waste—saponification itself (Clare began as a soapmaking enterprise) takes animal fat and ashes and renders from it soap. The rise of Clare is a parable about the diminishment of wonder over such natural abundance in favor of mercenary exploitation. Even as we manage the natural world into commodities—when Laura inventories her own closets, she finds them crowded with Clare products—we sanction its eventual mismanagement as bottom-line anxieties thin our respect for it. Eventually such estrangement leads Clare to promote synthetic products that baldly distort scientific data, to sell products that promise to defy the natural consequences of time—artificial dyes, home perms, skin care creams, insecticides, chemical defoliants, phosphate detergents, furniture restorers, cosmetics—in an effort to deny our place in the natural world itself.

Thus even as Laura spirals downward into her too-early death, even as we share the agonies of her chemical scourings, she is involved with the world from which Clare retreats. Powers has maintained since *Prisoner's Dilemma* that delight belongs to those willing to engage the world and, despite such open eyes, to maintain wonder. The regret, Powers offers, is that it takes the advent of harsh closure for Laura to see her world for what it has been even as she hurried about her busy days. In the earned lucidity of her final days, Laura spends her every painful moment taking in her bedroom, its every angle, its every shadow. Laura's life, unexamined, appears to confirm the worst of Whitman's fears, that life is simply a crossing from nowhere to nowhere. But, as in Frank Capra's *It's a Wonderful Life,* which Laura watches with her family on her last Christmas Eve, she comes to see the unsuspected glory of a world each of us can only begin to appreciate in the splinter of time we are given to relish its feel. Thus Laura does what the character Richard Powers cannot—engages the natural world, participates in that bruising enterprise, without seeking the sweet shelter of the imagination.

PLOWING THE DARK

The twinned narrative threads that make up Powers's seventh novel, *Plowing the Dark,* take place almost entirely within two tiny rooms. In one, a white-walled chamber, a "glorified walk-in closet" nicknamed the Cavern (an acronym for computer-assisted virtual environment), is converted with cutting-edge virtual reality software into a three-dimensional environment in which familiar works of art are given surface, depth, nuance, and sound. Magically, flat artifacts become interactive worlds as fully realized as any theme park attraction. Save for the cumbersome goggles and wirings required by participants, such spectacular playscapes prove remarkably accessible. Adie Klarpol, a graphics designer who ten years earlier had abandoned a promising art career, is enlisted by a software giant to lend her aesthetic expertise to creating the virtual reality prototype. She is stunned by the power of computer technology and by the comforting insulation of actually escaping into works of art. One of the first experiments the team undertakes is to recreate Henri Rousseau's haunting jungle canvas *The Dream.* When Adie completes the work on the software and first steps into the painting, she is stunned by the simulation and responds in vocabulary that recalls Eden:

Here is the shape of reforestation, eons in germinating. Till this novel test patch, more flexible than the original starter bed. Speed the green revolution. . . . Fuse the fact of the branch to its depiction. Join stump and symbol into a single thing, a tree you can walk around, prune, replicate. The tree you came down from. The one you'd happily climb up again. . . . Here you can shed your wood skeleton and travel at will through groves of pure notion. Here you can gather up the pieces of something that shattered once, long ago, in childhood's childhood. Here you can reassemble all lost growth, and even back it up onto magnetic tape.

She is revived by the experience—a voluntary celibate, she conducts a passionate affair with a colleague and even makes a difficult peace with an estranged dying ex-husband. After her most ambitious programming achievement, she soars—virtually—about the vaulted dome of a stone-by-stone true-scale simulation of the Hagia Sophia, the great domed Turkish church. It is the triumph of the imagination sought since the cleaning woman in *Three Farmers on Their Way to a Dance,* technology finally empowering the imagination to fashion actual worlds apart. Adie is crushed, however, to learn that the software she has helped develop has been marketed to the Defense Department and is part of the spectacle of the Gulf War, whose joystick execution she watches in horror. Brutalized by the intrusive cut of the real, she opts to disappear—she abandons both the project and the colleague she had come to love—another of Powers's virtual suicides.

But, in a contrapuntal narrative, we follow the revival of another such virtual suicide. After a tempestuous eight-year relationship finally collapses, Chicagoan Taimur Martin accepts, in a gesture of radical disengagement, an eight-month position to teach English in Beirut. He wants only to be alone, even when his former girlfriend, Gwen, calls Beirut to tell him she may be pregnant. When local terrorists, believing him to be a CIA operative, kidnap Taimur,

he endures isolation for more than four years, blindfolded, chained for twenty-three and a half hours a day to a radiator in an unfurnished room that, in its spartan appointments, clearly parallels Adie's Cavern.

Taimur gradually rediscovers the only energy not diminished by the routine indignities of imprisonment: the imagination. Like Max, he makes his exile resplendent. Blindfolded, he plows the dark. Initially, he merely reconstructs memories or meticulously retells novels he studied years earlier. As time slips into irrelevancy, Taimur moves to more accomplished exertions of the imagination, including an elaborate reconstruction of a long-ago visit to the Chicago Art Institute that complements Adie's extravagant technological projects. Taimur and Gwen had been captivated by a Van Gogh painting. Now, years later and chained to a Beirut radiator, he reconstructs that canvas and imagines stepping into its warm sunshine, stepping into a virtual reality entirely fashioned by his unassisted imagination. Like all artists, Taimur conjures without assurance of audience, conjures (like Max) to make tolerable an oppressive immediate to which he must inevitably return.

It is a familiar posture. Indeed, to this point Powers's fictions have only tapped the isolating power of the imagination, characters left unchallenged within their private spaces. Before closing out this first stage of his career, however, Powers attempts to show in *Plowing the Dark* how the imagination can forge a virtual community, by audaciously bringing together Adie and Taimur although they are separated by time and space.

At a heartbreaking moment of his absurd captivity, when he is certain, three years into his torment, that he will never be released, Taimur closes his blindfolded eyes and for a brief moment in that twice-darkness imagines he is in the entranceway of an ornate temple. On impulse, he looks up and spies in its vast dome a beautiful angel hanging for a moment before dropping down, not sweetly but in inexplicable terror. That mesmerizing, mysterious vision sustains Taimur for what turns out to be another full year of confinement. Under entirely different circumstances, Adie Klarpol is also despairing. Unable to accept the military applications of the technology she has helped devise, she prepares to abandon her work after indulging in one last tour of her Hagia Sophia. She straps on her goggles and soars into the dome. Suddenly, she spies far below her a movement, a shadow she did not program. Startled, she clumsily shifts the wand, the device that enables her to move within the virtual space, and feels herself plummet earthward. She departs Seattle haunted by the apparition. We understand that in a lexical feat of razzle-dazzle Adie and Taimur have met in the vast protective space of the imagination, apart yet a part. Like readers of the same book or visitors to the same art gallery or strangers sitting side by side in a theater, Adie and Taimur collide, suddenly, wonderfully, within the tight world of the imagination.

But even that fantastic connection is not sufficient to deny validity to the world itself. We last glimpse Taimur getting ready, finally, to rejoin the real world, preparing to meet Gwen, who has championed his release, and a daughter he has never met. As the novel ends, Taimur heads uncertainly across a tarmac toward those who love him best of all, a tearful Gwen and a young girl who clutches a crayoned picture as a gift. Taimur stands on that tarmac much like the rest of us stand every morning: uncertain of the next step, grateful only that we are able to take it. Comforted, indeed sustained by an imagination that has taught him about his own complicated heart, he is as ready as any of us to reengage the real world, ready to commence what will surely be a relationship necessarily invented moment to moment; rocked by disappointment; sustained by expectations; and, inevitably, ended by the gentle cut of death—in short, he prepares to engage the life we all must.

It is a risky ending that borders (as all of Powers's novels do) on the sentimental. Critics have long been wary of Powers's evident optimism; such affirmation, uncut by irony, is not only out of sync with contemporary literary fiction but is claimed to be unseemly for a writer of Powers's evident intelligence, as if intellect and affirmation cannot coexist. Powers has steadfastly refused to concede to the bugaboos that have haunted serious fiction of the latter half of the twentieth century. Against the fear that our technology has robbed us of our humanity, Powers reassures that we are far more complicated than any machine we assemble; against the disheartening discovery again and again of the sheer futility of love, he shows that it is love's very impossibility that sustains our driving need for each other; against the jeremiads concerning the steady destruction of our ecosystem, Powers recovers a natural world compelled by the furious energy of generation and bursting with uncountable species, from the thinnest scratch of bacterial life upward; against the fears of the tedious grind of the routine, Powers affirms that the ordinary is simply the extraordinary unexamined, that the most assimilated facts, considered for a moment, would blow us away with their complexity; and against the terror of our inevitable death, Powers asserts that the terror of mortality is unsustainable amid a world where every ending is a beginning, a species-wide system that operates relentlessly in the black.

For Powers, then, it is the work of the imagination to remind us to relish our capacity, singular among animal species, not merely to be aware of the unfolding processes of living and dying but to record those processes. Narratives serve to remind us that matter matters. Thus we depart a Powers novel revived. Despite critical caveats, Powers actually resists happy endings—and unhappy endings, for that matter.

He rejects endings entirely, in favor of improvisational narratives that invite us to continue the story, to step within the ever changing virtual-reality hideaway that is the novel, and to join in the play until (like Max) it is time for us to head home.

Selected Bibliography

WORKS OF RICHARD POWERS

FICTION

Three Farmers on Their Way to a Dance. New York: Beech Tree/Morrow, 1985.

Prisoner's Dilemma. New York: Beech Tree/Morrow, 1988.

The Gold Bug Variations. New York: Morrow, 1991.

Operation Wandering Soul. New York: Morrow, 1993.

Galatea 2.2. New York: Farrar, Straus & Giroux, 1995.

Gain. New York: Farrar, Straus & Giroux, 1998.

Plowing the Dark. New York: Farrar, Straus & Giroux, 2000.

BIBLIOGRAPHY

Dodd, David. "Richard Powers: A Bibliography" (http://arts.ucsc.edu/ GDead/AGDL/powers. html). University of California, Santa Cruz, Division of the Arts, December 2000. Revised January 17, 2001.

CRITICAL AND BIOGRAPHICAL STUDIES

Birkerts, Sven. "American Fictions: Mapping the New Reality." *Wilson Quarterly* 16:102–110 (spring 1992).

Dewey, Joseph. "Dwelling in Possibility: The Fiction of Richard Powers." *Hollins Critic* 33:2–16 (April 1996).

———. "'Humming the (In)Sufficient Heart Out': Richard Powers' *The Gold Bug Variations.*" In his *Novels from Reagan's America: A New Realism.* Gainesville: University Press of Florida, 1999.

Hayles, N. Katherine. "The Posthuman Body: Inscription and Incorporation in *Galatea 2.2* and *Snow Crash.*" *Configurations* 5:241–266 (1997). (Slightly revised version appears as Chapter 10 in her *How We Became Posthuman: Virtual Bodies in Cybernetics, Literature, and Informatics.* Chicago: University of Chicago Press, 1999.)

Herman, Luc, and Geert Lernout. "Genetic Coding and Aesthetic Clues: Richard Powers's *Gold Bug Variations.*" *Mosaic* 31:151–163 (December 1998).

Hermanson, Scott. "Chaos and Complexity in Richard Powers's *The Gold Bug Variations.*" *Critique* 38:38–52 (fall 1996).

Hurt, James. "Narrative Powers: Richard Powers as Storyteller." *Review of Contemporary Fiction* 18:24–41 (fall 1998).

Labinger, Jay. "Encoding an Infinite Message: Richard Powers's *The Gold Bug Variations.*" *Configurations* 1:79–93 (1995).

Lantos, John D. "Stories of Biology and Medicine: The Novels of Richard Powers." *Hastings Center Report* 26:17–20 (May/June 1996).

LeClair, Tom. "The Prodigious Fiction of Richard Powers, William Vollman, and David Foster Wallace." *Critique* 38:12–37 (fall 1996).

Lindner, April. "Narrative as Necessary Evil in Richard Powers's *Operation Wandering Soul.*" *Critique* 38:68–80 (fall 1996).

Marsh, Kelly. "The Neo-Sensation Novel: A Contemporary Genre in the Victorian Tradition." *Philological Quarterly* 74:99–123 (winter 1995).

Pancake, Ann. "'The Wheel's Worst Illusion': The Spatial Politics of *Operation Wandering Soul.*" *Review of Contemporary Fiction* 18:72–83 (fall 1998).

Saltzman, Arthur M. "The Poetics of Elsewhere: *Prisoner's Dilemma* and *The MacGuffin.*" In his *The Novel in the Balance.* Columbia: University of South Carolina Press, 1993.

———. "The Trope in the Machine." In his *This Mad "Instead": Governing Metaphors in Contemporary American Fiction.* Columbia: University of South Carolina Press, 2000. (Discussion of *Galatea 2.2.*)

Scott, A. O. "A Matter of Life and Death: Richard Powers's *Gain*." *New York Review of Books,* December 17, 1998, pp. 38, 40, 41–42.

Snyder, Sharon. "The Gender of Genius: Scientific Experts and Literary Amateurs in the Fiction of Richard Powers." *Review of Contemporary Fiction* 18:84–96 (fall 1998).

Updike, John. "Novel Thoughts." *The New Yorker,* August 21/28, 1995, pp. 105–114. (Review of *Galatea 2.2.*)

INTERVIEWS

Archer, Neil. "Mapping the Here and Now: An Interview with Richard Powers." *Tamaqua* 5:10–23 (fall 1995).

Berube, Michael. "Urbana Renewal: A Conversation with the Powers That Be." *Voice Literary Supplement,* June 6, 1995, pp. 8–10.

Birkerts, Sven. "An Interview with Richard Powers." *Bomb,* summer 1998, pp. 59–63.

"A Dialogue: Richard Powers and Bradford Morrow." *Conjunctions* (http://www.conjunctions.com/archives/c34-rp.htm), spring 2000. (Published by Bard College, Annandale-on-Hudson, N.Y.)

Miller, Laura. "The *Salon* Interview: Richard Powers." *Salon* (http://www.salon.com/books/int/1998/07covsi23inta.html), July 1998.

Neilson, Jim. "An Interview with Richard Powers." *Review of Contemporary Fiction* 18:13–23 (fall 1998).

Stites, Janet. "Bordercrossings: A Conversation in Cyberspace." *Omni,* November 1993, pp. 39+. (E-mail interview with UCLA literary critic N. Katherine Hayles, California Institute of Technology chemistry professor Jay Labinger, and Powers.)

Williams, Jeffrey. "The Last Generalist: An Interview with Richard Powers." *Cultural Logic* (http://www.eserver.org/clogic/2-2), spring 1999.

—JOSEPH DEWEY

Henry Roth

1906–1995

*I*N THE AUTUMN of 1956, *The American Scholar* published a symposium titled "The Most Neglected Books of the Past Twenty-five Years." Among several candidates nominated by the eminent literary critics whom the magazine solicited, only one book, *Call It Sleep,* was mentioned more than once. Although it had generally received very favorable reviews, Henry Roth's first novel had gone out of print when its publisher went bankrupt shortly after bringing the book out in 1934. In the symposium twenty-two years later, Alfred Kazin praised the unfamiliar work as "a wonderful novel about a little boy's first years in a Brooklyn jungle" and "the deepest and most authentic, and certainly the most unforgettable, example of this much-tried subject that I know." Nor had Leslie Fiedler forgotten what he called the "sheer virtuosity" of *Call It Sleep.* "No one has reproduced so sensitively the terror of family life in the imagination of a child caught between two cultures," he insisted. "To let another year go by without reprinting it would be unforgivable."

In fact, *Call It Sleep* was reprinted, without much reaction, in 1960. But when a paperback edition appeared in 1964, it made—and reshaped—American literary history. Reviewing the new edition on the front page of the *New York Times Book Review* (October 25, 1964), Irving Howe proclaimed it a masterpiece, "one of the few genuinely distinguished novels written by a 20th-century American." *Call It Sleep* became a belated best-seller of more than one million copies, and its author an overnight success (if three decades can be thought a long, dark night). Amid newfound fascination with

American Jewish authors, the reading public anointed Henry Roth an exemplary ancestor to Saul Bellow, Bernard Malamud, and Philip Roth. Although *Call It Sleep* was preceded by Mary Antin's *The Promised Land* (1912), Abraham Cahan's *The Rise of David Levinsky* (1917), and Samuel Ornitz's *Haunch, Paunch, and Jowl* (1923), it had by the end of the twentieth century become the earliest book by a Jewish author to enter the canon of American literature. At the age of fifty-eight, Roth abruptly became famous for being unknown. Thirty years after its publication, *Call It Sleep* was rediscovered as the classic of immigration fiction, a brilliant attempt to adapt Joycean techniques and Freudian insights to American experience, the finest of the proletarian novels of the 1930s, and a harbinger of the flowering of American Jewish literature after World War II. Roth himself was thrust out of obscurity as a duck and geese farmer in Maine and into the literary pantheon, a figure revered by readers and scholars not just in the United States but in Italy, Spain, Germany, Israel, and many other countries as well.

After failing to make a mark with his first novel, Roth abandoned the literary life, ostensibly becoming a textbook demonstration of F. Scott Fitzgerald's quip that American lives lack second acts. But the belated acclaim for Roth's novel reawakened his creative ambitions, and after several false starts he eventually published his second novel, *A Star Shines over Mt. Morris Park,* in 1994, sixty years after his first. In his eighties and suffering from rheumatoid arthritis so severe that creating prose became not just a psychological challenge but a physical one,

Roth managed to overcome the longest writer's block of any notable American author. His life is a case study in the fickleness of literary renown and in the redemptive powers of verbal art. Although he was born in Europe and spent most of his adult life in Maine and New Mexico, Roth became the twentieth century's preeminent laureate of the ethnic tumult of New York City.

CHILDHOOD AND YOUTH

Henry Roth was born on February 8, 1906, in Tsymenica, Galicia, a town at the edge of the Carpathian Mountains that was then part of the Austro-Hungarian Empire and eventually became part of Ukraine. A year after emigrating to the United States in 1902, his father, Herman Roth, returned to Tsymenica and married Leah Farb in 1905. In 1907 Herman went off alone to America again, but his wife and only son joined him in New York City in 1908. They formed part of the vast wave of immigration, mostly from eastern and southern Europe, that within the first decade of the twentieth century added nine million newcomers to the population of the United States, which in 1900 stood at only seventy-six million. One of the strengths of *Call It Sleep,* which draws directly from its author's own early childhood, is its ability to render the historic national experience of massive dislocation and absorption. New York City was the most common port of entry, and it was there, within sight of the Statue of Liberty, that young Henry Roth, along with most of the other two million Jewish greenhorns who abandoned Europe between the assassination of Czar Alexander II in 1881 and the outbreak of World War I in 1914, confronted America.

The family settled in Brownsville, an inexpensive area in Brooklyn, but in 1910 they moved to Avenue D and East 9th Street on Manhattan's Lower East Side. It was a crowded, bustling neighborhood of cheap, crude tenements inhabited mostly by working-class Jews recently arrived from Europe. Herman Roth, a querulous, domineering figure, held a series of jobs as a printer, a milkman, and a waiter. In 1914 the Roths moved to East 114th Street, in a largely Jewish section of Harlem, to be near Leah's parents and siblings, who had recently arrived in the United States. But they soon moved again, to East 119th Street, a part of Harlem then populated mostly by Irish and Italians. Although he declared himself an atheist at fourteen, Roth would for much of his life regret the Roths' abandonment of the Lower East Side when he was in only the third grade, depriving him at an impressionable age of membership in a vibrant Jewish community, one that he considered essential to his work as a writer. As a pupil receiving after-school religious instruction on the Lower East Side, Roth had barely begun his formal initiation into Judaism, and he would later also lament that the move to Harlem forever severed this vital connection as well.

Roth attended the City College of New York, a free public institution, with ambitions of becoming a biology teacher. However, an assignment in a freshman English class resulted in his first publication and early intimations of a literary calling. "Impressions of a Plumber" drew on Roth's own experience in a summer job as a plumber's assistant, and despite receiving a "D" for not responding to the assignment, it was recommended by his instructor for publication in *Lavender,* the City College literary magazine. At about the same time Lester Winter, a former classmate at DeWitt Clinton High School, introduced Roth to Eda Lou Walton, a faculty member at New York University who was both Winter's instructor in freshman English and his lover. Walton, who was twelve years older than Winter and Roth, was an energetic and unconventional figure active as poet, critic, essayist, and mentor. She regularly befriended, nurtured, and fell in love with promising young men, and Roth soon became a protégé, displacing Winter in her affections. Walton introduced Roth to the works of James Joyce, T. S. Eliot, and other moderns, and it was at her Greenwich Village apartment that the uncouth undergraduate met many of the city's leading artists and intellectuals, including Léonie Adams, Ruth Benedict, Louise Bogan, Kenneth Burke, Hart Crane, Horace Gregory, Margaret Mead, and Thomas Wolfe. In 1928, the year that he graduated (belatedly, due to poor grades) from City College, Roth moved in with Walton.

Although she openly maintained sexual relationships with other men even while sharing her bed with him, Walton supported Roth psychologically and financially. In 1930, in pencil and on empty blue books that Walton had on hand to administer exams at NYU, Roth began writing what he at first planned as an autobiography. Insulated by Walton's generosity from the hardships of the Depression, Roth worked for three-and-a-half years on his manuscript, both in their Greenwich Village apartment and in a farmhouse in Maine, where he rented a room during the summer of 1932. Although he concentrated on the childhood experiences of an immigrant Jewish boy, David Schearl, who was much like himself, Roth increasingly fictionalized his account. For example, although Roth had a younger sister, Rose, who was born in New York City two years after her brother's birth, David is depicted as an only child. Through David's eyes his father, Albert, looms as an overbearing monster, although Roth's own father, Herman, was five feet one inch tall and scrawny, albeit no less oppressive to his son.

Insecure about his artistry, the novice author showed his work in progress to no one until it was finished. But when Walton finally read Roth's book, she was enormously impressed and prevailed on another of her lovers, David Mandel, a labor lawyer who later married her, to get it published by Robert O. Ballou, a small company that also published John Steinbeck and Meyer Levin and in which Mandel was a partner. *Call It Sleep* is dedicated to Walton, and its deeply resonant title was chosen out of exasperation. When earlier possibilities, including "Ankle Deep in Lightning" and "East Side Inferno," were rejected, Roth, who was traveling to and from California while Walton handled details of publication in New York City, wrote her: "About that damned title again, just call it anything you like from A Pain in the Neck to Sleep. I'm too thoroughly confused and demoralized about it to know what I like anymore." They, of course, ended up calling it *Call It Sleep.*

CALL IT SLEEP

The novel begins with a short prologue, set in May 1907, that describes the arrival of two-year-old David Schearl and his mother Genya at the busy immigration center on Ellis Island. David's father had already settled in America, and suspicious about the date of birth of a son he had not seen before, offers a harsh reception to the new arrivals. The prologue serves to alert its reader to the fact that this is to be a story about outsiders, a dysfunctional immigrant family in which the young son seeks refuge in his mother's arms from the hostility of his father.

Call It Sleep consists of four sections, each defined by a different image: "The Cellar," "The Picture," "The Coal," and "The Rail." A coming-of-age story about a hypersensitive Jewish boy who is forced to cope alone with the mysteries of sex, religion, and love, the novel focuses on David's troubling experiences during the years from 1911 through 1913 as a stranger in a strange land. Not the least of his troubles is the enmity of his father, Albert, a surly, abusive man who is embittered by disappointment. Albert is forever falling out with fellow workers and forced to seek new employment, as a printer and then as a milkman, and he is particularly harsh toward David, about whose paternity he has doubts.

A bead of water falling ominously from the kitchen faucet is the first image in the first chapter, and throughout the book what might otherwise seem casual details are magnified by refraction through the mind of an anxious child. Roth uses stream of consciousness to intensify the sense of an unformed mind trying to assimilate the varied sensations that assault it. The family apartment on the crowded Lower East Side is a haven for David, as long as his father is not home and his doting mother can lavish her affections on him. When the boy ventures out into the clamorous streets of New York City, he encounters threats from both rats and humans. He is frightened and confused by sexual advances from a little girl named Annie and, later, by the attempts of an older Christian boy named Leo to use him to gain access to David's female cousins in order to "play dirty" with them.

David is sent to cheder, a drab religious school where Jewish boys are given rote instruction in a Hebrew Bible they cannot understand, and he is both confused and inspired by Isaiah's account of the angel with a burning coal. Eavesdropping on fragments of a conversation, mixing Polish and Yiddish, between his mother and her sister Bertha, he misconstrues an explanation for why Genya, disgraced after being jilted by a Gentile, married Albert. Out of Genya's account of her forbidden romance in eastern Europe, young David, a protonovelist, concocts a sensational story of his own origins. And when the Polish boy, Leo, persuades David to introduce him to his cousin Esther, David is overwhelmed by shock and guilt over the sexual liberties that his older friend takes. He is also fascinated by Leo's rosary and crucifix and by the symbolism of Christian salvation. By the final section of the novel, intricately constructed by crosscutting among different characters who ultimately converge and collide, Albert's sim-

mering rancor toward David is dramatically intensified. Esther's father, complaining about David's collusion with Leo, arrives at the apartment at the same time as David's cheder teacher, who has come to investigate the boy's fantastic claim that he is an orphan. When Albert then sees David holding an alien rosary, he erupts in violent rage. Fleeing his brutal father, David is shocked into unconsciousness after touching the live rail of a streetcar. Faced, like the reader, with sensory overload, David might as well call it sleep, embracing temporary oblivion as restoration after a long, disorienting day.

To explore the tensions among Albert, Genya, and David, a clanging family triangle rife with resentments and recriminations, Roth appropriates the then-recent theories of Sigmund Freud, particularly in describing the powerful oedipal bond between mother and son as well as the almost patricidal strife between Albert and David. The authority of James Joyce asserts itself, not only in that Roth's account of David Schearl, a surrogate for the author himself, is in effect another portrait of the artist as a young man, but also in his lavish use of consciousness and his meticulous, symbolist deployment of recurrent imagery. A pattern of images of radiance, as well as of biblical allusions, supports the story of a little boy who manages to transcend the shocks and horrors of everyday life into mystical illumination.

Call It Sleep records the traumas experienced when the Old World meets the New, as it did for millions of new Americans during the four decades surrounding the turn of the twentieth century. Particularly remarkable is the character of Reb Yidel Pankower, the cheder instructor who might have been an illustrious scholar in the old country but is convinced that he is wasting his life in a New York City slum trying to teach savage boys who are indifferent to the riches of Jewish tradition. Within his dreary classroom, Pankower is a pedant and a tyrant who earns the contempt of the children in his charge, provoking both fear and ridicule. But through an interior monologue in which he reflects on his own blighted opportunities, Pankower becomes a pathetic and even sympathetic figure. Many of Roth's immigrants are inspired by the American Dream of enlarged opportunity, while others are repulsed by an urban nightmare. Call it, too, sleep.

Although the Schearls are Polish Jews, the eclectic slum in which they live also serves as home to immigrants and natives from many other backgrounds. Not the least of Roth's accomplishments is his success at rendering the diversity of David's environs. *Call It Sleep* is attentive to physical details of life among the tenements of the Lower East Side, a tumult of conflicting impressions that make it easy for little David Schearl to become lost when he wanders just a few blocks away from home and cannot make himself understood to the kindly Irish cop who tries to help him out. But the book is most memorable as a cacophonous record of culture clash, one that makes its English into a subtle instrument for rendering the collision of languages.

Yiddish is the first language of the Schearls, but English, German, Hebrew, Italian, and Polish are also spoken, and in varying registers, by characters in the story. In a novel designed for an Anglophonic reader, it would be misleading and demeaning to put fractured English into the mouths or minds of fluent Yiddish speakers when they are assumed to be using their native tongue. Instead, Roth fashions English prose supple enough to represent the varying speech and thoughts of those who speak and think in other languages and dialects. In his afterword to the 1964 paperback edition, the British critic Walter Allen, noting the many disparate voices that clamor throughout the work, observes that *Call It Sleep* "must be the *noisiest* novel ever written." Roth, whose own first language was Yiddish, remained sensitive to the unique ways in which particular languages refract experience

and thus to the arbitrariness of verbal expression. The title he gave to the first manuscript version of his final work, the four-volume *Mercy of a Rude Stream* (1994–1998), was "Advanced English for Foreigners." In a sense, Roth's texts are always meant to be read as if in translation, as if the words are never entirely transparent or spontaneous.

Not inconsistent with the serious artistic ambitions of *Call It Sleep* is the humor that pervades a novel in which outsiders are continually blundering their way through circumstances they do not quite understand. The most notable comic figure in the book is Bertha, Genya's younger sister, who stays with the Schearls for a while after arriving alone in New York. While Genya and Albert are, for different reasons, withdrawn, sharp-tongued Bertha is exuberant and loquacious, and even during her clumsy attempts to find a husband, she is a vibrant presence amid the dismal tenements. An episode in which Bertha, along with her nephew David, ventures uptown to visit the labyrinthine Metropolitan Museum of Art is a comic gem. Exhausted and lost within the building's endless galleries and corridors, Bertha, thinking to find her way out by following a couple who seem more at ease in this American temple to high culture, discovers they are just as bewildered as she.

Call It Sleep is significant sociologically; it reflects a momentous phenomenon that transformed the United States into a multicultural nation, a phenomenon that was ignored by most of Roth's respectable literary contemporaries. But in its vivid rendition of a child's-eye view, its dramatic exposure of family tensions, and its creation of a rich linguistic texture, Roth's first novel is also an artistic triumph.

FLIGHT FROM THE LITERARY LIFE

Most reviewers were enthusiastic about the novice author's literary achievement. Writing in the *New York Herald Tribune,* Fred T. Marsh hailed *Call It Sleep* as "the most compelling and moving, the most accurate and profound study of an American slum childhood that has yet appeared in this day when, be it said to the credit of our contemporary critics, economic color-lines are no longer drawn in our literature." The few negative reactions to the novel came from the then-influential Marxist press, which faulted its young author for ignoring important social issues in favor of aesthetic self-indulgence. "It is a pity that so many young writers drawn from the proletariat can make no better use of their working class experience than as material for introspective and febrile novels," complained the reviewer for *New Masses.* By 1934 Roth had joined the American Communist Party and, in common with many of the most notable intellectuals and artists of the period, was determined to use his talents to serve its utopian cause. He was hurt by the accusation that his first novel distracted from the global struggle for social justice. Under contract to Scribner's and under the supervision of its legendary editor, Maxwell Perkins, he began a second novel very different from his first one: the story of an illiterate German-American laborer from Cincinnati who loses his right hand in an industrial accident and is converted to Marxism. However, after about 125 pages Roth, whose strongest creative impulses were always autobiographical, found himself unable to continue writing about a tough Midwestern Gentile whose life was so remote from the author's own experience. Although part of the aborted novel was eventually published in 1936 as a story called "If We Had Bacon," Roth burned most of the rest in May 1936, on the same day that he got his nose broken during an effort to organize longshoremen on the New York docks.

Discouraged and unfocused, Roth split from Walton in 1938 when, during a summer at Yaddo, the artists' colony in Saratoga Springs,

New York, he met Muriel Parker, a gifted composer and pianist. After the couple married in 1939, Roth worked for two years in New York City as a substitute high school teacher. Taking advantage of a World War II industrial training program, he became a precision metal grinder and labored at that trade, first in New York City and then in Providence and Boston, until 1946, when he purchased inexpensive land in Maine. Although Roth at first made sporadic efforts to continue his writing and even succeeded in placing a few short stories in *The New Yorker,* by the end of the 1940s he had essentially abandoned his literary ambitions. He lost contact with the authors and intellectuals he knew in New York City and gave himself up to an obscure rural existence under relatively primitive conditions. Apprehensive about persecution during the anti-Communist purges of the period, he even took most of his manuscripts out to a hilltop and burned them. *Call It Sleep* was long out of print and generally forgotten, and the people around Augusta, Maine, had no reason to think of Roth except as a crusty, thrifty neighbor.

Muriel had studied piano in Paris under the legendary Nadia Boulanger. However, she abandoned her own promising career and became a teacher to provide basic financial support for the family, which now included two sons: Jeremy, who was born in 1941, and Hugh, who was born in 1943. Her affluent old-line Protestant family broke with her when she married an indigent, immigrant Communist Jew. After a brief, unhappy experience teach- ing in a one-room schoolhouse, Roth helped out by chopping wood, picking blueberries, gathering maple syrup, fighting forest fires, tutoring Latin and math, and serving as an attendant at a mental hospital. From 1953 to 1963 he ran a waterfowl operation out of their house near Augusta, raising and slaughtering geese and ducks. Out of discarded washing machines, burners, stoves, and metal shelves that he salvaged from an Augusta junkyard, he constructed the only plant in Maine equipped to slaughter and pluck geese and ducks. Convinced that his artistry was dead, Roth, mired in personal depression, became an artist of death, the self-taught scourge of waterfowl. In 1954, fourteen years after his last publication—a short story called "Many Mansions," published in *Coronet* (September 1940)—Roth appeared in the *Magazine for Ducks and Geese* (August 1954). His article, "Equipment for Pennies," is a brief primer on how he created a viable business in waterfowl out of abandoned metal scraps.

Roth despised the work, especially the killing. It was as far as he could imagine from the humane task of writing prose that could change the world. But immediately after the rediscovery of *Call It Sleep* in 1964, Roth resented the wide attention he received. He was indignant over journalistic attempts to portray him as a literary freak, and he was anxious over questions about his future as a writer. Now a celebrity, he could no longer evade what seemed his calling by immersing himself in menial rustic labor. The ambitions that led to the creation of *Call It Sleep* thirty years before gradually began to revive. In 1965 he traveled to Spain to do research for a novel about the Inquisition. The novel was never completed, but the trip resulted in a short story, "The Surveyor," that was published in *The New Yorker* (August 6, 1966). In June 1967 Roth was still exploring Spanish persecution of crypto Jews in Guadalajara, Mexico, when, avidly following news of the Six-Day War in the Middle East, he became obsessed with the drama of Israel's survival. The war traumatized him and made him a Zionist. Rejecting the Marxist universalism that he had embraced for more than thirty years as well as the Communist Party's pro-Arab stance, he now saw his identity inextricably bound with that of the Jewish people. Roth would later claim that his alienation from the Jewish community, which began with his family's move from the Lower East Side to Harlem, was responsible for his silence after *Call It Sleep*. He complained that he had lost the cultural continuity with his own people that would have sustained his career beyond a single book and would have enabled him to take his protagonists beyond the childhood of David Schearl. Roth's identification with the Jewish state in 1967 marked the beginning of his redemption as a writer.

SHIFTING LANDSCAPE

In 1968 Roth accepted an invitation from the University of New Mexico to spend the summer at the 160-acre D. H. Lawrence ranch near Taos. He and Muriel liked the area so much that they abandoned Maine for a mobile home in Albuquerque. There, far from the gritty urban landscape in which he grew up and that had provided the raw materials for his most compelling fictions, Roth began to reemerge as an active presence in American literature. Mario Materassi, a young, admiring scholar from the University of Florence who had translated *Call It Sleep* into Italian, visited its author in New Mexico and became a trusted friend. After persuading Roth to allow publication of his short, uncollected work, Materassi put together a volume of miscellaneous texts, *Shifting Landscape: A Composite, 1925–1987* (1987). The title reflects the kaleidoscopic discontinuities in Roth's career. Arranged chronologically according to when the sections were written or first published, the book consists of thirty-one pieces. They include Roth's short stories and essays, as well as excerpts from letters and interviews, with running commentary by Materassi that establishes the context for each contribution. *Shifting Landscape* was designed to satisfy readers who knew Roth only as the author of *Call It Sleep* and were curious to know what else he had written and what direction his life had taken since 1934. It might have served as Roth's autobiography, at least until the publication of *Mercy of a Rude Stream.*

Shifting Landscape begins with Roth's first published piece of writing, "Impressions of a Plumber," the account of a summer job he had written for an English class at City College. The volume also contains "If We Had Bacon," a portion of the novel about a tough proletarian from Cincinnati that Roth had abandoned. The fragment survived only because it was published separately in 1936 in a small magazine called *Signatures: Works in Progress.* Also in the volume are three short stories, "Broker," "Somebody Always Grabs the Purple," and "Many Mansions," that were published in commercial magazines during the fallow period after Roth broke up with Walton. Roth's sojourn in Maine is represented in the collection by his article for the *Magazine for Ducks and Geese.* The beginnings of a literary comeback are apparent in "Petey and Yotsee and Mario," a short story that first appeared in *The New Yorker* on July 14, 1956, about a Jewish boy growing up in Harlem who is sensitive to the anti-Semitism of his three Gentile friends. In "At Times in Flight: A Parable," published in *Commentary* in July 1959, Roth, who almost always derives his fiction from autobiography, recounts an incident that occurred in 1938 during his residence at an artists' colony he calls Z but which very much resembles Yaddo. While courting a musician he calls Martha but who very much resembles Muriel, the narrator takes her to watch a horse race on the track adjoining the colony. Roth's description of how one horse suddenly breaks its leg and has to be shot is meant as an analogy to the death of Pegasus, to the demise of literary ambition within the author himself.

However, the steady, if not prodigious, output of short fiction over the lean times represented in *Shifting Landscape* demonstrates that, even during the years of obscurity before the rediscovery of *Call It Sleep,* Roth's artistic aspiration and inspiration were never entirely extin-

guished. "The Surveyor," the story that he wrote and published in 1966 in the wake of belated acclaim for his first book, reflects Roth's renewed determination to write another novel. Set in Seville, the story concerns an American Jew who insists on laying a wreath in memory of *conversos* martyred by the Inquisition for their refusal to renounce the faith of their ancestors. The surname he gave to the protagonist of his story, Stigman, is the same as the name of his alter ego in *Mercy of a Rude Stream,* the formidable sequence of novels that he did manage to complete just before his death.

Also included in *Shifting Landscape* are occasional essays that reflect Roth's evolving attitudes toward his identity and his art and that offer some clues to the mystery of his legendary silence as a novelist between 1934 and 1994. "Where My Sympathy Lies," a brief statement published in 1937, endorsed Joseph Stalin's efforts to purge Soviet society of Trotskyite dissidents and reflects the ideological commitment that made Roth question whether *Call It Sleep* was sufficiently revolutionary. One revealing thread in the nonfiction selections included in *Shifting Landscape* is the change in Roth's perspective on his Jewishness. As late as March 1963, in a contribution to a symposium on Diaspora culture published in the American Zionist magazine *Midstream,* he still espoused the universalist aversion to ethnic particularism that he had embraced as a Communist thirty years before. Impatient with such parochial symposia, Roth, known then as an obscure American Jewish novelist, if at all, proclaimed: "I can only say, again, that I feel that to the great boons Jews have already conferred upon humanity, Jews in America might add this last and greatest one: of orienting themselves toward ceasing to be Jews" (*Shifting Landscape*). Yet four years later, traumatized by the possibility that Arab armies would overwhelm and exterminate the Jews of Israel, Roth expressed solidarity with his threatened people, the victors of the

Six-Day War. "I felt at last that Jews had redeemed themselves by self-sacrifice and sheer valor," he explained. "From that point on, and there were other reasons, I experienced a resurgence of my long dormant literary vocation."

Far from ceasing to be a Jew, Roth now took pride in and inspiration from his ethnic identity. His new sense of community even caused him to repudiate James Joyce, the novelist who had most influenced the style and texture of *Call It Sleep*. Roth's reverence for the author of *A Portrait of the Artist as a Young Man* and *Ulysses* had been evident not only in explicit statements but in his adaptation of the stream-of-consciousness technique and in his celebration of the sensitive, alienated individual. The later selections in *Shifting Landscape* rejected Joyce, who abandoned his native Ireland for artistic cosmopolitanism, as a dangerous model. In its authorial commentary, Roth's final, redemptive fictional project, *Mercy of a Rude Stream,* would explicitly condemn Joyce, blaming his influence for Roth's own artistic impasse. And he would at last embrace the untidy details of an American Jewish life that spanned much of the twentieth century.

FINAL OPUS

In 1979 Roth began writing a vast fictional sequence that was a very thinly disguised version of his own life, closely paralleling his own experiences growing up in Harlem, attending City College, and becoming involved with Eda Lou Walton. A woman very much like Walton is named Edith Welles, and the narrator, an aging, autobiographical novelist living in Albuquerque, calls his wife M instead of Muriel, his older son Jess instead of Jeremy, his younger son Herschel instead of Hugh. Roth does not even bother to change his mother's maiden name, Farb. Although he names his protagonist Ira Stigman rather than David Schearl, the new work is in effect a continuation of *Call It Sleep*.

Among the most elusive of literary figures, Roth—who withdrew from public attention by moving to Maine and then New Mexico—is also one of the most confessional, and he deemed the material in his final opus so sensitive and potentially painful to those he loved that he did not intend to publish it, at least as long as his wife Muriel was still alive. Because of failing health that sent him to the hospital several times, Roth expected Muriel to survive him; in fact, his beloved wife of fifty-one years died of congestive heart failure in 1990, a loss that plunged him into profound depression and drove him to attempt suicide. Ultimately his resolve to conclude his final literary task was strengthened, and he also felt free to publish the work while he still lived.

In an Albuquerque house designed in the 1930s as a funeral parlor, the former Latin teacher composed a fictional sequence, *Mercy of a Rude Stream,* whose acronym, MORS, means death and whose tone throughout is valedictory. Roth appropriated the title itself from a soliloquy in act 3, scene 2, of Shakespeare's *Henry VIII*. In the passage, which Roth appropriates as an epigraph to his novel, Cardinal Wolsey describes himself, "weary and old with service," as abandoned "to the mercy of a rude stream that must for ever hide me." Yet, suggesting the theme of redemption that is central to his final fiction if not his entire career, Roth concludes the epigraph by commenting that: "The rude stream did show me Mercy." *Mercy of a Rude Stream* is the redeeming legacy of a troubled man who was touched by what *Requiem for Harlem* (1998), the last volume of the work, calls "that unique, unutterable afflatus of creativity." That touch returned sixty years after the publication of his first book.

Suffering from rheumatoid arthritis so crippling that it was agony even to hold a pencil, Roth found the keyboard of a personal computer more hospitable to his physical frailties. With the aid of a young assistant who served as a copyeditor and general factotum, the ailing octogenarian managed to turn out 3,200 manuscript pages before his death in Albuquerque at the age of eighty-nine, on October 13, 1995. In his preface to the 1960 edition of *Call It Sleep,* Harold Ribalow quotes Roth as telling him: "There is one theme I like above all others, and that is redemption." Redemption is certainly a recurring theme within Roth's final work, as it is in the twilight revival of his literary powers.

The first two volumes of *Mercy of a Rude Stream—A Star Shines over Mt. Morris Park* and *A Diving Rock on the Hudson*—were published in 1994 and 1995, respectively, before their author's death. Robert Weil, who served as Roth's editor at St. Martin's Press, carved two more volumes out of his final manuscripts and published them as *From Bondage* in 1996 and *Requiem for Harlem* in 1998. Left unpublished from the author's final literary outpouring was enough material to constitute two additional volumes. "You are not required to finish," declares the Talmudic dictum that Roth, struggling against the failure of his body if not his spirit as he tapped out every word, adapted as the epigraph to *Requiem for Harlem* even as he refuted it. This authorization for insufficiency, from Mishnah Abot 2:16, appears at the outset of *Requiem for Harlem.* His provisional title for it was "Portrait of the Artist as an Old Fiasco," and in an unpublished letter to Robert Manning, the editor of the *Atlantic Monthly,* dated May 6, 1969, its despondent author slighted his last, autumnal effort as "a rambling, interminable multivolume opus." Yet Roth was the Rip Van Winkle of modern authors, a major figure in both the 1930s and the 1990s, and it was not hyperbole for *Vanity Fair* in 1994 to have hailed his resurgence as "the literary comeback of the century."

For all his notorious procrastination, Roth was an artist of exitry; the prose lullaby that closes *Call It Sleep* is one of the most plangent finales in all of American literature:

It was only toward sleep one knew himself still lying on the cobbles, felt the cobbles under him, and over him and scudding ever toward him like a black foam, the perpetual blur of shod and running feet, the broken shoes, new shoes, stubby, pointed, caked, polished, buniony, pavement-beveled, lumpish, under skirts, under trousers, shoes, over one and through one, and feel them all and feel, not pain, not terror, but strangest triumph, strangest acquiescence. One might as well call it sleep. He shut his eyes.

Requiem for Harlem, too, concludes with the beginning of a dream. Like *A Portrait of the Artist as a Young Man,* Roth's parting tetralogy ends with the start of a writing career. "Ira boarded the train, his cold fingers still aching, and strait was the route, and strait the rails—the IRT swerved, squealing on the tracks of the long curve westward as it repaired downtown and the hell out of Harlem."

A STAR SHINES OVER MT. MORRIS PARK

The first volume of Roth's autobiographical tetralogy begins in 1914, on the eve of World War I, when his protagonist and alter ego, Ira Stigman, is eight years old. When Ira's mother's parents arrive in New York City from Galicia, Ira, Chaim (Herman), and Leah Stigman move from the Lower East Side to live near the newcomers in a Jewish section of Harlem. However, because Leah is unhappy with their rear apartment, the Stigmans soon move again, to a cold-water flat in a largely Irish area of Harlem. Ira is tormented by local anti-Semitic bullies, but when he visits his old neighborhood on the Lower East Side the boy realizes that he no longer belongs there either. He also feels estranged from his newly arrived relatives, who speak Yiddish and do not adapt to American ways.

Rambling and anecdotal, *A Star Shines over Mt. Morris Park* introduces members of Ira's extended family, including its patriarch, his grandfather, Ben Zion Farb. After being drafted into the army, Uncle Moe returns as a local hero from combat in Europe. Uncle Louie, a socialist postman, impresses Ira as "a real American, a Yankee," but does not impress Leah Stigman enough to reciprocate his romantic attentions while her husband is away in St. Louis looking for a job. Ira's truculent father, Chaim, avoids the war by finding brief employment as a streetcar conductor, which is classified as essential work, before taking a position as a waiter. As ineffectual a provider as he is a father, Chaim Stigman is, like Albert Schearl, a moody, menacing figure to his young son, who finds he must make his way in an ominous world alone.

Because of their move out of a Jewish neighborhood and because of the family's limited means, Ira does not attend Hebrew school. Although he does, at thirteen, undergo bar mitzvah, a ritual initiation into the community of Jewish men, Ira feels no meaningful connection to it. He is convinced that "he was only a Jew because he *had* to be a Jew; he hated being a Jew; he didn't want to be one, saw no virtue in being one, and realized he was caught, imprisoned in an identity from which there was no chance of his ever freeing himself." In the eighth grade, when he gets a job as a stock boy at Park & Tilford, gourmet grocers, he feels liberated by exposure to nonkosher foods. Delivering expensive baskets to wealthy customers, Ira is also initiated into the intricacies of American social stratification.

A Star Shines over Mt. Morris Park follows Ira into the early 1920s, but it alternates between the experiences of its young protagonist and miscellaneous commentary, in different and smaller type, by a weary, octogenarian Ira. To this and the three subsequent volumes in the series, Roth appends a glossary of Yiddish terms to assist the Anglophonic reader in making sense of expressions his immigrant characters employ. Looking back on his life, the older Ira Stigman, who, like Roth himself, suffers from rheumatoid arthritis and lives in Albuquerque, addresses his computer directly, personifying it and naming it Ecclesias. Many of the critics who reviewed the novel when it appeared in 1994 faulted these authorial interpolations for being superfluous and tendentious. While marveling at Roth's astonishing return to book-length fiction after a silence of sixty years, many were disappointed by what seemed an artistic chasm between *A Star Shines over Mt. Morris Park* and *Call It Sleep*. Written in a straightforward, naturalistic style consistent with Roth's deliberate rejection of Joycean flourishes, the new novel seemed episodic and inconclusive. Before the publication of the remaining three volumes, it was difficult to discern the achievement in this first installment of Roth's tetralogy.

A DIVING ROCK ON THE HUDSON

The second volume of *Mercy of a Rude Stream,* like the first, alternates between the aged, ailing Ira Stigman speaking to Ecclesias and episodes from his youth more than seventy years earlier. It begins with facing charts of Ira's paternal and maternal family trees. At the outset of *A Diving Rock on the Hudson,* the year is 1921, and its protagonist is just entering Stuyvesant High School. In the novel's final pages the year is 1925, and although he receives a "D" in his college English class, Ira, a student at City College, is encouraged to continue writing when an essay he produces on assignment, "Impressions of a Plumber," is published in the literary magazine, *The Lavender.*

In *A Star Shines over Mt. Morris Park,* Ira is an only child, but a sister two years his junior named Minnie suddenly and sensationally appears in the second volume of *Mercy of a Rude Stream*—as Ira's partner in incest. So, too, is his younger cousin, Stella. "This is a work of fiction," announces the book's copyright page. "This novel is certainly not an autobiography, nor should it be taken as such." But because *A*

Diving Rock on the Hudson seems so patently derived directly from Henry Roth's life, the apparent disclosure by its venerable, elderly, "fictional" author of sexual transgressions during his adolescence immediately brought its actual author more attention than he had received for anything else since 1964. It was reasonable to speculate that paralyzing guilt over incest was—in addition to alienation from the Jewish community as well as Marxist allegiances that failed to elicit his most powerful emotions—one of the reasons for his notorious writer's block. If Roth, whose fictional inspiration was almost always autobiographical, were to continue beyond *Call It Sleep,* he would have to take his protagonist through adolescence. And if he were to be true to his own experience, he would be obliged to confront his own shameful behavior with his sister and his cousin. Roth was not prepared to do that until he was in his eighties and embracing his own extinction, when most of the people who could be hurt by his shocking revelations were gone. Although his sister, Rose, was still alive, Roth paid her an indemnity of $10,000 for the right to divulge dark family secrets.

Like much of the rest of the tetralogy, *A Diving Rock on the Hudson* is a document of self-loathing in which the aging narrator finds many reasons to despise his awkward, erring younger self and welcomes his own imminent demise. The novel derives its title from a moment in which young Ira, caught stealing fountain pens at school, is tempted to drown himself in the Hudson River. He becomes convinced that his father's contempt for him is justified and that he is an unworthy companion to Farley Hewin, a celebrated track star who was his loyal friend until Ira, disgraced, stopped seeing him. Nor does his friendship with Billy Green, an energetic Protestant who seems to lack Ira's Jewish neuroses and with whom he enjoys boating and camping, survive their high school graduation. Friendship with Larry Gordon lasts a bit longer

and introduces Ira, a blue-collar immigrant who spends his summers hawking soft drinks at the Polo Grounds and Yankee Stadium, to the ways of a stable, middle-class family. When Ira is a student at City College, Larry, who is enrolled at New York University, introduces his friend to his teacher and lover, Edith Welles. And that is just the beginning of more torment and more text.

FROM BONDAGE

The third volume of *Mercy of a Rude Stream* begins and concludes with allusions to Samuel Taylor Coleridge, under the sign of the Ancient Mariner. It starts with an epigraph from the famous poem about an aging, obsessive storyteller and ends with a discussion of the line, "He prayeth best, who loveth best." Like Coleridge's Wedding Guest, readers will be spellbound by ancient Ira's vivid evocations of assignations, conversations, and job assignments seventy years earlier.

The opening scene of *From Bondage* recalls an exhilarating summer that Ira spent sharing a cottage in Woodstock, New York, with Edith and Larry. Ira covets his buddy's lover, although he fears that shabby domestic lechery has rendered him unworthy of the older, more sophisticated Gentile. Ira envies Larry's facile talents, as well as his assimilation into middle-class America. "Larry could relate his adventures; they slipped easily through regular channels. His didn't, his were deformed, fitted no channel, could never be told." They are told, of course, many years later, in *From Bondage,* a novel very much like the one that Ira, dying, struggles over in his agonizing, solitary sessions with Ecclesias. It is a book that, more than Larry's kind of conventional writing, overpowers with the force of delayed revelation and the hope of ultimate but earthly redemption. Although he expects Edith to tire of the shallow Larry, who suffers from premature ejaculation, he does not count on her involvement with other men, including Lewlyn Craddock, a sociology instructor and Anglican priest. Ira is both delighted and dismayed to find himself treated as a neutral confidant, a mere and mediocre undergraduate made privy to remarkable romantic triangulations within Edith's cosmopolitan circle of artists and intellectuals.

Before Edith and Ira become lovers, Edith serves as the uncouth young Jew's mentor, initiating him into the mysteries of James Joyce and T. S. Eliot, whose arcane texts he admires and then despises for their emotional sterility. Despite their dazzling stylistic virtuosity, the modernist masters abandoned, Ira comes to realize, the common people from whom art derives its power. His initial rapture over *Ulysses,* an outlawed work that he reads in a copy that Edith smuggles back from Europe, is undercut by his recognition that the novel was "an evasion of history; its author resolved to perceive nothing of the continuing evolution of Ireland, refusing to discover anything latent within the seeming inane of a day in 1904. History may have been a nightmare, but the ones who could have awakened him were the very ones he eschewed: his folk."

Ira resents his feckless father, Chaim, a failed milkman turned waiter, for having forced the family to move away from the Jewish community of the Lower East Side. Although he flirted with Marxist abstractions, the older Ira comes to understand that he can overcome his creative aridity only by returning to the kindred ordinary Jews whom he has sought to transcend and some of whom he has sexually abused. Late in life, he realizes that incest is a symptom of the arrested development that enabled him to devise a child's-eye masterpiece but obstructed other writing. Ira attributes his inability to achieve a sexual relationship with a mature woman outside his family to the same cause that prevented him from following up on his youthful novel of prepubescence: "his contin-

ued, his prolonged infantilism." *From Bondage* diagnoses the emotional captivity from which Ira learns to liberate himself only much later, through his writing.

Like Roth himself, Ira puzzles over the "grave and disabling discontinuity" following the publication of his ambitious first novel. Although both the author and his fictional alter ego have for decades been trying to explain to others and themselves why they failed to follow up on an early masterpiece, Ira spends much of *From Bondage* attempting to justify this shocking, shameful book. He asks himself: "Why was he doing this, demeaning himself—and perhaps jews, the multitude of jews who had transformed one previous novel into a shrine, a child's shrine at that—to the extent he was?" Is writing this lacerating good for the Jews? From an initial ambition to transcend the limitations of his origins in a poor family of immigrant Jews, Ira eventually learns that the only way to attain the universal for which he yearns is through embrace of the parochial. He credits the renewal of literary creativity in his eighties to his belated identification with the Jewish people, particularly with the revived Jewish state, what he calls "the midwife of his rebirth: Israel." He explains that "it was Israel that had rescued him from Joyce, had rescued him from alienation, modified him even to tolerating the Diaspora. It was late in happening, true, but it *had* happened, and it succeeded in altering the orientation of the once withdrawn individual." From an individualist aesthete, Ira sees himself transformed into a voice for his people, and it is by discovering and cultivating that voice that he is able to overcome his artistic and human obstructions, to write a novel very like the one that Roth constructs about him.

From Bondage is not nearly as schematic or tendentious as this outline might suggest. It immerses its reader in the felt life of an earnest bounder, compelled to move beyond the meager cold-water tenement of his uneducated parents into the enchanted intellectual bohemia that he imagines Edith inhabiting. A tense nocturnal scene in Aunt Mamie's apartment, in which Ira slinks past Zaida—his pious grandfather—and Mamie after an illicit tryst with his cousin Stella, is consummately constructed. Also memorable is a sequence in which Ira accompanies Edith to the pier in Hoboken—to see her lover Lewlyn off to England, where he intends to join another woman—and returns to sleep chastely beside Edith in her Greenwich Village bed. Ira's menial jobs as a clerk in a fancy candy shop and as a grease monkey on a repair crew of the New York subway system are vividly rendered. So is the old man's frank desire for death; the Cumaean Sibyl's announcement, "Apothanein thelo" ("I wish to die"), is what the aging author asks to be inscribed and hung in his study in New Mexico. Yet suffusing and exalting all is Ira's literary mission and his love for M, the musician he met at Yaddo so long ago, from whom he has been widowed for five years, and who is the object of what, in the novel's final words, Ira refers to as "the passionate homage he now so keenly felt."

REQUIEM FOR HARLEM

Requiem for Harlem concludes the four-volume *Künstlerroman* (artist-novel) that serves as Roth's scathing portrait of the artist as young wretch. Even more than the previous installments, this book both recounts and enacts its protagonist's humiliation, with Ira as the literary voodoo doll for his tormented author, Roth.

Roth's novel begins in gluttony and dyspepsia, wallows in revulsion, and concludes with the prospect of redemption. Yet its title, *Requiem for Harlem*, suggests nostalgia for a troubled adolescence in the lowly uptown neighborhood on which the final pages close the book. It is an elegy for anguished youth. The year is 1927, and Ira Stigman, twenty-one years old, is attending his senior year at City College. The opening pages recount Ira's arduous journey—with weary feet and, after gorging himself on pasta, a bloated stomach—from Harlem, in upper Manhattan, all the way down to Greenwich Village, near the lower tip of the island. When he arrives at Edith Welles's apartment, she is occupied with another man, and Ira returns to his room up on East 119th Street. However, in the final pages of *Requiem for Harlem*, he again makes his way down to Edith's house, to stay. In the novel's parting, plangent words, Ira, brooding on infernal guilt, takes a squealing subway "downtown and the hell out of Harlem." He has, at least, been transported into purgatory.

A college exam on *Paradise Lost* forces the immigrant scholar, afflicted with his own "sinister cyst of guilt that was within the self, denigrating the *yontif* [holiday], denigrating everything within reach, exuding ambiguity, anomaly, beyond redemption now," to ponder the vile connections between Satan and his daughter Sin. Yet Ira, who had earlier ceased sexual relations with his younger sister, Minnie, begun when she was only ten, continues his incestuous relationship with his sixteen-year-old cousin, Stella, even as his sentimental apprenticeship to Edith, who is older and more accomplished, deepens into something resembling mature love. After one last brazen act of self-degradation, Ira moves out of his family's Harlem flat and into a Greenwich Village apartment with Edith.

With a narrower palette of character and incident than the other volumes, *Requiem for Harlem* offers an excruciating focus on Ira's guilty desperation after learning that Stella might be pregnant. Anxiety and shame cause him to break, rudely, with Larry Gordon, by spurning his beneficent invitation to Thanksgiving dinner. The novel also provides revelations about further foulness within the Stigman family, about vile actions by Ira's father. Although they are fewer and shorter than in the previous three volumes, occasional interludes describe an elderly Ira, "goofiest of all scriveners," struggling, like Roth himself, to record his lacerating memories on his word processor, Ecclesias.

Requiem for Harlem is a document of the 1920s that happens to have been written seventy years later, in a style by turns supple and wooden, that recalls both Yiddish melodrama and the audacity of the post–World War I avant-garde. The narrative adopts the form by which the elder Ira imagines life itself: "full of chaotic fragments, discreet, in the mathematical sense, disparate, often dull and banal, but often fiercely engrossing, disparate but often desperate. And as often unexpected and unforeseen." But the book acquires intensity from its searing focus on Ira's dreadful burden, and from its confinement to a single week in November 1927. In the days preceding Thanksgiving, Ira concentrates his energies on freeing himself from the toxic snares of family.

While trying to study Milton at the kitchen table, Ira is helpless witness to the ferocious squabbles between his mother and his father. Like Albert Schearl in *Call It Sleep,* Chaim Stigman is a violent bundle of festering resentments, a man possessed of a permanent sense of personal abuse. Disappointed in his ambitions, unsuccessful in his business schemes in Galicia, St. Louis, and New York, Ira's father cannot hold a job for very long before he antagonizes his latest employer. He tyrannizes and terrorizes his only son, who sees him as "a mean, stingy, screwy little louse" yet is afraid to cross him. It is difficult for Ira to understand why his long-suffering mother did not leave her abusive husband many years ago.

It is easier for Ira to guess why Zaida, his maternal grandfather, moves away from Aunt Mamie's apartment in Manhattan in order to live with other relatives in Queens. In *From Bondage,* Ira, concluding a late-night visit to Mamie's place, had brazenly had his way with Cousin Stella within a few feet of their grandfather's bedroom door. Ambiguous statements uttered by Zaida lead Ira to conclude that the pious old man knew exactly what was going on between his two grandchildren and was too horrified to remain within that polluted household any longer. Ira begins to panic at the possibility that the entire family will soon learn of his depravity.

His most immediate concern, however, is over the fact that Stella, a pudgy girl who does not even appeal to him either physically or intellectually, is four days late for her menstrual period. Ira confides his fears to Edith, who has earlier aborted the fetus resulting from her own affair with the married Lewlyn, and she generously arranges to have her physician examine Stella. When Ira arrives at Stella's secretarial school in order to escort her to her appointment, she informs him that the pregnancy was a false alarm. Ira's elation at this unexpected news soon turns to lust and its satisfaction. Compounding the author Ira's revulsion over his sordid relations with his cousin is the memory of how deliverance from the horror of Stella's pregnancy was not enough to cure him of his incestuous compulsions.

Like Zaida's decision to move out of Mamie's apartment, Ira's departure from the Stigman household in Harlem is—albeit belated—an assertion of will, the feckless young man's emergence, as suggested in the title to volume 3, *From Bondage.* Ira's continuing servitude to family—his mother and his cousin—has infantilized him, and his departure for Greenwich Village marks a coming-of-age. Under the tutelage of the Gentile Edith, a mature woman and a writer, he can look forward to advancing outside the constrictive circle of Jewish immigrants and to developing the literary talents already manifested in his college compositions. The elder Ira looks back on a successful first novel that sounds very much like *Call It Sleep,* even as he struggles to write the cathartic new book whose awful secrets kept him for sixty years from extending his literary career and whose successful completion will provide him with "the Promethean catalytic exercising of his consciousness."

In the final pages of the cycle's final book, *Requiem for Harlem,* Ira bids farewell to his dysfunctional, debilitating family and his loathsome sexual compulsions by moving down to Greenwich Village to live with Edith. The apprentice artist is finally ready to write a novel very much like *Call It Sleep.* And, after disburdening himself of excruciating secrets, the eighty-nine-year-old Roth was finished writing and prepared at last to call it sleep.

REQUIEM FOR ROTH

After the rediscovery of *Call It Sleep,* Roth was the recipient of many prestigious honors. In 1965, in addition to a grant from the National Institute of Arts and Letters, he was given a medal for outstanding achievement by an alumnus of City College, the institution from which he had graduated, barely, with mediocre grades, in 1928. In 1994 Roth even collected an honorary doctorate from the University of New Mexico. The celebrity and esteem he attracted, if not enjoyed, at the end offered a stark contrast to the obscurity in which, even after publishing his extraordinary first novel, Roth lived for most of his eighty-nine years. He offers a dramatic lesson in the vicissitudes of reputation, in how fallible and changeable are an era's assessments of literary merit.

Roth was a harsher judge of himself than any reader is likely to be. Shame is the engine that drives much of his later fiction, and a quest for continuity is the only thread he found to link the episodes of a patchy life. So disappointed in himself that he welcomed death, Roth used his later fiction to exorcise his revulsion. From Galicia to New York to Maine to Albuquerque, the arc of Roth's eighty-nine years was classically Greek in both abomination and cathartic

redemption. His final, excruciating effort at expression gave life to his self-loathing, even as it put to rest an old man's mortal pain.

Selected Bibliography

WORKS OF HENRY ROTH

NOVELS

Call It Sleep. New York: Robert O. Ballou, 1934.

A Star Shines over Mt. Morris Park. New York: St. Martin's, 1994. (Vol. 1 of *Mercy of a Rude Stream.*)

A Diving Rock on the Hudson. New York: St. Martin's, 1995. (Vol. 2 of *Mercy of a Rude Stream.*)

From Bondage. New York: St. Martin's, 1996. (Vol. 3 of *Mercy of a Rude Stream.*)

Requiem for Harlem. New York: St. Martin's, 1998. (Vol. 4 of *Mercy of a Rude Stream.*)

NONFICTION

Nature's First Green. New York: William Targ, 1979.

Shifting Landscape: A Composite, 1925–1987. Edited by Mario Materassi. Philadelphia: Jewish Publication Society, 1987.

MANUSCRIPTS

Sixty-eight boxes of Henry Roth's papers are housed at the archives of the American Jewish Historical Society in New York City. The manuscript of *Call It Sleep* is held in the Berg Collection of the New York Public Library.

CRITICAL AND BIOGRAPHICAL STUDIES

Adams, Stephen J. "'The Noisiest Novel Ever Written': The Soundscape of Henry Roth's *Call It Sleep.*" *Twentieth Century Literature* 35:43–64 (spring 1989).

Allen, Walter. Afterword to *Call It Sleep,* by Henry Roth. London: M. Joseph, 1964.

Altenbernd, Lynn. "An American Messiah: Myth in Henry Roth's *Call It Sleep.*" *Modern Fiction Studies* 35:673–687 (winter 1989).

Diamant, Naomi. "Linguistic Universes in Henry Roth's *Call It Sleep.*" *Contemporary Literature* 27:336–355 (fall 1986).

Halkin, Hillel. "Henry Roth's Secret." *Commentary,* May 1994, pp. 44–47.

Howe, Irving. "Life Never Let Up." *New York Times Book Review,* October 25, 1964, pp. 1, 60.

Kellman, Steven G. "Requiem for Henry Roth." *USA Today Magazine,* March 2000, pp. 75–76.

————. "'The Midwife of His Rebirth': Henry Roth and Zion." *Judaism* 49:342–351 (summer 2000).

Lesser, Wayne. "A Narrative's Revolutionary Energy: The Example of Henry Roth's *Call It Sleep.*" *Criticism* 23:155–176 (spring 1981).

Lyons, Bonnie. "After *Call It Sleep.*" *American Literature* 45:610–612 (January 1974).

————. *Henry Roth: The Man and His Work.* New York: Cooper Square, 1976.

Marsh, Fred T. "A Great Novel about Manhattan Boyhood." *New York Herald Tribune,* February 17, 1935, p. 6.

Materassi, Mario. "The Return of Henry Roth: An Inside View." In *Their Own Words: European Journal of the American Ethnic Imagination* 1:47–55 (1983).

Mehegan, David. "Call It Writer's Block." *Boston Globe,* February 1, 1994, pp. 49, 52.

Michaels, Leonard. "The Long Comeback of Henry Roth: Call It Miraculous." *New York Times Book Review,* August 15, 1993, pp. 19–21.

Redding, Mary Edrich. "Call It Myth: Henry Roth and *The Golden Bough.*" *Centennial Review* 18:180–195 (spring 1974).

Ribalow, Harold. Preface to *Call It Sleep,* by Henry Roth. Paterson, N.J.: Pageant Books, 1960.

Rifkind, Donna. "Call It Irresponsible." *The New Criterion* 6:75–76 (February 1988).

Rosen, Jonathan. "The 60-Year Itch." *Vanity Fair,* February 1994, pp. 36–46.

Samet, Tom. "Henry Roth's Bull Story: Guilt and Betrayal in *Call It Sleep.*" *Studies in the Novel* 7:569–583 (winter 1975).

Studies in American Jewish Literature (University Park, Pa.) 5 (spring 1979). (The issue is devoted entirely to studies of Henry Roth.)

Wirth-Nesher, Hana, ed. *New Essays on Call It Sleep.* New York: Cambridge University Press, 1996.

———— "Henry Roth." In *Contemporary Jewish-American Novelists: A Bio-Critical Sourcebook.* Edited by Joel Shatzky and Michael Taub. Westport, Conn.: Greenwood, 1997. Pp. 327–334.

INTERVIEWS

Bronsen, David. "A Conversation with Henry Roth." *Partisan Review* 36:265–280 (spring 1969).

Freedman, William. "Henry Roth in Jerusalem: An Interview." *Literary Review* 23:5–23 (fall 1979).

Friedman, John S. "On Being Blocked and Other Literary Matters: An Interview." *Commentary,* August 1977, pp. 27–38.

Lyons, Bonnie. "An Interview with Henry Roth." *Shenandoah* 25:48–71 (fall 1973).

—STEVEN G. KELLMAN

James Salter

1925–

JOSEPH CAMPBELL WROTE in *The Power of Myth* (1988):

> People say that what we're all seeking is a meaning for life. I don't think that's what we're really seeking. I think that what we're seeking is an experience of being alive, so that our life experiences on the purely physical plane will have resonances within our innermost being and reality, so that we actually feel the rapture of being alive.

Any serious student, or even casual reader, of the life and works of James Salter will recognize that Salter has long held a similar belief.

EARLY YEARS AND PREP SCHOOL

James Salter was born James Horowitz on June 10, 1925 in Passaic, New Jersey. He was the only child of Louis George Horowitz and Mildred Scheff. In his *Burning the Days: Recollections* (1997), Salter described the day of his birth as being the hottest imaginable, although the evening brought welcome relief in the form of a fierce thunderstorm. He wrote, "I would like to think I somehow remember it and that my love of all storms proceeded from that first one, but more likely I was sleeping." In later life, Salter was fond of the fantasy that perhaps, given the date and location of his birth, he was delivered by the renowned poet and doctor William Carlos Williams. In fact, the doctor attending his mother was named Carlisle.

George Horowitz (Salter has written that his father never liked his first name and preferred to be called George) earned degrees from the U.S. Military Academy at West Point and MIT.

He was a moderately successful builder in New Jersey when he married Mildred Sheff in 1924. The birth of their son stirred Horowitz to seek greater financial rewards, and he moved his family to New York City in 1927. There, Salter grew up in a series of apartment buildings, moving from one to another as the rise and fall of his father's fortunes as a real estate broker allowed or necessitated. The family was Jewish, but that religion played a minor, if any, role in their lives. Indeed, Christmas was celebrated in grand style, complete with tree, presents, and parties. "Then as now, the best weeks of the year were at Christmas," Salter wrote in *Burning the Days*. "Colored by those Christmases, perhaps, others have all seemed to me exciting, like some glamorous invitation."

In 1929, the year of the Great Crash on Wall Street, Salter's father suffered a financial catastrophe presaging those that would ruin his health and bring about his death thirty years later. A man named Lignante convinced Horowitz to join him in a venture, the building of Hampshire House on Central Park South. For a share in the completed building, Horowitz loaned Lignante seventy-five thousand dollars with no collateral. The stock market crash destroyed Lignante and his hopes of Hampshire House. The money was never repaid. Somehow, the Horowitz family survived this tremendous loss and, by the time Salter began grammar school, had taken up residence on the Upper East Side, only a few blocks from the Metropolitan Museum of Art and Central Park.

In spite of the family's financial upheavals, Salter appears to have enjoyed a relatively carefree childhood. He did well in grammar school and was usually at the head of his class. He was liked by his peers and enjoyed the camaraderie of summer camp and trips to the beach at Atlantic City. In addition, a large and colorful extended family of grandparents, aunts, uncles, and cousins dispelled the loneliness that sometimes attends an only child. Salter also took pleasure in the private pastimes of drawing and reading. His reading ability was such that, in 1930, his mother bought him a six-volume set of books from a door-to-door saleswoman. The set, *My Bookhouse,* was a richly illustrated collection of classic literature modified for young readers. Here Salter read Charles Dickens, Leo Tolstoy, the Bible, poetry, and folktales. A poem by Rudyard Kipling, "Ballad of East and West," made a lasting impression on the young boy with its story of heroism and danger, virtue and fortitude.

Salter attended Horace Mann, a prep school in the northern outskirts of New York City, from 1938 to 1942. The curriculum was demanding, based on the classics and required courses in Latin. In addition, the students, all males, were taught a tough ethic of personal responsibility. Salter recalled in *Burning the Days,* "We were not what unknown forces made of us but rather what we made of ourselves." He enjoyed a well-rounded life at Horace Mann, writing for school publications, playing football, and going to parties with girls from Horace Mann's sister school, Lincoln. Another boy who submitted work to the school's literary magazine and played on the football team was Jack Kerouac. Salter knew him then but, as Kerouac was three years older, a tremendous span for adolescent boys, they were not friends. His best friend at Horace Mann was Wink Jaffee. An added attraction to this friendship was Jaffee's mother, Ethel Reiner, a woman of great beauty and style. Salter wrote of her in *Burning the Days:*

> She was a regal figure to me, affected but smiling, her ash-blonde hair heaped on her head, the silk of her dresses whispering. I never saw her in the kitchen—there was a cook—or with a vacuum cleaner in her hand or even changing a shoe, legs crossed, slipping it off and putting on another. Perhaps there were weekend mornings when, in a peignoir with fur cuffs she might scramble eggs to put on a breakfast tray and carry down the hallway to her husband. She suggested the sumptuous.

Clearly, she was an early inspiration and model for the exotic, beautiful women who appear in Salter's novels. In the 1950s Jaffee, who had become a successful stockbroker, advised Salter on how best to invest his money. As a result, he tripled the amount he had received from the movie sale of his first novel, *The Hunters* (1956).

WEST POINT

Salter graduated from Horace Mann in 1942, winning the School Poet award. Although no collection of Salter's poetry has been published, there does exist a privately printed poem to New York City entitled *Still Such* (1992). The poem is a rapid-fire list of recollections that moves like a speeding taxi through Manhattan. Salter had been accepted at Stanford but his father, who had graduated first in his class at West Point, arranged a second alternate's appointment at his alma mater for his son. Salter took the exam as a favor to his father but felt his chances of attending West Point were remote. He was spending the summer working on a farm in Connecticut, daydreaming about life on the West Coast, when word came that, against all odds, the principal appointee had failed the physical and the first alternate had failed the written exam. Salter knew that this was his father's "dream come true" and accepted the appointment. He wrote in *Burning the Days,* "Seventeen, vain, and spoiled by poems, I prepared to enter a remote West Point. I would succeed there, it was hoped, as he had."

Initially, however, success seemed unlikely. Salter rebelled against the rigid demands of cadet life and, in his first year, his name appeared on the punishment lists several times a week. He felt himself divided, split in two. One half was the boy who was fond of literature and wrote poetry and the other half was the unquestioning figure he knew he had to become to survive and succeed at West Point. "I began to change, not what I was truly but what I seemed to be. Dissatisfied, eager to become better, I shed as if they were old clothes the laziness and rebellion of the first year and began anew."

Early in 1944 Salter passed the examinations required for acceptance into flight training and was sent to Pine Bluff, Arkansas. Though less formal, the regimen was every bit as demanding as it was at West Point. A trainee was expected to be able to fly solo after no less than four and no more than eight hours of instruction in open cockpit airplanes, with the instructor seated in the rear and the trainee in the front. If the trainee could not solo after eight hours, he was dismissed and returned to West Point. In addition to hands-on instruction, there were weeks of classes and briefings. Within the required hours, Salter experienced the exaltation of solo flight, an experience he had longed for since reading Antoine de Saint-Exupéry's *Wind, Sand, and Stars* (1939).

Returning to West Point in the fall of 1944, Salter encountered an experience as exhilarating as flying: his first serious love affair. She, the eighteen-year-old daughter of a prosperous New York family, had known Salter before he entered West Point, and it was difficult for her to accept the man he had become. Eventually, however, Salter prevailed. They based their romance on a recently published and popular novel of young love and passion during World War II: *Shore Leave* (1944), by Frederic Wakeman. They enjoyed football weekends and dances together. Other, more amorous activities were enacted in borrowed rooms. During the uncertain times of the war years young couples, most in their late teens, were rushing to the altar. No one knew what tomorrow might bring and an opportunity postponed might very well be an opportunity lost. Salter received a telegram from his sweetheart that went straight to the question: Would he or would he not marry her? Salter's answer was indecisive and she, as she had threatened to do, married his rival. This had a tremendous impact on Salter, who has written that he realized he had turned his back on marriage, money, and the past, never to face them wholeheartedly again. Indeed, he has expressed the feeling that all he has experienced since sometimes seems less vital than the brief passion he shared with this girl.

When Salter graduated from West Point in 1945, the war in Europe had ended. Although he had missed the opportunity to prove himself in that war's great forge, an incident occurred that required every flying skill he had mastered. In May 1945, on a routine night navigation flight out of Stewart Field near West Point, he became lost. As darkness fell, he desperately tried to establish his position. With his fuel tanks almost empty, Salter flew low, looking for any open area where he might land. Over the outskirts of Great Barrington, Massachusetts, he found a dark area that he knew was small for an emergency landing, but his fuel was gone and he had no choice. As the plane neared the ground, one of its wings struck a tree and Salter crashed into a house. Fortunately, the residents had come outside, thinking that the low-flying plane was honoring a family member, a recently returned prisoner of war, and no one was hurt. The plane was demolished but, since the gas tanks were empty, there was no explosion and Salter escaped with only minor injuries.

Salter received more flight training throughout the summer of 1945 and entered the Army Air Force as a second lieutenant. In January of the following year, with the war in the Pacific over, he was assigned to fly transport planes there. For most of the next two years he was based at Hickam Field, Hawaii. Although Salter dedicated himself completely to the Air Force, he never gave up his long-held desire to become a writer. While in the Pacific, he read widely and worked on writing his first novel. Since such pursuits were likely to mark him as a maverick, he wrote during the night and on weekends and adopted a nom de plume, James Salter. He explained his choice in *Burning the Days*: "Salter was as distant as possible from my own name. It was essential not to be identified and jeopardize my career. . . . I wanted to be admired but not known." There were two other reasons for the new name; first, he sought to avoid military censorship, and second, he did not want to be stereotyped as a Jewish-American writer. Such identification, he felt, would create certain expectations in the reading public, limiting the scope of his work. The first reason seems plausible but does not explain why, as a teenager, he wrote poetry under the name James Arnold. Perhaps that merely fulfilled an adolescent boy's wish to distance himself from his father. The second reason is a bit more difficult to understand. In his review of *Burning the Days* for the *New York Review of Books,* A. Alvarez opined, "Being a Jew called Horowitz can't have made his difficult life any easier, though he doesn't mention it because Jewishness was not something he had been brought up to think important." Indeed, while at West Point, Salter attended a few services for Jewish cadets on Friday nights but in the end he opted to attend Sunday morning chapel with the majority of the corps. Salter sent a letter to Alvarez expressing his appreciation for the review. In it he attempted to answer the name change question this way: "The really Great Jews, Singer, Bellow, Malamud, Mailer, Roth, and in their wake many lesser, Heller, Potok, Levin, Brodkey had overwhelmed American literature, and I didn't belong, in any sense, among them. It wasn't my category."

Salter returned to the United States in 1948 and as an officer entered Georgetown University in Washington, D.C. That same year he submitted the manuscript of the novel he had been working on for the past two years to Harper Brothers. It was not accepted, but Salter was encouraged by their expressed desire to see future work.

After earning his master's degree in international affairs at Georgetown, Salter made his first trip to Europe in 1951. A fellow officer and West Pointer, Kelton Farris, who was stationed in Wiesbaden, had written to Salter extolling the glories of Paris. Salter joined Farris and, together with another officer, made a car trip to that city. Paris did not, as it had so many other American writers, enchant Salter on his first visit. He found it, in its postwar condition, dark, grimy, and somewhat disheveled. A few years later, in a small tobacco shop, Salter discovered a display of books unavailable in America. They were books of highly charged eroticism, such as *Our Lady of the Flowers* (1949), *Tropic of Cancer* (1934), *The Ginger Man* (1955), and *The Story of O* (1954). The stories were a revelation to Salter; they presented a new vision of living and loving and writing.

FIRST MARRIAGE AND KOREA

In 1951 Salter married Ann Altemus, whom he had met when she was visiting Honolulu. He had little to say in *Burning the Days* about her or their nearly twenty-four years of married life other than that his mother and her father disapproved of the union. He added that although friends thought she was perfect for him and had great hopes for their future, he felt that the marriage would last five years at most. Nevertheless, the couple married in the chapel at Fort Meyer, Virginia. At this time Salter was serving as an aide-de-camp to General Robert M. Lee. Lee was instrumental in securing an assignment for Salter in a fighter squadron at Presque Isle, Maine. There he found his true calling, flying the best combat plane the Air Force had at that time, the F-86. When the opportunity presented itself, Salter and his classmate and fellow flyer, William Wood, volunteered for combat duty in Korea. Nearly twenty-seven-years old and having missed out on active duty during World War II, Salter felt that chances to achieve glory were passing him by. When he arrived in the Korean arena, he was determined to prove himself. From February to July 1952, Salter flew in over one hundred combat missions against the Russian-made MIG-15s. Despite the number of sorties, Salter downed only one plane and disabled another, a total short of the five "kills" necessary to become an "ace." When Salter ended his tour of duty and returned to a fighter squadron in the United States, he was greatly disappointed with himself. In 1954 he was assigned to duty in Germany, where he served as a squadron operations officer and led an acrobatic team. The long-sought glorious achievements seemed far beyond his reach.

FIRST CHILD AND FIRST NOVEL

In 1955 Salter's first child, a girl the couple named Allan, was born. Also that year, Salter completed his Korean War novel *The Hunters*. He submitted the manuscript to Harper Brothers, where it was accepted and published in 1956. (The names and scenes described here will be from the slightly revised, more readily available 1997 Counterpoint Press edition.)

All the desires and disappointments that Salter experienced in Korea are embodied in the novel's protagonist, Cleve Connell. Cleve arrives in Korea determined to achieve the legendary goal of downing five enemy aircraft and thereby earning recognition as an ace. His reputation as a skilled flyer has preceded him and he is soon made a flight commander. However, successful encounters with the enemy elude him, and his dismay is further exacerbated by the seemingly effortless conquests of a brash,

cocky younger pilot named Pell. Cleve feels that Pell's arrogant disregard for the tactical rules of aerial combat is endangering the other flyers. Nevertheless, as Pell's number of kills increases, so does his celebrity among the men and officers. Finally, the day comes when Cleve shoots down an enemy aircraft and earns a mark on the group tally board. Although he is far behind many others, Cleve marks the occasion by taking a celebratory trip to Tokyo with his friend DeLeo.

The lyricism of the Tokyo interlude stands in marked contrast to the stoic, Spartan existence that has dominated the first half of the novel and provides a glimpse of the writer Salter would become. Cleve and DeLeo waste no time diving headfirst into the many pleasures that were to be found in Tokyo in the years following World War II. Determined visits to brothels and bars give way to more muted pleasures when Cleve pays a visit to a brother of a friend of his father's, the painter, Mr. Miyata. The two days Cleve spends with Miyata and Eiko, Miyata's shy, virginal nineteen-year-old daughter, are intellectually and emotionally stimulating for him. When he hears Miyata's story of losing all of his paintings to Allied bombing raids during World War II, he is impressed by the courage it took for the painter to start over. Cleve enjoys a chaste dalliance with Eiko by an idyllic lakeside. He is reluctant to leave, but duty calls. He and DeLeo learn that there has been a fierce air battle in Korea during their holiday, and he abruptly packs up and heads back to the action, leaving a hastily written note for Eiko.

With the time of his tour of duty running out, Cleve is desperate to prove himself. Pell has surpassed him in kills and has become an ace. Cleve realizes that his achieving five kills in the time he has left is unlikely, but he still dreams of a greater prize: downing the enemy pilots' champion, a brilliant Russian flyer nicknamed Casey Jones. On a mission with his wingman, Billy Hunter, Cleve encounters Casey Jones, stunningly outmaneuvers him, and shoots him down. The battle and the long flight back to the air base seriously deplete their fuel supply and Hunter is killed when his plane crashes short of the runway. Cleve lands unhurt, but without Hunter's confirmation of the downing of Casey Jones, he has no proof of victory. Pell is contemptuous of Cleve's claim that their renowned enemy has been eliminated, citing lack of any kind of proof. Hunter is dead and the camera in Cleve's plane has malfunctioned.

> Cleve looked at them, one by one. Nothing was real. He heard a short, insane cough of contempt leave his lips. He did not know what he was thinking, only that he was far removed, farther than he had ever believed possible.
>
> "Oh yes, there is," he said blindly.
>
> "Who?"
>
> "I can confirm it." He drew a sudden breath. "Hunter got him." It had come out almost subconsciously. Malice had brought it, and protest, and the sweeping magnanimity that accompanies triumph, but, as soon as he said the words, he realized there were no others that would have made it right. Billy Hunter would have his day as a hero, and in memory be never less of a man than he had been on his last flight. Cleve could give him that, at least—a name of his own. It was strange. In all that had passed, he had never imagined anything faintly like it, to have searched the whole heavens for his destiny and godliness, and in the end to have found them on earth.

This could have been the book's final chapter, with Salter-Cleve realizing that his "destiny and godliness" are not to be found in the Air Force, but Salter took the next step. Thoughts of resigning his commission may have been in his mind when he killed his fictional self in a final, vicious air battle. On a routine mission, Cleve is suddenly surrounded by enemy aircraft and cut off from his wingman.

> For Cleve, the war had ended in those final minutes of solitude he had always dreaded. He was carried as "missing in action." If there had been a last cry, electrically distilled through air, it had gone unheard as he fell to the multitudes he feared. They had overcome him in the end, tenaciously, scissoring past him, taking him down. Their heavy shots had splashed into him, and they had followed all the way, firing as they did, with that contagious passion peculiar to hunters.

George Barrett had this to say about the novel in the *New York Times Book Review*: "James Salter, a West Pointer who went to Korea as a jet fighter pilot, has written a novel of that Far Eastern event that has none of the hokum that (for the sake of specific comparison with recent popular Korean war tales) marks James Michener's output." Hollywood's Dick Powell produced and directed a film version of *The Hunters* starring Robert Mitchum and Robert Wagner. Although the screenplay by Wendell Mayes bore little resemblance to Salter's story, the movie brought Salter to the attention of a wider audience.

RESIGNATION, A SECOND NOVEL, AND DOCUMENTARIES

Encouraged by the publication and warm critical reception of *The Hunters* (and the $60,000 he received from Paramount for the movie rights), Salter resigned his commission in the Air Force with the rank of major on June 10, 1957, his thirty-second birthday. The decision was difficult and acting on it was even harder. He had been in uniform since the age of seventeen, nearly half his life. He wandered the Pentagon, stalling, feeling ill, before he submitted his papers. Salter has said it felt like a divorce and that he was the spouse who had failed.

With his wife and Allan and a second daughter, Nina, who was born in 1957, Salter settled into uneasy suburban life in the town of Grandview, north of New York City. In 1958 the family moved to a more rural setting, New City, in Rockland County, New York. Salter found it difficult to write in his busy home so he rented a room for himself in the Peck Slip neighborhood of southeastern Manhattan. He commuted daily to this threadbare room for the solitude he needed to work on his second novel, *The Arm of Flesh* (1961). The neighborhood housed other writers and artists. One in particular became a good friend, the sculptor, Mark di Suvero.

Salter submitted the manuscript of *The Arm of Flesh* to Harper Brothers in 1959 and returned to life in the Hudson Valley. While awaiting publication, Salter supplemented his income by selling swimming pools. This seemingly unrewarding venture (Salter recalls selling only three pools) brought him into contact with Lane Slate, a television writer who lived in nearby Piermont, New York. The two men, finding they were kindred spirits, formed a production company and made documentary films. Their first effort was a social commentary on New York City titled "Daily Life in Ancient Rome," but it was never finished. They did, however, complete several others. One in particular, a twelve-minute documentary about college football titled *Team Team Team,* released in 1959, surprised its creators by winning first prize at the Venice Film Festival in 1960. Encouraged, the pair went on to produce a series on the circus for PBS and a film on contemporary American painters for CBS.

Although Salter had resigned his commission in the Air Force, he remained active in the Air National Guard, flying on weekends and attending summer camps in Virginia and Cape Cod. In 1961, at the height of the Berlin crisis, Salter's unit was called up for service. For the next ten months he was stationed in France. While there, Salter met the man who was to be a major influence on his life as a writer, the American literary lion, Irwin Shaw. Salter and Shaw had the same agent, Max Wilkinson, who suggested to Shaw that he should meet the promising newcomer. Shaw invited Salter to join him for a drink at the Hotel Plaza Athénée

in Paris, and a friendship began that lasted until Shaw's death twenty-eight years later. Salter devoted an entire chapter, "Forgotten Kings," in *Burning the Days* to their relationship. Indeed, their closeness was such that Salter named one of his children Theo Shaw.

A TWICE-TOLD TALE

While Salter was in France, making notes for what would become his third novel, Harper published *The Arm of Flesh* (1961). For this novel Salter again used his Air Force experiences to provide the plot. Set in Germany in the 1950s, it tells the story of the lives and loves of members of a peacetime American fighter squadron, their wives, mistresses, and others. Salter employs a technique used by William Faulkner in *As I Lay Dying* (1930), that of using numerous narrators. Each of the seventeen narrators provides his or her perspective of daily events. Without the sustained suspense of combat found in *The Hunters, The Arm of Flesh* is essentially a novel about boredom. Everyone seems to be waiting for something to happen and, except for several tense scenes of low-fuel landings on fog-enshrouded runways and a trip to Africa for gunnery practice, nothing of much consequence does. Although reviewers reacted favorably to the book, Salter, always his own harshest critic, considered it a failure. He felt that so strongly that he refused requests from such publishers as North Point and Counterpoint to reissue it. Although he abandoned the novel, he did not abandon the story. In the foreword to *Cassada* (2000), he wrote:

> This novel about flying is drawn from another, earlier one, *The Arm of Flesh,* published in 1961 and largely a failure. . . . I had revised *The Hunters* slightly for its second appearance. *The Arm of Flesh,* however, had serious faults and needed to be rewritten completely. Even the title deserved to be changed to, in this case, one of the principal characters. It may have been a mistake to try to

stand on its feet again a failed book, but there were elements in it that continued to be interesting. . . . This new version, then, is meant to be the book the other might have been.

In *Cassada,* Salter added some new characters and changed the names of others, but the most striking difference between the two versions is the dropping of the multi-narrator device in favor of a crisp, straightforward narrative. Other changes are less evident but important to note. A good example can be found by comparing the following scene from both novels. Captain Isbell realizes he must eject from his plane or he is sure to die in an unavoidable crash. Just as Salter had found acting on his decision to resign his commission in the Air Force as difficult as making the decision in the first place, Isbell hesitates to take the action that will release him from certain death. In *The Arm of Flesh,* the passage reads,

> I sit there, trying to think. There is noise I don't hear. There are things I don't see. I've taken hold of the forked grip. I barely start to squeeze when there's another pause, mortal, abrupt. With a surge though it catches again. My fingers tightening, I force my head back against the plate, tense my legs, bring them close, then before I know what has happened, with a shock, a hunching jolt, I am—my fist still holding the two leaves together, the pale lights vanished beneath me—gone. Departed. Into the black air.

The same scene in *Cassada* reads,

> He sits there trying to think. He has hold of the forked ejection grip and is beginning to squeeze when there's another hesitation, mortal, abrupt. A surge as the engine catches again. The last of the fuel. He forces his head back against the heavy plate, tenses his legs bringing them close, and before he knows what had happened, with a shock, a hunching jolt, his fist holding the two leaves tight together, he is gone, through the darkness, into the black air.

Although the two versions are equally suspenseful, the writing in *Cassada* is leaner, more descriptive.

The story concerns the trials and tribulations of a new member of the Forty-fourth Air Force Fighter Squadron stationed in postwar Germany. The newcomer, Lieutenant Robert Cassada, is out of step with the seasoned veterans of the squadron. He loses his breakfast on his initial flight and is mildly ridiculed by the squadron commander, Major Davis Dunning, for preferring tea to coffee. However, Captain Isbell sees promise in the new man. Clearly, Cassada has skill and ambition and only needs the discipline of good leadership. Isbell is determined to provide that and shape Cassada into the pilot Isbell knows he can be. He fails. Nearing their home airfield on a return flight from an assignment in Tripoli, Cassada and Isbell encounter low clouds. The runway lights are not visible to the two pilots. Isbell's plane loses radio contact with the squadron's air tower and Cassada must take the lead in his plane and guide Isbell to a safe landing. After three botched attempts Isbell, low on fuel, loses sight of Cassada and must bail out. Cassada makes another attempt to land but is unsuccessful and is killed. The novel ends with Isbell leaving Germany at the end of his tour of duty. He carries with him the sense that he will someday be haunted by the memory of Cassada, the pilot who tried his best to achieve acceptance and failed. "It was too soon for him to reappear; that would come years after when all of it was sacred and he had slipped in with all the other romantic figures, the failed brother, the brilliant alcoholic friend, the rejected lover, the solitary boy who scorned the dance."

This story could be read as just another account of military life with a sad ending, but what Salter has done is provide a picture of the essence of leadership. He separates the posturing, career military men from those who have the qualities and characteristics of true leaders; those officers who are willing and able to give all that they have to those whom they command. Richard Bernstein, in a review in the *New York Times,* wrote of the "quiet power of this wonderful little book." Bernstein states that

> *Cassada* naturally brings to mind the best of Antoine de Saint-Exupéry, a writer to whom Mr. Salter has been compared before, especially the Saint-Exupéry of *Night Flight* (in which we find the phrase, "We always act as if something had an even greater price than life." Which is consistent with Mr. Salter's vision). But while *Night Flight* is about loneliness and danger, *Cassada* is about the company of men and the Sophoclean notion of character as tragedy.

> Mr. Salter is a master at delineating the pressures, the rejections, the mockery and the cruelty that spin within the male community; especially within a male community whose members are competitive, cliquish and defensive and live with a heightened possibility of death.

TWINS AND SCREENWRITING

Salter returned home after his tour of duty in Germany and found that his family was about to increase by two. In 1962 he became the father of twins, a daughter named Claude and a son, James Owen. Now with four children and a wife to support, Salter returned to documentary work with Lane Slate. Salter's first opportunity to write a screenplay for a feature film came in 1963 at the request of Howard Rayfiel, a junior member of Weissburger and Frosch, a law firm that specialized in the theatrical arts. His effort, "Goodbye, Bear," was not filmed, but the screenplay attracted the attention of a new talent on Broadway, Robert Redford. The two met for lunch and discussed the possibility of working together on a film. The possibility became a reality when Salter was hired in 1968 to write the screenplay for a movie about an American ski team, with Redford starring as the central character. Salter and Redford traveled with the U.S. ski team and attended the 1968 Winter Olympics in Grenoble, France, researching all aspects of the lives of competitive skiers.

The character Salter created for Redford, David Chapplett, has characteristics similar to those of Connell and Cassada. In the movie, *Downhill Racer* (1969), Chapplett is called to Europe to replace an injured member of the U.S. team. Chapplett arrives filled with egotism and a determination to excel but has little success and returns home to Colorado. The remainder of the movie follows Chapplett for two more years as he struggles with his coach, teammates, girlfriends, and rival skiers to win the gold medal. The movie concludes with Chapplett achieving his goal. Salter's screenplay ended quite differently. Salter had the not entirely admirable Chapplett finish an outstanding and, to that point, winning run down the mountainside to the finish line. As Chapplett raises in arms in triumph and the American team begins its victory celebration, a little-known competitor from the Austrian team streaks down the slope and beats Chapplett's time. Salter had hoped that this ending would show what he called "the justice of sport," and celebrate the type of modest hero who has almost vanished from sports in this country. Hollywood, however, had another idea. In its version the quiet, talented, unknown Austrian crashes before crossing the finish line and the brash, swaggering American egoist takes home the gold. Salter was disappointed in the final version but he learned a valuable lesson about the limits of attention paid to the screenwriter's vision. Despite his misgivings, *Downhill Racer* was a popular success and drew a positive review from critic Pauline Kael in her book *Deeper into Movies: The Essential Kael Collection from '69 to '72* (1973).

Undeterred, Salter continued to write screenplays. Only three of them became finished films: *The Appointment* (1969), directed by Sidney Lumet and starring Omar Sharif and Anouk Aimée; *Three* (1969), directed by Salter and starring Sam Waterston and Charlotte Rampling;

and finally, *Threshold* (1981), directed by Richard Pearce and starring Donald Sutherland and Jeff Goldblum.

Screenwriting certainly held attractions for Salter: the money was good (he was well paid even if his scripts never made it to the screen), he traveled throughout Europe in style, and he worked with the best and brightest and most glamorous in the business. Eventually, however, it lost its allure. After more than ten years of it, Salter decided to take another direction.

> There was another final script, which in fact ascended a bit before crashing as the result of a director's unreasonable demands, and I suppose there might have been another and another, but at a certain point one stands on the isthmus and sees clearly the Atlantic and Pacific of life. There is the destiny of going one way or the other and you must choose.
>
> And so the phantom, which in truth I was, passed from sight.

Movie offers continued to come his way, however. To fend off these temptations, Kay Eldredge, a journalist Salter met in 1976 and who would eventually become his second wife, had business cards printed in 1980 that read, "Mr. James Salter regrets he is far too occupied to: Write a Movie Script. Polish a Movie Script. Read a Movie Script. Take a Meeting." His disdain for motion pictures is perhaps best expressed in an interview published in the summer 1993 issue of the *Paris Review*. In it he said:

> If you have been writing movies you have been accommodating other people. . . . I tend to talk about them disrespectfully, but no matter what is said they have assumed the paramount position in American culture. They are unquestionably the enemy of writing, and this is something that is unresolvable. That is the way it is.

A SPORT AND A PASTIME

Of course, the screenwriting and documentary work of the 1960s and late 1970s did not keep Salter from more literary pursuits. In his *Paris Review* interview he said, "At that period of life I felt I could write anything: a sonnet, a libretto, a play." In 1961, while stationed in France, Salter met a young French woman who would become a central character in what many consider his best novel. Together they toured the French countryside, visiting sites of architectural splendor, dining in provincial restaurants, and living in small hotels. They parted company when Salter returned to the United States.

In 1964 Salter rented a ground-floor room on Downing Street in Greenwich Village with a film editor, Ed Nielsen, and from the notes he had taken in France, began to write what would become *A Sport and a Pastime* (1967). The title comes from chapter fifty-seven, line nineteen, in the Koran that reads: "Remember that the life of this world is but a sport and a pastime . . ."

The story begins in September with an unnamed narrator, who is vacationing in France, leaving Paris by train to visit and photograph the town of Autun. His Paris friends, Billy and Cristina Wheatland, have loaned him their house there, deep in the heart of what the narrator considers "the real France." He settles immediately and contentedly into the life and atmosphere of the town. "A town still rich with bicycles. In the morning they flow softly past. In the streets there's the smell of bread." Waking early on his first morning in Autun, he lies in bed and listens to the bells of the countryside ringing the three-quarter hour: "They flood over me, drawing me out of myself. I know where I am suddenly: part of this town and happy."

The narrator returns to Paris briefly to attend a dinner party. There he is introduced to a young American, Phillip Dean, who is traveling through Europe with his family. Dean, who has been in Spain and is on his own, expresses some interest in the area where the narrator is living. They exchange some dinner party pleasantries and part. The narrator is surprised when, a few weeks later, Dean arrives at his door. Dean is driving a splendid automobile loaned to him by a friend. It is a 1952 Delage, a product of a rather exclusive French manufacturer. Only thirty-eight thousand were made between 1905 and 1953, when production ceased. The car is important to the story. It lends an aura of independence and wealth to Dean, neither of which he has, and it provides greater mobility to the narrator, who has been quite content to travel the countryside on foot. Before Dean even sets foot in the narrator's house, the two go for a drive around the town, stopping at a café for a drink and then on to a hotel for dinner. Thus begins a pattern of drinking and dining that continues until Dean meets a young lady and a new element is added to the routine.

The narrator readily agrees to let Dean stay with him for a few days. He stays much longer, using the house in Autun as his home base for several months. This young man, who he learns has quit Yale University twice because it was too easy for him, fascinates the narrator.

> He had always been extraordinary in math. He had a scholarship. He knew he was exceptional. Once he took the anthropology final when he hadn't taken the course. He wrote that at the top of the page. His paper was so brilliant the professor fell in love with him. Dean was disappointed, of course. It only proved how ridiculous everything was.

They drive to Dijon one night to enjoy some drinks and music at a bar, La Rotonde. There the narrator sees an attractive young French woman at a table with several black American soldiers. "Suddenly I am in anguish, I don't know why—she obviously cares nothing—but somehow because of her predicament. She looks sixteen. Her young arms flash softly in the gloom." However, he says nothing of his concern about the safety of this vulnerable girl to Dean and they drive home. Several days later Dean announces that he has a surprise for the narrator and whisks him away to dinner in town.

There to join them is the young woman from the bar in Dijon, Anne-Marie Costallat.

It becomes evident that the narrator is in love with the girl. He dotes upon her every move. However, he does not challenge Dean's obvious intention to possess her. Perhaps it is the age difference that causes the narrator to stand aside; Dean is twenty-four and the narrator is ten years older. Perhaps he is reluctant to participate in any physical relationship, preferring to be an observer instead. He tells the reader, "I am only the servant of life. He is an inhabitant." It is important to note that the narrator is a photographer by profession. He has come to France on an impulse, inspired by the photographs of a now-vanished Paris made by Eugène Atget in the early 1900s. Like Atget, he is a man who creates pictures in which he is not included. For the remainder of the novel, roughly the last three-fourths of the story, the narrator presents the reader with images of the liaisons between Dean and Anne-Marie that he has developed in the darkroom of his imagination. Indeed, he goes so far as to state that everything he is relating is make-believe. "None of this is true," he claims, adding: "I am not telling the truth about Dean, I am inventing him. I am creating him out of my own inadequacies, you must always remember that." This is puzzling. Asked in the *Paris Review* interview about the narrator's role, Salter said,

> This book would have been difficult to write in the first person—that is to say if it were Dean's voice. It would be quite interesting written from Anne-Marie's voice, but I wouldn't know how to attempt that. On the other hand, if it were in the third person, the historic third, so to speak, it would be a little disturbing because of the explicitness, the sexual descriptions. The question was how to paint this, more or less. I don't recall how it came to me, but the idea of having a third person describe it, somebody who is really not an important part of the book but merely serving as an intermediary between the book and the reader, was perhaps the thing that was going to make it

possible; and consequently, I did that. I don't know who the narrator is. You could say it's me; well, possibly. But truly, there is no such person. He's a device. He's like the figure in black that moves the furniture in a play, so to speak, essential, but not part of the action.

He approached the question again in his introduction to the 1995 Modern Library edition of the book:

> The question of the novel's narrator is often posed, and how much of what he relates is invented or imagined. Very little, in my opinion. I am impressed by his powers of observation and tend to trust his description of scenes. If he—and he is almost certainly not the author—expresses a degree of disbelief and longing, I can understand it in view of the position in which he has been placed. He has many of my sentiments but the experience is his own.

Neither of these statements adequately addresses the question of how the narrator could know the very intimate details of Dean and Anne-Marie's adventure. Reynolds Price has commented: "I think *Sport* is one of the finest of all American novels, though almost nobody ever seems to comment on how mysterious it is. . . . The narrator apparently invents all the narration of the young couple's love affair—otherwise how could he know the details?"

In the first phase of their mutual enchantment, Dean and Anne-Marie travel in the Delage throughout France, visiting sites of architectural or historical significance, planning where to stay, deciding what to eat. What keeps this from becoming a tedious slide show for the reader is the inclusion of that which is forbidden: a voyeuristic view of the couple's erotic explorations and experimentation.

Their romance takes off like a bottle rocket and they enjoy long days and nights of mutual gratification for several months before the brilliance inevitably fades. Dean's money begins to run out and he borrows from his father, his sister, and his sister's friend and finally sells his return flight ticket to fund the life without consequences he leads with Anne-Marie. However, Anne-Marie begins to annoy him: she shuts the door of the Delage too hard; she wears too much lipstick; her feet are dirty. Eventually, he decides to return home to America. He tells the narrator that he must go back to "organize myself a little. I've even been thinking about going back to school." The narrator loans him the money for his plane fare and agrees to look after the Delage, which is packed with things Dean does not want to take with him. Dean meets with Anne-Marie for the last time, promising to return for her when he has raised some money. Anne-Marie knows better. They part silently the morning of his departure.

The narrator learns that soon after his arrival in America, while driving to visit his sister, Dean was killed in an automobile accident. Anne-Marie meets the narrator in a café and he expresses his concern about her future. She is clearly in shock and responds to his questions and offers of help in flat monosyllables.

At the novel's end the Delage sits under the trees near the narrator's house, "like a very old man fading, it has already begun to crumble before one's eyes." Salter gives the novel this sad, somewhat ironic closing: "As for Anne-Marie, she lives in Troyes now, or did. She is married. I suppose there are children. They walk together on Sundays, the sunlight falling upon them. They visit friends, talk, go home in the evening, deep in the life we all agree is so greatly to be desired."

Salter offered *A Sport and a Pastime* to Harper Brothers but they refused it, saying it was repetitive and uninteresting. Other refusals followed. Salter was ready to give up hope of ever seeing it published when a friend, William Becker, showed it to George Plimpton, the editor of the *Paris Review*. Plimpton eagerly accepted the book, and in 1967 Doubleday published it as one of its *Paris Review* editions.

Webster Schott wrote this in his review for the *New York Times Book Review*: "It's a tour de force in erotic realism, a romantic cliff-hanger, an opaline vision of Americans in France. . . . *A Sport and a Pastime* succeeds, as Art must. It tells us about ourselves." Doubleday, however, did not know quite what to make of the book. It was not well publicized. It sold only a few thousand copies in that edition. Bantam, followed by Penguin, then published it, and for the next eighteen years the novel circulated among writers and curious readers, creating a cult of admirers. In 1985 North Point Press published it as a trade paperback, and in 1995 The Modern Library recognized the novel's importance by adding it to its list of literary classics and publishing a hardcover edition. One of the novel's greatest admirers was Reynolds Price, who in a review for the *New York Times Book Review* wrote, "Of living novelists, none has produced a book I admire more than *A Sport and a Pastime,* by James Salter. In its peculiar compound of lucid surface and dark interior, it's as nearly perfect as any American fiction I know."

LIFE IN THE SOUTH OF FRANCE

In 1967 Salter booked passage on the *France* for himself, his wife, their four young children, and the family cat and dog. Salter intended to spend a year in France writing. An old, unheated, sparsely furnished stone farmhouse, La Moutonne, near the village of Grasse in Provence, was available for lease and Salter wrote to its previous tenants, Robert Penn Warren and his wife, Eleanor Clarke, for their assessment of the dwelling. Clarke responded that it was paradise with a distant view of the sea. She added that he would enjoy the most wonderful year of his life there if he could avoid freezing to death. The farmhouse had a resident white goat named Lily, who was a source of delight and companionship for the children as well as a provider of fresh milk. Except for the cold, the Salters found the place ideal and extended their stay an additional year.

In this idyllic setting Salter wrote outside at a table he placed on the second-floor balcony. He was still working on screenplays at this time but he also began to write short stories. The *Paris Review* had published a chapter of *A Sport and a Pastime* as a story, "Sundays," in 1966, and they published four new stories over the next six years: "Am Strand von Tanger" (1968), "The Cinema" (1970), "The Destruction of the Goetheanum" (1971), and "Via Negativa" (1972). Another story from this period, "Cowboys," later changed to "Dirt," was published in the *Carolina Quarterly* in 1971.

LIGHT YEARS AND DIVORCE

When the Salters returned to America in 1969, they settled in Aspen, Colorado, where they owned a small house that had been used for summer visits since 1962. Here Salter put aside short stories for a while and turned his attention to writing *Light Years* (1975), his novel about conjugal life. Coming as it did directly after *A Sport and a Pastime,* it is tempting to read *Light Years* as a sequel to that equally lyrical and episodic book. It could be considered the story of "the life we all agree is so greatly to be desired."

Indeed, in this novel of surface appearances and the dark depths beneath, the life of Nedra and Viri (Vladimir) Berland seems quite desirable. In 1958, when the novel opens, Viri is a thirty-year-old architect who yearns for that one glorious project that will bring him fame. His wife, Nedra, is stunningly attractive and intelligent. They have two daughters, Franca and Danny, and live on an estate in a large Victorian house on the banks of the Hudson River with a variety of animals and family pets. They indulge themselves in the best: the best books, the best art and music, the best shops that sell the best food and wine. Even their friends are the best sort: artistic, exotic, foreign. The children are loved and loving, and the house is filled with the joys of parties, holiday gatherings, birthdays. The security and happiness of this marriage seems unassailable. However, there is one unavoidable attacker poised to disrupt all this perfection and contentment: the passage of time. What was once spontaneous becomes a routine and boredom sets in.

Viri drifts into a briefly satisfying but ultimately humiliating affair with a young woman from his office. Nedra, in her turn, has a longer-lasting and more satisfying involvement with a family friend, Jivan. Time and familiarity bring it to an end. "In Jivan she noticed for the first time things which were small but clear, like the faint creases in his face which she knew would be furrows one day; they were the tracings of his character, his fate. . . . She would always have affection for him, but the summer had passed." She coolly brings the affair to an end. While shopping for wineglasses with a friend, she proclaims her strength and courage, saying, "The only thing I'm afraid of are the words, 'ordinary life.'"

Nedra soon begins another affair—this time with the poet, André Orlosky, whom she has met at Jivan's home. Viri's suspicions about her relationship with André and his concerns about the effect that their mother's open infidelity may have on Franca and Danny are answered by Nedra:

> "Viri," she said through the doorway, "but isn't it better to be someone who follows her true life and is happy and generous, than an embittered woman who is loyal? Isn't that so?"
>
> He did not answer.
>
> "Viri?"
>
> "What?" he said. "I'm afraid it makes me ill."
>
> "It all evens out in the end, really."
>
> "Does it?"

> "It doesn't make that much difference," she said.

Despite her emotional distance from Viri, Nedra accompanies him on a vacation to England. Their two weeks together only reinforce Nedra's need to be away from her husband, and she tells him that she does not want to go back to their old life.

They live together a few more months until the divorce is final. Nedra, now forty, leaves for Europe, where she dines with interesting men and reads Madame de Staël. Viri stays in the house with his daughters, who are now grown and involved in questionable relationships. He tries to hold his life together by doing those things he had done with his wife. He goes to a performance of Ibsen's *The Master Builder*. He drinks too much at dinner parties and guests ask, "Who is that pathetic man?" However, he is unable to hold the pieces of his old life together, so he sells the house and flees to Rome, hoping to start fresh. Soon after arriving, he meets and soon marries a beautiful and desperately needy younger woman who works as a receptionist for an architectural firm. Although her dependence upon him and her constant desire to satisfy his every sexual wish annoy him, she helps him survive the torturous process of forgetting what had passed from his life.

Nedra, after her short time in Europe, returns to New York City and lives in an apartment near the Metropolitan Museum. "She formed her life day by day, taking as its materials the emptiness and panic as well as the rushes, like fever, of contentment. I am beyond fear of solitude, she thought, I am past it. The idea thrilled her. I am beyond it and I will not sink." However, in the spring of her forty-seventh year, she becomes ill:

> A voice of illness had spoken to her. Like the voice of God, she did not know its source, she only knew what she was bidden, which was to

taste everything, to see everything with one long, final glance. A calm had come over her, the calm of a great journey ended.

She leaves the city and takes a small house near the sea where Franca comes to visit. They sit in the dunes, drink wine, and Franca reads a life of Tolstoy to her mother. Nedra realizes happiness is not to be found in "that sumptuous love which makes one drunk. . . . But to be close to a child, for whom one spent everything, whose life was protected and nourished by one's own, to have that child beside one, at peace, was the real, the deepest, the only joy." She dies the following autumn. Her daughters and a few friends attend her funeral.

In the novel's final chapter, Viri returns alone to the scene of his finest days. He wanders the grounds near his old home. Amid the decaying reminders of the full life once lived there—rotten branches, worm-eaten tools, the children's fort collapsed in the tall grass—he discovers an old tortoise, once a family pet, on whose shell he can still make out initials carved there many years ago. He walks to the river's edge and realizes, "It happens in an instant. It is all one long day, one endless afternoon, friends leave, we stand on the shore. Yes, he thought, I am ready, I have always been ready, I am ready at last."

As with *A Sport and a Pastime,* Salter had difficulty finding a publisher for *Light Years.* Farrar Straus and Scribners turned it down. Finally, Random House editor Joe Fox, the editor for such authors as Paul Bowles and Truman Capote, accepted the book and it was published in 1975. Critical reviews ranged from adoration to sarcastic contempt. Although James Wolcott in *Esquire* called it "an unexpectedly moving ode to beautiful lives frayed by time," Robert Towers announced in the *New York Times Book Review* that it was "an overwritten, chi-chi, and rather silly novel." Sales were disappointing, but the book never went out of print and eventually found itself in Harold Bloom's modern canon.

DIVORCE AND *SOLO FACES*

In 1975 the Salters' twenty-four-year marriage ended in divorce. The following year Salter began sharing his life with playwright and journalist Kay Eldredge. In about 1969 Robert Redford discussed with Salter a screenplay about mountain climbing. Salter, never an armchair expert, took up the sport seriously, climbing with and interviewing experts in the United States and Europe. Redford did not like the screenplay and it was shelved until Robert Ginna, a good friend and the editor-in-chief at Little, Brown, offered Salter fifty-thousand dollars to transform the screenplay into a novel.

Salter based *Solo Faces* (1979) on the exploits of Gary Hemming, an American mountain climber who was famous in the 1950s and 1960s. When Salter began his research, Hemming had been dead for a year from a self-inflicted gunshot. He relied on interviews with Hemming's friends and a careful study of his voluminous correspondence to create Vernon Rand.

A loner and drifter, Rand has one passion, mountain climbing. Women find him mysterious and attractive and, indeed, Rand enjoys the pleasures of several, but gives his heart only to the next climb. He travels to Europe, supporting himself by menial jobs, in search of greater challenges to his skills. In France he encounters fellow climber and friendly rival, John Cabot. Together they complete an extremely difficult climb up the West Face of the Dru, a forbidding mountain near the town of Chamonix, France. Few climbers have successfully scaled the Dru from that direction, and when Rand and Cabot arrive back in town, a reporter from a Geneva newspaper who has heard of their daring attempt comes to interview them. His story turns the pair into minor celebrities. Soon thereafter, Cabot and Rand part company. Rand makes a few solo climbs in the region. During one of these, he learns that two Italian climbers, a man and a woman, are trapped high on the West Face of the Dru. A rescue party has been trying to reach them by taking the far easier ascent on the North Face, but Rand knows this will take too long. The couple has been stranded on a narrow ledge for days already. Rand enlists three other amateur climbers, leads them on a direct climb up the West Face, and rescues the injured man and his fiancée. "When he woke he was famous. His face poured off the presses of France." He is the toast of Paris. People recognize him on the street. If he stops to speak to someone, a crowd gathers. Women take him to their beds. Soon, however, he returns to the mountains feeling old, out of shape, and discarded.

Rand attempts another solo climb but something has gone out of him. He loses his courage and turns back. He tells reporters watching his climb that he has not prepared well and would perhaps return to America for a rest. One of the reporters tells him that he had heard that Cabot was seriously injured in a fall while climbing in Wyoming. Rand makes his way back to California and finds his old friend paralyzed from the waist down and confined to a wheelchair.

Rand stays with Cabot and his wife for a few days, refusing to accept Cabot's physical condition. He insists that it is only a lack of will and courage that keeps Cabot from standing and walking. After a night of drunken gunplay, Rand borrows Cabot's car and disappears into the realm of legend. Over the years there are stories told of a lone climber who resembles Rand seen in Yosemite and Baja and Colorado. "They talked of him, however, which was what he had always wanted. The acts themselves are surpassed but the singular figure lives on."

Rand achieved the glory that escaped Cleve Connell and Robert Cassada, but like Nedra and Viri Berland he fell victim to the powers of time and nature. Reviews of the novel, particularly that of Vance Bourjaily in the *New York Times Book Review,* were favorable, and it became Salter's best-selling book.

THE SHORT STORIES

The 1980s were a time when Salter's literary output took the form of short stories and journalistic pieces. It was also a time of overwhelming personal tragedy. The decade began with the accidental death of his oldest daughter, Allan. Salter found her lying in the shower of his Colorado home. The cause of death was electrocution. She was in her mid-twenties. Salter left Aspen, the town he had called home since 1969, and returned to New York. In *Burning the Days* he wrote, "At the end of the summer of 1980 we drove East. I had been living, toward the end divorced, in Colorado and after the death of my daughter decided, more or less, to go home. I was drawing a line beneath ten years."

In 1982 Salter received the prestigious American Academy and Institute of Arts and Letters Award, and in 1985 Theo Shaw Salter, son of Salter and Eldredge, was born. The couple had carefully planned a trip to Paris so that their child would be born there. Construction was completed on their home in Bridgehampton, Long Island, in 1986. During this time of great change and challenge, Salter saw six of his short stories published. Three appeared in *Esquire*: "Foreign Shores" (1983), "The Fields at Dusk" (1984), and "American Express" (1988). The other three were published in *Grand Street*: "Akhnilo" (1981), "Lost Sons" (1983), and "Twenty Minutes" (1988). These six, together with four of the five previously published in the *Paris Review* (all but "Sundays") and "Dirt" from the *Carolina Quarterly,* were published as *Dusk and Other Stories* in 1988.

Each story in the collection has what Salter has called the three essentials of greatness: style, structure, and authority. These compact, lean tales are as memorable as the best of Chekhov, Hemingway, or Isaac Babel. Salter's personal favorite is "American Express." It tells the story of two young New York City lawyers, Frank and Alan, who achieve success and wealth by abandoning their ethics. They engage in nothing criminal, no overt scandalous behavior; they just allow themselves those small betrayals of the heart and conscience that so often lead to moral corruption. On vacation in Europe, they pick up a schoolgirl, Eda, who agrees to travel with them. She clearly belongs to Frank, but at the story's end he offers to share her with Alan, who is showing signs of dismay. Alan is ashamed but takes her to his bed. Early the next morning, looking out the window of the hotel room, he sees a man leaving on an errand. "He was going to get the rolls for breakfast. His life was simple. The air was pure and cool. He was part of that great, unchanging order of those who live by wages, whose world is unlit and who do not realize what is above." What the reader brings to this story will determine if Alan is contemptuous of the man or envious.

The most unusual story in the collection is "Dirt," unusual in that it is not set in New York City or Europe as the others are, but in the desert Southwest. The two main characters, old Harry Mies and his helper Billy, are day laborers who hire out to do odd jobs. They are poor but exceptionally skilled and make enough money to get by. Their satisfaction in life is the knowledge they have done a job well, and have received fair pay for their efforts, and that once in a while there is a cold beer waiting for them at the end of a hot day. When Harry dies after finishing a long, difficult job, the most valuable thing he leaves behind is the stories of his life he has shared with Billy. A. R. Gurney, in his review of *Dusk and Other Stories* in the *New York Times Book Review,* wrote, "Lest it seem that Mr. Salter confines himself only to the concerns of the privileged, it should be added that the final story, 'Dirt,' is about a relationship that is cemented through common manual labor, and evokes in some ways the world of Robert Frost." Indeed, reading Frost's "Two Tramps in Mud Time" (1936) or "The Death of the Hired Man" (1914) after reading Salter's "Dirt" is a

revelation. Salter exhibits in this collection a profound sympathy and understanding for all people in all walks of life. *Dusk and Other Stories* brought Salter more critical acclaim than any of his previous books, and in 1989 it won the PEN/Faulkner Award.

BURNING THE DAYS

Over the years, Salter had supplemented his income by writing articles for several different magazines and accepting teaching positions at Vassar, the Iowa Writers' Workshop, the University of Houston, and Williams College. In the 1970s Salter interviewed Vladimir Nabokov and Graham Greene for *People* magazine. It was the death of a very close friend, the man he calls Leland in *Burning the Days,* that prompted Salter to write the autobiographical essay "The Captain's Wife," which appeared in *Esquire* in June 1986. He had considered making a piece of fiction of the story of his relationship with the captain ("Leland") and the captain's wife ("Paula"), but in the end decided to tell their story truthfully. When Joe Fox, Salter's editor at Random House, saw the piece in 1986, he encouraged Salter to write similar pieces about the world he had known. Salter reluctantly agreed. His reluctance was based in part on his private nature; however, his military training, in which one is taught that the self counts for nothing, certainly played a part as well. He took his time revisiting places of personal history, interviewing old friends, and pouring over his vast correspondence. The result, *Burning the Days,* was published by Random House in 1997, eight years after the originally contracted publication date. He wrote in the preface, "Wearied by self-revelation, I would stop for months before starting in again."

What is contained in this recollection is the story of a life lived fully. The sheer number of people he knew, adventures he pursued, dangers he challenged, losses he survived, rivals those of anyone who ever lived including Hemingway, who perhaps only had better press coverage. Salter's own words provide the best description of the book:

> If you can think of life, for a moment, as a large house with a nursery, living and dining rooms, bedrooms, study, and so forth, . . . the chapters which follow are, in a way, like looking through the windows of this house. Certain occupants will be glimpsed only briefly. Visitors come and go. At some windows you may wish to stay longer, but alas. As with any house, all within cannot be seen.

The book was well received by critics, though some, who may have expected a racy confessional, were, as Richard Bernstein wrote in the *New York Times,* "annoyed by his secretiveness."

THE DAYS YET TO BURN

Salter and Eldredge postponed getting married until they could have the service performed in Paris. The forty-day residency requirement was a stumbling block, but they held fast to their desire for twenty-two years and were wed in Paris in 1998. That same year, Salter was presented the Edith Wharton Citation of Merit from the New York State Writers Institute and the John Steinbeck Award. In 2001 Salter and his wife still lived in the heart of a literary community on Long Island, occasionally getting away to Aspen, Colorado.

The idea of retirement is foreign to most writers. In a phone conversation on January 5, 2001, Salter, then seventy-five years old, said that he was working on another collection of short stories and a new novel. The answer to why he continues to work on what Hemingway called "the roughest trade of all" can be found at the conclusion of a *Paris Review* interview. The interviewer, poet Edward Hirsch, asked Salter, "What do you think is the ultimate impulse to write?" Salter answered,

To write? Because all this is going to vanish. The only thing left will be the prose and poems, the books, what is written down. Man was very fortunate to have invented the book. Without it the past would completely vanish, and we would be left with nothing, we would be naked on earth.

Selected Bibliography

WORKS OF JAMES SALTER

NOVELS
The Hunters. New York: Harper, 1956.
The Arm of Flesh. New York: Harper, 1961.
A Sport and a Pastime. Garden City, New York: Doubleday, 1967.
Light Years. New York: Random House, 1975.
Solo Faces. Boston: Little, Brown, 1979.
Cassada. Washington, D.C.: Counterpoint, 2000.

SHORT STORIES
"Sundays." *Paris Review* 38:140–148 (summer 1966).
Dusk and Other Stories. San Francisco: North Point, 1988.
"Comet." *Esquire,* July 1993, pp. 74–76.
"My Lord You." *Esquire,* September 1994, pp. 150–156.

POETRY
Still Such. New York: William Drenttel, 1992.

NONFICTION
"The Captain's Wife." *Esquire,* June 1986, pp. 130–135.
Tasting Paris: An Intimate Guide. Hopewell, N.J.: Ecco Press, 1996.
Burning the Days: Recollections. New York: Random House, 1997.

CRITICAL AND BIOGRAPHICAL STUDIES
Alvarez, A. "High Flier." *New York Review of Books,* January 15, 1998, pp. 37–39.

Barrett, George. "Death's Equals." *New York Times Book Review,* March 4, 1956, p. 36.

Bernstein, Richard. "Many Rooms in the Life of a True Writer's Writer." *New York Times,* August 25, 1997, p. B6.

———. "A Writer's First Effort Gets a New (and Altered) Life." *New York Times,* January 5, 2001, p. B45.

Bourjaily, Vance. "Different Points of View." *New York Times Book Review,* August 5, 1979, p. 11.

Dowie, William. *James Salter.* New York: Twayne Publishers, 1998.

Gurney, A. R. "Those Going Up and Those Going Down." *New York Times Book Review,* February 21, 1988, pp. 9, 11.

Hynes, Samuel. "A Teller of Tales Tells His Own." *New York Times Book Review,* September 7, 1997, p. 9.

Kael, Pauline. *Deeper into Movies: The Essential Kael Collection from '69 to '72.* Boston: Atlantic Monthly Press, 1973.

Price, Reynolds. "Famous First Words: Well Begun Is Half Done." *New York Times Book Review,* June 2, 1985, p. 3.

Schott, Webster. "Toujours l'amour." *New York Times Book Review,* April 2, 1967, p. 47.

Smith, Dinitia. "A Fighter Pilot Who Aimed for Novels but Lives on Films." *New York Times,* August 30, 1997, pp. 13–14.

Towers, Robert. "For Devotees of Scott Fitzgerald? Edward Fitzgerald?" *New York Times Book Review,* July 27, 1975, pp. 6–7.

Wolcott, James. "Great Escapes." *Esquire,* July 1982, pp. 119–120.

———. "Me, Myself, and I." *Vanity Fair,* October 1997, pp. 212+.

INTERVIEWS

Baker, Charles R. Letter from James Salter. December 21, 2000.

———. Telephone conversation with James Salter. January 5, 2001.

Hirsch, Edward. "James Salter: The Art of Fiction: CXXXIII." *Paris Review* 127:54–100 (summer 1993).

Stern, Daniel. "Writers Talk: George Plimpton, James Salter, Daniel Stern." *Hampton Shorts* 2:252–276 (1997).

FILMS BASED ON SCREENPLAYS BY JAMES SALTER

The Appointment. Screenplay by James Salter. Directed by Sidney Lumet. MGM, 1969.

Downhill Racer. Screenplay by James Salter. Directed by Michael Ritchie. Paramount, 1969.

The Hunters. Screenplay by Wendell Mayes. Directed by Dick Powell. Paramount, 1957. (Based on Salter's novel of the same name.)

Three. Screenplay by James Salter. Directed by James Salter. United Artists, 1969.

Threshold. Screenplay by James Salter. Directed by Richard Pearce. Twentieth Century Fox, 1981.

—*CHARLES R. BAKER*

Louis Simpson

1923–

Louis Simpson, poet, critic, memoirist, translator, and novelist, won the Pulitzer Prize for poetry in 1964 for his collection *At the End of the Open Road* (1963). He is best known for his work as a poet, and his writing often is divided by critics into three major phases. In the decades of the 1940s and 1950s, Simpson wrote and published primarily formal poems about his experiences as a soldier in World War II and about love. These poems are collected in his first three volumes, *The Arrivistes: Poems 1940–1949* (1949), *Good News of Death and Other Poems* (1955), and *A Dream of Governors* (1959).

As the decade of the 1950s wound down, he began a major shift in his aesthetic approach, however. The formal decorum of his earlier poems is abandoned in favor of free verse and a more conversational voice. Simpson was influenced at the time by the translations and poetry of Robert Bly, who, along with James Wright, pioneered a body of striking new American poetry in the early 1960s referred to as "deep imagism." These changes bore fruit in *At the End of the Open Road*.

Critics have pointed out that Simpson at this time felt a need to reenvision America. This re-envisioning was, in part, a consequence of the poet's reaction to Walt Whitman's exuberant view of America, as expressed in *Leaves of Grass* (1855). As a Jamaican who immigrated to the United States, Simpson always has had a keen eye and ear for his adopted country. The title of his fourth collection is a variant of the title of Whitman's poem "Song of the Open Road." By the end of the 1950s, Simpson recognized that the open roads Whitman had praised were paved over and that the prairie had become a subdivision or shopping mall. He captures these ironies in his poem "Walt Whitman at Bear Mountain" and in many of the other poems in this collection.

As Hank Lazer has noted in his essay "Louis Simpson and Walt Whitman: Destroying the Teacher," "His encounter with Whitman is pivotal in Simpson's development from an Audenesque, formal, ironic poet into a writer of free verse, dramatic narratives of ordinary life." This transformation continued throughout the 1960s and became refined through the influence of the Russian dramatist and short story writer Anton Chekhov and the Romantic poet William Wordsworth, writers whom Simpson read closely.

Simpson especially admired Chekhov's short stories and his tragicomic vision of life. In an essay entitled "Rolling Up" (*A Company of Poets*, 1981), the poet notes:

> I have tried to bring into poetry the sense of life, the gestures that Chekhov got in prose. . . . I have mixed humorous and sad thoughts in my poems, because this is the way life is. People want the sights and sounds of life; they ask for life in poetry. They ask for bread, but instead they have been given stones.

Simpson admires Wordsworth for his emotional intensity and for "writing with the sound of speech." In his short essay "To Make Words Disappear," also published in *A Company of Poets*, Simpson discusses the rationale for this approach to writing poetry: "Emotional intensity—this, as far as I can tell, is what poetry consists of." In the same essay, he goes on to say:

> I would like to write poems that made people laugh or made them want to cry, without their thinking that they were reading poetry. The poem would be an experience—not just talking about life, but life itself. I think that the object of writing is to make words disappear.

The three collections that followed *At the End of the Open Road* reflected these influences on Simpson's work. In *Adventures of the Letter I* (1971), the poet explores his mother's Russian ancestry and Chekhovian storytelling abilities. In *Searching for the Ox* (1976), Simpson applies the Wordsworthian emphasis on the poetry of common speech to his earlier life in the tropics and to the experiences of urban and suburban Americans. In *Caviare at the Funeral* (1980), he combines several of these elements, writing poems about the old country, Russia, and the New World, America.

In the third phase of Simpson's career, which covers the decades of the 1980s and 1990s, the poet increasingly emphasized the narrative quality of his verse. In "The Death of the Lyric: The Achievement of Louis Simpson," the contemporary poet-critics Mark Jarman and Robert McDowell praise Simpson as "an American original" because of his narratives of suburban American life. Simpson's late work has spurred critical discussion that places him in the American narrative tradition of Edwin Arlington Robinson and Robert Frost.

SIMPSON'S FORMATIVE EDUCATION

Louis Aston Marantz Simpson was born in Kingston, Jamaica, in the British West Indies on March 27, 1923. His father, Aston, who was of Scottish ancestry, was a lawyer and a sportsman. Simpson's mother, Rosalind Marantz, was a Russian Jew whose family had immigrated to the United States. Rosalind, who had worked in the garment district of New York City and later became an actress, went to Jamaica "on location" for a film, where she met Aston. He followed her back to New York and returned to Kingston with her as his wife.

When he was about six, Simpson's parents divorced. His father remarried several years later and moved with Simpson's stepmother to Bournemouth, an area to the east of Kingston. At the age of nine, Simpson began attending Munro College, a private preparatory school in the mountains that his older brother Herbert also attended. The school was a hundred miles to the west of Kingston, where Simpson attended Anglican services twice a day and became an avid reader. Simpson's mother left the island. She moved to Toronto, then traveled for the Helena Rubenstein company, selling cosmetics.

In 1940, following the death of his father and his graduation from Munro College, Simpson left Jamaica for New York City and enrolled in Columbia College. There he studied with the professors Lionel Trilling and Mark Van Doren. He took Trilling's humanities course, which emphasized the great books, ranging from works by Homer to those of Franz Kafka. In his memoir, *The King My Father's Wreck* (1995), he credits this course with having "made a great difference," broadening and deepening his knowledge of Western literature and culture and, at the same time, sharpening his critical perspective on modern and contemporary literature. Simpson preferred Van Doren, however, who was a poet and expressed a spontaneous love for literature in the classroom.

Simpson's years at Columbia were interrupted by World War II. He enlisted in the U.S. Army in 1942, served with the 101st Airborne in Europe until 1945, and received the Purple Heart and was twice awarded a Bronze Star. After the war Simpson returned to Columbia University, where he received his bachelor of science degree in 1948 and a master of arts degree in 1950. Meanwhile, Simpson had married Jeanne Rogers in 1949. The couple had one child, Matthew, and divorced in 1954. His wartime experiences had a major impact on his work as a poet. Many of the poems he published in his first three books grew out of his experiences of combat.

The poet's wartime experiences also helped shape his aesthetics and, in particular, his theory of poetic language. In his essay "Lessons of the Body," printed in *The King My Father's Wreck,* he notes that "words to me were pale in comparison with experience, mattered only in so far as they transmitted experience." As a result, Simpson was distrustful of poststructuralist literary theory. In the same essay, he criticized "those who have taken their text from [the Swiss linguist Ferdinand de] Saussure and who teach that there is no direct connection between words and life, only between one word and another, one 'sign' and another."

POEMS OF WAR AND LOVE

Simpson's first collection of poetry, *The Arrivistes: Poems 1940–1949,* is distinguished by a number of striking poems of war and love. One of the more famous of these early poems, "Carentan O Carentan," written in the form of a ballad, describes a dream where he is "walking with other shadowy figures along what seemed to be the bank of a canal, when bullets slashed the trees and shells were falling" ("Lessons of the Body"). This dream occurred a few years after the war, while Simpson was living in Paris. One effect of his combat experience had been to block memories of the war. But upon awakening from this dream, he wrote it down and realized that it was an event which really had happened. The scene of the carnage had once been peaceful and serene:

> Trees in the old days used to stand
> And shape a shady lane
> Where lovers wandered hand in hand
> Who came from Carentan.

The idyllic innocence described in this stanza, however, is disrupted violently by the ambush of an American platoon. Machine guns "aimed between the belt and boot / And let the barrel climb." The fire shatters the calm and maims and kills the speaker's fellow soldiers. It is a poem of initiation into the horrors of warfare and the resultant loss of innocence, summarized in the poem's concluding stanza:

> Carentan O Carentan
> Before we met with you
> We never yet had lost a man
> Or known what death could do.

The poem's simple diction and its depth of emotion and clarity of statement continued to characterize Simpson's poetry, but he came to see the ballad form as too restrictive.

As an infantryman in combat, Simpson had seen the dead and dying all around him. He was all too familiar with the precarious existence of a foot solider, and, in his memoir *The King My Father's Wreck,* he describes his feet freezing in a foxhole. In another poem from *The Arrivistes,* "Arm in Arm," he writes of the dead lying in a ditch in Holland, where the 101st Airborne had fought:

> Arm in arm in the Dutch dyke
> Were piled both friend and foe
> With rifle, helmet, motor-bike:
> Step over as you go.

This poem, like "Carentan O Carentan," is written in carefully constructed quatrains with a regular *abab* rhyme scheme. The carnage the speaker observes, however, stands in sharp contrast to the neat and orderly stanzas. Early in his career Simpson employed form to bear testimony to the tragedies of war. The lyrical quality of each stanza belies the brutality of the scene, yet at the same time it works to emphasize through the use of end rhyme the pathos of the fallen dead. Simpson often employs form in his early war poems as an ironic counterpoint to the tragic fate of the victims, who, like the fallen Captain in this poem, can no longer be of use:

> O, had the Captain been around
> When trenching was begun,
> His bright binoculars had found
> The enemy's masked gun!

While several other poems in this first collection address Simpson's wartime experiences, the volume also contains witty love poems. In the frequently anthologized "Song: 'Rough Winds Do Shake the Darling Buds of May,'" the poet evokes the sexual awakening of a sixteen-year-old girl. Formally, the poem is strikingly different from all the other poems in the collection. It is composed primarily of triadic stanzas, arranged on the page like many of William Carlos Williams's free verse poems. It is one of Simpson's early experiments in free verse. Of the subject's erotic awakening, he writes:

> She is sixteen
>   sixteen
>   and her young lust
> Is like a thorn
>   hard thorn
>   among the pink
> Of her soft nest.

In the poem "Summer Storm" Simpson also writes about sexual awakening, but he reverts to the traditional quatrains of several other poems in *The Arrivistes*:

> In that so sudden summer storm they tried
> Each bed, couch, closet, carpet, car-seat, table,
> Both river banks, five fields, a mountain side,
> Covering as much ground as they were able.

He describes the "couple" just about everywhere possible, including parks and fields. Yet for all their libidinous activity, the sonnet concludes on a note of domestication: "God rest them well, and firmly shut the door. / Now they are married Nature breathes once more." In these two poems Simpson seems more interested in sexuality than he is in romantic love.

In a third love poem, "A Witty War," the poet speaks to the chasms that can develop between lovers. A relationship that begins in kisses and closeness develops into something far more treacherous: "Between us two a silent treason grows. / Our eyes are empty, or they meet with tears."

The Arrivistes, the publication of which was paid for by the poet, was met with generally favorable reviews. Randall Jarrell, writing in a 1950 issue of *Partisan Review,* noted that "Louis Simpon is as promising a new poet as I've read in some time."

From 1950 to 1955 Simpson worked as an associate editor for the Bobbs-Merrill Publishing Company, where his job was to review submitted manuscripts. He had been divorced and was renting an apartment in the East Fifties.

Good News of Death and Other Poems was the second volume published in Scribner's Poets of Today series, edited by John Hall Wheelock. A few months before the publication of the volume, Simpson received a letter dated July 25, 1955, from Mark Van Doren, his former teacher at Columbia. In this correspondence (quoted in Ronald Moran, *Louis Simpson*), Van Doren notes: "*Good News of Death* is better than ever. I mean the whole collection, though I mean the pastoral too. You have a wonderful wit that never, I swear, stops playing. It is the seed of your seriousness, but meanwhile a joy forever; and so I know you will always be a fine poet, however many changes you go through." Although Simpson's poetry underwent many "changes," for now he seemed content to build upon the formal poems of his earlier volume and pursue the subjects of war and love.

One of the strongest poems in Simpson's second collection is "The Battle," a poem composed of four tightly constructed quatrains. In this poem the poet evokes in powerful detail the terror of combat, again seen from the perspective of an infantryman. The poem's second stanza describes their digging of foxholes:

They halted and they dug. They sank like moles
Into the clammy earth between the trees.
And soon the sentries, standing in their holes,
Felt the first snow. Their feet began to freeze.

No matter how intent the soldiers may be on living, the poet registers the inevitable devastation of war in the following stanza:

At dawn the first shell landed with a crack.
Then shells and bullets swept the icy woods.
This lasted many days. The snow was black.
The corpses stiffened in their scarlet hoods.

"The Battle" is an account of the 101st Airborne's defense of Bastogne. The English poet and critic Thom Gunn praised "The Battle" in a 1957 *Spectator* review, in which he wrote: "I know of almost no other poem about war which, soberly, without either hysteria or irony, is as convincing." Gunn also notes that the formal control of the poem adds to its emotional depth. The poet's second collection contains several other striking war poems, including "Memories of a Lost War," "The Heroes," and "The Ash and the Oak."

Although poems of love and war dominate the poet's second collection, one can see in the poems "West," "Mississippi," "American Preludes," and "Islanders" the inception of Simpson's poetic absorption with his adopted country, America. His interest in the culture and people of America never abated, and later volumes, especially *At the End of the Open Road,* largely comprise such poems.

Reviewers, including John Ciardi, Phillip Booth, and Donald Hall, praised Simpson's second volume. Mona Van Duyn, writing in the August 1956 issue of *Poetry,* notes: "These are suave and polished poems, very fine ones. One would have to search hard to find any stumbling in metrics or imagery. To describe them, one thinks of such terms as intellectual, witty, understated."

In 1955 Simpson began teaching at Columbia University. That year he also married his second wife, Dorothy M. Roochvarg, in a union that lasted twenty-four years and produced two children, Anne and Anthony. His reputation as a poet was growing, and in 1957 he was appointed a Hudson Review Fellow in Poetry and was awarded a Prix de Rome fellowship, which led to his spending the year 1957–1958 in Rome. While in Italy, the poet wrote his doctoral dissertation, *James Hogg: A Critical Study,* published in 1962. After the year abroad, Simpson returned to Columbia University to complete the requirements for his doctorate in comparative literature, which he received in 1959. This proved to be a very successful year for the poet, during which he published his third book of poems, *A Dream of Governors,* and was appointed to a position in the Department of English at the University of California, Berkeley.

In several important ways, *A Dream of Governors* more fully anticipated the new direction of Simpson's poetry. The volume contains a group of poems entitled "My America," important not only for its individual poems but also because, as a group, they deepen the poet's ongoing imaginative engagement with America. Two of these poems, "To the Western World" and "Hot Night on Water Street," later were placed by the poet in "A Discovery of America," one of seven thematic groupings in *People Live Here: Selected Poems 1949–1983* (1983). A third poem, "The Boarder," became the initial poem in a section entitled "Modern Lives" in *People Live Here.* In addition to these poems about America, *A Dream of Governors* is distinguished by "The Runner," a long blank verse narrative; "The

Bird," a shorter narrative about the Holocaust; and several poignant antiwar lyrics.

"To the Western World" and "Hot Night on Water Street," companion poems, are written in carefully constructed rhyming stanzas. The subject of the first of these poems is the European conquest of the Americas:

> We crossed the sea from Palos where they came
> And saw, enormous to the little deck,
> A shore in silence waiting for a name.

To the conquistadors and later the settlers and explorers of North America, the lands before them seemed both uninhabited and unnamed. The concluding four lines of "To the Western World" express the tragic consequences of conquest:

> In this America, this wilderness
> Where the axe echoes with a lonely sound,
> The generations labor to possess
> And grave by grave we civilize the ground.

The deaths of those who "civilize the ground" give it a history and a value. This process is a tragic one.

"Hot Night on Water Street" addresses this legacy of settlement. It is an autobiographical lyric about the poet's impressions of a small town on the border of West Virginia and describes in a wry and humorous way the poet's encounter with the place. He is out walking on "a hot midsummer night on Water Street," where he observes teenagers flirting with one another. Water Street has "three hardware stores, a barbershop, a bar" and a movie theatre, where the poet has gone to watch *The Star,* a Western film. Simpson writes:

> Some day, when this uncertain continent
> Is marble, and men ask what was the good
> We lived by, dust may whisper "Hollywood."

In "Hot Night on Water Street," Simpson's ironic observations of small-town American life are epitomized by a western film that valorizes the "dream of horses" and the settlement of the West.

Simpson's first three volumes of poetry are characterized primarily by finely tuned lyrics, yet in these two poems about America we find the germ of narrative. It is telling that as his career developed, Simpson increasingly turned to writing narrative poems. Two of the strongest of these, "The Runner" and "The Bird," are World War II poems published in his third collection of poetry.

"The Runner" is a long blank verse narrative about the twists in fortune of a character named Dodd, who is a runner, or messenger carrier, during the war. In his note to the poem, Simpson tells the reader that the poem is a fiction but is based upon the story of a solider of the 101st Airborne division of the U.S. Army. Simpson himself was wounded and yet still carried out his duties as a runner, much like the character Dodd in the poem. Simpson describes his own experiences as a runner during the war in two essays: "The Making of a Soldier USA," published in *Harper's Magazine* in 1966, and "In the Forest," from his memoir *The King My Father's Wreck.* Dodd, however, is a fictional character who represents the vicissitudes of war. He is seen as a hero and then as a goat by his fellow soldiers. He performs bravely under duress early in the poem and dishonorably in a later section of the poem. He is relegated to the humiliating task of digging latrines, yet toward the end of the poem he seems to regain respect.

"The Runner" is an important poem because of its ambition to tell a war story in blank verse. Robert McDowell and Mark Jarman, in their essay in *The Reaper Essays* entitled "The Death of the Lyric," praise "The Runner" as a "highly dramatic" poem that successfully adheres to narrative conventions in "dialogue, description, and characterization." It must be noted, however, that "The Runner" has not fared nearly as well as Simpson's more recent free verse narrative poems. Perhaps the most stinging critique of the poem was made by Robert Bly, who commented in his journal *Sixties* that "The Runner" "gives the impression of an experience of great depth, brought up into very awkward poetry." He goes on to say, "The effect is of an unfinished work." Bly's criticism of "The Runner" and other formalist poems by Simpson influenced the poet to make his break with form in his next book.

NEW POETIC FORMS

After the publication of his third book, Simpson moved to California to begin teaching at the University of California, Berkeley. His apprenticeship as a poet was now over. His work was widely published, both in little magazines and prestigious quarterlies like the *American Scholar* and *Hudson Review*. By the late 1950s, *The New Yorker* had signed a first-reading contract with Simpson, whereby the magazine retained the first right of refusal on Simpson's poetry. He had begun to receive major awards for his work and was ready to launch a long and successful academic career.

Despite his professional successes, Simpson continued to seek a new form of expression for his poetry. Of the change in his work at this time, Simpson told Steven Schneider in an interview:

I was developing and changing. Few poets stay the way they were. I decided I needed to change in order to get a different voice and material into my poetry. I felt that I could no longer fit into the traditional poems I had written. I was developing a more individual, colloquial voice.

The poet's fourth volume was written largely in free verse, and some of its most memorable poems take as their subject the poet's relationship to the land and people of America.

Simpson's friendships with Robert Bly and James Wright also played a role in his transformation as a poet. As early as 1958, Bly had commented in his journal *Fifties* that Simpson should "search for a form as fresh as his content." By this time, Simpson was corresponding with both Bly and Wright, and together with them and several other poets he formed a loose association of poets whose aesthetics became known as "deep imagism."

Although Simpson's work became associated with this movement, it was Robert Bly who was its leading theorist. In Bly's reviews and essays published in *Fifties* and *Sixties,* he cajoled American poets into considering the influence of South American surrealistic poets, such as César Vallejo and Pablo Neruda. Bly called for a new poetry based upon inwardness and the Jungian notion of the collective unconscious. The deep image, according to Bly and others, would arise from the depths of the psyche.

The opening poem of Simpson's *At the End of the Open Road* establishes the focus and tone for the volume. "In California" is an account of the poet's perceptions of the "dream coast," where he had moved to teach. Out of place with his "New York face" among the realtors and tennis players, the poet addresses his muse, the epic bard of America: "Lie back, Walt Whitman, / There, on the fabulous raft with the King and the Duke!" The reference here echoes the earlier poem, "Mississippi," where the poet invoked Huck Finn's river raft, only now the poetic lines are more relaxed and colloquial. Just as in the earlier poem, Simpson laments the loss of pastoral innocence:

Lie back! We cannot bear
The stars any more, those infinite spaces.
Let the realtors divide the mountain,
For they have already subdivided the valley.

The poet laments that we have lost our ability to contemplate "those infinite spaces" between stars that the French mathematician and philosopher Blaise Pascal had described. Whitman's expansive vision of America has been "contracted," literally and figuratively, by the realtors who are parceling out the subdivisions of the California landscape. The pioneering spirit has been transformed into gross materialism and the bulldozing of natural landscapes. "In California" introduces a "dark preoccupation" of the poet, one that he will take up elsewhere in the volume.

One of his best known poems, "Walt Whitman at Bear Mountain," also registers the poet's disappointment in how the American Dream has played itself out in the middle of the twentieth century. The poem begins with the poet describing a statue of Whitman at Bear Mountain State Park in New York State. In keeping with a long line of American poets who have felt compelled to come to terms with Whitman, the speaker of the poem, presumably Simpson, addresses the statue:

> "Where is the Mississippi panorama
> And the girl who played the piano?
> Where are you, Walt?
> The Open Road goes to the used-car lot."

Simpson laments the contraction of Whitman's expansive vision of America. Simpson's reading of America has produced a very different interpretation than Whitman's, and the "open road" that Whitman used as a metaphor for expansiveness has been transformed by Simpson into simply another road down the path of commercialism.

In "Walt Whitman at Bear Mountain," Simpson does not blame Whitman for the decadence found in American society. Indeed, the problem may be that the "pickpockets, salesmen, and the actors" have turned a "deaf ear" to Whitman's idealism in selling out to a materialistic version of the American Dream. The poem's concluding stanza, with its mysterious reference to "the angel in the gate . . . imagining red," lifts the poem from its narrative base to a more imaginative transrational dimension, reflecting the influence of surrealism and Jungian psychology:

> The clouds are lifting from the high Sierras,
> The Bay mists clearing.
> And the angel in the gate, the flowering plum,
> Dances like Italy, imagining red.

The poet has suggested that the final image, which critics have puzzled over, is one of the grace that comes with acceptance of "the given" world and realization that the dream of empire is dangerous and illusory.

"Walt Whitman at Bear Mountain" unquestionably stands out as one of Louis Simpson's major poems. It bears the signature of his quest to come to terms with America and represents the synthesis of many stylistic elements that would henceforth characterize his work. Both the poetic line and stanza have been relaxed, and the poet's voice is colloquial, the tone more casual. Simpson learned to perfect these features in the many collections of his work that followed this one.

At the End of the Open Road contains many other poems that have become "contemporary classics." Simpson's short poem "American Poetry" serves as the introduction to one of the most well-known anthologies of post–World War II American poetry, *Contemporary American Poetry,* edited by Al Poulin Jr. The first stanza of the poem speaks to the nature of American poetry in the latter half of the twentieth century:

> Whatever it is, it must have
> A stomach that can digest
> Rubber, coal, uranium, moons, poems.

Although much of Simpson's fourth collection focuses on American life, it also has one of the strongest of the poet's war poems, "A Story about Chicken Soup." This poem is divided into three sections, each separated by an asterisk, a typographical device Simpson came to depend on to indicate transitions in his free-form narrative poems. The first section of "A Story about Chicken Soup" recalls "talk of the old country" in Simpson's grandmother's house. The "old country" is Russia, where Simpson's maternal grandmother had lived. The first section ends with the recollection that the Germans had killed those relatives left behind in Russia.

In the poem's second section, the poet recalls seeing a young German girl whose brothers had been killed by American soldiers. She is described as "all skin and bones— / Not even enough to make chicken soup." In the concluding section of the poem, the poet reflects on the legacy of such tragedies, and though the sun is shining, presumably in California, he knows that he must "live in the tragic world forever." "A Story about Chicken Soup," like "Walt Whitman at Bear Mountain," has been anthologized often and is a pivotal poem in the corpus of Simpson's work.

At the End of the Open Road received many strong reviews and was awarded the Pulitzer Prize for poetry in 1964. Writing in a May 1964 issue of *Poetry,* William Stafford notes that "again and again the poems confront new, grim aspects of America's formative traditions. It is as if treasured documents like the Declaration of Independence should glow under a certain light and reveal odd skeletons." Duane Locke, in an article in the journal *dust* entitled "New Directions in Poetry," comments upon the stylistic changes evidenced in this collection:

> In *Open Road* the style loosens, the lines become uneven, and the movement of the natural voice and phrasal breaks replace preconceived measurement. The imagery tends toward inwardness, and the result is a more phenomenal poetry, one in which the subjective imagination transforms by its own operations the objective into what constitutes genuine reality.

Adventures of the Letter I, Simpson's fifth collection of poetry, develops the poet's inheritance from his mother of Jewish storytelling—he did not know of his Jewish ancestry until he moved from Jamaica to New York City and met his mother's family—and his continuing commitment to write poems about America and its people. He discussed his mother's influence on his work in a *New York Times Book Review* essay, "My Beginnings," reprinted in *The Character of the Poet* (1986):

> I trace my beginnings as a writer to the stories my mother read to me—Oscar Wilde's "The Happy Prince" was one of her favorites—and the stories she told about her childhood in Russia. She spoke of Cossacks and wolves, of freezing in winter, and rats. In Volhynia rats carried the typhus bacilli that had killed her sister Lisa and almost killed her.

The first section of *Adventures of the Letter I* is inspired by the stories his mother told him about Russia. Mostly fictional, they describe life in Volhynia, the part of Russia where his mother was born. There Jews who had been drafted into the czar's army hid under mattresses and inside ovens to escape searches by the police. These poems, "Adam Yankev," "A Son of the Romanovs," "A Night in Odessa," "Isidor," and others, form a cluster of poems linked thematically by their evocation of life in the Russian Jewish Pale. The characters in these poems are imagined by Simpson, yet they are inspired by stories told to him by his mother and the experiences she shared about the life of his maternal grandmother in Russia. Each character lives a life of great pathos.

In "A Son of the Romanovs," Avram, the "cello-mender," who is "the only Jewish sergeant / in the army of the Tsar," marries "a rich widow / who lived in a house in Odessa." The speaker of the poem relates this story: "One night in the middle of a concert / they heard a knock at the door." It turned out to be a beggar who claimed to be the natural son of the "Grand Duke Nicholas." He stays with Avram and his wife for years, working as a footman. The poem's humorous tone is undercut, however, by the arrival of the Germans, who march them off to the death chambers, including Nicholas, who they saw as feebleminded.

In "Dvonya" the poet imagines a romantic relationship with a cousin twice removed. They drink tea together in the garden and talk about the plays of Chekhov. As quickly as the poet imagines this lovely encounter, he soon acknowledges that "this is only a dream." Simpson's Volyhnia poems are both humorous and tragic, much like the fiction of Chekhov that Simpson admired.

His poem "The Foggy Lane" is perhaps the clearest expression of this poetry collection's aesthetic, which blends tragicomic elements. In the poem he declares: "I try to keep my attention fixed / on the uneven, muddy surface." This is a metaphor for the poet's sense of life, with its ruts, mud puddles, and unevenness. Life, as Simpson suggests in "The Foggy Lane," is not to be idealized or politicized. He rejects the view of the radical in the poem, who says that "everything is corrupt" and wants to live in a pure world. The world, as Simpson describes it, is rather like a bottle of sludge with all the various components mixed together, not distilled and separated. He has learned this from Chekhov, whose characters experience life as bitter and sweet.

While Chekhov looms as an influence behind many of the poems in *Adventures of the Letter I,* the volume also has strong imaginative poems about America. These include "Indian Country" and "American Dreams." In the first of these two poems, Simpson addresses the tragedies perpetrated against Native Americans in the name of Manifest Destiny. He describes senseless acts of violence against innocent victims, like old Black Kettle, who was shot at the massacre of Sand Creek while "tying the Stars and Stripes to his tent pole."

The poem "American Dreams" has been published frequently in antiwar anthologies and was twice published in 1966 in publications addressing America's involvement in Vietnam. Curiously, the poem was written in 1960, long before the escalation of America's involvement there. The poem was Simpson's warning shot against what he saw as America's increasing hegemony over Russia and Asia, yet it proved to be prescient in predicting America's tragic war in Vietnam.

Later, in the 1970s, the poet published his sixth collection of poetry, *Searching for the Ox.* By this point in his career he had made the transition from formalist poet to free verse poet. In addition to Whitman and Chekhov, Simpson found William Wordsworth to be an important figure in helping him refine his treatment of the people who inhabited America's cities and suburbs. In his essay "Rolling Up" (*A Company of Poets*), Simpson wrote that Wordsworth "shows the way to the future, a community built on human feeling and sympathy." He also suggests that Wordsworth "wished to reveal the deep springs that join one man to another and constitute a real nation." Subsequently, in a 1982 interview with Steven Schneider published in *The Wordsworth Circle,* Simpson explained that like Wordsworth, he "bases poetry in experience and in common life. I have been putting a lot of people into my poems and a lot of human situations."

In *Searching for the Ox,* he entitled one section of poems "The Company of Flesh and Blood," a phrase borrowed from Wordsworth, who wrote in his 1802 "Preface" to *Lyrical Ballads*: "I have wished to keep my reader in the company of flesh and blood." In a letter written in 1982, Simpson stated that "The Middleaged Man" and the other poems in this section "are an attempt to find poetry in the life of the average man." Tim Flanagan, who is the subject of "The Middleaged Man," is referred to by friends as "Fireball," because "every night he does the rocket-match trick." "'Ten, nine, eight . . .' On zero / p f f t! It flies through the air." Simpson walks with Flanagan to the subway and learns that he lives with his sister in Queens. The poet imagines Flanagan's life, with its moments of loneliness, staying up late to watch television, looking out the window at deserted streets, "wearing an old pair of glasses / with a wire bent around the ear / and fastened to the frame with tape." Flanagan, a sympathetic and lonely character, is representative of several other characters who peopled Simpson's work in the third stage of his poetic development.

Although the poet increasingly put other people into his poems, some of his strongest poems continued to be first-person autobiographical narratives. One of the strongest of these is the title poem of his sixth collection, "Searching for the Ox." The poet reflects in each of the five sections of this poem on his journey through life, which is symbolized by the poem's title. In Buddhism the ox represents transcendence and Enlightenment. In "Searching for the Ox" Simpson thinks back on those he has encountered on the journey: urban "ghosts" who single him out to tell him their stories, engineers and lawyers whose technical expertise propels their careers, cultists and survivalists who live underground, and women seen in the cafes of Alexandria, the city where C. P. Cavafy wrote his poetry. All of these experiences, however, are fleeting and illusory from the Buddhist perspective, which teaches that true knowledge resides within oneself.

In the concluding section of the poem, the poet contemplates the path of Buddhism and discovers, paradoxically, that in "Following in the Way / that 'regards sensory experience as relatively unimportant'" and teaches the renouncement of attachments, his awareness of the world has increased. The poem ends with a transcendent epiphany, wherein the poet achieves a heightened receptivity to the relative world by virtue of his learning how to transcend it. He has come to understand the Buddhist drawing of searching for the ox: "I seem to understand what the artist / was driving at; every

leaf stands clear / and separate." Ever since childhood, the poet has "always felt that there is a power and intelligence in things" ("My Beginnings"). In "Searching for the Ox" he discovers a way to heighten his already acute sense of the physical world.

Although Simpson's career is most distinguished by his work as a poet, he also published a novel, *Riverside Drive* (1962); a critical study of the Scottish writer James Hogg; two critical studies of modern poetry; an autobiography, *North of Jamaica* (1972); and a memoir, *The King My Father's Wreck.* In addition, several of his shorter essays on being a poet and on the craft of poetry, along with numerous book reviews, can be found in various collections of his prose writings, most notably *A Company of Poets, The Character of the Poet,* and *Ships Going into the Blue: Essays and Notes on Poetry* (1994).

Simpson's first forays as a prose writer were made as a schoolboy living in Jamaica, where he won prizes for his essays and short stories. It was not until after he had published three volumes of poetry that his first and only novel was published. *Riverside Drive* is the story of Duncan Bell, a writer of fiction and translator of the works of the French dramatist Jean Racine. Simpson describes the novel as being "thinly autobiographical," yet the parallels between Duncan, the narrator-protagonist, and Simpson are striking. Duncan comes to New York City from Jamaica, enrolls in a university there, serves in the 101st Airborne during World War II, suffers a mental breakdown upon his return, spends a year abroad, and returns to work in a New York publishing house. Moreover, the relationships treated in the novel, especially the loveless marriage between Duncan and Libby, mirror the circumstances of Simpson's first marriage.

There are significant differences between Duncan and Simpson, most strikingly that his fictional protagonist is a "loser" who fails to make his mark in the world. The novel is valuable in that it takes up several of Simpson's ideas about war and life in America. Reviewers of the novel discovered in it several qualities that also distinguish Simpson's poetry. John K. Hutchens, writing in the *New York Herald Tribune,* commented on the novel's "firm intelligence, a spare, intense way with words, a gift for images used with a difference." The poet learned from his only novel that his true genius was best expressed in poetry, although the narrative impulse was still strong.

Simpson's doctoral thesis, *James Hogg: A Critical Study,* was published the same year as his novel. Hogg was a Scotsman who wrote poems, stories, and novels at the beginning of the nineteenth century. Simpson was particularly impressed by Hogg's only novel, *The Private Memoirs and Confessions of a Justified Sinner* (1824), which Simpson describes as a "masterpiece."

Simpson published two additional critical studies. The first of these, entitled *Three on the Tower: The Lives and Works of Ezra Pound, T. S. Eliot, and William Carlos Williams* (1975), is an important study of three major figures of literary modernism. This volume was followed by *A Revolution in Taste: Studies of Dylan Thomas, Allen Ginsberg, Sylvia Plath, and Robert Lowell* (1978). In this book Simpson examined the shift toward a more direct kind of writing, a poetry in which the maker was no longer detached from the poem.

The best accounts of Simpson's life as a writer are chronicled in *North of Jamaica* and *The King My Father's Wreck.* The former book, an autobiography, covers his early years in Jamaica, his university days at Columbia University, his wartime experiences, and his development as a poet up through his years of teaching at the University of California at Berkeley. It is especially insightful about his formative years in Jamaica and contains many revealing anecdotes about his literary friend-

ships and teaching career. Although it is less comprehensive in scope, *The King My Father's Wreck* also is a colorful treatment of some of the key events in Simpson's life, including the death of the poet's mother; memorable excursions the poet took with his third wife, Miriam Butensky Bachner, whom the poet married in 1985 (and divorced in 1998); and additional insights into his poetry.

Caviare at the Funeral, Simpson's seventh collection of poetry, won the Jewish Book Council award for poetry in 1981. The collection is composed of four sections. The first contains such poems as "Working Late" and "Sway," about the poet's early life. "Sway" is a narrative about a beautiful waitress with whom Simpson flirts and to whom he reads poetry. It is one of the strongest of his autobiographical poems. Mark Jarman and Robert McDowell, in their essay "The Death of the Lyric," single out this poem for its narrative strengths and for linking Simpson to a tradition of American narrative poetry that dates back to Edwin Arlington Robinson. They praise the "richness of Sway's characterization" and "the originality of Simpson's narrative style." The memorable character study, the compression of time, the intimate sense of humor and understatement, and the vivid locale of this and other narrative poems are strengths that have been admired by numerous other critics as well.

The second section of *Caviare at the Funeral* includes the poems "American Classic" and "The Beaded Pear," which reflect the poet's ongoing commentary on American life. "The Beaded Pear" is representative of many of the poems that portray life in the American suburbs, where shopping at the mall is a family ritual, daydreams of living someplace exotic are common, and watching television is a cultural pastime.

While narrative poems like "The Beaded Pear" and "Sway" are characteristic of Simpson's fascination with modern American lives, poems from the third section of this collection, such as "Typhus" and "The Art of Storytelling," return the reader to the Russia of Simpson's mother's family. He explains this interest quite clearly at the beginning of the poem "Why Do You Write About Russia?" He notes: "When I was a child / my mother told stories about the country / she came from." One of the stories Rosalind told her son was about the time she almost died during a typhus epidemic. In "Typhus," Simpson tells us that she takes to her bed and is nursed back to life by "the woman who lived next door / who cooked for her and watched by the bed." Afterward, she is taken to Odessa, where she stays with relatives. The most memorable part of this poem is the train ride back from Odessa, when the poet's mother has to eat a basket of plums she bought as a present for her family, to prevent them from spoiling in the heat. Rosalind's sister, Lisa, is not so fortunate; she dies of typhus and is carried to the cemetery in a box that is later returned to the family because they are so poor.

If the poem "Typhus" speaks to the tragic nature of his family's life in Russia, the poem "The Art of Storytelling" addresses the more comic side of their existence. This short lyric contains the germ of a larger story, as do so many of Simpson's poems. The narrator, presumably one of Simpson's relatives who has made it to the New World, recalls the story of a shocket, or kosher butcher, who is impressed into the navy, sails around the world, and eventually makes it back to the village, where he resumes his occupation as a butcher. Toward the end of the account, the storyteller says: "This shocket-sailor / was one of our relatives, a distant cousin."

The poem turns on the gloss the poet provides on the art of storytelling, in the final stanza of the poem:

> It was always so, they knew they could depend
>   on it.

> Even if the story made no sense,
> the one in the story would be a relative—
> a definite connection with the family.

Simpson's connection to his mother's family and the stories he heard as a young boy in Jamaica and later from relatives gathered around the dinner table on Friday nights in New York City have continued to inspire some of his most interesting work.

THE LATTER PHASE OF THE POET'S CAREER

Caviare at the Funeral was followed in 1983 by *People Live Here* and *The Best Hour of the Night*. *People Live Here* is especially revealing because of its thematic organization, which groups together Simpson's best poems on the subject of war, his discovery of America and the people who inhabit it, and Russian Jewish family life. In the volume's afterword, the poet explains his reasons for writing poetry: "With poetry I could express an idea or tell a story in a brief space, and it would hang together. Besides, I loved the rhythm and the sound of words for their own sake."

The Best Hour of the Night builds on the poet's previous efforts to evoke life in the American suburbs. More so than previous collections, however, this one focuses on characters, who, in the words of Henry David Thoreau, live lives of "quiet desperation." The diminishment of the American Dream into materialism has irked Simpson since *At the End of the Open Road*. In his eighth major collection of poetry, the poet seems especially interested in the various strategies used by his characters to overcome boredom and loneliness.

In the poem "Quiet Desperation," Simpson describes the life of a suburbanite, whose wife is angry with the wife of a friend because she has disclosed damaging confidential information about a mutual friend. In the protagonist's living room, his son is watching television, a movie about the battle of Iwo Jima. The television is often a symbol of quiet desperation in Simpson's poems, and the father has seen the film and walks out of the room. He has a feeling of desperation, triggered by a sense that his life is passing quickly by him, as his son sits alone watching a rerun of an old film the father has seen. At the beginning of the next section, Simpson writes a group of lines that might work equally well in describing several of his characters in this book:

> A feeling of pressure . . .
> There is something that needs to be done
> immediately.
> But there is nothing,
> only himself. His life is passing,
> And afterwards there will be eternity,
> silence, and infinite space.

The sense that one must *do* something without knowing exactly what to do characterizes several of these suburban portraits. The characters feel an internal pressure because their lives seem to be passing away without meaning. Simpson describes this experience as "unfocused anxiety" in an interview, "Off the Cuff," published in *The Character of the Poet.* He says: "You suddenly realize you're getting old, that you're alone in the universe, that between you and space there is nothing, and your pulse starts to accelerate for no reason really."

In this poem the protagonist, out of desperation, goes outside to cut a pile of firewood, and then returns and "looks around for something else to do / to relieve the feeling of pressure." He seizes upon the dog and takes it for a walk along a cove, where he observes litter along the beach. He cannot find solace in his activity or his environment, and the poem ends with "the trees and houses vanishing / in quiet every day." The quiet they vanish into is the restless consciousness of Simpson's isolated suburban characters.

In poem after poem in this collection Simpson presents the reader with the quirks and anxieties of living in the suburbs. In "Physical Universe" the protagonist is another husband and father, who awakens at five in the morning and reads through his son's science book while the rest of the family sleeps. The poem hinges upon the dramatic description in the book of how the universe came into being, juxtaposed against the more mundane recollection that the garbage needs to be taken out.

He dutifully carries the garbage can out to the street, empties the wastebaskets in the house, and then makes a second trip outside to empty trash into the can once again. Having fulfilled his obligation, he climbs back into bed, where his wife, half-asleep, inquires whether he has taken out the garbage. He replies affirmatively and asks her a question about evolution, triggered by the reading of his son's textbook. She does not acknowledge his question but shoots back again with the query; "Did you take out the garbage?" The poem concludes with the husband pondering whether her question, like a zen koan, has something of the sublime in it. The "suburban sublime," however, has been reduced to taking out the garbage and leaves little room for contemplating the mysteries of the physical universe.

While many of the poems in this collection are mid-length narratives or shorter lyrics that contain the germ of narrative, the volume includes a long narrative poem entitled "The Previous Tenant" that runs fourteen pages. It is the story of Hugh McNeil, a physician at Mercy Hospital who has an affair with the wife of one of his patients. The narrator is the current tenant of the cottage McNeil had rented after his separation from his wife. McNeil, the "previous tenant," has left town after being mugged by the brothers of Irene Davis, the woman with whom he has been having the affair.

This poem is a sordid tale of suburban sexual intrigue and snobbish WASP culture, filtered through the consciousness of the narrator, who is a second-rate novelist. Published in the early

1980s, the poem has been important in terms of its influence on a younger generation of "new narrative" poets. "New narrative" is an umbrella term for a revival of interest in narrative poetry by contemporary American poets. Since the early 1980s, leading proponents of this movement, like Robert McDowell, Dick Allen, and Dana Gioia, have argued for a more expansive narrative poetry, with emphasis upon telling other people's stories. In the 1980s and 1990s, these poets looked to Simpson as a poet who pioneered a new kind of narrative of the American suburb.

The decade of the 1980s also saw the publication of Simpson's *Collected Poems* (1988). This volume is organized chronologically, with poems that Simpson selected from each of his previous eight collections of poetry, including *The Best Hour of the Night.* In a note at the head of the volume's table of contents, Simpson writes: "These are not all my poems—they are the poems I would like to be remembered by." For this reason the collection is particularly valuable.

In the 1990s, Simpson published his ninth and tenth collections of poetry, *In The Room We Share* (1990) and *There You Are* (1995). Of these two books, *There You Are* has fared better among reviewers than *In The Room We Share,* which drew criticism for being "uneven." Genevieve Stuttaford, writing for *Publishers Weekly,* suggests that "some poems remain little more than dressed-up anecdotes; others are superficial character sketches."

The poet's mother is again the subject of many of the poems in the first section of *In the Room We Share.* Simpson is fond of retelling in these poems the story of how his mother was "discovered" by a motion picture producer while working as a seamstress for seventy-five cents a day in New York City.

Both the opening section of poems and the concluding prose piece, "Villa Selene," are about family. The latter poem is a long account of a trip Simpson took with his third wife, Miriam, to Italy to visit his ninety-two-year-old mother, who was bedridden. The tone of this essay is nostalgic, just as the poems in the opening section are reminiscent of the poet's childhood in Jamaica.

In the middle two sections of the book, "Something Human" and "Homeland," the poet strikes a nostalgic, reminiscent tone of a different sort when he writes about peace marches in Berkeley during the 1960s in "The Peace March" or gives his reflections on being a family man in "The People Next Door." In "Pursuit of Happiness" the poet muses about his failed attempt to achieve lasting happiness. He describes trying transcendental meditation, becoming bored with it, and then joining a fitness center, only to grow tired of the machines. He accounts for other seekers' attempts to find happiness, including Jimmy, who ascends every morning over Aspen, Colorado, "in a balloon with colored panels." In this and other poems in the collection, the poet, now entering the latter stage of his life, is meditative about the pursuit of happiness, which he suggests may be experienced temporarily but is often elusive.

In *There You Are* Simpson regained his earlier mastery of narrative poetry and drew on his experiences in publishing and academia and his travels. The title poem of this collection, however, is about the Holocaust, a subject he has returned to again and again. "There You Are" describes the dramatic turn of events that led to the Jews of Paris being rounded up and put on trains that eventually would take them to Auschwitz. "There You Are" appears in the first section of the book, "Objects of the Storm," which also contains "Remembering the Sixties," a poem in which the poet recalls "the voice of Mario Savio" and the Free Speech movement.

Simpson's teaching days in Berkeley have long been a source of material for him, both in his prose writings and in his poetry. In "An Academic Story," a poem that appears in the concluding section of *There You Are,* the narrator tells the story of an assistant professor of English, Henry, who is married and having an affair with a student, Merridy. They attend a departmental party, after which they sleep together. Henry and Merridy travel to a Modern Language Association convention, where they enjoy dinners and the theater. When it comes time for Henry to be considered for tenure, he is denied it, because the host of the departmental party, who had made both pot and acid available to the partygoers, complains that Henry cannot be trusted. The poem is a rich blend of satire and humor, a scathing critique of English department politics. It is one of the strongest dramatic poems in a collection that contains many, including "The Indian Student," another wry commentary on the life of an English professor.

The middle section of the book, "The Walker on Main Street," is testimony to Simpson's ongoing Wordsworthian commitment to record the life of ordinary men and women, characters whom the poet meets in his daily life. "The Dental Assistant," for example, records a conversation between him and his hygienist about the problems she is having with her boyfriend. In "The Iverson Boy," Simpson describes his encounters with Tommy Iverson, a slow-witted thirty-year-old man whose father is an admirer of Richard Nixon and whose mother is a television game show fanatic. These are the characterizations of "American Lives" Simpson created throughout the 1980s and 1990s.

The concluding poem in *There You Are,* "A Clearing," is as memorable as earlier, widely anthologized autobiographical poems like "Walt Whitman at Bear Mountain" and "Searching for the Ox." It is an account of the poet's trip to Australia, the record of his attempt to start a new life after a divorce, and his impressions of the people and the countryside. Toward the end of the poem the poet walks out from a party late one night into a clearing in the trees.

There, looking up at the sky "glittering / with unknown constellations," he seems to merge with infinite space. He writes: "Everything I had ever known / seemed to have disappeared." The concluding lines of the poem describe this "clearing" of the mind, an experience of transcendence reminiscent of his poem "Searching for the Ox":

> there has been a place in my mind,
> a clearing in the shadows,
> and above it, stars and constellations
> so bright and thick they seem to rustle.
> And beyond them . . . infinite space,
> eternity, you name it.

Louis Simpson has always been a seeker of truth in his poetry. In his essay "Rolling Up," Simpson writes, "There was never as great a need for the poetry of feeling as there is in the United States at the present time. By this I mean poetry that addresses itself to the human condition, a poetry of truth, not dreams." The poetic truth Simpson has pursued has led him to poetry of emotional intensity, written in the words of common speech, evoking the bittersweet nature of life and its mysteries.

Simpson retired from his full-time teaching position in the English department at the State University of New York at Stony Brook in 1992, which he joined in 1967 after choosing to leave Berkeley because of his preference to live and teach on the East Coast. He continues to publish poems, however, in the *American Poetry Review,* the *Hudson Review,* and many other prestigious journals. He has become a consummate master of the contemporary narrative poem and the brief, yet poignant lyric that tells a short and revealing story about someone the poet has met. One of the finest of these is "Grand Forks," a poem published in the spring 2001 issue of *Critical Quarterly.* The poet describes a woman he met who cares for a variety of wounded animals. She once performed in the musical *Hello Dolly!* on Broadway but now lives alone in Grand Forks, South Dakota. He concludes the poem by writing:

The old woman who lives
out here all alone,
who has seen and known so much,
is taking a course in writing.
She told me so herself.
In this place it is clear that the word
is with us, and nowhere else.

Louis Simpson, the poet who has loved words for their own sake, continues to dedicate himself to poems of human sympathy in common speech, poetry that distinguishes him as one of our great social commentators.

Selected Bibliography

WORKS OF LOUIS SIMPSON

POETRY

The Arrivistes: Poems 1940–1949. New York: Fine Editions Press, 1949.

Good News of Death and Other Poems. New York: Scribners, 1955.

A Dream of Governors. Middletown, Conn.: Wesleyan University Press, 1959.

At the End of the Open Road. Middletown, Conn.: Wesleyan University Press, 1963.

Selected Poems. New York: Harcourt, Brace, & World, 1965.

Adventures of the Letter I. New York: Harper & Row, 1971.

Searching for the Ox. New York: William Morrow, 1976.

Caviare at the Funeral. New York: Franklin Watts, 1980.

People Live Here: Selected Poems 1949–1983. Brockport, N.Y.: BOA Editions, 1983.

The Best Hour of the Night. New Haven, Conn.: Ticknor & Fields, 1983.

Collected Poems. New York: Paragon House, 1988.

In the Room We Share. New York: Paragon House, 1990.

There You Are. Brownsville, Ore.: Story Line Press, 1995.

TRANSLATIONS

Modern Poets of France: A Bilingual Anthology. Ashland, Ore.: Story Line Press, 1997.

François Villon's "The Legacy" and "The Testament." Ashland, Ore.: Story Line Press, 2000.

LITERARY CRITICISM

James Hogg: A Critical Study. New York: St. Martin's, 1962.

Three on the Tower: The Lives and Works of Ezra Pound, T. S. Eliot, and William Carlos Williams. New York: William Morrow, 1975.

A Revolution in Taste: Studies of Dylan Thomas, Allen Ginsberg, Sylvia Plath, and Robert Lowell. New York: Macmillan, 1978.

A Company of Poets. Ann Arbor: University of Michigan Press, 1981.

The Character of the Poet. Ann Arbor: University of Michigan Press, 1986.

Ships Going into the Blue: Essays and Notes on Poetry. Ann Arbor: University of Michigan Press, 1994.

AUTOBIOGRAPHIES

Air with Armed Men. London: London Magazine Editions, 1972. Republished as *North of Jamaica*. New York: Harper & Row, 1972.

The King My Father's Wreck. Brownsville, Ore.: Story Line Press, 1995.

OTHER WORKS

New Poets of England and America. Edited by Louis Simpson, Donald Hall, and Robert Pack. New York: Meridian, 1957.

Riverside Drive. New York: Atheneum, 1962.

An Introduction to Poetry. Edited by Louis Simpson. New York: St. Martin's, 1986.

CRITICAL AND BIOGRAPHICAL STUDIES

Bly, Robert. "The Work of Louis Simpson." *Fifties* 1:22–25 (1958).

———. "Louis Simpson's New Book." *Sixties* 4:58–61 (fall 1960).

Cox, C. B. "The Poetry of Louis Simpson." *Critical Quarterly* 8:72–83 (spring 1966). Reprinted in *On Louis Simpson: Depths beyond Happiness.* Ann Arbor: University of Michigan Press, 1988. Pp. 193–208.

Dunn, Douglas. "Poetry of Inclusion." *Times Literary Supplement,* June 5, 1981, p. 645 (Review of *Caviare at the Funeral*). Reprinted in *On Louis Simpson: Depths beyond Happiness.* Ann Arbor: University of Michigan Press, 1988. Pp. 143–146.

Gray, Yohma. "The Poetry of Louis Simpson." *Tri-Quarterly* 5:33–39 (spring 1963). Reprinted in *On Louis Simpson: Depths beyond Happiness.* Ann Arbor: University of Michigan Press, 1988. Pp. 173–192.

Gunn, Thom. "American Examples." *Spectator,* March 27, 1957, p. 442.

Hungerford, Edward, ed. *Poets in Progress: Critical Prefaces to Thirteen Modern American Poets.* Evanston, Ill.: Northwestern University Press, 1967.

Hutchens, John K. "Riverside Drive." *New York Herald Tribune,* May 9, 1962, p. 27. Reprinted in *On Louis Simpson: Depths beyond Happiness.* Ann Arbor: University of Michigan Press, 1988. Pp. 50–51.

Jarman, Mark, and Robert McDowell. "The Death of the Lyric: The Achievement of Louis Simpson." In their *The Reaper Essays.* Brownsville, Ore.: Story Line Press, 1996.

Jarrell, Randall. "Poetry Unlimited." *Partisan Review* 17:189 (February 1950). Reprinted in *On Louis Simpson: Depths beyond Happiness.* Ann Arbor: University of Michigan Press, 1988. P. 27.

Lazer, Hank. "Louis Simpson and Walt Whitman: Destroying the Teacher." *Walt Whitman Quarterly Review* 1:1–21 (December 1983).

———, ed. *On Louis Simpson: Depths Beyond Happiness.* Ann Arbor: University of Michigan Press, 1988.

Lensing, George S., and Ronald Moran. *Four Poets and the Emotive Imagination: Robert Bly, James Wright, Louis Simpson, and William Stafford.* Baton Rouge: Louisiana State University Press, 1976.

Locke, Duane. "New Directions in Poetry: The Work of Louis Simpson." *dust* 1:67–69 (fall 1964). Reprinted in *On Louis Simpson: Depths beyond*

Happiness. Ann Arbor: University of Michigan Press, 1988. Pp. 63–65.

Moran, Ronald. *Louis Simpson.* New York: Twayne, 1972.

Plumly, Stanley. "Showing a Story." *American Poetry Review* 5:42–43 (July/August 1976). Reprinted in *On Louis Simpson: Depths beyond Happiness.* Ann Arbor: University of Michigan Press, 1988. Pp. 120–123.

Poulin, Al, Jr., and Michael Waters, eds. *Contemporary American Poetry,* 7th ed. Boston: Houghton Mifflin, 2001.

Roberson, William H. *Louis Simpson: A Reference Guide.* New York: G. K. Hall, 1980.

Smith, Dave. "A Child of the World." *American Poetry Review* 8:11–15 (January/February 1979). Reprinted in *On Louis Simpson: Depths beyond Happiness.* Ann Arbor: University of Michigan Press, 1988. Pp. 258–274.

Stafford, William. "From 'Terminations, Revelations.'" *Poetry* 104:104–105 (May 1964). Reprinted in *On Louis Simpson: Depths beyond Happiness.* Ann Arbor: University of Michigan Press, 1988. Pp. 61–62.

Stitt, Peter. *The World's Hieroglyphic Beauty: Five American Poets.* Athens: University of Georgia, 1985.

Stuttaford, Genevieve. Review of *In the Room We Share. Publishers Weekly,* January 12, 1990, p. 55.

Van Duyn, Mona. *Poetry* 88:332–333 (August 1956).

Wojahn, David. "'I Might Live Here Myself': On Louis Simpson." *Tar River Poetry* 24:41–51 (fall 1984).

INTERVIEWS

Dodd, Wayne, and Stanley Plumly. "Capturing the World as It Is: An Interview with Wayne Dodd and Stanley Plumly." *Ohio Review* 14:34–51 (spring 1973). Reprinted in *A Company of Poets.* Ann Arbor: University of Michigan Press, 1981. Pp. 223–251.

Josephi, Beate. "A Race That Has Not Yet Arrived: An Interview with Beate Josephi." *Opinion* 8 (May 1979). Reprinted in *A Company of Poets.* Ann Arbor: University of Michigan Press, 1981. Pp. 328–338.

Keller, Edith. "Off the Cuff." *Minetta Review* 3 (1984). Reprinted in *The Character of the Poet*. Ann Arbor: University of Michigan Press, 1986. Pp. 166–171.

Rompf, Kraft. "Everyone Knows But the Poet (What Poetry Is)" *Falcon* 7 (spring 1976). Reprinted in *A Company of Poets*. Ann Arbor: University of Michigan Press, 1981. Pp. 273–305.

Schneider, Steven P. "An Interview with Louis Simpson." *The Wordsworth Circle* 13:99–104 (spring 1982).

Smith, Lawrence R. "A Conversation with Louis Simpson." *Chicago Review* 27:99–109 (summer 1975).

—STEVEN P. SCHNEIDER

Gerald Stern

1925–

Describing his poetic technique in a 1998 interview, Gerald Stern referred to his "associative way of writing. . . . I begin with an image or an idea or a concept or a group of words and just move along as the spirit, if you will, takes me. God knows what that spirit is. Call it the muse, call it unconsciousness, guilt, shame, love, hope, memory." In part because of this approach to writing, Stern's poetry possesses a startling immediacy and emotional urgency. Elsewhere he has cited Judaism and the political ideals of the Left as major influences; these can be seen in his concern for justice and for the ways in which collective history and one's personal past shape one's life.

"Loss," "polarities," "nostalgia," "the Sabbath," and "caves" are key terms for understanding Stern's work. Each of the essays in the series collectively titled "Notes from the River" (1983, 1984, 1987) examines one of these terms as a grand theme winding its way through Stern's books. In the first essay, on "loss," the poet describes what he calls "two kingdoms," the earthly life of the present time and paradise. He says he writes a poetry of loss, lamenting the loss of paradise, the second kingdom. The essay on "polarities" gives a context to his twin themes of loss and paradise. Stern depicts a scene of a poor African American woman gathering dandelion weeds for soup and a white man in a window watching her. From this scene the poet extrapolates a system of contraries that define the world as he sees it. The man, as a "god at the window . . . is opposed to the goddess on the hillside." The man represents

> punctuality, love of form, skill in planning, use of reason, love of abstraction, foresight, capacity for organization, tolerance, willingness to delay, ruthlessness, equability, consistency, skill in record keeping, ability to live in the future, efficiency, addiction to logic, belief in the mind, distrust of aims, dependence on technology, dislike of mystery, indifference to religion, uniformity, denial.

The woman, by contrast, represents

> Belief in emotions, living by the senses, commitment to the heart, concordance with nature, indifference to time, love of religion and mystery, adaptability, sensitivity to weather, suspicion of the law, secrecy, addiction to children, love of singing, friendliness, practicality, generosity, love of beauty, willingness to share, sensuality, fear of machines, passion, concrete knowledge, terror of paper, love of family, kinship with other women, deep intelligence.

The poles represented by these two figures contextualize, and so explain, Stern's poetic vision. They define the world in which he lives; his poetry cannot help but grow out of them.

In the third "Notes from the River" essay, Stern turns his attention to "the pain of separation." This pain, nostalgia, comes from the loss of paradise itself: "I think nostalgia is not, in its profoundest sense, unprogressive. I don't think it prevents revolution or change." From Stern's perspective, to live in the modern world is to be at once in exile from paradise and firmly dedicated to creating paradise anew. If, for Stern, the modern world of polarities is a fall from paradise, it is also the source of justice itself: the desire to make paradise once more. In a figurative, metaphorical way, then, Stern makes himself and his readers Jewish. For exile—the consummate Jewish theme—is also, says Stern, the theme of contemporary life. It explains the social urge to create a just world. Fittingly, then, when Stern describes paradise he chooses the Sabbath as his figure: "The Sabbath can be seen not only as an anticipation of Messianic time but as a nostalgic reminder of Gardenic time, the time before the expulsion."

Thus, as influences, the Left represents Stern's attraction to an egalitarian urge to establish justice for all, and Judaism represents his persistent fascination with exile, paradise, the Sabbath. In his final essay in the "Notes from the River" series, he turns to the "caves" of his life, the places he has lived in and the pockets of time he particularly remembers. A few facts from Stern's biography offer a fuller sense of those "caves."

Born the second of two children in Pittsburgh, Pennsylvania, on February 22, 1925, Gerald Stern grew up in that city's rougher neighborhoods. In a 1984 interview with Mark Hillringhouse he told the story of his early life: his mother, Ida Barach Stern, was born in Bialstock, "a city in what is now Poland and was then Polish Russia, but which the Jews identify with ancient Lithuania, in their crazy archaic way." In Bialstock, Stern's maternal grandfather was a kosher butcher and a learned man: he "wrote essays on Tolstoi and Goethe." Stern's father, Harry Stern, was born on a farm in the Ukraine. As he explained in a 1993 essay titled "What I Have to Defend, What I Can't Bear Losing," his father was a manager and buyer for a men's and boy's clothing department in a credit store. "My father was a Truman democrat," Stern writes. "He was a manager but he loved unions and always respected working men and women. I never heard him express words of bigotry or racial or religious hatred." Stern went to religious school every day from the age of five until his bar mitzvah. He lived for a memorable time under the supervision of his observant grandmother, attending synagogue both Friday night and Saturday. But, as Stern remarks, "I was raised Orthodox and quit when I was thirteen years and one day."

In his early years he was subjected to anti-Semitic slurs and suffered from physical abuse on account of his faith. Of all the childhood events that would affect him, by far the most awful and life-transforming was his sister's death, at age nine, of spinal meningitis. Stern was only eight. In "Some Secrets," he recalls that his mother would hold him in bed, crying his sister's name while his father worked late on Saturday nights: "If anything came close to being a direct influence over me it was this, and it caused me the most pain and confusion, although I still don't fully understand its connection with my writing."

The Great Depression did not take a heavy toll on the Stern family's lifestyle. "We had a maid, owned our own house, bought a new car every two or three years, saved money, and had some hopeful and vague plans for my future," he remarked in "What I Have to Defend." In fact, Stern did not expect to go to college. He claims that he discovered the University of Pittsburgh only by mistake when he came across a line of students waiting to register for class. Despite the scholarly interests of his grandfather (who in any case rarely spoke of them), aside from prayer books Stern did not grow up in a house of books. At college he did not major in English but rather chose philosophy and political science, expecting a career in either the latter or labor law. In "Notes from the River" Stern admits, "I had come to my 'place' without training or support or any kind of preparation or conditioning."

During his freshman year at Pittsburgh he wrote his first poems. As Stern wrote in "Some Secrets," "I don't think I knew what a bohemian was. I did carry a little notebook around with me in which I wrote my poems. . . . I wore white shirts, ties, wing-tip shoes, double-breasted suits. I was on the football team, then the debate team. I played nine-ball. I didn't know one was or could be an actual poet." He was also immersed in political issues, explaining in "What I Have to Defend": "The 'natural' sentiment, for me and my friends, was for the left, and the left then meant two things only—pro-labor stance and an anti-fascist state. We hated the bosses, whom we never saw, and we loved the workers, whose children, if we were Jewish, often treated us with contempt, hatred and violence. . . . I made a kind of package out of my belief in justice, my unspeakable naivete, and my hope for perfection."

In 1946 Stern joined the U.S. Army Air Corps, where a conflict with a provost-sergeant led to a court-martial. In "Notes from the River," he says this eventually led to a "stint in the guard house." His job was hauling garbage cans of dead animals to an underground incinerator. He later labored ten to twelve hours a day breaking fieldstone with a sledgehammer under the watch of an armed guard. During this time Stern found that he had begun "to think a little like a poet." Although he had been writing poetry since he was a freshman, only now did it take on the resonance of art.

Following his army days, he met a young artist, Patricia Miller, the woman he would eventually marry; she had gone to college at what is now Carnegie-Mellon University in Pittsburgh. Stern took the GI Bill's offer of "twenty dollars a week for fifty-two weeks" to read and educate himself in a literary way. As he puts it in "Notes from the River": "My dear President [Harry Truman], the little scholar from Missouri, gave me twenty dollars a week to read old books and transform my life."

After that year, Stern enrolled at Columbia University in New York City and in 1949 received his master's degree. Following his graduation, he traveled to Europe with Jack Gilbert and Richard Hazley, two Pittsburgh friends from his college debating team days. Significantly, both men were poets. Stern's journey,

which led him for a time to graduate work at the Sorbonne, would prove to be a rich seedbed for his future poetry. Poetry, Stern said, "had become our religion."

It was during his year in Paris that Stern wrote his first serious poem, an epic entitled "Ishmael's Dream." He sent it to the poet W. H. Auden, who responded by inviting Stern to visit upon Stern's return to New York. Stern naturally assumed that an invitation from so famous and important a poet was going to be an auspicious event. But, as Stern told Gary Pacernick, it proved otherwise, with the topics of discussion being mainly "theater and cheese. . . . I knew Velveeta cheese. I mean, what did I know about cheese, coming from Pittsburgh. . . . Finally I said to him, 'Mr Auden, what about my poem?' He looked at me, and he said, 'Oh, I really liked the last ten lines.' A kind of a lyric at the end of the poem. And I was furious at him for years after that." Despite Auden's dismissal and Stern's frustration, this first serious effort laid the thematic groundwork for his future poetry. In "Some Secrets," he says: "The subject, which I never consciously thought about, was the regeneration and transformation of the world, and myself as religio-politico-linguistic hero, a common enough theme for a first generation American Jew only son."

After returning to New York, Stern enrolled in the Ph.D. program at Columbia. There he studied with the renowned literary scholar Lionel Trilling. After one year, however, he left the program and began supporting himself by teaching. His first job was as headmaster of a private school in New York. But in 1953 Stern, by then married, decided to make another trip to Europe, this time with his wife. They stayed three years, eventually settling in Glasgow, Scotland, where Stern taught high school.

When Stern returned to the United States, he began a career of teaching in colleges and universities: seven years at Temple University in Philadelphia (1956–1963), five years at

Indiana University of Pennsylvania (1963–1967), fourteen years at Somerset County College in Somerset, New Jersey (1968–1982). He also held numerous visiting professorships and chairs in creative writing throughout the country. Stern and his wife had two children, David and Rachel.

In addition to his teaching and writing careers, Stern led the life of a politically committed activist. He wrote in "What I Have to Defend":

> I suppose I was myself a latterday utopian socialist; although part of me was a good social democrat . . . I fought tooth and nail, with three college presidents, with committees, with department chairmen, with deans. I lost tenure once and was threatened twice more because of my political activities. . . . I fought the governor of Pennsylvania . . . when he censored a deeply moving photography exhibition on the walls of the state house. . . . I organized and led civil rights marches in Indiana, Pennsylvania. . . . I headed a teacher's union in the state of New Jersey. I wrote contracts, I negotiated, and led two strikes.

Stern's activist life waned, however, as his poetic career waxed. Eventually, in 1982, he was offered a position in the nation's oldest and most prestigious creative writing program, the Writer's Workshop at the University of Iowa. He taught there until his retirement in 1995. Stern was divorced from his wife in the 1980s. A shooting that occurred during a holdup in Newark, New Jersey, nearly killed Stern, and for the rest of his life he would carry a bullet in his neck as a frightening reminder of the attack.

As the disappointing meeting with Auden had ironically foretold, Stern would define his poetic voice through lyric rather than through epic forms. The road to that lyric paradise, however, would be hard won as Stern learned to combine—as Auden's own verse combines—the intellectual, the political, and the passionate in his work. Eventually, thirty years after that first meeting, Stern wrote about his early mentor in the poem "In Memory of W. H. Auden" (in

Paradise Poems, 1984). There, Stern casts himself as Caliban and Auden as Prospero. He laments their first meeting when "the stick / of that old Prospero would never rest / on my poor head." Nonetheless, now that he has become a poet, Stern can admit that Auden was just the "magician" he needed. In the poem Stern looks to Auden and says that he "could release me now, whom I release and remember."

LOSS AND RUIN: THE FIRST POEMS, 1950–1971

Stern had high hopes that his first major publication, an epic entitled "The Pineys," would be his ticket to Mount Parnassus. The poem, in four sections, establishes a mythic contest between good and evil set in the context of American history. In the 1984 interview with Hillringhouse, Stern explained:

> I deal with two poles. It's a poem about . . . the White House and the 'Black House.' The White House is a perfect example of . . . the age of reason, the age of order. And just behind and under all that order is chaos and destruction and disorganization and timelessness and simplicity and primitivism and childlessness. . . . I think of the Pineys, the so-called inhabitants of the Pine Barrens of southern New Jersey . . . as the symbol of the one order and the White House, or its inhabitants, as the symbol of the other.

By the end of the poem, Stern sets his landscape ablaze and concludes in a kind of ecstatic apocalypse: "Plunged the house in blazing ferocious incandescence."

If the poem did not make his reputation, it was for no other reason than Stern's own loss of faith in it. In "Some Secrets," he notes:

> One day, while rewriting the very last section, I realized the poem was a failure, that it was indulgent, that it was tedious, that it no longer interested me. It was either 1964 or '65; I was going on forty, living in Indiana, Pa., and teaching at

the state college there. I was devastated. I had been a practicing poet for almost two decades and I had nothing to show. I suddenly was nowhere; I had reached the bottom.

From this crisis would emerge the lyrical, prophetic, ecstatic voice that readers have to come to identify as Stern's own. Stern understood that he had to start over. He began a series of lyrics that would ultimately be published in his first book, *Rejoicings: Selected Poems, 1966–1972* (1973). Intriguingly, rather than put "The Pineys" away and never look back, the poet returned to it several years after his creative crisis, publishing it in 1969. Describing this decision in "Some Secrets," he says that after he "got rid of a lot of dead wood . . . it didn't look that bad. Wasn't it just the last stage of an endless series of rejections and abandonments that had plagued me since my early twenties?" Stern's first significant poem, then, must be read as if it were already an abandoned site. His first poem, like his first subjects, is itself a ruin, a step on the way to paradise.

VISIONS OF PARADISE: *REJOICINGS, LUCKY LIFE,* AND *THE RED COAL*

Responding to a query from *Contemporary Authors* (1978), Stern wrote: "If I had to explain my art I would talk about it in terms of staking out a place that no one else wanted, because it was not noticed, because it was abandoned or overlooked." He then elaborates: "I am talking about weeds, and waste places and lovely pockets, and in my poems I mean it on a literal as well as on a psychological and symbolic level." Stern asks that his poetry be understood as a nostalgic look into the past, as well as a present examination of the loss and ruin such a look back reveals. Rather than provoke despair, however, such nostalgia often prods him into founding, if not finding, paradise.

Stern's first book, *Rejoicings,* should be read in light of this theme. The book was published in three different editions (the first a fine-arts press limited edition entitled *The Naming of Beasts,* the second and third trade editions under the title *Rejoicings.*) This collection marks the first appearance of what would become his poetic persona, a voice at once overly—even outrageously—emotional and profoundly intellectual and critical. Stern takes his title from the name of the tractate on mourning in the Talmud, where "rejoicings" refers to loss and bereavement, an ironic twist to the standard English dictionary definition of the term. Jane Somerville, in a book-length study of Stern's poetry, says that Stern's speaker attempts "to reconcile the extremes of intellect and emotion, mind and body. His reverence for learnedness is a strong presence throughout the corpus, but his respect for the physical/emotional is just as serious."

The title poem, set on the beach in Atlantic City, begins:

> I put the sun behind the Marlborough Blenheim
> so I can see the walkers settling down
> to their evening of relaxation
> over the slimy piers.

In these lines, Stern organizes his world; he "puts" the sun in its place. Yet even as he watches others enjoy themselves, he is aware of "the slimy piers," of the equal proportion of muck and flowers. Later in the poem, Stern draws a figure on the sand. Again, the speaker is attempting to achieve a certain order and control, but emotion is given its place:

> a good circle before digging
> so I can close the world in my grip
> and draw my poor crumbling man
> so that his tears fall within the line.

The "crumbling man" is Stern's friend Robert Summers, a playwright, who died in the 1970s. In the poem Stern calls his friend "Nietzsche," identifying the man with the German philosopher. But the speaker has more to do at the shore than to bury his friend, or to memorialize his tears:

> After twenty years of dull loyalty
> I have come back one more time to the shore,
> like an old prisoner—like a believer—
> to squeeze the last poetry out of the rubbish.

He is determined to redeem the ritual of going to the sea's edge, to make sense of his double vision of the rubbish (or "the slimy piers") and the beauty that can be culled from it.

At the end of "Rejoicings," Stern writes: "I am burying our Nietzsche; / I am touching his small body for the last time." An angry, wild prophet/philosopher—and a friend keenly missed—is now ritually buried, properly mourned. For it is out of such a ritual farewell that one expects a rebirth, and the poems in this volume represent Stern's coming into his own as a lyric poet.

Stern sent *Rejoicings* to Robert Bly, an important American poet and editor. Bly, along with W. S. Merwin, James Wright, and Louis Simpson, had been advocating the use of a more spiritually intense poetic image. Eventually, he would herald a new poetic movement known as Deep Image Poetry. Bly was enthusiastic about Stern's lyrics and encouraged him to write more.

As it happened, the first two editions of *Rejoicings* received no substantial reviews; even the trade publication was printed in an edition of less than 500 copies. Therefore, when Stern's second book, *Lucky Life,* appeared in 1977, it seemed as if he had burst on the scene from out of nowhere, fully formed. In theme and style the two books are very similar. Published by Houghton Mifflin, *Lucky Life* won the Academy of American Poets' Lamont Prize, which recognizes achievement by a poet in a second published collection, and earned Stern a secure place in the American poetry world.

Particularly striking in *Lucky Life* are the New Jersey beach poems: "I Need Help," "On the Island," the title poem, and the last poem,

"Something New." Each of these poems announces Stern's desire to find paradise, to find some measure of peace and mercy in a world of ruins. As he puts it in "This Is It": "Everyone is into my myth! The whole countryside / is studying weeds, collecting sadness, dreaming."

In the title poem, as in "Rejoicings," Stern's speaker is on the beach, on the margins, once more. He addresses the waves:

> Dear waves, what will you do for me this year?
> Will you drown out my scream?
> Will you let me rise through the fog?
> Will you fill me with that old salt feeling?

Through six more lines he asks questions, but rather than finding some kind of "poetic" answer, he lets his questions float over the surf. In the concluding stanza of the poem, he simply praises the fact that he can even ask such questions at all:

> Lucky life is like this. Lucky there is an ocean to
>   come to.
> Lucky you can judge yourself in this water.
> Lucky the waves are cold enough to wash out the
>   meanness.
> Lucky you can be purified over and over again.
> Lucky there is the same cleanliness for everyone.
> Lucky life is like that. Lucky life. Oh lucky life.
> Oh lucky lucky life. Lucky life.

Asking questions, feeling pain and hope for a hint of redemption, of paradise, makes him a lucky man. Here, Stern addresses himself as "you" rather than the reader and, as a result, enters into a dialogue with himself—a turn inward that enables him to confront his own personal nostalgia, his own losses and gains.

Some of Stern's most well-regarded and well-known poems appear in this book: "Lucky Life," "Straus Park," "At Bickfords," "Behaving Like a Jew." Indeed, "Behaving Like a Jew" is perhaps Stern's "signature" poem, the most anthologized and discussed of all of his works. As if to underline its importance, Stern, in *This*

Time (1998), a volume of new and selected poems, placed the poem as the first in the *Lucky Life* section, whereas in the original volume it was the thirty-eighth.

The poem describes the moment when Stern finds a dead opossum on the side of the road. He takes it and throws it into the woods. Following this act, Stern says: "I am sick of the spirit of Lindbergh over everything / that joy in death, that philosophical / understanding of carnage." He declares that he will "be unappeased at the opossum's death." He says: "I am going to behave like a Jew / and touch his face, and stare into his eyes." In the 1998 interview with Pacernick, Stern recalled the poem's origin:

> I was in a waiting room in a hospital . . . and I was reading a greasy *Reader's Digest,* and there was an essay, an article by [Charles] Lindbergh about death. . . . I had just passed, driving my wife to the hospital, a dead opossum on the road with a bullet hole in its head and had helped it off the road. Reading the article by Lindbergh, I thought of the opossum as a kind of Jew. Perfectly absurd. And I thought of Lindbergh's anti-Semitism, and I thought of the whole view of death that's expressed in that *Reader's Digest* article, almost a kind of mystic love of death, as being totally alien to Judaism.

The poem's Jewish view of death is a refusal: "I am not going to . . . / praise the beauty and the balance." To be Jewish one must refuse certain conventions: the speaker refuses to "lose [him]self in the immortal lifestream." Instead, he will forgo mystical connection in favor of a frank recognition of the physical brutality of death: "My hands are still a little shaky / from his stiffness and his bulk."

The book, and particularly the poems "Lucky Life" and "Behaving Like a Jew," met with widespread enthusiasm, from the influential *New York Times Book Review* to obscure literary journals. In the *Georgia Review,* Peter Stitt offered a prayer: "Thank God, or Houghton Mifflin, for Gerald Stern." Writing in *Harper's,* the poet Hayden Carruth also praised Stern: "Because he is close to the dailiness of American life he speaks for us all in our own voices." The poet Patricia Hampl went even further, declaring that "*Lucky Life* is the most beautiful and genuine new book I've read in a long time."

Despite this chorus of praise, however, there were also dissenters. Indeed, certain complaints would dog Stern throughout his career. In *Parnassus,* for example, the reviewer Lawrence Kramer attacked Stern's relentlessly emotional, even excessive poetic voice, writing that his "investment in himself is arbitrary, justified perhaps only by a certain ruthless candor; it therefore seems sentimental." Stern's raw emotionalism, so new when compared to the poetry of the 1970s, was celebrated by some but rejected by others. Undeniably, however, he had established a unique voice and would remain true to it.

Stern published a third collection, *The Red Coal,* in 1981. It continues Stern's exploration of ruin, justice, loss, and paradise. The book's cover featured a photograph of Stern and his friend, the poet Peter Gilbert, walking down a street in Paris in 1950, foretelling the nostalgic urgency of the poems within. The photograph is the focus of the book's title poem:

> Sometimes I sit in my blue chair trying to remember
> what it was like in the spring of 1950
> before the burning coal entered my life.

"The burning coal" is his symbol for poetry; it is also a metaphor for the kind of life he has chosen: a life of intensity, imagination, profound meditation, and passion. Stern now adds poetry to his sense of "paradise." The poem also connects Stern and Gilbert to the generation of the modernist poets William Carlos Williams and Ezra Pound. Stern compares the Paris photograph to one of Williams visiting Pound at St. Elizabeth's Hospital in Washington, D.C., where Pound had been confined in lieu of going to trial for treason after World War II.

"The Red Coal" is one of Stern's more complex and difficult works because of its many resonances and polarities: here poetry opposes politics, public life opposes private art. The poem is also a journey of self-discovery: Stern goes back to a time when he made his choice to accept "the red coal." If his time in Europe was a mix of paradise and exile—a life of poetry and a rejection of the 1950s professional and corporate ideal for making a living—Stern's poetics of nostalgia assumes that everyone is, on some level, also in exile from paradise. The book makes clear that, at age 56, the poet is willing to embrace the choices he had made twenty-five years earlier.

Stern's poetic images often have a personal resonance that makes them surreal. They retain their emotional intensity even while being bizarre or indecipherable. One poem from *The Red Coal,* "For Night to Come," begins, "I am giving instructions to my monkey / on how to plant a pine tree," and goes on to describe how the monkey is trained for the task. Through the image of the monkey Stern explores a basic polarity between bestial instinct and civilized behavior, between nature and art. By treating his seemingly absurd subject without ironic distance, Stern presses the opposition under scrutiny to its limits.

In addition to its affecting lyrics, *The Red Coal* is also a triumph of Stern's narrative imagination. In long poems such as "The Shirt Poem," "Joseph Pockets," "The Angel Poem," "The Poem of Liberation," and "The Red Coal," the twin themes of loss and paradise clash. In "The Shirt Poem," for example, Stern brings to life a series of shirts in a closet: "they shake their empty arms / and grow stiff as they wait for the light to come." These surreal dancing shirts allow Stern to enter the lost world of labor organizers and to conceive political dreams of social justice: "I want to write it down before it's forgotten, / how we lived, what we believed in." The connection is as public as it is personal:

"What is my life if not a substitute for yours, / and my dream a substitute for your dream?"

In "Joseph Pockets," Stern recalls another paradise—not of social justice, but of familial love, remembering tender moments with his sister. From memories of her death emerges a long, meandering meditation on many subjects. In "The Angel Poem," Stern's speaker is a fallen angel who finds himself wandering in New York City. And in "The Poem of Liberation," Stern contrasts a public garden in New York City with the biblical garden to be found outside New York's Cathedral of St. John the Divine. Paradise is as likely to be stumbled upon on the next block as summoned from the personal past of a fifty-something-year-old poet.

Compared to Walt Whitman, praised for his spirituality and his range of subjects, Stern also met with renewed criticism. The poet Mary Jo Salter found Stern's poems "baffling" and his references "wearying." Vernon Shetley, reviewing the book in the *New York Times Book Review,* summarized it thus:

> Intensely personal without being autobiographical, Stern's poems lay bare his emotions while revealing almost nothing about their origins. Alternating between conversational speech and slightly surreal outbursts, Stern's work achieves its effects through accumulations of rhetorical weight or sudden flashes of disjunctive imagery. . . . The first person pronoun is ubiquitous, the free verse rarely strays far from a loose iambic. Famous names appear frequently, but more as part of Stern's mental furniture than as a test of the reader's erudition.

Stern's embrace of polarities, his placing intellectual allusions and personal stories side by side, was a stylistic trademark; moreover, it signaled the poet's refusal to follow what he saw as unsatisfactory poetic conventions.

Acknowledging the complaints about Stern's style, the poet David Wojahn wrote: "While some may find the bewildering accumulation of details and events in Stern's poems meandering and bothersome, a careful reading will reveal their function: everything Stern sees is filtered through the process of memory, and in doing so is given clarity and integration." He added that "it's Stern's *spirit* that makes him a significant figure, and with this collection he's become one of the finest poets of his generation, a group that includes such formidable figures as Philip Levine and James Wright." Stern was having a very real impact on a younger generation of poets, Wojahn himself included. To a new group of poets Stern represented a commitment to unadulterated emotionalism in poetry. He showed that one could be passionate in poetry without being either sentimental or anti-intellectual.

The critic Sanford Pinsker argued that Stern's themes and techniques are particular to Jewish tradition, specifically "East European, rather than . . . American." Raising another sort of polarity that appears in Stern's work, Pinsker adds: "Stern is either tagged as an urban (read: Jewish) poet who lives in the country, or a country poet who often writes about the city." Pinsker sees the poet as both urban and rural in a particular sense: "Stern is unashamedly bookish, but at the same time he gives himself freely to the senses; he is half bourgeois . . . half proletarian hero." Pinsker, like many of Stern's admirers, appreciates the way in which Stern, in his poetry and in his personal life, embraces and even embodies the contradictions of his poetry.

FINDING PARADISE: "FATHER GUZMAN" AND *PARADISE POEMS*

Following *The Red Coal,* Stern published a long poem, "Father Guzman," in the *Paris Review.* It won that journal's Bernard F. Conners Poetry Prize (1982). In three sections, this long poem relates a dialogue between a boy and a Jesuit priest. It begins with the two characters in a swamp at a port in Venezuela; they are watching a cruise ship depart the harbor. In the sur-real dialogue that constitutes the poem, the boy and the priest symbolize sexuality and spirituality, the city and nature, earthly politics and heavenly dreams.

Throughout the poem, the characters debate various forms of paradise, of utopian society. As if allegorizing Stern's own nostalgic obsessions, the boy expresses youth's carnality and desire for justice, while the older man thinks only of ruin, of what has been lost. At one point the boy even blesses, out of a kind of pity, the priest who no longer believes:

> Oh dearest precious man, oh lovely priest,
> oh brother of mine, oh brother and father and teacher,
> so worn out from your life, so sad and exhausted;
> you I love more than my own flesh and blood.

In the second section, Father Guzman admits: "I do long for a world / where souls can live with other souls / . . . / without authority or subordination." The poem goes on to take a sur-real, allegorical turn, moving through complex identity shifts and power relationships; finally, it returns to its main theme, the search for paradise. Near the end of the poem, Stern alludes to his earlier image of "the red coal." The two characters had been discussing how the Spaniards confused the mythical paradise of El Dorado with a sacred lake of an Indian tribe. The priest says of that lake:

> . . . Do you know
> it was a giant meteor dropping out of the sky
> that made the hole in the first place? Think of that!
> The myth of paradise begun by a hot stone
> hitting the ground. . . .

Stern suggests that without that fiery stone, without the descent of God into the material plane, there would be no paradise at all.

It should come as no surprise that Stern called his fourth book *Paradise Poems* (1984). In this book the familiar places of ruin, loss, and oc- casional redemption are now almost singularly praised for revealing paradise, if only tempo- rarily. Here are poems that take place in New York City: "The Same Moon above Us," "Three Skies," "The Expulsion"; and in Pittsburgh and Raubsville, Pennsylvania: "Christmas Sticks," "Leaving Another Kingdom," "Groundhog Lock," "Fritz." Here, too, are poems set in Stern's new home of Iowa City: "Dubuque Street" and "Sycamore." The book is also pep- pered with verses on places like Mexico ("Clay Dog"), the American Southwest ("One Bird to Love Forever"), Crete ("John's Mysteries"), Alabama ("Red Bird"), and California ("Berkeley"). Paradise, such a geographical range suggests, does not exist in one specific place.

"Sycamore" is perhaps the poem most repre- sentative of the complexity involved in locating paradise in present times here on earth. Set in Iowa City, the poem addresses a sycamore tree outside the poet's window. He says: "I want to live here / beside my tree and watch it change." Using images of rebirth and spring, Stern's poem then enacts a moment of paradise in his life. It is at once a tour of his own personal "promised lands" (New York City, Pennsyl- vania) and a more general cultural meditation on the American "errand into the wilderness," of America as every immigrant's imagined promised land. By the end of the poem, Stern becomes the tree, naturalizing himself:

> . . . I am
> the only one in this house, I do my reclining
> all alone, I howl when I want, and I am,
> should anyone come in, a crooked tree
> leaning far out, I am a hundred feet tall,
> I am a flowering figure. . . .

Meanwhile, as if to prove just how necessary paradise is—and to make sure that no one, least of all the poet himself, confuses a glimpse of it with the eradication of hell—Stern includes a harrowing series of Holocaust poems: "The Dancing," "Soap," "Adler." Indeed, "Soap," with "Behaving Like a Jew," has since become one of Stern's best-known poems. Referring to gruesome reports that the Germans had made soap out of the corpses of murdered Jews, Stern imagines a store stocked with such Jewish goods: "Here is a green Jew / with thin black lips. / I stole him from the men's room." In the second stanza, he says: "And here is a blue Jew. / It is his color, you know." This long discursive poem concludes in a strange dialogue with the soap that he ultimately buys.

This poem sparked a small controversy, with some critics indicting it as self-serving rather than honoring the dead or coping with past evil. But the Holocaust poems must not be seen merely as attempts to deal with "survivor's guilt"; they should be seen also as engaged responses to the horrors that make the need for paradise so urgent.

AFTER PARADISE: PROSE AND THE LYRICS OF LOVESICK

Throughout the 1980s the literary community paid a great deal of attention to Stern's work. Numerous interviews and critical assessments appeared. In this decade Stern published many prose pieces, including the essay series "Notes from the River," autobiographical pieces, and analyses of his own poems. In an apt assess- ment, an article by Frederick Garber in Ameri- can Poetry Review identified Stern's major theme as "the purest possible rendering of the conditions of the self," with one's place and one's language constituting fundamental features of a person's identity.

By concentrating on the poetic speaker of Stern's work, Garber touched on a controversy that characterized American poetry in the 1980s. The problem of voice divided critics from poets and poets from each other. Competing ideas of the self, of what constituted identity in the first place, caused many critics and poets to deny each other's claims to be writing poetry at all. If one did not accept someone else's philosophical premise about selfhood, then the poetry dependent on that premise was rejected out of hand. The argument, in effect, depended as much on theories of language as on theories of the self, of "personality." Essentialism, the belief that a fundamental core or "soul" lay at the root of human existence, particularly divided poets and critics. The more experimental and avant-garde camp rejected the very idea of an "essence," finding in such mostly religious beliefs a political agenda that often excluded entire categories of people who did not share similar ideas about "the soul," "the sacred," or "essence" itself. To the avant-garde community, in particular, poetry that relies on a single voice speaking from "the heart," is considered more often pernicious and exclusionary than inclusive and welcoming.

In the final panel discussion of a literary symposium held in the late 1980s on the subject of voice in poetry, Stern described poetry as "a sacred state," adding: "I'll use that word, if you'll forgive me, a sacred state." That he felt the need to apologize for using the word "sacred" shows what it meant to be writing his sort of poetry in those years. This sense of the sacred also drives his essay series "Notes from the River," as well as his two major autobiographical essays: "Some Secrets" (1983) and "What Is This Poet?" (1987).

Stern published his fifth collection, *Lovesick,* in 1987, reflecting on his own divorce, as well as on a new lover, to whom this collection is dedicated. Like its predecessor, *Paradise Poems,* this book takes joy as its dominant theme. Several of the poems recreate the thrill of listening to music: "Stopping Schubert," "I Am in a Window" (about Franz Liszt), "Béla" (about Bartok), "A Slow and Painful Recovery" (about Richard Strauss). In this book people are more likely to sing and dance than they are to weep and wail. Nonetheless, given its ecstatic tone, it is still very much a private, sealed, even hermetic collection of lyrics.

In an essay about the poem "I Am in Love," Stern reveals the details behind its "secret language." Describing his general poetic strategy, he writes: "If anything characterizes *my* mode it is the absence of sections; and it is seeing the poem through, pursuing the logic, even as it's a trap." Writing poetry, in other words, is an act of self-discovery. Writing "I Am in Love" teaches him about himself, about the nature of love, as he follows it through.

On the surface, "I Am in Love" is a strange love poem. There is no one but Stern in the poem. It begins with the poet standing in front of a library's card catalog: "My scholarship / is hectic, I can start with an O and stray / to everything in sight." From there, the poem really does "stray," moving from Italy to Pennsylvania until, at the end, Stern admits: "I have / a helpless fascination with myself." Then, in the very last line, Stern declares—"I am in love." So elusive does this "love" seem to be that one might conclude he is speaking of self-love, or love of life in general. Stern himself (in "A Few Words on Form," *Poetry East,* 1986), claims that the poem is very much about Diane Freund, to whom the book is dedicated: "I remember I was sitting alone in Diane's living room. . . . I was [being] super sensitive and melodramatic towards everything I did. The line, 'I have a helpless fascination with myself' is a quotation from Diane." According to Stern, the poem is really his way of asking for her forgiveness. By putting the line she had uttered into the verse, "I merely threw it back at her, as I asked forgiveness in the poem," the poet explained. Stern then admits that the poem's last line—"I am in love"—"surprised me when it happened. . . . And the reason it worked as a title for the whole poem, and as a subject, was that the state of soul, I suddenly realized, was not so different in the first part [of the poem] as it was in the second."

Such is the sort of emotional logic Stern's poetry had begun to teach.

Another representative poem from this collection, "A Song for the Romeos," is about a particular kind of shoe called the Romeo. It illustrates just how simple the occasion for joy can be. In the second stanza, Stern writes:

I'm wearing my romeos
with the papery thin leather
and the elastic side bands.
they are made for sitting,
or a little walking into the kitchen and out,
a little tea in the hands,
a little Old Forester or a little Schenley in the tea.

Dedicated to two poets, James Wright and Richard Hugo, the poem is also a larger celebration of their world and their people—hard-pressed, working-class America—and of a bygone, longed-for era in American life. In these lines one can see how nostalgia, for Stern, is often a return to a lost paradise:

I'm singing a song for the corner store
and the empty shelves;
for the two blocks of flattened buildings
and broken glass;
for the streetcar that still rounds the bend
with sparks flying through the air.

In the final stanza, in a characteristic embrace of opposites, he praises "the woman with a shopping bag, / and the girl with a book / walking home one behind the other."

Such emotionally invested lyrics are usually combined with intellectual themes, as in the poem "Knowledge Forwards and Backwards." This poem, illustrative of Stern's discursive method, shows just how fundamental his theme is to his style. Since knowledge and passion define his sense of paradise, it only makes sense that his meandering poetic lines and occasionally surreal imagery should be necessary to get him there.

In a 1989 interview with David Hamilton, recorded shortly after this book was published, Stern defined poetry:

It's a faith in life. It's a faith in the presence of the meaningful things, even if temporarily meaningless. Even if transient, even if they'll not be understood ever again, even if they won't ever reappear in that same order. There was order. There was form. There was love. There was joy. There was meaning. There was life, whether for a minute or a year or a century. And that's enough. That's about all we're going to get of Paradise.

WORKS SINCE 1990

In 1990 Stern published *Leaving Another Kingdom: Selected Poems* and *Two Long Poems* (a reprint of both "The Pineys" [1969] and "Father Guzman" [1982]). Also in 1990 the first scholarly book on Stern's poetry, Jane Somerville's *Making the Light Come: The Poetry of Gerald Stern,* appeared. By this time Stern's poetic voice, and a number of his poems in particular, had become central to contemporary American poetry.

Somerville takes a thematic approach to Stern's first five collections (through *Lovesick*), arguing for the importance of his poetic speaker's emotionalism. To her, "Stern's eccentric speaker" has "a voice and character which I see as the controlling principle in a poetry of performance." Somerville chooses to read the voice as a character and not as Stern speaking autobiographically. Discussing that voice's literary influences, Somerville writes that "biblical literature, in particular the kabbalistic and Hassidic reinterpretations of Talmud and the Midrashim" are more central than any particular poet or poetic tradition: "Thus the Bible—and more importantly the commentaries that readjust and even reverse biblical material—can be taken as his precursor." Specifically, Somerville examines four major images alive in each of Stern's books: the garden, the rabbi, the wanderer, and the angel.

Around the time he published *Lovesick,* Stern was shot in the neck during a holdup in Newark, New Jersey. He has never been willing to say much about the shooting; he has acknowledged that his reticence on the subject was to avoid the pitfalls of self-pity. The traumatic experience may explain why, after *Lovesick,* his poetry becomes less and less interested in distinct polarities. Having experienced firsthand the thin line between life and death, Stern was perhaps more willing to find unity, not disparity, and kinship, not opposition, in his poetry. After 1990 Stern's work is concerned with what he identifies as "pre-Socratic philosophy"—knowledge mixed with love and desire. Rather than become the isolated "man in the window" watching a woman who is different from him in enumerated ways, Stern now becomes even more a poet of paradise. In his later books, the man and the woman are increasingly joined as one.

Beginning with *Bread without Sugar* (1992), each of Stern's books manifests an interest in an emotional, passionate knowledge. These books also contain more and more long poems. The new narrative urge allows him to combine the two spheres, passion and knowledge, so that they no longer clash but complement one another. (This sixth new collection of poetry also, for the first time, divides his poems into numbered sections).

Of the poems in *Bread without Sugar,* "Sylvia," an elegy to his sister, and "The Bull-Roarer," an elegy to his father, stand out. "The Bull-Roarer" recalls a childhood visit to an uncle's farm in Pennsylvania. It recreates the time when Stern's father, uncle, and other men butchered a calf and played with the calf's tail. The tail is then compared to a child's toy, a "bull-roarer," which Stern saw years later in Italy. Looking back on the experience and using the toy as his metaphor, Stern writes:

> I saw children throwing it over their heads
> as if they were in central Australia
> or ancient Europe somewhere, in a meadow,
> forcing the gods to roar. They call it Uranic,
> a heavenly force, sometimes almost a voice,
> locked up in that whirling stone, dear father.

These lines are emotionally charged and at the same time intellectually rich.

Stern himself tells his readers about this new direction in "The Thought of Heaven." The poem begins as a meditation on "one blossom on my redwood table." Eventually, it queries Stern's own intellectual commitments:

> . . . I have
> to find the pre-Socratic, that is for me
> what thought should be, I am a sucker still
> for all of it to hang together, I want
> one bundle still. . . .

In these lines, Stern tells his readers two things. First, thought needs to be understood as at once an emotive and a rational phenomenon. Second, polarities are no longer interesting to him: unity is his real subject, how things "hang together."

The poems in this collection contain elements of the surreal, as in his earlier work. In "The Founder," for example, a bronze head of a "captain of industry" exerts a powerful, mysterious hold on the poet and his friends. Others launch typically Sternian voyages into the past. One such poem, "The Age of Strolling," returns to a lost decade, the 1930s, and muses on American ideals of social justice. It concludes: "I spent / a lifetime doing this, grieving and arguing."

Several characters, themselves "bundles" of both heart and mind, people the poems: friends, fellow poets, and Stern's new lover, Judy Rock, to whom the book is dedicated. The title poem, "Bread without Sugar," a long discursive elegy to his father, is an inquiry into the emotional logic of his relationship to his father. As the poem proceeds it becomes a means of understanding his own children's relationship to him.

Reactions to *Bread without Sugar* noted its attention to intellectual subjects and the ever-weaker basis for comparing Stern's work, with its self-questioning and its urgency, to Whitman. David Baker summed things up in a pithy remark: "This poet drives without brakes." On the other side of the critical divide, the poet Calvin Bedient, identified Stern's embrace of an anti-Enlightenment, anti-rational, "pre-Socratic" tradition as a flaw in his work and an undesirable path for American poetry to follow.

To make the case for the pre-Socratic tradition, Stern himself published two important essays in the early 1990s. One offers an extended treatment of Jewish American poetry (in *Jewish-American History and Culture: An Encyclopedia*, 1992), while the other is an autobiographical reflection on his influences. In "What I Have to Defend," Stern says Matthew Arnold taught him, when he was still a young man, that art was compatible with the need for social justice. In Arnold, Stern found a definition of culture, of literature that "should have as its purpose, the 'love of perfection,' that is motivated not merely, or primarily, by the passion for pure knowledge, but also by the moral and social passion for doing good." Also, says Stern, this lesson related to his sense of Judaism: "I think it is the idea of the Jew I cling to . . . I think *what I have to defend, what I can't bear losing,* is either contained or symbolized, in a significant way, in that idea." For Stern, in other words, neither art nor Jewishness can be understood only in the harsh light of reason or only in the more sympathetic light of the heart. Stern's poetry is also a hybrid, mixing heart and mind.

In 1995 Stern published *Odd Mercy,* his seventh collection of new poems. The following year *Odd Mercy* won the prestigious and lucrative Ruth Lilly Poetry Prize. Half of the volume is devoted to one poem, "Hot Dog." At forty-five pages and more than a thousand lines, it is by far Stern's longest poetic work. While many

other poems deserve attention and analysis ("Odd Mercy," "Ida," "Only Elegy," "Blacker than Ever," and "Sixteen Minutes" in particular), "Hot Dog" must be treated as his masterpiece. In keeping with Stern's turn to a poetry that fuses knowledge with an impassioned plea for social justice, "Hot Dog" also resembles a prophetic book of the Bible. In this poem, Stern suffers and records suffering: he is like Job and Amos.

In seventeen sections, Stern's poem travels backward and forward in time. He moves from Iowa to New York to Pennsylvania and New Jersey, sometimes without so much as a line break. Each section of the poem tells a specific story, with its own plot, based on a specific event. At once personal and public, the seventeen distinct episodes, when taken together, form a larger story. "The poem," Stern declared in 1995, "is about salvation. It's about God. It's about redemption. It's a comic poem too."

In the first section, for example, Stern, in lower Manhattan around Tompkins Square Park, centers his meditation on an African American woman—a street person named Hot Dog. She becomes for him the consummate image of exile, of social wrongs, of the need for both mercy and justice. In sections two and three, the poem meditates on biblical strictures—the laws of Kashruth, or keeping kosher, of distinguishing the sacred from the profane—as well as on two men—Saint Augustine and Walt Whitman. These two figures come to measure how such needs as justice and mercy are to be met. In section four Stern writes:

> Augustine
> fought one battle—although he fought many—we all
> fight one battle, one a life—I think
> that's mostly right. Whitman fought one. For which
> he is denounced. Sometimes. I'm amazed
> at my own battle. . . .

Stern takes his place alongside Augustine and Whitman and, as he suggests all of their associations with Hot Dog, makes of his poem a moral meditation; it becomes an ode on ethics and justice.

In many ways this is a capstone poem: here one finds Stern's narrative gift wedded to his lyric impulse, while bringing his characters, particularly marginalized figures like Hot Dog, to life. Equally at home in frank realism as in more outrageous flights of surrealism, "Hot Dog" is a compendium of what is best in Stern's work. It reiterates Stern's lifelong poetic journey from ruin to paradise. As the poet Delmore Schwartz once said, "It is always darkness before delight." The poem ends in delight with Stern declaring:

> . . . I
> felt young today, what with the rain what with
> the wind what with a rolling bottle that won't
> let me alone and yesterday morning's news
> still underfoot and all those trees still bare
> but starting to turn a little and two or three birdlets
> getting ready again for the next eternity.

Describing the poem in the 1998 interview, Stern commented: "It is the longest poem I've ever written, and it's as if I have been preparing to write that poem all my life."

Mark Hillringhouse suggested that "Hot Dog" depended on a struggle between "two opposite poles, from self-burial, or some low form of animal death, to rebirth on a higher plane." Referring to the philosophical implication of "Hot Dog," Hillringhouse wrote: "He seems to want to return to the foundations of philosophy, to the pre-Socratics, when it was possible to reduce matter and existence to a single permanent substance." In *Uncertainty and Plenitude: Five Contemporary Poets* (1997), Peter Stitt argues that Stern's poetry is a plea for mythic order, for meaning, and so poses a challenge to the new orthodoxy in intellectual life that reads only uncertainty and chance in the world of nature and humanity. Stern's work, Stitt suggests, is finally a grand attempt to resolve such

uncertainty. However, in 1997 Jonathan Barron argued that this uncertainty was not resolved in Stern's poetry but was, in fact, also a part of it. Barron demonstrates how Stern's poetry incorporates uncertainty as part of the ancient Jewish textual tradition of commentary known as midrash.

In 1998 Stern published *This Time: New and Selected Poems.* It contains representative poems from each of his previous volumes, including *Odd Mercy,* and adds fourteen "new poems," the title poem among them. Reading the new poems, one is struck by their familiar themes and images, but also by their renewed social and political interests. "December 1, 1994," "Swan Legs," and "Personal" are pointed poems on matters of social justice. Several of the poems are even more self-revealing than previous work and specifically autobiographical. "Eggshell" is a moving elegy to a poet friend, Larry Levis, and, invoking Walt Whitman's elegy to Abraham Lincoln ("When Lilacs Last in the Dooryard Bloomed"), Stern offers his own "Lilacs for Ginsberg," an elegy for the poet Allen Ginsberg, who died in 1997.

This Time won the 1998 National Book Award in poetry, a prize that essentially recognized Stern's entire career. Notably, the book sold extremely well, no mean feat for a volume of poetry published in the United States. Its success points to the immediacy of Stern's poetry, but more than that, to its emotional truth. As Deborah Garrison wrote, "It isn't often you come across poetry that makes you want to turn to the stranger next to you on the bus, grab him by the collar, and say, 'You have to read this.' But that's how I felt." As a sign of Stern's popularity, three times in 1999 Stern was invited to be a guest on National Public Radio's *Weekend Edition.*

Stern's *Last Blue,* published in 2000, contains fifty-two new poems divided into six sections. It opens with "One of the Smallest," a visionary, even apocalyptic, tale of death, rebirth, and regeneration. A four-page poem, it concludes with an ecstatic declaration: "I turned / garish for a while and burned." In the poems that follow, readers are invited into this fire, where Stern, now in his mid-seventies, looks backward and forward, weeps, wails, and sings.

Of the book's themes, one of the most central is announced in "Someone to Watch Over Me," where Stern states, "I am taking care of the things I love." One can read these poems as examples of how Stern "takes care." In them, he alternately blesses, praises, curses, and angrily defends "the things I love," sometimes doing all at once. In "Against the Crusades," for example, he depicts a paradise of inclusion, not exclusion:

> God bless the Lucca Cafe. God bless the green
>   benches
> in Father Demo Square and the dear Italian lady
> carrying a huge bouquet of red and white roses

Not all is "sweetness and light." Here, too, one finds the poetry of loss, ruin, and alienation. In "Visiting My Own House in Iowa City," he visits the house that he has rented to the poet Mark Doty. Arriving too early to take charge of his own home, and finding that Doty is absent but that his dogs are there, Stern looks in the window and then simply returns to his hotel room "to watch the telephone blinking." A poignant poem of self-reflection, it is also a meditation on the meaning of "home." Perhaps the most delightful "care" taken in the book, however, is the series of love poems to Anne Marie Macari, to whom the book is dedicated.

To understand the ways in which Stern's most recent work carries his poetic project full circle, one has only to look at the book's Paris poems: "Whatever Paris Meant," "The Sorrows," and "Paris." Stern read "Paris" on National Public Radio and designated it for inclusion in an anthology of Jewish American poetry. The poem begins in nostalgia, as Stern recalls a dinner he shared with Peter Gilbert at a Paris restaurant.

It then tells the story of how Stern sold an Underwood typewriter to a Polish victim of the Germans—"whose teeth the Germans had smashed / at Auschwitz." He remarks that he and the man "had the same / name in Hebrew." This memory feeds into another: "I went / to Italy on that money, it was my first / grant." Thinking of his time in Italy, Stern recalls it as a time when he "practiced deprivation . . . ketchup / with beans, seven pounds of lamb for a dollar, / bread eight cents a loaf." He concludes:

> . . . It was
> more loyal that way, I was so stubborn I did it
> ten years too long, maybe twenty, it was
> my only belief, what I went there for.

The specific memory that began the poem has, by the end, transformed into a visionary choice proudly made. The poem becomes a celebration and a defense of his poetic life. He insisted on "deprivation"—he had the courage to believe in the purity and power of art, of its ability to transform.

Beyond the centrality of two Jews—him and the man to whom he was selling black market goods—to the poem, and its taking place in a Jewish restaurant, "the poem is Jewish in a deeper sense," Stern wrote: "in the passionate and even obstinate devotion to an idea in which one's whole life is committed, or sacrificed, or put at risk much in the manner of Talmudic devotion" (*Jewish American Poetry*). Stern's fidelity to this idea was so strong that he felt the need to "sacrifice" to unite "with Him who is the God of poetry and Him who is the God of Mercy. Or Her." As it was in 1950, so too in 2000: for Stern, poetry is a sacred art.

Defining poetry in a brief essay for *American Poetry Review* (1999), Stern wrote: "Poetry helps people live their lives through its music." What is poetry's music? Stern answers this question: "It's the exquisite interpenetration of these two things, moral force and tenderness, or brute power and tenderness." Although he is speaking of poetry in general, the words aptly describe his own work. Stern has throughout his poetic career been faithful to the notion that poetry is a sacred act, that by participating in his spiritual journeys, the reader will experience his or her own. His poetry invites each reader to seek a wonderful and necessary paradise, at once deeply personal, worldly, and profoundly spiritual—a glimpse of the world to come.

Selected Bibliography

WORKS OF GERALD STERN

POETRY

The Naming of Beasts, and Other Poems. West Branch, La.: Cummington Press, 1972. Reprinted as *Rejoicings: Selected Poems, 1966–1972.* Fredericton, New Brunswick: Fiddlehead Poetry Books, 1973. Reprinted as *Rejoicings: Poems, 1966–1972.* Los Angeles: Metro Book Co., 1984.

Lucky Life. Boston: Houghton Mifflin, 1977.

The Red Coal. Boston: Houghton Mifflin, 1981.

Paradise Poems. New York: Random House, 1984.

Lovesick. New York: Harper & Row, 1987.

Leaving Another Kingdom: Selected Poems. New York: Harper & Row, 1990.

Two Long Poems. Pittsburgh: Carnegie-Mellon, 1990. (Contains "The Pineys," 1969, and "Father Guzman," 1982.)

Bread without Sugar. New York: Norton, 1992.

Odd Mercy. New York: Norton, 1995.

This Time: New and Selected Poems. New York: Norton, 1998.

Last Blue. New York: Norton, 2000.

ESSAYS

"Gerald Stern." In *Contemporary Authors.* Vols. 81–84. Detroit: Gale Research, 1978. Pp. 535–536.

"Some Secrets." In *In Praise of What Persists.* Edited by Stephen Berg. New York: Harper & Row, 1983. Pp. 257–258.

"Notes from the River." *American Poetry Review* 12, no. 1:20–22 (1983). (This essay is about the meaning of loss.)

"Notes from the River." *American Poetry Review* 12, no. 3:42–44 (1983). (This essay is about the meaning of polarities.)

"Notes from the River." *American Poetry Review* 12, no. 5:36–38 (1983). (This essay is about the meaning of nostalgia.)

"Notes from the River." *American Poetry Review* 13, no. 1:17–19 (1984). (This essay is about the meaning of the Sabbath.)

"'Sycamore': Poem and Commentary." *Poesis* 5, no. 4:1–11 (1984).

"For Night to Come." In *45 Contemporary Poems: The Creative Process.* Edited by Alberta T. Turner. New York: Longman, 1985. Pp. 213–218. (This is Stern's analysis of the poem.)

"A Few Words on Form." *Poetry East* 20–21:146–150 (1986). (This is Stern's analysis of his poem "I Am in Love.")

"Notes from the River." *American Poetry Review* 16, no. 3:41–46 (1987). (This is an autobiography; it uses the figure of caves.)

"What Is This Poet?" In *What Is a Poet?: Essays from the Eleventh Alabama Symposium on England and American Literature.* Edited by Hank Lazer. Tuscaloosa: University of Alabama Press, 1987. Pp. 145–156. (Also includes panel discussion, pp. 185–225.)

"Living in Ruin." *Poetry East* 26:21–31 (1988). (This is Stern's analysis of his poems "Delaware East" and "East of Kilmer.")

"Poetry." In *Jewish-American History and Culture: An Encyclopedia.* Edited by Jack Fischel and Sanford Pinsker. New York: Garland, 1992. Pp. 485–497.

"What I Have to Defend, What I Can't Bear Losing." *New England Review* 15, no. 2:94–103 (1993).

"How Poetry Helps People to Live Their Lives." *American Poetry Review* 28, no. 5:21–28 (1999).

"'Paris': Poem and Commentary." In *Jewish American Poetry.* Edited by Jonathan N. Barron and Eric Murphy Selinger. Hanover, N.H.: University Press of New England/Brandeis, 2000.

CRITICAL AND BIOGRAPHICAL STUDIES

Baker, David. "Ecstasy and Irony." *Poetry* CLXI, no. 2:99–113 (1992). (Review of *Bread without Sugar.*)

Barron, Jonathan N. "New Jerusalems: Contemporary Jewish American Poets and the Puritan Tradition." In *The Calvinist Roots of the Modern Era.* Edited by Aliki Barnstone, Michael Tomasek Manson, and Carol J. Singley. Hanover, N.H.: University Press of New England, 1997. Pp. 231–249.

———. "At Home in the Margins: The Jewish American Voice Poem in the 1990s." *College Literature* 24, no. 3:104–123 (1997).

Bedient, Calvin. "American Latitude." *Southern Review* 29, no. 4:782–787 (1993). (Review of *Bread without Sugar.*)

Behrendt, Stephen C. Review of *Paradise Poems. Prairie Schooner* 60, no. 1:109–111 (1986).

Boruch, Marianne. "Comment: The Feel of a Century." *American Poetry Review* 19, no. 4:17–18 (1990). (Review of *Leaving Another Kingdom.*)

Carruth, Hayden. "The Passionate Few." *Harper's* 256, no. 1537:86–88 (1978). (Review of *Lucky Life.*)

Chess, Richard. "Stern's Holocaust." *Poetry East* 26:150–158 (1988).

Clewell, David. "In Blue Light." *The Chowder Review* 10–11:159–162 (1978). (Review of *Lucky Life.*)

Daniels, Kate. "Boys to Men: Recent Poetry in Review." *Southern Review* 34, no. 4:736–753 (1998). (Review of *This Time.*)

deNiord, Chard. "Gerald Stern." In vol. 105 of *Dictionary of Literary Biography.* Edited by R. S. Gwynn. Columbia, S.C.: Bruccoli, Layman, Clark, 1991. Pp. 231–240.

Garber, Frederick. "Pockets of Secrecy, Places of Occasion: On Gerald Stern." *American Poetry Review* 15, no. 4:38–47 (1986).

Garrison, Deborah. "Lyricism Unpluggled: A Dazzling Poet Comes to the Fore." *The New Yorker* 74, no. 35:103–104 (1998). (Review of *This Time.*)

Gregorson, Linda. *Poetry* 105, no. 3:233–236 (1980). (Review of *Lovesick.*)

Grosholz, Emily. "Family Ties." *Hudson Review* 37, no. 4:647–655 (1984–1985). (Review of *Paradise Poems.*)

Gwynn, R. S. "Subject Matters." *Hudson Review* 52, no. 2:323–327 (1999). (Review of *This Time.*)

Hampl, Patricia. *Ironwood* 12:103–107 (1978). (Review of *Lucky Life.*)

Hillringhouse, Mark. "The Poetry of Gerald Stern." *Literary Review* 40, no. 2:346–358 (1997).

Hirsch, Edward. "A Late Ironic Whitman." *The Nation* 240, no. 2:55–58 (1985). (Review of *Paradise Poems.*)

Kitchen, Judith. "For the Moment: Essential Disguises." *Georgia Review* 46, no. 3:554–566 (1992). (Review of *Bread without Sugar.*)

Kramer, Lawrence. "In Quiet Language." *Parnassus* 6, no. 2:101–117 (1978). (Review of *Lucky Life.*)

McDowell, Robert. *Hudson Review* 40, no. 4:677–680 (1988). (Review of *Lovesick.*)

Michaels, Leonard. "Talk and Laments." *New York Times Book Review,* October 9, 1977, pp. 15, 34. (Review of *Lucky Life.*)

Miller, Jane. "Working Time." *American Poetry Review* 17, no. 3:9–16 (1988). (Review of *Lovesick.*)

Pinsker, Sanford. *New England Review* 4, no. 3:494–497 (1982). (Review of *The Red Coal.*)

———. "Weeping and Wailing: The Jewish Songs of Gerald Stern." *Studies in Jewish American Literature* 9, no. 2:186–196 (1990).

"The Poetry of Gerald Stern." *Poetry East* 26 (fall 1988). (This issue contains 15 essays and poems about Stern's work. It also contains an essay by Stern and an interview with the poet.)

Salter, Mary Jo. "Poetry." *Washington Post Book World* 11, no. 27:7, 10 (1981). (Review of *The Red Coal.*)

Sandy, Stephen. "Experienced Bards." *Poetry,* August 1982, pp. 293–303. (Review of *The Red Coal.*)

Schulman, Grace. "Dance, Song and Light." *The Nation* 266, no. 17:49–50 (1998). (Review of *This Time.*)

Shetley, Vernon. "Nature and the Self." *New York Times Book Review,* May 10, 1981, pp. 12, 41. (Review of *The Red Coal.*)

Siedlecki, Peter A. "Gerald Stern's Mediation of the I and the I." In *World, Self, Poem: Essays on Contemporary Poetry from the "Jubilation of Poets."* Edited by Leonard M. Trawick. Kent, Oh.: Kent State University Press, 1990. Pp. 110–119.

Simpson, Louis. "Facts and Poetry." *Gettysburg Review* 1, no. 1:158–160 (1988). (Review of *Lovesick.*)

Somerville, Jane. "Gerald Stern among the Poets: The Speaker as Meaning." *American Poetry Review* 17, no. 6:11–19 (1988).

———. "Gerald Stern and the Return Journey." *American Poetry Review* 18, no. 5:39–46 (1989).

———. *Making the Light Come: The Poetry of Gerald Stern.* Detroit: Wayne State University Press, 1990.

Stitt, Peter. Review of *Lucky Life. Georgia Review* 32, no. 1:243–248 (1978).

———. "Engagements with Reality." *Georgia Review* 35, no. 4:874–881 (1981). (Review of *The Red Coal.*)

———. "My Fingers Clawing the Air: Versions of Paradise in Contemporary American Poetry." *Georgia Review* 39, no. 1:188–193 (1985). (Review of *Paradise Poems.*)

———. "To Enlighten, To Embody." *Georgia Review* 11, no. 4:800–812 (1987). (Review of *Lovesick.*)

———. "Gerald Stern: Weeping and Wailing and Singing for Joy." In *Uncertainty and Plenitude: Five Contemporary Poets.* Iowa City: University of Iowa Press, 1997. Pp. 119–144.

Vollmer, Judith. *Prairie Schooner* 73, no. 3:139–143 (1999). (Review of *Odd Mercy.*)

Wojahn, David. *Poetry East* 6:96–102 (1981). (Review of *The Red Coal.*)

INTERVIEWS

Abbate, Francesca, Karin Schalm, and Robert Firth. "Five Questions: An Interview with Gerald Stern." *Cutbank* 43:88–102 (1995).

Hamilton, David. "An Interview with Gerald Stern." *Iowa Review* 19, no. 2:32–65 (1989).

Hillringhouse, Mark. "Gerald Stern: An Interview." *American Poetry Review* 13, no. 2:26–30 (1984).

Kelen, Leslie. "Explaining, Explaining: A Conversation with Gerald Stern," part one. *Boulevard,* spring 1992, pp. 100–115.

———. "Explaining, Explaining: A Conversation with Gerald Stern," part two. *Boulevard,* fall 1992, pp. 193–210.

Knight, Elizabeth. "A Poet of the Mind: An Interview with Gerald Stern." *Poetry East* 26:32–48 (1988).

Pacernick, Gary. *American Poetry Review* 27, no. 4:41–48 (1998).

Pinsker, Sanford. "An Interview with Gerald Stern." *Missouri Review* 5, no. 2:53–67 (1981–1982).

Zwerdling, Daniel. *Weekend Edition,* National Public Radio (NPR), March 27–28, 1999; May 2, 1999.

—*JONATHAN N. BARRON*

Jean Toomer

1894–1967

*L*IKE ITS PREDECESSOR, W. E. B. Du Bois's *The Souls of Black Folk* (1903), Jean Toomer's *Cane* (1923) evokes the lives and souls of African Americans living in the rural and poor South. In a collection of sketches, epigraphs, poems, short stories, and songs, *Cane* animates a world that is beautiful and violent, earthy and mystical. Today, *Cane* defies categorization, as it did in its own time. Composed of fifteen poems, six prose vignettes, seven stories, and a closet drama, *Cane* has been called a novel, a prose poem, and even a short story cycle. More accurately, it is an artist's search for a form that will capture the humanity, the yearning for meaning, the diversity, and the collective voice of the African American "folk." As such, the work weaves spirituals, vernacular stories, blues myths, imagist poetry, and expressionistic drama into a lyrical tapestry. The variety of genres used in the text necessitates its modernist collage, or montage, but it also honors the African American literary and musical traditions that have always been marked by their hybridity.

Unlike other portraits of the South with which most Americans at the time were familiar, *Cane* presented a picture that was free of stereotypical sentimentality. Toomer depicted the harshness and the turmoil of the land and its people. He wrote realistically of relationships between men and women and of the dangers that African American men, in particular, faced in the South. Toomer's impetus for *Cane* was to capture a culture on the verge of change. He referred to *Cane* as his "swan song" for the South and a way of life rooted in the traditions of the African American past. Encroaching modernization, the destruction of agrarian life, and the depletion of

the land were all inevitably leading to the end of a time and a place. The work could be considered a communal autobiography of an era and a culture on the edge of collapse.

Cane appeared shortly after T. S. Eliot's *The Waste Land* (1922), a work that is also about cultural loss. Like Eliot, Toomer returns to the past of a people in order to find ways to combat the anomie of a modern world that is losing its normative forms and traditions. By recovering the past and traditions of the African American South, Toomer also is recovering himself. Toomer's identity as a biracial young man, who did not learn of his African American ancestry until he was a young adult, determines the tone of *Cane*. The imminent loss of the past echoes Toomer's own fear that he will never fully know the part of himself that was hidden for most of his life. Toomer's African American heritage tied him to a father he never knew and to a powerful, but enigmatic grandfather. In trying to find his African American identity, Toomer also was trying to recover relationships with the most important men in his life.

Toomer was determined to confront the burden of the past, one that continued to enslave African Americans through oppression, poverty, feelings of mental inferiority, and racial violence. He believed that African Americans could fully reach their potential and realize their dreams only by addressing their painful history—thereby surviving the present and salvaging the future. By embracing a new artistic form in *Cane,* Toomer sought a way to offer African Americans a new cultural myth that celebrated their history and identity. He presented this "new story" in a manner that freed

African Americans to reflect on their individual desires and dreams and gave them license to pursue them. It is no wonder that *Cane* was an important text to Harlem Renaissance writers and also to the artists, students, and scholars of the Black Arts movement of the 1960s, who would rediscover and reclaim *Cane* and Toomer.

Like other experimental works of its era, including Sherwood Anderson's *Winesburg, Ohio* (1919), Hart Crane's *The Bridge* (1930), Gertrude Stein's *Three Lives* (1909), and Edgar Lee Masters's *Spoon River Anthology* (1915), *Cane* sparked literary debates over its content (including the exploration of sexuality in women) and its form. But unlike those works, *Cane* went out of print and remained largely unread for many years despite its stated importance to the development of modern and contemporary African American literature. The poet and critic Arna Bontemps, a contemporary of Toomer's, credited *Cane* with igniting the Harlem Renaissance in his essay "The Negro Renaissance: Jean Toomer and the Harlem of the 1920s." He suggested that the work "marked an awakening" in young African American writers. The poets Countee Cullen and Claude McKay corresponded with Toomer, and Langston Hughes admitted to knowing *Cane*. Whatever the degree of its impact, it is clear that *Cane* helped liberate the African American artist by paving the way for exploring new forms and new voices, by revisiting past traditions, and by describing through poetry, rather than propaganda, the richness and humanity of African American life.

Even after the book went out of print, the African American scholar and philosopher Alain Locke declared in his essay "From Native Son to Invisible Man" that *Cane,* along with Richard Wright's *Native Son* (1940) and Ralph Ellison's *Invisible Man* (1952), was one of the three most important historical events in African American fiction. The contemporary African American novelist Alice Walker, in her work *In Search of Our Mothers' Gardens* (1983), confessed that Toomer was one of the writers most responsible for her own development. In *Cane* she found women such as she had known growing up, who embodied the pain and the strength of the African American female in the South. Despite the amount of study that *Cane* generated, Toomer never saw another major work published in his lifetime. A few poems and essays found distribution, but the critical success of *Cane* was not matched.

While the moral ambiguities of the work and its complex form were the center of critical controversy and disagreement in his own time, later scholarship focuses a great deal of attention on Toomer's own ambiguity and ambivalence about his racial identity. After the publication of *Cane,* Toomer struggled with his African American heritage, uncomfortable with being considered a "Negro" writer. Refusing to "choose" either his European or African roots, he later disavowed his "blackness" and argued that he was of a "new race" of human being that was neither black nor white. He once wrote that he was "divided." Like many of his characters and the images in *Cane,* Toomer's life manifests the double consciousness, "the divided self," of African Americans so poignantly described by Du Bois in *The Souls of Black Folk.*

CHILDHOOD AND YOUTH

Nathan Eugene Pinchback Toomer was born in Washington, D.C., on December 26, 1894, to Nathan Toomer and Nina Pinchback Toomer. A year later, Nathan Toomer, who fancied himself a gentleman planter, deserted the family. Toomer never saw his father again. Toomer's maternal grandfather, Pinckney Benton Stewart (known as P. B. S.) Pinchback had opposed the marriage, yet he took his daughter and grandson into his home when Nathan Toomer left the family. Pinchback was a wealthy man and had once been the acting lieutenant governor of Louisiana during Reconstruction. Life in the Pinchback household was difficult for mother and son. By most accounts, Pinchback was a domineering figure, who early on decided to take over responsibility for young Jean. Pinchback was also a compulsive gambler and by 1904 had lost most of his fortune. The family moved around often, living in many different types of neighborhoods, some white and upper class and others middle class African American or racially mixed.

In 1905 Toomer's mother remarried. Nathan Toomer was biracial (the illegitimate son of a white man), but Nina Pinchback Toomer's second husband was white. At this time, Toomer was unaware of his mother's own mixed racial identity. The newly married couple moved to Brooklyn, New York, taking the young Toomer with them. Toomer was miserable in his stepfather's home, but he enjoyed and excelled in school. In 1909 his mother died from complications of an appendectomy. Toomer returned to live with his grandparents in Washington, D.C., where he attended an African American high school, Dunbar High (then M Street High). Apparently, it was during these adolescent years that Pinchback revealed to his grandson that Nathan Toomer had been biracial and that Pinchback himself had African ancestry. Pinchback had embraced this heritage before Toomer was born. Toomer later claimed that his grandfather had fabricated this lineage in order to gain political standing during the time of Reconstruction in the South. Pinchback's "passing" threw into question Toomer's own identity. This question plagued Toomer for the rest of his life, whether it was asked by him or by the outside world.

Toomer lived a short while with his Uncle Bismark, an intellectual and a scholar. Bismark influenced Toomer early on, suggesting to him that a person could earn a living "laying in bed" reading books. Stimulated by his uncle's life-style, Toomer began to read voraciously. Throughout his life, Toomer pursued varied disciplines and interests, largely because of his insatiable intellectual curiosity. After he graduated from high school in 1914, Toomer could not settle on a single path. He attended the University of Wisconsin, Madison, where he worked on a degree in agriculture. He was inspired by his love of nature but also by his desire to better understand his father, who had been a farmer. He dropped out the next semester and returned the following fall, only to drop out again at the end of 1915.

In 1916 he began a course of study at the University of Chicago. Believing that he wanted to be a medical doctor, Toomer enrolled in biology courses but grew tired of this discipline and left the university. Before that, he had enrolled at the American College of Physical Training. Toomer had always loved gymnastics and bodybuilding. During this time, he discovered yoga and meditation and pored over volumes of philosophy and psychology.

His years in Chicago provided material for the short story "Bona and Paul" in *Cane*. Like Paul, he began a relationship with a white girl that was complicated by racial differences. It was also at this time that Toomer had difficulty with the Catholicism that he had known as a boy. For a time, he declared himself an atheist. He likewise denounced capitalism and embraced socialist doctrine. Unable to believe that he would be happy being a physical education instructor the rest of his life, he left Chicago and moved to New York City. There, in 1917, he registered for sociology classes at New York University. Within a short time, however, he abandoned these courses and began studying history and then psychology at the City College of New York. By then, America had become involved in World War I. Toomer was at first fearful that he would have to fight but then was disappointed when he could not join the armed forces because of a hernia. In 1918 he switched to courses in pre-law at City College. Shortly afterward, Toomer dropped out of college for the final time.

His inability to decide on a course of study and stick with it did little to improve his already strained relationship with his grandfather. Pinchback decided that Toomer should get a job. Toomer worked for a few months in New York City and, for a time, sold cars in Chicago. Then he moved to Milwaukee, where he became a substitute physical education instructor. These moves from city to city and job to job took place within a few short months. By the fall of 1918, he was settled in Milwaukee, working the substitute job, studying music and literature on his own, writing, and lecturing at local youth groups about "improving" oneself. Overworked and exhausted, and possessed by a manic need to find a vocation that would satisfy his mind and soul as well as his grandfather's wishes, Toomer had a nervous breakdown.

After recuperating in Washington, D.C., with his grandparents, Toomer moved to New Jersey to become a shipyard worker. He believed that he could organize his fellow workers in the socialist cause. The job lasted a week. Toomer continued to practice and study music, deciding that he could become a composer. His grandfather supported Toomer's musical endeavors, and, for this reason, Toomer returned to New York. Within a few short months, however, he met a group of people who would change his life by encouraging him to pursue writing full time.

CANE

While he was always interested in writing, Toomer had never considered it a career option until his move to New York City. There he was introduced to Lola Ridge, the editor of *Broom* magazine; Waldo Frank, the author of *Our America* (1919); and Edwin Arlington Robinson. Each proved to have a profound influence as editors and inspirations for Toomer's work. It was also at this time that Toomer decided on the name Jean Toomer. He had been known at various times as Eugene Toomer and Eugene Pinchback, as well as by a host of other nicknames. "Jean Toomer" sounded like a writer's name to him. These various names and acts of naming represent Toomer's problems with identity throughout his life. The process of establishing his own identity indicated for Toomer that he had finally wrestled away control of his own life from his grandfather. Moreover, by reclaiming "Toomer," he established a link to his unknown father.

To prepare for a career as a writer, Toomer dove into reading as he never had before. He consumed everything: Sigmund Freud, Victor Hugo, Johann Wolfgang von Goethe, Edgar Lee Masters, Carl Sandburg, Robert Frost, George Bernard Shaw, Robinson, James Joyce, Theodore Dreiser, Sinclair Lewis, Walt Whitman, imagist poetry, philosophy, and anything on the occult. He also read the major literary magazines of the day, in many of which he later published his own work. In the years between 1920 and 1922, he immersed himself in writings about race. In any way he could, he explored the African American consciousness.

In 1920 Toomer was forced to return to Washington, D.C., when his grandfather fell ill. Once an imposing figure and the dominating force in Toomer's life, Pinchback was now reduced to a physically and mentally frail man. The effect devastated Toomer, but rather than deal openly with his grandfather's deterioration, he lost himself in writing and reading. He studied Sherwood Anderson's *Winesburg, Ohio,* which, he later admitted to Anderson, greatly influenced his own writing. He spent the rest of his time caring for his grandparents—nursing his ill grandfather and tending to family finances and household duties. The strain was immeasurable. Soon Toomer needed an escape, and the family needed money. Rescue came in the form of a job opportunity.

Late in the summer of 1921, Toomer was asked to act as the temporary head of an agricultural school for African Americans in Sparta, Georgia. Toomer jumped at the chance. The job combined his interests in teaching and agriculture. Moreover, it would take him to Georgia, away from the burdens of the Pinchback household and to the birthplace of both Pinchback and Toomer's father.

The trip back to his ancestral soil transformed Toomer and his art. Here he found the lyrical substance of African American life. He wrote in a letter to Anderson (quoted in *Cane: An Authoritative Text, Backgrounds, Criticism*): "My seed was planted in the cane-and-cotton fields, in the souls of the black and white people in the small southern town. My seed was planted in myself down there. Roots have grown and strengthened. They have extended out." Yet Toomer was also profoundly saddened by a culture that he perceived was dying out. He stated that it was the first time he ever heard folk songs and spirituals. Moved by what he saw and heard, Toomer discovered the roots of his tradition and realized that the past was in danger of being lost.

Toomer stayed only a few months in Sparta, and before he left he sent the poem "Georgia Dusk" to *The Liberator*. On the train home, he began several other sketches and poems that later found their way into *Cane*. He returned to Washington, D.C., in late November and devoted all of his energy, beyond his family responsibilities, to completing the work that he had started in Georgia. Shortly afterward, he traveled to Georgia again with Waldo Frank, who was collecting material for his own writing. Toomer worked feverishly on the sketches and poems. He finished the last draft of *Cane*'s closet drama, "Kabnis," the day before his grandfather died. Pinchback never saw his grandson achieve the success that he had always hoped for him.

Toomer returned to his work with renewed passion and dedication. By September of 1922, parts of *Cane* had been published by *The Double Dealer, The Crisis, Little Review, Broom*, and *Modern Review*. Many of the pieces had elicited high praise from reviewers, including Anderson. During this time, Toomer also helped his uncle manage the Howard University theater, a job that gave him material for the story "Theater" in *Cane*. By the beginning of 1923, the publisher Boni and Liveright solicited the manuscript from Toomer that came to be known as *Cane*.

Written during the period of American history that saw Prohibition, the rise in prominence of the Ku Klux Klan, and an increase in lynching and riots following the return of African American soldiers from World War I, *Cane* is an answer to a country that still could not openly accept the humanity of all of its citizens. Five hundred copies of *Cane* were printed. The book was reprinted in 1927 and then went out of print until 1967. Despite the small number of volumes available, the work summoned response from writers and reviewers from all quarters. Frank wrote the foreword to the first printing, complimenting his friend on depicting the beauty of the South and bringing attention to its themes. African American poets and critics were also positive. Countee Cullen, Arna Bontemps, William Stanley Braithwaite, and Charles S. Johnson (the editor of *Opportunity*) all praised the work and believed that Toomer was the new voice of the race. Alain Locke included two sketches from *Cane* in his anthology called *The New Negro* (1925).

Toomer's most urgent objective was to capture the spirit and essence of the folk and the art that was dying in the South. In a letter to Frank (quoted in *Cane: An Authoritative Text, Backgrounds, Criticism*), he mourned that loss: "The Negro of the folk song has all but passed away: the Negro of the emotional church is fading. A hundred years from now these Negroes, if they exist at all will live in art." Toomer's "swan song" to the past sought, artistically, to preserve that way of life.

Cane begins with the following lines:

Oracular.
Redolent of fermenting syrup,
Purple of the dusk,
Deep-rooted cane.

Many of these images repeat and reverberate throughout the text. Toomer reveals that the words of his text are "oracular," or prophetic. Printed on the book's title page, they act as an ancient signpost foretelling imminent danger. Unless we pay attention and read on, the past (the "deep roots") will be lost. The sugarcane is certainly the most important image of the text. Its purple hue, sweet taste, and sometimes acrid smell (when it is being processed) seep into the work. The cane fields and the factory are the places where most of the violence occurs, where most of the blood in the work is shed. But the cane fields are also open spaces of immeasurable beauty. The fields act as an "objective correlative" of the African American traditions and life in the South that not only survived the painful days of slavery but even transformed those experiences into divine art, full of both the beauty and the bloodshed of the past. Toomer wanted to illustrate that the past, though painful, also held moments of hope and joy, embodied by the connections between the land and African Americans and by the traditions that had sustained the race during slavery. The cane is one of the many images in the text that have double, if not several, associations. In fact, doubleness is itself a trope.

Divisions are central to *Cane*. Barriers are found in all the stories—physical and mental, between men and women, between classes, between races. Humankind's inability to cross the barriers to communication and interaction is usually at the center of the descriptions. The work also reflects the Du Boisian notion of double consciousness. Nearly all of the African American men and northerners suffer from the division. This is emphasized in the women by their biracial identity or by their double status in the community, as in the case of Becky (in the short story "Becky").

Other images also are imbued with a double quality. Trees in the South are beautiful figures of nature, but they are all symbols of terrible violence, haunted with the bodies of African American men. The soil denotes the life that has bled into the ground as well as the place of ancestry. Water gives life and drowns. Purple is the color of the cane and the sky as well as of deep contusions and bleeding wounds. Hazy mornings and evenings are the result of either the burning cane or a burning man, and the work is set in two opposite locales: the South and the North. The South is rich with its folk and is characterized through pastoral pictures of nature, intuition, and ripe sexuality. In the North, people are cut off from the land, imprisoned by streets, houses, buildings, and their own minds. Reason and middle-class morality keep people in the North from truly knowing themselves or each other or nature. These settings serve as opposite and double locales for African American life.

The work's multiple genres echo in its structure. A tripartite division separates *Cane*. The first section takes place in the South (though its narrator is from the North), and the next section is set in the northern cities of Chicago and Washington, D.C. (though many of its characters are southern immigrants). The action of the final section, "Kabnis," takes the reader back to the South. Here both Kabnis and Lewis are northerners. There is a tension throughout each of the three parts between the locale and the observers. They are always regionally opposed. *Cane* is printed with three different arcs that appear before the beginning of each section. Toomer told Frank that the curve indicated the "design" of the book. The arcs represent the movements between North and South. According to Toomer (quoted in *Cane: An Authoritative Text, Backgrounds, Criticism*), the circular design drawn by the arcs is also essential to the work's structure: "*Cane*'s design is a circle. Aesthetically from simple forms to complex ones, and back to simple forms. Regionally from the South, up into the North, and back into the South again. Or, from the North down into the South, and then a return North."

The circle implies the communal voices that permeate the text as well, and the three-part structure signifies the African American musical tradition that Toomer encountered on his trip to the South. The blues stanza is a three-line form (AAB) distinguished by repetition and revision. Character types repeat in *Cane,* and some are revised. The work as a whole resembles a jazz piece in its variations on a theme. The critic Barbara Bowen points out that *Cane* shares other characteristics with African American music. She asserts that the work is a "record of Toomer's discovery that call and response—the drama of finding authority through communal voice—has enabled the creation of a distinctively Afro-American literary form."

Cane is also a modernist text, replete with the period's celebration of sexuality and primitivism. With Toomer, unlike many of his European American contemporaries, primitivism is not a sideshow that sells tickets to a privileged white audience. It is a celebration of peasant life, orality, and folk tradition. As a harbinger of the Harlem Renaissance, *Cane* exemplifies the artistic and polemic qualities that mark that movement. There are also references to Africa. At the time, few writers of African American ancestry publicly characterized Africa as a source of artistic racial pride. African Americans are at the center of the stories (in fact, only two stories in *Cane* have any white characters). Like

other works of the Harlem Renaissance, it protests, sometimes subtly, sometimes openly, the treatment of African Americans. It is also frank in its treatment of the folk.

The first sketch in the work embodies many of these characteristics. Set in the South (all the stories in the first section are set in the fictional town of Sempter, Georgia), the story provides a brief glimpse of Karintha, the title character whose beauty is as "perfect as dusk when the sun goes down." Throughout *Cane* women are characterized by their relationship to nature. They are compared to images of the cane fields, the sun, cotton. Women's intuition and spirituality in the work are linked to the character's ties to nature. In almost every instance, it is the woman who is the most spiritual, emotional, and, hence, natural. Alice Walker's assessment of women in *Cane* suggests this same idea: "When the poet Jean Toomer walked through the South in the early twenties, he discovered a curious thing: black women whose spirituality was so intense, so deep, so *unconscious,* that they were themselves unaware of the richness they held." This is certainly true of the portrait of Karintha. It is this deep connection to the land and to her own soul that separates Karintha from men; they do not understand "that the soul of her was a growing thing ripened too soon. They will bring their money; they will die not having found it out." Men in "Karintha" fail to realize her true beauty and know only that they want to possess something, in the same way that they do not understand the land (yet want to own it), their history, or their own hearts. Karintha grows up too soon, giving birth to a child in the woods, onto a "bed of pine-needles." This image illuminates Karintha's naturalness but also her isolation from the community.

Karintha, like other women in the text, is an example of a "blues" woman, a figure popularized in ballads and blues songs, especially in the years that Toomer was conceiving and writing *Cane*. These women suffered (usually at the hands of men) but survived the circumstances of their lives. One of the poems that follows "Karintha," "November Cotton Flower," implies a similar theme. The cotton flower blooms despite the drought, the boll weevil, and the surrounding desolation. Karintha is described as a November cotton flower, and the flower in this poem is said to have "brown eyes that loved without a trace of fear." Like Karintha, the flower survives the harshest circumstances and retains its beauty. This poem is a counterpoint to "Reapers," which precedes it. If "November Cotton Flower" paints the resilience and beauty of nature, "Reapers" portrays its violent and indifferent temperament. The reapers kill a rat while harvesting, and the observer tells us that he sees "the blade, / Blood-stained, continue cutting weeds and shade." The reapers also seem to be victims of the system of the South. Their movements are mechanical. They are referred to only as "the reapers"; they have no separate identity. Taken together, "November Cotton Flower" and "Reapers" represent Toomer's double imagery and his structural arc. Both are poems of the fall or harvest months, yet each represents an opposite picture of the South and of the cane fields.

"Becky" is also a "blues woman." In this story, Becky is an isolated figure; she lives in a house deep in the woods, cast off from the community. Her offense is that she is the mother of two boys whose fathers were African American men, and she is white. The boys, too, are estranged from the community. Finally, after shooting two men, the boys leave town, and their mother. Becky is thought by some to be a "hant," or ghost. Nobody has seen her for years, but they know that she is still there in the woods by the smoke emanating from the chimney. The narrator of the story and his friend, Barlo, are even a little frightened about approaching her house in the woods. When the house collapses, presumably killing her, Barlo tosses a Bible on the rubble, and the narrator tells us that they "got away." The community's description of Becky and of Barlo and the narrator's attitude imply that Becky is some sort of ghost. Like other women in the work, she represents the South, the land, haunted by the past and by its racial tensions.

"Cotton Song" follows "Becky" and, like the previous poems, acts as a transition between or comments on the longer works thematically. "Cotton Song" is Toomer's rendition of a slave spiritual. It speaks of a "Judgment Day" and is populated by images of "cotton bales" and "shackles." Certainly, Toomer is trying to preserve the folk culture that he feels is being lost in the South, but another layer of the poem, which echoes some of the themes of "Becky," is the specter of the past that still haunts the South. Why should workers in the 1920s still be singing work songs replete with slave imagery? Toomer argues that the answer lies in the South's inability to treat its African American citizens as human. They are considered by some to be little more than the rat killed in the fields by the reapers.

The short prose piece "Carma" traces the difficult relationships between men and women on a more intimate scale than we have seen previously in *Cane*. Carma's husband has had to take a job out of town, and in his absence, Carma takes a series of lovers. Upon her husband's discovery of her infidelity, the two fight. Carma runs into the cane fields, where she makes it seem as if she has killed herself. Her husband becomes enraged when he figures out that she has deceived him again, and he tries to kill another man. He is put on a chain gang for his crime. The narrator holds Carma responsible, but the rest of the community does not ostracize her. It is suggested that Carma's indiscretion is natural. It is the narrator, the northerner, who is judgmental, calling her story the "crudest melodrama." He does not comprehend Carma, her connection to the land or to the past: "Her body is a song. She is in the forest, dancing. Torches flare . . . juju men, greegree, witch-doctors . . . torches go out. . . . The Dixie Pike has grown from a goat path in Africa." Carma is connected in a direct line from her ancestors to America, signified by the image of the Dixie Pike growing from the goat path.

One of the most significant pieces in the collection is the "Song of the Son," the poem that follows "Carma." Thematically, its images echo Toomer's overall intent in *Cane*. The poet describes an "epoch's sun" declining, but "though the sun is setting on / A song-lit race of slaves, it has not set." Toomer's remarks to Frank about the work being a "swan song" reverberate here. The poet realizes that traditions are passing away, though they are not completely lost. The poet also says of this song:

> Passing, before they stripped the old tree bare
> One plum was saved for me, one seed becomes
> An everlasting song, a singing tree,
> Caroling softly souls of slavery,
> What they were, and what they are to me.

Toomer receives the "seed," the songs of the past that tell the stories of slavery, which he must preserve and pass along to others. While the poem is a lament for what is being lost, it is also a guide to the ways in which the artist can recover the past and history, even in the face of pain. The tree is not simply the place from where the seed comes; it also symbolizes the suffering of the slaves' past. The tree has been "stripped . . . bare," and it sings "souls of slavery." In these lines, the tree symbolizes the slave. We also should see the tree in the context of Toomer's time as haunted by the victims of lynching. Again, Toomer uses an image to represent the dual character of the South. The tree is the thing that will save African American traditions and, at the same time, a painful reminder of the more horrific moments of the African American past.

Religious imagery punctuates "Fern." Fern is described as biracial, in terms that might imply that she is African American and Jewish. (When the narrator first sees Fern he is reminded of a Jewish cantor, and her last name is Rosen.) Besides the image of the cantor, there is also a story about a black Madonna, and Fern has fainting spells and visions. It is during these moments that Fern cries out to Christ. Fern's relationship to religion or spirituality is never clear, but it is evident that she is in touch with the sacred. It is important to note that Fern's visions occur when she is out in the woods. When she is in town, she has a vacant look and seems uninterested, as if she lives for those moments when she can return to nature and experience the divine. When she looks at the sunset, the narrator imagines that "God" and the "countryside" "flow into" Fern's eyes. It is only through nature that Fern connects to the world around her. Because of her almost divine relationship with nature, men "idolize" or "fear" her, since they cannot comprehend her essence. The narrator wants to take care of her, but he is unable to express why. All he can offer her, he realizes, is "talk." Like other male figures in the work, the narrator is too rational and too isolated from himself and his surroundings to connect to the woman in the story.

In her story, Esther, too, suffers from visions, though not quite of the same religious nature as Fern's. There are religious allusions to the Virgin Mary, and the story of the black Madonna is repeated here, but Esther, more than any of the other female characters, is distanced from nature. She dreams about motherhood and Barlo, a member of her community. Esther first sees Barlo when he stumbles into the street while he is in the grip of a quasi-religious vision of an African past. Esther is only nine years old, but she is drawn to him. The narrator implies that it is because Esther is a "near white" African American and Barlo is "Black. Magnetically so." Ambivalent about her heritage, Esther imagines that her baby by Barlo will be "black, singed, woolly." Her dreams of motherhood continue throughout the work, over a period of years. Barlo leaves town after Esther first sees him, and he does not return until she is twenty-seven years old. Her life has been wasted waiting for the image that Barlo represents and the well-defined identity that she believes he will bring her. When she grasps Barlo's true character—that he drinks too much and womanizes—she loses hope and wanders out into the empty streets. A typical "tragic mulatta" figure, Esther is isolated from both worlds, unable to find love or acceptance in either. The baby stands as her need for love and identity. She is left at the end with no connection to the world or the people around her.

The poem "Portrait in Georgia" comes after "Esther" and develops the patterns of violence that have been latent in the text thus far. Most of the violence has been hinted at or alluded to, but this poem draws our attention directly to the history of lynching in the South. The braided hair of a woman is "coiled like a lyncher's rope." We see further descriptions of this woman in the poem: her breath smells of cane and her body is as "white as the ash / of black flesh after flame." Clearly, the lines suggest miscegenation and lynching, the history of the South that must be dealt with in recovering past traditions. The poem's violence and its symbolic representation in the land and in the lives of men and women also stand in the foreground of the last story of the first section of *Cane,* "Blood-Burning Moon."

"Blood-Burning Moon" takes place in Toomer's present, but the setting is a mill that was an antebellum cotton factory. On the evening that the story unfolds, while she is walking home, Louisa notices the "blood-burning moon," an omen of death. The images of the cotton factory and the moon indicate that the violence of the past continues to haunt the present. Louisa vaguely feels that the omen speaks directly to her and her two lovers, Tom Burwell and Bob Stone. She is secretly seeing both men. Stone is a white man, the son of the owners of the factory, and Burwell is an African American who works at the factory. Like Louisa, we sense menace in the picture of the moon. Women in the fields and on their porches begin singing folk songs that will ward off the danger of the omen. Some characters in the story might scoff at the superstition, as might the reader, but in Toomer's South, where myth and history breathe in the very soil of the land, it is clear that the power and the reality of an ancient way of seeing the world will prevail. Louisa strains to pull herself away from such feelings of dread. We understand quickly that she is an independent woman, eager for the community to afford her the same privileges as any man, in this case, the freedom to have more than one lover and to embrace her sexuality. We realize, even if Louisa does not, that she will pay for her modern conceptions of male/female relationships. One of Toomer's projects throughout the book is to find ways to free his female characters from society's controls over their sexuality.

As in many of Toomer's stories, it is the man who remains fixed to the rules of the community governing sexual behavior. Carma's husband is such a character, as are characters in later sketches. Here both Burwell and Stone react to Louisa's independence with violent behavior. Their reactions, however, are dictated in part not only by gender roles but also by the complicated fusion of race and sexuality. The history of these forces in the South, the reader senses, will be the sources of the "blood-burning moon." The red soil of Georgia and the red in the moon foreshadow the violence we realize will come. The cane in the fields and their roots symbolically remind us that the roots of racism, of lynching, and of bloodshed in the South reside in the factory, where cotton was processed during the days of slavery.

The echoes of slavery and its aftermath directly affect the relationship that Louisa has with Burwell and Stone. Both men are angered when they hear rumors that Louisa has been with the other. Each man is as upset about the race of the other as he is about the fact that Louisa has been with another man. Stone, in particular, is disgusted by the possibility that any woman he is with, even if she is African American, would be with an African American man. Stone's anger over Burwell and Louisa's relationship is heightened by further contemplation of how far his family has fallen. They now depend on northern financial support, and they have lost the aristocratic standing they once had in the community. Of course, Stone was not alive when his family owned slaves, but he bemoans the past, at least his version of how good things used to be. The description of his visit to Louisa even reads like an account of a master going to the slave quarters to sleep with one of his female slaves. The past continues to define how people in the South interact with one another, even in their personal relationships.

Burwell confronts Louisa about her relationship, but she offers little explanation of her behavior. It is her life, and she intends to do what she wishes. When Stone arrives at her home, however, he sees Burwell and recognizes the truth. Unable to live with the "scandal," he attacks Burwell. In the ensuing fight, Burwell "slashes" Stone. Stone crawls into the streets to proclaim Burwell as his murderer, and the result is not surprising to students of history. White men in the community capture Burwell, who has not yet left the scene of the crime, because he feels "rooted" to the place. He is dragged to the factory, tied to a stake, and burned alive. The murder happens at the site of the past, and Burwell is its sacrificial victim (as are Stone and Louisa, to a lesser degree).

Toomer's double imagining is evident in this story as well. The color red, seen earlier in the story in the soil and in the moon, is found again in the flames that kill Burwell, an emblem of the forces of passion and destruction. Toomer's careful managing of these images argues that it is not Louisa's desires that ignite the tragedy, but the past and the ghosts that still haunt the South.

The second part of *Cane* arcs away from the South to the North and provides a counterpoint to the images and themes of the first section. The two sections each represent a region and act as a reflection of each other, serving as another reminder of Toomer's duality in the work. The first section focuses on the inner lives of women, while the second concentrates on the inner lives of men. The differences between men's reactions and women's reactions in these two sections further emphasize Toomer's interest in doubles and dichotomies. Men in the North are unable to act upon their feelings. This is clear even in the first section, when we consider that the narrator for most of stories (the one, for example, who cannot do anything but talk to Fern) is from the North. Men in the North are paralyzed by thought, preferring analysis to human interaction.

Because men are so disconnected from their feelings, they are unable to express their true desires. Women in the South seem very cognizant of their desires. The difficulty for the reader is that what these women want is unknown or mysterious to the narrator, so we are left with ambiguous sketches that rarely get to the essence of each woman. We probably comprehend Louisa the best, and it is noteworthy that this is one of the few third-person narratives in *Cane*, uninterrupted by an authorial voice. The narrator's confusion over women is missing in "Blood-Burning Moon." Male characters in the second section of the book are not any better at understanding women in the North than they were at comprehending women in the South. A primary difference that distinguishes women in the North is that they are cut off from the land and from nature and as such are much less aware of their inner selves. Middle-class values and the rules of society thwart self-knowledge for women as well as for men in the North.

Images of containment amplify the constraints of society in the second section. The stories, poems, and sketches are rife with metallic houses, gates, locked windows and doors, and "box" seats. In fact, Dan Moore in "Box Seat" sees the community governed by "zoo-restrictions" and "keeper-taboos." The world here is categorized by confinement and man-made works that cause the characters to feel disconnected from their surroundings. Many critics argue that this is evidence of Toomer's modernism. The alienation that the characters feel is a sign of the times. In terms of African American history, however, this feeling of isolation is much more.

Millions of African Americans arrived in the North during the "Great Migration" that occurred between the years following World War I and leading up to World War II. Many writers of the Harlem Renaissance describe characters that have made such a journey from the South only to find that their community, their past, and their sense of self have been left behind. With all the promises that the North seemed to offer, nothing could replace the soil or the "roots" that many African Americans associated with the South. This feeling of alienation worsened when many immigrants realized that the "Promised Land" of northern cities was an illusion. These images appear in the work of such writers as Langston Hughes, Richard Wright, and Ralph Ellison. Toomer's work was no exception. His grandfather had lived in the South and moved to Washington, D.C., the site of most of the stories in the second section of *Cane.* In fact, many of the northern stories, like their southern counterparts, have autobiographical elements. The southern immigrants, already shown to have problems communicating in the South, fare much worse in the North, where the city complicates, confines, and distorts their lives.

"Seventh Street," the first sketch of this section, is such a "Great Migration" portrait. There are images of the city, jazz, World War I, theaters, clubs, and alcohol. These pictures capture the spirit of the age and emphasize the difference between the pastoral, if less than ideal, world we left behind in the first section. Images of blood flow through the street. Unlike the blood that soaks into the soil in Georgia, this blood tries to penetrate the "soggy wood." This wood is not from the trees of the South but is the processed wood of the North. The blood also serves as a transition between "Blood-Burning Moon," the final tale of the first section, and this section. Here, however, the blood does not return to the land; instead it is wasted along the streets. While the blood is always a violent image in the southern section, it is also the "life" of the African American. Here that life "eddies" into corners. Toomer's doubling usually provides us with two ways of seeing something, but we are not allowed this perspective within the boundaries of this single story. We have to connect the image between sections, which makes us realize how northern life is both dependent on and isolated from its southern roots.

The short piece "Rhobert" furthers the depiction of life in the North, especially isolation and middle-class sensibility. Rhobert is an individual figuratively defined by his separation from the land and nature and his association with the city. He is described as wearing his house on his head. It is a "dead thing that weights him down." He is mentally a prisoner of those values that make the house the center of his universe. The house and what it represents consume him to the extent that he neglects his family. Other images indicate that Rhobert is in some way starving; the rules of the middle class control him to the point that a part of him is hungry. Toomer's other portraits of the city suggest that Rhobert is most hungry for spiritual fulfillment. This vignette is full of water imagery. The speaker refers to water's life-giving qualities, and by the end of the sketch, the house seems to "drown" Rhobert. The speaker says that we should sing the spiritual "Deep River" as Rhobert sinks. The image of water expresses the duality that Toomer has been interested in elsewhere. The water can be a source of life and the river a symbol of a spiritual journey or baptism—these are the associations that the speaker wants to invoke by singing the spiritual, but in the North the characters are too removed from the source of the river.

The narrator in "Avey" also wishes that someone would sing "Deep River." When he hears only silence, he starts to hum a folk tune. The music represents a need in the narrator to reconnect to the South, to the land. Other images in the story suggest this desire in the narrator, including his attraction to Avey. As we have seen elsewhere, women are associated with the land and often are used to symbolize humankind's need to reconnect to nature. Avey is described as smelling like clover, and the narrator associates her with a cow. At first this seems like a derogatory comment, but it is a pastoral image, and her sleepiness and vagueness, which the narrator complains about, seem like the ease in which many of the women in the South lived. He tells us that Avey is not ambitious, that she is indifferent to him, and that she has had many lovers—all characteristics that could easily be applied to someone like Karintha or Fern. The narrator looks for the "crimson-splashed beauty of the dawn" in her face, but removed as she is from nature, it should not surprise us that Avey has become "pale." It is the narrator's isolation in the North, accompanied by his middle-class value system, that truly separates him from Avey. Earlier, we are told, the narrator and the neighborhood boys used to whittle the young trees that were planted in boxes alongside his street. The images of the trees and the boys being "boxed" in, or controlled, contrast with images of trees that we saw in the South. They serve as tools for the boys, who strip the trees of all of their representations, negative and positive.

The narrator feels that Avey should be interested in him, especially when he proves his masculine prowess. When she does not return his attentions in the manner he wishes, he implies that she is "simple." Because Avey will not fit his definitions, he begins to criticize her. Then the narrator, again embracing a middle-class vision of how men and women should interact, begins to believe he will save Avey from her life. This is emphasized when Avey falls asleep in the park. Like the prince in "Sleeping Beauty," the man assumes that he is the only one who can awaken her.

The picture of Avey's sleepiness contrasts sharply with the tone of the short poem that follows, "Beehive." The busyness of bees represents the lives of the city habitants, and their silver color reminds us of the metallic contours of the city. The speaker associates himself with the bees, calling himself a "drone" and wishing that he could fly off past the moon to some country flower. The narrator's need for reconnection to the land is emphasized even in this short lyric.

Images of the need of characters to remember their southern roots are explored further in "Theater." John, a theater manager's brother, becomes attracted to Dorris, a dancer who is practicing her routines. In her movements and her singing he is reminded of "canebrake loves." Her dance releases natural sexual impulses that are found in the first section of *Cane*. John and Dorris's thoughts are expressed about each other in the manner of a drama. Even with the help of stage directions, they are unable truly to communicate. They are not capable of breaking the barriers imposed by their middle-class morality: Dorris's dreams of marriage and stability and John's own divided feelings. The lights of the theater depict John's double consciousness: "One half his face is orange. . . . One half his face is in shadow." The action in the theater emphasizes the illusions of the northern characters' lives and the roles that they are forced to play.

The theater is a significant setting in "Box Seat" as well. Dan Moore tells us that he was born in a "canefield." He sees himself in spiritual terms, sensing the relationship between nature and God. Moore resembles the women of the South in this realization, and he clearly does not fit into his surroundings. The beginning of the story illustrates this through the images of metallic, glass, or closed houses, bolted seats, and iron gates. The source of these images of confinement is the community as well as the man-made structures. Cut off from nature, northern African Americans have embraced middle-class values. Mrs. Pribby, the owner of the boarding house where Muriel lives, best exemplifies this attitude. Dan is attracted to Muriel, because the "zoo-restrictions" have not yet affected her. But she tells him that the "Mrs. Pribbys" of the world will not let her love him. Muriel has become a slave to convention; she is afraid even to take her hat off in the theater, because teachers are not supposed to "have bobbed hair." Dan has fought against such conventions by remembering spirituals in his head. The music keeps him connected to the South and to his true self.

Dan follows Muriel to the theater to show her how to break free from society. The theater was often the site of congregation for southern immigrants, and Dan realizes that many of his race need to be saved from the social conventions that have enslaved them in the North. He wants to "reach up and grab the girders of this building and pull them down."

He notices another woman in the theater, who, like Dan, has remained connected to the South. A "soil-soaked fragrance comes from her. Through the cement floor her strong roots sink down. They spread under the asphalt streets . . . her strong roots sink down and spread under the river and disappear in blood-lines that waver south." But even this woman does not acknowl-

edge Dan. The community is separated, symbolized by their bolted-down "box seats." Dan roars to the crowd that "JESUS WAS ONCE A LEPER." Instead of understanding the implications of society's role in Christ's isolation and death, patrons in the theater threaten Dan. In the end, Dan (to an extent like Christ) remains an outsider, with a message that few people want to hear.

"Prayer," which follows "Box Seat," also comments on the lack of self-understanding of people in the North. The poem is characterized by images of division, especially between the body and the soul. The body and soul are "opaque" to each other. Without this mutual understanding, the characters of *Cane* cannot comprehend their inner desires.

In the next story, "Bona and Paul," Paul also suffers from a lack of self-awareness caused by his double consciousness. A southerner living in the North, he is hiding his biracial identity. His consciousness is still in the South. In his mind, he sees the sun on the hills of Georgia and hears folk songs. He follows the image of the sun "into himself." A young woman at school, Bona, is attracted to Paul. The relationship is complicated by Paul's ambiguity about his racial identity and by the fact that Bona is white. The two have trouble communicating; they find understanding only through their intimate dance at a club while they are on a date. Paul has mixed feelings for Bona but leaves with her to consummate their passion. As they go outside, Paul feels compelled to explain himself and his attraction to Bona to an African American doorman. By the time he returns to Bona, she has left. In *The Negro Novel in America*, Robert Bone argues that it is "not his race consciousness which terminates the relationship, as one critic has suggested, but precisely [Paul's] 'whiteness,' his desire for knowledge, his philosophical bent. If he had been able to assert his Negro self—that which attracted Bona to him in the first place—he might have held her love."

The problems of double consciousness also plague the main character of the drama "Kabnis" in the final section of *Cane*. The third section completes Toomer's arc, taking the action back to the South. The voice shifts to an omniscient point of view. In Toomer's philosophy, our dualities should find resolution, and this final section is the synthesis of the themes and images presented in the first two, opposing sections. The action of the drama concerns Kabnis's inability to reconcile his feelings about the South. A northerner, he has willingly moved to the South. While he finds a connection to the soil, he is also horrified at southern history. He does not know how to deal with the history of slavery and the legacy of racism in this country. The work is an account of Kabnis's quest for identity and peace. He unconsciously returns to the South, his racial homeland, to discover himself and to understand his past better.

Early on, Kabnis is so disconnected from nature and history that he fears both. The winds "sing" to him, telling stories of burned black children. The spiritual aura that Toomer creates here emphasizes Kabnis's sense that everything in the South is deadly. Kabnis hears something outside and imagines that "they" have come for him. Or he hears ghosts, who, since they do not have chains, "drag trees." The images of the ghost and the tree, yoked together here, convey how slavery and lynching haunt the South. Kabnis looks under the bed and "sees" a rope. While the South is indeed full of the terrors that Kabnis fears, it is so much more. Kabnis's inability to see this further alienates him from the community, the nature around him, and even himself.

Kabnis is introduced to another visitor from the North, Lewis. Lewis has had trouble with the white population of the town, because he has not "bowed" to them. The possibility of being lynched is stronger for Lewis (though, of course, no one is safe). Nonetheless, Lewis accepts the paradox of the past and the South and his own duality. Lewis is described as a man who is a "stronger" version of Kabnis and in a sense "resembles" him. Lewis comprehends Kabnis's fears and tries to help him reconcile his double consciousness as well as his inability to see the South beyond its horrors:

> KABNIS: My ancestors were Southern blue-bloods—
>
> LEWIS: And black.
>
> KABNIS: Aint much difference between blue an black.
>
> LEWIS: Enough to draw a denial from you. Cant hold them, can you? Master; slave. Soil; and the overarching heavens. Dusk; dawn. They fight and bastardize you.

Lewis realizes that Kabnis cannot face his own duality and therefore does not comprehend or accept the duality of the South.

In the drama Lewis is one instrument of salvation for Kabnis. The other two are Carrie and Father John. An important female figure in the text, Carrie is similar to other female characters in her intuition and naturalness, but she is controlled more by a middle-class sensibility. We see in her a synthesis of images from the first two sections of *Cane*. She helps bring Kabnis out of the darkness at the end of the work. It is her light that leads him out of his fears and may eventually lead him to other types of enlightenment. Father John, who lives in a basement, is a symbol of the African American past. Practically mute, his inability to speak represents the imminent loss of the "voice" of tradition. Unless Kabnis connects to him and helps him speak, this voice will be lost. The fact that Father John is kept in the basement implies that Toomer's present is isolated from, or ashamed of, its past. Kabnis ends up in the basement as well, and his brief and mysterious communication with Father John, followed by Carrie's tenderness and help in leading him out, signal the artist's uncovering and revealing of traditions and the past. For Kabnis, it suggests that he is going to come to self-awareness.

AFTER *CANE*

Despite the critical success of *Cane,* the work generated only moderate sales. It also drew unwanted attention to Toomer's racial identity. He told Waldo Frank and his publishers that he was uncomfortable with questions about his race. In 1922 he spoke openly about being composed of "seven blood mixtures," including "Negro." But within a few years he announced that "though I am interested in and deeply value the Negro, I am not a Negro" (quoted in Turner, *In a Minor Chord: Three Afro-American Writers and Their Search for Identity*). Toomer's disassociation from his African American heritage may have hurt his career in an era when Harlem Renaissance authors enjoyed popularity.

Further complicating his career problems, Toomer became a follower of Georges Gurdjieff, the Russian founder of unitism. Gurdjieff and his Institute for the Harmonious Development of Man provided Toomer with a method for unifying the "differences in oneself," but Gurdjieff's principles also began to influence his work. According to many critics, Toomer's voice and style were consumed by the philosophy. His characters were little more than mouthpieces.

While Toomer was at a Gurdjieff commune, he met the writer Margery Latimer. They married in 1931. The wedding caused controversy when *Time* magazine brought attention to their interracial marriage in an article titled "Just Americans." America was still not comfortable with either the lifestyle or the marriage of the Toomers. The prevalent conservative attitudes of the time did further damage to Toomer's career. Within a year, however, Toomer had more to deal with than his failing career. His wife, Margery, died in 1932 while giving birth to their daughter, Margery.

Toomer wrote constantly during these years, even if his work did not reach a wide audience. Many of these works, including "Withered Skin of Berries," a short story, "Earth Being," an unfinished autobiographical piece, and "The Sacred Factory," an incomplete play, are now available in collections. Some short stories and poems found publishers, and he privately printed *Essentials: Definitions and Aphorisms* in 1931. His long poem "Blue Meridian" was the only other significant work published in his lifetime. Appearing in 1936, the 739-line poem is heavily indebted to Walt Whitman and Hart Crane. The work describes a "new America" and a "new race." This new race was the "blue man / the purple man," which was a spiritual mixture of the old races. The poem emphasized Toomer's growing refusal to choose his racial identity. Instead, he created a new one. The poem also illustrated Toomer's hunger for spiritual fulfillment. He broke from Gurdjieff in 1936. In 1934 Toomer married Marjorie Content. The two traveled to India in 1939, where Toomer studied spirituality. In the same year he returned to America, moving to Bucks County, Pennsylvania, where he began attending Quaker meetings. He lived the rest of his life in relative seclusion. He never again seemed to capture the imagination of his readers as he had with *Cane.* After a long illness, Toomer died of arteriosclerosis on March 30, 1967.

Selected Bibliography

WORKS OF JEAN TOOMER

SHORT STORIES, POETRY, DRAMA, AND APHORISMS
Cane. New York: Boni and Liveright, 1923. Reprinted as *Cane: An Authoritative Text, Backgrounds, Criticism.* Edited and with an introduction by Darwin T. Turner, New York: Norton, 1988.

Essentials: Definitions and Aphorisms. Chicago: Lakeside Press, 1931. Reprint, edited by Rudolph P. Byrd, Athens: University of Georgia Press, 1991.

COLLECTED WORKS

The Wayward and the Seeking: A Collection of Writings by Jean Toomer. Edited and with an introduction by Darwin T. Turner. Washington, D.C.: Howard University Press, 1980.

The Collected Poems of Jean Toomer. Edited by Robert B. Jones and Margery Toomer Latimer. Chapel Hill: University of North Carolina Press, 1988.

A Jean Toomer Reader: Selected Unpublished Writings. Edited by Frederik L. Rusch. New York: Oxford University Press, 1993.

MANUSCRIPT PAPERS

The personal archives of Jean Toomer, including drafts of his autobiography, are held at the Beinicke Rare Book and Manuscript Library of Yale University.

CRITICAL AND BIOGRAPHICAL STUDIES

Baker, Houston A., Jr. "Journey toward Black Art: Jean Toomer's *Cane.*" In *Afro-American Poetics: Revisions of Harlem and the Black Aesthetic.* Madison: University of Wisconsin Press, 1988. Pp. 11–44.

Benson, Brian Joseph, and Mabel Mayle Dillard. *Jean Toomer.* Boston: Twayne, 1980.

Bone, Robert. *The Negro Novel in America.* New York: Knopf, 1965.

Bontemps, Arna. "The Negro Renaissance: Jean Toomer and the Harlem of the 1920's." In *Anger and Beyond: The Negro Writer in the United States.* Edited by Herbert Hill. New York: Harper & Row, 1966. Pp. 20–36.

Bowen, Barbara E. "Untroubled Voice: Call and Response in *Cane.*" In *Black Literature and Literary Theory.* Edited by Henry Louis Gates Jr. New York: Methuen, 1984. Pp.187–203.

Byrd, Rudolph. "Jean Toomer and the Afro-American Literary Tradition." *Callaloo* 8, no. 2:310–319 (summer 1985).

———. *Jean Toomer's Years with Gurdjieff: Portrait of an Artist, 1923–1936.* Athens: University of Georgia Press, 1990.

Christensen, Peter. "Sexuality and Liberation in Jean Toomer's 'Withered Skin of Berries.'" *Callaloo* 11, no. 3:616–626 (summer 1988).

Davis, Charles T. "Jean Toomer and the South: Region and Race as Elements within a Literary Imagination." In *Harlem Renaissance Reexamined.* Rev. ed., Edited by Victor A. Kramer and Robert A. Russ. Troy, N.Y.: Whitson Publishing, 1997. Pp. 215–227.

Durham, Frank, ed. *The Merrill Studies in Cane.* Columbus, Ohio: Merrill, 1971.

Fabre, Geneviève, and Michel Feith. *Jean Toomer and the Harlem Renaissance: Dream Fluted Cane.* New Brunswick: Rutgers University Press, 2000.

Foley, Barbara. "Jean Toomer's Washington and the Politics of Class: From 'Blue Veins' to Seventh-Street Rebels." *Modern Fiction Studies* 42, no. 2:289–321 (summer 1996).

———. "'In the Land of the Cotton': Economics and Violence in Jean Toomer's *Cane.*" *African American Review* 32, no. 2:181–198 (summer 1998).

Gates, Henry Louis, Jr. "The Same Difference: Reading Jean Toomer, 1923–1982." In *Figures in Black: Words, Signs, and the "Racial" Self.* New York: Oxford University Press, 1987. Pp. 196–224.

Hajek, Friederike. "The Change of Literary Authority in the Harlem Renaissance: Jean Toomer's *Cane.*" In *The Black Columbiad: Defining Moments in African American Literature and Culture.* Edited by Werner Sollors and Maria Diedrich. Cambridge, Mass.: Harvard University Press, 1994. Pp. 185–190.

Hutchinson, George B. "Jean Toomer and American Racial Discourse." *Texas Studies in Literature and Language* 35, no. 2:226–250 (summer 1993).

Jones, Robert B. "Jean Toomer's Lost and Dominant: Landscape of the Modern Waste Land." *Studies in American Fiction* 18, no. 1:77–86 (spring 1990).

———. *Jean Toomer: Selected Essays and Literary Criticism.* Knoxville: University of Tennessee Press, 1996.

Kerman, Cynthia Earl, and Richard Eldridge. *The Lives of Jean Toomer: A Hunger for Wholeness.*

Baton Rouge: Louisiana State University Press, 1987.

Larson, Charles R. *Invisible Darkness: Jean Toomer and Nella Larsen.* Iowa City: University of Iowa Press, 1993.

Locke, Alain. "From *Native Son* to *Invisible Man*: A Review of the Literature for 1952." *Phylon* 14, no. 1:34–44 (spring 1953).

MacKethan, Lucinda H. "Jean Toomer's *Cane*: A Pastoral Problem." *Mississippi Quarterly* 35, no. 4:423–434 (fall 1975).

McKay, Nellie Y. *Jean Toomer, Artist: A Study of His Literary Life and Work, 1894–1936.* Chapel Hill: University of North Carolina Press, 1984.

McKeever, B. F. "*Cane* as Blues." *Negro American Literature Forum* 4:61–64 (July 1970).

O'Daniel, Therman B., ed. *Jean Toomer: A Critical Evaluation.* Washington, D.C.: Howard University Press, 1988.

Rusch, Frederik L. "Form, Function, and Creative Tension in *Cane*: Jean Toomer and the Need for the Avant-Garde." *Melus* 17:15–28 (winter 1991–1992).

Solard, Alain. "Myth and Narrative Fiction in *Cane*: 'Blood-Burning Moon.'" *Callaloo* 8, no. 3:551–560 (fall 1985).

Turner, Darwin T. *In a Minor Chord: Three Afro-American Writers and Their Search for Identity.* Carbondale: Southern Illinois University Press, 1971.

Wagner, Linda Martin. "Toomer's *Cane* as Narrative Sequence." In *Modern American Short Story Sequences: Composite Fictions and Fictive Communities.* Edited by J. Gerald Kennedy. New York: Cambridge University Press, 1995. Pp. 19–34.

Walker, Alice. *In Search of Our Mothers' Gardens: Womanist Prose.* New York: Harcourt Brace Jovanovich, 1983.

Woodson, Jon. *To Make a New Race: Gurdjieff, Toomer, and the Harlem Renaissance.* Jackson: University Press of Mississippi, 1999.

—*TRACIE CHURCH GUZZIO*

David Wagoner

1926–

As a poet David Wagoner is strongly identified with the Pacific Northwest, where he has lived and taught for most of his adult life. It is fair to say that in the decades he has been publishing poetry set in that part of the country he has helped to define its literary identity, yet at the same time his work has found a worldwide audience. As a novelist, however, Wagoner reaches back to the geography of his childhood, placing his fiction in the Midwest. The contrast between the two regions represents the contrast between the two poles of Wagner's sensibility.

David Russell Wagoner was born June 5, 1926, in the small town of Massillon, Ohio. At the age of seven he moved with his family to Whiting, Indiana, near Gary, where his father worked in a steel mill. Industrial Indiana contrasted sharply with rural Ohio, and Wagoner felt a great loss. He also sensed the contrast between his father's education and his career: Walter Wagoner, although a mill worker, had graduated magna cum laude from Washington and Jefferson College with a bachelor of arts degree in classical languages. In a 1986 autobiographical piece, David Wagoner described his father as short-tempered and taciturn, and his mother, Ruth Banyard Wagoner, as—perhaps in compensation—"almost pathologically self-effacing."

From 1944 to 1946 David Wagoner was a midshipman in the Naval Reserve Officer Training Corps. He earned his bachelor of arts degree in English from Pennsylvania State University in 1947 and his master of arts degree in creative writing from Indiana University in 1949. At Penn State, Wagoner attended a poetry writing workshop taught by Theodore Roethke, who later won the Pulitzer Prize for *The Waking* (1953). In *The World of David Wagoner* (1997), Ron McFarland discusses Roethke's influence on Wagoner's poetry. However, Richard Hugo, another student of Roethke's and a close friend of Wagoner's, says that Wagoner deliberately stepped out of his teacher's shadow.

Roethke did influence Wagoner to familiarize himself with the work of his predecessors. In an interview with Richard Wakefield, Wagoner explained that Roethke, upon learning that Wagoner was working on a poem about Chicago, asked if he had read any of a number of poems about cities; Wagoner admitted that he had not. Roethke, directing him to the library, said, "Your assignment this term is to read the bulk of poetry written in English." Wagoner demands the same of his own students. In 1949 and 1950 Wagoner was an instructor at DePauw University and from 1950 to 1954 at Penn State. In 1950 he married Elizabeth Arensman; they were divorced in 1953. In the latter year he published his first book, *Dry Sun, Dry Wind,* poems that show Roethke's influence but all of which Wagoner would later exclude from his *Collected Poems: 1956–1976* (1976).

In 1954 Wagoner was invited to come to the University of Washington, in Seattle, through the influence of Roethke, who was teaching there. The Pacific Northwest was a revelation, Wagoner would say later, in an interview with Nicholas O'Connell: "Where I grew up there was no natural place, everything was either dying or already dead. So I had to come to terms with other growing things for the first time—nonhuman growing things."

323

Although Wagoner does not define himself as a Northwest poet, the environment of the Pacific Northwest pervades his work. Sometimes the prolific vegetation is almost animate, as in the opening of "Standing Halfway Home" (from *Traveling Light: Collected and New Poems*), written soon after his arrival:

> At the last turn in the path, where locust thorns
> Halter my sleeve, I suddenly stand still
> For no good reason, planting both my shoes.

The pun on "planting" suggests his kinship and his commitment.

The year he arrived in Seattle, Wagoner's first novel, *The Man in the Middle* (1954), was published, beginning his parallel careers as poet and novelist. (Unlike his poetry, however, none of his novels is set in the Northwest.). In the next few years he published two more novels—*Money, Money, Money* (1955) and *Rock* (1958)—and in 1956 won a Guggenheim Fellowship in fiction, which allowed him to travel to England, France, and Spain. Around this time, however, he also published another collection of poems, *A Place to Stand* (1958), and although his fiction earned respectful reviews, his poetry brought greater recognition.

In 1961 Wagoner married Patricia Lee Parrott; their marriage would last over twenty years. He became friends with other Northwest poets, including Richard Hugo and Nelson Bentley. Wagoner wrote plays and won a Ford Foundation Fellowship in drama in 1964, and was playwright in residence at the Seattle Repertory Theater. However, he was viewed primarily as a poet, and his third collection, *The Nesting Ground* (1963), earned the admiration of prominent critics, including the poet Richard Howard.

Wagoner's 1965 novel *The Escape Artist,* which draws upon his lifelong interest in magic, became his biggest commercial success. In his poem "Filling Out a Blank," he remembers listing career preferences on a high school

achievement form: "1) Chemist 2) Stage Magician. . . ." (*Collected Poems, 1956–1976*). In 1980 the novel was made into a film, but the movie was not a commercial success.

In 1966 Wagoner published *Staying Alive,* was promoted to full professor, and became the editor of *Poetry Northwest,* a post that earned him a Fels Prize in editing in 1975 from the Coordinating Council of Literary Magazines. These achievements indicate the breadth of Wagoner's contribution to poetry as writer, editor, and teacher.

Poetry magazine awarded Wagoner its Zabel Prize in 1967, and since then the various aspects of his work have frequently been recognized for excellence: a National Council on the Arts grant in 1969; the Blumenthal-Leviton-Blonder Prize, from *Poetry* magazine, for poetry, in 1974; a Fels Prize for poetry (in addition to the prize the same year for editing) in 1975; a Pushcart Prize, the Tietjens Prize from *Poetry* magazine, for poetry, and a nomination for the National Book Award (for *Collected Poems 1956–1976*), all in 1977; election as one of twelve chancellors of the Academy of American Poets in 1978; a second nomination for the National Book Award (for *In Broken Country*) in 1979; the Sherwood Anderson Award for fiction and the English-Speaking Union Award from *Poetry* magazine, both in 1980; a second Pushcart Prize in 1983; and the Charles Agnoff Prize in poetry from *Literary Review* in 1985.

In June 1982 Wagoner and his second wife divorced, and the following month he married Robin Seyfried, a poet and his coeditor at *Poetry Northwest.* They have two daughters.

THE POETRY: *A PLACE TO STAND* AND *THE NESTING GROUND*

From his two volumes of collected poems, Wagoner omits all of the poems from his first book, *Dry Sun, Dry Wind* (1953). Although John Ciardi reviewed it favorably, it has little connection with the bulk of Wagoner's work.

In the 1950s so-called confessional poetry, by such writers as Robert Lowell, won acclaim with its focus on the darker emotions. *A Place to Stand* (1958), while by no means light, avoids the excesses of confessional poetry, largely because Wagoner's language play conveys delight even when the subject matter is dour. Wagoner says in the O'Connell interview that "the sound and rhythm come first; everything else is secondary," and the music of his "'Tan Ta Ra, Cries Mars . . .'" (the title quotes Thomas Weelkes, a seventeenth-century composer of English madrigals) illustrates his conviction. While indulging a love of pure sound, the poem also links sound with image:

> . . . The mace
> And halberd, jostled together, ring on the cobble-
> stones,
> While straight with the horde, blue flies and pieces
> of wings
> Sail to the war. . . .

The sound of weapons against cobblestones echoes in the consonants; the parallel verb phrases ("ring on the cobblestones" and "sail to the war") give order to a chaotic scene.

"Words above a Narrow Entrance" expresses Wagner's emotional commitment to the Northwest. The first of two perfectly balanced stanzas begins, "The land behind your back / Ends here . . ." and explores images of death, concluding,

> The country that seemed
> Malevolence itself
> Has gone back from the heart.

The second stanza begins, "Beyond this gate, there lies / The land of the different mind. . . ." He acknowledges that the ominous images will remain part of him, but he concludes that something better lies ahead: "Nothing will be at ease, / Nothing at peace, but you."

Wagoner's next collection establishes the Northwest as his inner landscape. The title poem of *The Nesting Ground* (1963) tells of two people drawn by the cry of birds protecting a nest. They glimpse two chicks but cannot find the nest, and the adult birds lead them away. Suddenly the birds fly back to where the people had searched for the nest, and the family of birds is reunited as "The young spring out of cover, / Piping one death was over."

Wagoner does not analyze the mystery of instinct and survival; rather, he stands in awe of it. Only in glimpses (like the glimpse of the chicks) does he suggest a larger meaning: The people seeking the nest feel a need "to stir what we love"; the birds, having led the people away "by pretending injuries," take flight "To sail back to the source." The two people recognize that the nest is a manifestation of love, and that the birds' return is to some "source" of human love as well.

"A Guide to Dungeness Spit" further explores the sources and expressions of love. Dungeness Spit, extending seven miles from the mountainous Olympic Peninsula into the Strait of Juan de Fuca, is a wildlife refuge almost unchanged from when George Vancouver first described it, in 1792, as teeming with countless varieties of birds. "First, put your prints to the sea, / Fill them, and pause there," our guide tells us, and then directs our attention both to the nearby wildlife and to his own knowledge of it: "Those whistling overhead are Canada geese; / Some on the waves are loons."

Unlike "The Nesting Ground," "A Guide to Dungeness Spit" overtly ponders the meaning of the landscape and people's place in it. The walk through the nesting grounds is a passage through life: "Those are called ships. We are called lovers. / There lie the mountains." These seemingly obvious statements, uttered in short, declarative sentences verging on the incantatory, express the wonderment that the speaker of the poem finds in their very simplicity. An earlier line refers to the ocean as "the spit and image of our guided travels," the pun on "spit" suggesting that their journey into love corresponds to their exploration of their surroundings.

Of a bird that dies he says, "the others touch him with webfoot or with claws, / Treading him for the ocean," suggesting that death cannot hinder the birds from their course. The lovers reach their destination, not the ocean itself but the lighthouse at the end of the spit:

> All our distance
> Has ended in the light. We climb to the light in
> spirals,
> And look, between us we have come all the way,
> And it never ends
> In the ocean. . . .

Unlike the birds that will trample their dead in pushing to the sea, these people will ascend together toward enlightenment.

STAYING ALIVE AND NEW AND SELECTED POEMS

The poet and critic Richard Howard comments in *Alone with America* that in *Staying Alive* (1966) Wagoner finds "the true Northwest Passage this explorer has been looking for." In these poems life, language, and landscape are fully integrated.

"The Words" specifically addresses the limits and latitude of language: In "half of what I write," he says, "the same six words recur": "Wind, bird, and tree, / Water, grass, and light." He ponders how much these words omit, but he finally celebrates their power: "I set loose, like birds / In a landscape, the old words." Words, "like birds," have great freedom.

The other "half" of what he writes is the human presence, which readers must provide in their experience of the poem. "Staying Alive" extends the human presence into Wagoner's beloved wilderness, which, like a poem, must be completed by our experience of it. We survive by discovering our own harmony with our surroundings:

> It may be best to learn what you have to learn
> without a gun,
> Not killing but watching birds and animals go
> In and out of shelter
> At will. Following their example, build for a
> whole season.

A "whole season" means a season of wholeness; from nature (and perhaps from a poem) we learn to be whole.

"Water Music for the Progress of Love in a Life-Raft Down the Sammamish Slough" adds another note to this harmony. Instead of the solitary soul of "Staying Alive," two people ride an "inflated life-raft" along the slough (pronounced "slew," a channel, not a swamp or bog) beside which Wagoner and his wife Pat once lived. The poet rows and therefore faces backward, dependent on his companion's guidance: "My love, upstream, / Be the eyes behind me, saying yes and no." From navigating the slough they will learn to live together:

> We begin our lesson here, our slight slow progress,
> Sitting face to face,
> Able to touch our hands or soaking feet
> But not to kiss
> As long as we must wait at opposite ends,
> Keeping our balance . . .

Wagoner's first retrospective collection also includes new poems that focus more sharply on domestic life (and strife). The earlier poem, "Water Music," acknowledged marital tension but also its resolution; in *New and Selected Poems* (1969), "From Hell to Breakfast" paints a less hopeful picture of a couple at breakfast after a fight. The third-person narrative distances the poet from the poem, but the people in the poem also use a distancing device: "they seem / To remember someone screaming. / Was it next door? In the street?" The speaker of the poem uses the third person as a window to look in on himself; so the couple in the poem cast their own fight as having happened between others.

Here Wagoner's wordplay becomes sardonic. As the couple sits down to breakfast we are told that "She put her face on straight, / He had a close shave" and that they "got in / On the wrong side of bed. . . ." They leave the house through "a brief passage of arms." Far from making light of the situation, Wagoner's verbal play perfectly suits his subject, as his twists of language mirror the couple's effort to keep up appearances while every word carries multiple meanings.

Another subject largely new with this book is the Native American. Wagoner once told an interviewer that as he came to feel at home in the Northwest he also became aware of those who had lived there before him. "Searching in the Britannia Tavern" translates into contemporary terms Clallam Indian myths of the passage to the land of the dead. Addressing an Indian man in a tavern, the poet says this unlikely place can be the beginning of his passage. He must go "To the curb, across the sidewalk, stumbling, to the hunting ground." The city can be traversed, the "hunting ground" reached. But as the poem continues, myth and reality collide more than they integrate. A phantasmagoria of images reflects the Indian's intoxication, suggesting that alcohol is a poor substitute for the old myths.

In "Getting Out of Jail on Monday," as the poet goes to pay a fine for "driving and walking crooked," he sees an Indian man just being released from jail. He accompanies "this husky, bowlegged, upright, sockless Indian / Who's singing, going downhill as straight as an arrow." They spend the day in taverns, the poet paying and observing the Indian (for example, his "flat obsidian eyes") and the workaday world ("Machines are cranking mimeographed Tuesdays") That afternoon the poet leaves to fulfill his original errand: "I put the touch on myself and start uphill, / A solid citizen, going to pay on time."

In this poem the wordplay sometimes seems glib, not integral to the subject, as it is in, say, "From Hell to Breakfast." The irony of "going downhill as straight as an arrow," for example, seems to be at the Indian's expense. Perhaps, however, irony is the only tone suitable for a poem about someone in an environment so foreign to his sensibilities.

RIVERBED AND *COLLECTED POEMS: 1956–1976*

In his book on Pacific Northwest writers Sanford Pinsker writes that in *Riverbed* (1972) the dominant emotion is "surprise." Ron McFarland, in his work on Wagoner, calls it "astonishment." We might better use one of Wagoner's words: "wonder." Indeed, as *Riverbed* went to press he was at work on his novel, *The Road to Many a Wonder* (1974).

"The Inexhaustible Hat" looks with wonder at a magician's revitalization of a hackneyed trick. "The incomparable Monsieur Hartz in 1880" pulls objects "from a borrowed hat": lighted lamps, scarves and other articles of clothing, empty boxes, a cage containing "a lovely, stuffed, half-cocked canary," and "lastly a grinning skull." The poet concludes, "Oh Monsieur Hartz, / You were right, you were absolutely right! Encore!" The flurry of vanities has led to a memento mori, and the magician's performance is itself a poem. "Encore!" is plaintive; the reality that the trick represents—the journey to death—allows no encore.

In "The Middle of Nowhere," the poet is lost in that journey. "To be here, in the first place, is sufficiently amazing," Wagoner writes. The phrase "in the first place" revitalizes a cliché (as "Monsieur Hartz" revitalized the old magic trick), suggesting that wonder transports us to a primordial "first place." The means of finding one's literal way are useless: maps, compasses, sextants, angles of the sun. "The middle of nowhere / Is portable, reusable, and indispensable." Not physical, it is a place in the heart, and "the problem of being / Here is not deducible." McFarland points to the effect of the line break after "the problem of being": any "Here" is as mysterious as any other.

Although different in tone, Wagoner echoes Walt Whitman, in section 29 of "Song of Myself": "To be in any form, what is that?" And like Whitman, Wagoner hears truths that cannot be reduced to words. Whitman's mystical poem concludes with the cry of a hawk; Wagoner's poem ends with the "squawk" of a bird:

> This is the place where we must be ready to take
> The truths or consequences
> Of which there are none to be filched or mastered
>   or depended on,
> Not even, as it was in the beginning, the Word
> Or, here, the squawk of a magpie.

The syntax mimics the disorienting experience and, like the experience, returns the reader to the beginning ("the first place"), at truths beyond paraphrase.

In "Lost," the poet rediscovers the Native Americans' view of the puzzle of being. "Wherever you are is called Here," he says, and when we respect "Here" it reveals wonders Drawing on Indian myths, the poet suggests we emulate "Raven" and "Wren," who recognize the individuality of every tree and branch.

> If what a tree or a bush does is lost on you,
> You are surely lost. Stand still. The forest knows
> Where you are. You must let it find you.

Here we see Wagoner's continuing fascination with the Northwest Indians, who experienced nature as an equal. As McFarland points out, in Wagoner's poems we are truly lost when we believe we can live apart from nature.

The critic James K. Robinson has said that *Sleeping in the Woods* (1974) records Wagoner's

greatest harmony with nature and his rage at those who exploit it. "Talking to Barr Creek," in which the poet asks the creek to "Teach me your spirit, going yet staying, being / Born, vanishing, enduring," expresses that harmony, and "Report from a Forest Logged by the Weyerhaeuser Company," which concludes "I mourn with my back against a stump," voices the rage.

However, the book is also about poetry. Each of its four sections begins with a poem about the poet's art. Introducing the first section, "The Singing Lesson" compares poetry with music:

> For your full resonance
> You must keep your inspiring and expiring moments
> Divided but equal. . . .

Poetry, a form of song, becomes a metaphor for life, and the phrase "inspiring and expiring" foreshadows the poems that follow. In "The Bad Fisherman," the poet gives up fishing after a rainbow trout in his hands literally expires; in "The First Place," two lovers wade in icy water, "singing, welcoming the wonder / Of the river," and are inspired by the realization that they are "*not alone.*"

The final section, "Seven Songs for an Old Voice," explores the ethos of the Native Americans. Among them, "Song for the First People" expresses the poet's awe for the Native Americans' unity with nature: "Change me. Forgive me. I will learn to crawl, stand, or fly / Anywhere among you, forever, as though among great elders."

Collected Poems: 1956–1976 (1976), published in the year of Wagoner's fiftieth birthday, looks forward as well as back. In addition to its twenty-year retrospective, it includes four groups of new poems, two of which groups would be included later in *Who Shall Be the Sun? Poems Based on the Lore, Legends, and Myths of the Northwest Coast and Plateau Indians* (1978), the book that most fully realizes what Robert Cording calls Wagoner's "Indian cosmology." Another of the new poems, "Traveling Light," provides the title for a volume of collected poems almost a quarter-century later.

"Waiting in a Rain Forest" describes the receptive passivity that Wagoner poses as the proper attitude toward nature. Its setting is the Olympic rain forest, where the air is so humid that the "rain does not fall" but rather "stands in the air around you / Always, drifting from time to time like breath." We would do well, the poem suggests, to learn to "drift . . . from time to time."

Plants grow as spontaneously as the rain condenses:

> . . . Whatever lies down, like you or a fallen nurse-
> log,
> Will . . . learn without fear or favor
> This gentlest of undertakings. . . .

The play on "undertakings" acknowledges the presence of death, while "gentlest" softens it. "A fallen nurse-log," itself a human metaphor for something found in nature, is further compared to a person lying down, thus enhancing the sense that life is a continuity.

"Tracking" develops some of the imagery from Wagoner's 1975 novel, *Tracker.* Observing nature, living, and writing are forms of "tracking" something undefinable. Wagoner offers guidance:

> Not even long excursions across bedrock
> Should trick your attention.
> If you come to running water, head upstream:
> Everything human
> Climbs as it runs away and goes to ground later.

Like the lovers in "A Guide to Dungeness Spit" who climb toward the light, we ascend even though we must eventually go "to ground." Our lives are spent pursuing some unseen "other," perhaps *deus absconditus,* the god who hides:

> The other, staring
> Back to see who's made this much of his foot-
> prints,

To study your dead-set face
And find out whether you mean to kill him, join him,
Or simply to blunder past.

WHO SHALL BE THE SUN? AND THROUGH THE FOREST: NEW AND SELECTED POEMS, 1977–1987

The Author's Note for *Who Shall Be the Sun?* (1978) states Wagoner's intention to express the ethos of the Native Americans, who "did not place themselves above their organic and inorganic companions on earth." The book is dedicated to Franz Boas, a nineteenth-century ethnographer of Pacific Northwest Indians who asserted that civilized and so-called primitive peoples do not differ fundamentally in their thinking. In these poems, Wagoner seeks the commonality that Boas claimed is possible.

The title poem recounts the efforts of Raven, Hawk, Coyote, and Snake to be the sun. The first three, unable to be anything but themselves, fail. Snake succeeds, however, because in shedding his skin he renews himself, much as the sun renews itself:

> Slowly he shed the Red Skin of Dawn,
> The Skin of the Blue Noontime, the Skin of Gold,
> And last the Skin of Darkness, and the People
> Slept in their lodges, safe, till he coiled again.

Snake's way of knowing is important: He learned of his ability to be the sun in dream. He knows his place not through logic, but by intuition.

"Song for the Coming of Smallpox" and "Song of a Man Who Rushed at the Enemy" recount the European conquest, but the conquerors are as indistinct as a virus, and as deadly. Both poems refer to "the Iron People," whose weapons are "harder than bone." That is, their weapons are harder than the bone tools of the native people, and also harder than the bones of the Indians themselves.

In "Song for the Coming of Smallpox," these weapons

> . . . burn, making holes
> As deep as bone,
> Setting fire to our bodies.

Whether done by a gun, a knife, or a disease, the devastation is the same. Yet even in death, the Indians retain their identity with nature. In "Song for a Man Who Rushed at the Enemy," a man refuses to flee before the Iron People's "smoke and firesticks, . . . their splitting stones," and he thus affirms his kinship with "Bear Mother and Badger / Who know already how to sleep under the ground."

Wagoner published three books between 1978 and 1987—*In Broken Country* (1979), *Landfall* (1981), and *First Light* (1983)—all largely incorporated into *Through the Forest: New and Selected Poems, 1977–1987* (1987), along with approximately thirty new poems. The book indirectly recounts much of what was happening in Wagoner's life. Now in his early sixties, he had married for the third time and had lost his parents. His friend and fellow poet, Richard Hugo, had died in 1982.

In "My Father's Ghost," Wagoner reflects on his father's life in the steel mills. He tries to

> Recall him burned by splashing steel each shift
> Of his unnatural life . . .
> . . . his eyes half-blinded
> . . . his ears deafened,

but he will not return in that form. Instead,

> . . . I dream him
> Returning unarmed, unharmed. Words, words. I hold
> My father's ghost in my arms in his dark doorway.

As any honest reconciliation must do, this poem acknowledges the estrangement, albeit obliquely. The "half-blinded" eyes and the "deafened" ears were the toll of Walter Wagoner's work, but they also symbolize his disengagement from his son's life. The phrase "unnatural life" further establishes how far apart father and son were, the father a mill worker, the son a nature poet. The rhyming pair "unarmed, unharmed" suggests that the father would be unable to harm his son had he not borne the harm done to him by his life. "Words, words" may be the poet's dismissal of his own profession, and yet at the poem's conclusion he succeeds; the necessary step was to move beyond words, the poet's medium, as he wishes his father could have moved beyond the limits of his own life.

"Elegy for My Mother" describes a woman who focused entirely on others: "life after life / Kept happening to others, but not to her." Wagoner sees a sad harmony between her life and her death:

> And it was no surprise to forget herself
> One morning, to misplace wherever she was,
> Whoever she was, and become a ghostly wonder

He sees that as her vitality waned she lost her hold on her self, tentative to begin with.

Although Hugo and Wagoner write in different modes, both poets linger upon the natural landscape of the Pacific Northwest. In "Eulogy for Richard Hugo (1923–1982)," Wagoner does not write in Hugo's key, but he does depart from his own most familiar manner. The poem is written in rhymed couplets of iambic pentameter, a rare instance of Wagoner's using consistent meter.

Like "Elegy for My Mother," the poem discovers parallels between a way of life and the ensuing death. As a poet Hugo had developed a persona or mask with which he faced the world, and he had learned to be alert to the danger of words used carelessly. Now, as he lies near death, Wagoner visits, and the masks are literal:

We both wore masks. Mine over my mouth
Was there to catch each word, each dangerous
  breath
Before it reached the man sitting in bed
And found its way through his defenseless blood.

Wagoner describes what lay beneath Hugo's figurative mask: "For thirty years I'd known a starving child / Inside him, tough and subtle, shrewd and squalid." He enumerates the "struggling selves" of Hugo's poetry, "beggar boys and family ghosts" among them, and in the final stanza lists the things Hugo eschewed: "The gibberish of God, grudge-matching wit, / The urge to pose or maunder, prattle or preach." By letting these various selves speak, leaving out egotism and didacticism, Hugo

> . . . sang blunt beautiful American speech
> In voices none of us had heard before,
> Whose burden was "We can grow up through
>   fear."

"Burden" means both the theme of a poem and a heavy load. The equivocation works. Hugo carried the weight of his fears but also made them the material of his poetry; moreover, the sentence "We can grow up through fear," through the equivocation of the word "through," allows two equally appropriate meanings: that we grow *past* fear and that we grow *because* of it.

WALT WHITMAN BATHING

In a quieter, much less bumptious voice than Whitman's, Wagoner also seeks the confluence of the human and the natural worlds. But unlike Whitman, he rarely asserts a conclusion, almost never reduces his findings to a lesson. His poem in tribute to Whitman is in Wagoner's mode but is faithful to the themes they share.

The title poem in *Walt Whitman Bathing* (1996) describes Whitman after he was partly paralyzed by a stroke. He

> . . . would walk into the woods
> On sunny days and take off all his clothes
> Slowly, one plain shoe
> And one plain sock at a time.

He bathes in a pond and then emerges, shuffling awkwardly, all the while "murmuring / And singing quietly." Wagoner suggests that Whitman's poetry poured through him even when he was no longer able to write; his greatest poem was his way of being in the world. Wagoner, although still vigorous at seventy, was at the age when Whitman had been in his final decline, and here he looks at an aging poet's life through and beyond his verse.

Wagoner rarely writes about his children, but it is fitting that in a book named for Walt Whitman he includes "Walking around the Block with a Three-Year-Old." In Whitman's "Song of Myself" a child asks what the grass is, and the search for an answer is a theme of that poem. In Wagoner's poem the child sees not grass but a dead starling, then a dead earthworm: "*What's wrong with them?* she says. I tell her they're dead." The child does not understand, and they continue around the block, the child asking further questions that touch on the timeless themes of poetry:

> She stomps on a sewer grid where the slow rain
> Is vanishing. *Do you want to go down there?*
> I tell her no. *Neither do I,* she says.

The grown man cannot miss the metaphorical weight of the vanishing rainwater, or the child's unintentional allusion to mortality when she asks if he wants "*to go down there.*" After they circle the block the dead bird is gone. She asks, "*Where did it go?*" and speculates, "*I think it's lost.*" She asks him if he can find it: "I tell her I don't think so." In reply to the grownup's fatalism, she suggests that they go look for it. The conclusion is an image of compensation: "I show her my empty hands, and she takes one." Showing her his empty hands is a gesture of helplessness in the face of the absolute, but her spontaneous affection contradicts it.

This small revelation is complemented later by one on a scale nearer Whitman's. In "On a Mountainside" the poet gazes from a height he has attained with much effort. Instead of "Wagnerian grandeur" (a self-referential pun), he feels

> That the earth is much more stony than motherly.
> That the closer you come
> To any mountain, the harder it is to see.
> That lightheadedness is not illumination.

Yet all this bleak observation gives way at the end of the poem, when

> The late afternoon sun comes rushing and skimming
> Toward you, through your eyes,
> And through your trembling, stiffening fingers
> In a dazzle of light, a burnt-gold avalanche.

Like the child's affection that refuted his gesture of futility, the sunset does, ironically, bring illumination to his dark musings.

THE NOVELS: *THE MAN IN THE MIDDLE* AND *MONEY, MONEY, MONEY*

Like his verse, Wagoner's fiction has a deceptively natural sound that arises, not surprisingly, from scrupulous effort. Because his language never seems forced or contrived, it gives an impression of spontaneity. However, in both modes he indulges in subtle word play and striking musicality. Despite these similarities, his fiction, unlike his poetry, often portrays people who live out of harmony with nature and, therefore, out of harmony with their own nature.

Published in 1954, *The Man in the Middle* is an accomplished novel in which Wagoner's style is fully developed, austere but expressive. Although the novels generally recognized as important in that era tended to be social in their focus, pondering, for example, the loss of shared belief, Wagoner follows a single, insular character who shows little sign of ever having had any ideals.

His protagonist—certainly not a hero—is Charlie Bell, a middle-aged man who works as a night guard at a railroad crossing. The opening establishes Charlie's emptiness as he stares at the rubble-strewn landscape. As the result of an accident in which his legs were broken, he can no longer work on the trains themselves, and their power contrasts with his weakness. Ready for a change, he will prove incapable of rising to the challenge of the change that comes.

Charlie is too pathetic to be a comic figure, but he never rises high enough for his failure to be tragic. In his lack of introspection beyond his vague sense of discontent, he is more like the trains than he suspects: put into motion by forces beyond his control or comprehension, trapped in meaningless repetition. In this sense Charlie has much in common with the characters in the naturalistic novels of an earlier era, such as the title characters in Theodore Dreiser's *Sister Carrie* (1900) and Frank Norris's *McTeague* (1899).

Charlie sees, on a passing train, a woman being beaten up by a man as she struggles to keep a briefcase from him. She and the briefcase fall from the train, and the man apparently judges that it is too dangerous to jump after her. As Charlie helps the woman and gathers up the scattered contents of the briefcase, he is caught in an underworld conflict that he never comprehends. In each episode he thinks he will soon be through with her: "He'd get her to the phone, then fade out," but he fails to extricate himself.

Charlie learns that he now possesses evidence of criminal involvement in politics, but his only impulse is to go to a bar where "he wished he were somebody else. Somebody bigger, different, who had fists like jugs and legs like fireplugs, who wasn't afraid of trains and things." Yet he is drawn along as surely as a train along a track: "When he saw the telephone on the far wall, he didn't know at first that he'd already started to think." Two hundred pages later he will continue to be borne along without conscious intent, wishing he were "able to cancel a couple days and hand them back for a refund."

The novel concludes back at the shanty where Charlie had been a crossing guard, and he has exerted no influence on his own life. At the end of the novel, as he approaches the point at which he began, "The train went a little faster, jerking itself from side to side, like a dream that wouldn't go the way you wanted it to."

Within a year after *The Man in the Middle,* Wagoner, not yet thirty years old, published his second novel, *Money, Money, Money* (1955). Beyond its clean, workmanlike prose, the novel has strong similarities to his first. Willy Grier, the protagonist, though far more likable than Charlie Bell (and even admirable, as Charlie is not), is also a man nearing middle age who is drawn unwittingly into corruption, and like Charlie, he never fully understands it. But unlike Charlie, Willy has no desire for a change.

Willy is simpleminded, perhaps mildly retarded, although various critics have noted that his mental capacity is inconsistent. He usually thinks at the level of a grade-schooler. In the opening scene, for example, as he goes for a swim, he runs his hands over his body and is relieved to find he isn't growing fat: "Some big people got flabby," he thinks. Willy is physically big, but by "big people" he means adults. The attraction of swimming is that he can feel "the pleasant chill take his body away from him."

Yet in other situations Willy shows an adult intelligence. At one point, as he tries to think of a word, he reflects "it was often in the newspapers like a mistaken anagram for *yeoman* or *woman* or *no one,*" and some of his favorite reading is the encyclopedia. McFarland suggests that these inconsistencies can be reconciled

if we assume that his retardation, or mental age, is a psychological adaptation to the traumatic death of his parents when he was a child. Willy lives on the income from an inherited trust fund but does not understand money. He works without pay, tending the trees in a neighborhood park, and he routinely treats the local children to soda and ice cream. An early scene in which the children go into a frenzy at the refreshment stand as their selections are added to Willy's tab foreshadows the avarice that motivates nearly everyone he encounters. Only Willy, with his intense pleasure in the immediacy of the physical world ("The discovery of an itch was more meaningful than a department store") is immune to avarice.

Willy is disgusted at the ways in which people degrade themselves with greed. In the first scene, as he goes for his swim, he finds the body of a man who he later learns was murdered—for money—and the decay of the dead body mirrors the corruption of greed. Later, in a bank, he feels even more revulsion than at the sight of the dead body: "He realized with a shock that this was a real bank, one of those awful places that made money or did something equally foreign and astonishing." We hear the contradiction in Willy's character, the childlike "real" along with the sophisticated "equally foreign and astonishing"; more important, we have the visceral "awful."

Later, caught up in a scheme, he rebels and holds the conspirators at gunpoint. As he throws a pile of cash from a boat, his speech is ineffectual: "You lie all the time and you hate people, and nobody listens to anybody. I think you're all crazy, and if you happen to want some money, there it is." Underscoring his ineffectuality, he discovers the gun is not loaded, and although he escapes, he is wounded and nearly delirious by the time he gets back to his beloved park. Like Charlie Bell, Willy ends up where he began. He has, however, learned the power of money, as real as the blood flowing into his "cupped fingers."

ROCK, THE ESCAPE ARTIST, AND BABY, COME ON INSIDE

Rock, published in 1958, is Wagoner's first novel wholly composed after his move to the Pacific Northwest. Wagoner has discussed the ways in which his new home influenced him, and those influences seem to be at work in *Rock.* As Wagoner told Nicholas O'Connell, in the area where he grew up (and which is the setting for *Rock*), "everything has a great deal of difficulty making it to adulthood." When he arrived in the Northwest, however, he found himself in "a place where almost anything would grow, where growing things had a kind of furious life about them, a kind of lavishness that I admired a lot"; he describes his experience as "a real crossing of a threshold, a real change of consciousness," including "the discovery of the ability to love."

Where Charlie Bell and Willy Grier end up even less able to make it "to adulthood," Max Fallon in *Rock* flourishes. Max has returned to his native Chicago suburb after a divorce, leaving a business career behind. Still only twenty-eight years old, he is in many ways similar to Biff Loman, the older son in Arthur Miller's *Death of a Salesman*: uncertain of his role in life; disillusioned with the pointlessness and hypocrisy of the world; and yearning for his childhood, when he was the family's pride.

He works as a lifeguard, a boy's job. Symbolizing the choice he must make between adulthood and childhood are Della, a teenage girl who openly flirts with him, and Kate, a divorced woman, about Max's age, with a six-year-old daughter. He also observes a man named O'Tool, older than Max but pathetically fixated on remaining an adolescent.

Max's infatuation with Della creates conflict with his younger brother, who angrily destroys

the mementos of Max's actual youth: diaries, pictures, model airplanes. Similarly, a gang of teenagers burns his lifeguard tower. The cutting of Max's ties to his youth sets him free, and when he transfers his affection to Kate, he chooses to recommence the life that his divorce truncated. The ending, while not unambiguously happy, is optimistic. Max discovers his "ability to love."

The most comic of his novels up to this point, *The Escape Artist* (1965) is Wagoner's only book to have been made into a motion picture, and it draws heavily upon his lifelong interest in magic, which (like writing) is based upon illusion and requires an audience's willingness to believe.

Sixteen-year-old Danny Masters, an accomplished magician, has to choose how much he will be corrupted by the adult world; although his specialty is illusion, it is an illusion distinct from falsehood, whereas the world is steeped in lies. An orphan, he comes to an unnamed Midwestern city to develop his art and to find an adult he can respect.

The novel opens with Danny's observation of an inept magician. No one will listen to his criticism, so as a gesture of contempt he lifts the man's wallet only to find later that it contains thousands of dollars. It is far too much money for the man to have obtained honestly, Danny knows. Danny stole the wallet to demonstrate his prowess, not out of greed, but this small act of dishonesty draws him into sordidness.

Much later Stu, the man from whom he stole the wallet, becomes his mentor. He may not be much of a magician, but he knows the ways of the world and he manipulates Danny into helping in a scam. Introducing him by an assumed name, Stu says of him, ironically, "A completely honest kid, believe it or not, one of the wonders of nature."

Danny is attracted to Stu in part because of the contrast between him and Danny's Uncle Burke. He came to the city in the first place to find his uncle and aunt, a pair of third-rate magicians, but Burke's lack of talent is exceeded only by his cynicism and his alcoholism. "You think you score any points being able to do that stuff? Try to impress somebody. Go up to the first person you meet and start doing all that for him and see what it gets you." Back in the first scene of the novel, of course, it got Danny a wallet full of money, although Burke does not know that; it also tainted the pure art of his magic.

The novel concludes with Danny's severing his ties to both men. Having hidden in a mailbox from Stu, he frees himself with his lock-picking tools and emerges into morning light that symbolizes his rebirth. He is determined to pursue his art without Burke's cynicism or Stu's greed, and the novel suggests that he will succeed. Like Max in *Rock,* Danny has touched corruption without becoming corrupt.

Popsy Meadows, the protagonist of Wagoner's fifth novel, *Baby, Come on Inside* (1968), is another kind of performer, a popular singer who has returned to his native Midwestern city in pursuit of a woman and to celebrate his fiftieth birthday. Deteriorating physically, artistically, and emotionally, he hands out money to placate those he offends. Even his parents, from whom he has been estranged for thirty years, accept his cash in place of emotion. He has only one friend, a comedian: "They could put their arms around each other's shoulders, on camera or off, without checking for knife holes later. You could even call them friends, and they'd both done it from time to time."

Popsy stays drunk throughout his visit. When he impulsively phones one of his three ex-wives to tell her "something's wrong . . . something's breaking up inside me," she makes a diagnosis: "Maybe it's that glass heart. It wouldn't show up on an X-ray."

He attempts to reconnect with his parents, asking his father, "Can't we start over from scratch?" but he learns that his parents adopted a boy who is now twenty years old, the age at which Popsy left home. There is no room for the son who left them.

Popsy tries desperately to mend whatever is "breaking up inside" and finally impulsively marries an aspiring singer half his age. At their honeymoon hotel she warns him not to "expect too much"—because they are drunk? because their marriage is a sham?—and he promises not to: "But he did, he always did."

The book is funny and bleak. Popsy's reckless desperation leads him to cynical gestures, like inviting the audience at a cabaret to a nonexistent birthday party for himself. It is a gesture of affection, but unsustainable: "The good feeling, which he couldn't trust, which he was learning to be scared of, was dwindling fast now and turning screwy, turning mucky in his chest like imitation bronchitis." Unlike Danny Masters, Popsy Meadows never earns the reader's affection or respect.

NOVELS OF THE AMERICAN WEST

Beginning with *Where Is My Wandering Boy Tonight?* (1970), Wagoner wrote four novels set in the American West of the nineteenth century, first-person narratives by young men in their late teens and with whom we empathize. Yet despite their differences from the earlier novels, these stories, too, are about the perils of venality; the protagonists come through largely unsullied, but they see their share of corruption.

Junior Holcomb, of *Where Is My Wandering Boy Tonight?,* is the son of a judge in the town of Slope, Wyoming, in the 1890s. His father's greed and violence recall Huck Finn's Pap, and Junior's innocence and quick wit likewise recall Huck. Junior's friend, Fred Haskell, is the son of the town preacher, a man as abusive as the judge. So, as in much American literature, the representatives of law and religion are discredited. Junior and Fred will be guided not by rules but by their own native decency.

Only two adults, a banker named Flint and an old cowboy named Greasy Brown, are honest but also savvy. Two despicable characters, Pinkus and Mauger, are hired to tutor Junior and Fred, but their real education comes from observing the rapacious behavior of their fathers. Like Huck Finn, Junior learns that the more he can discard the more free he becomes: "So I used my brains and headed for the depot, traveling light, with nothing but what I stood up in, no horse, no bicycle, no home, no old man, and nothing to worry about except the future."

Junior's father disappears, and Junior finds him living in a brothel and married to a prostitute. He learns that Mauger is his illegitimate half-brother and that Pinkus is Fred's. Even Junior's name is a sham: the con man Mauger is the direct continuation of their father. Junior chooses Greasy as his true forebear, learning from him to be a cowboy. When Mauger claims the family wealth, Junior says, "You're welcome to it. . . . I'm going to make something for my own self." Junior and Fred "headed out west of town to start scraping the green off our horns." Here, the West is a new world, uncorrupted by greed. Like Huck Finn lighting out for the territories, Junior embodies the optimism of youth in a young country.

Ike Bender, protagonist of *The Road to Many a Wonder* (1974), has Junior's optimism and integrity, and considerably more foresight. (He is also nineteen or twenty, a few years older than Junior.) As the novel begins, in the spring of 1859, Ike's abusive father has sold the family farm in the Nebraska Territory and is about to take the family to Missouri, which they left only five years before. Ike, however, has other plans. He has been working as a well digger, getting stronger to go west in search of gold and his brother Kit. Setting out with a wheelbarrow to haul his few belongings, Ike seeks adventure more than gold, and this distinguishes him from almost everyone he meets.

Others are undone by their greed, while Ike seems protected by his good heart. He is not immune to trouble, but obstacles yield to his simple determination to keep going. Two robbers blunder so badly that one accidentally shoots the other, and Ike, instead of losing what little he has, ends up with their plunder.

But human frailty is not the only wonder Ike sees; he also finds devotion and warmth. His girlfriend, Millie, whom he left behind, catches up and proposes marriage, saying, "'I aim to sleep in your arms.'" Ike thinks, "Miss Wilkerson, when she was teaching the both of us, claimed there wasn't but Seven Wonders of the World, but she must of quit counting too soon."

Ike himself is one of the wonders. When they meet Indians, Ike sizes up their leader as intending no harm: "There was just something too manly about him, and I think that's what he was looking for in me." By reciting poetry Ike and Millie inspire wonder in the Indians, but what really saves them is the Indians' respect for Ike's bravery. Ike hadn't suspected his own courage, and this discovery is another wonder. When he and Millie strike it rich, the gold is incidental: "And the mystery of it has stuck with me strong as any wonder: now that I went and found gold, I feel like I ought to be able to go back and do my journey all over and *not* find gold and feel just as good and grand and full of spring and summer sweetness."

Eli Clendennon, the protagonist of *Tracker* (1975), is a seventeen-year-old orphan working as a stable hand in Sheepshank, Colorado, in 1889. One morning, as he practices his harmonica in a hayloft, the nearby bank explodes and causes a shower of coins. Eli scoops up a few, but his nonchalance distinguishes him from the other townsfolk. Seeing a boy grovel for coins as if he "had been turned out to pasture in the Promised Land," Eli thinks, "Well, I'd felt like that about coins once, so I didn't blame him none. But I got over it, same as you quit sucking your thumb when you finally figure out you ain't going to get what you want out of it."

What Eli wants is knowledge, especially of the natural world. Even though he knows who the robbers are, he lets the sheriff form a posse (which will include Lud and Sooger Worley, the robbers), and goes to get Tracker Boyd, who has promised to teach his secrets to Eli.

Like Ike Bender, Eli seeks his own kind of treasure. As Tracker explains the signs that enable him to track across bare rock, Ike tells us, "I followed every word and kept my eye on everything he pointed at and knelt down when he knelt and was having a grand time shoveling all this information into my long tom where I'd be washing it down for gold for many a year." That is the gold Eli seeks.

Eli learns not only about nature, but also about how the destruction of nature mirrors human degradation. A beautiful young woman is involved in the robbery and attempts to swindle her own father. The sheriff, the embodiment of order, is also corrupt.

But those who live close to nature escape degradation. *Tracker* was written about the same time that Wagoner was working on his book of poems *Who Shall Be the Sun?* (1978), which draws on American Indian lore. In the novel an Indian saves Eli's life and tends Tracker's wounds, and we learn that Tracker learned his skills from the Indians. "This here's Arapaho land," Tracker says, "and you better do some thinking like them or you won't find nothing up here but a bellyful of flint."

Eli and Tracker literally ride off into the sunset, "not needing no crock of gold at the end of a rainbow but holding up one end of it our own selves and taking it along." Nature's beauty outweighs the gold for which people degrade themselves and nature.

The last of Wagoner's novels about young protagonists up against the vicissitudes of the West, *Whole Hog* (1976) also has the most sinister villain and the most violence. Zeke

Hunt, twenty years old, is accompanying his mother and father, herding hogs from Missouri to California. His antagonist is a Bible-quoting shape-shifter called "the buckskin man" who sees himself as an agent of God. Although he is glad to line his pockets with gold (or fill his belly with pork), his attacks on Zeke and his family are, in his mind, divine retribution— although for what is never clear.

The buckskin man is not alone in his biblical allusions. As the family prepares to cross the Platte River, Zeke objects because of the danger to the hogs, but his father insists that they continue. Zeke's reaction is that "if it'd been the River Jordan and us and them [the hogs] the Lost Tribes, it might of made some sense." His mother admonishes him, "'You'd best starting reading the Ten Commandments.'" The next moment brings their first meeting with the buckskin man and his gang, as if they are a manifestation of the family's strife.

In crossing the river Zeke's parents die (or are murdered—Zeke, knocked unconscious when a bullet fired by one of the gang members grazes his head, does not know for sure). He is on his own, like all of Wagoner's Western heroes. He never finds his parents' bodies, but he rounds up a few surviving hogs and continues, soon meeting a kindly, worldly-wise whiskey dealer named Casper. Zeke's father never touched whiskey, but Casper solemnly advises the young man that "'whiskey stops a whole lot more turmoil than it starts, and it's less expensive.'" In contrast to Zeke's father, Casper spreads peace.

Soon after meeting this kindly father figure, Zeke tells us, "I felt like a newborn baby that's just been swatted and might not like it but was squalling for his own good. I valued my life better than ever and most everybody's and everything else's life too." McFarland has pointed out that most of Wagoner's protagonists have abusive, immoral fathers or no father at all. Unlike Zeke's real father, Casper does not care about wealth: "'I don't want to be rich, boy . . . I want to be smart. Which means I want to find out why I was born.'" Although Zeke thinks this sounds "stupid," Casper will guide him into his new life.

Zeke falls in love with Peggy, a prostitute, and loses his virginity to her. But before he can propose to "make an honest woman out of her," the buckskin man reappears. At crucial moments in Zeke's journey he meets this nemesis. Zeke comments, "He smelt of burnt gunpowder (or was my nose just trying to turn him into a devil?)." Zeke learns that the buckskin man murdered his parents and intends to do the same to him.

After the buckskin man captures Zeke, Casper attempts to rescue him but fails; Zeke must save himself. The buckskin man takes Zeke to an Indian camp, intending to establish himself as their ruler, but the Indians kill him and mean to kill Zeke as well. When Zeke sees that they intend to butcher one of his hogs, he unleashes a hog call that brings the animal running; the Indians, impressed with Zeke's "special kind of power," release him and the hog.

Having passed the test of physical self-preservation, Zeke must pass another test. He finds Casper and Peggy and learns that Peggy has a wagonload of stolen jewels and cash. She offers herself and the plunder to Zeke if he will defend her from the outlaws from whom she stole it; Casper wants no part of the loot. Zeke must choose between Peggy and Casper, and Casper advises him, "'You'd best pick your poison very, very careful, boy.'" Zeke wants to save Peggy, but he does not want the riches: "'I'd be glad to defend you,' I says. 'But I'm not going to defend that trash you're hauling.'" She refuses to leave it and goes with the outlaws.

Zeke has chosen wisely. He had thought Casper's desire to be smart rather than rich was stupid, but no longer. Zeke has wrestled with the devil and kept his integrity.

THE HANGING GARDEN

Like Wagoner's other protagonists, Simon Burrows in *The Hanging Garden* (1980) is trying to create an emotional nexus for which he has no model. At the age of forty-nine, Simon has resigned as mayor of an unnamed city and is divorcing his wife, who in turn is running for the office Simon has just vacated.

Simon is starting over. He has bought a place in the country where he intends to breed show dogs, a complete departure from his recent past. And he begins a relationship with a woman half his age. The country place, which he says he bought because it reminded him of his "grandmother's place in the country," and the woman are ways of obliterating twenty-five years of emotional isolation. But as he reveals, his childhood was no more fulfilling than his adulthood. His abusive, alcoholic father was a judge; Simon says, "'I had to face a drunken judge every night for years. He made some very bad decisions and imposed some very strange sentences on me.'" Ironically, his emotional estrangement will become part of his bond with Diane, a part-time caterer and professional dog handler who has severed ties with her family. He asks if her parents are dead, and she replies, "'Yes, but they don't think so.'"

They meet a sinister knot of people in and around the little town near Simon's country place. Dorff, the caretaker, is an alcoholic. Dorff's son, Scratch, the local dog catcher, is a sadist who is also involved in some way with Mrs. Cutter, head of the historical society, and her daughter, Amy. These four turn out to be interrelated, but even before their relationships become explicit they are a revolting parody of family. Simon and Diane must find emotional sustenance without guidance from their own pasts and in a world of grotesquely distorted families.

Simon and Diane define themselves against a world that thrives on the perversion and misuse of emotion. After the miscreants are dealt with, Simon asks Diane if she wants to leave. Her answer:

"I couldn't leave the dogs. I want to go on being useful. I want to stay here. I don't want to go back to helping other people have a good time and teaching pedigreed pooches how to hold still and behave. I don't mind doing the dirty work, but from now on I want something to be *clean* after I do it."

Simon wants that too. They will take care of homeless animals: "'All right. An animal shelter. And I promise you won't have to cater to me, and I also promise not to be too obedient.'"

The provisionally happy ending in *The Hanging Garden* signals a convergence between Wagoner's fiction and his poetry. Throughout his novels we meet characters who are distracted from the natural life by the influence of a materialistic society; in his poetry, on the other hand, we hear the voice of someone either very close to nature or very aware of the need to be close. When, at the end of *The Hanging Garden,* Simon and Diane resolve to make a life together taking care of homeless animals, they effectively turn their backs on avarice and turn instead toward nature, becoming in spirit very much like the persona of Wagner's poetry.

Selected Bibliography

WORKS OF DAVID WAGONER

POETRY

Dry Sun, Dry Wind. Bloomington: Indiana University Press, 1953.

A Place to Stand. Bloomington: Indiana University Press, 1958.

The Nesting Ground: A Book of Poems. Bloomington: Indiana University Press, 1963.

Staying Alive. Bloomington: Indiana University Press, 1966.

New and Selected Poems. Bloomington: Indiana University Press, 1969.

Riverbed. Bloomington: Indiana University Press, 1972.

Sleeping in the Woods. Bloomington: Indiana University Press, 1974.

Collected Poems: 1956–1976. Bloomington: Indiana University Press, 1976.

Who Shall Be the Sun? Poems Based on the Lore, Legends, and Myths of the Northwest Coast and Plateau Indians. Bloomington: Indiana University Press, 1978.

In Broken Country: Poems. Boston: Atlantic-Little, Brown, 1979.

Landfall: Poems. Boston: Little, Brown, 1981.

First Light: Poems. Boston: Little, Brown, 1983.

Through the Forest: New and Selected Poems, 1977–1987. New York: Atlantic Monthly Press, 1987.

Walt Whitman Bathing: Poems. Urbana: University of Illinois Press, 1996.

Traveling Light: Collected and New Poems. Urbana: University of Illinois Press, 1999.

NOVELS

The Man in the Middle. New York: Harcourt Brace, 1954.

Money, Money, Money. New York: Harcourt Brace, 1955.

Rock: A Novel. New York: Viking, 1958.

The Escape Artist: A Novel. New York: Farrar, Straus & Giroux, 1965.

Baby, Come on Inside. New York: Farrar, Straus & Giroux, 1968.

Where Is My Wandering Boy Tonight? New York: Farrar, Straus & Giroux, 1970.

The Road to Many a Wonder: A Novel. New York: Farrar, Straus & Giroux, 1974.

Tracker. Boston: Little, Brown, 1975.

Whole Hog. Boston: Little, Brown, 1976.

The Hanging Garden. Boston: Little, Brown, 1980.

AUTOBIOGRAPHY

"David Wagoner." In vol. 3 of *Contemporary Authors Autobiography Series.* Edited by Adele Sarkissian. Detroit: Gale Research, 1986. Pp. 397–412.

CRITICAL AND BIOGRAPHICAL STUDIES

Carruth, Hayden. "Poetic Tradition and Individual Talent." *Harper's,* May 1979, pp. 88–90.

Ciardi, John. *New York Times Book Review,* June 26, 1953, p. 10.

Cording, Robert K. "David Wagoner." In vol. 5, part 2 of *Dictionary of Literary Biography.* Edited by Donald J. Greiner. Detroit: Gale Research, 1980. Pp. 348–355.

Howard, Richard. *Alone with America: Essays on the Art of Poetry in the United States since 1950.* New York: Atheneum, 1969.

Hugo, Richard. *The Triggering Town: Lectures and Essays on Poetry and Writing.* New York: Norton, 1979.

McFarland, Ron. *The World of David Wagoner.* Moscow, Idaho: University of Idaho Press, 1997.

Pinsker, Sanford. *Three Pacific Northwest Poets: William Stafford, Richard Hugo, and David Wagoner.* Boston: Twayne, 1987.

Robinson, James K. "Sassenachs, Palefaces, and a Redskin: Graves, Auden, MacLeish, Hollander, Wagoner, and Others." *Southern Review* 14:348–358 (spring 1978).

Sale, Roger. "Fooling Around, and Serious Business." *Hudson Review* 27:623–635 (winter 1974).

Stitt, Peter. "Knowledge, Belief, and Bubblegum." *Georgia Review* 33:699–706 (fall 1979).

INTERVIEWS

O'Connell, Nicholas. "David Wagoner." In *At the Field's End: Interviews with 20 Pacific Northwest Writers.* Seattle, Wash.: Madrona Publishers, 1987. Pp. 39–57.

Wagoner, David. Unpublished interview by Richard Wakefield. August 18, 2000.

FILM BASED ON A WORK BY DAVID WAGONER

The Escape Artist. Screenplay by Melissa Matheson and Stephen Zito. Directed by Caleb Deschanel. Zoetrope Studios, 1982.

—RICHARD WAKEFIELD

Index

Index

*Arabic numbers printed in bold-face type refer
to extended treatment of a subject.*